IDEAS FOR BEYOND THE FINAL EXAM

1. How Much Does It Really Cost?

2. Attempts to Repeal the Laws of Supply and Demand—The Market Strikes Back

3. The Surprising Principle of Comparative Advantage

4. Trade Is a Win-Win Situation

5. The Importance of Thinking at the Margin

6. Externalities—A Shortcoming of the Market Cured by Market Methods

7. The Trade-Off Between Efficiency and Equality

8. Government Policies Can Limit Economic Fluctuations—But Don't Always Succeed

9. The Short-Run Trade-Off Between Inflation and Unemployment

10. Productivity Growth Is (Almost) Everything in the Long Run

ECONOMICS
Principles and Policy
Tenth Edition 2007 Update

William J. Baumol

New York University and Princeton University

Alan S. Blinder

Princeton University

THOMSON

SOUTH-WESTERN

Australia · Brazil · Canada · Mexico · Singapore · Spain · United Kingdom · United State

THOMSON

SOUTH-WESTERN

Economics: Principles and Policy, 10ᵗʰ Edition 2007 Update
William J. Baumol and Alan S. Blinder

VP/Editorial Director:
Jack W. Calhoun

Editor-in-Chief:
Alex von Rosenberg

Sr. Acquisitions Editor:
Mike Worls

Developmental Editor:
Katie Yanos

Sr. Marketing Manager:
John Carey

Content Project Manager:
Starratt Alexander

Manager of Technology, Editorial:
John Barans

Technology Project Manager:
Deepak Kumar

Sr. Manufacturing Coordinator:
Sandee Milewski

Production House:
Pre-PressPMG

Printer:
Courier Kendallville, Inc.
Kendallville, IN

Sr. Art Director:
Michelle Kunkler

Cover and Internal Designer:
Lisa Albonetti
Cincinnati, OH

Cover Image:
© Getty Images, Inc.

Photography Manager:
Deanna Ettinger

Photo Researcher:
Terri Miller

Library of Congress Control Number:
2007926998

For more information about our products,
contact us at:

Thomson Learning Academic Resource
Center

1-800-423-0563

Thomson Higher Education
5191 Natorp Boulevard
Mason, OH 45040
USA

ABOUT THE AUTHORS

WILLIAM J. BAUMOL

William J. Baumol was born in New York City and received his BSS at the College of the City of New York and his Ph.D. at the University of London.

He is the Harold Price Professor of Entrepreneurship and Academic Director of the Berkley Center for Entrepreneurial Studies at New York University, where he teaches a course in introductory microeconomics; and the Joseph Douglas Green, 1895, Professor of Economics Emeritus and Senior Economist at Princeton University. He is a frequent consultant to the management of major firms in a wide variety of industries in the United States and other countries, as well as to a number of governmental agencies. In several fields, including the telecommunications and electric utility industries, current regulatory policy is based on his explicit recommendations. Among his many contributions to economics are research on the theory of the firm, the contestability of markets, the economics of the arts and other services—the "cost disease of the services" is often referred to as "Baumol's disease"—and economic growth, entrepreneurship and innovation. In addition to economics, he taught a course in wood sculpture at Princeton for about 20 years, and is an accomplished painter (you may view some of the paintings at http://pages.stern.nyu.edu/~wbaumol/)

Alan Blinder and Will Baumol

Professor Baumol has been president of the American Economic Association and three other professional societies. He is an elected member of the National Academy of Sciences, created by the U.S. Congress, and of the American Philosophical Society, founded by Benjamin Franklin. He is also on the board of trustees of the National Council on Economic Education and of the Theater Development Fund. He is the recipient of eleven honorary degrees.

Baumol is the author of more than 35 books and hundreds of journal and newspaper articles. His writings have been translated into more than a dozen languages.

ALAN S. BLINDER

Alan S. Blinder was born in New York City and attended Princeton University, where one of his teachers was William Baumol. After earning a master's degree at the London School of Economics and a Ph.D. at MIT, Blinder returned to Princeton, where he has taught since 1971, including teaching introductory macroeconomics since 1977. He is currently the Gordon S. Rentschler Memorial Professor of Economics and co-director of Princeton's Center for Economic Policy Studies, which he founded.

In January 1993, Blinder went to Washington as part of President Clinton's first Council of Economic Advisers. Then, from June 1994 through January 1996, he served as vice chairman of the Federal Reserve Board. He thus played a role in formulating both the fiscal and monetary policies of the 1990s, topics discussed extensively in this book. Blinder has also consulted for a number of the country's largest financial institutions.

For more than 10 years, he wrote newspaper and magazine columns on economic policy, and his op-ed pieces still appear periodically in various newspapers. He also appears frequently on CNN, CNBC, and Bloomberg TV, and is a regular commentator on PBS's "Nightly Business Report."

Blinder has been president of the Eastern Economic Association, vice president of the American Economic Association, and is a member of both the American Philosophical Society and the American Academy of Arts and Sciences. He has two grown sons, two grandsons, and lives in Princeton with his wife, where he plays tennis as often as he can.

BRIEF CONTENTS

TABLE OF CONTENTS

■ PART VII   FISCAL AND MONETARY POLICY   603

PREFACE

Over the years we have come to recognize that a textbook is a living thing. It is never in final shape. Comments from readers, both solicited and unsolicited, provide us with new ideas, showing us desirable and often essential changes. Moreover, outside events modify priorities. For example, what we are led to emphasize during a period of recession is different from the primary focus when inflation is the problem of the day. Finally, we ourselves change. Whether that change represents growth or deterioration of our faculties is an open question, but it means that we insist on revising the contents and emphasis of the book each time we embark on a new edition.

And here we are, with the update to the Tenth Edition, which adds up to nearly thirty years of existence and modification of this book. We had not planned many substantial changes in the Tenth Edition, but this resolution, like most, was easier to make than to keep. Some changes were made to clarify exposition or to bring out the previously missing end of the story. Others were adopted because of some modification of our ideas that we thought was important.

In the responses to a survey, it became clear that a number of chapters were generally not covered by instructors for lack of time, although the material is of considerable interest to students and is not—or need not be—technically demanding. So we simplified several such chapters further—notably Chapter 9 on the stock and bond markets, Chapter 13 on regulation and antitrust, Chapter 17 on environmental economics, and Chapter 21 on poverty and inequality—to make it practical for an instructor to assign any or all of them to the students for reading entirely by themselves.

In the opening section, we have restored what is now Chapter 2 ("The Economy: Myth and Reality") as a descriptive and factual basis for all that follows. This chapter had appeared in several previous editions but was omitted from the Ninth Edition to save space. It is now back by popular demand. Like several of the chapters mentioned in the previous paragraph, this chapter is meant to be read by students on their own.

In the micro sections of the book, we added a number of new materials in response to requests by correspondents. For example, in the material on the static-optimality properties of perfect competition, we added a diagrammatic discussion of the maximization of consumers' and producers' surpluses (Chapter 14). In Chapter 12, on monopolistic competition and oligopoly, the discussion of the kinked demand curve was abbreviated and simplified and much material was added on game theory, including concepts such as dominant strategies, Nash equilibria, repeated games, and zero-sum games.

There also was a major change in the section on microeconomics (Part IV), on the virtues and limitations of markets. It has become increasingly clear to us that the main accomplishment of the free-market economy is not its static efficiency, which is traditionally emphasized but, rather, its historically unprecedented record of innovation and growth. Moreover, it is obvious on consideration that these accomplishments have a substantial underpinning in the activities of firms and individuals and the incentives they face. That is, they have a critical microeconomic component. And, surely, outside the world of elementary textbooks, most observers would agree that in this arena one finds by far the most important, most desired, and most politically significant accomplishment of the market. Accordingly, in Chapter 16 we set about trying to close this critical gap, sometimes on the basis of research by the authors. We may note that one of us has already used the materials in this chapter twice in teaching, to spontaneous acclaim by the students.

In the macroeconomic portions of the book, we tried to make the links between the short run and the long run clearer and more explicit. For example, the culmination of the construction of the basic macro model in Chapter 27 has been reorganized substantially with this goal in mind. Specifically, we moved the section on "Applying the Model to a Growing Economy," which used to come six chapters later, up to this chapter. Doing so enables students to see from the beginning how the analysis of short-run business cycles and long-run growth relate to one another. This link is now also emphasized in other chapters. The change offers the further benefit of shortening the Phillips Curve chapter which, we know, many instructors found difficult to squeeze into their courses.

Chapter 23 on economic growth now includes more material on developing countries—another change requested by several users. The discussion of tax multipliers in Chapter 28 has been greatly simplified. The treatment of monetary policy and the Federal Reserve in Chapters 29 and 30 is not only simplified but also made more realistic by shifting the emphasis from the abstract "money market" to something much more concrete: the federal funds market. Reflecting the end of the brief era of budget surpluses, Chapter 32 now reemphasizes the consequences of large budget deficits, modernizing the discussion along the way. Finally, the most difficult material in Chapter 34 on international trade has been moved into an appendix.

We end this section of the preface by singling out the critical contribution of one colleague and friend of amazingly long duration, not leaving it to the later point in the preface in which we note the very long list of persons to whom we are indebted. Sue Anne Batey Blackman has been working with us now through ten editions of this book; for all practical purposes, she has become a coauthor. Indeed, Chapter 17 on environmental matters is now largely her product. Her creative mind has guided our efforts; her eagle eyes have caught our errors; and her stimulating and pleasant company has kept us going. Perhaps most important, we like her and value her most profoundly. What more is there to be said?

NOTE TO THE STUDENT

May we offer a suggestion for success in your economics course? Unlike some of the other subjects you may be studying, economics is cumulative: Each week's lesson builds on what you have learned before. You will save yourself a lot of frustration—and a lot of work—by keeping up on a week-to-week basis.

To assist you in doing so, we provide a chapter summary, a list of important terms and concepts, and a selection of questions to help you review the contents of each chapter. Making use of these learning aids will help you to master the material in your economics course. For additional assistance, we have prepared student supplements to help in the reinforcement of the concepts in this book and provide opportunities for practice and feedback. The following list indicates the ancillary materials and learning tools that have been designed specifically to be helpful to you. If you believe any of these resources could benefit you in your course of study, you may want to discuss them with your instructor. Further information on these resources is available at http://baumol.swlearning.com.

We hope our book is helpful to you in your study of economics and welcome your comments or suggestions for improving student experience with economics. Please write to us in care of Baumol and Blinder, Editor for Economics, Thomson Business and Economics, 5191 Natorp Boulevard, Mason, Ohio, 45040, or through the book's Web site at http://baumol.swlearning.com.

Baumol Xtra! Site

This Web site, available to be packaged with the textbook provides access to a robust set of online learning tools:

Master the Learning Objectives: Step-by-step instructions associated with each learning objective guide you systematically through all available text and Xtra! multimedia tools to deepen your understanding of that particular concept. Each tool is accompanied by icons that identify the learning styles (print, aural, tactile, haptic, interactive, visual) for which it is most appropriate so you can choose the most appropriate tools to support your learning style.

Graphing Workshop: The Graphing Workshop is a one-stop learning resource for help in mastering the language of graphs, one of the more difficult aspects of an economics course for many students. It enables you to explore important economic concepts through a unique learning system made up of tutorials, interactive drawing tools, and exercises that teach how to interpret, reproduce, and explain graphs.

Ask the Instructor Video Clips: Streaming video explains and illustrates difficult concepts from each chapter. These video clips are extremely helpful review and clarification tools if you have had trouble understanding an in-class lecture or if you are a visual learner.

Xtra! Quizzing: In addition to the open-access chapter-by-chapter quizzes found at the Baumol Product Support Web site (http://baumol.swlearning.com), Baumol Xtra! offers you the opportunity for more practice.

Economic Applications: EconNews Online, EconDebate Online, EconData Online, and EconLinks Online can help to deepen your understanding of theoretical concepts through hands-on exploration and analysis of the latest economic news stories, policy debates, and data.

■ InfoTrac® College Edition with InfoMarks™

This fully searchable database gains you anytime, anywhere access to reliable resources including more than twenty years' worth of full-text articles (not abstracts) from almost five thousand diverse sources, such as top academic journals, newsletters, and up-to-the-minute periodicals including *Time, Newsweek, Science, Forbes,* and *USA Today.*

■ Study Guide

The study guide assists you in understanding the text's main concepts. It includes learning objectives, lists of important concepts and terms for each chapter, quizzes, multiple-choice tests, lists of supplementary readings, and study questions for each chapter—all of which help you test your understanding and comprehension of the key concepts.

■ Business & Company Resource Center

The Business & Company Resource Center supplies online access to a wide variety of global business information, including competitive intelligence, career and investment opportunities, business rankings, company histories, and much more. Take a guided tour of the Business & Company Resource Center at http://www.gale.com/BusinessRC.

■ IN GRATITUDE

Finally, we are pleased to acknowledge our mounting indebtedness to the many who have generously helped us in our efforts through the more than quarter century of existence of this book. We often have needed help in dealing with some of the many subjects that an introductory textbook must cover. Our friends and colleagues Charles Berry, *Princeton University*; Rebecca Blank, *University of Michigan*; William Branson, *Princeton University*; Gregory Chow, *Princeton University*; Avinash Dixit, *Princeton University*; Susan Feiner, *University of Southern Maine*, Claudia Goldin, *Harvard University*; Ronald Grieson, *University of California, Santa Cruz*; Daniel Hamermesh, *University of Texas*; Yuzo Honda, *Osaka University*; Peter Kenen, *Princeton University*; Melvin Krauss, *Stanford University*; Herbert Levine, *University of Pennsylvania*; Burton Malkiel, *Princeton University*; Edwin Mills, *Northwestern University*; Janusz Ordover, *New York University*; David H. Reiley Jr., *University of Arizona*; Uwe Reinhardt, *Princeton University*; Harvey Rosen, *Princeton University*; Laura Tyson, *University of California, Berkeley*; and Martin Weitzman, *Harvard University* have all given generously of their knowledge in particular areas over the course of ten editions. We have learned much from them, and have shamelessly relied on their help.

Economists and students at colleges and universities other than ours offered numerous useful suggestions for improvements, many of which we have incorporated into this tenth edition. We wish to thank Donald M. Atwater, *Pepperdine University*; Mohsen Bahmani-Oskooee, *University of Wisconsin-Milwaukee*; Laurie J. Bates, *Bryant College*; Mary Bumgarner; *Kennesaw State University*; James Casey, *Washington and Lee University*; Ray Cohn, *Illinois State University*; Sean Corcoran, *California State University, Sacramento*; Lawrence DeBrock, *University of Illinois*, Robert Dunn, *George Washington University*; Barry Falk, *Iowa State University*; Mark Frascatore, Clarkson University; George Hoffer, *Virginia Commonwealth University*; Jack W. Hou, *California State University, Long Beach*; Louise Keely, *University of Wisconsin*; Kirk Kim, *University of Wisconsin- Whitewater*; Doug Kinnear, *Colorado State University*; Edward T. Merkel, *Troy State University*; Carrie A. Meyer, *George Mason University*; Sang Lee, *University of Florida*; Evelyn Lehrer, *University of Illinois, Chicago*; Una Okonkwo Osili, *Indiana-University-Purdue Univ at Indianapolis*; Thomas F. Pogue, *University of Iowa*; Fernando Quijano, *Dickinson State University*; David Ridley, *Duke University*; Robby Rosenman, *Washington State University*; Patricia K. Smith, *University of Michigan-Dearborn*; Michael Smitka, *Washington and Lee University*; Blake Sorem, *Pierce College*; Edward Stuart, *Northeastern Illinois University*; Chuck Thompson, *Troy State University*; John Tiernstra, *Calvin College*; Sandra R. Trejos, *Indiana University-Purdue University Indianapolis*; Hendrick Van den Berg, *University of Nebraska-Lincoln*; Kristin A. Van Gaasbeck, *California State University, Sacramento*; Doug Walker, *Louisiana State University*; Stephan Weiler, *Colorado State University*; Jonathan B. Wight, *University of Richmond*; Bob Williams, *Guilford College*; Mark Witte, *Northwestern University*; and Jason Zimmerman, *South Dakota State University* for their insightful reviews. In addition, we thank Thomas Rhoads, Towson University, and Ronald Elkins, Central Washington University, for their careful review of the graphs and figures for accuracy.

To determine which of the many strong suggestions made by reviewers we should incorporate into this edition, we performed a survey of those currently using our text and appreciated the responses of the following instructors:

W. David Allen	Aimee Dimmerman
Mary Allender	Didar Erdinic
Nestor M Arguea	Christi Essex
Don Atwater	Frederick Floss
Sudeshna Bandyopadhyay	Prem Gandhi
Charles Callahan	Elena Goldman
Carl Campbell	Mike Gunderson
Amber Casolari	George Heitmann
Gene Chang	Martha Hensley
I-Ming Chiu	Stella Koutoumanes Hofrenning
Sean Corcoran	Farrokh Hormozi
Everand Cowan	Kathleen Hurley
Eleanor Craig	John Isbister

Alexei Izyumov
Brad Kamp
Michael Karadanopoulos
Sharmila King
Tolga Koker
Janet Koscianski
Pradeep Kotamraju
Christopher Laincz
Gary Langer
Sam Laposata
Tom Larson
Pareena Lawrence
Evelyn Lehrer
Marie Livingston
Kristina Lybecker
Carrie A. Meyer
Ida Mirzaie
Aparajita Nandi
Ingmar Nyman
William O'Dea
David O'Hara
Maria Pia Olivero
Kwang Woo Park
Walter Park

Don Peppard
Jennie Popp
Hamideh Ramjerdi
Malcolm Robinson
Robert Rosenthal
Joseph Seneca
Tim Smeeding
Mike Smitka
Lynnette Smyth
Blake Sorem
Rebecca Stein
Charles M. Templeton
Manjuri Talukdar
Betty Tao
Robert Tokle
Joseph Uhl
David Vail
Kristin A. Van Gaasback
Cathleen Whiting
Katherine Willey-Wolfe
Mark Witte
Siew Wong
Sourushe Zandvakili
Jason Zimmerman

Obviously, the book you hold in your hands was not produced by us alone. An essential role was played by the staff at Thomson Business and Economics including Dave Shaut and Alex von Rosenberg, Editors-in-Chief; Michael Worls, Senior Acquisitions Editor; Brian Joyner and John Carey, Senior Marketing Managers; Sarah Dorger and Katie Yanos, Developmental Editors; Emily Gross and Starratt Alexander, Senior Content Project Managers; Peggy Buskey and Deepak Kumar, Technology Project Managers; Michelle Kunkler, Senior Art Director; Deanna Ettinger, Photo Manager; and Sandee Milewski, Senior Manufacturing Coordinator. It was a pleasure to deal with them, and we appreciate their understanding of our approaches, our goals, and our idiosyncrasies. We also thank our intelligent and delightful secretaries and research coworkers at Princeton University and New York University, Kathleen Hurley and Janeece Roderick Lewis, who struggled successfully with the myriad tasks involved in completing the manuscript.

And, finally, we must not omit our continuing debt to our wives, Hilda Baumol and Madeline Blinder. They have now suffered through ten editions and the inescapable neglect and distraction the preparation of each new edition imposes. Their tolerance and understanding has been no minor contribution to the project.

William J. Baumol
Alan S. Blinder

To my fine grandchildren, Naomi and Alex.

W.J.B.

To my beloved grandchildren, Malcom and Levi, who demand little and supply so much joy.

A.S.B.

GETTING ACQUAINTED WITH ECONOMICS

Welcome to economics! Some of your fellow students may have warned you that "Econ is boring." Don't believe them—or at least, don't believe them too much. It is true that studying economics is hardly pure fun. But a first course in economics can be an eye-opening experience. There is a vast and important world out there—the economic world—and this book is designed to help you understand it.

Have you ever wondered whether jobs will be plentiful or scarce when you graduate? Or why a college education becomes more and more expensive? Should the government be suspicious of big firms? Why can't pollution be eliminated? How did the U.S. economy manage to grow so rapidly in the 1990s while Japan's economy stagnated? If any of these questions have piqued your curiosity, read on. You may find economics to be more interesting than you had thought!

The four chapters of Part I introduce you to both the subject matter of economics and some of the methods that economists use to study their subject.

WHAT IS ECONOMICS?

Why does public discussion of economic policy so often show the abysmal ignorance of the participants? Why do I so often want to cry at what public figures, the press, and television commentators say about economic affairs?

ROBERT M. SOLOW, WINNER OF THE 1987 NOBEL PRIZE IN ECONOMICS

Economics is a broad-ranging discipline, both in the questions it asks and the methods it uses to seek answers. Many of the world's most pressing problems are economic in nature. The first part of this chapter is intended to give you some idea of the sorts of issues that economic analysis helps to clarify and the kinds of solutions that economic principles suggest. The second part briefly introduces the tools that economists use—tools you are likely to find useful in your career, personal life, and role as an informed citizen, long after this course is over.

CONTENTS

IDEAS FOR BEYOND THE FINAL EXAM

Elephants may never forget, but people do. We realize that most students inevitably forget much of what they learn in a course—perhaps with a sense of relief—soon after the final exam.

Nevertheless, we hope that you *will* remember some of the most important economic ideas and, even more important, the ways of thinking about economic issues that are taught in this course. To help you identify some of the most crucial concepts, we have selected ten from the many in this book. Some offer key insights into the workings of the economy. Several bear on important policy issues that appear in newspapers. Others point out common misunderstandings that occur among even the most thoughtful lay observers. Most of them indicate that it takes more than just good common sense to analyze economic issues effectively. As the opening quote of this chapter suggests, many learned judges, politicians, and university administrators who failed to understand basic economic principles could have made wiser decisions than they did.

Try this one on for size. Imagine you own a widget manufacturing company that rents a warehouse. Your landlord raises your rent by $10,000 per year. Should you raise the price of your widgets to try to recoup some of your higher costs? Or should you do the opposite—lower your price to try to sell more and spread the so-called overhead costs over more products? In fact, as we shall see in Chapter 8, both answers are probably wrong!

IDEAS FOR BEYOND THE FINAL EXAM

Each of the ten *Ideas for Beyond the Final Exam*, many of which are counterintuitive, will be sketched briefly here. More important, each will be discussed in depth when it occurs in the course of the book, where it will be called to your attention by a special icon in the margin. So don't expect to master these ideas fully now. But do notice how some of the ideas arise again and again as we deal with different topics. By the end of the course you will have a better grasp of when common sense works and when it fails. And you will be able to recognize common fallacies that are all too often offered as pearls of wisdom by public figures, the press, and television commentators.

Idea 1: How Much Does It Really Cost?

Because no one has infinite riches, people are constantly forced to make choices. If you purchase a new computer, you may have to give up that trip you had planned. If a business decides to retool its factories, it may have to postpone its plans for new executive offices. If a government expands its defense program, it may be forced to reduce its outlays on school buildings.

Economists say that the true costs of such decisions are not the number of dollars spent on the computer, the new equipment, or the military, but rather *the value of what must be given up in order to acquire the item*—the vacation trip, the new executive offices, and the new schools. These are called **opportunity costs** because they represent the *opportunities* the individual, firm, or government must forgo to make the desired expenditure. Economists maintain that rational decision making must be based on opportunity costs, not just dollar costs (see Chapters 3, 8, 14, and 15).

The cost of a college education provides a vivid example. How much do you think it *costs* to go to college? Most people are likely to answer by adding together your expenditures on tuition, room and board, books, and the like, and then deducting any scholarship funds you may receive. Suppose that amount comes to $15,000.

Economists keep score differently. They first want to know how much you would be earning if you were not attending college. Suppose that salary is $16,000 per year. This may seem irrelevant, but because you *give up* these earnings by attending college, they must be added to your tuition bill. You have that much less income because of your education. On the other side of the ledger, economists would not count *all* of the university's bill for room and board as part of the costs of your education. They would want to know how much *more* it costs you to live at school rather than at home. Economists would count only these *extra* costs as an educational expense because you

The **opportunity cost** of some decision is the value of the next best alternative that must be given up because of that decision (for example, working instead of going to school).

would have incurred these costs whether or not you attend college. On balance, college is probably costing you much more than you think.

Idea 2: Attempts to Repeal the Laws of Supply and Demand—The Market Strikes Back

When a commodity is in short supply, its price naturally tends to rise. Sometimes disgruntled consumers badger politicians into "solving" this problem by making the high prices illegal—by imposing a ceiling on the price. Similarly, when supplies are abundant—say, when fine weather produces extraordinarily abundant crops—prices tend to fall. Falling prices naturally dismay producers, who often succeed in getting legislators to impose price floors.

But such attempts to repeal the laws of supply and demand usually backfire and sometimes produce results virtually the opposite of those intended. Where rent controls are adopted to protect tenants, housing grows scarce because the law makes it unprofitable to build and maintain apartments. When price floors are placed under agricultural products, surpluses pile up because people buy less.

As we will see in Chapter 4 and elsewhere in this book, such consequences of interference with the price mechanism are no accident. They follow inevitably from the way in which free markets work.

Idea 3: The Surprising Principle of Comparative Advantage

China today produces many products that Americans buy in huge quantities—including toys, textiles, and electronic equipment. American manufacturers often complain about Chinese competition and demand protection from the flood of imports that, in their view, threatens American standards of living. Is this view justified?

Economists think not. They maintain that both sides normally gain from international trade. But what if the Chinese were able to produce *everything* more cheaply than we can? Wouldn't Americans be thrown out of work and our nation be impoverished?

A remarkable result, called the law of *comparative advantage*, shows that, even in this extreme case, the two nations can still benefit by trading and that each can gain as a result! We will explain this principle first in Chapter 3 and then more fully in Chapter 34. But for now a simple parable will make the reason clear.

Suppose Sally grows up on a farm and is a whiz at plowing. But she is also a successful country singer who earns $4,000 per performance. Should Sally turn down singing engagements to leave time to work the fields? Of course not. Instead, she should hire Alfie, a much less efficient farmer, to do the plowing for her. Sally may be better at plowing, but she earns so much more by singing that it makes sense for her to specialize in that and leave the farming to Alfie. Although Alfie is a less skilled farmer than Sally, he is an even worse singer.

So Alfie earns his living in the job at which he at least has a *comparative* advantage (his farming is not as inferior as his singing), and both Alfie and Sally gain. The same is true of two countries. Even if one of them is more efficient at everything, both countries can gain by producing the things they do best *comparatively*.

Idea 4: Trade Is a Win-Win Situation

One of the most fundamental ideas of economics is that *both* parties must expect to gain something in a *voluntary* exchange. Otherwise, why would they both agree to trade? This principle seems self-evident. Yet it is amazing how often it is ignored in practice.

For example, it was widely believed for centuries that in international trade one country's gain from an exchange must be the other country's loss (Chapter 34). Analogously, some people feel instinctively that if Ms. A profits handsomely from a deal with Mr. B then Mr. B must have been exploited. Laws sometimes prohibit mutually beneficial exchanges between buyers and sellers—as when a loan transaction is banned because the interest rate is "too high" (Chapter 19), or when a willing worker is condemned to remain unemployed because the wage she is offered is "too low" (Chapter 20), or when the resale of tickets to sporting events ("ticket scalping") is outlawed even though the buyer is happy to get the ticket that he could not obtain at a lower price (Chapter 4).

In every one of these cases—and many more—well-intentioned but misguided reasoning blocks the mutual gains that arise from voluntary exchange, and thereby interferes with one of the most basic functions of an economic system (see Chapter 3).

Idea 5: The Importance of Thinking at the Margin

We will devote many pages of this book to explaining and extolling a type of decision-making process called *marginal analysis* (see especially Chapters 5, 7, 8, and 14), which we can best illustrate through an example.

Suppose an airline is told by its accountants that the full average cost of transporting one passenger from Los Angeles to New York is $300. Can the airline profit by offering a reduced fare of $200 to students who fly on a standby basis? The surprising answer is probably yes. The reason is that most of the costs of the flight must be paid whether the plane carries 20 passengers or 120 passengers.

Costs such as maintenance, landing rights, and ground crews are irrelevant to the decision of whether to carry *additional* standby passengers at reduced rates. The only costs that *are* relevant are the *extra* costs of writing and processing additional tickets, the food and beverages consumed by these passengers, the additional fuel required, and so on. These so-called *marginal costs* are probably quite small in this example. Any passenger who pays the airline more than its marginal cost adds something to the company's profit. So it probably is more profitable to let students ride at low fares than to leave the seats empty.

In many real cases, a failure to understand marginal analysis leads decision makers to reject advantageous possibilities like the reduced fare in our example. These people are misled by using *average* rather than *marginal* cost figures in their calculations—an error that can be quite costly.

Idea 6: Externalities—A Shortcoming of the Market Cured by Market Methods

Markets are very adept at producing the goods that consumers want and in just the quantities they desire. They do so by rewarding those who respond to what consumers want and who produce these products economically. This all works out well as long as each exchange involves only the buyer and the seller—and no one else. But some transactions affect third parties who were not involved in the decision. Examples abound. Electric utilities that generate power for Midwestern states also produce pollution that kills freshwater fish in upstate New York. A farmer sprays crops with toxic pesticides, but the poison seeps into the groundwater and affects the health of neighboring communities.

Such social costs are called *externalities* because they affect parties *external* to the economic transactions that cause them. Externalities escape the control of the market mechanism because no financial incentive motivates polluters to minimize the damage they do—as we will learn in Chapters 15 and 17. So business firms make their products as cheaply as possible, disregarding any environmental harm they may cause.

Yet Chapters 15 and 17 will point out a way for the government to use the market mechanism to control undesirable externalities. If the electric utility and the farmer are charged for the clean air and water they use up, just as they are charged for any coal and fertilizer they consume, then they will have a financial incentive to reduce the amount of pollution they generate. Thus, in this case, economists believe that market methods are often the best way to cure one of the market's most important shortcomings.

Idea 7: The Trade-Off between Efficiency and Equality

Wages and income have grown more unequal in the United States since the late 1970s. Highly skilled workers have pulled away from low-skilled workers. The rich have grown richer while the poor have become (relatively) poorer. Yet U.S. unemployment has been much lower than that in Europe for many years. And in many European countries inequality has not grown more extreme.

Many economists see these phenomena as two sides of the same coin. Europe and the United States have made different choices regarding how best to balance the conflicting claims of greater economic efficiency (more output and jobs) versus greater equality.

Roughly speaking, the American solution is to let markets work to promote efficiency—something they are very good at doing—with only minimal government interferences to reduce economic inequalities. (Some of these interferences are studied in Chapter 21.) But much of continental Europe takes a different view. They find it scandalous that many Americans work for less than $6 per hour, with virtually no fringe benefits and no job security. European laws mandate not only relatively high minimum wages but also substantial fringe benefits and employment protections. Of course, European taxes must be much higher to pay for these programs.

As economists see it, each system's virtue is also its vice. There is an agonizing *trade-off* between the *size* of a nation's output and the degree of *equality* with which that output is distributed. European-style policies designed to divide the proverbial economic pie more equally inadvertently can cause the size of the pie to shrink. American-style arrangements that promote maximal efficiency and output may permit or even breed huge inequalities. Which system is better? There is no clear answer, but we will examine the issue in detail in Chapter 21.

■ Idea 8: Government Policies Can Limit Economic Fluctuations—But Don't Always Succeed

One of the most persistent problems of market economies has been their tendency to go through cycles of boom and bust. The booms, as we shall see, often bring inflation. The busts always raise unemployment. Years ago, economists, business people, and politicians viewed these fluctuations as inevitable: There was nothing the government could or should do about them.

That view is now considered obsolete. As we will learn in Part VI, and especially Part VII, modern governments have an arsenal of weapons that they can and do deploy to try to mitigate fluctuations in their national economies—to limit both inflation and unemployment. Some of these weapons constitute what is called *fiscal policy*: control over taxes and government spending. Others come from *monetary policy*: control over money and interest rates.

But *trying* to tame the business cycle is not the same as *succeeding*. Economic fluctuations remain with us, and one reason is that the government's fiscal and monetary policies sometimes fail—for both political and economic reasons. As we will see in Part VII, policymakers do not always make the right decisions. And even when they do, the economy does not always react as expected. Furthermore, for reasons we will explain later, it is not always clear what the "right" decision is.

■ Idea 9: The Short-Run Trade-Off between Inflation and Unemployment

The U.S. economy was lucky in the second half of the 1990s. A set of fortuitous events—falling energy prices, tumbling computer prices, a rising dollar, and so on—pushed inflation down even while unemployment fell to its lowest level in almost 30 years. During the 1970s and early 1980s, the United States was not so fortunate. Skyrocketing prices for food and, especially, energy sent both inflation and unemployment up to extraordinary heights. In both episodes, then, inflation and unemployment moved in the same direction.

But economists maintain that neither of these two episodes was "normal." When we are experiencing neither unusually good luck (as in the 1990s) nor exceptionally bad luck (as in the 1970s), there is a *trade-off between inflation and unemployment*—meaning that low unemployment normally makes inflation rise and high unemployment normally makes inflation fall. We will study the mechanisms underlying this trade-off in Parts VI and VII, especially in Chapter 33. It poses one of the fundamental dilemmas of national economic policy.

■ Idea 10: Productivity Growth Is (Almost) Everything in the Long Run

In Geneva, Switzerland, today, a worker in a watch factory turns out more than 100 times as many mechanical watches per year as her ancestors did three centuries earlier. The *productivity* of labor (output per hour of work) in cotton production has probably gone up more than 1,000-fold in 200 years. It is estimated that rising labor productivity has increased the standard of living of a typical American worker more than sevenfold in the past century. (See Chapters 16 and 24.)

Other economic issues such as unemployment, monopoly, and inequality are important to us all and will receive much attention in this book. But in the long run, nothing has as great an effect on our material well-being and the amounts society can afford to spend on hospitals, schools, and social amenities as the rate of growth of productivity—the amount that an average worker can produce in an hour. Chapter 24 points out that what appears to be a small increase in productivity growth can have a huge effect on a country's standard of living over a long period of time because productivity compounds like the interest on savings in a bank. Similarly, a slowdown in productivity growth that persists for a substantial number of years can have a devastating effect on living standards.

■ Epilogue

These ideas are some of the more fundamental concepts you will find in this book—ideas that we hope you will retain beyond the final exam. There is no need to master them right now, for you will hear much more about each as you progress through the book. By the end of the course, you may be amazed to see how natural, or even obvious, they will seem.

■ INSIDE THE ECONOMIST'S TOOL KIT

We turn now from the kinds of *issues* economists deal with to some of the tools they use to grapple with them.

■ Economics as a Discipline

Although economics is clearly the most rigorous of the social sciences, it nevertheless looks decidedly more "social" than "scientific" when compared with, say, physics. An economist must be a jack of several trades, borrowing modes of analysis from numerous fields. Mathematical reasoning is often used in economics, but so is historical study. And neither looks quite the same as when practiced by a mathematician or a historian. Statistics play a major role in modern economic inquiry, although economists had to modify standard statistical procedures to fit their kinds of data.

■ The Need for Abstraction

Some students find economics unduly abstract and "unrealistic." The stylized world envisioned by economic theory seems only a distant cousin to the world they know. There is an old joke about three people—a chemist, a physicist, and an economist—stranded on an desert island with an ample supply of canned food but no tools to open the cans. The chemist thinks that lighting a fire under the cans would burst the cans. The physicist advocates building a catapult with which to smash the cans against some boulders. The economist's suggestion? "Assume a can opener."

Economic theory *does* make some unrealistic assumptions; you will encounter some of them in this book. But some abstraction from reality is necessary because of the incredible complexity of the economic world, not because economists like to sound absurd.

Compare the chemist's simple task of explaining the interactions of compounds in a chemical reaction with the economist's complex task of explaining the interactions of people in an economy. Are molecules motivated by greed or altruism, by envy or ambition? Do they ever imitate other molecules? Do forecasts about them influence their behavior? People, of course, do all these things and many, many more. It is therefore vastly more difficult to predict human behavior than to predict chemical reactions. If economists tried to keep track of every feature of human behavior, they would never get anywhere. Thus:

Abstraction from unimportant details is necessary to understand the functioning of anything as complex as the economy.

An analogy will make clear why economists **abstract** from details. Suppose you have just arrived for the first time in Los Angeles. You are now at the Los Angeles Civic Center—the point marked *A* in Maps 1 and 2, which are alternative maps of part of Los Angeles. You want to drive to the Los Angeles County Museum of Art, point *B* on each map. Which map would be more useful?

Map 1 has complete details of the Los Angeles road system. This makes it hard to read and hard to use as a way to find the art museum. For this purpose, Map 1 is far too detailed, although for some other purposes (for example, locating some small street in Hollywood) it may be far better than Map 2.

In contrast, Map 2 omits many minor roads—you might say they are *assumed away*—so that the freeways and major arteries stand out more clearly. As a result of this simplification, several routes from the Civic Center to the Los Angeles County Museum

SOURCE: From *The Wall Street Journal*. Permission, Cartoon Features Syndicate.

"Yes, John, we'd all like to make economics less dismal . . ."

Note: The 19th-century British writer, Thomas Carlyle, described economics as the "dismal science," a label that stuck.

Abstraction means ignoring many details so as to focus on the most important elements of a problem.

MAP 1   Detailed Road Map of Los Angeles

Map © by Rand McNally, R.L.04-S-14. Reprinted by permission.

Note: Point A marks the Los Angeles Civic Center and Point B marks the Los Angeles County Museum of Art.

| MAP 2 | Major Los Angeles Arteries and Freeways |

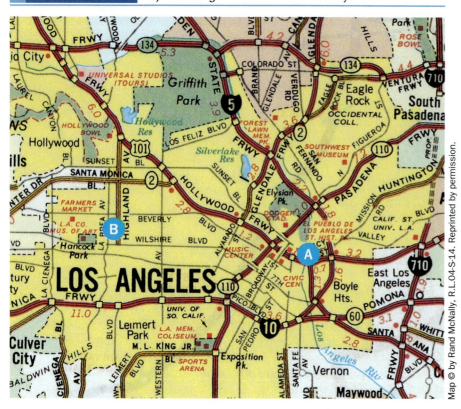

Map © by Rand McNally, R.L.04-S-14. Reprinted by permission.

| MAP 3 | Greater Los Angeles Freeways |

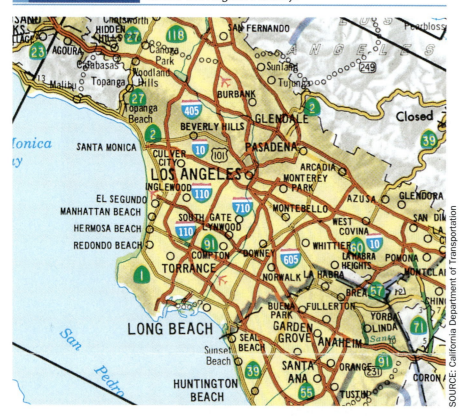

SOURCE: California Department of Transportation

of Art emerge. For example, we can take the Hollywood Freeway west to Alvarado Boulevard, go south to Wilshire Boulevard, and then head west again. Although we *might* find a shorter route by poring over the details in Map 1, most strangers to the city would be better off with Map 2. Similarly, economists try to *abstract* from a lot of confusing details while retaining the essentials.

Map 3, however, illustrates that simplification can go too far. It shows little more than the major interstate routes that pass through the greater Los Angeles area, and therefore will not help a visitor find the art museum. Of course, this map was never intended to be used as a detailed tourist guide, which brings us to an important point:

There is no such thing as one "right" degree of abstraction and simplification for all analytic purposes. The proper degree of abstraction depends on the objective of the analysis. A model that is a gross oversimplification for one purpose may be needlessly complicated for another.

Economists are constantly seeking analogies to Map 2 rather than Map 3, treading the thin line between useful generalizations about complex issues and gross distortions of the pertinent facts. For example, suppose you want to learn why some people are fabulously rich while others are abjectly poor. People differ in many ways, too many to enumerate, much less to study. The economist must ignore most of these details to focus on the important ones. The color of a person's hair or eyes is probably not important for the problem but, unfortunately, the color of his or her skin probably is because racial discrimination can depress a person's income. Height and weight may not matter, but education probably does. Proceeding in this way, we can pare Map 1 down to the manageable dimensions of Map 2. But there is a danger of going too far, stripping away some of the crucial factors, so that we wind up with Map 3.

The Role of Economic Theory

Some students find economics "too theoretical." To see why we can't avoid it, let's consider what we mean by a **theory.**

To an economist or natural scientist, the word *theory* means something different from what it means in common speech. In science, a theory is *not* an untested assertion of alleged fact. The statement that aspirin provides protection against heart attacks is not a theory; it is a *hypothesis*, which will prove to be true or false once the right sorts of experiments have been completed. Instead, a theory is a deliberate simplification (abstraction) of reality that attempts to explain how some relationships work. It is an *explanation* of the mechanism behind observed phenomena. Thus, gravity forms the basis of theories that describe and explain the paths of the planets. Similarly, Keynesian theory (discussed in Parts VI and VII) seeks to describe and explain how government policies affect unemployment and prices in the national economy.

People who have never studied economics often draw a false distinction between *theory* and *practical policy*. Politicians and business people, in particular, often reject abstract economic theory as something that is best ignored by "practical" people. The irony of these statements is that:

It is precisely the concern for policy that makes economic theory so necessary and important.

To analyze policy options, economists are forced to deal with *possibilities that have not actually occurred.* For example, to learn how to shorten periods of high unemployment, they must investigate whether a proposed new policy that has never been tried can help. Or to determine which environmental programs will be most effective, they must understand how and why a market economy produces pollution and what might happen if the government taxed industrial waste discharges and automobile emissions. Such questions require some *theorizing*, not just examination of the facts, because we need to consider possibilities that have never occurred.

The facts, moreover, can sometimes be highly misleading. Data often indicate that two variables move up and down together. But this statistical **correlation** does not prove that either variable *causes* the other. For example, when it rains, people drive their cars more slowly and there are also more traffic accidents. But no one thinks that it is the slower driving that causes more accidents when it's raining. Rather, we understand that both phenomena are caused by a common underlying factor—more rain. How do we know this? Not just by looking at the correlation between data on accidents and driving speeds. Data alone tell us little about cause and effect. We must use some simple *theory* as part of our analysis. In this case, the theory might explain that drivers are more apt to have accidents on rain-slicked roads.

Similarly, we must use theoretical analysis, and not just data alone, to understand *how*, if at all, different government policies will lead to lower unemployment or *how* a tax on emissions will reduce pollution.

Statistical correlation need not imply causation. Some theory is usually needed to interpret data.

What Is an Economic Model?

An **economic model** is a representation of a theory or a part of a theory, often used to gain insight into cause and effect. The notion of a "model" is familiar enough to children; and economists—like other scientists—use the term in much the same way that children do.

A child's model airplane looks and operates much like the real thing, but it is much smaller and simpler, so it is easier to manipulate and understand. Engineers for Boeing also build models of planes. Although their models are far larger and much more elaborate than a child's toy, they use them for much the same purposes: to observe the workings of these aircraft "up close" and to experiment with them to see how the models behave under different circumstances. ("What happens if I do this?") From

A **theory** is a deliberate simplification of relationships used to explain how those relationships work.

Two variables are said to be **correlated** if they tend to go up or down together. Correlation need not imply causation.

An **economic model** is a simplified, small-scale version of some aspect of the economy. Economic models are often expressed in equations, by graphs, or in words.

SOURCE: Science Museum/Science & Society Picture Library

A. W. Phillips built this model in the early 1950s to illustrate Keynesian theory.

these experiments, they make educated guesses as to how the real-life version will perform.

Economists use models for similar purposes. The late A. W. Phillips, the famous engineer-turned-economist who discovered the "Phillips curve" (discussed in Chapter 33), was talented enough to construct a working model of the determination of national income in a simple economy by using colored water flowing through pipes. For years this contraption has graced the basement of the London School of Economics. Although we will explain the models with words and diagrams, Phillips's engineering background enabled him to depict the theory with tubes, valves, and pumps.

Because many of the models used in this book are depicted in diagrams, for those of you who need review, we explain the construction and use of various types of graphs in the appendix to this chapter. Don't be put off by seemingly abstract models. Think of them as useful road maps. And remember how hard it would be to find your way around Los Angeles without one.

■ Reasons for Disagreements: Imperfect Information and Value Judgments

"If all the earth's economists were laid end to end, they could not reach an agreement," the saying goes. Politicians and reporters are fond of pointing out that economists can be found on both sides of many public policy issues. If economics is a science, why do economists so often disagree? After all, astronomers do not debate whether the earth revolves around the sun or vice versa.

This question reflects a misunderstanding of the nature of science. Disputes are normal at the frontier of any science. For example, astronomers once did argue vociferously over whether the earth revolves around the sun. Nowadays, they argue about gamma-ray bursts, dark matter, and other esoterica. These arguments go mostly unnoticed by the public because few of us understand what they are talking about. But economics is a *social* science, so its disputes are aired in public and all sorts of people feel competent to join economic debates.

Furthermore, economists actually agree on much more than is commonly supposed. Virtually all economists, regardless of their politics, agree that taxing polluters is one of the best ways to protect the environment (see Chapters 15 and 17), that rent controls can ruin a city (Chapter 4), and that free trade among nations is usually preferable to the erection of barriers through tariffs and quotas (see Chapter 34). The list could go on and on. It is probably true that the issues about which economists agree *far* exceed the subjects on which they disagree.

Finally, many disputes among economists are not scientific disputes at all. Sometimes the pertinent facts are simply unknown. For example, you will learn in Chapter 17 that the appropriate financial penalty to levy on a polluter depends on quantitative estimates of the harm done by the pollutant. But good estimates of this damage may not be available. Similarly, although there is wide scientific agreement that the earth is slowly warming, there are disagreements over how costly global warming may be. Such disputes make it difficult to agree on a concrete policy proposal.

Another important source of disagreements is that economists, like other people, come in all political stripes: conservative, middle-of-the-road, liberal, radical. Each may have different values, and so each may hold a different view of the "right" solution to a public policy problem—even if they agree on the underlying analysis. Here are two examples:

1. We suggested early in this chapter that policies that lower inflation are likely to raise unemployment. Many economists believe they can measure the amount of unemployment that must be endured to reduce inflation by a given amount. But they disagree about whether it is worth having, say, three million more people out of work for a year to cut the inflation rate by 1 percent.

2. In designing an income tax, society must decide how much of the burden to put on upper-income taxpayers. Some people believe the rich should pay a disproportionate share of the taxes. Others disagree, believing it is fairer to levy the same income tax rate on everyone.

Economists cannot answer questions like these any more than nuclear physicists could have determined whether dropping the atomic bomb on Hiroshima was a good idea. The decisions rest on moral judgments that can be made only by the citizenry through its elected officials.

Although economic science can contribute theoretical and factual knowledge on a particular issue, the final decision on policy questions often rests either on information that is not currently available or on social values and ethical opinions about which people differ, or on both.

SUMMARY

1. To help you get the most out of your first course in economics, we have devised a list of ten important ideas that you will want to retain *Beyond the Final Exam*. Briefly, they are the following:

   a. **Opportunity cost** is the correct measure of cost.

   b. Attempts to fight market forces often backfire.

   c. Nations can gain from trade by exploiting their *comparative advantages*.

   d. Both parties gain in a voluntary exchange.

   e. Good decisions typically require *marginal analysis* that weighs incremental costs against incremental benefits.

   f. Externalities may cause the market mechanism to malfunction, but this defect can be repaired by market methods.

   g. Governments have tools that can mitigate cycles of boom and bust, but these tools are imperfect.

   h. There is a trade-off between efficiency and equality. Many policies that promote one damage the other.

   i. In the short run, policy makers face a trade-off between inflation and unemployment. Policies that reduce one normally increase the other.

   j. In the long run, *productivity* is almost the only thing that matters for a society's material well-being.

2. Common sense is not always a reliable guide in explaining economic issues or to making economic decisions.

3. Because of the great complexity of human behavior, economists are forced to *abstract* from many details, to make generalizations that they know are not quite true, and to organize what knowledge they have in terms of some theoretical structure called a "model."

4. Correlation need not imply causation.

5. Economists use simplified models to understand the real world and predict its behavior, much as a child uses a model railroad to learn how trains work.

6. Although these models, if skillfully constructed, can illuminate important economic problems, they rarely can answer the questions that confront policy makers. Value judgments are needed for this purpose, and the economist is no better equipped than anyone else to make them.

KEY TERMS

Opportunity cost 4

Abstraction 9

Theory 11

Correlated 11

Economic Model 11

DISCUSSION QUESTIONS

1. Think about how you would construct a model of how your college is governed. Which officers and administrators would you include and exclude from your model if the objective were one of the following:

   a. To explain how decisions on financial aid are made

   b. To explain the quality of the faculty

   Relate this to the map example in the chapter.

2. Relate the process of abstraction to the way you take notes in a lecture. Why do you not try to transcribe every word uttered by the lecturer? Why don't you write down just the title of the lecture and stop there? How do you decide, roughly speaking, on the correct amount of detail?

3. Explain why a government policy maker cannot afford to ignore economic theory.

APPENDIX A *Using Graphs: A Review*[1]

As noted in the chapter, economists often explain and analyze models with the help of graphs. Indeed, this book is full of them. But that is not the only reason for studying how graphs work. Most people will deal with graphs in the future, perhaps frequently. You will see them in newspapers. If you become a doctor, you will use graphs to keep track of your patients' progress. If you join a business firm, you will use them to check profit or performance at a glance. This appendix introduces some of the techniques of graphic analysis—tools you will use throughout the book and, more important, very likely throughout your working career.

■ GRAPHS USED IN ECONOMIC ANALYSIS

Economic graphs are invaluable because they can display a large quantity of data quickly and because they facilitate data interpretation and analysis. They enable the eye to take in at a glance important statistical relationships that would be far less apparent from written descriptions or long lists of numbers.

■ TWO-VARIABLE DIAGRAMS

Much of the economic analysis found in this and other books requires that we keep track of two **variables** simultaneously.

A variable is something measured by a number; it is used to analyze what happens to other things when the size of that number changes (varies).

For example, in studying how markets operate, we will want to keep one eye on the *price* of a commodity and the other on the *quantity* of that commodity that is bought and sold.

For this reason, economists frequently find it useful to display real or imaginary figures in a two-variable diagram, which simultaneously represents the behavior of two economic variables. The numerical value of one variable is measured along the horizontal line at the bottom of the graph (called the *horizontal axis*), starting from the **origin** (the point labeled "0"), and the numerical value of the other variable is measured up the vertical line on the left side of the graph (called the *vertical axis*), also starting from the origin.

The "0" point in the lower-left corner of a graph where the axes meet is called the origin. Both variables are equal to zero at the origin.

Figures 1(a) and 1(b) are typical graphs of economic analysis. They depict an imaginary *demand curve*, represented by the blue dots in Figure 1(a) and the heavy blue line in Figure 1(b). The graphs show the price of natural gas on their vertical axes and the quantity of gas people want to buy at each price on the horizontal axes.

The dots in Figure 1(a) are connected by the continuous blue curve labeled *DD* in Figure 1(b).

Economic diagrams are generally read just as one would read latitudes and longitudes on a map. On the demand curve in Figure 1, the point marked *a* represents a hypothetical combination of price and quantity of natural gas demanded by customers in St. Louis. By drawing a horizontal line leftward from that point to the vertical axis, we learn that at this point the average price for gas in St. Louis is $3 per thousand cubic feet. By dropping a line straight down to the horizontal axis, we find that consumers want 80 billion cubic feet per year at this price, just as the statistics in Table 1 show. The other points on the graph give similar information. For example, point *b*

| FIGURE 1 | A Hypothetical Demand Curve for Natural Gas in St. Louis |

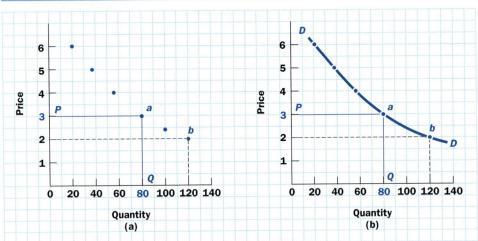

Note: Price is in dollars per thousand cubic feet; quantity is in billions of cubic feet per year.

---

[1] Students who have some acquaintance with geometry and feel quite comfortable with graphs can safely skip this appendix.

TABLE 1

Quantities of Natural Gas Demanded at Various Prices

Price (per thousand cubic feet)	$2	$3	$4	$5	$6
Quantity demanded (billions of cubic feet per year)	120	80	56	38	20

indicates that if natural gas in St. Louis costs only $2 per thousand cubic feet, quantity demanded would be higher—it would reach 120 billion cubic feet per year.

Notice that information about price and quantity is *all* we can learn from the diagram. The demand curve will not tell us what kinds of people live in St. Louis, the sizes of their homes, or the condition of their furnaces. It tells us about the quantity demanded at each possible price—no more, no less.

A diagram abstracts from many details, some of which may be quite interesting, so as to focus on the two variables of primary interest—in this case, the price of natural gas and the amount of gas that is demanded at each price. All of the diagrams used in this book share this basic feature. They cannot tell the reader the "whole story," any more than a map's latitude and longitude figures for a particular city can make someone an authority on that city.

■ THE DEFINITION AND MEASUREMENT OF SLOPE

One of the most important features of economic diagrams is the rate at which the line or curve being sketched runs uphill or downhill as we move to the right. The demand curve in Figure 1 clearly slopes downhill (the price falls) as we follow it to the right (that is, as consumers demand more gas). In such instances, we say that the curve has a negative slope, or is negatively sloped, because one variable falls as the other one rises.

The **slope of a straight line** is the ratio of the vertical change to the corresponding horizontal change as we move to the right along the line or, as it is often said, the ratio of the "rise" over the "run."

The four panels of Figure 2 show all possible types of slope for a straight-line relationship between two unnamed variables called Y (measured along the vertical axis) and X (measured along the horizontal axis). Figure 2(a) shows a *negative slope*, much like our demand curve in the previous graph. Figure 2(b) shows a *positive slope*, because variable Y rises (we go uphill) as variable X rises (as we move to the right). Figure 2(c) shows a *zero slope*, where the value of Y is the same irrespective of the value of X. Figure 2(d) shows an *infinite slope*, meaning that the value of X is the same irrespective of the value of Y.

Slope is a numerical concept, not just a qualitative one. The two panels of Figure 3 show two positively sloped straight lines with different slopes. The line in Figure 3(b) is clearly steeper. But by how much? The labels should help you compute the answer. In Figure 3(a) a horizontal movement, AB, of 10 units (13 − 3) corresponds to a vertical movement, BC, of 1 unit (9 − 8). So the slope is $BC/AB = 1/10$. In Figure 3(b), the same horizontal movement of 10 units corresponds to a vertical movement of 3 units (11 − 8). So the slope is 3/10, which is larger—the rise divided by the run is greater in Figure 3 (b).

By definition, the slope of any particular straight line remains the same, no matter where on that line we choose to measure it. That is why we can pick any horizontal distance, AB, and the corresponding slope triangle, ABC, to measure slope. But this is not true for curved lines.

Curved lines also have slopes, but the numerical value of the slope differs at every point along the curve as we move from left to right.

FIGURE 2   Different Types of Slope of a Straight-Line Graph

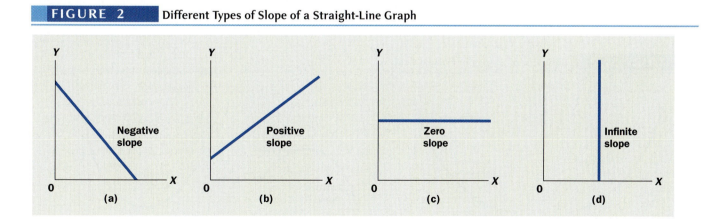

FIGURE 3   How to Measure Slope

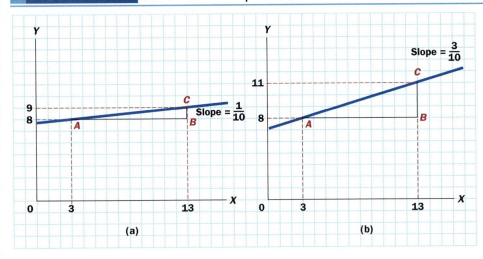

(a)

(b)

$$= \frac{(1 - 5)}{(3 - 1)} = \frac{-4}{2} = -2$$

A similar calculation yields the slope of the curve at point *R*, which, as we can see from Figure 5, must be smaller numerically. That is, the tangent line *rr* is less steep than line *tt*:

Slope at point *R* = Slope of line *rr*

$$= \frac{(5 - 7)}{(8 - 6)} = \frac{-2}{2} = -1$$

EXERCISE Show that the slope of the curve at point G is about 1.

The four panels of Figure 4 provide some examples of *slopes of curved lines.* The curve in Figure 4(a) has a negative slope everywhere, and the curve in Figure 4(b) has a positive slope everywhere. But these are not the only possibilities. In Figure 4(c) we encounter a curve that has a positive slope at first but a negative slope later on. Figure 4(d) shows the opposite case: a negative slope followed by a positive slope.

We can measure the slope of a smooth curved line numerically *at any particular point* by drawing a *straight* line that *touches*, but does not *cut*, the curve at the point in question. Such a line is called a **tangent** to the curve.

The slope of a curved line at a particular point is defined as the slope of the straight line that is tangent to the curve at that point.

Figure 5 shows tangents to the blue curve at two points. Line *tt* is tangent at point *T*, and line *rr* is tangent at point *R*. We can measure the slope of the curve at these two points by applying the definition. The calculation for point *T*, then, is the following:

Slope at point *T* = Slope of line *tt*

$$= \frac{\text{Distance BC}}{\text{Distance BA}}$$

What would happen if we tried to apply this graphical technique to the high point in Figure 4(c) or to the low point in Figure 4(d)? Take a ruler and try it. The tangents that you construct should be horizontal, meaning that they should have a slope exactly equal to zero. It is always true that where the slope of a *smooth* curve changes from positive to negative, or vice versa, there will be at least one point whose slope is zero.

Curves shaped like smooth hills, as in Figure 4(c), have a zero slope at their *highest* point. Curves shaped like valleys, as in Figure 4(d), have a zero slope at their *lowest* point.

■ RAYS THROUGH THE ORIGIN AND 45° LINES

The point at which a straight line cuts the vertical (*Y*) axis is called the *Y*-intercept.

The *Y*-intercept of a line or a curve is the point at which it touches the vertical axis (the *Y*-axis). The *X*-intercept is defined similarly.

For example, the *Y*-intercept of the line in Figure 3(a) is a bit less than 8.

FIGURE 4   Behavior of Slopes in Curved Graphs

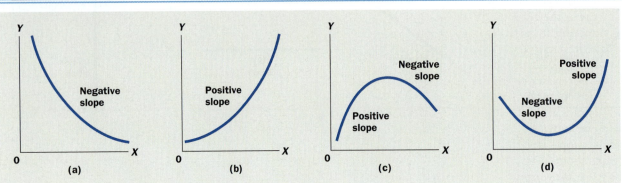

(a)

(b)

(c)

(d)

How to Measure Slope at a Point on a Curved Graph

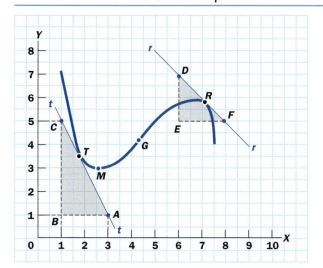

$$\text{Slope} = \frac{\text{Vertical change}}{\text{Horizontal change}} = 1$$

This implies that the vertical change and the horizontal change are always equal, so the two variables must always remain equal. Any point along that ray (for example, point A) is exactly equal in distance from the horizontal and vertical axes (length DA = length CA)—the number on the X-axis (the abscissa) will be the same as the number on the Y-axis (the ordinate).

Rays through the origin with a slope of 1 are called 45° lines because they form an angle of 45° with the horizontal axis. A 45° line marks off points where the variables measured on each axis have equal values.[2]

If a point representing some data is above the 45° line, we know that the value of Y exceeds the value of X. Similarly, whenever we find a point below the 45° line, we know that X is larger than Y.

■ SQUEEZING THREE DIMENSIONS INTO TWO: CONTOUR MAPS

Sometimes problems involve more than two variables, so two dimensions just are not enough to depict them on a graph. This is unfortunate, because the surface of a sheet of paper is only two-dimensional. When we study a business firm's decision-making process, for example, we may want to keep track simultaneously of three variables: how much labor it employs, how much raw material it imports from foreign countries, and how much output it creates.

Luckily, economists can use a well-known device for collapsing three dimensions into two—a *contour map*. Figure 7 is a contour map of the summit of the highest mountain in the world, Mt. Everest, on the border of

FIGURE 6   Rays Through the Origin

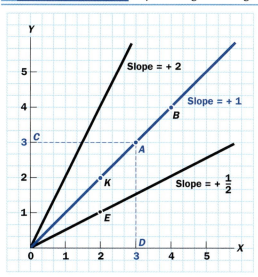

Lines whose Y-intercept is zero have so many special uses in economics and other disciplines that they have been given a special name: a **ray through the origin**, or a **ray**.

Figure 6 shows three rays through the origin, and the slope of each is indicated in the diagram. The ray in the center (whose slope is 1) is particularly useful in many economic applications because it marks points where X and Y are equal (as long as X and Y are measured in the same units). For example, at point A we have $X = 3$ and $Y = 3$; at point B, $X = 4$ and $Y = 4$. A similar relation holds at any other point on that ray.

How do we know that this is always true for a ray whose slope is 1? If we start from the origin (where both X and Y are zero) and the slope of the ray is 1, we know from the definition of slope that

SOURCE: Mount Everest. Alpenvereinskarte. Vienna: Kartographische Anstalt Freytag-Berndt und Artaria, 1957, 1988.

FIGURE 7   A Geographic Contour Map

---

[2] The definition assumes that both variables are measured in the same units.

Nepal and Tibet. On some of the irregularly shaped "rings" on this map, we find numbers (like 8500) indicating the height (in meters) above sea level at that particular spot on the mountain. Thus, unlike the more usual sort of map, which gives only latitudes and longitudes, this contour map (also called a topographical map) exhibits *three* pieces of information about each point: latitude, longitude, and altitude.

Figure 8 looks more like the contour maps encountered in economics. It shows how some third variable, called Z (think of it as a firm's output, for example), varies as we change either variable X (think of it as a firm's employment of labor) or variable Y (think of it as the use of imported raw material). Just like the map of Mt. Everest, any point on the diagram conveys three pieces of data. At point A, we can read off the values of X and Y in the conventional way (X is 30 and Y is 40), and we can also note the value of Z by finding out on which contour line point A falls. (It is on the $Z = 20$ contour.) So point A is able to tell us that 30 hours of labor and 40 yards of cloth produce 20 units of output per day. The contour line that indicates 20 units of output shows the various combinations of labor and cloth a manufacturer can use to produce 20 units of output. Economists call such maps **production indifference maps.**

A production indifference map is a graph whose axes show the quantities of two inputs that are used to produce some output. A curve in the graph corresponds to some given

FIGURE 8   An Economic Contour Map

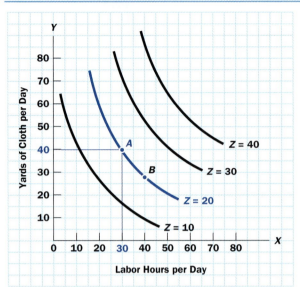

quantity of that output, and the different points on that curve show the different quantities of the two inputs that are just enough to produce the given output.

Although most of the analyses presented in this book rely on the simpler two-variable diagrams, contour maps will find their applications, especially in the appendixes to Chapters 5 and 7.

SUMMARY

1. Because graphs are used so often to portray economic models, it is important for students to acquire some understanding of their construction and use. Fortunately, the graphics used in economics are usually not very complex.

2. Most economic models are depicted in two-**variable** diagrams. We read data from these diagrams just as we read the latitude and longitude on a map: each point represents the values of two variables at the same time.

3. In some instances, three variables must be shown at once. In these cases, economists use contour maps, which, as the name suggests, show "latitude," "longitude," and "altitude" all at the same time.

4. Often, the most important property of a line or curve drawn on a diagram will be its **slope,** which is defined as the ratio of the "rise" over the "run," or the vertical change divided by the horizontal change. Curves that go uphill as we move to the right have positive slopes; curves that go downhill have negative slopes.

5. By definition, a straight line has the same slope wherever we choose to measure it. The slope of a curved line changes, but the slope at any point on the curve can be calculated by measuring the slope of a straight line tangent to the curve at that point.

KEY TERMS

Variable 14

Origin (of a graph) 14

Slope of a straight (or curved) line 15

Tangent to a curve 16

Y-intercept 16

Ray through the origin, or ray 17

45° line 17

Production indifference map 18

TEST YOURSELF

1. Portray the following hypothetical data on a two-variable diagram:

Academic Year	Total Enrollment	Enrollment in Economics Courses
1994–1995	3,000	300
1995–1996	3,100	325
1996–1997	3,200	350
1997–1998	3,300	375
1998–1999	3,400	400

Measure the slope of the resulting line, and explain what this number means.

2. From Figure 5, calculate the slope of the curve at point M.

3. Colin believes that the number of job offers he will get depends on the number of courses in which his grade is B+ or better. He concludes from observation that the following figures are typical:

Number of grades of B+ or better	0	1	2	3	4
Number of job offers	1	3	4	5	6

Put these numbers into a graph like Figure 1(a). Measure and interpret the slopes between adjacent dots.

4. In Figure 6, determine the values of X and Y at point K and at point E. What do you conclude about the slopes of the lines on which K and E are located?

5. In Figure 8, interpret the economic meaning of points A and B. What do the two points have in common? What is the difference in their economic interpretation?

THE ECONOMY: MYTH AND REALITY

E pluribus unum (Out of many, one)

MOTTO ON U.S. CURRENCY

This chapter introduces you to the U.S. economy and its role in the world. It may seem that no such introduction is necessary, for you have probably lived your entire life in the United States. Every time you work at a summer or part-time job, pay your college bills, or buy a slice of pizza, you not only participate in the American economy—you also observe something about it.

But the casual impressions we acquire in our everyday lives, though sometimes correct, are often misleading. Experience shows that most Americans—not just students—either are unaware of or harbor grave misconceptions about some of the most basic economic facts. One popular myth holds that the United States is inundated with imported goods, mostly from China. Another is that business profits account for something like a third of the price we pay for a typical good or service. Also, "everyone knows" that federal government jobs have grown rapidly over the past few decades. In fact, none of these things is true.

So, before we begin to develop theories of how the economy works, it is useful to get an accurate picture of what our economy is really like.

CONTENTS

■ THE AMERICAN ECONOMY: A THUMBNAIL SKETCH

"And may we continue to be worthy of consuming a disproportionate share of this planet's resources."

Inputs or **factors of production** are the labor, machinery, buildings, and natural resources used to make outputs.

Outputs are the goods and services that consumers and others want to acquire.

The U.S. economy is the biggest national economy on earth, for two very different reasons. First, there are a lot of us. The population of the United States is just over 300 million—making it the third most populous nation on earth after China (1.3 billion) and India (1.1 billion). That vast total includes children, retirees, full-time students, institutionalized people, and the unemployed, none of whom produce much output. But the *working population* of the United States numbers about 150 million. As long as they are reasonably productive, that many people are bound to produce vast amounts of goods and services. And they do.

But population is not the main reason why the U.S. economy is by far the world's biggest. After all, India has nearly four times the population of the United States, but its economy is considerably smaller than that of Texas. The second reason why the U.S. economy is so large is that we are a very rich country. Because American workers are among the most productive in the world, our economy produces more than $40,000 worth of goods and services for every living American—over $80,000 for every *working* American. If each of the 50 states was a separate country, California would be the fifth largest national economy on earth!

Why are some countries (like the United States) so rich and others (like India) so poor? That is one of the central questions facing economists. It is useful to think of an economic system as a machine that takes **inputs,** such as labor and other things we call **factors of production,** and transforms them into **outputs,** or the things people want to consume. The American economic machine performs this task with extraordinary

U.S. Share of World GDP—It's Nice To Be Rich

The nearly 6.5 billion people of the world produced approximately $41 trillion worth of goods and services in 2004. The United States, with only 4.5 percent of that population, turned out just under 30 percent of total output. As the accompanying graph shows, the United States is still the leader in goods and services, with about $40,000 worth of GDP produced per person (or per capita). Just seven major industrial economies (the United States, Japan, Germany, France, Italy, the United Kingdom, and Canada—which account for just under 12 percent of global population) generated 64 percent of world output.

SOURCE: International Monetary Fund, *World Economic Outlook Database, April 2005 and April 2006,* http://www.imf.org, accessed October 2006. Note: Foreign GDPs are converted to U.S. dollars using exchange rates.

2004 Gross Domestic Product (GDP) per Capita in 7 Industrial Countries

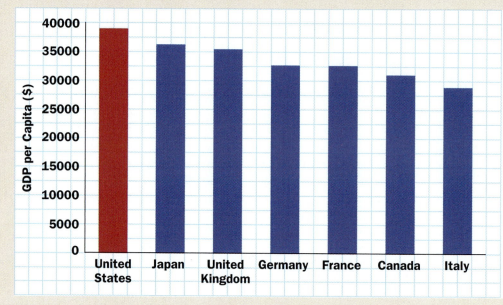

efficiency, whereas the Indian machine runs quite inefficiently (though it is improving rapidly). Learning why this is so is one of the chief reasons to study economics.

Thus, what makes the American economy the center of world attention is our unique combination of prosperity and population. There are other rich countries in the world, like Switzerland, and there are other countries with huge populations, like India. But no nation combines a huge population with high per-capita income the way the United States does. Japan, with an economy well under half the size of ours, is the only nation that comes close—although China, with its immense population, is moving up rapidly.

Although the United States is a rich and populous country, the 50 states certainly were not created equal. Population density varies enormously—from a high of about 1,200 people per square mile in crowded New Jersey to a low of just one person per square mile in the wide-open spaces of Alaska. Income variations are much less pronounced. But still, the average income in West Virginia is only about half that in Connecticut.

■ A Private-Enterprise Economy

Part of the secret of America's economic success is that free markets and private enterprise have flourished here. These days more than ever, private enterprise and capitalism are the rule, not the exception, around the globe. But the United States has taken the idea of the free market further than almost any other country. It remains the "land of opportunity."

Every country has a mixture of public and private ownership of property. Even in the darkest days of communism, Russians owned their own personal possessions. In our country, the post office and the electricity-producing Tennessee Valley Authority are enterprises of the federal government, and many cities and states own and operate mass transit facilities and sports stadiums. But the United States stands out among the world's nations as one of the most "privatized." Few industrial assets are publicly owned in the United States. Even many city bus companies and almost all utilities (such as electricity, gas, and telephones) are run as private companies in the United States. In Europe, they are often government enterprises, though there is substantial movement toward transfer of government firms to private ownership.

The United States also has one of the most "marketized" economies on earth. The standard measure of the total output of an economy is called **gross domestic product** (or **GDP**), a term that appears frequently in the news. The share of GDP that passes through markets in the United States is enormous. Although government purchases of goods and services amount to about 18 percent of GDP, much of that is purchased from private businesses. Direct government *production* of goods is extremely rare in our society.

Gross domestic product (GDP) is a measure of the size of the economy—the total amount it produces in a year. *Real GDP* adjusts this measure for changes in the purchasing power of money, that is, it corrects for inflation.

■ A Relatively "Closed" Economy

All nations trade with one another, and the United States is no exception. Our annual exports exceed $1.3 trillion and our annual imports exceed $2 trillion. That's a lot of money. But America's international trade often gets more attention than it deserves. The fact is that we still produce most of what we consume and consume most of what we produce, although the shares of imports and exports have been growing, as Figure 1 shows. In 1959, the average of exports and imports was only about 4 percent of GDP, a tiny fraction of the total. It has since gone up to about 13 percent. This is no longer negligible, but it still means that about 87 percent of what Americans buy every year is made in the United States.

Among the most severe misconceptions about the U.S. economy is the myth that this country no longer manufactures anything but, rather, imports everything from, say, China. In fact, only about 16 percent of U.S. GDP is imported, with imports from China making up about one seventh of this—or a little over 2 percent of GDP. It may surprise you to learn that we actually import far more merchandise from Canada than we do from China.

Economists use the terms *open* and *closed* to indicate how important international trade is to a nation. A common measure of "openness" is the average of exports and

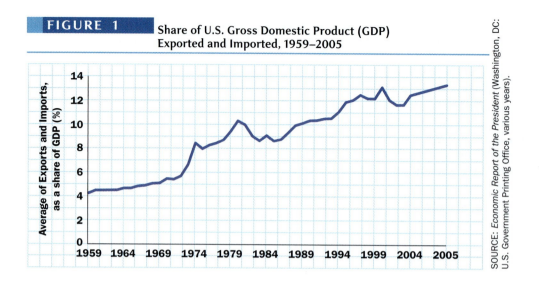

FIGURE 1   Share of U.S. Gross Domestic Product (GDP) Exported and Imported, 1959–2005

SOURCE: *Economic Report of the President* (Washington, DC: U.S. Government Printing Office, various years).

An economy is called relatively **open** if its exports and imports constitute a large share of its GDP.

An economy is considered relatively **closed** if they constitute a small share.

imports, expressed as a share of GDP. Thus, the Netherlands is considered an extremely **open economy** because it imports and exports about 59 percent of its GDP. (See Table 1.) By this criterion, the United States stands out as among the most **closed economies** of the advanced, industrial nations. We export and import a smaller share of GDP than nearly all of the countries listed in the table.

◼ A Growing Economy . . .

The next salient fact about the U.S. economy is its growth; it gets bigger almost every year (see Figure 2). Gross domestic product in 2005 was around $12.5 trillion; as noted earlier, that's over $40,000 per American. Measured in dollars of constant purchasing power,[1] the U.S. GDP was about 5 times as large in 2005 as it was in 1959. Of course, there were many more people in America in 2005 than there were 46 years earlier. But even correcting for population growth, America's real GDP *per capita* was about 2.7 times higher in 2005 than in 1959. That's still not a bad performance: Living standards nearly tripled in 46 years.

A **recession** is a period of time during which the total output of the economy falls.

TABLE 1	
Openness of Various National Economies, 2005	
	Openness
Netherlands	59%
Germany	33
Canada	33
Mexico	32
China	31
Russia	25
United Kingdom	19
United States	13
Japan	11

Note: Openness calculated as the average of imports and exports as a percentage of GDP.

SOURCE: For United States, *Economic Report of the President, 2006* (Washington, DC: U.S. Government Printing Office, Feb. 2006). For other countries, Central Intelligence Agency, *The World Factbook*, http://www.cia.org, accessed October 2006.

◼ But with Bumps along the Growth Path

Although the cumulative growth performance depicted in Figure 2 is impressive, America's economic growth has been quite irregular. We have experienced alternating periods of good and bad times, which are called *economic fluctuations* or sometimes just *business cycles*. In some years—five since 1959, to be exact—GDP actually declined. Such periods of *declining* economic activity are called **recessions.**

The bumps along the American economy's historic growth path are barely visible in Figure 2. But they stand out more clearly in Figure 3, which displays the same data in a different way. Here we plot not the *level* of real GDP each year but, rather, its *growth rate*—the percentage change from one year to the next. Now the booms and busts that delight and distress people—and swing elections—stand out clearly. From 1983 to 1984, for example, real GDP grew by

[1] This concept is called *real* GDP.

FIGURE 2   Real Gross Domestic Product (GDP) Since 1959

SOURCE: *Economic Report of the President* (Washington, DC: U.S. Government Printing Office, various years).

Note: Real (inflation-adjusted) GDP figures are in 2000 dollars.

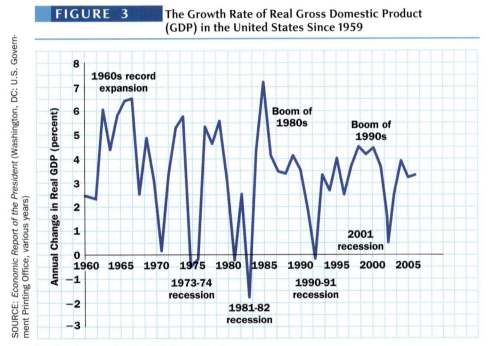

FIGURE 3   The Growth Rate of Real Gross Domestic Product (GDP) in the United States Since 1959

SOURCE: *Economic Report of the President* (Washington, DC: U.S. Government Printing Office, various years).

Note: Growth rates are for 1959–1960, 1960–1961, and so on.

over 7 percent, which helped ensure Ronald Reagan's landslide reelection. But from 1990 to 1991, real GDP actually fell slightly, which helped Bill Clinton defeat (the first) George Bush.

One important consequence of these ups and downs in economic growth is that *unemployment* varies considerably from one year to the next (see Figure 4). During the Great Depression of the 1930s, unemployment ran as high as 25 percent of the workforce. But it fell to barely over 1 percent during World War II. Just within the past few years, the national unemployment rate has been as high as 6.3 percent (in June 2003) and as low as 3.8 percent (in April 2000). In human terms, that 2.5 percentage point difference represents nearly four million jobless workers. Understanding why joblessness varies so dramatically, and what we can do about it, is another major reason for studying economics.

| FIGURE 4 | The Unemployment Rate in the United States, 1929–2006 |

SOURCE: *Economic Report of the President* (Washington, DC: U.S. Government Printing Office, various years); and Bureau of the Census, *Historical Statistics of the United States, Colonial Times to 1970* (Washington, DC: U.S. Government Printing Office, 1975).

THE INPUTS: LABOR AND CAPITAL

Let's now return to the analogy of an economy as a machine turning inputs into outputs. The most important input is human labor: the men and women who run the machines, work behind the desks, and serve you in stores.

Unemployment Rates in Europe

For roughly the first quarter-century after World War II, unemployment rates in the industrialized countries of Europe were significantly lower than those in the United States. Then, in the mid-1970s, rates of joblessness in Europe leaped, with double digits becoming common. And they have been higher than U.S. unemployment rates more or less ever since. Where employment is concerned, the U.S. economy has become the envy of Europe—with the exception of the United Kingdom. Put on a comparable basis by the U.S. Bureau of Labor Statistics, unemployment rates in the various countries in the summer of 2006 were:

U.S.	4.7%
Canada	5.5
Australia	4.9
Japan	4.2
France	8.8
Germany	10.3
Italy	7.1*
Sweden	6.3*
United Kingdom	5.6*

*Italy 2nd quarter 2006 data; Sweden 2nd quarter 2005 data; United Kingdom June 2006 data; all others August 2006 data.

■ The American Workforce: Who Is in It?

We have already mentioned that about 150 million Americans hold jobs. Almost 54 percent of these workers are men; 46 percent are women. This ratio represents a drastic change from two generations ago, when most women worked only at home (see Figure 5). Indeed, the massive entrance of women into the paid labor force was one of the major social transformations of American life during the second half of the twentieth century. In 1950, just 29 percent of women worked in the marketplace;

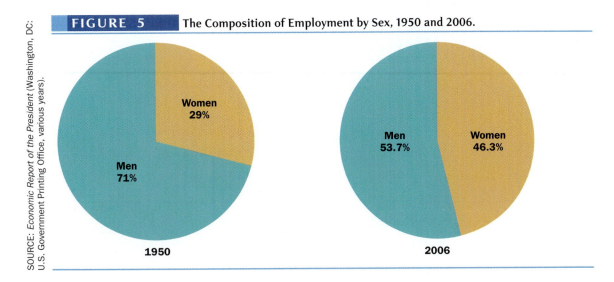

| FIGURE 5 | The Composition of Employment by Sex, 1950 and 2006. |

SOURCE: *Economic Report of the President* (Washington, DC: U.S. Government Printing Office, various years).

now about 60 percent do. As Figure 6 shows, the share of women in the labor forces of other industrial countries has also been growing. The expanding role of women in the labor market has raised many controversial questions—whether they are discriminated against (the evidence suggests that they are), whether the government should compel employers to provide maternity leave, and so on.

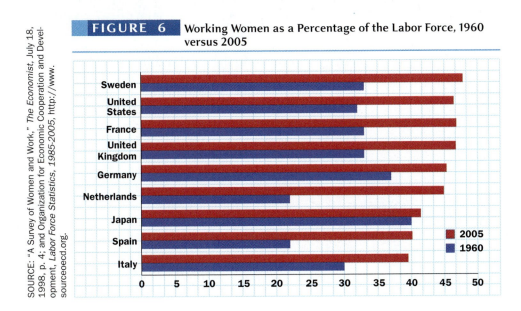

| FIGURE 6 | Working Women as a Percentage of the Labor Force, 1960 versus 2005 |

SOURCE: "A Survey of Women and Work," *The Economist*, July 18, 1998, p. 4; and Organization for Economic Cooperation and Development, *Labor Force Statistics, 1985-2005*, http://www.sourceoecd.org.

In contrast to women, the percentage of teenagers in the workforce has dropped significantly since its peak in the mid-1970s (see Figure 7). Young men and women aged 16 to 19 accounted for 8.6 percent of employment in 1974 but only 4.8 percent in 2006. As the baby boom gave way to the baby bust, people under 20 became

FIGURE 7   Teenage Employment as a Percentage of Total Employment, 1950–2006

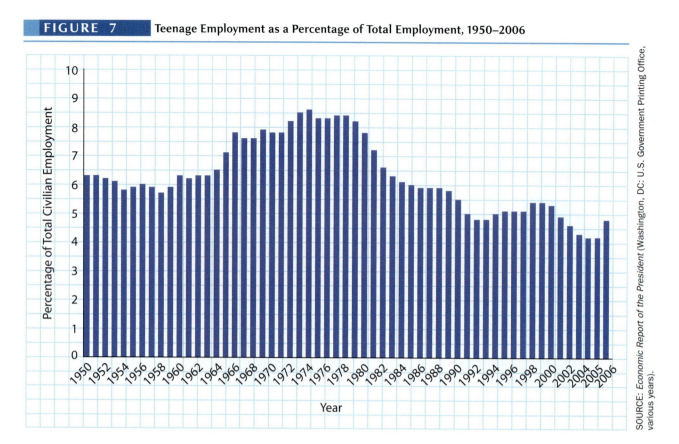

SOURCE: *Economic Report of the President* (Washington, DC: U.S. Government Printing Office, various years).

scarce resources! Still, about seven million teenagers hold jobs in the U.S. economy today—a number that has been pretty stable in the past few years. Most teenagers fill low-wage jobs at fast-food restaurants, amusement parks, and the like. Relatively few can be found in the nation's factories.

FIGURE 8   Civilian Employment by Sector, 2005

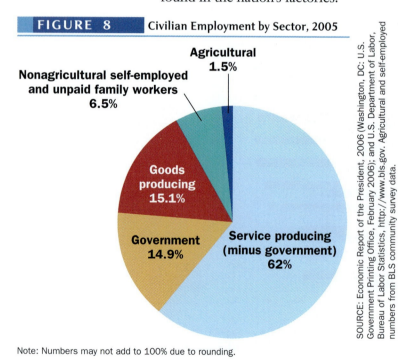

Note: Numbers may not add to 100% due to rounding.

SOURCE: Economic Report of the President, 2006 (Washington, DC: U.S. Government Printing Office, February 2006); and U.S. Department of Labor, Bureau of Labor Statistics, http://www.bls.gov. Agricultural and self-employed numbers from BLS community survey data.

The American Workforce: What Does It Do?

What do these 150 million working Americans do? The only real answer is: almost anything you can imagine. In 2005, America had 96,740 architects, 389,090 computer programmers, more than 935,920 carpenters, more than 2.5 million truck drivers, 529,190 lawyers, roughly 3.8 million secretaries, 171,290 kindergarten teachers, 26,400 pediatricians, 58,850 tax preparers, 5,680 geological engineers, 282,180 fire fighters, and 12,470 economists.[2]

Figure 8 shows the breakdown by sector. It holds some surprises for most people. The majority of American workers—like workers in all developed countries—produce services, not goods. In 2005, over 62 percent of all workers in the United States were employed by private service industries,

[2] Source: U.S. Bureau of Labor Statistics, *Occupational Employment and Wages, May 2005*, http://www.bls.gov, accessed December 2006.

whereas only than 15 percent produced goods. These legions of service workers included about 17.3 million in educational and health services, 17 million in business and professional services, and about 14 million in retail trade. (The biggest single employer in the country is Wal-Mart.) By contrast, manufacturing companies in the United States employed under 14.5 million people, and almost a third of those worked in offices rather than in the factory. The popular image of the typical American worker as a blue-collar worker—Homer Simpson, if you will—is really quite misleading.

Federal, state, and local governments employed about 22 million people but, contrary to another popular misconception, few of these civil servants work for the *federal* government. Federal *civilian* employment is about 2.7 million—and has been declining for about 15 years. (The armed forces employ about another 1.4 million men and women in uniform.) State and local governments provide about 19 million jobs—or about seven times the number of federal government jobs. Finally, approximately 2.2 million Americans work on farms and about 10.4 million are self-employed.

As Figure 9 shows, *all* industrialized countries have become "service economies." To a considerable degree, this shift to services reflects the arrival of the "Information Age." Activities related to computers, to research, to the transmission of information by teaching and publication, and other information-related activities are providing many of the new jobs. This means that, in the rich economies, workers who moved out of manufacturing jobs into the service sectors have not gone predominantly into low-skill jobs such as dishwashing or housecleaning. Many found employment in service jobs in which education and experience provide a great advantage. At the same time, technological change has made it possible to produce more and more manufactured products using fewer and fewer workers. Such labor-saving innovation in manufacturing has allowed a considerable share of the labor force to move out of goods-producing jobs and into services.

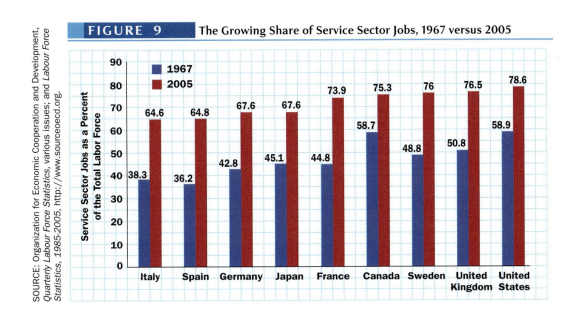

FIGURE 9 The Growing Share of Service Sector Jobs, 1967 versus 2005

SOURCE: Organization for Economic Cooperation and Development, *Quarterly Labour Force Statistics*, various issues; and *Labour Force Statistics, 1985-2005*, http://www.sourceoecd.org.

■ The American Workforce: What It Earns

Altogether, these workers' wages account for over 70 percent of the income that the production process generates. That figures up to an average hourly wage of almost $17—plus fringe benefits like health insurance and pensions, which can contribute an additional 30 to 40 percent for some workers. Because the average workweek is about 34 hours long, a typical weekly paycheck in the United States is about $580 before taxes (but excluding the value of benefits). That is hardly a princely sum, and most college graduates can expect to earn substantially more.[3] But it is typical of average wage rates in a rich country like the United States.

Wages throughout northern Europe are similar. Indeed, workers in a number of other industrial countries now receive higher compensation than American workers do—a big change from the situation a few decades ago. According to the U.S. Bureau of Labor Statistics, in 2004 workers in U.S. manufacturing industries made less than those in Germany, Belgium, and the Netherlands (see Figure 10). However, U.S. compensation levels still remain well above those in Japan, the United Kingdom, Italy, and many other countries.

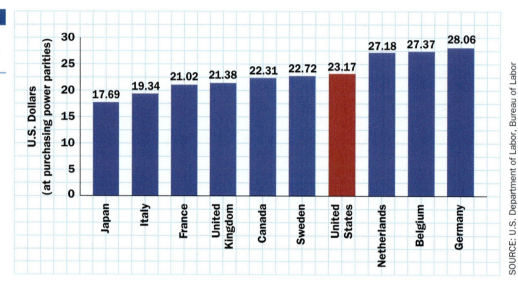

SOURCE: U.S. Department of Labor, Bureau of Labor Statistics, Division of Foreign Labor Statistics, http://www.bls.gov.

FIGURE 10

Average Hourly Compensation Rates in Manufacturing, 2004

◼ Capital and Its Earnings

The rest of national income (after deducting for the sliver of income that goes to the owners of land and natural resources) mainly accrues to the owners of *capital*—the machines and buildings that make up the nation's industrial plant.

The total market value of these business assets—a tough number to estimate—is believed to be in the neighborhood of $30 trillion. Because that capital earns an average rate of return of about 10 percent before taxes, total earnings of capital come to about $3 trillion. Of this, corporate profits are less than half; the rest is mainly interest.

Public opinion polls routinely show that Americans have a distorted view of the level of business profits in our society. The man and woman on the street believe that profits account for about 30 percent of the price of a typical product (see the box "Public Opinion on Profits" on the next page). The right number is closer to 9 percent.

◼ THE OUTPUTS: WHAT DOES AMERICA PRODUCE?

What does all this labor and capital produce? Consumer spending accounts for about 70 percent of GDP. And what an amazing variety of goods and services it buys. American households spend roughly 60 percent of their budgets on services, with housing

---

[3] These days, male college graduates typically earn almost 80 percent more than men with only high school diplomas, and female college grads almost 75 percent more than high-school-educated women. Source: *The State of Working America, 2006/2007*, Economic Policy Institute, http://www.epinet.org, accessed December 2006.

Public Opinion on Profits

Most Americans think corporate profits are much higher than they actually are. One public opinion poll years ago found that the average citizen thought that corporate profits *after taxes* amounted to 32 percent of sales for the typical manufacturing company. The actual profit rate at the time was closer to 4 percent!* Interestingly, when a previous poll asked how much profit was "reasonable," the response was 26 cents on every dollar of sales—more than six times as large as profits actually were.

*This poll was conducted in 1986. Corporate profit rates increased considerably in the 1990s and 2000s.

SOURCE: "Public Attitudes toward Corporate Profits," *Public Opinion Index* (Princeton, NJ: Opinion Research Corporation, June 1986).

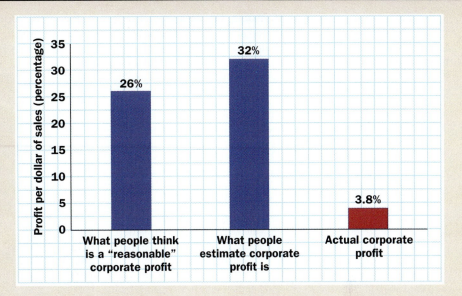

commanding the largest share. They also spend $130 billion annually on their telephone bills, $30 billion on airline tickets, and $75 billion on dentists. The other 40 percent of American budgets goes for goods—ranging from $100 billion per year on new cars to $50 billion on shoes.

This leaves about 30 percent of GDP for all *nonconsumption* uses. That includes government services (buying such things as airplanes, guns, and the services of soldiers, teachers, and bureaucrats), business purchases of machinery and industrial structures, and consumer purchases of new houses.

■ THE CENTRAL ROLE OF BUSINESS FIRMS

Calvin Coolidge once said that "the business of America is business." Although this statement often has been ridiculed, he was largely right. When we peer inside the economic machine that turns inputs into outputs, we see mainly private companies. Astonishingly, the United States has more than 25 million business firms—about one for every 12 people!

The owners and managers of these businesses hire people, acquire or rent capital goods, and arrange to produce things consumers want to buy. Sound simple? It isn't. Over 80,000 businesses fail every year. A few succeed spectacularly. Some do both. Fortunately for the U.S. economy, however, the lure of riches induces hundreds of thousands of people to start new businesses every year—against the odds.

A number of the biggest firms do business all over the world, just as foreign-based *multinational corporations* do business here. Indeed, some people claim that it is now impossible to determine the true "nationality" of a multinational corporation—which may have factories in ten or more countries, sell its wares all over the world, and have stockholders in dozens of nations. (See the accompanying box "Is That an American Company?") Most of General Motors' profits are generated abroad, for example, and the Honda you drive was probably assembled in Ohio.

Is That an American Company?

Robert Reich, who was Secretary of Labor in the Clinton administration, argued some years ago that it was already nearly impossible to define the nationality of a multinational company. Although many scholars think Reich exaggerated the point, no one doubts that he had one—nor that the nationalities of corporations have become increasingly blurred since then. He wrote in 1991:

What's the difference between an "American" corporation that makes or buys abroad much of what it sells around the world and a "foreign" corporation that makes or buys in the United States much of what it sells? . . . The mind struggles to keep the players straight. In 1990, Canada's Northern Telecom was selling to its American customers telecommunications equipment made by Japan's NTT at NTT's factory in North Carolina.

If you found that one too easy, try this: Beginning in 1991, Japan's Mazda would be producing Ford Probes at Mazda's plant in Flat Rock, Michigan. Some of these cars would be exported to Japan and sold there under Ford's trademark.

A Mazda-designed compact utility vehicle would be built at a Ford plant in Louisville, Kentucky, and then sold at Mazda dealerships in the United States. Nissan, meanwhile, was designing a new light truck at its San Diego, California, design center. The trucks would be assembled at Ford's Ohio truck plant, using panel parts fabricated by Nissan at its Tennessee factory, and then marketed by both Ford and Nissan in the United States and in Japan. Who is Ford? Nissan? Mazda?

SOURCE: AP / Wide World Photos

SOURCE: Robert B. Reich, *The Work of Nations* (New York: Knopf, 1991), pp. 124, 131.

Firms compete with other companies in their *industry*. Most economists believe that this *competition* is the key to industrial efficiency. A sole supplier of a commodity will find it easy to make money, and may therefore fail to innovate or control costs. Its management is liable to become relaxed and sloppy. But a company besieged by dozens of competitors eager to take its business away must constantly seek ways to innovate, to cut costs, and to build a better mousetrap. The rewards for business success can be magnificent. But the punishment for failure is severe.

■ WHAT'S MISSING FROM THE PICTURE? GOVERNMENT

Thus far, we have the following capsule summary of how the U.S. economy works: More than 25 million private businesses, energized by the profit motive, employ about 150 million workers and about $30 trillion of capital. These firms bring their enormously diverse wares to market, where they try to sell them to over 300 million consumers.

Households and businesses are linked in a tight circle, depicted in Figure 11. Firms use their receipts from sales to pay wages to employees and interest and profits to the people who provide capital. These income flows, in turn, enable consumers to purchase the goods and services that companies produce. This circular flow of money and goods lies at the center of the analysis of how the national economy works. All these activities are linked by a series of interconnected markets, some of which are highly competitive and others of which are less so.

All very well and good. But the story leaves out something important: the role of *government*, which is pervasive even in our decidedly free-market economy. Just what does government do in the U.S. economy—and why?

FIGURE 11   The Circular Flow of Goods and Money

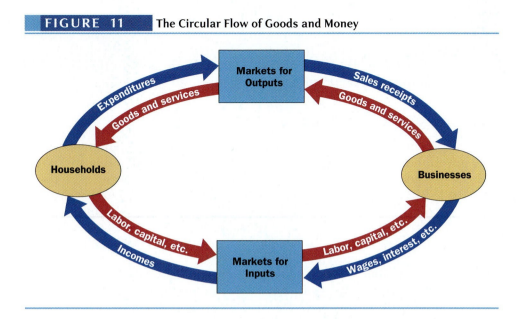

Although an increasing number of tasks seem to get assigned to the state each year, the traditional role of government in a market economy revolves around five jobs:

- Making and enforcing the laws
- Regulating business
- Providing certain goods and services such as national defense
- Levying taxes to pay for these goods and services
- Redistributing income

Every one of these tasks is steeped in controversy and surrounded by intense political debate. We conclude this chapter with a brief look at each.

The Government as Referee

For the most part, power is diffused in our economy, and people "play by the rules." But, in the scramble for competitive advantage, disputes are bound to arise. Did Company A live up to its contract? Who owns that disputed piece of property? In addition, some unscrupulous businesses are liable to step over the line now and then—as we saw spectacularly in the series of scandals that rocked corporate America at the beginning of the twenty-first century.

Enter the government as rule maker, referee, and arbitrator. Congress and state and local legislatures pass the laws that define the rules of the economic game. The executive branches of all three governmental levels share the responsibility for enforcing them. And the courts interpret the laws and adjudicate disputes.

The Government as Business Regulator

Nothing is pure in this world of ours. Even in "free-market" economies, governments interfere with the workings of free markets in many ways and for myriad reasons. Some government activities seek to make markets work better. For example, America's *antitrust laws* are used to protect competition against possible encroachment by monopoly. Some regulations seek to promote social objectives that unfettered markets do not foster—environmental regulations are a particularly clear case. But, as critics like to point out, some economic regulations have no clear rationale at all.

We mentioned earlier that the American belief in free enterprise runs deep. For this reason, the regulatory role of government is more contentious here than in most other countries. After all, Thomas Jefferson said that government is best that governs least. Two hundred years later, Presidents Reagan, Bush (both of them), and Clinton all pledged to dismantle inappropriate regulations—and sometimes did.

■ Government Expenditures

The most contentious political issues often involve taxing and spending because those are the government's most prominent roles. Democrats and Republicans, both in the White House and in Congress, have frequently battled fiercely over the federal budget. In 1995 and 1996, such disputes even led to some temporary shutdowns of the government. Under President Bill Clinton, the federal government managed to achieve a sizable surplus in its budget—meaning that tax receipts exceeded expenditures. But it didn't last long. Today the federal budget is deeply in the red, and prospects for getting it balanced are poor.

During fiscal year 2005, the federal government spent nearly $2.5 *trillion*—a sum that is literally beyond comprehension. Figure 12 shows where the money went. Over 35 percent went for *pensions and income security* programs, which include both social insurance programs (such as Social Security and unemployment compensation) and programs designed to assist the poor. About 20 percent went for *national defense*. Another 22 percent was absorbed by *health-care* expenditures, mainly on Medicare and Medicaid. Adding in *interest on the national debt*, these four functions alone accounted for about 85 percent of federal spending. The rest went for a miscellany of other purposes including education, transportation, agriculture, housing, and foreign aid.

Government spending at the state and local levels was about $1.8 trillion in 2003. Education claimed the largest share of state and local government budgets (34 percent), with health and public welfare programs a distant second (17 percent). Despite this vast outpouring of public funds, many observers believe that serious social needs remain unmet. Critics claim that our public infrastructure (such as bridges and roads) is adequate, that our educational system is lacking, that we are not spending enough on homeland defense, and so on.

Although the scale and scope of government activity in the United States is substantial, it is quite moderate when we compare it to other leading economies. Figure 13 is a bar graph showing government expenditure as share of GDP for ten rich countries. We see that the share of government in the U.S. economy is the lowest in this group of countries.

FIGURE 12   The Allocation of Government Expenditures

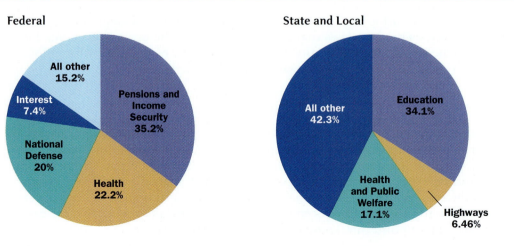

SOURCE: *Economic Report of the President, 2006* (Washington, DC: U.S. Government Printing Office, February 2004).

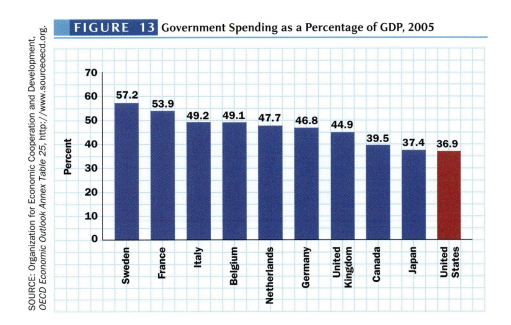

FIGURE 13 Government Spending as a Percentage of GDP, 2005

SOURCE: Organization for Economic Cooperation and Development, *OECD Economic Outlook Annex Table 25,* http://www.sourceoecd.org.

■ Taxes in America

Taxes finance this array of goods and services, and sometimes it seems that the tax collector is everywhere. We have income and payroll taxes withheld from our paychecks, sales taxes added to our purchases, property taxes levied on our homes; we pay gasoline taxes, liquor taxes, and telephone taxes.

Americans have always felt that taxes are both too many and too high. In the 1980s and 1990s, antitax sentiment became a dominant feature of the U.S. political scene. The old slogan "no taxation without representation" gave way to the new slogan "no new taxes." Yet, by international standards, Americans are among the most lightly taxed people in the world. Figure 14 compares the fraction of income paid in taxes in the United States with those paid by residents of other wealthy nations. The tax share in the United States has fallen notably during the presidency of George W. Bush.

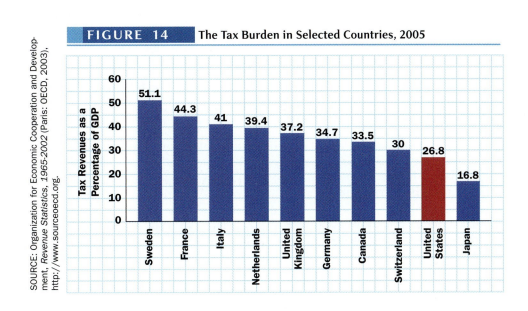

FIGURE 14   The Tax Burden in Selected Countries, 2005

SOURCE: Organization for Economic Cooperation and Development, *Revenue Statistics, 1965-2002* (Paris: OECD, 2003), http://www.sourceoecd.org.

■ The Government as Redistributor

In a market economy, people earn incomes according to what they have to sell. Unfortunately, many people have nothing to sell but unskilled labor, which commands a paltry price. Others lack even that. Such people fare poorly in unfettered markets. In extreme cases, they are homeless, hungry, and ill. Robin Hood transferred money from the rich to the poor. Some think the government should do the same; others disagree.

If poverty amid riches offends your moral sensibilities—a personal judgment that each of us must make for ourselves—two basic remedial approaches are possible. The socialist idea is to force the distribution of income to be more equal by overriding the decisions of the market. "From each according to his ability, to each according to his needs" was Marx's ideal. In practice, things were not quite so noble under socialism. But there is little doubt that incomes in the old Soviet Union were more equally distributed than those in the United States.

The liberal idea is to let free markets determine the distribution of *before-tax* incomes, but then to use the tax system and **transfer payments** to reduce inequality—just as Robin Hood did. This is the rationale for, among other things, **progressive taxation** and the antipoverty programs colloquially known as "welfare." Americans who support redistribution line up solidly behind the liberal approach. But which ways are the best, and how much is enough? No simple answers have emerged from debate on these highly contentious questions.

Transfer payments are sums of money that certain individuals receive as outright grants from the government rather than as payments for services rendered.

A tax is **progressive** if the ratio of taxes to income rises as income rises.

■ CONCLUSION: IT'S A MIXED ECONOMY

Ideology notwithstanding, all nations at all times blend public and private ownership of property in some proportions. All rely on markets for some purposes, but all also assign some role to government. Hence, people speak of the ubiquity of **mixed economies.** But mixing is not homogenization; different countries can and do blend the state and market sectors in different ways. Even today, the Russian economy is a far cry from the Italian economy, which is vastly different from that of Hong Kong.

When most of you were very young children, a stunning historical event occurred: Communism collapsed all over Europe. For years, the formerly socialist economies suffered through a painful transition from a system in which private property, free enterprise, and markets played subsidiary roles to one in which they are central. These nations have changed the mix, if you will—and dramatically so. To understand why this transformation is at once so difficult and so important, we need to explore the main theme of this book: *What does the market do well, and what does it do poorly?* This task begins in the next chapter.

A **mixed economy** is one with some public influence over the workings of free markets. There may also be some public ownership mixed in with private property.

SUMMARY

1. The U.S. economy is the biggest national economy on earth, both because Americans are rich by world standards and because we are a populous nation. Relative to most other advanced countries, our economy is also exceptionally "privatized" and **closed**.

2. The U.S. economy has grown dramatically over the years. But this growth has been interrupted by periodic **recessions,** during which unemployment rises.

3. The United States has a big, diverse workforce whose composition by age and sex has been changing substan-

tially. Relatively few workers these days work in factories or on farms; most work in service industries.

4. Employees take home most of the nation's income. Most of the rest goes, in the forms of interest and profits, to those who provide the capital.

5. Governments at the federal, state, and local levels employ one-sixth of the American workforce (including the armed forces). These governments finance their expenditures by taxes, which account for about 27 percent of GDP. This percentage is one of the lowest in the industrialized world.

6. In addition to raising taxes and making expenditures, the government in a market economy serves as referee and enforcer of the rules, regulates business in a variety of ways, and redistributes income through taxes and **transfer payments.** For all these reasons, we say that we have a **mixed economy,** which blends private and public elements.

KEY TERMS

Factors of Production, or Inputs   22

Outputs   22

Gross domestic product (GDP)   23

Open economy   24

Closed economy   24

Recession   24

Transfer payments   36

Progressive tax   36

Mixed economy   36

DISCUSSION QUESTIONS

1. Which are the two biggest national economies on earth? Why are they so much bigger than the others?

2. What is meant by a "factor of production?" Have you ever sold any on a market?

3. Why do you think per-capita income in Connecticut is nearly double that in West Virginia?

4. Roughly speaking, what fraction of U.S. labor works in factories? In service businesses? In government?

5. Most American businesses are small, but most of the output is produced by large businesses. That sounds paradoxical. How can it be true?

6. What is the role of government in a mixed economy?

THE FUNDAMENTAL ECONOMIC PROBLEM: SCARCITY AND CHOICE

Our necessities are few but our wants are endless.

INSCRIPTION ON A FORTUNE COOKIE

U nderstanding what the market system does well and what it does badly is this book's central task. But to address this complex question, we must first answer a simpler one: What do economists expect the market to accomplish?

The most common answer is that the market resolves what is often called *the* fundamental economic problem: how best to manage the resources of society, doing as well as possible with them, despite their scarcity. All decisions are constrained by the scarcity of available resources. A dreamer may envision a world free of want, in which everyone, even in Africa and Central America, drives a BMW and eats caviar, but the earth lacks the resources needed to make that dream come true. Because resources are scarce, all economic decisions involve *trade-offs*. Should you use that $5 bill to buy pizza or a new notebook for Econ class? Should General Motors invest more money in assembly lines or in research? A well-functioning market system facilitates and guides such decisions, assigning each hour of labor and each kilowatt-hour of electricity to the task where, it is hoped, the input will best serve the public.

This chapter shows how economists analyze choices like these. The same basic principles, based on the concept of *opportunity cost*, apply to the decisions made by business firms, governments, and society as a whole. Many of the most basic ideas of economics, such as *efficiency, division of labor, comparative advantage, exchange,* and *the role of markets* appear here for the first time.

CONTENTS

? ISSUE: *What to Do about the Budget Deficit?*

For roughly 15 years, from the early 1980s until the late 1990s, the top economic issue of the day was how to reduce the federal budget deficit. Presidents Ronald Reagan, George H. W. Bush, and Bill Clinton all battled with Congress over tax and spending *priorities*. Which programs should be cut? What taxes should be raised?

Then, thanks to a combination of strong economic growth and deficit-reducing policies, the budget deficit melted away like springtime snow and actually turned into a budget *surplus* for a few fiscal years (1998 through 2001). For a while, the need to make agonizing *choices* seemed to disappear—or so it seemed. But it was an illusion. Even during that brief era of budget surpluses, hard choices still had to be made. The U.S. government could not afford *everything*. Then, as the stock market collapsed, the economy slowed, and President George W. Bush pushed a series of tax cuts through Congress, the budget surpluses quickly turned back into deficits again—the largest deficits in our history.

SOURCE: ©Photodisc Green/Getting Images

The fiscal questions in the 2006 mid-term election campaign were the familiar ones of the 1980s and 1990s. Which spending programs should be cut and which ones should be increased? Which, if any, of the Bush tax cuts should be repealed? Even a government with an annual budget of over $2.5 *trillion* was forced to set priorities and make hard choices.

Even when resources are quite generous, they are never unlimited. So everyone must still make tough choices. An *optimal* decision is one that chooses the most desirable alternative *among the possibilities permitted by the available resources*, which are always scarce in this sense.

■ SCARCITY, CHOICE, AND OPPORTUNITY COST

Resources are the instruments provided by nature or by people that are used to create goods and services. Natural resources include minerals, soil, water, and air. Labor is a scarce resource, partly because of time limitations (the day has only 24 hours) and partly because the number of skilled workers is limited. Factories and machines are resources made by people. These three types of resources are often referred to as *land, labor,* and *capital.* They are also called *inputs* or *factors of production.*

One of the basic themes of economics is scarcity: the fact that **resources** are always limited. Even Philip II, of Spanish Armada fame and ruler of one of the greatest empires in history, had to cope with frequent rebellions in his armies when he could not meet their payrolls or even provide basic provisions. He is reported to have undergone bankruptcy an astonishing eight times during his reign. In more recent years, the U.S. government has been agonizing over difficult budget decisions even though it spends more than two and a half trillion dollars—that's $2,500,000,000,000—annually.

But the scarcity of *physical resources* is more fundamental than the scarcity of funds. Fuel supplies, for example, are not limitless, and some environmentalists claim that we should now be making some hard choices—such as keeping our homes cooler in winter and warmer in summer and living closer to our jobs. Although energy may be the most widely discussed scarcity, the general principle applies to all of the earth's resources—iron, copper, uranium, and so on. Even goods produced by human effort are in limited supply because they require fuel, labor, and other scarce resources as inputs. We can manufacture more cars, but the increased use of labor, steel, and fuel in auto production will mean that we must cut back on something else, perhaps the production of refrigerators. This all adds up to the following fundamental principle of economics, which we will encounter again and again in this text:

> Virtually all resources are *scarce*, meaning that humans have less of them than we would like. Therefore, choices must be made among a *limited* set of possibilities, in full recognition of the inescapable fact that a decision to have more of one thing means that we will have less of something else.

In fact, one popular definition of economics is the study of how best to use *limited* means to pursue *unlimited* ends. Although this definition, like any short statement, cannot possibly cover the sweep of the entire discipline, it does convey the flavor of the economist's stock in trade.

To illustrate the true cost of an item, consider the decision to produce additional cars, and therefore to produce fewer refrigerators. Although the production of a car may cost $15,000 per vehicle, or some other money amount, *its real cost to society is the refrigerators that society must forgo to get an additional car*. If the labor, steel, and energy needed to manufacture a car are sufficient to make 30 refrigerators, the **opportunity cost** of a car is 30 refrigerators. The principle of opportunity cost is so important that we will spend most of this chapter elaborating on it in various ways.

> **HOW MUCH DOES IT REALLY COST? The Principle of Opportunity Cost** Economics examines the options available to households, businesses, governments, and entire societies, given the limited resources at their command. It studies the logic of how people can make **optimal decisions** from among competing alternatives. One overriding principle governs this logic— a principle we introduced in Chapter 1 as one of the *Ideas for Beyond the Final Exam:* With limited resources, a decision to have *more* of one thing is simultaneously a decision to have *less* of something else. Hence, the relevant *cost* of any decision is its *opportunity cost*—the value of the next best alternative that is given up. **Optimal decision** making must be based on opportunity-cost calculations.

■ Opportunity Cost and Money Cost

Because we live in a market economy where (almost) everything has its price, students often wonder about the connection or difference between an item's *opportunity cost* and its *market price*. What we just said seems to divorce the two concepts: The true opportunity cost of a car is not its market price but the value of the other things (like refrigerators) that could have been made or purchased instead.

But isn't the opportunity cost of a car related to its money cost? The normal answer is yes. The two costs are usually closely tied because of the way in which a market economy sets prices. Steel, for example, is used to manufacture both automobiles and refrigerators. If consumers value items that can be made with steel (such as refrigerators) highly, then economists would say that the *opportunity cost* of making a car is high. But, under these circumstances, strong demand for this highly valued resource will bid up its market price. In this way, a well-functioning price system will assign a high price to steel, which will therefore make the *money cost* of manufacturing a car high as well. In summary:

> If the market functions well, goods that have high opportunity costs will also have high money costs. In turn, goods that have low opportunity costs will also have low money costs.

Yet it would be a mistake to treat opportunity costs and explicit monetary costs as identical. For one thing, sometimes the market does not function well, and hence assigns prices that do not accurately reflect opportunity costs.

Moreover, some valuable items may not bear explicit price tags at all. We encountered one such example in Chapter 1, where we noted that the opportunity cost of a

The **opportunity cost** of any decision is the value of the next best alternative that the decision forces the decision maker to forgo.

An **optimal decision** is one that best serves the objectives of the decision maker, whatever those objectives may be. It is selected by explicit or implicit comparison with the possible alternative choices. The term *optimal* connotes neither approval nor disapproval of the objective itself.

IDEAS FOR BEYOND THE FINAL EXAM

"O.K., who can put a price on love? Jim?"

college education may differ sharply from its explicit money cost. Why? Because one important item is typically omitted from the money-cost calculation: the *market value of your time*, that is, the wages you could earn by working instead of attending college. Because you give up these potential wages, which can amount to $15,000 per year or more, so as to acquire an education, they must be counted as a major part of the opportunity cost of going to college.

Other common examples where money costs and opportunity costs diverge are goods and services that are given away "free." For example, some early settlers of the American West destroyed natural amenities such as forests and buffalo herds, which had no market price, leaving later generations to pay the opportunity costs in terms of lost resources. Similarly, you incur no explicit monetary cost to acquire an item that is given away for free. But if you must wait in line to get the "free" commodity, you incur an opportunity cost equal to the value of the next best use of your time.

■ *Optimal* Choice: Not Just *Any* Choice

How do people and firms make decisions? There are many ways, some of them based on hunches with little forethought; some are even based on superstition or the advice of a fortune teller. Often, when the required information is scarce and the necessary research and calculations are costly and difficult, the decision maker will settle on the first possibility that he can "live with"—a choice that promises to yield results that are not too bad, and that seem fairly safe. The decision maker may be willing to choose this course even though he recognizes that there might be other options that are better, but are unknown to him. This way of deciding is called "satisficing."

In this book, like most books on economic theory, we will assume that decision makers seek to do better than mere satisficing. Rather, we will assume that they seek to reach decisions that are optimal, in other words, decisions that do better in achieving the decision maker's goals than any other possible choice. We will assume that the required information is available to the decision maker and study the procedures that enable her to determine which of the possible choices is optimal to her.

An optimal decision is one that is selected after implicit or explicit comparison of the consequences of each of the possible choices and that is shown by analysis to be the one that most effectively promotes her goals.

We will study optimal decision making by various parties: by consumers, by producers, and by sellers, in a variety of situations. The methods of analysis for determining what choice is optimal in each case will be remarkably similar. So, if you understand one of them, you will already be well on your way to understanding them all. A technique called "marginal analysis" will be used for this purpose. But one fundamental idea underlies any method used for optimal decision making: To determine whether a possible decision is or is not optimal, its consequences must be compared with those of each of the other possible choices.

■ SCARCITY AND CHOICE FOR A SINGLE FIRM

The **outputs** of a firm or an economy are the goods and services it produces.

The **inputs** used by a firm or an economy are the labor, raw materials, electricity and other resources it uses to produce its outputs.

The nature of opportunity cost is perhaps clearest in the case of a single business firm that produces two **outputs** from a fixed supply of **inputs**. Given current technology and the limited resources at its disposal, the more of one good the firm produces, the less of the other it will be able to make. Unless managers explicitly weigh the desirability of each product against the other, they are unlikely to make rational production decisions.

Consider the example of Jones, a farmer whose available supplies of land, machinery, labor, and fertilizer are capable of producing the various combinations of soybeans and wheat listed in Table 1. Obviously, devoting more resources to soybean production means that Jones will produce less wheat.

TABLE 1		
Production Possibilities Open to a Farmer		
Bushels of Soybeans	Bushels of Wheat	Label in Figure 1
40,000	0	A
30,000	38,000	B
20,000	52,000	C
10,000	60,000	D
0	65,000	E

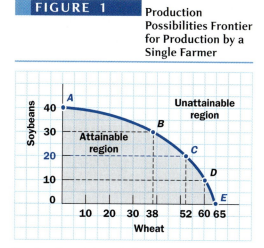

FIGURE 1 Production Possibilities Frontier for Production by a Single Farmer

Note: Quantities are in thousands of bushels per year.

Table 1 indicates, for example, that if Jones grows only soybeans, the harvest will be 40,000 bushels. But if he reduces his soybean production to 30,000 bushels, he can also grow 38,000 bushels of wheat. Thus, *the opportunity cost of obtaining 38,000 bushels of wheat is 10,000 fewer bushels of soybeans.* Put another way, the opportunity cost of 10,000 more bushels of soybeans is 38,000 bushels of wheat. The other numbers in Table 1 have similar interpretations.

The Production Possibilities Frontier

Figure 1 presents this same information graphically. Point *A* indicates that one of the options available to the farmer is to produce 40,000 bushels of soybeans and zero wheat. Thus, point *A* corresponds to the first line of Table 1, point *B* to the second line, and so on. Curves similar to *AE* appear frequently in this book; they are called **production possibilities frontiers.** Any point *on or inside* the production possibilities frontier is attainable. Points *outside* the frontier cannot be achieved with the available resources and technology.

Because resources are limited, the production possibilities frontier always slopes downward to the right. The farmer can *increase* wheat production (move to the right in Figure 1) only by devoting more land and labor to growing wheat. But this choice simultaneously *reduces* soybean production (the curve must move downward) because less land and labor remain available for growing soybeans.

Notice that, in addition to having a negative slope, our production possibilities frontier *AE* has another characteristic; it is "bowed outward." What does this curvature mean? In short, as larger and larger quantities of resources are transferred from the production of one output to the production of another, the additions to the second product decline.

Suppose farmer Jones initially produces only soybeans, using even land that is comparatively most productive in wheat cultivation (point *A*). Now he decides to switch some land from soybean production into wheat production. Which part of the land will he switch? If Jones is sensible, he will use the part relatively most productive in growing wheat. As he shifts to point *B*, soybean production falls from 40,000 bushels to 30,000 bushels as wheat production rises from zero to 38,000 bushels. A sacrifice of only 10,000 bushels of soybeans "buys" 38,000 bushels of wheat.

Imagine now that this farmer wants to produce still more wheat. Figure 1 tells us that the sacrifice of an additional 10,000 bushels of soybeans (from 30,000 bushels to 20,000 bushels) will yield only 14,000 more bushels of wheat (see point *C*). Why? The main reason is that *inputs tend to be specialized.* As we noted at point *A*, the farmer was using resources for soybean production that were relatively more productive in growing

A **production possibilities frontier** shows the different combinations of various goods that a producer can turn out, given the available resources and existing technology.

wheat. Consequently, their relative productivity in soybean production was low. When these resources are switched to wheat production, the yield is high.

But this trend cannot continue forever, of course. As more wheat is produced, the farmer must utilize land and machinery with a greater productivity advantage in growing soybeans and a smaller productivity advantage in growing wheat. This is why the first 10,000 bushels of soybeans forgone "buys" the farmer 38,000 bushels of wheat, whereas the second 10,000 bushels of soybeans "buys" only 14,000 bushels of wheat. Figure 1 and Table 1 show that these returns continue to decline as wheat production expands: The next 10,000-bushel reduction in soybean production yields only 8,000 bushels of additional wheat, and so on.

As we can see, the *slope* of the production possibilities frontier graphically represents the concept of *opportunity cost*. Between points C and B, for example, the opportunity cost of acquiring 10,000 additional bushels of soybeans is shown on the graph to be 14,000 bushels of forgone wheat; between points B and A, the opportunity cost of 10,000 bushels of soybeans is 38,000 bushels of forgone wheat. In general, as we move upward to the left along the production possibilities frontier (toward more soybeans and less wheat), the opportunity cost of soybeans in terms of wheat increases. Looking at the same thing the other way, as we move downward to the right, the opportunity cost of acquiring wheat by giving up soybeans increases—more and more soybeans must be forgone per added bushel of wheat and successive addition to wheat output occur.

The Principle of Increasing Costs

The **principle of increasing costs** states that as the production of a good expands, the opportunity cost of producing another unit generally increases.

We have just described a very general phenomenon with applications well beyond farming. The **principle of increasing costs** states that as the production of one good expands, the opportunity cost of producing another unit of this good generally increases.

This principle is not a universal fact—exceptions do arise. But it does seem to be a technological regularity that applies to a wide range of economic activities. As our farming example suggests, the principle of increasing costs is based on the fact that resources tend to be at least somewhat specialized. So we lose some of their productivity when those resources are transferred from doing what they are relatively *good* at to what they are relatively *bad* at. In terms of diagrams such as Figure 1, the principle simply asserts that the production possibilities frontier is bowed outward.

Perhaps the best way to understand this idea is to contrast it with a case in which no resources are specialized so costs do not increase as output proportion changes. Figure 2 depicts a production possibilities frontier for producing black shoes and brown shoes. Because the labor and machinery used to produce black shoes are just as good at producing brown shoes, the frontier is a straight line. If the firm cuts back its production of black shoes by 10,000 pairs, it can get 10,000 additional pairs of brown shoes, no matter how big is the shift between these two outputs. It loses no productivity in the switch because resources are not specialized.

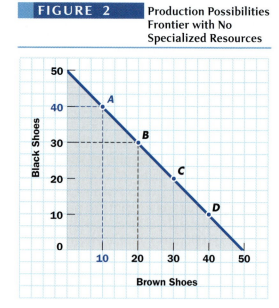

FIGURE 2   Production Possibilities Frontier with No Specialized Resources

Note: Quantities are in thousands of pairs per week.

More typically, however, as a firm concentrates more of its productive capacity on one commodity, it is forced to employ inputs that are better suited to making another commodity. The firm is forced to vary the proportions in which it uses inputs because of the limited quantities of some of those inputs. This fact also explains the typical curvature of the firm's production possibilities frontier.

SCARCITY AND CHOICE FOR THE ENTIRE SOCIETY

Like an individual firm, the entire economy is also constrained by its limited resources and technology. If the public wants more aircraft and tanks, it will have to give up some boats and automobiles. If it wants to build more factories and stores, it will have to build fewer homes and sports arenas. In general:

The position and shape of the production possibilities frontier that constrains society's choices are determined by the economy's physical resources, its skills and technology, its willingness to work, and how much it has devoted in the past to the construction of factories, research, and innovation.

Because so many nations have so long debated whether to reduce or augment military spending, let us illustrate the nature of society's choices by the example of deciding between military might (represented by missiles) and civilian consumption (represented by automobiles). Just like a single firm, the economy as a whole faces a production possibilities frontier for missiles and autos, determined by its technology and the available resources of land, labor, capital, and raw materials. This production possibilities frontier may look like curve BC in Figure 3. If most workers are employed in auto plants, car production will be large, but the output of missiles will be small. If the economy transfers resources out of auto manufacturing when consumer demand declines, it can, by congressional action, alter the output mix toward more missiles (the move from D to E). However, something is likely to be lost in the process because physical resources are specialized. The fabric used to make car seats will not help much in missile production. The principle of increasing costs strongly suggests that the production possibilities frontier curves downward toward the axes.

We may even reach a point where the only resources left are not very useful outside of auto manufacturing. In that case, even a large sacrifice of automobiles will get the economy few additional missiles. That is the meaning of the steep segment, FC, on the frontier. At point C, there is little additional output of missiles as compared to point F, even though at C automobile production has been given up entirely.

FIGURE 3   Production Possibilities Frontier for the Entire Economy

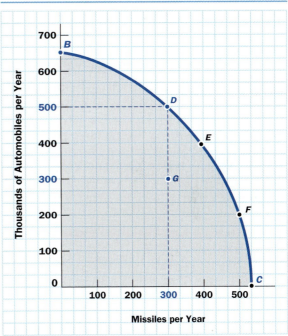

The downward slope of society's production possibilities frontier implies that hard choices must be made. Civilian consumption (automobiles) can be increased only by decreasing military expenditure, not by rhetoric or wishing. The curvature of the production possibilities frontier implies that, as defense spending increases, it becomes progressively more expensive to "buy" additional military strength ("missiles") in terms of the resulting sacrifice of civilian consumption.

Scarcity and Choice Elsewhere in the Economy

We have emphasized that limited resources force hard choices on business managers and society as a whole. But the same type of choices arises elsewhere—in households, universities, and other nonprofit organizations, as well as the government.

Hard Choices in the Real World

Two excerpts from recent newspaper stories bring home the realities of scarcity and choice:

"Bush Offers Budget Stressing Military and Security Spending," Washington, Feb. 2—President Bush proposed a $2.4 trillion budget for 2005 today, calling for big increases in military and domestic-security spending and for trims in many domestic programs. The budget for the fiscal year that begins on Oct. 1 proposes a 7 percent increase in military spending, a 10 percent increase in domestic security spending, and a hold-the-line increase of just one-half percent for a vast array of domestic programs....
(Source: David Stout, New York Times, February 2, 2004, available at http://www.nytimes.com).

"National Parks to Cut Back Services; More Volunteers, Higher Fees Expected," April 18—Visitors to national parks and monuments this summer could see higher fees, fewer educational programs and more volunteers doing what once was park rangers' work. That's because the parks are killing some programs while straining to keep others running in the face of stagnant operating budgets and cutbacks in staff nationwide. ..."That's the job, to try and do the very best with what you've got," said Chas Cartwright, superintendent of Dinosaur National Monument in northwestern Colorado. ...As at other national parks, job vacancies at Dinosaur are going unfilled. The fossil-rich park has only three law-enforcement officers and three nature interpreters—far short of ideal—and the budget has remained flat at $2.7 million since 2002. Dinosaur officials also have cut their vehicle fleet, ratcheted down utility use and trimmed construction materials and office supplies.
(Source: Monte Whaley, Times-Picayune, April 18, 2004, available at http://web.lexis-nexis.com).

SOURCE: ©James L. Amos/Corbis

This photo shows a Park Service staff member excavating dinosaur bones at Dinosaur National Monument in Colorado.

The nature of opportunity cost is perhaps most obvious for a household that must decide how to divide its income among the goods and services that compete for the family's attention. If the Simpson family buys an expensive new car, it may be forced to cut back sharply on some other purchases. This fact does not make it unwise to buy the car. But it does make it unwise to buy the car until the family considers the full implications for its overall budget. If the Simpsons are to utilize their limited resources most effectively, they must recognize the opportunity costs of the car—the things they will forgo as a result—perhaps a vacation and an expensive new TV set.

? ISSUE REVISITED: *Coping with the Budget Deficit*

As already noted, even a rich and powerful nation like the United States must cope with the limitations implied by scarce resources. The necessity for choice imposed on governments by the limited amount they feel they can afford to spend is similar in character to the problems faced by business firms and households. For the goods and services that it buys from others, a government must prepare a budget similar to that of a very large household. For the items it produces itself—education, police protection, libraries, and so on—it faces a production possibilities frontier much like a business firm does. Even though the U.S. government spent over $2.3 trillion in 2004, some of the most acrimonious debates between President Bush and his critics arose from disagreements about how the government's limited resources should be allocated among competing uses. Even if unstated, the concept of opportunity cost is central to these debates.

THE CONCEPT OF EFFICIENCY

So far, our discussion of scarcity and choice has assumed that either the firm or the economy always operates on its production possibilities frontier rather than *below* it. In other words, we have tacitly assumed that, whatever the firm or economy decides to do, it does so **efficiently**.

A set of outputs is said to be produced **efficiently** if, given current technological knowledge, there is no way one can produce larger amounts of any output without using larger input amounts or giving up some quantity of another output.

Economists define efficiency as the absence of waste. An efficient economy wastes none of its available resources and produces the maximum amount of output that its technology permits.

To see why any point on the economy's production possibilities frontier in Figure 3 represents an efficient decision, suppose for a moment that society has decided to produce 300 missiles. The production possibilities frontier tells us that if 300 missiles are to be produced, then the maximum number of automobiles that can be made is 500,000 (point D in Figure 3). The economy is therefore operating efficiently only if it produces 500,000 automobiles rather than some smaller amount such as 300,000 (as at point G).

Point D is efficient, but point G is not, because the economy is capable of moving from G to D, thereby producing 200,000 more automobiles without giving up any missiles (or anything else). Clearly, failure to take advantage of the option of choosing point D rather than point G constitutes a wasted opportunity—an inefficiency.

Note that the concept of efficiency does not tell us which point on the production possibilities frontier is *best*. Rather, it tells us only that any point *below* the frontier cannot be best, because any such point represents wasted resources. For example, should society ever find itself at a point such as G, the necessity of making hard choices would (temporarily) disappear. It would be possible to increase production of *both* missiles *and* automobiles by moving to a point such as E.

Why, then, would a society ever find itself at a point below its production possibilities frontier? Why are resources wasted in real life? The most important reason in today's economy is *unemployment*. When many workers are unemployed, the economy must be at a point such as G, below the frontier, because by putting the unemployed to work, some in each industry, the economy could produce both more missiles *and* more automobiles. The economy would then move from point G to the right (more missiles) and upward (more automobiles) toward a point such as E on the production possibilities frontier. Only when no resources are wasted is the economy operating on the frontier.

Inefficiency occurs in other ways, too. A prime example is assigning inputs to the wrong task—as when wheat is grown on land best suited to soybean cultivation. Another important type of inefficiency occurs when large firms produce goods that smaller enterprises could make better because they can pay closer attention to detail, or when small firms produce outputs best suited to large-scale production. Some other examples are the outright waste that occurs because of favoritism (for example, promotion of an incompetent brother-in-law to a job he cannot do very well) or restrictive labor practices (for example, requiring a railroad to keep a fireman on a diesel-electric locomotive where there is no longer a fire to tend).

A particularly deplorable form of waste is caused by discrimination against African-American, Hispanic, native American or female workers. When a job is given, for example, to a white male in preference to an African-American woman who is more qualified, society sacrifices potential output and the entire community is apt to be affected adversely. Every one of these inefficiencies means that the community obtains less output than it could have, given the available inputs.

■ THE THREE COORDINATION TASKS OF ANY ECONOMY

Allocation of resources refers to the society's decisions on how to divide up its scarce input resources among the different outputs produced in the economy and among the different firms or other organizations that produce those outputs.

In deciding how to **allocate its scarce resources,** every society must somehow make three sorts of decisions:

- First, as we have emphasized, it must figure out *how to utilize its resources efficiently;* that is, it must find a way to reach its production possibilities frontier.
- Second, it must decide *which of the possible combinations of goods to produce*—how many missiles, automobiles, and so on; that is, it must select one specific point on the production possibilities frontier.
- Third, it must decide *how much of the total output of each good to distribute to each person,* doing so in a sensible way that does not assign meat to vegetarians and wine to teetotalers.

There are many ways in which societies can and do make each of these decisions—to which economists often refer as *how, what,* and *to whom?* For example, a central planner may tell people how to produce, what to produce, and what to consume, as the authorities used to do, at least to some extent, in the former Soviet Union. But in a market economy, no one group or individual makes all such resource allocation decisions explicitly. Rather, consumer demands and production costs allocate resources *automatically* and *anonymously* through a system of prices and markets. As the formerly socialist countries learned, markets do an impressively effective job in carrying out these tasks. For our introduction to the ways in which markets do all this, let's consider each task in turn.

■ SPECIALIZATION FOSTERS EFFICIENT RESOURCE ALLOCATION

Production efficiency is one of the economy's three basic tasks, and societies pursue it in many ways. But one source of efficiency is so fundamental that we must single it out for special attention: the tremendous productivity gains that stem from *specialization.*

■ The Wonders of the Division of Labor

Division of labor means breaking up a task into a number of smaller, more *specialized* tasks so that each worker can become more adept at a particular job.

Adam Smith, the founder of modern economics, first marveled at how **division of labor** raises efficiency and productivity when he visited a pin factory. In a famous passage near the beginning of his monumental book, *The Wealth of Nations* (1776), he described what he saw:

SOURCE: ©Bettmann/Corbis

> One man draws out the wire, another straightens it, a third cuts it, a fourth points it, a fifth grinds it at the top for receiving the head. To make the head requires two or three distinct operations; to put it on is a peculiar business, to whiten the pins is another; it is even a trade by itself to put them into the paper.[1]

Smith observed that by dividing the work to be done in this way, each worker became quite skilled in a particular specialty, and the productivity of the group of workers as a whole was greatly enhanced. As Smith related it:

---

[1] Adam Smith, *The Wealth of Nations* (New York: Random House, 1937), p. 4.

I have seen a small manufactory of this kind where ten men only were employed. . . . Those ten persons . . . could make among them upwards of forty-eight thousand pins in a day. . . . But if they had all wrought separately and independently . . . they certainly could not each of them have made twenty, *perhaps not one pin in a day.*[2]

In other words, through the miracle of division of labor and specialization, ten workers accomplished what might otherwise have required thousands. This was one of the secrets of the Industrial Revolution, which helped lift humanity out of the abject poverty that had been its lot for centuries.

■ The Amazing Principle of Comparative Advantage

But specialization in production fosters efficiency in an even more profound sense. Adam Smith noticed that *how* goods are produced can make a huge difference to productivity. But so can *which* goods are produced. The reason is that people (and businesses, and nations) have different abilities. Some can repair automobiles, whereas others are wizards with numbers. Some are handy with computers, and others can cook. An economy will be most efficient if people specialize in doing what they do best and then trade with one another, so that the accountant gets her car repaired and the computer programmer gets to eat tasty and nutritious meals.

This much is obvious. What is less obvious—and is one of the great ideas of economics—is that two people (or two businesses, or two countries) can generally gain from trade *even if one of them is more efficient than the other in producing everything.* A simple example will help explain why.

Some lawyers can type better than their administrative assistants. Should such a lawyer fire her assistant and do her own typing? Not likely. Even though the lawyer may type better than the assistant, good judgment tells her to concentrate on practicing law and leave the typing to a lower-paid assistant. Why? Because the *opportunity cost* of an hour devoted to typing is an hour less time spent with clients, which is a far more lucrative activity.

This example illustrates the principle of **comparative advantage** at work. The lawyer specializes in arguing cases despite her advantage as a typist because she has a *still greater* advantage as an attorney. She suffers some direct loss by leaving the typing to a less efficient employee, but she more than makes up for that loss by the income she earns selling her legal services to clients.

Precisely the same principle applies to nations. As we shall learn in greater detail in Chapter 34, comparative advantage underlies the economic analysis of international trade patterns. A country that is particularly adept at producing certain items—such as aircraft manufacturing in the United States, coffee growing in Brazil, and oil extraction in Saudi Arabia—should specialize in those activities, producing more than it wants for its own use. The country can then take the money it earns from its exports and purchase from other nations items that it does not make for itself. And this is still true if one of trading nations is the most efficient producer of almost everything.

The underlying logic is precisely the same as in our lawyer-typist example. The United States might, for example, be better than South Korea at manufacturing both computers and television sets. But if the United States is vastly more efficient at producing computers, but only slightly more efficient at making TV sets, it pays for the United States to specialize in computer manufacture, for South Korea to specialize in TV production, and for the two countries to trade.

This principle, called the *law of comparative advantage,* was discovered by David Ricardo, one of the giants in the history of economic analysis, almost 200 years ago. It is one of the *Ideas for Beyond the Final Exam* introduced in Chapter 1.

One country is said to have a **comparative advantage** over another in the production of a particular good *relative to other goods* if it produces that good less inefficiently than it **produces** other goods, as compared with the other country.

---

[2] Ibid., p. 5.
[3] This particular example is considered in detail in Chapter 34, which examines international trade.

IDEAS FOR BEYOND THE FINAL EXAM

THE SURPRISING PRINCIPLE OF COMPARATIVE ADVANTAGE Even if one country (or one worker) is worse than another country (or another worker) in the production of *every* good, it is said to have a *comparative advantage* in making the good at which it is *least inefficient*—compared to the other country. Ricardo discovered that two countries can gain by trading even if one country is more efficient than another in the production of *every* commodity. Precisely the same logic applies to individual workers or to businesses.

In determining the most efficient patterns of production and trade, it is comparative advantage that matters. Thus, a country can gain by importing a good from abroad even if that good can be produced more efficiently at home. Such imports make sense if they enable the country to specialize in producing those goods at which it is *even more efficient.*

SPECIALIZATION LEADS TO EXCHANGE

The gains from specialization are welcome, but they create a problem: With specialization, people no longer produce only what they want to consume themselves. The workers in Adam Smith's pin factory had no use for the thousands of pins they produced each day; they wanted to trade them for things like food, clothing, and shelter. Similarly, the administrative assistant has no personal use for the legal briefs she types. Thus, specialization requires some mechanism by which workers producing pins can *exchange* their wares with workers producing such things as cloth and potatoes, and office workers can turn their typing skills into things they want to consume.

Without a system of exchange, the productivity miracle achieved by comparative advantage and the division of labor would do society little good. With it, standards of living have risen enormously. As we observed in Chapter 1, such exchange benefits *all* participants.

IDEAS FOR BEYOND THE FINAL EXAM

TRADE IS A WIN-WIN SITUATION Mutual Gains from Voluntary Exchange Unless someone is deceived or misunderstands the facts, a *voluntary* exchange between two parties must make both parties better off—or else why would each party agree? Trading increases production by permitting specialization, as we have just seen. But even if no additional goods are produced as a result of the act of trading, the welfare of society is increased because each individual acquires goods that are more suited to his or her needs and tastes. This simple but fundamental precept of economics is another of our *Ideas for Beyond the Final Exam.*

Although people can and do trade goods for other goods, a system of exchange works better when everyone agrees to use some common item (such as pieces of paper with unique markings printed on them) for buying and selling things. Enter *money.* Then workers in pin factories, for example, can be paid in money rather than in pins, and they can use this money to purchase cloth and potatoes. Textile workers and farmers can do the same.

A **market system** is a form of economic organization in which resource allocation decisions are left to individual producers and consumers acting in their own best interests without central direction.

These two phenomena—specialization and exchange (assisted by money)—working in tandem led to vast improvements in humanity's well-being. But what forces induce workers to join together so that society can enjoy the fruits of the division of labor? And what forces establish a smoothly functioning system of exchange so that people can first exploit their comparative advantages and then acquire what they want to consume? One alternative is to have a central authority telling people what to do. Adam Smith explained and extolled yet another way of organizing and coordinating economic activity—markets and prices can coordinate those activities.

MARKETS, PRICES, AND THE THREE COORDINATION TASKS

Smith noted that people are adept at pursuing their own self-interests, and that a **market system** harnesses this self-interest remarkably well. As he put it—with clear religious overtones—in doing what is best for themselves, people are "led by an invisible hand" to promote the economic well-being of society as a whole.

Those of us who live in a well-functioning market economy like that found in the United States tend to take the achievements of the market for granted, much like the daily rising and setting of the sun. Few bother to think about, say, what makes Hawaiian pineapples show up daily in Vermont supermarkets. Although the process by which the market guides the economy in such an orderly fashion is subtle and complex, the general principles are well known.

The market deals with efficiency in production through the profit motive, which discourages firms from using inputs wastefully. Valuable resources (such as energy) command high prices, giving producers strong incentives to use them efficiently. The market mechanism also guides firms' output decisions, matching quantities produced to consumer preferences. A rise in the price of wheat because of increased demand for bread, for example, will persuade farmers to produce more wheat and devote less of their land to soybeans.

SOURCE: ©Robert W. Ginn/PhotoEdit

Finally, a price system distributes goods among consumers in accord with their tastes and preferences, using voluntary exchange to determine who gets what. Consumers spend their incomes on the things they like best (among those they can afford). But the ability to buy goods is hardly divided equally. Workers with valuable skills and owners of scarce resources can sell what they have at attractive prices. With the incomes they earn, they can purchase generous amounts of goods and services. Those who are less successful in selling what they own receive lower incomes and so can afford to buy less. In extreme cases, they may suffer severe deprivation.

This, in broad terms, is how a market economy solves the three basic problems facing any society: how to produce any given combination of goods efficiently, how to select an appropriate combination of goods to produce, and how to distribute these goods sensibly among people. As we proceed through the following chapters, you will learn much more about these issues. You will see that they constitute the central theme that permeates not only this text, but the work of economists in general. As you progress through this book, keep in mind two questions:

- What does the market do well?
- What does it do poorly?

There are numerous answers to both questions, as you will learn in subsequent chapters.

Society has many important goals. Some of them, such as producing goods and services with maximum efficiency (minimum waste), can be achieved extraordinarily well by letting markets operate more or less freely.

Free markets will not, however, achieve all of society's goals. For example, they often have trouble keeping unemployment low. In fact, the unfettered operations of markets may even run counter to some goals, such as protection of the environment. Many observers also believe that markets do not necessarily distribute income in accord with ethical or moral norms.

But even in cases in which markets do not perform well, there may be ways of harnessing the power of the market mechanism to remedy its own deficiencies, as you will learn in later chapters.

LAST WORD: DON'T CONFUSE ENDS WITH MEANS

Economic debates often have political and ideological overtones. So we will close this chapter by emphasizing that the central theme we have just outlined is neither a *defense of* nor an *attack on* the capitalist system. Nor is it a "conservative" position. One does not have to be a conservative to recognize that the market mechanism can be an extraordinarily helpful instrument for the pursuit of economic goals. Most of the formerly socialist countries of Europe have been working hard to "marketize" their economies, and even the communist People's Republic of China has made huge strides in that direction.

The point is not to confuse ends with means in deciding how much to rely on market forces. Liberals and conservatives surely have different goals. But the means chosen to pursue these goals should, for the most part, be chosen on the basis of how effective the selected means are, not on some ideological prejudgments.

Even Karl Marx emphasized that the market is remarkably efficient at producing an abundance of goods and services that had never been seen in precapitalist history. Such wealth can be used to promote conservative goals, such as reducing tax rates, or to facilitate goals favored by liberals, such as providing more generous public aid for the poor.

Certainly, the market cannot deal with every economic problem. Indeed, we have just noted that the market is the *source* of a number of significant problems. Even so, the evidence accumulated over centuries leads economists to believe that most economic problems are best handled by market techniques. The analysis in this book is intended to help you identify both the objectives that the market mechanism can reliably achieve and those that it will fail to promote, or at least not promote very effectively. We urge you to forget the slogans you have heard—whether from the left or from the right—and make up your own mind after learning the material in this book.

SUMMARY

1. Supplies of all **resources** are limited. Because resources are **scarce**, an **optimal decision** is one that chooses the best alternative among the options that are possible with the available resources.

2. With limited resources, a decision to obtain more of one item is also a decision to give up some of another. What we give up is called the **opportunity cost** of what we get. The opportunity cost is the true cost of any decision. This is one of the *Ideas for Beyond the Final Exam*.

3. When markets function effectively, firms are led to use resources efficiently and to produce the things that consumers want most. In such cases, opportunity costs and money costs (prices) correspond closely. When the market performs poorly, or when important, socially costly items are provided without charging an appropriate price, or are given away free, opportunity costs and money costs can diverge.

4. A firm's **production possibilities frontier** shows the combinations of goods it can produce, given the current technology and the resources at its disposal. The frontier is usually bowed outward because resources tend to be specialized.

5. The **principle of increasing costs** states that as the production of one good expands, the opportunity cost of producing another unit of that good generally increases.

6. Like a firm, the economy as a whole has a production possibilities frontier whose position is determined by its technology and by the available resources of land, labor, capital, and raw materials.

7. A firm or an economy that ends up at a point below its production possibilities frontier is using its resources inefficiently or wastefully. This is what happens, for example, when there is unemployment.

8. Economists define **efficiency** as the absence of waste. It is achieved primarily by the gains in productivity brought about through **specialization** that exploits **division of labor** and **comparative advantage** and by a system of exchange.

9. Two countries (or two people) can gain by specializing in the activity in which each has a *comparative* advantage and then trading with one another. These gains from trade remain available even if one country is inferior at producing everything. This so-called principle of comparative advantage is one of our *Ideas for Beyond the Final Exam*.

10. If an exchange is voluntary, both parties must benefit, even if no additional goods are produced. This is another of the *Ideas for Beyond the Final Exam*.

11. Every economic system must find a way to answer three basic questions: How can goods be produced most efficiently?

How much of each good should be produced? How should goods be distributed among users?

12. The **market system** works very well in solving some of society's basic problems, but it fails to remedy others and may, indeed, create some of its own. Where and how it succeeds and fails constitute the central theme of this book and characterize the work of economists in general.

KEY TERMS

Resources 40	Inputs 42	Allocation of resources 48
Opportunity cost 41	Production possibilities frontier 43	Division of labor 48
Optimal decision 41	Principle of increasing costs 44	Comparative advantage 49
Outputs 42	Efficiency 47	Market system 50

TEST YOURSELF

1. A person rents a house for which she pays the landlord $12,000 per year. The house can be purchased for $100,000, and the tenant has this much money in a bank account that pays 4 percent interest per year. Is buying the house a good deal for the tenant? Where does opportunity cost enter the picture?

2. Graphically show the production possibilities frontier for the nation of Stromboli, using the data given in the following table. Does the principle of increasing cost hold in Stromboli?

Stromboli's 2002 Production Possibilities	
Pizzas per Year	Pizza Ovens per Year
75,000,000	0
60,000,000	6,000
45,000,000	11,000
30,000,000	15,000
15,000,000	18,000
0	20,000

3. Consider two alternatives for Stromboli in 2002. In case (a), its inhabitants eat 60 million pizzas and build 6,000 pizza ovens. In case (b), the population eats 15 million pizzas but builds 18,000 ovens. Which case will lead to a more generous production possibilities frontier for Stromboli in 2003?

4. Jasmine's Snack Shop sells two brands of potato chips. Brand X costs Jasmine 60 cents per bag, and Brand Y costs her $1. Draw Jasmine's production possibilities frontier if she has $60 budgeted to spend on potato chips. Why is it not "bowed out"?

DISCUSSION QUESTIONS

1. Discuss the resource limitations that affect:

   a. the poorest person on earth

   b. Bill Gates, the richest person on earth

   c. a farmer in Kansas

   d. the government of Indonesia

2. If you were president of your college, what would you change if your budget were cut by 10 percent? By 25 percent? By 50 percent?

3. If you were to leave college, what things would change in your life? What, then, is the opportunity cost of your education?

4. Raising chickens requires several types of feed, such as corn and soy meal. Consider a farm in the former Soviet Union. Try to describe how decisions on the number of chickens to be raised, and the amount of each feed to use in raising them, were made under the old communist regime. If the farm is now privately owned, how does the market guide the decisions that used to be made by the central planning agency?

5. The United States is one of the world's wealthiest countries. Think of a recent case in which the decisions of the U.S. government were severely constrained by scarcity. Describe the trade-offs that were involved. What were the opportunity costs of the decisions that were actually made?

SUPPLY AND DEMAND:
AN INITIAL LOOK

The free enterprise system is absolutely too important to be left to the voluntary action of the marketplace.

FLORIDA CONGRESSMAN RICHARD KELLY, 1979

I n this chapter, we study the economist's most basic investigative tool: the mechanism of supply and demand. Whether your Econ course concentrates on macroeconomics or microeconomics, you will find that the so-called law of supply and demand is a fundamental tool of economic analysis. Economists use supply and demand analysis to study issues as diverse as inflation and unemployment, the effects of taxes on prices, government regulation of business, and environmental protection. Supply and demand curves—graphs that relate price to quantity supplied and quantity demanded, respectively—show how prices and quantities are determined in a free market.[1]

A major theme of the chapter is that governments around the world and throughout recorded history have tampered with the price mechanism. As we will see, these bouts with Adam Smith's "invisible hand" have produced undesirable side effects that often surprised and dismayed the authorities. The invisible hand fights back!

CONTENTS

---

[1] This chapter, like much of the rest of this book, uses many graphs like those described in the appendix to Chapter 1. If you have difficulties with these graphs, we suggest that you review that material before proceeding.

PUZZLE: *What Happened to Oil Prices?*

Since 1949, the dollars of purchasing power that a buyer had to pay to buy a barrel of oil has remained remarkably steady, and gasoline has continued to be a bargain. But there were two exceptional time periods—one from about 1975 through 1985, and one beginning in 2003—when oil prices exploded, and filling up the automobile gas tank became painful to consumers. Clearly, supply and demand changes must have been behind these developments. But what led them to change so much and so suddenly? Later in the chapter, we will provide excerpts from a newspaper story about the more recent oil crisis that describes some dramatic events behind suddenly shifting supply, and will help to bring the analysis of this chapter to life.

SOURCE: © Kim Kulish/Corbis

■ THE INVISIBLE HAND

The **invisible hand** is a phrase used by Adam Smith to describe how, by pursuing their own self-interests, people in a market system are "led by an invisible hand" to promote the well-being of the community.

Adam Smith, the father of modern economic analysis, greatly admired the price system. He marveled at its accomplishments—both as an efficient producer of goods and as a guarantor that consumers' preferences are obeyed. Although many people since Smith's time have shared his enthusiasm for the concept of the **invisible hand**, many have not. Smith's contemporaries in the American colonies, for example, were often unhappy with the prices produced by free markets and thought they could do better by legislative decree. Such attempts failed, as explained in the accompanying box, "Price Controls at Valley Forge." In countless other instances, the public was outraged by the prices charged on the open market, particularly in the case of housing rents, interest rates, and insurance rates.

Attempts to control interest rates (which are the price of borrowing money) go back hundreds of years before the birth of Christ, at least to the code of laws compiled under the Babylonian king Hammurabi in about 1800 B.C. Our historical legacy also includes a rather long list of price ceilings on foods and other products imposed in the reign of Diocletian, emperor of the declining Roman Empire. More recently, Americans have been offered the "protection" of a variety of price controls. Laws have placed ceilings on some prices (such as rents) to protect buyers, whereas legislation has placed floors under other prices (such as farm products) to protect sellers. Yet, somehow, everything such regulation touches seems to end up in even greater disarray than it was before. Despite rent controls, rents in New York City have soared. Despite laws against "scalping," tickets for popular shows and sports events sell at tremendous premiums—tickets to the Super Bowl, for example, often fetch thousands of dollars on the "gray" market. To understand what goes wrong when we tamper with markets, we must first learn how they operate unfettered. This chapter takes a first step in that direction by studying the machinery of supply and demand. Then, at the end of the chapter, we return to the issue of price controls.

Every market has both buyers and sellers. We begin our analysis on the consumers' side of the market.

Price Controls at Valley Forge

George Washington, the history books tell us, was beset by many enemies during the winter of 1777–1778, including the British, their Hessian mercenaries, and the merciless winter weather. But he had another enemy that the history books ignore—an enemy that meant well but almost destroyed his army at Valley Forge. As the following excerpt explains, that enemy was the Pennsylvania legislature:

In Pennsylvania, where the main force of Washington's army was quartered . . . the legislature . . . decided to try a period of price control limited to those commodities needed for use by the army. . . . The result might have been anticipated by those with some knowledge of the trials and tribulations of other states. The prices of uncontrolled goods, mostly imported, rose to record heights. Most farmers kept back their produce, refusing to sell at what they regarded as an unfair price. Some who had large families to take care of even secretly sold their food to the British who paid in gold.

After the disastrous winter at Valley Forge when Washington's army nearly starved to death (thanks largely to these well-intentioned but misdirected laws), the ill-fated experiment in price controls was finally ended. The Continental Congress on June 4, 1778, adopted the following resolution:

"Whereas . . . it hath been found by experience that limitations upon the prices of commodities are not only ineffectual

Valley Forge.

for the purposes proposed, but likewise productive of very evil consequences . . . resolved, that it be recommended to the several states to repeal or suspend all laws or resolutions within the said states respectively limiting, regulating or restraining the Price of any Article, Manufacture or Commodity."

SOURCE: Robert L. Schuettinger and Eamonn F. Butler, *Forty Centuries of Wage and Price Controls* (Washington, D.C.: Heritage Foundation, 1979), p. 41. Reprinted by permission.

■ DEMAND AND QUANTITY DEMANDED

People commonly think of consumer demands as fixed amounts. For example, when product designers propose a new computer model, management asks: "What is its market potential?" That is, just how many are likely to be sold? Similarly, government bureaus conduct studies to determine how many engineers or doctors the United States will require (demand) in subsequent years.

Economists respond that such questions are not well posed—that there is no single answer to such a question. Rather, they say, the "market potential" for computers or the number of engineers that will be "required" depends on a great number of influences, including the price charged for each.

The quantity demanded of any product normally depends on its price. Quantity demanded also depends on a number of other determinants, including population size, consumer incomes, tastes, and the prices of other products.

Because prices play a central role in a market economy, we begin our study of demand by focusing on how quantity demanded depends on price. A little later, we will bring the other determinants of quantity demanded back into the picture. For now, we will consider all influences other than price to be fixed. This assumption, often expressed as "other things being equal," is used in much of economic analysis. As an example of the relationship between price and demand, let's think about the quantity of milk demanded. If the price of milk is very high, its "market potential" may be very small. People will find ways to get along with less milk, perhaps by switching to fruit juice or soda. If the price of milk declines, people will tend to drink more milk. They may give their children larger portions or switch away from juices and sodas. Thus:

There is no one demand figure for milk, or for computers, or for engineers. Rather, there is a different quantity demanded at each possible price, all other influences being held constant.

The **quantity demanded** is the number of units of a good that consumers are willing and can afford to buy over a specified period of time.

■ The Demand Schedule

A **demand schedule** is a table showing how the quantity demanded of some product during a specified period of time changes as the price of that product changes, holding all other determinants of quantity demanded constant.

A **demand curve** is a graphical depiction of a demand schedule. It shows how the quantity demanded of some product will change as the price of that product changes during a specified period of time, holding all other determinants of quantity demanded constant.

Table 1 shows how such information for milk can be recorded in a **demand schedule.** It indicates how much milk consumers in a particular area are willing and able to buy at different possible prices during a specified period of time, other things held equal. Specifically, the table shows the quantity of milk that will be demanded in a year at each possible price ranging from $1.50 to $0.90 per quart. At a relatively low price, such as $1 per quart, customers wish to purchase 70 billion quarts per year. But if the price were to rise to, say, $1.40 per quart, quantity demanded would fall to 50 billion quarts.

Common sense tells us why this happens.[2] First, as prices rise, some customers will reduce the quantity of milk they consume. Second, higher prices will induce some customers to drop out of the market entirely—for example, by switching to soda or juice. On both counts, quantity demanded will decline as the price rises.

TABLE 1		
Demand Schedule for Milk		
Price per Quart	Quantity Demanded	Label in Figure 1
$1.50	45	A
1.40	**50**	**B**
1.30	55	C
1.20	60	E
1.10	65	F
1.00	**70**	**G**
0.90	75	H

Note: Quantity is in billions of quarts per year.

As the price of an item rises, the quantity demanded normally falls. As the price falls, the quantity demanded normally rises, all other things held constant.

FIGURE 1

Demand Curve for Milk

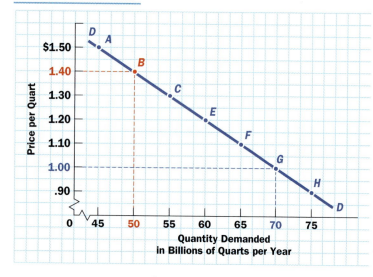

Quantity Demanded in Billions of Quarts per Year

■ The Demand Curve

The information contained in Table 1 can be summarized in a graph like Figure 1, which is called a **demand curve.** Each point in the graph corresponds to a line in the table. This curve shows the relationship between price and quantity demanded. For example, it tells us that to sell 70 billion quarts per year, the price must be $1.00. This relationship is shown at point *G* in Figure 1. If the price were $1.40, however, consumers would demand only 50 billion quarts (point *B*). Because the quantity demanded declines as the price increases, the demand curve has a negative slope.[3]

Notice the last phrase in the definitions of the demand schedule and the demand curve: "holding all other determinants of quantity demanded constant." What are some of these "other things," and how do they affect the demand curve?

■ Shifts of the Demand Curve

The quantity of milk demanded is subject to a variety of influences other than the price of milk. Changes in population size and characteristics, consumer incomes and tastes, and the prices of alternative beverages such as soda and orange juice presumably change the quantity of milk demanded, even if the price of milk does not change.

Because the demand curve for milk depicts only the relationship between the quantity of milk demanded and the price of milk, holding all other factors constant, a change in milk price moves the market for milk from one point on the demand curve

---

[2] This common-sense answer is examined more fully in later chapters.

[3] If you need to review the concept of slope, refer back to the appendix to Chapter 1

to another point on the same curve. However, a change in any of these other influences on demand causes a **shift of the entire demand curve.** More generally:

> *A change in the price of a good produces a movement* along *a fixed demand curve. By contrast, a change in any other variable that influences quantity demanded produces a shift of the* entire *demand curve.*

If consumers want to buy more milk at every given price than they wanted previously, the demand curve shifts to the right (or outward). If they desire less at every given price, the demand curve shifts to the left (or inward toward the origin).

Figure 2 shows this distinction graphically. If the price of milk falls from $1.30 to $1.10 per quart, and quantity demanded rises accordingly, we move along demand curve D_0D_0 from point C to point F, as shown by the red arrow. If, on the other hand, consumers suddenly decide that they like milk better than they did formerly, or if more children are born who need more milk, the entire demand curve shifts outward from D_0D_0 to D_1D_1, as indicated by the blue arrows, meaning that at *any* given price consumers are now willing to buy more milk than before. To make this general idea more concrete, and to show some of its many applications, let us consider some specific examples of those "other things" that can shift demand curves.

Consumer Incomes   If average incomes rise, consumers will purchase more of most goods, including milk, even if the prices of those goods remain the same. That is, increases in income normally shift demand curves outward to the right, as depicted in Figure 3(a), where the demand curve shifts outward from D_0D_0 to D_1D_1, establishing a new price and output quantity.

Population   Population growth affects quantity demanded in more or less the same way as increases in average incomes. For instance, a larger population will presumably want to consume more milk, even if the price of milk and average incomes do not change, thus shifting the entire demand curve to the right, as in Figure 3(a). The equilibrium price and quantity both rise.

A **shift in a demand curve** occurs when any relevant variable other than price changes. If consumers want to buy *more* at any and all given prices than they wanted previously, the demand curve shifts to the right (or outward). If they desire *less* at any given price, the demand curve shifts to the left (or inward).

FIGURE 2

Movements along versus Shifts of a Demand Curve

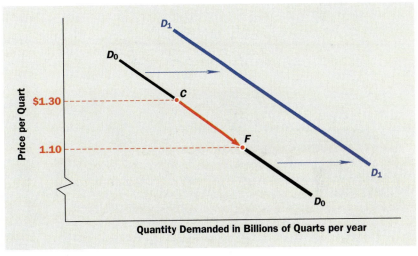

Increases in particular population segments can also elicit shifts in demand—for example, the United States experienced a miniature population boom between the late 1970s and mid-1990s. This group (which is dubbed Generation Y and includes most users of this book) has sparked higher demand for such items as cell phones and video games.

In Figure 3(b), we see that a decrease in population should shift the demand curve for milk to the left from D_0D_0 to D_2D_2.

Consumer Preferences   If the dairy industry mounts a successful advertising campaign extolling the benefits of drinking milk, families may decide to buy more at any given price. If so, the entire demand curve for milk would shift to the right, as in Figure 3(a). Alternatively, a medical report on the dangers of kidney stones may persuade consumers to drink less milk, thereby shifting the demand curve to the left, as in Figure 3(b). Again, these are general phenomena:

> *If consumer preferences shift in favor of a particular item, its demand curve will shift outward to the right, as in Figure 3(a).*

FIGURE 3

Shifts of the Demand
Curve

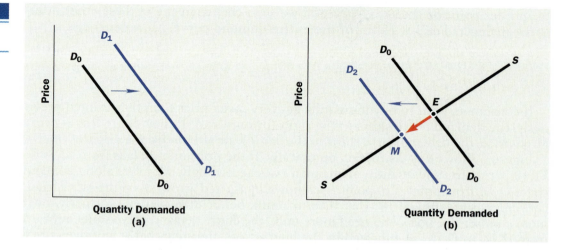

An example is the ever-shifting "rage" in children's toys—be it Yu-Gi-Oh! cards, electronic "Elmo" dolls, or the latest video games. These items become the object of desperate hunts as parents snap them up for their offspring, and stores are unable to keep up with the demand.

Prices and Availability of Related Goods   Because soda, orange juice, and coffee are popular drinks that compete with milk, a change in the price of any of these other beverages can be expected to shift the demand curve for milk. If any of these alternative

Volatility in Electricity Prices

The following newspaper story excerpt shows the dramatic effect on prices that can sometimes result from a shift in a demand curve. The source of the accompanying graph is Enron Corporation, the former energy trading and commodities company that has been labeled one of the worst offenders in the corporate scandals that came to light in the last few years. Although Enron was found to have distorted many relevant facts, what is reported in this excerpt from the *New York Times* is generally true. What *is* left out, however, is how Enron is said to have manipulated the market and distorted market prices to favor people in top management at the expense of consumers and company employees. Such a scenario demonstrates how a powerful firm can distort the supply-demand mechanism and manipulate its results.

"Because no one can stockpile electricity . . . prices have proved to be extremely volatile at times of high demand like a recent summer's heat waves. Here is the *Cinergy-Power Markets Week* daily index, in dollars per megawatt hour. When heat waves blistered much of the country in June and July of 1998, utility customers in cities like Dallas ran fans and air conditioners nonstop, and power demand soared. So the price of electricity exploded, as the graph demonstrates."

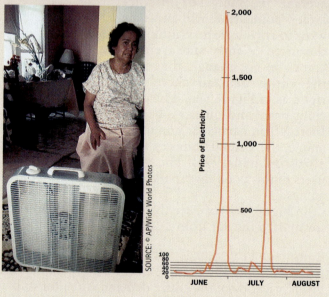

NOTE: Quantity is in billions of quarts per year.

SOURCES: *New York Times*, Business Section, August 23, 1998, p. 4 (text). Scatter Graph showing power prices from July to August from "A 20,000% Bounce: Now That's Volatility" by A.R. Myerson, *The New York Times*, Business Section, August 8, 1998, p. 4. Copyright © 1998 by The New York Times. Reprinted by permission; Enron Corporation (graph).

drinks becomes cheaper, some consumers will switch away from milk. Thus, the demand curve for milk will shift to the left, as in Figure 3(b). Other price changes may shift the demand curve for milk in the opposite direction. For example, suppose that cookies, which are often consumed with milk, become less expensive. This may induce some consumers to drink more milk and thus shift the demand curve for milk to the right, as in Figure 3(a). In general:

> Increases in the prices of goods that are substitutes for the good in question (as soda is for milk) move the demand curve to the right. Increases in the prices of goods that are normally used together with the good in question (such as cookies and milk) shift the demand curve to the left.

This is just what happened when a frost wiped out almost half of Brazil's coffee bean harvest in 1995. The three largest U.S. coffee producers raised their prices by 45 percent, and, as a result, the demand curve for alternative beverages such as tea shifted to the right. Then in 1998, coffee prices dropped about 34 percent, which in turn caused the demand curve for tea to shift toward the left (or toward the origin).

Although the preceding list does not exhaust the possible influences on quantity demanded, we have said enough to suggest the principles followed by demand and shifts of demand. Let's turn now to the supply side of the market.

■ SUPPLY AND QUANTITY SUPPLIED

Like quantity demanded, the quantity of milk that is supplied by business firms such as dairy farms is not a fixed number; it also depends on many things. Obviously, we expect more milk to be supplied if there are more dairy farms or more cows per farm. Cows may give less milk if bad weather deprives them of their feed. As before, however, let's turn our attention first to the relationship between the price and quantity of milk supplied.

Economists generally suppose that a higher price calls forth a greater **quantity supplied.** Why? Remember our analysis of the principle of increasing cost in Chapter 3 (page 44). According to that principle, as more of any farmer's (or the nation's) resources are devoted to milk production, the opportunity cost of obtaining another quart of milk increases. Farmers will therefore find it profitable to increase milk production only if they can sell the milk at a higher price—high enough to cover the additional costs incurred to expand production.

In other words, it normally will take higher prices to persuade farmers to raise milk production. This idea is quite general and applies to the supply of most goods and services.[4] As long as suppliers want to make profits and the principle of increasing costs holds:

> As the price of any commodity rises, the quantity supplied normally rises. As the price falls, the quantity supplied normally falls.

*The **quantity supplied** is the number of units that sellers want to sell over a specified period of time.*

■ The Supply Schedule and the Supply Curve

Table 2 shows the relationship between the price of milk and its quantity supplied. Tables such as this one are called **supply schedules;** they show how much sellers are willing to provide during a specified period at alternative possible prices. This particular supply schedule tells us that a low price like $1.00 per quart will induce suppliers to provide only 40 billion quarts, whereas a higher price like $1.30 will induce them to provide much more—70 billion quarts.

*A **supply schedule** is a table showing how the quantity supplied of some product changes as the price of that product changes during a specified period of time, holding all other determinants of quantity supplied constant.*

---

[4] This analysis is carried out in much greater detail in later chapters.

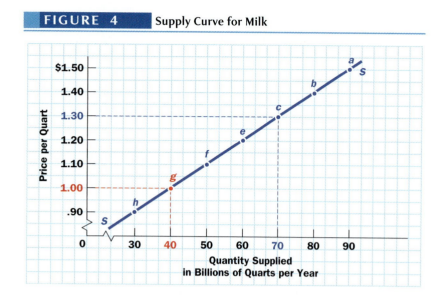

FIGURE 4   Supply Curve for Milk

Price per Quart (vertical axis): $1.50, 1.40, 1.30, 1.20, 1.10, 1.00, .90

Quantity Supplied in Billions of Quarts per Year (horizontal axis): 0, 30, 40, 50, 60, 70, 80, 90

TABLE 2		
Supply Schedule for Milk		
Price per Quart	Quantity Supplied	Label in Figure 4
$1.50	90	a
1.40	80	b
1.30	70	c
1.20	60	e
1.10	50	f
1.00	40	g
0.90	30	h

Note: Quantity is in billions of quarts per year.

A **supply curve** is a graphical depiction of a supply schedule. It shows how the quantity supplied of some product will change as the price of that product changes during a specified period of time, holding all other determinants of quantity supplied constant.

As you might have guessed, when such information is plotted on a graph, it is called a **supply curve.** Figure 4 is the supply curve corresponding to the supply schedule in Table 2, showing the relationship between the price of milk and the quantity supplied. It slopes upward—it has a positive slope—because quantity supplied is higher when price is higher. Notice again the same phrase in the definition: "holding all other determinants of quantity supplied constant." What are these "other determinants"?

■ Shifts of the Supply Curve

Like quantity demanded, the quantity supplied in a market typically responds to many influences other than price. The weather, the cost of feed, the number and size of dairy farms, and a variety of other factors all influence how much milk will be brought to market. Because the supply curve depicts only the relationship between the price of milk and the quantity of milk supplied, holding all other influences constant, a change in any of these other determinants of quantity supplied will cause the entire supply curve to shift. That is:

> A change in the price of the good causes a movement *along* a fixed supply curve. Price is not the only influence on quantity supplied, however. If any of these other influences change, the *entire* supply curve shifts.

Figure 5 depicts this distinction graphically. A rise in price from $1.10 to $1.30 will raise quantity supplied by moving along supply curve $S_0 S_0$ from point f to point c. Any rise in quantity supplied attributable to an influence other than price, however, will shift the *entire* supply curve outward to the right from $S_0 S_0$ to $S_1 S_1$, as shown by the blue arrows. Let us consider what some of these other influences are and how they shift the supply curve.

Size of the Industry   We begin with the most obvious influence. If more farmers enter the milk industry, the quantity supplied at any given price will increase. For example, if each farm provides 600,000 quarts of milk per year at a price of $1.10 per quart, then 100,000 farmers would provide 60 billion quarts, but 130,000 farmers would provide 78 billion. Thus, when more farms are in the industry, the quantity of milk supplied will be greater at any given price—and hence the supply curve will move farther to the right.

Figure 6(a) illustrates the effect of an expansion of the industry from 100,000 farms to 130,000 farms—a rightward shift of the supply curve from S_0S_0 to S_1S_1. Figure 6(b) illustrates the opposite case: a contraction of the industry from 100,000 farms to 62,500 farms. The supply curve shifts inward to the left from S_0S_0 to S_2S_2. Even if no farmers enter or leave the industry, results like those depicted in Figure 6 can be produced by expansion or contraction of the *existing* farms.

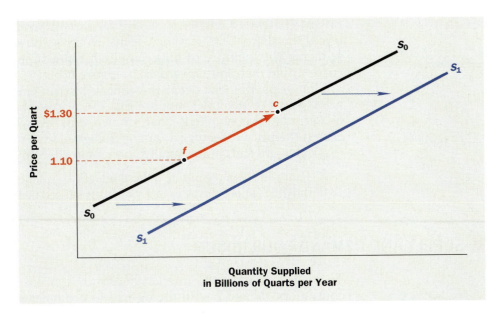

FIGURE 5

Movements along versus Shifts of a Supply Curve

Technological Progress   Another influence that shifts supply curves is technological change. Suppose some enterprising farmer invents a new milking machine that uses much less electricity. Thereafter, at any given price, farms will be able to produce more milk; that is, the supply curve will shift outward to the right, as in Figure 6(a). This example, again, illustrates a general influence that applies to most industries:

> **Technological progress that reduces costs will shift the supply curve outward to the right.**

Automakers, for example, have been able to reduce production costs since industrial technology invented robots that can be programmed to work on several different car models. This technological advance has shifted the supply curve outward.

Prices of Inputs   Changes in input prices also shift supply curves. Suppose a drought raises the price of animal feed. Farmers will have to pay more to keep their cows alive and healthy and consequently will no longer be able to provide the same quantity of milk at each possible price. This example illustrates that:

> **Increases in the prices of inputs that suppliers must buy will shift the supply curve inward to the left.**

FIGURE 6   Shifts of the Supply Curve

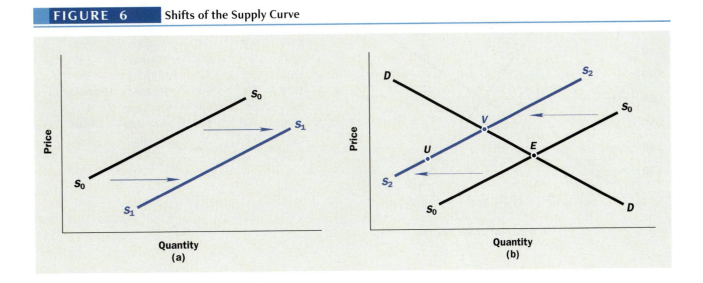

Prices of Related Outputs   Dairy farms sell products other than milk. If cheese prices rise sharply, farmers may decide to use some raw milk to make cheese, thereby reducing the quantity of milk supplied. On a supply-demand diagram, the supply curve would then shift inward, as in Figure 6(b).

Similar phenomena occur in other industries, and sometimes the effect goes the other way. For example, suppose that the price of beef goes up, which increases the quantity of meat supplied. That, in turn, will raise the number of cowhides supplied even if the price of leather does not change. Thus, a rise in the price of beef will lead to a rightward shift in the supply curve of leather. In general:

> A change in the price of one good produced by a multiproduct industry may be expected to shift the supply curves of other goods produced by that industry.

SUPPLY AND DEMAND EQUILIBRIUM

A **supply-demand diagram** graphs the supply and demand curves together. It also determines the equilibrium price and quantity.

To analyze how the free market determines price, we must compare the desires of consumers (demand) with the desires of producers (supply) to see whether the two plans are consistent. Table 3 and Figure 7 help us do this.

Table 3 brings together the demand schedule from Table 1 and the supply schedule from Table 2. Similarly, Figure 7 puts the demand curve from Figure 1 and the supply curve from Figure 4 on a single graph. Such graphs are called **supply-demand diagrams,** and you will encounter many of them in this book. Notice that, for reasons already discussed, the demand curve has a negative slope and the supply curve has a positive slope. That is generally true of supply-demand diagrams.

In a free market, price and quantity are determined by the intersection of the supply and demand curves. At only one point in Figure 7, point *E*, do the supply curve and the demand curve intersect. At the price corresponding to point *E*, which is $1.20 per quart, the quantity supplied and the quantity demanded are both 60 billion quarts per year. This means that at a price of $1.20 per quart, consumers are willing to buy exactly what producers are willing to sell.

At a lower price, such as $1.00 per quart, only 40 billion quarts of milk will be supplied (point *g*) whereas 70 billion quarts will be demanded (point *G*). Thus, quantity

---

FIGURE 7

Supply-Demand Equilibrium

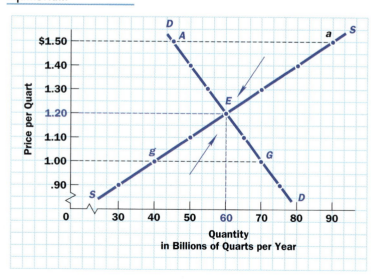

TABLE 3

Determination of the Equilibrium Price and Quantity of Milk

Price per Quart	Quantity Demanded	Quantity Supplied	Surplus or Shortage?	Price Direction
$1.50	45	90	**Surplus**	**Fall**
1.40	50	80	Surplus	Fall
1.30	55	70	Surplus	Fall
1.20	60	60	**Neither**	**Unchanged**
1.10	65	50	Shortage	Rise
1.00	70	40	**Shortage**	**Rise**
0.90	75	30	Shortage	Rise

demanded will exceed quantity supplied. There will be a **shortage** equal to 70 minus 40, or 30 billion quarts. Price will thus be driven up by unsatisfied demand. Alternatively, at a higher price, such as $1.50 per quart, quantity supplied will be 90 billion quarts (point *a*) and quantity demanded will be only 45 billion (point *A*). Quantity supplied will exceed quantity demanded—creating a **surplus** equal to 90 minus 45, or 45 billion quarts.

Because $1.20 is the price at which quantity supplied and quantity demanded are equal, we say that $1.20 per quart is the equilibrium price (or the "market clearing" price) in this market. Similarly, 60 billion quarts per year is the equilibrium quantity of milk. The term **equilibrium** merits a little explanation, because it arises so frequently in economic analysis.

An equilibrium is a situation in which there are no inherent forces that produce change. Think, for example, of a pendulum resting at its center point. If no outside force (such as a person's hand) comes to push it, the pendulum will remain exactly where it is; it is therefore in equilibrium.

If you give the pendulum a shove, however, its equilibrium will be disturbed and it will start to move. When it reaches the top of its arc, the pendulum will, for an instant, be at rest again. This point is not an equilibrium position, for the force of gravity will pull the pendulum downward. Thereafter, gravity and friction will govern its motion from side to side. Eventually, the pendulum will return to its original position. The fact that the pendulum tends to return to its original position is described by saying that this position is a *stable* equilibrium. That position is also the only equilibrium position of the pendulum. At any other point, inherent forces will cause the pendulum to move.

The concept of equilibrium in economics is similar and can be illustrated by our supply-and-demand example. Why is no price other than $1.20 an equilibrium price in Table 3 or Figure 7? What forces will change any other price?

Consider first a low price such as $1.00, at which quantity demanded (70 billion quarts) exceeds quantity supplied (40 billion quarts). If the price were this low, many frustrated customers would be unable to purchase the quantities they desired. In their scramble for the available supply of milk, some would offer to pay more. As customers sought to outbid one another, the market price would be forced up. Thus, a price below the equilibrium price cannot persist in a free market because a shortage sets in motion powerful economic forces that push the price upward.

Similar forces operate if the market price exceeds the equilibrium price. If, for example, the price should somehow reach $1.50, Table 3 tells us that quantity supplied (90 billion quarts) would far exceed the quantity demanded (45 billion quarts). Producers would be unable to sell their desired quantities of milk at the prevailing price, and some would undercut their competitors by reducing price. Such competitive price cutting would continue as long as the surplus remained—that is, as long as quantity supplied exceeded quantity demanded. Thus, a price above the equilibrium price cannot persist indefinitely.

We are left with a clear conclusion. The price of $1.20 per quart and the quantity of 60 billion quarts per year constitute the only price-quantity combination that does not sow the seeds of its own destruction. It is thus the only equilibrium for this market. Any lower price must rise, and any higher price must fall. It is as if natural economic forces place a magnet at point *E* that attracts the market, just as gravity attracts a pendulum.

The pendulum analogy is worth pursuing further. Most pendulums are more frequently in motion than at rest. However, unless they are repeatedly buffeted by outside forces (which, of course, is exactly what happens to economic equilibria in reality), pendulums gradually return to their resting points. The same is true of price and quantity in a free market. They are moved about by shifts in the supply and demand curves that we have already described. As a consequence, markets are not always in equilibrium. But, if nothing interferes with them, experience shows that they normally move toward equilibrium.

A **shortage** is an excess of quantity demanded over quantity supplied. When there is a shortage, buyers cannot purchase the quantities they desire at the current price.

A **surplus** is an excess of quantity supplied over quantity demanded. When there is a surplus, sellers cannot sell the quantities they desire to supply at the current price.

An **equilibrium** is a situation in which there are no inherent forces that produce change. Changes away from an equilibrium position will occur only as a result of "outside events" that disturb the status quo.

The **law of supply and demand** states that in a free market the forces of supply and demand generally push the price toward the level at which quantity supplied and quantity demanded are equal.

The Law of Supply and Demand

In a free market, the forces of supply and demand generally push the price toward its equilibrium level, the price at which quantity supplied and quantity demanded are equal. Like most economic "laws," some markets will occasionally disobey the law of supply and demand. Markets sometimes display shortages or surpluses for long periods of time. Prices sometimes fail to move toward equilibrium. But the "law" is a fair generalization that is right far more often than it is wrong.

EFFECTS OF DEMAND SHIFTS ON SUPPLY-DEMAND EQUILIBRIUM

Figure 3 showed how developments other than changes in price—such as increases in consumer income—can shift the demand curve. We saw that a rise in income, for example, will shift the demand curve to the right, meaning that at any given price, consumers—with their increased purchasing power—will buy more of the good than before. This, in turn, will move the equilibrium point, changing both market price and quantity sold.

This market adjustment is shown in Figure 8(a). It adds a supply curve to Figure 3(a) so that we can see what happens to the supply-demand equilibrium. In the example in the graph, the quantity demanded at the old equilibrium price of $1.20 increases from 60 billion quarts per year (point E on the demand curve D_0D_0) to 75 billion quarts per year (point R on the demand curve D_1D_1). We know that $1.20 is no longer the equilibrium price, because at this price quantity demanded (75 billion quarts) exceeds quantity supplied (60 billion quarts). To restore equilibrium, the price must rise. The new equilibrium occurs at point T, where the price is $1.30 per quart and both quantities demanded and supplied are 70 billion quarts per year. This example illustrates a general result, which is true when the supply curve slopes upward:

Any influence that makes the demand curve shift outward to the right, and does not affect the supply curve, will raise the equilibrium price and the equilibrium quantity.[5]

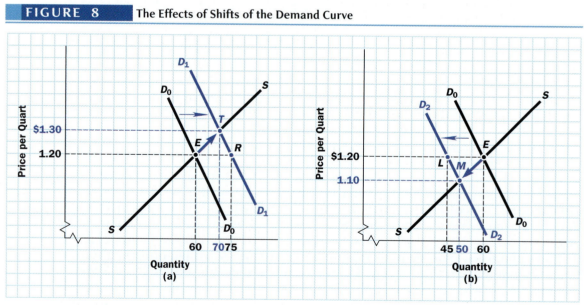

FIGURE 8   The Effects of Shifts of the Demand Curve

Note: Quantity is in billions of quarts per year.

---

[5] For example, when incomes rise rapidly, in many developing countries the demand curves for a variety of consumer goods shift rapidly outward to the right. In Japan, for example, the demand for used Levi's jeans and Nike running shoes from the United States skyrocketed in the early 1990s as status-conscious Japanese consumers searched for outlets for their then-rising incomes.

The Ups and Downs of Milk Consumption

The following excerpt from a U.S Department of Agriculture publication discusses some of the things that have affected the consumption of milk in the last century.

"In 1909, Americans consumed a total of 34 gallons of fluid milk per person—27 gallons of whole milk and 7 gallons of milks lower in fat than whole milk, mostly buttermilk....Fluid milk consumption shot up from 34 gallons per person in 1941 to a peak of 45 gallons per person in 1945. War production lifted Americans' incomes but curbed civilian production and the goods consumers could buy. Many food items were rationed, including meats, butter and sugar. Milk was not rationed, and consumption soared. Since 1945, however, milk consumption has fallen steadily, reaching a record low of just under 23 gallons per person in 2001 (the latest year for which data are available). Steep declines in consumption of whole milk and buttermilk far outpaced an increase in other lower fat milks. By 2001, Americans were consuming less than 8 gallons per person of whole milk, compared with nearly 41 gallons in 1945 and 25 gallons in 1970. In contrast, per capita consumption of total lower fat milks was 15 gallons in 2001, up from 4 gallons in 1945 and 6 gallons in 1970. These changes are consistent with increased public concern about cholesterol, saturated fat, and calories. However, decline in per capita consumption of fluid milk also may be attributed to competition from other beverages, especially carbonated soft drinks and bottled water, a smaller percentage of children and adolescents in the U.S., and a more ethnically diverse population whose diet does not normally include milk."

SOURCE: Judy Putnam and Jane Allshouse, "Trends in U.S. Per Capita Consumption of Dairy Products, 1909 to 2001," *Amber Waves: The Economics of Food, Farming, Natural Resources and Rural America,* June 2003, U.S. Department of Agriculture, available at http://www.usda.gov.

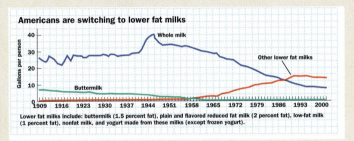

Americans are switching to lower fat milks

Lower fat milks include: buttermilk (1.5 percent fat), plain and flavored reduced fat milk (2 percent fat), low-fat milk (1 percent fat), nonfat milk, and yogurt made from these milks (except frozen yogurt).

Everything works in reverse if consumer incomes fall. Figure 8(b) depicts a leftward (inward) shift of the demand curve that results from a decline in consumer incomes. For example, the quantity demanded at the previous equilibrium price ($1.20) falls from 60 billion quarts (point E) to 45 billion quarts (point L on the demand curve D_2D_2). The initial price is now too high and must fall. The new equilibrium will eventually be established at point M, where the price is $1.10 and both quantity demanded and quantity supplied are 50 billion quarts. In general:

Any influence that shifts the demand curve inward to the left, and that does not affect the supply curve, will lower both the equilibrium price and the equilibrium quantity.

SUPPLY SHIFTS AND SUPPLY-DEMAND EQUILIBRIUM

A story precisely analogous to that of the effects of a demand shift on equilibrium price and quantity applies to supply shifts. Figure 6 described the effects on the supply curve of milk if the number of farms increases. Figure 9(a) now adds a demand curve to the supply curves of Figure 6 so that we can see the supply-demand equilibrium. Notice that at the initial price of $1.20, the quantity supplied after the shift is 78 billion quarts (point I on the supply curve S_1S_1), which is 30 percent more than the original quantity demanded of 60 billion quarts (point E on the supply curve S_0S_0). We can see from the graph that the price of $1.20 is too high to be the equilibrium price; the price must fall. The new equilibrium point is J, where the price is $1.10 per quart and the quantity is 65 billion quarts per year. In general:

Any change that shifts the supply curve outward to the right, and does not affect the demand curve, will lower the equilibrium price and raise the equilibrium quantity.

FIGURE 9   Effects of Shifts of the Supply Curve

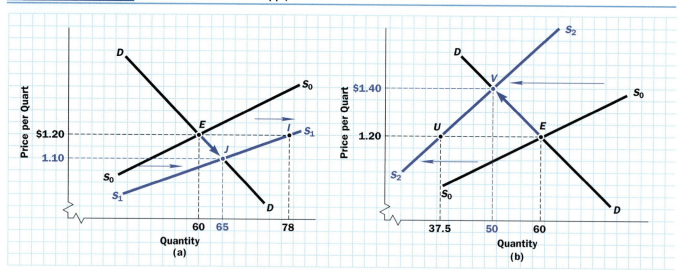

This must always be true if the industry's demand curve has a negative slope, because the greater quantity supplied can be sold only if the price is decreased so as to induce customers to buy more.[6] The cellular phone industry is a case in point. As more providers have entered the industry, the cost of cellular service has plummeted. Some cellular carriers have even given away telephones as sign-up bonuses.

Figure 9(b) illustrates the opposite case: a contraction of the industry. The supply curve shifts inward to the left and equilibrium moves from point E to point V, where the price is $1.40 and quantity is 50 billion quarts per year. In general:

Any influence that shifts the supply curve to the left, and does not affect the demand curve, will raise the equilibrium price and reduce the equilibrium quantity.

Many outside forces can disturb equilibrium in a market by shifting the demand curve or the supply curve, either temporarily or permanently. In 1998, for example, gasoline prices dropped because recession in Asia reduced demand, and a reduction in use of petroleum resulted from a mild winter. In the summer of 1998, severely hot weather and lack of rain damaged the cotton crop in the United States. Often these outside influences change the equilibrium price and quantity by shifting either the supply curve or the demand curve. If you look again at Figures 8 and 9, you can see clearly that any event that causes either the demand curve or the supply curve to shift will also change the equilibrium price and quantity.

Those Leaping Oil Prices: PUZZLE RESOLVED

The disturbing recent behavior of the price of gasoline, and of the oil from which it is made, is attributable to large shifts in both demand and supply conditions. Americans are, for example, driving more and are buying gas-guzzling vehicles, and the resulting upward shift in the demand curve raises price. Hurricanes Katrina and Rita disrupted pipeline operations on the U.S. Gulf Coast in 2005 and continuing instability in the Middle East and Russia has undermined supply—all of which also raised prices. We have seen the results at the gas pumps. The following newspaper story describes some of the most sensational sorts of changes in supply conditions:

---

[6] Graphically, whenever a positively sloped curve shifts to the right, its intersection point with a negatively sloping curve must always move lower. Just try drawing it yourself.

BAGHDAD, July 5, 2004—Oil prices rose Monday after attacks on Iraqi oil lines forced the country to reduce its exports by half. News of Russian giant Yukos Oil Co.'s expanding legal and financial troubles added to traders' anxiety.

Iraqi repair crews worked to fix one of two key southern crude oil pipelines, officials in the state-run South Oil Co. said. The disruption, about two weeks after exports were halted because of attacks on the two export lines, heightened concern among traders and analysts about the security of Iraq's oil flow.

The shutdown cut exports of crude oil from Basra to about 960,000 barrels a day, roughly half the postwar levels there. . . . In London, contracts of North Sea Brent crude for August delivery were trading at $36.30 per barrel, up 38 cents on the International Petroleum Exchange, before closing at $35.92. . . .

The current Iraqi disruption began Saturday when the line was breached, reportedly by smugglers, an oil company official said on condition of anonymity. On Sunday, saboteurs blasted another strategic line running from the north to the south, but South Oil officials said that line had not been used extensively for years, so exports would not be affected.

Also Monday, Russia's Yukos came a step closer to bankruptcy after a group of Western banks signaled they might call in a $1 billion loan to the company. . . .Yukos has been ordered to pay a 99.4-billion-ruble ($3.4 billion) back-taxes bill by Thursday. Its bank accounts were ordered frozen last week, and a freeze on its assets remains in place, giving the company no way to raise money. With a daily output of about 1.72 million barrels, or nearly one in every five that Russia extracts, Yukos is the country's largest oil producer.

Source: Tarek El-Tablawy, "Pipeline Sabotage In Iraq Helps Send Oil Prices Skyward," as appeared in *Washington Post*, July 5, 2004. Copyright 2005 Associated Press. All rights reserved. Distributed by Valeo IP. Reprinted by permission.

◼ Application: Who Really Pays That Tax?

Supply and demand analysis offers insights that may not be readily apparent. Here is an example. Suppose your state legislature raises the gasoline tax by 10 cents per gallon. Service station operators will then have to collect 10 additional cents in taxes on every gallon they pump. They will consider this higher tax as an addition to their costs and will shift it to you and other consumers by raising the price of gas by 10 cents per gallon. Right? No, wrong—or rather, partly wrong.

The gas station owners would certainly *like* to shift the entire tax to buyers, but the market mechanism will allow them to shift only *part* of it—perhaps 6 cents per gallon. They will then be stuck with the remainder—4 cents in our example. Figure 10, which is just another supply-demand graph, shows why.

The demand curve is the red curve *DD*. The supply curve before the tax is the black curve $S_0 S_0$. Before the new tax, the equilibrium point is E_0 and the price is $1.54. We can interpret the supply curve as telling us at what price sellers are willing to provide any given quantity. For example, they are willing to supply quantity $Q_1 = 50$ million gallons per year if the price is $1.54 per gallon.

So what happens as a result of the new tax? Because they must now turn 10 cents

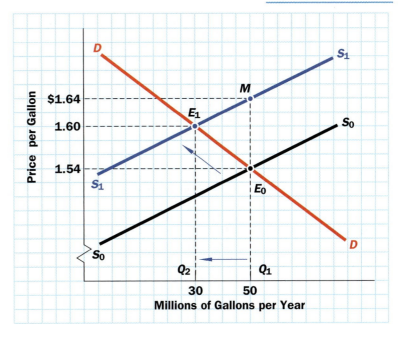

FIGURE 10

Who Pays for a New Tax on Products?

per gallon over to the government, gas station owners will be willing to supply any given quantity only if they get 10 cents more per gallon than they did before. Therefore, to get them to supply quantity $Q_1 = 50$ million gallons, a price of \$1.54 per gallon will no longer suffice. Only a price of \$1.64 per gallon will now induce them to supply 50 million gallons. Thus, at quantity $Q_1 = 50$, the point on the supply curve will move up by 10 cents, from point E_0 to point M. Because firms will insist on the same 10-cent price increase for any other quantity they supply, the *entire* supply curve will shift up by the 10-cent tax—from the black curve S_0S_0 to the new blue supply curve S_1S_1. And, as a result, the supplydemand equilibrium point will move from E_0 to E_1 and the price will increase from \$1.54 to \$1.60.

The supply curve shift may give the impression that gas station owners have succeeded in passing the entire 10-cent increase on to consumers—the distance from E_0 to M—but look again. The *equilibrium* price has only gone up from \$1.54 to \$1.60. That is, the price has risen by only 6 cents, not by the full 10-cent amount of the tax. The gas station will have to absorb the remaining 4 cents of the tax.

Now this really *looks* as though we have pulled a fast one on you—a magician's sleight of hand. After all, the supply curve has shifted upward by the full amount of the tax, and yet the resulting price increase has covered only part of the tax rise. However, a second look reveals that, like most apparent acts of magic, this one has a simple explanation. The explanation arises from the *demand* side of the supply-demand mechanism. The negative slope of the demand curve means that when prices rise, at least some consumers will reduce the quantity of gasoline they demand. That will force sellers to give up part of the price increase. In other words, firms must absorb the part of the tax—4 cents—that consumers are unwilling to pay. But note that the equilibrium quantity Q_1 has fallen from 50 million gallons to $Q_2 = 30$ million gallons—so both consumers and suppliers lose out in some sense.

This example is not an oddball case. Indeed, the result is almost always true. The cost of any increase in a tax on any commodity will usually be paid partly by the consumer and partly by the seller. This is so no matter whether the legislature says that it is imposing the tax on the sellers or on the buyers. Whichever way it is phrased, the economics are the same: The supply-demand mechanism ensures that the tax will be shared by both of the parties.

■ BATTLING THE INVISIBLE HAND: THE MARKET FIGHTS BACK

IDEAS FOR BEYOND THE FINAL EXAM

As we noted in our *Ideas for Beyond the Final Exam* in Chapter 1, lawmakers and rulers have often been dissatisfied with the outcomes of free markets. From Rome to Reno, and from biblical times to the space age, they have battled the invisible hand. Sometimes, rather than trying to adjust the workings of the market, governments have tried to raise or lower the prices of specific commodities by decree. In many such cases, the authorities felt that market prices were, in some sense, immorally low or immorally high. Penalties were therefore imposed on anyone offering the commodities in question at prices above or below those established by the authorities. Such legally imposed constraints on prices are called "price ceilings" and "price floors." To see their result, we will focus on the use of price ceilings.

■ Restraining the Market Mechanism: Price Ceilings

A **price ceiling** is a maximum that the price charged for a commodity cannot legally exceed.

The market has proven itself a formidable foe that strongly resists attempts to get around its decisions. In case after case where legal **price ceilings** are imposed, virtually the same series of consequences ensues:

1. *A persistent shortage develops because quantity demanded exceeds quantity supplied.* Queuing (people waiting in lines), direct rationing (with everyone getting a fixed allotment), or any of a variety of other devices, usually inefficient and unpleasant, must substitute for the distribution process provided

POLICY DEBATE

Economic Aspects of the War on Drugs

For years now, the U.S. government has engaged in a highly publicized "war on drugs." Billions of dollars have been spent on trying to stop illegal drugs at the country's borders. In some sense, interdiction has succeeded: Federal agents have seized literally tons of cocaine and other drugs. Yet these efforts have made barely a dent in the flow of drugs to America's city streets. Simple economic reasoning explains why.

When drug interdiction works, it shifts the supply curve of drugs to the left, thereby driving up street prices. But that, in turn, raises the rewards for potential smugglers and attracts more criminals into the "industry," which shifts the supply curve back to the right. The net result is that increased shipments of drugs to U.S. shores replace much of what the authorities confiscate. This is why many economists believe that any successful antidrug program must concentrate on reducing demand, which would lower the street price of drugs, not on reducing supply, which can only raise it.

Some people suggest that the government should go even further and legalize many drugs. Although this idea remains a highly controversial position that few are ready to endorse, the reasoning behind it is straightforward. A stunningly high fraction of all the violent crimes committed in America—especially robberies and murders—are drug-related. One major reason is

SOURCE: Chris Brown/Picturequest/Stock Boston

that street prices of drugs are so high that addicts must steal to get the money, and drug traffickers are all too willing to kill to protect their highly profitable "businesses."

How would things differ if drugs were legal? Because South American farmers earn pennies for drugs that sell for hundreds of dollars on the streets of Los Angeles and New York, we may safely assume that legalized drugs would be vastly cheaper. In fact, according to one estimate, a dose of cocaine would cost less than 50 cents. That, proponents point out, would reduce drug-related crimes dramatically. When, for example, was the last time you heard of a gang killing connected with the distribution of cigarettes or alcoholic beverages?

The argument against legalization of drugs is largely moral: Should the state sanction potentially lethal substances? But there is an economic aspect to this position as well: The vastly lower street prices of drugs that would surely follow legalization would increase drug use. Thus, while legalization would almost certainly reduce crime, it may also produce more addicts. The key question here is, How many more addicts? (No one has a good answer.) If you think the increase in quantity demanded would be large, you are unlikely to find legalization an attractive option.

by the price mechanism. Example: Rampant shortages in Eastern Europe and the former Soviet Union helped precipitate the revolts that ended communism.

2. *An illegal, or "black," market often arises to supply the commodity.* Usually some individuals are willing to take the risks involved in meeting unsatisfied demands illegally. Example: Although most states ban the practice, ticket "scalping" (the sale of tickets at higher than regular prices) occurs at most popular sporting events and rock concerts.

3. *The prices charged on illegal markets are almost certainly higher than those that would prevail in free markets.* After all, lawbreakers expect some compensation for the risk of being caught and punished. Example: Illegal drugs are normally quite expensive. (See the accompanying Policy Debate box, "Economic Aspects of the War on Drugs.")

4. A substantial portion of the price falls into the hands of the illicit supplier instead of going to those who produce the good or perform the service. Example: A constant complaint during the public hearings that marked the history of theater-ticket price controls in New York City was that the "ice" (the illegal excess charge) fell into the hands of ticket scalpers rather than going to those who invested in, produced, or acted in the play.

5. *Investment in the industry generally dries up.* Because price ceilings reduce the monetary returns that investors can legally earn, less capital will be invested in industries that are subject to price controls. Even fear of impending price controls can have this effect. Example: Price controls on farm products in Zambia have prompted peasant farmers and large agricultural conglomerates alike to cut back production rather than grow crops at a loss. The result has been thousands of lost jobs and widespread food shortages.

■ Case Study: Rent Controls in New York City

These points and others are best illustrated by considering a concrete example involving price ceilings. New York is the only major city in the United States that has continuously legislated rent controls in much of its rental housing, since World War II. Rent controls, of course, are intended to protect the consumer from high rents. But most economists believe that rent control does not help the cities or their residents and that, in the long run, it leaves almost everyone worse off. Elementary supply-demand analysis shows us why.

Figure 11 is a supply-demand diagram for rental units in New York. Curve *DD* is the demand curve and curve *SS* is the supply curve. Without controls, equilibrium would be at point *E*, where rents average $2,000 per month and 3 million housing units are occupied. If rent controls are effective, the ceiling price must be below the equilibrium price of $2,000. But with a low rent ceiling, such as $1,200, the quantity of housing demanded will be 3.5 million units (point *B*) whereas the quantity supplied will be only 2.5 million units (point *C*).

The diagram shows a shortage of 1 million apartments. This theoretical concept of a "shortage" manifests itself in New York City as an abnormally low vacancy rate—typically about half the national urban average. Naturally, rent controls have spawned a lively black market in New York. The black market raises the effective price of rentcontrolled apartments in many ways, including bribes, so-called key money paid to move up on a waiting list, or the requirement that prospective tenants purchase worthless furniture at inflated prices.

According to Figure 11, rent controls reduce the quantity supplied from 3 million to 2.5 million apartments. How does this reduction show up in New York? First, some property owners, discouraged by the low rents, have converted apartment buildings into office space or other uses. Second, some apartments have been inadequately maintained. After all, rent controls create a shortage, which makes even dilapidated apartments easy to rent. Third, some landlords have actually abandoned their buildings rather than pay rising tax and fuel bills. These abandoned buildings rapidly become eyesores and eventually pose threats to public health and safety.

An important implication of these last observations is that rent controls—and price controls more generally—harm consumers in ways that offset part or all of the benefits to those who are fortunate enough to find and acquire at lower prices the product that the reduced prices has made scarce.

FIGURE 11

Supply-Demand Diagram for Rental Housing

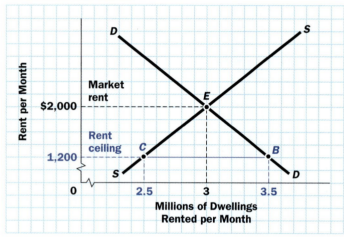

"If you leave me, you know, you'll never see this kind of rent again."

Tenants must undergo long waits and undertake time-consuming searches to find an apartment, the apartment they obtain is likely to be poorly maintained or even decrepit, and normal landlord services are apt to disappear. Thus, even for the lucky beneficiaries, rent control is always far less of a bargain than the reduced monthly payments make them appear to be. The same problems generally apply with other forms of price control as well.

With all of these problems, why does rent control persist in New York City? And why do other cities sometimes move in the same direction?

Part of the explanation is that most people simply do not understand the problems that rent controls create. Another part is that landlords are unpopular politically. But a third, and very important, part of the explanation is that not everyone is hurt by rent controls—and those who benefit from controls fight hard to preserve them. In New York, for example, many tenants pay rents that are only a fraction of what their apartments would fetch on the open market. They are, naturally enough, quite happy with this situation. This last point illustrates another very general phenomenon:

Virtually every price ceiling or floor creates a class of people that benefits from the regulations. These people use their political influence to protect their gains by preserving the status quo, which is one reason why it is so difficult to eliminate price ceilings or floors.

■ Restraining the Market Mechanism: Price Floors

Interferences with the market mechanism are not always designed to keep prices low. Agricultural price supports and minimum wage laws are two notable examples in which the law keeps prices *above* free-market levels. Such **price floors** are typically accompanied by a standard series of symptoms:

A **price floor** is a legal minimum below which the price charged for a commodity is not permitted to fall.

1. *A surplus develops as sellers cannot find enough buyers.* Example: Surpluses of various agricultural products have been a persistent—and costly—problem for the U.S. government. The problem is even worse in the European Union (EU), where the common agricultural policy holds prices even higher. One source estimates that this policy accounts for half of all EU spending.[7]
2. *Where goods, rather than services, are involved, the surplus creates a problem of disposal.* Something must be done about the excess of quantity supplied over quantity demanded. Example: The U.S. government has often been forced to purchase, store, and then dispose of large amounts of surplus agricultural commodities.
3. *To get around the regulations, sellers may offer discounts in disguised—and often unwanted—forms.* Example: Back when airline fares were regulated by the government, airlines offered more and better food and more stylishly-uniformed flight attendants instead of lowering fares. Today, the food is worse, but tickets cost much less.
4. *Regulations that keep prices artificially high encourage overinvestment in the industry.* Even inefficient businesses whose high operating costs would doom them in an unrestricted market can survive beneath the shelter of a generous price floor. Example: This is why the airline and trucking industries both went through painful "shakeouts" of the weaker companies in the 1980s, after they were deregulated and allowed to charge market-determined prices.

Once again, a specific example is useful for understanding how price floors work.

---

[7] *The Economist*, February 20, 1999.

■ Case Study: Farm Price Supports and the Case of Sugar Prices

America's extensive program of farm price supports began in 1933 as a "temporary method of dealing with an emergency"—in the years of the Great Depression, farmers were going broke in droves. These price supports are still with us today, even though farmers account for less than 2 percent of the U.S. workforce.[8]

One of the consequences of these price supports has been the creation of unsellable surpluses—more output of crops such as grains than consumers were willing to buy at the inflated prices yielded by the supports. Warehouses were filled to overflowing. New storage facilities had to be built, and the government was forced to set up programs in which grain from the unmanageable surpluses was shipped to poor foreign countries to combat malnutrition and starvation in those nations. Realistically, if price supports are to be effective in keeping prices above the equilibrium level, then *someone* must be prepared to purchase the surpluses that invariably result. Otherwise, those surpluses will somehow find their way into the market and drive down prices, undermining the price support program. In the United States (and elsewhere), the buyer of the surpluses has usually turned out to be the government, which makes its purchases at the expense of taxpayers who are forced to pay twice—once through taxes to finance the government purchases, and a second time in the form of higher prices for the farm products bought by the American public.

One of the more controversial farm price supports involves the U.S. sugar industry. Sugar producers receive low-interest loans from the federal government and a guarantee that the price of sugar will not fall below a certain level.

In a market economy such as that found in the United States, Congress cannot simply set prices by decree; rather, it must take some action to enforce the price floor.

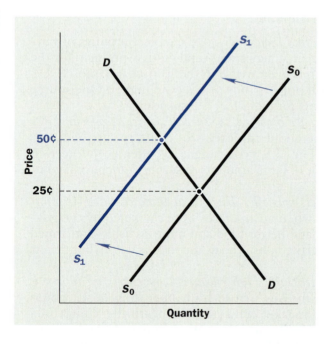

FIGURE 12

Supporting the Price of Sugar

In the case of sugar, that "something" is limiting both domestic production and foreign imports, thereby shifting the supply curve inward to the left. Figure 12 shows the mechanics involved in this price floor. Government policies shift the supply curve inward from S_0S_0 to S_1S_1 and drive the U.S. price up from 25¢ to 50¢ per pound. The more the supply curve shifts inward, the higher the price.

The sugar industry obviously benefits from the price-control program. But consumers pay for it in the form of higher prices for sugar and sugar-filled products such as soft drinks, candy bars, and cookies. Although estimates vary, the federal sugar price support program appears to cost consumers approximately $1.5 billion per year.

---

[8] Under major legislation passed in 1996, many agricultural price supports were supposed to be phased out over a seven-year period. In reality, many support programs, especially that for sugar, have changed little.

If all of this sounds a bit abstract to you, take a look at the ingredients in a U.S.-made soft drink. Instead of sugar, you will likely find "high-fructose corn syrup" listed as a sweetener. Foreign producers generally use sugar, but sugar is simply too expensive to be used for this purpose in the United States.

■ A Can of Worms

Our two case studies—rent controls and sugar price supports—illustrate some of the major side effects of price floors and ceilings, but barely hint at others. Difficulties arise that we have not even mentioned, for the market mechanism is a tough bird that imposes suitable retribution on those who seek to evade it by government decree. Here is a partial list of other problems that may arise when prices are controlled.

Favoritism and Corruption
When price ceilings or floors create shortages or surpluses, someone must decide who gets to buy or sell the limited quantity that is available. This decision-making process can lead to discrimination along racial or religious lines, political favoritism, or corruption in government. For example, many prices were held at artificially low levels in the former Soviet Union, making queuing for certain goods quite common. Even so, Communist Party officials and other favored groups were somehow able to purchase the scarce commodities that others could not get.

Unenforceability
Attempts to limit prices are almost certain to fail in industries with numerous suppliers, simply because the regulating agency must monitor the behavior of so many sellers. People will usually find ways to evade or violate the law, and something like the free-market price will generally reappear. But there is an important difference: Because the evasion process, whatever its form, will have some operating costs, those costs must be borne by someone. Normally, that someone is the consumer who must pay higher prices to the suppliers for taking the risk of breaking the law.

Auxiliary Restrictions
Fears that a system of price controls will break down invariably lead to regulations designed to shore up the shaky edifice. Consumers may be told when and from whom they are permitted to buy. The powers of the police and the courts may be used to prevent the entry of new suppliers. Occasionally, an intricate system of market subdivision is imposed, giving each class of firms a protected sphere in which others are not permitted to operate. For example, in New York City, there are laws banning conversion of rent-controlled apartments to condominiums.

Limitation of Volume of Transactions
To the extent that controls succeed in affecting prices, they can be expected to reduce the volume of transactions. Curiously, this is true regardless of whether the regulated price is above or below the free-market equilibrium price. If it is set above the equilibrium price, the quantity demanded will be below the equilibrium quantity. On the other hand, if the imposed price is set below the free-market level, the quantity supplied will be reduced. Because sales volume cannot exceed either the quantity supplied or the quantity demanded, a reduction in the volume of transactions is the result.[9]

---

[9] See Discussion Question 4 at the end of this chapter.

Misallocation of Resources   Departures from free-market prices are likely to result in misuse of the economy's resources because the connection between production costs and prices is broken. For example, Russian farmers used to feed their farm animals bread instead of unprocessed grains because price ceilings kept the price of bread ludicrously low. In addition, just as more complex locks lead to more sophisticated burglary tools, more complex regulations lead to the use of yet more resources for their avoidance.

Economists put it this way: Free markets are capable of dealing efficiently with the three basic coordination tasks outlined in Chapter 3: deciding what to produce, how to produce it, and to whom the goods should be distributed. Price controls throw a monkey wrench into the market mechanism. Although the market is surely not flawless, and government interferences often have praiseworthy goals, good intentions are not enough. Any government that sets out to repair what it sees as a defect in the market mechanism runs the risk of causing even more serious damage elsewhere. As a prominent economist once quipped, societies that are too willing to interfere with the operation of free markets soon find that the invisible hand is nowhere to be seen.

A SIMPLE BUT POWERFUL LESSON

Astonishing as it may seem, many people in authority do not understand the law of supply and demand, or they act as if it does not exist. For example, a few years ago the *New York Times* carried a dramatic front-page picture of the president of Kenya setting fire to a large pile of elephant tusks that had been confiscated from poachers. The accompanying story explained that the burning was intended as a symbolic act to persuade the world to halt the ivory trade.[10] One may certainly doubt whether the burning really touched the hearts of criminal poachers, but one economic effect was clear: By reducing the supply of ivory on the world market, the burning of tusks forced up the price of ivory, which raised the illicit rewards reaped by those who slaughter elephants. That could only encourage more poaching—precisely the opposite of what the Kenyan government sought to accomplish.

SUMMARY

1. An attempt to use government regulations to force prices above or below their equilibrium levels is likely to lead to **shortages** or **surpluses,** to black markets in which goods are sold at illegal prices, and to a variety of other problems. The market always strikes back at attempts to repeal the law of supply and demand.

2. The quantity of a product that is demanded is not a fixed number. Rather, **quantity demanded** depends on such factors as the price of the product, consumer incomes, and the prices of other products.

3. The relationship between quantity demanded and price, holding all other things constant, can be displayed graphically on a **demand curve.**

4. For most products, the higher the price, the lower the quantity demanded. As a result, the demand curve usually has a negative slope.

5. The quantity of a product that is supplied depends on its price and many other influences. A **supply curve** is a graphical representation of the relationship between **quantity supplied** and price, holding all other influences constant.

6. For most products, supply curves have positive slopes, meaning that higher prices lead to supply of greater quantities.

7. A change in quantity demanded that is caused by a change in the price of the good is represented by a movement *along* a fixed demand curve. A change in quantity demanded that is caused by a change in any other determinant of quantity demanded is represented by a **shift of the demand curve.**

8. This same distinction applies to the supply curve: Changes in price lead to movements along a fixed supply curve;

---

[10] *The New York Times*, July 19, 1989.

changes in other determinants of quantity supplied lead to shifts of the entire supply curve.

9. A market is said to be in **equilibrium** when quantity supplied is equal to quantity demanded. The equilibrium price and quantity are shown by the point on the supply-demand graph where the supply and demand curves intersect. The **law of supply and demand** states that price and quantity tend to gravitate to this point in a free market.

10. Changes in consumer incomes, tastes, technology, prices of competing products, and many other influences lead to shifts in either the demand curve or the supply curve and produce changes in price and quantity that can be determined from **supply-demand diagrams.**

11. A tax on a good generally leads to a rise in the price at which the taxed product is sold. The rise in price is generally less than the tax, so consumers usually pay less than the entire tax.

12. Consumers generally pay only part of a tax because the resulting rise in price leads them to buy less and the cut in the quantity they demand helps to force price down.

KEY TERMS

Invisible hand 56

Quantity demanded   57

Demand schedule 58

Demand curve 58

Shift in a demand curve   59

Quantity supplied   61

Supply schedule   61

Supply curve   62

Supply-demand diagram   64

Shortage   65

Surplus   65

Equilibrium   65

Law of supply and demand   66

Price ceiling   70

Price floor   73

TEST YOURSELF

1. What shapes would you expect for demand curves for the following:

   a. A medicine that means life or death for a patient

   b. French fries in a food court with kiosks offering many types of food

2. The following are the assumed supply and demand schedules for hamburgers in Collegetown:

Demand Schedule		Supply Schedule	
Price	Quantity Demanded per Year (thousands)	Price	Quantity Supplied per Year (thousands)
$2.25	12	$2.25	30
2.00	16	2.00	28
1.75	20	1.75	26
1.50	24	1.50	24
1.25	28	1.25	22
1.00	32	1.00	20

   a. Plot the supply and demand curves and indicate the equilibrium price and quantity.

   b. What effect would a decrease in the price of beef (a hamburger input) have on the equilibrium price and quantity of hamburgers, assuming all other things remained constant? Explain your answer with the help of a diagram.

   c. What effect would an increase in the price of pizza (a substitute commodity) have on the equilibrium price and quantity of hamburgers, assuming again that all other things remain constant? Use a diagram in your answer.

3. Suppose the supply and demand schedules for bicycles are as they appear below.

   a. Graph these curves and show the equilibrium price and quantity.

Price	Quantity Demanded per Year (millions)	Quantity Supplied per Year (millions)
$160	40	24
200	36	28
240	32	32
280	28	36
320	24	40
360	20	44

   b. Now suppose that it becomes unfashionable to ride a bicycle, so that the quantity demanded at each price falls by 8 million bikes per year. What is the new equilibrium price and quantity? Show this solution graphically. Explain why the quantity falls by less than 8 million bikes per year.

   c. Suppose instead that several major bicycle producers go out of business, thereby reducing the quantity supplied by 8 million bikes at every price. Find the new equilibrium price and quantity, and show it graphically. Explain again why quantity falls by less than 8 million.

   d. What are the equilibrium price and quantity if the shifts described in Test Yourself Questions 3(b) and 3(c) happen at the same time?

4. The following table summarizes information about the market for principles of economics textbooks:

Price	Quantity Demanded per Year	Quantity Supplied per Year
$40	4,200	200
50	2,200	600
60	1,200	1,200
70	700	2,000
80	550	3,000

a. What is the market equilibrium price and quantity of textbooks?

b. To quell outrage over tuition increases, the college places a $50 limit on the price of textbooks. How many textbooks will be sold now?

c. While the price limit is still in effect, automated publishing increases the efficiency of textbook production. Show graphically the likely effect of this innovation on the market price and quantity.

5. How are the following demand curves likely to shift in response to the indicated changes?

a. The effect of a drought on the demand curve for umbrellas

b. The effect of higher popcorn prices on the demand curve for movie tickets

c. The effect on the demand curve for coffee of a decline in the price of Coca-Cola

6. The two accompanying diagrams show supply and demand curves for two substitute commodities: tapes and compact discs (CDs).

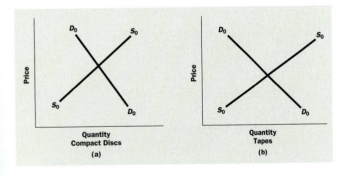

(a) Quantity Compact Discs   (b) Quantity Tapes

a. On the right-hand diagram, show what happens when rising raw material prices make it costlier to produce tapes.

b. On the left-hand diagram, show what happens to the market for CDs.

7. Consider the market for milk discussed in this chapter (Tables 1 through 4 and Figures 1 and 8). Suppose that the government decides to fight kidney stones by levying a tax of 40 cents per quart on sales of milk. Follow these steps to analyze the effects of the tax:

a. Construct the new supply schedule (to replace Table 2) that relates quantity supplied to the price that consumers pay.

b. Graph the new supply curve constructed in Test Yourself Question 7(a) on the supply-demand diagram depicted in Figure 7. What are the new equilibrium price and quantity?

c. Does the tax succeed in its goal of reducing the consumption of milk?

d. How much does the equilibrium price increase? Is the price rise greater than, equal to, or less than the 40-cent tax?

e. Who actually pays the tax, consumers or producers? (This may be a good question to discuss in class.)

8. (More difficult) The demand and supply curves for T-shirts in Touristtown, U.S.A., are given by the following equations:

$$Q = 24,000 - 500P \qquad Q = 6,000 + 1,000P$$

where P is measured in dollars and Q is the number of T-shirts sold per year.

a. Find the equilibrium price and quantity algebraically.

b. If tourists decide they do not really like T-shirts that much, which of the following might be the new demand curve?

$$Q = 21,000 - 500P \qquad Q = 27,000 - 500P$$

Find the equilibrium price and quantity after the shift of the demand curve.

c. If, instead, two new stores that sell T-shirts open up in town, which of the following might be the new supply curve?

$$Q = 4,000 + 1,000P \qquad Q = 9,000 + 1,000P$$

Find the equilibrium price and quantity after the shift of the supply curve.

DISCUSSION QUESTIONS

1. How often do you rent videos? Would you do so more often if a rental cost half as much? Distinguish between your demand curve for home videos and your "quantity demanded" at the current price.

2. Discuss the likely effects of the following:

a. Rent ceilings on the market for apartments

b. Floors under wheat prices on the market for wheat

Use supply-demand diagrams to show what may happen in each case.

3. U.S. government price supports for milk led to an unceasing surplus of milk. In an effort to reduce the surplus about a decade ago, Congress offered to pay dairy farmers to slaughter cows. Use two diagrams, one for the milk market and one for the meat market, to illustrate how this policy should have affected the price of meat. (Assume that meat is sold in an unregulated market.)

4. It is claimed in this chapter that either price floors or price ceilings reduce the actual quantity exchanged in a market. Use a diagram or diagrams to test this conclusion, and explain the common sense behind it.

5. The same rightward shift of the demand curve may produce a very small or a very large increase in quantity, depending on the slope of the supply curve. Explain this conclusion with diagrams.

6. In 1981, when regulations were holding the price of natural gas below its free-market level, then-Congressman Jack Kemp of New York said the following in an interview with the *New York Times*: "We need to decontrol natural gas, and get production of natural gas up to a higher level so we can bring down the price."[11] Evaluate the congressman's statement.

7. From 1990 to 1997 in the United States, the number of working men grew by 6.7 percent; the number of working women grew by 11 percent. During this time, average wages for men grew by 20 percent, while average wages for women grew by 25 percent. Which of the following two explanations seems more consistent with the data?

   a. Women decided to work more, raising their relative supply (relative to men).

   b. Discrimination against women declined, raising the relative (to men) demand for female workers.

---

[11] *The New York Times*, December 24, 1981.

THE BUILDING BLOCKS OF DEMAND AND SUPPLY

II

T he next four chapters describe and analyze the basic building blocks with which economists analyze markets and their two essential elements, buyers (consumers) and sellers (producers). As in a piece of machinery, all the parts of a market operate simultaneously together, so there is no logical place to begin the story. Furthermore, the heart of the story is not found in the individual components, but in the way they fit together. The four central microeconomics chapters start off with the separate components, but then assemble them into a working model of how firms determine price and output simultaneously. Then Chapter 9 deals with stocks and bonds as tools that help business firms obtain the finances they need to operate and as earnings opportunities for potential investors in firms.

5

CONSUMER CHOICE: INDIVIDUAL AND MARKET DEMAND

Everything is worth what its purchaser will pay for it.

PUBLILIUS SYRUS (IST CENTURY B.C.)

Y ou are about to start a new year in college, and your favorite clothing store is having a sale. So you decide to stock up on jeans. How do you decide how many pairs to buy? How is your decision affected by the price of the jeans and the amount of money you earned in your summer job? How can you get the most for your money? Economic analysis provides some rational ways to make these decisions. Do you think about your decision as an economist would, either consciously or unconsciously? Should you? By the end of the chapter, you will be able to analyze such purchase decisions using concepts called "utility" and "marginal analysis."

Chapter 4 introduced you to the idea of supply and demand and the use of supply and demand curves to analyze how markets determine prices and quantities of products sold. This chapter will investigate the underpinnings of the demand curve, which, as we have already seen, shows us half of the market picture.

CONTENTS

PUZZLE: *Why Shouldn't Water Be Worth More Than Diamonds?*

When Adam Smith lectured at the University of Glasgow in the 1760s, he introduced the study of demand by posing a puzzle. Common sense, he said, suggests that the price of a commodity must somehow depend on what that good is worth to consumers—on the amount of *utility* that the commodity offers. Yet, Smith pointed out, some cases suggest that a good's utility may have little influence on its price.

Smith cited diamonds and water as examples. He noted that water has enormous value to most consumers; indeed, its availability can be a matter of life and death. Yet water often sells at a very low price or is even free of charge, whereas diamonds sell for very high prices even though few people would consider them necessities. We will soon be in a position to see how marginal analysis, the powerful method of analysis introduced in this chapter, helps to resolve this paradox.

SOURCE: © L. Clarke/Corbis

SOURCE: © Thinkstock/Getting Images

■ SCARCITY AND DEMAND

When economists use the term "demand," they do not mean mere wishes, needs, requirements, or preferences. Rather, "demand" refers to actions of consumers who, so to speak, put their money where their mouths are. "Demand" assumes that consumers *can* pay for the goods in question and that they are also *willing* to pay out the necessary money. Some of us may, for example, dream of owning a racehorse or a Lear jet, but only a few wealthy individuals can turn such fantasies into effective demands.

Any individual consumer's choices are subject to one overriding constraint that is at least partly beyond that consumer's control: The individual has only a limited income available to spend. This scarcity of income is the obvious reason why less affluent consumers demand fewer computers, trips to foreign countries, and expensive restaurant meals than wealthy consumers do. The scarcity of income affects even the richest of all spenders—the government. The U.S. government spends billions of dollars on the armed services, education, and a variety of other services, but governments rarely, if ever, have the funds to buy everything they want.

Because income is limited (and thus is a scarce resource), any consumer's purchase decisions for different commodities must be *interdependent*. The number of movies that Jane can afford to see depends on the amount she spends on new clothing. If John's parents have just sunk a lot of money into an expensive addition to their home, they may have to give up a vacation trip. Thus, no one can truly understand the demand curves for movies and clothing, or for homes and vacation trips, without considering demand curves for alternative goods.

The quantity of movies demanded, for example, probably depends not only on ticket prices but also on the prices of clothing. Thus, a big sale on shirts might induce Jane to splurge on several, leaving her with little or no cash to spend on movies. So, an analysis of consumer demand that focuses on only one commodity at a time leaves out an essential part of the story. Nevertheless, to make the analysis easier to follow, we begin by considering products in isolation. That is, we employ what is called "partial analysis," using a standard simplifying assumption. This assumption requires that all other variables remain unchanged. Later in the chapter and in the appendix, we will tell a fuller story.

■ UTILITY: A TOOL TO ANALYZE PURCHASE DECISIONS

In the American economy, millions of consumers make millions of decisions every day. You decide to buy a movie ticket instead of a paperback novel. Your roommate decides to buy two tubes of toothpaste rather than one tube or three tubes. How do people make these decisions?

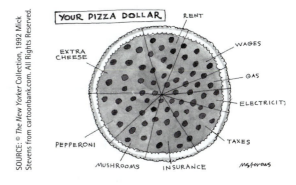

Economists have constructed a simple theory of consumer choice based on the hypothesis that each consumer spends her or his income in the way that yields the greatest amount of satisfaction, or *utility*. This seems to be a reasonable starting point, because it says only that people do what they prefer. To make the theory operational, we need a way to measure utility.

A century ago, economists envisioned utility as an indicator of the pleasure a person derives from consuming some set of goods, and they thought that utility could be measured directly in some kind of psychological units (sometimes called *utils*) after somehow reading the consumer's mind. Gradually, they came to realize that this was an unnecessary and, perhaps, impossible task. How many utils did you get from the last movie you saw? You probably cannot answer that question because you have no idea what a util is. Neither does anyone else.

But you may be able to answer a different question like, "How many hamburgers would you give up to get that movie ticket?" If you answer "three," no one can say how many utils you get from seeing a film, but they can say that you get more from the movie than from a single hamburger. When economists approach the issue in this manner, hamburgers, rather than the more vague "utility," become the unit of measurement. They can say that the utility of a movie (to you) is three hamburgers.

Early in the twentieth century, economists concluded that this indirect way of measuring consumer benefit gave them all they needed to build a theory of consumer choice. One can measure the benefit of a movie ticket by asking how much of some other commodity (like hamburgers) you are willing to give up for it. Any commodity will do for this purpose, but the simplest, most commonly used choice, and the one that we will use in this book, is money.[1]

■ The Purpose of Utility Analysis: Analyzing How People *Behave*, Not What They *Think*

Here, a very important warning is required: Money (or hamburgers, for that matter) can be a very imperfect measure of utility. The reason is that measuring utility by means of money is like measuring the length of a table with a rubber yardstick. The value of a dollar changes—sometimes a great deal—depending on circumstances. For example, if you win $10 million in the lottery, an additional dollar can confidently be expected to add much less to your well-being than it would have one week earlier. After you hit the jackpot, you may not hesitate to spend $9 on a hamburger, whereas before you would not have spent more than $3. This difference does not mean that you now love hamburgers three times as much as before. Consequently, although we use

---

[1] Note to Instructors: You will recognize that, although not using the terms, we are distinguishing here between neoclassical *cardinal utility* and *ordinal utility*. Moreover, throughout the book, *marginal utility in money terms* (or *money marginal utility*) is used as a synonym for the *marginal rate of substitution* between money and the commodity.

money as an indicator of utility in this book, it should not be taken as an indicator of the consumer's psychological attitude toward the goods he or she buys.

So why do we use the concept of money utility? There are two good reasons. First, we do know how to approach *measuring* it (see next section), but we do not know how to measure what is going on inside the consumer's mind. Second, and much more important, it is extremely useful for analyzing demand behavior—what consumers will spend to buy some good, even though it is *not* a good indicator of what is going on deep inside their brains.

Total Versus Marginal Utility

The **total utility** of a quantity of a good to a consumer (measured in money terms) is the maximum amount of money that he or she is willing to give up in exchange for it.

Thus, we define the **total monetary utility** of a particular bundle of goods to a particular consumer as *the largest sum of money that person will voluntarily give up in exchange for those goods.* For example, imagine that you love pizza and are planning to buy four pizzas for a party you are hosting. You are, as usual, a bit low on cash. Taking this into account, you decide that you are willing to buy the four pies if they cost up to $52 in total, but you're not willing to pay more than $52. As economists, we then say that the *total utility* of four pizzas to you is $52, the maximum amount you are willing to spend to have them.

Total monetary utility (from which we will drop the word "monetary" from here on) measures your dollar evaluation of the benefit that you derive from your total purchases of some commodity during some selected period of time. *Total* utility is what really matters to you. But to understand which decisions most effectively promote total utility, we must make use of a related concept, **marginal** (monetary) **utility.** This concept is not a measure of the amount of benefit you get from your purchase decision but, rather, provides *a tool* with which you can analyze how much of a commodity that you must buy to make your total utility as large as possible. Your marginal utility of some good, X, is defined as *the addition to total utility that you derive by consuming one more unit of X.* If you consumed two pizzas last month, marginal utility indicates how much additional pleasure you would have received by increasing your consumption to three pizzas. Before showing how marginal utility helps to find what quantity of purchases makes total utility as large as possible, we must first discuss how these two figures are calculated and just what they mean.

The **marginal utility** of a commodity to a consumer (measured in money terms) is the maximum amount of money that she or he is willing to pay for *one more unit* of that commodity.

Table 1 helps to clarify the distinction between marginal and total utility and shows how the two are related. The first two columns show how much *total* utility (measured in money terms) you derive from various quantities of pizza, ranging from zero to eight per month. For example, a single pizza pie is worth (no more than) $15 to you, two are worth $28 in total, and so on. The *marginal* utility is the *difference* between any two successive total utility figures. For example, if you have consumed three pizzas (worth $40.50 to you), an additional pie brings your total utility to $52. Your marginal utility is thus the difference between the two, or $11.50.

Remember: Whenever we use the terms *total utility* and *marginal utility*, we define them in terms of the consumer's willingness to part with *money* for the commodity, not in some unobservable (and imaginary) psychological units.

TABLE 1
Your Total and Marginal Utility for Pizza This Month

(1)	(2)	(3)	(4)
Quantity (Q) Pizzas per Month	Total Utility (TU)	Marginal Utility (MU) = (ΔTU/ΔQ)	Point in Figure 1
0	$0.00		
		$15.00	A
1	15.00		
		13.00	B
2	28.00		
		12.50	C
3	**40.50**		
		11.50	D
4	**52.00**		
		8.00	E
5	60.00		
		5.00	F
6	65.00		
		3.00	G
7	68.00		
		0.00	H
8	68.00		

Note: Each entry in Column (3) is the difference between successive entries in Column (2). This is what is indicated by the zigzag lines.

The "Law" of Diminishing Marginal Utility

With these definitions, we can now propose a simple hypothesis about consumer tastes:

The more of a good a consumer has, the less *marginal* utility an additional unit contributes to overall satisfaction, if all other things remain unchanged.

Economists use this plausible proposition widely. The idea is based on the assertion that every person has a *hierarchy* of uses for a particular commodity. All of these uses are valuable, but some are more valuable than others. Take pizza, for example. Perhaps you consider your *own* appetite for pizza first—you buy enough pizza to satiate your own personal taste for it. But pizza may also provide you with an opportunity to satisfy your social needs. So instead of eating all the pizza you buy, you decide to have a pizza party. First on your guest list may be your boyfriend or girlfriend. Next priority is your roommate, and, if you feel really flush, you may even invite your economics instructor! So, if you buy only one pizza, you eat it yourself. If you buy a second pizza, you share it with your friend. A third is shared with your roommate, and so on.

The point is: Each pizza contributes something to your satisfaction, but each *additional* pizza contributes less (measured in terms of money) than its predecessor because it satisfies a lower-priority use. This idea, in essence, is the logic behind the **"law" of diminishing marginal utility,** which asserts that the more of a commodity you already possess the smaller the amount of (marginal) utility you derive from acquisition of yet another unit of the commodity.

The third column of Table 1 illustrates this concept. The marginal utility (abbreviated MU) of the first pizza is $15; that is, you are willing to pay *up to* $15 for the first pie. The second is worth no more than $13 to you, the third pizza only $12.50, and so on, until you are willing to pay only $5 for the sixth pizza (the MU of that pizza is $5).

Figure 1, a marginal utility curve, shows a graph of the numbers in the first and third columns of Table 1. For example, point *D* indicates that the MU of a fourth pizza is $11.50. So, at any higher price, you will not buy a fourth pizza.

Note that the curve for marginal utility has a negative slope; it also illustrates how marginal utility diminishes as the quantity of the good rises. Like most laws, however, the "law" of diminishing marginal utility has exceptions. Some people want even more of some good that is particularly significant to them as they acquire more, as in the case of addiction. Stamp collectors and alcoholics provide good examples. The stamp collector who has a few stamps may consider the acquisition of one more to be mildly amusing. The person who has a large and valuable collection may be prepared to go to the ends of the earth for another stamp. Similarly, an alcoholic who finds the first beer quite pleasant may find the fourth or fifth to be absolutely irresistible. Economists generally treat such cases of increasing marginal utility as anomalies. For most goods and most people, marginal utility declines as consumption increases.

Table 1 illustrates another noteworthy relationship. Observe that as someone buys more and more units of the commodity—that is, as that person moves further down the table—the *total* utility numbers get larger and larger, while the *marginal* utility numbers get smaller and smaller. The reasons should now be fairly clear. The marginal utility numbers keep declining, as the "law" of diminishing marginal utility tells us they will. But *total* utility keeps rising so long as marginal utility remains positive. A person who owns ten compact disks, other things being equal, is better off (has higher total utility) than a person who possesses only nine, as long as the MU of the tenth CD is positive. In summary:

As a rule, as a person acquires more of a commodity, total utility increases and marginal utility from that good decreases, all other things being equal. In particular, when a commodity is very scarce, economists expect it to have a high marginal utility, even though it may provide little total utility because people have so little of the item.

The **"law" of diminishing marginal utility** asserts that additional units of a commodity are worth less and less to a consumer in money terms. As the individual's consumption increases, the marginal utility of each additional unit declines.

SOURCE: © 2001 Robert Mankoff from cartoonbank.com. All Rights Reserved.

FIGURE 1

A Marginal Utility (or Demand) Curve: Your Demand for Pizza This Month

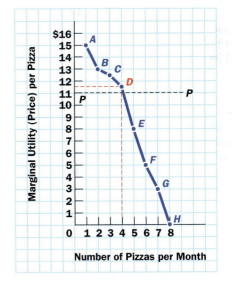

"It's been fun, Dave, but I think we're entering the diminished marginal utility phase of our relationship."

Using Marginal Utility: The Optimal Purchase Rule

Now let us use the concept of marginal utility to analyze consumer choices. Consumers must always choose among the many commodities that compete for their limited supply of dollars. How can you use the idea of utility to help you understand the purchase choices permitted by those dollars that best serve your preferences?

You can obviously choose among many different quantities of pizza, any of which will add to your total utility. But which of these quantities will yield the greatest net benefits? If pizza were all that you were considering buying, in theory the choice would involve a simple calculation. We would need a statistical table that listed all of the alternative numbers of pizzas that you may conceivably buy. The table should indicate the *net* utility that each possible choice yields. That is, it should include the total utility that you would get from a particular number of pizzas, minus the utility of the other purchases you would forego by having to pay for them—their opportunity cost. We could then simply read your optimal choice from this imaginary table—the number of pizzas that would give you the highest net utility number.

Even in theory, calculating optimal decisions is, unfortunately, more difficult than that. No real table of net utilities exists; an increase in expenditure on pizzas would mean less money available for clothing or movies, and you must balance the benefits of spending on each of these items against spending on the others. All of this means that we must find a more effective technique to determine optimal pizza purchases (as well as purchases of clothing, entertainment, and other things). That technique is **marginal analysis.**

Marginal analysis is a method for calculating optimal choices—the choices that best promote the decision maker's objective. It works by testing whether, and by how much, a small change in a decision will move things toward or away from the goal.

To see how marginal analysis helps consumers determine their optimal purchase decisions, first recall our assumption that you are trying to maximize the total *net* utility you obtain from your pizza purchases. That is, you are trying to select the number of pies that maximizes the total utility the pizzas provide you *minus the total utility you give up with the money you must pay for them.*

We can compare the analysis of the optimal decision-making process to the process of climbing a hill. First, imagine that you consider the possibility of buying only one pizza. Then suppose you consider buying two pizzas, and so on. If two pizzas give you a higher total net utility than one pizza, you may think of yourself as moving higher up the total net utility hill. Buying more pizzas enables you to ascend that hill higher and higher, until at some quantity you reach the top—*the optimal purchase quantity*. Then, if you buy any more, you will have overshot the peak and begun to descend the hill.

Figure 2 shows such a hill and describes how your total net utility changes when you change the number of pizzas you buy. It shows the upward-sloping part of the hill, where the number of purchases has not yet brought you to the top. Then it shows the point (*M*) at which you have bought enough pizzas to make your net utility as large as possible (the peak occurs at four pizzas). At any point to the right of *M*, you have overshot the optimal purchase. You are on the downward side of the hill because you have bought more than enough pizzas to best serve your interests; you have bought too many to maximize your net utility.

How does marginal analysis help you to find that optimal purchase quantity, and how does it warn you if you are planning to purchase too little (so that you are still on the ascending portion of the hill) or too much (so that you are descending)? The numerical example in Table 1 will help reveal the answers. The marginal utility of, for example, a third pizza is $12.50. This means that the total utility you obtain from three pizzas ($40.50) is exactly $12.50 higher than the total utility you get from two pizzas ($28). As long as marginal utility is a positive number, the more you purchase, the more total utility you will get.

That shows the benefit side of the purchase. But such a transaction also has a debit side—the amount you must pay for the purchase. Suppose that the price is $11 per pizza. Then the marginal *net* utility of the third pizza is marginal utility minus price, $12.50 minus $11, or $1.50. This is the

---

FIGURE 2

Finding Your Optimal Pizza Purchase Quantity: Maximizing Total Net Utility

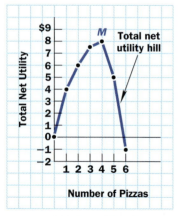

Total Net Utility equals Total Utility minus Total Expenditure (Price X Quantity)

amount that the third pizza adds to your total net utility. (See the third and fourth lines of Table 1.) So you really *are* better off with three pizzas than with two.

We can generalize the logic of the previous paragraph to show how marginal analysis solves the problem of finding the optimal purchase quantity, given the price of the commodity being purchased.

IDEAS FOR BEYOND THE FINAL EXAM

RULE 1: If marginal net utility is positive, the consumer must be buying too small a quantity to maximize total net utility. Because marginal utility exceeds price, the consumer can increase total net utility further by buying (at least) one more unit of the product. In other words, since marginal net utility (which is marginal utility minus price) tells us how much the purchase of an additional unit raises or lowers total net utility, a positive marginal net utility means that total net utility is still going uphill. The consumer has not yet bought enough to get to the top of the hill.

RULE 2: No purchase quantity for which marginal net utility is a negative number can ever be optimal. In such a case, a buyer can get a higher total net utility by cutting back the purchase quantity. The purchaser would have climbed too far on the net utility hill, passing the topmost point and beginning to descend.

This leaves only one option. The consumer cannot be at the top of the hill if marginal net utility (MU − P) is greater than zero—that is, if MU is greater than P. Similarly, the purchase quantity cannot be optimal if marginal net utility at that quantity (MU − P) is less than zero—that is, if MU is less than P. The purchase quantity can be optimal, giving the consumer the highest possible total net utility, only if:

Marginal net utility = MU − P = 0; that is, if MU = P

Consequently, the hypothesis that the consumer chooses purchases to make the largest net contribution to total utility leads to the following *optimal purchase rule:*

It always pays the consumer to buy more of any commodity whose marginal utility (measured in money) exceeds its price, and less of any commodity whose marginal utility is less than its price. When possible, the consumer should buy a quantity of each good at which price (P) and marginal utility (MU) are exactly equal—that is, at which

MU = P

because only these quantities will maximize the *net total utility* that the consumer gains from purchases, given the fact that these decisions must divide available money among all purchases.[2]

Notice that, although the consumer really cares about maximizing total *net* utility (and marginal utility is not the goal), we have used marginal analysis as a *guide* to the optimal purchase quantity. Marginal analysis serves only as an analytic method—as a means to an end. This goal is maximization of total net utility, not marginal utility or marginal net utility. In Chapter 8, after several other applications of marginal analysis, we will generalize the discussion to show how thinking "at the margin" allows us to make optimal decisions in a wide variety of fields besides consumer purchases.

Let's briefly review graphically how the underlying logic of the marginal way of thinking leads to the optimal purchase rule, MU = P. Refer back to the graph of marginal utilities of pizzas (Figure 1). Suppose that Paul's Pizza Parlor currently sells pizzas at a price of $11 (the dashed line *PP* in the graph). At this price, five pizzas (point *E*) is *not* an optimal purchase because the $8 marginal utility of the fifth pizza is less than its $11 price. You would be better off buying only four pizzas because that choice would save $11 with only a $8 loss in utility—a net gain of $3—from the decision to buy one less pizza.

---

[2] Economists can equate a dollar price with marginal utility only because they measure marginal utility in money terms (or, as they more commonly state, because they deal with the marginal rate of substitution of money for the commodity). If marginal utility were measured in some psychological units not directly translatable into money terms, a comparison of *P* and MU would have no meaning. However, MU could also be measured in terms of any commodity other than money. (Example: How many pizzas are you willing to trade for an additional ticket to a basketball game?)

You should note that, in practice, there may not exist a number of pizzas at which MU is *exactly* equal to *P*. In our example, the fourth pizza is worth $11.50, whereas the fifth pizza is worth $8—neither of them is *exactly* equal to their $11 price. If you could purchase an appropriate (in-between) quantity (say, 4.38 pizzas), then MU would, indeed, exactly equal *P*. But Paul's Pizza Parlor will not sell you 4.38 pizzas, so you must do the best you can. You buy four pizzas, for which MU comes as close as possible to equality with *P*.

The rule for optimal purchases states that you should not buy a quantity at which MU is higher than price (points like *A*, *B*, and *C* in Figure 1) because a larger purchase would make you even better off. Similarly, you should not end up at points *E*, *F*, *G*, and *H*, at which MU is below price, because you would be better off buying less. Rather, you should buy four pizzas (point *D*), where *P* = MU (approximately). Thus, marginal analysis leads naturally to the rule for optimal purchase quantities.

> The decision to purchase a quantity of a good that leaves marginal utility greater than price cannot maximize total net utility, because buying an additional unit would add more to total utility than it would increase cost. Similarly, it cannot be optimal for the consumer to buy a quantity of a good that leaves marginal utility less than price, because then a reduction in the quantity purchased would save more money than it would sacrifice in utility. Consequently, the consumer can maximize total net utility only if the purchase quantity brings marginal utility as close as possible to equality with price.

Note that price is an objective, observable figure determined by the market, whereas marginal utility is subjective and reflects consumer tastes. Because individual consumers lack the power to influence the price, they must adjust purchase quantities to make their subjective marginal utility of each good equal to the price given by the market.

■ From Diminishing Marginal Utility to Downward-Sloping Demand Curves

We will see next that the marginal utility curve and the demand curve of a consumer who maximizes total net utility are one and the same. The two curves are identical. This observation enables us to use the optimal purchase rule to show that the "law" of diminishing marginal utility implies that demand curves typically slope downward to the right; that is, they have negative slopes.[3] To do this, we use the list of marginal utilities in Table 1 to determine how many pizzas you would buy at any particular price. For example, we see that at a price of $8, it pays for you to buy five pizzas, because the MU of the fifth pizza ordered is $8. Table 2 gives several alternative prices and the optimal purchase quantity corresponding to each price derived in just this way. (To make sure you understand the logic behind the optimal purchase rule, verify that the entries in the right column of Table 2 are, in fact, correct.) This *demand schedule* appears graphically as the *demand curve* shown in Figure 1. This demand curve is simply the blue marginal utility curve. This is true, because at any given price, the consumer will find it best to buy the quantity at which marginal utility is equal to the given price. So at any given quantity of the commodity, the price at which it will be bought will equal its marginal utility. That is, at each quantity, the curve tells us the price at which it will be bought, so it is a demand curve. But the curve also tells us the marginal utility at any such quantity, so it is also a marginal utility curve. You can also see its negative slope in the graph, which is a characteristic of demand curves.

TABLE 2

List of Optimal Quantities of Pizza for You to Purchase at Alternative Prices

Price	Quantity of Pizzas Purchased per Month
$ 3.00	7
5.00	6
8.00	5
11.50	**4**
12.50	3
13.00	2
15.00	1

Note: For simplicity of explanation, the prices shown have been chosen to equal the marginal utilities in Table 1. In-between prices would make the optimal choices involve fractions of pizzas (say, 2.6 pizzas).

---

[3] If you need to review the concept of slope, refer to the Chapter 1 Appendix discussion on graphic analysis.

Let's examine the logic underlying the negatively sloped demand curve a bit more carefully. If you are purchasing the optimal number of pizzas, and then the price falls, you will find that your marginal utility for that product is now *above* the newly reduced price. For example, Table 1 indicates that at a price of $12.50 per pizza, you would optimally buy three pizzas, because the MU of the fourth pizza is only $11.50. If price falls below $11.50, it then pays to purchase more—it pays to buy the fourth pizza because its MU now exceeds its price. The marginal utility of the next (fifth) pizza is only $8. Thus, if the price falls below $8, it would pay you to buy that fifth pizza. So, the lower the price, the more the consumer will find it advantageous to buy, which is what is meant by saying that the demand curve has a negative slope.

Note the critical role that the "law" of diminishing marginal utility plays here. If *P* falls, a consumer who wishes to maximize total utility must buy more, to the point that MU falls correspondingly. According to the "law" of diminishing marginal utility, the only way to do this is to increase the quantity purchased.

Although this explanation is a bit abstract, we can easily rephrase it in practical terms. We have noted that individuals put commodities to various uses, each of which has a different priority. For you, buying a pizza for your date has a higher priority than using the pizza to feed your roommate. If the price of pizzas is high, it makes sense for you to buy only enough for the high-priority uses—those that offer high marginal utilities. When price declines, however, it pays to purchase more of the good—enough for some lower-priority uses. The same general assumption about consumer psychology underlies both the "law" of diminishing marginal utility and the negative slope of the demand curve. They are really two different ways of describing consumers' assumed attitudes.

Do Consumers Really Behave "Rationally" and Maximize Utility?

It may strike you that this chapter's discussion of the consumer's decision process—equating price and marginal utility—does not resemble the thought processes of any consumer you have ever met. Buyers may seem to make decisions much more instinctively and without any calculation of marginal utilities or anything like them. That is true—yet it need not undermine the pertinence of the discussion.

When you give a command to your computer, you actually activate some electronic switches and start some operations in what is referred to as *binary code*. Most computer users do not know they are having this effect and do not care. Yet they are activating binary code nevertheless, and the analysis of the computation process does not misrepresent the facts by describing this sequence. In the same way, if a shopper divides her purchasing power among various purchase options in a way that yields the largest possible utility for her money, she *must* be following the rules of marginal analysis, even though she is totally unaware of this choice.

A growing body of experimental evidence, however, has pointed out some persistent deviations between reality and the picture of consumer behavior provided by marginal analysis. Experimental studies by groups of economists and psychologists have turned up many examples of behavior that seem to violate the optimal purchase rule. For instance, one study offered two groups of respondents what were really identical options, presumably yielding similar marginal utilities. Despite this equality, depending on differences in some irrelevant information that was also provided to the respondents, the two groups made very different choices.

One group of subjects received the information in parentheses, and the other received the information in brackets. . . .

[*Problem 1*]. Imagine that you are about to purchase . . . a calculator for ($15)[$125]. The calculator salesman informs you that the calculator you wish to buy is on sale for ($10)[$120] at the other branch of the store, located a 20-minute drive away. Would you make the trip to the other store?

The responses to the two versions of this problem were quite different. When the calculator cost $125 only 29 percent of the subjects said they would make the trip, whereas 68 percent said they would go when the calculator cost only $15.

Thus, in this problem *both* groups were really being told they could save $5 on the price of a product if they took a 20-minute trip to another store. Yet, depending on an irrelevant fact, whether the product was a cheap or an expensive model, the number of persons willing to make the same trip to save the same amount of money was very different. The point is that human purchase decisions are affected by the environment in which the decision is made, and not only by the price and marginal utility of the purchase.

SOURCE: Courtesy of Texas Instruments Incorporated.

SOURCE: Richard H. Thaler, *Quasi Rational Economics* (New York: Russell Sage Foundation, 1992), pp. 148–150.

CONSUMER CHOICE AS A TRADE-OFF: OPPORTUNITY COST

We have expressed the optimal purchase rule as the principle guiding a decision about how much of *one* commodity to buy. However, we have already observed that the scarcity of income lurking in the background turns every decision into a trade-off. Given each consumer's limited income, a decision to buy a new car usually means giving up some travel or postponing furniture purchases. The money that the consumer gives up when she makes a purchase—her expenditure on that purchase—is only one measure of the true underlying cost to her.

IDEAS FOR BEYOND THE FINAL EXAM

HOW MUCH DOES IT REALLY COST?   The real cost is the *opportunity cost* of the purchase—the commodities that she must give up as a result of the purchase decision. This opportunity cost calculation has already been noted in one of our *Ideas for Beyond the Final Exam*—we must always consider the real cost of our purchase decisions, which take into account how much of *other* things they force us to forgo. Any decision to buy implies some such trade-off because scarcity constrains all economic decisions. Although their dilemmas may not inspire much pity, even billionaires face very real trade-offs: Invest $200 million in an office building, or go for the $300 million baseball team?

This last example has another important implication. The trade-off from a consumer's purchase decision does not always involve giving up another *consumer good.* This is true, for example, of the choice between consumption and saving. Consider a high school student who is deciding whether to buy a new car or to save the money to pay for college. If he saves the money, it can grow by earning interest, so that the original amount plus interest earned will be available to pay for tuition and board three years later. A decision to cut down on consumption now and put the money into the bank means that the student will be wealthier in the future because of the interest he will earn. This, in turn, will enable the student to afford more of his college expenses at the future date when those expenses arise. So the opportunity cost of a new car today is the forgone opportunity to save funds for the future. We conclude:

> From the viewpoint of economic analysis, the true cost of any purchase is the opportunity cost of that purchase, rather than the amount of money that is spent on it.

The opportunity cost of a purchase can be either higher or lower than its price. For example, if your computer cost you $1,800, but the purchase required you to take off two hours from your job that pays $20 per hour, the true cost of the computer—that is, the opportunity cost—is the amount of goods you could have bought with $1,840 (the $1,800 price plus the $40 in earnings that the purchase of the computer required you to give up). In this case, the opportunity cost ($1,840, measured in money terms) is higher than the price of the purchase ($1,800). (For an example in which price is higher than opportunity cost, see Test Yourself Question 4 at the end of the chapter.)

Consumer's Surplus: The Net Gain from a Purchase

The optimal purchase rule, MU (approximately) = *P,* assumes that the consumer always tries to maximize the money value of the total utility from the purchase *minus* the amount spent to make that purchase.[4] Thus, any difference between the price consumers *actually* pay for a commodity and the price they would be *willing* to pay for that item represents a net utility gain in some sense. Economists give the name **consumer's surplus** to that difference—that is, to the net gain in total utility that a purchase brings to a buyer. The consumer is trying to make the purchase decisions that maximize

Consumer's surplus is difference between the value to the consumer of the quantity of Commodity *X* purchased and the amount that the market requires the consumer to pay for that quantity of *X.*

Consumer's surplus = Total utility (in money terms) − Total expenditure

---

[4] Again, in practice, the consumer can often only approximately equate MU and *P.*

Thus, just as economists assume that business firms maximize total profit (equal to total revenue minus total cost), they assume that consumers maximize consumer's surplus, that is, the difference between the total utility of the purchased commodity and the amount that consumers spend on it.

The concept of *consumer's surplus* seems to suggest that the consumer gains some sort of free bonus, or *surplus*, for every purchase. In many cases, this idea seems absurd. How can it be true, particularly for goods whose prices seem to be outrageous?

We hinted at the answer in Chapter 1, where we observed that both parties must gain from a voluntary exchange or else one of them will refuse to participate. The same must be true when a consumer makes a *voluntary* purchase from a supermarket or an appliance store. If the consumer did not expect a net gain from the transaction, he or she would simply not bother to buy the good. Even if the seller were to "overcharge" by some standard, that would merely reduce the size of the consumer's net gain, not eliminate it entirely. If the seller is so greedy as to charge a price that wipes out the net gain altogether, the punishment will fit the crime: The consumer will refuse to buy, and the greedy seller's would-be gains will never materialize. The basic principle states that every purchase that is not on the borderline—that is, every purchase except those about which the consumer is indifferent—must yield *some* consumer's surplus.

But how large is that surplus? At least in theory, it can be measured with the aid of a table or graph of marginal utilities (Table 1 and Figure 1). Suppose that, as in our earlier example, the price of a large pizza is $11 and you purchase four pizzas. Table 3 reproduces the marginal utility numbers from Table 1. It shows that the first pizza is worth $15 to you, so at the $11 price, you reap a net gain (surplus) of $15 minus $11, or $4, by buying that pizza. The second pizza also brings you some surplus, but less than the first one does, because the marginal utility diminishes. Specifically, the second pizza provides a surplus of $13 minus $11, or $2. Reasoning in the same way, the third pizza gives you a surplus of $12.50 minus $11, or $1.50. It is only the fourth serving—the last one that you purchase—that offers little or no surplus because, by the optimal purchase rule, the marginal utility of the last unit is approximately equal to its price.

We can now easily determine the total consumer's surplus that you obtain by buying four pizzas. It is simply the sum of the surpluses received from each pizza. Table 3 shows that this consumer's total surplus is

$$\$4 + \$2 + \$1.50 + \$0.50 = \$8$$

This way of looking at the optimal purchase rule shows why a buyer must always gain some consumer's surplus if she buys more than one unit of a good. Note that the price of each unit remains the same, but the marginal utility diminishes as more units are purchased. The last unit bought yields only a tiny consumer's surplus because MU (approximately) = P. But all prior units must have had marginal utilities greater than the MU of the last unit because of diminishing marginal utility.

We can be more precise about the calculation of the consumer's surplus with the help of a graph showing marginal utility as a set of bars. The bars labeled *A*, *B*, *C*, and *D* in Figure 3 come from the corresponding points on the marginal utility curve (demand curve) in Figure 1. The consumer's surplus from each pizza equals the marginal utility of that pizza minus the price you pay for it. By representing consumer's surplus graphically, we can determine just how much surplus you obtain from your entire purchase by measuring the area between the marginal utility curve and the horizontal line representing the price of pizzas—in this case, the horizontal line *PP* represents the (fixed) $11 price.

TABLE 3

Calculating Marginal Net Utility (Consumer's Surplus) from Your Pizza Purchases

Quantity	Marginal Utility	Price	Marginal Net Utility (Surplus)
0			
	$15.00	$11.00	$4.00
1			
	13.00	11.00	2.00
2			
	12.50	11.00	1.50
3			
	11.50	11.00	0.50
4			
Total			$8.00

FIGURE 3

Graphic Calculation of
Consumer's Surplus

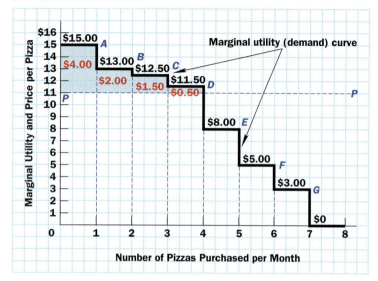

Number of Pizzas Purchased per Month

In Figure 3, the bar whose upper-right corner is labeled *A* represents the $15 marginal utility you derive from the first pizza; the same interpretation applies to the bars *B, C,* and *D.* Clearly, the first serving that you purchase yields a consumer's surplus of $4, indicated by the shaded part of bar *A.* The height of that part of the bar is equal to the $15 marginal utility minus the $11 price. In the same way, the next two shaded areas represent the surpluses offered by the second and third pizzas. The fourth pizza has the smallest shaded area because the height representing marginal utility is (as close as you can get to being) equal to the height representing price. Sum up the shaded areas in the graph to obtain, once again, the total consumer's surplus ($4 + $2 + $1.50 + $0.50 = $8) from a four-pizza purchase.

The consumer's surplus derived from buying a certain number of units of a good is obtained graphically by drawing the person's demand curve as a set of bars whose heights represent the marginal utilities of the corresponding quantities of the good, and then drawing a horizontal line whose height is the price of the good. The sum of the heights of the bars above the horizontal line—that is, the area of the demand (marginal utility) bars above that horizontal line—measures the *total* consumer's surplus that the purchase yields.

Resolving the Diamond–Water Puzzle

We can now use marginal utility analysis to analyze Adam Smith's paradox (which he was never able to explain) that diamonds are very expensive, whereas water is generally very cheap, even though water seems to offer far more utility. The resolution of the diamond–water puzzle is based on the distinction between marginal and total utility.

The *total* utility of water—its role as a necessity of life—is indeed much higher than that of diamonds. But price, as we have seen, is not related directly to *total* utility. Rather, the optimal purchase rule tells us that price tends to equal *marginal* utility. We have every reason to expect the marginal utility of water to be very low, whereas the marginal utility of a diamond is very high.

Given normal conditions, water is comparatively cheap to provide, so its price is generally quite low. Consumers thus use correspondingly large quantities of water. The principle of diminishing marginal utility, therefore, pushes down the marginal utility of water for a typical household to a low level. As the consumer's surplus diagram (Figure 3) suggests, this also means that its *total* utility is likely to be high.

In contrast, high-quality diamonds are scarce (partly because a monopoly keeps them so). As a result, the quantity of diamonds consumed is not large enough to drive down the MU of diamonds very far, so buyers of such luxuries must pay high prices for them. As a commodity becomes more scarce, its *marginal* utility and its market price rise, regardless of the size of its *total* utility. Also, as we have seen, because so little of the commodity is consumed, its *total* utility is likely to be comparatively low, despite its large *marginal* utility.

Thus, like many paradoxes, the diamond–water puzzle has a straightforward explanation. In this case, all one has to remember is that:

Scarcity raises price and *marginal* utility, but it generally reduces *total* utility. And although total utility measures the benefits consumers get from their consumption, it is marginal utility that is equal (approximately) to price.

Income and Quantity Demanded

Our application of marginal analysis has enabled us to examine the relationship between the *price* of a commodity and the quantity that will be purchased. But things other than price also influence the amount of a good that a consumer will purchase. As an example, we'll look at how quantity demanded responds to changes in *income*.

To be concrete, consider what happens to the number of ballpoint pens a consumer will buy when his real income rises. It may seem almost certain that he will buy more ballpoint pens than before, but that is not necessarily so. A rise in real income can either increase or decrease the quantity of any particular good purchased.

Why might an increase in income lead a consumer to buy fewer ballpoint pens? People buy some goods and services only because they cannot afford anything better. They may purchase used cars instead of new ones. They may use inexpensive ballpoint pens instead of finely crafted fountain pens or buy clothing secondhand instead of new. If their real incomes rise, they may then drop out of the used car market and buy brand-new automobiles or buy more fountain pens and fewer ballpoint pens. Thus, a rise in real income will reduce the quantities of cheap pens and used cars demanded. Economists have given the rather descriptive name **inferior goods** to the class of commodities for which quantity demanded falls when income rises.

The upshot of this discussion is that economists cannot draw definite conclusions about the effects of a rise in consumer incomes on quantity demanded. But for most commodities, if incomes rise and prices do not change, quantity demanded will increase. Such an item is often called a *normal good*.

> An **inferior good** is a commodity whose quantity demanded falls when the purchaser's real income rises, all other things remaining equal.

▪ FROM INDIVIDUAL DEMAND CURVES TO MARKET DEMAND CURVES

So far in this chapter, we have studied how *individual demand curves* are obtained from the logic of consumer choice. But to understand how the market system works, we must derive the relationship between price and quantity demanded *in the market as a whole*—the **market demand curve.** It is this market demand curve that plays a key role in the supply-demand analysis of price and output determination that we studied in Chapter 4.

> A **market demand curve** shows how the total quantity of some product demanded by *all* consumers in the market during a specified period of time changes as the price of that product changes, holding all other things constant.

▪ Market Demand as a Horizontal Sum

If each individual pays no attention to other people's purchase decisions when making his or her own, we can easily derive the market demand curve from consumers' individual demand curves: As we will see next, we simply *add* the individual consumers' demand curves, as shown in Figure 4. The figure gives the individual demand curves *DD* and *ZZ* for two people, Alex and Naomi, and the total (market) demand curve, *MM*. Alex and Naomi are both consumers of the product.

We can derive this market demand curve in the following straightforward way:

Step 1: Pick any relevant price, say, $10.

Step 2: At that price, determine Alex's quantity demanded (9 units) from his demand curve in Panel (a) of Figure 4 and Naomi's quantity demanded (6 units) from her demand curve in Panel (b) of Figure 4. Note that these quantities are indicated by the line segment labeled *AA* for Alex and that labeled *NN* for Naomi.

Step 3: Add Naomi's and Alex's quantities demanded at the $10 price (segment *AA* + segment *NN* = 9 + 6 = 15) to yield the total quantity demanded by the market at that price. This gives segment *CC*, with total quantity demanded equal to 15 units, in Panel (c) of Figure 4. Notice that the addition constitutes a *horizontal* movement in the graph because we are adding quantities purchased and those quantities are measured by horizontal distances from the zero point of the graph.

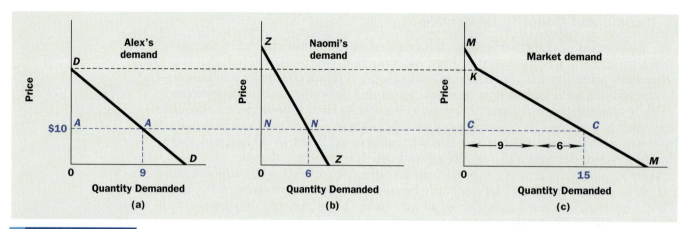

FIGURE 4

The Relationship
Between Total Market
Demand and the
Demand of Individual
Consumers Within That
Market

Now repeat the process for each alternative price to obtain other points on the market demand curve until the shape of the entire curve *MM* appears. (The sharp angle at point *K* on the market curve occurs because that point corresponds to the price at which Alex, whose demand pattern is different from Naomi's, first enters the market. At any higher price, only Naomi is willing to buy anything.) That is all there is to the adding-up process. (Question: What would happen to the market demand curve if, say, another consumer entered the market?)

■ The "Law" of Demand

Just as for the case of an individual's demand curve, we expect the total quantity demanded by the market to move in the opposite direction from price. Economists call this relationship the **"law" of demand.**

The **"law" of demand**
states that a lower price
generally increases the
amount of a commodity
that people in a market are
willing to buy. Therefore, for
most goods, market demand
curves have negative slopes.

Notice that we have put the word *law* in quotation marks. By now you will have observed that economic laws are not always obeyed, and we shall see in a moment that the "law" of demand is not without exceptions. But first let us see why the "law" usually holds.

Earlier in this chapter, we explained that individual demand curves usually slope downward because of the "law" of diminishing marginal utility. If individual demand curves slope downward, then the preceding discussion of the adding-up process implies that market demand curves must also slope downward. This is just common sense; if every consumer in the market buys fewer pizzas when the price of pizza rises, then the total quantity demanded in the market must surely fall.

But market demand curves may slope downward even if individual demand curves do not, because not all consumers are alike. Consider two examples where the individual's demand curve does not slope downward. If a bookstore reduces the price of a popular novel, it may draw many new customers, but few of the customers who already own a copy will buy a second one, despite the reduced price. Similarly, true devotees of pizza may maintain their pizza purchases unchanged even if prices rise to exorbitant levels, whereas others would not eat pizza even if you gave it to them free of charge. But the market prices of books and pizzas can still have a negative slope. As the price of pizza rises, less enthusiastic pizza eaters may drop out of the market entirely, leaving the expensive pie to the more devoted consumers. Thus, the quantity demanded declines as price rises, simply because higher prices induce more people to give up pizza completely. And for many commodities, lower prices encourage new customers to come into the *market* (for example, new book buyers) , and it is these "fair weather" customers (rather than the negative slope of *individual* demand curves) that can be most important for the "law" of demand.

This is also illustrated in Figure 4, in which only Naomi will buy the product at a price higher than *D*. At a price lower than *D*, Alex will also purchase the product. Hence, below point *K*, the market demand curve lies farther to the right than it would have if Alex had not entered the market. Put another way, a rise in price from a level below D to a level above D would cut quantity demanded for two reasons: (1) because Naomi's demand curve has a negative slope and (2) because it would drive Alex out of the market.

We conclude, therefore, that the "law" of demand stands on fairly solid ground. If individual demand curves slope downward, then the market demand curve surely will, too. Furthermore, the market demand curve may slope downward, even when individual demand curves do not.

■ Exceptions to the "Law" of Demand

Some exceptions to the "law" of demand have been noted. One common exception occurs when people judge quality on the basis of price—they perceive a more expensive commodity as offering better quality. For example, many people buy name-brand aspirin, even if right next to it on the drugstore shelf they see an unbranded, generic aspirin with an identical chemical formula, selling at half the price. The consumers who do buy the name-brand aspirin may well use comparative price to judge the relative qualities of different brands. They may prefer Brand X to Brand Y *because* X is slightly more expensive. If Brand X were to reduce its price below that of Brand Y, consumers might assume that it was no longer superior and actually reduce their purchases of X.

Another possible cause of an upward-sloping demand curve is snob appeal. If part of the reason for purchasing a $300,000 Rolls-Royce is to advertise one's wealth, a decrease in the car's price may actually reduce sales, even if the quality of the car remains unchanged. Other types of exceptions have also been noted by economists. But, for most commodities, it seems quite reasonable to assume that demand curves have negative slopes, an assumption that is supported by the data.

This chapter has begun to take us behind the demand curve, to discuss how it is determined by the preferences of individual consumers. Chapter 6 will explore the demand curve further by examining other things that determine its shape and the implications of that shape for consumer behavior.

SUMMARY

1. Economists distinguish between **total and marginal utility**. Total utility, or the benefit a consumer derives from a purchase, is measured by the maximum amount of money he or she would give up to obtain the good. Rational consumers seek to maximize (net) total utility, or **consumer's surplus**: the total utility derived from a commodity minus the value of the money spent in buying it.

2. Marginal utility is the maximum amount of money that a consumer is willing to pay for an *additional* unit of a particular commodity. *Marginal* utility is useful in calculating the set of purchases that maximizes net *total* utility. This illustrates one of our *Ideas for Beyond the Final Exam*.

3. The **"law" of diminishing marginal utility** is a psychological hypothesis stating that as a consumer acquires more and more of a commodity, the marginal utility of additional units of the commodity decreases.

4. To maximize the total utility obtained by spending money on Commodity X, given the fact that other goods can be purchased only with the money that remains after buying X, the consumer must purchase a quantity of X such that the price equals (or approximately equals) the commodity's marginal utility (in monetary terms).

5. If the consumer acts to maximize utility, and if her marginal utility of some good declines when she purchases larger quantities, then her demand curve for the good will have a negative slope. A reduction in price will induce her to purchase more units, leading to a lower marginal utility.

6. Abundant goods tend to have low prices and low marginal utilities regardless of whether their total utilities are high or low. That is why water can have a lower price than diamonds despite its higher total utility.

7. An **inferior good**, such as secondhand clothing, is a commodity of which consumers buy less when they get richer, all other things held equal.

8. Consumers usually earn a surplus when they purchase a commodity voluntarily. This means that the quantity of the good that they buy is worth more to them than the money they give up in exchange for it. Otherwise they would not buy it. That is why consumer's surplus is normally positive.

9. As another of our *Ideas for Beyond the Final Exam*, "How much does it really cost?", tells us, the true economic cost of the purchase of a commodity, X, is its opportunity cost—that is, the value of the alternative purchases that the acquisition of X requires the consumer to forgo. The

money value of the opportunity cost of a unit of good X can be higher or lower than the price of X.

10. A rise in a consumer's income can push quantity demanded either up or down. For normal goods, the effect of a rise in income raises the quantity demanded; for inferior goods, which are generally purchased in an effort to save money, a higher income reduces the quantity demanded.

11. The demand curve for an entire market is obtained by taking a horizontal sum of the demand curves of all individuals who buy or consider buying in that market. This sum is obtained by adding up, for each price, the quantity of the commodity in question that every such consumer is willing to purchase at that price.

KEY TERMS

Total utility   86

Marginal utility   86

The "law" of diminishing marginal utility   87

Marginal analysis   88

Consumer's surplus   92

Inferior good   95

Market demand curve   95

The "law" of demand   96

TEST YOURSELF

1. Which gives you greater *total* utility, 12 gallons of water per day or 20 gallons per day? Why?

2. At which level do you get greater *marginal* utility: 12 gallons per day or 20 gallons per day? Why?

3. Which of the following items are likely to be normal goods for a typical consumer? Which are likely to be inferior goods?

   a. Expensive perfume

   b. Paper plates

   c. Secondhand clothing

   d. Overseas trips

4. Emily buys an air conditioner that costs $600. Because the air in her home is cleaner, its use saves her $150 in curtain cleaning costs over the lifetime of the air conditioner. In money terms, what is the opportunity cost of the air conditioner?

5. Suppose that strawberries sell for $2 per basket. Jim is considering whether to buy zero, one, two, three, or four baskets. On your own, create a plausible set of total and marginal utility numbers for the different quantities of strawberries (as we did for pizza in Table 1) and arrange them in a table. From your table, calculate how many baskets Jim would buy.

6. Draw a graph showing the consumer's surplus Jim would get from his strawberry purchase in Test Yourself Question 5 and check your answer with the help of your marginal utility table.

7. Consider a market with two consumers, Jasmine and Jim. Draw a demand curve for each of the two consumers and use those curves to construct the demand curve for the entire market.

DISCUSSION QUESTIONS

1. Describe some of the different ways you use water. Which would you give up if the price of water were to rise a little? If it were to rise by a fairly large amount? If it were to rise by a very large amount?

2. Suppose that you wanted to measure the marginal utility of a commodity to a consumer by directly determining the consumer's psychological attitude or strength of feeling toward the commodity rather than by seeing how much money the consumer would give up for the commodity. Why would you find it difficult to make such a psychological measurement?

3. Some people who do not understand the optimal purchase rule argue that if a consumer buys so much of a good that its price equals its marginal utility, she could not possibly be behaving optimally. Rather, they say, she would be better off quitting while she was ahead, or buying a quantity such that marginal utility is much greater than price. What is wrong with this argument? (*Hint:* What opportunity would the consumer then miss? Is it maximization of marginal or total utility that serves the consumer's interests?)

4. What inferior goods do you purchase? Why do you buy them? Do you think you will continue to buy them when your income is higher?

APPENDIX *Analyzing Consumer Choice Graphically: Indifference Curve Analysis*

The consumer demand analysis presented in this chapter, although correct as far as it goes, has one shortcoming: By treating the consumer's decision about the purchase of each commodity as an isolated event, it conceals the fact that consumers must *choose* among commodities because of their limited budgets. The analysis so far does not explicitly indicate the hard choice behind every purchase decision—the sacrifice of some goods to obtain others.

The idea is included implicitly, of course, because the purchase of any commodity involves a trade-off between that good and money. If you spend more money on rent, you have less to spend on entertainment. If you buy more clothing, you have less money for food. But to represent the consumer's *choice* problem explicitly, economists have invented two geometric devices, the *budget line* and the *indifference curve*, which are described in this appendix.

■ GEOMETRY OF AVAILABLE CHOICES: THE BUDGET LINE

Suppose, for simplicity, that only two commodities are produced in the world: cheese and rubber bands. The decision problem of any household is then to allocate its income between these two goods. Clearly, the more it spends on one, the less it can have of the other. But just what is the trade-off? A numerical example will answer this question and introduce the graphical device that economists use to portray the trade-off.

Suppose that cheese costs $2 per pound, boxes of rubber bands sell at $3 each, and a consumer has $12 at his disposal. He obviously has a variety of choices, as displayed in Table 4. For example, if he buys no rubber bands, the consumer can go home with six pounds of cheese, and so on. Each of the combinations of cheese and rubber bands that the consumer can afford can be shown in a diagram in which the axes measure the quantities purchased of each commodity. In Figure 5, pounds of cheese are measured along the vertical axis, the number of boxes of rubber bands is measured along the horizontal axis, and a labeled point represents each of the combinations enumerated in Table 4. This budget line *AE* shows the possible combinations of cheese and rubber bands that the consumer can buy with $12 if cheese costs $2 per pound and a box of rubber bands costs $3. For example, point *A* corresponds to spending everything on cheese; point *E* corresponds to spending everything on rubber bands. At intermediate points on the budget line (such as *C*), the consumer buys some of both goods (at *C*, two boxes of rubber bands and three pounds of cheese), which together use up the $12 available.

If a straight line connects points *A* through *E*, the blue line in the diagram, it traces all possible ways to divide the $12 between the two goods. For example, at point *D*, if the consumer buys three boxes of rubber bands, he will have enough money left to purchase only 11/2 pounds of cheese. This is readily seen to be correct from Table 4. Line *AE* is therefore called the **budget line.**

The **budget line** for a household graphically represents all possible combinations of two commodities that it can purchase, given the prices of the commodities and some fixed amount of money at its disposal.

TABLE 4

Alternative Purchase Combinations for a $12 Budget

Boxes of Rubber Bands (at $3 each)	Expenditure on Rubber Bands	Remaining Funds	Pounds of Cheese (at $2 each)	Label in Figure 5
0	$0	$12	6	A
1	3	9	4.5	B
2	6	6	3	C
3	9	3	1.5	D
4	12	0	0	E

FIGURE 5   A Budget Line

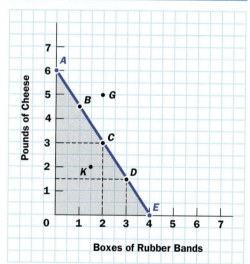

■ Properties of the Budget Line

Let us now use *r* to represent the number of boxes of rubber bands purchased by the consumer and *c* to indicate the amount of cheese that he acquires. Thus, at $2 per pound, he spends on cheese a total of $2 times the number of pounds of cheese bought, or $2c. Similarly, the consumer spends $3r on rubber bands, making a total of

$2c$ plus $3r$, which must equal $12 if he spends the entire $12 on the two commodities. Thus, $2c + 3r = 12$ is the equation of the budget line. It is also the equation of the straight line drawn in the diagram.[5]

Note also that the budget line represents the *maximum* amounts of the commodities that the consumer can afford. Thus, for any given purchase of rubber bands, it indicates the greatest amount of cheese that his money can buy. If the consumer wants to be thrifty, he can choose to end up at a point *below* the budget line, such as K. Clearly, then, the choices he has available include not only those points on the budget line, AE, but also any point in the shaded triangle formed by that line and the two axes. By contrast, points above the budget line, such as G, are not available to the consumer, given his limited budget. A bundle of five pounds of cheese and two boxes of rubber bands would cost $16, which is more than he has to spend.

Changes in the Budget Line

The position of the budget line is determined by two types of data: the prices of the commodities purchased and the income at the buyer's disposal. We can complete our discussion of the graphics of the budget line by examining briefly how a change in either prices or income affects the location of that line.

Obviously, any increase in the income of the household increases the range of options available to it. Specifically, *increases in income produce parallel shifts in the budget line*, as shown in Figure 6. The reason is simple: An increase in available income of, say, 50 percent, if spent entirely on these two goods, would permit the consumer's family to purchase exactly 50 percent more of *either* commodity. Point A in Figure 5 would shift upward by 50 percent of its distance from the origin, whereas point E would move to the right by 50 percent.[6] Figure 6 shows three such budget lines corresponding to incomes of $9, $12, and $18, respectively.

Finally, we can ask what happens to the budget line when the price of some commodity changes. In Figure 7, when the price of the rubber bands *decreases*, the budget line moves outward, but the move is no longer parallel because the point on the cheese axis remains fixed. Once

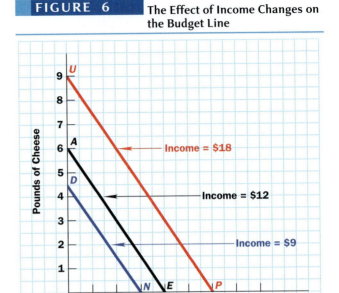

FIGURE 6 The Effect of Income Changes on the Budget Line

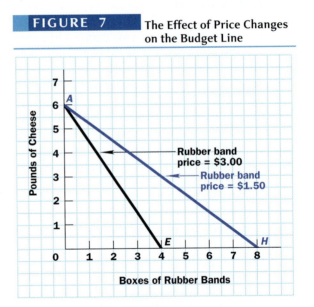

FIGURE 7 The Effect of Price Changes on the Budget Line

---

[5] You may have noticed one problem that arises in this formulation. If every point on the budget line, AE, is a possible way for the consumer to spend his money, he must be able to buy *fractional* boxes of rubber bands. Perhaps the purchase of 1½ boxes can be interpreted to include a down payment of $1.50 on a box of rubber bands to be purchased on the next shopping trip!

[6] An algebraic proof is simple. Let M (which is initially $12) be the amount of money available to the consumer's household. The equation of the budget line can be solved for c, obtaining $c = -(3/2)r + M/2$. This equation corresponds to a straight line with a slope of $-3/2$ and a vertical intercept of $M/2$. A change in M, the quantity of money available, will not change the *slope* of the budget line; rather, it will lead to parallel shifts in that line.

again, the reason is fairly straightforward. A 50 percent reduction in the price of rubber bands (from $3.00 to $1.50) permits the consumer to buy twice as many boxes of rubber bands with his $12 as before: Point E moves rightward to point H, where the buyer can obtain eight boxes of rubber bands. However, since the price of cheese has not changed from point A, the amount of cheese that can be bought for $12 is unaffected. This gives the general result that *a reduction in the price of one of the two commodities swings the budget line outward along the axis representing the quantity of that item while leaving the location of the other end of the line unchanged.* Thus a fall in the price of rubber bands from $3.00 to $1.50 swings the price line from AE to blue line AH. This happens because at the higher price,

$12 buys only four boxes of rubber bands, but at the lower price, it can buy eight boxes.

WHAT THE CONSUMER PREFERS: PROPERTIES OF THE INDIFFERENCE CURVE

The budget line indicates what choices are *available* to the consumer, given the size of his income and the commodity prices fixed by the market. Next, we must examine the consumer's *preferences* to determine which of these available possibilities he will choose.

After much investigation, economists have determined what they believe to be the minimum amount of information they need about a purchaser in order to analyze his choices. Economists need know only how a consumer *ranks* alternative bundles of available commodities, deciding which bundle she likes better, but making no effort to find out *how much* more she likes the preferred bundle. Suppose, for instance, that the consumer can choose between two bundles of goods, Bundle *W*, which contains three boxes of rubber bands and one pound of cheese, and Bundle *T*, which contains two boxes of rubber bands and three pounds of cheese. The economist wants to know for this purpose only whether the consumer prefers *W* to *T* or *T* to *W*, or whether he is *indifferent* about which one he gets. Note that the analysis requires no information about the *degree* of preference—whether the consumer is wildly more enthusiastic about one of the bundles or just prefers it slightly.

Graphically, the preference information is provided by a group of curves called **indifference curves** (Figure 8).

*An **indifference curve** is a line connecting all combinations of the commodities that are equally desirable to the consumer.*

Any point on the diagram represents a combination of cheese and rubber bands. (For example, point *T* on indifference curve I_b represents two boxes of rubber bands and three pounds of cheese.) Any two points on the same indifference curve (for example, *S* and *W*, on indifference curve I_a) represent two combinations of the goods that the consumer likes equally well. If two points, such as *T* and *W*, lie on different indifference curves, the consumer prefers the one on the higher indifference curve.

But before we examine these curves, let us see how to interpret one. A single point on an indifference curve says nothing about preferences. For example, point *R* on curve I_a simply represents the bundle of goods composed of four boxes of rubber bands and 1/2 pound of cheese. It does *not* suggest that the consumer is indifferent between 1/2 pound of cheese and four boxes of rubber bands. For the curve to indicate anything, one must consider at least two of its points—for example, points *S* and *W*. An indif-

ference curve, by definition, represents all such combinations that provide equal utility to the consumer.

We do not know yet which bundle, among all of the bundles he can afford, the consumer will choose to buy; this analysis indicates only that a choice between certain bundles will lead to indifference. Before using indifference curves to analyze the consumer's choice, one must examine a few of its properties. Most important is the fact that:

As long as the consumer desires more *of each of the goods in question, every point on a higher indifference curve (that is, a curve farther from the origin in the graph) will be preferred to any point on a lower indifference curve.*

In other words, among indifference curves, *higher is better*. The reason is obvious. Given two indifference curves, say, I_b and I_c in Figure 8, the higher curve will contain points lying above and to the right of some points on the lower curve. Thus, point *U* on curve I_c lies above and to the right of point *T* on curve I_b. This means that the consumer gets more rubber bands *and* more cheese at *U* than at *T*. Assuming that he desires both commodities, the consumer must prefer *U* to *T*.

Because every point on curve I_c is, by definition, equal in desirability to point *U*, and the same relation holds for point *T* and all other points along curve I_b, the consumer will prefer *every* point on curve I_c to *any* point on curve I_b.

This at once implies a second property of indifference curves: *They never intersect*. This is so because if an indifference curve, say, I_b, is anywhere above another indifference curve, say, I_a, then I_b must be above I_a everywhere, because every point on I_b is preferred to every point on I_a.

Another property that characterizes the indifference curve is its *negative slope*. Again, this holds only if the

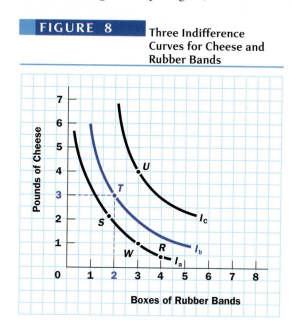

FIGURE 8 Three Indifference Curves for Cheese and Rubber Bands

Pounds of Cheese (vertical axis)

Boxes of Rubber Bands (horizontal axis)

consumer wants more of both commodities. Consider two points, such as S and R, on the same indifference curve. If the consumer is indifferent between them, one point cannot represent more of *both* commodities than the other point. Given that point S represents more cheese than point R does, R must offer more rubber bands than S does, or the consumer would not be indifferent about which he gets. As a result, any movement toward the point with the larger number of rubber bands implies a decrease in the quantity of cheese. The curve will always slope downhill toward the right, giving a negative slope.

A final property of indifference curves is the nature of their curvature—the way *they round toward the axes*. They are drawn "bowed in"—they flatten out (they become less and less steep) as they extend from left to right. To understand why this is so, we must first examine the economic interpretation of the slope of an indifference curve.

■ THE SLOPES OF INDIFFERENCE CURVES AND BUDGET LINES

In Figure 9, the average slope of the indifference curve between points M and N is represented by RM/RN.

> The **slope of an indifference curve**, referred to as the **marginal rate of substitution (MRS) between the commodities,** **represents the maximum amount of one commodity that the consumer is willing to give up in exchange for one more unit of another commodity.**

RM is the quantity of cheese that the consumer gives up in moving from M to N. Similarly, RN is the increased number of boxes of rubber bands acquired in this move. Because the consumer is indifferent between bundles M and N, the gain of RN rubber bands must just suffice to compensate him for the loss of RM pounds of cheese. Thus, the ratio RM/RN represents the terms on which the consumer is just willing—*according to his own preference*—to trade one good for the other. If RM/RN equals 2, the consumer is willing to give up (no more than) two pounds of cheese for one additional box of rubber bands.

The **slope of the budget line,** *BB*, in Figure 9 is also a rate of exchange between cheese and rubber bands. But it no longer reflects the consumer's subjective willingness to trade. Rather, the slope represents the rate of exchange that *the market* offers to the consumer when he gives up money in exchange for cheese and rubber bands. Recall that the budget line represents all commodity combinations that a consumer can get by spending a fixed amount of money. The budget line is, therefore, a curve of constant expenditure. At current prices, if the consumer reduces his purchase of cheese by amount DE in Figure 9, he will save just enough money to buy an additional amount, EF, of rubber bands, be-

cause at points D and F he is spending the same total number of dollars.

> The **slope of a budget line** is the amount of one commodity that the market requires an individual to give up to obtain one additional unit of another commodity without any change in the amount of money spent.

The slopes of the two types of curves, then, are perfectly analogous in their meaning. The slope of the indifference curve indicates the terms on which the *consumer* is willing to trade one commodity for another, whereas the slope of the budget line reports the *market* terms on which the consumer can trade one good for another.

It is useful to carry our interpretation of the slope of the budget line one step further. Common sense suggests that the market's rate of exchange between cheese and rubber bands should be related to their prices, pc and pr, and it is easy to show that this is so. Specifically, the slope of the budget line is equal to the ratio of the prices of the two commodities. To see why, note that if the consumer gives up one box of rubber bands, he has pr more dollars to spend on cheese. But the quantity of cheese this money will enable him to buy is *inversely* related to its price; that is, the lower the price of cheese, the more cheese that money can buy—each dollar permits him to buy $1/pc$ pounds of cheese. So the additional pr dollars the consumer has available when he forgoes the purchase of one box of rubber bands permit him to buy pr times $1/pc = pr/pc$ more pounds of cheese. Thus, the slope of the budget line, which indicates how much additional cheese the consumer can buy when he gives up one box of rubber bands, is pr/pc.

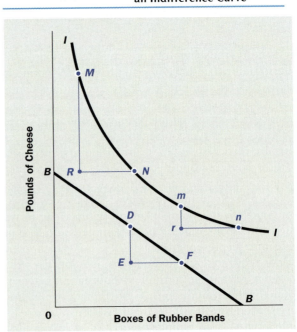

FIGURE 9   Slopes of a Budget Line and an Indifference Curve

Before returning to our main subject, the study of consumer choice, we pause briefly and use our interpretation of the slope of the indifference curve to discuss the third of the properties of the indifference curve—its characteristic curvature—which we left unexplained earlier. The shape of indifference curves means that the slope decreases with movement from left to right. In Figure 9, at point *m*, toward the right of the diagram, the consumer is willing to give up far less cheese for one more box of rubber bands (quantity *rm*) than he is willing to trade at point *M*, toward the left. This situation occurs because at *M* the consumer initially has a large quantity of cheese and few rubber bands, whereas at *m* his initial stock of cheese is low and he has many rubber bands. In general terms, the curvature premise on which indifference curves are usually drawn asserts that consumers are relatively eager to trade away some part of what they own of a commodity of which they have a large amount but are more reluctant to trade away part of the goods of which they hold small quantities. This psychological premise underlies the curvature of the indifference curve.

We can now use our indifference curve apparatus to analyze how the consumer chooses among the combinations that he can afford to buy—that is, the combinations of rubber bands and cheese shown by the budget line. Figure 10 brings together in the same diagram the budget line from Figure 5 and the indifference curves from Figure 8.

■ Tangency Conditions

Because, according to the first of the properties of indifference curves, the consumer prefers higher curves to lower ones, he will go to the point on the budget line that lies on the highest indifference curve attainable. This will be point *T* on indifference curve I_b. He can afford no other point that he likes as well. For example, neither point *K* below the budget line nor point *W* on the budget line puts the consumer on such a high indifference curve. Further, any point on an indifference curve above I_b, such as point *U*, is out of the question because it lies beyond his financial means. We end up with a simple rule of consumer choice:

Consumers will select the most desired combination of goods obtainable for their money. The choice will be that point on the budget line at which the budget line is tangent to an indifference curve.

We can see why only the point of tangency, *T* (two boxes of rubber bands and three pounds of cheese), will give the consumer the largest utility that his money can buy. Suppose that the consumer were instead to consider buying 3½ boxes of rubber bands and one pound of cheese. This would put him at point *W* on the budget line and on the indifference curve I_a. But then, by

buying fewer rubber bands and more cheese (a move upward and to the left on the budget line), he could get to another indifference curve, I_b, that would be higher and therefore more desirable without spending any more money. It clearly does not pay to end up at *W*. Only the point of tangency, *T*, leaves no room for further improvement.

At a point of tangency, where the consumer's benefits from purchasing cheese and rubber bands are maximized, the slope of the budget line equals the slope of the indifference curve. This is true by the definition of a point of tangency. We have just seen that the slope of the indifference curve is the marginal rate of substitution between cheese and rubber bands, and that the slope of the budget line is the ratio of the prices of rubber bands and cheese. We can therefore restate the requirement for the optimal division of the consumer's money between the two commodities in slightly more technical language:

Consumers will get the most benefit from their money when they choose combinations of commodities whose marginal rates of substitution equal the ratios of their prices.

It is worth reviewing the logic behind this conclusion. Why is it not advisable for the consumer to stop at a point such as *W*, where the marginal rate of substitution (slope of the indifference curve) is less than the price ratio (slope of the budget line)? By moving upward and to the left from W along his budget line, he can instead take advantage of market opportunities to obtain a commodity bundle that he likes better. This will always be true, for example, if the amount of cheese the consumer is *personally* willing to exchange for a box of rubber bands (the slope of the indifference curve) is greater than the amount of cheese for which the box of rubber bands trades *on the market* (the slope of the budget line).

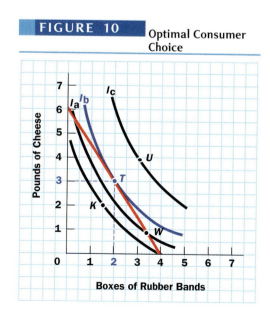

FIGURE 10 Optimal Consumer Choice

Boxes of Rubber Bands

Consequences of Income Changes: Inferior Goods

Now consider what happens to the consumer's purchases after a rise in income. We know that a rise in income produces a parallel outward shift in the budget line, such as the shift from *BB* to *CC* in Figure 11. The quantity of rubber bands demanded rises from three to four boxes, and the quantity demanded of cheese increases as well. This change moves the consumer's equilibrium from tangency point *T* to tangency point *E* on a higher indifference curve.

A rise in income may or may not increase the demand for a commodity. In Figure 11, the rise in income does lead the consumer to buy more cheese *and* more rubber bands, but indifference curves need not always be positioned in a way that yields this sort of result. In Figure 12, as the consumer's budget line rises from *BB* to *CC*, the tangency point moves leftward from *H* to *G*. As a result, when his income rises, the consumer actually buys *fewer* rubber bands. This implies that for this consumer rubber bands are an *inferior good*.

Consequences of Price Changes: Deriving the Demand Curve

Finally, we come to the main question underlying demand curves: How does a consumer's choice change if the price of one good changes? We explained earlier that a reduction in the price of a box of rubber bands causes the budget line to swing outward along the horizontal axis while leaving its vertical intercept unchanged. In Figure 13, we depict the effect of a decline in the price of rubber bands on the quantity of rubber

FIGURE 12   Effects of a Rise in Income When Rubber Bands Are an Inferior Good

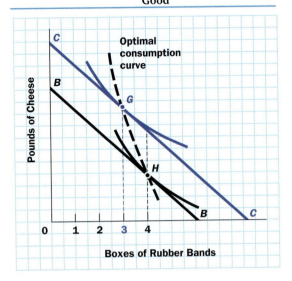

bands demanded. As the price of rubber bands falls, the budget line swings from *BC* to *BD*. The tangency points, *T* and *E*, also move in a corresponding direction, causing the quantity demanded to rise from two to three boxes. The price of rubber bands has fallen and the quantity demanded has risen, so the demand curve for rubber bands has a negative slope. The desired purchase of rubber bands increases from two to three boxes, and the desired purchase of cheese also increases, from three pounds to 3¾ pounds.

The demand curve for rubber bands can be constructed directly from Figure 13. Point *T* shows that the consumer will buy two boxes of rubber bands when the price of a box is $3.00. Point *E* indicates that when the price falls to $1.50, quantity demanded rises to three boxes of rubber

FIGURE 11   Effects of a Rise in Income When Neither Good Is Inferior

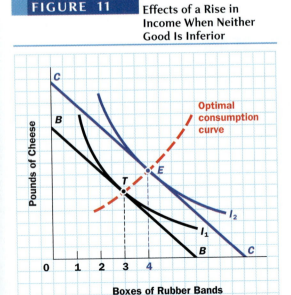

FIGURE 13   Consequences of Price Changes

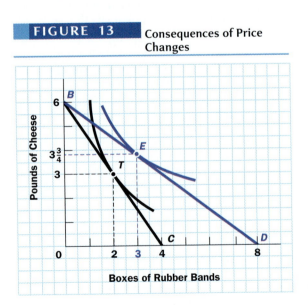

bands.[7] These two pieces of information are shown in Figure 14 as points *t* and *e* on the demand curve for rubber bands. By examining the effects of other possible prices for rubber bands (other budget lines emanating from point *B* in Figure 13), we can find all the other points on the demand curve in exactly the same way. The demand curve is derived from the indifference curve by varying the price of the commodity to see the effects of all other possible prices.

The indifference curve diagram also brings out an important idea that the demand curve does not show. A change in the *price of rubber bands* also has consequences for the *quantity of cheese demanded* because it affects the amount of money left over for cheese purchases. In the example illustrated in Figure 13, the decrease in the price of rubber bands increases the demand for cheese from 3 to 3¾ pounds.

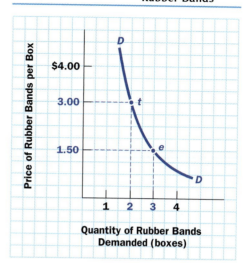

FIGURE 14 Deriving the Demand Curve for Rubber Bands

---

[7] How do we know that the price of rubber bands corresponding to the budget line *BD* is $1.50? Because the $12.00 total budget will purchase at most eight boxes (point *D*), the price per box must be $12.00/8 = $1.50.

SUMMARY

1. Indifference curve analysis permits economists to study the interrelationships of the demands for two (or more) commodities.

2. The basic tools of indifference curve analysis are the consumer's **budget line** and **indifference curves.**

3. A budget line shows all combinations of two commodities that the consumer can afford, given the prices of the commodities and the amount of money the consumer has available to spend.

4. The budget line is a straight line whose slope equals the ratio of the prices of the commodities. A change in price changes the **slope of the budget line.** A change in the consumer's income causes a parallel shift in the budget line.

5. Two points on an indifference curve represent two combinations of commodities such that the consumer does not prefer one combination over the other.

6. Indifference curves normally have negative slopes and are "bowed in" toward the origin. The **slope of an indifference curve** indicates how much of one commodity the consumer is willing to give up to get an additional unit of the other commodity.

7. The consumer will choose the point on her budget line that gets her to the highest attainable indifference curve. Normally this will occur at the point of tangency between the two curves. This point indicates the combination of commodities that gives the consumer the greatest benefits for the amount of money she has available to spend.

8. The consumer's demand curve can be derived from her indifference curve.

KEY TERMS

Budget line   99

Indifference curve   101

Slope of an indifference curve (marginal rate of substitution)   102

Slope of a budget line   102

TEST YOURSELF

1. John Q. Public spends all of his income on gasoline and hot dogs. Draw his budget line under several conditions:

   a. His income is $80, and one gallon of gasoline and one hot dog each cost $1.60.

   b. His income is $120, and the two prices remain the same.

   c. His income is $80, hot dogs cost $1.60 each, and gasoline costs $2.00 per gallon.

2. Draw some hypothetical indifference curves for John Q. Public on a diagram identical to the one you constructed for Test Yourself Question 1.

   a. Approximately how much gasoline and how many hot dogs will Mr. Public buy?

   b. How will these choices change if his income increases to $120? Is either good an inferior good?

   c. How will these choices change if gasoline price rises to $2.00 per gallon?

3. Explain the information that the *slope* of an indifference curve conveys about a consumer's preferences. Use this relationship to explain the typical U-shaped curvature of indifference curves.

6

DEMAND AND ELASTICITY

A high cross elasticity of demand [between two goods indicates that they] compete in the same market. [This can prevent a supplier of one of the products] from possessing monopoly power over price.

U.S. SUPREME COURT, DUPONT CELLOPHANE DECISION, 1956

I n this chapter, we continue our study of demand and demand curves, which we began in the previous chapter. Here we explain the way economists *measure* how much quantity demanded responds to price changes, and what such responsiveness implies about the revenue that producers will receive if they change prices. In particular, we introduce and explain an important concept called *elasticity* that economists use to examine the relationship between quantity demanded and price.

CONTENTS

ISSUE: *Will Taxing Cigarettes Make Teenagers Stop Smoking?*

Public health experts believe that increased taxes on cigarettes can be a major weapon in the battle to cut teenage smoking. Imagine yourself on a panel of consultants helping a congressional committee draft new legislation to deal with this issue. As the youngest member of the group, you are asked for your opinion about how effective a big tax increase on cigarettes would be in persuading young people to stop smoking. How would you respond? What sorts of statistical data, if any, would you use to help find your answer? And how might you go about analyzing the relevant numbers?

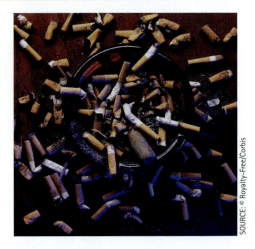

This chapter will help you answer such questions. As often happens in economics, we will see that careful investigation brings some surprises. This is true in the case of taxes to discourage teenage smoking. A tax on cigarettes may actually benefit teenagers'—and other citizens'—health. And it will, of course, benefit government finances by bringing in more tax money. Nothing surprising so far. Instead, the surprise is this: The more effective the tax is in curbing teenage smoking, the less beneficial it will be to the government's finances, and vice versa; the more the tax benefits the government, the less it will contribute to health. The concept of elasticity of demand will make this point clearer.

ELASTICITY: THE MEASURE OF RESPONSIVENESS

Governments, business firms, supermarkets, consumers, and law courts need a way to measure how responsive demand is to price changes—for example, will a 10 percent cut in the price of commodity X increase quantity of X demanded a little or a lot? Economists measure the responsiveness of quantity demanded to price changes via a concept called *elasticity*. Marketers sometimes use estimates of elasticity to decide how to price their products or whether to add new product models. A relatively flat demand curve like Figure 1(a) indicates that consumers respond sharply to a change in

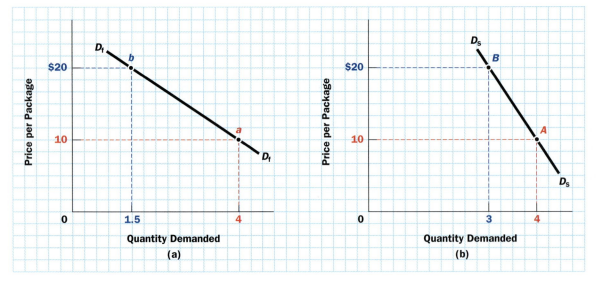

FIGURE 1

Hypothetical Demand Curves for Film

Note: Quantities are in millions of packages of film per year.

price—the quantity they demand falls by 2.5 units (from 4 units to 1.5 units) when price rises $10. That is, they demand or buy much less of the product when price rises even a little bit. Such a "touchy" curve is called *elastic* or *highly elastic*. A relatively steep demand curve like Figure 1(b), which indicates that consumers respond hardly at all to a price change, is called *inelastic*. In this graph, a $10 price rise cuts quantity demanded by only 1 unit.

The precise measure used for this purpose is called the **price elasticity of demand,** or simply the **elasticity of demand.** We define elasticity of demand as the ratio of the *percentage* change in quantity demanded to the associated *percentage* change in price.

Demand is called *elastic* if, say, a 10 percent rise in price reduces quantity demanded by *more* than 10 percent. Demand is called *inelastic* if such a rise in price reduces quantity demanded by *less* than 10 percent.

Why do we need these definitions to analyze the responsiveness to price shown by a particular demand curve? At first, it may seem that the *slope* of the demand curve conveys the needed information: Curve D_sD_s is much steeper than curve D_fD_f in Figure 1, so any given change in price appears to correspond to a much smaller change in quantity demanded in Figure 1(b) than in Figure 1(a). For this reason, it is tempting to call demand in Panel (a) "more elastic." But slope will not do the job, because the slope of any curve depends on the particular units of measurement, and economists use no standardized units of measurement. For example, cloth output may be measured in yards or in meters, milk in quarts or liters, and coal in tons or hundredweights. Figure 2(a) brings out this point explicitly. In this graph, we return to the pizza example from Chapter 5, measuring quantity demanded in terms of pizzas and price in dollars per pizza. A fall in price from $15 to $11 per large pizza (points *A* and *B*) raises quantity demanded at Paul's Pizza Parlor from 280 pizzas to 360 per week— that is, by 80 pizzas.

Now look at Figure 2(b), which provides *exactly* the same information, but measures quantity demanded in *slices* of pizza rather than whole pizzas (with one pizza yielding eight slices). Here, the same price change as before increases quantity demanded, from $8 \times 280 = 2{,}240$ slices to $8 \times 360 = 2{,}880$ slices—that is, by 640 slices, rather than by 80 pizzas.

Visually, the increase in quantity demanded looks eight times as great in Panel (b) as in Panel (a), but all that has changed is the unit of measurement. The 640-unit increase

The **(price) elasticity of demand** is the ratio of the *percentage* change in quantity demanded to the *percentage* change in price that brings about the change in quantity demanded.

| FIGURE 2 |

The Sensitivity of Slope to Units of Measurement at Paul's Pizza Parlor

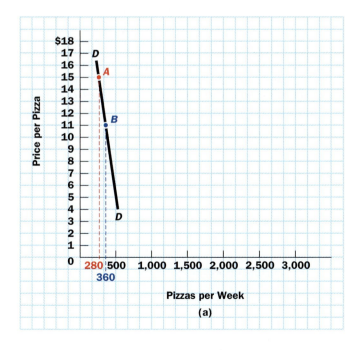

(a)

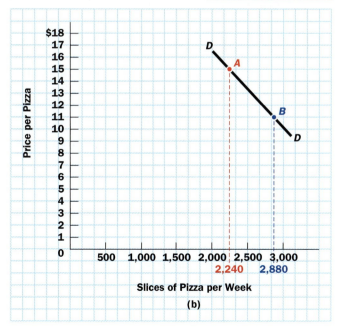

(b)

in Figure 2(b) represents the same increase in quantity demanded as the 80-unit increase in Figure 2(a). Just as you get different numbers for a given rise in temperature, depending on whether you measure it in Celsius or Fahrenheit, so the slopes of demand curves differ, depending on whether you measure quantity in pizzas or in pizza slices. Clearly, then, slope does not really measure responsiveness of quantity demanded to price, because the measure changes whenever the units of measurement change.

Economists created the elasticity concept precisely in response to this problem. Elasticity measures responsiveness on the basis of *percentage* changes in price and quantity rather than on *absolute* changes. The elasticity formula solves the units problem because percentages are unaffected by units of measurement. If the government defense budget doubles, it goes up by 100 percent, whether measured in millions or billions of dollars. If demand for pizza trebles, it rises by 200 percent, whether we measure the quantity demanded in number of pies or slices. The elasticity formula given earlier therefore expresses both the change in quantity demanded and the change in price as *percentages*.[1]

Furthermore, elasticity calculates the change in quantity demanded *as a percentage of the average of the two quantities*: the quantity demanded *before* the change in price has occurred (Q_0) and the quantity demanded *after* the price change (Q_1). In our example, the "before" pizza purchase is 280 (Q_0), the quantity sold after the price fall is 360 (Q_1), and the average of these two numbers is 320. The increase in number of pizzas bought is 80 pizzas, which is 25 percent of the 320 average of the sales before and after the price change. So 25 percent is the number we use as the purchase increase measure in our elasticity calculation. This procedure is a useful compromise between viewing the change in quantity demanded (80 pizzas) as a percentage of the initial quantity (280) or as a percentage of the final quantity (360).

Similarly, the change in price is expressed as a percentage of the average of the "before" and "after" prices, so that, in effect, it represents elasticity at the price halfway between those two prices. That is, the price falls by $4 (from $15 to $11). Because $4 is (approximately) 33 percent of the average of $14 ($P_0$) and $10 ($P_1$) (that is, $12), we say that in this case a 33 percent fall in price led to a 25 percent rise in quantity of pizza demanded.

To summarize, the elasticity formula has two basic attributes:

- Each of the changes with which it deals is measured as a *percentage* change.
- Each of the percentage changes is calculated in terms of the average values of the before and after quantities and prices.

In addition, economists often adjust the price elasticity of demand formula in a third way. Note that when the price *increases*, the quantity demanded usually *declines*. Thus, when the price change is a positive number, the quantity change will normally be a negative number; when the price change is a negative number, the quantity change will normally be a positive number. As a consequence, the ratio of the two percentage changes will be a negative number. We customarily express elasticity as a positive number, however. Hence:

- Each percentage change is taken as an "absolute value," meaning that the calculation drops all minus signs.[2]

---

[1] The remainder of this section involves fairly technical computational issues. On a first reading, you may prefer to go directly to the new section that begins on the next page.

[2] This third attribute of the elasticity formula—the removal of all minus signs—applies only when the formula is used to measure the responsiveness of *quantity demanded* of product X to a change in the *price* of product X. Later in the chapter, we will show that similar formulas are used to measure the responsiveness between other pairs of variables. For example, the elasticity of supply uses a similar formula to measure the responsiveness of quantity supplied to price. In such cases, it is not customary to drop minus signs when calculating elasticity. The reasons will become clearer later in the chapter.

We can now state the formula for price elasticity of demand, keeping all three features of the formula in mind:

Price elasticity of demand = Change in quantity demanded, expressed as a percentage of the average of the before and after quantities *divided by* the corresponding percentage change in price.

In our example:

Elasticity of demand for pizzas =

$$\frac{(Q_1 - Q_0)/\text{average of } Q_0 \text{ and } Q_1}{(P_1 - P_0)/\text{average of } P_0 \text{ and } P_1} = \frac{80/320}{4/13} = \frac{25\%}{31\%} = 0.8 \text{ (approximately)}$$

■ Price Elasticity of Demand and the Shapes of Demand Curves

We noted earlier that looks can be deceiving in some demand curves because their units of measurement are arbitrary. Economists have provided the elasticity formula to overcome that problem. Nonetheless, the shape of a demand curve does convey some information about its elasticity. Let's see what information some demand curve shapes give, with the aid of Figure 3.

1. Perfectly Elastic Demand Curves Panel (a) of Figure 3 depicts a horizontal demand curve. Such a curve is called *perfectly elastic* (or *infinitely elastic*). At any price higher than $0.75, quantity demanded will drop to zero; that is, the comparative change in quantity demanded will be infinitely large. Perfect elasticity typically occurs when many producers sell a product and consumers can switch easily from one seller to another if any particular producer raises his price. For example, suppose you and the other students in your economics class are required to buy a newspaper every day to keep up with economic events. If news dealer X, from whom you have been buying the newspaper, raises the price from 75 cents to 80 cents, but the competitor, Y, across the street keeps the old price, then X may lose all her newspaper customers to Y. This situation is likely to prevail whenever an acceptable rival product is available at the going price (75 cents in the diagram). In cases in which no one will pay more than the going price, the seller will lose all of her customers if she raises her price by even a penny.

FIGURE 3

Demand Curves with Different Elasticities

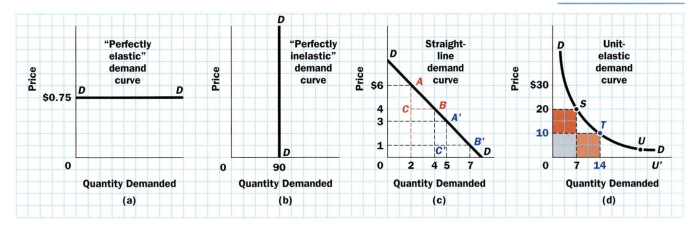

Quantity Demanded
(a) (b) (c) (d)

2. Perfectly Inelastic Demand Curves

Panel (b) of Figure 3 shows the opposite extreme: a completely vertical demand curve. Such a curve is called *perfectly inelastic* throughout because its elasticity is zero at every point on the curve. Because quantity demanded remains at 90 units no matter what the price, the percentage change in quantity is always zero, and hence the elasticity (which equals percentage change in quantity divided by percentage change in price) is always zero. In this case, consumer purchases do not respond at all to any change in price.

Vertical demand curves such as the one shown in Panel (b) of Figure 3 occur when a commodity is very inexpensive. For example, you probably will not buy more rubber bands if their prices fall. The demand curve may also be vertical when consumers consider the item in question to be an absolute necessity. For example, if your roommate's grandfather has a heart attack, the family will buy whatever medicine the doctor prescribes, regardless of the price, and will not purchase any more even if the price falls.

3. (Seemingly Simple) Straight-Line Demand Curves

Panel (c) of Figure 3 depicts a case between these two extremes: a *straight-line* demand curve that runs neither vertically nor horizontally. Note that, although the *slope* of a straight-line demand curve remains constant throughout its length, its *elasticity* does not. For example, the elasticity of demand between points A and B in Figure 3(c) is:

$$\frac{\text{Change in } \textbf{\textit{Q}} \text{ as a percentage of average } \textbf{\textit{Q}}}{\text{Change in } \textbf{\textit{P}} \text{ as a percentage of average } \textbf{\textit{P}}} = \frac{2/3}{2/5} = \frac{66.67\%}{40\%} = 1.67$$

The elasticity of demand between points A' and B' is:

$$\frac{2 \text{ as a percentage of } 6}{2 \text{ as a percentage of } 2} = \frac{33.33 \text{ percent}}{100 \text{ percent}} = 0.33$$

The general point is that:

> Along a straight-line demand curve, the price elasticity of demand grows steadily smaller as you move from left to right. That is so because the quantity keeps getting larger, so that a given *numerical* change in quantity becomes an ever-smaller *percentage* change. But, simultaneously, the price keeps going lower, so that a given numerical change in price becomes an ever-larger percentage change. So, as one moves from left to right along the demand curve, the numerator of the elasticity fraction keeps falling and the denominator keeps growing larger; thus the fraction that is the elasticity formula keeps declining.

A **demand curve** is **elastic** when a given percentage price change leads to a larger percentage change in quantity demanded.

A **demand curve** is **inelastic** when a given percentage price change leads to a smaller percentage change in quantity demanded.

A demand curve is **unit-elastic** when a given percentage price change leads to the same percentage change in quantity demanded.

4. Unit-Elastic Demand Curves

If the elasticity of a straight-line demand curve varies from one part of the curve to another, what does a demand curve with the same elasticity throughout its length look like? For reasons explained in the next section, it has the general shape indicated in Figure 3(d). That panel shows a curve with elasticity equal to 1 throughout (a *unit-elastic* demand curve). A unit-elastic demand curve bends in the middle toward the origin of the graph—at either end, it moves closer and closer to the axes but never touches or crosses them.

As we have noted, a curve with an elasticity greater than 1 is called an **elastic demand curve** (one for which the percentage change in quantity demanded will be greater than the percentage change in price); a curve whose elasticity is less than 1 is known as an **inelastic curve.** When elasticity is exactly 1, economists say that the curve is **unit-elastic.**

Real-world price elasticities of demand seem to vary considerably from product to product. Because people can get along without them, moderately luxurious goods, such as expensive vacations, are generally more price elastic—people give them up more readily when their prices rise—than goods such as milk and shirts, which are considered necessities. Products with close substitutes, such as Coke and Pepsi, tend to have relatively high elasticities because if one soft drink becomes expensive, consumers will switch to the other. Also, the elasticities of demand for goods that business firms buy, such as raw materials and machinery, tend to be higher on the whole than those for consumers' goods. This is because competition forces firms to buy their supplies wherever they can get them most cheaply. The exception occurs when a firm requires a particular input for which no reasonable substitutes exist or the available substitutes are substantially inferior. Table 1 gives actual statistical estimates of elasticities for some industries in the economy.

TABLE 1
Estimates of Price Elasticities

Product	Price Elasticity
Industrial chemicals	0.4
Shoe repairs and cleaning	0.4
Food, tobacco, and beverages	0.5
Newspapers and magazines	0.5
Data processing, precision and optical instruments	0.7
Medical care and hospitalization insurance	0.8
Metal products	1.1
Purchased meals (excluding alcoholic beverages)	1.6
Electricity (household utility)	1.9
Boats, pleasure aircraft	2.4
Public transportation	3.5
China, tableware	8.8

SOURCES: H. S. Houthakker and Lester D. Taylor, *Consumer Demand in the United States*, 2d ed. (Cambridge, Mass.: Harvard University Press, 1970), pp. 153–158; and Joachim Möller, "Income and Price Elasticities in Different Sectors of the Economy—An Analysis of Structural Change for Germany, the U.K., and U.S." (University of Regensburg, December 1998).

■ PRICE ELASTICITY OF DEMAND: ITS EFFECT ON TOTAL REVENUE AND TOTAL EXPENDITURE

Aside from its role as a measure of the responsiveness of demand to a change in price, elasticity serves a second, very important purpose. As a real illustration at the end of this chapter will show, a firm often wants to know whether an increase in price will increase or decrease its total revenue—the money it obtains from sales to its customers. The price elasticity of demand provides a simple guide to the answer:

If demand for the seller's product is elastic, a price *increase* will *actually decrease* total revenue. If demand is exactly unit-elastic, a rise in price will leave total revenue unaffected. If demand is inelastic, a rise in price will raise total revenue. The opposite changes will occur when price falls.

A corresponding story must be true about the expenditures made by the *buyers* of the product. After all, the expenditures of the buyers are exactly the same thing as the revenues of the seller.

These relationships between elasticity and total revenue hold because total revenue (or expenditure) equals price times quantity demanded, $P \times Q$, and because a drop in price has two opposing effects on that arithmetic product. It decreases P, and, if the demand curve is negatively sloped, it increases Q. The first effect *decreases* revenues by cutting the amount of money that consumers spend on each unit of the good. The second effect *increases* revenues by raising the number of units of the good that the firm sells.

The net effect on total revenue (or total expenditure) depends on the elasticity. If price goes down by 10 percent and quantity demanded increases by 10 percent (a case of *unit elasticity*), the two effects just cancel out: $P \times Q$ remains constant. In contrast, if price goes down by 10 percent and quantity demanded rises by 15 percent (a case of *elastic* demand), $P \times Q$ increases. Finally, if a 10 percent price fall leads to only a 5 percent rise in quantity demanded (*inelastic* demand), $P \times Q$ falls.

We can easily see the relationship between elasticity and total revenue in a graph. First, note that:

The total revenue (or expenditure) represented by any point on a demand curve (any price—quantity combination), such as point *S* in Figure 4, equals the area of the rectangle under that point (the area of rectangle O*RST* in the figure). This is true because the area of a rectangle equals its height times width, or O*R* × *RS* in Figure 4. Clearly, that is price times quantity, which is exactly total revenue.

FIGURE 4

An Elastic Demand Curve

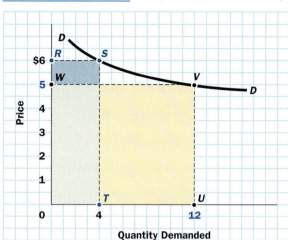

To illustrate the connection between elasticity and consumer expenditure, Figure 4 shows an elastic portion of a demand curve, *DD*. In this figure, when price falls, quantity demanded rises by a greater percentage, increasing total expenditure. At a price of $6 per unit, the quantity sold is four units, so total expenditure is 4 × $6 = $24, represented by the vertical rectangle whose upper-right corner is point *S*. When price falls to $5 per unit, 12 units are sold. Consequently, the new expenditure ($60 = $5 × 12), measured by the rectangle 0*WVU*, exceeds the old expenditure.

In contrast, Figure 3(d), the unit-elastic demand curve, shows constant expenditures even though price changes. Total spending is $140 whether the price is $20 and 7 units are sold (point *S*) or the price is $10 and 14 units are sold (point *T*).

This discussion also indicates why a unit-elastic demand curve must have the shape depicted in Figure 3(d), hugging the axes closer and closer but never touching or crossing them. When demand is unit-elastic, total expenditure must be the same at every point on the curve. That is, it must equal $140 at point *S* and point *T* and point *U* in Figure 3(d). Suppose that at point *U* (or some other point on the curve), the demand curve were to touch the horizontal axis, meaning that the price would equal zero. Then total expenditure would be zero, not $140. Therefore, if the demand curve remains unit-elastic along its entire length, it can never cross the horizontal axis (where *P* = 0). By the same reasoning, it cannot cross the vertical axis (where *Q* = 0). Because the slope of the demand curve is negative, any unit-elastic curve simply must get closer and closer to the axes as it moves away from its middle points, as illustrated in Figure 3(d). But it will never touch either axis.

We can now see why demand elasticity is so important for business decisions. A firm should not jump to the conclusion that a price increase will automatically add to its profits, or it may find that consumers take their revenge by cutting back on their purchases. For example, when Heinz's Pet Products Company raised the price of its 9-Lives cat food some years ago, its market share plummeted from 23 percent to 15 percent as customers flocked to other brands. In fact, if its demand curve is elastic, a firm that raises price will end up selling so many fewer units that its total revenue will actually fall, even though it makes more money than before on each unit it sells.

Price *cuts* can also be hazardous—if the elasticity of demand is low. For example, among adult smokers, cigarettes have an estimated price elasticity of between 0.25 and 0.50, meaning that we can expect a 10 percent drop in price to induce only a 2.5 percent to 5 percent rise in demand.[3] This relationship may explain why, when Philip Morris cut the price of Marlboros by about 18 percent, the company's profits dropped by 25 percent within months. Thus, the strategic value to a business firm of a price rise or a price cut depends very much on the elasticity of demand for its product. But elasticity tells us only how a price change affects a firm's revenues; we must also consider the effect of costs on the firm's output decisions, as we will do in Chapter 8.

? ISSUE REVISITED: *Will a Cigarette Tax Decrease Teenage Smoking Significantly?*

We're back to the issue with which we began this chapter: Will a tax on cigarettes, which increases their price, effectively reduce teenage smoking? We can express the answer to this question in terms of the price elasticity of demand for

---

[3] Source: F.J. Chaloupka, K.M. Cummings, C.P. Morley, and J.K. Horan, "Tax, Price and Cigarette Smoking," *Tobacco Control*, Vol. 11, 2002, pp. 62–72; and Craig A. Gallet and John A. List, "Cigarette Demand: A Meta-Analysis of Elasticities," *Health Economics*, Vol. 12, 2003, pp. 821–835.

cigarettes by teenagers. If that demand elasticity is high, the tax will be effective, because a small increase in cigarette taxes will lead to a sharp cut in purchases by teenagers. The opposite will clearly be true if this demand elasticity is small.

It turns out that young people *are* more sensitive to price increases than adult smokers. Teenagers' price elasticity of demand for cigarettes is estimated to be about 1.4.[4] This means that if, for example, a tax on cigarettes raises their price by 10 percent, the number of teenage smokers will fall by about 14 percent. Adults have been found to have a price elasticity of demand for cigarettes of between 0.25 and 0.50—their response to the 10 percent increase in the price of cigarettes will be a decrease of only 2.5 to 5 percent in the number of adult smokers. So we can expect that a substantial tax on cigarettes that resulted in a significant price increase would cause a higher percentage of teenagers than adults to stop smoking.

We said earlier in the chapter that if a cigarette tax program failed to curb teen smoking, it would benefit the government's tax collectors a great deal. On the other hand, if the program successfully curbed teenage smoking, then government finances would benefit only a little. The logic of this argument should now be clear. If teen cigarette demand were inelastic, the tax program would fail to make a dent in teen smoking. That would mean that many teenagers would continue to buy cigarettes and government tax revenue would grow as a result of the rise in tax rate. But when elasticity is high, a price rise *decreases* total revenue (in this case, the amount of tax revenues collected) because quantity demanded falls by a greater percentage than the price rises. That is, with an elastic demand, relatively few teen smokers will remain after the tax increase, so there will be few of them to pay the new taxes. The government will "lose out." Of course, in this case the tax seeks to change behavior, so the government would no doubt rejoice at its small revenues!

■ WHAT DETERMINES DEMAND ELASTICITY?

What kinds of goods have elastic demand curves, meaning that quantity demanded responds strongly to price? What kinds of goods have inelastic demand curves? Several influences affect consumers' sensitivity to price changes.

1. Nature of the Good   *Necessities*, such as basic foodstuffs, normally have relatively inelastic demand curves, meaning that the quantities consumers demand of these products respond very little to price changes. For example, people buy roughly the same quantity of potatoes even when the price of potatoes rises. One study estimated that the price elasticity of demand for potatoes is just 0.3, meaning that when their price rises 10 percent, the quantity of potatoes purchased falls only 3 percent. In contrast, many *luxury goods*, such as restaurant meals, have rather elastic demand curves. One estimate found that the price elasticity of demand for restaurant meals is 1.6, so that we can expect a 10 percent price rise to cut purchases by 16 percent.

2. Availability of Close Substitutes   If consumers can easily obtain an acceptable substitute for a product whose price increases, they will switch readily. Thus, when the market offers close substitutes for a given product, its demand will be more elastic. Substitutability is often a critical determinant of elasticity. The demand for gasoline is inelastic because we cannot easily run a car without it, but the demand for

---

[4] Source: See footnote 3.

any particular brand of gasoline is extremely elastic, because other brands will work just as well. This example suggests a general principle: The demand for narrowly defined commodities (such as romaine lettuce) is more elastic than the demand for more broadly defined commodities (such as vegetables).

3. Share of Consumer's Budget   The share of the consumer's budget represented by the purchase of a particular item also affects its elasticity. Very inexpensive items that absorb little of a consumer's budget tend to have inelastic demand curves. Who is going to buy fewer paper clips if their price rises 10 percent? Hardly anyone. But many families will be forced to postpone buying a new car, or will buy a used car instead, if auto prices go up by 10 percent.

4. Passage of Time   The time period is relevant because the demand for many products is more elastic in the long run than in the short run. For example, when the price of home heating oil rose in the 1970s, some homeowners switched from oil heat to gas heat. Very few of them switched immediately, however, because they needed to retrofit their furnaces to accommodate the other fuel. So, the short-term demand for oil was quite inelastic. As time passed and more homeowners had the opportunity to purchase and install new furnaces, the demand curve gradually became more elastic.

Selling Short

"Why does it have to be us who prove that price elasticity really works?"

ELASTICITY AS A GENERAL CONCEPT

So far we have looked only at how quantity demanded responds to price changes—that is, the *price* elasticity of demand. But elasticity has a more general use in measuring how any one economic variable responds to changes in another. From our earlier discussion, we know that a firm will be keenly interested in the price elasticity of its demand curve, but its interest in demand does not end there. As we have noted, quantity demanded depends on other things besides price. Business firms will be interested in consumer responsiveness to changes in these variables as well.

◼ 1. Income Elasticity

For example, quantity demanded depends on consumer incomes. A business firm's managers will, therefore, want to know how much a change in consumer income will affect the quantity of its product demanded. Fortunately, an elasticity measure can be helpful here, too. An increase in consumer incomes clearly raises the amounts of most goods that consumers will demand. To measure the response, economists use the **income elasticity of demand,** which is the ratio of the percentage change in quantity demanded to the percentage change in income. For example, foreign travel is quite income elastic, with middle-income and higher-income people traveling abroad much more extensively than poor people do. In contrast, blue jeans, worn by rich and poor alike, show little demand increase as income increases.

Income elasticity of demand is the ratio of the percentage change in quantity demanded to the percentage change in income.

■ 2. Price Elasticity of Supply

Economists also use elasticity to measure other responses. For example, to measure the response of quantity *supplied* to a change in price, we use the *price elasticity of supply*—defined as the ratio of the percentage change in quantity supplied to the percentage change in price, for example, by what percent the supply of wheat increases when the price (at the time of planting) goes up by, say, 7 percent. The logic and analysis of all such elasticity concepts are, of course, perfectly analogous to those for price elasticity of demand.

■ 3. Cross Elasticity of Demand

Consumers' demands for many products are substantially affected by the quantities and prices of *other* available products. This brings us to the important concept called *cross elasticity of demand*, which measures how much the demand for product X is affected by a change in the price of another good, Y.

This elasticity number is significantly affected by the fact that some products make other products *more* desirable, but some products *decrease* consumer demand for other products. There are some products that just naturally go together. For example, cream and sugar increase the desirability of coffee, and vice versa. The same is true of mustard or ketchup and hamburgers. In some extreme cases, neither product ordinarily has any use without the other—automobiles and tires, shoes and shoelaces, and so on. Such goods, each of which makes the other more valuable, are called **complements.**

The demand curves of complements are interrelated. That is, a rise in the price of coffee is likely to reduce the quantity of sugar demanded. Why? When coffee prices rise, people drink less coffee and therefore demand less sugar to sweeten it. The opposite will be true of a fall in coffee prices. A similar relationship holds for other complementary goods.

At the other extreme, some goods make other goods *less* valuable. These products are called **substitutes.** Ownership of a motorcycle, for example, may decrease one's desire for a bicycle. If your pantry is stocked with cans of tuna fish, you are less likely to rush out and buy cans of salmon. As you may expect, demand curves for substitutes are also related, but in the opposite direction. When the price of motorcycles falls, people may desire fewer bicycles, so the quantity of bicycles demanded falls. When the price of salmon goes up, people may eat more tuna.

Economists use **cross elasticity of demand** to determine whether two products are substitutes or complements. This measure is defined much like the ordinary price elasticity of demand, except that instead of measuring the responsiveness of the quantity demanded of, say, coffee, to a change in its own price, cross elasticity of demand measures how quantity demanded of one good (coffee) responds to a change in the price of another, say, sugar. For example, if a 20 percent rise in the price of sugar reduces the quantity of coffee demanded by 5 percent (a change of *minus* 5 percent in quantity demanded), then the cross elasticity of demand will be:

$$\frac{\text{Percentage change in quantity of coffee demanded}}{\text{Percentage change in sugar price}} = \frac{-5\%}{20\%} = -0.25$$

Obviously, cross elasticity is important for business firms, especially when rival firms' prices are concerned. American Airlines, for example, knows all too well that it will lose customers if it does not match price cuts by Continental or United. Coke and Pepsi provide another clear case in which cross elasticity of demand is crucial. But firms other than direct competitors may well take a substantial interest in cross elasticity. For example, the prices of DVD players and DVD rentals may profoundly affect the quantity of theater tickets that consumers demand.

Two goods are called **complements** if an increase in the quantity consumed of one increases the quantity demanded of the other, all other things remaining constant.

Two goods are called **substitutes** if an increase in the quantity consumed of one cuts the quantity demanded of the other, all other things remaining constant.

The **cross elasticity of demand** for product X to a change in the price of another product, Y, is the ratio of the percentage change in quantity demanded of X to the percentage change in the price of Y that brings about the change in quantity demanded.

The cross elasticity of demand measure underlies the following rule about complements and substitutes:

If two goods are substitutes, a rise in the price of one of them tends to increase the quantity demanded of the other; so their cross elasticities of demand will normally be positive. If two goods are complements, a rise in the price of one of them tends to decrease the quantity demanded of the other item so their cross elasticities will normally be negative. Notice that, because cross elasticities can be positive or negative, we do *not* customarily drop minus signs as we do in a calculation of the ordinary price elasticity of demand.

This result is really a matter of common sense. If the price of a good rises and buyers can find a substitute, they will tend to switch to the substitute. If the price of Japanese-made cameras goes up and the price of American-made cameras does not, at least some people will switch to the American product. Thus, a *rise* in the price of Japanese cameras causes a *rise* in the quantity of American cameras demanded. Both percentage changes are positive numbers and so their ratio—the cross elasticity of demand—is also positive.

However, if two goods are complements, a rise in the price of one will discourage both its own use and use of the complementary good. Automobiles and car radios are obviously complements. A large increase in automobile prices will depress car sales, and this in turn will reduce sales of car radios. Thus, a positive percentage change in the price of cars leads to a negative percentage change in the quantity of car radios demanded. The ratio of these numbers—the cross elasticity of demand for cars and radios—is therefore negative.

In practice, courts of law often evaluate cross elasticity of demand to determine whether particular business firms face strong competition that can prevent them from overcharging consumers—hence, the quotation from the U.S. Supreme Court at the beginning of this chapter. The quotation is one of the earliest examples of the courts using the concept of cross elasticities. It tells us that if two substitute (that is, rival) products exhibit a high cross elasticity of demand (for example, between McDonald's and Burger King), then neither firm can raise its price much without losing customers to the other. In such a case, no one can legitimately claim that either firm has a monopoly. If a rise in Firm X's price causes its consumers to switch in droves to a Firm Y's product, then the cross elasticity of demand for Firm Y's product with respect to the price of Firm X's product will be high. That, in turn, means that competition is really powerful enough to prevent Firm X from raising its price arbitrarily. This relationship explains why cross elasticity is used so often in litigation before courts or government regulatory agencies when the degree of competition is an important issue, because the higher the cross-elasticity of demand between two products, the stronger must be the competition between them. So cross elasticity is an effective measure of the strength of such competition.

The cross elasticity issue keeps coming up whenever firms are accused of acting like monopolists. For example, in 1997 a dispute arose between Litton and Honeywell, the two main manufacturers of the mechanisms that guide the flight of aircraft. In 1998, the issue reappeared in a lawsuit in which Rolite, an ash recycling firm, sued Waste Management, a waste removal company, charging monopolistic behavior by the latter. (See "How Large Is A Firm's Market Share? Cross Elasticity as a Test," on page 119, for more on cross elasticity.)

CHANGES IN DEMAND: *MOVEMENTS ALONG* THE DEMAND CURVE VERSUS *SHIFTS IN* THE DEMAND CURVE

Demand is a complex phenomenon. We have studied in detail the dependence of quantity demanded on price, and we have noted that quantity demanded depends also on *other* variables such as consumers' incomes and the prices of complementary and substitute products. Because of changes in these *other* variables (which we formerly

How Large Is a Firm's Market Share? Cross Elasticity as a Test

A firm's "market share" is often a crucial element in antitrust lawsuits (see Chapter 13) for a simple reason. If the firm supplies no more than, say, 20 percent of the industry's output, courts and regulators presume that the firm is not a monopoly, as its customers can switch their business to competitors if the firm tries to charge too high a price. On the other hand, if the defendant firm in the lawsuit accounts for 90 percent of the industry's output, courts may have good reason to worry about monopoly power (which we cover in Chapter 11).

Such court cases often provide lively debates in which the defendant firms try to prove that they have very small market shares, and the plaintiffs seek to establish the opposite. Each side knows how much the defendant firm actually produces and sells, so what do they find to argue about? The dispute is about *the size of the total relevant market,* which clearly affects the magnitude of the firm's market *share.* Ambiguity arises here because different firms do not produce identical products. For instance, are Rice Krispies in the same market as Cheerios? And how about Quaker Oatmeal, which users eat hot? What about frozen waffles? Are all of these products part of the same market? If they are, then the overall market is large, and each seller therefore has a smaller share. If these products are in different markets, the opposite will be true.

Many observers argue, as the Supreme Court did in the famous DuPont cellophane case (and, more recently, as was argued when Rolite sued Waste Management in 1998), that one of the proper criteria for determining the borders of the relevant market is *cross elasticity of demand.* If two products have a high and positive cross elasticity, they must be close enough substitutes to compete closely; that is, they must be in the same market. But how large must the cross elasticity be before the court decides that two products are in the same market? Although the law has not established a clear elasticity benchmark to determine whether a particular firm is in a relevant market, several courts have determined that a very high cross elasticity number clearly indicates effective competition between two products, meaning that the two items must be in the same market.

SOURCE: © Laura Dwight/Corbis

held constant when we studied only the effect of changes in price), demand curves often do not keep the same shape and position as time passes. Instead, they shift about. Chapter 4 showed that shifts in demand curves affect both quantity and price predictably.

Public policy and business discussions often make vague references to "changes in demand." By itself, this expression does not mean anything. Recall from our discussion in Chapter 4 that we must distinguish between a response to a price change—*which shows up as a movement along the demand curve*—and a change in the relationship between price and quantity demanded—*which produces a shift in the demand curve* (in effect, it moves the curve itself).

When price falls, quantity demanded generally rises. This change represents a movement *along* the demand curve. In contrast, an effective advertising campaign may result in people buying more goods at *any given price.* This case involves a rightward *shift* of the demand curve. Such a shift can be caused by a change in the value of any of the variables other than price that affect quantity demanded. Although the distinction between a shift in a demand curve and a movement along it may at first seem trivial, the difference is very significant in practice. Let us pause for a moment to consider how changes in some of these other variables shift the demand curve.

■ Demand Shifters

As an example, consider the effect of a change in consumer income on the demand curve for sweaters. In Figure 5(a), the black curve D_0D_0 is the original demand curve

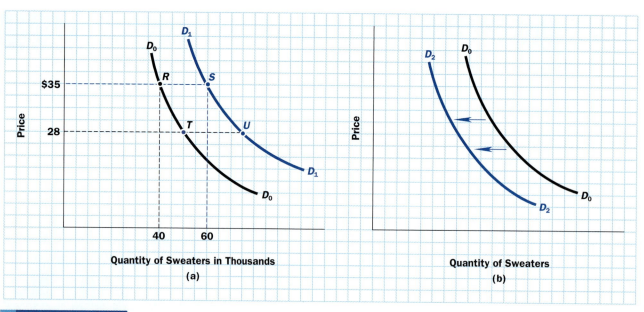

FIGURE 5

Shifts in a Demand Curve

for sweaters. Now suppose that parents start sending more money to their needy sons and daughters in college. If the price of sweaters remains the same, those students are likely to use some of their increased income to buy more sweaters. For example, if the price remains at $35, quantity demanded might rise from 40,000 sweaters (point *R*) to 60,000 (point *S*). Similarly, if price had been $28 and remained at that level, the rise in income might produce a corresponding change from *T* to *U*. In other words, we would expect the rise in income to *shift* the entire demand curve to the right from $D_0 D_0$ to $D_1 D_1$. In exactly the same way, a fall in consumer income can be expected to lead to a leftward shift in the demand curve for sweaters, as shown in Figure 5(b).

We can analyze other variables that affect quantity demanded in the same way. For example, increased television advertising for sweaters may lead to a rightward (outward) shift in the demand curve for sweaters, as in Figure 5(a). The same thing might occur if the price of a substitute product, such as jackets, increased, because it would put sweaters at a competitive advantage. If two goods are substitutes, a rise in the price of one of them will tend to shift the demand curve for the other one outward (to the right). Similarly, if a complementary product (perhaps matching pants to go with the sweaters) became more expensive, we would expect the demand curve for sweaters to shift to the left, as in Figure 5(b). In summary:

> We expect a demand curve to shift to the right (outward) if consumer incomes rise, if tastes change in favor of the product, if substitute goods become more expensive, or if complementary goods become cheaper. We expect a demand curve to shift to the left (inward) if any of these influences changes in the opposite direction.

THE TIME PERIOD OF THE DEMAND CURVE AND ECONOMIC DECISION MAKING

One more important feature of a demand curve does not show up on a graph. A demand curve indicates, at each possible price, the quantity of the good that is demanded *during a particular time period.* That is, all of the alternative prices considered in a demand curve must refer to the *same* time period. Economists do not compare a price of $10 for commodity X in January with a price of $8 in September.

This feature imparts a peculiar character to the demand curve and complicates statistical calculations. For obvious reasons, actual observed data show different prices and quantities only for different dates. Statistical data may show, for example, the one price that prevailed in January and another that occurred at a later date, when that price had changed. Why, then, do economists adopt the apparently peculiar approach of dealing in a demand curve only with the prices that may conceivably occur (as alternative possibilities) in one and the same time period? The answer is that the demand curve's strictly defined time dimension arises inescapably from the logic of decision making and attempts to reach an **optimal decision**—the decision that moves the decision maker as close to her goal as is possible under the circumstances she faces.

When a business seeks to price one of its products for, say, the following six months, it must consider the range of *alternative* prices available for that six-month period and the consequences of each of these possible prices. For example, if management is reasonably certain that the best price for the six-month period lies somewhere between $3.50 and $5.00, it should perhaps consider each of four possibilities—$3.50, $4.00, $4.50, and $5.00—and estimate how much it can expect to sell at each of these potential prices during that given six-month period. The result of these estimates may appear in a format similar to that of the following table:

> An **optimal decision** is one that best serves the objectives of the decision maker, whatever those objectives may be. It is selected by explicit or implicit comparison with the possible alternative choices. The term *optimal* connotes neither approval nor disapproval of the objective itself.

Potential Six-Month Price	Expected Quantity Demanded
$3.50	75,000
4.00	73,000
4.50	70,000
5.00	60,000

This table supplies managers with the information that they need to make optimal pricing decisions. Because the price that will be selected will be the one at which goods are sold *during the period in question*, all the prices considered in that decision must be alternative possible prices for that same period. The table therefore also contains precisely the information an economist uses to draw a demand curve.

> The demand curve describes a set of hypothetical quantity responses to a set of potential prices, but the firm can actually charge only one of these prices. All of the points on the demand curve refer to alternative possibilities for the *same time period*—the period for which the decision is to be made.

Thus, a demand curve of the sort just described is not just an abstract notion that is useful primarily in academic discussions. Rather, it offers precisely the information that businesses or government agencies need to make rational decisions. However, the fact that all points on the demand curve are hypothetical possibilities for the same period of time causes problems for statistical estimation of demand curves. These problems are discussed in the appendix to this chapter.

■ REAL-WORLD APPLICATION: POLAROID VERSUS KODAK[5]

Let's look at an example from the real world to show how the elasticity concept helps to resolve a concrete problem rather different from those we have been discussing. In 1989, a lengthy trial in a U.S. district court resulted in a judgment against the photographic products manufacturing company Eastman-Kodak for patent infringement of technology that rival firm Polaroid had designed. The court then set out to determine the amount of money Kodak owed Polaroid for its patent infringement during the ten-year period 1976 to 1986, when Kodak had sold very similar instant cameras and film. The key issue was how much profit Polaroid had lost as a result of Kodak's entry into the field of instant photography, because that would determine how much Kodak would be required to pay Polaroid. Both price elasticity of demand and cross elasticity of demand played crucial roles in the court's decisions.

The court needed accurate estimates of the price elasticity of demand to determine whether the explosive growth in instant camera sales between 1976 and 1979 was mainly attributable to the fall in price that resulted from Kodak's competition, or was attributable to Kodak's good reputation and the resulting rise in consumer confidence

---

[5] Here it should be pointed out that William Baumol was a witness in this court case, testifying on behalf of Kodak.

in the quality of instant cameras. If the latter were true, then Polaroid might actually have *benefited* from Kodak's entry into the instant camera market rather than *losing* profits, because Kodak's presence in the market would have increased the total number of potential customers aware of and eager to try instant cameras.

After 1980, instant camera and film sales began to drop sharply. On this issue, the *cross elasticity of demand* between instant and conventional (35-millimeter) cameras and film was crucial to the explanation. Why? Because the decline in the instant camera market occurred just as the prices of 35-millimeter cameras, film, developing, and printing all began to fall significantly. So, if the decline in Polaroid's overall sales was attributable to the decreasing cost of 35-millimeter photography, then Kodak's instant photography activity was *not* to blame. And, in that case, the amount that Kodak would be required to pay to Polaroid would decrease significantly. But if the cross elasticity of demand between 35-millimeter photography prices and the demand for instant cameras and film was low, then the cause of the decline in Polaroid's sales might well have been Kodak's patent-infringing activity—thus *adding* to the damage compensation payments to which Polaroid was entitled.

On the basis of its elasticity calculations, Polaroid at one point claimed that Kodak was obligated to pay it $9 *billion* or more. Kodak, however, claimed that it owed Polaroid something in the neighborhood of $450 million. A lot of money was at stake. The judge's verdict came out with a number very close to Kodak's figure.

■ IN CONCLUSION

In this chapter, we have continued our study of the demand side of the market. Rather than focusing on what underlies demand formation, as we did in Chapter 5, we applied demand analysis to business decisions. Most notably, we described and analyzed the economist's measure of the responsiveness of consumer demand to changes in price, and we showed how this assessment determines the effect of a firm's price change on the revenues of that enterprise. We illustrated how these concepts throw light not only on business sales and revenues, but also on a number of rather different issues, such as smoking and health, the effectiveness of competition among business firms as studied by courts of law, and the determination of penalties for patent infringement. In the next chapter, we turn to the supply side of the market and move a step closer to completing the framework we need to understand how markets work.

SUMMARY

1. To measure the responsiveness of the quantity demanded to price, economists calculate the **elasticity of demand,** which is defined as the percentage change in quantity demanded divided by the percentage change in price, after elimination of the minus sign.

2. If demand is **elastic** (elasticity is greater than 1), then a rise in price will reduce total expenditures. If demand is **unit-elastic** (elasticity is equal to 1), then a rise in price will not change total expenditures. If demand is **inelastic** (elasticity is less than 1), then a rise in price will increase total expenditure.

3. Demand is not a fixed number. Rather, it is a relationship showing how quantity demanded is affected by price and other pertinent influences. If one or more of these other variables change, the demand curve will shift.

4. Goods that make each other more desirable (hot dogs and mustard, wristwatches and watch straps) are called **complements.** When two goods are such that when consumers get more of one of them, they want less of the other (steaks and hamburgers, Coke and Pepsi), economists call those goods **substitutes.**

5. **Cross elasticity of demand** is defined as the percentage change in the quantity demanded of one good divided by the percentage change in the price of another good. Two substitute products normally have a positive cross elasticity of demand. Two complementary products normally have a negative cross elasticity of demand.

6. A rise in the price of one of two substitute products can be expected to *shift the demand curve* of the other product to the right. A rise in the price of one of two complementary

goods tends to shift the other good's demand curve to the left.

7. All points on a demand curve refer to the *same time period*—the time during which the price that is under consideration will be in effect.

KEY TERMS

(Price) elasticity of demand   109

Elastic, inelastic, and unit–elastic demand curves   112

Income elasticity of demand   116

Complements   117

Substitutes   117

Cross elasticity of demand   117

Optimal decision   121

TEST YOURSELF

1. What variables other than price and advertising are likely to affect the quantity demanded of a product?

2. Describe the probable shifts in the demand curves for:

   a. Airplane trips when airlines' on-time performance improves

   b. Automobiles when airplane fares increase

   c. Automobiles when gasoline prices increase

   d. Electricity when the average temperature in the United States rises during a particular year (*Note:* The demand curve for electricity in Maine and the demand curve for electricity in Florida should respond in different ways. Why?)

3. Taxes on particular goods discourage their consumption. Economists say that such taxes "distort consumer demands." In terms of the elasticity of demand for the commodities in question, what sort of goods would you choose to tax to achieve the following objectives?

   a. Collect a large amount of tax revenue

   b. Distort demand as little as possible

   c. Discourage consumption of harmful commodities

   d. Discourage production of polluting commodities

4. Give examples of commodities whose demand you would expect to be elastic and commodities whose demand you would expect to be inelastic.

5. A rise in the price of a certain commodity from $15 to $20 reduces quantity demanded from 20,000 to 5,000 units. Calculate the price elasticity of demand.

6. If the price elasticity of demand for gasoline is 0.3, and the current price is $1.20 per gallon, what rise in the price of gasoline will reduce its consumption by 10 percent?

7. Which of the following product pairs would you expect to be substitutes, and which would you expect to be complements?

   a. Shoes and sneakers

   b. Gasoline and sport utility vehicles

   c. Bread and butter

   d. Instant camera film and regular camera film

8. For each of the product pairs given in Test Yourself Question 7, what would you guess about the products' cross elasticity of demand?

   a. Do you expect it to be positive or negative?

   b. Do you expect it to be a large or small number? Why?

DISCUSSION QUESTIONS

1. Explain why elasticity of demand is measured in *percentages*.

2. Explain why the elasticity of demand formula normally eliminates minus signs.

3. Explain why the elasticity of a straight-line demand curve varies from one part of the curve to another.

4. A rise in the price of a product whose demand is elastic will reduce the total revenue of the firm. Explain.

5. Name some events that will cause a demand curve to shift.

6. Explain why the following statement is true: "A firm with a demand curve that is inelastic at its current output level can always increase its profits by raising its price and selling less." (*Hint:* Refer back to the discussion of elasticity and total expenditure/total revenue on pages 113–115.)

APPENDIX *How Can We Find a Legitimate Demand Curve from Historical Statistics?*

The peculiar time dimension of the demand curve, in conjunction with the fact that many variables other than price influence quantity demanded, makes it surprisingly difficult to derive a product's demand curve from historical statistical data. Specialists can and often do derive such estimates, but the task is full of booby traps and usually requires advanced statistical methods and interpretation. This Appendix seeks to warn you about the booby traps. It implies, for example, that if you become the marketing manager of a business firm after you graduate from college, and you need demand analysis, you will need experts to do the job. This Appendix will also show you some mistakes to look for as you interpret the results, if you have reason to doubt the qualifications of the statisticians you hire to calculate or forecast your demand curve. It also gives an intuitive explanation of the legitimate ways in which demand curves may be determined from the statistics.

The most obvious way to go about estimating a demand curve statistically is to collect a set of figures on prices and quantities sold in different periods, like those given in Table 2. These points can then be plotted on a diagram with price and quantity on the axes, as shown in

Figure 6. We can then draw a line (the dashed line *TT*) that connects these points (labeled Jan., Feb., and so on), and connects them reasonably well, to represent the prices and quantities sold in the months indicated. This line may appear to approximate the demand curve, but unfortunately line *TT*, which summarizes the data for different points of time, may bear no relationship to the true demand curve. Let us see why, and what can be done about it.

You may notice at once that the prices and quantities represented by the historical points in Figure 6 refer to different periods of time, and that each point on the graph represents an *actual* (not hypothetical) price and quantity sold at a particular period of time (for example, one point gives the data for January, another for February, and so on). The distinction is significant. Over the entire period covered by the historical data (January through May), the true demand curve, which is what an economist really needs to analyze decision problems, may well have shifted because of changes in some of the other variables affecting quantity demanded.

The actual events may appear as shown in Figure 7. In January, the demand curve was given by *JJ*, but by February the curve had shifted to *FF*, by March to *MM*, and so on. This figure shows a separate and distinct demand curve for each of the relevant months, and none of them needs to resemble the plot of historical data, *TT*.

In fact, the slope of the historical plot curve, *TT*, can be very different from the

TABLE 2

Historical Data on Price and Quantity

	January	February	March	April	May
Quantity Sold	95,000	91,500	95,000	90,000	91,000
Price	$7.20	$8.00	$7.70	$8.00	$8.20

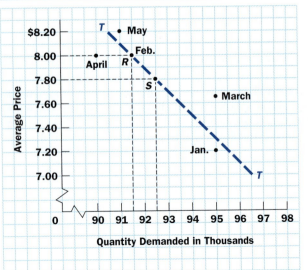

FIGURE 6 Plot of Historical Data on Price and Quantity

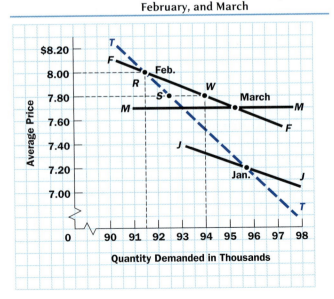

FIGURE 7 Plot of Historical Data and True Demand Curves for January, February, and March

slopes of the true underlying demand curves, as is the case in Figure 7. As a consequence, the decision maker can be seriously misled if she selects her price on the basis of the historical data. She may, for example, think that demand is quite insensitive to changes in price (as line *TT* seems to indicate), so she may conclude that a price reduction is not advisable. In fact, the true demand curves show that a price reduction would increase quantity demanded substantially, because they are much more elastic than the shape of the estimated curve in Figure 6 would suggest.

For example, if the decision maker were to charge a price of $7.80 rather than $8.00 in February, the historical plot would lead her to expect a rise in quantity demanded of only 1,000 units. (Compare point *R*, with sales of 91,500 units, and point *S*, with sales of 92,500 units, in Figure 6.) The true demand curve for February (line *FF* in Figure 7), however, indicates an increase in sales of 2,500 units (from point *R*, with sales of 91,500 units, to point *W*, with sales of 94,000 units). A manager who based her decision on the historical plot, rather than on the true demand curve, might be led into serious error. Nevertheless, it is astonishing how often people make this mistake in practice, even when using apparently sophisticated techniques.

AN ILLUSTRATION: DID THE ADVERTISING PROGRAM WORK?

Some years ago, one of the largest producers of packaged foods in the United States conducted a statistical study to judge the effectiveness of its advertising expenditures, which amounted to nearly $100 million per year. A company statistician collected year-by-year figures on company sales and advertising outlays and discovered, to his delight, that they showed a remarkably close relationship to one another: Quantity demanded rose as advertising rose. The trouble was that the relationship seemed just too perfect. In economics, data about demand and any one of the elements that influence it almost never show such a neat pattern. Human tastes and other pertinent influences are just too variable to permit such regularity.

Suspicious company executives asked one of the authors of this book to examine the analysis. A little thought showed that the suspiciously close statistical relationship between sales and advertising expenditures resulted from a disregard for the principles just presented. The investigator had, in fact, constructed a graph of *historical* data on sales and advertising expenditure, analogous to *TT* in Figures 6 and 7 and therefore not necessarily similar to the truly relevant relationship.

It transpired, after study of the situation, that the stability of the relationship actually arose from the fact that, in the past, the company had based its advertising spending on its sales, automatically allocating a fixed percentage of its sales revenues to advertising. The *historical* relationship between advertising and demand therefore described only the company's budgeting practices, not the effectiveness of its advertising program. If the firm's management had used this curve in planning future advertising campaigns, it might have made some regrettable decisions. *The moral of the story:* Avoid the use of purely historical curves like *TT* in making economic decisions.

HOW CAN WE FIND A LEGITIMATE DEMAND CURVE FROM THE STATISTICS?

The trouble with the discussion so far is that it tells you only what you *cannot* legitimately do. But business executives and economists often need information about demand curves—for example, to analyze a pricing decision for next April. How can the true demand curves be found? In practice, statisticians use complex methods that go well beyond what we can cover in an introductory course. Nevertheless, we can (and will) give you a feeling for the advanced methods used by statisticians via a simple illustration in which a straightforward approach helps to locate the demand curve statistically.

The problem described in this Appendix occurs because demand curves and supply curves (like other curves in economics) shift from time to time. They do not shift for no reason, however. As we saw in the chapter, they shift because quantity demanded or supplied is influenced by variables other than price, such as advertising, consumer incomes, and so forth. Recognizing this relationship can help us track down the demand curve—if we can determine the "other things" that affect the demand for, say, widgets, and observe when those other things changed and when they did not, we can infer when the demand curve may have been moving and when it probably wasn't.

Consider the demand for umbrellas. Umbrellas are rarely advertised and are relatively inexpensive, so neither advertising nor consumer incomes should have much effect on their sales. In fact, it is reasonable to assume that the quantity of umbrellas demanded in a year depends largely on two influences: their price and the amount of rainfall. As we know, a change in price will lead to a movement *along the demand curve* without shifting it. Heavy rains will *shift the demand curve* outward, because people will need to buy more umbrellas, whereas the curve will shift inward in a drought year. Ideally, we would like to find some dates *when the demand curve stayed in the same position but the supply curve shifted*, so that we can obtain a number of different equilibrium points, all of which lie on or near the same demand curve.

Suppose that rainfall in St. Louis was as given in Table 3 for the period 1993–2001 and that prices and quantities

TABLE 3								
Hypothetical Annual Rainfall in St. Louis, 1993–2001								
Year	1993	1994	1995	1996	1997	1998	1999	2000	2001
Inches of rain	26	18	28	29	35	20	32	27	34

FIGURE 8 — Legitimate Demand Curve Estimation from Statistical Data

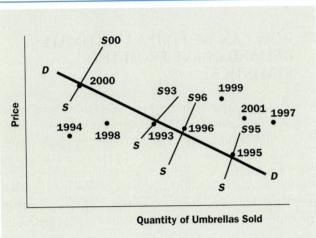

of umbrellas sold in those years were as indicated by the dots in Figure 8. Notice, first, that in years in which rainfall was highest, such as 1997 and 2001, the dots in the graph lie farthest to the right, whereas the dots for low-rain years lie toward the left, meaning that in rainier years more umbrellas were sold, as our hypothesis about the effect of rain on sales suggests. More important for our purposes, for the four years 1993, 1995, 1996, and 2000, rainfall was about the same—nearly 27 inches. Thus, the demand curve did *not* shift from one of these years to the next. It is reasonable to conclude that the dots for these four years fell close to the same true demand curve.

But the dots for those four years are quite far apart from one another. This separation means that in those years, with the demand curve in the same position, the supply curve must have been shifting. So, if we wish, we can check this supposition statistically, by observing that the supply curve can be expected to shift when there is a change in the cost of the raw materials that go into the production of umbrellas—cloth, steel for the ribs, and plastic for the handles. Changes in this cost variable can be expected to shift the supply curve but not the demand curve, because consumers do not even know these cost numbers. So, just as the rainfall data indicated in what years the demand curve probably moved and when it did not, the input price data can give us such information about the supply curve.

To see this, imagine that we have a year-by-year table for those input costs similar to the table for rainfall (the cost table is not shown here); and suppose it tells us that in the four years of interest (1993, 1995, 1996, and 2000), those costs were very different from one another. We can infer that the supply curves in those years were quite different even though, as we have just seen, the demand curve was unchanging in the same years. Accordingly, the graph shows line *DD* drawn close to these four dots, with their four supply curves—*SS93, SS95, SS96,* and *SS00*—also going through the corresponding points, which are the equilibrium points for those four years. We can therefore interpret *DD* as a valid statistical estimate of the true demand curve for those years. We derived it by recognizing as irrelevant the dots for the years with much higher or much lower rainfall amounts, in which the demand curve can be expected to have shifted, and by drawing the statistical demand curve through the relevant dots—those that, according to the data on the variables that shift the curves, were probably generated by different supply curves but a common demand curve.

The actual methods used to derive statistical demand curves are far more complex. The underlying logic, however, is analogous to that of the process used in this example.

7

PRODUCTION, INPUTS, AND COST: BUILDING BLOCKS FOR SUPPLY ANALYSIS

Of course, that's only an estimate. The actual cost will be higher.

AUTO MECHANIC TO CUSTOMER

Suppose you take a summer job working for Al's Building Contractors, a producer of standardized, inexpensive garages. On your first day of work, you find that Al has bought or signed contracts to buy enough lumber, electric wiring, tools, and other materials to meet his estimated needs for the next two years. The only input choice that has not been made is the number of carpenters that he will hire. So Al is left with only one decision about input purchases: How many carpenters should he sign up for his company? In this chapter, we explore this kind of decision and answer the following question: What input choice constitutes the most profitable way for a business firm to produce its output?

When firms make their supply (output) decisions, they examine the likely demand for the products they create. We have already studied demand in the last two chapters. But to understand the firm's decisions about the supply side of its markets, we must also study its production costs. A firm's costs depend on the quantities of labor, raw materials, machinery, and other inputs that it buys, and on the price it pays for each input. This chapter examines how businesses can select optimal input combinations—that is, the combinations that enable firms to produce whatever output they decide on at the minimum cost for that output. We will discuss the firm's profit-seeking decisions about output and price in Chapter 8.

To make the analysis of optimal input quantities easier to follow, we approach this task in two stages, based on a very important economic distinction: the short run and the long run. We begin the chapter with the simpler, short-run case, in which the firm can vary the quantity of only one input, while all other input quantities are already determined. This assumption vastly simplifies the analysis and enables us to answer two key questions:

- How does the quantity of input affect the quantity of output?
- How can the firm select the optimal quantity of an input?

After that, we deal with the more realistic case where the firm simultaneously selects the quantities of several inputs. We will use the results of that analysis to deduce the firm's cost curves.[1]

CONTENTS

---

[1] Some instructors may prefer to postpone discussion of this topic until later in the course.

PUZZLE: *How Can We Tell If Large Firms Are More Efficient?*

Modern industrial societies enjoy cost advantages as a result of automation, assembly lines, and sophisticated machinery, all of which often reduce production costs dramatically. But in industries in which equipment with such enormous capacity requires a very large investment, small companies will be unable to reap many of these benefits of modern technology. Only large firms will be able to take advantage of the associated cost savings. When firms can take advantage of such *economies of scale*, as economists call them, production costs per unit will decline as output expands.

But this relationship between large size and low costs does not always fit every industry. Sometimes the courts must decide whether a giant firm should be broken up into smaller units. The most celebrated case of this kind involved American Telephone and Telegraph Company (AT&T), which had a monopoly over most of the phone service in the United States for nearly 50 years.[2] Government agencies and analysts who urged a breakup of AT&T argued that such a giant firm has great economic power and deprives consumers of the benefits of competition. Opponents of the breakup, including AT&T itself, pointed out that if AT&T's large size brought significant economies of scale, then smaller firms would be much less efficient producers than the larger one and costs to consumers would have to be correspondingly higher. Who was right? To settle the issue, the courts needed to know whether AT&T had significant economies of scale.

Sometimes data like those shown in Figure 1 are offered to the courts when they consider such cases. The data in the figure, which were provided by AT&T, indicate that as the volume of telephone messages rose after 1942, the capital cost of long-distance communication by telephone dropped enormously and eventually fell below 8 percent of its 1942 level. But economists maintain that this graph does *not* constitute legitimate evidence, one way or another, about the presence of economies of scale. Why do they say this? At the end of this chapter, we will study precisely what is wrong with the evidence presented in Figure 1 and consider what sort of evidence really would legitimately have determined whether AT&T had economies of scale.

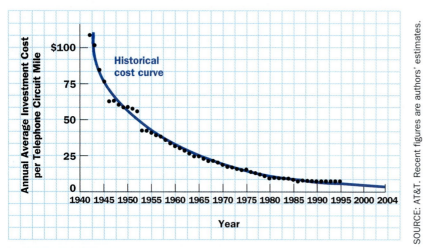

SOURCE: AT&T. Recent figures are authors' estimates.

FIGURE 1

Historical Costs for Long-Distance Telephone Transmissions

Note: Figures are in dollars per year.

SHORT-RUN VERSUS LONG-RUN COSTS: WHAT MAKES AN INPUT VARIABLE?

As firms make input and output decisions, their actions are limited by previous commitments to equipment, plant, and other production matters. At any point in time, many input choices are *precommitted* by past decisions. If, for example, a firm purchased machinery a year ago, it has committed itself to that production decision for the remainder of the machine's economic life, unless the company is willing to take

---

[2] AT&T is a descendant of the original Bell Telephone Company, affectionately known as "Ma Bell." The company relinquished the use of the name "Bell" when it was forced by the courts to divest itself of its twenty-two regional companies in 1982. These companies were reorganized into the "Baby Bells"—seven regional phone companies called Nynex, Bell Atlantic, Ameritech, BellSouth, Southwestern Bell, USWest, and Pacific Telesis Group. In the 1990s several of these "Baby Bells" merged once again (Bell Atlantic, for example, bought Nynex). Since then, there have been more consolidations: in 2000, Bell Atlantic bought GTE and MCI, and changed its name to Verizon. And in 2005, Southwestern Bell (SBC Communications) merged with the parent company, AT&T (along with Cingular), and is now known as AT&T Inc.

the loss involved in replacing that equipment sooner. An economist would say that these temporarily unalterable capital commitments are not variable for the time period in question. Firms that employ unionized labor forces may also incur costs that are temporarily not variable if labor contracts commit the firms to employing a certain number of employees or to using employees for a required number of weeks per year. Costs are not variable for some period if they are set by a longer-term financial commitment, such as a contract to buy a raw material, lease a warehouse, or invest in equipment that cannot be resold or transferred without substantial loss of the investment. Even if the firm has not paid for these commitments ahead of time, legally it must still pay for the contracted goods or services.

■ The Economic Short Run Versus the Economic Long Run

A two-year-old machine with a nine-year economic life can be an inescapable commitment and therefore represent a cost that is not variable for the next seven years. But that investment is not an unchangeable commitment in plans that extend *beyond* those seven years, because by then it may benefit the firm to replace the machine in any case. Economists summarize this notion by speaking of two different "runs" (or periods of time) for decision making: the **short run** and the **long run.**

These terms recur time and again throughout this book. In the short run, firms have relatively little opportunity to change production processes so as to adopt the most efficient way of producing their current outputs, because plant sizes and other input quantities have largely been predetermined by past decisions. Managers may be able to hire more workers to work overtime and buy more supplies, but they can't easily increase factory size, even if sales turn out to be much greater than expected. Over the long run, however, all such inputs, including plant size, become adjustable.

As an example, let's examine Al's Building Contractors and consider the number of carpenters that it hires, the amount of lumber that it purchases, and the amounts of the other inputs that it buys. Suppose the company has signed a five-year rental contract for the warehouse space in which it stores its lumber. Ultimately—that is, in the long run—the firm may be able to reduce the amount of warehouse space to which it is committed, and if warehouse space in the area is scarce in the long run, more can be built. But once he has signed the warehouse contract, Al has relatively little immediate discretion over its capacity. Over a longer planning horizon, however, Al will need to replace the original contract, and he will be free to decide all over again how large a warehouse to rent or construct.

Much the same is true of large industrial firms. Companies have little control over their plant and equipment capacities in the short run. But with some advance planning, they can acquire different types of machines, redesign factories, and make other choices. For instance, General Motors continued producing the Chevrolet Caprice and other big, rear-wheel-drive cars at its plant in Arlington, Texas, for the 1995 and 1996 model years even though the vehicles were not selling well. That was partly because the company knew that it would need time to convert the plant to manufacture its popular full-size pickup trucks, which were in short supply. By the 1997 model year, however, GM engineers were able to convert the plant to truck production.

Note that the short run and the long run do not refer to the same time periods for all firms; rather, those periods vary in length, depending on the nature of each firm's commitments. If, for example, the firm can change its workforce every week, its machines every two years, and its factory every twenty years, then twenty years will be the long run, and any period less than twenty years will constitute the short run.

The **short run** is a period of time during which some of the firm's cost commitments will *not* have ended.

The **long run** is a period of time long enough for all of the firm's current commitments to come to an end.

■ Fixed Costs and Variable Costs

This distinction between the short run and the long run also determines which of the firm's costs rise or fall with a change in the amount of output produced by the firm. Some costs cannot be varied, *no matter how long the period in question.* These are called

A **fixed cost** is the cost of an input whose quantity does not rise when output goes up, one that the firm requires to produce any output at all. The total cost of such indivisible inputs does not change when the output changes. Any other cost of the firm's operation is called a **variable cost.**

fixed costs, and they arise when some types of inputs can be bought only in big batches or when inputs have a large productive capacity. For example, there is no such thing as a "mini" automobile assembly line capable of producing two cars per week, and, except for extreme luxury models, it is impractical to turn out automobiles without an assembly line. For these reasons, the fixed cost of automobile manufacturing includes the cost of the smallest (least expensive) assembly line that the firm can acquire. These costs are called *fixed* because the total amount of money spent in buying the assembly line does not vary, whether it is used to produce 10 cars or 100 cars each day, so long as the output quantity does not exceed the assembly line's capacity.

In the short run, some other costs behave very much as fixed costs do; in other words, they are predetermined by previous decisions and are *temporarily* fixed. But in the longer run, firms can change both their capital and labor commitments. So, in the long run, more costs become **variable.** We will have more to say about fixed and variable costs as we examine other key input and cost relationships.

PRODUCTION, INPUT CHOICE, AND COST WITH ONE VARIABLE INPUT

In reality, all businesses use many different inputs. Nevertheless, we will begin our discussion with the short-run case in which there is *only a single input that is variable*—that is, in which the quantities of all other inputs will not be changed. In doing so, we are trying to replicate in our theoretical analysis what physicists or biologists do in the laboratory when they conduct a *controlled* experiment: changing just one variable at a time to enable us to see the influence of that one variable in isolation. Thus, we will study the effects of variation in the quantity of one input under the assumption that all other things remain unchanged—that is, other things being equal.

Total, Average, and Marginal Physical Products

TABLE 1

Total Physical Product Schedule for Al's Building Company

(1)	(2)
Number of Carpenters	Total Product (Garages per Year)
0	0
1	4
2	12
3	24
4	32
5	35
6	30

We begin the analysis with the first of the firm's three main questions: what is the relationship between the quantity of inputs utilized and the quantity of production? Al has studied how many of its inexpensive standardized garages his firm can turn out in a year, depending on the number of carpenters it uses. The relevant data are displayed in Table 1.

The table begins by confirming the common-sense observation that garages cannot be built without labor. Thus, output is zero when Al hires zero labor input (see the first line of the table). After that, the table shows the rising total garage outputs that additional amounts of labor yield, assuming that the firm's employees work on one garage at a time and, after it is finished, move on to the next garage. For instance, with a one-carpenter input, total output is 4 garages per year; with two carpenters helping one another and specializing in different tasks, annual output can be increased to 12 garages. After five carpenters are employed in building a garage, they begin to get in one another's way. As a result, employment of a sixth carpenter actually reduces output from 35 to 30 garages.

Total Physical Product   The data in Table 1 appear graphically in Figure 2, which is called a **total physical product (TPP)** curve. This curve reports how many garages Al can produce with different quantities of carpenters, holding the quantities of all other inputs constant.

Average Physical Product   To understand more about how the number of carpenters contributes to output, Al can use two other physical product relationships given in Table 2. The **average physical product (APP)** measures output per unit of input; it is simply the total physical product divided by the quantity of variable input used. For Al's firm, it is the total number of garages produced in a year divided by the number of carpenters hired. APP is shown in Column (5) of Table 2. For example, because four carpenters can turn out 32 garages annually, the APP of four carpenters is 32/4, or 8 garages per carpenter.

The firm's **total physical product (TPP)** is the amount of output it obtains in total from a given quantity of input.

The **average physical product (APP)** is the total physical product (TPP) divided by the quantity of input. Thus, APP = TPP/X where X = the quantity of input.

TABLE 2				
Al's Product Schedules: Total, Average, and Marginal Physical Product and Marginal Revenue Product				
(1)	(2)	(3)	(4)	(5)
Number of Carpenters	Total Physical Product (Garages per year)	Marginal Physical Product (Garages per added carpenter)	Marginal Revenue Product (Thousands of $ per added carpenter)	Average Physical Product (Garages per carpenter)
0	0			0
1	4	4	$ 60	4
2	12	8	120	6
3	24	12	180	8
4	32	8	120	8
5	35	3	45	7
6	30	−5	−75	5

Note: Each entry in Column (3) is the difference between successive entries in Column (2). This is what is indicated by the zigzag lines.

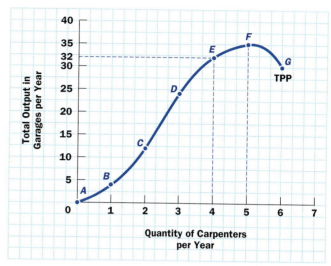

Marginal Physical Product To decide how many carpenters to hire, Al should know how many *additional* garages to expect from each *additional* carpenter. This concept is known as **marginal physical product (MPP),** and Al can calculate it from the total physical product data using the same method we introduced to derive marginal utility from total utility in Chapter 5. For example, the marginal physical product of the fourth carpenter is the total output when Al uses four carpenters *minus* the total output when he hires only three carpenters. That is, the MPP of the fourth carpenter = 32 − 24 = 8 garages. We calculate the other MPP entries in the third column of Table 2 in exactly the same way. Figure 3 displays these numbers in a graph called a *marginal physical product curve.*

FIGURE 2

Total Physical Product with Different Quantities of Carpenters Used by Al's Firm

The **marginal physical product (MPP)** of an input is the increase in total output that results from a one-unit increase in the input quantity, holding the amounts of all other inputs constant.

▪ Marginal Physical Product and the "Law" of Diminishing Marginal Returns

The shape of the marginal physical product curve in Figure 3 has important implications for Al's garage building. Compare the TPP curve in Figure 2 with the MPP curve in Figure 3. The MPP curve can be described as the curve that reports the *rate* at which the TPP curve is changing. MPP is equal to the *slope* of the TPP curve[3] because it tells us how much of an increase in garage output results from each additional carpenter Al hires. Thus, until input reaches three carpenters, the marginal physical product of carpenters *increases* when Al hires more of them. That is, TPP increases at an increasing rate (its slope becomes steeper) between points *A* and *D* in Figure 2. Between three carpenters and five carpenters, the MPP *decreases* but still has *positive* values throughout (that is, it lies above the horizontal axis). Consequently, in this range, TPP is still increasing (its slope, MPP, is greater than zero), but it is increasing more slowly (its slope, MPP, is still positive, but is a declining positive number). That is, in this region, between points *D* and *F* in Figure 2, each additional carpenter contributes garage output, but adds less than the

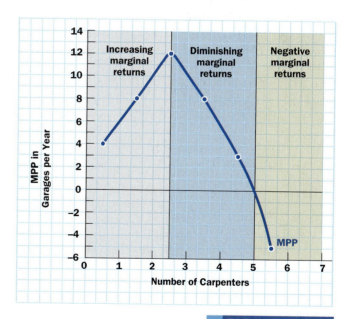

FIGURE 3

Al's Marginal Physical Product (MPP) Curve

---

[3] The same is true of any total and marginal curves: at any output level the marginal is the slope of the total curve. For example, the slope of an individual's total utility curve when he has 5 apples is the change in his total utility when he acquires a sixth apple. But that, by definition, is the marginal utility of the sixth apple.

previous carpenter added. Beyond five carpenters, to the right of point *F* in Figure 2, the MPP of carpenters actually becomes *negative:* The total physical product curve starts to decrease as additional carpenters get in one another's way.

Figure 3 is divided into three zones to illustrate these three cases. Note that the marginal returns to additional carpenters increase at first and then diminish. This is the typical pattern, and it parallels what we had to say about the utility of consumption in Chapter 5. Each additional unit adds some production, but at a decreasing rate. In the leftmost zone of Figure 3 (the region of increasing marginal returns), each additional carpenter adds more to TPP than the previous one did.

**IDEAS FOR
BEYOND THE
FINAL EXAM**

The "law" of diminishing marginal returns, which has played a key role in economics for two centuries, states that an increase in the amount of any one input, *holding the amounts of all others constant,* ultimately leads to lower marginal returns to the expanding input.

This so-called law rests simply on observed facts; economists did not deduce the relationship analytically. Returns to a single input usually diminish because of the "law" of variable input proportions. When the quantity of one input increases while all others remain constant, the variable input whose quantity increases gradually becomes more and more abundant relative to the others, and gradually becomes overabundant. (For example, the proportion of labor increases and the proportions of other inputs, such as lumber, decrease.) As Al uses more and more carpenters with fixed quantities of other inputs, the proportion of labor time to other inputs becomes unbalanced. Adding yet more carpenter time then does little good and eventually begins to harm production. At this last point, the marginal physical product of carpenters becomes *negative.*

Many real-world cases seem to follow the law of variable input proportions. In China, for instance, farmers have been using increasingly more fertilizer as they try to produce larger grain harvests to feed the country's burgeoning population. Although its consumption of fertilizer is four times higher than it was fifteen years ago, China's grain output has increased by only 50 percent. This relationship certainly suggests that fertilizer use has reached the zone of diminishing returns.

■ The Optimal Quantity of an Input and Diminishing Returns

We can now address the second question that all firms must ask as they make production decisions: How can the firm select the optimal quantity of an input? To answer this question, look again at the first and third columns of Table 2, which show the firm's marginal physical product schedule. We will assume for now that a carpenter is paid $50,000 per year, and that Al can sell his inexpensive garages for $15,000 each.

Now suppose that Al is considering using just one carpenter. Is this choice optimal? That is, does it maximize his profits? To answer this question we have to consider not only how many garages an additional carpenter provides but also the money value of each garage; that is, we must first translate the marginal *physical* product into its money equivalent. In this case, the monetary evaluation of TPP shows that the answer is no, one carpenter is not enough to maximize profit, because the marginal physical product of a second carpenter is 8 garages per year, the second entry in marginal physical product Column (3) of Table 2. At a price of $15,000 per garage, this extra output would add $120,000 to total revenue. Because the added revenue exceeds the $50,000 cost of the second carpenter, the firm comes out ahead by $120,000 − $50,000, or $70,000 per year.

The **marginal revenue product (MRP)** of an input is the additional revenue that the producer earns from the increased sales when it uses an additional unit of the input.

Marginal Revenue Product and Input Prices   The additional *money revenue* that a firm receives when it increases the quantity of some input by one unit is called the input's **marginal revenue product (MRP).** If Al's garages sell at a fixed price, say, $15,000, the marginal revenue product of the input equals its marginal physical product multiplied by the output price:

$$\text{MRP} = \text{MPP} \times \text{Price of output}$$

For example, we have just shown that the marginal revenue product of the second carpenter is $120,000, which we obtained by multiplying the MPP of 8 garages by the price of $15,000 per garage. The other MRP entries in Column (4) of Table 2 are calculated in the same way. The MRP concept enables us to formulate a simple rule for the optimal use of any input. Specifically:

When the marginal revenue product of an input exceeds its price, it pays the firm to use more of that input. Similarly, when the marginal revenue product of the input is less than its price, it pays the firm to use less of that input.

Let's test this rule in the case of Al's garages. We have observed that two carpenters cannot be the optimal input because the MRP of a second carpenter ($120,000) exceeds his wages ($50,000). What about a third carpenter? Table 2 shows that the MRP of the third carpenter (12 × $15,000 = $180,000) also exceeds his wage; thus, stopping at three carpenters also is not optimal. The same is true for a fourth carpenter, because his MRP of $120,000 still exceeds his $50,000 price. The situation is different with a fifth carpenter, however. Hiring a fifth carpenter is not a good idea because his MRP, which is 3 × $15,000 = $45,000, is less than his $50,000 cost. Thus, the optimal number of carpenters for Al to hire is four, yielding a total output of 32 garages.

Notice the crucial role of diminishing returns in this analysis. When the marginal *physical* product of carpenter begins to decline, the money value of that product falls as well—that is, the marginal *revenue* product also declines. The producer always profits by expanding input use until diminishing returns set in and reduce the MRP to the price of the input. So Al should stop *increasing* his carpenter purchases when MRP *falls* to the price of a carpenter.

A common expression suggests that it does not pay to continue doing something "beyond the point of diminishing returns." As we see from this analysis, quite to the contrary, it normally *does* pay to do so! The firm has employed the proper amount of input only when diminishing returns reduce the marginal revenue product of the input to the level of its price, because then the firm will be wasting no opportunity to *add* to its total profit. Thus, the optimal quantity of an input is that at which MRP equals its price (*P*). In symbols:

$$MRP = P \text{ of input}$$

The logic of this analysis is exactly the same as that used in our discussion of marginal utility and price in Chapter 5. Al is trying to maximize *profits*—the difference between the *total* revenue yielded by his carpenter input and the *total* cost of buying that input. To do so, he must increase his carpenter usage to the point where its price equals its marginal revenue product, just as an optimizing consumer keeps buying until price equals marginal utility.

■ MULTIPLE INPUT DECISIONS: THE CHOICE OF OPTIMAL INPUT COMBINATIONS[4]

Up to this point we have simplified our analysis by assuming that the firm can change the quantity of only one of its inputs and that the price the product can command does not change, no matter how large a quantity the producer offers for sale (the fixed price is $15,000 for Al's garages). Of course, neither of these assumptions is true in reality. In Chapter 8, we will explore the effect of product quantity decisions on prices by bringing in the demand curve. But first we must deal with the obvious fact that a firm must decide on the quantities of each of the many inputs it uses, not just one input at a time. That is, Al must decide not only how many carpenters to hire, but how much lumber and how many tools to buy. Both of the latter decisions clearly depend on the number of carpenters in his team. So, once again, we must examine the two

[4] Instructors may want to teach this part of the chapter (up to page 135) now, or they may prefer to wait until they come to Chapters 19 and 20 on the determination of wages, interest rates, profit, and rent.

Closer to Home: The Diminishing Marginal Returns to Studying

The "law" of diminishing marginal returns crops up a lot in ordinary life, not just in the world of business. Consider Jason and his study habits: He has a tendency to procrastinate and then cram for exams the night before he takes them, pulling "all-nighters" regularly. How might an economist describe his payoff from an additional hour of study in the wee hours of the morning, relative to Colin's efforts (who studies for two hours every night)?

SOURCE: © Mark Richards/PhotoEdit

basic and closely interrelated issues: production levels and optimal input quantities. But this time, we will allow the firm to select the quantities of *many* inputs. By expanding our analysis in this way, we can study a key issue: how a firm, by its choice of production method (also called its production technology), can make up for decreased availability of one input by using more of another input.

■ Substitutability: The Choice of Input Proportions

Just as we found it useful to start the analysis with physical output or product in the one-variable-input case, we will start with physical production in the multiple-variable-input case. Firms can choose among alternative types of technology to produce any given product. Many people mistakenly believe that management really has very little choice when selecting its input proportions. Technological considerations alone, they believe, dictate such choices. For example, a particular type of furniture-cutting machine may require two operators working for an hour on a certain amount of wood to make five desks—no more and no less. But this way of looking at the possibilities is an overly narrow view of the matter. Whoever first said that there are many ways to "skin a cat" saw things more clearly.

In reality, the furniture manufacturer can choose among several alternative production processes for making desks. For example, simpler and cheaper machines might be able to change the same pile of wood into five desks, but only by using more than two hours of labor. Or, the firm might choose to create the desks with simple hand tools, which would require many more workers and no machinery at all. The firm will seek the method of production that is *least costly.*

In advanced industrial societies, where labor is expensive and machinery is cheap, it may pay to use the most automated process. For example, Caterpillar, a U.S. heavy-vehicle and machinery producer, curbed its high labor costs by investing in computers that enabled it to manufacture twice as many truck engines with the same number of people. But in less developed countries, where machinery is scarce and labor is abundant, making things by hand may be the most economical solution. An interesting example can be found in rural India, where company records are often still hand-written, not computerized, as is widely true in the United States.

We conclude that firms can generally substitute one input for another. A firm can produce the same number of desks with less labor, *if* it is prepared to sink more money into machinery. But whether it *pays* to make such a substitution depends on the relative costs of labor and machinery. Several general conclusions follow from this discussion:

- Normally, a firm can choose among different technological options to produce a particular volume of output. Technological considerations rarely fix input proportions immutably.

- Given a target production level, a firm that cuts down on the use of one input (say, labor) will normally have to increase its use of another input (say, machinery). This trade-off is what we mean when we speak of *substituting* one input for another.
- The combination of inputs that represents the *least costly* way to produce the desired level of output depends on the relative prices of the various inputs.

The Marginal Rule for Optimal Input Proportions

Choosing the input proportions that minimize the cost of producing a given output is really a matter of common sense. To understand why, let us turn, once again, to marginal analysis of the decision. As before, Al is considering whether to buy more expensive tools that will enable him to produce his garages using fewer carpenters or to do the reverse. The two inputs, tools and carpenters, are substitutes; if the firm spends more on tools, it needs fewer carpenters. *But the tools are not perfect substitutes for labor.* Tools need carpenters to operate them, and tools are not endowed with the judgment and common sense that are needed if something goes wrong. Of course, a carpenter without tools is also not very productive, so Al gains a considerable benefit by acquiring balanced relative quantities of the two inputs. If he uses too much of one and too little of the other, the output of the firm will suffer. In other words, it is reasonable to assume *diminishing returns* to excessive substitution of either input for the other. As he substitutes more and more labor for expensive machinery, the marginal physical product of the added labor will begin to decline.

How should Al decide whether to spend more on tools and less on labor, or vice versa? The obvious—and correct—answer is that he should compare what he gets for his money by spending, say, $100 more on labor or on tools. If he gets more (a greater marginal revenue product) by spending this amount on labor than by spending it on tools, clearly it pays Al to spend that money on labor rather than on tools. As a matter of fact, in that case it pays him to spend somewhat less on tools than he had been planning to do, and to transfer the money he thereby saves to purchasing more carpenter labor. So we have the following three conclusions:

1. If the marginal revenue product of the additional labor that Al gets by spending, say, a dollar more on carpenters is greater than the marginal revenue product he receives from spending the same amount on tools, he should change his plans and devote more of his spending to labor than he had planned and less to tools.
2. If the marginal revenue product of an additional dollar spent on labor is less than the marginal revenue product of an additional dollar spent on tools, Al should increase his spending on tools and cut his planned spending on labor.
3. If the marginal revenue products of an additional dollar spent on either labor or tools are the same, Al should stick to his current purchase plans. There is nothing to be gained by switching the proportions of his spending on the two inputs.[5]

There is only one more step. Suppose, for example, that the MRP per dollar is greater for labor than that for tools. Then, as we have just seen, Al should spend more money on labor than originally planned, and less on tools. But where should this switch in spending stop? Should the transfer of funds continue until Al stops spending on tools altogether, because the MRP per dollar is greater for labor than for tools? Such an answer makes no sense—a worker without tools is not very productive. The correct answer is that, by the "law" of diminishing returns, when Al buys more and more carpenter time, the initially higher MRP of carpenters will decline. As he spends less and less

---

[5] Calculation of the marginal revenue product per dollar spent on an input is easy if we know the marginal revenue product of the input and the price of the input. For example, we know from Table 2 that the MRP of a third carpenter is $180,000, and his wage is $50,000. Thus, his MRP per dollar spent on his wages is $180,000/$50,000 = $3.60. More generally, the MRP per dollar spent on any input, X, is the MRP of X divided by the price of X.

Beyond Farms and Firms: The General Rule for Optimal Input Proportions

We have just discussed how a firm can determine the most economical input combination for any given level of output. This analysis does not apply only to business enterprises. Nonprofit organizations such as your own college are interested in finding the least costly ways to accomplish a variety of tasks (for example, maintaining the grounds and buildings); government agencies (sometimes) seek to meet their objectives at minimum costs; even in the home, we can find many ways to "skin a cat." Thus, our present analysis of *cost minimization* is widely applicable.

SOURCE: © Michael Malyszko/Taxi/Getty Images

on tools, tools will become scarcer and more valuable and their initially lower MRP will rise. So, as Al transfers more money from tools to carpenters, the MRPs per dollar for the inputs will get closer and closer to one another, and they will eventually meet. That, then, is when the proportions of Al's spending allocated to the two inputs will have reached the optimal level. At that point, there is no way he can get more for his money by changing the proportions of those inputs that he hires or buys.

Changes in Input Prices and Optimal Input Proportions

The common-sense reasoning behind the rule for optimal input proportions leads to an important conclusion. Let's say that Al is producing seven garages at minimum cost. Suppose that the wage of a carpenter falls, but the price of tools remains the same. This means that a dollar will now buy a larger quantity of labor than before, thus increasing the marginal revenue product *per dollar* spent on carpenters—a dollar will now buy more carpenter labor and more of its product than it did before. But because tool prices have not changed, the marginal revenue product obtainable by spending an additional dollar on tools will also be unchanged. So, if Al had previously devoted the right proportions to spending on carpenters and spending on tools, that will no longer be true. If, previously, the marginal revenue product per dollar spent on carpenters equaled the marginal revenue product per dollar spent on tools, now this relationship will have changed so that

Marginal revenue product per dollar spent on carpenters > marginal revenue product per dollar spent on tools

That is, the proportion between the two inputs will no longer be optimal. Clearly, Al will be better off if he increases his spending on carpenters and reduces his spending on tools.

Looked at another way, to restore optimality, the MRP per dollar spent on carpenters must fall to match the MRP per dollar spent on tools. But, by the "law" of diminishing returns, the MRP of carpenters will *fall* when the use of carpenters is increased. Thus, a fall in the price of carpenters prompts Al to use *more* carpenter time. And if the increase is sufficiently large, it will restore equality in the marginal revenue products per dollar spent on the two inputs. In general, we have the common-sense result that:

Input Substitution in the Logging Industry

After Congress outlawed logging in much of the Redwood National Forest, Louisiana Pacific Corporation (one of the world's largest lumber producers) lost access to one of its essential inputs: old-growth timber from which the company made building materials. But CEO Harry Merlo was pragmatic about the situation, and turned his attention to trees that were not under the watchful eye of conservationists. One likely candidate, the aspen—a so-called *waste-species*—immediately came to his attention. Aspens grow quickly and they appear plentifully in forests stretching across the whole of North America. Fortunately, Merlo had kept himself abreast of the latest technology in the building industry.

Canadian lumber mills have long had the capability of trimming small trees into sheets and then gluing and pressing the sheets together. Merlo observed this process, and he conceived some innovative ideas of his own. He correctly figured that alternating the grain of the layered sheets would add to overall strength. The result was waferwood, which turned out to be cheaper and stronger than plywood. It could be used as siding and, when combined with other engineered lumber, used to create I-beams for floor joists and roof rafters.

SOURCE: © Taxi/Getty Images

Thus, when Louisiana Pacific was forced out of the market for its old input (old-growth timber), it substituted a new input, aspen wood, for one that was no longer available.

SOURCE: "Let's Go for Growth," *Fortune*, March 7, 1994, p. 60.

As any one input becomes more costly relative to competing inputs, the firm is likely to substitute one input for another—that is, to use less of the input that has become more expensive and to use more of competing inputs.

This general principle of input substitution applies in industry just as it does in Al's firm. For a real-world application of the analysis, see the accompanying box, "Input Substitution in the Logging Industry."

COST AND ITS DEPENDENCE ON OUTPUT

Having analyzed how the firm decides on its input quantities, we now take the next step toward our analysis of the implications for pricing and output quantity of the product it sells to consumers. For this purpose, the firm needs to know, among other things, how much it will cost to produce different output quantities. Clearly, this cost—the amount of money that the firm spends on production—will depend on how much it produces, and what quantities of input it will need to do the job. How do we measure the cost relationships?

Input Quantities and Total, Average, and Marginal Cost Curves

So, we must turn now to the third of the three main questions that a firm must ask: How do we derive the firm's cost relationships from the input decisions that we have just explained? We will use these cost relationships when we analyze the firm's output and pricing decisions in Chapter 8, in which we will study the last of the main components of our analysis of the market mechanism: How much of its product or service should the profit-maximizing firm produce?

The most desirable output quantity for the firm clearly depends on the way in which costs change when output varies. Economists typically display and analyze such information in the form of *cost curves*. Indeed, because we will use marginal analysis again in our discussion, we will need three different cost curves: the *total cost curve*, the *average cost curve*, and the *marginal cost curve*.

These curves follow directly from the nature of production. The technological production relationships for garage-building dictate the amount of carpenter time, the type and quantity of tools, the amount of lumber, and the quantities of the other inputs that Al uses to produce any given number of garages. This technological relationship for carpenters appeared earlier in Figure 2 (p. 131). From these data on carpenter usage and the price of a carpenter, plus similar information on tools, lumber, and other inputs, and the decision on the optimal proportions among those inputs, Al can determine how much it will cost to produce any given number of garages. Therefore, the relevant cost relationships depend directly on the production relationships we have just discussed. The calculation of the firm's total costs from its physical product schedule that we will use here assumes that the firm cannot influence the market price of carpenters or the prices of other inputs, that these are fixed by union contracts and other such influences. Using this assumption, let us begin with the portion of the cost calculation that applies to carpenters.

The method is simple: For each quantity of output, record from Table 1 or Figure 2 the number of carpenters required to produce it. Then multiply that quantity of carpenters by the assumed annual average wage of $50,000.

Total Costs   In addition to the cost of carpenters, Al must spend money on his other inputs, such as tools and lumber. Furthermore, his costs must include the *opportunity costs* of any inputs that Al himself contributes—such as his own labor, which he could instead have used to earn wages by taking a job in another firm, and his own capital that he has invested in the firm, which he could instead have invested, say, in interest-paying government bonds. The costs of the other inputs are calculated, essentially, in the same manner as the cost of carpenters—by determining the quantity of each input that will optimally be used in producing any given number of garages, and then multiplying that input quantity by its price. To calculate the total cost Al must cover to build, say, four garages per year, we have the following very simple formula:

> **The total cost of four garages =
> (the number of carpenters used ×
> the wage per carpenter) +
> (the amount of lumber that will be used ×
> the price of lumber) +
> (the number of pounds of nails that will be
> used × the price of nails) + . . .**

Using this calculation and data such as those in Table 1, we obtain directly the total costs for different output quantities shown in Table 3. For example, Row (4), Column (2), of Table 3 indicates that if he wants to produce three garages per year, Al needs to purchase quantities of labor time, lumber, and other inputs whose total cost is $54,000. The other numbers in the second column of Table 3 are to be interpreted similarly. To summarize the story:

The marginal product relationships enable the firm to determine the input proportions and quantities needed to produce any given output at lowest total cost. From those input quantities and the prices of the inputs, we can determine the total cost *(TC) of producing*

TABLE 3

Al's (Variable) Cost Schedules

(1) Total Product (Garages per year)	(2) Total Variable Cost (Thousands of $ per year)	(3) Marginal Variable Cost (Thousands of $ per added garage)	(4) Average Variable Cost (Thousands of $ per garage)
0	$ 0		$ 0
1	28	$28	28
2	44	16	22
3	54	10	18
4	62	8	15.5
5	68	6	13.6
6	75	7	12.5
7	84	9	12
8	100	16	12.5
9	132	32	14.7 (approx.)
10	178	46	17.8

any level of output. Thus, the relationship of total cost to output is determined by the technological production relationships between inputs and outputs and by input prices.

Total, Average, and Marginal Cost Curves

Two other cost curves—the average cost (AC) and marginal cost (MC) curves—provide information crucial for our analysis. We can calculate these curves directly from the total cost curve, just as Table 2 calculated average and marginal physical product from total physical product.

For any given output, *average cost* is defined as total cost divided by quantity produced. For example, Table 3 shows that the total cost of producing seven garages is $84,000, so the average cost is $84,000/7 or $12,000 per garage.

Similarly, we define the *marginal cost* as the increase in total cost that arises from the production of an additional garage. For example, the marginal cost of the fifth garage is the difference between the total cost of producing five garages, $68,000, and the total cost of producing four garages, $62,000. That is, the marginal cost of the fifth garage is $6,000. Figure 4 shows all three curves—the total, average, and marginal cost curves. The TC curve is generally assumed to rise fairly steadily as the firm's output increases. After all, Al cannot expect to produce eight garages at a lower total cost than he can produce five, six, or seven garages. The AC curve and the MC curve both look roughly like the letter U—first going downhill, then gradually turning uphill again. We will explore the reason for and implications of this U-shape later in the chapter.

So far, we have taken into account only the *variable* costs of Al's garage-building, or the costs that depend on the number of garages his firm builds. That's why these costs are labeled as "variable" in the table and the graph. But there are other costs, such as the rent Al pays for the company office, that are fixed; that is, they stay the same in total, no matter how many garages he produces, at least within some limits. Of course, Al cannot obtain these fixed-cost inputs for free. Their costs, however, are constants—they are positive numbers and not zero.

Total Fixed Cost and Average Fixed Cost Curves

Although variable costs are only part of combined total costs (which include both fixed and variable costs), the total and average cost curves that include both types of costs have the same general shape as those shown in Figure 4. In contrast, the curves that record *total fixed costs* (TFC) and *average fixed costs* (AFC) have very special shapes, illustrated in Figure 5. By definition, TFC remains the same whether the firm produces a little or a lot—so long as it produces anything at all. As a result, any TFC curve is a horizontal straight line like the one shown in Figure 5(a). It has the same height at every output.

Average fixed cost, however, gets smaller and smaller as output increases, because AFC (which equals TFC/Q) (where Q represents quantity of output) falls as output (the denominator) rises for constant TFC. Businesspeople typically put the point another way: Any increase in output spreads the fixed cost (which they often call "overhead") among more units, meaning that less of it is

FIGURE 4

Al's Total Variable Cost, Average Variable Cost, and Marginal Variable Cost

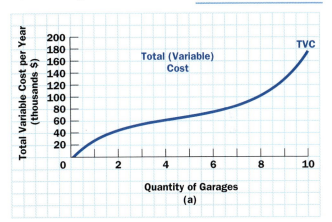

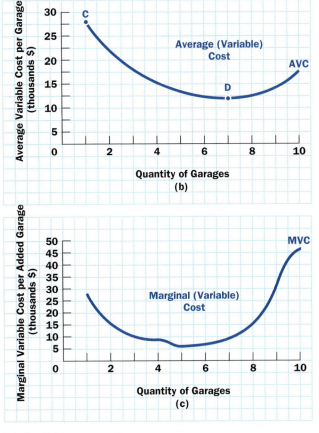

Note: Quantity is in garages per year.

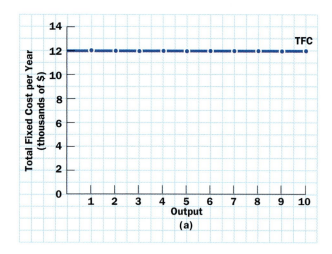

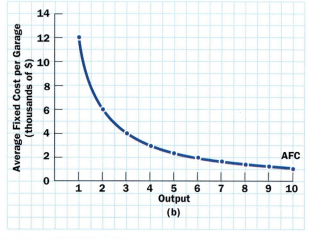

FIGURE 5

Fixed Costs: Total and Average

Note: Output is in garages per year.

carried by any one unit. For example, suppose that Al's garage operation's total fixed cost is $12,000 per year. When he produces only two garages, the entire $12,000 of fixed cost must be borne by those two garages; that is, the average fixed cost is $6,000 per garage. But if Al produces three garages, the fixed cost per garage falls to $4,000 = $12,000/3 (Table 4).

AFC can never reach zero. Even if Al were to produce 1 million garages per year, each garage would have to bear, on the average, one-millionth of the TFC—which is still a positive number (although minuscule). It follows that the AFC curve gets lower and lower as output increases, moving closer and closer to the horizontal axis but never crossing it. This pattern appears in Figure 5(b).

Finally, we may note that marginal fixed costs exhibit a very simple behavior: *Marginal fixed costs are always zero.* Building an additional garage does not add a penny to Al's annual office rent, which is fixed at $12,000 by the lease he and his landlord have signed. Looked at another way, because the total fixed cost stays unchanged at $12,000, no matter how many garages are produced, the marginal fixed cost of, say, a fifth garage is the total fixed cost of five garages minus the total fixed cost of four garages = $12,000 − $12,000 = 0.

Having divided costs into fixed costs (FC) and variable costs (VC), we can express corresponding rules for total average and marginal costs:

$$TC = TFC + TVC$$
$$AC = AFC + AVC$$
$$MC = MFC + MVC$$
$$= 0 + MVC$$
$$= MVC$$

■ The Law of Diminishing Marginal Productivity and the U-Shaped Average Cost Curve

The preceding discussion of fixed and variable costs enables us to consider the configuration of the average cost curve and the production implications of its typical U-shape. The typical curve looks like that in Figure 4(b) and is roughly U-shaped: The left-hand portion of the curve is downward-sloping and the right-hand portion is upward-sloping. AC declines when output increases in the left-hand portion of the curve for two reasons.

The first reason makes intuitive sense and pertains to the fixed-cost portion of AC and the fact that these fixed costs are divided over more units of product as output increases. As Figure 5(b) shows, the average *fixed* cost curve always falls as output increases, and it falls very sharply at the left-hand end of the AFC curve. Because AC equals AFC plus average variable costs (AVC), the AC curve for virtually any product contains a fixed-cost portion,

TABLE 4

Al's Fixed Costs

(1)	(2)	(3)	(4)
	Total Fixed Cost		Average Fixed Cost
Number of Garages	(Thousands of $ per year)	Marginal Fixed Cost	(Thousands of $ per garage)
0	$12		–
1	12	$0	$12
2	12	0	6
3	12	0	4
4	12	0	3
5	12	0	2.4
6	12	0	2
7	12	0	1.7
8	12	0	1.5
9	12	0	1.33
10	12	0	1.2

AFC, which falls steeply at first when output increases. So, as these fixed costs are spread over more units as output increases, the AC curve for any product should have a downward-sloping portion such as *CD* in Figure 4(b), which is characterized by decreasing average cost.

The second reason why AC curves have a downward-sloping section relates to changing input proportions. As the firm increases the quantity of one input while holding other inputs constant, the marginal physical product relationship tells us that MPP will first rise. As a result, average costs will decrease. For example, if Al is using very few carpenters relative to the amounts of other inputs, a rise in the quantity of carpenters will, at first, yield increasing additions to output (in the range of increasing marginal physical product of carpenters illustrated in the left-hand part of Figure 3). As the quantity produced increases, the average cost of output falls.

Now look at any point to the right of point *D* in Figure 4(b). Average cost rises as output increases along this section of the curve. Why does the portion of the curve with decreasing AC end? Although it may not seem very important in our simple example, increasing administrative costs are a major source of increasing average cost in practice. Sheer size makes firms more complicated to run. Large firms tend to be relatively bureaucratic, impersonal, and costly to manage. As a firm becomes very large and loses top management's personal touch, bureaucratic costs ultimately rise disproportionately. Typically, this change ultimately drives average cost upward.

The output at which average costs stop decreasing and begin to rise varies from industry to industry. Other things being equal, the greater the relative size of fixed costs, the higher the output at which the switch-over occurs.[6] For example, it occurs at a much larger volume of output in automobile production than in farming, which is why no farms are as big as even the smallest auto producer. Automobile producers must be larger than farms because the fixed costs of automobile production are far greater than those in farming, so spreading the fixed cost over an increasing number of units of output keeps AC falling far longer in auto production than in farming. Thus, although firms in both industries may have U-shaped AC curves, the bottom of the U occurs at a far larger output in auto production than in farming.

The AC curve for a typical firm is U-shaped. We can attribute its downward-sloping segment to increasing marginal physical products and to the fact that the firm spreads its fixed costs over ever-larger quantities of outputs. Similarly, we can attribute the upward-sloping segment primarily to the disproportionate rise in administrative costs that occurs as firms grow large.

■ The Average Cost Curve in the Short and Long Run

At the beginning of this chapter, we observed that some inputs are variable and some are precommitted, depending on the pertinent time horizon. It follows that:

The average (and marginal and total) cost curve depends on the firm's planning horizon—how far into the future it tries to look when making its plans. The average (and total) cost curve for the long run differs from that for the short run because, in the long run, input quantities generally become variable.

We can, in fact, be much more specific about the relationships between the short-run and long-run average cost curves. Consider, as an example, the capacity of Naomi's poultry farm. In the short run, she can choose to raise, at most, only the number of chickens that she can crowd into her coops' current capacity. Of course, she can always build more chicken coops. However, if it turns out that the coops are much larger than she needs, Naomi cannot simply undo the excessive space and get

---

[6] Empirical evidence confirms this view, although it suggests that the bottom of the U is often long and flat. That is to say, a considerable range of outputs often fall between the regions of decreasing and increasing average cost. In this intermediate region, the AC curve is approximately horizontal, meaning that, in this range, AC does not change when output increases.

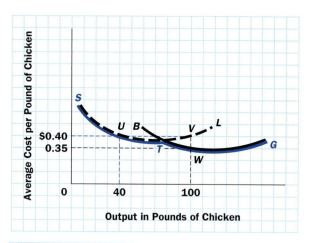

FIGURE 6

Short-Run and
Long-Run Average
Cost Curves

back the money that she has spent on it. But, in the long run, after they are sufficiently old to need replacement, she can choose among new coops of different sizes.

If she constructs a smaller coop, Naomi's AC curve looks like curve *SL* in Figure 6. That means that if she is pleasantly surprised as sales grow to 100 pounds of chicken per week, average cost will be $0.40 per pound of chicken (point *V*). She may then wish she had built bigger coops with an AC curve of *BG*, which would have enabled her to cut the cost per pound of chicken to $0.35 (point *W*). In the short run, though, Naomi can do nothing about this decision; the AC curve remains *SL*. Similarly, had she built the larger coops, the short-run AC curve would be *BG*, and the farm would be committed to this cost curve even if her sales were to decline sharply.

In the long run, however, Naomi must replace the coops, and she is free to decide all over again how big they should be. If Naomi expects sales of 100 pounds of chicken per week, she will construct larger coops and have an average cost of $0.35 per pound of chicken (point *W*). If she expects sales of only 40 pounds of chicken per week, she will arrange for smaller buildings with an average cost of $0.40 per pound of chicken (point *U*).

In sum, in the long run, a firm will select the plant size (that is, the short-run AC curve) that is most economical for the output level that it expects to produce. The long-run average cost curve therefore consists of all of the *lower* segments of the short-run AC curves. In Figure 6, this composite curve is the blue curve, *STG*. The long-run average cost curve shows the lowest possible short-run average cost corresponding to each output level.

ECONOMIES OF SCALE

We have now put together the basic tools we need to address the question posed at the beginning of this chapter: Does a large firm benefit from substantial economies of scale that allow it to operate more efficiently than smaller firms? To answer this question, we need a precise definition of this concept.

An enterprise's scale of operation arises from the quantities of the various inputs that it uses. Consider what happens when the firm doubles its scale of operations. For example, suppose Al's garage-building firm were to double the number of carpenters, the amount of lumber, the number of tools, and the quantity of every other input that it uses. Suppose as a result that the number of garages built per year increased from 12 to 26; that is, output more than doubled. Because output goes up by a greater percentage than the increase in each of the inputs, Al's production is said to be characterized by **increasing returns to scale** (or **economies of scale**), at least in this range of input and output quantities.

Economies of scale affect operations in many modern industries. Where they exist, they give larger firms cost advantages over smaller ones and thereby foster large firm sizes. Automobile production and telecommunications are two common examples of industries that enjoy significant economies of scale. Predictably, firms in these industries are, indeed, huge.

Technology generally determines whether a specific economic activity is characterized by economies of scale. One particularly clear example of a way in which this can happen is provided by warehouse space. Imagine two warehouses, each shaped like a perfect cube, where the length, width, and height of Warehouse 2 are twice as large as the corresponding measurements for Warehouse 1. Now remember your high-school geometry. The surface area of any side of a cube is equal to the square of its length. Therefore, the amount of material needed to build Warehouse 2 will be 2^2, or

Production is said to involve **economies of scale,** also referred to as **increasing returns to scale,** if, when all input quantities are increased by X percent, the quantity of output rises by *more* than X percent.

four times as great as that needed for Warehouse 1. However, because the volume of a cube is equal to the cube of its length, Warehouse 2 will have 2^3, or eight times, as much storage space as Warehouse 1. Thus, in a cubic building, multiplying the input quantities by four leads to eight times the storage space—an example of strongly increasing returns to scale.

This example is, of course, oversimplified. It omits such complications as the need for stronger supports in taller buildings, the increased difficulty of moving goods in and out of taller buildings, and the like. Still, the basic idea is correct, and the example shows why, up to a point, the very nature of warehousing creates technological relationships that lead to economies of scale.

Our definition of economies of scale, although based on the type of production, relates closely to the shape of the *long-run* average cost curve. Notice that the definition requires that a doubling of *every* input must bring about more than a doubling of output. If all input quantities are doubled, total cost must double. But if output *more* than doubles when input quantities are doubled, then cost per unit (average cost) must decline when output increases. In other words:

Production relationships with economies of scale lead to long-run average cost curves that decline as output expands.

Figure 7(a) depicts a decreasing average cost curve, but shows only one of three possible shapes that the long-run average cost curve can take. Panel (b) shows the curve for *constant* returns to scale. Here, if all input quantities double, both total cost (TC) and the quantity of output (Q) double, so average cost (AC = TC/Q) remains *constant*. There is a third possibility. Output may also increase, but less than double, when all inputs double. This case of *decreasing* returns to scale leads to a *rising* long-run average cost curve like the one depicted in Panel (c). The figure reveals a close association between the slope of the AC curve and the nature of the firm's returns to scale.

Note that the same production function can display increasing returns to scale in some ranges, constant returns to scale in other ranges, and decreasing returns to scale in yet others. This is true of all the U-shaped average cost curves we have shown, such as that shown in Figure 4(b).

■ The "Law" of Diminishing Returns and Returns to Scale

Earlier in this chapter, we discussed the "law" of diminishing marginal returns. Is there any relationship between economies of scale and the phenomenon of diminishing returns? At first, the two ideas may seem contradictory. After all, if a producer gets diminishing returns from her inputs as she uses more of each of them, doesn't it follow that by using more of *every* input, she must encounter decreasing returns to scale? In fact, the two principles do not contradict one another, for they deal with fundamentally different issues.

FIGURE 7

Three Possible Shapes for the Long-Run Average Cost Curve

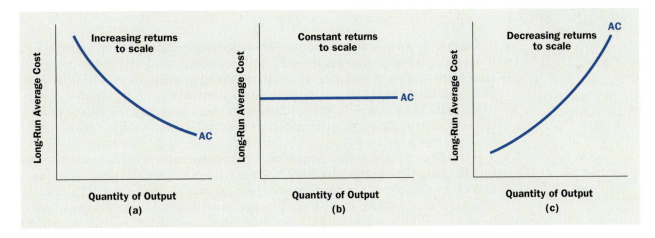

(a) Increasing returns to scale — Long-Run Average Cost — Quantity of Output

(b) Constant returns to scale — Long-Run Average Cost — AC — Quantity of Output

(c) Decreasing returns to scale — AC — Long-Run Average Cost — Quantity of Output

- *Returns to a single input.* This analysis asks the question, How much does output expand if a firm increases the quantity of just *one* input, *holding all other input quantities unchanged?*
- *Returns to scale.* Here the question is, How much does output expand if *all* inputs are increased *simultaneously* by the same percentage?

The "law" of diminishing returns pertains to the first question, because it examines the effects of increasing only one input at a time. It is plausible that the firm will encounter diminishing returns as this one input becomes relatively overabundant as compared to the quantities of the firm's other inputs. Thus, for example, the addition of too much carpenter time relative to a given quantity of lumber will contribute relatively little to total garage production, yielding diminishing returns. To get the most benefit out of the hiring of an additional carpenter, the firm needs to acquire more tools and raw materials.

Returns to scale pertain to proportionate increases in *all* inputs and therefore answer the second question. If Al doubles carpenter time and all other inputs as well, the carpenters, clearly, need not become redundant. But increasing the amount of one input without expanding any other inputs clearly threatens redundancy of the expanded item even in a factory where simultaneous expansion of *all* inputs will lead to a very big jump in output. Thus, the "law" of diminishing returns (to a single input) is compatible with *any* sort of returns to scale. In summary:

Returns to scale and returns to a single input (holding all other inputs constant) refer to two distinct aspects of a firm's technology. A production function that displays diminishing returns to *a single input* may show diminishing, constant, or increasing returns when *all input quantities are increased proportionately.*

■ Historical Costs Versus Analytical Cost Curves

In Chapter 5, we noted that all points on a demand curve pertain to the *same* period of time. Decision makers must use this common time period for the analysis of an optimal decision for a given period, because the demand curve describes the alternative choices available *for the period of time to which the decision will apply* . The same is true of a cost curve. All points on a cost curve pertain to exactly the same time period, because the graph examines the cost of each alternative output level that the firm can choose for that period, thus providing the information needed to compare the alternatives and their consequences, and thereby to make an optimal decision for that period.

It follows that a graph of historical data on prices and quantities at *different points in time* is normally *not* the cost curve that the decision maker needs. This observation will help us resolve the problem posed at the beginning of the chapter, which raised the question whether declining historical costs were evidence of economies of scale as information needed to decide on the optimal size of the firm in question.

All points on any of the cost curves used in economic analysis refer to the same period of time.

One point on an auto manufacturer's cost curve may show, for example, how much it would cost the firm to produce 2.5 million cars during 2007. Another point on the same curve may show what would happen to the firm's costs if, *instead*, it were to produce 3 million cars in that same year. Such a curve is called an *analytical cost curve* or, when there is no possibility of confusion, simply a cost curve. This curve must be distinguished from a diagram of *historical costs*, which shows how costs have changed from year to year.

The different points on an analytical cost curve represent *alternative possibilities*, all for the same time period. In 2007, the car manufacturer will produce either 2.5 million or 3 million cars (or some other amount), but certainly not both. Thus, at most, only one point on this cost curve will ever be observed. The company may, indeed, produce 2.5 million cars in 2007 and 3 million cars in 2008, but the 2008 data are not relevant to the 2007 cost curve, which is to be used to analyze the 2007 output decision. By the time 2008 comes around, the cost curve may have shifted, so the 2008 cost figure will not apply to the 2007 cost curve.

A different sort of graph can, of course, indicate year by year how costs and outputs vary. Such a graph, which gathers together the statistics for a number of different periods, is not, however, a *cost curve* as that term is used by economists. An example of such a diagram of historical costs appeared in Figure 1 on page 128.

Why do economists rarely use historical cost diagrams and instead deal primarily with analytical cost curves, which are more abstract, more challenging to explain, and more difficult to estimate statistically? The answer is that analysis of real policy problems—such as the desirability of having a single supplier of telephone services for the entire market—leaves no choice in the matter. Rational decisions require analytical cost curves. Let's see why.

Resolving the Economies of Scale Puzzle

Recall the problem that we introduced early in the chapter. We examined the divestiture of AT&T's components and concluded that, to determine whether it made sense to break up such a large company, economists would have to know whether the industry provided economies of scale. Among the data offered as evidence was a graph that showed a precipitous drop in the capital cost of long-distance communications as the volume of calls rose after 1942. But we did not answer a more pertinent question: Why didn't this information constitute legitimate evidence about the presence or absence of economies of scale?

It all boils down to the following: To determine whether a single large firm can provide telephone service more cheaply in, say, 2007 than a number of smaller firms can, we must compare the costs of *both large-scale and small-scale production in 2007*. It does no good to compare the cost of a large supplier in 2007 with its own costs as a smaller firm back in 1942, because that cannot possibly provide the needed information. The cost situation in 1942 is irrelevant for today's decision between large and small suppliers, because no small firm today would use the obsolete techniques employed in 1942.

Since the 1940s, great technical progress has taken the telephone industry from ordinary open-wire circuits to microwave systems, telecommunications satellites, coaxial cables of enormous capacity, and fiber optics. As a result, the *entire* analytical cost curve of telecommunications must have shifted downward quite dramatically from year to year. Innovation must have reduced not only the cost of large-scale operations, *but also the cost of smaller-scale operations*. Until decision makers compare the costs of large and small suppliers *today*, they cannot make a rational choice between single-firm and multifirm production. It is the analytical cost curve, all of whose points refer to the same period, that, by definition, supplies this information.

Figures 8 and 9 show two extreme hypothetical cases, one that entails true economies of scale and one that does not. Both are based on the same historical cost data (in black) with their very sharply declining costs. (This curve is reproduced from Figure 1.) They also show (in blue and red) two possible average cost curves, one for 1942 and one for 2007.

In Figure 8, the analytical AC curve has shifted downward very sharply from 1942 to 2007, as technological change reduced all costs. Moreover, both of the AC curves slope downward to the right, meaning that, in either year, a larger firm has lower average costs. Thus, the situation shown in Figure 8 really does entail scale economies, so that one large

FIGURE 8

Declining Historical Cost Curve with the Analytical Average Cost Curve Also Declining in Each Year

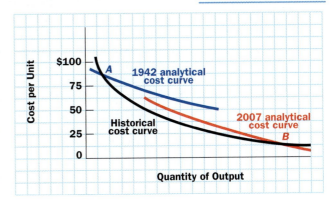

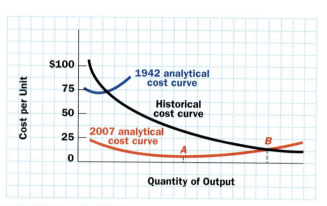

FIGURE 9

Declining Historical
Cost Curve with
U-Shaped Analytical
Cost Curves in Each
Year

firm can serve the market at lower cost than many small ones.

Now look at Figure 9, which shows exactly the same historical costs as Figure 8. Here, however, both analytical AC curves are U-shaped. In particular, the 2007 AC curve has its minimum point at an output level, *A*, that is less than one-half of the current output, *B*, of the large supplier. Thus, the shape of the analytical cost curves does *not* show economies of scale. This means that, for the situation shown in Figure 9, a smaller company can produce more cheaply than a large one can. In this case, one cannot justify domination of the market by a single large firm on the grounds that its costs are lower—despite the sharp downward trend of historical costs.

In sum, the behavior of historical costs reveals nothing about the cost advantages or disadvantages of a single large firm. More generally:

> Because a diagram of historical costs does not compare the costs of large and small firms *at the same point in time,* it cannot be used to determine whether an industry provides economies of large-scale production. Only the analytical cost curve can supply this information.

In the case of telephone service, some estimates indicate that economies of large-scale production do indeed exist. Presumably because of this influence, 25 years after the Bell telephone system's breakup, the typical firm providing traditional long-distance telephone service is still very large, with AT&T and Verizon dominating the industry. Yet half a dozen or so other smaller firms still compete in this arena. It is perhaps ironic that a substantial portion of the "Baby Bell" local telephone companies that were pulled away from AT&T by the courts in 1982 have recombined, in order to obtain cost and other advantages of larger size. Cellular and internet-based long-distance service have also gained ground at a rapid pace.

Cost Minimization in Theory and Practice

Lest you be tempted to run out and open a business, confident that you now understand how to minimize costs, we should point out that business decisions are a good deal more complicated than we have indicated here. Rare is the business executive who knows for sure the exact shapes of his or her marginal physical product schedules, or the precise nature of his or her cost curves. No one can provide an instruction book for instant success in business. What we have presented here is, instead, a set of principles that constitutes a guide to the logic of good decision making.

Business management has been described as the art of making critical decisions on the basis of inadequate information, and our complex and ever-changing world often leaves people no alternative but to make educated guesses. Actual business decisions will at best approximate the cost-minimizing ideal outlined in this chapter. Certainly, practicing managers will make mistakes, but when they do their jobs well and the market system functions smoothly, the approximation may prove amazingly good. Although no system is perfect, inducing firms to produce the output they select at the lowest possible cost is undoubtedly one of the jobs the market system does best.

POLICY DEBATE

Should Water Be Provided to Western Farmers at Subsidized Prices?

Farmers in the western United States use a great deal of water. Because most of the area's climate is high desert, agriculture there requires artificial irrigation—indeed, water is critical. In California, for example, farmers use 30 million acre-feet of water a year (almost 10 trillion gallons) to irrigate their crops—about 80 percent of that state's developed water supply. Yet western farmers and ranchers have traditionally paid very low prices for the water they use. Government controls have kept the price of water used for agriculture artificially low, so that California farmers pay only a small fraction of the price that urban residents pay for water. Even during droughts, farmers in that state continued to use vast quantities of water, while residents in the cities were forced to ration.

This situation has given rise to an intense debate between farmers and environmentalists. There is no question that water is scarce in the western states, and there are predictions of a looming shortage of disastrous proportions. It is also clear that farmers pay a price that is much lower than the true marginal cost of water, particularly because that cost includes a very high *opportunity cost*—that is, the value of the other uses of water that must be forgone as a result of its extensive employment in agriculture.

As analysis in this chapter shows, a low price for an input increases the amount that producers use, and there is little doubt that the low price of water substantially increases its consumption by western farmers. Environmentalists and economists have joined forces in arguing that western water users should pay prices that cover its true marginal cost. Indeed, it has been suggested that at such a price any shortage would simply disappear.

But the farmers argue that long practice entitles them to continued low water prices and that low prices in the past induced them to invest extensively in their agricultural properties, so that a price increase now would be tantamount to confiscating their investments. Recent small price increases for water have, in fact, encouraged farmers to utilize water-saving methods such as drip irrigation, with some farmers now eager to sell their resulting surplus water to California cities. State water authorities are working toward creating a market for farmers, cities and private businesses to buy and sell water. This shows how higher prices can sometimes benefit society, but it also illustrates how it can raise issues of fairness to some of the persons affected.

SOURCE: © Bob Rowan; Progressive Image/Corbis

SOURCES: James Flanigan, "Creating a Free-Flowing Market to Buy, Sell Water," *Los Angeles Times*, October 24, 2001, www.latimes.com; "California's Economy: The Real Trouble," *The Economist*, July 28, 2001, p. 31; and California Department of Water Resources, http://www.owue.water.ca.gov.

SUMMARY

1. A firm's total cost curve shows its lowest possible cost of producing any given quantity of output. This curve is derived from the input combination that the firm uses to produce any given output and the prices of the inputs.

2. The **marginal physical product** (MPP) of an input is the increase in total output resulting from a one-unit increase in that input, holding the quantities of all other inputs constant.

3. The "law" of diminishing marginal returns states that if a firm increases the amount of one input (holding all other input quantities constant), the marginal physical product of the expanding input will eventually begin to decline.

4. To maximize profits, a firm must purchase an input up to the point at which diminishing returns reduce the input's **marginal revenue product** (MRP) to equal its price (P = MRP = MPP × price).

5. Average and marginal variable cost curves tend to be U-shaped, meaning that these costs decline up to a certain level of output, and then begin to rise again at larger output quantities.

6. The **long run** is a period sufficiently long for the firm's plant to require replacement and for all of its current contractual commitments to expire. The **short run** is any period briefer than the long run.

7. **Fixed costs** are costs whose total amounts do not vary when output increases. All other costs are called **variable costs**. Some costs are variable in the long run but not in the short run.

8. At all levels of output, the total fixed cost (TFC) curve is horizontal and the average fixed cost (AFC) curve declines toward the horizontal axis but never crosses it.

9. TC = TFC + TVC; AC = AFC + AVC; MFC = 0.

10. It is usually possible to produce the same quantity of output in a variety of ways by substituting more of one input for less of another input. Firms normally seek the

combination of inputs that is the least costly way to produce any given output.

11. A firm that wants to minimize costs will select input quantities at which the ratios of the marginal revenue product of each input to the input's price—its MRP per dollar—are equal for all inputs.

12. If a doubling of all the firm's inputs just doubles its output, the firm is said to have constant returns to scale. If a doubling of all inputs leads to more than twice as much output, it has **increasing returns to scale** (or **economies of scale**). If a doubling of inputs produces less than a doubling of output, the firm has decreasing returns to scale.

13. With increasing returns to scale, the firm's long-run average costs are decreasing; constant returns to scale are associated with constant long-run average costs; decreasing returns to scale are associated with increasing long-run average costs.

14. Economists cannot tell if an industry offers economies of scale (increasing returns to scale) simply by inspecting a diagram of historical cost data. Only the underlying analytical cost curve can supply this information.

KEY TERMS

Short run   129

Long run   129

Fixed cost   130

Variable cost   130

Total physical product (TPP)   130

Average physical product (APP)   130

Marginal physical product (MPP)   131

Marginal revenue product (MRP)   132

Economies of scale (increasing returns to scale)   142

TEST YOURSELF

1. A firm's total fixed cost is $360,000. Construct a table of its total and average fixed costs for output levels varying from zero to 6 units. Draw the corresponding TFC and AFC curves.

2. With the following data, calculate the firm's AVC and MVC and draw the graphs for TVC, AVC, and MVC. Why is MVC the same as MC?

Quantity	Total Variable Costs
1	$40,000
2	80,000
3	120,000
4	176,000
5	240,000
6	360,000

3. From the data in Test Yourself Questions 1 and 2, calculate TC and AC for each of the output levels from 1 to 6 units and draw the two graphs.

4. If a firm's commitments in 2006 include machinery that will need replacement in 5 years, a factory building rented for 12 years, and a 3-year union contract specifying how many workers it must employ, when, from its point of view in 2006, does the firm's long run begin?

5. If the marginal revenue product of a gallon of oil used as input by a firm is $1.20 and the price of oil is $1.07 per gallon, what can the firm do to increase its profits?

6. A firm hires two workers and rents 15 acres of land for a season. It produces 150,000 bushels of crop. If it had doubled its land and labor, production would have been 325,000 bushels. Does it have constant, decreasing, or increasing returns to scale?

7. Suppose that wages are $20,000 per season per person and land rent per acre is $3,000. Calculate the average cost of 150,000 bushels and the average cost of 325,000 bushels, using the figures in Test Yourself Question 6. (Note that average costs increase when output increases.) What connection do these figures have with the firm's returns to scale?

8. Naomi has stockpiled a great deal of chicken feed. Suppose now that she buys more chicks, but not more chicken feed, and divides the feed she has evenly among the larger number of chickens. What is likely to happen to the marginal physical product of feed? What, therefore, is the role of input proportions in the determination of marginal physical product?

9. Labor costs $10 per hour. Nine workers produce 180 bushels of product per hour, while ten workers produce 196 bushels. Land rents for $1,000 per acre per year. With ten acres worked by nine workers, the marginal physical product of an acre of land is 1,400 bushels per year. Does the farmer minimize costs by hiring nine workers and renting ten acres of land? If not, which input should he use in larger relative quantity?

10. Suppose that Al's total costs increase by $5,000 per year at every output level. Show in Table 2 how this change affects his total and average costs.

1. A firm experiences a sudden increase in the demand for its product. In the short run, it must operate longer hours and pay higher overtime wage rates to satisfy this new demand. In the long run, the firm can install more machines instead of operating fewer machines for longer hours. Which do you think will be lower, the short-run or the long-run average cost of the increased output? How is your answer affected by the fact that the long-run average cost includes the new machines the firm buys, while the short-run average cost includes no machine purchases?

APPENDIX *Production Indifference Curves*

To describe a production function—that is, the relationship between input combinations and the size of a firm's total output—economists use a graphic device called the **production indifference curve**. Each indifference curve indicates *all* combinations of input quantities just capable of producing a *given* quantity of output; thus, a separate indifference curve corresponds to each possible quantity of output. These production indifference curves are perfectly analogous to the consumer indifference curves discussed in the appendix to Chapter 5.

> A production indifference curve (sometimes called an *isoquant*) is a curve showing all the different quantities of two inputs that are just sufficient to produce a given quantity of output.

Figure 10 represents different quantities of labor and capital capable of producing given amounts of wheat. The figure shows three indifference curves: one for the production of 220,000 bushels of wheat, one for 240,000 bushels, and one for 260,000 bushels. The indifference curve labeled 220,000 bushels indicates that a farm can generate an output of 220,000 bushels of wheat using *any one* of the combinations of inputs represented by points on that curve. For example, it can employ ten years of labor and 200 acres of land (point *A*) or the labor–land combination shown by point *B* on the same curve. Because it lies considerably below and to the right of point *B*, point *A* represents a productive process that uses more labor and less land.

Points *A* and *B* can be considered *technologically* indifferent because each represents a bundle of inputs just capable of yielding the same quantity of finished goods. However, the word "indifference" in this sense does not mean that the producer will be unable to decide between input combinations *A* and *B*. Input prices will permit the producer to arrive at a decision.

The production indifference curves in a diagram such as Figure 10 show for each combination of inputs how much output can be produced. Because production indifference curves are drawn in two dimensions, they represent only two inputs at a time. In more realistic situations, firms are likely to need more than two inputs, so, to study the subject, economists must conduct an algebraic analysis. Even so, all the principles we need to analyze such a situation can be derived from the two-variable case.

■ CHARACTERISTICS OF THE PRODUCTION INDIFFERENCE CURVES, OR ISOQUANTS

Before discussing input pricing and quantity decisions, we first examine what is known about the shapes of production indifference curves.

Characteristic 1: *Higher curves correspond to larger outputs.* Points on a higher indifference curve represent larger quantities of *both* inputs than the corresponding points on a lower curve. Thus, a higher curve represents a larger output.

Characteristic 2: *An indifference curve will generally have a negative slope.* It goes downhill as we move toward the right. Thus, if a firm reduces the quantity of one input, and if it does not want to cut production, it must use more of another input.

Characteristic 3: *An indifference curve is typically assumed to curve inward toward the origin near its middle.* This shape reflects the "law" of diminishing returns to a single input. For example, in Figure 10, points *B*, *D*, and *A* represent three different input combinations

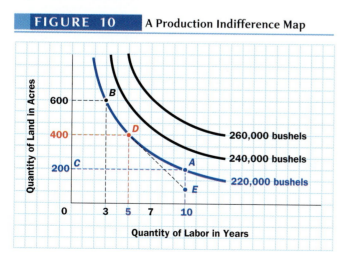

FIGURE 10   A Production Indifference Map

capable of producing the same quantity of output. At point *B*, the firm uses a large amount of land and relatively little labor, whereas the opposite is true at point *A*. Point *D* is intermediate between the two.

Now consider the choice among these input combinations. When the farmer considers moving from point *B* to point *D*, he gives up 200 acres of land and instead hires two additional years of labor. Similarly, the move from *D* to *A* involves giving up another 200 acres of land. This time, however, hiring an additional two years of labor does not make up for the reduced use of land. Diminishing returns to labor as the farmer hires more and more workers to replace more and more land means that the farm now needs a much larger quantity of additional labor—five person-years rather than two—to make up for the reduction in the use of land. Without such diminishing returns, the indifference curve would have been a straight line, *DE*. The curvature of the indifference curve through points *D* and *A* reflects diminishing returns to substitution of inputs.

■ THE CHOICE OF INPUT COMBINATIONS

A production indifference curve describes only the input combinations that *can* produce a given output; it indicates just what is technologically possible. To decide which of the available options suits its purposes best, a business needs the corresponding cost information: the relative prices of the inputs.

The **budget line** in Figure 11 represents all equally costly input combinations for a firm. For example, if farmhands are paid $9,000 per year and land rents for $1,000 per acre per year, then a farmer who spends $360,000 can hire 40 farmhands but rent no land (point *K*), or he can rent 360 acres but have no money left for farmhands (point *J*). It is undoubtedly more sensible to

pick some intermediate point on his budget line at which he divides the $360,000 between the two inputs. The slope of the budget line represents the amount of land the farmer must give up if he wants to hire one more worker without increasing his budget.

> A budget line is the locus of all points representing every input combination of inputs that the producer can afford to buy with a given amount of money and given input prices.

If the prices of the inputs do not change, then the slope of the budget line will not change anywhere in the graph. It will be the same at every point on a given budget line, and it will be the same on the $360,000 budget line as on the $400,000 budget line or on the budget line for any other level of spending. For if the price of hiring a worker is nine times as high as the cost of renting an acre, then the farmer must rent nine fewer acres to hire an additional farmhand without changing the total amount of money he spends on these inputs. Thus, the slope will be acres given up per added farmhand = −9/1 = −9.

So, with the input prices given, the slope of any budget line does not change and the slopes of the different budget lines for different amounts of expenditures are all the same. Two results follow: (1) the budget lines are straight lines because their slopes remain the same throughout their length, and (2) because they all have the same slope, the budget lines in the graph will all be parallel, as in Figure 12.

A firm that is seeking to minimize costs does not necessarily have a fixed budget. Instead, it wants to produce a given quantity of output (say, 240,000 bushels) with *the smallest possible budget.*

Figure 12 combines the indifference curve for 240,000 bushels from Figure 10 with a variety of budget lines similar to *JK* in Figure 11. The firm's task is to find the

---

FIGURE 11   A Budget Line

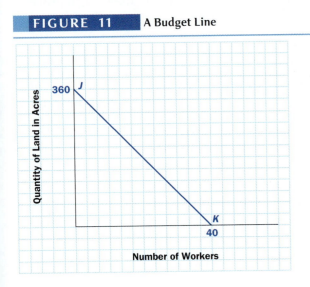

FIGURE 12   Cost Minimization

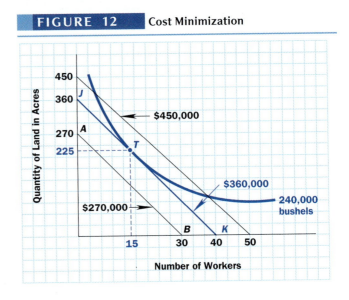

lowest budget line that will allow it to reach the 240,000-bushel indifference curve. Clearly, an expenditure of $270,000 is too little; no point on the budget line, *AB*, permits production of 240,000 bushels. Similarly, an expenditure of $450,000 is too much, because the firm can produce its target level of output more cheaply. The solution is at point *T* where the farmer uses 15 workers and 225 acres of land to produce the 240,000 bushels of wheat. That budget line, the one that is tangent to the relevant indifference curve, is evidently the lowest budget line that meets the indifference curve anywhere, so it represents the lowest-cost input combination capable of producing the desired output. In general:

> The least costly way to produce any given level of output is indicated by the point of tangency between a budget line and the production indifference curve corresponding to that level of output.

■ COST MINIMIZATION, EXPANSION PATH, AND COST CURVES

Figure 12 shows how to determine the input combination that minimizes the cost of producing 240,000 bushels of output. The farmer can repeat this procedure exactly for any other output quantity, such as 200,000 bushels or 300,000 bushels. In each case, we draw the corresponding production indifference curve and find the lowest budget line that permits the farm to produce that much. For example, in Figure 13, budget line *BB* is tangent to the indifference curve for 200,000 units of output; similarly, budget line *JK* is tangent to the indifference curve for 240,000 bushels; and budget line *B'B'* is tangent to the indifference curve for 300,000 units of output. This gives us three tangency points: *S*, which gives the input combination that produces a 200,000-bushel output at lowest cost; *T*, which gives the same information for a 240,000-bushel output; and *S'*, which indicates the cost-minimizing input combination for the production of 300,000 bushels.

This process can be repeated for as many other levels of output as we like. For each such output we draw the corresponding production indifference curve and find its point of tangency with a budget line. The blue curve *EE* in Figure 13 connects all of the cost-minimizing points; that is, it is the locus of *S*, *T*, *S'*, and all other points of tangency between a production indifference curve and a budget line. Curve *EE* is called the firm's **expansion path.**

> The expansion path is the locus of the firm's cost-minimizing input combinations for all relevant output levels.

Point *T* in Figure 12 shows the quantity of output (given by the production indifference curve through that point) and the total cost (shown by the tangent budget line). Similarly, we can determine the output and total cost for every other point on the expansion path, *EE*, in Figure 13. For example, at point *S*, output is 200,000 bushels and total cost is $270,000. These data are precisely the sort of information we need to find the firm's total cost curve; that is, they are just the sort of information contained in Table 3, which is the source of the total cost curve and the average and marginal cost curves in Figure 4. Thus:

> The points of tangency between a firm's production indifference curves and its budget lines yield its expansion path, which shows the firm's cost-minimizing input combination for each pertinent output level. This information also yields the output and total cost for each point on the expansion path, which is just what we need to draw the firm's cost curves.

Suppose that the cost of renting land increases and the wage rate of labor decreases. These changes mean that the budget lines will differ from those depicted in Figure 12. Specifically, with land becoming more expensive, any given sum of money will rent fewer acres, so the intercept of each budget line on the vertical (land) axis will shift *downward*. Conversely, with cheaper labor, any given sum of money will buy more labor, so the intercept of the budget line on the horizontal (labor) axis will shift to the *right*. Figure 14 depicts a series of budget lines corresponding to a $1,500 per acre rental rate for land and a $6,000 annual wage for labor. If input prices change, the combination of inputs that minimizes costs will normally change. In this diagram, the land rent at $1,500 per acre is more than it was in Figure 12, whereas labor costs $6,000 per year (less than in Figure 12). As a result, these budget lines are less steep than those shown in Figure 12, and point *E* now represents the least costly way to produce 240,000 bushels of wheat.

To assist you in seeing how things change, Figure 15 combines, in a single graph, budget line *JK* and tangency

| FIGURE 13 | The Firm's Expansion Path |

FIGURE 14 Optimal Input Choice at a Different Set of Input Prices

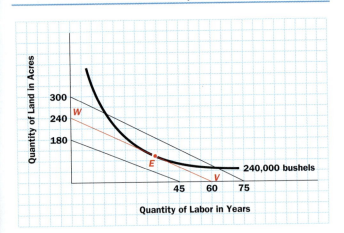

FIGURE 15 How Changes in Input Prices Affect Input Proportions

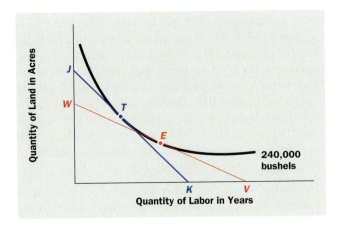

point T from Figure 12 with budget line WV and tangency point E from Figure 14. When land becomes more expensive and labor becomes cheaper, the budget lines (such as JK) become less steep than they were previously (see WV). As a result, the least costly way to produce 240,000 bushels shifts from point T to point E, at which the firm uses more labor and less land. As common sense

suggests, when the price of one input rises in comparison with that of another, it will pay the firm to use less of the more expensive input and more of the other input.

In addition to substituting one input for another, a change in the price of an input may induce the firm to alter its level of output. We will cover this subject in the next chapter.

SUMMARY

1. A production relationship can be described by a series of **production indifference curves**, each of which shows all input combinations capable of producing a specified amount of output.

2. As long as each input has a positive marginal physical product, production indifference curves will have negative slopes and the higher curves will represent larger amounts of output than the lower curves. Because of diminishing returns, these curves characteristically bend toward the origin near the middle.

3. The optimal input combination for any given level of output is indicated by the point of tangency between a **budget line** and the corresponding production indifference curve.

4. The firm's **expansion path** shows, for each of its possible output levels, the combination of input quantities that minimizes the cost of producing that output.

5. Total cost for each output level can be derived from the production indifference curves and the budget lines tangent to them along the expansion path. These figures can be used to determine the firm's total cost, average cost, and marginal cost curves.

6. When input prices change, firms will normally use more of the input that becomes relatively less expensive and less of the input that becomes relatively more expensive.

KEY TERMS

TEST YOURSELF

1. Compound Consolidated Corporation (CCC) produces containers using two inputs: labor and glue. If labor costs $10 per hour and glue costs $5 per gallon, draw CCC's budget line for a total expenditure of $100,000. In this same diagram, sketch a production indifference curve indicating that CCC can produce no more than 1,000 containers with this expenditure.

2. With respect to Test Yourself Question 1, suppose that wages rise to $20 per hour and glue prices rise to $6 per gallon. How are CCC's optimal input proportions likely to change? (Use a diagram to explain your answer.)

3. What happens to the location of the expansion path of the firm in Test Yourself Question 2?

OUTPUT, PRICE, AND PROFIT: THE IMPORTANCE OF MARGINAL ANALYSIS

Business is a good game. . . . You keep score with money.

NOLAN BUSHNELL, FOUNDER OF ATARI (AN EARLY VIDEO GAME MAKER)

Suppose you become president of a firm that makes video games. One of your most critical decisions will be how many video games to produce and at what price to offer them for sale. The owners of the company want to make as much profit as possible. This chapter explores the logic underlying the decisions that lead to achievement of this goal.

With this chapter, we cap off our discussion of the fundamental building blocks of microeconomics. Chapters 5 and 6 dealt with the behavior of consumers. Then Chapter 7 introduced the other main participant in microeconomics, the firm. The firm's two main roles are, first, to produce its product efficiently and, second, to sell that product at a profit. Chapter 7 described production decisions. Now we turn to the selling decisions. Then, in Chapter 9, we will discuss stocks and bonds as instruments that enable business firms to obtain the money to finance their activities and as an earnings opportunity for individuals who consider investing in firms.

Throughout Part II, we have described how firms and consumers can make *optimal decisions*, meaning that their decisions go as far as possible, given the circumstances, to promote the consumer's and producer's goals. In this chapter, we will continue to assume that business firms seek primarily to maximize total profit, just as we assumed that consumers maximize utility. (See the box, "Do Firms Really Maximize Profits?" on the following page, for a discussion of other objectives of business firms.)

CONTENTS

Do Firms Really Maximize Profits?

Naturally, many people question whether firms really try to maximize profits to the exclusion of all other goals. But businesspeople are like other human beings: Their motives are varied and complex. Given the choice, many executives may prefer to control the *largest* firm rather than the most profitable one. Some may be fascinated by technology and therefore spend so much on research and development that it cuts down on profit. Some may want to "do good" and therefore give away some of the stockholders' money to hospitals and colleges. Different managers within the same firm may not always agree with one another on goals, so that it may not even make sense to speak about "the" goal of the firm. Thus, any attempt to summarize the objectives of management in terms of a single number (profit) is bound to be an oversimplification.

In addition, the exacting requirements for maximizing profits are tough to satisfy. In deciding how much to invest, what price to set for a product, or how much to allocate to the advertising budget, the range of available alternatives is enormous. Also, information about each alternative is often expensive and difficult to acquire. As a result, when a firm's management decides on, say, an $18 million construction budget, it rarely compares the consequences of that decision in any detail with the consequences of all possible alternatives—such as budgets of $17 million or $19 million. But unless all the available possibilities are compared, management cannot be sure that it has chosen the one that brings in the highest possible profit.

Often, management's concern is whether the decision's results are likely to be acceptable—whether its risks will be acceptably low, whether its profits will be acceptably high—so that the company can live satisfactorily with the outcome. Such analysis cannot be expected to bring in the maximum possible profit. The decision may be good, but some unexplored alternative may be even better.

Decision making that seeks only solutions that are acceptable has been called *satisficing*, to contrast it with optimizing (profit maximization). Some analysts, such as the late Nobel Prize winner Herbert Simon of Carnegie-Mellon University, have concluded that decision making in industry and government is often of the satisficing variety.

Even if this assertion is true, it does not necessarily make profit maximization a bad assumption. Recall our discussion of abstraction and model building in Chapter 1. A map of Los Angeles that omits hundreds of roads is no doubt "wrong" if interpreted as a literal description of the city. Nonetheless, by capturing the most important elements of reality, it may help us understand the city better than a map that is cluttered with too much detail. Similarly, we can learn much about the behavior of business firms by assuming that they try to maximize profits, even though we know that not all of them act this way all of the time.

"It's true that more is not necessarily better, Edward, but it frequently is."

An optimal decision is one which, among all the decisions that are actually possible, best achieves the decision maker's goals. For example, if profit is the sole objective of some firm, the price that makes the firm's profit as large as possible is optimal for that company.

As in the previous three chapters, marginal analysis helps us to determine what constitutes an **optimal decision.** Because that method of analysis is so useful, this chapter summarizes and generalizes what we have learned about the methods of marginal analysis, showing also how this analysis applies in many other situations in which optimality is an issue.

Marginal analysis leads to some surprising conclusions that show how misleading unaided "common sense" can sometimes be. Here's an example. Suppose a firm suffers a sharp increase in its rent or some other fixed cost. How should the firm react? Some would argue that the firm should raise the price of its product to cover the higher rent; others would argue that it should cut its price so as to increase its sales enough to pay the increased rent. We will see in this chapter that both of these answers are incorrect! A profit-maximizing firm faced with a rent increase should neither raise nor lower its price if it does not want to reduce its net earnings.

PUZZLE: *Can a Company Make a Profit by Selling Below its Costs?*

Price and output decisions can sometimes perplex even the most experienced businesspeople. The following real-life illustration seems to show that it is possible for a firm to make a profit by selling at a price that is apparently below its cost.[1]

In a recent legal battle between two manufacturers of pocket calculators, Company B accused Company A of selling ten million sophisticated calculators at a price of $12, which Company A allegedly knew was too low to cover costs. Company B claimed that Company A was cutting its price simply to drive Company B out of business. At first, Company A's records, as revealed to the court, appeared to confirm Company B's accusations. The cost of materials, labor, advertising, and other direct costs of the calculators came to $10.30 per calculator. Company A's accountants also assigned to this product its share of the company's annual expenditure on overhead—such items as general administration, research, and the like—which amounted to $4.25 per calculator. The $12 price clearly did not cover the $14.55 cost attributed to each calculator. Yet economists representing Company A were able to convince the court that, at the $10.30 price, manufacturing the calculator was a profitable activity for Company A, so there was no basis on which to conclude that its only purpose was to destroy B. At the end of the chapter, we'll see how ordinary good sense is not necessarily the best guide in business decisions and how marginal analysis helped solve this problem.

■ PRICE AND QUANTITY: ONE DECISION, NOT TWO

When your company introduces a new line of video games, the marketing department has to decide what price to charge and how many games to produce. These crucial decisions strongly influence the firm's labor requirements, the consumer response to the product, and, indeed, the company's future success.

When the firm selects a *price* and a *quantity* of output that maximize profits, it seems that it must choose two numbers. In fact, however, the firm can pick only one. Once it has selected the *price*, the *quantity* it can sell is up to consumers. Alternatively, the firm may decide how many units it would like to sell, but then the market will determine the *price* at which this quantity can be sold. The firm's dilemma explicitly illustrates the powerful role that consumers play in the market. Management gets two numbers by making only one decision because the firm's demand curve tells it, for any quantity it may decide to market, the highest possible price its product can bring.

To illustrate, we return to Chapter 7's garage-building example. Al's Building Contractors sells garages to individual home owners, and Al is trying to figure out how best to make money on his building operation. To do this, he must estimate his *firm's demand curve*. The firm's demand curve is different from the demand curves we encountered in earlier chapters—the demand curve of an individual consumer and the market demand curve (which is the combined demand of all consumers in the market). Now we are dealing with a single firm (Al's Building Contractors) that is only one among possibly many firms that serve the market. The demand curve of any one supplier depends on the number and activities of the other firms in the market, as each competes for its share of total market demand. The demand curve of a single firm is actually a complicated matter that we will deal with several times in subsequent chapters.[2] For now, suffice it to say that Al's demand curve will lie closer to the market demand curve (meaning that

---

[1] The following case is disguised to protect the confidentiality of the firms involved.

[2] In one case, the relation between market demand and firm demand is very easy. That is the case where the firm has no competitors—it is a *monopoly*. Since it has the entire market to itself, its demand curve and the market demand curve are one and the same. We deal with monopoly in Chapter 11. Another fairly straightforward case, called perfect competition, will be studied in Chapter 10.

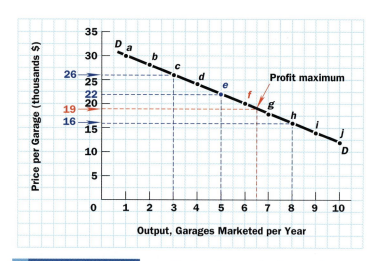

FIGURE 1

Demand Curve for Al's
Garages

Each point on the demand curve represents a price–quantity pair. The firm can pick any such pair. It can never pick the price corresponding to one point on the demand curve and the quantity corresponding to another point, however, because such an output cannot be sold at the selected price.

Al has a greater share of the market), the better his service, the more effective his advertising, the stronger his reputation for quality, and so on.

Suppose Al faces the demand curve for his garages shown as *DD* in Figure 1. The curve depicts the quantity demanded at each price. For example, the curve shows that at a price of $22,000 per garage (point *e*), Al's customers will demand five garages. If Al gets greedy and tries to charge the higher price of $26,000 per garage (point *c* on the curve), he can sell only three garages. If he wants to sell eight garages, he can find the required number of customers only by offering the garages at the lower price of $16,000 each (point *b*). In summary:

For this reason, we will not discuss price and output decisions separately throughout this chapter, for they are actually two different aspects of the same decision. To analyze this decision, we will make an imperfectly realistic assumption about the behavior of business firms—the assumption that firms strive for the largest possible total profit to the exclusion of any other goal. We will therefore assume throughout this chapter (and for most of the book) that the firm has only one objective: It wants to make its total profit as large as possible. Our analytic strategy will seek to determine what output level (or price) achieves this goal. But you should keep in mind that many of our results depend on this simplifying assumption, so the conclusions will not apply to every case. Our decision to base the analysis on the profit-maximizing assumption gives us sharper insights, but we pay for it with some loss of realism.

The **total profit** of a firm is its net earnings during some period of time. It is equal to the total amount of money the firm gets from sales of its products (the firm's total revenue) minus the total amount that it spends to make and market those products (total cost).

TOTAL PROFIT: KEEP YOUR EYE ON THE GOAL

Total profit, then, is the firm's assumed goal. By definition, total profit is the difference between what the company earns in the form of sales revenue and what it pays out in the form of costs:

Total profit = Total revenue − Total cost (including opportunity cost)

IDEAS FOR
BEYOND THE
FINAL EXAM

OPPORTUNITY COST AND PROFIT   Total profit defined in this way is called economic profit to distinguish it from an accountant's definition of profit. The two concepts of profit differ because an economist's total cost counts the *opportunity cost* of any capital, labor, or other inputs supplied by the firm's owner. For example, let's say that Naomi, who owns a small business, earns just enough to pay her the money that her labor and capital could have earned if they had been sold to others (say, $60,000 per year). Then, as we saw in Chapter 3, economists say that she is earning zero economic profit. (Naomi is just covering all her costs, including her opportunity costs.) In contrast, most accountants would say her profit is $60,000, referring to the difference between her gross receipts and her gross costs.

ECONOMIC PROFIT AND OPTIMAL DECISION MAKING

Why do economists use this apparently strange definition of profits, in which they subtract not only the costs that would ordinarily be deducted from total revenue, but also the opportunity costs? The answer is that doing so tells us directly whether the firm has made an *optimal* decision, in other words, whether the firm has chosen the price and quantity that maximizes profits. Specifically:

1. If economic profit is positive, then the firm's decisions are optimal; that is, its price and output yield a profit larger than any alternative prices and outputs.
2. If economic profit is zero, then the firm's choices are still satisfactory, because its price and output yield as much profit as the best available alternative.
3. If economic profit is negative, then the choice is not optimal; there exists at least one alternative price-output combination that is more profitable.

This reasoning explains why we pay so much attention to opportunity cost: because it helps us to determine whether or not a decision is optimal. And it works for all decisions, not only those about prices and quantities. But how does it do so? An example will make it clear. Suppose a firm has $100,000 to spend on either packaging or advertising. Suppose further that if the $100,000 is spent on packaging, it will bring in an accounting profit (that is, a profit as ordinarily defined: total revenue minus total ordinary cost, leaving out opportunity cost) of $20,000. If, instead, the (accounting) profit it could obtain from a $100,000 investment in advertising is $X, then by definition, $X is the opportunity cost of the decision to invest in packaging. In other words, $X is the earnings that could have been obtained from the alternative opportunity that the firm gives up by investing in packaging. So, for that decision:

Economic **profit = Accounting profit − opportunity cost = $20,000 − $X.**

This immediately illustrates our three conclusions above, because:

1. If $X < $20,000, then economic profit > 0, and packaging is the more profitable investment choice,
2. If $X = $20,000, then economic profit = 0, and the two investment options are equally profitable, and
3. If $X > $20,000, then the economic profit of packaging ($20,000 − $X) is negative, and advertising is a more profitable investment than packaging.

The reason economic profit performs this test is simple:

Economic profit of the decision in question = its accounting profit − its opportunity cost = accounting profit of the decision in question − accounting profit of the best available alternative. So, the economic profit of the decision in question will be positive only if it is more profitable (in the accountant's measurement) than the alternative, and so on.

Economic profit equals net earnings, in the accountant's sense, minus the *opportunity costs* of capital and of any other inputs supplied by the firm's owners.

◼ Total, Average, and Marginal Revenue

To see how total profit depends on output, we must study how the two components of total profit, total revenue (TR) and total cost (TC), behave when output changes. It should be obvious that both total revenue and total cost depend on the output–price combination the firm selects; we will study these relationships presently.

We can calculate **total revenue** directly from the firm's demand curve because, by definition, it is the product of price times the quantity that consumers will buy at that price:

$$TR = P \times Q$$

The **total revenue** of a supplier firm is the total amount of money it receives from the purchasers of its products, without any deduction of costs.

Table 1 shows how we derive the total revenue schedule from the demand schedule for Al's garages. The first two columns simply express Figure 1's demand curve in tabular form. The third column gives, for each quantity, the product of price times quantity. For example, if Al sells seven garages at a price of $18,000 per garage, his annual sales revenue will be 7 garages × $18,000 per garage = $126,000.

Figure 2 displays Al's total revenue schedule in graphic form as the black TR curve. This graph shows precisely the same information as the demand curve in Figure 1,

TABLE 1

Demand for Al's Garages: His Total Revenue Schedule, and His Marginal Revenue Schedule

(1)	(2)	(3)	(4)
	Price = Average Revenue per Garage (in thousands)	Total Revenue per Year (in thousands)	Marginal Revenue per Added Garage (in thousands)
Garages per Year			
0	—	$ 0	
1	$30	30	$30
2	28	56	26
3	26	78	22
4	24	96	18
5	22	110	14
6	20	120	10
7	18	126	6
8	16	128	2
9	14	126	−2
10	12	120	−6

The **average revenue (AR)** is total revenue (TR) divided by quantity.

Marginal revenue (MR) is the addition to total revenue resulting from the addition of one unit to total output. Geometrically, marginal revenue is the slope of the total revenue curve at the pertinent output quantity. Its formula is $MR_1 = TR_1 - TR_0$, and so on.

but in a somewhat different form. For example, point f on the demand curve in Figure 1, which shows a price–quantity combination of $P = \$20,000$ per garage and $Q = 6$ garages per year, appears as point F in Figure 2 as a total revenue of $120,000 per year ($20,000 per garage × 6 garages). Similarly, each other point on the TR curve in Figure 2 corresponds to the similarly labeled point in Figure 1.

We can speak of the relationship between the demand curve and the TR curve in a slightly different and more useful way than that shown in Figure 1. Because the product price is the revenue per unit that the firm receives, we can view the demand curve as an **average revenue (AR)** curve. To see why this is so, observe that average revenue and total revenue are, by definition, related to one another by the formula $AR = TR/Q$ and, as we have seen, $TR = P \times Q$. Therefore,[3]

$$AR = TR/Q = P \times Q/Q = P$$

As you can see, average revenue and price are just different names for the same thing. The reason should be clear. If a supermarket sells candy bars *at the same price*—say, $1—to each and every customer who wants one, then the average revenue that the store derives from each sale of these candy bars must also be $1.

Finally, the last column of Table 1 shows the **marginal revenue (MR)** for each level of output. Marginal revenue provides us with an analytic tool that we will explain presently. This concept (analogous to marginal utility and marginal cost) refers to the *addition* to total revenue that results from raising output by one unit. Thus, in Table 1, we see that when output rises from two to three garages, total revenue goes up from $56,000 to $78,000, so marginal revenue is $78,000 minus $56,000, or $22,000.

Total, Average, and Marginal Cost

The revenue side is, of course, only half of the firm's profit picture. We must turn to the cost side for the other half. As we saw in Chapter 7, average cost (AC) and marginal cost (MC) are obtained directly from total cost (TC) in exactly the same way

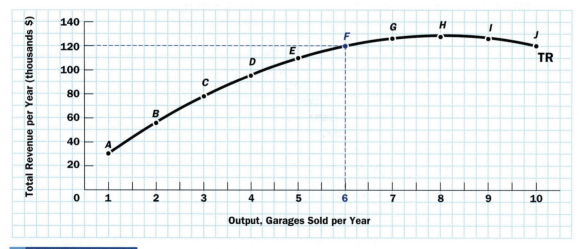

FIGURE 2

Total Revenue Curve for Al's Garages

[3] See the appendix to this chapter for a general discussion of the relationship between totals and averages.

TABLE 2

Al's Total, Average, and Marginal Costs

(1) Garages per Year	(2) Total Cost per Year (in thousands)	(3) Marginal Cost per Added Garage (in thousands)	(4) Average Cost per Garage (in thousands)
0	$ 12		—
		$28	
1	40		$40
		16	
2	56		28
		10	
3	66		22
		8	
4	74		18.5
		6	
5	80		16
		7	
6	87		14.5
		9	
7	96		13.7 (approx.)
		16	
8	112		14
		32	
9	144		16
		46	
10	190		19

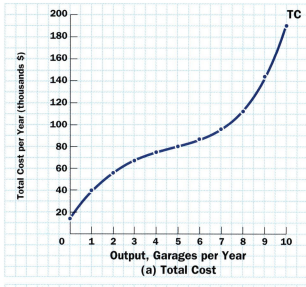

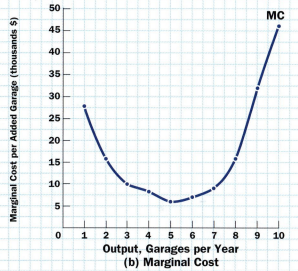

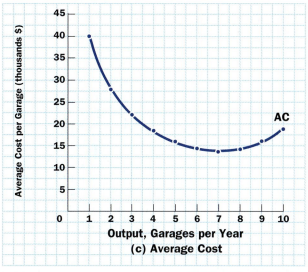

NOTE: Output is in garages per year.

that average and marginal revenue are calculated from total revenue.

Figure 3 plots the numbers in Table 2 and thus shows the total, average, and marginal cost curves for Al's garage-building operation. As we learned in Chapter 7, the U-shapes of the average cost and marginal cost curves depicted here are considered typical. The shapes mean that, in any given industry, there is some size of firm that is most efficient in producing the output. Smaller enterprises lose any advantages that derive from a large volume of production, and so their average cost (the cost per unit of output) will be greater than that of a firm operating at the most efficient size of output. Similarly, firms that are too large will suffer from difficulties of supervision and coordination, and perhaps from bureaucratic controls, so that their costs per unit of output will also be higher than those of a firm of the most efficient size.

■ Maximization of Total Profit

We now have all the tools we need to answer our central question: What combination of output and price will yield the largest possible total profit? To study how total profit depends on output, Table 3 brings together the total revenue and total cost schedules from Tables 1 and 2. The fourth column in Table 3—called, appropriately enough, total profit—is just the difference between total revenue and total cost at each level of output.

Because we assume that Al's objective is to maximize profits, it is simple enough to determine the level of production he will choose. The table indicates that by producing and selling six garages per year, Al's garage-building operation earns the highest level of profits it is capable of earning—$33,000 per year (actually, we will see

FIGURE 3

Cost Curves for Al's Garages

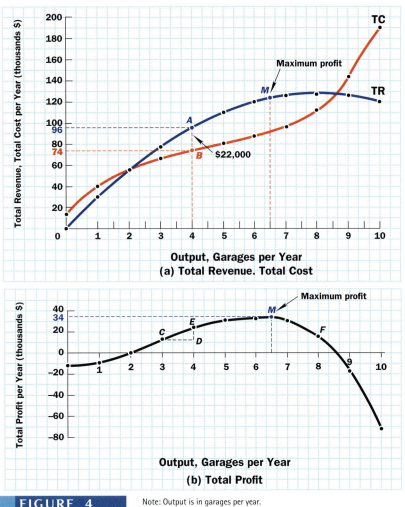

FIGURE 4

Profit Maximization:
A Graphical
Interpretation

Note: Output is in garages per year.

TABLE 3

Total Revenues, Costs, and Profit for Al's Garages

(1)	(2)	(3)	(4)	(5)
Garages per Year	Total Revenue (TR) (in thousands)	Total Cost (TC) (in thousands)	Total Profit (TR − TC) (in thousands)	Marginal Profit (in thousands)
0	$ 0	$ 12	$−12	$ 2
1	30	40	−10	10
2	56	56	0	12
3	78	66	12	10
4	96	74	22	8
5	110	80	30	3
6	120	87	33	−3
7	126	96	30	−14
8	128	112	16	−34
9	126	144	−18	−52
10	120	190	−70	

in a moment that it pays Al to produce a little more than this amount). Any higher or lower rate of production would lead to lower profits. For example, profits would drop to $30,000 if output were increased to seven garages. If Al were to make the mistake of producing ten garages per season, he would actually suffer a net loss.

■ Profit Maximization: A Graphical Interpretation

We can present the same information on a graph. In Panel (a) of Figure 4, we bring together into a single diagram the relevant portion of the total revenue curve from Figure 2 and the total cost curve from Figure 3. Total profit, which is the difference between total revenue and total cost, appears in the diagram as the vertical distance between the TR and TC curves. For example, when output is four garages, total revenue is $96,000 (point *A*), total cost is $74,000 (point *B*), and total profit is the distance between points *A* and *B*, or $22,000.

In this graphical view of the problem, Al wants to maximize total profit, which is the vertical distance between the TR and TC curves. Panel (b) of Figure 4 plots these vertical differences derived from Panel (a) and so it shows the curve of total profit—that is, TR − TC. We see that it reaches its maximum value of about $34,000 (point M) at an output level of six and one-half garages per year—that is, 13 garages every two years. This graph shows that the conclusion we reached by looking at Table 3 was approximately right, but not perfectly accurate. Why? Because the table did not consider the possibility that the labor and material it pays Al to acquire may make it profitable to start on the construction of yet another garage after the first six are completed, with this garage being finished in the next year. We will consider this possibility in more detail in a few paragraphs.

The total profit curve in Figure 4(b) is shaped like a hill. Although such a shape is not inevitable, we expect a hill shape to be typical for the following reason: If a firm produces nothing, it certainly earns no profit. At the other extreme, a firm can produce so much output that it swamps the market, forcing price down so low that it loses money. Only at intermediate levels of output—something between zero and the amount that floods the market—will the company earn a positive profit. Consequently, the total profit curve will rise from zero (or negative) levels at a very small output to positive levels at intermediate outputs; finally, it will fall to negative levels when output gets too large.

■ MARGINAL ANALYSIS AND MAXIMIZATION OF TOTAL PROFIT

We see from Figure 4 and Table 3 that many levels of output may yield a positive profit, but the firm is not aiming for just any level of profit. Instead, it wants the largest possible profit. If management knew the exact shape of its profit hill, choosing the optimal level of output would be a simple task indeed. It would merely have to locate the point, such as *M* in Figure 4(b), that defined the top of its profit hill. However, management rarely, if ever, has so much information, so a different technique for finding the optimum is required. That technique is marginal analysis—the same set of tools we used to analyze the firm's input purchase decisions in Chapter 7 and the consumer's buying decisions in Chapters 5 and 6.

This time we will use a concept known as **marginal profit** to solve Al's problem. Referring back to Table 3, we see that an increase in Al's output from three to four garages would raise total profit from $12,000 to $22,000; that is, it would generate $10,000 in additional profit, as shown in the last column of Table 3. We call this amount the marginal profit resulting from the addition of the fourth garage. Similarly, marginal profit from the seventh garage would be:

Marginal profit is the addition to total profit resulting from one more unit of output.

Total profit from 7 garages − Total profit from 6 garages =
$30,000 − $33,000 = −$3,000

The marginal rule for finding the optimal level of output is easy to understand:

If the marginal profit from increasing output by one unit is positive, then output should be increased. If the marginal profit from increasing output by one unit is negative, then output should be decreased. Thus, an output level can maximize total profit only if marginal profit is neither positive nor negative—that is, if it equals zero at that output.

For Al's Building Contractors, the marginal profit from the sixth unit of output (a sixth garage) is $3,000. This means that building six garages is not enough. Because marginal profit is still positive at six garages per year, it pays to produce more than six garages per year. However, marginal profit from the seventh garage is $30,000 −$33,000, or −$3,000, so the firm should produce less than seven garages because production of the seventh garage would reduce total profit by $3,000. Only at something between six and seven garages, where marginal profit is neither positive nor negative (as is approximately true for 6.5 garages), can total profit be as big as possible, because neither increasing nor reducing output can add to total profit.

The marginal profit numbers in Table 3 indicate one way in which marginal analysis helps to improve decisions. If we had looked only at the total profit figures in the fourth column of the table, we

SOURCE: © Royalty-Free/Corbis

might have concluded that six garages is the profit-maximizing output for Al. The marginal profit column (column 5) tells us that this is not so. We see that the marginal profit of a seventh garage is −$3,000, so Al should, indeed, produce fewer than seven garages per year. But *the marginal profit of the sixth garage is +$3,000, so it pays Al to produce **more** than six garages.* Thus, a production level somewhere between six and seven garages per year really maximizes profits, as the total profit graph confirms.

The profit hill in Figure 4(b) is a graphical representation of the condition stating that to maximize profit, marginal profit should be zero (or as close to zero as possible). Marginal profit is defined as the additional profit that accrues to the firm when output rises by one unit. For example, when output is increased, say, from three units to four units, or the distance *CD* in Figure 4(b), total profit rises by $10,000 (the distance *DE*) and marginal profit is therefore *DE/CD* (see the triangle *CDE* in the graph). This is precisely the definition of the slope of the total profit curve between points *C* and *E*. In general:

Marginal profit at any output is the slope of the total profit curve at that level of output.

With this geometric interpretation in hand, we can easily understand the logic of the marginal profit rule. At a point such as *C* in Figure 4(b), where the total profit curve is rising, marginal profit (which equals slope) is positive. Profit cannot be maximal at such a point, because we can increase profits by moving farther to the right. A firm that decided to stick to point *C* would be wasting the opportunity to increase profits by increasing output. Similarly, the firm cannot be maximizing profits at a point such as *F*, where the slope of the curve is negative, because there marginal profit (which, again, equals slope) is negative. If it finds itself at a point such as *F*, the firm can raise its profit by decreasing its output.

Only at a point such as *M* in Figure 4(b), where the total profit curve is neither rising nor falling, can the firm possibly be at the top of the profit hill rather than on one of the sides of the hill. Point *M* is precisely where the slope of the curve—and hence the marginal profit—is zero. Thus:

An output decision cannot be optimal unless the corresponding marginal profit is zero.

It is important to recognize that the firm is *not* interested in marginal profit for its own sake, but rather for what it implies about total profit. Marginal profit is like the needle on the temperature gauge of a car: The needle itself is of no concern to anyone, but failure to watch it can have dire consequences.

One common misunderstanding about marginal analysis is the idea that it seems foolish to go to a point where marginal profit is zero. "Isn't it better to earn a positive marginal profit?" This notion springs from a confusion between the quantity one is seeking to maximize (total profit) and the gauge that indicates whether such a maximum has actually been attained (marginal profit). Of course, it is better to have a positive *total* profit than a zero total profit. In contrast, a zero value on the marginal profit gauge merely indicates that all is well—that total profit is at its maximum.

IDEAS FOR BEYOND THE FINAL EXAM

THE IMPORTANCE OF THINKING AT THE MARGIN   *Marginal Analysis*: You are likely to have noticed a recurrent theme in this chapter, which is a cornerstone of any economic analysis and thus one of our *Ideas for Beyond the Final Exam*. In any decision about whether to expand an activity, it is always the marginal cost and marginal benefit that are the relevant factors. A calculation based on average data is likely to lead the decision maker to miss all sorts of opportunities, some of them critical.

More generally, if one wants to make optimal decisions, marginal analysis should be used in the planning calculations. This is true whether the decision applies to a business firm seeking to maximize total profit or minimize the cost of the output it has selected, to a consumer trying to maximize utility, or to a less-developed country striving to maximize per-capita output. It applies as much to decisions on input proportions and advertising as to decisions about output levels and prices.

Marginal Revenue and Marginal Cost: Guides to Optimization

An alternative version of the marginal analysis of profit maximization can be derived from the cost and revenue components of profit. For this purpose, refer back to Figure 4, where we used total revenue (TR) and total cost (TC) curves to construct the profit hill. There is another way of finding the profit-maximizing solution.

We want to maximize the firm's profit, which is measured by the vertical distance between the TR and TC curves. This distance, we see, is not maximal at an output level such as three units, because there the two curves are growing farther apart. If we move farther to the right, the vertical distance between them (which is total profit) will increase. Similarly, we have not maximized the vertical distance between TR and TC at an output level such as eight units, because there the two curves are coming closer together. We can add to profit by moving farther to the left (reducing output). The conclusion from the graph, then, is that total profit—the vertical distance between TR and TC—is maximized only when the two curves are neither growing farther apart nor coming closer together—that is, when their slopes are equal (in the case of Al's Building Contractors in Figure 4, at 6.5 garages).

Marginal revenue and marginal cost curves, which we learned about earlier in the chapter, will help us understand this concept better. For precisely the same reason that marginal profit is the slope of the total profit curve, marginal revenue is the slope of the total revenue curve—because it represents the increase in total revenue resulting from the sale of one additional unit. Similarly, marginal cost is equal to the slope of the total cost curve. This interpretation of marginal revenue and marginal cost, respectively, as the slopes of the total revenue and total cost curves permits us to restate the geometric conclusion we have just reached in an economically significant way:

Profit can be maximized only at an output level at which marginal revenue is (approximately) equal to marginal cost. In symbols:

$$MR = MC$$

The logic of the MR = MC rule for profit maximization is straightforward.[4] When MR is not equal to MC, profits cannot possibly be maximized because the firm can increase its profits by either raising or reducing its output. For example, if MR = $22,000 and MC = $10,000 (Table 4), an additional unit of output adds $22,000 to revenues but only $10,000 to costs. Hence, the firm can increase its net profit by $12,000 by producing and selling one more unit. Similarly, if MC exceeds MR, say, MR = $6,000 and MC = $9,000, then the firm loses $3,000 on its marginal unit, so it can add $3,000 to its profit by reducing output by one unit. Only when MR = MC (or comes as close as possible to equaling MC) is it impossible for the firm to add to its profit by changing its output level.

Table 4 reproduces marginal revenue and marginal cost data for Al's Building Contractors from Tables 1 and 2. The table shows, as must be true, that the MR = MC rule leads us to the same conclusion as Figure 4 and Table 3. If he wants to maximize his profits, Al should produce more than six but fewer than seven garages per year. The marginal revenue of the sixth garage is $10,000 ($120,000 from the sale of six garages less $110,000 from the sale of five garages), whereas the marginal cost is only $7,000 ($87,000 − $80,000). Therefore, MR > MC and the firm

TABLE 4		
Al's Marginal Revenue and Marginal Cost		
(1)	(2)	(3)
Garages per Year	Marginal Revenue (in thousands)	Marginal Cost (in thousands)
0	—	—
1	$30	$28
2	26	16
3	22	10
4	18	8
5	14	6
6	10	7
7	6	9
8	2	16
9	−2	32
10	−6	46

---

[4] You may have surmised by now that just as total profit = total revenue − total cost, it must be true that marginal profit = marginal revenue − marginal cost. This is, in fact, correct. It also shows that when marginal profit = 0, we must have MR = MC.

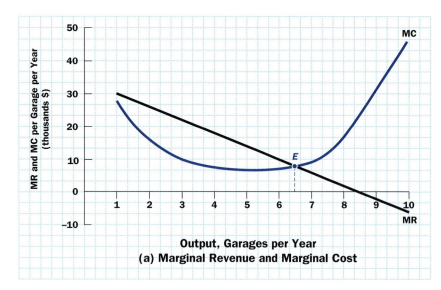

(a) Marginal Revenue and Marginal Cost

Output, Garages per Year

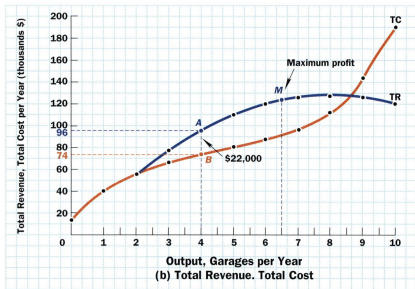

(b) Total Revenue. Total Cost

Output, Garages per Year

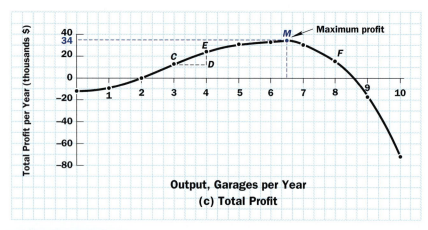

(c) Total Profit

Output, Garages per Year

Note: Output is in garages per year.

FIGURE 5

**Profit Maximization:
Another Graphical
Interpretation**

should produce more than the sixth unit. The seventh garage, however, brings in only $6,000 in marginal revenue and its marginal cost is $9,000—clearly a losing proposition. Only at about six and one-half units of output does MR equal MC *exactly*.

Because the graphs of marginal analysis will prove so useful in later chapters, Figure 5(a) shows the MR = MC condition for profit maximization graphically. The black curve labeled MR in the figure is the marginal revenue schedule from Table 4. The blue curve labeled MC is the marginal cost schedule. The two curves intersect at point *E*, which is therefore the point where marginal revenue and marginal cost are equal. The optimal output for Al is six and one-half units.[5] Panels (b) and (c) in Figure 5, respectively, reproduce the TR and TC curves from Figure 4(a) and the total profit curve from Figure 4(b). Note how MC and MR intersect at the same output at which the distance of TR above TC is greatest, which is also the output at which the profit hill reaches its peak.

■ Finding the Optimal Price from Optimal Output

At the beginning of this chapter, we set two goals: to determine the profit-maximizing output and to find the profit-maximizing price, and emphasized that once we know either of these, it can automatically tell us the other. So far, we have identified the profit-maximizing output, the output level at which MR = MC (6.5 garages per year in our garage-building example). That leaves us with the task of determining the profit-maximizing price.

Fortunately, this task requires only one more easy step. As we said earlier, once the firm has selected the output it wants to produce and sell, the demand curve determines the price it

---

[5] We must note one important qualification. Sometimes marginal revenue and marginal cost curves do not have the nice shapes depicted in Figure 5(a), and they may intersect more than once. In such cases, although it remains true that MR = MC at the output level that maximizes profits, there may be other output levels at which MR = MC but at which profits are not maximized.

POLICY DEBATE

Profit and the New Market Economies

The failure of communism to produce economic abundance has led the nations of Eastern Europe, and even China, to turn to the market mechanism. These countries hope that the market will soon bring them the sort of prosperity achieved by the industrialized countries.

The market, as we know, is driven by the profit motive. In a free market, profits are not determined by a government agency but rather by demand and cost conditions, as described by the demand and cost curves. Many citizens of these new market economies are appalled by the sizes of the profits that the free market affords to successful businesspeople, and they are upset by the greed that these entrepreneurs display. There are pressures to put limits on these profits.

The same thing happened in the United Kingdom and elsewhere as firms formerly owned by the government were sold to private individuals and returned to the market. In the United Kingdom, a number of the privatized firms were initially monopolies, and the government chose to protect consumers by putting ceilings on prices but not on profits to provide the firms with appropriate incentives. Yet when some of these firms proved to be quite profitable, the British government agencies reduced the price ceilings so as to cut those profits, a move that was attacked sharply not only by the firms themselves but also by some British economists. The debate in the United Kingdom and elsewhere amounts to this: Should severe limits be placed on profits as a matter of fairness and to improve the ethical climate of society, or should such measures be avoided because ceilings on profits undermine the incentives for business success and therefore prevent the market mechanism from delivering the economic abundance of which it is capable?

"Please stand by, we are switching to a free-market economy"

must charge to induce consumers to buy that amount of product. Consequently, if we know that the profit-maximizing output is 6.5 garages, the demand curve in Figure 1 (on page 158) tells us what price Al must charge to sell that profit-maximizing output. To sell an average of 6.5 garages per year (that is, 13 garages every two years), he must price each garage at $19,000 (between points *f* and *g*). The demand curve tells us that this amount is the only price at which this quantity will be demanded by customers.

Once the profit-maximizing output quantity has been determined with the help of the MR = MC rule, it is easy to find the profit-maximizing price with the help of the demand curve. Just use that curve to find out at what price the optimal quantity will be demanded.

◼ GENERALIZATION: THE LOGIC OF MARGINAL ANALYSIS AND MAXIMIZATION

The logic of marginal analysis of profit maximization that we have just studied can be generalized, because essentially the same argument was already used in Chapters 5 and 7 and will recur in a number of chapters later in this book. To avoid having to master the argument each time all over again, it is useful to see how this concept can be applied in problems other than the determination of the firm's profit-maximizing output.

The general issue is this: Decision makers often are faced with the problem of selecting the magnitude of some variable, such as how much to spend on advertising, or how many bananas to buy, or how many school buildings to construct. Each of these acts brings benefits, so that the larger the number selected by the decision maker, the larger the total benefits that will be derived. Unfortunately, as larger numbers are selected, the associated costs also grow. The problem is to take the trade-off properly into account and to calculate at what point the net gain—the difference between the total benefit and the total cost—will be greatest. Thus, we have the following general principle:

If a decision is to be made about the quantity of some variable, then to maximize

Net benefit = Total benefit − Total cost,

the decision maker must select a value of the variable at which

Marginal benefit = (approximately) Marginal cost

For example, if a community were to determine that the marginal benefit from building an additional school was greater than the cost of an additional school, it would clearly be better off if it built another school. But if the community were planning to build so many schools that the marginal benefit was less than the marginal cost, it would be better off if it switched to a more limited construction program. Only if the marginal benefit and cost are as close as possible to being equal will the community have the optimal number of schools.

We will apply this same concept in later chapters. Again and again, when we analyze a quantitative decision that brings together both benefits and costs, we conclude that the optimal decision occurs at the point where the marginal benefit equals the marginal cost. The logic is the same whether we are considering the net gains to a firm, to a consumer, or to society as a whole.

■ Application: Fixed Cost and the Profit-Maximizing Price

We can now use our analytic framework to offer an insight that is often unexpected. Suppose there is a rise in the firm's fixed cost; for example, imagine that the property taxes on Al's Building Contractors double. What will happen to the profit-maximizing price and output? Should Al raise his price to cover the increased cost, or should he produce a larger output even if it requires a drop in price? The answer is surprising: Neither!

When a firm's fixed cost increases, its profit-maximizing price and output remain completely unchanged, so long as it pays the firm to stay in business.

In other words, there is nothing that the firm's management can do to offset the effect of the rise in fixed cost. Management must just put up with it. This is surely a case where common sense is not a reliable guide to the right decision.

Why is this so? Recall that, by definition, a fixed cost does not change when output changes. The increase in Al's fixed costs is the same whether business is slow or booming, whether production is 2 garages or 20. This idea is illustrated in Table 5, which also reproduces Al's total profits from Table 3. The third column of the table shows that total fixed cost has risen (from zero) to $10,000 per year. As a result, total profit is $10,000 less than it would have been otherwise—no matter what the firm's output. For example, when output is four units, we

TABLE 5			
Rise in Fixed Cost: Total Profit Before and After			
(1)	(2)	(3)	(4)
Garages per Year	Total Profit Before (in thousands)	Rise in Fixed Cost (in thousands)	Total Profit After (in thousands)
0	$−12	$10	$−22
1	−10	10	−20
2	0	10	−10
3	12	10	2
4	22	10	12
5	30	10	20
6	33	10	23
7	30	10	20
8	16	10	6
9	−18	10	−28
10	−70	10	−80

see that total profit falls from $22,000 (second column) to $12,000 (last column).

Because profit is reduced by the same amount at every output level, whatever output was most profitable before the increase in fixed costs must still be most profitable. In Table 5, we see that $23,000 is the largest entry in the last column, which shows profits after the rise in fixed cost. This approximately highest possible profit is attained, as it was before, when output is at six units. The actual profit-maximizing output will remain at 6.5 garages, exactly as before. In other words, the firm's profit-maximizing price and quantity remain unchanged.

This is shown graphically in Figure 6, which displays the firm's total profit hill before and after the rise in fixed cost (reproducing Al's initial profit hill from Figure 4). We see that the cost increase simply moves the profit hill straight downward by $10,000, so the highest point on the hill is just lowered from point M to point N. But the top of the hill is shifted neither toward the left nor toward the right. It remains at the 6.5 garage output level.[6]

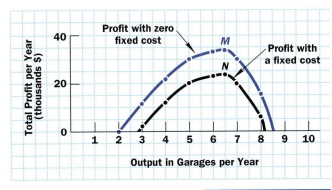

FIGURE 6

Fixed Cost Does Not Affect Profit-Maximizing Output

PUZZLE RESOLVED: *Using Marginal Analysis to Unravel the Case of the "Unprofitable" Calculator*

We can now put the marginal analysis of profit determination to work to solve the puzzle with which we began this chapter. The example was drawn from reality, and reality never works as neatly as a textbook illustration with a mechanical application of the MR = MC rule. However, we will see that the underlying reasoning does shed useful light on real problems.

Our "unprofitable" calculator puzzle concerned a firm that produced a number of electronic items, including calculators. The company was apparently losing money on calculator sales because the $12 price was less than the $14.55 average cost that the company's bookkeepers assigned to the product. This $14.55 figure included $10.30 of (marginal) costs caused directly by manufacture and marketing of each additional calculator, plus a $4.25 per-calculator share of the company's overall general expenses ("overhead") such as compensation of the company president. When it was accused in a court of law of trying to drive a competitor out of business by deliberately selling below cost, the company turned to marginal analysis to show that the charge was untrue and that the calculators were indeed a profitable line of business.

To demonstrate this fact, a witness for the company explained that if selling the calculators really were unprofitable, then the company could increase its earnings by *ceasing* their production altogether. But, in fact, had the company done so, it would have lowered its profits.

To see why, let's look at the numbers again. If the company gave up the sale of 10 million calculators, its revenues would be reduced by $12 (the price of each calculator) × 10 million units sold—a (marginal) revenue reduction of $120 million. But how much cost would it save by giving up those sales? The answer is that the cost outlay actually caused by the production of each calculator was only the $10.30 in direct cost. Even if it stopped selling the calculators (which were just one part of its product line), the company would still have to continue to pay for costs like the salary of the company president and general advertising expenditures. In other words, none of the company's fixed overhead costs would be saved by ending calcu-

---

[6] EXERCISE: Does the added fixed cost change the marginal cost? Explain. What does this imply for optimal output?

lator production. Rather, the (marginal) cost saving would be the direct cost of $10.30 per calculator × the 10 million calculator output—a total cost saving of just $103 million.

The bottom line was that eliminating calculators from the product line would have reduced total profit by $17 million per year—the $120 million in forgone revenue minus the $103 million cost. So, continued production of the calculators was not causing losses; on the contrary, it was contributing $17 million in profits every year, because each unit of output was bringing in $12 in revenue − $10.30 in marginal cost = $1.70. The court concluded that this reasoning was correct and used this conclusion in its decision.

This case illustrates a point that is encountered frequently. The calculator manufacturer was selling its product at a price that appeared not to cover the costs but really did. The appearance stems from the fact that the cost attributable to any one of a company's products is essentially its *marginal* cost—the cost the firm must pay to add the item to its product line. But bookkeepers usually don't think in terms of marginal costs, and in their calculations they often include other types of cost that that are not affected by reducing the output of the product or by eliminating its production.

The same sort of issue faces airlines that offer discounted fares to students (or to senior citizens, or some other group), when those fares are lower than the average cost (including fuel cost, salaries of personnel, and so on) per passenger. If the discounted fares have the effect of filling up seats that would otherwise have flown empty, and if the fares cover more than their *marginal cost* (which consists only of the additional cost of selling the tickets and providing the students with a snack), then those fares clearly are adding to the airline's profits. Nevertheless, such fare discounts sometimes lead to lawsuits by competitors of the airlines that offer such discounted fares.

CONCLUSION: THE FUNDAMENTAL ROLE OF MARGINAL ANALYSIS

IDEAS FOR BEYOND THE FINAL EXAM

THE IMPORTANCE OF THINKING AT THE MARGIN We saw in Chapter 7 how marginal analysis helps us to understand the firm's input choices. Similarly, in Chapters 5 and 6, it cast indispensable light on the consumer's purchase decisions. In this chapter, it enabled us to analyze output and pricing decisions. The logic of marginal analysis applies not only to economic decisions by consumers and firms, but also to decisions made by governments, universities, hospitals, and other organizations. In short, this type of analysis applies to any individual or group that must make optimal choices about the use of scarce resources. Thus, one of the most important conclusions that can be drawn from this chapter, and a conclusion brought out vividly by the examples we have just discussed, is the importance of thinking "at the margin"—one of our *Ideas for Beyond the Final Exam.*

Another real-life example far removed from profit maximization will illustrate how marginal criteria are useful in decision making. For some years before women were first admitted to Princeton University (and to several other colleges), administrators cited the cost of the proposed admission of women as a major obstacle. They had decided in advance that any women coming to the university would constitute a net addition to the student body because, for a variety of reasons involving relations with alumni and other groups, it was not feasible to reduce the number of male students. Presumably on the basis of a calculation of average cost, some critics spoke of cost figures as high as $80 million.

To economists, it was clear that the relevant figure was actually the *marginal cost,* or the addition to total cost that would result from the admission of the additional students. The women students would, of course, bring additional tuition fees (marginal revenues) to Princeton. If these fees were just sufficient to cover the amount that they would add to costs, the admission of the women would leave the university's financial picture unaffected.

A careful calculation showed that the admission of women would add far less to the university's financial problems than the average cost figures indicated. One reason was that women's course preferences at that time were characteristically different from men's, and hence women frequently selected courses that were undersubscribed in exclusively male institutions. Therefore, the admission of 1,000 women to a formerly all-male institution could be expected to require fewer additional classes than if 1,000 more men had been admitted.[7] More important, it was found that a number of classroom buildings were underutilized. The cost of operating these buildings was nearly fixed—their total utilization cost would be changed only slightly by the influx of women. The marginal cost for classroom space was therefore almost zero and certainly well below the average cost (the cost per student).

For all of these reasons, it turned out that the relevant marginal cost was much smaller than the figures that had been considered earlier. Indeed, this cost was something like one-third of the earlier estimates. There is little doubt that this careful marginal calculation played a critical role in the admission of women to Princeton at that time and to some other institutions that subsequently made use of the calculations in the Princeton analysis. More recent data, incidentally, confirmed that the marginal calculations were amply justified.

■ THE THEORY AND REALITY: A WORD OF CAUTION

We have now completed two chapters describing how business managers can make optimal decisions. Can you go to Wall Street or Main Street and find executives calculating marginal cost and marginal revenue to decide how much to produce? Not very often—although in some important applications they do. Nor can you find consumers in stores using marginal analysis to decide what to buy. Like consumers, successful businesspeople often rely heavily on intuition and "hunches" that cannot be described by any set of rules. In fact, in a 1993 survey of CEOs conducted by *Inc.* magazine, nearly 20 percent of the respondents admitted to using guesswork to price their products or services.

Note that we have not sought to provide a literal description of business behavior but rather a model to help us analyze and predict this behavior. The four chapters that we have just completed constitute the core of microeconomics. We will find ourselves returning again and again to the principles learned in these chapters.

SUMMARY

1. A firm can choose the quantity of its product that it wants to sell or the price that it wants to charge, but it cannot choose both because price affects the quantity demanded.

2. In economic theory, we usually assume that firms seek to maximize **profits**. This assumption should not be taken literally but rather interpreted as a useful simplification of reality.

3. The demand curve of a firm is determined from the market demand curve by the strength of the competitive efforts of the rival firms in the market.

4. **Marginal revenue** is the additional revenue earned by increasing quantity sold by one unit. Marginal cost is the additional cost incurred by increasing production by one unit.

---

[7] See Gardner Patterson, "The Education of Women at Princeton," *Princeton Alumni Weekly 69* (September 24, 1968).

5. Maximum profit requires the firm to choose the level of output at which marginal revenue is equal to (or most closely approximates) marginal cost.

6. Geometrically, the profit-maximizing output level occurs at the highest point on the total profit curve. There the slope of the total profit curve is zero (or as close to zero as possible), meaning that **marginal profit** is zero.

7. A change in fixed cost will not change the profit-maximizing level of output.

8. It will generally pay a firm to expand its output if it is selling at a price greater than marginal cost, even if that price happens to be below average cost.

9. **Optimal decisions** must be made on the basis of marginal cost and marginal revenue figures, not average cost and average revenue figures. This concept is one of the *Ideas for Beyond the Final Exam.*

KEY TERMS

Optimal decision   156

Total profit   158

Economic profit   159

Total revenue (TR)   159

Average revenue (AR)   160

Marginal revenue (MR)   160

Marginal profit   163

TEST YOURSELF

1. Suppose that the firm's demand curve indicates that at a price of $12 per unit, customers will demand 2 million units of its product. Suppose that management decides to pick both price and output; the firm produces 3 million units of its product and prices them at $20 each. What will happen?

2. Suppose that a firm's management would be pleased to increase its share of the market, but if it expands its production the price of its product will fall. Will its profits necessarily fall? Why or why not?

3. Why does it make sense for a firm to seek to maximize *total* profit rather than to maximize *marginal* profit?

4. A firm's marginal revenue is $133 and its marginal cost is $90. What amount of profit does the firm fail to pick up by refusing to increase output by one unit?

5. Calculate average revenue (AR) and average cost (AC) in Table 3. How much profit does the firm earn at the output at which AC = AR? Why?

6. A firm's total cost is $800 if it produces one unit, $1,400 if it produces two units, and $1,800 if it produces three units of output. Draw up a table of total, average, and marginal costs for this firm.

7. Draw an average and marginal cost curve for the firm in Question 6 above. Describe the relationship between the two curves.

8. A firm has the demand and total cost schedules given in the following table. If it wants to maximize profits, how much output should it produce?

Quantity	Price	Total Cost
1	$6	$ 1.00
2	5	2.50
3	4	6.00
4	3	7.00
5	2	11.00

DISCUSSION QUESTION

1. "It may be rational for the management of a firm not to try to maximize profits." Discuss the circumstances under which this statement may be true.

APPENDIX *The Relationships Among Total, Average, and Marginal Data*

You may have surmised that there is a close connection between the average revenue curve and the marginal revenue curve and that there must be a similar relationship between the average cost curve and the marginal cost curve. After all, we derived our average revenue figures from the total revenues and also calculated our marginal revenue figures from the total revenues at the various possible output levels; a similar relationship applied to costs. In fact:

Marginal, average, and total figures are inextricably bound together. From any one of the three figures, the other two can be calculated. The relationships among total, average, and marginal data are exactly the same for any variable—such as revenue, cost, or profit—to which the concepts apply.

To illustrate and emphasize the wide applicability of marginal analysis, we switch our example from profits, revenues, and costs to a noneconomic variable. As we are about to see, the same concepts can be applied to human body weights. We use this example because calculation of weights is more familiar to most people than calculation of profits, revenues, or costs, and we can use it to illustrate several fundamental relationships between average and marginal figures.

In Table 6, we begin with an empty room. (The total weight of occupants is equal to zero.) A person weighing 100 pounds enters; total, marginal and average weight are all, then, 100 pounds. If the person is followed by a person weighing 140 pounds (marginal weight equals 140 pounds), the total weight increases to 240 pounds, average weight rises to 120 pounds (240/2), and so on.[8]

The rule for converting totals to averages, and vice versa, is:

Rule 1a. Average weight equals total weight divided by number of persons.
Rule 1b. Total weight equals average weight times number of persons.

This rule naturally applies equally well to cost, revenue, profit, or any other variable.

We calculate marginal weight from total weight by working with the same subtraction process already used to calculate marginal cost and marginal revenue. Specifically:

Rule 2a. The marginal weight of, say, the third person equals the total weight of three people minus the total weight of two people.

For example, when the fourth person enters the room, total weight rises from 375 to 500 pounds, and hence the corresponding marginal weight is $500 - 375 = 125$ pounds, as is shown in the second column of Table 6. We can also do the reverse—calculate total from marginal weight—through an addition process.

Rule 2b. The total weight of, say, three people equals the (marginal) weight of the first person who enters the room plus the (marginal) weight of the second person, plus the (marginal) weight of the third person.

You can verify Rule 2b by referring to Table 6, which shows that the total weight of three persons, 375 pounds, is indeed equal to $100 + 140 + 135$ pounds, the sum of the preceding marginal weights. A similar relation holds for any other total weight figure in the table, a fact that you should verify.

In addition to these familiar arithmetic relationships, there are two other useful relationships.

Rule 3. With an exception (fixed cost) that was discussed in Chapter 7, the marginal, average, and total figures for the first person must all be equal.

That is, when there is only one person in the room whose weight is X pounds, the average weight will obviously be X, the total weight must be X, and the marginal weight must also be X (because the total must have risen from zero to X pounds). Put another way, when the marginal person is alone, he or she is obviously the average person and also represents the totality of all relevant persons.

Our final and very important relationship is:

Rule 4. If marginal weight is lower than average weight, then average weight must decrease when the number of persons increases. If marginal weight exceeds average weight, average weight must increase when the number of

TABLE 6

Weights of Persons in a Room (in pounds)

Number of Persons in a Room	Marginal Weight	Total Weight	Average Weight
0		0	—
	100		
1		100	100
	140		
2		240	120
	135		
3		**375**	125
	125		
4		**500**	**125**
	100		
5		600	120
	60		
6		660	110

[8] In this illustration, "persons in room" is analogous to units of output, "total weight" is analogous to total revenue or cost, and "marginal weight" is analogous to marginal revenue or cost in the discussions of marginal analysis in the body of the chapter.

persons increases. If marginal and average weight are equal, the average weight must remain constant when the number of persons increases.

These three possibilities are all illustrated in Table 6. Notice, for example, that when the third person enters the room, the average weight increases from 120 to 125 pounds. That increase occurs because this person's (marginal) weight is 135 pounds, which is above the average and therefore pulls up the average, as Rule 4 requires. Similarly, when the sixth person—who is a 60-pound child—enters the room, the average decreases from 120 to 110 pounds because marginal weight, 60 pounds, is below average weight and so pulls the average down.

It is essential to avoid a common misunderstanding of this rule. It does *not* state, for example, that if the average figure is rising, the *marginal* figure must be *rising*. When the average rises, the marginal figure may rise, fall, or remain unchanged. The arrival of two persons, both well above the average weight, will push the average up in two successive steps even if the second new arrival is lighter than the first. We see such a case in Table 6, where average weight rises successively from 100 to 120 to 125 pounds, while the marginal weight falls from 140 to 135 to 125 pounds.

GRAPHICAL REPRESENTATION OF MARGINAL AND AVERAGE CURVES

We have shown how, from a curve of total profit (or total cost or total anything else), we can determine the corresponding marginal figure. In the chapter, we noted repeatedly that the marginal value at any particular point is equal to the slope of the corresponding total curve at that point. But for some purposes, it is convenient to use a graph that records marginal and average values directly rather than deriving them from the curve of totals.

We can obtain such a graph by plotting the data in a table of average and marginal figures, such as Table 6. The result looks like the graph shown in Figure 7. In that graph, the number of persons in the room appears on the horizontal axis and the corresponding average and marginal figures appear on the vertical axis. The solid dots represent average weights; the small circles represent marginal weights. For example, point *A* shows that when

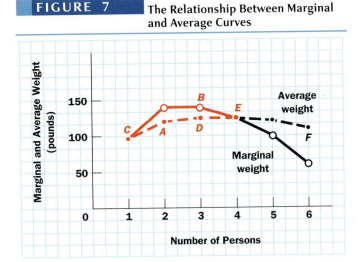

FIGURE 7   The Relationship Between Marginal and Average Curves

two persons are in the room, their average weight is 120 pounds, as recorded on the third line of Table 6. Similarly, point *B* on the graph represents information provided in the next column of the table—that is, that the marginal weight of the third person who enters the room is 135 pounds. We have connected these points into a marginal curve and an average curve, represented, respectively, by the solid and the broken curves in the diagram. This is the representation of marginal and average values economists most frequently use.

Figure 7 illustrates two of our rules. Rule 3 says that for the first unit, the marginal and average values will be the same; that is precisely why the two curves start out together at point *C*. The graph also depicts Rule 4 between points *C* and *E*: Where the average curve is rising, the marginal curve lies above the average. (Notice that over part of this range, the marginal curve falls even though the average curve is rising; Rule 4 says nothing about the rise or fall of the *marginal* curve.) We see also that over range *EF*, where the average curve is falling, the marginal curve is below the average curve, again in accord with Rule 4. Finally, at point *E*, where the average curve is neither rising nor falling, the marginal curve meets the average curve; the average and marginal weights are equal at that point, so that the marginal weights to not pull the average weight either upward or downward.

TEST YOURSELF

1. Suppose that the following table is your record of exam grades in your Principles of Economics course:

Use these data to make up a table of total, average, and marginal grades for the five exams.

Exam Date	Grade	Comment
September 30	65	A slow start
October 28	75	A big improvement
November 26	90	Happy Thanksgiving!
December 13	85	Slipped a little
January 24	95	A fast finish!

2. From the data in your exam-grade table in Test Yourself Question 1 above, illustrate each of the rules mentioned in this appendix. Be sure to point out an instance where the marginal grade falls but the average grade rises.

INVESTING IN BUSINESS: STOCKS AND BONDS

A bargain that is going to become a greater bargain is no bargain.

MARTIN SHUBIK, YALE UNIVERSITY

A firm does more than select inputs, outputs, and prices—which were the topics of previous chapters. In this chapter, we discuss how real firms finance their activities—notably with stocks and bonds. These days, a very large proportion of the nation's college graduates invests money in the stock and bond markets. You probably will as well, if you don't already. For this reason, it is important to understand something about how these markets work. But please do not think that this chapter will turn you into a super speculator who can beat the market consistently. Too many investors have thought that way and ended up losing their life's savings. Indeed, the main lesson of this chapter is that, for good reason, the future behavior of the stock market is virtually unpredictable. As you look toward the future, the stock market will undoubtedly go up and undoubtedly go down, but the unanswerable question is: When? History repeatedly teaches us that lesson, and as philosopher George Santayana once wrote, "Those who cannot remember the past are condemned to repeat it"—as many stock-market investors have done.[1]

CONTENTS

[1] George Santayana, *The Life of Reason, or, The Phases of Human Progress, Vol. I*, New York: C. Scribner's Sons, 1905-06.

PUZZLE #1: *What in the World Happened to the Stock Market?*

Sometimes a picture really *is* worth a thousand words. Figure 1 shows the remarkable behavior of share prices on the NASDAQ stock market (which we will describe later in the chapter) between 1990 and 2006. It looks a bit like the Rocky Mountains, rising spectacularly from the autumn of 1998 to early 2000, and then falling dramatically back down to earth. The numbers on the scale tell you that the index soared from about 1,600 in October 1998 to about 4,800 in March 2000—an astonishing gain of 200 percent in less than a year and a half! But by the fall of 2001, the index was back to about where it had been in October 1998. All in all, it was one of the most spectacular booms and busts in stock market history.

DATA SOURCE: http://www.freelunch.com

FIGURE 1

NASDAQ Stock Market Composite Index, 1990–2006

What in the world happened? In all honesty, most of the world's best economists and leading financial experts were left puzzled by this episode. As we will learn in this chapter, the value of a share of stock is supposed to reflect the current and future profits of the company that issues the stock. But that theory of stock prices will not explain why shares of Amazon.com, the online retailer, once sold for about $105 per share and then plunged to around $6 (it was about $39 as this book went to press), or why shares of Priceline.com (which sells airline tickets and books hotel reservations online) once sold for about $165 per share and dropped to around $4 (as against $44 at press time).

Alan Greenspan, the chairman of the Federal Reserve, once called the phenomenon that gripped America in the boom years "irrational exuberance"—and it was certainly that. One of the authors of this book called the upside of Figure 1 the "Wile E. Coyote stock market," after that old nemesis in Road Runner cartoons, who would run off cliffs and yet somehow manage to remain in the air—until he looked down.

Apparently, investors in U.S. technology stocks "looked down" around March 2000. But why then? Why not before? And what made stock prices rise so high in the first place? As we said, the answers to such questions remain shrouded in mystery. Even so,

PUZZLE #2: *The Stock Market's Unpredictability*

The stock market is obviously something of an enigma. No other economic activity is reported in such detail in so many newspapers and other media and followed with such concern by so many people. Yet few activities have so successfully eluded prediction of their future. There is no shortage of well-paid "experts" prepared to forecast the future of the market or the price of a particular stock or the earnings of the company to which the stock price is related. But there are real questions about what these experts deliver.

For example, a famous study of leading stock market analysts' predictions of company earnings (on which they based their stock-price forecasts) reports:

> [W]e wrote to 19 major Wall Street firms . . . among the most respected names in the investment business.
>
> We requested—and received—past earnings predictions on how these firms felt earnings for specific companies would behave over both a one-year and a five-year period. These estimates . . . were . . . compared with actual results to see how well the analysts forecast short-run and long-run earnings changes. . . .
>
> Bluntly stated, the careful estimates of security analysts (based on industry studies, plant visits, etc.) do very little better than those that would be obtained by simple extrapolation of past trends. . . .
>
> For example . . . the analysts' estimates were compared [with] the assumption that every company in the economy would enjoy a growth in earnings approximating the long-run rate of growth of the national income. It often turned out that . . . this naïve forecasting model . . . would make smaller errors in forecasting long-run earnings growth than . . . [did] the professional forecasts of the analysts. . . .
>
> When confronted with the poor record of their five-year growth estimates, the security analysts honestly, if sheepishly, admitted that five years ahead is really too far in advance to make reliable projections. They protested that, although long-term projections are admittedly important, they really ought to be judged on their ability to project earnings changes one year ahead.
>
> Believe it or not, it turned out that their one-year forecasts were even worse than their five-year projections.[2]

It has been said that an investor may as well pick stocks by throwing darts at the stock market page—it is far cheaper to buy a set of darts than to obtain the apparently useless advice of a professional analyst. Indeed, there have been at least two experiments, one by a U.S. senator and one by *Forbes* magazine, in which stocks picked by dart-throwing actually outperformed the mutual funds, the stocks of which are selected by experts.

Later in this chapter we will suggest an explanation for this poor performance.

◼ CORPORATIONS AND THEIR UNIQUE CHARACTERISTICS

Stocks and bonds are created by *corporations* and are among the primary tools that these companies use to acquire the funds they need to operate. Corporations play a crucial role in the U.S. economy. Revenues of the top 500 corporations totaled $9.1 trillion in 2005, or nearly 75 percent of the country's gross domestic product (GDP). And some of them are true industrial giants. Exxon Mobil alone generated $340 billion in revenues in 2005, and Wal–Mart Stores and General Motors took in $316 billion and $193 billion, respectively. The combined revenues of just these three firms amounted to considerably more than the gross domestic product (GDP) of Australia (and Belgium, the Netherlands, Norway, Switzerland, and many, many other countries).

But only 20 percent of American firms are incorporated, because most firms are small. Even many corporations are quite small—40 percent have business receipts of less than $100,000 per year.[3] That said, almost all *large* American firms are corporations. It's a word you've heard used many times. But what, exactly, is a "corporation"?

A **corporation** is a type of firm that is defined by law and to which the law assigns special privileges and special obligations. Three noteworthy features that their legal status entails are the following:

A **corporation** is a firm that has the legal status of a fictional individual. This fictional individual is owned by a number of persons, called its *stockholders,* and is run by a set of elected officers and a board of directors, whose chairman is often also in a powerful position.

---

[2] Burton G. Malkiel, *A Random Walk Down Wall Street* (New York: W. W. Norton; 1990), pp. 140–141.

[3] "Fortune 500: The 500 Largest U.S. Corporations," *Fortune* magazine, April 5, 2004, p. 289; and Organization for Economic Cooperation and Development, *OECD in Figures, 2004,* http://new.sourceoecd.org.

- Special limits are placed on the losses that may be suffered by those who invest in these firms.
- These firms are subjected to types of taxation from which other firms are exempt.
- The corporation is considered to be an entity that is distinct from any of its owners or its management, so that the corporation can outlast the association of any and all of the individuals who are currently connected with the firm.

Let us consider the logic behind these three features. To begin with, although it may seem strange, a *corporation* is considered an *individual* in the eyes of the law. Therefore, its earnings, like those of other individuals, are taxed. Thus the legal status leads to what is called "double taxation" of the stockholders. Unlike the earnings of other firms, corporate earnings are taxed twice—once when they are earned by the company and a second time when they go to investors in the form of dividends (and are subject to the personal income tax).

This disadvantage is counterbalanced by an important legal advantage, however: Any corporate debt is regarded as that fictitious individual's obligation, not any one stockholder's liability. In this way, stockholders benefit from the protection of **limited liability**—they can lose no more money than they have invested in the firm. In contrast, if you are part or sole owner of a firm that is not a corporation, and it loses money and cannot repay its debts, you can be sued by the people to whom the money is owed, who may be able to force you to pay them out of your own bank account or by selling your vacation home.

Limited liability is the main secret of the success of the corporate organizational form, and the reason that some corporations grow so big. Thanks to that provision, individuals throughout the world are willing to invest money in firms whose operations they do not understand and whose management personnel they do not know. Each shareholder receives in return a claim on the firm's profits and, at least in principle, a portion of the company's ownership.

> **Limited liability** is a legal obligation of a firm's owners to pay back company debts only with the money they have already invested in the firm.

The corporate form is a boon to investors because their liability for loss is limited to their investments. There is also a major disadvantage to this form of business organization: Corporate income is taxed twice.

■ FINANCING CORPORATE ACTIVITY: STOCKS AND BONDS

When a corporation needs money to add to its plant or equipment, or to finance other types of investment, it may reinvest its own earnings (rather than paying them out as dividends to stockholders), or print and sell new stock certificates or new bonds, or take out a loan. Stocks and bonds, in the last analysis, are pieces of paper printed by the firm under a variety of legal safeguards. If it can find buyers, the firm can sell these pieces of paper to the investing public when it wants to obtain more money to invest in its operations.

How can a firm obtain money in exchange for such printed paper as a stock or bond certificate? Doesn't the process seem a bit like counterfeiting? If done improperly, there are indeed grounds for the suspicion. But, carried out appropriately, it is a perfectly reasonable economic process. First, let's define our terms.

Common stock represents partial ownership of a corporation. For example, if a company issues 100,000 shares, then a person who owns 1,000 shares owns 1 percent of the company and is entitled to 1 percent of the company's *dividends*, the corporation's annual payments to stockholders. This shareholder's vote also normally counts for 1 percent of the total votes in an election of corporate officers or in a referendum on corporate policy.

Bonds differ from stocks in several ways. First, the purchaser of a corporation's stock *buys* a share of its ownership and some control over its affairs, whereas a bond purchaser simply *lends* money to the firm and obtains no part of its ownership. Second, whereas

> A **common stock** (also called a share) of a corporation is a piece of paper that gives the holder of the stock a share of the ownership of the company.

> A **bond** is simply an IOU sold by a corporation that promises to pay the holder of the bond a fixed sum of money at the specified *maturity* date and some other fixed amount of money (the *coupon* or *interest payment*) every year up to the date of maturity.

stockholders have no idea how much they will receive when they sell their stocks or how much they will receive in dividends each year, bondholders know with a high degree of certainty how much money they will be paid if they hold their bonds to maturity (the date the firm has promised to repay the loan). For instance, a bond with a face value of $1,000 and an $80 *coupon* (the firm's annual interest payment to the bondholder) that matures in 2010 will provide $80 per year every year until 2010, and the firm will repay the bondholder's $1,000 in 2010. Unless the company goes bankrupt, this repayment schedule is guaranteed. Third, bondholders legally have a *prior claim* on company earnings, which means the stockholders receive no money until the firm has paid its bondholders. For all these reasons, bonds are considered less risky investments than stocks.[4]

To return to the question we asked earlier, a new issue of stocks and bonds is generally not like counterfeiting. As long as the funds obtained from the sale of the new securities[5] are used effectively to increase a firm's profit-earning capacity, these funds will automatically yield any required repayment and appropriate interest and dividends to purchasers. Occasionally this payout does not happen. One of the favorite practices of the more notorious nineteenth-century market manipulators was "watering" company stocks—issuing stocks with little or nothing to back them up. The term is originally derived from the practice of some cattle dealers who would force their animals to drink large quantities of water just before bringing them to be weighed for sale.

Similarities Between Stocks and Bonds   In reality, the differences between stocks and bonds are not as clear-cut as just described. Two relevant misconceptions are worth noting. First, the ownership represented by a few shares of a company's stock may be more symbolic than real. A person who holds 0.02 percent of IBM Corporation stock—which, by the way, is a *very large* investment—exercises no real control over IBM's operations.

In fact, many economists believe that the ownership of large corporations is so diffuse that stockholders or stockholder groups rarely have *any* effective control over management. In this view, a corporation's management is a largely independent decision-making body; as long as it keeps enough cash flowing to stockholders to prevent discontent and *organized* rebellion, management can do anything it wants within the law. Looked at in this way, stockholders, like bondholders, merely provide loans to the company. The only real difference between the two groups, according to this interpretation, is that stockholders' loans are riskier and therefore entitled to higher payments.

Second, bonds actually *can* be a very risky investment. People who try to sell their bonds before maturity may find that the market price happens to be low; so if they need to raise cash in a hurry, they may incur substantial losses. Also, bondholders may be exposed to losses from inflation. Whether the $1,000 promised to the bondholder at the 2010 maturity date represents substantial (or very little) purchasing power depends on what happens to the general price level in the meantime (that is, how much price **inflation** occurs). No one can predict the price level this far in advance with any accuracy. Finally, a firm can issue bonds with little backing; that is, the firm may own little valuable property that it can use as a guarantee of repayment to the lender—the bondholder. This is often true of "junk bonds," and it helps to explain their high risk.

Bond Prices and Interest Rates   What makes bond prices go up and down? A straightforward relationship exists between bond prices and current *interest rates:* Whenever one goes up, the other *must* go down. The term **interest rate** refers to the amount that borrowers currently pay to lenders per dollar of the money borrowed—it is the current market price of a loan.

For example, suppose that J.C. Penney issued some 15-year bonds when interest rates were comparatively low, so the company had to pay only 6 percent to sell the bonds. People who invested $1,000 in those bonds received a contract that promised

Inflation occurs when prices in an economy rise rapidly. The rate of inflation is calculated by averaging the percentage growth rate of the prices of a selected sample of commodities.

The **interest rate** is the amount that borrowers currently pay to lenders per dollar of the money borrowed—it is the current market price of a loan.

---

[4] An important exception involves so-called junk bonds—very risky bonds that became popular in the 1980s. They were used heavily by people trying to purchase enough of a corporation's stock to acquire control of that firm.

[5] Stocks and bonds are also called securities.

them $60 per year for 15 years plus the return of their $1,000 at the end of that period. Suppose, however, that interest rates *rise*, so that new 15-year bonds of similar companies now pay 12 percent. An investor with $1,000 can now buy a bond that offers $120 per year. Obviously, no one will now pay $1,000 for a bond that promises only $60 per year. Consequently, the market price of the old J.C. Penney bonds must fall.

This example is not entirely hypothetical. Until a few years ago, bonds issued much earlier—at interest rates of 6 percent or lower—were still in circulation. In the 1980s' markets, when interest rates were well *above* 6 percent, such bonds sold for prices far below their original values.

> When interest rates *rise*, the prices of previously issued bonds with lower interest earnings must fall. For the same reason, when interest rates *fall*, the prices of previously issued bonds must rise.

It follows that as interest rates change because of changes in government policy or other reasons, bond prices fluctuate. That is one reason why bonds can be a risky investment.

Corporate Choice Between Stocks and Bonds

If a corporation chooses to finance the construction of new factories and equipment through the issue of new stocks or bonds, how does it determine whether bonds or stocks best suit its purposes?

Two considerations are of prime importance. Although issuing bonds generally exposes a firm to more risk than issuing stocks, the corporation usually expects to pay more money to stockholders over the long run. In other words, to the firm that issues them, bonds are cheaper but riskier. The decision about which is better for the firm therefore involves a trade-off between the two considerations of expense and risk.

Why are bonds risky to a corporation? When it issues $20 million in new bonds at 10 percent, a company commits itself to pay out $2 million every year of the bond's life, whether business is booming or the firm is losing money. If the firm is unable to meet its obligation to bondholders in some year, bankruptcy may result.

Stocks do not burden the company with any such risk, because the firm does not promise to pay stockholders *any* fixed amount. Stockholders simply receive whatever is left of the company's net earnings after the firm makes its payments to bondholders. If nothing is left to pay the new stockholders in some years, legally speaking, that is just their bad luck. The higher risk faced by stockholders is the reason they normally obtain higher average payments than bondholders.

> To the firm that issues them, bonds are riskier than stocks because they commit the firm to make a fixed annual payment, even in years when it is losing money. For the same reason, stocks are riskier than bonds to the buyers of securities. Therefore, stockholders expect to be paid more money than bondholders.

■ Plowback, or Retained Earnings

Plowback (or **retained earnings**) is the portion of a corporation's profits that management decides to keep and reinvest in the firm's operations rather than paying out as dividends to stockholders.

The final major source of funds for corporations, in addition to loans and the issue of stocks and bonds, is **plowback** or **retained earnings.** For example, if a company earns $30 million after taxes and decides to pay only $10 million in dividends to its stockholders and reinvest the remaining $20 million in the firm, that $20 million is called "plowback."

When business is profitable, corporate managers will often prefer plowback to other sources of funding. For one thing, plowback usually involves lower risk. Also, plowback, unlike other sources of funding, does not come under the scrutiny of the Securities and Exchange Commission (SEC), the government agency that regulates stocks.[6] And, of course, plowback does not depend on the availability of eager customers for new company stocks and bonds. An issue of new securities can be a disappointment if there is little public demand when they are offered, but plowback runs no such risk.

---

[6] The Securities and Exchange Commission, established in 1934, protects the interests of people who buy securities. It requires firms that issue stock and other securities to provide information about their financial condition, and it regulates the issue and trading of securities.

Above all, a plowback decision generally does not call attention to the degree of success of management's operations, as a new stock issue does. When stock is issued, the SEC, potential buyers, and their professional advisers may all scrutinize the company carefully. No management has a perfect record, and the process may reveal things management would prefer to be overlooked.

Another reason for plowback's attractiveness is that issuing new stocks and bonds is usually an expensive and lengthy process. The SEC requires companies to gather masses of data in a *prospectus*—a document that describes a company's financial condition—before any new issue is approved.

Figure 2 shows the relative importance of each of the different funding sources to U.S. corporations. Of the $986 billion in corporate funding in 2005, new bond issues and other forms of debt supplied about 30 percent. Sales of stock actually contributed a *negative* amount of funding (about -40 percent), because corporations reduced the number of their stocks in the public's hands by buying some back. Plowback was thus by far the most important source of corporate financing, constituting over 100 percent of total corporate financing in 2005. New bond issues and other forms of debt supplied about 15 percent of the total, and stock sales actually contributed a *negative* amount of funding (about −6 percent), because corporations reduced the number of their stocks in the public's hands by buying some back.

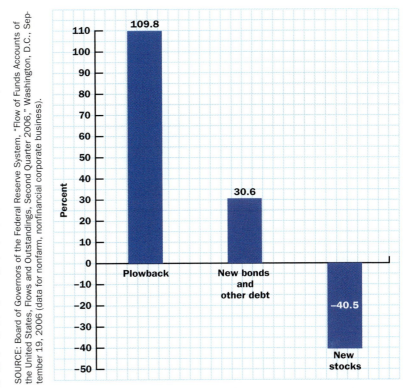

SOURCE: Board of Governors of the Federal Reserve System, "Flow of Funds Accounts of the United States, Flows and Outstandings, Second Quarter 2006," Washington, D.C., September 19, 2006 (data for nonfarm, nonfinancial corporate business).

FIGURE 2

Sources of New Funds for U.S. Corporations, 2005

What Determines Stock Prices? The Role of Expected Company Earnings

People invest in stocks because they believe (and hope) that the prices of the stocks they have purchased will rise. But will they? To answer that question, one should understand just what determines the price of a stock—but we do not really know the answer. We do know that, as with other things sold in markets, prices are determined by supply and demand. That merely raises the next question: What explains the behavior of supply and demand? That answer depends on the actions and expectations of the people who have stocks to sell or who wish to buy.

There is one apparently logical answer, although later we will see that there are reasons to question that explanation. This answer is that a stock is simply a share of the ownership of the firm that has issued it. The stock will therefore be valuable if the firm earns a good deal of money in the future, and it will rise in price if the firm earns more than investors had expected. The stock will fall in price if the earnings of the firm are poor or disappointing. That is why professional stock analysts who sell their advice to investors devote most of their efforts to studying individual firms and their markets, hoping to gain some insights into each company's future earnings prospects.

BUYING STOCKS AND BONDS

Although investors can purchase stocks and bonds through any brokerage firm, not all brokers charge the same fees. Bargain brokerage houses advertise in the newspapers'

"To hell with a balanced portfolio. I want to sell my Fenwick Chemical and sell it now."

financial pages, offering investors very little service—no advice, no research, no other frills—other than merely buying or selling what the customer wants them to, at lower fees than those charged by higher-service brokerage firms. And during the late 1990s, it became possible to buy and sell shares over the Internet at very low cost—and millions of Americans did so.

Many investors are not aware of the various ways in which they can purchase (or sell) stocks. Two noteworthy arrangements are (1) a *market order* purchase, which simply tells the broker to buy a specified quantity of stock at the best price the market currently offers, and (2) a *limit order*, which is an agreement to buy a given amount of stock when its price falls to a specified level. If the investor offers to buy at $18, then the broker will purchase shares if and when the market price falls to $18 per share or less.

A 2002 shareowners' survey estimated that there were 84 million individual stockholders in the United States (nearly one out of every three Americans). Of these, 89 percent owned stock mutual funds, 38 percent held both stock mutual funds and individual stocks, and 11 percent owned only individual stocks.[7]

◼ Selecting a Portfolio: Diversification

Perhaps the first rule of safe investing is: Always diversify—never put all your eggs in one basket.[8] A person or an organization's holdings of securities from several different corporations is called a *portfolio* of investments. A portfolio tends to be far less risky than any of the individual securities it contains because of the benefits of **portfolio diversification**. Let's see why.

If, for example, Alex divides his holdings among Companies A, B, and C, then his portfolio may perform satisfactorily overall even if Company A goes broke. Moreover, suppose that Company A specializes in producing luxury items, which do well in prosperous periods but very badly during recessions, whereas Company B sells cheap clothing, whose cyclical demand pattern differs greatly from that of Company A. If Alex holds stock in both companies, his overall risk is obviously less than if he owned stock in only one. All other things being equal, a portfolio containing many different types of securities tends to be less risky than a portfolio with fewer types of securities.

Increasingly, institutional investors, such as **mutual funds,** have adopted portfolios composed of broad ranges of stocks typifying those offered by the entire stock market. Mutual funds now are among the largest U.S. investors in securities. They offer their customers portfolios of various groups of domestic stocks, foreign stocks, and bonds. Small investors can easily put their money into these funds, thereby reducing the risks of owning individual stocks and ensuring that the overall market does not significantly outperform their portfolios. Mutual fund transactions can be carried out by telephone or over the internet, and investors can also easily check on the past performance of the different funds and obtain other pertinent information. Investors purchasing mutual fund shares should check on the fees charged by different funds, because fees vary surprisingly widely from one fund to another—and the difference can have a large effect on the relative earnings of an investment in a fund.

Portfolio diversification means inclusion of a number and variety of stocks, bonds, and other such items in an individual's portfolio. If the individual owns airline stocks, for example, diversification requires the purchase of a stock or bond in a very different industry, such as breakfast cereal production.

A **mutual fund,** in which individual investors can buy shares, is a private investment firm that holds a portfolio of securities. Investors can choose among a large variety of mutual funds, such as stock funds, bond funds, and so forth.

---

[7] Investment Company Institute and Securities Industry Association, *Equity Ownership in America, 2002,* available at http://www.sia.com.

[8] This was a bitter lesson for employees of Enron, the giant firm that went bankrupt so spectacularly in 2001. Many of its workers invested much of their savings in high-priced Enron stocks and lost virtually everything when the price of Enron stock later plunged.

One kind of mutual fund, called an **index fund,** buys the securities used in one of the standard **stock price indexes** (such as Standard & Poor's 500—known as the S&P 500—or the broader Wilshire 5000 Index). A stock price index is an average of the prices of a group of stocks—weighted by the size of each company—that are believed to be representative of the overall stock market (or some specialized segment, such as Far Eastern stocks). When you invest in an index fund, the return on your money will therefore reflect the performance of the entire market, rather than any one or a few securities that you or your broker might have selected instead.

Institutional money managers increasingly use computer programs to decide on their portfolios and to buy or sell huge portfolios of stocks simultaneously and rapidly. Since 1982, some traders have also allowed their computers to decide when to jump in and make massive sales or purchases. This practice is called *program trading.* In 2003, program trading accounted for about 40 percent of the total New York Stock Exchange volume and a considerable amount of the volume in other stock exchanges. Program trading was heavily criticized for aggravating price fluctuations and contributing to the stock market crash of October 1987. Restrictions are now in place that curb program trading when stock markets decline sharply.

> An **index fund** is a mutual fund that chooses a particular stock price index and then buys the stocks (or most of the stocks) that are included in the index. The value of an investment in an index fund depends on what happens to the prices of all stocks in that index.
>
> A **stock price index,** such as the S&P 500, is an average of the prices of a large set of stocks. These stocks are selected to represent the price movements of the entire stock market, or some specified segment of the market, and the chosen set is rarely changed.

■ Following a Portfolio's Performance

To enable you to keep track of your investments and how they are performing, newspapers carry daily information on stock and bond prices. Investors also use this information as a basis for decisions on purchase and sale of stocks and bonds. Figure 3 is an excerpt from the stock market page of the *New York Times.* The figure highlights the stock listing for the clothing retailer Gap, Inc. In the first two columns, before the company name, the report gives the stock's highest and lowest prices in the last year. Gap's stock is reported to have ranged between $25.72 and $16.99. After the stock's name, the annual dividend per share ($0.09) appears. Following that is the yield, or the dividend as a percentage of the closing price (0.5 percent).

The next column reports the *price-to-earnings* (P/E) ratio (16 for Gap, Inc.). This figure is the price per share divided by the company's net earnings per share in the previous year, and it is often taken as a basic measure indicating whether the stock's current price overvalues or undervalues the company. However, no simple rule enables us to interpret the P/E figures—for example, a very risky firm or a slowly growing firm with a low P/E ratio may be considered overvalued, whereas a safe, rapidly growing firm with a high P/E ratio may still be a bargain.

The next column indicates the number of shares traded on the previous day (4,745,300), an indication of whether that stock is actively traded. Finally, the last four figures indicate yesterday's highest price ($19.19), lowest price ($18.90), the price of the last transaction of the day ($18.99), and the change in that price from the previous day (+0.02).

Figure 4 gives similar information about bonds. Notice that a given company may have several different bonds differing in maturity date and coupon (annual interest payment). For example, AT&T

52-Week High	Low	Stock	Div	Yld %	P/E	Sales 100s	High	Low	Last	Chg
51.52	36.84	Gallaher	2.14 e	4.6	...	121	46.16	45.81	46.05	+0.05
19.05	14.13	GameStp	...	...	17	1649	18.18	17.65	18.17	+0.39
91.38	77.20	Gannett	1.08 f	1.3	18	9983	84.51	83.42	83.61	–1.05
25.72	16.99	Gap	.09	0.5	16	47453	19.19	18.90	18.99	+0.02
30.30	19.95	GardDen	...	...	18	743	27.58	26.79	27.05	–0.05
13.75	10.70	Gartner	...	...	58	1935	11.65	11.35	11.65	+0.17
13.06	10.54	GartnrB	...	...	57	69	11.42	11.30	11.42	+0.08
6.79	3.64	Gateway	...	...	dd	9783	4.60	4.46	4.60	+0.10
32.70	23.80	GaylrdEnt	...	...	dd	2377	31.04	30.85	31.00	+0.02
14.01	8.75	GenCorp	.06 j	...	dd	7098	13.70	13.50	13.51	–0.08
68.25	38.15	Genentch s	...	...	88	21966	52.70	51.60	52.14	+0.12
31.74	27.40	GAInv	.61 e	0.1	q	90	29.43	29.34	29.40	–0.04
11.14	6.79	GnCable	...	...	dd	4172	10.55	10.30	10.46	+0.12
101.94	76.49	GenDyn	1.44	1.4	18	8442	100.22	99.27	100.13	–0.02
34.57	27.37	GenElec	.80	2.4	22	139227	33.58	33.28	33.45	+0.14
35.30	23.63	GnGrthP s	1.44 f	4.7	25	15718	31.24	30.78	30.80	–0.04
35.69	11.20	GnMarit	...	...	10	2267	34.93	34.05	34.59	+0.49
50.00	43.51	GenMills	1.24	2.8	16	11801	45.13	44.40	45.09	+0.29
55.55	40.04	GnMotr	2.00	4.9	5	34201	41.36	40.90	41.10	–0.15
25.67	14.30	Gensco	...	...	14	2335	23.80	23.10	23.78	+0.86
26.10	15.34	GenWyo s	...	...	19	860	25.19	24.80	25.04	+0.04
40.20	30.03	GenuPrt	1.20	3.2	17	2033	37.77	37.43	37.67	+0.17
23.99	18.75	Genworth n	.26	1.1	...	6050	22.76	22.50	22.73	+0.13
29.79	25.00	Genwth un	1.50	5.3	...	4001	28.65	28.33	28.47	–0.08
24.69	16.94	GeoGroup	...	...	17	182	20.42	20.04	20.32	–0.07
44.67	23.15	GaGulf	.32	0.7	26	8253	45.09	43.38	43.70	–0.75
38.60	23.17	GaPacif	.50	1.4	15	15770	35.30	34.78	34.87	–0.28

SOURCE: *New York Times,* September 30, 2004, Business Section, p. W3.

FIGURE 3

Excerpt from a Stock-Price Table

Company	Cur. Yld	Vol	Price	Chg
AES Cp 4 1/2 05	cv	10	100 1/4	+ 1/8
AMR 9s16	14.5	321	62	...
AT&T 7s05	6.8	5	102 23/32	+13/16
AT&T 7 1/2 06	7.1	90	105 5/8	– 1/2
AT&T 7 3/4 07	7.3	119	106 3/8	...
AT&T 6s09	5.9	925	101 3/4	+ 1/8
AT&T 6 1/2 13	6.6	95	98 1/2	– 7/8
AT&T 8.35s25	8.2	85	102 3/8	– 1/8
Alcan 4 7/8 12	4.8	25	101 1/4	+2 3/8
BellsoT 6 3/4 33	6.6	36	101 1/2	– 1/4
BellsoT 7 5/8 35	7.3	10	105 1/8	...
CarnCp 7.2s23	6.6	1	108 1/2	+1 3/8
Chiq 10.56s09	9.8	2	108	...
FordCr 6 3/8 08	6.1	10	105 1/4	– 5/8
GMA 6 1/8 08	5.8	146	105 1/4	– 1/8
GMA dc6s11	6.0	28	100	– 1/4
GMA zr12	...	22	59 5/8	+2 3/8
GMA zr15	...	29	49 5/8	+1 7/8
GoldmS 7.35s09	6.4	5	114 1/2	– 3/4

SOURCE: *New York Times,* September 30, 2004, Business Section, p. W8.

FIGURE 4

Excerpt from a Bond-Price Table

"What Is a Share of Google Worth?"

It almost goes without saying that Google is one of the world's leading brands. Its Internet search engine is so ubiquitous that its very name is a verb for looking up information about someone or something.

So when its founders decided to "go public" and offer shares of the company for the public to buy, the announcement set off tremendous speculation about what the company would be worth. Google itself predicted a jaw-dropping price range of $108 to $135 for its shares, which would have translated into a company value of $36 billion dollars. That would put Google right up there with the bluest of the "blue chip" stocks—of the thousands of publicly listed companies in the United States, only about 70 companies have a market value that high.

On August 19, 2004, Google made its debut on the NASDAQ stock market. Trading under the ticker symbol GOOG (you can "google it," if you like), the stock opened at $100, which was almost 18 percent higher than its initial offering price of $85. More than 22 million shares changed hands on that first day of trading, with Google selling a total of 19.6 million shares, thus raising about $1.2 billion for the company. That price implied a market value of $27.2 billion. Not bad for an idea conceived by two Stanford University grad students!

(As the updated version of this book went to press, Google was selling for about $475 a share, after hitting a high of $513 in November 2006.)

SOURCE: © Kim Kulish/Corbis

SOURCES: Paul R. La Monica, "Google Jumps 18% in Debut," CNN Money, August 19, 2004, http://money.cnn.com; Ben Berkowitz, "Is Google Worth $135 a Share?," *MSN Money*, July 26, 2004, http://msn.com; Ben Elgin, "Commentary: Google This: Investor Beware," *Business Week Online*, August 9, 2004, http://www.businessweek.com; "Financial Release: Google Inc. Prices Initial Public Offering of Class A Common Stock," August 18, 2004, http://investor.google.com; and "2004 Leaders: The Business Week Global 1000," *Business Week*, July 26, 2004, http://www.businessweekonline.com.

Corporation offers six different bonds. The highlighted one is labeled AT&T 7½ 06, meaning that these bonds pay an annual interest rate of 7.5 percent (the coupon) on their face value and that their maturity (redemption) date is 2006. Next, the current yield is reported as 7.1 percent; it is simply the coupon divided by the price. Because that yield, 7.1 percent, is slightly lower than the coupon, 7.5 percent, the bond must be selling at a price a little higher than its face value, so the return per dollar is correspondingly lower. The remaining information in Figure 4, like that in Figure 3, tells us the trading volume for the bond, the previous day's closing price, and the change in price from the day before.

Investors can also find information about the performance of stocks and bonds (and other kinds of investment) on the Internet. For example, an investor who visits the web site, http://cnnmoney.com, will find all the information just described, and a lot more. The difference will be that each individual stock and bond usually has to be viewed separately, whereas the print newspapers allow one to look at large lists of securities and quickly compare them.

◼ STOCK EXCHANGES AND THEIR FUNCTIONS

The New York Stock Exchange (NYSE)—"The Big Board"—is perhaps the world's most prestigious stock market. Located on Wall Street in New York City, it is "*the* establishment" of the securities industry. The NYSE deals with only the best-known and most heavily traded securities—2,672 companies in all at the end of 2005. Leading brokerage firms hold 1,366 "seats" on the stock exchange, which enable them to trade directly on the exchange floor. (In the NYSE's early years, members sat in assigned seats during roll call; the term lost its literal meaning with the advent of continuous trading in 1871.) Seats are traded on the open market. On September 29, 2004, for example, a seat on the exchange went for $1.2 million.

The NYSE handles a little over half of all stock market transactions in the United States (measured in *dollar* volume). A number of *regional* exchanges—such as the Chicago, Pacific, Philadelphia, Boston, and Cincinnati Stock Exchanges—deal in many of the stocks handled on the NYSE but mainly serve large institutional customers such as banks, insurance companies, and mutual funds. These regional exchanges together with the American Stock Exchange (located a few blocks away from the NYSE) handle less than 10 percent of the total stock traded.[9]

The remainder of all stock transactions are carried by NASDAQ (also known as the Nasdaq Stock Market), which draws its name from the National Association of Securities Dealers.[10] It is the home of most of the "tech" stocks that soared in the late 1990s, plummeted in 2000–2002, and have now returned to their pre-boom levels. Unlike the NYSE, NASDAQ has no physical trading floor, although it does have an outdoor display at its headquarters in New York City's Times Square, where a spectacular eight-story LED screen runs a continuous stock ticker, delivers market news, and shows advertisements and logos of NASDAQ member companies. All of its transactions are carried out on a computer network, with NASDAQ handling the stocks of approximately 3,300 companies, including such giants as Intel and Microsoft.

In recent years, the established stock markets have faced competition from another source. With the rapid growth of the Internet, people are now buying and selling stocks directly through their home computers. It is estimated that the number of on-line trading accounts at major U.S. brokerages increased from 1.5 million in 1997 to 19.7 million at the end of 2001, and topped 50 million in 2004.[11]

You Are There: An Event on the Trading Floor of the New York Stock Exchange

You are standing on the trading floor of the New York Stock Exchange, a crowded and noisy set of rooms cluttered with people, hundreds of computer monitors, and other electronic paraphernalia. It is a high-tech space in a 93-year-old architectural relic of bygone days. Around the floor are seventeen stations, or "trading posts," presided over by *specialists,* each assigned responsibility for trading a particular set of stocks.

Suddenly the floor's frenetic activity focuses on one specialist's post. News has just come in that one of the companies whose stock she handles has earned more in the previous quarter than was expected. Brokers crowd around her, calling out orders to buy and sell the company's stock, as its price rises rapidly in the wake of the good news. Deals are completed verbally, as clerks record the trades and enter them into the computerized tape, making the information instantly available all over the globe.

SOURCE: Murray Teitelbaum, Communications Division, New York Stock Exchange.

[9] New York Stock Exchange, http://www.nyse.com.

[10] The NASD and Nasdaq have been separated legally.

[11] *The New York Times 2004 Almanac* (John W. Wright, ed.), New York: Penguin Group, 2003, p. 342, which cites Gómez, Inc., an Internet research firm in Lincoln, Massachusetts; and *Wall Street Journal,* "Trading Stocks Online," http://investing.wsj.com, which cites Forrester Research in Cambridge, Massachusetts.

◼ Regulation of the Stock Market

Both the government and the industry itself regulate the U.S. securities markets. At the base of the regulatory pyramid, stock brokerage firms maintain compliance departments to oversee their own operations. At the next level, the NYSE, the American Stock Exchange, NASDAQ, and the regional exchanges are responsible for monitoring their member firms' business practices, funding adequacy, compliance, and integrity. They also use sophisticated computer surveillance systems to scrutinize trading activity. The Securities and Exchange Commission (SEC) is the federal government agency that oversees the market's self-regulation.

One example of these self-imposed rules involves the steps that markets adopted after the October 1987 stock market crash to cushion future price falls. Starting in 1988, with amendments since then, the NYSE and other stock markets adopted a series of rules called *circuit breakers*, which now halt all trading for one hour, two hours, or the remainder of the trading day when the Dow Jones Industrial Average (a widely followed average price of a sample of stocks) declines below its previous day's closing value by defined percentage amounts (which are adjusted every quarter). These restrictions on trading vary with the severity of the drop in the Dow and with the time of day when the drop occurs. Circuit breakers were designed to head off panics among market participants and forestall crashes like the ones in October 1929 and October 1987.

◼ Stock Exchanges and Corporate Capital Needs

Although corporations often raise needed funds by selling stock, they do not normally do so through the stock exchanges. New stock issues are typically handled by a special type of bank, called an *investment bank*. In contrast, the stock markets trade almost exclusively in "secondhand securities"—stocks in the hands of individuals and others who bought them earlier and now wish to sell them. Thus, the stock market does not provide funds to corporations needing financing to expand their productive activities. The markets provide money only to persons who already hold previously issued stocks.

Nevertheless, stock exchanges perform two critically important functions for corporate financing. First, by providing a secondhand market for stocks, they make individual investment in a company much less risky. Investors know that if they need money, they can always sell their stocks to other investors or to stock market specialists at the current market price. This reduction in risk makes it far easier for corporations to issue new stocks. Second, the stock market determines the current price of the company's stocks. That, in turn, determines whether it will be difficult or easy for a corporation to raise money by selling new stocks.

Some people believe that a company's stock price is closely tied to its operational efficiency, its effectiveness in meeting consumer demands, and its diligence in going after profitable innovation. According to this view, firms that use funds effectively will usually have comparatively high stock prices, and that will enable the firms to raise more money when they issue new stocks through their investment banks and sell them at the high prices determined by the stock market. In this way, the stock market tends to channel the economy's funds to the firms that can make best use of the money. In sum:

> If a firm has a promising future, its stock will tend to command a high price on the stock exchanges. Its high stock price will increase the firm's ability to raise capital by permitting it to amass a large amount of money through the sale of a comparatively small number of new stock shares. Thus, *the stock market helps to allocate the economy's resources to firms that can best use those resources.*

Other people voice skepticism about the claim that the price of a company's stock is closely tied to efficiency. These observers believe that the demand for a stock is

Corporate Scandals

Excerpted from the *The Economist* magazine, the following account provides details of some of the scandals that erupted in the corporate world in the early 2000s.

"... After a tumultuous few years in which a series of corporate America's best-known names admitted to wrongdoing of one sort or another—the roll-call includes Enron, WorldCom, Qwest, Adelphia, Rite Aid, Tyco and Xerox—the focus shifted to Wall Street's banks and fund managers, giving industrial companies some breathing space. They are also relieved that the latest scandals—the billions missing from Italy's biggest dairy company, Parmalat, and questionable accounting at Adecco, a Swiss-based company that is the world's biggest temping agency—are unfolding thousands of miles away. ...

Right now, the pack following the demise of one-time corporate titans is enraptured by the trial of Dennis Kozlowksi, former chief executive, and Mark Swartz, former chief financial officer, of Tyco. ... [S]hareholders were appalled by revelations of excess, including $6,000 spent on a shower curtain and more than $100,000 on a mirror at a posh company apartment where Mr. Kozlowski lived. Prosecutors have alleged that Mr. Kozlowski and Mr. Swartz stole $170 million from the company, illegally gained $430 million from selling stock, and used dubious accounting to hide their actions—allegations the men have denied. ...

So far, of the senior Enron executives, only [Andrew Fastow, former finance chief], has been indicted. The man who set up a series of offshore partnerships that disguised huge liabilities had pleaded not guilty to charges of fraud, money laundering and conspiracy to inflate Enron's profits. ... His wife, also a former Enron employee, was last week offered a deal under which she would plead guilty to a charge of filing a false tax return. ...

February is scheduled to bring two trials, that of Scott Sullivan, former chief financial officer of WorldCom, and that of John Rigas, founder of Adelphia Communications, a cable television company. WorldCom is the holder of the record for the most deceptive accounts, to the tune of an estimated $11 billion over several years. Mr. Sullivan is charged with masterminding the fraud, though he denies this. ...

While the rash of scandals did subside somewhat in 2003, another of the best-known corporate personalities of the late 1990s fell from grace. Dick Grasso resigned as chairman and chief executive of the New York Stock Exchange after a furore erupted over his $140 million pay packet (later revealed to have been $188m in total). ...

"Our financial officer won't be at work today—he just called in guilty."

SOURCE: "A Trying Year," The Economist, January 13, 2004, http://www.economist.com.

---

disproportionately influenced by short-term developments in the company's profitability and that the market pays little attention to management decisions affecting the firm's long-term earnings growth. These critics sometimes suggest that the stock market is similar to a gambling casino in which hunch, rumor, and superstition have a critical influence on prices. (We will learn more about this view later in the chapter.)

Whether or not stock prices are an accurate measure of a company's efficiency, if a company's stock price is very low in comparison with the value of its plant, equipment, and other assets, or when a company's earnings seem low compared to their potential level, that company becomes a tempting target for a **takeover** attempt. Perhaps the firm's current management is believed not to be very competent and those who seek to take control of the company believe that they can do better. Alternatively, if the demand for a company's stocks is believed to be inordinately influenced by short-term developments, such as temporarily low profits, others may believe that it is a bargain in terms of the low current price of the stock and its more promising future earnings prospects.

A takeover occurs when a group of outside financiers buys a sufficient amount of company stock to gain control of the firm. Often, the new controlling group will simply fire the current management and substitute a new chairman, president, and other top officers.

A **takeover** is the acquisition by an outside group (the raiders) of a controlling proportion of a company's stock. When the old management opposes the takeover attempt, it is called a *hostile takeover attempt.*

How to Lose Billions: Betting on Derivatives

Derivatives, one of the fastest growing areas of finance, are complex financial instruments so named because they "derive" their value from the price movements of an underlying investment, such as a group of stocks, bonds, or commodities. Businesses buy these contracts in an effort to hedge or insure against sudden changes in interest rates or currency values. But they also can be used to speculate in the markets.

A number of recent spectacular financial failures have been closely tied to the use of derivatives. First was the nearly $2 billion loss and resulting bankruptcy of Orange County, California. Then came the collapse of a 233-year-old British investment bank, Barings PLC, after one of its employees (a 28-year-old "rogue" futures trader named Nicholas Leeson) "bet the ranch" on the movement of the Japanese stock market and lost $1.46 billion. But the grandest episode of them all involved the meltdown of a private investment fund called Long-Term Capital Management, the management of which happened to include two Nobel Prize–winning economists. The firm was a so-called hedge fund that used derivatives to place

SOURCE: Digital image © 2002 Getty Images/PhotoDisc

multi-million-dollar bets on movements in such financial instruments as Russian treasury bonds and Danish mortgages. In the fall of 1998, the firm was reported to have lost more than $4 billion (and had to be bailed out by its bankers) when its statistical models failed to predict the movement of global markets.

SOURCE: "Wall Street Struggles to Save Big Fund," *Washington Post*, September 24, 1998.

■ SPECULATION

Individuals who engage in **speculation** deliberately invest in risky assets, hoping to obtain profits from future changes in the prices of these assets.

Securities dealings are sometimes viewed with suspicion because they are thought to be an instrument of **speculation.** When something goes wrong in the stock market—when, say, prices suddenly fall—observers often blame speculators. Editorial writers, for example, often use the word *speculators* as a term of strong disapproval, implying that those who engage in the activity are parasites who produce no benefits for society and often cause considerable harm. (See "How to Lose Billions: Betting on Derivatives" above for a description of a particularly risky speculative instrument, the *derivative.*)

Economists disagree vehemently with this judgment. They argue that speculators perform two vital economic functions:

- Speculators sell *protection from risk* to other people, much as a fire insurance policy offers protection from risk to a homeowner.
- Speculators help to smooth out price fluctuations by purchasing items when they are abundant (and cheap) and holding them and reselling them when they are scarce (and expensive). In that way, speculators play a vital economic role in helping to alleviate and even prevent shortages.

Some examples from outside the securities markets will help clarify the role of speculators. Imagine that a Broadway ticket broker attends a preview of a new musical comedy and suspects it will be a hit. He decides to speculate by buying a large block of tickets for future performances. In that way, he takes over part of the producer's risk, while the play's producer reduces her inventory of risky tickets and receives some hard cash. If the show opens and is a flop, the broker will be stuck with the tickets. If the show is a hit, he can sell them at a premium, if the law allows (and he will be denounced as a speculator or a "scalper").

Similarly, speculators enable farmers (or producers of metals and other commodities whose future price is uncertain) to decrease their risk. Let's say Jasmine and Jim have planted a large crop of wheat but fear its price may fall before harvest time. They can protect themselves by signing a contract with a speculator for future delivery of the crop at an agreed-upon price. If the price then falls, the speculator—not Jasmine and Jim—will suffer the loss. Of course, if the price rises, the speculator will reap the rewards—but that is the nature of risk bearing. The speculator who has agreed to buy the crop at a preset price, regardless of market conditions at the time of the sale, has, in effect, sold an insurance policy to Jasmine and Jim. Surely this is a useful function.

The speculators' second role is perhaps even more important. In effect, they accumulate and store goods in periods of abundance and make goods available in periods of scarcity. Suppose that a speculator has reason to suspect that next year's crop of a storable commodity will not be nearly as abundant as this year's. She will buy some of the crop now, when it is cheap, for resale when it becomes scarce and expensive. In the process, she will smooth out the swing in prices by adding her purchases to the total market demand in the low-price period (which tends to bring the price up at that time), and bringing in her supplies during the high-price period (which tends to push this later-period price down).[12]

Thus, the successful speculator will help to relieve matters during periods of extreme shortage. Speculators have sometimes even helped to relieve famine by releasing supplies they had deliberately hoarded for such an occasion. Of course, speculators are cursed for their high prices when this happens. But those who curse them do not understand that prices would have been even higher if the speculators' foresight and avid pursuit of profit had not provided for the emergency. On the securities market, famine and severe shortages are not an issue, but the fact remains that successful speculators tend to reduce price fluctuations by increasing demand for stocks when prices are low and contributing to supply when prices are high.

> Far from aggravating instability and fluctuations, to earn a profit speculators *iron out* fluctuations by buying when prices are low and selling when prices are high.

PUZZLE #2 RESOLVED: *Unpredictable Stock Prices as "Random Walks"*

In one of the puzzles at the beginning of this chapter, we cited evidence indicating that the best professional securities analysts have a forecasting record so miserable that investors may do as well predicting earnings by hunch, superstition, or any purely random process as they would by following professional advice. (See "Giving Up on Stock Gimmicks" on the next page to learn about some crazy ways of "predicting" the stock market's performance.)

Does this mean that analysts are incompetent people who do not know what they are doing? Not at all. Rather, there is fairly strong evidence that they have undertaken a task that is basically impossible.

How can this be so? The answer is that to make a good forecast of *any* variable—be it GDP, population, fuel usage, or stock market prices—there must be something in the past whose behavior is closely related to the future behavior of the variable whose path we wish to predict. If a 10 percent rise in this year's consumption always produces a 5 percent rise in next year's GDP, this fact can help us predict future GDP on the basis of current observations. But if we want to forecast the future of a variable whose behavior is completely unrelated to the behavior of *any* current or past variable, there is no objective evidence that can help us make that forecast. Throwing darts or gazing into a crystal ball are no less effective than analysts' calculations.

A mass of statistical evidence indicates that the behavior of stock prices is largely unpredictable. In other words, the behavior of stock prices is essentially *random;* the paths they follow approximate what statisticians call **random walks.** A random walk is like the path followed by a sleepwalker. All we know about his position after his next step is that it will be given by his current position plus whatever random direction his next haphazard step will carry him. The relevant feature of randomness, for

The time path of a variable such as the price of a stock is said to constitute a **random walk** if its magnitude in one period (say, May 2, 2005) is equal to its value in the preceding period (May 1, 2005) plus a completely random number. That is: Price on May 2, 2005 = Price on May 1, 2005 + Random number, where the random number (positive or negative) can be obtained by a roll of dice or some such procedure.

---

[12] For a diagrammatic analysis of this role of speculation, see Discussion Question 3 at the end of this chapter.

our purposes, is that it is by nature *unpredictable*, which is just what the word *random* means.

> If the evidence that stock prices approximate a random walk stands up to research in the future as it has so far, it is easy enough to understand why stock market predictions are so poor. Analysts are trying to forecast behavior that is basically random; in effect, they are trying to predict the unpredictable.

Two questions remain. First, does the evidence that stock prices follow a random walk mean that investment in stocks is a pure gamble and never worthwhile? Second, how does one explain the random behavior of stock prices?

To answer the first question, it is wrong to conclude that investment in stocks is generally not worthwhile. The statistical evidence is that, over the long run, stock prices *as a whole* have followed a fairly marked upward trend, perhaps reflecting the long-term growth of the economy. Thus, the random walk does not proceed in just any direction—rather, it represents a set of erratic movements *around a basic upward trend in stock prices.*

Moreover, it is not in the *overall* level of stock prices that the most pertinent random walk occurs, but in the performance of one company's stock as compared with

Giving Up on Stock Gimmicks

For a New Year's resolution, I'm giving up stock market forecasting gimmicks.

The Super Bowl indicator. The January barometer. Others so numerous I can't think of them all right now. It won't be easy to do this cold turkey. The indicators are often ingenious, occasionally quite persuasive, and nearly always fun. They appeal to my yearning for a simple answer to a complicated problem.

The first indicator I bid goodbye to, the Super Bowl stock market predictor, is the easiest to forswear. It has suddenly and completely stopped functioning, breaking down like a rusty old car. That's too bad, because it added some zest to the National Football League championship extravaganza, which more than once has needed it.

The idea is this: If a team from the original National Football League before its 1970 merger with the American Football League won the Super Bowl, a good year for the stock market was in store. Conversely, if a team with AFL origins triumphed, tough times lay ahead.

An awareness of this pattern would have been especially helpful in the bear-market years 1969, 1970, 1973, 1974, and 1981, all of which began with wins by a team from the wrong side of the tracks. So what if everybody knew there was no possible causal link between football and the stock market?

As the years rolled by, though, the novelty of the Super Bowl indicator wore off, especially as analysts picked it apart looking for corollaries. Was the margin of victory important? What about which team scored first? Then along came John Elway to knock the whole thing down with a barrage of his famous bullet passes. The Denver Broncos quarterback led his team, a product of the AFL, to victories in '98 and '99, and yet the stock market boomed anyway.

While Super Bowl indicator fans struggled to formulate the "Elway exception," the St. Louis Rams recaptured the Super Bowl in 2000 for the NFL originals. Contrarily, the stock market then dropped. . . .

A seasonal indicator with a stronger rationale, the January barometer long espoused by investment advisor Yale Hirsch, gave a

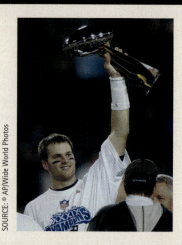

SOURCE: © AP/Wide World Photos

better performance in 2000. In line with Hirsch's doctrine that "as January goes, so goes the year," it foreshadowed a down year for the market when the stock-price averages posted minus signs for the first month.

By Hirsch's reckoning, this rule has seen only three glaring exceptions since 1950. Most years, I readily confess, I find myself checking in January to see how it's shaping up.

But when the time comes to figure out how to put it into use, I'm at a loss. Trading on it seems impractical. Any long-term investor who sits out each January to await a signal misses a lot of gains: Measuring by the Standard & Poor's 500 Index, 3.3 percent in 1996, 6.1 percent in 1997, 1 percent in 1998 and 4.1 percent in 1999. . . .

Maybe you've got some favorite indicators of your own. If so, you're welcome to them. From now on, I never touch the stuff.

SOURCE: Chet Currier, "Investing: Giving Up on Stock Gimmicks," from *Newsday*, January 7, 2001, p. F13. Reprinted by permission of Tribune Media Services.

another firm's stock. For this reason, professional advice may be able to predict that investment in the stock market is likely to be a good thing over the long haul. But, if the random walk evidence is valid, there is no way professionals can tell us *which* of the available stocks is most likely to increase in price—that is, which combination of stocks is best for the investor to buy.

The only appropriate answer to the second question of how to account for the random behavior of stock prices is that no one is sure of the explanation. There are two widely offered hypotheses—each virtually the opposite of the other. The first asserts that stock prices are random because clever professional speculators are able to foresee almost perfectly every influence that is *not* random. For example, suppose that a change occurs that makes the probable earnings of some company higher than had previously been expected. Then, according to this view, the professionals will instantly become aware of this change and immediately buy enough shares to raise the price of the stock accordingly. Then the only thing for that stock price to do between this year and next is wander randomly, because the professionals cannot predict random movements, and hence they cannot force current stock prices to anticipate them.

SOURCE: © 1990 Cartoonists & Writers Syndicate/cartoonweb.com

"Just a normal day at the nation's most important financial institution . . . "

The second explanation of the random behavior of stock prices is at the opposite extreme from the view that all nonrandom movements are wiped out by super-smart professionals. This is the view that people who buy and sell stocks have learned that they cannot predict future stock prices. As a result, they react to *any* signal, however irrational and irrelevant it appears. If the president catches cold, stock prices fall. If an astronaut's venture is successful, prices go up. According to this view, investors are, in the last analysis, trying to predict not the prospects of the economy or of the company whose shares they buy, but the supply and demand behavior of other investors, which will ultimately determine the course of stock prices. Because all investors are equally in the dark, their groping around can only result in the randomness that we observe.

The classic statement of this view of stock market behavior was provided in 1936 by the English economist John Maynard Keynes, a successful professional speculator himself:

Professional investment may be likened to those newspaper competitions in which the competitors have to pick out the six prettiest faces from a hundred photographs, the prize being awarded to the competitor whose choice most nearly corresponds to the average preferences of the competitors as a whole; so that each competitor has to pick not those faces which he himself finds prettiest, but those which he thinks likeliest to catch the fancy of the other competitors, all of whom are looking at the problem from the same point of view. It is not a case of choosing those which, to the best of one's judgment, are really the prettiest, nor even those which average opinion genuinely thinks the prettiest. We have reached the third degree where we devote our intelligences to anticipating what average opinion expects the average opinion to be. And there are some, I believe, who practice the fourth, fifth and higher degrees.[13]

---

[13] John Maynard Keynes, *The General Theory of Employment, Interest, and Money* (New York: Harcourt Brace; 1936), p. 156.

PUZZLE #1 REDUX: *The Boom and Bust of the U.S. Stock Market*

This last quotation leads to some insights into the remarkable behavior of the U.S. stock market during the late 1990s and early 2000s—a phenomenon we mentioned at the start of this chapter. (Refer back to Figure 1.)

First, many people who buy stocks—both professionals and amateurs—do so for speculative purposes. They may not care (or even know!) what the company does; they care only that its stock price goes up. Second, in a speculative world, where people buy stocks in order to sell them later, a share of stock is basically worth what *someone else* will pay for it. So even if Smart Susan is convinced that Dotcon.com has poor business prospects, it may still be rational for her to buy the stock at $50 per share if she is convinced that she will be able to sell it to Foolish Frank next year for $100 per share. (This idea has been called the "greater fool" theory of investing: It makes sense to buy a stock at a foolishly high price if you can sell it at an even higher price—to an even greater fool!) Third, once something attains the status of a fad, waves of buying can drive prices up to ridiculous levels, as has happened many times in history. Fourth, America undoubtedly fell in love both with information technology (especially the Internet) and the stock market (especially Internet-related stocks) in the late 1990s.

All this set the stage for what is commonly called a financial "bubble." The metaphor is meant to conjure up images of things like balloons and soap bubbles that blow up and up and up . . . until they burst. Indeed, legions of economists were warning about a stock market bubble in 1998, in 1999, and into 2000. The problem is simply stated: No one ever knows when a bubble will burst. And for stock market speculators, timing is everything. Look back at Figure 1 again. Those who claimed in mid-1999 that technology stocks were overvalued looked pretty silly when stock prices doubled in less than one year. (Of course, they subsequently looked pretty smart when prices collapsed!) Technology enthusiasts ignored them as the stock market partied on. The only thing that is truly predictable about a bubble is that it will burst—*eventually*. But no one ever knows when. As a result, no one could say definitively that *now* was the time to sell technology stocks. As the saying goes, the rest is history.

SUMMARY

1. Most U.S. manufactured goods are produced by **corporations**.

2. Investors in corporations have greater risk protection than those who put their money into other types of firm because the corporate form gives them **limited liability**—they cannot be asked to pay more of the company's debts than they have invested in the firm.

3. Higher taxation of corporate earnings tends to limit the things in which corporations can invest and may lead to inefficiency in resource allocation.

4. A **common stock** is a share in a company's ownership. A **bond** is an IOU for money lent to a company by the bondholder. Many observers argue that a stock purchase really amounts to a loan to the company—a loan that is riskier than a bond purchase.

5. If **interest rates** rise, bond prices will fall. In other words, if some bond amounts to a contract to pay 8 percent and the market interest rate goes up to 10 percent, people will no longer be willing to pay the old price for that bond.

6. Corporations finance their activities mostly by **plowback** (that is, by retaining part of their earnings and reinvesting the funds in the company). They also obtain funds by selling stocks and bonds and by taking out more traditional loans.

7. If stock prices correctly reflect the future prospects of different companies, it is easier for promising firms to raise money because they are able to sell each stock issue at favorable prices.

8. Bonds are relatively risky for the firms that issue them, but they are fairly safe for their buyers, because they are a commitment by those firms to pay fixed annual amounts to the bondholders whether or not the companies make money that year. Stocks, which do not promise any fixed payment, are relatively safe for the companies but risky for their owners.

9. A portfolio is a collection of stocks, bonds, and other assets of a single owner. The greater the number and variety of securities and other assets a portfolio contains, the less risky it generally is.

10. A **takeover** of a corporation occurs when an outside group buys enough stock to get control of the firm's decisions. Takeovers are a useful way to get rid of incompetent management or to force management to be more efficient. However, the process is costly and leads to wasteful defensive and offensive activities.

11. **Speculation** affects stock market prices, but (contrary to widespread belief) it actually tends to reduce the frequency and size of price fluctuations. Speculators are also useful to the economy because they undertake risks that others wish to avoid, thereby, in effect, providing others with insurance against risk.

12. Statistical evidence indicates that individual stock prices behave randomly (in other words, unpredictably).

KEY TERMS

Corporation   179

Limited liability   180

Common stock   180

Bond   180

Inflation   181

Interest rate   181

Plowback (retained earnings)   182

Portfolio diversification   184

Mutual fund   184

Index fund   185

Stock price index   185

Takeover   189

Speculation   190

Random walk   191

TEST YOURSELF

1. Suppose that interest rates are 6 percent in the economy and a safe bond promises to pay $3 per year in interest forever. What do you think the price of the bond will be? Why?

2. Suppose that in the economy described in Test Yourself 1, interest rates suddenly fall to 3 percent. What will happen to the price of the bond that pays $3 per year?

3. For whom are stocks riskier than bonds? For whom are bonds riskier than stocks?

4. If the price of a company's stock constitutes a random walk, next year its price will equal today's price plus what?

5. Company A sells heaters and Company B sells air conditioners. Which is the safer investment, Company A stock, Company B stock, or a portfolio containing half of each?

6. If you make a lucky prediction about the prices of the stocks of the two companies in question 5 will you earn more or less if you invest in that company rather than the portfolio?

DISCUSSION QUESTIONS

1. If you hold shares in a corporation and management decides to plow back the company's earnings some year instead of paying dividends, what are the advantages and disadvantages to you?

2. If you want to buy a stock, when might it pay you to use a market order? When will it pay to use a limit order?

3. Show in diagrams that if a speculator were to buy when price is high and sell when price is low, he would increase price fluctuations. Why would it be in his best interest *not* to do so? (*Hint:* Draw two supply-demand diagrams, one for the high-price period and one for the low-price period. How would the speculator's activities affect these diagrams?)

4. If stock prices really do take a random walk, can you nevertheless think of good reasons for getting professional advice before investing?

5. Hostile takeovers often end up in court when management attempts to block such a maneuver and raiders accuse management of selfishly sacrificing the stockholders' interests. The courts often look askance at "coercive" offers by raiders—an offer to buy, say, 20 percent of the company's stock by a certain date from the first stockholders who offer to sell. By contrast, they take a more favorable attitude toward "noncoercive" offers to buy any and all stock supplied at announced prices. Do you think the courts are right to reject "coercive offers" but prevent management from blocking "noncoercive" offers? Why?

6. In program trading, computers decide when to buy or sell stocks on behalf of large, institutional investors. The computers then carry out those transactions with electronic speed. Critics claim that this practice is a major reason why stock prices rose and fell sharply in the 1980s. Is this idea plausible? Why or why not?

MARKETS AND THE PRICE SYSTEM

So far, we have talked only about firms in general without worrying about the sorts of markets in which they operate. To understand the different types of competition a firm can face, it is necessary, first, to explain clearly what we mean by the word "market." Economists do not reserve this term for only an organized exchange, such as the London stock exchange, operating in a specific location. In its more general and abstract usage, *market* refers to a set of sellers and buyers whose activities affect the price at which a *particular commodity* is sold. For example, two separate sales of General Motors stock in different parts of the country can be considered to take place in the same market, whereas sales of bread in one stall of a market square and sales of compact disks in the next stall may, in our sense, occur in totally different markets.

Economists distinguish among different kinds of markets according to how many firms they include, whether the products of the different firms are identical or different, and how easy it is for new firms to enter the markets. *Perfect competition* is at one extreme (many small firms selling an identical product, with easy entry into the market), and *pure monopoly* (a single firm dominating the market) is at the other extreme. In between are hybrid forms—called *monopolistic competition* (many small firms, each selling slightly different products) and *oligopoly* (a few large rival firms)—that share some of the characteristics of both perfect competition and monopoly.

Perfect competition is far from the typical market form in the U.S. economy. Indeed, it is quite rare. Pure monopoly—literally *one* firm—is also infrequently encountered. Most of the products you buy are no doubt supplied by oligopolies or monopolistic competitors—terms that we will define precisely in Chapter 12.

10

THE FIRM AND THE INDUSTRY UNDER PERFECT COMPETITION

Competition . . . brings about the only . . . arrangement of social production which is possible. . . . [Otherwise] what guarantee [do] we have that the necessary quantity and not more of each product will be produced, that we shall not go hungry in regard to corn and meat while we are choked in beet sugar and drowned in potato spirit, that we shall not lack trousers to cover our nakedness while buttons flood us in millions?

FRIEDRICH ENGELS (THE FRIEND AND COAUTHOR OF KARL MARX)

I ndustries differ dramatically in the number and typical sizes of their firms. Some, such as commercial fishing, encompass a great many very small firms. Others, like automobile manufacturing, are composed of a few industrial giants. This chapter deals with a very special type of market structure—called *perfect competition*—in which firms are numerous and small. We begin by comparing alternative market forms and defining perfect competition precisely. First, as usual, we set out our puzzle.

CONTENTS

PUZZLE: *Pollution Reduction Incentives That Actually Increase Pollution*

Many economists and other citizens concerned about the environment believe that society can obtain cleaner air and water cheaply and effectively by requiring polluters to pay for the damages they cause. (See Chapter 17 for more details.) Yet people often view pollution charges as just another *tax*, and that word can translate into political poison. Some politicians—reasoning that you can move a donkey along just as effectively by offering it a carrot as by poking it with a stick—have proposed *paying* firms to cut down on their polluting emissions.

At least some theoretical and statistical evidence indicates that such a system of bribes (or, to use a more palatable word, subsidies) does work, *at least up to a point*. Individual polluting firms will, indeed, respond to government payments for decreased emissions by reducing their pollution. But, over the long haul, it turns out that society may well end up with more pollution than before! Subsidy payments to the firms can actually exacerbate pollution problems. How is it possible that subsidies induce each firm to pollute less but in the long run lead to a rise in total pollution? The analysis in this chapter will supplement your own common sense sufficiently to supply the answer.

■ PERFECT COMPETITION DEFINED

Perfect competition
occurs in an industry when that industry is made up of many small firms producing homogeneous products, when there is no impediment to the entry or exit of firms, and when full information is available.

You can appreciate just how special perfect competition is by considering this comprehensive definition. A market is said to operate under **perfect competition** when the following four conditions are satisfied:

1. *Numerous small firms and customers.* Competitive markets contain so many buyers and sellers that each one constitutes a negligible portion of the whole—so small, in fact, that each player's decisions have no effect on price. This requirement rules out trade associations or other collusive arrangements in which firms work together to influence price.

2. *Homogeneity of product.* The product offered by any seller is identical to that supplied by any other seller. (For example, No. 1 red winter wheat is a homogeneous product; different brands of toothpaste are not.) Because products are homogeneous, consumers do not care from which firm they buy, so competition is more powerful.

3. *Freedom of entry and exit.* New firms desiring to enter the market face no impediments that previous entrants can avoid. So new firms can easily come in and compete with older firms. Similarly, if production and sale of the good proves unprofitable, no barriers prevent firms from leaving the market.

4. *Perfect information.* Each firm and each customer is well informed about available products and prices. They know whether one supplier is selling at a lower price than another.

These exacting requirements are rarely, if ever, found in practice. One example that comes close to the perfectly competitive standard is a market for common stocks. On any given day, literally millions of buyers and sellers trade AT&T stock; all of the shares are exactly alike; anyone who wishes to sell his or her AT&T stock can enter the market easily; and most relevant company and industry information is readily available (and virtually free of charge) in the daily newspapers or on the Internet. Many farming and fishing industries also approximate perfect competition. But it is difficult to find many other examples. Our interest in the perfectly competitive model surely does not lie in its ability to describe reality.

Why, then, do we spend time studying perfect competition? The answer takes us back to the central theme of this book. Under perfect competition the market mechanism in many ways performs best. If we want to learn what markets do well, we can put the market's best foot forward by beginning with perfect competition.

As Adam Smith suggested some two centuries ago, perfectly competitive firms use society's scarce resources with maximum efficiency. Also, as Friedrich Engels (Karl Marx's closest friend and coauthor) suggested in the opening quotation of this chapter, only perfect competition can ensure that the economy turns out just those varieties and relative quantities of goods that match consumer preferences. By studying perfect competition, we can learn some of the things an *ideally functioning* market system can accomplish. This is the topic of this chapter and Chapter 14. In Chapters 11 and 12, we will consider other market forms and see how they deviate from the perfectly competitive ideal. Still later chapters (especially Chapter 15 and the chapters in Parts IV and V) will examine many important tasks that the market does *not* perform well, even under perfect competition. All these chapters combined should provide a balanced assessment of the virtues and vices of the market mechanism.

■ THE PERFECTLY COMPETITIVE FIRM

To discover what happens in a perfectly competitive market, we must deal separately with the behavior of *individual firms* and the behavior of the *industry* that is constituted by those firms. One basic difference between the firm and the industry under competition relates to *pricing*:

> **Under perfect competition, the firm has no choice but to accept the price that has been determined in the market. It is therefore called a "price taker" (rather than a "price maker").**

The idea that no firm in a perfectly competitive market can exert any control over product price follows from our stringent definition of perfect competition. The presence of a vast number of competitors, each offering identical products, forces each firm to meet but not exceed the price charged by the others, because at any higher price all of the firm's customers would leave it and move their purchases to its rivals.

With two important exceptions, analysis of the behavior of the firm under perfect competition is exactly as we described in Chapters 7 and 8. The two exceptions relate to the special shape of the perfectly competitive firm's demand curve and the freedom of entry and exit, along with their effects on the firm's profits. We will consider each of these special features of perfect competition in turn, beginning with the demand curve.

■ The Firm's Demand Curve under Perfect Competition

In Chapter 8, we always assumed that the firm faced a downward-sloping demand curve. That is, if a firm wished to sell more (without increasing its advertising or changing its product specifications), it had to reduce its product price. The perfectly competitive firm is an exception to this general principle.

> **A perfectly competitive firm faces a *horizontal* demand curve. This means that it can sell as much as it wants at the prevailing market price. It can double or triple its sales without reducing the price of its product.**

How is this possible? The answer is that the perfectly competitive firm is so insignificant relative to the market as a whole that it has absolutely no influence over price. The farmer who sells his corn through a commodities exchange in Chicago must accept the current quotation that his broker reports to him. Because there are thousands of farmers, the Chicago price per bushel will not budge because farmer Jasmine decides she doesn't like the price and stores a truckload of corn rather than taking it to the grain elevator.

Thus, the demand curve for Jasmine's corn is as shown in Figure 1(a). As we can see, the price she is paid in Chicago will be $3 per bushel whether she sells one truckload

*Under perfect competition, the firm is a **price taker**. It has no choice but to accept the price that has been determined in the market.*

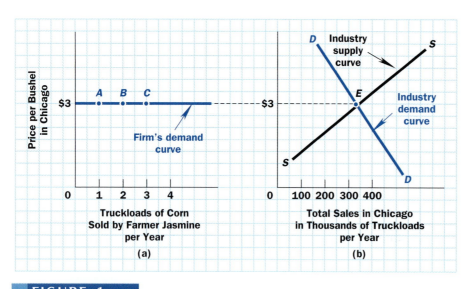

FIGURE 1

Demand Curve for a
Firm under Perfect
Competition

(point *A*) or two (point *B*) or three (point *C*). This is because that $3 price is determined by the intersection of the *industry's* supply and demand curves shown in the right-hand portion of the graph, Panel (b).

Notice that, in the case of perfect competition, the downward-sloping industry demand curve in Figure 1(b) leads to the horizontal demand curve for the individual firm in Figure 1(a). Also notice that the height of that horizontal firm demand curve will be the height of the intersection point, *E*, of the industry supply and demand curves. So the firm's demand curve will generally not resemble the demand curve for the industry.

■ Short-Run Equilibrium for the Perfectly Competitive Firm

We already have sufficient background to study the decisions of a firm operating in a perfectly competitive market. Recall from Chapter 8 that profit maximization requires the firm to pick an output level that makes its *marginal cost equal to its marginal revenue:* MC = MR. The only feature that distinguishes the profit-maximizing equilibrium for the perfectly competitive firm from that of any other type of firm is its horizontal demand curve. We know from Chapter 8 that the firm's demand curve is also its average revenue curve because the average revenue a firm gets from selling a commodity is equal to the price of the commodity. That is, if it sells 100 shirts at a price of $18 each, then obviously, the average revenue it obtains from the sale of each shirt will be $18. Because the demand curve tells us the price at which the supplier can sell a given quantity, this means it also tells us the average revenue it gets per unit sold when it sells that given quantity. So the firm's demand curve and its average revenue curve are identical. The same curve does two jobs. But it also does a third job.

Because this demand curve is horizontal, the competitive firm's *marginal* revenue curve is a horizontal straight line that also coincides with its demand curve; hence, MR = Price (*P*). It is easy to see why this is so. If the price does not depend on how much the firm sells (which is exactly what a horizontal demand curve means), then each *additional* unit sold brings in an amount of additional revenue (the *marginal* revenue) exactly equal to the market price. So marginal revenue always equals price under perfect competition because the firm is a price taker.

Under perfect competition the firm's demand curve, average revenue curve and marginal revenue curve are all the same.

As in Chapter 8, once we know the shape and position of a firm's marginal revenue curve, we can use this information and the marginal cost curve to determine its optimal output and profit, as shown in Figure 2. As usual, the profit-maximizing output is that at which MC = MR (point *B*). The demand curve, *D* = MR = AR, is horizontal because the firm's output is too small to affect market price, as we just saw.

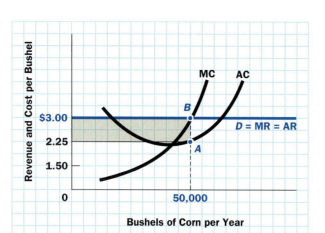

FIGURE 2

Short-Run Equilibrium
of the Perfectly
Competitive Firm

This particular competitive firm produces 50,000 bushels of corn per year—the output level at which MC and MR both equal the market price, $3. Thus:

Because it is a price taker, the *equilibrium* of a profit-maximizing firm in a perfectly competitive market must occur at an output level at which marginal cost equals price = AR = MR. This is because a horizontal demand curve makes price and MR equal and, therefore, both must equal marginal cost according to the profit-maximizing principle. In symbols:

MC = MR = P.

This idea is illustrated in Table 1, which gives the firm's total and marginal revenue, total and marginal cost, and total profit for different output quantities. We see from Column (6) that total profit is maximized at an output of about 50,000 bushels where total profit is $37,500. An increase in output from 40,000 to 50,000 bushels incurs a marginal cost ($26,500) that most nearly equals the corresponding marginal revenue ($30,000), confirming that 50,000 bushels is the profit-maximizing output.[1]

TABLE 1

Revenues, Costs, and Profits of a Perfectly Competitive Firm

(1) Total Quantity	(2) Total Revenue	(3) Marginal Revenue	(4) Total Cost	(5) Marginal Cost	(6) Total Profit
0	$ 0				
		$30			
10	30		$ 32		$ −2
		30		$ 24	
20	60		56		4
		30		11.5	
30	90		67.5		22.5
		30		18.5	
40	120		86		34
		30		26.5	
50	**150**		**112.5**		**37.5**
		30		56.5	
60	180		169		11
		30		93	
70	210		262		−52

Note: Quantity is in thousands of bushels; dollars are in thousands.

▪ Short-Run Profit: Graphic Representation

Our analysis so far tells us how a firm can pick the output that maximizes its profit. It may even be able to earn a substantial profit. But sometimes, even if it succeeds in maximizing profit, the firm may conceivably find itself in trouble because market conditions may make the highest possible profit a *negative* number. If the demand for its product is weak or its costs are high, even the firm's most profitable option may lead to a loss. In the short run, the demand curve can either be high or low relative to costs. To determine whether the firm is making a profit or incurring a loss, we must compare *total* revenue (TR = P × Q) with *total* cost (TC = AC × Q). Because the output (Q) is common to both of these amounts, this equation tells us that the process is equivalent to comparing price (P) with average cost (AC). If P > AC, the firm will earn a profit, and if P < AC, it will suffer a loss.

We can therefore show the firm's profit in Figure 2, which includes the firm's *average cost* curve. By definition, profit per unit of output is revenue per unit (P) minus cost per unit (AC). We see in Figure 2 that average cost at 50,000 bushels per year is only $2.25 per bushel (point A), whereas *average revenue* (AR) is $3 per bushel (point B). The firm makes a profit of AR − AC = $0.75 per bushel, which appears in the graph as the vertical distance between points A and B.

Notice that, in addition to showing the *profit per unit*, Figure 2 can be used to show the firm's *total profit*. Total profit is the profit per unit ($0.75 in this example) times the number of units (50,000 per year). Therefore, total profit is represented by the *area* of the shaded rectangle whose height is the profit per unit ($0.75) and whose width is the number of units (50,000).[2] In this case, profits are $37,500 per year. In general, total profit at any output is the area of the rectangle whose base equals the level of output and whose height equals AR − AC.

The MC = *P* condition gives us the output that maximizes the perfectly competitive firm's profit. It does not, however, tell us whether the firm is making a profit or incurring a loss. To make this determination, we must compare price (average revenue) with average cost.

---

[1] Marginal cost is not precisely equal to marginal revenue, because to calculate marginal costs and marginal revenues with perfect accuracy, we would have to increase output one bushel at a time instead of proceeding in leaps of 10,000 bushels. Of course, that would require too much space! In any event, our failure to make a more careful calculation in terms of individual bushels explains why we are unable to find the output at which MR and MC are *exactly* equal.

[2] Recall that the formula for the area of a rectangle is Area = Height × Width.

The Case of Short-Term Losses

The market is obviously treating the farmer in Figure 2 rather nicely. But what if the corn market were not so generous in its rewards? What if, for example, the market price were only $1.50 per bushel instead of $3? Figure 3 shows the equilibrium of the firm under these circumstances. The cost curves are the same in this diagram as they were in Figure 2, but the demand curve has shifted down to correspond to the market price of $1.50 per bushel. The firm still maximizes profits by producing the level of output at which marginal costs (MC) is equal to price (P) - (MC = P = MR)—point B in the diagram. But this time "maximizing profits" really means minimizing losses, as shown by the shaded rectangle.

At the optimal level of output (30,000 bushels per year), average cost is $2.25 per bushel (point A), which exceeds the $1.50 per bushel price (point B). The firm therefore incurs a loss of $0.75 per bushel times 30,000 bushels, or $22,500 per year. This loss, which is represented by the area of the gold rectangle in Figure 3, is the best the firm can do. If it selected any other output level, its loss would be even greater.

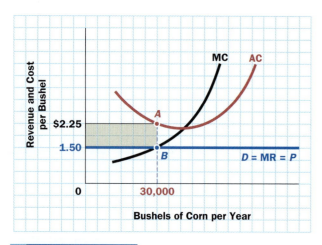

FIGURE 3

Short-Run Equilibrium of the Perfectly Competitive Firm with a Lower Price

A **variable cost** is a cost whose total amount changes when the quantity of output of the supplier changes.

Shutdown and Break-Even Analysis

Of course, any firm will accept only a limited amount of loss before it stops production. If losses get too big, the firm can simply go out of business. To understand the logic of the choice between shutting down and remaining in operation, we must return to the distinction between **costs** that are **variable** in the short run and those that are not. Recall from Chapter 7 that costs are not variable if the firm cannot escape them in the short run, either because of a contract (say, with a landlord or a union) or because it has already bought the item whose cost is not variable (for example, a machine).

If the firm stops producing, then its revenue and its short-run variable costs will fall to zero. But its costs that are not variable will remain. If the firm is losing money, sometimes it will be better off continuing to operate until its obligations to pay the nonvariable costs expire; sometimes it will do better by shutting down immediately and producing nothing. That obviously depends on whether or not by shutting down immediately, the costs it can avoid *immediately* are greater that the revenue it gives up by having nothing to sell any longer. More explicitly, two rules govern the decision:

Rule 1. The firm will make a loss if total revenue (TR) is less than total cost (TC). In that case, it should plan to shut down, either in the short run or in the long run.

Rule 2. The firm should continue to operate in the short run if TR exceeds total short-run variable cost (TVC).

The first rule is self-evident. If the firm's revenues do not cover its total costs, then it surely will lose money and, sooner or later, it will have to close. The second rule is a bit more subtle. Suppose that TR is less than TC. If our unfortunate firm continues in operation, it will lose the difference between total cost and total revenue:

Loss if the firm stays in business = TC − TR

However, if the firm stops producing, both its revenues and short-run variable costs become zero, leaving only the *nonvariable* costs to be paid:

Loss if the firm shuts down = Nonvariable costs = TC − TVC

Hence, it is best to keep operating as long as: its loss if it stays in business is less than its loss if it shuts down:

$$TC - TR < TC - TVC$$

or

$$TVC < TR$$

That is Rule 2.

We can illustrate Rule 2 with the two cases shown in Table 2. Case A deals with a firm that loses money but is better off staying in business in the short run. If it shuts down, it will lose its entire $60,000 worth of short-run nonvariable cost. If it continues to operate, its total revenue of $100,000 will exceed its total variable cost (TVC = $80,000) by $20,000. That means continuing operation contributes $20,000 toward meeting nonvariable costs and reduces losses to $40,000. In Case B, in contrast, it pays the firm to shut down because continued operation merely adds to its losses. If the firm operates, it will lose $90,000 (the last entry in Table 2); if it shuts down, it will lose only the $60,000 in nonvariable costs, which it must pay whether it operates or not.

TABLE 2
The Shutdown Decision

	Case A	Case B
Total revenue (TR)	$100	$100
Total variable cost (TVC)	80	130
Short-run nonvariable cost	60	60
Total cost (TC)	140	190
Loss if firm shuts down (= Short-run nonvariable cost)	60	60
Loss if firm does not shut down	40	90

Note: Figures are in thousands of dollars.

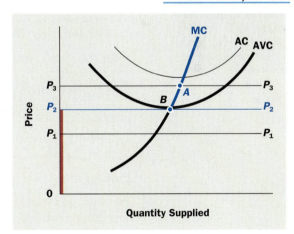

FIGURE 4
Shutdown Analysis

We also can analyze the shutdown decision graphically. In Figure 4, the firm will run a loss whether the price is P_1, P_2, or P_3, because none of these prices is high enough to reach the minimum level of average cost (AC). We can show the *lowest* price that keeps the firm from shutting down by introducing one more short-run cost curve: the average variable cost (AVC) curve. Why is this curve relevant? Because, as we have just seen, it pays the firm to remain in operation if its total revenue (TR) exceeds its total short-run variable cost (TVC). If we divide both TR and TVC by quantity (Q), we get TR/Q = P and TVC/Q = AVC. So, we can state the condition for continued operation equivalently as the requirement that price must exceed AVC. The conclusion is:

The firm will produce nothing unless price lies above the minimum point on the AVC curve.

In Figure 4, price P_1 is below the minimum average variable cost. With this price, the firm cannot even cover its variable costs and is better off shutting down (producing zero output). Price P_3 is higher. Although the firm still runs a loss if it sets MC = P at point A (because AC exceeds P_3), it allows the firm to at least cover its short-run variable costs, so it pays to keep operating in the short run. Price P_2 is the borderline case. If the price is P_2, the firm is indifferent between shutting down and staying in business and producing at a level where MC = P (point B). P_2 is thus the *lowest* price at which the firm will produce anything. As we see from the graph, P_2 corresponds to the minimum point on the AVC curve.

The Garden State: Farm Income in a Competitive Market

Because farmers are *price takers,* they simply have to live with the price that is determined by the market's supply and demand. Here is an example.

With the month's first drops of rain on Monday, many farmers relaxed a bit about the year's longest and most intense dry spell, and got back to the problem that plagues them rain or shine: earning enough from their crops to stay afloat.

And that boils down to the farmer's golden rule: entwined as they are, prices are still far more variable than weather.

"The quality of the produce does not have anything to do with your income," explained Mark Malench, a 38-year-old farmer who grows lettuce, peppers, eggplant and more than a dozen other crops on his family's 60-acre spread in Vineland [New Jersey]. "It's supply and demand." . . . [And] it was competition, not weather, that almost ru-

SOURCE: © David H. Wells/Corbis

ined the blueberry market. . . . "There were just a lot of people out there with berries at the same time," said Dennis G. Doyle, the general manager of the Tru-Blu Cooperative in New Lisbon, where nearly half of New Jersey's 145 blueberry farmers sell. But, he said, that's just part of the high-risk business of farming. "We're near Atlantic City and people ask me if I go much," Mr. Doyle said. "I say no. The risk isn't great enough."

The bottom line for farmers is the price they sell their crops for, which varies not only because of the weather, but also according to competition from other growers.

SOURCE: Excerpted from "For Crop Prices, Competition Matters More than Rain" by Andrea Kannapell, *The New York Times,* August 16, 1998. Copyright © 1998 by the New York Times Co. Reprinted with permission.

■ The Perfectly Competitive Firm's Short-Run Supply Curve

The **supply curve of a firm** shows the different quantities of output that the firm would be willing to supply at different possible prices during some given period of time.

Without realizing it, we have now derived the **supply curve of the perfectly competitive firm** in the short run. Why? Recall that a supply curve summarizes in a graph the answers to questions such as, "If the price is so and so, how much output will the firm offer for sale?" We have now discovered two possibilities:

- In the short run, if the price exceeds the minimum AVC, then it pays a competitive firm to produce the level of output at which MC equals P. Thus, for any price above point B in Figure 4, we can read the corresponding quantity supplied from the firm's MC curve.
- If the price falls below the minimum AVC, then it pays the firm to produce nothing. Quantity supplied falls to zero, as indicated by vertical red line $0P_2$ in Figure 4.

Putting these two observations together, we conclude that:

The short-run supply curve of the perfectly competitive firm is that portion of its marginal cost curve that lies above the point where it intersects the average (short-run) variable cost curve—that is, above the minimum level of AVC. If price falls below this level, the firm's quantity supplied drops to zero.

■ THE PERFECTLY COMPETITIVE INDUSTRY

Now that we have completed the analysis of the perfectly competitive *firm's* supply decision, we turn our attention next to the perfectly competitive *industry.*

■ The Perfectly Competitive Industry's Short-Run Supply Curve

Once again, we need to distinguish between the short run and the long run, but the distinction is different here. The short run for the *industry* is defined as a period of

time too brief for new firms to enter the industry or for old firms to leave, so the number of firms is fixed. By contrast, the long run for the industry is a period of time long enough for any firm to enter or leave as it desires. In addition, in the long run each firm in the industry can adjust its output to its own long-run costs.[3] We begin our analysis of industry equilibrium in the short run.

With the number of firms fixed, it is a simple matter to derive the **supply curve of the perfectly competitive industry** from those of the individual firms. At any given price, we simply *add up* the quantities supplied by each of the firms to arrive at the industry-wide quantity supplied. For example, if each of 1,000 identical firms in the corn industry supplies 45,000 bushels when the price is $2.25 per bushel, then the quantity supplied by the industry at a $2.25 price will be 45,000 bushels per firm × 1,000 firms = 45 million bushels.

> The **supply curve of an industry** shows the different quantities of output that the industry would supply at different possible prices during some given period of time.

This process of deriving the *market* supply curve from the *individual* supply curves of firms is analogous to the way we derived the *market* demand curve from the *individual* consumers' demand curves in Chapter 6. Graphically, what we are doing is *summing the individual supply curves horizontally*, as illustrated in Figure 5. At a price of $2.25, each of the 1,000 identical firms in the industry supplies 45,000 bushels—point *c* in Panel (a)—so the industry supplies 45 million bushels—point *C* in Panel (b). At a price of $3, each firm supplies 50,000 bushels—point *e* in Panel (a)—and so the industry supplies 50 million bushels—point *E* in Panel (b). We can carry out similar calculations for any other price. By adding up the quantities supplied by each firm at each possible price, we arrive at the industry supply curve *SS* in Panel (b).

The supply curve of the competitive industry in the short run is derived by *summing* the short-run supply curves of all the firms in the industry *horizontally*.

FIGURE 5

Derivation of the Industry Supply Curve from the Supply Curves of the Individual Firms

This adding-up process indicates, incidentally, that the supply curve of the industry will shift to the right whenever a new firm enters the industry.

Notice that if the short-run supply curves of individual firms slope upward, then the short-run supply curve of the perfectly competitive industry will slope upward as well. We have seen that the firm's supply curve is its marginal cost curve (above the level of minimum average variable cost), so it follows that rising marginal costs lead to an upward-sloping short-run *industry* supply curve.

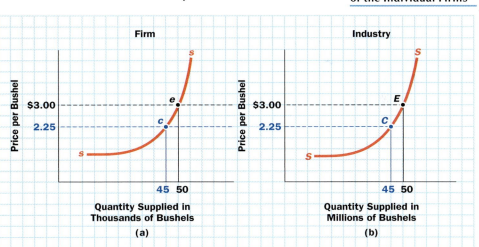

Industry Equilibrium in the Short Run

Now that we have derived the industry supply curve, we need only add a market demand curve to determine the price and quantity that will emerge in equilibrium. We do this for our illustrative corn industry in Figure 6, where the red industry supply curve, carried over from Figure 5(b), is *SS* and the demand curve is *DD*. The only equilibrium combination of price and quantity is a price of $3 and a quantity of 50 million bushels, at which the supply curve, *SS*, and the demand curve, *DD*, intersect (point *E*). At any lower price, such as $2.25, quantity demanded (72 million bushels,

---

[3] The relationship between short-run and long-run cost curves for the firm was discussed in Chapter 7, pages 141–142.

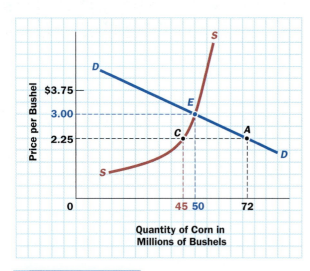

FIGURE 6

Supply-Demand
Equilibrium of a
Perfectly Competitive
Industry

as shown by point *A* on the demand curve) will be higher than the 45-million-bushel quantity supplied (point *C*). Thus, the price will be bid up toward the $3 equilibrium. The opposite will happen at a price such as $3.75, which is above equilibrium.

Note that for the perfectly competitive industry, unlike the perfectly competitive firm, the demand curve normally slopes downward. Why? Each firm by itself is so small that if it alone were to double its output, the effect would hardly be noticeable. But if *every* firm in the industry were to expand its output, that would make a substantial difference. Customers can be induced to buy the additional quantities arriving at the market only if the price of the good falls.

Point *E* is the equilibrium point for the perfectly competitive industry, because only at a price of $3 are sellers willing to offer exactly the amount that consumers want to purchase (in this case, 50 million bushels).

Should we expect price actually to reach, or at least to *approximate*, this equilibrium level? The answer is yes. To see why, we must consider what happens when price is not at its equilibrium level. Suppose that the price is lower—say, $2.25. This low price will stimulate customers to buy more; it will also lead firms to produce less than they would at a price of $3. Our diagram confirms that at a price of $2.25, quantity supplied (45 million bushels) is lower than quantity demanded (72 million bushels). Thus, the availability of unsatisfied buyers will probably lead sellers to raise their prices, which will force the price *upward* in the direction of its equilibrium value, $3.

Similarly, if we begin with a price higher than the equilibrium price, we may readily verify that quantity supplied will exceed quantity demanded. Under these circumstances, frustrated sellers are likely to reduce their prices, so price will be forced downward. In the circumstances depicted in Figure 6, in effect a magnet at the equilibrium price of $3 will pull the actual price in its direction, if for some reason the actual price starts out at some other level.

In practice, over a long period of time prices do move toward equilibrium levels in most perfectly competitive markets. Matters eventually appear to work out as depicted in Figure 6. Of course, numerous transitory influences can jolt any real-world market away from its equilibrium point—a workers' strike that cuts production, a sudden change in consumer tastes, and so on.

Yet, as we have just seen, powerful forces push prices back toward equilibrium—toward the level at which the supply and demand curves intersect. These forces are fundamentally important for economic analysis. If no such forces existed, prices in the real world would bear little resemblance to equilibrium prices, and there would be little reason to study supply-demand analysis. Fortunately, the required equilibrating forces do step in as appropriate to bring markets back toward equilibrium.

■ Industry and Firm Equilibrium in the Long Run

The equilibrium of a perfectly competitive industry in the long run may differ from the short-run equilibrium that we have just studied for two reasons. First, the number of firms in the industry (1,000 in our example) is not fixed in the long run. Second, as we saw in Chapter 7 (page 129), in the long run firms can vary their plant size and change other commitments that could not be altered in the short run. Hence, the firm's (and the industry's) long-run cost curves are not the same as the short-run cost curves. These differences can be very important, as we will see.

What will lure new firms into the industry or encourage old ones to leave? The answer is *profits*—economic profits (that is, any part of the firm's earnings that exceeds the average earnings of other firms in the economy and thus exceeds the firm's costs including its opportunity costs). Remember that when a firm selects its optimal level of output by setting MC = P, it may wind up with either a profit, as in Figure 2, or a loss, as in Figure 3. Such profits or losses must be *temporary* for perfectly competitive firms, because new firms are free to enter the industry if profits greater than the average that they can obtain by investing elsewhere are available in our industry. For the same reason, old firms will leave if they cannot cover their costs in the long run. Suppose that firms in the industry earn very high profits, in excess of the normal rates of return currently available. Then new companies will find it attractive to enter the business, and expanded production will force the market price to fall from its initial level. Why? Recall that the industry supply curve is the horizontal sum of

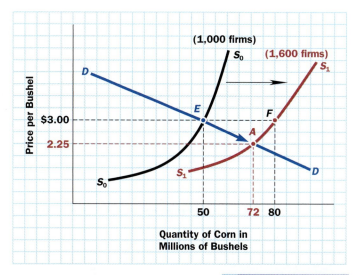

the supply curves of individual firms. Under perfect competition, new firms can enter the industry *on the same terms as existing firms.* Thus, new entrants will have the *same* individual supply curves as the old firms. If the market price did not fall, the entry of new firms would lead to an increased number of firms, with no change in output *per firm.* Consequently, the total quantity supplied to the market would be higher, and it would exceed quantity demanded—which, of course, would also drive prices down. Thus, the entry of new firms *must* push the price down.

Figure 7 shows how the entry process works. In this diagram, the demand curve *DD* and the original (short-run) supply curve S_0S_0 are carried over from Figure 6. The entry of new firms seeking high profits *shifts the industry's short-run supply curve outward to the right,* to S_1S_1. The new market equilibrium at point *A* (rather than at point *E*) indicates that price is $2.25 per bushel and that 72 million bushels are produced and consumed. The entry of new firms reduces price and raises total output.

If the price had not fallen, the quantity supplied after the new firms' entry would have been 80 million bushels—point *F.* Why must the price fall in this case? Because the demand curve for the industry slopes downward: Consumers will purchase the increased output only at a reduced price.

To see the point at which entry stops being attracted by high profits, we must consider how new firm entry affects existing firms' behavior. At first glance, this notion may seem to contradict the idea of perfect competition; perfectly competitive firms are not supposed to be affected by what competitors do, because no individual firm can influence the industry. Indeed, these corn farmers don't care about the entry of new firms. But they *do* care very much about the market price of corn and, as we have just seen, the entry of new firms into the corn-farming industry lowers the price of corn.

In Figure 8, we juxtapose the diagram of perfectly competitive firm equilibrium (Figure 2) with the perfectly competitive industry equilibrium diagram (Figure 7). Before the new firms' entry, the market price was $3, point *E* in Figure 8(b), and each of the 1,000 firms produced 50,000 bushels—the point where marginal cost and price were equal, point *e* in Figure 8(a). Each firm faced the horizontal demand curve D_0 in Figure 8(a). Firms within the industry enjoyed profits because average costs (AC) at 50,000 bushels per firm were less than price.

Now suppose that 600 new firms are attracted by these high profits and enter the industry. Each faces the cost structure indicated by the AC and MC curves in Figure 8(a). As a result of the new entrants' production, the industry supply curve in Figure 8(b) shifts to the right, and price falls to $2.25 per bushel. Because the height of the firm's horizontal demand curve is, as we have seen, equal to the industry price, the firm's demand curve must now move down to the blue line D_1 *corresponding to the reduced market price.* Firms in the industry react to this demand shift and its associated lower price. As we see in Figure 8(a), each firm reduces its output to 45,000 bushels

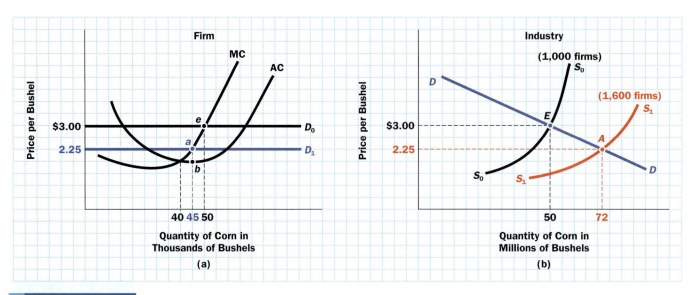

The Perfectly
Competitive Firm
and the Perfectly
Competitive Industry

(point *a*). But now there are 1,600 firms, so total industry output is 45,000 bushels ×
1,600 firms = 72 million bushels, point *A* in Figure 8(b).

At point *a* in Figure 8(a), some profits remain available because the $2.25 price still
exceeds average cost (point *b* is below point *a*). Thus, the entry process is not yet complete. New firms will stop appearing only when all profits have been competed away.
The two panels of Figure 9 show the perfectly competitive firm and the perfectly
competitive industry in long-run equilibrium. Only when entry shifts the industry
supply curve so far to the right—S_2S_2 in Figure 9(b)—that each individual firm faces a
demand curve that has fallen to the level of minimum average cost—point *m* in Figure 9(a)—will all profits be eradicated and entry cease.[4]

At the equilibrium point, *m*, in Panel (a), each firm picks its own output level to
maximize its profit. As a result, for each firm $P = MC$. But free entry also forces AC
to equal P in the long run—point *M* in Panel (b) of Figure 9—because if P were not
equal to AC, firms would either earn profits or suffer losses. That would mean, in

Long-Run Equilibrium
of the Perfectly
Competitive Firm
and Industry

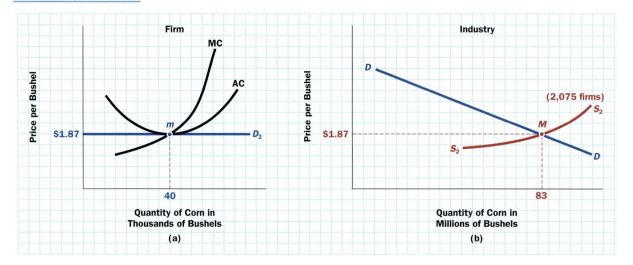

----

[4] If the original short-run equilibrium had involved losses instead of profits, firms would have exited from the industry, shifting the industry supply curve inward, until all losses were eradicated, and we would end up in a position exactly like Figure 9. *Exercise:* To test your understanding, draw the version of Figure 8 that corresponds to this case.

turn, that firms would find it profitable to enter or leave the industry, which is not compatible with industry equilibrium. Thus:

When a perfectly competitive industry is in long-run equilibrium, firms maximize profits so that P = MC, and entry forces the price down until it is tangent to the firm's long-run average cost curve (P = AC). As a result, in long-run perfectly competitive equilibrium it is always true that for each firm:

$$P = MC = AC$$

Thus, even though every firm earns zero profit, profits are at the maximum that is sustainable.[5]

Zero Economic Profit: The Opportunity Cost of Capital

Why would there be any firms in the industry *at all* if in the long run they could make no profits? The answer is that the zero profit concept used in economics does not mean the same thing that it does in ordinary, everyday usage. We have already encountered this and discussed its relevance in Chapter 8 (pages 158–159). Here we will explain this important point in a slightly different way.

We have noted repeatedly that when economists measure average cost, they include the cost of *all* of the firm's inputs, *including the opportunity cost of the capital (the funds) or any other inputs, such as labor, provided by the firm's owners.* Because the firm may not make explicit payments to some of the people who provide it with capital, this element of cost may not be picked up by the firm's accountants. So what economists call zero **economic profit** will correspond to a *positive* amount of profit as measured by conventional accounting techniques. For example, if investors can earn 15 percent by lending their funds elsewhere, then the firm must earn a 15 percent rate of return to cover its opportunity cost of capital. The chance for investors to earn 15 percent on their money by putting it into the firm is what attracts them to do so. True, the 15 percent return is no more than the investors can earn by putting their money elsewhere, but that does not make their 15 percent receipt unattractive.

> **Economic profit** equals net earnings, in the accountant's sense, minus the opportunity costs of capital and of any other inputs supplied by the firm's owners.

IDEAS FOR BEYOND THE FINAL EXAM

HOW MUCH DOES IT REALLY COST? *Opportunity Cost:* Because economists consider the 15 percent opportunity cost in this example to be the *cost of the firm's capital,* they include it in the AC curve. If the firm cannot earn at least 15 percent on its capital, funds will not be made available to it, because investors can earn greater returns elsewhere. To break even—to earn zero *economic profit*—a firm must earn enough not only to cover the cost of labor, fuel, and raw materials but also the cost of its funds, including the opportunity cost of any funds supplied by the owners of the firm.

An example will illustrate how economic profit and conventional accounting profit differ. Suppose that U.S. government bonds pay 8 percent interest, and the owner of a small shop earns 6 percent on her business investment. This shopkeeper might see a 6 percent profit, but an economist would see a 2 percent loss on every dollar she has invested in her business. By keeping her money tied up in her firm, the shop owner gives up the chance to buy government bonds and receive an 8 percent return. With this explanation of economic profit, we can understand the logic behind the zero-profit condition for the long-run industry equilibrium.

Zero profit in the economic sense simply means that firms are earning a return, but that return is just the same as the normal, economy-wide rate of profit in the accounting sense. This result is guaranteed, in the long run, under perfect competition by freedom of entry and exit.

---

[5] *Exercise:* Show what happens to the equilibrium of the firm and of the industry in Figure 9 if a rise in consumer income leads to an outward shift in the industry demand curve.

■ The Long-Run Industry Supply Curve

We have now seen basically what lies behind the supply-demand analysis that we first introduced in Chapter 4. Only one thing remains to be explained. Figures 5 through 8 depicted short-run industry supply curves and short-run equilibrium. However, because Figure 9 describes long-run perfectly competitive equilibrium, its industry supply curve must also pertain to the long run.

How does the long-run *industry* supply curve relate to the short-run supply curve? The answer is implicit in what we have just discussed. The long-run industry supply curve evolves from the short-run supply curve via two simultaneous processes. First, new firms enter or some existing ones exit, which shifts the short-run industry supply curve toward its long-run position. Second, and concurrently, as in the long run each firm in the industry is freed from its fixed commitments, the cost curves pertinent to its decisions become its long-run cost curves rather than its short-run cost curves. For example, consider a company that was stuck in the short run with a plant designed to serve 20,000 customers, even though it is now fortunate enough to have 25,000 customers. When it is time to replace the old plant, management will want to build a new plant that can serve the larger number of customers more conveniently, efficiently, and cheaply. The reduced cost that results from the larger plant is the pertinent cost to both the firm and the industry in the long run.

Finally, let us note that the long-run supply curve of the perfectly competitive industry (S_2S_2 in Figure 9) must be identical to the industry's long-run *average* cost curve. This is because in the long run, as we have seen, economic profit must be zero. The price the industry charges cannot exceed the long-run average cost (LRAC) of supplying that quantity because any excess of price over LRAC would constitute a profit opportunity that would have attracted new firms and driven price down to average cost. Similarly, price cannot be below LRAC because firms would then have refused to continue to supply that output at this price, output would have fallen, driving price up until it equaled average cost. Therefore, for each possible long-run quantity supplied, the price must equal the industry's long-run average cost. Thus, this long-run industry supply curve is the industry's average cost curve, and that is the cost curve relevant for determination of long-run equilibrium price and quantity in a standard supply-demand diagram.

These ideas are illustrated in Figure 10, in which the short-run industry supply curve, *SS*, lies above and to the left of the long-run average cost curve, LRAC. Consider any industry output—say, 70 million bushels of corn per year. At that output, the long-run average cost is $1.50 per bushel (point *A*). But if the price charged by farmers were given by the short-run supply curve for that output—that is, $2.62 per bushel (point *B*)—then the firms would earn $1.12 in economic profit on each and every bushel they sold.

Such economic profits would induce other firms to enter the industry, which would force prices downward as the industry supply curve shifted outward. So long as this shift did not take *SS* all the way down to LRAC, some economic profits would remain, and so entry would continue. Thus, *SS* must continue to fall until it reaches the position of the long-run average cost curve. Then and only then will entry of new firms cease and long-run equilibrium be attained.

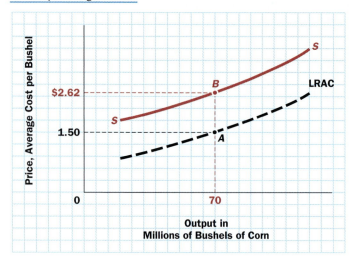

Output in Millions of Bushels of Corn

The long-run supply curve of the perfectly competitive industry is also the industry's long-run average cost curve. The industry is driven to that supply curve by the entry or exit of firms and by the adjustment of firms already in the industry.

POLICY DEBATE

Should Government Regulators Use Perfect Competition as a Guide?

As we have seen here and will discuss further in Chapter 14, perfect competition displays the market mechanism at its best. It prevents firms from earning excess profits, it forces firms to produce the output quantity at which AC is as low as possible, and it has other virtues as well.

As we will see in Chapters 11 and 12, markets where monopoly or oligopoly prevail are very different from perfect competition. In monopolistic or oligopolistic markets, a few large firms may charge high prices that yield large profits, and they may produce output quantities that do not match consumer preferences. Consequently (see Chapter 13), such industries are often *regulated* by government agencies.

But just what should regulation force monopoly or oligopoly firms to do? Should it force them to behave like perfectly competitive firms? Should it force their prices to equal marginal costs? Should it try to break them up into thousands of tiny enterprises?

No one believes that government regulation should go quite that far. Indeed, some

SOURCE: © Royalty-Free/Corbis

economists and others argue that perfect competition is an undesirable and, indeed, impossible goal for such regulated industries.

For example, if those industries are characterized by economies of scale, then breaking them into small firms will raise their costs and consumers will have to pay more, not less. Moreover, as we saw in Chapter 7, where there are economies of scale, the average cost curve must go downhill—the larger the firm's output, the lower its average cost. So marginal cost must be below average cost (see the appendix to Chapter 8 for a review), and a price equal to marginal cost must also be below average cost. Thus, where there are economies of scale, if the firm is forced to charge a price equal to marginal cost it will be forced to go bankrupt!

Even so, many regulators, economists, and others believe that perfect competition is so desirable a state of affairs that regulated firms should be required to come as close to it as possible in their behavior.

■ PERFECT COMPETITION AND ECONOMIC EFFICIENCY

Economists have long admired perfect competition as a thing of beauty, like one of King Tutankhamen's funerary masks. (And it's just as rare!) Adam Smith's invisible hand produces results that are considered *efficient* in a variety of senses that we will examine carefully in Chapter 14. But one aspect of the great efficiency of perfect competition follows immediately from the analysis we have just completed.

We saw earlier that when the firm is in long-run equilibrium, it must have $P = MC = AC$, as indicated by Figure 9(a). But we know that MC does not equal AC at any point on the AC curve that is moving either downhill or uphill (see the appendix to Chapter 8 if you need to be reminded why this is so). This implies that the long-run competitive equilibrium of the firm will occur at the lowest point (the horizontal point) on its long-run AC curve, which is also where that curve is tangent to the firm's horizontal demand curve.

In long-run perfectly competitive equilibrium, every firm produces at the minimum point on its average cost curve. Thus, the outputs of perfectly competitive industries are produced at the lowest possible cost to society.

An example will show why it is most efficient if each firm in a perfectly competitive industry produces at the point where AC is as small as possible. Suppose the industry is producing 12 million bushels of corn. This amount can be produced by 120 farms each producing 100,000 bushels, or by 100 farms each producing 120,000 bushels, or by 200 farms each producing 60,000 bushels. Of course, the job can also be done instead by other numbers of farms, but for simplicity let us consider only these three possibilities.

Suppose that the AC figures for the firm are as shown in Table 3. Suppose, moreover, that an output of 100,000 bushels corresponds to the lowest point on the AC curve, with an AC of 70 cents per bushel. Which is the cheapest way for the industry to produce its 12-million-bushel output? In other words, what is the cost-minimizing number of firms for the job? Looking at Column (5) of Table 3, we see that the industry's total cost of producing the 12-million-bushel output is as low as possible if 120 firms each produce the cost-minimizing output of 100,000 bushels.

Why is this so? The answer is not difficult to see. For any *given* industry output, Q, because Q is constant, *total* industry cost (= AC × Q) will be as small as possible if and only if AC (for *each* firm) is as small as possible—that is, if the number of firms doing the job is such that each is producing the output at which AC is as low as possible.

That this kind of cost efficiency characterizes perfect competition in the long run can be seen in Figures 8 and 9. Before full long-run equilibrium is reached (Figure 8), firms may not be producing in the least costly way. For example, the 50 million bushels being produced by 1,000 firms at points e and E in Figures 8(a) and 8(b) could be produced more cheaply by more firms, each producing a smaller volume, because the point of minimum average cost lies to the left of point e in Figure 8(a). This problem is rectified in the long run by the entry of new firms seeking profit. We see in Figure 9 that after the entry process is complete, every firm is producing at its most efficient (lowest AC) level—40,000 bushels.

As Adam Smith might have put it, even though each farmer cares only about his or her own profits, the corn-farming industry as a whole is *guided by an invisible hand* to produce the amount of corn that society wants at the lowest possible cost.

TABLE 3				
Average Cost for the Firm and Total Cost for the Industry				
(1)	(2)	(3)	(4)	(5)
Firm's Output	Firm's Average Cost	Number of Firms	Industry Output	Total Industry Cost
60,000	$0.90	200	12,000,000	$10,800,000
100,000	**0.70**	**120**	**12,000,000**	**8,400,000**
120,000	0.80	100	12,000,000	9,600,000

Note: Output is in bushels.

PUZZLE RESOLVED: *Which Is Better to Cut Pollution— The Carrot or the Stick?*

We end by returning to the puzzle with which the chapter began, because we now have all the tools needed to solve it. Remember that we asked: Should polluters be *taxed* on their emissions, or should they, instead, be offered *subsidies* to cut emissions? A subsidy—that is, a government payment to the firms that comply—would indeed induce firms to cut their emissions. Nevertheless, the paradoxical result is likely to be an *increase* in total pollution. Let us see now why this is so.

In Figure 11, we have drawn the industry long-run average cost curve (LRAC), *XX*. We now know that this must also be the industry's long-run supply curve, because if the supply curve lies above (to the left of) LRAC, then economic profits will be earned and entry will drive the supply curve to the right. The opposite would occur if the supply were below and to the right of LRAC.

Now, a tax on business firms clearly raises the long-run average costs of the industry. Suppose that it shifts the LRAC, and thus the long-run supply curve, upward from *XX* to *TT* in the graph. This change will move the equilibrium point from E to B and reduce polluting output from Q_e to Q_b. Similarly, a subsidy reduces average cost, so it shifts the LRAC and the long-run supply curve downward and to the right (from *XX* to *SS*). This change moves the equilibrium point from E to A and *raises polluting output to* Q_a.

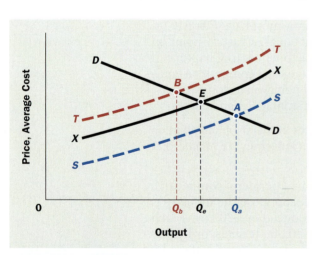

FIGURE 11

Taxes versus Subsidies as Incentives to Cut Pollution

Our paradoxical result follows from the presumption that the more *output* a polluting industry produces, the more *pollution* it will emit. Under the tax on emissions, equilibrium moves from E to B, so the polluting output falls from Q_e to Q_b. Thus, emissions will fall—just as common sense leads us to expect. But, with the subsidy, industry output will *rise* from Q_e to Q_a. Thus, contrary to intuition and despite the fact that each firm emits less, the industry must pollute more!

What explains this strange result? The answer is the *entry* of new firms. The subsidy will initially bring economic profits to the polluters, which will in turn attract even more polluters into the industry. In essence, a subsidy encourages more polluters to open up for business. But our graph takes us one step beyond this simple observation. It is true that we end up with more polluting firms, but each will be polluting less than before. Thus, we have one influence leading to more pollution and another influence leading to less pollution. Which of these forces will win out? The graph tells us that if a rise in the polluting good's output always increases pollution, then, in a perfectly competitive industry, subsidies *must* lead to increased pollution on balance.

"So that's where it goes! Well, I'd like to thank you fellows for bringing this to my attention."

SUMMARY

1. **Markets** are classified into several types depending on the number of firms in the industry, the degree of similarity of their products, and the possibility of impediments to entry.

2. The four main market structures discussed by economists are *monopoly* (single-firm production), *oligopoly* (production by a few firms), *monopolistic competition* (production by many firms with somewhat different products), and *perfect competition* (production by many firms with identical products and free entry and exit).

3. Few, if any, industries satisfy the conditions of **perfect competition** exactly, although some come close. Perfect competition is studied because it is easy to analyze and because it represents a case in which the market mechanism works well, so that it is useful as a yardstick to measure the performance of other market forms.

4. The demand curve of the perfectly competitive firm is horizontal because its output is such a small share of the industry's production that it cannot affect price. With a horizontal demand curve, price, average revenue, and marginal revenue are all equal.

5. The short-run equilibrium of the perfectly competitive firm is at the level of output that maximizes profits—that is, where MR = MC = price. This equilibrium may involve either a profit or a loss.

6. The short-run **supply curve** of the perfectly competitive firm is the portion of its marginal cost curve that lies above its average **variable cost** curve.

7. The industry's short-run supply curve under perfect competition is the horizontal sum of the supply curves of all of its firms.

8. In the long-run equilibrium of the perfectly competitive industry, freedom of entry forces each firm to earn zero **economic profit**, or no more than the firm's capital could earn elsewhere (the opportunity cost of the capital).

9. Industry equilibrium under perfect competition is at the point where the industry supply and demand curves intersect.

10. In long-run equilibrium under perfect competition, the firm chooses output such that average cost, marginal cost, and price are all equal. Output is at the point of minimum average cost. The firm's demand curve is tangent to its average cost curve at its minimum point.

11. The competitive industry's long-run supply curve coincides with its long-run average cost curve.

12. Both a tax on the emission of pollutants and a subsidy payment for reductions in those emissions induce firms to cut emissions. However, under perfect competition, a subsidy leads to the entry of more polluting firms and the likelihood of a net increase in total emissions by the industry.

KEY TERMS

Market   197

Perfect competition   200

Price taker   201

Variable cost   204

Firm's supply curve   206

Industry supply curve   207

Economic profit   211

TEST YOURSELF

1. Under what circumstances might you expect the demand curve of the firm to be:

   a. Vertical?

   b. Horizontal?

   c. Negatively sloping?

   d. Positively sloping?

2. Explain why $P = MC$ in the short-run equilibrium of the perfectly competitive firm, whereas in long-run equilibrium $P = MC = AC$.

3. Explain why it is not sensible to close a business firm if it earns zero economic profits.

4. If the firm's lowest average cost is $48 and the corresponding average variable cost is $24, what does it pay a perfectly competitive firm to do if:

   a. The market price is $49?

   b. The price is $30?

   c. The price is $8?

5. If the market price in a competitive industry were above its equilibrium level, what would you expect to happen?

DISCUSSION QUESTIONS

1. Explain why a perfectly competitive firm does not expand its sales without limit if its horizontal demand curve indicates that it can sell as much as it desires at the current market price.

2. Explain why a demand curve is also a curve of average revenue. Recalling that when an average revenue curve is neither rising nor falling, marginal revenue must equal average revenue, explain why it is always true that $P = MR = AR$ for the perfectly competitive firm.

3. Regarding the four attributes of perfect competition (many small firms, freedom of entry, standardized product, and perfect information):

   a. Which is primarily responsible for the fact that the demand curve of a perfectly competitive firm is horizontal?

   b. Which is primarily responsible for the firm's zero economic profits in long-run equilibrium?

4. We indicated in this chapter that the MC curve cuts the AVC (average variable cost) curve at the *minimum* point of the latter. Explain why this must be so. (*Hint:* Because marginal costs are, by definition, entirely composed of variable costs, the MC curve can be considered the curve of *marginal variable costs*. Apply the general relationships between marginals and averages explained in the appendix to Chapter 8.)

5. **(More difficult)** In this chapter we stated that the firm's MC curve goes through the lowest point of its AC curve and also through the lowest point of its AVC curve. Because the AVC curve lies below the AC curve, how can both of these statements be true? Why are they true? (*Hint:* See Figure 4.)

11

MONOPOLY

The price of monopoly is upon every occasion the highest which can be got.

ADAM SMITH[1]

I n Chapter 10, we described an idealized market system in which all industries are perfectly competitive, and in Chapters 14 and 16 we will describe the virtues of that system. In this chapter, we turn to one of the blemishes—the possibility that some industries may be monopolized—and to the consequences of such a flaw in the market system.

We will indeed find that monopolized markets do not match the ideal performance of perfectly competitive markets. Under monopoly, the market mechanism no longer allocates society's resources efficiently. This suggests that government actions to constrain monopoly may sometimes be able to improve the workings of the market—a possibility that we will study in detail in Chapter 13.

But, first, as usual, we start with a real-life puzzle.

CONTENTS

---

[1] But Adam Smith's statement is incorrect! See Discussion Question 4 at the end of the chapter.

PUZZLE: *What Happened to AT&T's "Natural Monopoly" in Telephone Service?*

We are all keenly aware of the strong competition in the market for telephone service. How can we miss it? A plethora of firms (old and new) offering telephone service of one kind or another besiege us with television commercials, internet advertisements, and mountains of "snail" mail. The days of "Ma Bell," the affectionate nickname for AT&T's ubiquitous Bell Telephone System—which used to be virtually the only provider of telephone service—are long gone and now seem as quaint and old-fashioned as the horse and buggy. What was it that allowed competition in this industry, which had always been considered by some as a classic example of a "natural monopoly" against which no competitor could be expected to survive (see a fuller definition below)? In this chapter you will learn about the causes and consequences of monopoly and, in the process, obtain insights about the answers to this question.

SOURCE: © H. Armstrong Roberts/Corbis.

MONOPOLY *DEFINED*

A **pure monopoly** is an industry in which there is only one supplier of a product for which there are no close substitutes and in which it is very difficult or impossible for another firm to coexist.

The definition of **pure monopoly** has rather stringent requirements. First, only one firm can be present in the industry—the monopolist must be "the only game in town." Second, no close substitutes for the monopolist's product may exist. Thus, even a city's sole provider of natural gas is not considered a pure monopoly, because other firms offer close substitutes such as heating oil and electricity. Third, there must be some reason why entry and survival of potential competitors is extremely unlikely. Otherwise, monopolistic behavior and its excessive economic profits could not persist.

These rigid requirements make pure monopoly a rarity in the real world. The telephone company and the post office used to be examples of one-firm industries that faced little or no effective competition, at least in some of their activities. But most firms face at least a degree of competition from substitute products. If only one railroad serves a particular town, it still must compete with bus lines, trucking companies, and airlines. Similarly, the producer of a particular brand of beer may be the only supplier of that specific product, but the firm is not a pure monopolist by our definition. Because many other beers are close substitutes for its product, the firm will lose much of its business if it tries to raise its price far above the prices of other brands.

There is another reason why the unrestrained pure monopoly of economic theory is rarely found in practice. We will learn in this chapter that pure monopoly can have a number of undesirable features. So in markets in which pure monopoly might otherwise prevail, the government has often intervened to prevent monopolization or to limit the discretion of the monopolist to set its price.

If we do not study pure monopoly for its descriptive realism, why *do* we study it? Because, like perfect competition, pure monopoly is a market form that is easier to analyze than the more common market structures that we will consider in the next chapter. Thus, pure monopoly is a stepping stone toward more realistic models. Also, we will understand the possible evils of monopoly most clearly if we examine monopoly in its purest form.

■ Sources of Monopoly: Barriers to Entry and Cost Advantages

The key requirement for preservation of a monopoly is exclusion of potential rivals from the market. One way to achieve this result is by means of some specific impediment that prevents the establishment of a new firm in the industry. Economists call such impediments **barriers to entry.** Here are some examples.

1. Legal Restrictions   The U.S. Postal Service has a monopoly position because Congress has given it one. Private companies that may want to compete with the postal service directly are prohibited from doing so by law. Local monopolies of various kinds are sometimes established either because government grants some special privilege to a single firm (for example, the right to operate a food concession in a municipal stadium) or prevents other firms from entering the industry (for instance, by licensing only a single cable television supplier).

Barriers to entry are attributes of a market that make it more difficult or expensive for a new firm to open for business than it was for the firms already present in that market.

2. Patents   Some firms benefit from a special, but important, class of legal impediments to entry called **patents.** To encourage inventiveness, the government gives exclusive production rights for a period of time to the inventors of certain products. As long as a patent is in effect, the firm has a protected position and holds a monopoly. For example, Xerox Corporation for many years had (but no longer has) a monopoly in plain-paper copying. Most pharmaceutical companies also obtain monopolies on the medicines they discover. The drugmaker Pfizer, for instance, has a patent on Norvasc, a blood pressure medication. This patent expires in 2007, which will open the door to competition from generic makers of the drug.

A **patent** is a privilege granted to an inventor, whether an individual or a firm, that for a specified period of time prohibits anyone else from producing or using that invention without the permission of the holder of the patent.

3. Control of a Scarce Resource or Input   If a certain commodity can be produced only by using a rare input, a company that gains control of the source of that input can establish a monopoly position for itself. Real examples are not easy to find, but the South African diamond syndicate used to come close.

4. Deliberately Erected Entry Barriers   A firm may deliberately attempt to make entry into the industry difficult for others. One way is to start costly lawsuits against new rivals, sometimes on trumped-up charges. Another is to spend exorbitant amounts on advertising, thus forcing any potential entrant to match that expenditure.

5. Large Sunk Costs   Entry into an industry will, obviously, be very risky if it requires a large investment, especially if that investment is *sunk*—meaning that it cannot be recouped for a considerable period of time. Thus, the need for a large sunk investment discourages entry into an industry. Many analysts therefore consider sunk costs to be the most important type of "naturally imposed" barrier to entry. For example, the high sunk costs involved in jet airplane production helped Boeing Corporation enjoy a monopoly in the top end of the long-range, wide-body jet airliner market for many years after the launch of the 747 jumbo jet. The rival aircraft manufacturer, Airbus, which with European governments' sponsorship has been able to afford the high investments, has since encroached on Boeing's territory.

Such barriers can keep rivals out and ensure that an industry is monopolized. But monopoly can also occur in the absence of barriers to entry if a single firm has substantial cost advantages over potential rivals. Two examples of attributes of production that create such advantages are technical superiority and economies of scale.

6. Technical Superiority A firm whose technological expertise vastly exceeds that of any potential competitor can, for a period of time, maintain a monopoly position. For example, IBM Corporation for many years had little competition in the computer business mainly because of its technological virtuosity. Of course, competitors eventually caught up. More recently, Microsoft Corporation has established a commanding position in the software business, especially for operating systems, through a combination of inventiveness and marketing wizardry.

7. Economies of Scale If mere size gives a large firm a cost advantage over a smaller rival, it is likely to be impossible for anyone to compete with the largest firm in the industry.

■ Natural Monopoly

This last type of cost advantage is important enough to merit special attention. In some industries, economies of large-scale production or economies of scope (from simultaneous production of a large number of related items, such as car motors and bodies, truck parts, and so on) are so extreme that the industry's output can be produced at far lower cost by a single large firm than by a number of smaller firms. In such cases, we say there is a **natural monopoly**. Once a firm becomes large enough relative to the size of the market for its product, its natural cost advantage may well drive the competition out of business whether or not anyone in the relatively large firm has evil intentions.

A monopoly need not be a large firm if the market is small enough. *What matters is the size of a single firm relative to the total market demand for the product.* Thus, a small bank in a rural town or a gasoline station at a lightly traveled intersection may both be natural monopolies, even though they are very small firms.

Figure 1 shows the sort of average cost (AC) curve that leads to natural monopoly. It has a negative slope throughout, meaning that the more a firm in this industry produces, the lower its average cost will be. Suppose that any firm producing video games has this AC curve and that, initially, there are two firms in the industry. Suppose also that the larger firm is producing 2 million games at an average cost of $2.50 (point *A*), and the smaller firm is producing 1 million games at an average cost of $3.00 (point *B*). Clearly, the larger firm can drive the smaller firm out of business if it offers its output for sale at a price below $3.00 (so the smaller firm can match the price only by running a loss) but above $2.50 (so it can still make a profit). Hence, a monopoly may arise "naturally," even in the absence of barriers to entry.

Once the monopoly is established (producing, say, 2.5 million video games—point *C*), the economies of scale act as a very effective deterrent to entry because no new entrant can hope to match the low average cost ($2.00) of the existing monopoly firm. Of course, the public interest may be well served if the natural monopolist uses its low cost to keep its prices low. The danger, however, is that the firm may raise its price once rivals have left the industry.

Many public utilities operate as *regulated* monopoly suppliers for exactly this reason. It is believed that the technology of producing or distributing their output enables them to achieve substantial cost reductions by producing large quantities. It is therefore often considered preferable to permit these firms to achieve lower costs by having the entire market to themselves, and then to subject them and their prices to regulatory supervision, rather than to break them up into a number of competing firms. We will examine the issues connected with regulation of natural monopolies in detail in Chapter 13. To summarize this discussion:

A **natural monopoly** is an industry in which advantages of large-scale production make it possible for a single firm to produce the entire output of the market at lower average cost than a number of firms, each producing a smaller quantity.

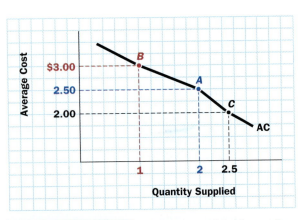

FIGURE 1
Natural Monopoly

Note: Average cost is in dollars per unit; quantity is in millions.

There are two basic reasons why a monopoly may exist: barriers to entry, such as legal restrictions and patents, and cost advantages of superior technology or large-scale operation that lead to natural monopoly. It is generally considered undesirable to break up a large firm whose costs are low because of scale economies. But barriers to entry are usually considered to be against the public interest except where they are believed to offer offsetting advantages, as in the case of patents.

The rest of this chapter analyzes how a monopoly can be expected to behave if its freedom of action is not limited by the government.

■ THE MONOPOLIST'S SUPPLY DECISION

A monopoly firm does not have a "supply curve," as we usually define the term. Unlike a firm operating under perfect competition, a monopoly is not at the mercy of the market; the firm does not have to accept the market's price as beyond its control and adjust its output level to that externally fixed price, as the supply curve assumes. Instead, it has the power to set the price, or rather to select the price-quantity combination on the demand curve that suits its interests best.

Put differently, a monopolist is not a *price taker* that must simply adapt to whatever price the forces of supply and demand decree. Rather, a monopolist is a *price maker* that can, if so inclined, raise the product price. Thus, the standard supply-demand analysis described in Chapter 4 does not apply to the determination of price or output in a monopolized industry. But it remains true that, for whatever price the monopolist selects, the demand curve for the product indicates how much consumers will buy.

The demand curve of a monopoly, unlike that of a perfectly competitive firm, is normally downward sloping, not horizontal. This means that a price rise will not cause the monopoly to lose *all* of its customers. But any increase will cost it *some* business. The higher the price, the less the monopolist can expect to sell.

The market cannot impose a price on a monopolist as it imposes a price on the price-taking perfectly competitive firm. But the monopolist cannot select both price and the quantity it sells. In accord with the demand curve, the higher the price it sets, the less it can sell.

Is the Software Industry a Natural Monopoly?

Some leading economists believe the software industry is prone to monopoly. Three influences may incline the industry in this direction, as an article in *InfoWorld* describes:

One factor is diminishing costs: while the first copy of a software program costs millions to produce, the cost to produce subsequent copies is negligible. The second factor is the network effect in which the value of software increases by the number of people using it and developers creating applications for it. The third factor is the lock-in effect, in which the cost of switching to another system (installation, training, application compatibility) persuades users to stick with current systems. . . . These forces create natural barriers to entry for newcomers, and Microsoft's operating-system dominance is a prime example.

SOURCE: Lynda Radosevich, "Top of the News: How the Software Industry Creates Monopolies," *InfoWorld* 20 (May 25, 1998).

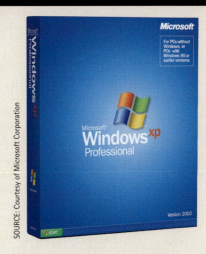

SOURCE: Courtesy of Microsoft Corporation

In deciding what price best serves the firm's interests, the monopolist must consider whether profits can be increased by raising or lowering the product's price. Because of the downward-sloping demand curve, the sky is not the limit in pricing by a monopolist. Some price increases are not profitable because they lead to disproportionately large reductions in sales of the products.

In our analysis, we will assume that the monopolist wants to maximize profits. That does not mean that a monopoly is guaranteed a positive profit. If the demand for its product is low, or if the firm is inefficient, even a monopoly may lose money and eventually be forced out of business. However, if a monopoly firm does earn a positive profit, it may be able to keep on doing so in the long run because there will be no entry that competes the profits away.

We can use the methods of Chapter 8 to determine which price the profit-maximizing monopolist will prefer. To maximize profits, the monopolist must compare marginal revenue (the addition to total revenue resulting from a one-unit rise in output) with marginal cost (the addition to total cost resulting from that additional unit). Figure 2 shows a marginal cost (MC) curve and a marginal revenue (MR) curve for a typical monopolist. Recall that the firm's demand curve (DD) is also its average revenue (AR) curve. That is because if a firm sells Q units of output, selling every unit of output at the price P, then the average revenue brought in by a unit of output must be the price, P, because the average of a bunch of equal numbers must be that same number. Because the demand curve gives the price at which any particular quantity can be sold, it also automatically indicates the AR (= price) yielded by that quantity.

Notice that the marginal revenue curve is always below the demand curve, meaning that MR is always less than price (P). This important fact is easy to explain. The monopoly firm charges the same price to all of its customers. If the firm wants to increase sales by one unit, it must decrease the price somewhat to all of its customers. When it cuts the price to attract new sales, all previous customers also benefit. Thus, the additional revenue that the monopolist takes in when sales increase by one unit (*marginal revenue*) is the price that the firm collects from the new customer *minus the revenue that it loses by cutting the price paid by all of its old customers.* This means that MR is necessarily less than price; graphically, it implies that the MR curve is below the demand curve, as in Figure 2.

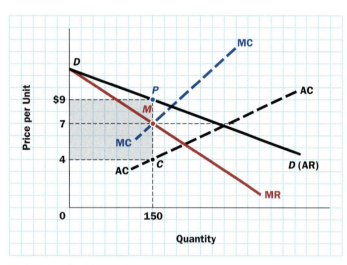

FIGURE 2

Profit-Maximizing Equilibrium for a Monopolist

Note: Price is in dollars per unit.

Determining the Profit-Maximizing Output

Like any other firm, the monopoly maximizes its profits by setting marginal revenue (MR) equal to marginal cost (MC). It selects point M in Figure 2, where output is 150 units. But point M does not tell us the monopoly price because, as we have just seen, price exceeds MR for a monopolist. To learn what price the monopolist charges, we must use the demand curve to find the price at which consumers are willing to purchase the profit-maximizing output of 150 units. The answer, we see, is given by the height of the demand curve at that output—it is given by point P directly above M. The monopoly price is $9 per unit. Not surprisingly, it exceeds both MR and MC (which are equal at $7).

The monopolist depicted in Figure 2 is earning a tidy profit. This profit is shown in the graph by the shaded rectangle whose height is the difference between price (point P) and average cost (point C) and whose width is the quantity produced (150 units). In the example, profits are $5 per unit, or $750.

To study the decisions of a profit-maximizing monopolist:

1. **Find the output at which MR equals MC to select the profit-maximizing output level.**

2. **Find the height of the demand curve *at that level of output* to determine the corresponding price.**

3. **Compare the height of the demand curve with the height of the AC curve at that output to see whether the net result is an economic profit or a loss.**

We also can show a monopolist's profit-maximization calculation numerically. In Table 1, the first two columns show the quantity and price figures that constitute this monopolist's demand curve. Column (3) shows total revenue (TR) for each output, which is the product of price times quantity. Thus, for 3 units of output, we have TR = $92 × 3 = $276. Column (4) shows marginal revenue (MR). For example, when output rises from 3 to 4 units, TR increases from $276 to $320, so MR is $320 − $276 = $44. Column (5) gives the monopolist's total cost for each level of output. Column (6) derives marginal cost (MC) from total cost (TC) in the usual way. Finally, by subtracting TC from TR for each level of output, we obtain total profit in Column (7).

The table brings out a number of important points. We note first in Columns (2) and (3) that a cut in price may increase or decrease total revenue. When output rises from 1 to 2 units, *P* falls from $140 to $107 and TR rises from $140 to $214. But when (between 5 and 6 units of output) *P* falls from $66 to $50, TR falls from $330 to $300. Next we observe, by comparing Columns (2) and (4), that after the first unit, price always exceeds marginal revenue (because the marginal revenue curve *must* lie below the downward-sloping demand [AR] curve). Finally, from Columns (4) and (6) we see that MC = MR = $44 when *Q* is between 3 and 4 units, indicating that this is the level of output that maximizes the monopolist's total profit. That is confirmed in Column (7) of the table, which shows that at this output profit reaches its highest level, $110, for any of the output quantities considered in the table.

TABLE 1

A Profit-Maximizing Monopolist's Price-Output Decision

		Revenue		Cost		Total Profit
(1) Q	(2) P	(3) TR = P × Q	(4) MR	(5) TC	(6) MC	(7) TR − TC
0	—	$ 0		$ 10		$−10
			$140		$60	
1	$140	140		70		70
			74		50	
2	107	214		120		94
			62		46	
3	92	276		166		110
			44		44	
4	80	320		210		110
			10		43	
5	66	330		253		77
			−30		45	
6	50	300		298		2

Comparing Monopoly and Perfect Competition

This completes our analysis of the monopolist's price-output decision. At this point, it is natural to wonder whether there is anything distinctive about the monopoly equilibrium. To find out, we need a standard of comparison. Perfect competition provides this standard because, as we will learn in Chapter 14, it is a theoretical benchmark of ideal performance against which other market structures can be judged. By comparing the results of monopoly with those of perfect competition, we will see why economists since Adam Smith have condemned monopoly as inefficient.

1. A Monopolist's Profit Persists
The first difference between competition and monopoly is a direct consequence of barriers to entry in monopoly. Profits such as those shown in Figure 2 would be competed away by free entry in a perfectly competitive market, because a positive profit would attract new competitors into the business. A competitive firm must earn *zero economic profit* in the long run; that is, it can earn only enough to cover its costs, including the opportunity cost of the owner's capital and labor. But higher **profit** *can* persist under **monopoly**—if the monopoly is protected from the arrival of new competitors by barriers to entry. This can, then, allow monopolists to grow wealthy at the expense of their consumers. But because people find such accumulations of wealth objectionable, monopoly is widely condemned. As a result, monopolies are generally regulated by government, which often limits the profits they can earn.

Monopoly profits are any excess of the profits earned persistently by a monopoly firm over and above those that would be earned if the industry were perfectly competitive.

2. Monopoly Restricts Output to Raise Short-Run Price

Excess monopoly profit can be a problem. But economists believe that the second difference between competition and monopoly is even more worrisome:

> Compared with the perfectly competitive ideal, the monopolist restricts output and charges a higher price.

To see that this is so, let us conduct the following thought experiment. Imagine that a court order breaks up the monopoly firm depicted in Figure 2 (and reproduced as Figure 3) into a large number of perfectly competitive firms. Suppose further that the industry demand curve is unchanged by this event and that the MC curve in Figure 3 is also the (horizontal) sum of the MC curves of all the newly created competitive firms. These may be unrealistic assumptions, as we will soon explain. However, they make it easy to compare the output-price combinations that would emerge in the short run under monopoly and perfect competition.

Before making our comparison, we must note that under monopoly, the firm and the industry are exactly the same entity. But under perfect competition, any one firm is just a small portion of the industry. So when we measure the performance of monopoly against that of perfect competition, we should compare the monopoly with the entire competitive industry, not with an individual competitive firm. In Figure 3, the monopolist's output is point M at which MC = MR. The long-run competitive output (point B) is greater than the monopoly's because it must be sufficiently large to yield zero economic profit (P = AR = AC).

It is self-evident and not very interesting to observe that the output of the monopolist is virtually certain to be larger than that of a tiny competitive *firm*. The interesting issue is how much of the entire industry's product gets into the hands of consumers under the two market forms—that is, how much output is produced by a monopoly as compared with the quantity provided by a similar competitive *industry*.

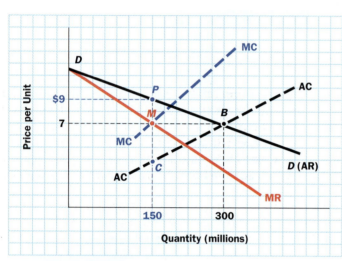

FIGURE 3

Comparison of a Monopoly and a Perfectly Competitive Industry

Note: Price is in dollars per unit.

3. Monopoly Restricts Output to Raise Long-Run Price

As we have seen, monopoly output is determined by the profit-maximization requirement that MC = MR (point M). But as we learned in Chapter 10, long-run perfectly competitive equilibrium occurs at point B in Figure 3, where price and average cost are equal and economic profit is zero.

By comparing point B with the monopolist's equilibrium (point M), we see that the monopolist produces fewer units of output than would a competitive industry with the same demand and cost conditions. Because the demand curve slopes downward, producing less output means that the industry gets away with a higher price. The monopolist's price, indicated by point P on the demand curve and directly above M, exceeds the price that would result from perfect competition at point B. This is the essence of the truth behind the popular view that unregulated monopolists "gouge the public." The monopolist deliberately cuts back the amount of output he produces in order to make the product scarcer and thereby force its price upward.

We should note that matters will *always* turn out that way if the average cost curve has a positive slope between the monopoly output level and the competitive output level. That is because we know, in this case, that the MC curve must lie above the AC curve (to review why, see pages 173–174 of Chapter 8). We also have just seen that the MR curve must lie below the demand (AR) curve. It is clear, then, that the point where the MR curve meets the MC curve (the monopoly output) must always lie to the left of the output at which AC and AR meet (the competitive industry output). Consequently, monopoly output will always be the smaller of the two when the curves of the competitive and monopoly industries are identical. With monopoly output lower, its price will always be higher.

4. Monopoly Leads to Inefficient Resource Allocation

We conclude, then, that a monopoly will charge a higher price and produce a smaller output than will a competitive industry with the same demand and cost conditions. Why do economists find this situation so objectionable? Because, as we will learn in Chapter 14, a competitive industry devotes "just the right amount" of society's scarce resources to the production of its particular commodity. Therefore, if a monopolist produces less than a competitive industry, it must be producing too little.

We will see in Chapter 14 that efficiency in resource allocation requires that the marginal utility (MU) of each commodity be equal to its marginal cost. Also, perfect competition guarantees that:

$$MU = P \text{ and } MC = P, \text{ so } MU = MC$$

Under monopoly, consumers continue to maximize their own welfare by setting MU equal to P. But the monopoly producer sets MC equal to MR. Because MR is *below* the market price, P, we conclude that in a monopolized industry:

$$MU = P \text{ and } MC = MR < P, \text{ so } MC < MU$$

Because MU exceeds MC, too small a share of society's resources is being used to produce the monopolized commodity. Consumers would have a net benefit of $MU - MC > 0$ if output were increased above the monopoly level by one unit because the added benefit would exceed the added cost. Under monopoly, Adam Smith's invisible hand is sending out the wrong signals. Consumers are willing to pay an amount for an additional unit of the good (its MU) that exceeds what it costs to produce that unit (its MC). But the monopoly refuses to increase production, because if it raises output by one unit, the additional revenue it will collect (MR) will be less than the price the consumer will pay for the additional unit (P). The monopolist does not increase production, and resources are allocated inefficiently. To summarize this discussion of the consequences of monopoly:

Because it is protected from entry, a monopoly firm may earn positive economic profits, that is, profits in excess of the opportunity cost of capital. At the same time, monopoly breeds inefficiency in resource allocation by producing too little output and charging too high a price. For these reasons, some of the virtues of the free market evaporate if an industry becomes monopolized.

■ Monopoly Is Likely to Shift Demand

This analysis need not always apply. For one thing, it has assumed that the market demand curve is the same whether the industry is competitive or monopolized. But is this usually so? The demand curve will be the same if the monopoly firm does nothing to expand its market, but that is hardly plausible.

Under perfect competition, purchasers consider the products of all suppliers in an industry to be identical, so

no single supplier has any reason to advertise. But if a monopoly takes over from a perfectly competitive industry, it may very well pay to advertise. If management believes that the creative touch of the advertising agency can make consumers rush to the market to purchase the product whose virtues have been extolled on television, then the firm will allocate a substantial sum of money to accomplish this feat. Take the Eastman Kodak Company, for example. Kodak enjoyed a near monopoly on U.S. film sales from the turn of the century until the 1980s, but that did not stop the company from spending a good deal on advertising. This type of expenditure should shift the demand curve outward. The monopoly's demand curve and that of the competitive industry will then no longer be the same.

The higher demand curve for the monopoly's product may induce it to expand production and therefore reduce the difference between the competitive and the monopolistic output levels indicated in Figure 3. But it may also make it possible for the monopoly to charge even higher prices, so the increased output may not constitute a net gain for consumers.

◾ Monopoly Is Likely to Shift Cost Curves

The advent of a monopoly also may shift the average and marginal cost curves. One reason for higher costs is the advertising we have just been discussing. Another reason is the sheer size of the monopolist's organization, which may lead to bureaucratic inefficiencies, coordination problems, and the like.

At the same time, a monopolist may be able to eliminate certain types of duplication that are unavoidable for a number of small, independent firms: One purchasing agent may do the input-buying job where many buyers were needed before; a few large machines may replace many small items of equipment in the hands of the competitive firms. In addition, the large scale of the monopoly firm's input purchases may permit it to take advantage of quantity discounts not available to small competitive firms.

If the consolidation achieved by a monopoly does shift the marginal cost curve downward, monopoly output will tend to move up closer to the competitive level. The monopoly price will then tend to move down closer to the competitive price.

◾ CAN ANYTHING GOOD BE SAID ABOUT MONOPOLY?

We conclude that our graphic comparison of monopoly and perfect competition is very artificial. It assumes that all other things will remain the same, even though that is unlikely to happen in reality. For that reason and others, at least in some cases monopoly may not be as damaging to the public interest as the previous discussion suggests. Let us consider some specific ways in which monopoly can offset some of its undesirable consequences.

◾ Monopoly May Aid Innovation

Some economists have emphasized that it is misleading to compare the cost curves of a monopoly and a competitive industry *at a single point in time*. Because it is protected from rivals and therefore sure to capture the benefits from any cost-saving methods and new products it can invent, a monopoly has particularly strong motivation to invest in research, these economists argue. If this research bears fruit, the monopolist's costs will be lower than those of a competitive industry in the long run, even if they are higher in the short run. Monopoly, according to this view, may be the handmaiden of innovation. Although the argument is an old one, it remains controversial. The statistical evidence is decidedly mixed.

Natural Monopoly: Where Single-Firm Production Is Cheapest

Second, we must remember that the monopoly depicted in Figure 2 is not a natural monopoly, because its average costs increase rather than decrease when its output expands. But some of the monopolies you find in the real world are "natural" ones. Where a monopoly is natural, costs of production would, by definition, be higher—possibly much higher—if the single large firm were broken up into many smaller firms. (Refer back to Figure 1.) In such cases, it may serve society's interests to allow the monopoly to continue because consumers benefit from the economies of large-scale production. But then it may be appropriate to regulate the monopoly by placing legal limitations on its ability to set its prices.

■ PRICE DISCRIMINATION UNDER MONOPOLY

So far we have assumed that a monopoly charges the same price to all of its customers, but that is not always true. In reality, monopoly firms can sell the same product to different customers at different prices, even if that price difference is unrelated to any special costs that affect some customers but not others. Such a practice is called **price discrimination.** Pricing is also said to be discriminatory if it costs more to supply a good to Customer A than to Customer B, but A and B are nonetheless charged the same price.

> **Price discrimination** is the sale of a given product at different prices to different customers of the firm, when there are no differences in the costs of supplying these customers. Prices are also discriminatory if it costs more to supply one customer than another, but they are charged the same price.

We are all familiar with cases of price discrimination. For example, suppose that Erik and Emily both mail letters from Lewisburg, Pennsylvania, but his goes to New York while hers goes to Hawaii. Both pay the same 37¢ postage even though Hawaii is much farther away from Lewisburg than New York is. Bargain airline fares are another example. Passenger C, who obtained a student discount, may find herself seated next to Passenger D, who has paid 25 percent more for the same flight and the same taste-free food.

The airline example shows that price discrimination occurs in industries that are not monopolies. Still, it is easier for a monopolist to charge discriminatory prices than it is for a firm that is affected by competition, because price discrimination means that sales to some customers are more profitable than sales to others. Such discrepancies in profitability tempt rivals, including new entrants into the industry, to charge the more profitable consumers somewhat lower prices in order to lure them away from the firm that is "overcharging" them. Price discriminators sneeringly call this type of targeted entry *cream skimming*, meaning that entrants go after the best-paying customers, leaving the low payers (the "skimmed milk") to the discriminator. But, whether desirable or not, such entry certainly makes it more difficult to charge higher prices to the more profitable customers.

Why do firms sometimes engage in price discrimination? You may already suspect the answer: to increase their profits. To see why, let us consider a simple example. Imagine a town with 100 rich families and 1,000 poor ones. The poor families are each willing to buy one video game but cannot afford to pay more than $25. The rich, however, are prepared to buy one per family as long as the price is no higher than $75.

If it cannot price-discriminate, the best the firm can do is to set the price at $25 for everyone, yielding a total revenue of $25 × 1,100 = $27,500. If it charged more, say, $75, it would sell only to the rich and earn just $7,500. If the added cost of producing the 1,000 games for the poorer families is less than the $27,500 − $7,500 = $20,000 in added revenues from the sales to the poor, then the $25 price must be more profitable than the $75 price.

But what if the game maker can charge different prices to the rich and to the poor—and can prevent the poor from reselling their low-priced merchandise to the rich at a markup? Then the revenue obtainable by the firm from the same 1,100 video game output becomes $25 \times 1,000 = $25,000 from selling to the poor plus $75 \times 100 = $7,500 from selling to the rich, for a total of $32,500. This is clearly a better deal for the firm than the $27,500 revenue obtainable without price discrimination. Profits are $5,000 higher. In general:

> When a firm charges discriminatory prices, profits are normally higher than when the firm charges nondiscriminatory (uniform) prices because the firm then divides customers into separate groups and charges each group the price that maximizes its profits from those customers.

We have constructed our simple example to make the two profit-maximizing prices obvious. In practice, that is not so; the monopolist knows that if it sets a price too high, quantity demanded and hence profits will be too low. The discriminating monopolist's problem is determining the different profit-maximizing prices to charge to different customer groups. The solution to this problem is given by another rule of marginal analysis. For simplicity, suppose that the seller proposes charging two different prices to two customer groups, A and B. Profit maximization requires that the price to Group A and the price to Group B are such that they yield the same *marginal* revenue, that is:

> The marginal revenue from a sale to a Group A customer must be the same as that from a sale to a Group B customer:

$$\text{MR}_a = \text{MR}_b$$

The reasoning is straightforward. Suppose that the sale of an additional video game to a Group A customer who lives in Richtown brings in $\text{MR}_a = $28 in revenue, whereas the corresponding sale to a Group B customer in Poorborough adds only $\text{MR}_b = $12. Such an arrangement cannot possibly be a profit-maximizing solution. By switching one unit of its shipments from Poorborough, with its B customers, and sending that unit instead to Richtown's A customers, the firm gives up $12 in revenue to gain $28—a net gain of $16 from the same total quantity of sales. Because a similar argument holds for any other pair of marginal revenues that are unequal, profit maximizing clearly requires that the marginal revenue from each group of customers be equal.

The equal-marginal-revenue rule enables us to determine the profit-maximizing prices and sales volumes for two such groups of customers diagrammatically. The two panels of Figure 4 show the demand curves and corresponding marginal revenue curves for customer groups A and B. Suppose that the firm is selling the quantity Q_a to Group A customers at price P_a. How much must the firm then sell to Group B customers, and at what price, to maximize profits? Our rule gives the answer. The marginal revenue from selling to Group A is equal to H—as we see from point J directly above Q_a on the MR curve in Panel (a). The rule tells us that the firm must charge a price to Group B customers that induces them to buy the quantity that yields the same marginal revenue, H. We find this quantity by drawing a horizontal line HH through point J from Panel (a) to Panel (b). The marginal revenues of the two customer groups will clearly be equal where HH cuts the Group B marginal revenue curve—at point W. The profit-maximizing sales volume to Group B will be Q_b, directly below point W. And at sales volume Q_b, the market B price is clearly given by the corresponding point on the market B demand curve, price P_b directly above Q_b.

> Given price and output in one of two markets (Figure 4a), to determine the profit-maximizing output and price in the other market (Figure 4b) under price discrimination, do the following:
>
> 1. Draw the demand and marginal revenue curves for the different customer groups (Group A and Group B) side by side.

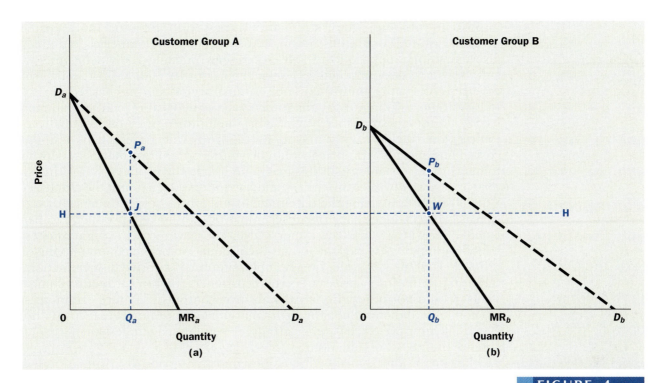

FIGURE 4

Prices and Quantities under Price Discrimination

2. For the first market (Group A, Figure 4a), draw a horizontal line through point J corresponding to the marginal revenue-quantity combination, which will set the price and quantity for Customer Group A at (P_a, Q_a).

3. Knowing the marginal revenue H and output (Q_a), point J, for the first market, find the profit-maximizing sales quantity for the second market where the horizontal line cuts the MR curve for the second group of customers, so that the MR levels are the same for both customer groups.

4. Knowing the marginal revenue H and point maximizing sales quantity Q_b for the second market, determine the second customer group's profit-maximizing price P_b, point W, by locating the point on the demand curve corresponding to the profit-maximizing quantity.

That is not quite the end of the story: We have not yet said anything about costs, and we know that profit maximization must take account of costs as well as revenues. But we can deal with the cost issue quite easily, at least if the marginal cost of a video game is the same whether supplied to an A customer or a B customer. Even under price discrimination, we still have the fundamental MR = MC rule for profit maximization in each market segment (see page 165 in Chapter 8). The extended profit-maximization rule under price discrimination then must be:

$$\text{MR}_a = \text{MR}_b = \text{MC}$$

■ Is Price Discrimination Always Undesirable?

Although the word *discrimination* is generally used to refer to reprehensible practices, *price* discrimination may not always be bad. Most people feel strongly that it is appropriate for the post office to charge the same price for all first-class letters going between two points in the United States, regardless of the differences in delivery costs. Similarly, most people approve of discounts on theater tickets sold to students or to senior citizens, even though those prices are obviously discriminatory. The same is widely agreed about lower doctor's fees for needy patients.

Other reasons, in addition to some standard of fairness or justice, may provide a defense for price discrimination in certain cases. One such case arises when it is impossible without price discrimination for a private firm to supply a product that customers want. For an illustration, go back to our first numerical example of price discrimination. Suppose that the total cost of producing 100 video games is $8,000, and the total cost of producing 1,100 video games is $30,000. Then our firm cannot cover its costs with a uniform, nondiscriminatory price. If it charged $75 to the 100 rich customers willing to pay that much, its $7,500 total revenue would fall short of its $8,000 total cost. Similarly, charging the uniform price of $25 to all 1,100 customers would yield total revenue of only $27,500, which is less than the $30,000 total cost. Thus, *any* uniform price would drive the firm out of business, depriving customers of the consumers' surplus from purchasing the product. But with discriminatory prices, we saw that the firm would earn $32,500, enabling the firm to cover the $30,000 cost of supplying the requirements of both sets of customers.

It is even possible that price discrimination can make a product cheaper than it would otherwise be for *all* customers—even those who pay the higher prices. As you may imagine, this can be true only if the production of the commodity involves significant economies of scale. For example, suppose that price discrimination permits the firm to offer lower prices to certain customers, thereby attracting some business that it would not otherwise have. The firm's output will therefore increase. Scale economies will then reduce the firm's marginal costs. If marginal cost falls enough, even the "high-priced" customer group may end up paying less than it would in the absence of price discrimination.

The conclusion from this discussion is not that price discrimination is always a good thing, but rather that it is *sometimes* desirable. In particular, we must recognize that a firm may be unable to cover its costs without price discrimination—a situation that some observers consider to be relatively common.

THE PUZZLE RESOLVED: *Competition in Telephone Service*

We conclude our discussion of monopoly by returning to the puzzle that began this chapter: Why are phone services around the country threatened by competition in an industry that was once considered the very definition of a natural monopoly? The answer has many parts, notably changes in the government's rules and new rulings by the courts. But the main development that made competition in the industry possible is the huge change in telephone service technology.

Until recently, the market for *local* telephone service was considered a natural monopoly. The primary reason was the need for very expensive transmission facilities, primarily the wires that had to enter every subscriber's home. Local and state governments even disallowed competition in these markets because they believed that it would lead to wasteful duplication of such costly equipment and that this expensive duplication would lead to higher prices. Instead, local utility commissions regulated these monopolies to ensure adequate service and reasonable prices. Because long distance calls also had to reach the home and office via those costly wires, the firm that owned them would have been in a position to control the industry and perhaps even to turn it into a monopoly once again, if government rules had not prevented it.

SOURCE: © AP/Wide World Photos.

Recent changes in communications technology have since made this market riper for competition. Computers and satellite technology have reduced the investment costs of providing phone service. Wherever you live, competition may be on the way, with mobile (cell) phones clearly needing no wires connecting to households. Voice message transmission via the internet is also growing, and is far less costly, rapidly improving, and easily supplied by rival providers. The local phone companies still have some near-monopoly power in their own geographic territories, but that power seems likely to erode before long.

SUMMARY

1. A **pure monopoly** is a one-firm industry producing a product for which there are no close substitutes.

2. Monopoly can persist only if there are important cost advantages to single-firm operation or **barriers to free entry**. These barriers may consist of legal impediments (**patents**, licensing), the special risks faced by a potential entrant resulting from the need to incur large sunk investments, or the result of "dirty tricks" designed to make things tough for an entrant.

3. One important case of cost advantages is **natural monopoly**—instances in which only one firm can survive because of significant economies of large-scale production.

4. A monopoly has no supply curve. It maximizes its profit by producing an output at which its marginal revenue equals its marginal cost. Its price is given by the point on its demand curve corresponding to that output.

5. In a monopolistic industry, if demand and cost curves are the same as those of a competitive industry, and if the demand curve has a negative slope and the competitive supply curve has a positive slope, then monopoly output will be lower and price will be higher than they will be in the competitive industry.

6. Economists consider the fact that monopoly output tends to be below the competitive level to constitute an (undesirable) inefficiency.

7. Advertising may enable a monopoly to shift its demand curve above that of a comparable competitive industry. Through economies such as large-scale input purchases, a monopoly may be able to shift its cost curves below those of a competitive industry.

8. A monopoly may be able to increase its profits by engaging in **price discrimination**—charging higher prices for the same goods to customers who are less resistant to price increases, or failing to charge higher prices to customers whom it costs more to serve.

9. The profit-maximizing discriminatory prices, and corresponding sales volumes, for a firm with several different customer groups can be determined with the help of an extended rule for profit maximization: that the *marginal revenue* from sales to *each* customer group must be equal to one another and to the firm's marginal cost.

10. Price discrimination can sometimes be damaging to the public interest, but at other times it can be beneficial. Some firms cannot survive without it, and price discrimination may even reduce prices to *all* customers if there are substantial economies of scale.

KEY TERMS

Pure monopoly   218

Barriers to entry   219

Patents   219

Natural monopoly   220

Monopoly profits   223

Price discrimination   227

TEST YOURSELF

1. Which of the following industries are pure monopolies?

   a. The only supplier of heating fuel in an isolated town

   b. The only supplier of IBM notebook computers in town

   c. The only supplier of digital cameras

   Explain your answers.

2. The following are the demand and total cost schedules for Company Town Water, a local monopoly:

Output in Gallons	Price per Gallon	Total Cost
50,000	$0.28	$ 6,000
100,000	0.26	15,000
150,000	0.22	22,000
200,000	0.20	32,000
250,000	0.16	46,000
300,000	0.12	64,000

How much output will Company Town Water produce, and what price will it charge? Will it earn a profit? How much? (*Hint:* First compute the firm's MR and MC schedules.)

3. Show from the table in Test Yourself Question 2 that for the water company, marginal revenue (per 50,000-gallon unit) is always less than price.

4. A monopoly sells Frisbees to two customer groups. Group A has a downward-sloping straight-line demand curve, whereas the demand curve for Group B is infinitely elastic. Draw the graph determining the profit-maximizing discriminatory prices and sales to the two groups. What will be the price of Frisbees to Group B? Why? How is the price to Group A determined?

DISCUSSION QUESTIONS

1. Suppose that a monopoly industry produces less output than a similar competitive industry. Discuss why this may be considered socially undesirable.

2. If competitive firms earn zero economic profits, explain why anyone would invest money in them. (*Hint:* What is the role of the opportunity cost of capital in economic profit?)

3. Suppose that a tax of $24 is levied on each item sold by a monopolist, and as a result, she decides to raise her price by exactly $24. Why may this decision be against her own best interests?

4. Use Figure 2 to show that Adam Smith was wrong when he claimed that a monopoly would always charge "the highest price which can be got."

5. MCI and Sprint have invested vast amounts of money in their fiber-optic networks, which are costly to construct but relatively cheap to operate. If both of them were to go bankrupt, why might this *not* result in a decrease in the competition facing AT&T? (*Hint:* At what price would the assets of the bankrupt companies be offered for sale?)

6. What does your answer to the previous question tell you about ease or difficulty of entry into telecommunications?

7. A firm cannot break even by charging uniform (nondiscriminatory) prices, but with price discrimination it can earn a small profit. Explain why in this case consumers *must* be better off if the firm is permitted to charge discriminatory prices.

8. It can be proved that, other things being equal, under price discrimination the price charged to some customer group will be higher the less elastic the demand curve of that group is. Why is that result plausible?

12

BETWEEN COMPETITION AND MONOPOLY

. . . neither fish nor fowl.

JOHN HEYWOOD (C. 1565)

Most productive activity in the United States, as in any advanced industrial society, falls somewhere between the two extreme market forms we have considered so far. So if we want to understand the workings of the market mechanism in a real, modern economy, we must look at hybrid market structures that fall somewhere between perfect competition and pure monopoly. There are two such market forms—*monopolistic competition* and *oligopoly*—that are analyzed extensively by economists and are extremely important in practice.

Monopolistic competition is a market structure characterized by many small firms selling somewhat different products. Here, each firm's output is so small relative to the total output of closely related and, hence, rival products that the firm does not expect its competitors to respond to or even to *notice* any changes in its own behavior.

Monopolistic competition, or something close to it, is widespread in retailing: shoe stores, restaurants, and gasoline stations are good examples. Most firms in our economy can be classified as monopolistic competitors, because even though they are small, such enterprises are abundant. We begin the chapter by using the theory of the firm described in Chapter 8 to analyze a monopolistically competitive firm's price-output decisions, then we consider the role of entry and exit, as we did in Chapter 10.

Finally we turn to oligopoly, a market structure in which a few large firms dominate the market. The steel, automobile, and airplane manufacturing industries are good examples of oligopolies, despite the increasing number of strong foreign competitors. Probably the largest share of U.S. economic output comes from oligopolists. Although they are fewer in number than monopolistic competitors, many oligopoly firms are extremely large, with annual sales exceeding the total outputs of most countries in the world and even of some of the smaller industrial European countries.

CONTENTS

One critical feature distinguishing an oligopolist from either a monopolist or a perfect competitor is that oligopolists care very much about what other individual firms in the industry do. The resulting *interdependence* of decisions, as we will see, makes oligopoly very difficult to analyze and results in a wide range of behavior patterns. Consequently, economic theory uses not just one but many models of oligopoly (some of which we will review in this chapter), and it is often hard to know which model to apply in any particular situation.

THREE PUZZLING OBSERVATIONS

We need to study the hybrid market structures considered in this chapter because many economic phenomena cannot be explained in terms of perfect competition or pure monopoly. Here are three examples:

Puzzle 1: Why Are There So Many Retailers? You have undoubtedly seen road intersections with gasoline stations on every corner. Often, two or three of them have no customers at the pumps. There seem to be more gas stations than the number of cars warrants, with a corresponding waste of labor, time, equipment, and other resources. Why—and how—do they all stay in business?

Puzzle 2: Why Do Oligopolists Advertise More Than "More Competitive" Firms? Many big companies use advertising as a principal weapon in their battle for customers, and advertising budgets can constitute very large shares of their expenditures. Such firms spend literally billons of dollars per year on advertising, seeking to leap ahead of their rivals. Procter & Gamble, for example, is reported to spend $4 billion on advertising (about 10 percent of its revenues in 2004).[1] Yet critics often accuse oligopolistic industries containing only a few giant firms of being "uncompetitive." Farming, in contrast, is considered as close to perfect competition as any industry in our economy, but few, if any, individual farmers spend anything at all on advertising.[2] Why do these allegedly "uncompetitive" oligopolists make such heavy use of combative advertising whereas very competitive farmers do not?

Puzzle 3: Why Do Oligopolists Seem to Change Their Prices So Infrequently? Many prices in the economy change from minute to minute. The very latest prices of commodities such as soybeans, pork bellies, and copper are available online twenty-four hours a day, seven days a week. If you want to buy one of these commodities at 11:45 A.M. today, you cannot use yesterday's price—or even the price from 11:44 A.M. today—because it has probably changed already. Yet prices of products such as cars and refrigerators generally change only a few times a year at most, even during fairly rapid inflation. Firms that sell cars and refrigerators know that product and input market conditions change all the time. Why don't they adjust their prices more often? This chapter will offer answers to each of these questions.

MONOPOLISTIC COMPETITION

For years, economic theory told us little about market forms in between the two extreme cases of pure monopoly and perfect competition. Then, during the 1930s, Edward Chamberlin of Harvard University and Joan Robinson of Cambridge

---

[1] "The Harder Hard Sell," *The Economist* magazine, June 24, 2004, http://www.economist.com; and http://www.pg.com.

[2] But farmers' associations, such as Sunkist and various dairy groups, do spend money on advertising.

University (working separately) partially filled this gap and helped to make economic theory more realistic. The market structure they analyzed is called **monopolistic competition.**

> **Monopolistic competition** refers to a market in which products are heterogeneous but which is otherwise the same as a market that is perfectly competitive.

■ Characteristics of Monopolistic Competition

A market is said to operate under conditions of monopolistic competition if it satisfies four requirements, three of which are the same as those for perfect competition:

- *Numerous participants*—that is, many buyers and sellers, all of whom are small
- *Freedom of exit and entry*
- *Perfect information*
- *Heterogeneous products*—as far as the buyer is concerned, each seller's product differs at least somewhat from every other seller's product

Notice that monopolistic competition differs from perfect competition in only the last respect. Perfect competition assumes that the products of different firms in an industry are identical, but under monopolistic competition products differ from seller to seller—in terms of quality, packaging, supplementary services offered (such as windshield washing at a gas station), or merely consumers' perceptions. The attributes that differentiate products need not be "real" in any objective or directly measurable sense. For example, differences in packaging or in associated services can and do distinguish otherwise identical products. However, although two products may perform quite differently in quality tests, if consumers know nothing about this difference, it is irrelevant.

In contrast to a perfect competitor, a monopolistic competitor's demand curve is negatively sloped. Because each seller's product is different, each caters to a set of customers who vary in their loyalty to the particular product. If the firm raises its price somewhat, it will drive *some* of its customers to competitors' offerings, but customers who strongly favor the firm's product will not switch. If one monopolistic competitor lowers its price, it may expect to attract some trade from rivals. But, because different products are imperfect substitutes, it will not lure away *all* of the rivals' business.

For example, if Harriet's Hot Dog House reduces its price slightly, it will attract those customers of Sam's Sausage Shop who were nearly indifferent between the two. If Harriet were to cut her prices further, she would gain some customers who have a slightly greater preference for Sam's product. But even a big cut in Harriet's price will not bring her the hard-core sausage lovers who hate hot dogs. Therefore, monopolistic competitors face a demand curve that is negatively sloped, like that of a monopolist, rather than horizontal, like that of a perfect competitor who will lose all of his business if he insists on a higher price than that charged by a rival.

Because consumers see each product as distinct from all others, a monopolistically competitive firm appears to have something akin to a small monopoly. Can we therefore expect it to earn more than zero economic profit? Like perfect competitors, perhaps monopolistic competitors will obtain economic profits in the short run. In the long run, however, high economic profits will attract new entrants into a monopolistically competitive market—not with products *identical* to an existing firm's, but with products sufficiently similar to absorb the excess economic profits.

If McDonald's is thriving at a particular location, it can confidently expect Burger King or some other fast-food outlet to open a franchise nearby shortly. When one seller adopts a new, attractive package, rivals will soon follow suit with slightly different designs and colors of their own. In this way, freedom of entry ensures that the monopolistically competitive firm earns no higher return on its capital in the long run than that capital could earn elsewhere. In other words, the firm earns no excess economic profits. Just as under perfect competition, competition will drive price

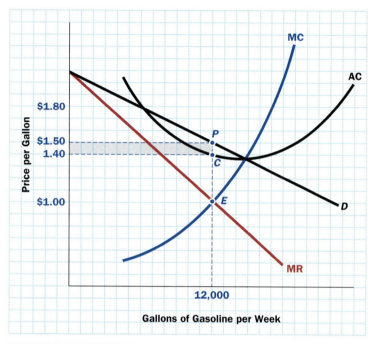

Gallons of Gasoline per Week

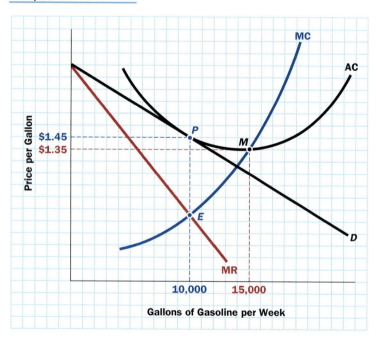

Gallons of Gasoline per Week

down to equal average cost, including the opportunity cost of capital. In this sense, although its product differs somewhat from everyone else's, the firm under monopolistic competition has no more monopoly *power* than one operating under perfect competition does.

Let us now examine the process that ensures that competition will drive economic profits down to zero in the long run, even under monopolistic competition, and see what prices and outputs that process fosters.

■ Price and Output Determination under Monopolistic Competition

The *short-run* equilibrium of the firm under monopolistic competition differs little from the equilibrium seen under monopoly. Because the firm faces a downward-sloping demand curve (labeled *D* in Figure 1), its marginal revenue (MR) curve will lie below its demand curve. Like any firm, a monopolistic competitor maximizes profits by producing the output at which marginal revenue equals marginal cost (MC). In Figure 1, the profit-maximizing output for a hypothetical gas station is 12,000 gallons per week, and it sells this output at a price of $1.50 per gallon (point *P* on the demand curve). The firm makes 10 cents per gallon in profits, as depicted by the vertical distance from *C* to *P*.

This analysis, you will note, looks much like Figure 2 in Chapter 11 for a monopoly. The main difference is that monopolistic competitors are likely to face a much flatter demand curve than pure monopolists do, because many products serve as close substitutes for the monopolistic competitor's product . If our gas station raises its price to $1.80 per gallon, most of its customers will go across the street. If it lowers its price to $1.00 per gallon, it will have long lines at its pumps.

The gas station depicted in Figure 1 is enjoying economic profits. Because average cost at 12,000 gallons per week is only $1.40 per gallon (point *C*), the station makes a profit of 10 cents per gallon on gasoline sales, or $1,200 per week in total, shown by the shaded rectangle. Under monopoly, such profits can persist. Under monopolistic competition, they cannot—because economic profits will entice new firms to enter the market. Although the new gas stations will not offer the identical product, they will offer products that are close enough to take away some business from our firm. (For example, they may sell Conoco or Shell gasoline instead of Exxon gasoline.)

When more firms enter the market, each firm's demand curve will shift downward (to the left). But how far will it shift? The answer is basically the same as it was under perfect competition: Market entry will cease only when the most that the firm can earn is zero economic profit—exactly the same return the firm can earn elsewhere.

Figure 2 depicts the same monopolistically competitive firm as in Figure 1 *after* the adjustment to the long-run equilibrium is complete. The demand curve—and hence also the MR curve—has been pushed down so far by the entry of new rivals that when the firm equates MC and MR in an attempt to maximize profits (point *E*), it simultaneously equates price *(P)* and average cost (AC) so that economic profits are zero (point *P*). As compared to the short-run equilibrium depicted in Figure 1, price in long-run equilibrium is *lower* ($1.45 cents per gallon versus $1.50), *more firms* participate in the industry, and each firm produces a *smaller* output (10,000 gallons versus 12,000 gallons) at a *higher* average cost per gallon ($1.45 versus $1.40).[3] In general:

Long-run equilibrium under monopolistic competition requires that the firm's output be at a level where its demand curve and its average cost curve meet, and there the two curves must be *tangent,* not crossing.

Why? Because if the demand curve were above the average cost curve or the two curves intersected, firms could produce output quantities at which price would exceed average cost, which means that participants would be earning economic profits, and that would draw an influx of new close-substitute products that would push down the demand curve. Similarly, if the average cost curve were above the demand curve at every point, the firm would incur an economic loss—it would be unable to obtain returns equal to those that its capital can get elsewhere, and firms would leave the industry.

This analysis of entry is quite similar to the perfectly competitive case. Moreover, the notion that firms under monopolistic competition earn exactly zero economic profits seems to correspond fairly well to what we see in the real world. Gas station operators, whose markets fit the characteristics of monopolistic competition, do not earn notably higher profits than do small farmers, who operate under conditions closer to perfect competition.

■ The Excess Capacity Theorem and Resource Allocation

One economically significant difference arises between perfect and monopolistic competition. Look at Figure 2 again. The tangency point between the average cost and demand curves, point *P*, occurs along the *negatively sloping portion* of the average cost curve, because *P* is the only point where the AC curve has the same (negative) slope as the demand curve. If the AC curve is U-shaped, the tangency point must therefore lie above and to the left of the *minimum point* on the average cost curve, point *M*. In other words, under monopolistic competition, the demand curve hits the average cost curve in a region where average costs are still declining. Average costs have yet to reach their lowest point. By contrast, the perfectly competitive firm's demand curve is horizontal, so tangency must take place at the minimum point on the average cost curve. You can easily confirm this by referring back to Figure 10-9(a). This difference leads to the following important conclusion:

Under monopolistic competition in the long run, the firm will tend to produce an output lower than that which minimizes its unit costs, and hence unit costs of the monopolistic competitor will be higher than necessary. Because the level of output that corresponds to minimum average cost is naturally considered to be the firm's optimal capacity, this result has been called the *excess capacity theorem of monopolistic competition.* Thus, monopolistic competition tends to lead firms to have unused or wasted capacity.

It follows that if every firm under monopolistic competition were to expand its output, cost per unit of output would be reduced. But we must be careful about jumping

---

[3] *Exercise:* Show that if the demand curve fell still further, the firm would incur a loss. What would then happen in the long run?

to policy conclusions from that observation. It does *not* follow that *every* monopolistically competitive firm *should* produce more. After all, such an overall increase in industry output means that a smaller portion of the economy's resources will be available for other uses; from the information at hand, we have no way of knowing whether that choice leaves us better or worse off in terms of social benefits.

Even so, the situation depicted in Figure 2 probably represents a substantial *inefficiency*. Although it is not clear that society would gain if *every* firm were to achieve lower costs by expanding its production, society *can* save resources if firms combine into *a smaller number of larger companies* that produce the *same total output*. For example, suppose that in the situation shown in Figure 2, 15 monopolistically competitive firms each sell 10,000 gallons of gasoline per week. The total cost of this output, according to the figures given in the diagram, would be:

$$\text{Number of firms} \times \text{Output per firm} \times \text{Cost per unit} =$$
$$15 \times 10,000 \times \$1.45 = \$217,500$$

If, instead, the number of stations was cut to 10 and each sold 15,000 gallons, total production would be unchanged. But total costs would fall to $10 \times 15,000 \times \$1.35 = \$202,500$, a net saving of \$15,000 *without any cut in total output*.

This result does not depend on the particular numbers that we used in our illustration. It follows directly from the observation that lowering the cost per unit must always reduce the total cost of producing *any* given industry output. That is, producing a *given* output, Q, always must have a lower total cost when average cost is lower: Specifically, if $AC_1 < AC_2$, it must obviously *always* be true that $TC_1 = Q \times AC_1 < Q \times AC_2 = TC_2$. Society must gain in the sense of getting the same total output, Q, as before but at a lower total cost. After all, which do you prefer—a dozen cans of soda for \$0.70 each or the same dozen cans for \$0.55 each?

1ST PUZZLE RESOLVED: *Explaining the Abundance of Retailers*

The excess capacity theorem explains one of the puzzles mentioned at the beginning of this chapter. The highway intersection with four gas stations, where two could serve the available customers with little increase in customer delays and at lower costs, is a real-world example of excess capacity.

The excess capacity theorem seems to imply that too many sellers participate in monopolistically competitive markets and that society would benefit from a reduction in their numbers. However, such a conclusion may be a bit hasty. Even if a smaller number of larger firms can reduce costs, society may not benefit from the change because it will leave consumers with a smaller range of choice. Because all products differ at least slightly under monopolistic competition, a reduction in the number of *firms* means that the number of different *products* falls as well. We achieve greater efficiency at the cost of greater standardization.

In some cases, consumers may agree that this trade-off represents a net gain, particularly if the variety of products available was initially so great that it only confused them. But for some products, most consumers would probably agree that the diversity of choice is worth the extra cost involved. After all, we would probably save money on clothing if every student were required to wear a uniform. But because the uniform is likely to be too hot for some students, too cool for other students, and aesthetically displeasing to almost everyone else, would the cost saving really be a net benefit?

"Why have we come? Because only Earth offers the rock-bottom prices and wide selection of men's, women's, and children's clothing in the styles and sizes we're looking for."

OLIGOPOLY

An **oligopoly** is a market dominated by a few sellers, at least several of which are large enough relative to the total market that they may be able to influence the market price.

In highly developed economies, it is not monopoly, but *oligopoly*, that is virtually synonymous with "big business." Any oligopolistic industry includes a group of giant firms, each of which keeps a watchful eye on the actions of the others. Under oligopoly, rivalry among firms takes its most direct and active form. Here one encounters such actions and reactions as frequent new-product introductions, free samples, and aggressive—if not downright nasty—advertising campaigns. A firm's price decision may elicit cries of pain from its rivals, and firms are often engaged in a continuing battle in which they plan strategies day by day and each major decision induces direct responses by rival firms.

Notice that the definition of oligopoly does not mention the degree of product differentiation. Some oligopolies sell products that are essentially identical (such as steel plate from different steel manufacturers), whereas others sell products that are quite different in consumers' eyes (for example, Chevrolets, Fords, and Hondas). Some oligopolistic industries also contain a considerable number of smaller firms (example: soft drink manufacturers), but they are nevertheless considered oligopolies because a few large firms carry out the bulk of the industry's business, and smaller participants must follow their larger rivals' lead to survive at the margins of the industry. Oligopolistic firms often seek to create unique products—unique, at least, in consumers' perceptions. To the extent that an oligopolistic firm can create a unique product in terms of features, location, or appeal, it protects itself from the pressures of competition that will force down its prices and eat into its sales.

Managers of large, oligopolistic firms who have occasion to study economics are somewhat taken aback by the notion of perfect competition, because it is devoid of all harsh competitive activity as they know it. Recall that under perfect competition firm managers make no price decisions—they simply accept the price dictated by market forces and adjust their output accordingly. As we observed at the beginning of the chapter, a perfectly competitive firm does not advertise; it adopts no sales gimmicks; it does not even know who most of its competitors are. But because oligopolists have some degree of influence on market forces, they do not enjoy the luxury of such anonymity. They worry about prices, spend fortunes on advertising (see "The Mad Scramble to Differentiate the Product" on the next page), and try to understand or even predict their rivals' behavior patterns.

An **oligopoly** is a market dominated by a few sellers, at least several of which are large enough relative to the total market to be able to influence the market price.

2ND PUZZLE RESOLVED: *Why Oligopolists Advertise but Perfectly Competitive Firms Generally Do Not*

The two reasons for such divergent behavior should be clear, and they explain the puzzling fact that oligopolists advertise far more than the supposedly far more competitive firms in perfectly competitive markets. First, a perfectly competitive firm can sell all it wants at the current market price, so why should it waste money on advertising? By contrast, General Motors (GM) and Toyota cannot sell all the cars they want at the current price. Because they face negatively sloped (and thus less than perfectly elastic) demand curves, if they want to sell more, they must either reduce prices (to move along the demand curve toward greater quantities) or advertise more (to shift their demand curves outward).

Second, because the public believes that the products supplied by firms in a perfectly competitive industry are identical, if Firm A advertises its product, the advertisement is just as likely to bring customers to Firm B. Under oligopoly, however, consumer products are often *not* identical. Ford advertises to convince consumers that its automobiles are better than GM's or Subaru's. If the advertising campaign succeeds, GM and Subaru will be hurt and probably will respond with more advertising of their own. Thus, the firms in an oligopoly with differentiated products must compete via advertising, whereas perfectly competitive firms gain little or nothing by doing so.

The Mad Scramble to Differentiate the Product

Competition is fierce in the world of business, and companies will go very far indeed to outdo their rivals. In the summer of 2000, Pizza Hut's advertising campaign was literally out of this world: The firm helped to bankroll Russia's space agency by putting a ten-meter-high, $1.25 million ad on a Proton booster rocket.

SOURCE: Courtesy of Pizza Hut

SOURCE: "Marketing: Guerrillas in Our Midst," *The Economist*, October 14, 2000, p. 80.

■ Why Oligopolistic Behavior Is So Difficult to Analyze

Firms in an oligopolistic industry—in particular, the largest of those firms—have some latitude in choosing their product prices and outputs. Furthermore, to survive and thrive in an oligopolistic environment, firms must take direct account of their rivals' responses. Both of these features complicate the analysis of the oligopolistic firm's behavior and prevent us from drawing unambiguous conclusions about resource allocation under oligopoly. Oligopoly is much more difficult to analyze than other forms of economic organization, because oligopolistic decisions are, by their very nature, *interdependent*. Oligopolists *recognize* that the outcomes of their decisions depend on their rivals' responses. For example, Ford managers know that their actions will probably lead to reactions by GM, which in turn may require a readjustment of Ford's plans, thereby modifying GM's response, and so on. Where such a sequence of moves and countermoves may lead is difficult enough to ascertain. But the fact that Ford executives recognize this possibility in advance, and may try to second-guess or predict GM's reactions as they initially decide on a marketing tactic, makes even that first step difficult to analyze and almost impossible to predict.

Truly, almost anything can and sometimes does happen under oligopoly. The early railroad kings went so far as to employ gangs of hoodlums who fought pitched battles to try to squelch rival lines' operations. At the other extreme, oligopolistic firms have employed overt or covert forms of collusion to avoid rivalry altogether—to transform an oligopolistic industry, at least temporarily, into a monopolistic one. In other instances, oligopolistic firms seem to have arranged to live and let live, via price leadership (discussed later) or geographic allocations, dividing up customers by agreement among the firms.

■ A Shopping List

Because oligopolies in the real world are so diverse, oligopoly models in the theoretical world should also come in various shapes and sizes. An introductory course cannot hope to explain all of the many oligopoly models. This section offers a quick review of some oligopolistic behavior models. In the remainder of the chapter, we turn our attention to a particularly interesting set of models that use methods such as game theory to analyze oligopolistic firm behavior.

1. Ignoring Interdependence   One simple approach to the problem of oligopolistic interdependence is to assume that the oligopolists themselves ignore it—that they behave as if their actions will not elicit reactions from their rivals. Perhaps an oligopolist, finding the "If they think that we think that they think . . . " chain of reasoning too complex, will decide to ignore rivals' behavior. The firm may then just seek to maximize profits, assuming that its decisions will not affect its rivals' strategies. In this case, economists can analyze oligopoly in the same way they look at monopoly, which we described in Chapter 11. Probably no oligopolist totally ignores all of its major rivals' decisions, but many of them seem to do so as they make their more routine decisions, which are nevertheless often quite important.

2. Strategic Interaction   Although *some* oligopolists may ignore interdependence *some* of the time, models based on such behavior probably do not offer a general explanation for *most* oligopoly behavior *most* of the time. The reason is simple: Because they operate in the same market, the price and output decisions of soap suds makers Brand X and Brand Y *really are* interdependent.

Suppose, for example, that Brand X, Inc. managers decide to cut their soap suds' price from $1.12 to $1.05, on the assumption that rival Brand Y, Inc. will ignore this move and continue to charge $1.12 per box. Brand X decides to manufacture 5 million boxes per year and to spend $1 million per year on advertising. It may find itself surprised when Brand Y cuts its price to $1.00 per box, raises production to 8 million boxes per year, and sponsors the Super Bowl! In such a case, Brand X's profits will suffer, and the company will wish it had not cut its price in the first place. Most important for our purposes, Brand X managers will learn not to ignore interdependence in the future.

For many oligopolies, then, competition may resemble military operations involving tactics, strategies, moves, and countermoves. Thus, we must consider models that deal explicitly with oligopolistic interdependence.

3. Cartels   The opposite of ignoring interdependence occurs when all firms in an oligopoly try to do something about their interdependence and agree to set price and output, acting as a monopolist would. In a **cartel,** firms collude directly to coordinate their actions to transform the industry into a giant monopoly.

A cartel is a group of sellers of a product who have joined together to control its production, sale, and price in the hope of obtaining the advantages of monopoly.

A notable cartel is the Organization of Petroleum Exporting Countries (OPEC), which first began making joint decisions on oil production in the 1970s. For a while, OPEC was one of the most spectacularly successful cartels in history. By restricting output, its member nations managed to quadruple the price of oil between 1973 and 1974. Unlike most cartels, which come apart because of internal bickering or other reasons, OPEC held together through two worldwide recessions and a variety of unsettling political events. It struck again with huge price increases between 1979 and 1980. In the mid-1980s, its members began to act in ways that did not promote the interest of the entire industry and oil prices tumbled, but prices have since risen and OPEC continues to dominate the world oil market. (See "OPEC Plans Another Cutback in Oil Production" on the next page for more recent news of OPEC and oil prices.)

OPEC's early success is hardly the norm. Cartels are difficult to organize and even more difficult to enforce. Firms struggle to agree on such things as the amount by which each will reduce its output in order to help push up the price. For a cartel to survive, each member must agree to produce no more output than that assigned to it by the group. Yet once the cartel drives up the price and increases profitability, each member faces the temptation to offer secret discounts that lure some of the very profitable business away from other members. When this happens, or even when members begin to suspect one another of doing so, collusive agreement often begins to come apart. Each member begins suspecting the others and is tempted to cut price first, before the others beat it to the punch.

For this reason, cartels usually adopt elaborate policing arrangements. In effect, they spy on each member firm to ensure that it does not sell more than it is supposed to or shave the price below that chosen by the cartel. This means that cartels are unlikely to succeed or to last very long if the firms sell many, varied products whose prices are difficult to compare and whose outputs are difficult to monitor. In addition, if firms frequently negotiate prices on a customer-by-customer basis and often offer special discounts, a cartel may be almost impossible to arrange.

Many economists consider cartels to be the worst form of market organization, in terms of efficiency and consumer welfare. A successful cartel may end up charging the monopoly price and obtaining monopoly profits. But because the firms do not actually combine operations, cartels offer the public no offsetting benefits in the form of economies of large-scale production. For these and other reasons, open collusion on prices and outputs among firms is illegal in the United States, as we will see in Chapter 13. Outright cartel arrangements rarely occur within the United States, although they are common in some other countries. Only one major exception occurs in the United States: Government regulations have sometimes forced industries such as railroads and gas pipeline transportation to behave as cartels. Regulations prohibited these firms from undercutting the prices set by the regulatory agencies—an exception that we will discuss in Chapter 13.

4. Price Leadership and Tacit Collusion   Overt collusion—in which firms actually meet or communicate directly in some other way to decide on prices and outputs—is quite rare. But some observers think that *tacit collusion*—where firms, without meeting together, try to do unto their competitors as they hope their competitors will do unto them—occurs quite commonly among oligopolists in our economy. Oligopolists

OPEC Plans Another Cutback in Oil Production

OPEC, whose member nations produce 40 percent of the world's oil, said yesterday it would cut output by 1.9 percent in February [2007]. . . .Production will be pared by 500,000 barrels a day as of Feb. 1, OPEC President Edmund Daukoru told journalists in Abuja, the Nigerian capital. The cut is in addition to the 1.2 million barrel-a-day reduction agreed upon by OPEC at its previous meeting on Oct. 20 in Doha, Qatar. The 11-member group, known formally as the Organization of the Petroleum Exporting Countries, is attempting to revive prices that have slid about 21 percent from a July [2006] record of $78.40 a barrel in New York. . . .Oil rose yesterday on speculation that OPEC's meeting would result in lower supplies, jumping $1.14, or 1.9 percent, to $62.51 a barrel on the New York Mercantile Exchange."

SOURCE: © Bettmann/Corbis

SOURCE: Excerpted from Andy Critchlow and Fred Pals, "OPEC Plans Another Cutback in Oil Production," *Washington Post*, December 15, 2006, http://www.washingtonpost.com.

POLICY DEBATE

Acting on Recognized Interdependence versus "Tacit Collusion"

Antitrust laws unequivocally prohibit price fixing—collusion among competitors in which they agree on their pricing policies (see Chapter 13). But suppose that the firms in an industry, recognizing their interdependence, simply decide to "go along with" each other's decisions? Is this collusion by long distance? Should it be declared illegal? Should the government require such a firm to "make believe" that it does not know how competitors will respond to its price moves? Must firms act as if they were not interdependent? If such requirements make no sense, what should the government require of oligopolistic firms?

The airline industry constantly illustrates this issue and its complexities. In 1992, American Airlines decided that the vast number of different airline fares and discounts hurt all airlines and that the industry needed a simplified fare structure. American offered a new, simplified pricing plan called "value pricing," in the hope that other airlines would copy that structure widely. But a few weeks later, Northwest Airlines introduced a special vacation travel deal that undercut American's pricing. This led to a price war, and American had to withdraw its plan, losing considerable money in the process. In this case, American's rivals did not go along with a price leader's decision.

In a more recent set of events, matters worked out differently. The airlines, which have lost money for years, have been seeking ways to cut costs by reducing wages, firing employees, and so on. As part of these cost-cutting efforts, Delta Airlines announced in early 1995 that it was capping payments to travel agents for each ticket sold. As it moved first to make the first such cut in ten years,

SOURCE: © Peter Christopher/Masterfile

Delta feared (as we know from its internal memoranda) that if the other airlines did not do the same, travel agents would stop booking passengers on Delta. Everything depended on whether other airlines would support Delta's new policy. They did. Within a week of Delta's announcement, the seven largest airlines each announced (apparently without consulting one another) that they would adopt Delta's ceiling on payments to travel agents. The travel agents sued, charging tacit collusion. The case was settled out of court with a compromise.

who do not want to rock a very profitable boat may seek to find some indirect way of communicating with one another, signaling their intentions and managing the market accordingly. Each tacitly colluding firm hopes that if it does not make things too difficult for its competitors, its rivals will return the favor. For example, three major makers of infant formula—Abbott Laboratories, Bristol-Myers Squibb, and American Home Products—were accused of conspiring against competitors by keeping their wholesale prices only a few cents apart. The formula makers denied any wrongdoing. (See "Acting on Recognized Interdependence versus 'Tacit Collusion'" above for another example.)

One common form of tacit collusion is **price leadership,** an arrangement in which one firm in the industry, in effect, makes pricing decisions for the entire group. Other firms are expected to adopt the prices set by the price leader, even though no explicit agreement exists—only tacit consent. Often, the price leader will be the largest firm in the industry. But in some price-leadership arrangements, the leadership role may rotate from one firm to another. For example, analysts suggested that for many years the steel industry conformed to the price-leadership model, with U.S. Steel and Bethlehem Steel assuming the leadership role at different times.

Under **price leadership,** one firm sets the price for the industry and the others follow.

In a **price war,** each competing firm is determined to sell at a price that is lower than the prices of its rivals, usually regardless of whether that price covers the pertinent cost. Typically, in such a price war, Firm A cuts its price below Firm B's price; B retaliates by undercutting A; and so on and on until some of the competitor firms surrender and let themselves be undersold.

Price leadership *does* overcome some problems for the firms that result from oligopolistic interdependence, although it does not provide the only possible way of doing so. If Brand X, Inc. acts as price leader for the soap suds industry, it can predict how Brand Y, Inc. will react to any price increases that it announces: Brand Y will match the increases. Similarly, Brand Z, Inc. executives will be able to predict Brand Y's behavior as long as the price-leadership arrangement holds up.

One problem besetting price leadership is that, although the oligopolists as an industry may benefit by avoiding a damaging **price war,** the *firms* may not benefit equally. The price-leading firm may be able to enhance its own profits more easily than any of the other firms in the group can. But if the price leader does not consider its rivals' welfare as it makes price decisions, it may find itself dethroned! Like cartels, such arrangements can easily break down.

◼ Sales Maximization: An Oligopoly Model with Interdependence Ignored

Early in our analysis of the firm we discussed the profit maximization hypothesis, and we noted that firms have other possible objectives. Among these alternative goals, one has attracted much attention: **sales maximization.**

A firm's objective is said to be **sales maximization** if it seeks to adopt prices and output quantities that make its total revenue (its "sales"), rather than its profits, as large as possible.

Modern industrial firms are managed by people who are not the owners of the companies. Paid executives manage the firms, working for the company on a full-time basis. These managers may begin to believe that whatever is good for them as individuals must be good for the company. The owners may be a large and diverse group of stockholders, most of whom own only a tiny fraction of the outstanding stock. They may take little interest in the company's day-to-day operations and may feel no real sense of ownership. In such a situation, managers' goals may influence company decisions more strongly than the owners' goal of profit maximization.

Some statistical evidence, for example, suggests that management's compensation often relates more directly to company *size*, as measured by sales volume, than to *profit*. The president of a large firm generally fetches a much higher salary—and bigger incentive rewards—than the president of a tiny company. Therefore, firm managers may select price-output combinations that maximize *sales* rather than profits. But does sales maximization lead to different outcomes than profit maximization? We shall see shortly that the answer is yes.

The graph in Figure 3 should be familiar by now. It shows the marginal cost (MC) and average cost (AC) curves for a soap suds firm—in this case Brand X, Inc.—along with its demand and marginal revenue (MR) curves. We have used such diagrams before and thus know that if the company wants to maximize profits, it will select point *A*, where MC = MR. Brand X will produce 2.5 million boxes of soap suds per year and sell them at $1 each (point *E* on the demand curve above *A*). Because average cost at this level of output is only 80 cents per box, X earns 20 cents economic profit per unit. Total profits are therefore $0.20 × 2,500,000 = $500,000 per year. This is the highest attainable profit level for Brand X.

But what if Brand X chooses to maximize total sales revenue instead? In this case, it will want to keep producing until MR falls to *zero*; that is, it will select point *B*. Why? By definition, MR is the *additional* revenue obtained by raising output by one unit. If the firm wishes to maximize total revenue, then whenever MR is positive, it will want to increase output further, and any time that MR becomes negative, X's management will want to decrease output. Only when MR = 0 can management possibly have maximized total sales revenue.[4]

---

[4] The logic here is exactly the same as the logic that led to the conclusion that a firm maximized profits by setting *marginal profit* equal to zero. If you need to review, consult Chapter 8, especially pages 163–164.

Thus, if Brand X is a sales maximizer, it will produce 3.75 million boxes of soap suds per year (point *B*), and charge 75 cents per box (point *F*). Because average costs at this level of production are only 69 cents per box, profit per unit is 6 cents and, with 3.75 million units sold, total profit is $225,000. Naturally, this profit is substantially less than what the firm can achieve if it reduces output to the profit-maximizing level. But that is not the goal of Brand X's management. The firm's sales revenue at point *B* is 75 cents per unit times 3.75 million units, or $2,812,500, whereas at point *A* it was only $2,500,000 (2.5 million units at $1.00 each). We conclude that:

If a firm is maximizing sales revenue, it will produce more output and charge a lower price than it would if it were maximizing profits.

Figure 3 clearly shows that this result holds for Brand X. But does it always hold? The answer is yes. Look again at Figure 3, but ignore the numbers on the axes. At point *A*, where MR = MC, marginal revenue must be positive because it equals marginal cost (which, we may assume, is *always* positive—output can normally not be increased at zero additional cost). At point *B*, MR is equal to zero. Because the marginal revenue curve slopes negatively, the point where it reaches zero (point *B*) must necessarily correspond to a higher output level than does the point where it cuts the marginal cost curve (point *A*). Thus, sales-maximizing firms always produce more than profit-maximizing firms and, to sell this greater volume of output, they must charge lower prices.[5]

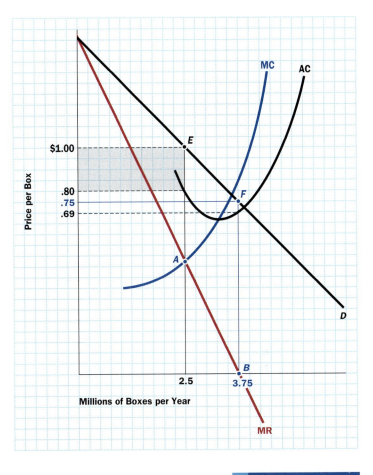

FIGURE 3

Sales-Maximization Equilibrium

3RD PUZZLE RESOLVED: *The Kinked Demand Curve Model*[6]

Another oligopoly analysis model accounts for the alleged "stickiness" in oligopolistic pricing, meaning that prices in oligopolistic markets change far less frequently than do competitive market prices—one of the puzzling phenomena with which we began this chapter. The prices of corn, soybeans, pork bellies, and silver—all commodities that trade in markets with large numbers of buyers and sellers—change second by second. But products supplied by oligopolists such as cars, televisions, and refrigerators usually change prices only every few months or even more rarely. These products seem to resist frequent price changes, even in inflationary periods.

---

[5] *Exercise:* In the graph, how much below maximum profit is total profit under sales maximization?

[6] Variants of this model were constructed by Hall and Hitch in England and by Sweezy in the United States. See R. L. Hall and C. J. Hitch, "Price Theory and Business Behavior," *Oxford Economic Papers* 2 (May 1939): 12–45; and P. M. Sweezy, "Demand under Conditions of Oligopoly," *Journal of Political Economy* 47 (August 1939): 568–573.

One reason for such "sticky" prices may be that when an oligopolist cuts its product's price, it can never predict how rival companies will react. One extreme possibility is that Firm Y will ignore Firm X's price cut; that is, Firm Y's price will not change. Alternatively, Firm Y may reduce its price, precisely matching that of Firm X. Accordingly, the model of oligopolistic behavior we discuss next uses two different demand curves. One curve represents the quantities a given oligopolistic firm can sell at different prices *if competitors match its price moves,* and the other demand curve represents what will happen if competitors stubbornly *stick to their initial price levels.*

Point *A* in Figure 4 represents our firm's initial price and output: 1,000 units at $8 each. Two demand curves, *DD* and *dd,* pass through point *A. DD* represents our company's demand if competitors keep their prices fixed, and *dd* indicates what happens when competitors match our firm's price changes.

The *DD* curve is the more elastic (flatter and more responsive) of the two, and a moment's thought indicates why this should be so. If our firm cuts its price from its initial level of $8 to, say, $7, and if competitors do not match this cut, we would expect our firm to get a large number of new customers—perhaps its quantity demanded will jump to 1,400 units. However, if its competitors respond by also reducing their prices, its quantity demanded will rise by less—perhaps only to 1,100 units (more inelastic demand curve *dd*).

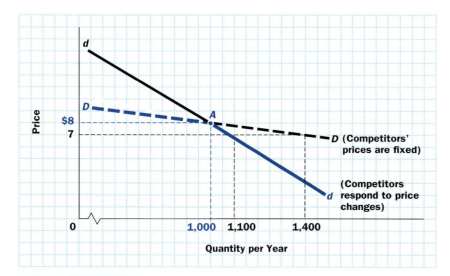

FIGURE 4

The Kinked Demand Curve

Similarly, when it raises its price, our firm may expect a larger sales flight if its rivals fail to match its increase, as indicated by the relative flatness (elasticity) of the curve *DD* in Figure 4, as compared to *dd,* the firm's demand curve when rivals do match our firm's price changes.

How does this relate to sticky oligopolistic prices? The economists who designed this model hypothesized that a typical oligopolistic firm has good reason to fear the worst. If it lowers its prices and its rivals do not, its sales will seriously cut into its competitors' volume, and so the rivals will *have* to match the price cut to protect themselves. The inelastic demand curve, *dd,* will therefore apply if our firm decides on a price *reduction* (points below and to the right of point *A*).

If, on the contrary, our company chooses to *increase* its price, management expects its rivals to respond differently than they will to a price cut. The price-raising firm will fear that its rivals will continue to sit at their old price levels, calmly collecting customers as they flee from X's higher prices. Thus, this time, for price increases, the relevant demand curve (above *A*) will be *DD.*

In sum, our firm will figure that it will face a segment of the elastic demand curve *DD* if it raises its price and a segment of the inelastic demand curve *dd* if it decreases its price. Its true demand curve will then be given by the heavy blue line, *DAd.* For obvious reasons, it is called a **kinked demand curve.**

The kinked demand curve represents a "heads you lose, tails you lose" proposition in terms of any potential price changes. If a firm raises its price, it will lose many customers (because in that case its demand is elastic); if it lowers its price, the sales increase will be comparatively small (because then its demand is inelastic). In these circumstances, management will vary its price only under extreme provocation—that is, only if its costs change enormously.

A **kinked demand curve** is a demand curve that changes its slope abruptly at some level of output.

Figure 5 illustrates this conclusion graphically. The two demand curves, *DD* and *dd*, are carried over precisely from Figure 4. The dashed line labeled MR is the marginal revenue curve associated with *DD*, while the solid line labeled *mr* is the marginal revenue curve associated with *dd*. The marginal revenue curve relevant to the firm's decision making is MR for any output level below 1,000 units, but mr for any output level above 1,000 units. Therefore, the composite marginal revenue curve facing the firm is shown by the gold-highlighted line DBCmr with two slopes.

The marginal cost curve drawn in the diagram cuts this composite marginal revenue curve at point *E*, which indicates the profit-maximizing combination of output and price for this oligopolist. Specifically, the quantity supplied at point *E* is 1,000 units, and the price is $8, which we read from the blue demand curve *DAd*.

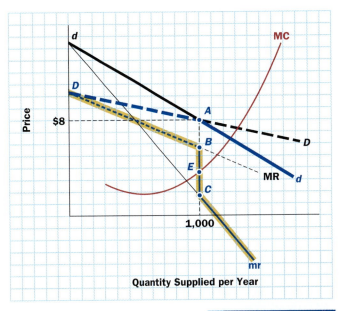

FIGURE 5

The Kinked Demand Curve and Sticky Prices

The unique aspect of this diagram is that the kinked demand curve leads to a marginal revenue curve that takes a sharp plunge between points *B* and *C*. Consequently, even if the MC curve shifts moderately upward or downward, it will still intersect the marginal revenue curve somewhere between *B* and *C* and thus will *not* lead the firm to change its output decision. Therefore, *the firm's price will remain unchanged.* (Try this for yourself in Figure 5.) Oligopoly prices are **"sticky,"** then, in the sense that they do not respond to minor cost changes. Only cost changes large enough to push the MC curve out of the *BC* range will lead to price changes.

If this is, in fact, the way oligopolists view their competitors' behavior, we can easily see why they may be reluctant to make frequent price changes. We can also understand why price leadership may arise. The price leader firm can raise prices at will, confident that the firm will not be left out on a limb (a kink?) by other firms' unwillingness to follow.

A price is called **sticky** if it does not change often even when there is a moderate change in cost.

The Game-Theory Approach

In 1944, the mathematician John von Neumann (1903–1957) and the economist Oskar Morgenstern (1902–1977) contributed a new approach to oligopoly analysis called *game theory*. Game theory is now economists' most widely used analysis of oligopoly behavior. The theory deals with the issue of interdependence directly, taking for granted that the managers of business firms make decisions on the assumption that rival managers are strategic decision makers. In this model, each oligopolist acts as a competing player in a strategic game.

Game theory uses two fundamental concepts: *strategy* and the **payoff matrix**. A strategy represents a participant's operational plan. In its simplest form, it may refer to just one possible decision, such as "Add a new car to my product line that features a DVD player for backseat passengers," or "Cut the price of my car to $19,500." For simplicity's sake, game-theory analysis often focuses on an oligopoly of two firms—a *duopoly.*

An example will help to explain game theory analysis. Imagine that the market for telecommunications on a low-income Caribbean island is about to be entered by two cell-phone service providers. Say that patent restrictions and other impediments mean that the two companies each have a choice between only one of two cell phones: (1) an expensive, high-tech phone that would have to be sold at a price that gives the

A **payoff matrix,** shows how much each of two competitors (players) can expect to earn, depending on the strategic choices each of them makes.

	Firm B Strategy	
	Low-tech	High-tech
Firm A Strategy Low-tech	$10m	$–2m
High-tech	$12m	$3m

seller a low profit margin or, (2) a cheaper, low-tech phone with a high profit margin. Furthermore, under this island government's rules, each firm is required to offer the same phone and price for two years. Table 1 illustrates the resulting payoff matrix for one of the two "players" in this game, Firm A.

This matrix shows how the profits that Firm A can expect to earn depend on the strategy that its sole rival, Firm B, adopts. The choice open to each firm is to select one of the two available strategies—either the "low-tech, high-markup" cell phone or the "high-tech, low-markup" cell phone—without knowing the strategy that the other will choose. The matrix is read like a mileage chart. It shows, for example, that if Firm A chooses the high-tech option (second row of the matrix) and Firm B selects the low-tech option (left-hand column), then A will earn $12 million (lower left-hand square).

■ Games with Dominant Strategies

How does game theory analyze Firm A's optimal strategic choice? There are a number of related methods. The most direct way is to search for what is called a **dominant strategy**. Such a strategy is defined as the one that gives the bigger payoff to the firm that selects it, *no matter which of the two strategies the competitor happens to choose.* As a general matter, not all games have such a dominant strategy. But the one illustrated in Table 1 does. Let us see how we know this.

Consider Firm A's decision. Either company can select either the high-tech or the low-tech strategy. Whichever choice B makes, there are two possible profit outcomes for A depending on which strategy it selects. For example, if B selects low-tech, A will either earn $10 million or $12 million, depending its strategy choice (see the left-hand column of Table 1). So the high-tech strategy, with its $12 million payoff, is clearly A's better decision if B selects low-tech. But what if B turns out to pick high-tech, instead? In that case, we see from the right-hand column of the matrix that if A offers the low-tech product, it will lose $2 million while, with that same choice by firm B, A could earn $3 million in profit by choosing high-tech (the lower right-hand entry). So high-tech is again the better choice for A. Clearly, the high-tech option is a *dominant strategy* for firm A, because it will give A a higher profit than the low-tech choice *no matter which option firm B selects.*

Now let us expand the payoff matrix to show simultaneously the earnings of both firms—not, as before, only those of Firm A. In Table 2, this combined payoff matrix reports the profits that each firm can expect to earn, given its own pricing choice and that of its rival. For example, the upper-left square indicates that if both firms decide to offer the low-tech, high-markup model, both A and B will earn $10 million. We also see that if one firm brings in the high-tech model, whereas the other does not, the high-tech supplier will actually raise its profit to $12 million (presumably by capturing more sales) and drive its rival to a $2 million loss. However, if both firms offer the high-tech model, each will be left with a modest $3 million profit.

Exercise: Use the same reasoning as above to show that high-tech is also the dominant strategy for Firm B.

Because both firms have a dominant strategy in this example, and it is the same for both, they can both be expected to select it. Each will therefore end up offering the high-tech cell phone, and each will earn $3 million per year.

This example has important implications for policy, because it shows just how competition can force business firms to behave in the way that most benefits consumers, even though it is not the most profitable for the firms. In this example, both firms would have profited most by offering the lower-quality, higher-markup equipment. If they had both chosen the low-tech strategy, they would each have earned $10 million,

A **dominant strategy** for one of the competitors in a game is a strategy that will yield a higher payoff than any of the other strategies that are possible for her, no matter what choice of strategy is made by her competitors.

	Firm B Strategy	
	Low-tech	High-tech
Firm A Strategy Low-tech	A gets $10m B gets $10m	A gets $–2m B gets $12m
High-tech	A gets $12m B gets $–2m	A gets $3m B gets $3m

but at the consumers' expense. However, the presence of a competitor, with its unknown choice, forces each firm to protect itself by offering the better (high-tech) product, even though they end up each earning only $3 million. Of course, if the market had been served by a profit-maximizing monopolist, the lone firm would have selected the more-profitable low-tech option, and the public would have been denied the better-quality product.

The Moral of the Story: A market that is a *duopoly,* **that is, a two-firm oligopoly, can serve the public interest better than a monopoly because of the competition between the two duopolists.**

Notice that each firm's fear of what its rival will do virtually forces it to offer the high-tech product and to forgo the higher ($10 million) profit that it could earn if it could trust the other to stick to a lower quality product. This example illustrates why many observers conclude that, particularly where the number of firms is small, companies should not be permitted to confer or exchange information on prices or product quality. If the two rivals were allowed to collude and act like a monopolist, consumers would be damaged in two ways: They would have to pay more in order to provide the resulting additional profits and, besides, as usually is expected to happen under monopoly, consumers would usually get smaller quantities of the products and the products might well be of lower quality.

Games whose payoff matrices have dominant strategies like that in Table 2 have many other interesting applications. They illustrate how people can get trapped into making both themselves and their rivals worse off. For example, a matrix with the same pattern of payoffs applies to people driving polluting cars in the absence of laws requiring emission controls. Each driver runs a polluting auto because she does not trust other drivers to install emission controls voluntarily. So if she alone goes to the expense of equipping her car with pollution controls, most of the pollution—that from all other cars—will remain in the air. She will have paid for the equipment but have gotten little or no cleaner air benefit. So they all end up with a low payoff (breathing polluted air), even though by getting together and all agreeing to do what is needed to cut emissions, they could all end up with a higher payoff in terms of better health, etc.[7]

Still another interpretation explains why the game in Table 2 is known as the "prisoners' dilemma." Instead of a two-firm industry, the prisoners' dilemma involves two burglary suspects who are captured by the police and interrogated in separate rooms. Each suspect has two strategy options: to deny the charge or to confess. If both deny it, both go free, because the police have no other evidence. But if one confesses and the other does not, the silent prisoner can expect the key to his cell to be thrown away while the talker gets off with a light sentence. The dominant solution for each prisoner, then, is to confess and receive the light sentence that results from this choice.

The prisoners' dilemma story confirms the important economic point we made earlier. The reason the two prisoners are both driven to confess, and to bring themselves to justice, is that they are not allowed to communicate. Otherwise, they would collude and promise each other not to confess. The same thing applies to a duopoly. The public interest requires that the duopolists be banned from colluding. If they were permitted to get together and agree on a high price and low-cost, low-quality products, they would earn monopoly profits and the public would suffer the consequences.

The Moral of the Story: It is damaging to the public interest to permit rival firms to collude and to make joint decisions on what prices to charge for their similar products and what quality of product to supply.

---

[7] *Exercise:* Make up a payoff matrix that tells this story.

Games Without Dominant Strategies

We have already observed that games need not offer dominant strategies. An example is easy to provide. For simplicity, Table 3 again shows only the payoffs for Firm A. But this time the hypothetical payoff numbers are different from those in Table 1.

With these new numbers, neither a low-tech nor a high-tech choice is a dominant strategy for A. Suppose A chooses to go with the low-tech product. Then, if B also happens to select low-tech, A will find itself better off (at a $10 million payoff) than if it had chosen a high-tech product (profit = $3 million). But if B goes the other way and offers the high-tech product, A's payoff will be worse ($7 million) with a low-tech product than with one that is high-tech ($8 million payoff). So which of the two options is better for A depends on B's unforeseeable strategy choice. Neither choice by A offers it fool-proof protection, so neither of A's possible strategies is dominant.

The decision for A in Table 3 is now much harder than it was before. How can it go about selecting a strategy? One solution proposed in game theory is called the **maximin criterion.** In this strategy, we may envision the management of Firm A reasoning as follows: "If I choose a low-tech strategy, the worst that can happen to me is that my competitor will select the high-tech counterstrategy, which will make my return $7 million (the blue number in the first row of the payoff matrix). Similarly, if I select a high-tech strategy, the worst possible outcome for me is a $3 million profit" (the blue minimum payoff in the second row of the matrix). How can the managers of Firm A best protect their company from trouble in these circumstances? Game theory suggests that it may be rational to select a strategy based on comparison of the *minimum* payoffs of the different strategies. If the firm's managers want to cut down the risk, they should pick what can be interpreted as an insurance-policy approach. They should select the strategy that will guarantee them the *highest* of these undesirable minimum payoffs. In other words, expecting the worst outcome for any strategy choice it makes, Firm A should pick the strategy that promises the best of those bad outcomes.. In this case, the maximin strategy for Firm A is to offer the low tech product, whose worst possible outcome is $7 million, while the worst outcome if it selects the high-tech product is a profit of only $3 million.

TABLE 3

Firm A's Payoff Matrix in a Game Without a Dominant Strategy

	Firm B Strategy	
	Low-tech	High-tech
Firm A Strategy Low-tech	$10m	$7m
High-tech	$3m	$8m

The **maximin criterion** requires you to select the strategy that yields the maximum payoff on the assumption that your opponent will do as much damage to you as he or she can.

Other Strategies: The Nash Equilibrium

We can interpret the maximin strategy as a pessimist's way to deal with uncertainty. A player who adopts this strategy assumes that the worst will always happen: No matter what move she makes, her opponent will adopt the countermove that does her the most damage. The maximin strategy neglects the possibility that opponents will not have enough information to find out the most damaging countermove. It also ignores the possibility of finding common ground, as when two competitors collude to extract monopoly profit from consumers.

Other strategies are less pessimistic, yet still rational. One of the most analytically useful strategies leads to what is called a **Nash equilibrium.** The mathematician John Nash devised this strategy, for which he won the Nobel Prize in economics in 1994 (after a long period of schizophrenia).[8] The basic idea is simple. In a two-player game, suppose that each firm is trying to decide whether to adopt a red or a blue package for its product. Assume that each firm earns a higher profit if it selects a package color that differs from the other's. Then, if Firm X happens to select a blue package, it will obviously be most profitable for Y to select a red package. Moreover, it will pay each

A **Nash equilibrium** results when each player adopts the strategy that gives her the highest possible payoff if her rival sticks to the strategy he has chosen.

---

[8] As described in the 2001 movie *A Beautiful Mind*, which was based on the book by Sylvia Nasar.

firm to stick with that choice, because red is Y's most profitable response to X's choice of blue, and vice versa.

In general, a Nash equilibrium describes a situation in which both players adopt moves such that each player's move is the most profitable response to the other player's move. Often, no such mutually accommodating solution is possible. But where it is possible, if both players realize this fact and act accordingly, they may both be able to benefit. For example, note how much worse off both firms would be in the preceding example if Firm Y were determined to damage Firm X, at whatever the cost to itself, and adopted a blue package, just like X's.

■ Zero-Sum Games

There is a special but significant situation involving a simple form of payoff matrix that has even been taken up in popular parlance. It is called a **zero-sum game**. The idea is a simple one and is a useful way to think about many issues. A zero-sum game is one in which whatever one player gains, the other must lose. Thus, when one adds up all the gains and losses, the sum is always zero. If I pick your pocket and find $80 in cash, you are $80 poorer and I am $80 richer, so that the sum of the positive gains and negative losses is clearly zero. But if the money was in a wallet with your driver's license and credit cards, and I take the money out and then throw the wallet into a river, it is evidently not zero-sum. You have lost not only the money but also the time and cost of replacing the license and credit cards, whereas I have gained only the money. The payoff matrix of a zero sum game has a very simple structure. Table 4 provides an example:

A **zero-sum game** is one in which exactly the amount one competitor gains must be lost by other competitors.

The special feature of this matrix is that the payoffs of the two firms add up to $10 million in each and every payoff square. For example, in the lower left-hand square of Table 4, Firm A's payoff is $4 million and Firm B's payoff is $6 million, for a total of $10 million. You can verify that the sum of the two payoffs is $10 million in each of the other three cells, as well.

The following example will bring out the importance of understanding the zero-sum case as a way to avoid fallacious analysis. It was once thought that international trade is a zero-sum game, because it was believed that each trading nation's objective was to get as much gold as possible from other countries in payment for their purchases. If Brazil ships coffee to France, and the French shippers pay 10,000 ounces of gold for the shipment, then on this view of the matter, Brazil has gained and France has lost exactly the same amount—making it a zero-sum transaction. But a little thought tells us that this view is naïve, because it leaves the coffee shipment itself out of the calculation. Trade is not just about money, but also about the goods and services that are traded. If France is too cold to grow good coffee, and Brazil is too hot to produce good wine, and the populations of both countries prefer coffee in the morning and wine in the evening, then it is clear that both will be better off as the result of an exchange of wine for coffee. The game of international trade is far from zero-sum. This is something that must be kept in mind when we consider contentious trade-related issues such as globalization and outsourcing, which will be discussed in Chapter 34.

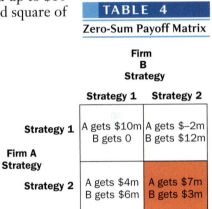

TABLE 4

Zero-Sum Payoff Matrix

	Firm B Strategy	
Firm A Strategy	Strategy 1	Strategy 2
Strategy 1	A gets $10m B gets 0	A gets $–2m B gets $12m
Strategy 2	A gets $4m B gets $6m	A gets $7m B gets $3m

■ Repeated Games

The scenarios described so far involve one-time transactions, as when a tourist passes through a city and makes a purchase at a store that he will never visit again. Most business transactions are different. A firm usually sells its products day after day, often to repeat buyers. It must continuously review its pricing decisions, knowing that its rivals are likely to gain information from any repeated behavioral patterns and adapt their response. The important concept of repeated games also offers significant additional insights about the competitive process under oligopoly.

Repeated games give all of the players the opportunity to learn something about each other's behavior patterns and, perhaps, to arrive at mutually beneficial arrangements. By adopting a fairly clear pricing behavior pattern, each firm can attain a reputation that elicits desired responses from competitors.

We return to the example of the product introduction war between Firm A and Firm B to show how this approach works. When we studied the payoff matrix for that game, we assumed that in a single play in which neither player knew anything about the other's behavior pattern, each player was likely to feel forced to adopt its dominant strategy. In other words, each firm offered the low-profit, high-tech product for fear that if it adopted the potentially more profitable low-tech product, its rival would adopt a high-tech product and take customers away. In that way, both firms would end up with low profits.

But when games are repeated, the players may be able to escape such a trap. For example, Firm A can cultivate a reputation for selecting a strategy called *"tit for tat."* Each time Firm B chooses a high-tech product, Firm A responds by also introducing a high-tech product, with its limited profit, next time. Firm A also follows a similar repeating strategy if B's product choice is low-tech. After a few repetitions, B will learn that A always matches its decisions. B will then see that it is better off sticking to a more profitable low-tech product. Firm A, too, benefits from its tit-for-tat approach, which will lead both, eventually, to stick permanently to the more profitable low-tech products.

In practice, this amounts to tacit collusion. The two competing firms never actually get together to reach a joint decision on product price and quality, behavior that is illegal. But they watch one another's behavior in their repeated game, and each eventually learns to adapt itself and go along with the other's behavior—which may be anticompetitive and damaging to consumer interests, but offers monopoly profits to the tacit colluders. The courts do not have a clear response to this behavior, because it is difficult to argue that firms should not consider all publicly and legitimately available information about its rivals, or that firms should not take this observed rival behavior into consideration when they make their own decisions.

Threats and Credibility

A player can also use *threats* to induce rivals to change their behavior. The trouble is that, if carried out, the threat may well damage both parties. For example, a retailer can threaten to double its output and drive prices down near zero if a rival imitates its product. However, the rival is unlikely to believe the threat, because such a low price harms the threatener as much as the threatened. Such a threat is simply not *credible*, with one exception.

The possibility can become a **credible threat** if the threatener takes steps that commit it to carry out the action. For example, if Firm A signed an irrevocable contract committing it to double its output if Firm B copied A's product, then the threat would become credible, and B would be forced to believe it. But A can make other commitments that make its threat credible. For example, it can build a large plant with plenty of excess capacity. The factory may be very expensive to build, but once built, that cost is irrevocable. If the additional cost of turning out the product, once the plant has been built, is very low, then it will pay A to expand its output of the product even at a very low price (if that price exceeds the marginal [variable] cost of the item). So, having built the large factory, the threat to expand output in response to entry becomes credible.

This last possibility leads directly to an important application of game theory: how firms inside an industry ("old firms") can decide strategically on ways to prevent *new* firms from entering into the industry. To create a credible threat to potential entrants, the old firm may well consider building a bigger factory than it would otherwise want.

Some hypothetical numbers and a typical game theory graph will make the story clear. The old firm faces two options: to build a small factory or a big one. Potential entrant firms also face two options: open for business (that is, enter the industry) or do not enter. Figure 6 shows the four resulting possible decision combinations and the corresponding profits or losses that the two firms may expect in each case.

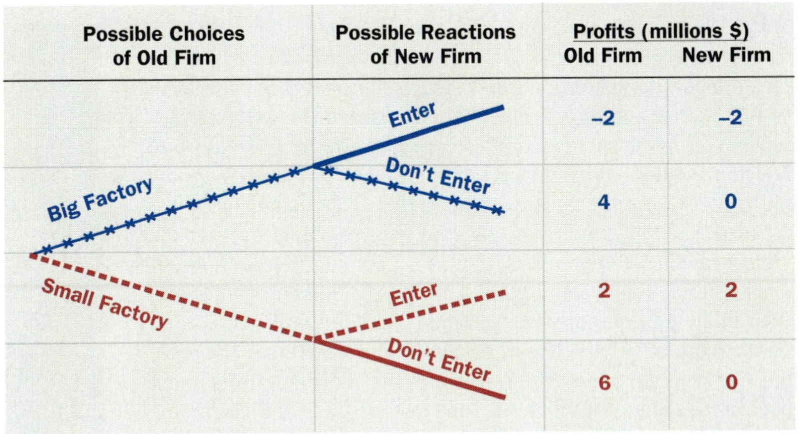

The graph shows that the best outcome for the old firm occurs when it builds a small factory and the new firm decides not to enter. In that case, the old firm will earn $6 million, whereas the new firm will earn nothing, because it never starts up.

However, if the old firm *does* decide to build a small factory, it can be fairly sure that the new firm *will* open up for business, because the new firm can then earn $2 million (rather than zero), as shown by the dashed lines. In the process, the old firm's profit will be reduced, also to $2 million.

But if the old firm builds a big factory, its increased output will depress prices and profits. The old firm will now earn

FIGURE 6

Entry and Entry-Blocking Strategy

Possible Choices of Old Firm	Possible Reactions of New Firm	Profits (millions $) Old Firm	New Firm
Big Factory → Enter		–2	–2
Big Factory → Don't Enter		4	0
Small Factory → Enter		2	2
Small Factory → Don't Enter		6	0

only $4 million if the new firm stays out, as shown by the asterisk line, whereas *each* firm will *lose* $2 million if the new firm enters. Obviously, if the old firm builds a big factory, the new firm will be better off staying out of the business rather than subjecting itself to a $2 million loss.

What size factory, then, should the old firm build? When we consider the firms' interactions, the old firm should clearly build the large factory with its excess capacity—because this decision will keep the new firm out of the industry, leaving the old firm with a $4 million profit. The moral of the story: "Wasting" money on excess capacity may not be wasteful to the oligopolist firm if it protects the firm's long-term interest.

Of course, game theory is a much richer topic than we have explained here. For example, game theory also provides tools for economists and business managers to analyze coalitions. It indicates, for cases involving more than two firms, which firms would do well to align themselves together against which others. People other than economists also have used game theory to analyze a variety of complicated problems outside the realm of oligopoly theory. Management training programs employ its principles, as do a number of government agencies (see "Application: Game Theory and FCC Auctions" on the next page). Political scientists and military strategists use game theory to formulate and analyze strategy.

MONOPOLISTIC COMPETITION, OLIGOPOLY, AND PUBLIC WELFARE

How well or poorly do monopolistically competitive or oligopolistic firms perform, from the viewpoint of the general welfare?

We have seen that their performance *can* leave much to be desired. For example, the excess capacity theorem showed us that monopolistic competition can lead to inefficiently high production costs. Similarly, because market forces may not sufficiently restrain their behavior, oligopolists' prices and outputs may differ substantially from socially optimal levels. In particular, when oligopolists organize themselves into a successful cartel, prices will be higher and outputs lower than those associated with their perfectly competitive counterparts. Moreover, some people believe that misleading advertising by corporate giants often distorts consumers' judgments, leading them to buy things they do not need and would otherwise not want. Many social critics feel that such corporate giants wield political power, economic power, and power over the

Application: Game Theory and FCC Auctions

Since 1994, the Federal Communications Commission (FCC) has conducted competitive bidding auctions of licenses to parts of the electromagnetic spectrum used for such communications services as cell phones and pagers. The FCC used game theory when it designed the online auctions of these so-called *rights to the airways*, and the bidding companies must figure out for themselves how much to offer for the right to service a particular region.

The FCC might simply have decided to price the licenses for the various available regions itself. But by conducting auctions, it places the decision-making onus on the bidding companies and their hired game-theorist consultants. The FCC prohibits collusion by the bidders, so each one must decide which sectors it can serve most efficiently, and each must anticipate its competitors' most likely moves and countermoves. The FCC runs these national online auctions continuously. For example, one recent auction offered licenses in the Automated Maritime Telecommunications System (AMTS) spectrum. AMTS is a specialized system of coast stations that provide integrated and interconnected marine voice and data communications, somewhat like a cellular phone system, for tugs, barges and other vessels on the waterways. Completed on September 15, 2004, the auction raised a total of $1,057,365 from four winning bidders for ten licenses.

SOURCE: © Paul A. Souders/Corbis

SOURCE: U.S. Federal Communications Commission, http://www.fcc.gov.

minds of consumers—power that undermines the benefits of Adam Smith's invisible hand.

Because oligopoly behavior varies so widely, the social welfare implications differ from case to case. Some recent economic analysis, however, provides one theoretical case in which oligopolistic behavior and performance quality can be predicted and judged unambiguously.[9] The analysis also can serve as a model for government agencies that are charged with the task of preventing harmful anticompetitive behavior by oligopolistic firms. In this theoretical case, called a **perfectly contestable** market, entry into or exit from the market is costless and unimpeded. Here, the constant threat of the possible entry by new firms forces even the largest existing firm to behave well—to produce efficiently and never overcharge. Otherwise, the firm will be threatened with replacement by an entrant that offers to serve customers more cheaply and efficiently.

A market is **perfectly contestable** if entry and exit are costless and unimpeded.

We define a market as perfectly contestable if firms can enter it and, if they choose, exit it without losing the money they invested. The crucial issue here is not the amount of capital required to enter the industry, but whether an entrant can withdraw the investment if it wishes. For example, if market entry requires investing in highly *mobile* capital (such as airplanes, trucks, or river barges—which can be moved around easily), the entrant may be able to exit quickly and cheaply.[10] For instance, if a barge operation decides to serve the lower Mississippi River but finds business disappointing, it can easily transfer its boats to, say, the Ohio River.

---

[9] See William J. Baumol, John C. Panzar, and Robert D. Willig, *Contestable Markets and the Theory of Industry Structure*, rev. ed. (San Diego: Harcourt Brace Jovanovich, 1988).

[10] Earlier it was thought that air transportation could be classified as a highly contestable industry, but recent evidence suggests that although this judgment is not entirely incorrect, it requires considerable reservations.

A profitable market that is also contestable therefore attracts *potential* entrants. Because no barriers to entry or exit exist, firms incur little risk by going into such a market. If their entry turns out to have been a mistake, they can move to another market without loss.

Because perfect competition requires a large number of firms, all of them small relative to the size of the industry, no industry with economies of large-scale production can be perfectly competitive. However, markets that contain a few relatively large firms may be highly contestable, although they are certainly not perfectly competitive. But no real-world industry is *perfectly* contestable, just as no industry is perfectly competitive.

The constant threat of entry forces oligopolists to perform well. Even monopolists must perform well if they do business in a highly contestable market. In particular, perfectly contestable markets have at least two socially desirable characteristics.

First, the freedom of entry eliminates any excess economic profits, so in this respect contestable markets resemble perfectly competitive markets. For example, if the current opportunity cost of capital is 12 percent while the firms in a contestable market are earning a return of 18 percent, then new firms will enter the market, expand the industry's outputs, and drive down the prices of its products to the point at which no firm earns any excess profit. To avoid this outcome, established firms must expand output to a level that precludes excess profit.

Second, inefficient enterprises cannot survive in a perfectly contestable industry because cost inefficiencies invite replacement of the existing firms by entrants that can provide the same outputs at lower cost and lower prices. Only firms operating at the lowest possible cost can survive. In sum, firms in a perfectly contestable market will be forced to operate as efficiently as possible and to charge prices as low as long-run financial survival permits.

The theory of contestable markets has been widely used by courts and government agencies concerned with the performance of business firms and provides workable guidelines for improved or acceptable behavior in industries in which economies of scale mean that only a small number of firms can or should operate.

■ A GLANCE BACKWARD: COMPARING THE FOUR MARKET FORMS

We have now completed the set of chapters that has taken us through the four main market forms: perfect competition, monopoly, monopolistic competition, and oligopoly. You have probably absorbed a lot of information about the workings of these market forms as you read through Chapters 10 through 12, but you may be confused by the details. Table 5 presents an overview of the main attributes of each of the market forms for comparison. It shows that:

- Perfect competition and pure monopoly are concepts useful primarily for *analytical* purposes—we find neither very often in reality. There are very many monopolistically competitive firms, and oligopoly firms account for the largest share of the economy's output.
- Profits are zero in long-run equilibrium under perfect competition and monopolistic competition because entry is so easy that high profits attract new rivals into the market.
- Consequently, AC = AR in long-run equilibrium under these two market forms. In equilibrium, MC=MR for the profit-maximizing firm under any market form. However, under oligopoly, firms may adopt the strategies described by game theory or they may pursue goals other than profits; for example, they may seek to maximize sales. Therefore, in the equilibrium of the oligopoly firm, MC may be unequal to MR.
- As we will confirm in Chapter 14, the behavior of the perfectly competitive firm and industry theoretically leads to an efficient allocation of resources that

maximizes the benefits to consumers, given the resources available to the economy. Monopoly, however, can misallocate resources by restricting output in an attempt to raise prices and profits. Under monopolistic competition, excess capacity and inefficiency are apt to result. And under oligopoly, almost anything can happen, so it is impossible to generalize about its vices or virtues.

TABLE 5
Attributes of the Four Market Forms

Market Form	Number of Firms in the Market	Frequency in Reality	Entry Barriers	Public Interest Results	Long-Run Profit	Equilibrium Conditions
Perfect competition	Very many	Rare (if any)	None	Good	Zero	$MC = MR = AC = AR = P$
Pure monopoly	One	Rare	Likely to be high	Outputs not optimal	May be high	$MR = MC$
Monopolistic competition	Many	Widespread	Minor	Inefficient	Zero	$MR = MC$ $AR = AC$
Oligopoly	Few	Produces large share of GDP	Varies	Varies	Varies	Varies

SUMMARY

1. Under **monopolistic competition**, there are numerous small buyers and sellers; each firm's product is at least somewhat different from every other firm's product—that is, each firm has a partial "monopoly" over some product characteristics, and thus a downward-sloping demand curve; there is freedom of entry and exit; and there is perfect information.

2. In long-run equilibrium under monopolistic competition, free entry eliminates economic profits by forcing the firm's downward sloping demand curve into a position of tangency with its average cost curve. Therefore, output will be below the point at which average cost is lowest. As a result, monopolistic competitors are said to have "**excess capacity**."

3. An oligopolistic industry is composed of a few large firms selling similar products in the same market.

4. Under **oligopoly**, each firm carefully watches the major decisions of its rivals and often plans counterstrategies. As a result, rivalry is often vigorous and direct, and the outcome is difficult to predict.

5. One model of oligopoly behavior assumes that oligopolists ignore interdependence and simply maximize profits or sales. Another model assumes that they join together to form a **cartel** and thus act like a monopoly. A third possibility is **price leadership**, where one firm sets prices and the others follow suit.

6. A firm that maximizes sales will continue producing up to the point where marginal revenue is driven down to zero. Consequently, a **sales maximizer** will produce more than a profit maximizer and will charge a lower price.

7. If a firm thinks that its rivals will match any price cut but fail to match any price increase, its demand curve becomes "kinked" and its price will be sticky—in other words, price will be adjusted less frequently than would be true under either perfect competition or pure monopoly.

8. **Game theory** provides new tools for the analysis of business strategies under conditions of oligopoly.

9. A **payoff matrix**, shows how much each of two competitors (players) can expect to earn, depending on the strategic choices each of them makes. It is used to analyze the reasoning that applies and the possible outcomes when the payoff to any oligopolist depends on what the other oligopolists in the market will do, so that they are all interdependent.

10. A **dominant strategy** for one of the competitors in a game is a strategy that will yield a higher payoff than any of the other strategies that are possible for her, no matter what choice of strategy is made by her competitors. So selection of a dominant strategy, where it is possible, is a good way for a competitor to avoid risk

11. In a **maximin** strategy, the player takes the strongest possible precautions against the worst possible outcome of any move it selects.

12. In a **Nash equilibrium**, each player adopts the move that yields the highest possible payoff to itself, given the move selected by the other player.

13. A **zero-sum** game is one in which exactly the amount one competitor gains must be lost by other competitors. The zero-sum game is a useful analytic concept, even it is rare in the real world.

14. In **repeated games**, a firm can seek to acquire a reputation that induces the other player to make decisions that do not damage its interests. It may also promote its goals by means of **credible threats**.

15. Monopolistic competition and oligopoly can be harmful to the general welfare. But because behavior varies widely, the implications for social welfare also vary from case to case.

KEY TERMS

Monopolistic competition 237	Kinked demand curve 248	Nash equilibrium 252
Oligopoly 241	Sticky price 249	Zero-sum game 253
Cartel 243	Payoff matrix 249	Repeated game 254
Price leadership 245	Dominant strategy 250	Credible threat 254
Price war 246	Maximin criterion 252	Perfectly contestable market 256
Sales maximization 246		

TEST YOURSELF

1. Using game theory, set up a payoff matrix similar to one that GM's management might employ in analyzing the problem presented in Discussion Question 5.

2. Test Yourself Question 4 at the end of Chapter 11 presented cost and demand data for a monopolist and asked you to find the profit-maximizing solution. Use these same data to find the sales-maximizing solution. In terms of the firm's MR explain why the answers are different.

3. In the payoff matrix Table 2, which is Firm B's dominant strategy? Show the calculation that leads to that conclusion.

4. You are given a payoff matrix for a *zero sum* game. You see that, for one pair of strategy choices by the two firms, A's payoff is 9 and B's payoff is 6. For a second set of strategy choices A's payoff is 5. What is B's payoff?

DISCUSSION QUESTIONS

1. How many real industries can you name that are oligopolies? How many that operate under monopolistic competition? Perfect competition? Which of these is most difficult to find in reality? Why do you think this is so?

2. Consider some of the products that are widely advertised on television. By what kind of firm is each produced—a perfectly competitive firm, an oligopolistic firm, or another type of firm? How many major products can you think of that are *not* advertised on TV?

3. In what ways may the small retail sellers of the following products differentiate their goods from those of their rivals to make themselves monopolistic competitors: hamburgers, radios, cosmetics?

4. Pricing of securities on the stock market is said to be carried out under conditions in many respects similar to perfect competition. The auto industry is an oligopoly. How often do you think the price of a share of Ford Motor Company's common stock changes? How about the price of a Ford Taurus? How would you explain the difference?

5. Suppose that General Motors hires a popular singer to advertise its compact automobiles. The campaign is very successful, and the company increases its share of the compact-car market substantially. What is Ford likely to do?

6. A new entrant, Bargain Airways, cuts air fares between Eastwich and Westwich by 20 percent. Biggie Airlines, which has been operating on this route, responds by cutting fares by 35 percent. What does Biggie hope to achieve?

7. If air transportation were perfectly contestable, why would Biggie Airlines (see Discussion Question 8) fail to achieve the ultimate goal of its price cut?

8. Which of the following industries are most likely to be contestable?

   a. Aluminum production

   b. Barge transportation

   c. Automobile manufacturing

   Explain your answers.

9. Since the deregulation of air transportation, a community served by a single airline is no longer protected by a regulatory agency from monopoly pricing. What market forces, if any, restrict the ability of the airline to raise prices as a pure monopolist would? How effective do you think those market forces are in keeping air fares down?

10. Explain, for a repeated game:

   a. Why it may be advantageous to have the reputation of being a tough guy who always takes revenge against anyone who harms your interests.

   b. Why it may be advantageous to have a reputation of irrationality.

13

LIMITING MARKET POWER: REGULATION AND ANTITRUST

. . . the one law you can't repeal is supply and demand.

WILLIAM SAFIRE, *NEW YORK TIMES*, JULY 13, 1998

To protect the interests of the public when industries are, or threaten to become, monopolistic or oligopolistic, government in the United States uses two basic tools. *Antitrust policy* seeks to prevent acquisition of *monopoly power* and to ban certain monopolistic practices. All business firms are subject to the antitrust laws. In addition, some industries are *regulated* by rules that constrain firms' pricing and other decisions. Generally, only firms suspected of having the power to act like monopolists are regulated in this way.

CONTENTS

■ THE PUBLIC INTEREST ISSUE: MONOPOLY POWER VERSUS MERE SIZE

Economies of scale are savings that are obtained through increases in quantities produced. Scale economies occur when an *X* percent increase in input use raises output by *more than X* percent, so that the more the firm produces, the lower its per-unit costs become.

Monopoly power (or market power) is the ability of a business firm to earn high profits by raising the prices of its products above competitive levels and to keep those prices high for a substantial amount of time.

In Chapters 11 and 12, we learned that when an industry is a monopoly or an oligopoly, the result may not be as desirable in terms of the public interest as it would be if the industry were perfectly competitive. Yet for many industries anything like perfect competition is an impossible goal, and perhaps even an undesirable one. This is true, notably, when the industry's technology provides **economies of scale,** meaning, as you will remember, that the more of its product a firm supplies, the lower the cost of supplying a unit of that product. Scale economies therefore mean that in competition between a large firm and a small one, the big one can usually win. As a result, industries with scale economies usually end up having a small number of firms, each of which has a large share of the industry's sales. In other words, such an industry is usually fated to be a monopoly or an oligopoly.

But what is so bad about that? The answer is that sometimes it is not bad at all, because economies of scale allow the larger firms to supply the public at lower cost. In other cases, the public interest will be threatened, because some or all of the firms in the industry will possess **monopoly power.** Monopoly power (or market power) is usually defined as the ability of a firm to earn high profits by raising and keeping the prices of its products substantially above the levels at which those products would be priced in competitive markets. That is, a firm with monopoly power can charge high prices and get away with it—the market will not punish it for doing so. In a competitive industry, in contrast, the market *will* punish a high-price firm by the loss of its customers to rivals with lower prices. Thus, monopoly power is undesirable for several reasons, some of them obvious:

- *High prices reduce the wealth of consumers.* The use of monopoly power is obviously undesirable to consumers because no one likes to pay high prices for purchased commodities. Such high prices may make the firm with monopoly power rich and make the consumers of its products poor. These effects on the distribution of wealth are generally considered undesirable.
- *High prices lead to resource misallocation.* Economists give greater emphasis to a second undesirable effect of prices that exceed the competitive level. Such prices tend to reduce the quantities of the products that consumers demand. In this case, smaller quantities of labor, raw materials, and other inputs will be devoted to production of these high-priced products relative to the quantities that would *best* serve consumer interests. More of those inputs will therefore be transferred to the products of competitive industries. The result will be *underproduction* of the products priced at monopoly levels and *overproduction* of the products of competitive industries. So, as a result of the exercise of monopoly power, the economy does not produce the mix of outputs that best serves the public interest.
- *Monopoly power creates an obstacle to efficiency and innovation.* A firm with monopoly power is a firm that does not face much effective competition—and consequently it does not have as much reason to fear loss of business to others. Where this is so, there is little incentive for management to make the effort to produce efficiently with a minimum of waste or to undertake the expense and risks of innovation. The result is that products may be of poorer quality than they would if the company possessed no monopoly power, and there will be waste in the production process.

The efficiency problems inherent in monopoly power are among the main reasons for governmental intervention controlling business firms' behavior and other attributes. The critical problem is control of monopoly power and prevention of acts by firms that are designed either to give them (or enhance) monopoly power, or to curb the use of that power to exploit the public.

There is a widespread misconception that all big firms have monopoly power, so that the primary purpose of antitrust or regulatory activity should be to break up as many large firms as possible and to constrain the pricing of all large firms that cannot be broken into smaller ones. But this is not a valid conclusion. It is true that firms that have a very small share of their industry's sales cannot wield market power. For reasons studied in Chapter 10, such small firms are price takers, not price makers. They must simply accept the price determined by supply and demand in a competitive market, or the prices determined by larger firms in their industry if those large firms do have market power. But although firms with small market shares never have market power, the converse is not true: Large firms do not always have market power.

Why? In an oligopoly characterized by fierce rivalry, each firm may be prevented by the actions of its competitors from raising its price above competitive levels. For example, Coca-Cola and Pepsi each have a very large share of the soft drink market. It is well known that there is no love between the two companies, so neither dares to raise its prices substantially for fear of driving customers into the arms of its unloved competitor.

Even a monopoly may have little or no monopoly power if entry into its industry is cheap and easy. Such a firm knows that it can retain its monopoly *only if its behavior is not monopolistic.* If it tries to raise its price to monopoly levels for any substantial period of time, then its rivals will have an opportunity to come in and take some or all of its business away. So in industries where entry is very easy, a large firm will have no monopoly power because the perpetual threat of potential entry will keep it from misbehaving. For this reason, government agencies concerned with monopoly issues explicitly avoid interfering with the actions of firms in industries where entry is cheap and easy.

The primary threat of monopoly and oligopoly to the public interest is monopoly power. This power can lead to excessive prices that exploit consumers, misallocation of resources, and inefficient and noninnovative firms. But firms that are big do not necessarily have market power.

In Part 1 of this chapter, we will discuss how regulation is used to deal with these issues. In Part 2, we turn to antitrust policy—a second way of dealing with the problems.

PART 1: REGULATION

We begin with regulation, one of the two traditional instruments used by government to protect consumers from exploitation by firms that are too powerful.

WHAT IS REGULATION?

"**Regulation** of industry" refers to the activities of a number of government agencies that enforce rules about business conduct enacted by Congress, or rules that the agencies themselves have adopted. When an industry is suspected of possessing monopoly power and, because of scale economies or for other reasons, it is not considered feasible or desirable to bring effective competition into its markets, the regulatory agency imposes restrictions designed to curb use of the monopoly power. For example, the agency may place ceilings on the prices the regulated firms can charge, or it may require the firm to submit any change it desires in any of its prices to the agency. Such changes, then, are not permitted until they have been approved by the agency, sometimes after extensive (and expensive) hearings (that is, trials) before the agency, in which the opponents and supporters of the proposed changes, as well as their lawyers and their witnesses, have the opportunity to present their opinions.

Regulations designed to limit market power, and economic behavior more generally, affect industries that together provide perhaps 10 percent of the gross domestic product (GDP) of the United States. The list includes telecommunications, railroads,

Regulation of industry is a process established by law that restricts or controls some specified decisions made by the affected firms; it is designed to protect the public from exploitation by firms with monopoly power. Regulation is usually carried out by a special government agency assigned the task of administering and interpreting the law. That agency also acts as a court in enforcing the regulatory laws.

"Won't all these new rules impact adversely on the viability of small businesses with fewer than fifty employees?"

electric utilities, oil pipelines, banks and the stock markets. Both the federal government and the states have regulatory agencies devoted to such tasks.

Despite its good intentions, regulation has been criticized as a cause of inefficiency and excessive costs to the consuming public. The basic fact about regulation and other forms of government intervention that are designed to affect the operations of markets is that *neither* markets *nor* governmental agencies always work perfectly. In an uncontrolled market, for example, monopoly power can damage the public interest, but excessive or poorly conceived regulations or antitrust decisions also can prove very harmful.

PUZZLE: *Why Do Regulators Often Raise Prices?*

Regulation sometimes forces consumers to pay *higher* prices than they would pay in its absence. For instance, before the airline industry was deregulated, the flight between New York City and Washington, D.C.—an interstate trip that was controlled by the federal government—was *more* expensive than the flight between San Francisco and Los Angeles—a trip that was not controlled by the federal government, because it took place entirely within the state of California. The California trip was nearly *twice* as long as the East Coast trip, and it did not have a substantially lower cost per passenger mile. So why did regulators, whose job is to protect the public interest, deliberately price the New York–Washington hop about 25 percent higher? Later in the chapter, you will be able to answer this question.

SOME OBJECTIVES OF REGULATION

Economists recognize a number of reasons that may justify the regulation of an industry.

FIGURE 1

Economies of Scale

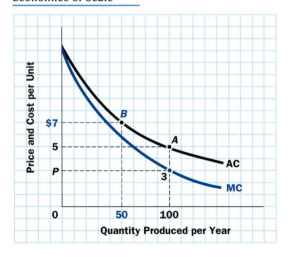

Quantity Produced per Year

Control of Market Power Resulting from Economies of Scale and Scope

As we noted at the beginning of this chapter, a major reason for regulation of industry is to prevent the use of or acquisition of market power by regulated firms. In some industries, it is far cheaper to have production carried out by one firm than by many, and the relatively large firms that result may gain market power. One cause is economies of large-scale production. Railroad tracks are a particularly good example of such economies of scale. The total cost of building and maintaining the tracks when 100 trains traverse them every day is not much higher than when only one train uses them. So substantial savings in average cost result when rail traffic increases. As we saw in Chapter 7, scale economies lead to an average cost (AC) curve that goes downhill as output increases (see Figure 1). This means that a firm with a large output can cover its costs at a price lower than a firm whose output is smaller. In the figure, point *A* represents the larger firm whose AC is $5, whereas point *B* is the smaller firm with an AC of $7.

A single, large firm also may have a cost advantage over a group of small firms when it is cheaper to produce a number of different commodities together rather than making each separately in a different firm. Savings made possible by simultaneous production of many different products by one firm are called **economies of scope.** One clear example of economies of scope is the manufacture of both cars and trucks by the same producer. The techniques employed in producing both commodities are similar, which provides a cost advantage to firms that produce both types of vehicles.

In industries characterized by great economies of scale and scope, costs will be much higher if government intervenes to preserve a large number of small, and therefore costly, firms. Moreover, where economies of scale and scope are strong, society will not be able to preserve free competition, even if it wants to. The large, multi-product firm will have so great a cost advantage over its rivals that the small firms simply will be unable to survive.

> Where monopoly production is cheapest, so that free competition is not sustainable, the industry is a natural monopoly. When monopoly is cheaper, society may not want to have competition; if free competition is not sustainable, it will not even have a choice in the matter.

Even if society reconciles itself to monopoly in such cases, it will generally not want to let the monopoly firm wield its market power without limits. Therefore, it will consider regulating the company's decisions on matters such as pricing. The first and most universal problem facing the regulator is how to prevent the regulated firm from pricing and taking other actions that exploit the public and undermine the efficiency of the market, but to do so in ways that do not destroy the regulated firm or prevent it from serving the public effectively.

■ Universal Service and Rate Averaging

A second type of problem in the analysis of regulation stems from another objective of regulation of the prices and other choices of firms in a regulated industry—the desire for "universal service." By this regulators mean the availability of service to everyone at "reasonable prices," particularly to impoverished consumers and small communities where the limited scale of operations may make costs extremely high. In such cases, regulators may encourage or require a public utility (such as an electric power supplier) to serve some consumers at a financial loss. This loss on some sales is financially feasible only when the regulated firm is permitted to make up for it by obtaining higher profits on its other sales. Charging higher prices to one set of customers to finance lower prices to another customer group is called **cross-subsidization.**

This sort of cross-subsidization is possible only if the regulated firm is protected from price competition and free entry of new competitors in its other, more profitable markets (in which it charges the higher prices that subsidize the financing of the mandated low prices). If no such protection is provided, potential competitors will sniff out these profit opportunities in the markets where service is supplied at prices well above cost. Many new firms will enter the business and drive prices down in those markets—a practice referred to as *cream skimming*. The entrants choose to enter only the profitable markets and skim away the "cream" of the profits for themselves, leaving the unprofitable markets (the skimmed milk?) to the supplier that had attempted to provide universal service. This phenomenon is one reason why regulatory rules, until recently, made it very difficult or impossible for new firms to enter when and where they saw fit.

Airlines and telecommunications are two industries in which these issues have arisen frequently. In both cases, it was feared that without regulation of entry and rates, or special subsidies, less populous communities would effectively become

Economies of scope are savings that are obtained through simultaneous production of many different products. They occur if a firm that produces many commodities can supply each good more cheaply than a firm that produces fewer commodities.

Cross-subsidization means selling one product of the firm at a loss, which is balanced by higher profits on another of the firm's products.

isolated, losing their airline services and obtaining telephone service only at cripplingly high rates. Many economists question the validity of this argument for regulation, which, they say, calls for hidden subsidies of rural consumers by everyone else. The airline deregulation act provided for government subsidies to help small communities attract airline service. In fact, this market has since been taken over to a considerable extent by specialized "commuter" airlines flying much smaller aircraft than the major airlines, which have withdrawn from many such routes.

A similar issue affects the U.S. Postal Service, which charges the same price to deliver a letter anywhere within the United States, regardless of the distance or the special difficulties and costs of a particular route. To maintain this pricing scheme, the law must protect the Postal Service from direct competition in many of its activities—otherwise, its extreme form of uniform pricing would soon deprive it of its most profitable routes. Thus, the goal of providing universal service leads to the regulation of entry into and exit from the affected industry, and not just price control.

TWO KEY ISSUES THAT FACE REGULATORS

Regulators around the world face (at least) two critical issues that are of fundamental importance for economic policy. They are at the heart of recent legal battles before regulatory agencies almost everywhere.

Setting Prices to Protect Consumers' Interests and Allow Regulated Firms to Cover Their Costs

When governments regulate prices, they usually want to prevent those prices from being so high that they bring monopoly profits to the firm. At the same time, governments want to set prices at levels that are "compensatory." That is, the prices must be sufficiently high to enable the firms to cover their costs and, consequently, to survive financially. Regulators also are asked to select prices that best serve the public interest. These goals, as we will see next, can often be at odds.

- *Prices intended to promote the public interest may cause financial problems for firms.* The discussion in Chapter 10 implied that the consumer's welfare is most effectively promoted by setting the price of a product equal to that product's marginal cost, and this will be further confirmed in Chapter 14. But as we will show presently, such a rule would condemn many regulated firms to bankruptcy. What should the regulator do in such a case?
- *Preventing firms with monopoly power from earning excessive profits without eliminating all incentives for efficiency and innovation may prove difficult.* The firm's incentive and reward for the effort and expenditure needed to improve efficiency and to innovate is the higher profit that it expects to obtain if it succeeds. But a frequent objective of regulation is to put a ceiling on profit to prevent monopoly earnings. How can monopoly profits be prevented without destroying incentives?

Let's now analyze these issues, which arise frequently in today's crucial regulatory policy debates.

Marginal versus Average Cost Pricing

Regulatory agencies often have the task of controlling the prices of regulated firms. Acrimonious debate over the proper levels for those prices has filled hundreds of thousands of pages of regulatory-hearing records and has involved literally hundreds of millions of dollars of expenditures in fees for lawyers, expert witnesses, and research. The central question has been: What constitutes the proper formula to set these prices?

Where it is feasible, most economists favor setting price equal to marginal cost because, as we will show in Chapter 14, this pricing policy provides the incentive for firms to produce output quantities that serve consumers' wants most efficiently. However, a serious practical problem often prevents use of marginal-cost pricing: In many regulated industries, the firms would go bankrupt if all prices were set equal to marginal costs!

This seems a startling conclusion, but it follows inescapably from three simple facts:

Fact 1. Many regulated industries are characterized by significant economies of large-scale production. As we pointed out earlier, economies of scale are one of the main reasons why certain industries were regulated in the first place.

Fact 2. In an industry with economies of scale, the long-run average cost curve is downward sloping. This means that the long-run average cost falls as the quantity produced rises, as was illustrated by the AC curve in Figure 1. Fact 2 is something we learned back in Chapter 7. The reason, to review briefly, is that where there are economies of scale, if all input quantities are doubled, output will *more than double.* But total costs will double only if input quantities double. Thus, total costs will rise more slowly than output and so average cost must fall. That is, average cost (AC) is simply total cost (TC) divided by quantity (Q), so with economies of scale, $AC = TC/Q$ must decline when Q increases because the denominator, Q, rises more rapidly than the numerator, TC.

Fact 3. If average cost is declining, then marginal cost must be below average cost. This fact follows directly from one of the general rules relating marginal and average data that were explained in the appendix to Chapter 8. Once again, the logic is simple enough to review briefly. If, for example, your average quiz score is 90 percent but the next quiz pulls your average down to 87 percent, then the grade on the most recent test (the marginal grade) must be below both the old and the new average quiz scores. That is, it takes a marginal grade (or cost) that is below the average to pull the average down.

Putting these three facts together, we conclude that in many regulated industries, marginal cost (MC) will be below average cost, as depicted in Figure 1. Now suppose that regulators set the price (or average revenue, AR) at the level of marginal cost. Because P then equals MC, $P (= AR)$ must be below AC and the firm must lose money, so "P equals MC" is simply not an acceptable option. What, then, should be done? One possibility is to set price equal to marginal cost and to use public funds to make up for the deficit. However, government subsidies to large regulated firms are not very popular politically and may also not be sensible.

A second option, which is quite popular among regulators, is to (try to) set price equal to average cost. But this method of pricing is, however, neither desirable nor possible to carry out except on the basis of arbitrary decisions. The problem is that almost no firm produces only a single commodity. Almost every company produces a number of different varieties and qualities of some product, and many produce thousands of different products, each with its own price. Even General Motors, a fairly specialized firm that produces many makes and sizes of cars and trucks, also sells home mortgages and quite a few other things. In a multiproduct firm, we cannot even define $AC = TC/Q$, because to calculate Q (total output), we would have to add up all of the apples and oranges (and all of the other different items) that the firm produces. Of course, we know that we cannot add up apples and oranges. Because we cannot calculate AC for a multiproduct firm, it is hardly possible for the regulator to require P to equal AC for each of the firm's products (although regulators sometimes think they can do so).

One way of dealing with the issue is the price cap approach that was invented by economists but is now widely employed in practice. The procedure and its logic will be described a little later in this chapter.

Preventing Monopoly Profit but Keeping Incentives for Efficiency and Innovation

Opponents of regulation claim that it seriously impairs the efficiency of American industry and reduces the benefits of free markets. One obvious source of inefficiency is the endless paperwork and complex legal proceedings that prevent the firm from responding quickly to changing market conditions.

In addition, economists believe that regulatory interference in pricing causes economic inefficiency. By forcing prices to differ from those that would prevail in a free, competitive market, regulations lead consumers to demand a quantity of the regulated product that does not maximize consumer benefits from the quantity of resources available to the economy. (This resource misallocation issue will be discussed in Chapter 15.)

A third source of inefficiency may be even more important. It occurs because regulators often are required to prevent the regulated firm from earning excessive profits, while at the same time offering it financial incentives for maximum efficiency of operation and allowing it enough profit to attract the capital it needs when growing markets justify expansion. It would seem to be ideal if the regulator would permit the firm to earn just the amount of revenue that covers its costs, including the cost of its capital. Thus, if the current rate of profits in competitive markets is 10 percent, the regulated firm should recover its costs plus 10 percent on its investment and not a penny more or less. The trouble with such a rule is that it removes all profit incentive for efficiency, responsiveness to consumer demand, and innovation. In effect, it guarantees just one standard rate of profit to the firm, no more and no less—regardless of whether its management is totally incompetent or extremely talented and hard-working.

Competitive markets do not work this way. Although under perfect competition the average firm will earn just the illustrative 10 percent, a firm with an especially ingenious and efficient management will do better, and a firm with an incompetent management is likely to go broke. It is the possibility of great rewards and harsh punishments that gives the market mechanism its power to cause firms to strive for high efficiency and productivity growth.

When firms are guaranteed fixed returns no matter how well or how poorly they perform, gross inefficiencies often result. For example, many contracts for purchases of military equipment have prices calculated on a so-called cost-plus basis, meaning that the supplier is guaranteed that its costs will be covered and that, in addition, it will receive some prespecified profit. Studies of such cost-plus arrangements have confirmed that they lead to enormous supplier inefficiencies. A regulatory arrangement that in effect guarantees a regulated firm its cost plus a "fair rate of return" on its investment obviously has much in common with a cost-plus contract. Fortunately, there are also substantial differences between the two, and so regulatory profit ceilings need not always have serious effects on the firm's incentives for efficiency.

How can one prevent regulated firms from earning excessive profits, but also permit them to earn enough to cover their legitimate costs, attract the capital they need and, above all, still allow rewards for superior performance and penalties for poor performance?

Price Caps as Incentives for Efficiency   A regulatory innovation designed to prevent monopoly profits while offering incentives for the firm to improve its efficiency is now in use in many countries—for electricity, telephones, and airport services in the United Kingdom, for example, and for telephone rates in the United States and elsewhere.

Under this program, regulators assign ceilings (called **price caps**) for the *prices* (not the profits) of the regulated firms. However, the price caps (which are measured in real, inflation-adjusted terms—in other words, they are adjusted for changes in the purchasing power of money) are reduced each year at a rate based on the rate of cost reduction (productivity growth) previously achieved by the regulated firm. Thus, if

A **price cap** is a ceiling above which regulators do not permit prices to rise. The cap is designed to provide an efficiency incentive to the firm by allowing it to keep part of any savings in costs it can achieve.

the regulated firm subsequently achieves cost savings (by innovation or other means) greater than those it obtained in the past, the firm's real costs will fall more rapidly than its real prices do, and it will be permitted to keep the resulting profits as its reward. Of course, there is a catch. If the regulated firm reduces its costs by only 2 percent per year, whereas in the past its costs fell 3 percent per year, the price cap will also fall at a 3 percent rate. The firm will therefore lose profits, although consumers will continue to benefit from falling real prices. So under this arrangement the firm is automatically punished if its cost-reduction performance does not keep up with what it was able to achieve in the past.

Thus, under price-cap regulation, management is constantly forced to look for ever more economical ways of doing things. This approach clearly gives up any attempt to limit the profit of the regulated firm—leaving the possibility of higher profits as an incentive for efficiency. At the same time, it protects the consumer by controlling the firm's prices. Indeed, it makes those prices lower and lower, in real terms.

THE PROS AND CONS OF "BIGNESS"

We have described several goals for regulation, including control of monopoly power and the provision of universal service. Is it desirable, in addition to these regulatory goals, to try to make big firms become smaller? In other words, are the effects of "bigness" always undesirable? We have already seen that only relatively large firms have any likelihood of possessing monopoly power. We also have seen that monopoly power can cause a number of problems, including undesirable effects on income distribution, misallocation of resources, and inhibition of efficiency and innovation.

But we also have seen that big firms, at least sometimes, do not possess monopoly power. More generally, there is another side of the picture. Bigness in industry can also, at least sometimes, benefit the general public. Again, this is true for a number of reasons.

Economies of Large Size

Probably the most important advantage of bigness is found in industries in which technology makes small-scale operation inefficient. One can hardly imagine the costs if automobiles were produced in little workshops rather than giant factories. The notion of a small firm operating a long-distance railroad does not even make sense, and a multiplicity of firms replicating the same railroad service would clearly be incredibly wasteful.

On these grounds, most policy makers have never even considered any attempt to eliminate bigness. Of course, it does not follow that every industry in which firms happen to be big is one in which big firms are best. Some observers argue that many firms, in fact, exceed the sizes required for cost minimization.

Required Scale for Innovation

Some economists have argued that only large firms have the resources and the motivation for really significant innovation. Many important inventions are still contributed by individuals. But, because it is often an expensive, complex, and large-scale undertaking to put a new invention into commercial production, often only large firms can afford the funds and bear the risks that such an effort demands.

Many studies have examined the relationships among firm size, industry competitiveness, and the level of expenditure on research and development (R&D). Although the evidence is far from conclusive, it does indicate that highly competitive industries composed of very small firms tend not to spend a great deal on research. Up to a point, R&D outlays and innovation seem to increase with size of the firm and the concentration of the industry. One reason for this is that many oligopolistic firms use innovation—new products and new processes—as their primary competitive "weapon," forcing them, as time passes, to maintain and even increase their spending on R&D and other innovative activities.

However, some of the most significant innovations introduced in the twentieth century have been contributed by firms that started very small. Examples include the airplane, alternating current (AC) electricity, the photocopier, and the electronic calculator. Yet, the important successive improvements in those products have characteristically come out of the research facilities of large, oligopolistic enterprises.

The bottom line is that bigness in business firms receives a mixed score. In some cases it can produce undesirable results, but in other cases it is necessary for efficiency and low costs and offers other benefits to the public. A rule requiring regulators to combat bigness per se, wherever it occurs, is likely to have undesirable results and would, in any event, be unworkable.

■ DEREGULATION

Because regulators have sometimes adopted rules and made decisions that were ill-advised and were demonstrably harmful to the public interest, and because the bureaucracy that is needed to enforce regulation is costly and raises business expenses, there have long been demands for reduced regulation. Beginning in the mid-1970s, Congress responded to such arguments by deregulating several industries, such as airlines and trucking, and eliminating most of the powers of the relevant regulatory agencies. In other industries, such as railroads and telecommunications, rule changes now give regulated firms considerably more freedom in decision making. This deregulation process is still under way.

■ The Effects of Deregulation

One way to deal with the regulation difficulties just discussed is to shut regulation down—that is, simply to leave everything to the free market and get rid of the regulators. Many observers think that would be a good idea in a number of cases, but sometimes it would be unacceptable, as in markets that are virtually pure monopolies. Thus, the move toward deregulation has proceeded slowly, by eliminating regulation in some fields and reducing it in others. Deregulation's effects in the United States are still being debated, but several conclusions seem clear.

1. Effects on Prices   There seems little doubt that deregulation has generally led to lower prices. Airline fares, railroad freight rates, and telephone rates have all declined on the average (again, in real, inflation-adjusted terms) after total or partial deregulation. At least in the case of the airlines, however, the rate of decline slowed abruptly toward the end of the 1980s. Still, observers conclude that most of these prices are well below the levels that would have prevailed under regulation.

2. Effects on Local Services   At first it was widely feared, even by supporters of deregulation, that smaller and more isolated communities would be deprived of services because small numbers of customers would make those services unprofitable. Some predicted that airlines, railroads, and telephone companies would withdraw from such communities once there was no longer any regulation to force them to stay. The outcome was not as serious as had been anticipated. For example, although larger airlines have left smaller communities, they have usually been replaced by smaller commuter airlines that have often provided more frequent service. In addition, the larger airlines inaugurated a new scheduling pattern called the "hub-and-spoke system" (see the discussion below), which enabled them to continue to serve less traveled destinations profitably.

3. Effects on Entry   As a result of deregulation, older airlines invaded one another's routes, several dozen new airlines sprang up, and about 10,000 new truck operators entered the market. Many of the trucking entrants have since dropped out of the industry, as profits and wages were driven down by competition. Almost all of the new airlines also ran into trouble and were sold to the older airlines. Since 1990, however, many small airlines have been launched and several are now the most profitable firms in the industry. A battle is now shaping up over whether the small airlines need special protection from tough competition by the larger airlines. Here it is also pertinent to note that although many of the small entrant airlines have perished, so have a number of very large carriers, including Eastern Airlines, Braniff, Pan Am, and TWA, all of which had once been major enterprises.

4. Effects on Unions   Deregulation has badly hurt unions such as the Teamsters (of the trucking industry) and the Airline Pilots Association. In the new, competitive climate, firms have been forced to make sharp cuts in their workforces and to resist wage increases and other costly changes in working conditions. Indeed, there has been strong pressure for retrenchment on all of these fronts. It should not be surprising, then, that unions often oppose deregulation.

5. Effects on Product Quality   The public has been unpleasantly surprised by another effect of deregulation. At least in the case of aviation, increased price competition has been accompanied by sharp reductions in "frills." To cut costs, airlines have made meals less elaborate (to put it mildly) and have limited the number of flights to avoid empty seats—which has increased crowding. To fill planes with more passengers, many airlines turned to "hub and spoke" systems (see Figure 2). Instead of running a flight directly from a low-demand airport, A, to another low-demand airport, B, the airline flies all passengers from Airport A to its "hub" at Airport H, where all passengers, from many points of origin, who are bound for the same destination, Airport B, are brought together and asked to reboard an airplane flying to B. This system clearly saves money and gives passengers more options as the number of flights between hubs and spokes increases. At the same time, it is less convenient for passengers than a direct flight from origin to destination. Critics of deregulation have placed a good deal of emphasis on the reductions in passenger comfort. Economists, however, argue that competition would not bring such results unless passengers as a group prefer the reduction in fares to the greater standards of luxury that preceded them.

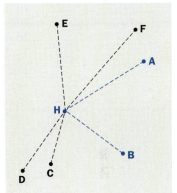

FIGURE 2

A "Hub and Spoke" Airline Routing Pattern

6. Effects on Safety   Also in the case of airline deregulation (though the issue can well arise elsewhere), some observers have been concerned that cost cutting after deregulation would lead to skimping on safety measures. As Figure 3 shows, deregulation seems not to have increased the rate of airline accidents. Even so, deregulation may require special vigilance to guard against neglect of safety as a cost-cutting measure. In late 2001, this concern led Congress to legislate a government role in protecting the public from terrorist attacks. Some observers suggest that the reduced profits that competition caused in truck transportation has led truckers to cut corners in terms of safety.

7. Effects on Profits and Wages   As the previous discussion suggested, deregulation has generally strengthened competition, and the increased power of competition has, in turn, tended to depress profits and wages. There is evidence that few airlines, including the largest carriers, have been able to earn profits as high as those in other competitive industries, on average, since the deregulation of the airlines more than two decades ago. Recent events such as the threat of terrorism and rising fuel prices have brought several large airlines to the brink of bankruptcy. This, of course, is just the other side of reduced prices to consumers. In some cases, the profit and wage cuts were very substantial and had significant consequences. The recent financial

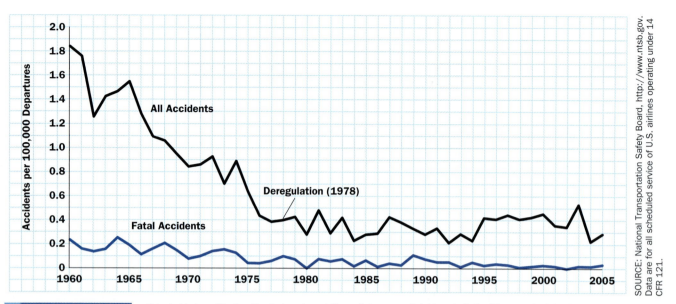

SOURCE: National Transportation Safety Board, http://www.ntsb.gov. Data are for all scheduled service of U.S. airlines operating under 14 CFR 121.

FIGURE 3

U.S. Airline Accident Rates, 1960–2005

Note: Accidents resulting from illegal acts, such as suicide or sabotage, are excluded from the National Transportation Safety Board's accident rate computations.

problems for airlines and trucking firms have already been noted, and the pressures for decreases in the very high earnings of airline pilots have prompted frequent confrontations between these workers and the airlines.

The general conclusion is that deregulation has usually worked out well, but hardly perfectly in promoting the welfare of consumers. Indeed, partial deregulation has sometimes proved to be disastrous, as illustrated by what happened in the electricity industry in California in 2001. There, *wholesale* prices were deregulated, but tight ceilings were imposed on *retail* prices. Firms that bought at wholesale and sold at retail incurred great losses when wholesale prices increased, with a brief period of significant power shortages being the predictable result.

The battle for deregulation is far from over. Even if those who wish for a return to the good old days of regulation (and there are some) do not succeed, many areas exist in which regulation of the old-time variety still retains its grip or has been reintroduced in disguised form.

THE PUZZLE REVISITED: *Why Regulators Often Push Prices Upward*

We can now return to the puzzle we posed earlier: Why would regulators, who are supposed to protect the interests of the public, raise prices? The answer is that regulators sometimes push for higher prices when they want to prevent the demise of any existing firms in an industry. Earlier, we saw that strong economies of scale and economies of scope may make it impossible for a number of firms to survive. The largest firm in an industry may have such a big cost advantage over its competitors that it can drive them out of the market while still operating at a profit.

Firms that are hurt by such competitive pressures often complain to regulatory commissions that the prices charged by a rival are "unfairly low." These commissions, afraid that unrestrained pricing will reduce the number of firms in the industry, then attempt to "equalize" matters by imposing price floors (below which prices cannot be set). Such price floors are designed to permit *all* the firms in the industry to operate profitably, including those that operate inefficiently and incur costs far higher than their competitors' costs. That is presumably why, under regulation, the New York–Washington, D.C., air fares were so high.

Many economists maintain that this approach to pricing is a perversion of the idea of competition. The virtue of competition is that, where it occurs, firms force one another to supply consumers with products of high quality at low prices. Any firm that cannot achieve this goal is driven out of business by market forces. A regulatory arrangement may allow efficient and inefficient firms to coexist only by preventing them from competing with one another, but this arrangement merely preserves the appearance of competition while destroying its substance, and it forces consumers to pay the higher prices necessary to keep the inefficient firms alive.

PART 2: ANTITRUST LAWS AND POLICIES

In Part 1 of this chapter, we described the process of regulation, which governments use to oversee monopoly or oligopoly firms that are deemed to have dangerous power to control their markets. In Part 2, we will analyze the second of government's instruments for protecting competition: **antitrust policy.** Antitrust policy refers to programs that preclude the deliberate creation of monopoly and prevent powerful firms from engaging in related "anticompetitive practices." Firms accused of violating the U.S. antitrust laws are likely to be sued by the federal government or other private firms. Antitrust suits seek to prevent such undesirable behavior from recurring, provide compensation to the victims, and punish offenders via fines or even imprisonment.

The antitrust agencies generally are not allowed to decide that a firm has violated the antitrust laws. They can only sue a company they suspect of violating those laws in the

Antitrust policy refers to programs and laws that preclude the deliberate creation of monopoly and prevent powerful firms from engaging in related "anticompetitive practices."

You Are There: An Antitrust Trial

The charming courtroom is old but recently refurbished, and the air conditioning is inadequate. It is often difficult to hear what is happening. The defendant firm has been accused of predatory pricing—that is, of charging very low prices in order to drive a competitor out of the market—and is defending itself against a judgment that can run into the billions of dollars.

For the past two months, both sides have called many witnesses—company executives, accountants, statisticians. The female lawyers are dressed in conservative outfits, the men in somewhat seedy two-piece suits. It would not do to appear too wealthy, for this is a jury trial, and the men and women jurors wear casual attire including sneakers, jeans, and sports clothes. Although determined to see justice done, they are having a hard time staying awake under a hurricane of technical arguments and contradictory figures.

The judge follows the proceedings closely, often interrupting with questions of her own. Sometimes she jokes with the witnesses.

The lawyers call in an expert witness who is a specialist in the field—in this case, an economist who has written on predatory pricing. He explains to the court and the jury the current thinking of the economics profession on the definition of predatory pricing and the standards by which one judges whether or not it has occurred. He is persuasive.

SOURCE: © Llewellyn/Uniphoto

But the judge and jury have already heard from another economist, equally distinguished, representing the other side. Their analyses, which were quite technical, reached opposite conclusions though they agree on analytic procedures. Which one are the jurors to believe, and on what basis?

The Size and Scope of an Antitrust Case

Alleged violations of the antitrust laws are usually dealt with by bringing the accused firm to court or by threatening to sue it in the hope that the accused firm will surrender and accept a compromise. Antitrust suits are frequently well-publicized affairs because the accused firms are often the giants of industry—such famous names as Standard Oil, U.S. Steel, the Aluminum Company of America (Alcoa), General Electric, International Business Machines (IBM), American Telephone and Telegraph (AT&T), and Microsoft all have appeared in such proceedings. Even some of the nation's most prestigious colleges and universities have been accused of engaging in a pricing conspiracy.

The magnitude of an antitrust suit is difficult to imagine. After the charges have been filed, it is not unusual for more than five years to elapse before the case even comes to trial. The parties spend this period laboriously preparing their cases. Dozens of lawyers, scores of witnesses, and hundreds of researchers are likely to participate in this process. The trial itself also can run for years. A major case produces literally thousands of volumes of material, and it can easily cost the defendant several hundred million dollars. In addition, if it loses, the defendant may have to pay billions of dollars in fines.

As you may imagine, the power of the government or another firm to haul a company into court on antitrust charges is an awesome one. Win, lose, or draw, such a case imposes a very heavy burden on the accused firm, draining its funds, consuming the time and attention of its management, and delaying business decisions until the outcome of the legal proceedings is determined.

courts and provide evidence supporting their allegations against the firm, seeking to get the court to punish the claimed misbehavior and prevent its continuation. Still, even the threat of such a lawsuit is a serious matter to the firm, because of the possible punishment if it loses the case and because fighting such a lawsuit can cost the firm hundreds of millions of dollars. What justifies investment of so much power in such government agencies as the Department of Justice and the Federal Trade Commission? What are the purposes of the antitrust laws? How well has antitrust policy succeeded? These are the issues that we will discuss in the remainder of the chapter.

■ MEASURING MARKET POWER: CONCENTRATION

■ Concentration: Definition and Measurement— The Herfindahl-Hirschman Index

It is generally agreed that a firm is not strong enough to violate the antitrust laws if it possesses no monopoly power—that is, no power to prevent entry of competitors and to raise prices substantially above competitive levels. So in antitrust lawsuits one issue that is almost invariably argued about is whether the accused company does or does not have monopoly power. In enforcing the antitrust laws, one piece of evidence that the U.S. Department of Justice and the Federal Trade Commission use to test whether a firm under investigation for antitrust violations is likely to possess monopoly power is the **concentration** of the markets in which the firm carries out its activities. A market or an industry is said to be *highly concentrated* if it contains only a few firms, most or all of which sell a large share of the industry's products. In contrast, an industry with many small firms is said to be *unconcentrated*. Thus, concentration is a useful index of the relative bigness of the firms in the industry. Earlier, we noted that big firms do not always have market power, whereas relatively small firms never (or almost never) do. Still, concentration is one useful piece of evidence in deciding whether market power exists in any case under investigation. In particular, if the accused firm can convince the court that it has no such power, the case is likely to be dismissed by the court.

Concentration is measured in a number of ways. The most straightforward method is to calculate what share of the industry's output is sold by some selected number of

Concentration of an industry measures the share of the total sales or assets of the industry in the hands of its largest firms.

Protection of Competition, Not Protection of Competitors

The courts have repeatedly emphasized that the antitrust laws are not intended to make life easier for individual firms that encounter difficulties coping with competitive market pressures. The following quotation from a recent decision of the U.S. Supreme Court makes this clear:

> The purpose of the Sherman Act is not to protect businesses from the workings of the market, it is to protect the public from the failure of the market.

SOURCE: *Spectrum Sports Inc. v. M.cQuillan*, US 122 L.Ed 2d 247 [1993], p. 506.

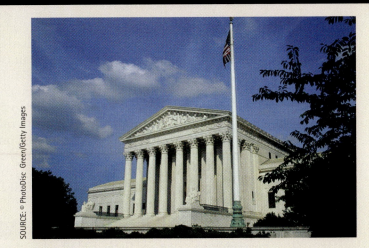

SOURCE: © PhotoDisc Green/Getty Images

the industry's firms. Most often a *four-firm* **concentration ratio** is used for this purpose. Thus, if the four largest firms in an industry account for, say, 58 percent of the industry's sales, we say that the four-firm concentration ratio is 0.58.

Another formula now widely used to measure concentration is the **Herfindahl-Hirschman Index (HHI).** This measure is used by the U.S. Department of Justice and the Federal Trade Commission, for example, to decide whether the proposed merger of two firms will lead to excessive concentration in a particular industry. The index is calculated by determining the market share of each of the firms in the industry, squaring each of these numbers and adding them together. To quote one of the government documents,

"For example, a market consisting of four firms with market shares of 30 percent, 30 percent, 20 percent, and 20 percent has an HHI of 2,600 (or, $30^2 + 30^2 + 20^2 + 20^2 = 2,600$). The HHI ranges from 10,000 (in the case of a pure monopoly) to a number approaching zero (in the case of [near perfect competition])."[1]

The government considers a market to be unconcentrated if its HHI number is less than 1,000, and highly concentrated if that number exceeds 1,800. The HHI offers at least two advantages over the four-firm concentration ratio. Unlike the latter ratio, HHI takes into account data on a much larger percentage of the firms in the market than just the top four. However, the calculation automatically magnifies the weight assigned to the market shares of the larger firms, because the square of a larger number is disproportionately larger than the square of a smaller number. This effect is considered desirable, because these larger firms are the reason the government worries about monopoly power in the market under consideration. It also explains why the HHI works as a measure of concentration. The HHI number rises when concentration grows because the larger the shares of the market's total sales held by the big firms, the disproportionately larger the squared values of those shares will be.

Ultimately, we care about concentration ratios if they are a good measure of market power. The question, then, is this: If an industry becomes more concentrated, will

A **concentration ratio** is the percentage of an industry's output produced by its four largest firms. It is intended to measure the degree to which the industry is dominated by large firms.

The **Herfindahl-Hirschman Index (HHI)** is an alternative and widely used measure of the degree of concentration of an industry. It is calculated, in essence, by adding together the squares of the market shares of the firms in the industry, although the smallest firms may be left out of the calculation because their small market share numbers have a negligible effect on the result.

---

[1] Department of Justice and Federal Trade Commission, *Horizontal Merger Guidelines*, Washington, D.C., 1993, page 8, footnote.

the firms necessarily increase their ability to price their products above competitive levels? Many economists have, in fact, concluded that although increased concentration *often* facilitates or increases market power, it does not *always* do so. Specifically, the following three conclusions are now widely accepted:

- If, after an increase in concentration, an industry still has a very low concentration ratio, then its firms are very unlikely to have any market power either before or after the rise in concentration.
- If circumstances in the industry are in other respects favorable for successful price collusion—that is, an agreement among the firms not to undercut one another's prices or not to compete "too much" in other ways—a rise in concentration will facilitate market power. It will do so by reducing the number of firms that need to be consulted in arriving at an agreement and by decreasing the number of firms that have to be watched to make sure they do not betray the collusive agreement.
- Where entry into and exit from the industry are easy and quite inexpensive, then even when concentration increases, market power will not be enhanced because an excessive price will attract new entrants that will soon force the price down.

TABLE 1

Concentration Ratios and Herfindahl-Hirschman Indexes for Selected Manufacturing Industries, 1997

Industry	Four-Firm Ratio	Herfindahl-Hirschman Index for 50 Largest Companies in the Industry
Precision-turned products	3.6	12.5
Cement and concrete products	9.2	48.1
Women's and girls' dresses	13.3	105.9
Fine jewelry	13.5	84.7
Bolts, nuts, screws, rivets, and washers	20.3	173.6
Computers and electronic products	20.8	170.7
Fluid milk	22.5	219.5
Sporting and athletic goods	24.1	191.6
Brooms, brushes, and mops	25.9	296.3
Musical instruments	32.3	462.1
Dolls and stuffed toys	33.0	452.5
Pharmaceutical preparations	37.1	489.1
Ship and boat building	43.1	578.7
Men's and boys' suits and coats	45.1	1,103.6
Fasteners, buttons, needles, and pins	49.1	1,049.3
Tortillas	58.4	1,881.7
Cookies and crackers	64.6	1,609.7
Tires	69.4	1,667.5
Aircraft	80.9	2,526.2
Breakfast cereal	86.7	2,773.7
Automobiles	87.4	2,725.0
Electric lamp bulbs and parts	89.7	Not disclosed
Guided missiles and space vehicles	91.6	Not disclosed
Cigarettes	98.9	Not disclosed

Note: Concentration ratios are percentage of output produced by the four largest firms in each industry. HHIs are calculated by summing the squares of the individual company percentages for the 50 largest companies or the entire universe of companies, whichever is lower. Where HHI is not disclosed, information is withheld to avoid disclosing data of individual companies.

SOURCE: U.S. Census Bureau, "Concentration Ratios in Manufacturing, 1997," *1997 Economic Census*, U.S. Department of Commerce, Economics and Statistics Administration, issued June 2001.

■ The Evidence of Concentration in Reality

Concentration data may be the best evidence that we have on the effectiveness of antitrust programs. Table 1 shows concentration ratios and Herfindahl-Hirschman Indexes in a number of industries in the United States. We see that concentration varies greatly from industry to industry: Automobiles, breakfast cereals, and aircraft are produced by highly concentrated industries, but the cement, jewelry, and women's and girls' clothing industries show very little concentration.

During the last century, concentration ratios in the United States, on the average, have remained remarkably constant. It has been estimated that, at the turn of the twentieth century, 32.9 percent of manufactured goods were produced by industries in which the concentration ratios were 50 percent or more (meaning that at least 50 percent of industry output was produced by the four largest firms). By 1997, the figure had risen only to 33.5 percent. These figures and those for other years are shown in Table 2. As we see, over the course of the twentieth century, concentration in individual U.S. industries has shown little tendency to increase.

Such information may suggest that the antitrust laws have to some degree been effective in inhibiting whatever trend toward bigness may actually exist. Even this very cautious conclusion has been questioned by some observers, who argue that the size of firms has been held down by market forces and technical developments (such as declining computer costs that make it easier for small firms to increase their efficiency, or the takeover of much of freight traffic from large railroads by small trucking firms). These observers argue that antitrust laws have made virtually no difference in the size and the behavior of American business.

A CRUCIAL PROBLEM FOR ANTITRUST: THE RESEMBLANCE OF MONOPOLIZATION AND VIGOROUS COMPETITION

One problem that haunts most antitrust litigation is that vigorous competition may look very similar to acts that *undermine* competition and support monopoly power. The resulting danger is that the courts will prohibit, or the antitrust authorities will prosecute, acts that *appear* to be anticompetitive but are really the opposite.

The difficulty occurs because effective competition by a firm is always tough on its rivals. It forces rivals to charge lower prices, to improve product quality, and to spend money on innovations that will cut their costs and improve their products. Competition will legitimately force competitors out of business if they are inefficient and therefore cannot keep their prices low or provide products of acceptable quality. When competition destroys a rival in this way, however, it is difficult to tell whether the firm was, so to speak, murdered or died of natural causes. In both cases, the surviving competitor bears some responsibility for its rival's failure. On the one hand, if the cause of the rival's demise is legitimate competition, consumers will benefit; on the other hand, if the end of the rival was part of a process of monopoly creation, then the public will end up paying. This very real issue constantly recurs in today's antitrust litigation.

TABLE 2
The Historical Trend in Concentration in Manufacturing Industries, 1901–1997

	Percentage of Value-Added in Industries with Four-Firm Concentration Ratios over 50 Percent
Circa 1901	32.9
1947	24.4
1954	29.9
1958	30.2
1963	33.1
1966	28.6
1970	26.3
1972	29.0
1982	25.2
1987	27.9
1992	26.4
1997	33.5

SOURCES: P. W. McCracken and T. G. Moore, "Competitive and Market Concentration in the American Economy," Subcommittee on Antitrust and Monopoly, U.S. Senate, March 29, 1973; F. M. Scherer, *Industrial Market Structure and Economic Performance* (Boston: Houghton Mifflin, 1980), p. 68; F. M. Scherer and David Ross, *Industrial Market Structure and Economic Performance*, 3rd ed. (Boston: Houghton Mifflin, 1990), p. 84; personal communication with Professor Frederick M. Scherer, March 10, 1993; and personal communication with Andrew W. Hait, Special Reports Branch, U.S. Bureau of the Census, December 2001.

ANTICOMPETITIVE PRACTICES AND ANTITRUST

A central purpose of the antitrust laws is to prevent "anticompetitive practices," which are actions by a powerful firm that threaten to destroy competitors, or force competitors to compete less vigorously, or prevent the entry of new rivals.

Predatory Pricing

Typical of accusations of anticompetitive behavior is the claim, made frequently in antitrust cases, that the defendant has adopted unjustifiably low prices in order to force other firms to lose money, thereby driving competitors out of business. This practice is called **predatory pricing.** Deciding whether pricing is "predatory" is difficult, both for economists and for courts of law, because low prices generally benefit consumers. Therefore, the courts do not want to discourage firms from cutting prices by being too eager to declare that lower prices are intended to destroy a rival.

One principle widely followed by the courts holds that prices are predatory only if they are below either marginal or average variable costs. The logic of this criterion as

Predatory pricing is pricing that threatens to keep a competitor out of the market. It is a price that is so low that it will be profitable for the firm that adopts it only if a rival is driven from the market.

a test for whether prices are "too low" is that even under perfect competition, prices will not, in the long run, fall below that level, but will equal marginal costs. But even in cases where prices are below marginal or average variable costs, they may be held to be predatory only under two conditions:

- If evidence shows that the low price would have been profitable *only* if it succeeded in destroying a rival or in keeping it out of the market.
- When there is a real probability that the allegedly predatory firm could raise prices to monopoly levels after the rival was driven out, thereby profiting from its venture in crime.

Many major firms—including AT&T, American Airlines, and Microsoft—have been accused of predatory pricing. The defendants typically argue that their low prices cover both marginal and average variable costs, that their prices are low because of superior efficiency, and that the lawsuit was brought to prevent the defendants from competing effectively. The courts have generally accepted these arguments. There have been many predatory pricing cases, but few convictions.

■ The Microsoft Case: Bottlenecks, Bundling, and Network Externalities

The recent litigation involving Microsoft Corporation illustrates two other practices that can conceivably be anticompetitive. Microsoft is the enormously successful supplier of computer operating systems that enable you to communicate with and control your personal computer; it also supplies other very popular computer programs. Microsoft's software sales are huge, and the company is clearly a tough and energetic competitor. The difficulty of distinguishing vigorously competitive behavior from anticompetitive acts is illustrated by the Microsoft antitrust case, in which the U.S. Department of Justice accused the firm of various anticompetitive practices.

The Microsoft case raises many issues, two of which are discussed here as illustrations.

Abuse via Bottlenecks   Microsoft's Windows, an operating system that runs on about 90 percent of all personal computers, is a prime example of a problem referred to as a "bottleneck"—a facility or product in the hands of a single firm, without which competitors find it difficult or even impossible to operate. To reach any substantial proportion of personal computer customers, the producer of any word processor, spreadsheet, or graphics program must use Windows, and there seems little likelihood that any alternative to Windows will soon capture a large share of customers.

The bottleneck exists in part because Windows is widely considered a good program, but even more because user compatibility is desirable—computer users need to communicate with one another, and that task is easier if all of them employ the same operating system. That is, there exists a network of users of computer products who want to be able to communicate easily with one another, and who therefore desire compatible software. This preference gives Microsoft a big advantage, because it already has so many users that a new purchaser who values such compatibility will be reluctant to buy a competing product that will make it more difficult to communicate with those many users of the Microsoft products. The bottleneck problem arises because Microsoft itself supplies not only Windows but also many applications (such as Word, a word-processing program; Excel, a spreadsheet program; and Internet Explorer, an Internet browser). There is nothing illegal about simply being the owner of a bottleneck. If company X is a railroad with the only train-bearing bridge over a river because no other rail line had the resources or the initiative to build its own bridge, that is surely not anticompetitive. The worry is that a bottleneck owner, like Microsoft, will use its bottleneck product, Windows, in a way that favors its own programs and handicaps programs supplied by its competitors.

Bundling: Legitimate and Illegitimate   Microsoft has promoted its own products by providing them more cheaply to computer manufacturers if these makers buy a *bundle* of Microsoft programs, rather than just Windows alone. This practice means that rival producers of word processors, spreadsheets, and Internet browsers are handicapped in selling their products to PC owners. The question is whether Microsoft's low bundle price is legitimate or if it constitutes a case of predatory pricing whose only purpose is to destroy competitors. Economists often take the position that a **bundling** discount is legitimate if it is less expensive for the firm to supply several products at once than to supply them one at a time, and if the price cut corresponds to the cost saving. However, they question the legitimacy of the bundle discount if the cost saving is considerably less than the difference between the bundled price and the sum of the prices of the included products (when bought individually). However, even here, it is argued that if the price of the bundle exceeds its marginal cost or its average variable cost, it is not predatory.

> **Bundling** refers to a pricing arrangement under which the supplier offers substantial discounts to customers if they buy several of the firm's products, so that the price of the bundle of products is less than the sum of the prices of the products if they were bought separately.

USE OF ANTITRUST LAWS TO PREVENT COMPETITION

Finally, let us turn to an issue that some observers consider very serious: the *misuse* of the antitrust laws to prevent competition. Many firms that have been unable to compete effectively on their own merits have turned to the courts to seek protection from their successful competitors—and some have succeeded.

Firms that try to protect themselves in this way always claim that their rivals have not achieved success through superior ability but rather by means that they call "monopolization." Sometimes the evidence is clear-cut, and the courts can readily discern whether an accused firm has violated the antitrust laws or whether it has simply been too efficient and innovative for the complaining competitor's tastes. In other cases, the issues are complicated, and only a long and painstaking legal proceeding offers any prospect of resolving them.

Various steps have been suggested to deal with the misuse of U.S. antitrust laws. In one proposal, if the courts decide that a firm has been falsely accused by another of violating the antitrust laws, then (as is done in other countries) the *accuser* will pay the legal costs of the innocent defendant. Another proposal is to subject such suits to prescreening by a government agency, as is done in Japan. But these issues are hardly open-and-shut, for there is no such thing as a perfect legal system. Anything that

Doonesbury   BY GARRY TRUDEAU

Can Antitrust Laws Be Used to *Prevent* Competition?

Many observers are concerned that the antitrust laws are often used by inefficient firms to protect themselves from the competition of more efficient rivals. When they are unable to win out in the marketplace, the argument goes, firms simply file lawsuits against their competitors claiming that those rivals have achieved success by means that violate the antitrust laws.

Not only do they seek protection from the courts against what they describe as "unfair competition" or "predatory practices," but they often sue for compensation that, under the law, can sometimes be three times as large as the damages that they claim to have suffered. Moreover, even if the defendant is found innocent, it must normally pay the very high costs of the litigation itself. Aside from the enormous waste that such lawsuits entail, observers worry that they represent a perversion of the antitrust laws, which were, after all, designed to promote competition, not to prevent it.

Two recent examples illustrate the nature of such litigation.* These cases also show that the courts are often wise enough to throw out such attempts to use the antitrust laws to prevent competition.

AMI VERSUS IBM

Allen-Myland, Inc. (AMI), is a small firm that specialized in the up-grading of computers, an activity that had earned it handsome profits in a period of time when expanding a computer's capacity was very laborious. Over time, technological progress by IBM transformed what was once a labor-intensive task requiring considerable skill into the routine installation of a small and highly reliable part. This change rendered obsolete many of the services offered by AMI. AMI then sued IBM, seeking to persuade the court to impose an artificial and expensive market niche for upgrading services, with AMI permanently protected from competitive pressures by high upgrading prices when the job was done by IBM. The court's decision completely rejected AMI's position (Eastern District of Pennsylvania, 1988).

*One of the authors of this book was involved as a witness in both cases.

SOURCE: AP/Wide World Photos

SEWELL PLASTICS VERSUS COCA-COLA, SOUTHEASTERN CONTAINER, ET AL.

The Sewell Plastics Company once had a preponderant market share in the manufacture of plastic soft-drink bottles in the United States, selling two-liter bottles for more than 30¢ each. A group of Coca-Cola bottlers in the Southeast considered the price too high and formed a cooperative firm (Southeastern Container) to manufacture their own plastic bottles.

Within five years, Southeastern had reduced its cost below 14¢ per bottle, and real retail prices of soft drinks fell as well. Despite rising national sales and profits, Sewell sued Southeastern, seeking to force its owners to sell the firm to Sewell or, as a possible alternative, to force Southeastern's customers to sign exclusive purchasing contracts with Sewell. In the spring of 1989, the judge dismissed Sewell's claims, holding that there was no need for a trial (U.S. District Court, Western District, North Carolina, April 1989).

restricts anticompetitive, private antitrust suits will almost certainly inhibit legitimate attempts by individual firms to defend themselves from genuine acts of monopolization by rival enterprises (for more on this issue, see "Can Antitrust Laws Be Used to *Prevent* Competition?" above).

■ CONCLUDING OBSERVATIONS

As we noted at the beginning of this chapter, monopoly and monopoly power are rightly judged to cause market failure—they prevent the market from serving consumer interests most effectively by providing the products the public desires at the lowest possible prices. The alternative is government intervention, and governments, too, sometimes make imperfect decisions. Thus, before deciding whether to regulate more or deregulate, whether to toughen antitrust laws or loosen them, informed citizens should carefully weigh the prospects for market failure against the possibility of government failure in terms of the contemplated change.

Certainly, monopolists have sometimes succeeded in preventing the introduction of useful new products. They have raised prices to consumers and held down product quality. In contrast, large firms have sometimes been innovative and their service to customers has in some cases been considered of high quality.

Government has suffered its own missteps. It has initiated costly lawsuits, sometimes on questionable grounds. It has forced regulated firms to adopt pricing rules that were clearly not beneficial to consumers, and it has handicapped the operations of industries—for example, arguably for a time almost destroying the nation's railroads. Yet government, too, has done useful things in influencing industry behavior, preventing various monopolistic practices, protecting consumers from impure foods and medications, and so on. Most economists believe that by the 1970s government intervention had clearly gone too far in some respects and that deregulation was, consequently, in the public interest. However, the general issue is hardly settled.

SUMMARY

1. Economic **regulation** is adopted to put brakes on the decisions of industries with **monopoly power.**

2. In the United States, regulation of prices and other economic decisions is generally applied only to large firms, including railroads, telecommunications, and gas and electricity supply.

3. In recent years, we have seen a major push toward reduction of regulation. Among the industries that have been deregulated in whole or in part are air, truck, and rail transportation.

4. Among the major reasons given for regulation are (a) **economies of scale** and **economies of scope,** which make industries into natural monopolies; and (b) the universal service goal, which refers to the provision of service to poor people and isolated areas where supply is unprofitable.

5. Regulators often reject proposals by regulated firms to cut their prices, and sometimes the regulators even force firms to *raise* their prices. The purposes of such actions are to prevent "unfair competition" and to protect customers of some of the firm's products from being forced to **cross-subsidize** customers of other products. Many economists disagree with most such actions, arguing that the result is usually to stifle competition and make all customers pay more than they otherwise would.

6. Economists generally agree that a firm should be permitted to cut its price as long as it covers its marginal cost. However, in many regulated industries, firms would go bankrupt if all prices were set equal to marginal costs.

7. By putting ceilings on profits to prevent monopoly earnings, regulation can eliminate the firm's incentive for efficiency and innovation. Price caps, which put (inflation-adjusted) ceilings on prices, rather than profits, are used widely to deal with this problem.

8. **Antitrust policy** includes those policies and programs designed to control the growth of monopoly and to prevent big business from engaging in "anticompetitive" practices.

9. **Predatory pricing** is pricing that is low relative to the marginal or average variable costs of the firm and so threatens to drive a competitor out of the market. For pricing to be considered predatory, there must also be a likelihood that if the prices do destroy a competitor, the firm will acquire market power enabling it to charge prices well above competitive levels.

10. **Bundling** refers to a price reduction given to customers who purchase several of the firm's products simultaneously. It is considered unobjectionable if it is cheaper for the firm to bundle its products so that the price cut merely passes the savings on to customers. However, bundling can be used to destroy competitors that sell only some of the bundled products.

11. The evidence indicates that no significant increase in the **concentration** of individual U.S. industries into fewer, relatively larger firms occurred during the twentieth century. Evidence as to whether antitrust laws have been effective in preventing monopoly is inconclusive, and observers disagree on the subject.

12. Unregulated monopoly is apt to distribute income unfairly, produce undesirably small quantities of output, and provide inadequate motivation for innovation.

13. Sometimes, however, only large firms may have funds sufficient for effective research, development, and innovation. Where economies of scale are available, large firms may also serve customers more cheaply than can small ones.

KEY TERMS

Economies of scale   264

Monopoly power   264

Regulation   265

Economies of scope   267

Cross-subsidization   267

Price cap   270

Antitrust policy   275

Concentration of industry   276

Concentration ratios   277

Herfindahl–Hirschman Index   277

Predatory pricing   279

Bundling   281

DISCUSSION QUESTIONS

1. Why is an electric company in a city often considered to be a natural monopoly? What would happen if two competing electric companies were established? How about telephone companies? How can changes in technology affect your answer?

2. Suppose that a 20 percent cut in the price of coast-to-coast telephone calls brings in so much new business that it permits a long-distance telephone company to cut its charges for service from Chicago to St. Louis, but only by 2 percent. In your opinion, is this practice equitable? Is it a good idea or a bad one?

3. In some regulated industries, regulatory agencies prevented prices from falling, and as a result many firms opened for business in those industries. In your opinion, is this kind of regulation competitive or anticompetitive? Is it a good idea or a bad one?

4. Regulators are highly concerned about the prevention of "predatory pricing." The U.S. Court of Appeals has, however, noted that "the term probably does not have a well-defined meaning, but it certainly bears a sinister connotation." How might one distinguish "predatory" from "nonpredatory" pricing? What would you do about it?

5. Do you think that it is fair or unfair for rural users of telephone service to be cross-subsidized by other telephone users?

6. To provide incentives for increased efficiency, several regulatory agencies have eliminated ceilings on the profits of regulated firms but instead put caps on their prices. Suppose that a regulated firm manages to cut its prices in half, but in the process it doubles its profits. Should rational consumers consider this to be a good or a bad development? Why?

7. A shopkeeper sells his store and signs a contract that restrains him from opening another store in competition with the new owner. The courts have decided that this contract is a reasonable restraint of trade. Can you think of any other types of restraint of trade that seem reasonable? Can you think of any that seem unreasonable?

8. Which of the following industries do you expect to have high concentration ratios: automobile production, aircraft manufacture, hardware production, pharmaceuticals, production of expensive jewelry? Compare your answers with the data in Table 1.

9. Why do you think the specific industries you selected in Review Question 8 are highly concentrated?

10. Do you think it is in the public interest to launch an antitrust suit that costs $1 billion? What leads you to your conclusion?

11. In Japan and a number of European countries, the antitrust laws were once much less severe than those in the United States. Do you think that this difference helped or harmed American industry in its efforts to compete with foreign producers? Why?

12. Can you think of some legal rules that may discourage the use of antitrust laws to prevent competition while at the same time not interfering with legitimate antitrust actions?

13. During the oil crisis in the 1970s, long lines at gas stations disappeared soon after price controls were removed and gas prices were permitted to rise. Should this event be interpreted as evidence that the oil companies have monopoly power? Why or why not?

14. Some economists believe that firms rarely attempt predatory pricing because it would be a very risky act even if it were legal. Why may this be so?

15. Firm X cuts its prices, and competing Firm Y soon goes out of business. How would you judge whether this price cut was an act of legitimate and vigorous competition or an anticompetitive act?

THE VIRTUES AND LIMITATIONS OF MARKETS

Like most institutions, the market has both shortcomings and benefits, and one of the goals of this book is to describe them both as dispassionately as we can. Chapter 14 describes and analyzes a snapshot picture of the market at its best, showing how remarkably well it can coordinate the vast number of activities and decisions that drive our economy. The next chapter, in contrast, investigates some of the important ways in which the market mechanism, if left entirely to itself, fails to serve the public interest well. In Chapter 15 as well as in Chapter 17, we examine what can be done to remedy these deficiencies—or at least to reduce their undesirable consequences. In Chapter 16, the growth chapter, we depict the economy in motion. There we will see the most incredible accomplishments of the market economy in its ability to bring remarkable increases in standards of living and innovative products that could hardly have been imagined by our ancestors. In short, growth performance of the market has totally outstripped anything our forebears could conceivably have expected. Finally, Chapter 18 introduces you to the tax system and the effects of the government on resource allocation.

14

THE CASE FOR FREE MARKETS I: THE PRICE SYSTEM

If there existed the universal mind that . . . would register simultaneously all the processes of nature and of society, that could forecast the results of their inter-reactions, such a mind . . . could . . . draw up a faultless and an exhaustive economic plan. . . . In truth, the bureaucracy often conceives that just such a mind is at its disposal; that is why it so easily frees itself from the control of the market.

LEON TROTSKY, A LEADER OF THE RUSSIAN REVOLUTION

O ur study of microeconomics focuses on two crucial questions: What does the market do well, and what does it do poorly? By applying what we learned about demand in Chapters 5 and 6, supply in Chapters 7 and 8, and the functioning of perfectly competitive markets in Chapter 10, we can provide a fairly comprehensive answer to the first part of this question. This chapter describes major tasks that the market carries out well—some, indeed, with spectacular effectiveness.

We begin by recalling two important themes from Chapters 3 and 4. First, because all resources are *scarce*, a society benefits by using them efficiently. Second, to do so, an economy must somehow coordinate the actions of many individual consumers and producers. Specifically, society must somehow choose:

- How much of each good to produce
- What input quantities to use in the production process
- How to distribute the resulting outputs among consumers

CONTENTS

As suggested by the opening quotation (from someone who was certainly in a position to know), these tasks are exceedingly difficult for a centrally planned economy. That overwhelming difficulty surely contributed to the fall of communism in the late 1980s, and the same difficulty shows up in the few remaining centrally planned economies such as North Korea and Cuba. But for the most part those same tasks appear to be rather simple for a market system. This is why observers with philosophies as diverse as those of Adam Smith and the Russian Revolution's Leon Trotsky have admired the market, and why even countries that maintain very strong central governments have now moved toward market economies.

Do not misinterpret this chapter as a piece of salesmanship. Here, we study the market mechanism at its theoretical very best—when every good is produced under the exacting conditions of perfect competition. Some industries in our economy are reasonable approximations of perfect competition, but many others are as different from this idealized world as the physical world is from a frictionless vacuum tube. Just as the physicist uses the vacuum tube to study the laws of gravity, the economist uses the theoretical concept of a perfectly competitive economy to analyze the virtues of the market. We will spend plenty of time in later chapters studying its vices.

PUZZLE: *Crossing the San Francisco–Oakland Bay Bridge: Is the Price Right?*

In California, the San Francisco–Oakland Bay Bridge is very heavily traveled. The large volume of toll-paying traffic has probably long since paid for the cost of building this bridge, although that is less likely for the nearby San Mateo–Hayward and Dumbarton bridges, which are less crowded. Yet economists argue that the price charged to use the San Francisco–Oakland Bay Bridge should be *higher* than the prices charged for use of the other two bridges. Why does that make sense? Before you have finished reading this chapter, you may even agree with this seemingly unfair proposition.

SOURCE: © Roger Allyn Lee/SuperStock

■ EFFICIENT RESOURCE ALLOCATION AND PRICING

The fundamental fact that inputs are scarce means that there are limits to the volume of goods and services that any economic system can produce. In Chapter 3 we illustrated the concept of scarcity with a graphic device called a production possibilities frontier, which we repeat here for convenience as Figure 1. The frontier, curve *BC*, depicts all combinations of missiles and milk that a hypothetical society can produce given the limited resources at its disposal. For example, if it decides to produce 300 missiles, it will have enough resources left over to produce no more than 500 billion quarts of milk (point *D*). Of course, it is possible, then, to produce *fewer* than 500 billion quarts of milk—at a point, such as *G*, below the production possibilities frontier. But if a society makes this choice, it is wasting some of its potential output; that is, it is not operating efficiently.

In Chapter 3 we defined efficiency rather loosely as the absence of waste. Because this chapter discusses primarily how a competitive market economy allocates resources efficiently, we now need a more precise definition. It is easiest to define an **efficient allocation of resources** by saying what it is not. For example, suppose that we could rearrange our resource allocation so that one group of people would get more of the things it wanted, while no one else would have to give up anything. Then,

An **efficient allocation of resources** is one that takes advantage of every opportunity to make some individuals better off in their own estimation while not worsening the lot of anyone else.

the failure to change the allocation of resources to take advantage of this opportunity would surely be wasteful—that is, inefficient. When society has taken advantage of *every* such opportunity for improvement, so that no such possibilities remain for making some people better off without making others worse off, we say that the allocation of resources is **efficient.**

To see what this implies for our analysis, let us see what an inefficient set of output quantities looks like in our graph. Because point *G* in Figure 1 is below the frontier, there must be points like *E* on the frontier that lie above and to the right of *G*. At point *E*, we get more of *both* outputs without any increase in input, so it is possible to make some people better off without harming anyone. Thus, no point below the frontier can represent an efficient allocation of resources. By contrast, every point on the frontier is efficient because, no matter where on the frontier we start, we cannot get more of one good without giving up some of the other.

This discussion also shows that, normally, many particular allocations of resources will be efficient; in the example, every combination of outputs that is represented by a point on frontier *BC* can be efficient. As a rule, the concept of efficiency cannot tell us which of these efficient allocations is best for society. Yet, as we shall see in this chapter, we can use the concept of efficiency to formulate surprisingly detailed rules to steer us away from situations in which resources would be wasted.

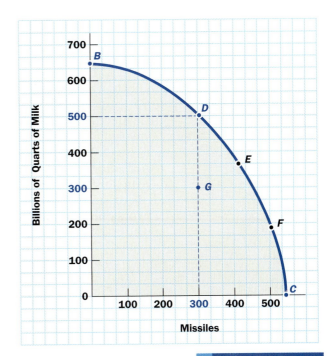

FIGURE 1
Production Possibilities Frontier and Efficiency

FIGURE 2
Toll Bridges of the San Francisco Bay Area

Pricing to Promote Efficiency: An Example

We can use the real example in our opening puzzle about the San Francisco–Oakland Bay Bridge to illustrate the connection between efficiency and the way prices can guide efficient choices. Prices can make all the difference between efficiency and inefficiency. We will see now that the prices (tolls) California transportation authorities charge drivers to use San Francisco Bay area bridges can save some of the time that the drivers spend commuting—that is, it can make the commuting process more efficient. But we also will see that people nonetheless may well reject the efficient solution, and may even have reasonable grounds for doing so.

Figure 2 shows a map of the San Francisco Bay area, featuring the five bridges that serve most of the traffic in and around the bay. A traveler going from a location north of Berkeley (point *A*) to Palo Alto (point *B*) can choose among at least three routes:

Route 1: Over the Richmond–San Rafael Bridge, across the Golden Gate Bridge, through San Francisco, and on southward via Highway 101.

Route 2: Across the bay on the San Francisco–Oakland Bay Bridge and on southward via Highway 101 as before.

Route 3: Down the eastern shore of the bay, across the San Mateo–Hayward Bridge or the Dumbarton Bridge, and then on to Palo Alto (shown in red in Figure 2).

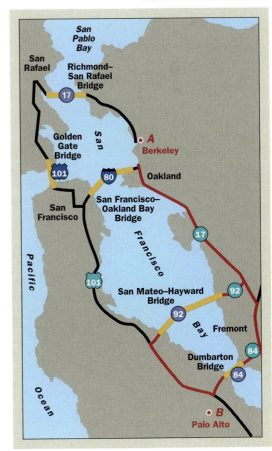

Let's consider which of these three choices uses society's resources—commuter time, gasoline, and so on—most efficiently. The San Francisco–Oakland Bay Bridge is by far the most crowded of the five bridges, carrying approximately 280,000 vehicles per day, followed by the Golden Gate Bridge, which carries about 100,000 per day. The San Mateo–Hayward, Dumbarton, and Richmond–San Rafael bridges carry approximately 90,000, 80,000, and 74,000 vehicles per day, respectively.

To achieve efficiency, any driver who is indifferent about the two routes should take the one using the least crowded bridges. This would help reduce the amount of travel time wasted by the population as a whole. Specifically, in our illustration, Route 1, using the Golden Gate Bridge, is not a socially desirable way for our driver to get to Palo Alto because it adds too many miles to the trip and because it requires two bridge crossings. Route 2, with its use of the San Francisco–Oakland Bay Bridge, is even worse because of the added delays it causes for everyone else. Route 3, for drivers who are indifferent about these options, is the best choice from the viewpoint of the public interest. This does not mean that it is socially efficient to equalize the traffic among the routes, but it certainly would help travelers get where they are going more quickly if transportation authorities could induce some drivers (those who care least about which of the routes they take) to leave the most crowded routes and switch over to some less crowded ones.

Appropriate prices can promote this sort of efficiency in bridge utilization. Specifically, if higher prices (very likely *substantially* higher prices) were charged for drivers to cross the most crowded bridges (on which space is a scarce resource), balanced by lower prices on the uncrowded bridges, then more drivers could be induced to use the uncrowded bridges. This is just the same reasoning that leads economists to advocate low prices for abundant natural resources and high prices for scarce ones.

■ Can Price Increases Ever Serve the Public Interest?

This discussion raises a point that people untrained in economics always find extremely difficult to accept: Low prices may not always serve the public interest! The reason is pretty clear. If a price, such as the toll charged for crossing a crowded bridge or the price of gasoline, is set "too low," then consumers will receive the "wrong" market signals. Low prices will encourage them to crowd the bridge even more or to consume more gasoline, thereby squandering society's precious resources.

A striking historical illustration brings out the importance of this role of prices. In 1834, a professor of economics at the University of Dublin named Mountifort Longfield lectured about the price system. He offered the following example:

> Suppose the crop of potatoes in Ireland was to fall short in some year [by] one-sixth of the usual consumption. If [there were no] increase of price, the whole . . . supply of the year would be exhausted in ten months, and for the remaining two months a scene of misery and famine beyond description would ensue. . . . But when prices [increase] the sufferers [often believe] that it is not caused by scarcity. . . . They suppose that there are provisions enough, but that the distress is caused by the insatiable rapacity of the possessors . . . [and] they have generally succeeded in obtaining laws against [the price increases] . . . which alone can prevent the provisions from being entirely consumed long before a new supply can be obtained.[1]

You may be intrigued to know that this talk was given some ten years before the great potato famine, which caused unspeakable misery and death by starvation and brought many people from Ireland to the United States. The story of the actual potato famine in Ireland is much more complex than Longfield's discussion indicates. Still, the implications of his lecture about the way the price system works are entirely valid.

---

[1] Mountifort Longfield, *Lectures on Political Economy Delivered in Trinity and Michaelmas Terms* (Dublin: W. Curry, Jr., and Company; 1834), pp. 53–56.

Using Economic Principles to Reduce Highway Congestion in Orange County, California

"91 Express Lanes" is a four-lane, ten-mile toll road built in the median of California's crowded Riverside Freeway (State Road 91). Opened in 1995, it was the first variable-priced and fully automated highway in the United States. By varying the price that drivers must pay to use these lanes, the traffic authorities control the congestion on the road and keep the traffic moving. For example, tolls in January 2007 ranged from $1.15 at the most uncongested times (like three o'clock in the morning) all the way up to $9.25 during the worst of the rush hour. Faced with high tolls during commuting hours, some drivers choose not to use the lanes at that time. The drivers who do use the lanes report an average time savings of thirty minutes per trip, with over thirty-two million hours of commuting time saved since 1995.

SOURCE: Orange County Transportation Authority, http://www.91expresslanes.com/learnabout/snapshot.asp.

SOURCE: © copyright 2007, Orange County Transportation Authority, www.OCTA.net.

We can perhaps rephrase Longfield's reasoning more usefully. If the crop fails, potatoes become scarcer. If society is to use its scarce resources efficiently, stretching out the potato supply to last until the next crop arrives, it must cut back on the consumption of potatoes during earlier months—which is just what rising prices will do automatically if free-market mechanisms are allowed to work. However, if the price is held artificially low, consumers will use society's resources inefficiently. In this case, the inefficiency shows up in the form of famine and suffering when people deplete this year's crop months before the next one is harvested.

It is not easy to accept the notion that higher prices can serve the public interest better than lower ones. Politicians who voice this view are in the position of the proverbial parent who, before spanking a child, announces, "This is going to hurt me much more than it hurts you!" Because advocacy of higher prices courts political disaster, the political system often rejects the market solution when resources suddenly become scarcer.

The way that airport officials price landing privileges at crowded airports offers a good example. Airports become particularly congested at "peak hours," just before 9 A.M. and just after 5 P.M. These times are when passengers most often suffer long delays. But many airports continue to charge bargain landing fees throughout the day, even at those crowded hours. That makes it attractive for small corporate jets or other planes carrying only a few passengers to arrive and take off at those hours, worsening the delays. Higher fees for peak-hour landings can discourage such overuse, but they are politically unpopular, and many airports are run by local governments. So we continue to experience late arrivals as a normal feature of air travel. (See "Using Economic Principles to Reduce Highway Congestion in Orange County, California" above for a successful example of pricing to reduce congestion.)

ATTEMPTS TO REPEAL THE LAWS OF SUPPLY AND DEMAND: THE MARKET STRIKES BACK
As we saw in our list of **Ideas for Beyond the Final Exam,** keeping prices low when an increase is appropriate can have serious consequences indeed. we have just observed that it can worsen the effects of shortages of food and other vital goods. We know that inappropriately low prices caused nationwide chaos in gasoline distribution after the sudden decline in Iranian oil exports in 1979. In times of war, constraints on prices have even contributed to the surrender of cities under military siege, deterring those who would otherwise have risked smuggling food supplies through enemy lines. Low prices also have discouraged housing construction in cities where government-imposed upper limits on rents made building construction a losing proposition. Of course, in some cases it is appropriate to resist price increases—when unrestrained monopoly would otherwise succeed in gouging the public, when taxes are imposed on products capriciously and inappropriately, and when rising prices fall so heavily on poor people that rationing becomes the more acceptable option. But before tampering with the market mechanism, we must carefully evaluate the potentially serious and even tragic consequences that artificial restrictions on prices can produce.

SCARCITY AND THE NEED TO COORDINATE ECONOMIC DECISIONS

Efficiency becomes a particularly critical issue when we concern ourselves with the workings of the economy as a whole, rather than with narrower topics such as choosing among bridge routes or deciding on the output of a single firm. We can think of an economy as a complex machine with literally millions of component parts. If this machine is to function efficiently, we must find some way to make the parts work in harmony.

A consumer in Madison, Wisconsin, may decide to purchase two dozen eggs, and on the same day thousands of shoppers throughout the country make similar decisions. None of these purchasers knows or cares about the decisions of the others. Yet scarcity requires that these demands must somehow be coordinated with the production process so that the total quantity of eggs demanded does not exceed the total quantity supplied. Consumers, supermarkets, wholesalers, shippers, and chicken farmers must somehow arrive at mutually consistent decisions; otherwise, the economic process will deteriorate into chaos, as will millions of other such decisions. A machine cannot run with a few missing parts.

In a planned or centrally directed economy, we can easily imagine how such coordination takes place—though implementation is far more difficult than conception. Central planners set production targets for firms and sometimes tell firms how to meet these targets. In extreme cases, consumers may even be told, rather than asked, what they want to consume.

In contrast, a market system uses prices to coordinate economic activity. High prices discourage consumption of the scarcest resources, whereas low prices encourage consumption of comparatively abundant resources. In this way, Adam Smith's invisible hand uses prices to organize the economy's production.

The invisible hand has an astonishing capacity to handle enormously complex coordination problems—even those that remain beyond computer capabilities. Like any mechanism, this one has its imperfections, some of them rather serious. But we should not lose sight of the tremendously demanding task that the market constantly does accomplish—unnoticed, undirected, and, in some respects, amazingly well. Let's look at just how the market goes about coordinating economic activity.

43

"Corporate leaders gather in a field outside Darien, Connecticut, where one of them claims to have seen the invisible hand of the marketplace."

◼ Three Coordination Tasks in the Economy

We recalled at the beginning of this chapter that any economic system, planned or unplanned, must find answers to three basic questions of resource allocation:

- *Output selection.* How much of each commodity should be produced?
- *Production planning.* What quantity of each of the available inputs should be used to produce each good?
- *Distribution.* How should the resulting products be divided among consumers?

These coordination tasks may at first appear to be tailor-made for a regime of government planning like the one that the former Soviet Union once employed. Yet most economists (even, nowadays, those in the formerly centrally planned economies) believe that it is in exactly these tasks that central direction performs most poorly and, paradoxically, the undisciplined free market performs best, even though no one directs its overall activities.

To understand how the unguided market manages the miracle of creating order out of what might otherwise be chaos, let's look at how each of these questions is answered by a system of free and unfettered markets—the method of economic organization that eighteenth-century French economists named **laissez-faire.** Under laissez-faire, the government acts to prevent crime, enforce contracts, and build roads and other types of public works; it does not set prices, however, and interferes as little as possible with the operation of free markets. How does such an unmanaged economy solve the three coordination problems?

Laissez-faire refers to a situation in which there is minimal government interference with the workings of the market system. The term implies that people should be left alone in carrying out their economic affairs.

Output Selection   A free-market system decides what should be produced via what we have called the "law" of supply and demand. Where there is a shortage (that is, where quantity demanded exceeds quantity supplied), the market mechanism pushes the price upward, thereby encouraging more production and less consumption of the commodity that is in short supply. Where a surplus arises (that is, where quantity supplied exceeds quantity demanded), the same mechanism works in reverse: The price falls, discouraging production and stimulating consumption.

As an example, suppose that millions of people wake up one morning with a change in taste, and thereafter want more omelets. As a result, for the moment, the quantity of eggs demanded exceeds the quantity supplied. But, within a few days, the market mechanism swings into action to meet this sudden change in demand. The price of eggs rises, which stimulates egg production. At first, farmers will simply bring more eggs to market by taking them out of storage. Over a somewhat longer time period, chickens that otherwise would have been sold for meat will be kept in the chicken coops laying eggs. Finally, if the high price of eggs persists, farmers will begin to increase their flocks, build more coops, and so on. Thus, a shift in consumer demand leads to a shift in society's resources; more eggs are wanted, so the market mechanism sees to it that more of society's resources are devoted to egg production and marketing.

Similar reactions follow if a technological breakthrough reduces the input quantities needed to produce some item. Electronic calculators are a marvelous example. Calculators used to be so expensive that they could be found only in business firms and scientific laboratories. Then advances in science and engineering reduced their cost dramatically, and the market went to work. With costs sharply reduced, prices fell and the quantity demanded skyrocketed. Electronics firms flocked into the industry to meet this demand, which is to say that more of society's resources were devoted to producing the calculators that were suddenly in such great demand. These examples lead us to conclude that:

Under laissez-faire, the allocation of society's resources among different products depends on consumer preferences (demands) and the production costs of the goods demanded. Prices (and the resulting profitability of the different products) vary so as to bring the quantity of each commodity produced into line with the quantity demanded.

Poland's Transition to a Free-Market Econony

Nearly twenty years have passed since communism collapsed all over Eastern Europe and the former Soviet Union, ending economic central planning and heralding the emergence of a free market in these countries. Nowhere were these changes as dramatic as in Poland, where radical economic reforms constituted no less than "shock therapy."

Poland's transformation into a market economy, though far from complete, has been nearly as drastic as the first post-communist government hoped. Poland had been saddled with a legendarily incompetent, old-fashioned, and badly managed economy, which in its depths managed to run out of things like matches and salt, its paltry living standards bequeathed by a centrally controlled economy. It reached out to the West for help in creating monetary, budget, trade, and legal regimes, and is now one of the most robust economies in central Europe, and, most recently, one of the newest members of the European Union. Poland is the only transition economy that has experienced substantial growth: Real GDP was 30 percent higher in 2002 than it was in 1990. Economic liberalization freed entrepreneurs to sell, within loose limits, anything they want at whatever price they can get. Today, there are more than 1.7 million independent firms and 75 percent of the country's GDP is produced in the private sector (up from just 16 percent in 1989).

Despite all the good news, Poland still has much work to do. Almost 50 percent of working-age individuals are out of work. Many of its publicly owned industries are still backward, business and personal life remains hampered by bureaucratic red tape and corruption, and Polish farming is antiquated and very inefficient—the agricultural sector produces only 3 percent of GDP but engages 20 percent of the population. Indeed, one observer writes that, from the air, it is easy to identify Poland's national boundary, because the patchwork of tiny fields in Poland is in such contrast to the sprawling expanses of arable land in adjacent countries.

SOURCES: Rudolf Herman, "Rural Poland: Ready for the Chop," *Central European Review*, 1, no. 10 (August 1999); Stanislaw Gomulka, "Macroeconomic Policies and Achievements in Transition Economies, 1989–1999," United Nations' Economic Commission for Europe Annual Seminar, Geneva (May 2, 2000); Michael P. Keane and Eswar S. Prasad, "Poland: Inequality, Transfers, and Growth in Transition," *Finance & Development*, 38, no. 1 (March 2001); and Organization for Economic Cooperation and Development, *OECD Economic Surveys 2004: Poland*, Paris: OECD, 2004, http://www.sourceoecd.org.

SOURCE: © Grochowiak Ewa/Corbis Sygma

SOURCE: © Raymond Gehman/Corbis

Notice that no bureaucrat or central planner arranges resource allocation. Instead, an unseen force guides allocation—the lure of profits, which is the invisible hand that guides chicken farmers to increase their flocks when eggs are in greater demand and guides electronics firms to build new factories when the cost of electronic products falls.

Production Planning   Once the market has decided on output composition, the next coordination task is to determine just how those goods will be produced. The production-planning problem includes, among other things, the division of society's scarce inputs among enterprises. Which farm or factory will get how much of which materials? How much of the nation's labor force? Of the produced inputs such as plant and machinery? Such decisions can be crucial. If a factory runs short of an essential input, the entire production process may grind to a halt.

In reality, no economic system can select inputs and outputs separately. The input distribution between the production of cars and the manufacture of washing machines determines the quantities of cars and washing machines that society can obtain. However, it is simpler to think of input and output decisions as if they occur one at a time.

Once again, under laissez-faire it is the price system that apportions labor, fuel, and other inputs among different industries in accord with those industries' requirements. The firm that needs a piece of equipment most urgently will be the last to drop out of the market for that product when prices rise. If millers demand more wheat than is currently available, the price will rise and bring quantity demanded back into line with quantity supplied, always giving priority to those users who are willing to pay the most for grain because it is most valuable to them. Thus:

> In a free market, inputs are assigned to the firms that can make the most productive (most profitable) use of them. Firms that cannot make a sufficiently productive use of some input will be priced out of the market for that item.

This task, which sounds so simple, is actually almost unimaginably complex. It is so complex that it has helped to bring down many centrally planned systems. We will return to it shortly, as an illustration of how difficult it is to replace the market by a central planning bureau. But first let us consider the third of our three coordination problems.

Distribution of Products Among Consumers

The third task of any economy is to decide which consumer gets each of the goods that has been produced. The objective is to distribute the available supplies to match differing consumer preferences as well as possible. Coffee lovers must not be flooded with tea, for example, while tea drinkers are showered with coffee.

The price mechanism solves this problem by assigning the highest prices to the goods in greatest demand and then letting individual consumers pursue their own self-interests. Consider our example of rising egg prices. As eggs become more expensive, people whose craving for omelets is not terribly strong will begin to buy fewer eggs. In effect, the price acts as a rationing device that apportions the available eggs among consumers who are willing to pay the most for them.

Thus, the price mechanism has an important advantage over other rationing devices: It can respond to individual consumer preferences. If a centrally planned economy rations eggs by distributing the same amount to everyone (say, two eggs per week to each person), then everyone ends up with two eggs whether he likes eggs or detests them. The price system, on the other hand, permits each consumer to set her own priorities. Thus:

> **THE TRADE-OFF BETWEEN EFFICIENCY AND EQUALITY** The price system carries out the distribution process by rationing goods on the basis of preferences and relative incomes. Notice the last three words of the previous sentence. The price system does favor the rich, and this is a problem to which market economies must face up.
>
> However, we may still want to think twice before declaring ourselves opposed to the price system. If equality is our goal, might not a more reasonable solution be to use the tax system to equalize incomes and then let the market mechanism distribute goods in accord with preferences? We take this idea up in Chapter 18, in which we discuss tax policy.

IDEAS FOR BEYOND THE FINAL EXAM

We have just seen, in broad outline, how a laissez-faire economy addresses the three basic issues of resource allocation: what to produce, how to produce it, and how to distribute the resulting products. Because it performs these tasks quietly, without central direction, and with no apparent concern for the public interest, many radical critics have predicted that such an unplanned system must degenerate into chaos. Yet unplanned, free-market economies are far from chaotic. Quite ironically, it is the centrally planned economies that have often ended up in economic disarray while the invisible hand seems to go about its business seamlessly. Perhaps the best way to appreciate the free market's accomplishments is to consider how a centrally planned system must cope with the coordination problems we have just outlined. Let us examine just one of them: production planning.

■ Input-Output Analysis: The Near Impossibility of Perfect Central Planning

Of the three coordination tasks of any economy, the assignment of input to specific industries and firms has claimed the most attention of central planners. Why? Because the production processes of the various industries are interdependent. Industry X cannot operate without Industry Y's output, but Industry Y, in turn, needs Industry X's product. The output decisions of the two industries cannot escape this (non-vicious) circle. The entire economy can grind to a halt if planners do not solve such production-planning problems satisfactorily. In recent years, failure to adapt to this kind of interdependence has had dire consequences in North Korea, one of the last remaining centrally planned economies. Breakdowns of key economic activities such as the electric supply grid, transportation systems, and other basic industries have each exacerbated the others' failures and created a terrible cycle of economic disaster, contributing to severe famine and cutting the life expectancy of North Koreans by more than six years in the 1990s.[2]

A simple example will further illustrate the point. Unless economic planners allocate enough gasoline to the trucking industry, products will not get to market. And unless planners allocate enough trucks to haul gasoline to gas stations, drivers will have no fuel. Thus, trucking activity depends on gasoline supply, but gasoline supply also depends on trucking activity. We see again that the decision maker is caught in a circle. Planners must decide both truck and gasoline outputs together, not separately.

Because the output required from any one industry depends on outputs from many other industries, planners can be sure that the production of the various outputs will be suffi-

Input-Output Equations: An Example

Imagine an economy with only three outputs: electricity, steel, and coal. Let E, S, and C represent the respective dollar values of these outputs. Suppose that to produce every dollar's worth of steel, $0.20 worth of electricity is used, so that the total electricity demand of steel manufacturers is 0.2S. Similarly, assume that coal manufacturers use $0.30 of electricity in producing $1 worth of coal, or a total of 0.3C units of electricity. Because E dollars of electricity are produced in total, the amount left over for consumers, after subtracting industrial demands for fuel, will be E (available electricity) minus 0.2S (used in steel production) minus 0.3C (used in coal production). Suppose further that the central planners have decided to supply $15 million worth of electricity to consumers. We end up with the electricity output equation:

$$E - 0.2S - 0.3C = 15$$

The planner will also need such an equation for each of the two other industries, specifying for each of them the net amount intended to be left for consumers after the industrial uses of the product. The full set of equations will then be similar to the following:

$$E - 0.2S - 0.3C = 15$$
$$S - 0.1E - 0.06C = 7$$
$$C - 0.15E - 0.4S = 10$$

These are typical equations in an input-output analysis. In practice, however, such an analysis has dozens and sometimes hundreds of equations with similar numbers of unknowns. This, then, is the logic of input-output analysis.

SOURCE: © Paul Hardy/Corbis

[2] "Life Expectancy Plummets, North Korea Says," *New York Times*, May 16, 2001, http://www.nytimes.com.

cient to meet both consumer and industrial demands only by taking explicit account of this interdependence among industries. If they change the output target for one industry, they must also adjust every other industry's output target. But those changes in turn are likely to require readjustment of the first target change that started it all, leading to still more target change requirements, and so on, indefinitely.

For example, if planners decide to provide consumers with more electricity, then more steel must be produced in order to build more electric generators. Of course, an increase in steel output requires more iron ore to be mined. More mining, in turn, means that still more electricity is needed to light the mines, run the elevators, perhaps operate some of the trains that carry the iron ore, and so on and on. Any single change in production triggers a chain of adjustments throughout the economy that require still more adjustments that lead to still more adjustments.

There is a solution to this seemingly intractable problem, at least in theory. To decide how much of each output an economy must produce, the planner must use statistics to form a set of equations, one equation for each product, and then solve those equations simultaneously. The simultaneous solution process prevents interdependence in the analysis—electricity output depends on steel production, but steel output depends on electricity production—from becoming a vicious circle. The technique used to solve these complicated equations—**input-output analysis**—was invented by the late economist Wassily Leontief, who won the 1973 Nobel Prize for his work.

The equations of input-output analysis illustrated in the box, "Input-Output Equations: An Example," opposite, take explicit account of the interdependence among industries by describing precisely how each industry's target output depends on every other industry's target. Only by solving these equations simultaneously for the required outputs of electricity, steel, coal, and so on can planners ensure a consistent solution that produces the required amounts of each product—including the amount of each product needed to produce every other product.

The illustrative input-output analysis that appears in the box is not provided to make you a master at using the technique yourself. Its real purpose is to help you imagine how very complicated the problems facing central planners can become. Their task, although analogous to the one described in the box, is enormously more complex. In any real economy, the number of commodities is far greater than the three outputs in the example! In the United States, some large manufacturing companies deal in hundreds of thousands of items, and the armed forces keep several million different items in inventory.

Planners must ultimately make calculations for each single item. It is not enough to plan the right number of bolts in total; they must make sure that the required number of each size is produced. (Try putting five million large bolts into five million small nuts.) To be sure that their plans will really work, they need a separate equation for every size of bolt and one for every size and type of nut. But then, to replicate the analysis described in the box, they would have to solve several million equations simultaneously! This task would strain even the most powerful computer's capability, but that is not even the main difficulty.

Worse still is the data problem. Each of our three equations requires three pieces of statistical information, making 3 × 3, or 9 numbers in total. The equation for electricity must indicate how much electricity is needed in steel production, how much in coal production, and how much is demanded by consumers, all on the basis of statistical

> **Input-output analysis** is a mathematical procedure that takes account of the interdependence among the economy's industries and determines the amount of output each industry must provide as inputs to the other industries in the economy.

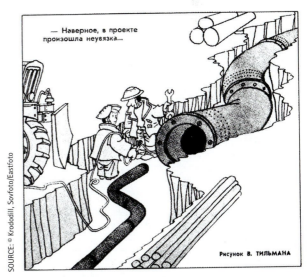

In this cartoon from a Soviet humor magazine, one construction worker comments to another, "A slight mistake in the plans, perhaps." It is interesting that there were many cartoons making fun of the inefficiencies of the Soviet economy in the humor magazines of the USSR before the collapse of communism.

information that is itself subject to error. Therefore, in a five-industry analysis, 5×5, or 25, pieces of data are needed; a 100-industry analysis requires 100×100, or 10,000, numbers, and a million-item input-output study might need 1 trillion pieces of information. Solving the data-gathering problems is no easy task, to put it mildly. Still other complications arise, but we have seen enough to conclude that:

> A full, rigorous central-planning solution to the production problem is a tremendous task, requiring an overwhelming quantity of information and some incredibly difficult calculations. Yet this very complex job is carried out automatically and unobtrusively by the price mechanism in a free-market economy.

◼ Which Buyers and Which Sellers Get Priority?

Because the supplies of all commodities are limited, some potential customers of a product will end up with none of it. And because demand is not infinite, some potential suppliers of a commodity will find no market available for them. So, which consumers get the scarce commodity, and which firms get to supply the goods? Again, the price mechanism comes to the rescue.

> Other things being equal, the price mechanism ensures that those consumers who want a scarce commodity most will receive it, and that those sellers who can supply it most efficiently will get to supply the commodity.

To illustrate, let's look at Figure 3, an ordinary supply-demand graph. For simplicity, suppose we are dealing here with a commodity such as a best-selling novel. We assume also that no one buys more than one copy of the book. The demand curve, *DD*, represents the preferences of 6,000 potential customers with widely differing preferences. The first 1,000 of them are willing to pay as much as $70 for the book, as shown by point *A* on the demand curve (though they would, of course, prefer to pay less). Point *B* shows a second group of 1,000 buyers who will purchase the book at a price of $60, but refuse to spend $70 on it (because they care less about the book than the point *A* consumers). Similarly, point *C* represents the demand of a third group of consumers, to whom the book is even less important, so that they are willing to spend only $50 for a copy. And points *E*, *F*, and *G* represent sets of consumers with successively lower desires for the book, until at point *G*, consumers are only willing to pay $20 for the book.

With *SS* as the supply curve, the equilibrium point is *E*, where *SS* and *DD* intersect. Under perfect competition, the market price of the book will be $40. Buyers at point *A*, to whom the book is worth $70, will be delighted to buy it for only $40. Similarly, buyers at points *B*, *C*, and *E* will also buy the book. But the consumers at points *F* and *G*, to whom the book is worth less than $40, will not buy the book. We can see in this example that the book will go to the consumers who value it most (in terms of money), and only those who value it least will be deprived of it.

> The price mechanism always ranks potential consumers of a good in the order of the intensity of their preference for the good, as indicated by the amount they are willing to spend for it.

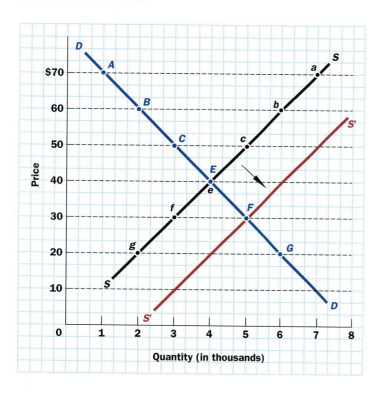

FIGURE 3

Supply-Demand Graph Showing That Price Excludes Only Buyers and Sellers Who Care the Least

Quantity (in thousands)

The price system's priority to those consumers who assign most importance to a good goes one step further. Suppose that supply increases, with the supply curve shifting to the right, from SS to S'S' in the figure. Which consumers will get the increased quantity supplied? Answer: Of those consumers in the group of people who were previously denied the commodity, those who want it most intensely will acquire the product. In the graph, the shift in supply moves the equilibrium point from E to F, so point F consumers will now be included in the group of buyers of the book (along with point A, B, C, and E consumers), but the point G consumers still do not purchase the book. The book is worth more to point F consumers ($30) than it is to point G consumers, who value it only at $20.

The price system seems to set the right priorities in deciding which prospective consumers of some specific good do receive some of it and which do not. Only one major imperfection arises in this argument, to which we will return in a moment.

First, however, let's look at Figure 3 again, this time from the supplying firm's point of view. Assume that SS is the long-run industry supply curve. Point G on this curve represents the amount that the industry will supply if the price is $20—that is, the amount that will be supplied by firms whose average cost is no higher than $20, so that the price will cover their cost. Similarly, point F represents the output of all firms whose average cost is no higher than $30, so that the group of suppliers now includes some firms that are less efficient (they have higher average cost) than those at point g. At point e, some of the suppliers will have average costs of $40, but none of the suppliers will have an average cost higher than that level. Using the same reasoning, as we move farther along SS to points C, B, and A, increasingly inefficient firms will be included among the suppliers.

Now we examine the supply-demand equilibrium point e, at which price is $40. Which suppliers will be able to market their products at this point? Answer: Those at points g, f, and e, but not firms at points c, b, and a, because no firm in the last three groups can cover its costs at the equilibrium price. Once again, the price mechanism does its job. It ranks firms in order of their efficiency, as measured by long-run average costs, and brings business to the more efficient firms, leaving out the least efficient potential suppliers.

This example illustrates yet another of the many desirable features of the price mechanism. But there is one fly in the ointment—at least on the demand side of the story. We saw that consumers in group G were likely to be denied the scarce commodity we are discussing, because they wanted it less than the other consumers. Group G consumers were willing to spend only $20 for the book, whereas the other consumers were willing to spend more for it. But what if some consumers in group G want the book very badly, but are also very poor? This is an important question—one we will encounter again and again. The price mechanism is like a democracy, but one in which the rule is not "one person, one vote," but rather, "one dollar, one vote." In other words, under the price mechanism rich consumers' preferences get much more attention than poor consumers' desires do.

■ HOW PERFECT COMPETITION ACHIEVES EFFICIENCY: A GRAPHIC ANALYSIS

We have indicated how the market mechanism solves the three basic coordination problems of any economy—what to produce, how to produce it, and how to distribute the goods to consumers. Also, we have suggested that these same tasks pose almost insurmountable difficulties for central planners. One critical question remains: Is the allocation of resources that the market mechanism selects *efficient*, according to the precise definition of efficiency presented at the start of this chapter? The answer, under the idealized circumstances of perfect competition, is *yes*. And a simple supply-and-demand diagram can be used to give us an intuitive view of why that is so.

Focusing on the market for a single commodity, let us ask whether either an increase or a decrease in the amount of output produced by the market mechanism can yield a greater total net benefit to consumers and producers. Suppose the current output level of swimming lessons in a swimming pool (number of people being taught) is 20 and the total net benefit to all involved in the activity can somehow be evaluated in money terms at $500 per week. Then, if any other number of students yields a total net benefit less than $500, clearly we have reason to conclude that 20 students is the optimum. We will show that, in equilibrium under perfect competition, the market unerringly and automatically will always drive toward an equilibrium exactly at that optimal output level, without any central direction, or explicit guidance, or planning by anyone. That is one of the remarkable accomplishments of the market mechanism.

To show this, let's begin by defining consumer and producer benefits sufficiently precisely so we can measure them. In Chapter 5 (page 91), we already have encountered the concept we need for the consumer benefits: consumer's surplus. And we will introduce a perfectly analogous concept, called producer's surplus, for the other side of the market. Suppose Anne would be willing to purchase a full week of swimming lessons at any price up to $140, but when she arrives at the gym she sees that the lessons are available for sale at a price of $90. Because swimming lessons are worth $140 to her, and she only has to spend $90 to obtain them, the purchase provides her with a net benefit of $140 − $90 = $50. If the lessons had been priced at $140, the result of the purchase would have been a wash—she would have given up $140 and received in exchange a service worth exactly $140 to her. But because the market price happens to be $90, she obtains a net gain worth $50 to her—a surplus—from the transaction. So, as we did in Chapter 5, we define:

> The **consumer's surplus** from a purchase is equal to the difference between the maximum amount the consumer would be willing, if necessary, to pay for the item bought, and the price that the market actually charges. In a purchase by a rational consumer, the surplus will never be a negative number, because if the price is higher than the maximum amount the potential purchaser is willing to pay, he will simply refuse to buy it.

Producer's surplus is defined exactly analogously. If Ben, a swimming instructor, is willing to provide a week of lessons at any price from $30 up, but the market price happens to be $90, he receives a $60 surplus from the transaction—and is delighted to make such a sale. So we have the definition:

> The **producer's surplus** from a sale is the difference between the market price of the item sold and the lowest price at which the supplier would be willing to provide the item.

Now that we know how the two surpluses are defined and how to measure them, our objective is to see how the total surplus to all buyers and sellers in a market is affected by the quantity produced and sold in the market. We will demonstrate a striking result: that at the perfectly competitive market output level—the output level at which the market supply and demand curves intercept—the total surplus for all participants is as large as possible. To do this, we must turn to our familiar supply-demand analysis, and use it to show explicitly the roles played by Anne, Ben, and the others involved in the market.

We begin with a table that assumes for simplicity that there are five potential buyers (Anne, Charles, Elaine, etc.) and five potential competing sellers (Ben, Debbie, etc.) in the market for swimming lessons. We see in Table 1 that at the weekly fee of $90 (third column in the table), Anne, to whom a week's lessons are worth $140 (first column) obtains a consumer's surplus of $50 = $140 − $90.

Similarly, at that price, Charles obtains a surplus of just $30. The consumer's surplus for these two customers is shown by the two light blue areas below the blue demand curve DD in Figure 4(a), corresponding to their purchases (two sets of lessons). For example, the left-most blue bar has its bottom at the price of $90 and its top at the $140 that the lessons are worth to Anne, so that the area of Anne's bar is equal to her surplus, $140 − $90 = 50.

The **consumer's surplus** from a purchase is equal to the difference between the maximum amount the consumer would be willing, if necessary, to pay for the item bought, and the price that the market actually charges.

The **producer's surplus** from a sale is the difference between the market price of the item sold and the lowest price at which the supplier would be willing to provide the item.

TABLE 1

Consumer's and Producer's Surplus in the Swimming Lesson Market (dollars)

Students	(1) Student's Acceptable Maximum Price	(2) Individual Consumer's Surplus	(3) Actual Price	(4) Cumulative Total Surplus	(5) Individual Producer's Surplus	(6) Instructor's Acceptable Minimum Price	Instructors
Anne	$140	$50	$90	$110 = 50 + 60	$60	$ 30	Ben
Charles	120	30	90	180 = 110 + 30 + 40	40	50	Debbie
Elaine	110	20	90	220	20	70	Frank
George	90	0	90	220	0	90	Harriet
Irene	80	−10	90	180	−30	120	Jack

Similarly, Table 1 shows the producer's surpluses that can be earned by the different potential instructors. For example, it shows that the $90 fee gives Ben a surplus of $60 = $90 − $30, because he would be willing to give the lessons even if the fee were as low as $30. In the same way, we see that Debbie obtains a surplus of $40. These two producers' surpluses are shown in Figure 4(a) by the areas of the first two light pink bars—the areas between the red supply curve SS and the $90 price line for those two sales. We also note that if both Anne and Charles received lessons, and both Ben and Debbie gave lessons, so that two sets of lessons were provided, the total surplus created by the market would be the sum of their four individual surpluses, $50 + 30 + 60 + 40 = $180—which is the second entry in the fourth column in the table. This is also shown by the area DRTUVS in Figure 4(a) that lies between the blue demand curve and the red supply curve when only two sets of lessons are provided.

But comparison of Figure 4(a) and Figure 4(b) shows us clearly that two lessons are not enough to make the total surplus generated by the market as large as possible. Specifically, if Elaine also takes lessons, and Frank provides them, this third transaction generates an additional consumer's surplus of $20 and an additional producer's surplus of $20, raising the total to $220. This larger total is shown by summing all the light blue and light pink areas between the demand and supply curves in Figure 4 (b). One more set of lessons, the number at which the supply and demand curves intersect at PP, contributes no net gain in surplus, because George and Harriet value the lessons at exactly the prevailing price of $90. In buying and selling the service, these

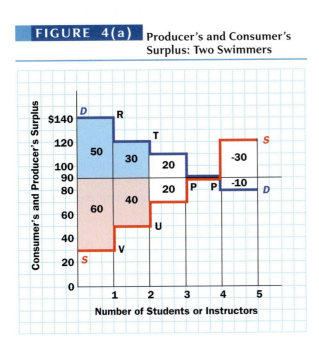

FIGURE 4(a) Producer's and Consumer's Surplus: Two Swimmers

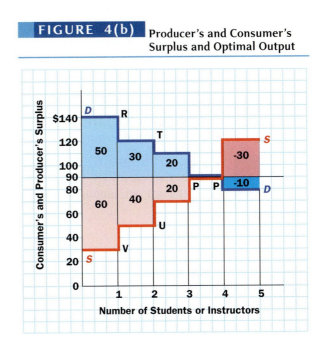

FIGURE 4(b) Producer's and Consumer's Surplus and Optimal Output

two people exchange money and services that are worth exactly the same to them. Increasing output further, by raising it to a fifth set of lessons will actually reduce total surplus, because Irene, the potential student, values the lessons at less than their $90 price while Jack, the potential instructor, considers his work worth $120. If Jack were to provide lessons to Irene, they both would obtain *negative* surpluses, represented by the dark pink and dark blue bars toward the right of the graph. These negative surpluses bring the total surplus down from $220 to $180 (the last two entries in column 4 of the table), clearly a net loss to the economy.

Now we come to the payoff from all this reasoning. Looking at Figure 4(a), we see that if total output stops short of the intersection of the supply and demand curve (interval PP), the light pink and blue areas will not be as large as possible. Similarly, if more than that quantity of swimming lessons is supplied, total surplus is decreased (Figure 4(b)). Only when the output quantity corresponds to the intersection of the supply and demand curves is the net surplus earned by both buyers and sellers as large as possible. Three conclusions follow:

1. Because under perfect competition the equilibrium output will be at the intersection of the supply and demand curves, a regime of perfect competition will select output levels that are optimal in terms of the public interest. They yield as large a sum of consumer's and producer's surpluses as possible.

2. If some influence such as monopoly forces output to be smaller (because price is higher) than that under perfect competition, the public interest will be damaged because the quantity of resources allocated to this market will be less than optimal.

3. If something like a government tax reduction induces suppliers to produce an output larger than the competitive level, that will also be a misallocation of resources damaging to the public welfare.

■ HOW PERFECT COMPETITION ACHIEVES OPTIMAL OUTPUT: MARGINAL ANALYSIS

There is a second way to look at the optimality of outputs under perfect competition's idealized circumstances, this time relating the discussion directly to the definition of efficiency given at the beginning of this chapter. Because a detailed proof of this assertion for all three coordination tasks is long and time-consuming, we will present the proof only for the task we have just been considering—*output selection*. We will show that, at least in theory, perfect competition does guarantee efficiency in determining the relative quantities of the different commodities that the economy produces.

The proof comes in two steps. First, we derive a criterion for efficient output selection—that is, a test that tells us whether production is being carried out efficiently. Second, we show that the prices that emerge from the market mechanism under perfect competition automatically pass this test.

Step 1: Rule for Efficient Output Selection   We begin by stating the rule for efficient output selection:

IDEAS FOR BEYOND THE FINAL EXAM

THE IMPORTANCE OF THINKING AT THE MARGIN *Marginal Analysis:* **Efficiency in the choice of output quantities requires that, for each of the economy's outputs, the marginal cost (MC) of the last unit produced be equal to the marginal utility (MU) of the last unit consumed.[3] In symbols:**

$$MC = MU$$

This rule is yet another example of the basic principle of marginal analysis that we learned in Chapter 8.

---

[3] Recall from Chapter 5 that we measure marginal utility in money terms—that is, the amount of money that a consumer is willing to give up for an additional unit of the commodity. Economists usually call this the marginal rate of substitution between the commodity and money.

> The efficient decision about output quantities is the one that maximizes the total benefit (total utility) to society, minus the cost to society of producing the output quantities that are chosen. In other words, the goal is to maximize the surplus that society gains—total utility minus total cost. But, as we saw in Chapter 8, to maximize the difference between total utility and total cost, we must find the outputs that equalize the corresponding marginal figures (marginal utility and marginal cost), as the preceding efficiency rule tells us.

An example will help us to see explicitly why resource allocation must satisfy this rule to be deemed efficient. Suppose that the marginal utility of an additional pound of beef to consumers is $8, but its marginal cost is only $5. Then the value of the resources that would have to be used up to produce one more pound of beef (its MC) would be $3 less than the money value that consumers would willingly pay for that additional pound (its MU). By expanding the output of beef by one pound, society could get more (in MU) out of the economic production process than it was putting in (in MC). We know that the output at which MU exceeds MC cannot be optimal, because society would be better off with an increase in that output level. The opposite is true if the MC of beef exceeds the MU of beef.

Thus, we have shown that, if any product's MU is not equal to MC—whether MU exceeds MC or MC exceeds MU—the economy must be wasting an opportunity to achieve a net improvement in consumers' welfare. This is exactly what we mean by saying society is using resources inefficiently. Just as was true at point G in Figure 1, if MC does not equal MU for some commodity, it is possible to rearrange production to make some people better off while harming no one else. It follows, then, that efficient output choice occurs only when MC equals MU for every good.[4]

Step 2: The Price System's Critical Role

Next, we must show that under perfect competition, the price system automatically leads buyers and sellers to behave in a way that equalizes MU and MC.

To see this, recall from Chapter 10 that under perfect competition it is most profitable for each beef-producing firm to produce the quantity at which the marginal cost equals the price (P) of beef:

$$MC = P$$

This must be so because, if the marginal cost of beef were less than the price, the farmer could add to his profits by increasing the size of the herd (or the amount of grain fed to the animals). The reverse would be true if the marginal cost of beef were greater than its price. Thus, under perfect competition, the lure of profits leads each producer of beef (and of every other product) to supply the quantity that makes $MC = P$.

We also learned, in Chapter 5, that each consumer will purchase the quantity of beef at which the marginal utility of beef in money terms equals the price of beef:

$$MU = P$$

If consumers did not do so, either an increase or a decrease in their beef purchases would leave them better off.

Putting these last two equations together, we see that the invisible hand enforces the following string of equalities:

$$MC = P = MU$$

But if the MC of beef and the MU of beef both equal the same price, P, then they must equal each other. That is, it must be true that the quantity of beef produced and consumed in a perfectly competitive market satisfies the equation:

$$MC = MU$$

---

[4] *Warning:* As described in Chapter 15, markets sometimes perform imperfectly because the decision maker faces a different marginal cost than the marginal cost to society. This situation occurs when the individual who creates the cost can make someone else bear the burden. Consider an example: Firm X's production causes pollution emissions that increase nearby households' laundry bills. In such a case, Firm X will ignore this cost and produce inefficiently large outputs and emissions. We study such problems, called externalities, in Chapters 15 and 17.

This is precisely our rule for efficient output selection. Because the same must be true of every other product supplied by a competitive industry:

Under perfect competition, producers and consumers will make uncoordinated decisions that we can expect automatically (and amazingly) to produce exactly the quantity of each good that satisfies the MC = MU rule for efficiency. That is, under the idealized conditions of perfect competition, the market mechanism, without any government intervention and without anyone else directing it or planning for it, is capable of allocating society's scarce resources efficiently.

The Invisible Hand at Work

This is truly an extraordinary result. How can the price mechanism automatically satisfy all of the exacting requirements for efficiency (that marginal utility equals marginal cost for each and every commodity)—requirements that no central planner can hope to handle because of the masses of statistics and the enormous calculations they entail? This seems analogous to a magician suddenly pulling a rabbit out of a hat!

But, as always, rabbits come out of hats only if they were hidden there in the first place. What really is the mechanism by which our act of magic works? The secret is that the price system lets consumers and producers pursue their own best interests—something they are probably very good at doing. Prices are the dollar costs of commodities to consumers, so in pursuing their own best interests, consumers will buy the commodities that give them the most satisfaction per dollar. Under perfect competition, the price the consumer pays is also equal to MC, because the market's incentives lead each supplier to supply that amount at which this is true.

Because $P = MC$ measures the resource cost (in every firm) of producing one more unit of the good, this means that when consumers buy the commodities that give them the most satisfaction for *their money*, they will automatically have chosen the set of purchases that yields the most satisfaction obtainable from the resources used up in producing those purchases. In other words, the market mechanism leads consumers to squeeze the greatest possible benefit out of the social resources used up in making the goods and services they buy. So, if resources are priced appropriately ($P = MC$), when consumers make the best use of their money, they must also be making the best use of society's resources. That is the way the market mechanism ensures economic efficiency.

When all prices are set equal to marginal costs, the price system gives correct cost signals to consumers. It has set prices at levels that induce consumers to use society's resources with the same care they devote to watching their own money, because the money cost of a good to consumers has been set equal to the opportunity cost of the good to society. A perfectly analogous explanation applies to the decisions of producers.

This is the magic of the invisible hand. Unlike central planners, consumers need not know how difficult it is to manufacture a certain product or how scarce the inputs required by the production process are. Everything consumers need to know about supply in making their decisions is embodied in the market price, which, under perfect competition, accurately reflects marginal costs. Similarly, producers do not need to know anything about the psychology and tastes of their individual customers— price movements tell them all they need to know when consumer preferences change.

Other Roles of Prices: Income Distribution and Fairness

So far we have stressed the role of prices that economists emphasize most: Prices guide resource allocation. But prices also command the spotlight in another role: Prices influence the distribution of income between buyers and sellers. For example, high rents often make tenants poorer and landlords richer.

This rather obvious role of prices draws the most attention from the public, politicians, and regulators, and we should not lose sight of it.[5] Markets serve only those demands that are backed up by consumers' desire and *ability to pay*. The market system may do well in serving poor families, because it gives them more food and clothing than a less efficient economy would provide. But the market system offers far more to wealthy families. Many people think that such an arrangement represents a great injustice, however efficient it may be.

Often, people oppose economists' recommendations for improving the economy's efficiency on the grounds that these proposals are *unfair*. For example, economists frequently advocate higher prices for transportation facilities at the times of day when the facilities are most crowded. Economists propose a pricing arrangement called "peak, off-peak pricing" under which prices for public transportation are higher during rush hours than during other hours.

The rationale for this proposal should be clear from our discussion of efficiency. A seat on a train is a much scarcer resource during rush hours than it is during other times of the day when the trains run fairly empty. Thus, according to the principles of efficiency outlined in this chapter, seats should be more expensive during rush hours to discourage those consumers with no set schedule from riding the trains during peak periods. The same notion applies to other services. Charges for long-distance telephone calls made at night are sometimes lower than those in the daytime. And in some places, electricity is cheaper at night, when demand does not strain the supplier's generating capacity.

Yet the proposal that transportation authorities should charge higher fares for public transportation during peak hours—say, from 8:00 A.M. to 9:30 A.M. and from 4:30 P.M. to 6:00 P.M.—often runs into stiff opposition. Opponents say that most of the burden of such higher fares will fall on lower-income working people who have no choice about the timing of their trips. For example, a survey in Great Britain of economists and members of Parliament found that, while high peak-period fares were favored by 88 percent of the economists, only 35 percent of the Conservative Party members of Parliament and just 19 percent of the Labour Party members of Parliament approved of this arrangement (see Table 2). We may surmise that these members of the British Parliament reflected the views of the public more accurately than did the economists. In this case, people simply found the efficient solution unfair, and so they refused to adopt it.

TABLE 2			
Replies to a Questionnaire			
Question: To make the most efficient use of a city's resources, how should subway and bus fares vary during the day?	Economists	Conservative Party Members of Parliament	Labour Party Members of Parliament
a. They should be relatively low during rush hour to transport as many people as possible at lower costs.	1%	0%	40%
b. They should be the same at all times to avoid making travelers alter their schedules because of price differences.	4	60	39
c. They should be relatively high during rush hour to minimize the amount of equipment needed to transport the daily travelers.	88	35	19
d. Impossible to answer on the data and alternatives given.	7	5	2

SOURCE: Excerpt from Samuel Brittan, *Is There an Economic Consensus?* p. 93. Copyright © 1973. Reproduced by permission of Samuel Brittan.

---

[5] Income distribution is the subject of Part V.

POLICY DEBATE

User Charges for Public Facilities

At a time when budget cutting is the way to popularity for a politician, the notion of charging users for the services that government once gave away for free is under debate. Economists have often advocated such charges for the use of roads, bridges, museums, educational facilities, and the like. Of course, it's true that if the services are provided for "free," the public has to pay for them anyway—just more indirectly through taxes. But if people are asked to pay directly for such services, it can make a big difference.

As an example, let's say a road is financed out of general taxes. In this circumstance, it does not matter how many times Sabrina, the owner of an independent trucking firm, uses the road. She pays the same amount whether she uses it twice a year or every day. But if Sabrina has to pay a toll every time she uses the road, she will have a strong incentive to avoid unnecessary use. That is why advocates of pricing to promote economic efficiency propose more substantial *user charges,* not only for roads and bridges but also for admission to national parks, for the use of publicly owned grazing lands, and for the use of the television and radio spectrums by broadcasters.

Opponents of user charges contend that these fees are unfair to poor people. Besides, it is argued, the use of public facilities such as libraries, museums, and schools should be encouraged rather than impeded by user charges. For instance, in New York there is no charge to cross the three deteriorating bridges that connect Brook-

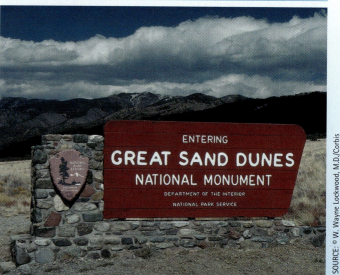

SOURCE: © W. Wayne Lockwood, M.D./Corbis

lyn and Queens with Manhattan. But each time user charges are proposed, they are met with the cry, "Should I have to pay an admission fee into my own city?!"

■ Yet Another Free-Market Achievement: Growth Versus Efficiency

This chapter has followed the economist's standard approach in evaluating the market mechanism. Economists usually stress efficiency in resource allocation and the role of the market in ensuring such efficiency—the division of resources among alternative uses in a way that misses no opportunity to increase consumer net benefits.

Some other admirers of the market do not place their main emphasis on the free market's efficiency accomplishments. A very diverse group, including businesspeople, politicians, economic historians, leaders in formerly communist economies such as Vladimir Putin, and even Marxists, appreciate the market primarily for a very different reason—the extraordinary growth in output that market economies have achieved and the historically unprecedented abundance that has resulted.

Historians have estimated that before the arrival of the capitalistic market mechanism, output per person grew with glacial slowness. But today, an average American can afford more than *seven* times the quantity of goods and services that an individual's income bought one hundred years ago. Undoubtedly, the failure to achieve substantial growth and prosperity (and not just inefficiencies in allocating goods) helped to bring about the fall of communism in eastern Europe. Even Karl Marx stressed this role of the market mechanism, waxing lyrical in his description of its accomplishments. Chapter 16 will return to this subject, indicating what a free-market economy can accomplish in terms of economic growth.

San Francisco Bridge Pricing Revisited

Our earlier example of the San Francisco Bay area bridges also raises fairness issues. Recall that we concluded from our analysis that efficient bridge use requires higher tolls on the more crowded bridges. Because this principle seems so clear and rational, it is surprising to find out what the actual bridge tolls are: $4 on all bridges, even though their average daily traffic varies, with the San Francisco–Oakland Bay Bridge by far the most crowded.[6]

From an efficiency point of view, this uniform toll seems irrational, with the relatively uncrowded bridges assigned the same toll as the most crowded bridge. The explanation lies in some widely held notions of fairness.

Many people feel that it is fair for those who travel on a particular bridge to pay for its costs. In this view, it would be unjust for those who use the crowded San Francisco–Oakland Bay Bridge to pay more in order to subsidize the relatively uncrowded Dumbarton Bridge. Naturally, a heavily traveled bridge earns more toll payments and so recoups its building, maintenance, and operating costs more quickly. On the other hand, it is felt that the relatively few users of a less crowded bridge should make a fair contribution toward its costs.

An economically irrational pattern of tolls does nothing to ease congestion on overcrowded bridges, and thereby contributes to inefficiency. But one cannot legitimately conclude that advocates of such prices are "stupid." Whether this pattern of tolls is or is not desirable must be decided, at least partly, on the basis of the public's sense of what constitutes fairness and justice in pricing. It also depends on the amount that people are willing to pay in terms of delays, inconvenience, and other inefficiencies to avoid apparent injustices.

Economics alone cannot decide the appropriate trade-off between fairness and efficiency. It cannot even pretend to judge which pricing arrangements are fair and which are unfair. But it can and should indicate whether a particular pricing decision, proposed because it is considered fair, will impose heavy inefficiency costs on the community. Economic analysis also can and should indicate how to appraise these costs, so that the issues can be evaluated on a rational, factual basis.

■ TOWARD ASSESSMENT OF THE PRICE MECHANISM

We do not mean to imply in our discussion of the case for free markets that the free-enterprise system is an ideal of perfection, without flaw or room for improvement. In fact, it has a number of serious shortcomings that we will explore in subsequent chapters. But recognition of these imperfections should not conceal the price mechanism's enormous accomplishments.

We have shown that, under the proper circumstances, prices are capable of meeting the most exacting requirements of allocative efficiency—requirements that go well beyond any central planning bureau's capacities. Even centrally planned economies use the price mechanism to carry out considerable portions of the task of allocation, most notably in the distribution of consumer goods. No one has invented an instrument for directing the economy that can replace the price mechanism, which no one ever designed or planned for, but which simply grew by itself, a child of the processes of history.

---

[6] Toll schedules and traffic volumes for the San Francisco Bay area bridges from California Department of Transportation, http://www.dot.ca.gov and Golden Gate Bridge Highway and Transportation District, http://www.goldengate.org and http://www.answers.com. Note that nowadays these bridge authorities do encourage efficiency by providing faster carpool lanes for buses and cars with three or more passengers: these categories of vehicle cross the five bridges free of charge during weekday rush hours. And the introduction of an electronic toll collection system (FasTrak) that can process almost three times as many vehicles per hour as the manual collection system has significantly improved efficiency and reduced congestion. Drivers who do not utilize FasTrak on the Golden Gate Bridge are charged an extra dollar to cross that bridge.

SUMMARY

1. Economists consider an **allocation of resources** to be inefficient if it wastes opportunities to change the use of the economy's resources in any way that makes at least some consumers better off without harming anyone. Resource allocation is considered efficient if there are no such wasted opportunities.

2. Under perfect competition, the free-market mechanism adjusts prices so that the resulting resource allocation is efficient. It induces firms to buy and use inputs in ways that yield the most valuable outputs per unit of input. It distributes products among consumers in ways that match individual preferences. Finally, it produces commodities whose value to consumers exceeds the cost of producing them and assigns the task of production to the potential suppliers who can produce most efficiently.

3. Resource allocation involves three basic coordination tasks:

   a. How much of each good to produce

   b. What quantities of available inputs to use in producing the different goods

   c. How to distribute the goods among different consumers

4. An optimal allocation of society's resources among the commodities the economy produces and consumes is one that maximizes the sum of the consumers' and producers' surpluses derived by everyone in the community. Perfectly competitive equilibrium achieves this goal, at least in theory.

5. Efficient decisions about what goods to produce require that the marginal cost (MC) of producing each good be equal to its marginal utility (MU) to consumers. If the MC of any good differs from its MU, then society can improve resource allocation by changing the amounts produced.

6. Because the market system induces firms to set MC equal to price, and it induces consumers to set MU equal to price, it automatically guarantees satisfaction of the condition that MC should equal MU.

7. Improvements in efficiency occasionally require some prices to increase so as to stimulate supply or to prevent waste in consumption. This is why price increases can sometimes be beneficial to consumers.

8. In addition to resource allocation, prices influence income distribution between buyers and sellers.

9. The price mechanism can be criticized on the ground that it is unfair because it accords wealthy consumers preferential treatment.

KEY TERMS

Efficient allocation of resources   288

Laissez-faire   293

Input–output analysis   297

Consumer's surplus   300

Producer's surplus   300

TEST YOURSELF

1. What possible social advantages of price increases arise in the following cases?

   a. Charging higher prices for electrical power on very hot days when many people use air conditioners

   b. Raising water prices in drought-stricken areas

2. In the discussion of Figure 3 on page 298, there is a set of numbers indicating how much different buyers would be willing to pay for a book. Construct a table for these buyers like the first three columns in Table 1, indicating their consumer's surpluses.

3. As in the previous question, use the numbers in Figure 3 to determine the producer's surpluses and complete your table to correspond to the remaining columns of Table 1.

4. Suppose that a given set of resources can be used to make either handbags or wallets. The MC of a handbag is $19 and the MC of a wallet is $10. If the MU of a wallet is $10 and the MU of a handbag is $30, what can be done to improve resource allocation? What can you say about the gain to consumers?

DISCUSSION QUESTIONS

1. Discuss the fairness of the two proposals included in Test Yourself Question 1.

2. Using the concepts of marginal cost (MC) and marginal utility (MU), discuss the nature of the inefficiency in each of the following cases:

   a. An arrangement that offers relatively little coffee and much tea to people who prefer coffee and does the reverse for tea lovers

   b. An arrangement in which skilled mechanics are assigned to ditch digging and unskilled laborers to repairing cars

   c. An arrangement that produces a large quantity of trucks and few cars, assuming that both cost about the same amount to produce and to run, but that most people in the community prefer cars to trucks

3. In reality, which of the following circumstances might give rise to each of the situations described in Discussion Question 2 above?

   a. Regulation of output quantities by a government

   b. Rationing of commodities

   c. Assignment of soldiers to different jobs in an army

4. We have said that the economy's three coordination tasks are output selection, production planning, and product distribution. Which of these is done badly in the cases described in Discussion Questions 2a, 2b, and 2c?

5. In a free market, how will the price mechanism deal with each of the inefficiencies described in Discussion Question 2?

6. In the early months after the end of communism in Eastern Europe, there seems to have been an almost superstitious belief that the free market could solve all problems. What sorts of problems do you think the leaders and the citizens of those countries had in mind? Which of those problems is there good reason to believe the market mechanism actually can deal with effectively? What disappointments and sources of disillusionment should have been expected? Which disappointments have resulted?

15

THE SHORTCOMINGS OF FREE MARKETS

When she was good
She was very, very good,
But when she was bad
She was horrid.

HENRY WADSWORTH LONGFELLOW

W hat does the market do well, and what does it do poorly? These questions are the focus of our microeconomic analysis, and we are well on our way toward finding their answers. In Chapters 10 and 14, we explained the workings of Adam Smith's invisible hand, the instrument by which a perfectly competitive economy allocates resources efficiently without any guidance from government. Of course, that perfectly competitive model is just a theoretical ideal, but our observations of the real world confirm the extraordinary accomplishments of the market mechanism. Free-market economies have achieved levels of output, productive efficiency, variety in available consumer goods, and general prosperity that are unprecedented in history—and are now the envy of the formerly planned economies. We will discuss that phenomenal record of production and growth in detail in Chapter 16.

Yet the market mechanism has its weaknesses. In Chapters 11 and 12, we examined one of these defects—the free market's vulnerability to exploitation by large and powerful business firms, which can lead to both an inappropriate concentration of wealth and resource misallocation. Now we take a more comprehensive view of market failures and study some of the steps that can be taken to remedy them. Clearly, the market does not do everything we want it to do. Amid the vast outpouring of products in our economy, we also find appalling poverty, cities choked by traffic and pollution, and hospitals, educational institutions, and artistic organizations in serious financial trouble. Although our economy produces an overwhelming abundance of material wealth, it seems far less capable of reducing social ills and environmental damage. We will examine the reasons for these failings and indicate why the price system *by itself* may not be able to deal with them.

Our recognition of the market's limitations does not imply that the public interest calls for abandoning the market. As we will see, many of the imperfections of this economic system are treatable within the market environment, sometimes even by making use of the market mechanism to cure its own deficiencies.

CONTENTS

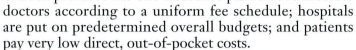

PUZZLE: *Why Are Health-Care Costs in Canada Rising?*

Long before the U.S. government made a serious (but ultimately unsuccessful) attempt in the early 1990s to grapple with the costs of health care, Canada adopted a universal health-care program intended to solve the same problem in that country. For this purpose, the Canadian government imposed strong controls over prices and fees. Each province has one insurance plan that reimburses doctors according to a uniform fee schedule; hospitals are put on predetermined overall budgets; and patients pay very low direct, out-of-pocket costs.

Many observers believe that Canada has created an efficient, user-friendly system, although some critics disagree. But Canadians clearly have *not* succeeded in containing costs. Despite the price controls, Canadian health-care costs have been rising persistently faster than the general inflation rate, just as they have in the United States, where there are no such national rules to rein in rising health-care prices. Moreover, some observers contend that Canadian health services are getting worse, with longer waits for diagnostic tests and elective surgery and tighter restrictions on treatments available to patients. Does this trend mean that Canadian health services are especially inefficient or corrupt? There is no evidence for such suspicions. Then why have the Canadians been unable to brake the growth of their health care costs? This chapter will help you to understand the answer to this question, with its important implications for U.S. policy.

SOURCE: © Jens Haas/Corbis

WHAT DOES THE MARKET DO POORLY?

Although we cannot list all of the market's imperfections, we can list some major areas in which it has been accused of failing:

1. Market economies suffer from severe business fluctuations.
2. The market distributes income unequally.
3. Where markets are monopolized, they allocate resources inefficiently.
4. The market deals poorly with the side effects of many economic activities.
5. The market cannot readily provide public goods, such as national defense.
6. The market may do a poor job of allocating resources between the present and the future.
7. The market mechanism makes public and personal services increasingly expensive, which often induces socially damaging countermeasures by government.

We discuss the first three items in the list elsewhere in this book. This chapter deals with the remaining four. To help us analyze these cases, we will first briefly review the concept of efficient resource allocation, discussed in detail in Chapter 14.

EFFICIENT RESOURCE ALLOCATION: A REVIEW

The basic problem of resource allocation is deciding how much of each commodity the economy should produce. At first glance, the solution may seem simple: the more, the better! But this is not necessarily so, as one of our *Ideas for Beyond the Final Exam* indicates.

HOW MUCH DOES IT REALLY COST? *Opportunity Costs:* Outputs are not created out of thin air. We produce them from scarce supplies of fuel, raw materials, machinery, and labor. If we use these resources to produce, say, more jeans, then we must take resources away from some other products, such as backpacks. To decide whether increasing the production of jeans is a good idea, we must compare the utility of that increase with the loss of utility in producing fewer backpacks. This, as you recall, means we must consider the opportunity cost of increased output. It is *efficient* to increase the output of jeans only if society considers the additional jeans more valuable than the forgone backpacks.

To illustrate this idea, we repeat a graph you have seen several times in earlier chapters—a *production possibilities frontier*—but we put it to a somewhat different use here. Curve *ABC* in Figure 1 is a **production possibilities frontier** showing the alternative combinations of jeans and backpacks that the economy can produce by reallocating its resources between production of the two goods. Suppose that point *B*, representing the production of 8 million backpacks and 60 million pairs of jeans, constitutes the *optimal* resource allocation. We assume this combination of outputs is the only one that best satisfies society's wants among all the possibilities that are *attainable* (given the technology and resources as represented by the production frontier). Two questions are pertinent to our discussion of the price system:

> 1. What prices will get the economy to select point *B*; that is, what prices will yield an *efficient* allocation of resources?
> 2. How can the wrong set of prices lead to a misallocation of resources?

We discussed the first question in detail in Chapter 14, where we saw that:

An efficient allocation of resources requires that each product's price be equal to its marginal cost; that is:

$$P = MC$$

The reasoning, in brief, goes like this: In a free market, the price of any good reflects the money value to consumers of an additional unit—that is, its *marginal utility* (MU). Similarly, if the market mechanism is working well, the *marginal cost* (MC) measures the value (the opportunity cost) of the resources needed to produce an additional unit of the good. That is, MC is the resources cost *caused* by producing another unit of the commodity. Hence, if prices are set equal to marginal costs, then consumers, by using *their own money* in the most effective way to maximize *their own* satisfaction, will automatically be using *society's resources* in the most effective way. In other words, as long as it sets prices equal to marginal costs, the market mechanism automatically satisfies the MC = MU rule for efficient resource allocation that we studied in Chapter 10.[1] In terms of Figure 1, this means that if *P* = MC for both goods, the economy will automatically gravitate to point *B*, which we assumed to be the optimal point.

This chapter is devoted mainly to the second question: How can the "wrong" prices cause a **misallocation of resources?** The answer to this question is not too difficult, and we can use the case of monopoly as an illustration.

The "law" of demand tells us that a rise in a commodity's price normally will reduce the quantity demanded. Suppose, now, that the backpack industry is a monopoly, so the price of backpacks exceeds their marginal cost.[2] This will decrease the quantity of backpacks demanded below the 8 million that we have assumed to be

The **production possibilities frontier** is a curve that shows the maximum quantities of outputs it is possible to produce with the available resource quantities and the current state of technological knowledge.

The Economy's Production Possibilities Frontier for the Production of Two Goods

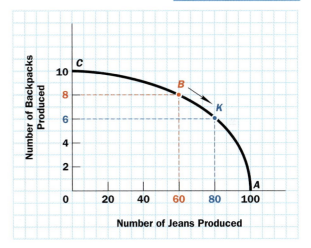

Number of Backpacks Produced

Number of Jeans Produced

Note: Numbers are in millions per year.

Resources are **misallocated** if it is possible to change the way they are used or the combination of goods and services they produce and thereby make consumers better off.

---

[1] If you need a review, consult Chapter 14, pages 304–306.

[2] To review why price under monopoly may be expected to exceed marginal cost, you may want to reread Chapter 11, pages 222–225.

socially optimal (point *B* in Figure 1). The economy will move from point *B* to a point such as *K*, where too few backpacks and too many pairs of jeans are being produced for maximal consumer satisfaction. By setting the "wrong" prices, then, the market induces individual consumers to buy quantities that are inconsistent with maximal welfare of all individuals as a group, and thereby prevents the most efficient use of the economy's resources.

> If a commodity's price is higher than its marginal cost, the economy will tend to produce less of that item than would maximize consumer benefits. The opposite will occur if an item's price is lower than its marginal cost.

In the rest of this chapter, we will encounter several other significant instances in which the market mechanism may set the "wrong" prices.

EXTERNALITIES: GETTING THE PRICES WRONG

We start with the fourth item on our list of market failures (since we have studied the first three in previous chapters): The market deals poorly with the *incidental* side effects of economic activities. This flaw is one of the least obvious yet most consequential of the price system's imperfections.

Many economic activities provide incidental *benefits* to others for whom they are not specifically intended. For example, homeowners who plant beautiful gardens in front of their homes incidentally and unintentionally provide pleasure to neighbors and passers-by, even though they receive no payment in return. Economists say that their activity generates a **beneficial externality.** That is, the activity creates benefits that are *external* to, or outside, the intentions and interests of those that are directly involved in the activity. Similarly, some activities incidentally and unintentionally impose *costs* on others. For example, the owners of a motorcycle repair shop create a lot of noise for which they pay no compensation to their neighbors. Economists say these owners produce a **detrimental externality.** Pollution is the classic illustration of a detrimental externality.

An activity is said to generate a **beneficial** or **detrimental externality** if that activity causes incidental benefits or damages to others not directly involved in the activity and no corresponding compensation is provided to or paid by those who generate the externality.

To see why externalities cause the price system to misallocate resources, you need only recall that the price system achieves efficiency by rewarding producers who serve consumers well—that is, at the lowest possible cost. This argument breaks down, however, as soon as some of the costs and benefits of economic activities are left out of the profit calculation.

When a firm pollutes a river, it uses up some of society's resources just as surely as when the firm burns coal. However, if the firm pays for coal but not for the use of clean water, we can expect the firm's management to be economical in its use of coal and wasteful in its use of water. By the same token, a firm that provides unpaid benefits to others is unlikely to be generous in allocating resources to the activity, no matter how socially desirable it may be.

In an important sense, the source of the market mechanism's difficulty here lies in society's rules about property rights. Coal mines are *private property;* their owners will not let anyone take coal without paying for it. Thus, coal is costly and so is not used wastefully. But waterways are not private property. Because they belong to everyone in general, they belong to no one in particular. Therefore, anyone can use waterways as free dumping grounds for wastes that spew poisons into the water and use up the water's oxygen that is vital for underwater life. Because no one pays for the use of the socially valuable dissolved oxygen in a public waterway, people will use that oxygen wastefully. The fact that waterways are exempted from the market's normal control procedures is therefore the source of a detrimental externality.

Externalities and Inefficiency

Using these concepts, we can see precisely why an externality has undesirable effects on the allocation of resources. In discussing externalities, it is crucial to distinguish between *social* and *private* marginal cost. We define **marginal social cost (MSC)** as the sum of two components: (1) **marginal private cost (MPC),** which is the share of an activity's marginal cost that is paid for by the persons who carry out the activity, plus (2) *incidental cost*, which is the share paid by others.

If an increase in a firm's output also increases the smoke its factory spews into the air, then, in addition to direct private costs (as recorded in the company accounts), the expansion of production imposes incidental costs on others. These costs take the form of increased laundry bills, medical expenditures, outlays for air conditioning and electricity, and the unpleasantness of living in a cloud of noxious fumes. These are all part of the activity's marginal *social* cost.

Where the firm's activities generate detrimental externalities, its marginal social cost will be greater than its marginal private cost, while the business firm will base its pricing only on its private cost because it does not pay the remainder of the social costs of its operation (and generally does not even know how large that remaining cost is). In symbols, MSC > MPC, whereas the price charged by the firm is based on MPC. Therefore, the firm's output must be too big because, in equilibrium, the market will yield an output at which consumers' marginal utility (MU) is equal to the firm's marginal private cost (MU = MPC < MPC). Where there are detrimental externalities, then, the marginal utility is *smaller* than the marginal *social* cost. In such a case, society would necessarily benefit if output of that product were *reduced*. It would lose the marginal utility but save the greater marginal social cost. We conclude that:

> Where a firm's activity causes detrimental externalities, marginal benefits will be less than marginal social costs in a free market. Smaller outputs than those that maximize profits will be socially desirable.

This relationship holds because private enterprise has no motivation to take into account any costs to others for which it does not have to pay. In fact, competition *forces* firms to produce at as low a private cost as possible, because if they don't, rivals will be able to take their customers away. Thus, competition *compels* firms to make extensive use of resources for which they are not required to pay or pay fully. As a result, goods that cause detrimental externalities will be produced in undesirably large amounts, because they have social costs that are not paid by the supplier firms.

The opposite, of course, holds for the case of external benefits. This situation is one where the **marginal social benefit (MSB)** is greater than the **marginal private benefit (MPB).** A clear example is an invention produced by Firm A that gives an idea for another new product or process to an engineer from a different firm, B. Firm B clearly benefits from Firm A's research and development (R&D) spending, and B does not pay anything to A for this gain. In that case, the social benefit—the sum of the benefits to the two firms together—will be greater than the private benefit to the inventor Firm A alone. Thus, the marginal private benefit to investment in R&D will be less than the marginal social benefit, and less R&D will be carried out under private enterprise than social optimality requires.

These principles can be illustrated with the aid of Figure 2. This diagram repeats the two basic curves needed for analysis of the firm's equilibrium: a marginal revenue curve and a marginal cost curve (see Chapter 8). These curves represent the *private* costs and revenues of a particular firm (in this case, a paper mill). The mill maximizes profits by providing 100,000 tons of output, corresponding to the intersection between the marginal private cost and marginal revenue curves (point *A*).

Now suppose that the factory's wastewater pollutes a nearby estuary, so that its production creates a detrimental externality for which the owners do not pay. Then marginal social cost must be higher than marginal

The **marginal social cost (MSC)** of an activity is the sum of its marginal private cost (MPC) plus its incidental costs (positive or negative) that are borne by others who receive no compensation for the resulting damage to their well-being.

The **marginal private cost (MPC)** is the share of an activity's marginal cost that is paid for by the persons who carry out the activity.

The **marginal social benefit (MSB)** of an activity is the sum of its marginal private benefit (MPB) plus its incidental benefits (positive or negative) that are received by others, and for which those others do not pay.

The **marginal private benefit (MPB)** is the share of an activity's marginal benefit that is received by the persons who carry out the activity.

FIGURE 2

Equilibrium of a Firm Whose Output Produces a Detrimental Externality (Pollution)

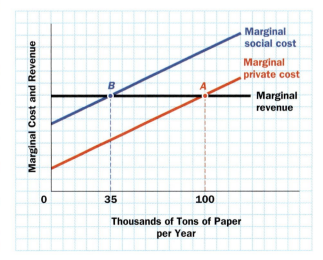

private cost, as shown in the diagram. The output of paper, which is governed by private costs, will be 100,000 tons (point *A*)—an excessive amount from the viewpoint of the public interest, given its environmental consequences.

If, instead of being able to impose the external costs on others, the paper mill's owners were forced to pay them, then their private marginal cost curve would correspond to the higher of the two cost curves. Paper output would then fall to 35,000 tons, corresponding to point *B*, the intersection between the marginal revenue curve and the marginal *social* cost curve.

The same sort of diagram shows that the opposite relationship will hold when the firm's activity produces beneficial externalities. The firm will produce less of its beneficial output than it would if it were rewarded fully for its activities' benefits. Thus:

Where the firm's activity generates beneficial externalities, free markets will produce too little output. Society would be better off with larger output levels.

We can also see these results with the help of a production possibilities frontier diagram similar to that in Figure 1. In Figure 3, we see the frontier for two industries: electricity generation, which causes air pollution (a detrimental externality), and tulip growing, which makes an area more attractive (a beneficial externality). We have just seen that detrimental externalities make marginal social cost greater than marginal private cost. Hence, if the electric company charges a price equal to its own marginal (private) cost, that price will be less than the true marginal social cost. Similarly, in tulip growing, a price equal to marginal private cost will be above the true marginal cost to society.

Earlier in the chapter, we saw that an industry that charges a price above marginal social cost will reduce quantity demanded through this high price, and so it will produce an output too small for an efficient allocation of resources. The opposite will be true for an industry whose price is below marginal social cost. In terms of Figure 3, suppose that point *B* again represents the efficient allocation of resources, involving the production of *E* kilowatt-hours of electricity and *T* dozen tulips.

Because the polluting electricity-generation company charges a price below marginal social cost, it will sell more than *E* kilowatt-hours of electricity. Similarly, because tulip growers generate external benefits and so charge a price above marginal social cost, they will produce less than *T* dozen tulips. The economy will end up with the resource allocation represented by point *K* rather than that at point *B*. There will be too much smoky electricity production and too little attractive tulip growing. More generally:

An industry that generates detrimental externalities will have a marginal social cost higher than its marginal private cost. If the price is equal to a firm's own marginal private cost, it will therefore be below the true marginal cost to society. In this way, the market mechanism tends to encourage inefficiently large outputs of products that cause detrimental externalities. The opposite is true of products that cause beneficial externalities; private industry will provide inefficiently small quantities of these products.

Externalities Are Everywhere

Externalities occur throughout the economy. Many are beneficial. A factory that hires unskilled or semiskilled laborers, for example, gives them on-the-job *training* and provides the external benefit of better workers to future employers. Benefits to others are also generated when firms *invent* useful but unpatentable products, or even patentable products that can be imitated by others to some degree. We will discuss the externalities of innovation further in Chapter 16.

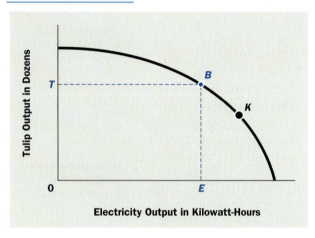

FIGURE 3

Externalities, Market Equilibrium, and Efficient Resource Allocation

Detrimental externalities are also widespread. Pollution by factories, cars, and trucks cause some of our most pressing environmental problems. The abandonment of buildings causes the quality of neighborhoods to deteriorate and is the source of serious externalities for cities. And these are only two of many significant examples.

Although the market mechanism, acting on its own, does nothing to cure externality problems, there is more to the story. Market economies often have dirty air and rivers and suffer from the effects of improperly disposed toxic wastes, but that does not mean that *non*market economies do any better. The communist countries of Eastern Europe and the Soviet Union long were known to have a dismal environmental record. When communism fell apart in those countries, the horrors of environmental degradation that were revealed were hard to believe. It became abundantly clear that central planning is not a guaranteed cure for environmental difficulties.

Moreover, the market mechanism does offer an effective way of dealing with such difficulties. Although markets hardly can be claimed to protect the environment automatically, they offer us a powerful tool for doing so, as we will see shortly.

◼ Government Policy and Externalities

Because of the market's inability to cope with externalities, governments support activities that are believed to generate external benefits. Governments subsidize education, not only because they know it helps promote equal opportunity for all citizens, but also because they believe it generates beneficial externalities. For example, educated people normally commit fewer crimes than uneducated people do, so the more we educate people, presumably the less we need to spend on crime prevention. Also, academic research that is a by-product of the educational system has often benefited the entire population and has, indeed, been a major contributor to the nation's economic growth. Biotechnology and advanced computing are just two major scientific breakthroughs that have stemmed from university research. We consequently believe that, if education were offered only by profit-making institutions, the outputs of these beneficial services would be provided at less than optimal levels.

Similarly, governments have begun to increase fines on companies that contribute heavily to air and water pollution. In the years just before George W. Bush's administration, the U.S. Environmental Protection Agency levied more criminal fines and civil penalties against violators than ever before. This is done, of course, as a disincentive for the creation of socially damaging externalities. In other words, it brings the amounts that business firms pay closer to covering all of the costs that their activities generate.

EXTERNALITIES: A SHORTCOMING OF THE MARKET CURED BY MARKET METHODS   Externalities are really just failures to price resources so that markets will allocate them efficiently. One effective way to deal with externalities may be to use taxes and subsidies, making polluters pay for the costs they impose on society and paying the generators of beneficial externalities for the incidental benefits of their activities (which can be considered as an offset or deduction from the social cost of the activity).

IDEAS FOR BEYOND THE FINAL EXAM

For example, firms that generate beneficial externalities should be given *subsidies* per unit of their output equal to the difference between their marginal social costs and their marginal private costs. Similarly, detrimental externalities should be *taxed* so that the firm will have to pay the entire marginal social cost. In terms of Figure 2, after paying the tax, the firm's marginal private cost curve will shift up until it coincides with its marginal social cost curve, so the market price will be set in a manner consistent with efficient resource allocation.

Although this approach works well in principle, it is often difficult to carry out in reality. Social costs are rarely easy to estimate, partly because they are so widely diffused throughout the community (everyone is affected by pollution) and partly because it is difficult to assess many of the costs and benefits (effects on health, unpleasantness of living in smog) in monetary terms. In Chapter 17, which focuses on environmental problems, we will continue our discussion of the pros and cons of the economist's approach to externalities and will outline alternative policies for their control.

PROVISION OF PUBLIC GOODS

A **public good** is a commodity or service whose benefits are *not depleted* by an additional user and from which it is generally difficult or *impossible to exclude* people, even if the people are unwilling to pay for the benefits.

A **private good** is a commodity characterized by both depletability and excludability.

A commodity is **depletable** if it is used up when someone consumes it.

A commodity is **excludable** if someone who does not pay for it can be kept from enjoying it.

A second area in which market failure occurs is the provision of what economists call **public goods.** Public goods are socially valuable commodities whose provision, for reasons we will explain, cannot be financed by private enterprise, or at least not at socially desirable prices. Thus, government must pay for public goods if they are to be provided at all. Standard examples of public goods include everything from national defense to coastal lighthouses.

It is easiest to explain the nature of public goods by contrasting them with **private goods,** which are at the opposite end of the spectrum. *Private goods are characterized by two important attributes.* One can be called **depletability.** If you eat an apple or use a gallon of gasoline, there is that much less fruit or fuel in the world available for others to use. Your consumption depletes the supply available for other people, either temporarily or permanently.

But a pure public good is like the legendary widow's jar of oil, which always remained full no matter how much oil was poured out. For example, once snow has been removed from a street, improved driving conditions are available to every driver who uses that street, whether ten or 1,000 cars pass that way. One passing car does not make the road less snow-free for the next driver. The same is true of spraying swamps near a town to kill malarial mosquitoes. The cost of spraying is the same whether the town contains 10,000 or 20,000 persons. A resident of the town who benefits from this service does not deplete its advantages to others.

The other property that characterizes private goods but not all public goods is **excludability,** meaning that anyone who does not pay for the good can be excluded from enjoying its benefits. If you do not buy a ticket, you are excluded from the basketball game. If you do not pay for an electric guitar, the storekeeper will not hand it over to you.

But some goods or services, once provided to anyone, automatically become available to many others whom it is difficult, if not impossible, to exclude from the benefits. When the street is cleared of snow, everyone who uses the street benefits, regardless of who paid for the snowplow. If a country provides a strong military, every citizen receives its protection, even persons who do not want it.

A public good is defined as a good that lacks depletability. Very often, it also lacks excludability. Notice two important implications:

First, because nonpaying users usually cannot be excluded from enjoying a public good, suppliers of such goods will find it *difficult or impossible to collect fees* for the benefits they provide. This is the so-called *free-rider* problem. How many people, for example, would *voluntarily* cough up close to $6,000 a year to support our national defense establishment? Yet this is roughly what it costs per American family. Services such as national defense and public health, which are not depletable and where excludability is simply impossible, *cannot* be provided by private enterprise because people will not pay for what they can get free. Because private firms are not in the business of giving services away, the supply of public goods must be left to government and nonprofit institutions.

The second implication we notice is that, because the supply of a public good is not depleted by an additional user, *the marginal (opportunity) cost of serving an additional user is zero.* With marginal cost equal to zero, the basic principle of optimal resource allocation (price equal to marginal cost) calls for provision of public goods and services to anyone who wants them *at no charge.* In other words, not only is it often *impossible* to charge a market price for a public good, it is often *undesirable* as well. Any nonzero price would discourage some users from enjoying the public good; but this would be inefficient, because one more person's enjoyment of the good costs society nothing. To summarize:

It is usually *not easily possible* to charge a price for a pure public good because people cannot be excluded from enjoying its benefits. It may also be *undesirable* to charge a price for it because that would discourage some people from benefiting, even though using a public good does not deplete its supply. For both of these reasons, government supplies many public goods. Without government intervention, public goods simply would not be provided.

Referring back to our example in Figure 1, if backpacks were a public good and their production were left to private enterprise, the economy would end up at point *A*, with zero production of backpacks and a far greater output of jeans than is called for by efficient allocation (point *B*). Usually, communities have not let that happen; today they devote a substantial proportion of government expenditure—indeed, the bulk of municipal budgets—to financing of public goods or services believed to generate substantial external benefits. National defense, public health, police and fire protection, and research are among the services governments provide because they offer beneficial externalities or are public goods.

ALLOCATION OF RESOURCES BETWEEN PRESENT AND FUTURE

A third area in which market failure occurs is the division of benefits between today and tomorrow. When a society invests, more resources are devoted to expanding its capacity to produce consumer goods in the future. But if we devote inputs to building new factories and equipment that will add to production tomorrow, those resources then become unavailable for consumption now. Fuel used to make steel for a factory cannot be used to heat homes or drive cars. Thus, the allocation of inputs between current consumption and investment—their allocation between present and future—influences how fast the economy grows. Investment in education has a similar role, because people who are educated today are likely to be more effective producers tomorrow, and if education enables them to contribute inventions, that may increase tomorrow's production even more. That is why economists refer to education as "investment in human capital," thereby thinking of more-educated people as analogous to machinery in the factory whose efficiency is increased by modernization.

In principle, the market mechanism should be as efficient in allocating resources between present and future uses as it is in allocating resources among different outputs at any one time. If future demands for a particular commodity, such as personal computers, are expected to be higher than they are today, it pays manufacturers to plan now to build the necessary plant and equipment so they will be ready to turn out the computers when the market expands. More resources are thereby allocated to future consumption.

We can analyze the allocation of resources between present and future with the aid of a production possibilities frontier diagram, such as the one in Figure 1. The question now is how much labor and capital to devote to producing consumers' goods and how much to devote to construction of factories to produce output in the future. Then, instead of jeans and backpacks, the graph will show consumers' goods and number of factories on its axes, but otherwise it will be exactly the same as Figure 1.

The profit motive directs the flow of resources between one time period and another, just as it handles resource allocation among different industries in a given period. The lure of profits directs resources to those products *and those time periods* in which high prices promise to make output most profitable. But at least one feature of the process of resource allocation among different time periods distinguishes it from the process of allocation among industries—the special role that the *interest rate* plays in allocation among time periods.

The Role of the Interest Rate

If receipt of a given amount of money is delayed until some future time, the recipient incurs an *opportunity cost*—the interest that the money could have earned if it had been received earlier and invested. For example, if the prevailing interest rate is 9 percent and you can persuade someone who owes you $100 to make that payment one year earlier than originally planned, you come out $9 ahead (because you can take the $100 and invest it at 9 percent). Put another way, if the interest rate is 9 percent and the payment of $100 is postponed for one year, you lose the opportunity to earn $9. Thus, the interest rate determines the opportunity cost to a recipient who gets money at some future date instead of now—the lower the interest rate, the lower the opportunity cost. For this reason, as we will see in greater detail in Chapter 19:

> Low interest rates will persuade people to invest more now in factories and equipment, because that will reduce the opportunity cost of these investments, which yield a large portion of their benefits in the future. Thus, more resources will be devoted to the future if interest rates are low. Similarly, high interest rates make durable investment less attractive, because it yields much of its benefit only in the future. Therefore, high interest rates tend to increase the use of resources for current output at the expense of reduced future outputs.

On the surface, it seems that the price system can allocate resources among different time periods in the way consumers prefer, because the supply of and demand for loans, which determine the interest rate—the price of a loan—reflects the public's preferences between present and future. Suppose, for example, that the public suddenly became more interested in future consumption (say, people wanted to save more for their retirement years). People would save more money, the supply of funds available for lending would increase, and interest rates would tend to fall. This would stimulate investment and add to the future output of goods at the expense of current consumption.

But economists have raised several questions about how effectively the market mechanism allocates resources among different time periods in practice.

■ How Does It Work in Practice?

One thing that makes economists uneasy is that the interest rate (which is the price that controls resource allocation over time) is also used for a variety of *other* purposes. For instance, sometimes the interest rate is used to deal with business fluctuations. It plays an analogous role in international monetary relations. As a result, governments frequently manipulate interest rates. For example, during the economic downturn in the early 2000s, the Federal Reserve Board—the organization that oversees the activities of banks in the United States—reduced interest rates repeatedly so as to make it cheaper for consumers and firms to borrow and buy consumers' goods or to invest in new plant and equipment. In doing so, policy makers seem to give little thought to the effects on resource allocation between present and future, so we may well worry whether the resulting interest rates were the most appropriate.

Second, some economists have suggested that, even when the government does not manipulate the interest rate, the market may devote too large a proportion of the economy's resources to immediate consumption. One British economist, A. C. Pigou, argued that people suffer from a "defective telescopic faculty"—that they are too shortsighted to give adequate weight to the future. A "bird in the hand" point of view leads people to spend too much on today's consumption and commit too little to tomorrow's investments.

A third reason why the free market may not invest enough for the future is that investment projects, such as the construction of a new factory, are much greater risks to the individual investor than to the community as a whole. Even if the original investor goes bankrupt and the factory falls into someone else's hands, it can continue turning out goods for the general public. Of course, the profits will not go to the original investor or to his or her heirs. Therefore, the loss to the individual investor will be far greater than the loss to society. For this reason, individual investment for the future may fall short of the socially optimal amounts, even though investments too risky to be worthwhile to any group of private individuals may nevertheless be advantageous to society as a whole.

Fourth, our economy shortchanges the future when it despoils irreplaceable natural resources, exterminates whole species of plants and animals, floods canyons, "develops" attractive areas into acres of potential slums, and so on. Worst of all, industry, the military, and individuals bequeath a ticking time bomb to the future when they leave behind lethal and slow-acting toxic residues. For example, nuclear wastes may remain dangerous for hundreds or even thousands of years, but their disposal containers are likely to fall apart long before the contents lose their lethal qualities. Such actions are essentially *irreversible*. If a factory is not built this year, the deficiency in facilities provided for the future can be remedied by building it next year. But a natural canyon, once destroyed, can never be replaced. For this reason:

Many economists believe that *irreversible decisions* have a special significance and must *not* be left entirely to the decisions of private firms and individuals—that is, to the market.

Some writers, however, have questioned the general conclusion that the free market will not invest enough for the future. They point out that our economy's prosperity has increased fairly steadily from one decade to the next, and that there is reason to expect future generations to have far higher real average incomes and an abundance of consumer goods. Pressures to increase future investment then may be like taking from the poor to give to the rich—a sort of backward Robin Hood redistribution of income.

■ SOME OTHER SOURCES OF MARKET FAILURE

We have now surveyed some of the most important imperfections of the market mechanism. But our list is not complete, and it can never be. In this imperfect world, nothing ever works out ideally. Indeed, by examining anything with a sufficiently powerful microscope, one can always detect more blemishes. However, some significant items were omitted from our list. We will conclude with a brief description of three of them and discuss a fourth of special current interest in somewhat greater detail.

■ Imperfect Information: "Caveat Emptor"

In our analysis of the virtues of the market mechanism in Chapter 14, we assumed that consumers and producers have all the information they need to make good decisions. In reality, this is rarely true. When buying a house or secondhand car or when selecting a doctor, consumers are vividly reminded of how little they know about what they are purchasing. The old cliché, "caveat emptor" (let the buyer beware), applies. Obviously, if participants in the market are ill-informed, they will not always make the optimal decisions described in our theoretical models. (For more on this issue, see "Asymmetric Information, 'Lemons,' and Agents," on the next page.)

Yet not all economists agree that imperfect information is really a failure of the market mechanism. They point out that information, too, is a commodity that costs money to produce. Neither firms nor consumers have complete information because it would be irrational for them to spend the enormous amounts needed to get it. As always, compromise is necessary. One should, ideally, stop buying information at the point where the marginal utility of further information is no greater than its marginal cost. With this amount of information, the business executive or the consumer would be able to make what we call "optimally imperfect" decisions.

■ Rent Seeking

An army of lawyers, expert witnesses, and business executives crowd our courtrooms and cause enormous costs to pile up through litigation. Business firms seem to sue each other at the slightest provocation, wasting vast resources and delaying business decisions. Why? Because it is possible to make money by such seemingly unproductive activities—through legal battles over profit-making opportunities.

Asymmetric Information, Lemons, and Agents

Have you ever wondered why a six-month-old car sells for so much less than a brand-new one? Economists offer one explanation, having to do with *imperfect information.* The problem is that some small percentage of new automobiles are "lemons" that are plagued by mechanical troubles. The new-car dealer probably knows no more than the buyer about whether a particular car is a lemon. The information known to the two parties, therefore, is said to be *symmetric,* and there is a low probability that a car purchased from a new-car dealer will turn out to be a lemon.

In the used-car market, however, information is *asymmetric.* The person selling the used car knows very well whether the car is a lemon, but the buyer does not. Moreover, a seller who wants to get rid of a relatively new car is likely to be doing so only because it *is* a lemon. Potential buyers realize that. Hence, if a person is forced to sell a good new car because of an unexpected need for cash, he will be stuck with a low price because he cannot *prove* that his car really works well. The moral is that asymmetric information also tends to harm the honest seller.

In addition, asymmetric information leads to the *principal-agent problems,* that are discussed in the text and whose analysis is a major concern of recent economic research. Principal-agent and asymmetric information problems are said to have played a major part in the much-publicized Enron debacle. When that huge energy-trading firm collapsed, stockholders (including Enron employees whose retirement money was invested in the firm) lost their savings. But Enron's management had already deserted the sinking ship with large bonus payments, having sold *their* company stocks while the

price was still high. Asymmetric information is crucial here. The principals know only *imperfectly* whether their agents are serving their interests faithfully and efficiently or are instead neglecting or even acting against the principals' interests to pursue selfish interests of their own. Misuse of the principals' property, embezzlement, and political corruption are extreme examples of such dereliction of duty by agents and, unfortunately, they seem to occur often. Stock options may help to deal with the asymmetric information problem here. If the earnings of corporate management are linked to company profits or based on the market value of company shares, then by promoting the welfare of stockholders, managers will make themselves better off. Shareholders, even though they know only imperfectly what management is doing, can have greater confidence that management will try to serve their interests well.

SOURCE: © Photopia

For example, suppose that a municipality awards a contract to produce electricity to Firm A, offering $20 million in profit. It may be worthwhile for Firm B to spend $5 million in a lawsuit against the municipality and Firm A, hoping that the courts will award it the contract (and thus the $20 million profit) instead.

Rent seeking refers to unproductive activity in the pursuit of economic profit—in other words, profit in excess of competitive earnings.

In general, any source of unusual profit, such as a monopoly, tempts firms to waste economic resources in an effort to obtain control of that source of profit. This process, called **rent seeking** (meaning that the firms hope to obtain earnings without contributing to production), is judged by some observers to be a major source of inefficiency in our economy. (For more on rent seeking, see pages 411–412 in Chapter 19.)

■ Moral Hazard

Moral hazard refers to the tendency of insurance to discourage policyholders from protecting themselves from risk.

Another widely discussed problem for the market mechanism is associated with insurance. Economists view insurance—which is the provision of protection against risk—as a useful commodity, like shoes or information. But insurance also encourages the very risks against which it provides protection. For example, if an individual has a valuable stamp collection that is fully insured against theft, she has little motivation to protect it against burglars. She may, for example, fail to lock it up in a safe-deposit box. This problem—the tendency of insurance to encourage the source of risk—is called **moral hazard,** and it makes a free market in insurance difficult to operate.

■ Principals, Agents, and Recent Stock Option Scandals

Yet another important area of concern about the performance of the unconstrained market is called the "principal-agent problem." The economy contains many activities so large and complex that it is out of the question for them to be organized and operated by those most directly concerned. The most striking example is provided by our representative democracy that is, in theory, run by "We the people." But it is obvious that it would be quite impractical to assemble all of the citizens of the country to discuss and decide on the details of proposed legislation on complex matters such as trade policy or rules for protection of the environment. So, instead, the U.S. Constitution requires us to hire politicians via the election process to run the country on our behalf. In economic terminology, we would say that the citizens are the **principals** in the activity of running the country, and the president and members of Congress are the **agents** who are hired by us, the principals, to operate the country on our behalf.

A second example, the one on which we will focus here, is the running of a corporation. A giant corporation such as Intel (the largest producer of microprocessors for computers) has thousands of stockholder-owners. And, like citizens of a country, they are also too numerous to run the firm day by day, making the thousands of required decisions. So these principals, too, hire agents—the corporate management—to do the job. The assigned task of the agents is to run the corporation in a way that best promotes the interests of the stockholders.

The main problem that besets this arrangement, like all principal-agent arrangements, is that the agents cannot always be trusted. All too often they put their own interests ahead of those of their principals, in clear dereliction of duty. Indeed, in just this decade so far, there has been what seems like a flood of corporate scandals, with managements having indiscriminately betrayed stockholders and employees while obtaining for themselves hundreds of millions of dollars as their supposedly merited rewards. (For examples, see the feature box in Chapter 9 on "Corporate Scandals.")

Economic analysis suggests a solution to the problem: Arrange for the amount that the agents are paid to depend on the degree to which their actions succeed in benefiting the principals. Pay the agents a lot if they achieve much for the principals, and pay them little if they don't. If such an incentive scheme is established, the agents can do well for themselves only by doing well for the stockholders.

The only trouble with this solution is that it is easier to describe on paper than to carry out in practice. First, it is not easy to measure what the agents have actually accomplished. If the company's sales increased, was that because of something management did, or was it largely an accident? The second problem is that unscrupulous managers can often find ways to get around such rules via legal maneuvers or by appointing friends and allies to the company's board of directors, rather than evenhanded appointees who can assure the honesty and competence of management.

One seemingly clever device was thought up to do the job of rewarding management for what they achieve: the employee stock option. But corruption within firms and irrational tax laws that undermine their effectiveness, among other impediments, have prevented stock options from doing the job they were intended to do. Let us see why.

A **stock option** is, in effect, a contract that allows the person who owns the option to buy a specified quantity of the company's stock at some date in the future that can be chosen, within specified limits, by the owner. But when he pays for the stock, he pays not the price on the day the stock is bought but, rather, the price of the stock on the day the option was obtained. For example, suppose the price of the stock was $40 on February 12, the day the option was acquired. On March 23, the owner considers using the option to buy the stock. If the price has fallen to $30, the option owner will decide not to buy any stock because, if he did, the option contract would require him to spend $40 for a stock worth only $30, clearly a losing proposition. But suppose the stock had gone in the other direction and, on the proposed purchase date, the share's price had risen to $60. Since this means that the option owner could acquire a stock worth $60 for only $40, it would give him an immediate $20 profit—a very good deal.

Agents are people hired to run a complex enterprise on behalf of **the principals,** those whose benefit the enterprise is supposed to serve.

A **stock option** is a contract that permits its owner to buy a specified quantity of stocks of a corporation at a future date, but at the price specified in the contract rather than the stock's market price at the date of purchase.

When the price of the company's stock goes down, stock options are not used. Thus, the owner of the option loses only what she paid for the option, if anything. But if the price of the stock rises, the owner can make a profit by "exercising the option;" that is, by using it to buy the stock and pocketing the difference between the price specified in the option and the value of the stock at the time it is bought.

If stock options are granted to a corporation's management under appropriate rules, they may well be a powerful way to deal with the principal-agent problem in corporations. For if managers who own stock options work harder to make the company successful, their actions can raise the market price of the corporation's stock, thereby benefiting the stockholders as well as themselves. In other words, a gift or sale of stock options to management can help align the interests of stockholders and management: They both want to stock price to rise. Few other instruments can ensure such compatibility between the interest of stockholders and managers.

However, the conditions under which stock options are now granted are far from this ideal. They can, for instance, lead management to focus on short-term gains in stock prices, rather than on the long-run performance of the firm. They reward management even when the firm's performance is worse than that of the industry and that of the stock market as a whole. And subservient boards of directors often provide staggering and probably undeserved managerial compensation in the form of huge gifts of stock options.

Unscrupulous managers have learned ways to manipulate stock options and undermine their benefits to stockholders. For instance, there have been cases in which management sent out misleading information indicating, falsely, that the company was about to make large profits. This raised the price of its stock temporarily, giving the holders of stock options an opportunity to use them quickly to buy the stocks at the low prices specified in the options and quickly sell the shares while their market price was still high, thus making a large profit for themselves. Such problems are best attacked directly by requiring the issue of stock options to management to satisfy provisions such as the following:

1. That exercise of those stock options should not be permitted for some substantial period of time, say five years, after they are initially offered;
2. That the stock options be performance-based, meaning that they are contingent on performance by the firm that exceeds that of comparable firms or of the firm's own past record, with the number of stock options granted to management proportioned to the magnitude of the superiority of the firm's performance;
3. That any such grant of options to management be subject to approval by vote of the firm's stockholders; and
4. That the sale of such shares by top management be made public promptly.

Stock options granted on these terms may well lead to a dramatic change in the incentives facing management—and in the desired direction. If the improved incentives created by options succeed in their purpose of fostering higher earnings, the gift of options to management may involve no cost to stockholders. On the contrary, earnings per share will be higher than they would otherwise have been, and both managers and shareholders will benefit.

But unfortunately, the existing rules do not contain such provisions to protect the interests of the shareholders (the principals). There are even rules that discourage some of those provisions. For example, under current tax rules, a company obtains some tax advantages if it uses stock options as part of management's compensation. But the law offers those advantages only if the grant of options is not made to depend on how well management performs for the company. Only if the options are given outright, with *no* difference in reward between cases where management performs its job well and where it does badly, do the current rules offer a tax benefit to the company.

■ MARKET FAILURE AND GOVERNMENT FAILURE

We have pointed out some of the invisible hand's most noteworthy failures. We seem forced to the conclusion that a market economy, if left entirely to itself, is likely to produce results that are, at least in some respects, far from ideal. We have noted in our discussion, either directly or by implication, some of the things that government can do to correct these deficiencies. But the fact that government often *can* intervene in the economy's operation in a constructive way does not always mean that it actually *will* succeed in doing so. Governments cannot be relied on to behave ideally, any more than business firms can be expected to do so.

It is difficult to make this point in a suitably balanced way. Commentators too often stake out one extreme position or the other. Some people think the market mechanism is inherently unfair and biased by the greed of those who run its enterprises and look to the government to cure all economic ills. Others deplore government intervention and consider the public sector to be the home of every sort of inefficiency, graft, and bureaucratic stultification. The truth, as usual, lies somewhere in between.

Governments, like humans, are inherently imperfect. The political process leads to compromises that sometimes bear little resemblance to rational decisions. For example, legislators' versions of the policies suggested by economic analysis are sometimes mere caricatures of the economists' ideas. (For a satirical editorial illustrating this point, see "The Politics of Economic Policy," below.)

Yet often the problems engendered by an unfettered economy are too serious to be left to the free market. The problems of inflation, environmental decay, and the

The Politics of Economic Policy

In 1978, Alfred Kahn, a noted economist who served in the administration of President Jimmy Carter, advocated reducing pollution by raising the tax on leaded gasoline and lowering the tax on unleaded gasoline. The *Washington Post*, in an editorial excerpted here, agreed that Kahn's idea was a sound one but worried about what might emerge from Congress:

SOURCE: Digital Image © The Museum of Modern Art/Licensed by SCALA/Art Resource, NY

If the administration adopts the Kahn plan, recent history offers a pretty clear view of the rest of the story. Mr. Kahn will draft a one-page bill to raise the tax on the one kind of gas and lower it on the other. But the White House political staff will immediately point out that his draft fails to address profound questions of social equity. What about the poor, who buy leaded gas because it's cheaper? What about young people driving old cars? What about the inhabitants of lower Louisiana, who need their outboard motors to get around the swamps and bayous? There will have to be a rebate formula. It will take into account each family's income, the number and ages of its various automobiles and the distance from its front doorstep to the bus stop. The legislative draftsmen at the Energy Department have had a lot of experience with that kind of formula and eventually the 53-page bill will be sent to Congress. . . .

The real fun will start when it arrives at the Senate Finance Committee. First the committee will add tuition tax credits for families with children in private schools. Then, warming to its work,

it will vote import quotas on straw hats from Hong Kong, beef from Argentina and automobiles from Japan. . . . [I]t will then add several obscure but pregnant provisions that seem to refer to the tax treatment of certain oil wells in the Gulf states. When the 268-page bill comes to the Senate floor, the administration will narrowly manage to defeat an amendment to improve business confidence by repealing the capital-gains tax and returning to the gold standard.

When the bill gets back to the House, liberal Democrats will denounce it as an outrage and declare all-out war. They will succeed in getting all references to gasoline taxes and the environment stricken—but not, unfortunately, the import quotas or the obscure tax changes for the oil wells. By the time the staff of the Joint Committee on Taxation has straightened out a few technical difficulties, the bill will run to 417 pages and Ralph Nader will be calling on President Carter to veto it. But the feeling at the White House will be that Congress has worked so long and hard on the bill that he has no choice but to sign it. By the time the bill is finally enacted, Mr. Kahn might well wish he had chosen some other instrument of policy.

SOURCE: Alfred E. Kahn, "The Politics of Economic Policy" from *Washington Post*, December 26, 1978. Reprinted by permission of Alfred E. Kahn, Robert Julius Thorne Professor of Political Economy, Emeritus, Cornell University.

provision of public goods are cases in point. In such instances, government intervention is likely to yield substantial benefits to the general public. However, even when *some* government action is clearly warranted, it may be difficult or impossible to calculate the *optimal* degree of governmental intervention. There is, then, the danger of intervention so excessive that the society might have been better off without it.

In other areas, the market mechanism is likely to work reasonably well, and small imperfections do not constitute adequate justification for government intervention. In any event, *even where government action is appropriate, we must consider market-like instruments as one possible way to correct market mechanism deficiencies.* The tax incentives described earlier in our discussion of externalities are an outstanding example of what we have in mind.

THE COST DISEASE OF SOME VITAL SERVICES IN THE ECONOMY

As our final example, we consider next a problem that is not strictly a *failure* of the market mechanism. Rather, it is a case where the market's behavior creates that illusion and often leads to ill-advised *government* action that threatens the general welfare. This problem concerns dramatically rising prices, as typified by college tuitions. As a reader of this book, you are well aware that your attendance at college is likely to cost as much as $40,000 per year. When the older of the two authors of this book attended graduate school, the fee was a little over $100 per year. That is a dramatic rise in cost, and it has not hit only college tuitions. In this section, we will examine the reasons for these rising prices and other disturbing developments in the affected segments of the economy.

Deteriorating Personal Services

Over the years, general standards of living have increased and our material possessions have multiplied. But at the same time, our communities have experienced a decline in the quality of a variety of public and private services. Not just in the United States, but throughout the world, streets and subways, for example, have grown increasingly dirty. Bus, train, and postal services have all been cut back. Amazingly

BY ROSE FOR BYRD NEWSPAPERS, FREDERICKSBURG, VA.

SOURCE: By Rose for Byrd Newspapers, Harrisburg, VA

enough, in the 1800s in suburban London, there were twelve mail deliveries per day on weekdays and one on Sundays! Today, mail service in the United Kingdom is hardly a subject of admiration anymore.

Parallel cutbacks have occurred in the quality of private services. Milk once used to be delivered to homes every day, and it was not necessary to push five buttons successively on the telephone to get to speak to a human being at the bank. Doctors almost never visit patients at home anymore. In many areas a house call, which fifty years ago was a commonplace event, now occurs only rarely. Another example, although undoubtedly a matter for less general concern, is the quality of food served in restaurants. Even some of the most elegant and expensive restaurants serve frozen and reheated meals—charging high prices for what amounts to little more than TV dinners.

■ Personal Services Are Getting More Expensive

Perhaps most distressing of all, and closely connected with the problems just described, is the persistent and dramatic rise in the *cost* of what we call *personal services*—services that require face-to-face, in-person interaction between the supplier and the consumer, such as health care and education. As a college student, you know how fast college tuitions have been increasing. But you may not realize that the cost of a hospital stay has been going up even more rapidly. Worse still, the cost of health care has denied adequate health services to a substantial portion of our population—the poor and even some members of the middle class. These cost increases have made health care a prime subject of debate in political contests, not only in the United States but in virtually every other industrialized country.

Consider these facts: Between 1948 and 2004, the Consumer Price Index (CPI) (an official measure of *overall* price rises in the economy) increased at an average rate of about 3.7 percent per year, whereas the price of physicians' services rose about 5.2 percent per year. This difference seems tiny, but compounded over those fifty-six years it had the effect of increasing the price of a doctor visit, measured in dollars of constant purchasing power, more than 130 percent. During this same period, the price of hospital care skyrocketed: The average price of inpatient hospital services increased at an annual rate of about 8 percent compounded. This amounts to more than a 1,000 percent increase since 1948, measured in constant dollars.[3]

Virtually every major industrial nation has tried to prevent health-care costs from rising faster than its economy's overall rate of inflation, but none has succeeded, as Figure 4 shows. In this graph, the bar for each country shows its average yearly rate of increase in real (inflation-adjusted) health-care spending per person between 1970 and 2004. In some countries, real health-care costs have grown even faster than in the United States.

The cost of education has a similar record—costs per pupil in the United States have increased at an average annual rate of almost 7 percent per year in the past fifty years. During the seventeen years between 1985 and 2002, U.S. increases in education costs were the highest among a group of seven top industrial countries, as shown in Figure 5.

These are remarkable statistics, particularly because doctors' earnings have barely kept up with the economy's overall inflation rate in the post–World War II time period, and teachers' salaries actually fell behind. Persistent cost increases have also plagued other services such as postal delivery and libraries. The soaring costs of education, health care, and police and fire protection place a terrible financial burden on municipal budgets.

■ Why Are These "In-Person" Services Costing So Much More?

What accounts for the ever-increasing costs? Are they attributable to inefficiencies in government management or to political corruption? Perhaps to some degree to both. But there is also another reason—one that cannot be avoided by any municipal administration no matter how pure its conduct and efficient its bureaucrats and one that

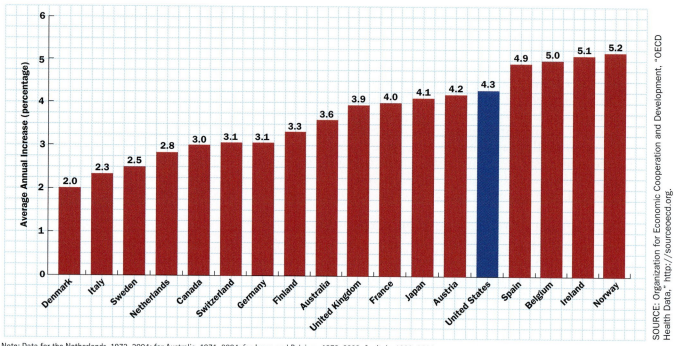

SOURCE: Organization for Economic Cooperation and Development, "OECD Health Data," http://sourceoecd.org.

Note: Data for the Netherlands, 1972–2004; for Australia, 1971–2004; for Japan and Belgium, 1970–2003; for Italy, 1988–2004.

FIGURE 4

Average Annual Growth Rates in Real (Inflation-Adjusted) Health-care Spending per Person between 1970 and 2004

The **cost disease of the personal services** is the tendency of the costs and prices of these services to rise persistently faster than those of the average output in the economy.

affects personal services provided by the private sector of the economy just as severely as it does the public sector. The common influence underlying all of these problems of rising cost and deterioration in service quality, which is *economic* in character and expected to grow even more serious with time, has been called the **cost disease of the personal services.**

This "cost disease" stems from the basic nature of personal services: they usually require face-to-face interaction between those who provide the service and those who consume it. Doctors, nurses, teachers, and librarians all engage in activities that require direct, in-person interaction. Moreover, the quality of the service deteriorates if less personal time is provided by doctors, teachers, and librarians to each user of their services.

■ Uneven Labor Productivity Growth in the Economy

In other parts of the economy, such as manufacturing, no direct personal contact between the consumer and the producer is required. For instance, the buyer of an automobile usually has no idea who worked on its assembly and could not care less how much labor time went

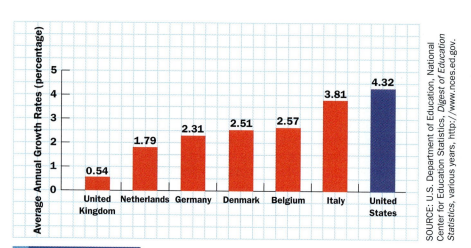

SOURCE: U.S. Department of Education, National Center for Education Statistics, *Digest of Education Statistics*, various years, http://www.nces.ed.gov.

FIGURE 5

Increased Education Spending per Pupil between 1985 and 2002

---

[3] These figures were derived from data provided by the U.S. Department of Labor, Bureau of Labor Statistics, available at http://www.bls.gov; and U.S. Department of Education, *Digest of Education Statistics*, available at http://nces.ed.gov.

into its production. A labor-saving innovation in auto production need not imply a reduction in product quality. As a result, over the years it has proved far easier for technological change to save labor in manufacturing than to save labor in providing many services. Labor productivity (output per worker) in U.S. manufacturing and agriculture has increased at an average rate of approximately 2 percent per year since World War II, whereas the productivity of college teaching (crudely measured by the number of students taught per teacher) has increased at a rate of only 1 percent per year during that period. And, in elementary and secondary education, labor productivity has actually *declined*—the average number of pupils per teacher fell from about 27 pupils per teacher in 1955 to 17 pupils per teacher in 1999, partly because classes have become smaller.[4]

These disparate productivity performances have grave consequences for prices. When manufacturing wages rise 2 percent, the cost of manufactured products need not rise because increased output per worker can make up for the rise in wages. But the nature of many personal services makes it very difficult to introduce labor-saving devices in those parts of the service sector. A 2 percent wage increase for teachers or police officers is not offset by higher productivity and must lead to an equivalent rise in municipal budgets. Similarly, a 2 percent wage increase for hairdressers must lead beauty salons to raise their prices.

In the long run, wages for all workers throughout the economy tend to go up and down together, for otherwise an activity whose wage rate falls seriously behind will tend to lose its labor force. So autoworkers and police officers will see their wages rise at roughly the same rate in the long run. But if productivity on the assembly line advances, while productivity in the police patrol car does not, then police protection grows ever more expensive, relative to manufacturing, as time goes on. Because productivity improvements are very difficult to achieve for most personal services, their costs can be expected to rise more rapidly, year in and year out, than the costs of manufactured products do. Over a period of several decades, this difference in the growth rate of costs of the two sectors adds up, making services enormously more expensive compared with manufactured goods. This imbalance explains why personal services have grown steadily more expensive compared to goods, and they are likely to continue to do so.

◾ A Future of More Goods but Fewer Services: Is It Inevitable?

If some services continue to get ever more expensive in comparison to goods, the implications for life in the future are profound indeed. The cost disease portends a world in which the typical home contains an abundance of goods—luxuries and furnishings that we can hardly imagine. But it is a home surrounded by garbage and perhaps by violence. The cost disease also portends a future in which the services of doctors, teachers, and police officers are increasingly mass produced and impersonal, and in which arts and crafts are increasingly supplied only by amateurs because the cost of professional work in these fields is too high.

But this future is by no means inevitable. To see why, we must first recognize that the problem's source, paradoxically, is the growth in our economy's productivity—or rather, the *unevenness* of that growth. Trash removal costs go up, not because garbage collectors become *less* efficient but because labor in automobile manufacturing becomes *more* efficient, thus enhancing the sanitation worker's potential value on the automotive assembly line. The sanitation worker's wages must go up to keep him at his garbage removal job.

But increasing productivity in goods manufacturing does *not* make a nation poorer. It does *not* make us unable to afford things that we could afford in the past. Indeed,

---

[4] U.S. Department of Education, *Digest of Education Statistics*, available at http://nces.ed.gov.

increasing productivity (that is, more output from each work-hour) means that we can afford more of *all* things—televisions, electric toothbrushes, cell phones, *and* medical care, education, and other services.

> The role of services in the nation's future depends on how we order our priorities. If we value services sufficiently, we can have more and better services—at some sacrifice in the growth rate of manufactured goods. Whether that is a good choice for society is not for economists to say. But society *does* have a choice, and if we fail to exercise it, matters may proceed relentlessly toward a world in which material goods are abundant and many things that most people now consider primary requisites for a high quality of life are scarce.

Government May Make the Problem Worse

How does the cost disease relate to the central topic of this chapter—the market's performance and its implications for the government's economic role? Here the problem is that the market *does* give the appropriate price signals, but government is likely to misunderstand these signals and to make decisions that do not promote the public interest most effectively.

Health care is a good example. The cost disease itself is capable of causing health-care costs (say, the price of a hospital stay) to rise more rapidly than the economy's inflation rate because medical care cannot be standardized enough to share in the productivity gains offered by automation and assembly lines. As a result, if we want to maintain standards of care in public hospitals, it is not enough to keep health-care budgets growing at the economy's prevailing inflation rate. Those budgets must actually grow *faster* to prevent a decline in quality. For example, when the inflation rate is 4 percent per year, hospitals' budgets may need to increase by 6 percent annually.

In these circumstances, something may seem amiss to a state legislature that increases its hospitals' budgets by only 5 percent per year. Responsible lawmakers will doubtless be disturbed by the fact that the budget is growing steadily, outpacing the inflation rate, and yet standards of quality at public hospitals continue to slip. If the legislators do not realize that the cost disease is causing the problem, they will look for villains—greedy doctors, corrupt or inefficient hospital administrators, and so on. The net result, all too often, is a set of wasteful rules that hamper the freedom of action of hospitals and doctors inappropriately or that tighten hospital budgets below the levels that demands and costs would require if they were determined by the market mechanism rather than by government.

In many cases, *price controls* are proposed for sectors of the economy affected by the cost disease—for medical services, insurance services, and the like. As we know, such price controls can, at best, merely eliminate the symptoms of the disease, and they often create problems that are sometimes more serious than the disease itself.[5]

THE PUZZLE RESOLVED: *Explaining the Rising Costs of Canadian Health Care*

This brings us back to the puzzle with which we began the chapter: Why have price controls failed to brake the rise in Canadian health-care costs? The answer is that the medical care system in Canada, like the health-care system in every other industrial country, is struggling with the effects of the cost disease of the personal services. As we have just seen, legislative fiat cannot abolish the productivity-growth patterns that force health-care costs to rise persistently and universally faster than the overall inflation rate. The government-imposed price controls on doctors' fees and hospital budgets have, in fact, led to long waiting lists for Canadians who need high-tech medical procedures and have reduced patients' access to high-priced

---

[5] See Chapter 4, pages 56–57 and 70–76.

specialists. The Canadian government has been forced to ease up somewhat on price controls, allowing health-care prices to adapt more closely to costs so as to prevent more serious erosion of medical-care services. The provincial governments are also trying to hold down costs by squeezing the list of services covered by public health insurance, dropping such things as vision tests and physical therapy, and forcing Canadians to pay for these things out of their own pockets. The overall quality of service apparently remains high, but the costs have risen persistently more rapidly than the overall inflation rate, just as in the United States.

SOURCE: From *The Wall Street Journal*—Permission, Cartoon Features Syndicate

"What really makes this heaven is our great healthcare plan."

Figure 4 showed that the U.S. record of increasing health-care costs is not out of line with the records of other industrialized countries. After correcting for differences in the overall inflation rates in the various countries (the U.S. record looks even better if this correction is omitted), we saw that the U.S. performance is by no means the best, but also not worst, in this sample of eighteen countries for the period 1970 to 2004. The conclusion is that, although a modification in the U.S. health-care system may or may not be desirable for other reasons, it is hardly a promising cure for the cost disease. Congress can declare both heart disease and the cost disease of the services to be illegal, but that will do little to cure either disease, and such a law may well impede more effective approaches to the problem.

In sum, the cost disease is not a case where the market performs badly. Rather, it is a case in which the market *appears* to misbehave by singling out certain sectors through particularly large cost increases. Because the market *seems* to be working badly here, government reactions that can be highly damaging to the public interest are likely. That is, "government failure" may occur.

THE MARKET SYSTEM ON BALANCE

This chapter, like Chapter 14 has deliberately offered a rather unbalanced assessment of the market mechanism. In Chapter 14, we extolled the market's virtues; in this chapter, we catalogued its vices. We come out, as in the nursery rhyme, concluding that the market is either very, very good or it is horrid.

There seems to be nothing *moderate* about the quality of performance of a market system. As a means of achieving efficiency in the production of ordinary consumer goods and responding to changes in consumer preferences, it is unparalleled. It is, in fact, difficult to overstate the accomplishments of the price system in these areas. By contrast, the market has proved itself incapable of coping with business fluctuations, income inequality, or the consequences of monopoly. It has proved to be a very poor allocator of resources among outputs that generate external costs and external benefits, and it has shown itself to be incapable of arranging for the provision of public goods. Some of the most urgent problems that plague our society—the deterioration of services in the cities, the despoilation of our atmosphere, the social unrest attributable to poverty—can be ascribed in part to one or another of these market system shortcomings.

Most economists conclude from these observations that although the market mechanism is virtually irreplaceable, the public interest nevertheless requires considerable modifications in the way it works. Proposals designed to deal directly with the problems of poverty, monopoly, and resource allocation over time abound in economic literature. All of them call for the government to intervene in the economy, either by supplying directly those goods and services that, it is believed, private enterprise does not supply in adequate amounts, or by seeking to influence the workings of the economy more indirectly through regulation. We discussed many of these programs in earlier chapters; we will explain others in future chapters.

■ EPILOGUE: THE UNFORGIVING MARKET, ITS GIFT OF ABUNDANCE, AND ITS DANGEROUS FRIENDS

As we said at the end of Chapter 14, economists' analysis of the free market's accomplishments, although valid enough, may fail to emphasize its central contribution. The same can be said of their analysis of the market's shortcomings.

The market's major contribution to the general welfare may well be its stimulation of *productivity*, which has yielded an abundance of consumer goods, contributed to increases in human longevity, created new products, expanded education, and raised standards of living to levels undreamed of in earlier societies. This is an accomplishment that is yet to be discussed (see Chapters 16, 32, and 33). The main shortcoming of the market, according to many observers, lies in the arena of justice and injustice, a subject that economists are no more competent to address than anyone else. The perception that markets are cruel and unjust springs from the very heart of the mechanism. The market mechanism has sometimes been described appropriately as the profit system, because it works by richly rewarding those who succeed in introducing attractive new products or in increasing efficiency sufficiently to permit sharp price reductions of other items. At the same time, it is unforgiving to those who fail, subjecting them to bankruptcy and perhaps to poverty.

Both the wealth awarded to those who succeed and the drastic treatment accorded to those who fail are main sources of the markets' productive power. But they also generate disenchantment and opposition. Consider what has happened in the newly "marketized" countries of Eastern Europe. Predictably, as enterprise in these countries was freed from government control, a number of wildly successful entrepreneurs have earned high incomes, leading to widespread resentment among the populace and calls for restrictions on entrepreneurial earnings. These critics do not seem to realize that a market without substantial rewards to successful entrepreneurs is a market whose engine has been weakened, if not altogether removed.

Indeed, efficient and effectively competitive markets often elicit support from groups that, at the same time, do their best to undermine that competition. For example, regulators who seek to prevent "excessive competition," and politicians in other countries who arrange for the sale of government enterprises to private owners only to constrain decision making by the new owners at every turn, are, in fact, doing their best to keep markets from working. When the general public demands price controls on interest rates, rents, and health-care services, it is expressing its unwillingness to accept the free market's decisions. Businesspeople who tirelessly proclaim their support for the market system, but who seek to acquire the monopoly power that can distort its activities, are doing the same thing. In short, the market has many professed supporters who genuinely believe in its virtues but whose behavior poses a constant threat to its effectiveness.

We cannot take for granted the success of the newly introduced market mechanism in Eastern Europe. The Russian economy, in its transition from communist government control, has come very slowly out of turmoil, as have other economies in Eastern Europe. Even in the older free-enterprise economies, we cannot simply assume that the market will emerge unscathed from the dangerous embrace of its most vocal supporters.

SUMMARY

1. At least seven major imperfections are associated with the market mechanism:

   a. Inequality of income distribution

   b. Fluctuations in economic activity (inflation and unemployment)

   c. Monopolistic output restrictions

   d. Beneficial and detrimental externalities

   e. Inadequate provision of public goods

   f. Misallocation of resources between present and future

   g. Deteriorating quality and rising costs of personal services

2. Efficient resource allocation is a matter of balancing the benefits of producing more of one good against the benefits of devoting the required inputs to some other good's production.

3. A detrimental **externality** occurs when an economic activity incidentally does harm to others who are not directly involved in the activity. A beneficial externality occurs when an economic activity incidentally creates benefits for others.

4. When an activity causes a detrimental externality, the activity's **marginal social cost** (including the harm it does to others) must be greater than the **marginal private cost** to those who carry on the activity. The opposite will be true when a beneficial externality occurs.

5. If a product's manufacture causes detrimental externalities, its price will generally not include all of the marginal social cost it causes, because part of the cost will be borne by others. The opposite is true for beneficial externalities.

6. The market will therefore tend to overallocate resources to the production of goods that cause detrimental externalities and underallocate resources to the production of goods that create beneficial externalities. This imbalance is one of the *Ideas for Beyond the Final Exam.*

7. A **public good** is a commodity (such as the guiding beam of a coastal lighthouse) that is not depleted by additional users. It is often difficult to exclude anyone from the benefits of a public good, even those who refuse to pay for it. A **private good**, in contrast, is characterized by both **excludability** and **depletability**.

8. Free-enterprise firms generally will not produce a public good, even if it is extremely useful to the community, because they cannot charge money for the use of the good.

9. Many observers believe that the market often shortchanges the future, particularly when it makes irreversible decisions that destroy natural resources.

10. Complex and large-scale enterprises such as huge corporations cannot be run day-to-day or effectively controlled directly by their owners, the **principals.** So they hire **agents** to run the enterprises on their behalf. The danger is that the agents will operate the enterprises so as to favor their own interests rather than those of the principals.

11. Because personal services—such as education, medical care, and police protection—are activities whose inherent value depends on face-to-face, in-person interaction, they are not amenable to labor-saving innovations, they suffer from a **cost disease.** That is, their costs tend to rise persistently and considerably more rapidly than costs in the economy as a whole, where faster productivity increases offset rising input costs. The result can be a distortion in the supply of services by government or the imposition of unwise price controls when the rising cost is misattributed to greed and mismanagement.

KEY TERMS

Production possibilities frontier   313

Resource misallocation   313

Externalities (detrimental and beneficial)   314

Marginal social cost (MSC)   315

Marginal private cost (MPC)   315

Marginal social benefit (MSB)   315

Marginal private benefit (MPB)   315

Public good   318

Private good   318

Depletability   318

Excludability   318

Rent seeking   322

Moral hazard   322

Principals   323

Agents   323

Stock options   323

Cost disease of the personal services   328

TEST YOURSELF

1. What is the opportunity cost to society of a 100-mile trip of a truck? Why may the price of the gasoline used by the truck not adequately represent that opportunity cost?

2. Suppose that, because of a new disease that attacks coffee plants, far more labor and other inputs are required to harvest a pound of coffee than before. How may that change affect the efficient allocation of resources between tea and coffee? How would the prices of coffee and tea react in a free market?

3. Give some examples of goods whose production causes detrimental externalities and some examples of goods whose production creates beneficial externalities.

4. Compare cleaning a dormitory room with cleaning the atmosphere of a city. Which is a public good and which is a private good? Why?

5. **(More difficult)** A firm holds a patent that is estimated to be worth $20 million. The patent is repeatedly challenged in the courts by a large number of (rent-seeking) firms, each hoping to grab away the patent. If anyone is free to challenge the patent so that there is free entry into the litigation process, how much will end up being spent in the legal battles? (*Hint:* Under perfect competition, should firms expect to earn any economic profit?)

DISCUSSION QUESTIONS

1. Give some other examples of public goods. In each case, explain why additional users do not deplete the good and why it is difficult to exclude people from using it.

2. Think about the goods and services that your local government provides. Which are "public goods" as economists use the term?

3. Explain why the services of a lighthouse are sometimes used as an example of a public good.

4. Explain why education is not a very satisfactory example of a public good.

5. In recent decades, college tuition costs have risen more rapidly than the general price level, even though the wages of college professors have failed to keep pace with the price level. Can you explain why?

16

THE CASE FOR FREE MARKETS II: INNOVATION AND GROWTH

Procter & Gamble has a world-class global research and development organization, with over 7,500 scientists working in 22 research centers in 12 countries around the world. This includes 1,250 Ph.D. scientists. For perspective, this is larger than the combined science faculties at Harvard, Stanford and MIT. . . .

PROCTER & GAMBLE [THE GIANT CONSUMER PRODUCTS COMPANY], http://www.pg.com.

An activity is said to generate a beneficial or detrimental **externality** if that activity causes incidental benefits or damages to others not directly involved in the activity, and no corresponding compensation is provided to or paid by those who generate the externality.

The past several chapters have tried to provide a balanced evaluation of the market, describing both its shortcomings and its accomplishments. Among its defects we have listed attributes such as vulnerability to monopoly power, **externalities** such as damage to the environment, and a propensity to underproduce public goods. On the virtuous side, we showed how the market can allocate resources more efficiently and more in accord with consumer desires than planning and central direction. But we have saved the best for last—the free market's incredible performance in terms of *innovation* and growth, in which it has far exceeded any other type of economy in history, whether ancient or recent.

Although growth is often viewed as a macroeconomic topic, inventions are provided by individuals or individual laboratories, and are brought to market by individual firms. So understanding innovation and its contribution to growth requires microeconomic analysis of the behavior of individual innovators and firms. This chapter will indicate the magnitude of the market's growth accomplishment and will use our microeconomic tools to analyze how the market has produced that achievement. Part of the discussion may be considered both as a review of some of the analytic tools we have used before and as an additional illustration of the wide variety of subjects they can be used to investigate.

CONTENTS

■ THE MARKET ECONOMY'S INCREDIBLE GROWTH RECORD

Per-capita income in an economy is the average income of all people in that economy.

In the free-market economies, the growth in **per-capita income** (average income per person) and **productivity** (output per hour of work) has been so enormous that we can hardly comprehend its magnitude. In contrast, average growth rates of per-capita incomes probably approximated *zero* for about 1,500 years before the **Industrial Revolution** (around the time of George Washington). In 1776, even the wealthiest consumers in England, then the world's richest country, could purchase perhaps only a half-dozen consumer goods that had not been available more than a thousand years earlier in ancient Rome. These new products included (highly inaccurate) hunting guns, (highly inaccurate) watches, paper with printed material on it, window glass, and very little else. No sounds had ever been recorded, so we can never hear Washington's voice. No one had traveled on land faster than on horseback. Messages delivered from the Old World to the New required weeks and even months, so that the battle of New Orleans was fought after the peace treaty had been signed. And Roman citizens enjoyed a number of amenities, such as hot baths and paved roads, that had practically disappeared long before the American Revolution.

The **productivity** of an economy is the value of all goods and services produced there, divided by the total labor time devoted to the economy's productive activities.

The **Industrial Revolution** is the stream of new technology and the resulting growth of output that began in England toward the end of the eighteenth century.

The economic conditions of the lower economic classes before the Industrial Revolution and for quite a period beyond it are difficult for us to grasp. Regular famines—at least once per decade on average, with starvation widespread and corpses littering the streets—only began to disappear in the eighteenth century. Still, famines continued occasionally well into the nineteenth, and not only in Ireland. For example, in relatively wealthy Belgium, "During the great crisis of 1846, the newspapers would tell daily of cases of death from starvation. . . .[In one town] cases became so frequent that the local policeman was given the job of calling at all houses each day to see if the inhabitants were still alive."[1] But even the living standards of the upper classes were far from enviable (see "Discomforts of the Rich a Few Centuries Ago" below).

Discomforts of the Rich a Few Centuries Ago

Earlier eras were characterized by miserable living conditions even for the wealthy and powerful. Their wealth did give them ostentatious clothing, exotic foods, and armies of servants. But the problem for them was that little of the technology of human comfort had yet been invented.

The standards of discomfort for the rich and powerful before the Industrial Revolution are illustrated by the oft-cited report by the Princess Palatine (German sister-in-law of the mighty French king Louis XIV) that in the winter of 1695, the wine froze in the glasses at the king's table in the Palace of Versailles! Even throughout the nineteenth century, in much of the United States it was expected that every winter the ink would freeze in the inkwells.

A description of the 1732 journey of the pregnant Wilhelmina, favorite sister of Frederick the Great, between Berlin and Bayreuth is also revealing:

"Ten strenuous, abnormally frigid days were spent upon roads, bad enough in summer, now deep with snow. On the second day the carriage in which Wilhelmina was riding turned over. She was

SOURCE: © Adam Woolfitt/Corbis

buried under an avalanche of luggage. . . . Everyone expected a miscarriage and wanted Wilhelmina to rest in bed for several days. . . . Mountains appeared after Leibzig had been passed. . . . Wilhelmina was frightened by the steepness of the roads and preferred to get out and walk to being whacked about as the carriage jolted from boulder to boulder.

Statistics and other pieces of evidence tell a story consistent with such anecdotes. Using genealogical records, it has been estimated that between 1550 and 1700 the average longevity for the general male and female population slightly exceeded that for members of the nobility for a substantial part of this period.

SOURCE: Fernand Braudel, *Civilization and Capitalism, 15th to 18th Century*, vol. 1, New York: Harper & Row, 1979, p. 299; Constance Wright, *A Royal Affinity*, London: Frederick Muller, 1965, p. 142; and Robert W. Fogel, "Nutrition and the Decline of Mortality since 1700: Some Preliminary Findings," in S. L. Engerman and R. E. Gallman, eds., *Long-Term Factors in American Economic Growth*, Chicago: University of Chicago Press, 1986.

---

[1] Adrien De Meeüs, *History of the Belgians*, New York: Frederick A. Praeger, 1962, p. 305.

By comparison, in the past two centuries, per-capita incomes in the typical **capitalist** economy have risen by amounts ranging from several hundred to several thousand percent. Recent decades have yielded an unmatched outpouring of new products and services: color television, the computer, jet aircraft, the VCR and DVD player, the microwave oven, the hand-held calculator, the cellular telephone, and so on and so on. And the flood of new products continues.[2] Surely part of the reason for the collapse of most of the world's communist regimes was their citizens' desire to participate in the growth miracle of the capitalist economies.

During the twentieth century, the real income of an average American grew by a factor of more than seven.[3] Looked at another way, an average American family living around 1900 could afford only *one seventh* the food, clothing, housing, and other amenities that constitute the standard of living today. The change is really incredible. Just try to imagine how your family's life would be changed if it lost more than six out of seven dollars from its consumption expenditure.

We can look at this enormous economic progress from another angle: by examining how much work it takes to acquire the things we purchase. For example, in 1919, the average U.S. worker had to labor nearly an hour to buy a pound of chicken. At today's wages and poultry prices, less than five minutes of labor is required for the purpose! Figure 1 (Minutes of Work) shows how much cheaper a variety of snack foods have become over the past century.

Food is not the only item that has become much less costly in terms of the labor time needed to pay for it. Figure 2 (Hours of Work) shows the great cost reductions of various types of electronic equipment—a cut of 98 percent in the cost of a color TV between 1954 and 1997, 96 percent in the cost of a VCR between 1972 and 1997, and 99 percent in the cost of a microwave oven between 1947 and 1997. Of course, the most sensational decrease of all has been in the cost of computers. Computer capability is standardized in terms of the number of MIPS (millions of instructions per second) that the computer is capable of handling. These days, it costs about 27 minutes of labor per 1 MIPS capacity. In 1984, it cost the wages of 52 *hours* of labor; in 1970, the cost was 1.24 *lifetimes* of labor; and in 1944, the price was a barely believable 733,000 *lifetimes* of

Capitalism is an economic system in which most of the production process is controlled by private firms operating in markets with minimal government control. The investors in these firms (called "capitalists") own the firms.

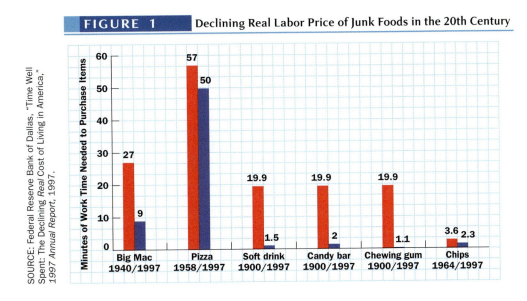

FIGURE 1   Declining Real Labor Price of Junk Foods in the 20th Century

SOURCE: Federal Reserve Bank of Dallas, "Time Well Spent: The Declining *Real Cost of Living in America," 1997 Annual Report,* 1997.

[2] "Could the Emperor Tiberius have eaten grapes in January? Could the Emperor Napoleon have crossed the Atlantic in a night? . . . Could Thomas Aquinas have . . . dispatched [a letter] to 1,000 recipients with the touch of a key, and begun to receive replies within the hour?" (J. Bradford DeLong, *The Economic History of the Twentieth Century: Slouching Toward Utopia?,* Chapter 2, p. 3, draft copy, http://www.j-bradford-delong.net.)

[3] Angus Maddison, *The Nature and Functioning of European Capitalism: A Historical and Comparative Perspective* (Groningen, Netherlands: University of Groningen, 1997), p. 34. Real income is not measured in actual dollars but in dollars whose purchasing power is kept unchanged.

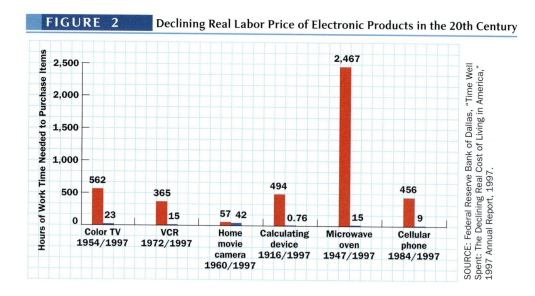

FIGURE 2   Declining Real Labor Price of Electronic Products in the 20th Century

SOURCE: Federal Reserve Bank of Dallas, "Time Well Spent: The Declining Real Cost of Living in America," 1997 Annual Report, 1997.

GDP (gross domestic product) is a measure of the total amount the economy produces domestically in a year.

labor.[4] In this chapter, we will investigate the free market's extraordinary record of growth and economic progress.

The history of the growth in income per person can be summed up with a graph depicting estimates of the United Kingdom's **GDP** per capita for five centuries (Figure 4: Real GDP per Capita). It is clear that the pattern of the graph is characterized by a rising slope that grows dramatically ever steeper.

THE BIG PUZZLE: *What Accounts for the Free Market's Incredible Growth Record?*

The conclusion from all this is that the explosion of growth and innovation of the past two centuries is the most sensational economic accomplishment of the free market economies. Its secret is what the developing countries would most like to learn from the experience of the world's wealthy nations. But that is the basic puzzle: How does one explain this extraordinary performance? The rest of the chapter seeks to describe the features of the market economy that played the primary role in that success story.

FIGURE 3

Work Time Needed to Buy a College Education, 1965 versus 1995

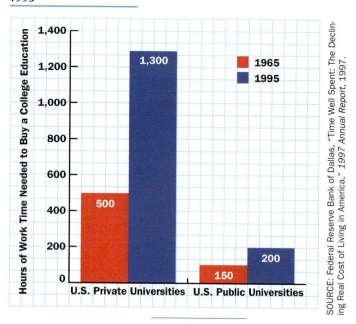

SOURCE: Federal Reserve Bank of Dallas, "Time Well Spent: The Declining Real Cost of Living in America," 1997 Annual Report, 1997.

■ **INNOVATION, NOT INVENTION, IS THE UNIQUE FREE-MARKET ACCOMPLISHMENT**

The search for explanations of the capitalist growth miracle must focus on its unprecedented outpouring of innovation, and to that we will soon turn. But first it is important to distinguish the key term "*innovation*," from the related word "in-

---

[4] But the magic of productivity growth has not yet succeeded in invading every sector of the U.S. economy. In particular, the process of college teaching seems to have been able to escape the cost-reducing ability of productivity growth. Figure 3 (Hours of Work) shows the consequences. Between 1965 and 1995, the cost of a college education rose 33 percent at public universities, whereas at private universities it went up by more than 150 percent, from 500 to 1,300 labor hours. All of these figures on changing labor-value prices are taken from Federal Reserve Bank of Dallas. 1997. *Time Well Spent: The Declining Real Cost of Living in America, 1997 Annual Report* (Dallas, Tex.).

| FIGURE 4 | Real GDP per Capita in the United Kingdom, 1500–1998 |

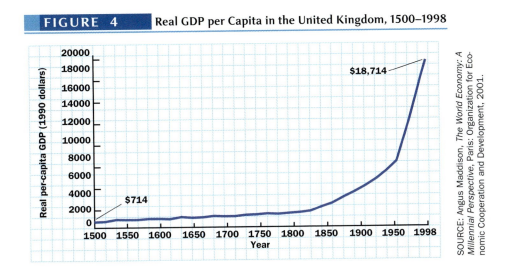

SOURCE: Angus Maddison, *The World Economy: A Millennial Perspective*, Paris: Organization for Economic Cooperation and Development, 2001.

vention." **Invention** is used by economists to mean what it usually does: the creation of new products or processes or at least the ideas that underlie them. But the term "**innovation**" means more than that; it refers to the entire extended process of which invention is only the initial step. Innovation includes development of the invention's design to the point at which it is ready for practical use, its introduction to the market, and its subsequent utilization by the economy. The distinction is critical here because it underlies much of the difference between the accomplishments of the capitalist economy and those of any and all of its predecessors, including those earlier economies with remarkable records of invention.

Invention is nothing new. Ancient China, for example, invented printing, paper, playing cards, the spinning wheel, an elaborate water clock, the umbrella and, of course, gunpowder, to name but a few. But despite China's talent for the creation of novel technology, its performance in adoption and utilization of these inventions was hardly outstanding. More than once inventions were diverted to amusement rather than productive use, or, like the wondrous water clock, soon forgotten.[5] Even in the Soviet Union, with its cadre of very capable scientists and engineers, there is evidence of a respectable record of invention, but a remarkably poor record of utilization of these inventions—except in military activity. The reason is that the economic institutions in both ancient China and the Soviet Union not only failed to offer incentives for innovative activity, but actually provided strong motivation for its determined avoidance. In China, inventions often were confiscated by the government, with no reward for the inventors. In the Soviet Union, factory managers resisted the installation of improved equipment or the adoption of improved products because the necessary retooling period could cut down the factory's production, on which the manager's reward was based. In short, although the free market's record of invention is noteworthy, it is its performance in innovation that is unique.

Invention is the creation of new products or processes or the ideas that underlie them.

Innovation is the process that begins with invention and includes improvement to prepare the invention for practical use and marketing of the invention or its products.

■ SOURCES OF FREE-MARKET INNOVATION: THE ROLE OF THE ENTREPRENEUR

There are many obvious sources of innovation. Some innovations are contributed by *universities* and *government research agencies*, which are not inherently market-driven. Then there are the well-known products of *individual inventors*, such as Thomas Edison and Alexander Graham Bell. Finally, there are the outputs of industrial laboratories in *giant corporations*. These last two sources—the private entrepreneur and the

---

[5] This persisted into a much more recent era. Westerners bringing mechanical clocks as gifts to the Chinese emperors found that timekeeping accuracy elicited little appreciation, but marching or dancing figures run by the clockworks were highly valued.

An **entrepreneur** is an individual who organizes a new business firm, particularly a firm that offers new products or new productive technology.

giant corporations—clearly are directly embedded in the workings of the market economy, and it is upon them that we will focus.

Here, we use the term **entrepreneur** to refer to an individual who organizes a new business firm. We will deal primarily with the creators of firms that offer new products or new productive technology, that is, with individuals who establish *innovative* firms. Until the end of the nineteenth century, invention was largely the work of independent inventors and their entrepreneur associates who brought the invention to market (though in a number of cases both roles were played by the same individual).

There have always been imaginative, enterprising, and risk-taking individuals who followed the most effective routes to acquisition of wealth, power, and prestige. But the methods they used for the purpose were very different from those that became the norm in the capitalist era. They often sought advancement through military careers supporting the ruling monarch, or as independent robber barons, or organized private armies as business enterprises and hired them out for money, or they undertook warfare on their own for the wealth they could capture. Sometimes the enterprising individuals sought economic success by way of careers in the government bureaucracy or in the church hierarchy. And such varied activities of enterprising individuals have not disappeared today: Who would deny that a high official in a dictatorial government or a godfather in a Mafioso organization can be enterprising and grow rich? But these forms of entrepreneurial activity rarely lead to increases in productivity of the economy.

In precapitalist societies, the more modern forms of productivity-increasing entrepreneurship were virtually prevented by regimes in which any property accumulated by commercial and productive activity was constantly threatened by government expropriation, and where organizations such as the medieval guilds could punish anyone who attempted to set up in business as a competitor, particularly if that person offered improved productive techniques or innovative products that threatened the guild's monopoly.[6] Until the century after Shakespeare's time, patent monopolies were often awarded by the monarchs, but were given to personal friends of the king and their relatives rather than the inventors. Only with the adoption of laws protecting property from expropriation, enforcing contracts, and providing patents only to inventors could modern entrepreneurship flourish. It is noteworthy that the U.S. founding fathers considered the patent system so important that they embodied it in the Constitution itself.

Breakthrough Invention and the Entrepreneurial Firm

Individual inventors and entrepreneurs continued to be the primary source of innovation in the market economies until the end of the nineteenth century, when large corporations began to play a critical role in the process. But the part played by large corporations is very different from that of the more freewheeling and flexible small enterprises. Research activity in large business organizations is inherently cautious and focuses on small, relatively limited improvements in current technology. The big established firms tend to avoid the great risks that revolutionary breakthroughs involve. The true breakthrough inventions, rather, are often still the domain of small or newly founded enterprises, guided by enterprising owners, although success of an invention can rapidly transform a startup firm into a business giant.

There is no clear boundary between inventions that can be considered revolutionary breakthroughs and those that are "merely" cumulative incremental improvements, but some inventions clearly fall into the former category. For example, the electric light, alternating electric current, the internal combustion engine, and the electronic computer must surely be deemed revolutionary. In contrast, successive models of washing machines and refrigerators—with each new model a bit longer-lasting, a bit less susceptible to breakdown, and a bit easier to use—clearly constitute a sequence of incremental improvements.

---

[6] In the Middle Ages, unions of employer craftsmen, called *guilds*, controlled various types of production in a community. An example is the Fishmongers' Guild of London.

There is a striking degree of asymmetry between small and large firms in their introduction of breakthrough versus incremental invention. The U.S. Small Business Administration has prepared a list of breakthrough innovations of the twentieth century for which small firms are responsible, and its menu of inventions literally spans the range from A to Z, from air conditioning to the zipper. Included in the list are the cotton picker, the electronic spreadsheet, FM radio, the helicopter, the integrated circuit, the instant camera, quick-frozen food, the vacuum tube and the photocopier, among a host of others, many of enormous significance for our economy (Table 1 reproduces part of the list).

So a high proportion of the revolutionary new ideas of the past two centuries have been, and are likely to continue to be, provided by independent innovators who operate small business enterprises. The small entrepreneurial firms have played a leading role in the portion of business **research and development (R&D)** activity that is engaged in the search for the revolutionary breakthroughs that are such a critical part of the growth machine that is provided by the market economy. What drives this activity and what is different about its operation in the market economy? To the extent one can generalize, inventor-entrepreneurs are driven by the prospect that by being first to come up with a better product or better productive technology they can (temporarily) beat out all competitors in the market for their product, and can thereby obtain monopoly profits. In a market economy, however, this source of wealth is only available temporarily, because current and prospective rivals in the market will constantly try to improve on the initial invention and recapture the market. Thus, there is no rest for the innovators. They can never afford to be satisfied with their past achievements if they want their stream of monopoly profits to continue. Yesterday's invention soon is ancient history, and unless successor inventions are introduced soon enough by the firm, rivals will succeed in entering the market and will dry up the initial entrepreneur's stream of profits. So the entrepreneurs have no choice. They must seek to generate a stream of innovations, and that is one key part of the free-market's success story—the market provides a mechanism designed to change innovation from an occasional happening with a large element of accident and chance into a systematic process that ensures, so far as ingenuity and current knowledge permit, the injection of a stream of inventions into the economy.[7]

Research and development (R&D) is the activity of firms, universities, and government agencies that seeks to invent new products and processes and to improve those inventions so that they are ready for the market or other users.

TABLE 1
Some Important Innovations by U.S. Small Firms in the 20th Century

Air Conditioning	Heart Valve	Pacemaker
Airplane	Helicopter	Personal Computer
Assembly Line	High Resolution CAT Scanner	Photo Typesetting
Audio Tape Recorder	Human Growth Hormone	Polaroid Camera
Biosynthetic Insulin	Hydraulic Brake	Portable Computer
Catalytic Petroleum Cracking	Integrated Circuit	Prefabricated Housing
Cotton Picker	Microprocessor	Quick-Frozen Food
Defribrillator	Nuclear Magnetic Resonance Scanner	Safety Razor
DNA Fingerprinting	Optical Scanner	Soft Contact Lens
Electronic Spreadsheet	Oral Contraceptives	Solid-Fuel Rocket Engine
FM Radio	Overnight National Delivery	Vacuum Tube
Geodesic Dome		Xerography
Gyrocompass		X-Ray Telescope
		Zipper

SOURCE: U.S. Small Business Administration, *The State of Small Business: A Report of the President, 1994*, Washington, DC: U.S. Government Printing Office, 1995, p. 114.

---

[7] The materials in this paragraph are a brief summary of the analysis of the late Joseph Schumpeter, who can be judged to have inaugurated the economics of innovation and growth in a book first published in 1911.

But what is there about modern free-market economy that allows this innovation process to flourish? The answer is primarily found in the new institutions that grew up along with the capitalist economy, perhaps partly as a historical accident. We have already mentioned such institutions as sanctity of property (prohibiting arbitrary expropriation by the king and his nobles), enforceability of contracts, and the patent system. These rules were quite new at the time of the Industrial Revolution, and for the first time they assured entrepreneurs and innovators that they could keep the wealth generated by their efforts. This assurance not only provided the incentives that attracted individuals into the struggle for innovation, it also served as an irresistible lure for the entry of competitors. The appearance of the early innovating entrepreneurs and their success brought in ever more entrepreneurs, but it also gave rise to ever-fiercer competition using innovation as a weapon. And this provided the driving force for innovation that is present and fully effective only in the market economies.

> The individual inventor and entrepreneur play a critical role in the provision of a constant stream of breakthrough innovations. If they succeed in marketing an innovation, they are rewarded by temporary monopoly profits. But, usually, the profits are soon eroded by competition. So if they want the accumulation of profit to continue, they must provide one innovation after another. This is all possible only in the market economy, with its institutions such as sanctity of property, enforceability of contracts, and the patent system.

This apparently critical and continuing innovative role of the entrepreneur and the small firm may seem to leave little scope for invention by the large enterprise. But that, as we will see next, is a very misleading conclusion.

■ The Large Enterprises and Their Innovation "Assembly Lines"

As we see in Figure 5, private investment in R&D has risen sharply in the last three decades (with only a few slowdowns in funding during those years). Increasingly, at least in the United States, the financing for innovation has been supplied by large oligopolistic enterprises, rather than by independent inventors or small, newly-founded entrepreneurial firms. Today private business pays for 64 percent of U.S. R&D (and performs 70 percent of it), with most of this outlay provided by the larger firms.[8]

FIGURE 5

Expenditures on Research and Development (R&D) by U.S. Business Firms (in real, inflation-adjusted terms), 1970–2004

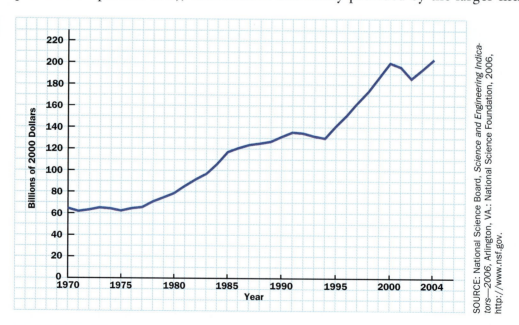

SOURCE: National Science Board, *Science and Engineering Indicators—2006*, Arlington, VA.: National Science Foundation, 2006, http://www.nsf.gov.

---

[8] For instance, the U.S. National Science Foundation reports that, in 2001, the 68 largest manufacturing firms (each employing 25,000 or more workers) accounted for 49 percent of R&D in the manufacturing sector of the economy (National Science Board, *Science and Engineering Indicators—2004*, Arlington, VA: National Science Foundation, 2004, http://www.nsf.gov).

Even seemingly "low-tech" companies like the consumer products giant Procter & Gamble (noted for outputs like cleaning and personal care products) employ small armies of R&D personnel, as evidenced in the quotation at the beginning of the chapter). These large firms are driven to do this by powerful market pressures of competitive innovation

Innovation has, in fact, become a prime weapon of choice for competitive battles in substantial sectors of the economy. Of course, prices are still important. But it is improved products and methods of production that really capture the attention of the firm's managers. Product lines as diverse as computers and computer software, automobiles, cameras, and machinery all feature constant improvements, which are instantly and widely advertised.

The result is a kind of innovation arms race in which no firm in a high-tech industry can afford to fall behind its rivals. Indeed, only by staying abreast of the others can the firm hope to preserve its place in the market. In its innovation, it is forced to run as fast as it can just to stand still—because its rivals are doing the same. Any firm that can come up with a better model than its rivals will gain a critical advantage.

Firms in many high-tech industries—such as computers, medical equipment, aeronautics, and even automobiles—struggle for market position in this way. The managers of firms cannot afford to neglect R&D activities. For if a firm fails to adopt the latest technology—even if the technology is created by others—then rival firms can easily take the lead and make disastrous inroads into the slower firm's sales. Often, for the firm, innovation is literally a matter of life and death.

Thus, especially in high-tech sectors, firms dare not leave innovation to chance, or to the haphazard contributions of independent inventors tinkering in their basements and garages. Rather, competitive markets force firms to take over the innovation process themselves and (in the immortal words of the great comedian, W. C. Fields) "to remove all elements of chance" from the undertaking.[9] Many business firms today routinely budget for R&D, hire scientists and engineers to do the job, and systematically decide how to promote and price their innovations.

This "arms-race" feature of an industry's innovation process probably plays a critical role in the continuing outpouring of innovations that characterize the market economy. The capitalist economy itself has become a giant innovation machine the predictable output of which is a stream of improved technology. Never in any other type of economy has there existed such an innovation machine—an assembly line that forces the economy to bring one invention after another from the drawing board all the way to the market.

We mentioned earlier that that there is a rather sharp differentiation between the contributions to the economy's innovation that are provided by entrepreneurs and those that are offered by established businesses, with their large internal R&D laboratories. In their effort to contain the risks inherent in the innovation process, large business firms have tended to slant their efforts toward incremental improvements rather than revolutionary breakthroughs. User friendliness, increased reliability, marginal additions to application, expansions of capacity, flexibility in design—these and many other types of improvement have come out of the industrial R&D facilities, with impressive consistency, year after year, and often preannounced and preadvertised.

The products of these innovative activities may often be individually modest, making very small improvements in products and productive processes. Nevertheless, taken in the aggregate, they have accomplished a great deal. An example is the airplane. The comfort, speed, and reliability of the modern passenger aircraft and the complexity and power of today's military flying machines clearly have turned the Wright brothers' original revolutionary device into a historical curiosity. Most of the sophistication, speed,

A **high-tech (high-technology)** firm or industry is one whose products, equipment and production methods utilize highly advanced technology that is constantly modified and improved. Examples are the aerospace, scientific instruments, computer, communications, and pharmaceutical industries.

---

[9] This phrase is uttered when Fields, playing a card shark, seeks to lure an unsuspecting novice into a card game, whereupon his intended victim questions the morality of "games of chance." Fields hastens to reassure him: "Young man, when you play with me, all elements of chance have been removed!"

and reliability of today's aviation equipment is probably attributable to the combined incremental additions made by routine research activities in corporate facilities.

There are even more startling examples of the magnitude of the innovative contributions of the large companies, whose incremental advances can compound to results of enormous magnitude. It is reported, for example, that between 1971 and 2003, the "clock speed" of Intel's microprocessor chips—that is, the number of instructions each chip can carry out per second—has increased by some *three million percent*, reaching about three billion computations per second today. And, between 1968 and 2003, the number of transistors embedded in a single chip has expanded more than *ten million percent*, and the number of transistors that can be purchased for a dollar has grown by *five billion percent*.[10] Added up, these advances surely contributed enormously more computing capacity than was provided by the original revolutionary breakthrough of the invention of the electronic computer. Of course, that initial invention was an indispensable necessity for all of the later improvements. But it is only the combined work of the two together that made possible the powerful and inexpensive apparatus that serves us so effectively today. Other careful observers have extended such examples and have concluded that incremental innovation activities of the large firms have been responsible for a very respectable share of the contribution of innovation to economic growth in the twentieth century.

Predicting the Future: A Feebleness of Imagination?

There is one area where futurists have suffered not from inflated hopes but from a feebleness of imagination: the information revolution. In an article titled "Brains That Click" in the March 1949 issue of *Popular Mechanics,* the author enthused over a state-of-the-art supercomputer called the ENIAC (for Electronic Numerical Integrator and Computer). But he knew it was just the beginning. "Where a calculator like the ENIAC today is equipped with 18,000 vacuum tubes and weighs 30 tons," he predicted, "computers in the future may have only 1,000 tubes and perhaps weigh only 1½ tons." Today's amused denizens of the Internet have used their laptops and desktop PCs—each vastly more powerful than the pitiful ENIAC—to lampoon the quotation on scores of pages across the World Wide Web. Also spreading like a virus through cyberspace are words attributed to I.B.M.'s former chairman Thomas J. Watson in 1943: that there is a world market for perhaps five computers. Back then it seemed sensible that only nations or the largest corporations would be able to afford such mammoth contraptions. Again and again, prognosticators made the mistake of assuming that computers would be like rocket ships or other ordinary machines. The mightier you wanted to make them, the bigger, more expensive and more energy-hungry they would have to be. It defied common sense to envision what exists today, a technology where making something smaller causes it to be more powerful, with denser skeins of circuitry squeezed into increasingly tinier spaces.

And that's just the beginning of the magic. As the parts become closer together they can exchange information more rapidly. Designers can take a circuit diagram and photograph it onto a silicon chip. As the focus of the projector grows sharper, the circuits become finer and more tightly packed. With a design in place, chips can be stamped out like pages on a printing press.

These devices—the most complex things produced by the human mind—can be made indefinitely small because of a crucial distinction. While ordinary machines work by manipulating stuff, computers manipulate information, symbols which are essentially weightless. A bit of information, a 1 or a 0, can be indicated by a pencil mark in a checkbox, by a microscopic spot on a magnetic disk or by the briefest pulse of electricity or scintilla of light.

According to Moore's famous law, the number of components that can be packed onto a single chip doubles every year or two. The latest Pentium chip contains 42 million transistors, each doing the job of one of ENIAC's glowing tubes but far more rapidly and efficiently.

The end is not in sight. By some estimates, the shrinking will continue over coming decades until each component is the size of a single atom, registering a bit of information by the position of an orbiting electron.

SOURCE: © Bettmann/CORBIS

SOURCE: Excerpted from George Johnson, "Out of Place—a Virtual Space Odyssey; This Time, the Future Is Closer Than You Think," *New York Times,* December 31, 2000, http://www.nytimes.com. Copyright © 2000 by the New York Times Co. Reprinted with permission.

---

[10] John Markoff, "Technology; Is There Life After Silicon Valley's Fast Lane?," *New York Times,* Business/Financial Desk, Section C, April 9, 2003, p. 1.

In the growth process, the individual entrepreneurs and the giant firms have played roles that are different, but are essential for one another. The breakthrough ideas have been contributed disproportionately by the entrepreneurs in their pursuit of the temporary monopoly profits that successful innovations promise. The giant firms have specialized in a constant stream of incremental improvements that protect them from destruction by competitors who constantly seek to beat them at the innovation game. Together, the contributions of the two groups have played a critical role in the growth of the market economies.

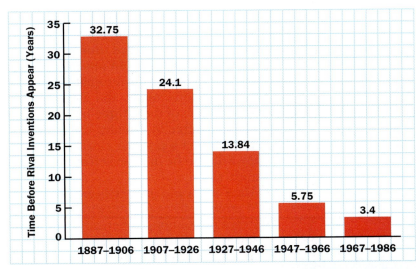

SOURCE: Rajshree Agarwal and Michael Gort "First Mover Advantage and the Speed of Competitive Entry, 1887–1986" (*Journal of Law and Economics* Vol. XLIV, April 2001, pp. 161–177).

FIGURE 6

Increased Speed with Which Competition of Similar Products Faces the Seller of an Innovative Product

The Market Economy and the Speedy Dissemination of New Technology

Another attribute of the market economy that is vital for its growth is the fact that new technology now spreads with impressive speed, meaning that obsolete products and processes do not long survive or hold back economic growth. The evidence indicates that dissemination is not only surprisingly rapid, but has also been growing more so with remarkable consistency for more than a century (see "The Speed-Up of Technology Dissemination" below).

What underlies this increase in the rapidity with which inventions spread? It may seem that when a business firm obtains a promising new invention, it will naturally do all it can to bar its competitors' access to the new technology so as to retain a competitive advantage over its rivals. In reality, this is often not so. If a firm can get a sufficiently high price by licensing others to use its technology, it may be just as profitable to do that as to reserve the innovations for itself. This is not just a theoretical possibility. Newspaper reports indicate, for example, that more than 20 percent of IBM's profits in 2000 were obtained from its technology licenses.

There is another incentive for firms to trade innovations with others, including their competitors. Fearing that their own laboratories may conceivably fail in all

The Speed-Up of Technology Dissemination

A recent study of 46 major product innovations found that, in less than a century, the average time between the commercial introduction of a new product and the time of entry of competitors supplying the same or similar products fell precipitously from almost 33 years at the inception of the 20th century to just 3.4 years in the period 1967–1986.* Moreover, as shown in Figure 6 above, the decline was remarkably steady and persistent.

* Rajshree Agarwal and Michael Gort, "First Mover Advantage and the Speed of Competitive Entry, 1887–1986" (*Journal of Law and Economics* Vol. XLIV, April 2001, pp. 161–177). The authors report that other studies support their results.

SOURCE: "Runner 2" by William J. Baumol.

R&D undertakings in a particular time period, while competitors may have better luck, firms often enter into agreements with a competitor to *share* all successful future innovations for a specified time period—say, the next five years. Such agreements reduce risk for *both* firms. In photography, for example, one camera manufacturer may introduce an improved automatic-focus device, a second firm may develop an automatic light adjustment, and a third may invent a way to make the camera more compact. Each of these three firms can keep its invention to itself. But if they get together and agree to produce cameras combining all their new features, they will be able to market a product clearly superior to what any could have produced alone. They will also be in a far better position to meet competition from another camera manufacturer.

Cross licensing of patents occurs when each of two firms agrees to let the other use some specified set of its patents, either at a price specified in their agreement or in return for access to the other firm's patents.

Many firms and industries engage in this practice of **cross licensing.** For example, IBM cross-licenses patents with *each* of its major competitors. One study of technology exchange among American steel minimills, which are now world leaders in steel productivity, found that *all but one* of the eleven firms regularly and routinely exchanged information with the others. Firms would sometimes train the employees of competing firms or send their own personnel to competing facilities to help set up unfamiliar equipment.[11]

Indeed, business firms provide their technology to others for a profit so commonly that MIT has run a seminar teaching firms how to earn more from their technology-rental business. There is even an international association of technology licensing firms—with thousands of members.

> Inventions are becoming available more quickly to other firms, including competitors of the firms that own them. Moreover, competitive pressures ensure that these innovations are rapidly put to use.

MICROECONOMIC ANALYSIS OF THE INNOVATIVE FIRM

Next, we turn from our description of the facts related to the market's accomplishments in innovation and economic growth and see what the tools of microeconomic analysis can help us to understand about these achievements.

Financing the Innovation "Arms Race": Firms with High R&D Costs and Low Marginal Costs

Large-scale innovative activity is expensive. Firms must spend substantial amounts of money, year after year. In some firms, the costs of R&D can account for as much as 40 percent of the company's total costs. If an innovative firm is to stay in business, the products it supplies must be priced so as to enable the firm to recover those expenditures.

This effort requires an approach to pricing that is very different from the one we studied in earlier chapters. There we concluded that, in a competitive market, prices tend to be set approximately equal to marginal costs, assuming this price would bring in enough revenue to keep the firm in business. To see the reason for the difference between this case and that of the innovative firm, consider the case of Jim—an organic wheat farmer—who decides to grow 1,000 more bushels of wheat than he did last year. That level of production will require him to rent x more acres of land, to buy y more bags of fertilizer and z more bags of seed, to hire h more hours of labor, and to borrow b more dollars from the bank. The prices of these inputs tell Jim how much he must spend to get the added output. If this added cost is divided by the 1,000 added bushels, we have an (approximate) calculation of the marginal cost of a bushel, including the marginal return to capital—Jim's loan payment to the bank. If the price

---

[11] Eric Von Hippel, The Sources of Innovation (New York: Oxford University Press, 1988), p. 79.

of organic wheat is set by the market so that it covers this amount, evidently price is equal to marginal cost and is also enough to keep the farm in business. It is enough to keep Jim's farm going because *all* of his costs, including the cost of renting more land, are costs of *adding* to his output—in essence, all of his costs take the form of marginal or added costs.

Contrast this case with a software firm that has just spent $20 million to create a valuable new computer program. If the firm supplies one more unit of the program (or even one thousand more units of the program), what is its added cost? The answer is nearly zero: just the cost of making a new CD, packaging it, and shipping it. One of the firm's main costs is that of R&D, but no *added* R&D cost is incurred when another purchaser acquires the already-designed program. So the firm's heavy R&D expenditure contributes nothing to *marginal* cost. A price that covers only the marginal cost of one more copy of the program can hardly amount to more than, say, $5. That price cannot begin to cover the $20 million in R&D cost—a cost the firm will probably have to replicate in the next year to keep the program up-to-date and up to competitive standards. So, pricing software—or any other products of a firm with high and continuing R&D costs—at marginal cost is a recipe for financial suicide. Prices of the products of innovating firms simply cannot follow the familiar formula: $P = MC$.

> Firms that are forced by competition to spend a great deal on research and development year after year, but that use the results of the R&D to improve a product whose marginal costs are low, cannot expect to recover their R&D costs if they set their prices equal or close to marginal costs, as occurs under perfect competition.

This pricing situation is troubling because it can mislead the government agencies charged with preventing firms from acting as monopolists. Many of the people who work in these agencies have been trained using textbooks such as this one, and they have come away from their studies with the valid (but possibly irrelevant) conclusion that under perfect competition price must equal marginal cost. So, when they encounter prices in innovative firms that are nowhere near marginal costs, their suspicions are sometimes aroused. Is this firm exploiting the public by charging prices higher than marginal costs? Should something be done to make the company price its products as wheat farmer Jim does? We see now that doing so may well bring innovative activity to a virtual standstill. Of course, most of the government authorities who are concerned with monopolistic behavior know better than that, but their suspicions are nevertheless aroused by finding cases of $P > MC$. In addition, some of them really do misunderstand the issue, and so constitute a threat to innovative activity by business.

The Profits of Innovation

Many discussions of innovation start off with the assumption that innovators can expect to earn very high profits. Indeed, huge rewards do often accrue to those who introduce unusually successful innovations. We have all heard of innovators like Thomas Edison, Alexander Graham Bell, and, more recently, Bill Gates, Steven Jobs, and others in the computer industry, who have acquired great riches from their ability to invent, or to bring innovations to market. Of course, for every successful innovator, many others have plowed their family savings into new gadgets and lost all they have spent. Quite possibly, inventors on average earn zero economic profits, or even lose money.

This possibility appears even more likely when we consider business investment in R&D. As we saw in Chapter 10, if an industry is perfectly competitive, entry will occur until economic profits are forced down to zero. Put another way, perfect competition permits firms to earn just what they need to pay investors for the funds they provide—no more and no less. This must be so because, if a typical firm in one industry earns more than firms in other industries, investors will put more money into the more profitable industry. Any excess economic profit will lead to an expansion of industry output, which will drive prices down and squeeze profits.

Because there are some barriers to entry into innovation, we cannot be certain that economic profits from invention will tend *exactly* toward zero, but we can expect them to be very low on average. In other words, although inventive activity sometimes pays off handsomely, large R&D investments also can fail spectacularly, so that the average economic profits comes out close to zero. In particular, a large firm with a big R&D division may work simultaneously on many possible innovations. The "law of averages" suggests that some of these efforts will fail and some will succeed. So we should not be surprised to find near-zero economic profit even in industries with a great deal of innovative activity.

Does this conclusion fit the facts? Although we have no systematic study of all inventive activities, high-tech industries provide a useful illustration—especially the computer industry, where many founders have made fortunes and received much publicity. According to corporate management guru Peter F. Drucker, "The computer industry hasn't made a dime . . . Intel and Microsoft make money, but look at all the people who were losing money all the world over. It is doubtful the industry has yet broken even."[12] But is it true? A recent study looked at companies that went public from 1975 to 1992, most of which were high-tech firms, and found their rate of return to be about average (that is, zero economic profit), once the researchers adjusted for risk and company size.[13]

How Much Will a Profit-Maximizing Firm Spend on Innovation?

The legendary "Eureka! I have found it!" scenario, in which the lone inventor working in a basement or garage happens to come up with a brilliant invention, may not be amenable to conventional economic analysis. But innovation in a modern corporation is easier to analyze by using the standard tools of the theory of the firm because R&D budgeting looks a lot like other business decisions, such as those about how much to produce or how much to spend on advertising. We can study all of these standard business decisions using the same tools of marginal analysis that we studied in Chapters 5, 7, and 8. The key questions are: How much can we expect firms to spend on R&D? How much can they expect to earn by doing so? And how will competition affect their innovative activity?

We have asked and answered similar questions before, when we studied how basic marginal analysis addresses business decision making. If the firm seeks to maximize its profits, it will expand its spending on R&D up to the point at which the marginal cost of additional R&D equals the marginal revenue.

By now, the logic should be familiar. A level of R&D spending (call it X dollars) at which marginal revenue (MR) is, for example, *greater* than marginal cost (MC) cannot possibly represent the profit-maximizing amount for the company to spend on R&D. For, if MR exceeds MC, the company can increase its profits by spending more than X dollars on R&D. The opposite will be true if MR < MC. In that case, the firm can increase its profits by *decreasing* R&D spending. So X dollars cannot be the optimal level of spending if, at that level of expenditure, either MR > MC or MR < MC. It follows that the profit-maximizing level of spending on R&D can only be an amount—say, Y dollars—at which MR = MC. You will recognize this argument, for we have repeated it many times in earlier chapters when we discussed other business decisions, such as those related to price and quantity of output.

This analysis simultaneously tells us everything, and nothing, about the R&D decision. It tells us everything because its conclusion is correct. If the firm is a profit maximizer, and if we know its MR and its MC curves for R&D investment, then the

[12] As cited in Jane Katz, "To Market, to Market: Strategy in High-Tech Business," *Federal Reserve Bank of Boston Regional Review*, Fall 1996, www.bos.frb.org.

[13] Alon Brav and Paul A. Gompers, "Myth or Reality? The Long-Run Underperformance of Initial Public Offerings: Evidence from Venture and Nonventure Capital-Backed Companies," *Journal of Finance* 52, no. 5 (December 1997): 1791–1821.

MR = MC rule does, in theory, tell us exactly how much the profit-seeking firm should invest in R&D. But the discussion so far tells us nothing about the shape of "typical" marginal revenue and marginal cost curves for R&D, nor does it tell us how the competitive pressures that play such an important role in R&D decisions affect those curves. We turn next to these crucial matters.

A Kinked Revenue Curve Model of Spending on Innovation

Our discussion thus far has left a basic question unanswered. If innovation is so expensive and so risky, and if the economic profits expected from innovation approach zero, why do firms do it? Why doesn't every firm refuse to participate in this unattractive game? The answer, at least in part, is that competitive markets leave them no choice. If firms do not keep up with their competitors in terms of product attractiveness and improved process efficiency that lowers costs, they will lose out to their rivals and end up losing money. Clearly, firms prefer *zero* economic profits—profits that yield only normal competitive returns to investors—to *negative* profits and investor flight.

This observation also enables us to investigate how much the firm will spend on R&D, using a microeconomic model very similar to one we encountered in Chapter 12—the kinked demand curve model that we used to explain why prices tend to be "sticky" in oligopoly markets. The underlying mechanism there was an asymmetry in the firm's expectations about its competitors. The firm hesitates to lower its price for fear that its rivals will match the price cut, causing the firm to end up with only a few new customers but dramatically reduced revenues. But the firm fears that if it *increases* its price, the others will *not* follow suit, so that it will be left all by itself with an overpriced product. A firm with such beliefs will want to set its price at the industry level—no more and no less—and leave it there unless the competitive situation changes drastically.

The innovation story is similar. Imagine an industry with, say, five firms of roughly equal size. Company X sees that each of the other firms in the industry spends approximately $20 million per year on R&D. It will not dare to spend much less than $20 million on its own R&D because, if it does so, its next model may lack new features as attractive as those of rival products. But Company X sees little point in raising the ante to, say, $30 million because it knows that its competitors will simply follow suit. So we can expect that as time passes the firms will hesitate to make *any* significant changes in the amount they spend on innovative activity.

But that's not the end of the story. All the firms in the industry will continue to invest the same amount as they have in the past, even if the cost of R&D shifts down moderately or some other minor change occurs, until one of them enjoys a research breakthrough leading to a wonderful new product. That fortunate firm will then expand its investment in the breakthrough product, because doing so will pay off *even if the other firms in the industry match the increase.* Thus the MR curve for the breakthrough firm will move to the right, and so will its profit maximizing R&D budget level—to an amount larger than $20 million. Other companies in the industry will then be forced to follow. So now the industry norm will no longer be a $20 million annual investment but some larger amount, say, $25 million per firm. No firm will be the first to drop back to the old $20 million level, fearing that its rivals would not follow such a retrenchment move. So the MR = MC equilibrium point will now be $25 million of R&D spending. Again, the common story of armaments races among countries parallels the story of innovation battles among firms.

The process we have just described assumes that competition forces firms in the industry to keep up with one another in their R&D investments. But once they have caught up, the investment level remains fairly constant until one firm breaks ranks and increases its spending. Then, all other firms follow suit, but none dares to drop back. Such an arrangement is described as a **ratchet,** in analogy to the mechanical device that prevents a wound-up spring from suddenly unwinding. This arrangement

A **ratchet** is an arrangement that permits some economic variable, such as investment or advertising, to increase, but prevents that variable from subsequently decreasing.

"You will never catch up with the new technology."

normally holds technological spending steady, sometimes permits it to move forward, but generally does not allow it to retreat. Thus, we can expect R&D spending to expand from time to time. Once the new level is reached, the ratchet—enforced by the competitive market—prevents firms from retreating to the previous lower level.[14]

Ratcheting acts as a critical part of the mechanism that produces the extraordinary growth records of free enterprise economies and differentiates them from all other known economic systems. Competitive pressures force firms to run as fast as they can in the innovation race just to keep up with the others.

■ Innovation as a Public Good

An innovation, once created, usually does not contribute only to the output of the firm that discovered the breakthrough. At little or no additional cost, the new technology can also add to the outputs produced by other enterprises, often in other industries. This public good property (for review of the concept of *public goods*, see Chapter 15, pages 318–319) of technical knowledge enables those who adopt the innovation (with or without the inventor's permission) to adopt it more cheaply.

In Chapter 15, we used the term "public good" to describe any input or output that is not depleted when used once, but rather can be used over and over by more users with little or no additional cost. Such goods can be costlessly available to the entire public, not just to a single individual. Analogously, R&D expenses need not be duplicated when firms use knowledge repeatedly to produce output. For instance, Thomas Edison and his colleagues worked for many months and used up much material before they finally found a way to create a viable light bulb. But they did not have to repeat that outlay to produce their second light bulb. Similarly, if Edison had permitted another firm to use the technology, that firm would not have needed to repeat the expensive research that yielded the first light bulb. Innovation is like the oil lamp in the ancient Hanukkah legend: a lamp that miraculously replenished its fuel and could provide light day after day without any additional oil.

That is one distinguishing feature of any knowledge. Both coal and technical knowledge contribute to output. But when a ton of coal is used as fuel, it cannot be used again. A second ton of coal must be mined and burned to run the engine longer. Once technical knowledge is created, however, it can be used over and over again without ever being depleted.

■ Effects of Process Research on Outputs and Prices

A **product innovation** is the introduction of a good or service that is entirely new or involves major modifications of earlier products.

A **process innovation** is an innovation that changes the way in which a commodity is produced.

As a last example of how standard analytic tools of microeconomic analysis can help us to deal with innovation, we turn to the effects of innovation on outputs and prices. We will consider a single monopoly firm that makes decisions independently of other enterprises' activities and decisions.

Innovation is often divided into two types: **product innovations**, which consist of the introduction of a new item (such as a photocopying machine or a video camera), and **process innovations**, which entail an improvement in the way in which commodities are produced, making them cheaper to buy. At this point, we will discuss only process innovations, because they are easier to analyze.

---

[14] This statement somewhat exaggerates the effectiveness of ratchets in preventing the economy from *ever* sliding backward in its R&D expenditures. After all, even in machinery, ratchets sometimes slip. Firms may, for example, be forced to cut back their R&D expenditure if business is extremely bad. They may also make mistakes in planning how much to spend on investment or become discouraged by repeated failures of their research division to come up with saleable products. The economy's ratchets are indeed imperfect, but they nevertheless exist. They cannot completely prevent backsliding in R&D expenditure, but they can be a powerful influence that is effective in resisting such retreats.

A successful process innovation can be expected to expand the output of the product that uses the process, and to reduce the product's price, for a very simple reason: A process innovation normally leads to a downward shift in the firm's marginal and average cost curves but, because it involves no change in the product, it should not cause any change in the demand and marginal revenue curves.

A standard graph familiar from earlier chapters can demonstrate these results. Figure 7 shows MR and DD (demand), the firm's marginal revenue and demand (average revenue) curves, respectively, for the production of widgets. The graph also shows MC_1, the marginal cost curve of widgets *before* the process innovation, and MC_2, the marginal cost curve *after* the innovation is adopted. MC_2 is naturally lower than MC_1 because the innovation has reduced the cost of making widgets. Before the innovation, the quantity produced by our profit-maximizing firm is Q_1, the quantity at which $MR = MC_1$ (at point E_1). The corresponding price is P_1, the point on the demand curve (DD) above quantity Q_1. After the process innovation, the marginal cost curve shifts downward to MC_2. That new marginal cost curve meets the downward-sloping MR curve at point E_2, which lies to the right of E_1. This means that the profit-maximizing output quantity must increase from Q_1 to Q_2, and, because of the downward slope of the demand curve, price must fall from P_1 to P_2. Thus, we have shown, as suggested earlier, that:

A cost-cutting process innovation increases the output and decreases the price of the product that a profit-making firm supplies with the help of the innovation.

DO FREE MARKETS SPEND ENOUGH ON R&D ACTIVITIES?

We have seen that today's market economies turn out innovations at a pace and complexity never seen before in human history. Business firms, the U.S. government, universities, and others spend a good deal on research and innovation. In 2004, more than $312 billion (about 2.7 percent of the United States' total GDP) was spent on these activities, with business firms funding 64 percent of that amount.[15] Yet we may well ask, is this amount too small or too large a share of GDP? That is, would the general public benefit or lose if more resources were devoted to innovation? Some economic analysis suggests that there is a fundamental reason for believing that, despite our impressive successes in this arena, we still do not spend enough.

As usual, there is a trade-off to spending more than we currently do. If we devote more resources to innovation this year, less will be left over to produce clothing, food, or new TV programs—goods and services that contribute primarily to today's consumption rather than tomorrow's. With smaller supplies of these items, their prices will rise. On the other hand, if we devote more resources to innovation, we will probably get better and cheaper products in the future. So, as with any investment,

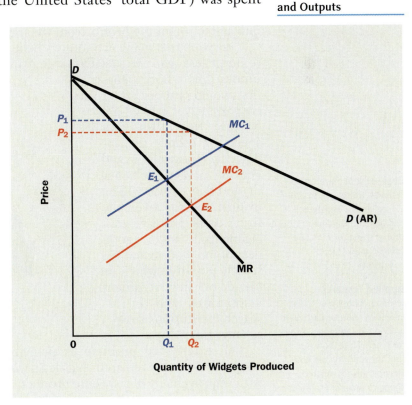

FIGURE 7

Effect of Process Innovations on Prices and Outputs

[15] National Science Board, *Science and Engineering Indicators—2006*, Arlington, VA.: National Science Foundation, 2006, http://www.nsf.gov.

R&D expenditures entail a trade-off between the present and the future. More R&D spending means that consumers get less to consume this year, but they get more and better products in the future. The question is, how much is enough?

■ Innovation as a Beneficial Externality

Many economists believe that private enterprise does *not* devote enough resources to innovation, because the acquisition of new technical knowledge generates large *externalities*. Recall from Chapter 15 that an externality is an effect of a business transaction that benefits or hurts persons other than those who directly take part in the transaction.[16] For example, if demand for air travel expands and more planes take off from the local airport, noise pollution affecting nearby residents will increase and they may feel it necessary to spend more money on insulation. Here, the air passengers and the airline are the participants in the transaction, and neighborhood homes suffer from the damaging externality. A detrimental externality is part of the true social cost of producing a commodity—air transport, in this example. This means that the airline will not pay all of the costs of its flights because, inadvertently or deliberately, it can shift part of the costs to others—which they pay in the form of higher spending on headache medicine or soundproofing. Because lower costs lead firms to produce higher outputs, the ability to escape part of the cost of its operation will lead the airline to overproduce air travel capacity. The result is excessive flight activity and too much noise pollution.

But sometimes externalities *benefit* innocent third parties, rather than harming them, and then those who carry out the transaction reap only part of the benefits. For example, suppose your roommate, an advanced engineering student, comes up with a more efficient battery that turns out to benefit laptop computer manufacturers, the makers of electric cars, and many others. Your roommate may get a prize for her work or may even receive a royalty payment from the companies that license her innovation. But she will not get all of the benefits. This is true of most innovations: They benefit the innovator to some degree, but large parts of the benefits also go to others. Such beneficial externalities mean that a firm that invests in R&D can expect to reap only a fraction of the profits from the innovation.

Consequently, many economists believe that the free market induces private firms to invest less than the socially optimal amount in innovation. They believe that many innovations whose benefits would exceed their costs are never carried out because any firm that spent the money to produce the innovation would get only part of the benefit, and that part would be insufficient to cover the firm's costs. Instead, governments finance a good deal of innovation and research activity, which is carried out in government laboratories and in research institutions such as universities.

"Oh, if only it were so simple."

Basic research refers to research that seeks to provide scientific knowledge and general principles rather than coming up with any specific marketable inventions.

Applied research is research whose goal is to invent or improve particular products or processes, often for profit. Note, however, that the military and government health-related agencies provide examples of not-for-profit applied research.

The externality problem is probably most severe for what is called **basic research**—that is, research that deals with science and general principles rather than with improvement of a specific product. (Research of the latter sort, which is directly related to commercial or other uses, is called **applied research**.) For example, research on the nature of electricity and magnetism may yield enormous economic

---

[16] For review, see Chapter 15, pages 314–319.

benefits in the near or distant future, but for the moment it satisfies only physicists' curiosity. Few business firms will finance such research. Of course, the economy would be much less productive in the long run if no one did it. That is why the governments of the United States and a number of other industrialized countries finance basic research, and why economists generally favor such funding.

■ Why the Shortfall in Innovation Spending May Not Be So Big After All

But the notion that we are spending far too small a share of GDP on innovation is not really very plausible. Looking about us, we see a flood of new products and processes, but certainly nothing that suggests a dearth of new technology. And a number of economists are now offering reasons that suggest why there may be no shortfall, or why any shortfall that occurs may be relatively limited.

Here only one of the reasons will be suggested: the existence of profitable markets in *licensing* of innovation to others. As we have seen, many firms permit others, even their closest competitors, to use their private technology—for a fee. That fee becomes the market price for a license to use the technology. To take this idea to its extreme, imagine that all innovating firms are successful in profitably licensing their technology to every firm and individual that can benefit from it. Then the externality problem would disappear. The reason is straightforward: A beneficial externality, after all, is simply a good deed for which the doer of the deed is not paid, or not paid adequately, for the benefit he or she creates. For this reason, the outputs that yield beneficial externalities can generally be expected to be too low from the general welfare point of view. But if the supplier can somehow arrange to be paid sufficiently, the incentive to supply an adequate amount of the beneficial product will plainly be restored. So a profitable market for technology licenses is said to help in "internalizing the externality," by getting the supplier paid for supplying the valuable innovation and by restoring the incentive for further innovation.

SOURCE: Courtesy of The Patent & License Exchange, Inc. http://www.pl-x.com

A related but lesser-known phenomenon occurs when many firms try to reduce their risks by **technology trading**—getting paid for another firm's use of its technology by receiving in exchange the right to use the other firm's technology. This type of deal can be thought of as bartering, rather than selling, technology licenses. Either way, the innovator firm receives some compensation for use of its technology by others.

The implication of all this is that, even if innovating firms do not receive full compensation for the benefits that their technology provides to others, those firms seem to have become quite adept at getting some substantial portion of the appropriate payment. The result is that the innovation externalities may not be nearly as serious a handicap to innovation as the theory may have led some observers to suspect.

Technology trading is an arrangement in which a firm voluntarily makes its privately owned technology available to other firms either in exchange for access to the technology of the second company or for an agreed-upon fee.

■ CONCLUSION: THE MARKET ECONOMY AND ITS INNOVATION ASSEMBLY LINE

Although we devoted a lot of attention to the virtues and vices of the market system in earlier chapters, those chapters barely mentioned what may be its greatest strength. Free-market capitalism has proved to be the most powerful engine of economic growth and innovation ever known. The increased creation, faster dissemination, and accelerated utilization of inventions is surely no accident. There is something about the way the modern economy works that makes it outstrip all of its predecessors in terms of the creation and utilization of new technology—and to do so with little let-up for more than two centuries.

Collaboration, Rather Than Competition, in Innovation

Even some of the largest companies in the world find that collaboration, rather than competition, can sometimes give them an advantage in the global economy. Cargill and Monsanto, two firms that are active in the global market for agricultural products, recently announced a joint venture that will produce and market better animal feeds around the world.

Cargill is a producer and marketer of agricultural products, pharmaceuticals, and food ingredients, with 79,000 employees in 72 countries. Monsanto is a global marketer of agricultural, food, and industrial products, with 21,000 employees around the world. Even though both of these companies are large by any measure, they decided to pool their strengths: Monsanto has relatively greater expertise in genomics and biotechnology, and Cargill has a comprehensive distribution and marketing network. Together they plan to use the latest in biotechnology research to create and market better animal feeds around the world.

The Monsanto-Cargill joint venture will allow the two firms to develop new products and introduce them more rapidly to the market, perhaps reducing hunger around the world—and earning greater profits, too.

SOURCE: © Joseph Sohm, Visions of America/Corbis

SOURCE: "Cargill and Monsanto Announce Global Feed and Processing Biotechnology Joint Venture," http://www.cargill.com.

TOWARD SOLUTION OF THE PUZZLE:
How the Market Achieved Its Unprecedented Growth

There can be no single answer to the question we posed earlier in the chapter: Why do all rival economic systems trail so far behind free-market growth rates? But several key features of the market economy seem clearly to constitute the major elements of the story. A critical difference between the modern market economy and all other types of economies in history, ancient or modern, is that the other economies had no built-in mechanisms that led to widespread *use* of the inventions. By contrast, market economies are built around a number of critical institutions that have made efforts to provide products and processes a very promising route to success. Primary among these from the point of view of growth are the legal institutions that prevent governments from arbitrary expropriation of the wealth acquired through innovation and production, the enforceability of contracts that prevent disorder in the transactions among firms, and between firms and consumers, and the patent system that most directly protects the interests of innovators, entrepreneurs and firms that deal in innovative properties. One consequence has been that vigorous competition now provides a strong incentive for innovative effort and often makes innovative effort a matter of life and death for the business firm. The result has been a kind of innovation arms race, which, in turn, underlies the growing inclusion of innovative activity as a standard part of the internal operations of modern business firms—an assembly line that turns out innovations routinely much as a meat packing plant turns out sausages.

The market economy *is* different to a substantial degree, and in ways that will make a major difference to economic well-being both now and in the foreseeable future. It is hardly perfection. The free market has brought more effective and fiercer competition, even as it has raised new problems for prevention or control of monopoly. It has led to more rapid resource depletion, but it has also provided ways to use natural resources more efficiently. It has left many other important economic problems unsolved, but it has raised standards of living and accelerated the rate of improvement of these economic standards in the wealthiest countries to a degree that could not have been imagined when the United States was founded. The free market of the capitalist economy has done this, and continues to do so, not through a series of lucky accidents, but rather through features built solidly into the economy that have turned it into a growth machine that contains and operates its very effective innovation assembly line.

SUMMARY

1. The growth records and **per-capita incomes** achieved by market economies far exceed those attained by any other form of economic organization. **Innovation** is one of the main sources of that economic growth.

2. Small firms created by **entrepreneurs** account for a substantial proportion of the economy's breakthrough inventions, while larger companies specialize in incremental improvements that over time often add up to very major advances.

3. Innovation in free-market economies is stimulated by competition among business firms, which try to outdo one another in terms of the attractiveness of their new and improved products and in the efficiency of their productive processes.

4. Innovative entrepreneurial firms are driven to provide a stream of innovations because otherwise rivals are likely to introduce substitute products that will erode the profits from any one innovation. Among large competing firms frequent innovation is a matter of life and death because a firm with obsolete products or processes will lose its customers to rivals.

5. The large amounts that competition forces many firms to spend on R&D and the low marginal costs of the consumer goods sometimes produced with the resulting inno-

vations often mean that if the firms set $P = MC$, as is done under perfect competition, the innovating firms will not be able to recover their costs.

6. As with any other decision, a profit-maximizing firm will invest in R&D up to the point at which the expected MR equals the MC of that expenditure.

7. Competition can force firms to set their R&D spending at levels corresponding to those of their rivals.

8. The typical level of R&D spending in an industry will sometimes increase, but it will rarely decline because no firm dares to be the first to cut back on such spending.

9. Firms often seek to reduce the risks of their R&D activities by entering into agreements with other firms to share one another's technology. They may also sell access to their technology to others.

10. Many economists believe that private investment in innovation will fall short of the socially optimal level, because the externalities from innovation mean that inventors do not obtain all of the benefits of their innovations.

11. **Process innovations** can be shown by MR = MC analysis to increase outputs and decrease prices, even in monopoly firms.

KEY TERMS

Externality   335

Per–capita income   336

Productivity   336

Industrial Revolution   336

Capitalism   337

GDP   338

Invention   339

Innovation   339

Entrepreneur   340

Research and development (R&D)   341

High-tech   343

Cross licensing   346

Ratchet   349

Product innovation   350

Process innovation   350

Basic research   352

Applied research   352

Technology trading   353

DISCUSSION QUESTIONS

1. To understand how much the free-enterprise economy has increased living standards, try to envision the daily life of a middle-class family in a major American city just after the Civil War, when the average purchasing power is estimated to have been less than one-ninth of today's. What do you think they ate? How much clothing did they own? What were their living quarters like? What share of their budget was available for vacations and entertainment?

2. Name five common products introduced since you were born.

3. Name some companies that advertise that their products are "new" or "improved."

4. Explain why firms in an industry that spends a large amount of money on advertising may feel locked into their current advertising budgets, with no one firm daring to cut its expenditure. Describe the analogy with competition in innovation.

5. Alexander Graham Bell beat Elisha Grey to the patent office by several hours, so that Bell obtained the patent on the telephone. Imagine how much that patent turned out to be worth. How much do you think Grey got for his effort and expenditure on development of the invention? How does that help explain the possibility that *average* economic profits from innovation are close to zero?

6. If average economic profits from investment in innovation are close to zero, why would many people be anxious to invest in innovation?

7. Explain how firms that share their technology with competitors benefit by improving their ability to compete against new entrants.

8. What are the possible advantages to the general welfare when firms make their technology automatically available to others (while, of course, charging a price for use of the technology)?

9. Why may it be unprofitable for a firm to spend much more on R&D than its competitors do?

10. Define the following terms:

    a. externality

    b. public good

    c. ratchet

    Explain the applicability of these concepts to the innovative economy.

11. From the point of view of the general welfare, do you think spending on R&D in the United States is too low? Too high? Just about right? Why?

17

EXTERNALITIES, THE ENVIRONMENT, AND NATURAL RESOURCES

Environmental taxes are perhaps the most powerful tool societies have for forging economies that protect human and environmental health.

DAVID MALIN ROODMAN, WORLDWATCH INSTITUTE

Economics is useful in pointing out both the accomplishments of the market and its shortcomings. But that is only half the battle. Economic analysis would be quite arid if it could not offer us any remedial suggestions for dealing with the market's shortcomings. In Chapter 13, we investigated one of the market's important imperfections: monopoly, or limited competition. In this chapter, we will look at another significant market imperfection studied by microeconomists: *externalities*. In Chapter 15, we learned that externalities—the incidental benefits or damages imposed on people not directly involved in an economic activity—can cause the market mechanism to malfunction. In Part 1 of this chapter, we study a particularly important application of this idea: externalities as a way to explain environmental problems. We will consider the extent to which the price mechanism bears responsibility for these problems and see how that same mechanism can be harnessed to help remedy them. In Part 2 of this chapter, we address a closely related subject: the depletion of natural resources. We will discuss fears that the world is quickly using up many of its vital natural resources and see how the price mechanism can help with this problem as well.

CONTENTS

PUZZLE: *Those Resilient Natural Resource Supplies*

It is a plain fact that the earth is endowed with only finite quantities of such vital resources as oil, copper, tin, and coal. This reality underlies many worried forecasts about the inevitable, and imminent, exhaustion of one resource or another. For instance, on page 372, "The Permanent Fuel Crisis" lists a number of bleak prophecies about oil production in the United States, all of which proved far off the mark.

In reality, far from running out, available supplies of many key minerals and fuels are *growing*. Known supplies of most minerals have grown at least as fast as production, and in many cases have far outstripped it. For example, in 1950 world reserves of tin were estimated at 6 million metric tons (mmt). Between 1950 and 2000, 11 mmt of tin were mined from the earth. Nonetheless, at the end of 2000 world reserves of tin had *increased* to 10 mmt. For iron ore (which is used to make steel), known reserves in 1950 were 19,000 mmt, and production between 1950 and 2000 amounted to about 38,000 mmt, but estimated world reserves at the end of 2000 had risen to 140,000 mmt. A similar odd story is true for zinc, copper, and many more minerals.[1] How is this possible? Aren't the quantities of these resources finite? Economic principles, as we will see later in this chapter, help to clear up these mysteries.

PART 1: THE ECONOMICS OF ENVIRONMENTAL PROTECTION

Environmental problems are not new. For example, in the Middle Ages, English kings repeatedly denounced the massive pollution of the river Thames, which, they reported, had grown so bad that it was impeding navigation of the tiny medieval ships! What *is* new and different is the attention we now give to environmental problems. Much of the increased interest stems from rising incomes, which have reduced our concerns about our most basic needs of food, clothing, and shelter and have allowed us the luxury of concentrating on the *quality* of life.

Economic thought on the subject of environmental degradation preceded the outburst of public concern by nearly half a century. In 1911, the British economist Arthur C. Pigou wrote a remarkable book called *The Economics of Welfare*, which for the first time explained environmental problems in terms of externalities. Pigou also outlined an approach to environmental policy that is still favored by most economists today and is gradually winning over lawmakers, bureaucrats, and even cautious environmentalists (as the opening quotation suggests). His analysis indicated that a system of monetary *pollution charges* can be an effective means to control pollution. In this way, the price mechanism can remedy one of its own shortcomings!

EXTERNALITIES: A CRITICAL SHORTCOMING OF THE MARKET MECHANISM

An activity is said to generate a beneficial or detrimental **externality** if that activity causes incidental benefits or damages to others not directly involved in the activity, and no corresponding compensation is provided to or paid by those who generate the externality.

In our discussion in Chapter 15, we emphasized that externalities are found throughout the economy. For example, pollution of the air and waterways is to a considerable degree contributed by factories and motor vehicles as an incidental byproduct of their activities that damages other members of society. Similarly, another car's entry onto an overcrowded highway adds to delays that other travelers must endure, thereby causing those drivers and passengers to suffer a *detrimental* **externality.** But externalities can also be *beneficial* to third parties. In Chapter 16, when discussing the microeconomics of innovation and growth, we emphasized that the vital innovative activities, to which society devotes huge quantities of resources, usually provide beneficial externalities to persons who neither invest in innovation nor work in any research and development establishments.

---

[1] U.S. Geological Survey, *Minerals Yearbook*, various years, http://minerals.usgs.gov/.

IDEAS FOR BEYOND THE FINAL EXAM

EXTERNALITIES: *A Shortcoming of the Market Cured by Market Methods*   Because those who create harmful externalities do not pay for the damage done to others, they have little incentive to desist. In this way, the market tends to create an undesired abundance of damaging externalities. Similarly, because those who create beneficial externalities are not compensated for doing so, they have little incentive to supply as large a quantity as will best serve the interests of society. Therefore, the market tends to supply an undesirably small amount of such beneficial externalities. In sum, economists conclude that unless something is done about it, the market will provide an overabundance of harmful externalities and an undersupply of desirable ones. Either case is far from ideal.

Externalities are one of our *Ideas for Beyond the Final Exam* because they have such important consequences for the welfare of society and the efficient functioning of the economy. They affect the health of the population and threaten our natural resource heritage. This chapter discusses the character and magnitude of the problem and the methods that can be used to contain its harmful consequences.

In this chapter, we focus on one of the most highly publicized externalities—pollution. Toxic fumes from a chemical plant affect not only the plant's employees and customers, but also other people not directly associated with the plant. Because the firm does not pay for this *incidental* damage, the firm's owners have no financial incentive to limit their emissions of pollution, particularly given that pollution controls cost money. Instead, the polluting firm will find it profitable to continue its toxic emissions as though the fumes caused no external damage to the community.

■ The Facts: Is the World Really Getting Steadily More Polluted?

First, let's see what the facts really are. The popular press often gives the impression that environmental problems have been growing steadily worse and that *all* pollution

Four-Legged Polluters

WHEN PIGS ROAMED BROADWAY

Broadway's affinity with ham has an enduring quality. In the 1860s, however, two species competed for attention in the heart of the city—one panting on stage, the other squealing and grunting in the streets. The pig in the city was a paradox—an element of rural culture transposed to urban life. Pigs roamed the streets rooting for food, the stink from their wastes poisoning the air. Because they ate garbage, the pigs were tolerated to a degree in the absence of adequate sanitation facilities. But this dubious contribution to municipal services was tiny in comparison with the nuisance they caused. From the nation's capital to Midwestern "porkopolis," we are told, squares and parks amounted to public hogpens. . . . in Kansas City the confusion and stench of patrolling hogs were so penetrating that Oscar Wilde observed, "They made granite eyes weep."

EQUINE SMELLS

In city streets clogged with automobiles, the vision of a horse and buggy produces strong nostalgia. A century ago it produced a different feeling—distress, owing to the horse for what he dropped and to the buggy for spreading it. Of the three million horses in American cities at the beginning of the twentieth century, New York had some 150,000, the healthier ones each producing between twenty and twenty-five pounds of manure a day. These dumplings were numerous on every street, attracting swarms of flies and radiating a powerful stench. The ambiance was further debased by the presence

on almost every block of stables filled with urine-saturated hay. During dry spells the pounding traffic refined the manure to dust, which blew "from the pavement as a sharp, piercing powder, to cover our clothes, ruin our furniture and flow up into our nostrils." . . . The steadily increasing production [of manure] caused the more pessimistic observers to fear that American cities would disappear like Pompeii—but not under ashes.

SOURCE: © Bettmann/CORBIS

SOURCE: Excerpted from Otto L. Bettman, *The Good Old Days—They Were Terrible!* (New York: Random House; 1974), pp. 2–3.

is attributable to modern industrialization and the profit system. The problems are, indeed, serious and some of them are extremely urgent. But it is nevertheless possible to exaggerate them.

For one thing, pollution is nothing new. Medieval cities were pestholes; streets and rivers were littered with garbage and the air stank of rotting wastes—a level of filth that was accepted as normal. Early in the twentieth century, the automobile was actually hailed for its major *improvement* in the cleanliness of city streets, which until then had fought a losing battle against the proliferation of horse dung (see "Four-Legged Polluters" on the previous page for more on this issue).

Since World War II, there has been marked progress in solving a number of pollution problems. Air quality has improved in U.S. cities during the past three decades, and concentrations of most air pollutants continue to decline. Most dramatic has been the nearly 100 percent decrease in ambient concentrations of lead since the 1970s. Figure 1 portrays the encouraging trends in national air pollution levels. With the exception of ozone, average concentrations are well below the national ambient air quality standards (NAAQS) established by the U.S. Environmental Protection Agency (EPA). Rapid declines in automobile pollution have played a large role in this improvement, along with decreases in emissions from power plants. There have also been some spectacular gains in water quality. In the Great Lakes region, where the Cuyahoga River once caught fire because of its toxic load and where Lake Erie was pronounced dead, tough pollution controls have gradually effected a recovery.

The Europeans have made progress as well. For example, the infamous killing fogs of London, once the staple backdrop of British mystery fiction, are a thing of the past

FIGURE 1

Air Quality Trends in the United States, 1975–2001

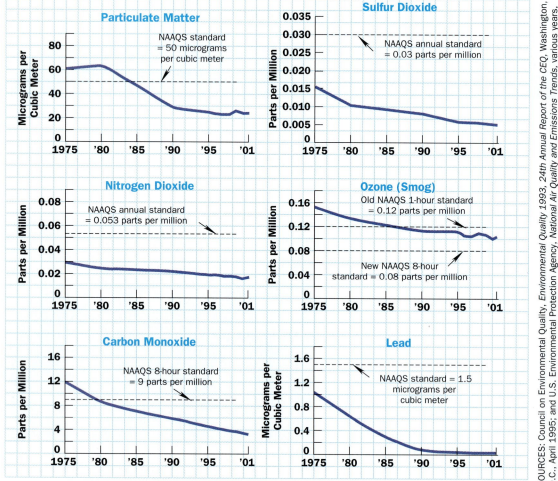

SOURCES: Council on Environmental Quality, *Environmental Quality 1993, 24th Annual Report of the CEQ*, Washington, D.C., April 1995; and U.S. Environmental Protection Agency, *National Air Quality and Emissions Trends*, various years, available at http://www.epa.gov. Special thanks to Joe Elkins of the U.S. Environmental Protection Agency for assistance in obtaining the latest air quality data.

NOTE: Measures are average ambient concentrations of the six pollutants for which the U.S. Environmental Protection Agency has established National Ambient Air Quality Standards (NAAQS). After 1987, particulate matter is measured by PM10 only, an indicator of those particles smaller than 10 micrometers.

because of the air quality improvement since 1950. The Thames River has been cleaned up enough to allow large-scale fishing of giant conger eels to resume after a 150-year hiatus. The point is that pollution problems are not a uniquely modern phenomenon, nor is every part of the environment deteriorating relentlessly.

Free-market economies certainly have no monopoly on pollution. Although it may seem that a centrally planned economy should be able to cope much better with the environmental problems caused by externalities, such economies have in reality been the *biggest* environmental disasters. China, the last large communist society, has some of the world's worst air pollution, mainly from the burning of low-quality, high-sulfur coal and a dearth of pollution control devices. Urban ozone levels in China are far greater than those in Los Angeles, a place that Americans tend to think invented smog.

Grave environmental problems also continue to plague Eastern Europe and the countries of the former Soviet Union. Poland, despite considerable improvement since 1989, continues to battle very serious air pollution problems. Particularly in the cities, high pollution levels contribute to health problems. The collapse of communism in the former Soviet Union revealed a staggering array of environmental horrors, including massive poisoning of air, ground, and water in the vicinity of industrial plants and the devastation of the Aral Sea, once the world's fourth largest inland sea, but now reduced to less than half its previous size. Many Russians live in environmentally hazardous conditions, and especially severe problems are found in Chechnya, where millions of barrels of oil have seeped into the ground from the region's black-market oil industry. Radioactive pollutants from fifty years of plutonium production, processing, and storage at the Mayak industrial complex have turned nearby Lake Karachay into one of the most polluted places on earth. The result has been widespread illness and countless premature deaths in these areas.[2]

Yet our own environment here in the United States is hardly free from problems. Despite improvements, many U.S. urban areas still suffer many days of unhealthful air quality, particularly during the summer months. According to the EPA, approximately 159 million Americans (more than half the population) were living in areas where pollution levels in 2004 still exceeded at least one of the national air quality standards adopted by the federal government.[3] Ozone (the presence of which high above the Earth protects humans from the fiercest part of the sun's ultraviolet radiation) is the most important component of serious ground-level urban air pollution—smog—and remains a pervasive problem in the United States. Even formerly pristine wilderness areas are threatened by air pollution (see "Visibility Impairment from Air Pollution at Canyonlands National Park" on the next page).

Our world is frequently subjected to new pollutants, some far more dangerous than those we have reduced, although less visible and less malodorous. Improperly dumped toxic substances—such as PCBs (polychlorinated biphenyls), chlorinated hydrocarbons, dioxins, heavy metals, and radioactive materials—can cause cancer and threaten life and health in other ways. The danger presented by some of these substances can persist for thousands of years, causing all but irreversible damage.

But all these problems pale when compared to a global environmental threat—the long-term warming of the earth's atmosphere. Scientists have demonstrated that the documented global warming of the past century, and especially in the past decade, is at least partly a consequence of human activities that have increased "greenhouse gases" in the atmosphere. Most climatologists agree that

---

[2] Central Intelligence Agency, *The World Factbook*, www.cia.gov; "Poland: Areas of Con-cern," Resource Renewal Institute, http://www.rri.org; and "Russia: Environmental Issues," U.S. Department of Energy, Energy Information Administration, http://www.eia.doe.gov.

[3] U.S. Environmental Protection Agency, Office of Air Quality Planning and Standards, "Report on Air Quality in Nonattainment Areas for 2003–2005 Covering Ozone, Particulate Matter, Carbon Monoxide, Sulfur Dioxide, Nitrogen Dioxide, and Lead," November 2006, Research Triangle Park, NC: U.S. EPA, November 2006.

Source:©Ashley Cooper/Corbis

This photo shows the significant glacial retreat in the Swiss Alps caused by global warming.

Visibility Impairment from Air Pollution at Canyonlands National Park

Even in such pristine and remote areas as Utah's Canyonlands National Park, air pollution degrades visibility, as these two photos show.

... a clear day

... a hazy day

SOURCE: Courtesy of USEPA

SOURCE: U.S. Environmental Protection Agency, Office of Air & Radiation, *Visibility Impairment,* http://www.epa.gov/oar/vis/canyonld.html.

the carbon dioxide buildup from the burning of fossil fuels such as oil, natural gas, and coal is a prime contributor to this problem. Forecasts of future warming range from 1.8° to 6.3° Fahrenheit by the year 2100, a dramatic change that may shift world rain patterns, disrupt agriculture, threaten coastal cities with inundation, and expand deserts (for more on this topic, see "Big Arctic Perils Seen in Warming, Survey Finds" on the next page).

> Although environmental problems are neither new nor confined to capitalist, industrialized economies, we continue to inflict damage on ourselves and our surroundings.

■ The Role of Individuals and Governments in Environmental Damage

Many people think of industry as the primary villain in environmental damage. But:

> Although business firms do their share in harming the environment, private individuals and government are also major contributors.

For example, individual car owners are responsible for much of the air pollution in cities. Wood-burning stoves and fireplaces are a source of particulate pollution (smoke). Wastes from flush toilets and residential washing machines also cause significant harm.

Governments, too, add to the problem. Municipal treatment plant wastes are a major source of water pollution. Military aircraft expel exhaust fumes and cause noise pollution. Obsolete atomic materials and by-products associated with chemical and nuclear weapons are among the most dangerous of all wastes, and their disposal remains an unsolved problem.

Governments have also constructed giant dams and reservoirs that flooded farmlands and destroyed canyons. Swamp drainage has altered local ecology, and canal building has diverted the flow of rivers. The U.S. Army Corps of Engineers has been accused of acting on the basis of a so-called *edifice complex.*

■ Pollution and the Law of Conservation of Matter and Energy

The physical law of conservation of matter and energy tells us that objects cannot disappear—at most they can be changed into something else. Petroleum, for instance, can be transformed into heat (and smoke) or into plastic—but it will never vanish. This means that after a raw material has been used, either it must be used again (recycled) or it becomes a waste product that requires disposal.

Big Arctic Perils Seen in Warming, Survey Finds

A comprehensive four-year study of warming in the Arctic shows that heat-trapping gases from tailpipes and smokestacks around the world are contributing to profound environmental changes, including sharp retreats of glaciers and sea ice, thawing of permafrost and shifts in the weather, the oceans and the atmosphere.

The study, commissioned by eight nations with Arctic territory, including the United States, [and conducted by 300 scientists] says the changes are likely to harm native communities, wildlife and economic activity but also to offer some benefits, like longer growing seasons. . . .

The report says that "while some historical changes in climate have resulted from natural causes and variations, the strength of the trends and the patterns of change that have emerged in recent decades indicate that human influences, resulting primarily from increased emissions of carbon dioxide and other greenhouse gases, have now become the dominant factor."

The Arctic "is now experiencing some of the most rapid and severe climate change on Earth," the report says, adding, "Over the next 100 years, climate change is expected to accelerate, contributing to major physical, ecological, social and economic changes, many of which have already begun. . . ."

Prompt efforts to curb greenhouse-gas emissions could slow the pace of change, allowing communities and wildlife to adapt, the report says. But it also stresses that further warming and melting are unavoidable, given the century-long buildup of the gases, mainly carbon dioxide. . . .

The potential benefits of the changes include projected growth in marine fish stocks and improved prospects for agriculture and timber harvests in some regions, as well as expanded access to Arctic waters.

But the list of potential harms is far longer.

The retreat of sea ice, the report says, "is very likely to have devastating consequences for polar bears, ice-living seals and local people for whom these animals are a primary food source."

Oil and gas deposits on land are likely to be harder to extract as tundra thaws, limiting the frozen season when drilling convoys can traverse the otherwise spongy ground, the report says. Alaska has already seen the "tundra travel" season on the North Slope shrink to 100 days from about 200 days a year in 1970.

The report concludes that the consequences of the fast-paced Arctic warming will be global. In particular, the accelerated melting of Greenland's two-mile-high sheets of ice will cause sea levels to rise around the world.

SOURCE: Andrew C. Revkin, "Big Arctic Perils Seen in Warming, Survey Finds," New York Times, October 30, 2004. Copyright© 2004 by the New York Times Co. Reprinted with permission.

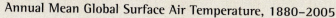

Annual Mean Global Surface Air Temperature, 1880–2005

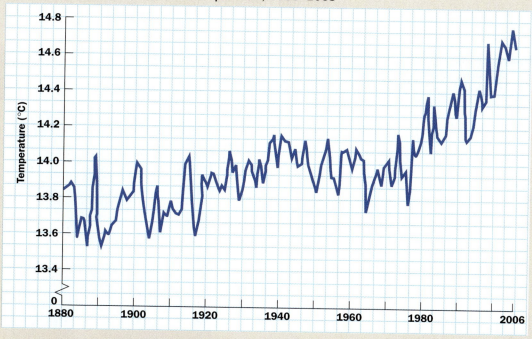

SOURCE: National Aeronautics and Space Administration, Goddard Institute for Space Studies. http://www.giss.nasa.gov

If it is not recycled, any input used in production must ultimately become a waste product. It may end up in some municipal dump; it may literally go up in smoke, contributing to atmospheric pollution; or it may be transformed into heat, warming up adjacent waterways and killing aquatic life. But the laws of physics tell us nothing can be done to make used inputs disappear altogether.

We create an extraordinary amount of solid waste—each American discards close to 4½ pounds of trash every *day*, despite our efforts to reduce this waste. Fortunately, in the face of this rising tide of garbage, recycling rates for many commonly used materials (such as aluminum, paper, and glass) are rising in the United States and many other industrial countries. In the United States, recycling has increased substantially—according to the EPA, Americans recycled 24 percent of municipal solid waste in 2005, a rate that has almost doubled during the past fifteen years. Switzerland recycles more than 20 percent of its municipal solid waste, and the statistics for Japan, Sweden, the Netherlands, Germany, and Spain are all in the 15 to 20 percent range.[4]

Our very existence makes some environmental damage inevitable. To eat and protect ourselves from the elements, people must inevitably use up the earth's resources and generate wastes.

Environmental damage cannot be reduced to zero. As long as the human race survives, eliminating such damage completely is impossible.

Why do economists believe that, although environmental damage cannot be reduced to zero, the *public interest* requires it to be reduced below its free-market level? Why do economists conclude that the market mechanism, which is so good at providing approximately the right number of hockey sticks and hair dryers, generates too much pollution? Pollution is an externality, which means that it results from a price mechanism malfunction that prevents the market from doing its usual effective job of carrying out consumers' wishes.

Here, the *failure of the pricing system* is caused by a pollution-generating firm's ability to use up some of the community's clean air or water without paying for the privilege. Just as the firm would undoubtedly use oil and electricity wastefully if they were available at no charge, so it will use "free" air wastefully, despoiling it with chemical fumes far beyond the level justified by the public interest. The problem is that *price* has not been permitted to play its usual role here. Instead of having to pay for the pure air that it uses up, a polluting firm gets that valuable resource free of charge.

Garbage! Economic Incentives to Create Less of It and Recycle More of It

The U.S. Environmental Protection Agency estimates that 9,000 American communities (covering about 20 percent of the U.S. population) operate "pay-as-you-throw" programs (also known as unit-pricing or variable-rate pricing), in which residents are charged for the collection of household garbage based on the *amount* they throw away. This creates a direct economic incentive to generate less garbage and to recycle more of what *is* generated. Rather than paying a flat fee for waste disposal (or simply receiving waste disposal services without any sense of what the cost is—as is true when a municipality provides trash collection services and pays for them out of general revenues), these programs require residents to pay for municipal waste disposal based on the number of bags or cans of trash placed at the curb or dropped off at a trash disposal facility. It is no surprise that it works! It has been shown that variable rate PAYT programs have substantially reduced the tonnage of waste shipped to disposal facilities. One recent study estimated that these programs have reduced residential disposal by a total of 16-17 percent, with 5-7 percent attributable to source reduction (less garbage generated), 5-6 percent attributable to increases in recycling, and 4-5 percent attributable to decreases in the amount of yard waste that residents put into their garbage cans.

SOURCE: © Bernard Wittich/Visuals Unlimited

SOURCE: "Measuring Source Reduction: Pay as You Throw/Variable Rates as an Example," Seattle, WA: Skumatz Economic Research Associates, Inc., May 13, 2000, available at http://www.epa.gov.

[4] U.S. Environmental Protection Agency, *Municipal Solid Waste Factbook—Internet Version*, available at http://www.epa.gov. We should point out that recycling is not always as benign as it seems. The very process of preparing materials for reuse often can produce dangerous emissions. The recycling of waste oil is a clear example, because used petroleum products are often combined with toxic chemicals that can be released in the recycling process.

Externalities play a crucial role affecting the quality of life. They show why the market mechanism, which is so efficient in supplying consumers' goods, has a much poorer record in terms of environmental effects. The problem of pollution illustrates the importance of externalities for public policy.

■ SUPPLY-DEMAND ANALYSIS OF ENVIRONMENTAL EXTERNALITIES

We can use basic supply-demand analysis to explain both how externalities lead to environmental problems and how these problems can be cured. As an illustration, consider the environmental damage caused by massive garbage generation.

Figure 2 shows a hypothetical demand curve, *DE*, for garbage removal. As usual, this curve has a negative slope, meaning that if garbage removal prices rise, people will demand less removal. They may create less waste, or take more waste to recycling centers, or reuse items rather than throwing them out after one use. (See "Garbage! Economic Incentives to Create Less of It and Recycle More of It" on the previous page for an example of financial incentives in action.)

The graph also shows the supply curve, *SS*, of an ideal market for garbage removal. As we saw in our analysis of competitive industries (Chapter 10), the position of the market's long-run supply curve is the average cost of garbage removal. If suppliers had to pay the full costs of removal—including costs (such as laundry and doctor's bills) of pollution caused when garbage is burned at the dump—the supply curve, showing the prices at which suppliers can be induced to provide any given quantity of output, would be comparatively high (as drawn in the graph). For the community depicted in the graph, the price of garbage removal is *P* dollars per ton, and 10 million tons are generated (point *A*).

But what if the community's government decides to remove garbage "for free"? Of course, the consumer still really pays for garbage removal through taxes, but not in a way that makes each household pay for the quantity of garbage it actually produces. The supply curve is then no longer *SS*. Rather it becomes the blue line *TT*, which lies along the horizontal axis, because any household can increase the garbage it throws away at no cost to itself. Now the intersection of the supply and demand curve is no longer point *A*. Rather it is point *E*, at which the price is zero, and the quantity of garbage generated is 25 million tons—a substantially greater amount.

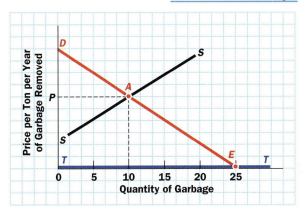

NOTE: Quantity is in millions of tons per year.

Similar problems occur if a community offers the dissolved oxygen in its waterways and its atmosphere's purity without charge. The amount wasted and otherwise used up is likely to be enormously greater than if users had to pay for the cost of their actions to society. That is a key reason for the severity of our environmental problems.

The magnitude of our pollution problems is largely attributable to the fact that the market lets individuals, firms, and government agencies deplete such resources as clean water and pure air without charging them any money for using up those resources.

It follows that one way of dealing with pollution problems is to charge those who emit pollution, and those who despoil the environment in other ways, a price commensurate with the costs they impose on society.

■ BASIC APPROACHES TO ENVIRONMENTAL POLICY

In broad terms, there are three ways to control activities that damage the environment:

- *Voluntary efforts*, such as nonmandatory investment in pollution-control equipment by firms motivated by social responsibility, or voluntary recycling of solid wastes by consumers.

- *Direct controls*, which either (1) impose legal ceilings on the amount any polluter is permitted to emit or (2) specify how particular activities must be carried out. For example, direct controls may prohibit backyard garbage incinerators or high-sulfur coal burning or require smokestack "scrubbers" to capture the emissions of power plants.
- *Taxes on pollution, tradeable emissions permits*, or the use of other monetary incentives or penalties to make it unattractive financially for pollution emitters to continue to pollute as usual.

As we will see next, all of these methods have useful roles.

1. Voluntarism

Voluntarism, though admirable, often has proved weak and unreliable. Some well-intentioned business firms, for example, have voluntarily made sincere attempts to adopt environmentally beneficial practices. Yet competition has usually prevented them from spending more than token amounts for this purpose. No business, whatever its virtues, can long afford to spend so much on "good works" that rivals can easily underprice it. As a result, voluntary business programs sometimes have been more helpful to the companies' public relations activities than to the environment.

Yet voluntary measures do have their place. They are appropriate where surveillance and, consequently, enforcement is impractical, as in the prevention of littering by campers in isolated areas, where appeals to people's consciences are the only alternative. And in brief but serious emergencies, which do not allow for time to plan and enact a systematic program, voluntary compliance may be the only workable approach.

Several major cities have, for example, experienced episodes of temporary but dangerous concentrations of pollutants, forcing the authorities to appeal to the public for drastic emissions cuts. Public response to appeals requiring cooperation for short periods often has been enthusiastic and gratifying, particularly when civic pride was a factor. During the 1984 Summer Olympic Games, for example, Los Angeles city officials asked motorists to carpool, businesses to stagger work hours, and truckers to restrict themselves to essential deliveries and to avoid rush hours. The result was an extraordinary decrease in traffic and smog, such that the 6,000-foot San Gabriel Mountains suddenly became visible behind the city.

Direct controls are government rules that tell organizations or individuals what processes or raw materials they may use or what products they are permitted to supply or purchase.

2. Direct Controls

Direct controls have traditionally been the chief instrument of environmental policy in the United States (the so-called command and control approach). The federal government, through the Environmental Protection Agency, formulates standards for air and water quality and requires state and local governments to adopt rules that will ensure achievement of those goals. For example, the standards for automobile emissions require new automobiles to pass tests showing that their emissions do not exceed specified amounts. As another example, localities sometimes prohibit industry's use of particularly "dirty" fuels or require firms to adopt processes to "clean" those fuels.

Pollution charges (taxes on emissions) are taxes that polluters are required to pay. The amount they pay depends on what they emit and in what quantities.

3. Taxes on Pollution Emissions

Most economists agree that relying exclusively on direct controls is a mistake and that, in most cases, *financial penalties*, or **pollution charges**, on polluters can do the same job more dependably, effectively, and economically.

The most common suggestion is that governments permit firms to pollute all they want but be forced to pay a tax for the privilege, in order to make them *want* to pollute less. Under such a plan, the quantity of the polluter's emissions is metered just like the use of electricity. At the end of the month the government sends the polluter a bill charging a stipulated amount for each gallon (or other unit) of emissions. (The amount can also vary with the emissions' quality, with a higher tax rate being imposed on emissions that are more dangerous or unpleasant.) Thus, in such a scheme, the more environmental damage done, the more the polluter pays. Emissions taxes are deliberately designed to *encourage* polluters to take advantage of the tax loophole—by polluting less, the polluter can reduce the amount of tax owed.

Making the Polluter Pay

In the Netherlands, a set of charges originally intended only to cover the costs of wastewater treatment has produced a classic demonstration of the pollution-preventing power of charges themselves. Since 1970, gradually rising fees for emissions of organic material and heavy metals into canals, rivers, and lakes have spurred companies to cut emissions, but without dictating how. Between 1976 and 1994, emissions of cadmium, copper, lead, mercury, and zinc plummeted 86–97 percent, primarily because of the charges, according to statistical analyses. . . . And demand for pollution control equipment has spurred Dutch manufacturers to develop better models, lowering costs and turning the country into a global leader in the market. The taxes have in effect sought the path of least economic resistance—of least cost—in cleaning up the country's waters.

Industrial Discharges of Selected Heavy Metals into Surface Waters of the Netherlands, 1976–1994

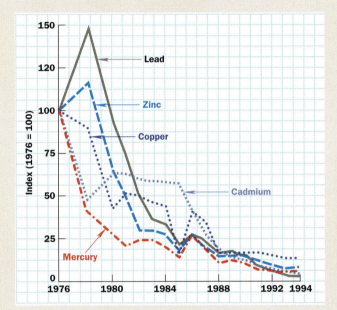

SOURCE: © Hill Creek Pictures/Index Stock Imagery, Inc.

SOURCE: David Malin Roodman, "Getting the Signals Right: Tax Reform to Protect the Environment and the Economy" from Worldwatch Institute, *Worldwatch Paper* 134, 1997, www.worldwatch.org. Reprinted by permission.

In terms of Figure 2, if the tax is used to increase the payment for waste emissions from zero (blue supply line TT) and instead forces the polluter to pay its true cost to society (line SS), then emissions will automatically be reduced from 25 million to 10 million tons.

Businesses *do* respond to such taxes. One well-known example is the Ruhr River basin in Germany, where emissions taxes have been used for many years. Although the Ruhr is a heavily concentrated industrial center, the rivers that are protected by taxes are clean enough for fishing and other recreational purposes. Firms have also found it profitable to avoid taxes by extracting pollutants from their liquid discharges and recycling them. (See "Making the Polluter Pay" for another example of the response to taxes.)

◼ Emissions Taxes versus Direct Control

It is important to see why taxes on emissions may prove more effective and reliable than direct controls. Direct controls rely on the criminal justice system for enforcement. But a polluter who violates the rules must first be caught. Then the regulatory agency must decide whether it has enough evidence to prosecute. Next, the agency must win its case in court. Finally, the court must impose a penalty strong enough to matter. If any *one* of these steps does not occur, the polluter gets away with the environmentally damaging activities.

Enforcement Issues   Enforcement of direct controls requires vigilance and enthusiasm by the regulatory agency, which must assign the resources and persons needed to carry out enforcement. But in many cases the resources devoted to enforcement are pitifully small. The effectiveness of direct controls also depends on the speed and rigor of the court system. Yet the courts are often slow and lenient. In the notorious case of the Reserve Mining Company, more than a decade of litigation was required to stop this company from pouring its wastes (which contain asbestos-like fibers believed to cause cancer) into Lake Superior, the drinking water source for a number of communities.

Finally, direct controls work only if the legal system imposes substantial penalties on violators. In the late 1990s, there were some significant penalties imposed in several cases (for instance, in 1998 Louisiana Pacific Corporation was fined a record $37 million for violations of the Clean Air Act; and in 1999 Royal Caribbean Cruises Ltd., one of the world's largest cruise lines, agreed to pay $18 million for dumping oil and hazardous chemicals in U.S. waters). Some polluters have even served prison terms for their misdeeds. Much more often, however, large firms have been convicted of polluting and fined amounts beneath the notice of even a relatively small corporation. The $37 million fine cited above looks pretty small next to the company's $2.5 billion in sales that year.[5] And, under the current administration, environmental fines and the prosecution of polluters has fallen off significantly.

> In contrast, pollution taxes are automatic and certain. No one need be caught, prosecuted, convicted, and punished. The tax bills are sent out automatically by the untiring tax collector. The only sure way for the polluter to avoid paying pollution charges is to pollute less.

Efficiency in Cleanup   A second important advantage of emissions taxes is that they tend to cost less than direct controls. Statistical estimates for several pollution control programs suggest that the cost of doing the job through direct controls can easily be twice as high as under the tax alternative. Why should there be such a difference? Under direct controls, emissions cutbacks are usually *not* apportioned among the various firms on the basis of ability to reduce pollution cheaply and efficiently.

Suppose it costs Firm A only 3 cents per gallon to reduce emissions, whereas Firm B must spend 20 cents per gallon to do the same job. If each firm spews out 2,000 gallons of pollution per day, authorities can achieve a 50 percent reduction in pollution by ordering both firms to limit emissions to 1,000 gallons per day. This may or may not be fair, but it is certainly not efficient. The social cost will be 1,000 × 3 cents (or $30) to Firm A, and 1,000 × 20 cents (or $200) to Firm B, a total of $230. If the government had instead imposed a tax of 10 cents per gallon, Firm A would have done all the cleanup work by itself, at a far lower total cost. Why? Firm A would have eliminated its emissions altogether, paying the 3 cents/gallon cost to avoid the 10 cents/gallon tax. Firm B would have gone on polluting as before, because the tax would be cheaper than the 20 cents/gallon cost of controlling its pollution. In this way, under the tax, *total daily emissions would still be cut by 2,000 gallons per day*, but the total daily cost of the program would be $60 (3 cents × 2,000 gallons) as opposed to $230 under direct controls.

> The secret of a pollution tax's efficiency is straightforward. Only polluters that can reduce emissions cheaply and efficiently can afford to take advantage of the built-in loophole—the opportunity to save on taxes by reducing emissions. The tax approach therefore assigns the job to those who can do it most effectively—and rewards them by letting them escape the tax.

---

[5] "$37 Million Fine Levied for Clean Air Violation," *The New York Times*, May 28, 1998, p. A22; "Royal Caribbean Gets Record Fine in Dumping Case," July 21, 1999, www.CNN.com.

Advantages and Disadvantages   Given all these advantages of the tax approach, why would anyone want to use direct controls?

In three important situations, direct controls have a clear advantage:

- *Where an emission is so dangerous that it must be prohibited altogether.*
- *Where a sudden change in circumstances—for example, a dangerous air-quality crisis—calls for prompt and substantial changes in conduct, such as temporary reductions in use of cars.* Tax rule changes are difficult and time-consuming, so direct controls will usually do a better job in such a case. The mayor of a city threatened by a dangerous air-quality crisis can, for example, forbid use of private passenger cars until the crisis passes.
- *Where effective and dependable pollution metering devices have not been invented or are prohibitively costly to install and operate.* In such cases, authorities cannot operate an effective tax program because they cannot determine the emissions levels of an individual polluter and so cannot calculate the tax bill. The only effective option may be to require firms to use "clean" fuel or install emissions-purification equipment.

◾ Another Financial Device to Protect the Environment: Emissions Permits

The basic idea underlying the emissions-tax approach to environmental protection is that financial incentives induce polluters to reduce their environmental damage. But at least one other form of financial inducement can accomplish the same thing: requiring polluters to buy **emissions permits** that authorize the emission of a specified quantity of pollutant. Such permits can be offered for sale in limited quantities fixed by the government authorities at prices set by demand and supply.

Under this arrangement, the environmental agency decides what quantity of emissions per unit of time (say, per year) is tolerable and then issues a batch of permits authorizing (altogether) just that amount of pollution. The permits are sold to the highest bidders, with the price determined by demand and supply. The price will be high if the number of permits offered for sale is small and many firms need permits to carry out their industrial activities. Similarly, the price of a permit will be low if authorities issue many permits but the quantity of pollution that firms demand is small.

Emissions permits basically work like a tax—they make it too expensive for firms to continue polluting as much as before. However, the permit approach has some advantages over taxes. For example, it reduces *uncertainty* about the *quantity* of pollution that will be emitted. Under a tax, we cannot be sure about this quantity in advance, because it depends on polluters' response to a given tax rate. In the case of permits, environmental authorities decide on an emissions ceiling in advance, then issue permits authorizing just that amount of emissions. When the U.S. EPA first introduced tradeable emissions permits in 1995, many people were outraged by the notion of such "licenses to pollute." Nowadays, one hears few complaints, because tradeable permit programs have turned out to be such a huge success. One of the best examples is the "acid rain" market for sulfur dioxide permits (in which the main players are the large electricity-generating utility companies). This "cap and trade" program (in which the EPA sets limitations on total SO_2 emissions and issues the number of tradeable permits, called allowances, that will keep emissions within those limits) has lowered pollution levels while saving billions of dollars in polluter costs. In 2003, more than 15 million SO_2 allowances were traded, the vast majority in private over-the-counter transactions, with the EPA providing online systems of allowance tracking, emissions tracking, and continuous emissions monitoring. The Chicago Board of Trade runs EPA's annual auction of a small percentage of allowances, which generates valuable information about the going price of allowances. These markets are open to anyone, so environmental activists can buy these permits and "retire" them, thereby improving the quality of the air (for example, during the 2004 auction, the Acid Rain Retirement Fund, a Portland, Maine–based nonprofit organization, bought 7 allowances at a price of $2,100; at the

Emissions permits are licenses issued by government specifying the maximum amount the license holder is allowed to emit. The licenses are restricted to permit a limited amount of emission in total. Often, they must be purchased from the government or on a special market.

EPA's Clean Air Markets

The Environmental Protection Agency's Clean Air Markets let participants in the sulfur dioxide (SO_2) and nitrogen oxide (NO_x) pollution permits markets record trades directly on the internet. A trading unit is called an allowance and is equivalent to one ton of air emissions. EPA's tracking systems record official SO_2 and NO_x allowance transfers under existing emission "cap and trade" programs. Anyone anywhere in the world can participate in the market, and hundreds of companies, brokers, and individuals are already engaged in trading.

Emissions "cap and trade" programs ensure that environmental goals are met (by setting a cap on emissions and allowing polluters to trade allowances among themselves), while providing companies with an alternative to the installation of costly pollution control technologies in complying with the law. This approach was first used nationally by EPA in its acid rain program to reduce SO_2 and then utilized by the Northeastern states to reduce NO_x. It has also been used in Southern California to reduce SO_2 and NO_x and in Chicago to reduce volatile organic compounds, the prime ingredient in the formation of ground-level ozone (smog). The cap and trade programs effectively reduce air pollution by setting a permanent cap on emissions,

SOURCE: © 2002 PhotoDisc

then allowing trading within that cap. As a prerequisite to trading, EPA requires rigorous monitoring and reporting standards, and mandates that companies pay automatic fees to the government for any emissions above the legal limit. Rigorous monitoring is essential to ensuring certainty and consistency in the program and to confirming that each allowance traded represents one ton of emissions, regardless of where it is generated. It is this certainty and consistency that enable creation of a robust market for allowances, free from the need for government review and approval of transactions. EPA emphasizes, however, that no matter how many allowances a utility holds, it will not be allowed to emit emissions levels that would violate the national or state atmospheric (ambient) health-protection standards.

Additional cap and trade programs have been proposed by Congress to reduce electricity industry emissions in the United States, and dozens of countries around the world are considering implementing such programs.

SOURCE: U.S. Environmental Protection Agency, "$20 Billion Emission Trading Market Goes Online," *EPA Newsroom*, www.epa.gov, December 4, 2001. The Clean Air Markets Web site is at http://www.epa.gov/airmarkets.

---

same time, Ohio-based American Electric Power bought 75,000 allowances for $20,813,800.).[6] (See "EPA's Clean Air Markets" above for more on the sulfur dioxide market and other programs involving tradeable emissions permits.)

Despite the good news about economic incentives in cap and trade for sulfur dioxide and other pollutants, it must be noted that politics can sometimes interfere with environmental programs. As this edition went to press, for example, the U.S. Supreme Court overturned a Bush administration attempt to relax Clean Air Act rules for aging electric power plants. And, in another decision on the same day (April 2, 2007), the court held that the Clean Air Act gives the U.S. Environmental Protection Agency the power to regulate carbon dioxide and other global-warming pollutants, contrary to arguments by the Bush administration.

■ TWO CHEERS FOR THE MARKET

In Part 1 of this chapter, we have learned that environmental protection cannot be left to the free market. Because of the large externalities involved, the market will systematically allocate insufficient resources to the job. However, this market failure does not imply that we should disregard the price mechanism. On the contrary, we have seen that a legislated market solution based on pollution charges may often be the best way to protect the environment. At least *in this case, the market mechanism's power can be harnessed to correct its own failings*.

We turn now, in the second half of this chapter, to the issue of natural resources, where the market mechanism also plays a crucial role.

---

[6] Source: http://epa.gov

▦ PART 2: THE ECONOMICS OF NATURAL RESOURCES

*Since Fuel is become so expensive, and will of course grow scarcer and dearer;
any new Proposal for saving the [fuel] . . . may at least be thought worth Consideration.*

BENJAMIN FRANKLIN, 1744

One of the most significant forms of environmental damage occurs when we waste natural resources. Earlier in this chapter, we saw that externalities can lead to just this sort of waste—as when governments, individuals, or business firms use up clean air and clean water without cost or penalty. There is a close analytic connection between the economics of environmental protection that we have just investigated and the economics of natural resources, to which we now turn.

Nearly thirty years ago, the world was rocked by a sudden "energy crisis." Oil prices shot up and consumers found themselves waiting in long lines to buy gasoline.

This event had profound effects throughout the world and ended the widespread assumption that the stock of natural resources was unlimited and simply ours for the taking. Indeed, back in the late 1970s and early 1980s, there was near-panic about the threatened exhaustion of many natural resources. The front page of a leading magazine even asked, "Are we running out of *everything*?"

Natural resources have always been scarce, and they have often been used wastefully. Nevertheless, we are *not* about to run out of the most vital resources. In many cases, substitutes are available, and many of the shortages of the 1970s can largely be ascribed to the folly of government programs rather than the imminent exhaustion of natural resources.

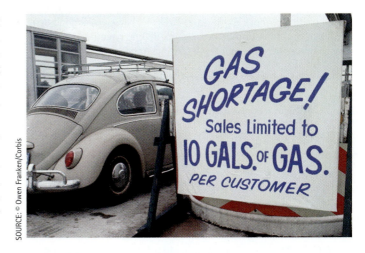

SOURCE: © Owen Franken/Corbis

■ ECONOMIC ANALYSIS: THE FREE MARKET AND PRICING OF DEPLETABLE RESOURCES

If statistics on known mineral reserves keep rising as surprisingly as those reported in the puzzle with which this chapter began, we may begin to regard them skeptically and question whether the statistics are wrong or whether we are really not running out of a number of valuable resources, despite their finite supply and their continued use. Is there another indicator of resource depletion that is more reliable? Most economists say there is one—*the price of the resource.*

■ Scarcity and Rising Prices

According to economic analysis, a better indicator of the degree of depletion of a resource is its price. As a resource becomes scarcer, we expect its price to rise for several reasons. One reason is that we do not deplete a resource simply by gradually using up a homogeneous product, every unit of which is equally available. Rather, we generally use up the most accessible and highest-quality deposits first; only then do we turn to less accessible supplies that are more costly to retrieve or deposits of lower purity or quality. Oil is a clear example. First, Americans relied primarily on the most easily found domestic oil. Then they turned to imports from the Middle East with their higher transport costs. At that point it was not yet profitable to embark on the dangerous and extremely costly process of bringing up oil from the floor of the North Sea. We know that the United States still possesses a tremendous amount of petroleum embedded in shale (rock), but so far this oil has been too difficult and, therefore, too costly to extract.

Increasing scarcity of a resource such as oil is not usually a matter of imminent and total disappearance. Rather, it involves exhaustion of the most accessible and cheapest sources so that new supplies become more costly.

■ Supply-Demand Analysis and Consumption

Growing scarcity also raises resource prices for the usual supply-demand reason. As we know, goods in short supply tend to become more expensive. To see just how this process works for natural resources, imagine a mythical mineral, "economite," consistent in quality, which has negligible extraction and transportation costs. How quickly will the reserves of this mineral be used up, and what will happen to its price as time passes?

The Permanent Fuel Crisis

Humanity has a long history of panicking about the imminent exhaustion of natural resources. In the thirteenth century, a large part of Europe's forests was cut down, primarily for use in metalworking (much of it for armor). Wood prices rose, and there was a good deal of talk about depletion of fuel stocks. People have been doing it ever since, as the accompanying table illustrates.

SOURCE: William M. Brown, "The Outlook for Future Petroleum Supplies," in Julian L. Simon and Herman Kahn, eds., *The Resourceful Earth: A Response to Global 2000* (Oxford, U.K.: Basil Blackwell; 1984), p. 362, who cite Presidential Energy Program, Hearings before the Subcommittee on Energy and Power of the Committee on Interstate and Foreign Commerce, House of Representatives, 1st session on the implication of the President's proposals in the Energy Independence Act of 1975, Serial No. 94–20, p. 643. February 17, 18, 20, and 21, 1975.

SOURCE: © Keith Wood/Stone/Getty Images

	Past Petroleum Prophecies (and Realities)		
Date	U.S. Production Rate	Prophecy	Reality
1866	0.005	Synthetics are available if oil production should end. *U.S. Revenue Commission*	In the next 82 years, the U.S. produces 37 billion barrels with no need for synthetics.
1891	0.05	Little or no chance for oil in Kansas or Texas. *U.S. Geological Survey*	Production exceeds 14 billion barrels in these two states since 1891.
1914	0.27	Total future production only 5.7 billion barrels. *Official of U.S. Bureau of Mines*	More than 34 billion barrels produced since 1914, or six times the prediction.
1920	0.45	U.S. needs foreign oil and synthetics; peak domestic production almost reached. *Director, U.S. Geological Survey*	1948 U.S. production exceeds consumption and is more than four times 1920 output.
1939	1.3	U.S. oil supplies will last only 13 years. *Radio Broadcasts by Interior Department*	New oil found since 1939 exceeds the 13 years' supply known at that time.
1947	1.9	Sufficient oil cannot be found in the United States. *Chief of Petroleum Division, State Department*	4.3 billion barrels found in 1948, the largest volume in history and twice U.S. consumption.
1949	2.0	End of U.S. oil supply almost in sight. *Secretary of the Interior*	Recent industry data show ability to increase U.S. production by more than 1 million barrels daily in the next five years.

NOTE: U.S. oil production rate in billions of barrels per year.

The basic law of pricing of a depletable resource tells us that as its stocks are used up, its price in a perfectly competitive market will rise every year by greater and greater dollar amounts.

Although we can predict the price of economite without knowing anything about its supply or consumer demand for it, we do need to know something about supply and demand to determine what will happen to economite's consumption—the rate at which it will be used up.

Figure 3(a) is a demand curve for economite, DD, which shows the amount people want to use up *per year* at various price levels. On the vertical axis, we show how the price must rise from year to year from $100 per ton in the initial year to $110 in the next year, and so on. Because of the demand curve's negative slope, it follows that consumption of this mineral will fall each year. That is, *if there is no shift in the demand curve, as in Panel (a)*, consumption will fall from 100,000 tons initially to 95,000 tons the next year, and so on.

In reality, such demand curves rarely stay still. As the economy grows and population and incomes increase, demand curves shift outward—a pattern that has probably been true for most scarce resources. Such shifts in the demand curve will offset at least part of the reduction in quantity demanded that results from rising prices. Nevertheless, rising prices do cut consumption growth relative to what it would have been if price had remained unchanged. Figure 3(b) depicts an outward shift in demand from curve D_1D_1 in the initial period to curve D_2D_2 a year later. If price had remained constant at the initial value, $100 per ton, quantity consumed per year would have risen from 100,000 tons to 120,000 tons. But because with a given supply curve price must rise, say to $110, quantity demanded will increase only to 110,000 tons. Thus, whether or not the demand curve shifts, we conclude:

FIGURE 3

Consumption over Time of a Depletable Resource

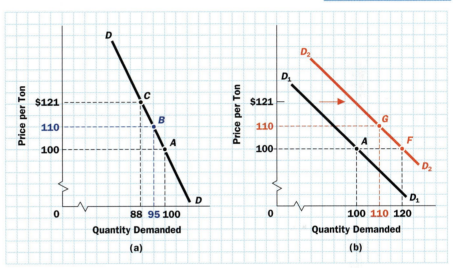

NOTE: Quantity is in thousands of tons per year.

The ever-rising prices accompanying increasing scarcity of a depletable resource discourage consumption (encourage conservation). Even if quantity demanded grows, it will not grow as much as it would if prices were not rising.

ACTUAL RESOURCE PRICES IN THE TWENTIETH CENTURY

How do the facts match up with this theoretical analysis? Not too well, as we will see now. Figure 4 shows the behavior of the prices of three critical metals—lead, zinc, and copper—since the beginning of the twentieth century. This graph shows the prices of these three resources relative to other prices in the economy (in other words, the *real* prices, after adjustment for any inflation or deflation that affected the purchasing power of the dollar). What we find is that instead of rising steadily, as the theory leads us to expect, zinc prices actually remained amazingly constant, as has the price of lead, even though both minerals are gradually being used up. The price of copper has been all over the map but also has shown no upward trend.

Figure 5 shows the real price of crude oil in the United States since 1949 (again, adjusted for inflation). It gives price at the wellhead—that is, at the point of production,

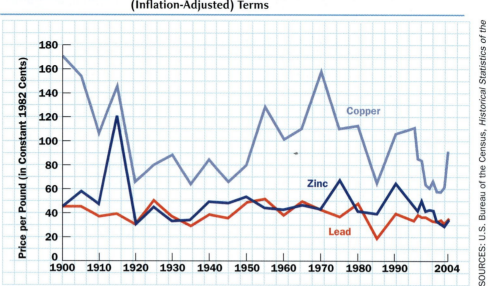

FIGURE 4   Prices of Lead, Zinc, and Copper, 1900–2004, in Real (Inflation-Adjusted) Terms

SOURCES: U.S. Bureau of the Census, *Historical Statistics of the United States, Colonial Times to 1970*, Washington, D.C.: 1975; *Statistical Abstract of the United States*, Washington, D.C.: various issues; U.S. Department of Labor, Bureau of Labor Statistics, http://www.bls.gov; and U.S. Geological Survey, http://www.usgs.gov.

NOTE: Prices are in constant 1982 cents, as deflated by the producer price index for all commodities.

with no transportation cost included. Notice how constant these prices were until the first "energy crisis" in 1973, when oil prices rose precipitously. A second and even more dramatic increase occurred in the late 1970s and early 1980s. After that, real oil prices remained well below their "energy crisis" levels, until 2003, when oil prices increased significantly again.

Interferences with Price Patterns

How does one explain this strange behavior in the prices of finite resources, which surely are being used up, even if only gradually? Although many things can interfere with the price patterns that theory leads us to expect, we will mention only three:

1. *Unexpected discoveries of reserves whose existence was previously not suspected.* If we were to stumble upon a huge and easily accessible reserve of economite, which came as a complete surprise to the market, the price of this mineral would

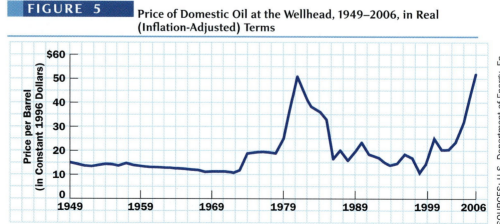

FIGURE 5   Price of Domestic Oil at the Wellhead, 1949–2006, in Real (Inflation-Adjusted) Terms

SOURCES: U.S. Department of Energy, Energy Information Administration, http://www.eia.doe.gov; and Department of Commerce, Bureau of Economic Analysis, http://www.bea.gov.

NOTE: Price is in constant 2000 dollars, as deflated with implicit GDP price deflators (first ten months only of 2006).

obviously fall. This situation is illustrated in Figure 6, where we see that people originally believed that the S_1S_1 curve represented available supply. The discovery of the new economite reserves leads them to recognize that the supply is much larger than previously thought. A rightward shift of the supply curve (curve S_2S_2) results, because the suppliers' cost of any given quantity is reduced by the discovery, so it will pay them to supply a larger quantity at any given price. Like any outward shift in a supply curve, this change can be expected to cause a price decrease (from P_1 to P_2).

A clear historical example was the Spaniards' sixteenth-century discovery of gold and silver in Mexico and South America, which led to substantial drops in European prices of these precious metals. The same effect can result from innovations that use the resources more efficiently. *If a new invention doubles the number of miles one can travel on a gallon of gasoline, that is tantamount to doubling the supply of petroleum that still remains in the ground.*

2. *The invention of new methods of mining or refining that may significantly reduce extraction costs.* This development can also lead to a rightward shift in the supply curve, as suppliers become able to deliver a larger quantity at any given price. The situation is therefore again represented by a diagram like Figure 6—only now a reduction in cost, not a new discovery of reserves, shifts the supply curve to the right. (See "Necessity is the Mother of Invention: Innovation Can Increase Resources" on the next page for a real-world example.)

3. *Price controls that hold prices down or decrease them.* A legislature can pass a law prohibiting the sale of the resource at a price higher than P^* (see Figure 7). Often this strategy doesn't work; in many cases an illegal black market emerges, where suppliers charge very high prices more or less secretly. But when price controls do work, shortages usually follow. Because the objective is to make the legal ceiling price, P^*, lower than the market equilibrium price, P, then at price P^* quantity demanded (5 million tons in the figure) will be higher than the free-market level (4 million tons). Similarly, we may expect quantity supplied (2 million tons in the figure) to be less than its free-market level (again, 4 million tons). Thus, as always happens in these cases, quantity supplied is less than quantity demanded, and a shortage results (measured in Figure 7 by the length of *AB*, or 3 million tons).

Many economists believe that this is exactly what happened after 1971 when President Nixon decided to experiment with price controls. It was then that the economy experienced a plague of shortages, and we seemed to be "running out of nearly everything." After price controls ended in 1974, most of the shortages disappeared.

We can explain each of our examples of minerals whose price did not rise by one or more of these influences. For example, copper and zinc have benefited from technological changes that lowered their extraction costs. In addition, the development of direct electroplating techniques has made copper production much more efficient. In the case

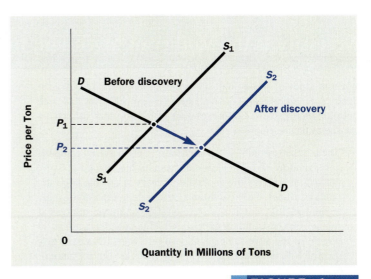

FIGURE 6

Price Effects of a Discovery of Additional Reserves

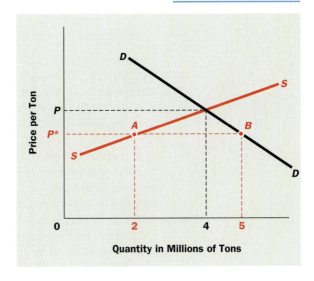

FIGURE 7

Controls on the Price of a Resource

Necessity Is the Mother of Invention: Innovation Can Increase Resources

A recent study of technological innovation in natural resource industries describes how economic necessity compels firms to search hard for ways to extract resources more efficiently, thereby increasing the available supply:

> "The U.S. petroleum industry faced a squeeze between competition from low-cost foreign producers and the upward pressure exerted on costs by the depletion of easily accessible domestic reserves. Under these conditions, it was imperative to develop techniques that would allow exploitation of known reserves at competitive costs. Initial extraction had removed as little as 30 percent of the oil in some abandoned reservoirs. This was largely because traditional vertical drilling methods limited the amount of oil that could be economically removed from reserves with complex structures. With the development of horizontal drilling, it became possible to approach a reservoir from any angle and thus to drain it more thoroughly."

SOURCE: R. David Simpson, ed., *Productivity in Natural Resource Industries: Improvement Through Innovation*, Washington, DC: Resources for the Future, 1999, pp. 17–18.

SOURCE: © AP Wide World

of lead, new mines in Missouri held abundant quantities of ore that were much easier to extract and much cheaper to refine than what had been available before. Obviously, real events are more complex than a naïve reading of theoretical models might lead us to believe.

■ Is Price Interference Justified?

Despite these influences, if a resource does become very scarce and costly to obtain, its price must ultimately rise unless government interferes. Moreover:

> In a free market, quantity demanded can never exceed quantity supplied, even if a finite resource is undergoing rapid depletion. The reason is simple: In any free market, price will automatically adjust to eliminate any difference between quantity supplied and quantity demanded.
>
> In theory, any shortage—any excess of quantity demanded over quantity supplied—must be artificial, ascribable to a decision to prevent the price mechanism from doing its job.

To say that the cause is artificial, of course, does not settle the basic issue—whether freedom of price adjustments is desirable when resources are scarce, or whether interference with the pricing process is justified.

Many economists believe that this is a case in which the disease—shortages and their resulting economic problems—is far worse than the cure—deregulation of prices. They hold that the general public is misguided in regarding these price rises as the problem, when in fact they are part of the (admittedly rather painful) cure.

It is, of course, easy to understand why no consumer loves a price rise. It is also easy to understand why many consumers attribute any such price increase to a conspiracy by greedy suppliers that somehow deliberately arrange for shortages to force prices upward. Sometimes, this view is even correct. For example, the members of the Organization of Petroleum Exporting Countries (OPEC) have openly and frankly tried to influence the flow of oil in order to increase its price. But it is important to recognize from the principles of supply and demand that when a resource grows scarce, its price will tend to rise automatically, even without any conspiracies or plots.

■ On the Virtues of Rising Prices

Rising prices help to control resource depletion in three basic ways:

- They discourage consumption and waste and provide an inducement for conservation.
- They stimulate more efficient resource use by industry, providing incentives for employment of processes that are more sparing in their use of the resource or that use substitute resources.
- They encourage innovation—the discovery of other, more abundant resources that can serve the same role and of new techniques that permit these other resources to be used economically.

Growing Reserves of Exhaustible Natural Resources: THE PUZZLE REVISITED

Earlier we saw, strangely enough, that reserves of many mineral resources have actually been increasing, despite growing world production that uses these resources. This paradox has a straightforward economic explanation: Rising mineral reserves are a tribute to the success of pricing and exploration activity. Minerals are not discovered by accident. Rather, exploration and discovery entail costly work requiring geologists, engineers, and expensive machinery. Industry does not consider this money worth spending when reserves are high and mineral prices are low.

In the twentieth century, every time some mineral's known reserves fell and its price tended to rise, exploration increased until the decline was offset. The law of supply and demand worked. In the 1970s, for example, the rising price of oil led to very substantial increases in oil exploration, which helped to build up reserves. Although, to protect ourselves from OPEC, it may not be wise for us to *consume* more oil from American sources, it certainly does seem prudent for us to increase our reserves through exploration. Increased profitability of exploration is perhaps the most effective way to achieve that goal.

SUMMARY

1. Pollution is as old as human history. Contrary to popular notions, some forms of pollution were actually decreasing even before government programs were initiated to protect the environment.

2. Both planned and market economies suffer from substantial environmental problems.

3. The production of commodities *must* cause waste disposal problems unless everything is recycled, but even recycling processes cause pollution (and use up energy).

4. Industrial activity causes environmental damage, but so does the activity of private individuals (as when people drive cars that emit pollutants). Government agencies also damage the environment (as when military airplanes emit noise and exhaust fumes or a hydroelectric project floods large areas).

5. Pollution is an **externality**—when a factory emits smoke, it dirties the air in nearby neighborhoods and may damage the health of persons who neither work for the factory nor buy its products. Hence, the public interest in pollution control is not best served by the free market. This conclusion is another of our *Ideas for Beyond the Final Exam*.

6. Pollution can be controlled by voluntary programs, **direct controls**, **pollution charges** (taxes on emissions), or other monetary incentives for emissions reduction.

7. Most economists believe that the monetary incentives approach is the most efficient and effective way to control damaging externalities.

8. The quantity demanded of a scarce resource can exceed the quantity supplied only if something prevents the market mechanism from operating freely.

9. As a resource grows scarce on a free market, its price will rise, inducing increased conservation by consumers, increased exploration for new reserves, and increased substitution of other items that can serve the same purpose.

10. In the twentieth century, the relative prices of many resources remained roughly constant, largely because of the discovery of new reserves and cost-saving innovations.

11. In the 1970s, OPEC succeeded in raising petroleum's relative price, but the price increase led to a substantial decline in world demand as well as to an increase in production in countries outside OPEC.

12. *Known reserves* of depletable scarce resources have not tended to fall with time, because as the price of the resource rises with increasing scarcity, increased exploration for new reserves becomes profitable.

KEY TERMS

Externality   358

Direct controls   366

Pollution charges (taxes on emissions)   366

Emissions permits   369

TEST YOURSELF

1. Production of Commodity X creates 10 pounds of emissions for every unit of X produced. The demand and supply curves for X are described by the following table:

Price	Quantity Demanded	Quantity Supplied
$10	80	100
9	85	95
8	90	90
7	95	85
6	100	80
5	105	75

What is the equilibrium price and quantity, and how much pollution will be emitted?

2. Using the data in Test Yourself Question 1, if the price of X to consumers is $9, and the government imposes a tax of $2 per unit, show that because suppliers get only $7, they will produce only 85 units of output, not the 95 units of output they would produce if they received the full $9 per unit.

3. With the tax described in Test Yourself Question 2, how much pollution will be emitted?

4. Compare your answers to Test Yourself Questions 1 and 3 and show how large a reduction in pollution emissions occurs because of the $2 tax on the polluting output.

DISCUSSION QUESTIONS

1. What sorts of pollution problems would you expect in a small African village? In a city in India? In the People's Republic of China? In New York City?

2. Suppose you are assigned the task of drafting a law to impose a tax on smoke emissions. What provisions would you put into the law?

   a. How would you decide the size of the tax?

   b. What would you do about smoke emitted by a municipal electricity plant?

   c. Would you use the same tax rate in densely and sparsely settled areas?

What information will you need to collect before determining what you would do about each of the preceding provisions?

3. Discuss some valid and some invalid objections to letting rising prices eliminate shortages of supplies of scarce resources.

4. Why may an increase in fuel prices lead to more conservation after several years have passed than it does in the months following the price increase? What does your answer imply about the relative sizes of the long-run and short-run elasticity of demand for fuel?

18

TAXATION AND RESOURCE ALLOCATION

The taxing power of the government must be used to provide revenues for legitimate government purposes. It must not be used to regulate the economy or bring about social change.

RONALD REAGAN

"Nothing is certain but death and taxes," proclaims an old adage. But, in recent decades, American politics has turned this aphorism on its head. It seems that the surest route to political death is to raise taxes—and the surest route to winning elections is to cut them.

Tax-cutting fever swept the nation during the presidency of Ronald Reagan—who won two landslide elections. After pledging not to raise taxes, President George Bush (the first) agreed to some small tax increases in 1990—a decision that some think cost him the 1992 election. Next came President Bill Clinton, who made income-tax increases for upper-income taxpayers a major component of his deficit-reduction plan in 1993. The next year, the Democrats were annihilated at the polls by a Republican party pledging to cut taxes. Clinton won reelection in 1996 anyway. But President George Bush (the second) defeated Al Gore in 2000 partly on the basis of his promise to cut taxes, and then won reelection in 2004 partly because John Kerry, like Clinton, proposed to repeal part of the Bush tax cuts.

Antitax sentiment is nothing new in America. Indeed, our country was born partly out of a tax revolt. But taxes are inevitable in any modern, mixed economy. Although the vast majority of economic activities in the United States are left to the private sector, some—such as provision of national defense and highways—are reserved for the government. And any such government spending requires tax revenues to pay the bills. So do transfer programs such as Social Security and unemployment insurance.

In addition, the government sometimes uses the tax system to promote some social goal. For example, we learned in the previous chapter that policy makers can use taxes to correct misallocations of resources caused by externalities.

This chapter discusses the types of taxes that are used to raise what President Reagan called "revenues for legitimate government purposes," the effects of taxes on resource allocation and income distribution, and the principles that distinguish "good" taxes from "bad" ones.

CONTENTS

ISSUE: *Were the Tax Cuts of 2001–2003 Sound Policy?*

President George W. Bush has been one of the biggest tax cutters in U.S. history. He proposed, and Congress passed, tax cuts in 2001, 2002, and 2003. These bills reduced personal income tax rates substantially, phased out the estate tax, and created a preferentially low tax rate on dividends—among other things. While most of the legislation made the various tax cuts temporary (with different "sunset" years), President Bush campaigned in 2004 on a promise to make all his tax cuts permanent—and still professes a desire to do that despite losing control of Congress in the 2006 election.

The Bush tax cuts have been controversial since their inception. Supporters credit them with the economy's rapid growth in 2003 and 2004. Critics blame them for ballooning the federal budget deficit and suggest that the tax cuts for upper-income households should be repealed because the nation cannot afford them. The debate continues to this day, as Congress seeks ways to reduce the budget deficit. In this chapter, you will learn the principles by which tax systems are judged. Then we will apply them to appraising the 2001–2003 tax cuts.

THE LEVEL AND TYPES OF TAXATION

Many Americans believe that taxes have been gobbling up an ever-increasing share of the U.S. economy. Figure 1, however, shows that this supposition is not true. By charting the behavior of both federal and state and local taxes *as a percentage of gross domestic product (GDP)* since 1929, we see that the share of federal taxes in GDP was rather steady from the early 1950s until a few years ago. It climbed from less than 4 percent in 1929 to 20 percent during World War II, fell back to 15 percent in the immediate postwar period, and fluctuated mainly in the 18 to 21 percent range until the Bush tax cuts pushed it down below 17 percent. Very recently, it has rebounded.

The share of GDP taken by state and local taxes climbed substantially from World War II until the early 1970s. But since then it, too, has remained remarkably stable—at about 10 to 11 percent. Whether these shares are too high or too low is a matter of some debate. But in any event:

The shares of GDP taken in taxes by the federal, state, and local governments were approximately constant for more than thirty years, but the federal share has dropped sharply in this decade.

FIGURE 1   Taxes as a Percentage of Gross Domestic Product

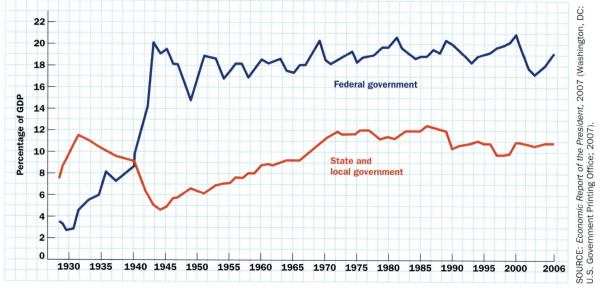

SOURCE: *Economic Report of the President, 2007* (Washington, DC: U.S. Government Printing Office; 2007).

Americans have always felt that taxes are both too many and too high. Sometimes it seems that the tax collector is everywhere. We have income and payroll taxes deducted from our paychecks, sales taxes added to our purchases, property taxes levied on our homes. We pay gasoline taxes, liquor taxes, cigarette taxes, and telephone taxes. Not surprisingly, tax cuts are more popular politically than are tax increases. Yet, as we noted in Chapter 2, by international standards Americans are among the most lightly taxed people in the world. (See Figure 14 of Chapter 2, on page 35.)

■ Progressive, Proportional, and Regressive Taxes

Economists classify taxes as *progressive*, *proportional*, or *regressive*. Under a **progressive tax** like the personal income tax, the fraction of income paid in taxes *rises* as a person's income increases. Under a **proportional tax** like the payroll tax, this fraction is constant. Under a **regressive tax** like the notorious *head tax*, which charges every person the same amount, the fraction of income paid to the tax collector *declines* as income rises.[1] Because the fraction of income paid in taxes is called the **average tax rate,** we can reformulate these definitions as they appear in the margin.

Often, however, the average tax rate is less interesting than the **marginal tax rate,** which is the fraction of each *additional* dollar that is paid to the tax collector. The reason, as we will see, is that the *marginal* tax rate, not the *average* tax rate, most directly affects economic incentives.

A **progressive tax** is one in which the average tax rate paid by an individual rises as income rises.

A **proportional tax** is one in which the average tax rate is the same at all income levels.

A **regressive tax** is one in which the average tax rate falls as income rises.

The **average tax rate** is the ratio of taxes to income.

The **marginal tax rate** is the fraction of each *additional* dollar of income that is paid in taxes.

■ Direct versus Indirect Taxes

Another way to classify taxes is to categorize them as either **direct taxes** or **indirect taxes.** Direct taxes are levied directly on *people*; primary examples are *income taxes* and *estate taxes.* In contrast, indirect taxes are levied on particular activities, such as buying cigarettes, gasoline, or using the telephone.

The federal government raises revenues mainly by direct taxes, whereas states and localities rely more heavily on indirect taxes. *Sales taxes* and *property taxes* are the most important indirect taxes in the United States, although many other countries including the members of the European Union (EU) rely heavily on the *value-added tax (VAT)*—a tax that has often been discussed, but never adopted, in the United States.

Direct taxes are taxes levied directly on people.

Indirect taxes are taxes levied on specific economic activities.

■ THE FEDERAL TAX SYSTEM

The *personal income tax* is the biggest source of revenue to the federal government. Few people realize that the *payroll tax*—a tax levied on wages and salaries up to a certain limit and paid by employers and employees—is the next biggest source. Furthermore, payroll taxes have been growing more rapidly than income taxes for decades. In 1960, payroll tax collections were just 36 percent as large as personal income tax collections; today, this figure is about 80 percent. In fact, most Americans today pay more in payroll taxes than they do in income taxes.

The rest of the federal government's revenues come mostly from the *corporate income tax* and from various excise (sales) taxes. Figure 2 shows the breakdown of federal revenues for the fiscal year 2006 budget. Let us now look at these taxes in more detail.

■ The Federal Personal Income Tax

The tax on individual incomes traces its origins to the Sixteenth Amendment to the U.S. Constitution in 1913, but it remained inconsequential until the beginning of

---

[1] In 1990, Prime Minister Margaret Thatcher caused riots in the United Kingdom by instituting a head tax.

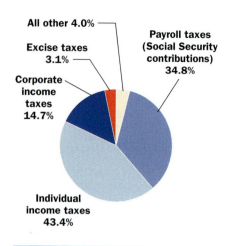

FIGURE 2

Sources of Federal Revenue

SOURCE: *Economic Report of the President, 2007* (Washington, DC: U.S. Government Printing Office; 2007).

TABLE 1

Federal Personal Income Tax Rates in 2004 for a Married Couple Filing Jointly

Taxable Income	Tax	Average Tax Rate	Marginal Tax Rate
$ 10,000	$ 1,000	10.0%	10.0%
25,000	3,035	12.1	15.0
50,000	6,785	13.6	15.0
100,000	18,475	18.5	25.0
150,000	31,958	21.3	28.0
250,000	63,525	25.4	33.0
1,000,000	324,643	32.5	35.0

A **tax loophole** is a special provision in the tax code that reduces taxation below normal rates (perhaps to zero) if certain conditions are met.

A particular source of income is **tax exempt** if income from that source is not taxable.

A **tax deduction** is a sum of money that may be subtracted before the taxpayer computes his or her taxable income.

World War II. Washington then raised the tax substantially to finance the war, and it has been the major source of federal revenue ever since.

Many taxpayers have little or no additional tax to pay when the April 15 day of reckoning comes around, because employers *withhold* income taxes from payrolls and forward those funds to the U.S. Treasury. In fact, many taxpayers are "over-withheld" during the year and receive refund checks from Uncle Sam. Nevertheless, most taxpayers (including the authors of this book!) dread the arrival of their Form 1040 because of its legendary complexity.

The personal income tax is *progressive.* That fact is evident in Table 1, which shows that average tax rates rise as income rises. Ignoring a few complications, the current tax law has six basic marginal rates, each of which applies within a specific tax bracket. As income rises above certain points, the marginal tax rate increases from 10 percent to 15 percent, then to 25 percent, 28 percent, and then finally to 33 percent and 35 percent on very high incomes (more than about $320,000 of taxable income for a married couple).

Actually, the income tax is less progressive than it seems because of a variety of **tax loopholes.** Let us examine a few major ones.

Tax-Exempt Status of Municipal Bond Interest

To help state and local governments and certain public authorities raise funds, Congress has made interest on their bonds **exempt** from federal income tax. Whether or not it was Congress's intent, this provision has turned out to be one of the biggest loopholes for the very rich, who invest much of their wealth in tax-free municipal bonds. Such tax-conscious investing has long been the principal reason why some multimillionaires pay so little income tax.

Tax Benefits for Homeowners

Among the sacred cows of the U.S. income tax system is the deductibility of payments that homeowners make for mortgage interest and property taxes. These **tax deductions** substantially reduce homeowners' tax bills and give them preferential treatment compared to renters. Clearly, Congress's intent is to encourage home ownership. However, because homeowners are, on the average, richer than renters, this loophole also erodes the progressivity of the income tax.

But why call this a "loophole," when other interest expenses and taxes (such as those paid by shopkeepers, for example) are considered legitimate deductions? The answer is that, unlike shopkeepers, homeowners do not pay taxes on the income they earn by incurring these expenses. The reason is that the "income" from owning a home accrues not in cash, but in the form of living rent-free.

An example will illustrate the point. Jack and Jill are neighbors. Each earns $60,000 per year and lives in a $200,000 house. The difference is that Jack owns his home, while Jill rents. Most observers would agree that Jack and Jill *should* pay the same income tax. Will they? Suppose Jack pays $4,000 per year in local property taxes and has a $160,000 mortgage at an 8 percent interest rate, which costs him $12,800 per year in interest. Both property taxes and mortgage interest are tax deductible, so he gets to deduct $16,800 in housing expenses. But Jill, who may pay $16,800 per year in rent, does not. Thus, Jill's tax burden is higher than Jack's.

We could go on listing more tax loopholes, but enough has been said to illustrate the main point:

Every tax loophole encourages particular patterns of behavior and favors particular types of people. Furthermore, because most loopholes mainly benefit the rich, they erode the progressivity of the income tax.

■ The Payroll Tax

The second most important tax in the United States is the payroll tax, the proceeds of which are earmarked to be paid into various "trust funds." These funds, in turn, are used mainly to pay for Social Security, Medicare, and unemployment benefits. The payroll tax is levied at a fixed percentage rate (now about 16 percent), shared about equally between employees and employers. For example, a firm paying an employee a gross monthly wage of $5,000 will deduct $400 (8 percent of $5,000) from that worker's check, add an additional $400 of its own funds, and send the $800 to the government.

On the surface, this tax seems to be *proportional*, but it is actually highly *regressive* for two reasons. First, only wages and salaries are subject to the tax; interest and dividends are not. Second, because Social Security benefits are subject to upper limits, earnings above a certain level (which changes each year) are exempted from the Social Security tax. In 2007, this level was $97,500 per year. Above this limit, the *marginal payroll tax rate* is zero.[2]

■ The Corporate Income Tax

The tax on corporate profits is also considered a "direct" tax, because corporations are fictitious "people" in the eyes of the law. All large corporations currently pay a basic marginal tax rate of 35 percent. (Firms with smaller profits pay a lower rate.) Because the tax applies only to *profits*—not to income—all wages, rents, and interest paid by corporations are deducted before the tax is applied. Since World War II, corporate income-tax collections have accounted for a declining share of federal revenue. But the high corporate profits of recent years have boosted this share to nearly 15 percent.

■ Excise Taxes

An excise tax is a sales tax on the purchase of a particular good or service. Although sales taxes are mainly reserved for state and local governments in the United States, the federal government does levy excise taxes on a hodgepodge of miscellaneous goods and services, including cigarettes, alcoholic beverages, gasoline, and tires.

Although these taxes constitute a minor source of federal government revenue, raising revenue is not their only goal. Some taxes seek to discourage consumption of a good by raising its price. For example, there are steep excise taxes on cigarettes and alcoholic beverages. But their main purpose is not to raise revenue. The clear intent is to discourage smoking and drinking.

■ The Payroll Tax and the Social Security System

In government statistical documents, payroll taxes are euphemistically called "contributions for social insurance," although these "contributions" are far from voluntary. The term signifies the fact that, unlike other taxes, the proceeds from this particular tax are set aside in "trust funds" to pay benefits to Social Security recipients and others.

But the standard notion of a trust fund does not apply. Some private pension plans *are* trust funds. You pay money into them while you are working, the trustees invest those savings for you, and you withdraw it bit by bit in your retirement years. The Social Security system does *not* function that way. For most of its history, the system has simply taken the payroll tax payments of current workers and handed them over to cur-

---

[2] However, the portion of the payroll tax that pays for Medicare is applied to all earnings, without limit.

POLICY DEBATE
Privatizing Social Security

According to the government's long-range projections, Social Security benefits that have already been promised exceed expected future payroll tax receipts by a wide margin. Thus, although Social Security faces no immediate financial problem, something must be done eventually to put the system on a sound financial footing.

You don't have to be an actuary to see that some combination of higher payroll taxes (or some other revenue source) and lower Social Security benefits will be needed to do the job. But both alternatives are politically unpalatable. So President Bush has suggested another way out: *privatizing* part of the Social Security System.

What does that mean? Simply that some portion of current payroll taxes would be diverted away from the Social Security Trust Fund and directed into private investment accounts, owned and controlled by individual workers. The idea is that these private

SOURCES: © AP/Wide World Photos

accounts would earn higher returns than the Social Security Trust Fund, which invests all of its money in U.S. government bonds. If so, the private accounts would grow rapidly, relieving the Trust Fund of some of the burden of paying future benefits. But critics worry that many individuals may not be wise investors.

In 2001, President Bush appointed a commission of experts to work out the details. But, when they reported three alternative plans for Congress to consider, he did not endorse any of them—and the matter was dropped until the 2004 presidential election campaign, when President Bush revived it. Early in 2005, the president presented his own privatization plan and began to press for it. But Congress would have none of it, even though it was then in Republican hands. It looks like Social Security reform will have to wait for another day.

rent retirees. The benefit checks that your grandparents receive each month are not, in any real sense, dividends on the investments they made while they worked. Instead, these checks are paid out of the payroll taxes that your parents (or you) pay each month.

For many years, this "pay as you go" system managed to give every generation of retirees more in benefits than it had contributed in payroll taxes. Social Security "contributions" were, indeed, a good investment. How was this miracle achieved? It relied heavily on growth—both population growth and wage growth. As long as the population grows, there are always more and more young people to tax in order to pay the retirement benefits of senior citizens. Similarly, as long as real wages keep rising, the same payroll tax *rates* permit the government to pay benefits to each generation in excess of that generation's contributions. Ten percent of today's average real wage, after all, is a good deal more than 10 percent of the real wages your grandfather earned fifty years ago.

Unfortunately, the growth magic stopped working in the 1970s, for several reasons. First, growth in real wages slowed dramatically, while Social Security benefits continued to grow rapidly. As a result, the burden of financing Social Security grew more onerous.

Second, population growth slowed significantly in the United States. Birthrates in this country were very high from the close of World War II until about 1960 (the postwar baby boom) and fell thereafter. As a result, the fraction of the U.S. population that is older than age 65 has climbed from only 7.5 percent in 1945 to 12.5 percent today, and it is certain to go much higher in the coming decades as baby boomers retire. Thus, there are fewer working people available to support each retired person.

Third, life expectancy keeps rising while the average retirement age keeps falling. These facts are undoubtedly good news for Americans, but they are bad news for the financial health of the Social Security system. The reason is simple: As people live longer and retire younger, they spend more and more years in retirement. When Congress set the normal Social Security retirement age at sixty-five, many Americans did not live that long. Nowadays most do, and many live twenty years or more beyond retirement.

With the growth magic over and the long-run funding of Social Security clearly at risk in 1983, Congress trimmed Social Security benefits (mainly by raising the normal retirement age to sixty-seven in stages) and increased payroll taxes to shore up the system's finances. Furthermore, Social Security abandoned its tradition of pay-as-you-go financing. Congress decided instead to start accumulating funds *in advance* so that the Social Security Administration would be able to pay the baby boomers' retirement benefits.

Since then, the trust fund has taken in more money than it has paid out. The Social Security surplus is now running at about $185 billion per year. If current projections of population, real wages, and retirement behavior prove reasonably accurate, these annual surpluses will accumulate into a huge trust fund balance in about ten years from now and then start to be drawn down. Unfortunately, the long-run funding problem has not been solved, for those same projections show the trust fund running out of money by about 2040. It is therefore clear that some combination of lower Social Security benefits and higher payroll taxes looms on the long-run horizon, unless some way is found to inject more money into the system. (See "Privatizing Social Security.")

■ THE STATE AND LOCAL TAX SYSTEM

Indirect taxes are the backbone of state and local government revenues, although most states also levy income taxes. *Sales taxes* are the principal source of revenue to the states, whereas cities and towns rely heavily on *property taxes*. Figure 3 shows the breakdown of state and local government receipts by source.

■ Sales and Excise Taxes

These days, all but five states, many large cities, and a few counties levy broad-based sales taxes on purchases of goods and services, with certain specific exemptions. For example, food is exempted from sales tax in many states. Overall sales tax rates typically run in the 5 to 8 percent range. In addition, most states impose special excise taxes on such things as tobacco products, liquor, gasoline, and luxury items.

■ Property Taxes

Municipalities raise revenue by taxing properties, such as houses and office buildings. Educational and religious institutions are normally exempt from these property tax levies. The usual procedure is to *assess* each taxable property based on its market value and then to place a tax rate on the community's total assessed value that yields enough revenue to cover expenditures on local services. Property taxes generally run between 1 and 3 percent of true market value.

Considerable political controversy has surrounded the property tax for years. Because local property taxes provide the main source of financing for public schools, wealthy communities with expensive real estate are able to afford higher-quality schools than poor communities. A simple arithmetical example will clarify why. Suppose real estate holdings in Richtown average $300,000 per family, whereas real estate holdings in Poortown average only $100,000 per family. If both towns levy a 2 percent property tax to pay for their schools, Richtown will generate $6,000 per family in tax receipts, but Poortown will generate only $2,000.

Glaring inequalities like this have led courts in many states to declare unconstitutional the financing of public schools by local property taxes, because doing so deprives children in poorer districts of an equal opportunity to receive high-quality education. These legal decisions, in turn, have created considerable political

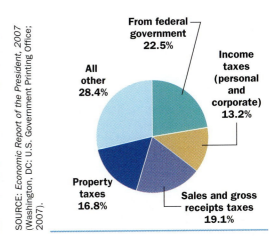

SOURCE: *Economic Report of the President, 2007* (Washington, DC: U.S. Government Printing Office; 2007).

FIGURE 3

Sources of State and Local Revenue

From federal government 22.5%

Income taxes (personal and corporate) 13.2%

Sales and gross receipts taxes 19.1%

Property taxes 16.8%

All other 28.4%

turmoil as state legislatures scrambled to find ways to fund their schools while complying with court rulings. Many states have been grappling with this problem for years.

Fiscal Federalism

Figure 3 points out an interesting fact: Grants from the federal government are a major source of revenue to state and local governments. In addition, grants from the states are vital to local governments. This system of transfers from one level of government to the next, which has a long history, is referred to as **fiscal federalism.**

Aid from this source has come traditionally in the form of *restricted grants*—that is, money given from one level of government to the next on the condition that it be spent for a specific purpose. For example, the U.S. government may grant funds to a state *if* that state promises to use the money to build highways. Or a state government may give money to a school district to spend on a specific educational program.

The system of grants from the federal government to the states has often been the subject of political controversy. Supporters of large grants see state governments as more flexible and closer to the people. They also view the states as "laboratories of democracy," where creative solutions to make government more efficient can be developed. Critics of grant programs argue that the history of state government gives little reason to see them as efficient providers of public services. These people worry that minimum national standards in welfare and health care might be sacrificed as states husband their limited financial resources.

> **Fiscal federalism** refers to the system of grants from one level of government to the next.

THE CONCEPT OF EQUITY IN TAXATION

Taxes are judged on two criteria: *equity* (Is the tax fair?) and *efficiency* (Does the tax interfere unduly with the workings of the market economy?). Although economists are mostly concerned with the second criterion, public discussions about tax proposals focus almost exclusively on the first. Let us, therefore, begin our discussion by investigating the concept of equitable taxation.

Horizontal Equity

> **Horizontal equity** is the notion that equally situated individuals should be taxed equally.

There are three distinct concepts of tax equity. The first, **horizontal equity,** simply asserts that *equally situated individuals should be taxed equally.* Few would quarrel with this principle. But because it is often difficult to apply in practice, violations of horizontal equity can be found throughout the tax code.

Consider, for example, the personal income tax. Horizontal equity calls for two families with the same income to pay the same tax. But what if one family has eight children and the other has just one? Well, you answer, we must define "equally situated" to include equal family sizes, so only families with the same number of children can be compared on grounds of horizontal equity. But what if one family has unusually high medical expenses, and the other has none? Are they still "equally situated"? By now, the point should be clear: Determining when two families are equally situated is no simple task. In fact, the U.S. tax code contains literally scores of requirements that must be met before two families are construed as equal.

Vertical Equity

> **Vertical equity** refers to the notion that differently situated individuals should be taxed differently in a way that society deems to be fair.
>
> The **ability-to-pay principle** of taxation refers to the idea that people with greater ability to pay taxes should pay higher taxes.

The second concept of fair taxation seems to flow naturally from the first. If equals are to be treated equally, it appears that *unequals should be treated unequally.* This precept is known as **vertical equity.**

Just saying this does not get us very far, however, because vertical equity is a slippery concept. Often it is translated into the **ability-to-pay principle,** which states that *those most able to pay should pay the highest taxes.* Unfortunately, this principle still leaves a definitional problem similar to the problem of defining "equally situated":

How do we measure ability to pay? The nature of each tax often provides a straightforward answer. In income taxation, we measure ability to pay by income; in property taxation, we measure it by property value, and so on.

But an even thornier problem arises when we try to translate this concept into concrete terms. Consider the three alternative income-tax plans listed in Table 2. Families with higher incomes pay higher taxes under all three plans, so all of them can claim to follow the ability-to-pay principle. Yet the three plans have radically different distributive consequences. Plan 1 is a progressive tax, like the individual income tax in the United States: The average tax rate is higher for richer families. Plan 2 is a proportional tax: Every family pays 10 percent of its income. Plan 3 is regressive: Because tax payments rise more slowly than income, the average tax rate for richer families is lower than that for poorer families.

TABLE 2						
Three Alternative Income-Tax Plans						
	Plan 1		Plan 2		Plan 3	
Income	Tax	Average Tax Rate	Tax	Average Tax Rate	Tax	Average Tax Rate
$ 10,000	$ 300	3%	$ 1,000	10%	$1,000	10%
50,000	8,000	16	5,000	10	3,000	6
250,000	70,000	28	25,000	10	7,500	3

Which plan comes closest to the ideal notion of vertical equity? Many people find that Plan 3, the regressive tax, offends their sense of fairness. But people agree much less over the relative merits of progressive versus proportional taxes. Some people take the notion of vertical equity to be synonymous with progressivity. Other things being equal, progressive taxes are seen as "good" taxes in some ethical sense, whereas regressive taxes are seen as "bad." On these grounds, advocates of greater equality support progressive income taxes and oppose regressive sales taxes. But other people disagree and find proportional taxes to be "fair."

The Benefits Principle

Whereas the principles of horizontal and vertical equity, for all their ambiguities and practical problems, at least do not conflict with one another, the final principle of fair taxation often violates commonly accepted notions of vertical equity. According to the **benefits principle** of taxation, those who reap the benefits from government services should pay the taxes.

The benefits principle is often used to justify earmarking the proceeds from certain taxes for specific public services. For example, receipts from gasoline taxes typically go to finance construction and maintenance of roads. Thus, those who use the roads pay the taxes—and roughly in proportion to their usage. Most people seem to find this system fair. But in other contexts—such as public schools and hospitals—the body politic has been loath to apply the benefits principle because it clashes so dramatically with common notions of fairness. (Should sick people pay for public hospitals?) So most public services are financed out of general tax revenues rather than by direct charges for their use.

The **benefits principle** of taxation holds that people who derive benefits from a service should pay the taxes that finance it.

THE CONCEPT OF EFFICIENCY IN TAXATION

Economic efficiency is among the most central concepts of economics. The economy is said to be *efficient* if it has used every available opportunity to make someone better off without making anyone else worse off. In this sense, taxes almost always introduce *inefficiencies*. That is, if the tax were removed, some people could be made better off without anyone being harmed.

However, that is not a terribly pertinent comparison. The government does, after all, need revenue to pay for the services it provides. So, when economists discuss the notion of "efficient" taxation, they are usually seeking taxes that cause the *least amount of inefficiency* for a given amount of tax revenue. Or, in the more colorful words of Jean-Baptiste Colbert, treasurer to King Louis IV of France, "The art of taxation consists in so plucking the goose to obtain the largest amount of feathers, with the least possible amount of hissing."

To explain the concept of efficient taxation, we need to introduce a new term. Economists define the **burden of a tax** as the amount the taxpayer would have to be given to be just as well off in the presence of the tax as in its absence. An example will clarify this notion and also make clear why:

The **burden of a tax** to an individual is the amount one would have to be given to be just as well off with the tax as without it.

The burden of a tax normally exceeds the revenue raised by the tax.

Suppose the government, in the interest of energy conservation, levies a high tax on the biggest gas-guzzling cars, with progressively lower taxes on smaller cars.[3] For example, a simple tax schedule might be the following:

Car Type	Tax
Hummer	$1,000
Chrysler 300	500
Toyota Prius	0

Harry has a taste for big SUVs and has recently been buying Hummers. Once the new tax takes effect, he has three options: He can still buy a Hummer and pay $1,000 in tax; he can switch to a Chrysler 300 and avoid half the tax; or he can switch to the hybrid Toyota Prius and avoid the entire tax.

If Harry sticks with the Hummer, we have a case in which the burden of the tax is exactly equal to the tax he pays. Why? Because if someone gave Harry $1,000, he would be in exactly the same position as he was before the tax was enacted. In general:

When a tax induces no change in economic behavior, the burden of the tax is measured accurately by the revenue collected.

However, this result is not what we normally expect to happen, and it is certainly not what the government intends by levying a tax on gas-guzzling vehicles. Normally, we expect taxes to induce some people to alter their behavior in ways that reduce or avoid tax payments. So let us look into Harry's other two options.

If Harry decides to purchase a Chrysler, he pays only $500 in tax. But that $500 *understates* his burden. Give Harry $500 and his tax bill will be covered, but he will still be chagrined by the fact that he no longer drives a Hummer. How much money would it take to make Harry just as well off as he was before the tax? Only Harry knows for sure. But we do know that it is more than the $500 tax that he pays. Whatever that (unknown) amount is, the amount by which it exceeds the $500 tax bill is called the **excess burden** of the tax.

The **excess burden** of a tax to an individual is the amount by which the burden of the tax exceeds the tax that is paid.

Harry's final option makes the importance of understanding excess burden even more clear. If he switches to a Prius, Harry will pay no tax. Are we therefore to say he has suffered no burden? Clearly not, for he longs for the Hummer that he no longer drives. The general principle is:

Whenever a tax induces people to change their behavior—that is, whenever it "distorts" their choices—the tax has an *excess burden*. In such a case, the revenue collected systematically understates the true burden of the tax.

The excess burdens that arise from tax-induced changes in economic behavior are precisely the *inefficiencies* we noted at the outset of this section. The basic precept of efficient taxation is to try to devise a tax system that *minimizes* these inefficiencies. In particular:

In comparing two taxes that raise the same total revenue, the one that produces less excess burden is the more efficient.

---

[3] A tax like the one described here has been in effect since 1984.

Notice the proviso that the two taxes being compared must yield the *same* revenue. We are really interested in the *total* burden of each tax. Because:

Total burden = Tax collections + Excess burden

we can unambiguously state that the tax with less *excess* burden is more efficient only when tax collections are equal.

Excess burdens arise when consumers and firms alter their behavior on account of taxation. So this precept of sound tax policy can be restated in a way that is reminiscent of President Reagan's statement at the beginning of this chapter:

In designing a tax system to raise revenue, the government should try to raise any given amount of revenue through taxes that induce the smallest changes in behavior.

Sometimes, however, a tax is levied not primarily as a revenue raiser, but as a way to induce individuals or firms to alter their behavior—in contrast to President Reagan's dictum. For example, we mentioned earlier that higher taxes on cigarettes are one way to reduce teen smoking. The possibility of using taxes to change consumer behavior will be discussed later in this chapter.

Tax Loopholes and Excess Burden

We noted earlier that loopholes make the income tax less progressive than it appears to be on paper. Now that we have learned that tax-induced changes in behavior lead to excess burdens, we can understand the second reason why tax specialists condemn tax loopholes: Loopholes make the income tax less *efficient* than it could be. Why? Because most loopholes involve imposing different tax rates on different types of income. Given a choice between paying, say, a 35 percent marginal tax rate on one type of income and a 15 percent rate on another, most rational taxpayers will favor the latter. Thus:

When different income-earning activities are taxed at different marginal rates, economic choices are distorted by tax considerations, which in turn impairs economic efficiency.

Our example is hardly hypothetical. Upper-bracket taxpayers in the United States now pay a 35 percent tax on income that comes in the form of wages or interest but only 15 percent on income that comes in the form of capital gains or dividends. It is no wonder, then, that such people shun interest and seek capital gains—often in the stock market.

One major objective shared by tax reformers is to enhance both the equity and efficiency of the personal income tax by closing loopholes and lowering tax rates. The Tax Reform Act of 1986—the pride and joy of tax reformers—did exactly that. But by now that law is ancient history. Since 1986, Congress has allowed a number of tax loopholes to reappear and has created some new ones. More seem to get legislated every year. During the 2004 presidential campaign, President Bush pledged to simplify the tax code and make it fairer—two goals that almost everyone supports. After his reelection he appointed a bipartisan commission which made numerous recommendations, but none of them were adopted.

SHIFTING THE TAX BURDEN: TAX INCIDENCE

When economists speak of the **incidence of a tax,** they are referring to who actually bears the burden of the tax. In discussing the tax on gas-guzzling autos, we adhered to what has been called the *flypaper theory of tax incidence*: that the burden of any tax sticks where the government puts it. In this case, the burden stays on Harry, our SUV fan. But often things do not work out this way.

Consider, for example, what will happen if the government levies a $1,000 tax on SUVs like Hummers. We learned how to deal with such a tax in a supply-and-demand

The **incidence of a tax** is an allocation of the burden of the tax to specific individuals or groups.

The American Way of Tax

The humorist Russell Baker discussed the problem of excess burden in this classic newspaper column. It seems that every time his mythical Mr. Figg took a step to avoid paying taxes and to satisfy the tax man, he became less and less happy.

New York—The Tax Man was very cross about Figg. Figg's way of life did not conform to the way of life several governments wanted Figg to pursue.

"What's the idea of living in a rental apartment over a delicatessen in the city, Figg?" he inquired.

Figg explained that he liked urban life. In that case, said the Tax Man, he was raising Figg's city sales and income taxes. "If you want them cut, you'll have to move out to the suburbs," he said.

Figg gave up the city and rented a suburban house but the Tax Man was not satisfied. He squeezed Figg until beads of blood popped out along the seams of Figg's wallet.

"Mercy, good Tax Man," Figg gasped. "Tell me how to live so that I may please my government, and I shall obey."

The Tax Man told Figg to quit renting and buy a house. The government wanted everyone to accept large mortgage loans from bankers. If Figg complied, it would cut his taxes.

Figg bought a house, which he did not want, in a suburb where he did not want to live, and he invited his friends and relatives to attend a party celebrating his surrender to a way of life that pleased his governments.

"I have had enough of this, Figg," the Tax Man declared. "Your government doesn't want you entertaining friends and relatives. This will cost you plenty."

Figg immediately threw out all of his friends and relatives, then asked the Tax Man what sort of people his government wished him to entertain. "Business associates," said the Tax Man. "Entertain plenty of business associates, and I shall cut your taxes."

To make the Tax Man and his government happy, Figg began entertaining people he didn't like in the house he didn't want in the suburb where he didn't want to live.

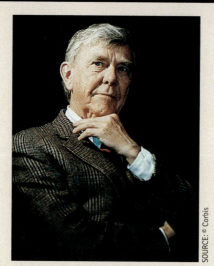

SOURCE: © Corbis

Then was the Tax Man enraged indeed. "Figg!" he thundered, "I will not cut your taxes for entertaining straw bosses, truck drivers and pothole fixers."

"Why not?" said Figg. "These are the people I associate with in my business."

"Which is what?" asked the Tax Man.

"Earning my pay by the sweat of my brow," said Figg.

"Your government is not going to bribe you for performing salaried labor," said the Tax Man. "Don't you know, you imbecile, that tax rates on salaried income are higher than on any other kind?"

And he taxed the sweat of Figg's brow at a ferocious rate.

"Get into business, or minerals, or international oil," warned the Tax Man, "or I shall make your taxes as the taxes of 10."

Figg went into business, which he hated, and entertained people he didn't like in the house he didn't want in the suburb where he did not want to live, and the Tax Man and all the governments and the nation were happy.

Figg began to make a profit. The Tax Man was outraged.

"What's the idea of making a profit, Figg?" he demanded, placing his iron grip on Figg's bank account.

"Spare me," Figg pleaded.

"Only if you sell your business!" roared the Tax Man.

"After forcing me to get into business, the Government now wants me to get out of business?" asked Figg.

"Exactly" said the Tax Man. "Sell, and I'll tax the profit from the sale at a delightfully low capital-gain rate of only 25 percent. Otherwise, I'll take the meat ax to those profits."

SOURCE: Excerpted from Russell Baker, "The American Way of Tax," from *The New York Times*, April 12, 1977, p. 27. Copyright © 1977 The New York Times Co. Reprinted by permission.

diagram back in Chapter 3: The supply curve shifts up by the amount of the tax—in this case, $1,000. Figure 4 shows such a shift by the movement from S_0S_0 to S_1S_1. If the demand curve DD does not shift, the market equilibrium moves from point A to point B. The quantity of SUVs declines as Harrys all over America react to the higher price by buying fewer SUVs. Notice that the price rises from $40,000 to $40,600, an increase of $600. People who continue buying these vehicles therefore bear a burden of only $600—less than the tax that they pay!

Does this mean that the tax imposes a *negative* excess burden? Certainly not. What it means is that consumers who refrain from buying the taxed commodity manage to *shift* part of the tax burden away from consumers as a whole, including those who continue to buy SUVs. Who are the victims of this **tax shifting?** There are two main candidates. First are the automakers or, more precisely, their stockholders. To the ex-

Tax shifting occurs when the economic reactions to a tax cause prices and outputs in the economy to change, thereby shifting part of the burden of the tax onto others.

tent that the tax reduces auto sales and profits, stockholders bear the burden. The other principal candidates are autoworkers. To the extent that reduced production leads to layoffs or lower wages, these workers bear part of the tax burden.

People who have never studied economics almost always believe in the flypaper theory of incidence, which holds that sales taxes are borne by consumers, property taxes are borne by homeowners, and taxes on corporations are borne by stockholders. Perhaps the most important lesson of this chapter is that:

The flypaper theory of incidence is often wrong.

Failure to grasp this basic point has led to all sorts of misguided tax legislation in which members of Congress or state legislatures, *thinking* they were placing a tax burden on one group of people, inadvertently placed it squarely on another. Of course, in some cases the flypaper theory of incidence is roughly correct. So let us consider some specific examples of tax incidence.

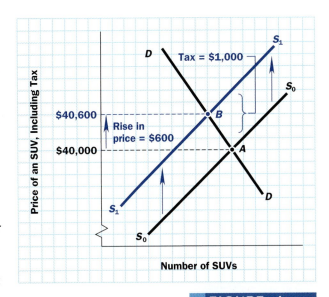

FIGURE 4

The Incidence of an Excise Tax

The Incidence of Excise Taxes

Excise taxes have already been covered by our SUV example, because Figure 4 could represent any commodity that is taxed. Our basic finding is that *part* of the burden will fall on consumers of the taxed commodity (including those who stop buying it because of the tax), and part will be borne by the firms and workers who produce the commodity.

How is the burden shared between buyers and sellers? It all depends on the slopes of the demand and supply curves. Intuitively speaking, if consumers are very loyal to the taxed commodity, they will continue to buy almost the same amount regardless of price. In that case, they will get stuck with most of the tax bill because they have left themselves vulnerable to it. Thus:

The more *inelastic* the demand for the product, the larger the share of the tax that consumers will pay.

Similarly, if suppliers are determined to offer the same amount of the product no matter how low the price, then they will wind up paying most of the tax. That is:

The more *inelastic* the supply curve, the larger the share of the tax that suppliers will pay.

One extreme case arises when no one stops buying SUVs when their prices rise. The demand curve becomes vertical, like the demand curve *DD* in Figure 5. Then no tax shifting can take place. When the supply curve shifts upward by the amount of the tax ($1,000), the price of an SUV (inclusive of tax) rises by the full $1,000—from $40,000 to $41,000. So consumers bear the entire burden.

The other extreme case arises when the supply curve is totally inelastic, as depicted by the vertical line *SS* in Figure 6. Because the number of SUVs supplied is the same at any price, the supply curve will not shift when a tax is imposed. Consequently, automakers must bear the full burden of any tax that is placed on their product. Figure 6 shows that the tax does not change the market price (including tax), which, of course, means that the price received by sellers must fall by the full amount of the tax.

FIGURE 5

An Extreme Case of Tax Incidence

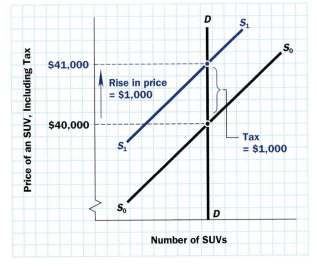

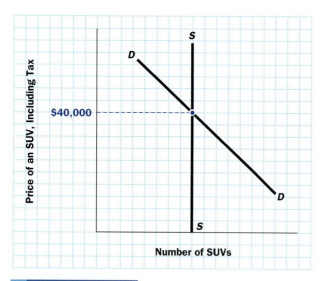

FIGURE 6

Another Extreme Case
of Tax Incidence

Demand and supply schedules for most goods and services are not as extreme as those depicted in Figures 5 and 6, so buyers and sellers share the burden. Precisely how it is shared depends on the elasticities of the supply and demand curves.[4]

The Incidence of the Payroll Tax

Economists view the payroll tax as an excise tax on the employment of labor. As mentioned earlier, the U.S. payroll tax comes in two parts: Half is levied on employees (via payroll deductions) and half on employers. A fundamental point, which people who have never studied economics often fail to grasp, is that:

The ultimate incidence of a payroll tax is the same whether it is levied on employers or on employees.

A simple numerical example will illustrate why this must be so. Consider an employee earning $100 per day with a 16 percent payroll tax that is shared equally between the employer and the employee, as under present U.S. law. To hire this worker, a firm must pay $100 in wages to the worker plus $8 in taxes to the government—for a total daily cost of $108. But how much does the worker receive? He gets $100 in wages paid by the employer less $8 deducted and sent to the government, or $92 per day. The difference between wages *paid* and wages *received* is $108 − $92 = $16, the amount of the tax.

Now suppose Congress tries to "shift" the burden of the tax entirely onto firms by raising the employer's tax to $16 while lowering the employee's tax to zero. At first, with the daily wage fixed at $100, the firm's total labor costs (including tax) rise to $116 per day, and workers' net income rises to $100 per day. Congress seems to have achieved its goal.

This achievement is fleeting, however, for what we have just described is not an equilibrium situation. With the daily cost of labor at $116 for firms, the quantity of labor *demanded* will be *less* than it was when labor cost only $108 per day. Similarly, with take-home pay up to $100 for workers, the quantity of labor *supplied* will be *more* than it was when the after-tax wage was only $92. Therefore, a *surplus of labor* on the market will develop (an excess of quantity supplied over quantity demanded), and this surplus will place downward pressure on wages.

How far will wages have to fall? We can easily see that an *after-tax* wage of $92 will restore equilibrium. If daily take-home pay is $92, the same as it was before the tax change, quantity supplied will be the same. From the firm's perspective, labor now costs $108 per day ($92 in wages plus $16 in taxes), just as it did before the tax change. Firms will, therefore, demand the same quantity of labor as they did when the payroll tax was shared. Thus, in the end, the market will completely frustrate the intent of Congress.

The payroll tax is an excellent example of a case in which Congress, misled by the flypaper theory of incidence, thinks it is "taxing firms" when it raises the employer's share and "taxing workers" when it raises the employee's share. In truth, who really pays the tax in the long run depends on the incidence of the payroll tax. But no lasting difference results from a change in the employee's and the employer's shares.

So who, in fact, bears the burden? Like any excise tax, the incidence of the payroll tax depends on the elasticities of the supply and demand schedules. In the case of labor, a large body of empirical evidence points to the conclusion that the quantity of labor supplied is not very responsive to price for most population groups. The supply curve is almost vertical, like that shown in Figure 6. The result: Workers as a group can shift little of the burden of the payroll tax to employees.

---

[4] For concrete examples, see Test Yourself Questions 3 and 4 at the end of this chapter.

But employers *can* shift it in most cases. To firms, their share of the payroll tax is an additional cost of using labor. When payroll taxes go up, firms try to substitute cheaper factors of production (such as capital) for labor wherever they can. This effort reduces the quantity of labor demanded, lowering the wage received by workers. Thus market forces shift part of the tax burden from firms to workers.

To the extent that the supply curve of labor has some positive slope, the quantity of labor supplied will fall when the wage goes down, allowing workers to shift some of the burden back onto firms. But firms, in turn, can shift that burden onto consumers by raising their prices. As we know from Part III, prices in competitive markets generally rise when costs (such as labor costs) increase. It is doubtful, therefore, that firms bear much of the payroll tax burden. The flypaper theory of incidence could not be farther from the truth. Even though the tax is collected by the firm, it is really borne by workers and consumers.

WHEN TAXATION CAN IMPROVE EFFICIENCY

We have spent much of this chapter discussing the inefficiencies and excess burdens that arise from taxation. Before we finish this discussion, we must point out two things.

First, economic efficiency is not society's only goal. For example, a tax on energy causes "inefficiencies" if it changes people's behavior patterns. But these changes may be just what the government intends. The government wants people to conserve energy and is willing to tolerate some economic inefficiency to accomplish this goal. We can, of course, argue whether the conservation achieved is worth the efficiency loss. But the general point is that:

Some taxes that introduce economic inefficiencies may nonetheless be good social policy if they help to achieve some other goal.

We have already mentioned the excise tax on cigarettes, which aims to change behavior. Another important example is the high tax on alcoholic beverages.

A second, and more fundamental, point is that:

Some taxes that change economic behavior may lead to efficiency gains, rather than to efficiency losses.

As you might suspect, this favorable outcome is possible only when the system has an inefficiency prior to the tax. In such a case, an appropriate tax may help set things right. One important example of this phenomenon was discussed at length in the previous chapter. Because firms and individuals who despoil clean air and water often do so without paying any price, these precious resources are used inefficiently. A corrective tax on pollution can remedy this problem.

EQUITY, EFFICIENCY, AND THE OPTIMAL TAX

In a perfect world, the ideal tax would raise the revenues the government needs, reflect society's views on equity in taxation, and induce no changes in economic behavior—and so have no excess burden. Unfortunately, there is no such tax.

Sometimes, in fact, the taxes with the smallest excess burdens are the most regressive. For instance, a head tax, which charges every person the same number of dollars, is incredibly regressive. But it is also perfectly efficient. Because no change in economic behavior will enable anyone to avoid it, no one has any reason to change behavior. As we have noted, the regressive payroll tax also seems to have small excess burdens.

Fortunately, however, there is a tax that, although not ideal, still scores highly on both the equity and efficiency criteria: a comprehensive personal income tax with few loopholes.

Although it is true that income taxes can be avoided by earning less income, we have already observed that in reality the supply of labor responds little to tax policy.

People also can reduce their tax bills by investing in relatively safe assets (such as government bonds) rather than riskier ones (such as common stocks), because safer assets pay lower rates of return. But it is not clear that the income tax actually induces such behavior. Why? Because although the government shares in the *profits* when investments turn out well, it also shares in the *losses* when investments turn sour. Finally, because an income tax reduces the return on saving, many economists have worried that it would discourage saving and thus retard economic growth.[5] Empirical evidence, however, does not suggest that such reactions happen to any great extent.

On balance, then, although unresolved questions remain and research is continuing:

Most of the studies that have been conducted to date suggest that a comprehensive personal income tax with no loopholes would induce few of the behavioral reactions that cause inefficiencies, and thus would have a rather small excess burden.

On the equity criterion, we know that personal income taxes can be made as progressive as society deems desirable, though if marginal tax rates on rich people get extremely high, some of the potential efficiency losses might become more serious than they are now. On both grounds, then, many economists—including both liberals and conservatives—view a comprehensive personal income tax as one of the best ways for a government to raise revenue. They differ, however, over how progressive the income tax should be, with some conservatives favoring a proportional tax.

ISSUE REVISITED: *The Pros and Cons of the Bush Tax Cuts*

How do the tax cuts enacted in 2001 and 2003 stack up against these criteria?

First, the Bush tax cuts concentrated on reducing *marginal* tax rates. They therefore can be expected to improve economic *efficiency*, at least modestly. That effect is a clear plus, which was—not surprisingly—touted by the president and the law's supporters during the debate.

Second, however, the tax cuts were skewed toward upper-bracket taxpayers, thereby reducing the *progressivity* of the tax system. Whether that change is a plus or a minus depends on your attitude toward inequality. Some Americans wondered why the very rich should get such large tax breaks. Others pointed out that the people who received the biggest tax cuts in 2001–2003 were the people who paid the highest taxes.

Third, a number of critics of the tax cuts worried about their large *magnitude*. Can we really afford such generosity, they asked, or does the government need the money for what President Reagan called "legitimate government purposes"? To answer this question back in 2001, President Bush argued that, with large budget *surpluses* looming, the government should return some of the money to the people who paid the (unneeded) taxes. But the surpluses evaporated quickly after September 11, 2001, and the government now has a huge budget deficit.

So where does this partial accounting of the pros and cons of the Bush tax cuts leave us? As usual in a serious public policy debate, with plenty of room for reasonable people to disagree! As we said back in Chapter 1, economics is not supposed to give you all the *answers*. It is supposed to teach you how to ask the right *questions*. You now know what they are.

SUMMARY

1. Taxes in the United States were quite constant as a percentage of gross domestic product from the early 1970s until the early 2000s. But the federal tax share fell sharply after 2001.

2. The U.S. government raises most of its revenue by **direct taxes,** such as the personal and corporate income taxes and the payroll tax. Of these taxes, the payroll tax is increasing most rapidly.

---

[5] For this reason, some economists prefer a tax on consumption to a tax on income.

3. For decades, the Social Security System relied successfully on pay-as-you-go financing. In recent years, however, it has been accumulating a large trust fund to be used to pay benefits to the baby boom generation when it retires. But experts do not think that trust fund will be enough.

4. State and local governments raise most of their tax revenues by **indirect taxes.** States rely mainly on sales taxes, whereas localities depend on property taxes.

5. Controversy has arisen over whether local property taxes are an equitable way to finance public education.

6. In our multilevel system of government, the federal government makes a variety of grants to state and local governments, and states in turn make grants to municipalities and school districts. This system of intergovernmental transfers is called **fiscal federalism.**

7. The three concepts of fair, or "equitable," taxation occasionally conflict. **Horizontal equity** simply calls for equals to be treated equally. **Vertical equity,** which calls for unequals to be treated unequally, has often been translated into the **ability-to-pay principle**—namely, that people who are better able to pay taxes should be taxed more heavily. The **benefits principle** of tax equity ignores ability to pay and seeks to tax people according to the benefits they receive.

8. The **burden of a tax** is the amount of money an individual would have to be given to be as well off with the tax as without it. This burden normally exceeds the taxes that are paid, and the difference between the two amounts is called the **excess burden** of the tax.

9. Excess burden arises whenever a tax induces some people or firms to change their behavior. Because excess burdens signal economic inefficiencies, the basic principle of efficient taxation is to utilize taxes that have small excess burdens.

10. When people change their behavior on account of a tax, they often **shift** the burden of the tax onto someone else. For this reason, the "flypaper theory of **incidence**"—the belief that the burden of any tax sticks where Congress puts it—is often incorrect.

11. The burden of a sales or excise tax normally is shared between suppliers and consumers. The manner in which it is shared depends on the elasticities of supply and demand.

12. The payroll tax works like an excise tax on labor services. Because the supply of labor is much less elastic than the demand for labor, workers bear most of the burden of the payroll tax—including both the employer's and the employee's shares.

13. Sometimes "inefficient" taxes—that is, taxes that cause a good deal of excess burden—are nonetheless desirable because the changes in behavior they induce further some other social goal.

14. When there are inefficiencies in the system for reasons other than the tax system (for example, externalities), taxation can conceivably improve efficiency.

KEY TERMS

Progressive, proportional, and regressive taxes   381

Average and marginal tax rates   381

Direct and indirect taxes   381

Personal income tax   381

Tax loopholes   382

Tax exempt   382

Tax deductions   382

Payroll tax   383

Corporate income tax   383

Excise tax   383

Social Security system   383

Property tax   385

Fiscal federalism   386

Horizontal and vertical equity   386

Ability-to-pay principle   386

Benefits principle of taxation   387

Economic efficiency   387

Burden of a tax   388

Excess burden   388

Incidence of a tax   389

Tax shifting   390

TEST YOURSELF

1. Using the following hypothetical income tax table, compute the marginal and average tax rates. Is the tax progressive, proportional, or regressive?

Income	Income Tax
$20,000	$2,000
30,000	2,700
40,000	3,200
50,000	3,500

2. Which concept of tax equity, if any, seems to be served by each of the following?

   a. The progressive income tax

   b. The excise tax on cigarettes

   c. The gasoline tax

3. Suppose the supply and demand schedules for cigarettes are as follows:

Price per Carton	Quantity Demanded	Quantity Supplied
$3.00	360	160
3.25	330	180
3.50	300	200
3.75	270	220
4.00	240	240
4.25	210	260
4.50	180	280
4.75	150	300
5.00	120	320

NOTE: Quantity is in millions of cartons per year.

a. What are the equilibrium price and equilibrium quantity?

b. Now the government levies a $1.25 per carton excise tax on cigarettes. What are the new equilibrium price paid by consumers, the price received by producers, and the quantity?

c. Explain why it makes no difference whether Congress levies the $1.25 tax on the consumer or the producer. (Relate your answer to the discussion of the payroll tax in the text.)

d. Suppose the tax is levied on the producers. How much of the tax are producers able to shift onto consumers? Explain how they manage to do so.

e. Will there be any excess burden from this tax? Why? Who bears this excess burden?

f. By how much has cigarette consumption declined on account of the tax? Why might the government be happy about this outcome, despite the excess burden?

4. Now suppose the supply schedule is instead:

Price per Carton	Quantity Supplied
$3.00	60
3.25	105
3.50	150
3.75	195
4.00	240
4.25	285
4.50	330
4.75	375
5.00	420

NOTE: Quantity is in millions of cartons per year.

a. What are the equilibrium price and equilibrium quantity in the absence of a tax?

b. What are the equilibrium price and equilibrium quantity in the presence of a $1.25 per carton excise tax?

c. Explain why your answer to part b differs from your answer to part b of the previous question, and relate this difference to the discussion of the incidence of an excise tax in this chapter.

5. The country of Taxmania produces only two commodities: rice and caviar. The poor spend all their income on rice, while the rich purchase both goods. Both demand for and supply of rice are quite inelastic. In the caviar market, both supply and demand are quite elastic. Which good would be heavily taxed if Taxmanians cared mostly about efficiency? What if they cared mostly about vertical equity?

DISCUSSION QUESTIONS

1. "Americans are overtaxed. The federal government should continue cutting taxes." Comment.

2. Soon after taking office in 2001, President Bush proposed a series of large tax cuts, including lower bracket rates and repeal of the estate tax. Critics argued that these tax cuts were excessive in magnitude and regressive in their distributional impact. Why did they say that? Do you agree?

3. Use the example of Mr. Figg (see the box, "The American Way of Tax" on page 390) to explain the concepts of efficient taxes and excess burden.

4. Think of some tax that you personally pay. What steps have you taken or could you take to reduce your tax payments? Is there an excess burden on you? Why or why not?

5. Discuss President Reagan's statement on taxes quoted on the first page of this chapter. Do you agree with him?

6. Use the criteria of equity and efficiency in taxation to evaluate the idea of taxing capital gains at a lower rate than other sources of income.

V

THE DISTRIBUTION OF INCOME

I n Part V, we examine how a market economy distributes its income, using the price mechanism, with the prices of the inputs to the production process determined by supply and demand—that is, we investigate what determines the share of total output that goes to workers, to landowners, to investors, etc. We will see that the market assigns a central role to the marginal productivity of each of these recipients—how much of a marginal contribution each makes to the economy's total output.

In Chapter 19, we will study the payments made for the use of capital (interest), land (rent), and the reward to entrepreneurs (profits). Because most people earn their incomes primarily from wages and salaries, and because these payments constitute nearly three-quarters of U.S. national income, our analysis of the payments to labor (wages) merits a separate chapter (Chapter 20). In Chapter 21, we turn to some important problems in the distribution of income—poverty, inequality, and discrimination.

19

PRICING THE FACTORS OF PRODUCTION

Rent is that portion of the produce of the earth which is paid to the landlord for use of the original and indestructible powers of the soil.

DAVID RICARDO (1772–1823)

Factors of production
are the broad categories—land, labor, capital, exhaustible natural resources, and entrepreneurship—into which we classify the economy's different productive inputs.

I n Chapter 15, we noted that the market mechanism cannot be counted on to distribute income in accord with ethical notions of fairness, and we listed this as one of the market's shortcomings. There is much more to say about how income is distributed in a market economy, and we turn to that subject in this chapter.

The market mechanism distributes income through its payments to the **factors of production.** Everyone owns some potentially usable factors of production—which are simply the inputs used in the production process. Many of us have only our own labor; but some of us also have funds that we can lend, land that we can rent, or natural resources that we can sell. We sell these factors on markets at prices determined by supply and demand. So the distribution of income in a market economy is determined by the prices of the factors of production and by the amounts that are employed. For example, if wages are low and unequal and unemployment is high, then many people will be poor.

CONTENTS

PUZZLE: *Why Does a Higher Return to Savings Reduce the Amounts Some People Save?*

The rate of interest is the price one obtains by saving some money and lending it to others—for example, lending the money to a bank (by depositing the money into a bank account) or lending the money to a corporation (by buying its bonds). We normally expect from the way the supply and demand mechanism works that a rise in the price of a loan (like the price of anything else) will reduce the quantity demanded and increase the quantity supplied. But the evidence is that many people who save their money and lend it to others do the opposite—they *reduce* the amount they lend when the rate of interest goes up. How can that make sense?

The same puzzle affects other factors of production, in a way that may hint at the explanation. For example, wages are the price of labor. But when wages rise, workers often decide to work less, for example, taking longer vacations. Why don't they work more when pay is better? A little thought may give you the answer, but we will provide a fuller explanation of this behavior later in the chapter.

Entrepreneurship is the act of starting new firms, introducing new products and technological innovations, and, in general, taking the risks that are necessary to seek out business opportunities.

It is useful to group the factors of production into five broad categories: land, labor, capital, exhaustible natural resources, and a rather mysterious input called **entrepreneurship.** In this chapter, we will look at three of them—the interest paid to capital, the rent of land, and the profits earned by entrepreneurs.

But first, because there is a great deal of misperception about the distribution of income among workers, suppliers of capital, and landlords, let's see how much these three groups actually earn. Of all the payments made to factors of production in the U.S. in 2006, interest payments accounted for about 4.5 percent; land rents were minuscule, making up only 0.7 percent; corporate profits accounted for 15 percent; and income of other business proprietors made up 9.4 percent. In total, the payments to all the factors of production that we deal with in this chapter amounted to about 30 percent of national factor income. Where did the rest of it go? The answer is that 70 percent of 2006 national factor income consisted of employee compensation—that is, wages and salaries.[1]

There are many other serious misunderstandings about the nature of income distribution and about what government can do to influence it, and discussions of the subject are often emotional. That's because the distribution of income is the one area in economics in which any one individual's interests almost inevitably conflict with the interests of someone else. By definition, if I get a larger slice of the total income pie, then you end up with a smaller slice.

THE PRINCIPLE OF MARGINAL PRODUCTIVITY

The **marginal physical product (MPP)** of an input is the increase in output that results from a one-unit increase in the use of the input, holding the amounts of all other inputs constant.

The **marginal revenue product (MRP)** of an input is the money value of the additional sales that a firm obtains by selling the marginal physical product of that input.

By now it should not surprise you to learn that economists analyze factor prices in terms of supply and demand. The supply sides of the markets for the various factors differ enormously, so we must discuss each factor market separately. But we can use one basic principle, the *principle of marginal productivity*, to explain how much of any input a profit-maximizing firm will *demand*, given the price of that input. To review the principle, we must first recall two concepts from Chapter 7: **marginal physical product (MPP)** and **marginal revenue product (MRP).**

Table 1 helps us review these two concepts in terms of Naomi's Natural Farm, which has to decide how much organic corn priced $10 per bag to feed its chickens. The *marginal physical product* (MPP) column tells us how many additional pounds of chicken each additional bag of corn will yield. For example, according to the table,

---

[1] *National Income and Product Accounts*, U.S. Department of Commerce, Bureau of Economic Analysis, available at http://www.bea.gov. (Note: This calculation consists of the Bureau of Economic Analysis categories, Compensation of Employees, Proprietors' Income with IVA and CCAdj., Rental Income of Persons with CCAdj., Corporate Profits with IVA and CCAdj., and Net Interest and Miscellaneous Payments, all as a percentage of Net National Factor Income.)

the fourth bag increases output by 34 pounds. The *marginal revenue product* (MRP) column tells us how many dollars this marginal physical product is worth. In Table 1, we assume Naomi's prized, natural chickens sell at 75 cents per pound, so the MRP of the fourth bag of corn is $0.75 per pound times 34 pounds, or $25.50 (last column of the table).

> The marginal productivity principle states that in competitive factor markets, the profit-maximizing firm will hire or buy the quantity of any input at which the marginal revenue product equals the price of the input.

The basic logic behind this principle is both simple and powerful. We know that the firm's profit from acquiring an additional unit of an input is the input's marginal revenue product minus its marginal cost (which is the price of the additional unit of input). If the input's marginal revenue product is greater than its price, it will pay the profit-seeking firm to acquire more of that input because an additional unit of input brings the firm revenue over and above its cost. The firm should purchase that input up to the amount at which diminishing returns reduce the MRP to the level of the input's price, so that further expansion yields zero further addition to profit. By similar reasoning, if MRP is less than price, then the firm is using too much of the input. We see in Table 1 that about seven bags is the optimal amount of corn for Naomi to use each week, because an eighth bag brings in a marginal revenue product of only $6.75, which is less than the $10 cost of buying the bag.

One corollary of the principle of marginal productivity is obvious: The quantity of any input demanded depends on its price. The lower the price of corn, the more it pays the farm to buy. In our example, it pays Naomi to use between seven and eight bags when the price per bag is $10. But if corn were more expensive—say, $20 per bag—that high price would exceed the value of the marginal product of either the sixth or seventh bag. It would, therefore, pay the firm to stop at five bags of corn. Thus, *marginal productivity analysis shows that the quantity demanded of an input normally declines as the input price rises.* The "law" of demand applies to inputs just as it applies to consumer goods.

	TABLE 1			
	\multicolumn{4}{c}{Naomi's Natural Farm Schedules for TPP, MPP, APP, and MRP of Corn}			

(1)	(2)	(3)	(4)	(5)
Corn Input (Bags)	TPP: Total Physical Product (chicken, lbs)	MPP: Marginal Physical Product per Bag	APP: Average Physical Product per Bag	MRP: Marginal Revenue Product per Bag
0	0.0 lbs		0.0 lbs	
		14.0 lbs		$10.50
1	14.0		14.0	
		22.0		16.50
2	36.0		18.0	
		30.0		22.50
3	66.0		22.0	
		34.0		25.50
4	100.0		25.0	
		30.0		22.50
5	130.0		26.0	
		26.0		19.50
6	156.0		26.0	
		19.0		14.25
7	175.0		25.0	
		9.0		6.75
8	184.0		23.0	
		1.4		1.05
9	185.4		20.6	
		−5.4		−4.05
10	180.0		18.0	
		−15.0		−11.25
11	165.0		15.0	
		−21.0		−15.75
12	144.0		12.0	

INPUTS AND THEIR DERIVED DEMAND CURVES

We can, in fact, be much more specific about how much of each input a profit-maximizing firm will demand. That's because the marginal productivity principle tells us precisely how to derive the demand curve for any input from its marginal revenue product (MRP) curve.

Figure 1 graphs the MRP schedule from Table 1, showing the marginal revenue product for corn (MRP_c) rising and then declining as Naomi feeds more and more corn to her chickens. In the figure, we focus on three possible prices for a bag of corn: $20, $15, and $10. As we have just seen, the optimal purchase rule requires Naomi to keep increasing her use of corn until her MRP begins to fall and eventually is reduced to the price of corn. At a price of $20 per bag, we see that the quantity demanded is about 5.6 bags of corn per week (point *A*); at that point, MRP equals price. Similarly, if the price of corn is $15 per bag, quantity demanded is about 6.8 bags per week (point *B*). Finally, at a price of $10 per bag, the quantity demanded would be about 7.7 bags per week (point *C*). Points *A*, *B*, and *C* are therefore three points on the demand curve for corn. By repeating this exercise for any other price, we learn that,

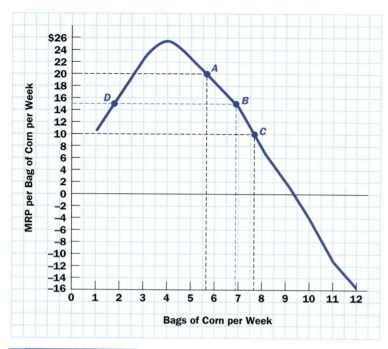

FIGURE 1

Marginal Revenue Product Graph for Naomi's Natural Farm

The **derived demand** for an input is the demand for the input by producers as determined by the demand for the final product that the input is used to produce.

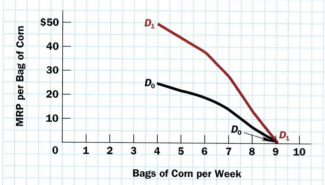

FIGURE 2

A Shift in the Demand Curve for Corn

because the profit-maximizing purchase of an input occurs at the point where the MRP has *fallen* down to the level of the input price:

> The demand curve for any input is the downward-sloping portion of its marginal revenue product curve.[2]

The demand for corn or labor (or for any other input) is called a **derived demand** because it is derived from the underlying demand for the final product (poultry in this case). For example, suppose that a surge in demand drives organic chicken prices to $1.50 per pound. Then, at each level of corn usage, the marginal revenue product will be twice as large as when poultry brought 75 cents per pound. This effect appears in Figure 2 as an upward shift of the (derived) demand curve for corn, from D_0D_0 to D_1D_1, even though the marginal physical product curves have not changed. Thus, an outward shift in demand for poultry leads to an outward shift in the demand for corn.[3] We conclude that, in general:

> An outward shift in the demand curve for any commodity causes an outward shift of the derived demand curve for all factors utilized in the production of that commodity.

Similarly, an inward shift in the demand curve for a commodity leads to inward shifts in the demand curves for factors used in producing that commodity.

This completes our discussion of the *demand* side of the analysis of input pricing. The most noteworthy feature of the discussion is the fact that the same marginal productivity principle serves as the foundation for the demand schedule for each and every type of input. In particular, as we will see in Chapter 20, the marginal productivity principle serves as the basis for the determination of the demand for *labor*—that crucial input whose financial reward plays so important a role in an economy's standard of living. On the demand side, one analysis fits all.

The supply side for each input, however, entails a very different story. Here we must deal with each of the main production factors individually. We must do so because, as we will see, the supply relationships of the different inputs vary considerably. We begin with *interest payments*, or the return on capital. First, we must define a few key terms.

---

[2] Why is the demand curve restricted to only the *downward-sloping portion* of the MRP curve? The logic of the marginal productivity principle dictates this constraint. For example, if the price of corn were $15.00 per bag, Figure 1 shows that MRP = P at two input quantities: (approximately) 1.75 bags (point D) and 6.8 bags (point B). Point D cannot be the optimal stopping point, however, because the MRP of a second bag ($16.50) is greater than the cost of the third bag ($15.00); that is, the firm makes more money by expanding its input use beyond 1.5 bags per week. A similar profitable opportunity for expansion occurs any time the MRP curve slopes upward at the current price, because an increase in the quantity of input used by the firm will raise MRP above the input's price. It follows that a profit-maximizing firm will always demand an input quantity that is in the range where MRP is diminishing.

[3] To make Figure 2 easier to read, the (irrelevant) upward-sloping portion and the negative portion of each curve have been omitted.

INVESTMENT, CAPITAL, AND INTEREST

Although people sometimes use the words *investment* and *capital* as if they were interchangeable, it is important to distinguish between them. Economists define **capital** as the *inventory* (or stock) of plant, equipment, and other productive resources held by a business firm, an individual, or some other organization. **Investment** is the amount by which capital *grows*. A warehouse owned by a firm is part of its capital. Expansion of the warehouse by adding a new area to the building is an investment. So, when economists use the word "investment," they do not mean just the transfer of money. The higher the level of investment, the *faster* the amount of capital that the investor possesses grows. The relation between investment and capital is often explained by analogy with filling a bathtub: The accumulated water in the tub is analogous to the *stock* of capital, whereas the flow of water from the faucet (which adds to the tub's water) is like the *flow* of investment. Just as the faucet must be turned on for more water to accumulate, the capital stock increases only when investment continues. If investment ceases, the capital stock stops growing (but does not disappear). In other words, if investment is zero, the capital stock does not fall to zero but remains constant (just as when you turn off the faucet the tub doesn't suddenly empty, but rather the level of the water stays the same).

The process of building up capital by investing and then using this capital in production can be divided into five steps, listed below and summarized in Figure 3:

Step 1. The firm decides to enlarge its stock of capital.

Step 2. The firm raises the funds to finance its expansion, either by tapping outside sources such as banks or by holding onto some of its own earnings rather than paying them out to company owners.

Step 3. The firm uses these funds to hire the inputs needed to build factories, warehouses, and the like. This step is the act of *investment*.

Step 4. After the investment is completed, the firm ends up with a larger stock of capital.

Step 5. The firm uses the capital (along with other inputs) either to expand production or to reduce costs. At this point, the firm starts earning *returns* on its investment.

Capital refers to an inventory (*stock*) of plant, equipment, and other (generally durable) productive resources held by a business firm, an individual, or some other organization.

Investment is the *flow* of resources into the production of new capital. It is the labor, steel, and other inputs devoted to the *construction* of factories, warehouses, railroads, and other pieces of capital during some period of time.

SOURCE: © *The New Yorker* Collection 1995, Robert Mankoff from cartoonbank.com. All Rights Reserved.

"I can't sleep. I just got this incredible craving for capital."

FIGURE 3   **The Investment Production Process**

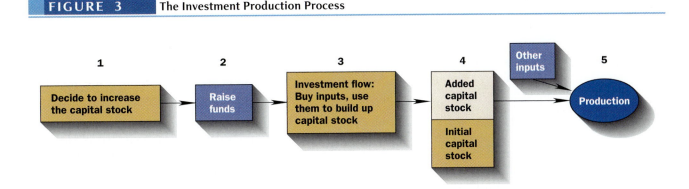

Notice that investors put *money* into the investment process—either their own or funds they borrow from others. Then, through a series of steps, firms transform the funds into physical inputs suitable for production use. If investors borrow the funds, they must someday return those amounts to the lender with some payment for their use. This payment is called **interest,** and it is calculated as an annual percentage of the amount borrowed. For example, if an investor borrows $1,000 at an interest rate of 12 percent per year, the annual interest payment is $120.

Interest is the payment for the use of funds employed in the production of capital; it is measured as the percent per year of the value of the funds tied up in the capital.

■ The Demand for Funds

The rate of interest is the *price* at which funds can be rented (borrowed). Just like other factor prices, interest rates are determined by supply and demand.

On the demand side of the market for loans are borrowers—people or institutions that, for one reason or another, wish to spend more than they currently have. Individuals or families borrow to buy homes or automobiles or other expensive products. Sometimes, as we know, they borrow because they want to consume more than they can afford, which can get them into financial trouble. But often, borrowing makes good sense as a way to manage their finances when they experience a temporary drop in income. It also makes sense to borrow money to buy an item such as a home that will be used for many years. This long product life makes it appropriate for people to pay for the item as it is used, rather than all at once when it is purchased.

Businesses use loans primarily to finance investment. To the business executive who borrows funds to finance an investment and pays interest in return, the funds really represent an intermediate step toward the acquisition of the machines, buildings, inventories, and other forms of physical capital that the firm will purchase.

The marginal productivity principle governs the quantity of funds demanded, just as it governs the quantity of corn demanded for chicken feed. Specifically:

Firms will demand the quantity of borrowed funds that makes the marginal revenue product of the investment financed by the funds just equal to the interest payment charged for borrowing.

One noteworthy feature of capital distinguishes it from other inputs, such as corn. When Naomi feeds corn to her chickens, the input is used once and then it is gone. But a blast furnace, which is part of a steel company's capital, normally lasts many years. The furnace is a *durable* good; because it is durable, it contributes not only to today's production but also to future production. This fact makes calculation of the marginal revenue product more complex for a capital good than for other inputs.

To determine whether the MRP of a capital good is greater than the cost of financing it (that is, to decide whether an investment is profitable), we need a way to compare money values received at different times. To make such comparisons, economists and business people use a calculation procedure called *discounting*. We will explain discounting in detail in the appendix to this chapter, but you need not master this technique in an introductory course. There are really only two important attributes of discounting to learn here:

- *A sum of money received at a future date is worth less than the same sum of money received today.*
- *This difference in values between money today and money in the future is greater when the rate of interest is higher.*

We can easily understand why this is so. To illustrate our first point, consider what you could do with a dollar that you received today rather than a year from today. If the annual rate of interest were 10 percent, you could lend it out (for example, by putting it in a savings account) and receive $1.10 in a year's time—your original $1.00 plus 10 cents interest. For this reason, money received today is worth more than the same number of dollars received later.

Now for our second point. Suppose the annual rate of interest is 15 percent rather than the 10 percent in the previous example. In this case, $1.00 invested today would grow to $1.15 (rather than $1.10) in a year's time, which means that $1.15 received a year from today would be equivalent to $1.00 received today, and so, when the interest rate is 15 percent, $1.10 a year in the future must now be worth less than $1.00 today. In contrast, when the interest rate is only 10 percent per year, $1.10 to be received a year from today *is* equivalent to $1 of today's money, as we have seen. This illustrates the second of our two points.

The rate of interest is a crucial determinant of the economy's level of investment. It strongly influences the amount of current consumption that consumers will choose to forgo in order to use the resources to build machines and factories that can increase the output of consumers' goods in the future. The interest rate is crucial in determining the allocation of society's resources between present and future—an issue that we discussed in Chapter 15 (pages 319–320). Let us see, then, how the market sets interest rates.

■ The Downward-Sloping Demand Curve for Funds

A rise in the price of borrowed funds, like a rise in the price of any item, usually increases quantity demanded. But the two attributes of discounting discussed above also help to explain why the demand curve for funds has a negative slope.

Recall that the demand for borrowed funds, like the demand for all inputs, is a *derived demand*, derived from the desire to invest in capital goods. But firms will receive part—perhaps all—of a machine or factory's marginal revenue product in the future. Hence, the value of the MRP *in terms of today's money* shrinks as the interest rate rises. Why? Because future returns on investment in a machine or factory must be *discounted* more when the rate of interest rises, as our illustration of the second point about discounting showed. As a consequence of this shrinkage, a machine that appears to be a good investment when the interest rate is 10 percent may look like a terrible investment if interest rates rise to 15 percent. That is, the higher the interest rate, the fewer machines a firm will demand, because investing in the machines would use up money that could earn more interest in a savings account. Thus, the demand curve for machines and other forms of capital will have a negative slope—the higher the interest rate, the smaller the quantity that firms will demand.

> As the interest rate on borrowing rises, more and more investments that previously looked profitable start to look unprofitable. The demand for borrowing for investment purposes, therefore, is lower at higher rates of interest.

Note that, although this analysis clearly applies to a firm's purchase of capital goods such as plant and equipment, it may also apply to the company's land and labor purchases. Firms often finance both of these expenditures via borrowed funds, and these inputs' marginal revenue products may accrue only months or even years after the inputs have been bought and put to work. (For example, it may take quite some time before newly acquired agricultural land will yield a marketable crop.) Thus, just as in the case of capital investments, a rise in the interest rate will reduce the quantity demanded of investment goods such as land and labor, just as it cuts the derived demand for investment in plant and equipment.

Figure 4 depicts a derived demand schedule for loans, with the interest rate on the vertical axis as the loan's cost to a borrower. Its negative slope illustrates the conclusion we have just stated:

> The higher the interest rate, the less people and firms will want to borrow to finance their investments.

FIGURE 4
The Derived Demand Curve for Loans

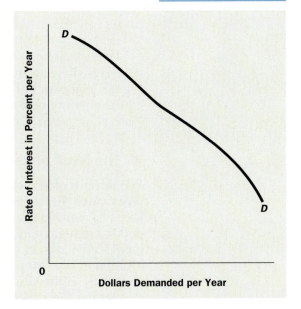

The Supply of Funds: THE PUZZLE RESOLVED

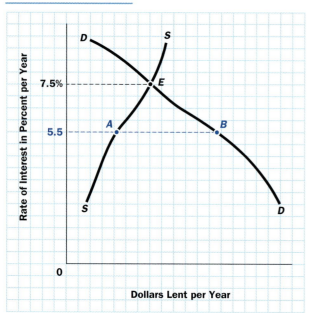

Somewhat different relationships arise on the supply side of the market for funds—where the suppliers or *lenders* are consumers, banks, and other business firms. Funds lent out are usually returned to the owner (with interest) only over a period of time. Loans will look better to lenders when they bear higher interest rates, so the supply schedule for loans rather naturally may be expected to slope upward—at higher rates of interest, lenders supply more funds. Such a supply schedule appears as the curve SS in Figure 5, where we also reproduce the demand curve, DD, from Figure 4. Here, the free-market interest rate is 7.5 percent.

However, not all supply curves for funds slope uphill to the right like curve SS. As we stated in the puzzle at the beginning of the chapter, sometimes a rise in the interest rate (the price of loans that is the financial reward for saving) will lead people to save *less*, rather than more. An example will help to explain the reason for this apparently curious behavior which, as we will see, can sometimes be sensible behavior. Say Jim is saving to buy a $10,000 used tractor in three years. If he lends money out at interest in the interim, suppose Jim must save $3,100 per year to reach his goal. If interest rates were higher, he could get away with saving less than $3,100 per year and still reach his $10,000 goal because every year, with the higher interest, he would get larger interest payments on his savings. Thus, Jim's saving (and lending) may decline as a result of the rise in interest rate. This argument applies fully only to savers, like Jim, with a fixed accumulation goal, but similar considerations affect the calculations of other savers. So when the rate of interest rises, some people save more but some save less.

Generally, we expect the quantity of loans supplied to rise at least somewhat when the interest reward rises, so the supply curve will have a positive slope, like SS in Figure 5. However, for reasons similar to those indicated in Jim's example, the increase in the economy's saving that results from a rise in the interest rate is usually quite small. That is why we have drawn the supply curve to be so steep. The rise in the amount supplied by some lenders is partially offset by a decline in the amounts lent by savers with fixed goals (like Jim, who is putting money away to buy a tractor, or Jasmine, who is saving for an expensive camera).

Having examined the relevant demand and supply curves, we are now in a position to discuss the determination of the equilibrium rate of interest. This is summed up in Figure 5, in which the equilibrium is, as always, at point E, where quantity supplied equals quantity demanded. We conclude, again, that the equilibrium interest rate on loans is 7.5 percent in the example in the graph.

■ The Issue of Usury Laws: Are Interest Rates Too High?

People have often been dissatisfied with the market mechanism's determination of interest rates. Fears that interest rates, if left unregulated, would climb to exorbitant levels have made usury laws (which place upper limits on money-lending rates) quite popular in many times and places. Attempts to control interest payments date back to biblical days, and in the Middle Ages the influence of the church even led to total prohibition of interest payments in much of Europe. The same is true today in Moslem countries. In the United States, the patchwork of state usury laws was mostly dismantled during the 1980s when the banking industry was deregulated.

Unscrupulous lenders often manage to evade usury laws, charging interest rates even higher than the free-market equilibrium rate. But even when usury laws are effective, they interfere with the operation of supply and demand and, as we will demonstrate, they may harm economic efficiency.

Look at Figure 5 again but, this time, assume it depicts the supply of bank loans to consumers. Consider what happens if a usury law prohibits interest rates higher than 5.5 percent per year on consumer loans. At 5.5 percent, the quantity supplied (point *A* in Figure 5) falls short of the quantity demanded (point *B*). This means that many applicants for consumer loans are being turned down even though banks consider them to be creditworthy.

Who gains and who loses from this usury law? The gainers are the lucky consumers who get loans at 5.5 percent even though they would have been willing to pay 7.5 percent. The losers come on both the supply side and the demand side: the consumers who would have been willing and able to get credit at 7.5 percent but who are turned down at 5.5 percent, and the banks that could have made profitable loans at rates of up to 7.5 percent if there were no interest-rate ceiling.

This analysis explains why usury laws can be politically popular. Few people sympathize with bank stockholders, and the consumers who get loans at lower rates are, naturally, pleased with the result of usury laws. Other consumers, who would like to borrow at 5.5 percent but cannot because quantity supplied is less than quantity demanded, are likely to blame the bank for refusing to lend, rather than blaming the government for outlawing mutually beneficial transactions.

Yet concern over high interest rates can be rational. It may, for example, be appropriate to combat homelessness by making financing of housing cheaper for poor people. Of course, it may be much more rational for the government to subsidize the interest on housing for the poor rather than to declare high interest rates illegal, in effect pretending that those costs can simply be legislated away, as a usury ceiling tries to do.[4]

THE DETERMINATION OF RENT

The second main factor of production is land. Rent, the payment for the use of land, is another price that, when left to the market, often seems to settle at politically unpopular levels. Rent controls are a popular solution. We discussed the effects of rent controls in Chapter 4 (page 72), and we will say a bit more about them later in this chapter. But our main focus here is the determination of rents by free markets.

The market for land is characterized by a special feature on the supply side. Land is a factor of production whose total quantity supplied is (roughly) unchanging and virtually unchangeable: The same quantity is available at every possible price. Indeed, classical economists used this notion as the working definition of land. And the definition seems to fit, at least approximately. Although people may drain swamps, clear forests, fertilize fields, build skyscrapers, or convert land from one use (a farm) to another (a housing development), human effort cannot change the total supply of land by very much.

What does this fact tell us about how the market determines land rents? Figure 6 helps to provide an answer. The vertical supply curve *SS* means that no matter what

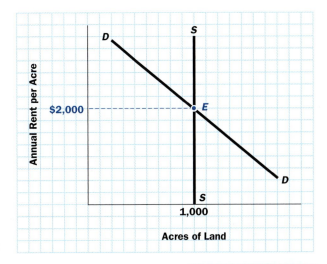

[4] The law also sometimes concerns itself with discrimination in lending against women or members of ethnic minority groups. Strong evidence suggests the existence of sex and race discrimination in lending. For example, married women have been denied loans without the explicit permission of their husbands, even where the women had substantial independent incomes.

FIGURE 6

Determination of Land Rent in Littleville

FIGURE 7

A Shift in Demand with a Vertical Supply Curve

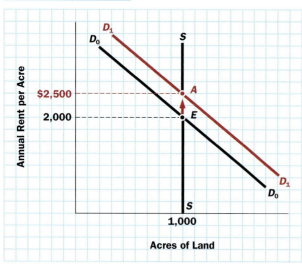

Acres of Land

the level of rents, there are only 1,000 acres of land in a small hamlet called Littleville. The demand curve *DD* slopes downward and is a typical marginal revenue product curve, predicated on the notion that the use of land, like everything else, is subject to diminishing returns. The free-market price is determined, as usual, by the intersection of the supply and demand curves at point *E*. In this example, each acre of land in Littleville rents for $2,000 per year. The interesting feature of this diagram is that, because quantity supplied is rigidly fixed at 1,000 acres whatever the price:

> The market level of rent is entirely determined by the market's demand side.

If, for example, a major university relocates to Littleville, attracting more people who want to live there, the *DD* curve will shift outward, as depicted in Figure 7. Equilibrium in the market will shift from point *E* to point *A*. The same 1,000 acres of land will be available, but now each acre will command a rent of $2,500 per acre. The landlords will collect more rent, even though society gets no more of the input—land—from the landlords in return for its additional payment.

The same process also works in reverse, however. If the university shuts its doors and the demand for land declines as a result, the landlords will suffer even though they did not contribute to the decline in the demand for land. (To see this simply reverse the logic of Figure 7. The demand curve begins at D_1D_1 and shifts to D_0D_0.)

This discussion shows the special feature of rent that leads economists to distinguish it from payments to other factors of production. An **economic rent** is an "extra" payment for a factor of production (such as land) that does not change the amount of the factor that is supplied. Society is not compensated for a rise in its rent payments by any increase in the quantity of land it obtains. Economic rent is thus the portion of the factor payment that exceeds the minimum payment necessary to induce that factor to be supplied.

As late as the end of the nineteenth century, the idea of economic rent exerted a powerful influence far beyond technical economic writings. An American journalist, Henry George, was nearly elected mayor of New York in 1886, running on the platform that all government should be financed by a "single tax" levied on landlords who, he said, are the only ones who earn incomes without contributing to the productive process. George said that landlords reap the fruits of economic growth without contributing to economic progress. He based his logic on the notion that landowners do not increase the supply of their factor of production—the quantity of land—when rents increase.

Economic rent is the portion of the earnings of a factor of production that exceeds the minimum amount necessary to induce that factor to be supplied.

■ Land Rents: Further Analysis

If all plots of land were identical, our previous discussion would be virtually all there is to the theory of land rent. But plots of land *do* differ—in geographical location, topography, nearness to marketplaces, soil quality, and so on. The classical economists took this disparity into account in their analysis of rent determination—a remarkable nineteenth-century piece of economic logic still considered valid today.

The basic notion is that capital invested in any piece of land must yield the same return as capital invested in any other piece that is actually in use. Why? If it were not so, capitalist renters would bid against one another for the more profitable pieces of land. This competition would go on until the rents they would have to pay for these parcels were driven up to a point that eliminated their advantages over other parcels.

Suppose that a farmer produces a crop on one piece of land for $160,000 per year in labor, fertilizer, fuel, and other non-land costs, while a neighbor who is no more efficient produces the same crop for $120,000 on a second piece of land. The rent on the second parcel must be *exactly* $40,000 per year higher than the rent on the first, because otherwise production on one plot would be cheaper than on the other. If, for example, the rent difference were only $30,000 per year, it would be $10,000 cheaper to produce on the second plot of land. No one would want to rent the first plot and every grower would instead bid for the second plot. Rent on the first plot would be forced down by the lack of customers, and rent on the second plot would be driven up by eager bidders. These pressures would come to an end only when the rent difference reached $40,000, so that both plots became equally profitable.

At any given time, some low-quality pieces of land are so inferior that it does not pay to use them at all—remote deserts are a prime example. Any land that is exactly on the borderline between being used and not being used is called **marginal land.** By this definition, marginal land earns no rent because if its owner charged any for it, no one would willingly pay to use it.

We combine these two observations—that the difference between the costs of producing on any two pieces of land must equal the difference between their rents and that zero rent is charged on marginal land—to conclude that:

> Rent on any piece of land will equal the difference between the cost of producing the output on that land and the cost of producing it on marginal land.

That is, competition for the superior plots of land will permit the landowners to charge prices that capture the full advantages of their superior parcels.

This analysis helps us to understand more completely the effects of an outward shift in the demand curve for land. Suppose population growth raises demand for land. Naturally, rents will rise. But we can be more specific than this statement. In response to an outward shift in the demand curve, two things will happen:

- *It will now pay to employ some land whose use was formerly unprofitable.* The land that was previously on the zero-rent margin will no longer be on the borderline, and some land that is so poor that it was formerly not even worth considering will now just reach the borderline of profitability. The settling of the American West illustrates this process strikingly. Land that once could not be given away is now quite valuable.
- *People will begin to exploit already-used land more intensively.* Farmers will use more labor and fertilizer to squeeze larger amounts of crops out of their acreage, as has happened in recent decades. Urban real estate that previously held two-story buildings will now be used for high-rise buildings.

These two events will increase rents in a predictable fashion. Because the land that is considered marginal *after* the change must be inferior to the land that was considered marginal previously, rents must rise by the difference in yields between the old and new marginal lands. Table 2 illustrates this point. In the table, we deal with three pieces of land: A, a very productive piece; B, a piece that was initially considered only marginal; and C, a piece that is inferior to B but nevertheless becomes marginal when the demand curve for land shifts upward and to the right.

The crop costs $80,000 more when produced on B than on A, and $12,000 more when produced on C than on B. Suppose, initially, that demand for the crop is so low that Farmer Jones does not plant crops in field C. Farmer Jones is on the fence about whether to plant crops in field B. Because field B is marginal, it is just on the margin between being used and being left idle—it will command no rent. We know that

Marginal land is land that is just on the borderline of being used—that is, any land the use of which would be unprofitable if the farmer had to pay even a penny of rent.

		TABLE 2		
	Nonrent Costs and Rent on Three Pieces of Land			
Type of Land		Nonland Cost of Producing a Given Crop	Total Rent	
			Before	After
A. A tract that was better than marginal before and after		$120,000	$80,000	$92,000
B. A tract that was marginal before but is attractive now		200,000	0	12,000
C. A tract that was previously not worth using but is now marginal		212,000	0	0

the rent on field A will be equal to the $80,000 cost advantage of A over B. Now suppose demand for the crop increases enough so that plot C becomes marginal land. Then field B commands a rent of $12,000, the cost advantage of B over C. Plot A's rent now must rise from $80,000 to $92,000, the size of its cost advantage over C, the newly marginal land.

In addition to the quality differences among pieces of land, a second influence pushes land rents up: increased intensity of use of land that is already under cultivation. As farmers apply more fertilizer and labor to their land, the marginal productivity of the land increases, just as factory workers become more productive when more is invested in their equipment. Once again, the landowner can capture this productivity increase in the form of higher rents. (If you do not understand why, refer back to Figure 7 and recall that the demand curves are marginal revenue product curves—that is, they indicate the amount that capitalists are willing to pay landlords to use their land.) Thus, we can summarize the theory of rent as follows:

As the use of land increases, landlords receive higher payments from two sources:

- Increased demand leads the community to employ land previously not good enough to use; the advantage of previously used land over the new marginal land increases, and rents go up correspondingly.

- Land is used more intensively; the marginal revenue product of land rises, thereby increasing the ability of the producer who uses the land to pay rent.

Generalization: Economic Rent Seeking

Economists refer to the payments for land as "rents," but land is not the only scarce input with a fixed supply, at least in the short run. Toward the beginning of the twentieth century, some economists realized that the economic analysis of rent can be applied to inputs *other* than land. As we will see, this extension yielded some noteworthy insights.

The concept of rent can be used to analyze such common phenomena as lobbying in the U.S. Congress (attempts to influence the votes of members of Congress) by

Land Prices Around the World

Supply and demand do not equalize prices when the commodity, such as land, cannot be transferred from one geographic market to another. In 2006, for example, real estate in Paris was selling for an average of $645 per square foot. In London, currently the priciest place to buy a home, prime residential property sold for around $2,300 per square foot, compared to $1,900 in New York City. Property in Montreal was going for around $250 per square foot, while it cost about $110 per square foot to buy in Bucharest, Romania.

SOURCE: © David Lawrence/Corbis

SOURCES: Stephanie Rosenbloom, "Buying Around the World," *International Herald Tribune*, February 22, 2006, and Arlane Bernard, "An American (and His Second Home) in Paris," *International Herald Tribune*, October 18, 2006, http://www.iht.com.

Dapper Dan would be willing to play basketball for $50,000 per year, rather than working as a hamburger flipper, the only other job for which he is qualified. But Dan knows he can do better than that. He estimates, quite accurately, that his presence on the team brings in $10 million of added revenue over and above what the team would obtain if Dan were replaced by a player of Willy's caliber. In that case, Dan and his agent ought to be able to obtain $10 million *more* per year than is paid to Willy. As a result, Dan obtains a salary of $10,050,000, of which $10 million is economic rent—exactly analogous to the previous rent example involving different pieces of land of unequal quality. Note that the team gets no more of Dapper Dan's working time in return for the rent payment. (See "A-Rod: Earning lots of Economic Rent" on the facing page, for a real-world example.)

Almost all inputs, including employees, earn some economic rent. What sorts of inputs earn no rent? Only those inputs that can be provided by a number of suppliers at constant cost and with identical quality earn no rents. For instance, no ball-bearing supplier will ever receive any rent on a ball bearing, at least in the long run, because any desired number of them, *of equal quality*, can be produced at (roughly) constant costs and can contribute equal amounts to the profits of those who use them. If one ball-bearing supplier tried to charge a price above their x-cent cost, another manufacturer would undercut the first supplier and take its customers away. Hence, the competitive price includes no economic rent.

Rent Controls: The Misplaced Analogy

Why is the analysis of economic rent important? Because only economic rent can be taxed away without reducing the quantity of the input supplied. Here common English gets in the way of sound reasoning. Many people feel that the *rent* they pay to their landlord is economic rent. After all, their apartments will still be there if they pay $1,500 per month, or $500, or $100. This view, although true in the short run, is quite shortsighted.

Like the ball-bearing producer, the owner of a building cannot expect to earn *economic rent* because too many other potential owners whose costs of construction are roughly the same as her own will also offer apartments. If the market price temporarily included some economic rent—that is, if price exceeded production costs plus the opportunity cost of the required capital—other builders would start new construction that would drive the price down. Thus, far from being in perfectly *inelastic* (vertical) supply, like raw land, buildings come rather close to being in perfectly *elastic* (horizontal) supply, like ball bearings. As we have learned from the theory of rent, this means that builders and owners of buildings cannot collect economic rent in the long run.

Because apartment owners collect very little economic rent, payments by tenants in a free market must be just enough to keep those apartments on the market (the very definition of zero economic rent). If rent controls push these prices down, the apartments will start disappearing from the market.[5] Among other unfortunate results, we can therefore expect rent controls to contribute to homelessness—though it is, of course, not the only influence behind this distressing phenomenon.

PAYMENTS TO ENTREPRENEURSHIP: ARE PROFITS TOO HIGH OR TOO LOW?

We turn next to business profits, the discussion of which often seems to elicit more passion than logic. With the exception of some economists, almost no one thinks that profit rates are at about the right level. Critics point accusingly to some giant corporations' billion-dollar profits and argue that they are unconscionably high; they then

---

[5] None of this is meant to imply that temporary rent controls in certain locations cannot have desirable effects in the short run. In the short run, the supply of apartments and houses really is fixed, and large shifts in demand can hand windfall gains to landlords—gains that are true, if temporary, economic rents. Controls that eliminate such windfalls should not cause serious problems. But knowing when the "short run" fades into the "long run" can be tricky. "Temporary" rent control laws have a way of becoming rather permanent.

call for much stiffer taxes on profits. On the other hand, the Chambers of Commerce, National Association of Manufacturers, and other business groups complain that regulations and "ruinous" competition keep profits too low, and they constantly petition Congress for tax relief.

The public has many misconceptions about the nature of the U.S. economy, but probably none is farther from reality than popular perceptions of what American corporations earn in profits. Try the following experiment. Ask five of your friends who have never had an economics course what fraction of the nation's income they imagine is pure profit to companies. Although the correct answer varies from year to year, business profits in 2006 made up 12.4 percent of gross domestic product (GDP) (before taxes).[6] A comparable percentage of the prices you pay represents before-tax profit. Most people think this figure is much, much higher (see "Public Opinion on Profits" on page 31 in Chapter 2).

As you have no doubt noticed by now, economists are reluctant to brand factor prices as "too low" or "too high" in some moral or ethical sense. Rather, they are likely to ask first: What is the market equilibrium price? Then they will ask whether there are any good reasons to interfere with the market solution. This analysis, however, is not so easily applied to the case of *profits*, because it is difficult to use supply and demand analysis when you do not know which factor of production earns profit.

In both a bookkeeping sense and an economic sense, *profits are the residual.* **They are what remains from the selling price after all other factors have been paid.**

But which production factor earns this reward? Which factor's marginal productivity constitutes the profit rate?

■ What Accounts for Profits?

Economic profit is the total revenue of a firm minus all of its costs, including the interest payments and opportunity costs of the capital it obtains from its investors.

Economic profit, as we learned in Chapter 10, is the amount a firm earns *over and above the payments for all inputs,* including the interest payments for the capital it uses and the opportunity cost of any capital provided by the owners of the firm. The payment that firm owners receive to compensate them for the opportunity cost of their capital (and that in common parlance *is* considered profit) is closely related to interest rates, but is not part of *economic profit.* In an imaginary (and dull) world in which everything was certain and unchanging, capitalists who invested money in firms would simply earn the market rate of interest on their funds. Profits beyond this level would be competed away. Payment for capital below this level could not persist, because capitalists would withdraw their funds from firms and deposit them in banks. Capitalists in such a world would be mere moneylenders.

But the real world is not at all like this. Some capitalists are much more than moneylenders, and the amounts they earn often exceed current interest rates by a huge margin (see "Entrepreneurship: Cleaning Up in Business, with a Mop" on the next page, for an example). These active capitalists who seek out or even create earnings opportunities are called *entrepreneurs.* We can credit such creative individuals for the constant change that characterizes business firms and for preventing operations of the firm from stagnating. Because entrepreneurs constantly seek to do something new, it is difficult to provide a general description of their activities. However, we can list three primary ways in which entrepreneurs can and do drive profits above "normal" interest rate levels.

1. Monopoly Power   If entrepreneurs can establish monopolies with some or all of their products, even for a short while, they can use that monopoly power to earn monopoly profits. We analyzed the nature of these monopoly earnings in Chapter 11.

---

[6] Source: *National Income and Product Accounts,* U.S. Department of Commerce, Bureau of Economic Analysis, available at http://www.bea.gov.

Entrepreneurship: Cleaning Up in Business, with a Mop

As a teenager working part-time at an animal hospital in Huntington, Long Island, where she grew up, Joy Mangano came up with an idea for a fluorescent flea collar to keep cats and dogs from getting hit by cars at night. A year later, Hartz Mountain introduced a similar product.

Ms. Mangano, now 44, says she learned a valuable lesson that day: "I told myself the next time I had a good idea, I would bring it to market." That next time occurred in 1989, and the better mousetrap she dreamed up was actually a better mop. By then, Ms. Mangano had grown disgruntled with ordinary household mops. "I found they didn't last very long," she recalled. "I'd constantly be throwing them out or using sponges or paper towels to get the floors really clean." And there was the added aggravation of "continually having to bend down and wring it out," she said.

Her solution was the Miracle Mop, a sturdy plastic mop with easy-to-grip interlocking handles that allow users to wring it out without getting their hands wet. The rest is history: Today, Ms. Mangano has sold five million Miracle Mops worldwide, and her company, Ingenious Designs, Inc., has toted up cumulative retail sales of more than $200 million.

SOURCE: Courtesy of Joy Mangano, President–Ingenious Designs LLC

SOURCE: Excerpted from Susan Konig, "Cleaning Up in Business, with a Mop," *New York Times*, February 11, 2001, http://www.nytimes.com.

2. Risk Bearing   Entrepreneurs often engage in financially risky activities. For example, when a firm prospects for oil, it must drill exploratory wells hoping to find petroleum at the bottom. Of course, many such exploratory wells end up as dry holes, and the costs then bring no return. Lucky investors, on the other hand, do find oil and are rewarded handsomely—more than the competitive return on the firm's capital. The extra income pays the firm for bearing risk.

A few lucky individuals make out well in this process, but many suffer heavy losses. How well can we expect risk takers to do, on the average? If one exploratory drilling out of ten typically pays off, do we expect its return to be exactly ten times as high as the interest rate, so that the *average* firm will earn exactly the normal rate of interest? The answer is that the payoff will be *more* than ten times the interest rate if investors dislike gambling—that is, if they prefer to avoid risk. Why? Because investors who are risk averse will not be willing to put their money into a business that faces such long odds—10 to 1—unless the market provides compensation for the financial peril.

In reality, nothing guarantees that things will always work out this way. Some people love to gamble and tend to be overly optimistic. They may plunge into projects to a degree unjustified by the odds. Average payoffs to such gamblers in risky undertakings may end up below the interest rate. The successful investor will still make a good profit, just like the lucky winner in Las Vegas. The average participant, however, will have to pay for the privilege of bearing risk.

3. Returns to Innovation   The third major source of profits is perhaps the most important of all for social welfare. The first entrepreneur able to innovate and market a desirable new product or employ a new cost-saving machine will garner a higher profit than what an uninnovative (but otherwise similar) business manager would earn. Innovation differs from invention. Whereas **invention** generates new ideas, **innovation** takes the next step by putting the new idea into practical use. Businesspeople are rarely inventors, but they are often innovators.

When an entrepreneur innovates, even if her new product or new process is not protected by patents, she will be one step ahead of her competitors. If the market likes

Invention is the act of generating an idea for a new product or a new method for making an old product.

Innovation also includes the next step, the act of putting the new idea into practical use.

her innovation, she will be able to capture most of the sales, either by offering customers a better product or by supplying the product more cheaply. In either case, she will temporarily find herself with some monopoly power as her competitors weaken, and she will receive monopoly profit for her initiative.

However, this monopoly profit—the reward for innovation—will only be temporary. As soon as the idea's success becomes evident to the world, other firms will find ways of imitating it. Even if they cannot turn out precisely the same product or the same process, they must find close substitutes in order to survive. In this way, new ideas spread through the economy, and in the process the innovator's special profits come to an end. The innovator can resume earning special profits only by finding still another promising idea.

> The market system forces entrepreneurs to keep searching for new ideas, to keep instituting innovations, and to keep imitating new ideas even if they did not originate those innovations or ideas. This process lies at the heart of the growth of the capitalist system. It is one of the secrets of its extraordinary dynamism.

We explored these issues of innovation and growth performance in free markets more fully in Chapter 16.

■ Taxing Profits

Thus, we can consider profits in excess of market interest rates to be the return on entrepreneurial talent. But this definition is not really very helpful, because no one can say exactly what entrepreneurial talent is. Certainly we cannot measure it; nor can we teach it in a college course, although business schools may try. We do not know whether the observed profit rate provides more than the minimum reward necessary to attract entrepreneurial talent into the market. This relationship between observed profit rates and minimum necessary rewards is crucial when we start to consider the policy ramifications of taxes on profits—a contentious issue, indeed.

Consider a profits tax levied on oil companies. If oil companies earn profits well above the minimum required to attract entrepreneurial talent, those profits contain a large element of economic rent. In that case, we could tax away these excess profits (rents) without fear of reducing oil production. In contrast, if oil company profits do not include economic rents, then a windfall profits tax can seriously curtail oil exploration and, hence, production.

This example illustrates the general problem of deciding how heavily governments should tax profits. Critics of big business who call for high, if not confiscatory, profits taxes seem to believe that profits are mostly economic rent. If they are wrong—if, in fact, most of the observed profits are necessary to attract people into entrepreneurial roles—then a high profits tax can be dangerous. Such a tax would threaten the very lifeblood of the capitalist system. Business lobbying groups claim, predictably enough, that current tax policy creates precisely this threat. Unfortunately, neither group has offered much evidence to support its conclusion.

■ CRITICISMS OF MARGINAL PRODUCTIVITY THEORY

The theory of factor pricing described in this chapter once again uses supply-demand analysis. Factor pricing theory also relies heavily on the principle of marginal productivity to derive the shape and position of the demand curve for various inputs. Indeed, some economists refer to the analysis (rather misleadingly) as the *marginal productivity theory of distribution*, when it is, at best, only a theory of the demand side of the pertinent market.

Over the years, factor pricing analysis has been subject to attack on many grounds. One frequent accusation, which is largely (but not entirely) groundless, is the assertion that marginal productivity theory merely attempts to justify the income distribution that the capitalist system yields—in other words, that it is a piece of pro-capitalist propaganda. According to this argument, when marginal productivity theory claims that each factor is paid exactly its marginal revenue product, it is only a sneaky way of saying that each factor is paid exactly what it deserves. These critics claim that the theory legitimizes the gross inequities of the system—the poverty of many and the great wealth of a few.

This argument is straightforward but wrong. First, payments are made not to factors of production, but rather to the people who happen to own them. If an acre of land earns $2,000 because that is its marginal revenue product, it does not mean, nor is it meant to imply, that the landlord *deserves* any particular payment, because he may even have acquired the land by fraud.

Second, an input's MRP does not depend only on "how hard it works" but also on how much of it happens to be employed—because, according to the "law" of diminishing returns, the more that is employed, the lower its MRP. Thus, a factor's MRP is not and cannot legitimately be interpreted as a measure of the intensity of its "productive effort." In any event, what an input "deserves," in some moral sense, may depend on more than what it does in the factory. For example, workers who are sick or have many children may be considered more deserving, even if they are no more productive than their healthy or childless counterparts.

On these and other grounds, no economist today claims that marginal productivity analysis shows that distribution under capitalism is either just or unjust. It is simply wrong to claim that marginal productivity theory is pro-capitalist propaganda. The marginal productivity principle is just as relevant to organizing production in a socialist society as it is in a capitalist one.

Other critics have attacked marginal productivity theory for using rather complicated reasoning to tell us very little about the really urgent problems of income distribution. In this view, it is all very well to say that everything depends on supply and demand and to express this idea in terms of many complicated equations (many of which appear in more advanced books and articles). But these equations do not tell us what to do about such serious distribution problems as malnutrition among the indigenous populations in Latin America or poverty among minority groups in the United States.

Although it does exaggerate the situation somewhat, there is some truth to this criticism. We have seen in this chapter that the theory provides some insights into real policy matters, though not as many as we would like. Later in the book, we will see that economists do have useful things to say about the problems of poverty and underdevelopment, but very little of what we can say about these issues arises out of marginal productivity analysis.

Perhaps, in the end, what should be said for marginal productivity theory is this: As the best model we have at the moment, marginal productivity theory offers us *some* valuable insights into the way the economy works, and until we find a more powerful model, we are better off using the tools that we do have.

SUMMARY

1. A profit-maximizing firm purchases the quantity of any input at which the price of the input equals its **marginal revenue product** (MRP). Consequently, the firm's demand curve for an input is (the downward-sloping portion of) that input's MRP curve.

2. **Investment** in a firm is the amount that is *added* to the firm's capital, which is its plant, equipment, inventory, and other productive inputs that tie up the company's money.

3. **Interest** rates are determined by the supply of and demand for funds. The demand for funds is a **derived demand**,

because these funds are used to finance business investment whose profitability depends on the demand for the final products turned out with the aid of such investment. In this way, the demand for funds depends on the marginal revenue productivity of capital.

4. A dollar obtainable sooner is worth more than a dollar obtainable later because of the interest that can be earned on that dollar in the interim.

5. Increased demand for a good that needs land to produce it will drive up the price of land either because inferior land

will be brought into use or because land will be used more intensively.

6. Rent controls do not significantly affect the supply of land, but they do tend to reduce the supply of buildings.

7. **Economic rent** is any payment to the supplier of a factor of production that is greater than the minimum amount needed to induce the factor to be supplied.

8. **Factors of production** that are unique in quality and difficult or impossible to reproduce will tend to be paid relatively high economic rents because of their scarcity.

9. Factors of production that are easy to produce at a constant cost and that are provided by many suppliers will earn little or no economic rent.

10. **Economic profits** over and above the cost of **capital** are earned (a) by exercise of monopoly power, (b) as payments for bearing risk, and (c) as the earnings of successful **innovation**.

11. The desirability of increased taxation of profits depends on the taxes' effects on the supply of entrepreneurial talent. If most profits are economic rents, then higher profits taxes will have few undesirable effects. If most profits are necessary to attract entrepreneurs into the market, then higher profits taxes can weaken the capitalist economy.

KEY TERMS

Factors of production   399

Entrepreneurship   400

Marginal physical product (MPP)   400

Marginal revenue product (MRP)   400

Derived demand   402

Capital   403

Investment   403

Interest   404

Economic rent   408

Marginal land   409

Economic profit   414

Invention   415

Innovation   415

TEST YOURSELF

1. Which of the following inputs do you think include relatively large economic rents in their earnings?

   a. Nuts and bolts

   b. Petroleum

   c. A champion racehorse

   Use supply-demand analysis to explain your answer.

2. Three machines are employed in an isolated area. They each produce 2,000 units of output per month, the first requiring $20,000 in raw materials, the second $25,000, and the third $28,000. What would you expect to be the monthly charge for the first and second machines if the services of the third machine can be hired at a price of $9,000 per month? Which parts of the charges for the first two machines are economic rent?

3. Economists conclude that a tax on the revenues of firms will be shifted in part to consumers of the products of those firms in the form of higher prices. However, they believe that a tax on the rent of land usually cannot be shifted and must be paid entirely by the landlord. What explains the difference? (Hint: draw the supply-demand graphs.)

4. Many economists argue that a tax on apartment buildings is likely to reduce the supply of apartments, but that a tax on all land, including the land on which apartment buildings stand, will not reduce the supply of apartments. Can you explain the difference? How is this answer related to the answer to Question 3?

5. Distinguish between investment and capital.

6. Explain the difference between an invention and an innovation. Give an example of each.

7. What is the difference between interest and profit? Who earns interest, in return for what contribution to production? Who earns economic profit, in return for what contribution to production?

DISCUSSION QUESTIONS

1. A profit-maximizing firm expands its purchase of any input up to the point where diminishing returns have reduced the marginal revenue product so that it equals the input price. Why does it not pay the firm to "quit while it is ahead," buying so small a quantity of the input that the input's MRP remains greater than its price?

2. If you have a contract under which you will be paid $10,000 two years from now, why do you become richer if the rate of interest falls?

3. Do you know any entrepreneurs? How do they earn a living? How do they differ from managers?

4. "Marginal productivity does not determine how much a worker will earn—it determines only how many workers will be hired at a given wage. Therefore, marginal productivity analysis is a theory of demand for labor, not a theory of distribution." What, then, do you think determines wages? Does marginal productivity affect their level? If so, how?

5. **(More difficult)** American savings rates are among the lowest of any industrial country. This has caused concern about our ability to finance new plants and equipment for U.S. industry. Some politicians and others have advocated lower taxes on saving as a remedy. Do you expect such a program to be very effective? Why?

6. If rent constitutes only 2 percent of the incomes of Americans, why may the concept nevertheless be significant?

7. Litigation in which one company sues another often involves costs for lawyers and other court costs literally amounting to hundreds of millions of dollars per case. What does rent have to do with the matter?

APPENDIX *Discounting and Present Value*

Frequently, in business and economic problems, it is necessary to compare sums of money received (or paid) at different dates. Consider, for example, the purchase of a machine that costs $11,000 and will yield a marginal revenue product of $14,520 two years from today. If the machine can be financed by a two-year loan bearing 10 percent interest, it will cost the firm $1,100 in interest at the end of each year, plus $11,000 in repayment of the principal (the amount originally borrowed) at the end of the second year. (See the table that follows.) Is the machine a good investment?

Costs and Benefits of Investing in a Machine		
	End of Year 1	End of Year 2
Benefits		
Marginal revenue product of the machine	$ 0	$14,520
Costs		
Interest	1,100	1,100
Repayment of principal on loan	0	11,000
Total Cost	1,100	12,100

The total costs of owning the machine over the two-year period ($1,100 + $12,100 = $13,200) are less than the total benefits ($14,520). But this is clearly an invalid comparison, because the $14,520 in future benefits is not worth $14,520 in terms of today's money. Adding up dollars received (or paid) at different dates is a bit like adding apples and oranges.

The process that has been invented for making the magnitudes of payments at different dates comparable to one another is called *discounting,* or *computing the present value.*

To illustrate the concept of present value, let us ask how much $1 received a year from today is worth *in terms of today's money.* If the rate of interest is 10 percent, the answer is about 91 cents. Why? Because if we invest 91 cents today at 10 percent interest, it will grow to 91 cents plus 9.1 cents in interest = 100.1 cents in a year. That is, at the end of a year a payment of $100 will leave the recipient about as well off as he would have been if he had instead received $91 now. Similar considerations apply to any rate of interest. In general:

If the rate of interest is *i*, the present value of $1 to be received in a year is:

$$\frac{\$1.00}{(1 + i)}$$

This is so, because in a year

$$\frac{\$1.00}{(1 + i)}$$

will grow to the original amount plus the interest payment, that is,

$$\frac{\$1.00}{(1 + i)} + \frac{\$1.00}{1 + i} \times i = \frac{\$1.00}{(1 + i)} \times (1 + i) = \$1$$

What about money to be received two years from today? Using the same reasoning, and supposing the interest rate is 10 percent so that $1 + i = 1.1$, $1.00 invested today will grow to $1.00 times (1.1) = $1.10 after one year and will grow to $1.00 times (1.1) times (1.1) = $1.00 times $(1.1)^2$ = $1.21 after two years. Consequently, the present value of $1.00 to be received two years from today is:

$$\frac{\$1.00}{(1 + i)^2} = \frac{\$1.00}{1.21} = 82.64 \text{ cents}$$

A similar analysis applies to money received three years from today, four years from today, and so on.

The general formula for the present value of $1.00 to be received *N* years from today when the rate of interest is *i* is:

$$\frac{\$1.00}{(1 + i)^N}$$

The present value formula is based on the two variables that determine the present value of any future flow of money: the rate of interest (*i*) and the amount of time you have to wait before you get it (*N*).

Let us now apply this analysis to our example. The present value of the $14,520 revenue is easy to calculate because it all comes two years from today. Because the rate of interest is assumed to be 10 percent ($i = 0.1$), we have:

$$\text{Present value of revenues} = \frac{\$14,520}{(1.1)^2}$$

$$= \frac{\$14,520}{1.21}$$

$$= \$12,000$$

The present value of the costs is a bit trickier in this example because costs occur at two different dates.

The present value of the first interest payment is:

$$\frac{\$1,100}{(1 + i)} = \frac{\$1,100}{1.1} = \$1,000$$

The present value of the final payment of interest plus principal is:

$$\frac{\$12,100}{(1 + i)^2} = \frac{\$12,100}{(1.1)^2} = \frac{\$12,000}{1.21} = \$10,000$$

Now that we have expressed each sum in terms of its present value, it is permissible to add them up. So the present value of all costs is:

$$\text{Present value of costs} = \$1,000 + \$10,000$$

$$= \$11,000$$

Comparing this figure to the $12,000 present value of the revenues clearly shows that the machine really is a good investment. We can use the same calculation procedure for all investment decisions.

SUMMARY

1. To determine whether a loss or a gain will result from a decision whose costs and returns will come at several different periods of time, we must discount all the figures represented by these gains and losses to obtain their **present value.**

2. For **discounting** purposes, we use the present value formula for X dollars receivable N years from now with an interest rate i:

$$\text{Present value} = \frac{X}{(1 + i)^N}$$

3. We then combine the present values of all the returns and all the costs. If the sum of the present values of the returns is greater than the sum of the present values of the costs, then the decision to invest will promise a net gain.

KEY TERM

Discounting, or computing the present value   419

TEST YOURSELF

1. Compute the present value of $1,000 to be received in three years if the rate of interest is 11 percent.

2. A government bond pays $100 in interest each year for three years and also returns the principal of $1,000 in the third year. How much is it worth in terms of today's money if the rate of interest is 8 percent? If the rate of interest is 12 percent?

20

LABOR: THE HUMAN INPUT

Octavius (a wealthy young Englishman): "I believe most intensely in the dignity of labor."

The chauffeur: "That's because you never done any."

GEORGE BERNARD SHAW, *MAN AND SUPERMAN*, ACT II

Labor costs account for by far the largest share of gross domestic product (GDP). As noted in Chapter 19, the earnings of labor amount to almost three quarters of national income. Wages also represent the primary source of personal income for the vast majority of Americans. For more than a century, wages were the centerpiece of the American dream. In almost every decade, the purchasing power of a typical worker's earnings grew substantially, and the U.S. working class evolved into a comfortable middle class—the envy of the world and an irresistible lure for millions of immigrants. Then, something changed fundamentally in ways economists do not yet fully understand.

Figure 1 shows that average real wages (adjusted for changes in the purchasing power of the dollar) stopped their upward march around 1973 and, by some (disputed) calculations, even declined. In contrast, hourly *compensation* (wages plus fringe benefits) did not fall. Fringe benefits include things like health insurance, retirement payments, and education subsidies that employers provide to their employees. But compensation *growth* did slow markedly.[1] The graph also shows that average hours worked per week have declined by almost 35 percent since the early 1900s, even when wages and compensation were increasing. (The big drop in hours worked during the 1930s was a consequence of the Great Depression, and the sharp rise in hours worked during the 1940s was attributable to World War II.) During most of the 1990s, average hours worked per week remained virtually constant, then after 2000 started to drop slowly once again.

CONTENTS

---

[1] The sharp increases in compensation over the years reflect, at least in part, the rising cost of services such as health care, rather than an increase in the quantity and quality of benefits provided to workers. We explored the reasons for the rising costs of services in Chapter 15.

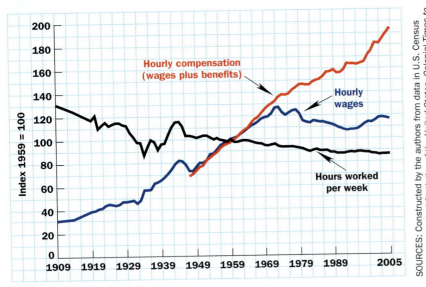

SOURCES: Constructed by the authors from data in U.S. Census Bureau, *Historical Statistics of the United States, Colonial Times to 1970* (Washington, D.C.: U.S. Government Printing Office; 1975); *Economic Report of the President* (Washington, D.C.: U.S. Government Printing Office; various years); and U.S. Bureau of Labor Statistics, http://www.bls.gov.

Slowing wage growth has been accompanied by an expanding *income gap* between the rich and the poor. These days, the ratio between high-income and low-income families in the United States is nearly 6.0—and the disparity is growing.[2] Figure 2 shows that, in 1967, the richest one fifth of U.S. households accounted for about 44 percent of all household income generated in the United States, whereas the poorest one fifth accounted for only 4 percent. By 2005, the income share of the poorest fifth of households had actually slipped a little to about 3.4 percent, and the richest fifth's income share had risen to about 50 percent.[3]

In Germany, by contrast, the ratio between low-wage and high-wage families is about 3.0. As one economist said of the United States, "We are the most unequal industrialized country in terms of income and wealth, and we're growing unequal faster than the other industrialized countries."[4] Almost one in six American children lives in poverty, a rate about twice as high as in the big economies of Western Europe.[5]

Along with this, the prospective gap between your income as a future college graduate and the incomes of your contemporaries who have not attended college has

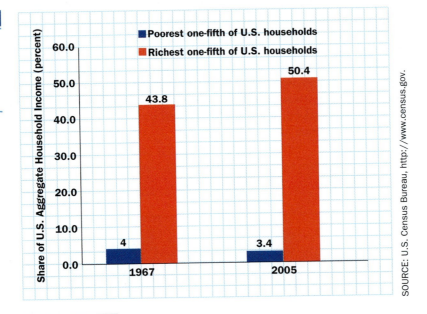

SOURCE: U.S. Census Bureau, http://www.census.gov.

[2] The ratio between high-income families (the 90th percentile) and low-income families (the 10th percentile) in the United States was 5.91 in 1997, compared to 2.13 for Finland and 3.17 for Germany (Source: Timothy M. Smeeding, Director, Luxembourg Income Study, "The Gap Between Rich and Poor: A Cross-National Perspective for Why Inequality Matters and What Policy Can Do to Alleviate It," March 21, 2001, available at http://www.sprc.unsw.edu.au/seminars/japan.pdf.

[3] U.S. Census Bureau, http://www.census.gov.

[4] "Studies Show Major Economic Division," Reuters, April 17, 1995 (from the *New York Times*). For more information on this issue, see Edward N. Wolff, *Top Heavy: A Study of Increasing Inequality of Wealth in America* (New York: Twentieth Century Fund; 1995).

[5] United Nations Children's Fund, "A League Table of Child Poverty in Rich Nations," *Innocenti Report Card*, Issue No. 1, Florence, Italy: Innocenti Research Center, June 2000; and U.S. Federal Interagency Forum on Child and Family Statistics, http://www.childstats.gov.

widened sharply. For instance, in 1973 male college graduates earned about 38 percent more than their high school-educated counterparts, and female college grads earned about 50 percent more than their high school-educated counterparts. By 2005, college educated men and women were earning about 80 percent more and 72 percent more, respectively, than men and women with only high-school educations.[6] This "college premium" is likely to give you a huge financial advantage in terms of your family life, leisure activities, health benefits, retirement conditions—in short, virtually every aspect of your existence.

These developments also have profound and distressing implications for the future of our society as a whole. We are not sure what is behind the trend in growing income inequality, nor do we quite know what can be done about it. But we will discuss some of the possible causes later in the chapter.

? ISSUE: *Do Cheap Foreign Labor and Technological Progress Contribute to Lagging Wages?*

Throughout the history of the successful free-enterprise economies, workers have usually identified two economic enemies: (1) the competition of underpaid foreign laborers and the underpriced exported products made by low-paid foreign workers, and (2) labor-saving technological progress that eliminates jobs. Either or both of these influences may be able to hold down wages in the United States and other industrial economies, and many economists believe that the peril is real (although they argue about which one poses the greater danger). Many workers worry about the future of their jobs and incomes, especially in light of trade legislation that seems to export jobs to other countries. But as obvious as these explanations of lagging wages may seem, as is often true in economics, things seem less straightforward when we dig beneath the surface.

For example, it is the much admired technical progress and labor-saving innovation that have raised productivity spectacularly—by definition, making it possible for fewer workers to produce a given amount of output. Is this change a great benefit or a major threat to jobs in the United States? These two issues—foreign competition and technological progress, and their effects on demand for labor—are among the most crucial that face economic analysis and policy. Although economists continue to gather valuable evidence, we are still a long way from having the complete answers to these questions. This chapter, however, will report some of the things we do know, or think we know, about the subject.

"Sorry boys, the production work is being shipped to the South Pole."

WAGE DETERMINATION IN COMPETITIVE LABOR MARKETS

To begin to understand labor issues, we must first investigate how wages are determined in a free-market economy. In a completely free labor market, wages (the price of labor) would be determined by supply and demand, just like any other price. On

---

[6] Lawrence Mishel, Jared Bernstein, and Sylvia Allegretto, *The State of Working America, 2006/2007*, Ithaca, NY: ILR Press, Cornell University Press, 2007, http://www.epi.org.

the demand side, we would find that the demand curve for labor is derived like the demand curve for any other input—by labor's marginal revenue product, in the manner described in Chapter 19. But the labor market has a number of distinctive features on the supply side.

The labor market is also generally far from perfectly competitive. Nonetheless, we start our investigation by describing the theory of competitive labor markets in which the buyers are large numbers of tiny firms and the sellers are individual workers who act independently of one another. In this model, both buyers and sellers are too small to have any choice but to accept the wage rate determined by the impersonal forces of supply and demand.

■ The Demand for Labor and the Determination of Wages

The **marginal revenue product of labor (MRP$_L$)** is the increase in the employer's total revenue that results when it hires an additional unit of labor.

Much of what we can say about the demand for labor was already said about the demand for inputs in general in earlier chapters. Workers are hired (primarily) by profit-maximizing firms, which hire an input quantity at which the input's price (the market wage) equals its marginal revenue product (MRP). In this chapter, we will use the symbol **MRP$_L$** as an abbreviation for the **marginal revenue product of labor.** Recall that the marginal revenue product is the addition to the firm's revenue that it obtains by hiring one additional unit of input—in this case, one additional worker. So, MRP$_L$ is equal to the additional amount that worker produces (the worker's marginal physical product, or MPP) multiplied by the price of that product. In other words, to determine how much additional money that worker brings in, we multiply the amount she produces by the price of the commodity she produces.[7]

If the MRP$_L$ exceeds the price of labor (the wage), by the usual reasoning of marginal analysis, the firm can increase its profit by hiring at least one more worker either to produce more output or to substitute for some other input. The reverse is true when the MRP$_L$ is less than its wage. Thus, the derived demand and, consequently, the demand curve for labor are determined by labor's marginal revenue product. Such a demand curve is shown as the red curve *DD* in Figure 3. The figure also includes a blue supply curve, labeled *SS*. In a competitive labor market, equilibrium will be established at the wage that equates the quantity supplied with the quantity demanded. In this figure, equilibrium occurs at point *E*, where demand curve *DD* crosses supply curve *SS*. The equilibrium wage is $300 per week and equilibrium employment is 500,000 workers. In this example, because 500,000 workers will be employed at a wage of $300 per week, the total income of the workers will be $300 × 0.5 million = $150 million.

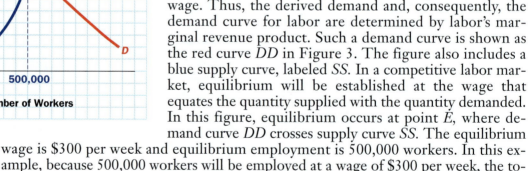

FIGURE 3

Equilibrium in a Competitive Labor Market

■ Influences on MRP$_L$: Shifts in the Demand for Labor

The conclusion that the demand curve for labor is one and the same as labor's MRP curve is merely the beginning of the story. The next question is: What influences affect MRP$_L$? The answers cast light on a number of important developments in the labor market.

Some obvious influences can change labor's MRP. For example, increased education can improve the ability of the labor force to follow complex instructions and to master difficult technology, thus raising a worker's MRP. Economists use the term **investment in human capital** to refer to spending on increased education and on

Investment in human capital is any expenditure on an individual that increases that person's future earning power or productivity.

---

[7] To review, see Chapter 7, pages 130–131.

other means to increase the knowledge and skills of the labor force. Such spending is analogous to investment in the firm's plant and equipment because both of them are outlays today that lead to more production both now *and in the future.*

Workers can also improve their skills through experience, called *on-the-job training,* and in a variety of other ways that add to the information they possess and increase their mental and physical dexterity.

Because the demand for labor is a *derived demand,* anything that improves the market for the goods and services that labor produces can shift the labor demand curve upward. In particular, in a period of economic prosperity consumers will have more to spend; their demand for products will shift upward, which in turn will raise the price of the worker's product, thereby shifting the MRP curve upward. The result will be a rise in the demand for labor. That, of course, is why unemployment is always low when the economy is enjoying a period of prosperity.

■ Technical Change, Productivity Growth, and the Demand for Labor

Another critical influence on the MRP_L is the quality and quantity of the *other* inputs used in the workers' productive activity. Especially important is the technology of the workers' equipment. Innovation that improves machinery, power sources, and other productive instruments adds to the amount that can be produced by a given amount of labor. Thus, technical change that increases labor productivity plays a crucial role in determining the level of wages and the level of employment.

Technical change that increases the worker's productivity has two effects that work in opposite directions. First, increased productivity clearly implies an increase in the worker's marginal physical product—the quantity of widgets that an additional worker can produce will rise. Second, because of the resulting reduction in labor cost and the increased output of widgets, we can expect that when productivity rises, widget prices will fall. Now recall that:

Marginal revenue product of labor in widget production = price of widgets multiplied by the worker's marginal widget output:

$$\text{MRP} = P \text{ (of widgets)} \times \text{MPP}$$

Because an increase in productivity raises MPP but reduces *P,* we cannot be sure of the net effect on MRP—that is, the net effect on the demand curve for labor.

However, experience shows us how an increase in productivity will affect both wages and the demand for labor. In the very short run, an increase in labor productivity (that is, of labor-saving technology) often causes a downward shift in the demand for labor, which holds down wages. If firms can meet the current demand for their products with 10 percent fewer workers than they needed last year, they will be tempted to "downsize," which is a polite way of saying that they will fire some workers. This does not always happen, but it does sometimes occur. Thus, workers' widespread fear of labor-saving technology is, to some degree, justified.

IDEAS FOR BEYOND THE FINAL EXAM

PRODUCTIVITY GROWTH: *Productivity Growth Is (Almost) Everything in the Long Run*   In the long run, rising productivity has always improved the standard of living for both workers and the owners of other factors of production. As we indicated in one of our *Ideas for Beyond the Final Exam,* in the long run nothing contributes more to the economic well-being of the nation than rising productivity. Today workers enjoy far longer lives, better health, more education, and more luxury goods than they did a century ago or in any previous period in history. The fact that an hour of labor today can produce a large multiple of what our ancestors could create in an hour increases everyone's average income, including the workers who constitute so large a part of it. In the short run, labor-saving technological change sometimes cuts employment and holds down wages. Historically, however, in the long run it has not reduced employment. It has raised workers' incomes and increased real wages spectacularly since the Industrial Revolution. In the United States, in the last century, productivity per hour of labor has been multiplied about eightfold, and the purchasing power of the wage a worker earns in an hour is estimated to have been multiplied nearly fivefold.

■ The Service Economy and the Demand for Labor

Although productivity growth has not led to any long-term upward trend in unemployment, it *has* cut jobs drastically in some parts of the economy, sending the labor force to other economic sectors for employment. Agriculture is the prime example. At the time of the American Revolution, by far the preponderant share of the U.S. labor force had agricultural jobs and eked out what today would be considered a meager standard of living. In Europe only a century earlier, farm productivity was so low that famines and starvation were frequent occurrences. Yet today, with a very small share of the nation's labor working on farms, the United States produces such a surplus of products that it sometimes seems unmanageable. This dramatic increase in farm productivity has forced farm employment to drop from about 90 percent to less than 3 percent of the labor force. At first, farm workers shifted to manufacturing, as growing U.S. incomes led to a sharp rise in demand for industrial products. Then productivity in manufacturing took off, and workers again had to look elsewhere for their jobs.

Today, the increased productivity in manufacturing has moved workers into the service sector of the economy. Indeed, it has transformed the United States into a "service economy," meaning that more than three-quarters of the labor force is employed in services such as telecommunications, software design, health care, teaching, and restaurant services.

Some observers have argued that this trend has occurred in the United States because other countries are stealing away our manufacturing business base. But the facts show that this statement is simply untrue. As Figure 4 reports, the service sector has become dominant in *all* the major industrial economies. No industrial economy has been able to avoid this development by stealing manufacturing markets away from the others. More relevant to our concerns here is another worry: that the workers driven from manufacturing into the service sector of the economy have predominantly become low-paid dishwashers and hamburger flippers. That is true in some cases, but the majority of new service jobs created in the past half-century are in the information sector of the economy, which includes computation, research, and teaching, among other jobs; all of these occupations require both education and specialized skills. Many economists attribute the rising relative compensation of college-educated workers to such developments.

FIGURE 4

The Growing Share of Service-Sector Jobs in Nine Countries, 1967 and 2003

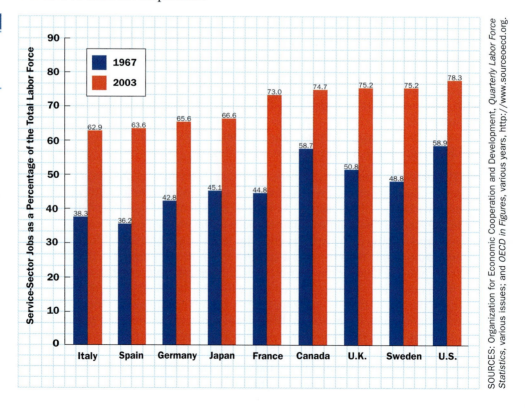

SOURCES: Organization for Economic Cooperation and Development, *Quarterly Labor Force Statistics*, various issues; and *OECD in Figures*, various years, http://www.sourceoecd.org.

◼ THE SUPPLY OF LABOR

Having discussed the demand for labor, we turn next to its supply. Several significant labor supply trends have characterized recent decades in the United States.

First, there has been a continuation of the expansion of the total labor force that has been going on throughout the country's history. Much of this expansion is ascribable to sheer growth of the nation's population through birth and immigration. With more people living in the country, the number of job seekers and jobholders has grown—from about 60 million jobholders right after World War II to about 150 million today.

Second, the proportion of the population with jobs has also grown, from about 58 percent after World War II to 66 percent today. This increase is referred to as a rise in *labor force participation*.

Third, new groups of workers have entered the labor force. This is particularly true of women, who today hold proportionately more jobs (46 percent of the workforce) than they did in earlier decades (except during wartime).

Finally, in addition to the trends in sheer numbers of workers, the labor supply picture has been affected by a protracted and substantial relative decline in union membership. That is, there has been a significant fall in the share of American workers who belong to unions, the organizations whose stated purpose is to protect their interests. Because unions seek to bargain for all the workers in a firm or an industry, thus eliminating competition among workers over jobs and wages, we will consider them later in this chapter, after we have finished our discussion of wage determination in labor markets that are fully competitive. First, we discuss some other supply-side influences.

◼ Rising Labor-Force Participation

One significant development in the supply of labor in the industrial countries is the increase in the number of family members who hold jobs. For instance, in 2004, 55 percent of the 59 million American married-couple families had *two* wage earners, compared with only 40 percent in 1970.[8] It used to be that the "head of the household" (usually the husband) was ordinarily the only breadwinner. Today, however, married women also hold jobs. This phenomenon is in part attributable to lagging wages, which means that both heads of the family are forced to seek gainful employment if the household's economic aspirations are to be realized. Rapidly rising medical costs and costs of education add to these financial pressures.

But participation in the labor force has increased for other reasons as well: the moves toward the liberation of women from their traditional role in the family, along with progress in the education of minorities that has increased their job opportunities. Not so long ago, an African-American executive in a major business firm was unheard of, and an employed wife was considered disgraceful because it implied that her husband could not support her properly. Today this has changed drastically, although discrimination is by no means a thing of the past. In many firms top jobs, beyond the "token black" and the "token woman," have gone to members of these groups. It is not unusual for women and minorities to hold positions superior to those of many employees who are white and male.

These changes have affected the labor market in several ways that, some observers have suggested, may have held back wages, at least for a time. First, the sheer increase in supply of workers tends to depress wages. This is, of course, an implication of standard supply-demand analysis. Just draw the usual supply-demand graph for a labor market, and you will readily confirm that when the supply curve of labor shifts to the right, the price of labor (that is, the wage) can be expected to fall. Second, it has been argued that a combination of discrimination and the initial lack of experience of these new entrants into the labor market (which temporarily reduced their MRP_L) had a

---

[8] U.S. Census Bureau, *Current Population Survey*, http://www.census.gov.

similar effect. Discrimination against women or African-American or Hispanic workers in the labor market means that to get jobs, workers from these groups must offer special incentives to prospective employers. This can force them to accept wages lower than those paid to white male employees with comparable ability for the performance of similar tasks. Lack of experience can have a similar effect, but for a reason that is less objectionable: If workers acquire skill through experience on the job (on-the-job training), then, on the average, inexperienced workers can be expected to have lower productivity than more experienced workers. Because their MRP_L is comparatively low, the demand curve for the inexperienced workers will also be low, and lower wages will tend to follow.

■ An Important Labor Supply Conundrum

For most commodities, an increase in their prices leads to an increase in the quantities supplied, whereas a price decline reduces the amounts supplied; that is, supply curves slope upward. But the striking historical trends in labor supply tell a very different story. Supply has tended to fall when wages rose and to rise when wages fell. Throughout the first three quarters of the 20th century, real wages rose, as Figure 1 clearly showed. Yet labor asked for and received *reductions* in the length of the workday and workweek. At the beginning of the century, the standard workweek was fifty to sixty hours (with virtually no vacations). Since then, labor hours have generally declined to an average workweek of about thirty-four hours.

But in the two most recent decades, as real wages have fallen, the number of family members who leave the home each day to earn wages has increased. And, in recent years there has been a rise in overtime work—that is, workers laboring more than the standard number of hours in their firms. Thus, reduced real wages appear to have induced people to increase the quantity of labor they supply.

Where has the common-sense view of this matter gone wrong? Why, as hourly wages rose for seventy-five years, did workers not sell more of the hours they had available instead of pressing for a shorter and shorter workweek? And why, in recent years, have they sold more of their labor time as real wage rates stopped rising?

To answer these questions it is helpful to follow the economic analysis of labor supply and make use of a simple observation: Given the fixed amount of time in a week, a person's decision to *supply labor* to firms is simultaneously a decision to *demand leisure* time for himself. The leisure time can be interpreted simply as the residue, what is left over after the time spent at work. Assuming that, after deducting the necessary time for eating and sleeping, a worker has ninety usable hours in a week, then a decision to spend forty of those hours working is simultaneously a decision to demand fifty of them for other purposes.

The interpretation of the supply of labor as the opposite of the worker's demand for leisure offers us a very substantial insight into the relationship between wages and labor supply. Economists say that a rise in wages has two effects on the worker's demand for leisure: the substitution effect and the income effect. We will see that they tell us a good deal about the labor market.

The **substitution effect** of a wage increase is the resulting incentive to work more because of the higher relative reward to labor.

1. Substitution Effect   The **substitution effect** of an increase in the price of any good is the resulting switch of customers to a substitute product whose price has not risen. An increase in the price of fish, for example, can lead consumers to buy more meat. The same is true of wages and the demand for leisure. When the wage rate rises, leisure becomes more expensive relative to other commodities that consumers can buy. For instance, if you decide not to work overtime this weekend, the price you pay for that increase in leisure (the opportunity cost) is the wage you have to give up as a result of the decision. So an increase in wages makes leisure more expensive. This leads us to expect that a wage increase will induce workers to buy *less* leisure time (and *more* of other things). Thus:

The substitution effect of higher wages leads most workers to want to work more.

2. Income Effect An increase in the price of any good, other things equal, clearly increases the real incomes of sellers of the good and reduces the real incomes of buyers of the good. That change in income affects the amount of the good (as well as the amounts of other items) that the individual demands. This *indirect* effect of a price change on demand, which is called the **income effect** of the price change, is especially important in the case of wages. Higher wages make consumers richer. We expect this increased wealth to raise the demand for most goods, *including leisure*. So:

The **income effect** of a rise in wages is the resulting rise of workers' purchasing power that enables them to afford more leisure.

> The income effect of higher wages leads most workers to want to work less (that is, demand more leisure), whereas the income effect of lower wages make them want to work more.

Putting these two effects together, we conclude that some workers may react to an increase in their wage rate by working more, whereas others may react by working less. Still others will have little or no discretion over their work hours. In terms of the market as a whole, therefore, higher wages can lead to either a larger or a smaller quantity of labor supplied.

Statistical studies of this issue in the United States have arrived at the following conclusions:

- The response of labor supply to wage changes is not very strong for most workers.
- For low-wage workers, the substitution effect seems clearly dominant, so they work more when wages rise.
- For high-wage workers, the income effect just about offsets the substitution effect, so they do not work more when wages rise.

Figure 5 depicts these approximate "facts." It shows labor supply rising (slightly) as wages rise up to point *A*, *as substitution effects outweigh income effects.* Thereafter, labor supply is roughly constant as wages rise and income effects become just as important as substitution effects up to point *B*. At still higher wages, above point *B*, income effects may overwhelm substitution effects, so that rising wages can even cut the quantity of labor supplied.

Thus, it is even possible that when wages are raised high enough, further wage increases will lead workers to purchase more leisure and therefore to work less (see "The Income Effect: Is Time More Precious Than Money?" on the next page). The supply curve of labor is then said to be **backward-bending,** as illustrated by the broken portion of the curve above point *B* in Figure 5.

Does this theory of labor supply apply to college students? A study of the hours worked by students at Princeton University found that it does.[9] Estimated substitution effects of higher wages on the labor supply of Princeton students were positive and income effects were negative, just as the theory predicts. Apparently, substitution effects outweighed income effects by a slim margin, so that higher wages attracted a somewhat greater supply of labor. Specifically, a 10 percent rise in wages increased the hours of work of the Princeton student body by about 3 percent.

■ The Labor Supply Conundrum Resolved

We can now answer our earlier question: Why is it that, historically, rising wages have reduced labor supply and falling wages have increased it? We know that any wage increase sets in motion *both* a substitution effect *and* an income effect. If only the

FIGURE 5

A Typical Labor Supply Schedule

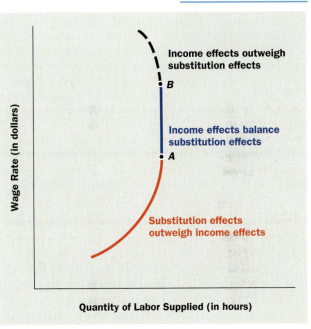

A supply curve of labor is **backward-bending** when a rise in an initially low wage leads to a rise in quantity of labor supplied, but a rise in a wage that was already high reduces the amount supplied.

[9] Mary P. Hurley, "An Investigation of Employment among Princeton Undergraduates during the Academic Year," senior thesis, Department of Economics, Princeton University, May 1975.

The Income Effect: Is Time More Precious Than Money?

Plagued by stress, a growing number of people say they think time is becoming more precious than money and they're trying to slow down. . . . Americans say they have become worn down. But the exhaustion represents a paradox. They are extraordinarily stressed out even though they make more money, have more leisure time, spend more on recreation and enjoy more time-saving and efficient technology than adults did a generation or two ago. The reasons underlying this paradox are varied. Many Americans, especially married women, are working longer at their jobs now than they were then—although they have cut back on the amount of work they do around their homes. The anxieties wrought by the increasingly competitive global economy also have put many on edge, not to mention the fact that work-related intrusions via fax, e-mail or cellular phones can take place anywhere, from a kitchen to the family minivan.

In addition, . . . there's the thesis of economist Steffan Linder, whose book called *The Harried Leisure Class* argued that affluence itself engendered "an increasing scarcity of time." His argument: Productivity increases the "value" of time spent at work, and folks who want to maximize their worth then feel they should work more.

Now, though, a growing number of citizens have begun to unplug their lives from a system they feel leaves them little or no time to recharge. They have begun to retreat . . . into their private corners and demand at least some quiet time. In a comprehensive new quality-of-life poll conducted by U.S. News and the advertising agency Bozell Worldwide Inc., half of all Americans say they have taken steps in the past five years that could simplify their lives—steps as dramatic as moving to communities with a less hectic way of life, cutting back their hours at work, lowering their commitments or expectations and declining promotions.

SOURCE: Excerpted from John Marks, "Time Out: Plagued by Stress, a Growing Number of People Say They Think Time Is Becoming More Precious Than Money and They're Trying to Slow Down," *U.S. News and World Report*, December 11, 1995, pp. 84–96.

substitution effect operated, then rising wages would indeed cause people to work longer hours because the high price of leisure would make leisure less attractive. But this reasoning leaves out the income effect.

Rising wages enable the worker to provide for her family with fewer hours of work. As a result, the worker can afford to purchase more leisure without suffering a cut in living standards. Thus, the income effect of increasing wages induces workers to work fewer hours. Similarly, falling wages reduce the worker's income. To preserve the family's living standard, she must seek additional hours of work; and the worker's spouse may have to leave their children in day care and take a job.

Thus, it is the strong income effect of rising wages that apparently accounts for the fact that labor supply has responded in the "wrong" direction, with workers working ever-shorter hours as real wages rose and longer hours as wages fell.

■ WHY DO WAGES DIFFER?

Earlier in the chapter, we saw how wages are determined in a free-market economy: In a competitive labor market, the equilibrium wage occurs where quantity supplied equals quantity demanded (refer back to Figure 3). In reality, of course, no single wage level applies to all workers. Some workers are paid very well, whereas others are forced to accept meager earnings. We all know that certain groups in our society (the young, the disadvantaged, the uneducated) earn relatively low wages and that some of our most severe social ills (poverty, crime, drug addiction) are related to this fact. But why are some wages so low while others are so high? The explanation is important, because it can help us determine what to do to help poorly paid workers increase their earnings and move up toward the income levels of the more fortunate suppliers of labor. Because the issue is so significant, we will discuss it in some detail.

In the most general terms, the explanation of wage differences is the fact that there is not one labor market but many—each with its own supply and demand curves and its own equilibrium wage. Supply-demand analysis implies that wages are relatively high in markets where demand is high relative to supply, as in Figure 6(a). This can happen if qualified workers are scarce or if the demand for a product is great (because labor demand is a derived demand). In contrast, wages are comparatively low in markets where labor supply is high relative to demand, as in Figure 6(b). This also can be true if product demand is weak or if workers are not very productive. This is hardly startling news, however, and it doesn't tell us what we need to know about wage differentials. To make the analysis useful, we must breathe some life into the supply and demand curves.

■ Labor Demand in General

We start with demand. Why is the demand for labor greater in some markets than in others? Because the marginal revenue product of workers depends on their *marginal physical product* (MPP), the variables that influence MPP_L will also influence wages. Each worker's MPP depends, of course, on his or her own *abilities* and *degree of effort* on the job. But, as we have seen, the influence of these characteristics is supplemented by the *other factors of production* that workers use to produce output. Workers in U.S. industry are more productive than workers in many other countries at least partly because they have generous supplies of machinery, natural resources, and technical know-how with which to work. As a consequence, they earn high wages. In other words, the marginal product of labor is raised by an abundance of efficient machinery and other inputs that increase the worker's effectiveness.

The marginal product of some workers can also be increased relative to that of others by superior education, training, and experience. We will go into greater detail later about the role of education in wage determination.

■ Labor Supply in General

Turning next to differences in the supply of labor to different areas, industries, or occupations, it is clear that the *size of the available working population relative to the magnitude of industrial activity* in a given area is of major importance. It helps explain why wages rose so high in sparsely populated Alaska when the Alaskan oil pipeline created

---

| FIGURE 6 | Wage Differentials |

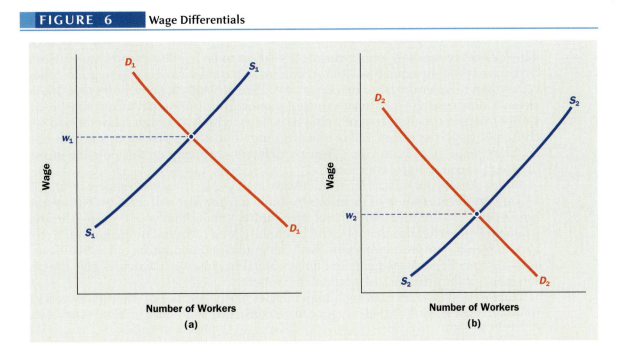

Number of Workers
(a)

Number of Workers
(b)

many new jobs, and why wages have been and remain so low in Appalachia, where industry is dormant.

The *nonmonetary* attractiveness of any job will also clearly influence the supply of workers to it. (The monetary attractiveness is the wage itself, which governs movements *along* the supply curve.) Jobs that people find pleasant and satisfying—such as teaching in suburban schools—will attract a large supply of labor and will consequently pay a relatively low wage. In contrast, a premium will have to be paid to attract workers to jobs that are onerous, disagreeable, or dangerous—such as washing the windows of skyscrapers.

Finally, the amount of ability and training needed to enter a particular job or profession is relevant to its supply of labor. Brain surgeons and professional ice skaters earn generous incomes because there are few people as highly skilled as they, and because it is time-consuming and expensive to acquire these skills even for those who have the ability.

■ Ability and Earnings: The Rent Component of Wages

In considering the effects of ability on earnings, it is useful to distinguish between skills that can be duplicated easily and skills that cannot. If Jill Jones has an ability that Sandra Smith cannot acquire, even if she undergoes extensive training, then the wages that Jones earns will contain an element of **economic rent.** We saw this to be true in the case of professional athletes in Chapter 19.[10]

Indeed, the salaries of professional athletes provide particularly clear examples of how economic rents can lead to huge wage differentials. Virtually anyone with moderate athletic ability can be taught to jump and shoot a basketball. But in most cases, no amount of training will teach the player to play basketball like Shaquille O'Neal, a star. His high salary is a reward for his unique ability.

But many of the abilities that the market rewards generously—such as those of doctors and lawyers—clearly can be duplicated. Here the theory of rent does not apply, and we need a different explanation of the high wages that these skilled professionals earn. Once again, however, part of our analysis from Chapter 19 finds an immediate application because the acquisition of skills, through formal education and other forms of training, has much in common with business investment decisions. Why? Because the decision to gain more education in the hope of increasing future earnings involves a sacrifice of *current* income for the sake of *future* gain—precisely the hallmark of an investment decision.

■ Investment in Human Capital

The idea that education is an investment is likely to be familiar even to students who have never thought explicitly about it. You made a conscious decision to go to college rather than to enter the labor market, and you are probably acutely aware that this decision is now costing you money—lots of money. Your tuition payments may be only a minor part of the total cost of going to college. Think of a high school friend who chose not to go to college and is now working. The salary that he or she is earning could, perhaps, have been yours. You are deliberately giving up this possible income in order to acquire more education.

In this sense, your education is an *investment* in yourself—a *human investment*. Like a firm that devotes some of its money to build a plant that will yield profits at some future date, you are investing in your own future, hoping that your college education will help you earn more than your high school-educated friend or enable you to find a more pleasant or prestigious job when you graduate. Economists call activities such as going to college investments in human capital because such activities give the person many of the attributes of a capital investment.

Doctors and lawyers earn such high salaries partly because of their many years of training. That is, part of their wages can be construed as a *return on their (educational)*

> **Economic rent** is any portion of the payment to labor or any other input that does not lead to an increase in the amount of labor supplied.

---

[10] See Chapter 19, pages 412–413.

investments, rather than as economic rent. Unlike the case of a star athlete, any number of people conceivably *could* become surgeons if they found the job sufficiently attractive to endure the long years of training that are required. Few, however, are willing to make such large investments of their own time, money, and energy. Consequently, the few who do become surgeons earn very generous incomes.

Economists have devoted quite a bit of attention to the acquisition of skills through human investment. An entire branch of economic theory—called **human capital theory**—analyzes an individual's decisions about education and training in exactly the same way as we analyzed a firm's decision to buy a machine or build a factory in the previous chapter. Although educational decisions can be influenced by love of learning, desire for prestige, and a variety of other factors, human capital theorists find it useful to analyze a schooling decision as if it were made purely as a business plan. The optimal length of education, from this point of view, is to stay in school until the marginal revenue (in the form of increased future income) of an additional year of schooling is exactly equal to the marginal cost.

> **Human capital theory** focuses on the expenditures that have been made to increase the productive capacity of workers via education or other means. It is analogous to investment in better machines as a way to increase their productivity.

One implication of human capital theory is that college graduates should earn substantially more than high school graduates to compensate them for their extra investments in schooling. Do they? Will your college investment pay off? Many generations of college students have supposed that it would, and recent data strongly confirm they were right. Indeed, as we noted earlier, the gap between the wages of workers with a college degree and those with a high school education has been widening. College graduates now earn nearly twice as much as their high school-educated peers.

The large income differentials earned by college graduates provide an excellent "return" on the tuition payments and sacrificed earnings that they "invested" while in school.

Human capital theory emphasizes that jobs that require more education *must* pay higher wages if they are to attract enough workers, because people insist on a financial return on their human investments. But the theory does not address the other side of the question: What is it about more-educated people that makes firms willing to pay them higher wages? Put differently, the theory explains why the supply of educated people is limited, but does not explain why the *demand* is substantial even at high wages.

Most human capital theorists complete their analyses by assuming that students in high schools and colleges acquire particular skills that are productive in the marketplace, thereby raising the marginal revenue products of those workers. In this view, educational institutions are factories that take less productive workers as their raw materials, apply doses of training, and create more productive workers as outputs. This view of what happens in schools makes educators happy and accords well with common sense. However, a number of social scientists doubt that this is quite how schooling raises earning power.

◼ Education and Earnings: Dissenting Views

Just why do jobs with stiffer educational requirements typically pay higher wages? The common-sense view that educating people makes them more productive is not universally accepted.

Education as a Sorting Mechanism   One alternative view denies that the educational process teaches students anything directly relevant to their subsequent performance on jobs. In this view, people differ in ability when they enter the school system and differ in more or less the same ways when they leave. What the educational system does, according to this theory, is to *sort* individuals by ability. Skills such as intelligence and self-discipline that lead to success in schools, it is argued, are closely related to the skills that lead to success in jobs. As a result, the abler individuals stay in school longer and perform better. Prospective employers recognize this, and consequently seek to hire those whom the school system has suggested will be the most productive workers.

The Dual Labor Market Theory   Another view of the linkages among education, ability, and earnings is part of a much broader theory of how the labor market operates—the theory of **dual labor markets.** Proponents of this theory suggest that there are two very different types of labor markets, with relatively little mobility between them.

The "primary labor market" is where most of the economy's "good jobs" are found—jobs such as business management, computer programming, and skilled crafts that are interesting and offer considerable possibilities for career advancement. The educational system helps decide which individuals get assigned to the primary labor market and, for those who make it, greater educational achievement does indeed offer financial rewards.

The privileged workers who wind up in the primary labor market are offered opportunities for additional training on the job; they augment their skills by experience and by learning from their fellow workers; and they progress in successive steps to more responsible, better-paying positions. Where jobs in the primary labor market are concerned, dual labor market theorists believe that education really is productive. But they also think that admission to the primary labor market depends in part on social position, and that firms probably care more about steady work habits and punctuality than they do about reading, writing, and arithmetic.

Everything is quite different in the "secondary labor market"—where we find all the "bad jobs." Jobs such as those in cleaning and fast-food services, which are often the only ones inner-city residents can find, offer low pay, few fringe benefits, and virtually no training to improve the workers' skills. They are dead-end jobs that offer little or no hope for promotion or advancement. As a result, lateness, absenteeism, and pilferage are expected as a matter of course, so that workers in the secondary labor market tend to develop the bad work habits that confirm the prejudices of those who assigned them to inferior jobs in the first place.

In the secondary labor market, increased education leads neither to higher wages nor to increased protection from unemployment—benefits generally offered elsewhere in the labor market. For this reason, workers in the secondary market have little incentive to invest in education.

In sum, we have a well-established fact—that people with more education generally earn higher wages—but little agreement on what accounts for this fact. Probably, there is some truth to all of the proposed explanations.

"As far as I'm concerned, they can do what they want with the minimum wage, just as long as they keep their hands off the maximum wage."

The Effects of Minimum Wage Legislation

As we have observed, the "labor market" is really composed of many submarkets for labor of different types, each with its own supply and demand curves. One particular labor market always seems to have higher unemployment than the labor force as a whole: the job market for teenagers.

Figure 7 shows that teenage unemployment rates have consistently been much higher than the overall unemployment rate, and black teenagers have fared worse than white teenagers. For the most part, however, the three unemployment rates have moved up and down together, as the figure shows. The graph indicates that whenever the unemployment rate for all workers goes up or down, the teenage (defined here as a person aged sixteen to nineteen years) unemployment rate almost always moves in the same direction, but more dramatically. Thus, when things are generally bad,

SOURCES: *Economic Report of the President* (Washington, D.C.: U.S. Government Printing Office; various years); and U.S. Bureau of Labor Statistics, http://www.bls.gov.

FIGURE 7   The Teenage Unemployment Problem

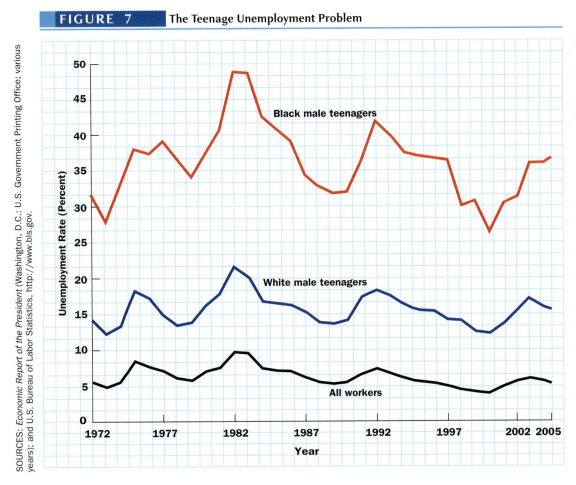

things are much, much worse for teenage workers, and especially for black teenage workers. Despite social and legislative pressures against race discrimination, efforts to improve the quality of education available to children in the inner cities, and many related programs, there has been no relative improvement in black teenage unemployment in recent years.

One reason is that teenagers generally have not completed their educations and have little job experience, so their marginal revenue products tend to be relatively low. Until recently, many economists argued that this fact, together with **minimum wage laws** that prevent teenagers from accepting wages commensurate with their low marginal revenue products, is the main cause of high teenage unemployment. The reasoning is that legally imposed high wages make it too expensive to hire teenagers. Recent studies suggest, however, that a rise in minimum wage produces little, if any, cut in demand for teen labor.

We should also note that over the years inflation has eaten into the real value of the minimum wage (the lowest hourly wage rate that the law permits employers to pay). Figure 8 shows clearly that after 54 years of sporadic increases in the nominal minimum wage rate, the real (inflation-adjusted) rate has actually been falling slowly for nearly 40 years.

A **minimum wage law** imposes a floor on wages and prohibits employers from paying their workers less than that amount.

UNIONS AND COLLECTIVE BARGAINING

Our analysis of competitive labor markets has so far not dealt with one rather distinctive feature of the markets for labor: The supply of labor is not at all competitive in many labor markets; instead it is controlled by a labor monopoly, a **labor union.**

Although they are significant, unions in the United States are not nearly as important as is popularly supposed. For example, most people who are unfamiliar with the

A **labor union** is an organization made up of a group of workers (usually with the same specialization, such as plumbing or costume design, or in the same industry). The unions represent the workers in negotiations with employers over issues such as wages, vacations, and sick leave.

FIGURE 8   The Minimum Wage, 1950–2006

Nominal rate

Real rate (adjusted for inflation)

SOURCES: U.S. Department of Labor, Employment Standards Administration, http://www.dol.gov, and Bureau of Labor Statistics, http://www.bls.gov.

Note: Nominal rates deflated by Consumer Price Index (1950 = 100).

SOURCES: U.S. Department of Labor, Bureau of Labor Statistics, *Employment and Earnings* (Washington, D.C.: Government Printing Office; January issues, various years); and http://www.bls.gov.

FIGURE 9

Unionization in the United States, 1930–2005

data are astonished to learn that less than 13 percent of American workers belong to unions. This percentage is about half of what it was in the heyday of unionism in the mid-1950s. Figure 9 shows that in 1930, unions had enrolled slightly less than 7 percent of the U.S. labor force, and by 1933 this figure had slipped to barely more than 5 percent. Since the 1950s, the unionization rate has fallen with few interruptions.

One reason unionization in the United States been declining is the shift of the U.S. labor force (like that experienced in every other industrial country) into service industries and out of manufacturing, where unions traditionally had their base. In addition, deregulation has forced airlines, trucking companies, and firms in other industries to compete more intensely, and it may thus have influenced the firms to hire less expensive nonunion labor.

In addition, American workers' preferences seem to have shifted away from unions. The increasing share of women in the labor force may have contributed to this trend, because women have traditionally been less prone than men to join unions.

Finally, American unions came under increasing pressure in the 1990s and early 2000s because of stronger competition both at home and abroad. In response, firm after firm has closed plants and eliminated jobs. This "downsizing" trend has made it even more difficult for unions to win concessions that improve the economic positions of their members. That, in turn, has reduced the attractiveness of union membership.

In the United States, union membership levels are much lower than in most other industrialized countries. For example, about 30 percent of German workers and over 80 percent of Danish workers belong to unions.[11] The differences are striking and doubtless have something to do with the American tradition of "rugged individualism." But there are also other influences involved. In the United States, growing conservatism has apparently led to to growing hostility toward unions. In addition, workers may well have greater fear of retaliation ever since President Reagan fired all the striking air traffic controllers in the early 1980s. Added to this, there was the movement of many factories away from traditional northern manufacturing states to the South and Southwest, where unionism was not as entrenched. Nevertheless, in at least a few industries that have the attention of politicians (such as oil and steel), unions retain considerable power.

The main sector of the U.S. economy in which the unions are still fairly healthy is government employment. City, state, and federal employees join unions in relatively large numbers (about 37 percent of public-sector workers are union members).[12] Perhaps this higher union participation arises because the job opportunities for public-sector employees are controlled by political forces, and politicians find it far more difficult to resist the unions than private firms do. Here, too, the unions are under siege as more and more government services are contracted out to private businesses. For example, the state of New Jersey used the threat of turning highway toll collection over to private enterprise as an effective bargaining chip in 1995 negotiations with the toll collectors' union.

Today, the character of American unionism is still somewhat unsettled. Unions are struggling very hard to make inroads into labor markets that by tradition have not been unionized—such as the agricultural and white-collar office markets. They have achieved notable successes in organizing teachers, government employees, and many other types of white-collar workers. In 2005, 5.6 million managerial and professional workers were union members.[13]

As noted, U.S. labor unions are very different from their counterparts in Europe and Japan. Besides the commitment of U.S. unions to capitalism and the rarity of their espousal of socialism (unlike their Western European counterparts), American unions also often see themselves as adversaries of management (unlike Japanese unions). This country's century-long tradition of hostile labor–management relations has impeded current attempts to emulate the Japanese model of labor–management cooperation. In general, U.S. labor may perhaps continue to feel, as it used to do, that American employers are all too likely to adopt unfair practices unless they are restrained by powerful unions

◼ Unions as Labor Monopolies

Unions require that we alter our economic analysis of the labor market in much the same way that monopolies required us to alter our analysis of the goods market (see Chapter 11). Recall that a monopoly seller of goods selects the point on its demand curve that maximizes its profits. Much the same idea applies to a union, which is, after all, a monopoly seller of labor. It too faces a demand curve—derived this time from the marginal revenue product schedules of firms—and can choose the point on that curve that suits it best.

The problem for the economist trying to analyze union behavior—and perhaps also for the union leader trying to select a course of action—is how to decide which point on the demand curve is "best" for the union and its members. There is no obvious single goal analogous to profit maximization that clearly determines what a union should do. Instead, there are a number of *alternative* goals that sound plausible.

---

[11] Small or declining membership may not necessarily be the same thing as declining influence, according to a recent report in *The Economist*. For example, union membership in France is lower than in the U.S., but unions are much more powerful because of their formal role the French welfare system (Source: "Déjà vu?: Special Report, Trade Unions," *The Economist* magazine, June 7, 2003, http://www.economist.com).

[12] U.S. Department of Labor, Bureau of Labor Statistics, http://www.bls.gov.

[13] U.S. Department of Labor, Bureau of Labor Statistics, http://www.bls.gov.

The Way It Was

The calamitous Triangle Shirtwaist Factory fire of 1911, in which 146 women and girls lost their lives, was a landmark in American labor history. It galvanized public opinion behind the movement to improve conditions, hours, and wages in the sweatshops. Pauline Newman went to work in the factory, located on what is now New York University's campus, at the age of eight. Many of her friends lost their lives in the fire. She went on to become an organizer and executive of the newly formed International Ladies Garment Workers' Union. In her words:

We started work at seven-thirty in the morning, and during the busy season we worked until nine in the evening. They didn't pay you any overtime and they didn't give you anything for supper money. . . .

The employers didn't recognize anyone working for them as a human being. You were not allowed to sing. . . . We weren't allowed to talk to each other. . . . If you went to the toilet and you were there longer than the floor lady thought you should be, you would be laid off for half a day and sent home. And, of course, that meant no pay. You were not allowed to have your lunch on the fire escape in the summertime. The door was locked to keep us in. That's why so many people were trapped when the fire broke out. . . .

You were expected to work every day if they needed you and the pay was the same whether you worked extra or not.

Conditions were dreadful in those days. We didn't have anything. . . . There was no welfare, no pension, no unemployment insurance. There was nothing. . . . There was so much feeling against unions then. The judges, when one of our girls came before him, said to her: "You're not striking against your employer, you know, young lady. You're striking against God," and sentenced her to two weeks.

I wasn't at the Triangle Shirtwaist Factory when the fire broke out, but a lot of my friends were. . . . The thing that bothered me was the employers got a lawyer. How anyone could have *defended* them! Because I'm quite sure that the fire was planned for insurance purposes. And no one is going to convince me otherwise. And when they testified that the door to the fire escape was open, it was a lie! It was never open. Locked all the time. One hundred and forty-six people sacrificed, and the judge fined Blank and Harris seventy-five dollars!

The Triangle Factory, now part of New York University

SOURCE: © AP/Wide World Photos.

THE PROBLEM PERSISTS

The following excerpt from *Time* magazine shows that unsafe working conditions continue to produce tragedies, even in this day and age:

Nobody who worked at the Imperial Food Products plant in Hamlet, North Carolina, had much love for the place. The job—cooking, weighing and packing fried chicken parts for fast-food restaurants—was hot, greasy and poorly paid. The conveyor belts moved briskly, and the rest breaks were so strictly timed that going to the bathroom at the wrong moment could lead to dismissal. But in the sleepy town of 6,200 there was not much else in the way of work. So most of the plant's 200 employees, predominantly black and female, were thankful just to have the minimum-wage job. Until last week, that is.

The morning shift had just started when an overhead hydraulic line ruptured, spilling its volatile fluid onto the floor. Gas burners under the frying vats ignited the vapors and turned the 30,000-sq.-ft. plant into an inferno of flame and thick, yellow smoke. Panicked employees rushed for emergency exits only to find several of them locked. "I thought I was gone, until a man broke the lock off," says Letha Terry, one of the survivors. Twenty-five of Terry's fellow employees were not so lucky. Their bodies were found clustered around the blocked doorways or trapped in the freezer.

The disaster brought to light the mostly invisible body count of the American workplace. By some estimates, more than 10,000 workers die each year from on-the-job injuries—about 30 every day. Perhaps 70,000 more are permanently disabled. The fire also exposed the weaknesses of measures for ensuring job safety. The 11-year-old Imperial Food Products plant had never been inspected. Like a lot of American workplaces, it fell through the gaping cracks of a system in which there are too few inspectors, penalties are mostly trifling and the procedures for reporting dangerous conditions can leave workers to choose between risking their jobs and risking their lives.

SOURCES: Excerpted from Joan Morrison and Charlotte Fox Zabusky, *American Mosaic: The Immigrant Experience in the Words of Those Who Lived It* (New York: E. P. Dutton; 1980), reprinted by permission of the publisher, E. P. Dutton, Inc.; and Richard Lacayo, "Death on the Shop Floor: A Murderous Fire in a North Carolina Poultry Plant Underscores the Dangers of America's Workplaces," *Time*, September 16, 1991, p. 28.

Alternative Union Goals   The union leadership may, for example, decide that the size of the union is more or less fixed and try to force employers to pay the highest wage they will pay without firing any of the union members. But this tactic is a high-risk strategy for a union. Firms forced to pay such high wages will be at a competitive disadvantage compared with firms that have nonunion labor, and they may even be forced to shut down. Alternatively, union leaders may assign priority to increasing the size of their union. They may even try to make employment as large as possible by accepting a wage just above the competitive level. One way, but certainly not the only way, to strike a balance between the conflicting goals of maximizing wages and maximizing employment is to maximize the total earnings of all workers taken together.

The basic conclusion of these alternative goals for unions is this: Even if unions, as monopoly sellers of labor, have the power to push wages above the competitive level, they can normally achieve such wage increases only by reducing the number of jobs, because the demand curve for labor is downward sloping. Just as monopolists must limit their outputs to push up their prices, so unions must restrict employment to push up wages.

In some exceptional cases, however, a union may be able to achieve wage gains without sacrificing employment. To do so, the union must be able to exercise effective control over the demand curve for labor. Figure 10 illustrates such a possibility. Union actions push the demand curve outward from D_0D_0 to D_1D_1, simultaneously raising both wages and employment. Typically, this is difficult to do. One possible approach involves *featherbedding*—forcing management to employ more workers than it really needs.[14] Quite the opposite technique is to institute a campaign to raise worker productivity, which some unions seem to have been able to do. Alternatively, the union can try to raise the demand for the company's product either by flexing its political muscle (for example, by obtaining legislation to reduce foreign competition) or by appealing to the public to buy union products.

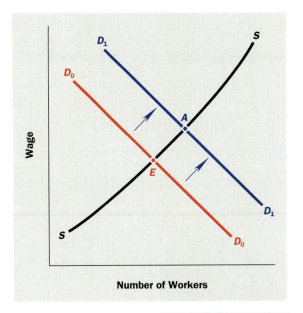

FIGURE 10

Union Control over the Demand Curve

Have Unions Really Raised Wages?   To what extent do union members actually earn higher wages than nonmembers? The consensus would probably surprise most people. Economists estimate that most union members' wages are about 20 percent higher than those of nonmembers who are otherwise identical (in skills, geographical locations, and so on). Although certainly not negligible, we can hardly consider this gap to be a huge differential. Narrowing the gap even further is the fact that nonunion workers do not have to pay the dues that are required of union members.

This 20 percent differential does not mean, however, that unions have raised wages no more than 20 percent. Some observers believe that union activity has also raised the wages of nonunion workers by forcing nonunion employers to compete more fiercely for their workers. If so, the differential between union and nonunion workers will be less than the amount by which unions raised wages overall. A recent study of this issue found that unions raise compensation, including wages and benefits, by about 28 percent, that is, they raise total compensation more than they increase wages. The study reported that the most sweeping advantage unionized workers obtain is in fringe benefits—unionized workers are more likely to receive paid leave, are 18 to 28 percent more likely to have employer-provided health insurance and are 23 to 54 percent more likely to be in employer-provided pension plans. The authors also reported that the impact of unions on total *nonunion* wages is almost as large as the impact on total *union* wages (with estimates ranging from 15 to 20 percent in the 1990s).[15]

■ Monopsony and Bilateral Monopoly

Our analysis thus far oversimplifies matters in several important respects. For one thing, it envisions a market situation in which one powerful union is dealing with

---

[14] The best-known example of featherbedding involved the railroad unions, which for years forced management to keep "firemen" in the cabs of diesel engines, in which there were no burning fires. Similarly, the musicians' union in New York City forces Broadway producers who use certain theaters to employ a minimum number of musicians— whether or not they actually play music. Of course, it is not only unionized labor that has tried to create an artificial demand for its services. Lawyers, doctors, and business firms, among others, have sought ways to induce consumers to buy more of their products and services. *Exercise:* Can you think of ways in which they have done so?

[15] Source: Lawrence Mishel with Matthew Walters, "How Unions Help All Workers," Economic Policy Institute, EPI Briefing Paper, August 2003, pp. 1–18.

many powerless employers: We have assumed that the labor market is monopolized on the selling side but is competitive on the buying side. Some industries more or less fit this model. The giant Teamsters' union negotiates with a trucking industry consisting of thousands of firms, most of them quite small and powerless. Similarly, most of the unions within the construction industry are much larger than the firms with which they bargain.

But many cases simply do not fit the model. The huge auto manufacturing corporations do not stand idly by while the United Automobile Workers (UAW) union picks its favorite point on the demand curve for autoworkers. Nor does the steelworkers' union sit across the bargaining table from representatives of a perfectly competitive industry. In these and other industries, although the union certainly has a good deal of monopoly power over labor supply, the firms also have some *monopsony* power over labor demand. (A **monopsony** is a buyer's monopoly—a case where sellers have only one purchaser for their products.) As a result, the firms may deliberately reduce the quantity of labor they demand as a way to force down the equilibrium level of wages. We can calculate the profit-maximizing restriction of the quantity of labor in the same way that we determined a monopolist's profit-maximizing restriction of output in Chapter 11.

> A **monopsony** is a market situation in which there is only one buyer.

Analysts find it difficult to predict the wage and employment decisions that will emerge when both the buying and selling sides of a market are monopolized—a situation called **bilateral monopoly.** The difficulties here are similar to those we encountered in considering the behavior of oligopolistic industries in Chapter 12. Just as one oligopolist is acutely aware that its rivals are likely to react to anything the oligopolistic employer does, so a union dealing with a monopsony employer knows that any move it makes will elicit a countermove by the firm. This knowledge makes the first decision that much more complicated. In practice, the outcome of bilateral monopoly depends partly on economic logic, partly on the relative power of the union and management, partly on the skill and preparation of the negotiators, and partly on luck.

> A **bilateral monopoly** is a market situation in which there is both a monopoly on the selling side and a monopsony on the buying side.

Still, we can be a bit more concrete about the outcome of the wage determination process under bilateral monopoly. A monopsonist employer unrestrained by a union will use its market power to force wages down below the competitive level, just as a monopoly seller uses its market power to force prices higher. It accomplishes this by reducing its demand for labor below what would otherwise be the profit-maximizing amount, thereby cutting both wages and the number of workers employed.

However, a union may be in a position to prevent this decline from happening. It can deliberately set a floor on wages, pledging its members not to work at all at any wage level below this floor. In this way, a union may force the monopsony employer to pay higher wages and, simultaneously, to hire more workers than the employer otherwise would.

Even though we can hardly find examples of industries that are pure monopsonists in their dealings with labor, these conclusions do have some important implications in reality. The fact is that large, oligopolistic firms do often engage in one-on-one wage bargaining with the unions of their employees, and there is reason to believe that the resulting bargaining process closely resembles the workings of the bilateral monopoly model that we just described.

■ Collective Bargaining and Strikes

The process by which unions and management settle on the terms of a labor contract is called **collective bargaining.** Unfortunately, nothing as straightforward as a supply-demand diagram can tell us what wage level will emerge from a collective bargaining session.

> **Collective bargaining** is the process of negotiation of wages and working conditions between a union and the firms in the industry.

Furthermore, actual collective bargaining sessions range over many more issues than just wages. For example, fringe benefits such as pensions, health and life insurance, overtime pay, seniority privileges, and work conditions are often crucial issues. Many labor contracts specify in great detail the rights of labor and management to set work conditions—and also provide elaborate procedures for resolving grievances and disputes. This list could go on and on. The final contract that emerges from collective bargaining may well run to many pages of fine print.

With the issues so varied and complex, and with the stakes so high, it is no wonder that both labor and management employ skilled professionals who specialize in preparing for and carrying out these negotiations. The bargaining in these sessions is often heated, with outcomes riding as much on the personalities and skills of the negotiators as on cool-headed logic and economic facts. Negotiations may last well into the night, with each side making threats and seeming to try to wear out the other side. Unions, for their part, generally threaten strikes or work slowdowns. Firms counter that they would rather face a strike than give in, or they may even threaten to close the plant without a strike (called a *lockout*).

Mediation and Arbitration   When the public interest is seriously affected, or when the union and firm reach an impasse, government agencies may well send in a **mediator,** whose job is to try to speed up the negotiation process. As an impartial observer, the mediator sits down with both sides separately to discuss their problems and then tries to persuade each to make concessions. At some stage, when an agreement looks possible, she or he may call the parties back together for another bargaining session in the mediator's presence. Mediators, however, have no power to force a settlement. Their success hinges on their ability to smooth ruffled feathers and to find common ground.

Sometimes in cases in which unions and firms simply cannot agree but neither wants a strike, differences are finally settled by **arbitration**—the appointment of an impartial individual empowered to settle the issues that negotiation could not resolve. This happens often, for example, in wage negotiations in professional sports or for municipal jobs such as police and firefighters. For instance, a federal arbitrator was called in to resolve a major labor dispute between American Airlines and its flight attendants' union. In fact, in some vital sectors in which a strike is deemed too injurious to the public interest, the labor contract or the law may stipulate that there must be *compulsory arbitration* if the two parties cannot agree. However, both labor and management are normally reluctant to accept this procedure.

Strikes   Most collective bargaining situations do not lead to strikes. But the right to strike, and to take a strike, remain fundamentally important tools in the bargaining process. Imagine, for example, a firm bargaining with a union that was prohibited from striking. The union's bargaining position would probably be quite weak. On the other hand, a firm that always capitulated rather than suffer a strike would be virtually at the mercy of the union. So strikes—or, more precisely, the possibility of strikes—serve an important economic purpose.

Fortunately, the incidence of strikes is not nearly so common as many people believe. Figure 11 reports the percentage of work time lost as a result of strikes in the United States from 1948 to 2004. This fraction has varied greatly from year to year, but has never been very large. One of the worst years for strikes was 1946, and it is probably no coincidence that the Taft-Hartley Act that placed constraints on union activity was enacted the following year. The fraction of total work time lost has been under one-tenth of 1 percent since 1979 and

> **Mediation** takes place during collective bargaining when a neutral individual is assigned the job of persuading the two parties to reach an agreement.

> **Arbitration** occurs during collective bargaining when a neutral individual is appointed with the power to decide the issues and force both parties to accept his decisions.

FIGURE 11

Work Time Lost in the United States Because of Strikes, 1948–2004

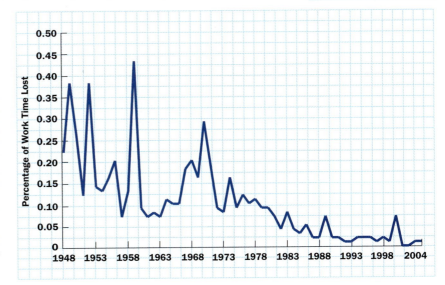

SOURCES: U.S. Department of Labor, Bureau of Labor Statistics, *Monthly Labor Review*, various issues, and http://www.bls.gov.

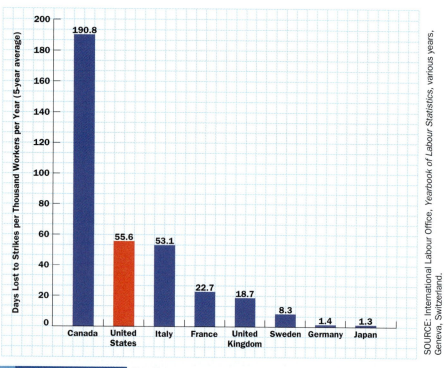

SOURCE: International Labour Office, *Yearbook of Labour Statistics*, various years, Geneva, Switzerland.

FIGURE 12

Incidence of Strikes in Eight Industrial Countries, 1996–2000

Note: Five-year averages: 1996–2000 for Italy, Canada, Sweden, Germany, and United States; 1995–1999 for United Kingdom, France, and Japan.

has dwindled to insignificance at *less than five-hundredths of one percent* since 2001. Despite the headline-grabbing nature of major national strikes, the total amount of work time lost to strikes is truly trivial—far less, for example, than the time lost to coffee breaks! Compared with other nations, the United States suffers more from strikes than, say, Japan, but it has many fewer strikes than Canada (see Figure 12).

Outsourcing is the hiring of workers in foreign counties by U.S. firms to do work formerly carried out in the U.S.

? ISSUE REVISITED: *Foreign Competition, Technology, and American Jobs: Are Union Fears Justified?*

Unions have actively taken up the issues we discussed at the beginning of this chapter. Early in the 1990s, trade agreements worldwide seemed to threaten U.S. workers' jobs—union jobs in particular. But historical evidence raises questions about whether these union fears were grounded in fact.

Careful analysis shows that there are two sides to the matter, and that overall American living standards are sometimes improved (but sometimes hurt) by practices such as **outsourcing**, that is, the hiring of workers in foreign counties by U.S. firms to do work formerly carried out in the U.S. First, we must recognize that although one effect of low-wage foreign employees may be to hold down American *dollar* wages, the availability of their inexpensive products also helps to raise *real* wages. Lower product prices mean that U.S. wages command more goods per dollar. If cars, televisions, and foods become cheaper because of imports, a given wage can buy larger quantities of these items. Besides, in comparison with most other industrial economies, the United States imports a relatively small proportion of its GDP, yet wages in those other countries have risen more quickly than those in the United States for many decades. Indeed, historically, real wages in the United States grew most rapidly when wages in the countries from which the United States received many of its imports were much farther behind U.S. wages than they are now. In other words, when foreign labor was really cheap, U.S. wages were growing most rapidly.

The second part of the story, related to technological progress, also raises questions. Labor-saving innovation has played a leading role in the economic history of the United States. In the course of the 20th century, the productivity of the U.S. labor force grew more than eightfold. This means that seven out of eight U.S. workers could have been fired without any loss in production. Yet unemployment in the United States has shown no rising trend over this period. Several years ago, the U.S. unemployment rate reached its lowest level in thirty years. Evidently, technological progress, which has stimulated the demand for products, has not cut the demand for the workers who turn out those products. In fact, by making goods and services cheaper and better, technical progress has always stimulated demand for improved commodities. Increased demand for goods and services, in turn, translates into a greater demand for labor. Thus, in terms of demand for labor, there are also two sides to technical progress. And in the long run, throughout U.S. history, its effects have generally included rising real wages, but no trend toward increased unemployment.

Still, even if this has been true in the past, it cannot just be assumed that it will always be true in the future. In the past, although some types of unfortunate workers did suffer severe wage cuts and job losses, "cheap foreign labor" did *not*, in the long run, hurt the American worker *on average*. But this mostly fortuitous result was made possible by the remarkable success of the United States in introducing new and better products and processes. To ensure that foreign competition is beneficial to us as well as to other countries, it may be dangerous for us just to sit back and hope for the best. There is reason to argue that we must take steps to ensure continuation of our past innovation and productivity performance.

SUMMARY

1. In a free market, the wage rate and the level of employment are determined by the interaction of supply and demand. Workers in great demand or short supply command high wages. Similarly, low wages go to workers who are in abundant supply or who have skills that are not in great demand.

2. The demand curve for labor, like the demand curve for any factor of production, is derived from the **marginal revenue product curve**. It slopes downward because of the "law" of diminishing marginal returns.

3. The demand curve for labor can be shifted upward by an increase in education or on-the-job training that raises the workers' marginal physical products or by an increase in demand for those products that raises *product* price and therefore also increases labor's MRP.

4. Labor-saving innovations may either raise or lower workers' wages and available jobs in the short run. Because they are tantamount to increased productivity, in the long run they generally raise the incomes of workers along with those of other members of the community.

5. The supply of labor is determined by free choices made by individuals. The supply curve can be shifted so that more labor is supplied at any given wage level if there are developments such as increased labor force participation, as when women find it more desirable to hold jobs.

6. Because of conflicting **income and substitution effects**, the quantity of labor supplied may rise or fall as a result of an increase in wages. Historical data show that hours of work per week have fallen as wages have risen, suggesting that income effects may be dominant in the long run.

7. Some valuable skills are virtually impossible to duplicate. People who possess such skills will earn **economic rents** as part of their wages.

8. Most skills can be acquired by means of **investment in human capital,** such as education.

9. **Human capital theory** assumes that people make educational decisions in much the same way as businesses make investment decisions, and it tacitly assumes that people learn things in school that increase their productivity in jobs.

10. Other theories of the effects of education on earnings deny that schooling actually raises productivity. For example, one view is that the educational system primarily sorts people according to their abilities.

11. According to the theory of **dual labor markets**, there are two distinct types of labor markets, with very little mobility between them. The primary labor market contains the "good" jobs where wages are high, prospects for advancement are good, and higher education pays off. The secondary labor market contains the "bad" jobs, which are characterized by low wages, little opportunity for promotion, and little return on education.

12. Only 13 percent of all U.S. workers belong to **unions**, which we can think of as monopoly sellers of labor. Compared with many other industrialized countries, unions in the United States have as members a smaller share of the labor force and are less radical politically.

13. For the most part, unions probably force wages to be higher and employment to be lower than they would be in a competitive labor market.

14. **Collective bargaining** agreements between labor and management are complex documents covering much more than employment and wage rates.

15. Strikes play an important role in collective bargaining as a way of dividing the fruits of economic activity between big business and big labor. But strikes are not nearly so common as is often supposed.

16. For about two decades Americans have experienced three noteworthy trends: (a) a decline in union membership of more than 30 percent, (b) a steady fall in real wages partly offset by rising fringe benefits, and (c) a rise in the income gap between well-paid and poorly paid workers.

KEY TERMS

Marginal revenue product of labor
(MRP_L)   424

Investment in human capital   424

Substitution effects   428

Income effects   429

Backward–bending supply curve   429

Economic rent   432

Human capital theory   433

Dual labor markets   434

Minimum wage law   435

Labor union   435

Monopsony   440

Bilateral monopoly   440

Collective bargaining   440

Mediation   441

Arbitration   441

Outsourcing   442

TEST YOURSELF

1. The following table shows the number of pizzas that can be produced by a large pizza parlor employing various numbers of pizza chefs.

Number of Chefs	Number of Pizzas per Day
1	40
2	64
3	82
4	92
5	100
6	92

a. Find the marginal physical product schedule of the pizza chefs.

b. Assuming a price of $9 per pizza, find the marginal revenue product schedule.

c. If chefs are paid $100 per day, how many chefs will this pizza parlor employ? How would your answer change if chefs' wages rose to $125 per day?

d. Suppose the price of pizza increases from $9 to $12. Show what happens to the derived demand curve for chefs.

2. Discuss the concept of the financial rate of return on a college education. If this return is less than the return on a bank account, does that mean you should quit college? Why might you want to stay in school anyway? Are there circumstances under which it might be rational not to go to college, even when the financial returns to college are very high?

3. In which of the following industries is wage determination most plausibly explained by the model of perfect competition? The model of pure monopoly? The model of bilateral monopoly?

   a. Odd-job repairs in private homes

   b. Manufacture of low-priced clothing for children

   c. Auto manufacturing

4. Can you think of some types of workers whose marginal products probably were raised by computerization? Are there any whose marginal products were probably reduced? Can you characterize the difference between the two types of jobs in general terms?

DISCUSSION QUESTIONS

1. Colleges are known to pay rather low wages for student labor. Can this trend be explained by the operation of supply and demand in the local labor markets? Is the concept of monopsony of any use? How might things differ if students formed a union?

2. College professors are highly skilled (or at least highly educated!) laborers, yet their wages are not very high. Is this a refutation of the marginal productivity theory?

3. It seems to be a well-established fact that workers with more years of education typically receive higher wages. What are some possible reasons for this trend?

4. Approximately what fraction of the U.S. labor force belongs to unions? (Try asking this question of a person who has never studied economics.) Why do you think this fraction is so low?

5. What are some reasonable goals for a union? Use the tools of supply and demand to explain how a union might pursue its goals, whatever they are. Consider a union that has been in the news recently. What was it trying to accomplish?

6. "Strikes are simply intolerable and should be outlawed." Comment on this statement.

7. In a bitter strike battle between Eastern Airlines and several of its unions, it was clear from the beginning that the airline was in serious financial trouble. The airline was, indeed, eventually forced to close down at the cost of many jobs. Discuss what might nevertheless have led the unions to hold out so tenaciously.

8. European labor unions have traditionally had a strong socialistic orientation. How would you guess this tradition is likely to be affected by the movement of countries in Eastern Europe toward market economies?

9. What, if anything, do you think is the effect of long-term unemployment on crime rates? What about short-term unemployment?

10. Since about 1980, GDP per capita (that is, the average real income per person) in the United States has risen fairly substantially. Yet real wages have failed to rise. What do you think may explain this phenomenon?

21

POVERTY, INEQUALITY, AND DISCRIMINATION

The white man knows how to make everything, but he does not know how to distribute it.

SITTING BULL

The last two chapters analyzed how factor prices—wages, rents, and interest rates—are determined in a market economy. One reason for concern about this issue is that these payments determine the *incomes* of the people who own the factors. The study of factor pricing, therefore, is an indirect way to learn about how the market *distributes income* among individuals.

In this chapter, we turn to the problem of income distribution more directly. Specifically, we seek answers to the following questions: How unequal are incomes in the United States, and why? How can society decide rationally on how much equality it wants? And, once this decision is made, what policies are available to pursue this goal?

CONTENTS

ISSUE: *Were the Bush Tax Cuts Unfair?*

Reducing taxes has been the cornerstone of President George W. Bush's economic policy. Tax cuts were passed in 2001, 2002, 2003, and 2004, amounting in total to a substantial reduction in the federal tax burden—or, as some critics have put it, a large reduction in the tax burdens of the rich. And that is precisely the fairness issue. One of the chief criticisms of the Bush tax cuts is that they are distributively *unfair*, that wealthy Americans have been the chief beneficiaries while people of modest means have received little. According to one estimate, the lower 60 percent of income earners—a majority of the population—received just 13.7 percent of the tax cuts while the top 1 percent received 24.2 percent.[1] To people concerned with income inequality, that is *prima facie* evidence that the tax cuts were unfair.

The president and his supporters respond to these criticisms in a variety of ways. One is to deny the unfairness. It is natural, they say, for upper-bracket taxpayers to get a disproportionate share of the tax cuts for a simple reason: They pay a disproportionate share of the taxes. But a second retort points out that lower tax rates improve incentives and enhance economic efficiency—topics that we addressed in Chapter 18. Fairness is in the eye of the beholder, they maintain, but one thing we do know is that lower tax rates improve economic performance.

Which side of this debate has it right? Should we worry more about the distributive consequences of the Bush tax cuts or welcome their efficiency effects? It's a good question, but one, as we shall see, without a clear answer.

IDEAS FOR BEYOND THE FINAL EXAM

As we will show in this chapter, the debate over the Bush tax cuts provides a classic example of the trade-off between equality and efficiency that we introduced in Chapter 1. Some conservatives seem so enamored of the efficiency gains from lower tax rates that they ignore, or even deny, the distributive consequences. Some liberals, by contrast, argue that tax cuts that are so "unfair" should be rejected regardless of their potential efficiency benefits.

Economists prefer to avoid such absolutes and to think in terms of trade-*offs* instead. To reap gains on one front, society often must make sacrifices on another. A policy is not necessarily ill conceived simply because it has an undesirable effect on income inequality, provided it makes a sufficiently important contribution to efficiency. But policies with very adverse distributive consequences may deserve to be rejected, even if they would raise the nation's total output.

Admitting that there is a *trade-off between equality and efficiency*—namely, that tax cuts that favor the rich may nonetheless enhance economic efficiency—may not be the best way to win votes. But it does face up to reality. And in that way, it helps us to think through the inherently political decisions about what should be done.

If we are to understand these complex issues, a good place to start is, as always, with the facts.

■ THE FACTS: POVERTY

In 1962, social critic Michael Harrington published a little book called *The Other America*, which had a profound effect on American society. Harrington's "other Americans" were the poor who lived in the land of plenty. Ill-clothed in the richest country on earth, inadequately nourished in a nation where obesity was a problem, infirm in a country with some of the world's highest health standards, these people lived an almost unknown existence in their dilapidated hovels, according to Harrington. To make matters worse, this deprivation often condemned the children of the

---

[1] See Isaac Shapiro and Joel Friedman, "Tax Returns: A Comprehensive Assessment of the Bush Administration Tax Cuts," Center on Budget and Policy Priorities, April 2004, p. 19.

The Poorest Place in America?

Pine Ridge [South Dakota] lies in the poorest county in America, with 75 percent unemployment and an average family income of $3,700 per year. The life expectancy for men is 48 years, 25 years below the national average. The infant mortality rate is the highest in the country. Bad health, disease, drugs and alcohol have ravaged the Oglala Sioux. Their culture has been diluted by television and their language is gradually dying out.

. . . [P]eople on the reservation . . . agree that the tribe's funds are chronically mismanaged, that nepotism rules job placement and that a handful of people are getting rich while the rest of the tribe struggles to survive. . . . But . . . hardly anyone outside the reservation knows what's going on at Pine Ridge.

SOURCE: Julie Winokur, "Bury the News at Wounded Knee," at http://www.salon.com/news/feature/2000/03/13/pine_ridge.

SOURCE: © Bob Rowan; Progressive Image/CORBIS

"other Americans" to repeat the lives of their parents. There was, Harrington argued, a "cycle of poverty" that could be broken only by government action.

The work of Harrington and others touched the hearts of many Americans who, it seemed, really had no idea of the abominable living conditions of some other people in the country. Within a few years, the growing outrage over the plight of the poor had crystallized into a "War on Poverty," which President Lyndon Johnson declared in 1964.

■ Counting the Poor: The Poverty Line

As part of this program, the government adopted an official definition of *poverty:* The poor were those families with incomes less than $3,000 in 1964. This dividing line between the poor and nonpoor was called the **poverty line,** and a goal was established: to get all Americans above the poverty line by the nation's bicentennial in 1976. (The goal was not met.) The poverty line was subsequently modified to account for differences in family size and other considerations, and it is now also adjusted each year to reflect changes in the cost of living. In 2005, the poverty line for a family of four was about $20,000 and 12.6 percent of all Americans remained in poverty by official definitions.

Who are the poor? Relative to their proportions in the overall population, they are more likely to be black than white and more likely to be female than male. They are less educated and in poorer health than the population as a whole. About 35 percent of the poor are children.

America made substantial progress toward eliminating poverty in the decade from 1963 to 1973; the percentage of people living below the poverty line dropped from 20 percent to 11 percent (see Figure 1). But thereafter, slower economic growth and cutbacks in social welfare programs reversed the trend. By 1983, the poverty rate was back to what it had been in the 1960s. After that, the poverty rate increased and decreased with no clear trend until the great economic boom of the 1990s restored it almost to its 1970s low. But poverty rose again when the economy slumped early in this decade.

High poverty rates worry many people, especially because poverty seems often to be associated with homelessness, illegitimacy, drug dependency, and ill health. However, some critics argue that the official data badly overstate the number of poor persons. Some even go so far as to claim that poverty would be considered a thing of the

The **poverty line** is an amount of income below which a family is considered "poor."

FIGURE 1   Progress in the War on Poverty

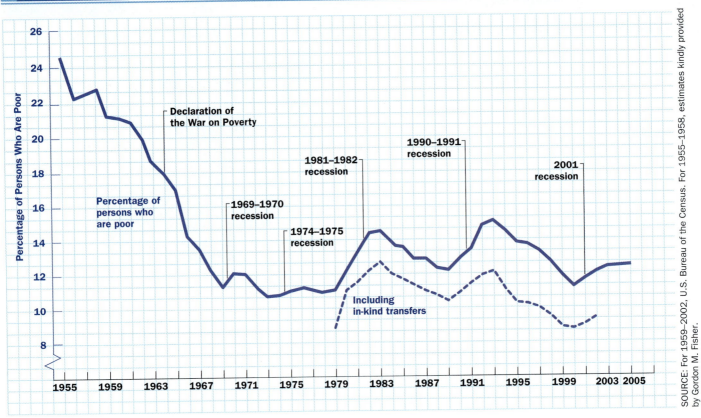

SOURCE: For 1959–2002, U.S. Bureau of the Census. For 1955–1958, estimates kindly provided by Gordon M. Fisher.

past if the official definition (based on cash income) were amended to include the many goods that the poor receive in kind: public education, public housing, health care, food, and the like.

These criticisms prompted the Census Bureau to develop several experimental measures of poverty that account for the value of goods given in kind. If these new measures are accepted as valid, fewer people are classified as poor, but the basic patterns of recent years remain the same: Poverty went up and down from the late 1970s until about 1993 with no clear trend and then declined until recently. (See the broken line in Figure 1.)

Absolute versus Relative Poverty

This debate raises a fundamental question: How do we define "the poor"? Continuing economic growth will eventually pull almost everyone above any arbitrarily established poverty line. Does this event mark the end of poverty? Some would say yes. But others would insist that the biblical injunction is right: "The poor ye have always with you."

We can define poverty two ways. The more optimistic definition uses an absolute concept of poverty: If you fall short of a certain minimum standard of living, you are poor; once you pass this standard, you are no longer poor. The more pessimistic definition relies on a relative concept of poverty: The poor are those who fall too far behind the average income.

Each definition has advantages and disadvantages. The basic problem with the absolute poverty concept is that it is arbitrary. Who sets the line? Most of the people of Bangladesh would be delighted to live a bit below the U.S. poverty line and would consider themselves quite prosperous. Similarly, the standard of living that we now call "poor" would probably not have been considered so in America in 1900, and certainly not in Europe during the Middle Ages. Different times and different places apparently call for different poverty lines.

Because the concept of poverty seems to be culturally—not physiologically—determined, it must be a relative concept. For example, the European Union (EU) places the poverty line at half the national average income—which means that the poverty line automatically rises as the EU grows richer.

Once we move from an absolute to a relative concept of poverty, any sharp distinction between the poor and the nonpoor starts to blur. At least in part, the poor are so poor because the rich are so rich. If we follow this line of thought far enough, we are led away from the narrow problem of *poverty* and toward the broader problem of *income inequality*.

■ THE FACTS: INEQUALITY

Nothing in the market mechanism guarantees equality of incomes. On the contrary, the market system tends to allow or even foster inequality because the basic source of its great efficiency is its system of rewards and penalties. The market is generous to those who succeed in operating efficient enterprises that respond to consumer demands, but it ruthlessly penalizes those who are unable or unwilling to satisfy consumer demands efficiently.

Its financial punishment of those who try and fail can be particularly severe. At times the market even brings down the great and powerful. Robert Morris, once perhaps the wealthiest resident of the American colonies, ended up in debtors' prison. Some of the greatest Ameican fortunes in the late nineteenth century were made in the railroads, most of which subsequently went bankrupt. When the Internet euphoria ended in 2000, many former multimillionaires (and a few former billionaires) found themselves jobless and nearly destitute.

Most people have a good idea that the gulf between the rich and the poor is wide. But few have any concept of where they stand in the income distribution. For example, during a 1995 congressional debate over tax cuts for "the middle class," one member of Congress with an annual income in excess of $150,000 declared himself a member of the "middle class," if not indeed of the "lower-middle class"!

Table 1 offers some statistics on the income distribution among U.S. households in 2005. But before looking at them, try the following experiment. First, write down what you think your household's before-tax income was in 2005. (If you do not know, take a guess.) Next, try to guess what percentage of American households had incomes *lower* than this amount. Finally, if we divide America into three broad income classes—rich, middle class, and poor—to which group do you think your household belongs?

Now that you have written down answers to these three questions, look at the income distribution data for 2005 in Table 1. If you are like most college students, these figures may surprise you. First, if we adopt the tentative definition that the lowest 20 percent are the "poor," the highest 20 percent are the "rich," and the middle 60 percent are the "middle class," many fewer of you belong to the celebrated "middle class" than thought they did. In fact, the cut-off point that defined membership in the "rich" class in 2005 was only about $92,000 before taxes, an income level exceeded by the parents of many college students. (Your parents may be shocked to learn that they are rich!)

Next, use Table 1 to estimate the fraction of U.S. households that have incomes lower than yours. (The

TABLE 1

Distribution of Household Income in the United States in 2003

Income Range	Households in This Range	Households in This and Lower Ranges
Less than $5,000	3.3%	3.3%
$5,000 to $9,999	5.0	8.3
$10,000 to $14,999	6.4	14.7
$15,000 to $24,999	12.4	27.1
$25,000 to $34,999	11.4	38.5
$35,000 to $49,000	14.9	53.4
$50,000 to $74,999	18.4	71.8
$75,000 to $99,999	11.1	82.9
$100,000 or more	17.2	100.0

Note: If your household income falls close to one of the end points of the ranges indicated here, you can approximate the fraction of households with income lower than yours by just looking at the last column. If your household's income falls within one of the ranges, you can interpolate the answer. Example: Your household's income was $60,000. This is 40 percent of the way from $50,000 to $75,000, so your household was richer than roughly 0.40 × 18.4 percent = 7.4 percent of the households in this class. Adding this to the percentage of households in lower classes (53.4 percent in this case) gives the answer—about 61 percent of all households earned less than yours.

SOURCE: U.S. Bureau of the Census at www.census.gov/hhes/income.html

TABLE 2				
Income Shares in Selected Years				
Income Group	2005	1990	1980	1970
Lowest fifth	3.4	3.9	4.3	4.1
Second fifth	8.6	9.6	10.3	10.8
Middle fifth	14.6	15.9	16.9	17.4
Fourth fifth	23.0	24.0	24.9	24.5
Highest fifth	50.4	46.6	43.7	43.3

SOURCE: U.S. Bureau of the Census

table caption has instructions to help you make this estimate.) Many students who come from households of moderate prosperity feel instinctively that they stand perhaps a bit above the middle of the income distribution. So they estimate that a little more than half of all families have lower incomes. In fact, the median income among American households in 2005 was only $46,300.

This exercise has perhaps brought us down to earth. America is not nearly as rich as Madison Avenue would like us to believe. Let us now look past the average level of income and see how the pie is divided. Table 2 shows the shares of income accruing to each fifth of the population in 2005, and several earlier years. In a perfectly equal society, all numbers in this table would be "20 percent," because each fifth of the population would receive one fifth of the income. In fact, as the table shows, reality is far from this perfect equality. In 2005, for example, the poorest fifth of all households had just 3.4 percent of the total income, whereas the richest fifth had 50.4 percent, almost 15 times as much.

These data for 2005 give us a snapshot of the U.S. income distribution. But to interpret them, we must know what the distribution looked like in earlier years or what it looks like in other countries. The historical data in Table 2 show that:

The distribution of income in the United States has grown substantially more unequal since about 1980.

Specifically, the share of the poorest fifth is now the lowest, and the share of the richest fifth is close to the highest since the government began collecting data in 1947. America is not a very class-conscious society, and for years only specialists paid much attention to data like those in Table 2. But income inequality has captured increasing public attention of late as more and more American families sense that they are losing ground to the people at the top. There is particular, and well-justified, concern that the real earnings of wage earners below the middle have fallen further and further behind the wages at the top. These trends toward widening income and wage disparities have been going on for over a quarter-century now, which is a long time.

Comparing the United States with other countries is much more difficult because no two nations use precisely the same definition of income distribution. The Luxembourg Income Study is the leading international effort to produce comparable data for many countries. In its latest comparison of the income distributions of twenty high-income (mostly European) countries, Sweden and Finland had the most equal income distributions, with Norway, The Netherlands, and Belgium close behind. The United States stood out as having the most inequality. Thus, it appears that:

The United States has rather more income inequality than most other industrialized countries.

"The poor are getting poorer, but with the rich getting richer it all averages out in the long run."

■ SOME REASONS FOR UNEQUAL INCOMES

Let us now begin to formulate a list of the *causes* of income inequality. Here are some that come to mind.

Differences in Ability Everyone knows that people have different capabilities. Some can run faster, ski better, do calculations more quickly, type more accurately, and so on. Hence, it should not be surprising that some people are more adept at earning in-

How Important Is the Bell Curve?

A decade ago, social critic Charles Murray and the late Richard Herrnstein, a psychologist, created a furor with a book claiming that genetically inherited intelligence is overwhelmingly important to economic success. The book's title, *The Bell Curve*, referred to the shape of the distribution of scores on conventional IQ tests (see chart), which shows most people clustered near the middle, with small minorities on either end.

Critics of government antipoverty efforts were attracted to the book's central message: that the poor are poor in large measure because they are not very smart. Among the most stunning claims made by Herrnstein and Murray was that much of the observed economic gap between blacks and whites could be attributed to the fact that blacks' IQ scores were, on average, lower than those of whites.

Although *The Bell Curve* received a blitz of media attention, social scientists generally gave the analysis low marks. No one doubts that intelligence contributes to economic success, nor that genetics has some bearing on intelligence. But the scientific evidence on the strength of each link is in great dispute. Many experts on IQ, for example, argue that environmental factors may be more important than genetics in determining intelligence and that "true" intelligence may differ from measured IQ. Furthermore, few if any economists believe that cognitive ability is the main ingredient in economic success.

The bottom line, according to most scholars, is that the black–white IQ gap does not go very far in explaining racial income inequalities. Nor can we be certain that much of the measured IQ gap is biologically, rather than culturally, determined.

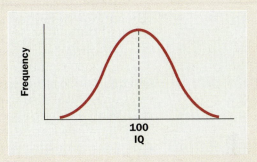

come. Precisely what sort of ability is relevant to earning income has been a matter of intense debate among economists, sociologists, and psychologists for decades. The talents that make for success in school seem to have some effect, but hardly an overwhelming one. The same is true of innate intelligence—"IQ" (see the box, "How Important Is the Bell Curve?"). It is clear that some types of inventiveness are richly rewarded by the market, as is that elusive characteristic called "entrepreneurial ability." Also, it is obvious that poor health often impairs earning ability.

Differences in Intensity of Work   Some people work longer hours than others, or labor more intensely when they are on the job. These disparities lead to income differences that are largely voluntary.

Risk Taking   Most people who acquire large sums of money do so by taking risks—by investing their money in the stock market, in a small start-up company, or in some other uncertain venture. Those who gamble and succeed become wealthy. Perhaps the most spectacular example is Bill Gates, believed to be the richest person in the world, who dropped out of Harvard to start a small company that we now know as Microsoft. Of course, those who try and fail often go broke. Most people prefer not to take such chances and end up somewhere in between. This is another way in which income differences arise voluntarily.

Compensating Wage Differentials   Some jobs are more arduous than others, or more dangerous, or more unpleasant for other reasons. To induce people to take these jobs, some sort of financial incentive normally must be offered. For example, factory workers who work the night shift normally receive higher wages than those who work during the day.

Schooling and Other Types of Training   Chapter 20 analyzed schooling and other types of training as "investments in human capital." As explained there, this term refers to the idea that people sacrifice current income to improve their skills so that their future incomes will be higher. When this is done, income differentials naturally rise. Although it is generally agreed that differences in schooling are an important cause of income differentials, this particular cause has both voluntary and involuntary aspects. Young men or women who choose not to go to college have made voluntary decisions that affect their incomes. But many never get the choice: Their parents simply cannot afford to send them. For them, the resulting income differential is not voluntary.

Work Experience   It is well known to most people and well documented by scholarly research that more experienced workers earn higher wages.

Inherited Wealth   Not all income is derived from work. Some represents the return on invested wealth, and part of this wealth is inherited. Although this cause of inequality applies to few people, many of America's superrich got that way through inheritance. Think of the Rockefellers or, more recently, the Waltons (of Wal-Mart fame). And financial wealth is not the only type of capital that can be inherited—so can human capital. In part, this inheritance happens naturally through genetics: High-ability parents tend to have high-ability children, although the link is an imperfect one. But it also happens partly for economic reasons: Well-to-do parents send their children to the best schools, thereby transforming their own financial wealth into human wealth for their children. This type of inheritance affects many more people than the financial type.

Luck   No observer of our society can fail to notice the role that chance plays in income inequalities. Some of the rich and some of the poor got there largely by good or bad fortune. Two skilled programmers work hard, but only one develops the "killer app" that makes him rich. A farmer digs for water, but strikes oil instead. A storekeeper near the World Trade Center disaster is driven out of business for lack of customers. The list could go on and on. Many large income differentials arise purely by chance.

■ THE FACTS: DISCRIMINATION

Some of the factors we have just listed lead to income differentials that are widely accepted as "just." For example, most people believe it is fair for people who work harder to receive higher incomes. Other factors on our list ignite heated debates. For example, some people view income differentials that arise purely by chance as perfectly acceptable, whereas others find these same differentials intolerable. However, almost no one is willing to condone income inequalities that arise from discrimination.

Economic discrimination occurs when equivalent factors of production receive different payments for equal contributions to output.

The facts about discrimination are not easy to come by. **Economic discrimination** is said to occur when equivalent factors of production receive different payments for equal contributions to output. But this definition is difficult to apply in practice because we cannot always tell when two factors of production are "equivalent."

Few people would call it "discrimination" if a woman with only a high school diploma receives a lower salary than a man with a college degree. Even if a man and a woman have the same education, the man may have ten more years of work experience than the woman does. If they receive different wages for this reason, is that discriminatory?

In principle, we should compare men and women with equal *productivities*. If women receive lower wages than men who do the same work, we would attribute the difference to discrimination. But discrimination normally takes much more subtle forms than paying unequal wages for equal work. For instance, employers can simply relegate women to inferior jobs, thereby justifying their lower salaries.

One clearly *incorrect* way to measure discrimination is to compare the different groups' typical incomes. Table 3 displays such data for white men, white women, black men, and black women in 2005. Virtually everyone agrees that the amount of discrimination is less than these differentials suggest, but far greater than zero. Precisely how much is a topic of continuing economic research. Several studies suggest that about half of the observed wage differential between black men and white men, and at least half of the differential between white women and white men, arises from discrimination in the labor market (although more might be due to discrimination in education, and so on). Other studies have reached somewhat different conclusions.

TABLE 3
Median Incomes in 2005

Population Group	Median Income	Percentage of White Male Income
White males	$32,179	100
Black males	22,653	70
White females	18,669	58
Black females	17,631	55

NOTE: For persons 15 years old and older.
SOURCE: U.S. Bureau of the Census

THE TRADE-OFF BETWEEN EQUALITY AND EFFICIENCY

We have noted that America has more income inequality than other wealthy nations, and we have observed that inequality in the U.S. has been on the rise for about twenty-five years. Should society try to reverse this trend? Here economics *alone* cannot provide an answer, although it can inform the discussion. Value judgments are needed to supplement the economic analysis.

Some people say, "That's the way the ball bounces." If the market mechanism happens to produce high and rising inequality, so be it. To these conservatives, government has no business intervening to reduce income inequalities. If it does, they argue, economic efficiency will be impaired. But others beg to differ. Their vision of a "good society" does not countenance high and rising inequality, especially when those at the bottom are so poor. These liberals want the government to promulgate policies that reduce income disparities, programs such as income support for the poor, antidiscrimination statutes, and progressive income and inheritance taxes.

Economic analysis cannot tell us how important it is to promote greater equality. That value-laden judgment falls more into the realm of political theory and philosophy, maybe even psychology. It is a question over which reasonable people can and do differ. But economics can tell us quite a bit about the costs, in terms of reduced efficiency, of alternative policies that promote greater equality. Specifically:

THE TRADE-OFF BETWEEN EQUALITY AND EFFICIENCY   Policies that redistribute income reduce the rewards of high-income earners while raising the rewards of low-income earners. Hence, such policies reduce the incentive to earn high income. Such incentive effects give rise to a trade-off that is one of the most fundamental in all of economics, and one of our **Ideas for Beyond the Final Exam.**

IDEAS FOR BEYOND THE FINAL EXAM

When we take measures to increase the amount of economic equality, we normally reduce economic efficiency—that is, we reduce society's total output. In trying to divide the pie more equally, we may inadvertently reduce its size.

But this stark fact does not mean that all attempts to reduce inequality are misguided. This is where the economic analysis comes in—to temper and inform our value judgments. Basic economic principles teach us two lessons on which we will elaborate in the balance of this chapter:

1. There are better and worse ways to promote equality. In pursuing further income equality (or fighting poverty), we should always seek policies that do the least possible harm to incentives and efficiency.

2. Equality is bought at a price. Thus, like any commodity, society must rationally decide how much to "purchase." We will probably want to spend some of our potential income on equality, but certainly not all of it.

The first lesson is obvious: *We should accomplish any desired redistribution by utilizing the most efficient redistributive policies*. By picking these policies, rather than less efficient ones, we can "buy" whatever degree of equality we want at a lower "price" in terms of lost output. In the rest of this chapter, we will discuss alternative policies and try to indicate which ones damage incentives least.

The second lesson is somewhat less obvious: *Neither complete laissez faire nor complete equality would normally be society's optimal choice*. To see why, let's take the argument in two pieces. At one extreme, it is easy to understand why we should not seek perfect equality. Ask yourself what would happen if we tried to achieve complete equality of incomes by putting a 100 percent income tax on all income and then dividing the tax receipts equally among the population. No one would have any incentive to work, to invest, to take risks, or to do anything else to earn money, because the rewards for all such activities would have disappeared. The nation's total production would fall drastically. Only someone with a fanatic desire for equality would favor such an outcome.

The argument at the other extreme is more subtle. Let's assume (a) that almost everyone would favor greater equality if nothing had to be sacrificed to achieve it, and (b) that complete *laissez faire* results in more inequality than society wants. There will presumably be some small redistributive policies that have essentially no adverse effects on incentives. Example: Levying a 0.1 percent tax on the income of multibillionaires, and giving the proceeds to poor children. In a democracy, policies like that would presumably receive nearly unanimous approval. It follows that society should always carry out *some* redistribution, even if it is minor.

We have therefore established our result: The socially optimal amount of equality is presumably *more* than the unfettered operation of free markets would produce, but *less* than complete equality. The government should therefore presumably undertake *some* redistribution of income, but not too much

It is astonishing how much confusion is caused by a failure to understand these two lessons. Proponents of greater equality often feel obliged to deny that the programs they advocate will hurt incentives at all. Sometimes these vehement denials are so patently unrealistic that they undermine the very case that the egalitarians are trying to make. Conservatives who oppose such policies also undercut the strength of their case by making outlandish claims about the efficiency losses from redistribution.

IDEAS FOR BEYOND THE FINAL EXAM

Neither side, it seems, is willing to acknowledge the fundamental trade-off between equality and efficiency. As a result, the debate generates more heat than light. Because these debates will likely continue for the rest of your lives, we hope that some understanding of this trade-off stays with you well *Beyond the Final Exam*.

The trade-off applies directly to the Bush tax cuts. They did worsen income inequality, but they also improved incentives and therefore contributed to greater economic efficiency. Depending on your value judgments, you might therefore approve or disapprove of the policies.

This case illustrates the point that merely understanding the trade-off will not tell you what to do. We know that the optimal amount of equality lies between two extremes, but we do not know what it actually is. Nor can we expect people to agree on the optimal degree of inequality because the answer depends on value judgments: Just how much is more equality worth to you?

Arthur Okun, one-time chairman of the Council of Economic Advisers, described the issue graphically. Imagine that

"There is a perfect example of what is wrong with this country today."

"There is a perfect example of what is wrong with this country today."

money is liquid, and that you have a bucket that can be used to move money from the rich to the poor. Unfortunately, the bucket leaks. As you move the money, some gets lost. (These are the efficiency losses from redistribution.) Will you use the bucket if only 1 cent is lost for each $1 you move? Almost everyone would say yes. But what if you lose 90 cents, so that each $1 taken from the rich results in only 10 cents for the poor? Only the most extreme egalitarians will still say yes. Now try the more difficult questions. What if 20 to 40 cents is lost for each $1 that you move? If you can answer questions such as these, you can decide how much equality you want, for you will have expressed your value judgments in quantitative terms.

◼ POLICIES TO COMBAT POVERTY

Let us take it for granted that the nation wants to reduce poverty, at least somewhat. Which policies promote this goal? Which of these does the least harm to incentives, and hence is most efficient?

◼ Education as a Way Out

Education is often advertised as one of the principal ways to escape from poverty. No doubt many people have used this route successfully, and still do.

However, delivering quality education to poor children is no simple matter. Many of them, especially in the inner cities, are ill-equipped to learn and attend schools that are ill-equipped to teach. Despite some gratifying progress in recent years, dropout rates remain dismayingly high. An astonishing number of youths leave the public school system without even acquiring basic literacy. All of these problems are familiar; none is easy to solve.

In truth, our educational system must serve many goals, and the alleviation of poverty is not the major one. If it were, we would certainly spend more money on preschool and inner-city children and less on college education than we do today. Furthermore, education is not an effective way to lift *adults* out of poverty. Its effects are delayed for a generation or more.

◼ The Welfare Debate and the Trade-Off

By contrast, a variety of programs collectively known as "welfare" are specifically designed to alleviate poverty, meant to help adults as well as children, and intended to have quick effects. The best known and most heavily criticized of these programs used to be *Aid to Families with Dependent Children (AFDC)*. AFDC provided direct cash grants to families that had children but no breadwinner, generally because the father was absent or unknown and the mother could not or did not work.

When Bill Clinton campaigned in 1992 on a promise to "end welfare as we know it," many Americans shared his dissatisfaction with the system. Why? Because AFDC was a classic example of an inefficient redistributive program. One major reason was that it provided no incentive for welfare mothers to earn income. Once monthly earnings passed a few hundred dollars, AFDC payments were reduced by $1 for each $1 that the family earned as wages. Thus, if a member of the family got a job, the family was subjected to a 100 percent marginal tax rate! Little wonder, then, that many welfare recipients did not look very hard for work. In addition, critics argued that "the welfare mess" was too bureaucratic, too expensive, and might even be hurting the very people it was designed to help—by, for example, encouraging out-of-wedlock births and fostering a culture of dependence on the state.

In 1996, Congress redeemed President Clinton's campaign pledge by replacing AFDC with a new welfare program: Temporary Assistance to Needy Families (TANF). TANF limits eligibility for welfare checks to two years at a time and five years over a person's lifetime. Before recipients reach these time limits, they are supposed to have found jobs. The new law also gave states much greater latitude to design their own welfare systems, thereby greatly reducing federal influence over welfare. And, indeed, the generosity of TANF now varies tremendously across the fifty states.

The new welfare law was highly controversial when it was enacted. Critics argued that it would throw many needy families to the wolves when their benefits ran out. Supporters argued that it would give them "a hand up, instead of a handout"—and would save the taxpayers money to boot. This debate offered another illustration of the trade-off between equality and efficiency, and how poorly understood it is. Critics of TANF argued that the new law was mean-spirited because it reduced the amount of income support that poor mothers could receive. Supporters argued that TANF provided better work incentives than AFDC.

From 1996 to 2000, the economy boomed, jobs were plentiful, and the welfare rolls shrank dramatically. So the new system was not put to the test until the economy slowed in 2000 and 2001, and jobs became scarcer. When the welfare rolls did *not* soar in the weak job market of 2001–2003, TANF passed its first test with flying colors. This success, supporters claimed, proved that the new system worked well. However, studies of the welfare population found very high poverty rates among those who had exited the TANF program. They also found that roughly half of the people eligible for TANF benefits were not receiving them. Furthermore, because many poor women cycle in and out of welfare, few had yet reached the five-year lifetime limit. For all of these reasons, the debate over welfare reform goes on.

Food Stamps   A second prominent welfare program is Food Stamps, which burgeoned in the 1970s and was cut back several times in the 1980s and 1990s. Under this program, poor families receive "stamps"—which nowadays are actually delivered via an electronic benefits card—that they can use to purchase food. The size of each family's Food Stamp benefit depends on its income: The poorer the family, the greater the benefit.

Transfers in Kind   In addition to TANF and Food Stamps, the government provides many poor people with a number of important goods and services, either at no charge or at prices that are well below market levels. Medical care under the Medicaid program and subsidized public housing are two notable examples.[2] These programs significantly enhance the living standards of the poor. However, most of them offer benefits that decline as family income rises. Taken as a whole, all of the antipoverty programs together put some poor families in a position where they are taxed extremely heavily if their earnings rise. When this situation occurs, the incentive to work becomes quite weak.

■ The Negative Income Tax

How can we do the job better? Can we design a simple structure that gets income into the hands of the poor without destroying their incentives to work? The solution suggested most frequently by economists is called the *negative income tax (NIT)*.

Table 4 illustrates how an NIT works. A particular NIT plan is defined by picking two numbers: a minimum income level below which no family is allowed to fall (the "guarantee") and a rate at which benefits are "taxed away" as income rises. The table considers a plan with a $12,000 guaranteed income and a 50 percent tax rate. Thus, a family with no earnings (top row) would receive a $12,000 payment (a "negative tax") from the government. A family earning $4,000 (second row) would have the basic benefit reduced by 50 percent of its earnings, or $2,000. Thus, it would receive $10,000 from the government plus the $4,000 earned income for a total income of $14,000.

---

[2] *Medicaid* programs pay for the health care of low-income people; *Medicare* is available to all seniors, regardless of income.

Notice in Table 4 that, with a 50 percent tax rate, the increase in total income as earnings rise is always *half* of the increase in earnings. Thus, recipients always have some incentive to work. Notice also that there is a level of income at which benefits cease—$24,000 in this example. This "break-even" level is not a third number that policy makers can select freely. Rather, it is dictated by the choices of the guarantee and the tax rate. In our example, $12,000 is the

TABLE 4		
Illustration of a Negative Income Tax Plan		
Benefits Earnings	Total Paid	Income
$ 0	$12,000	$12,000
4,000	10,000	14,000
8,000	8,000	16,000
12,000	6,000	18,000
16,000	4,000	20,000
20,000	2,000	22,000
24,000	0	24,000

maximum possible benefit, and benefits are reduced by 50 cents for each $1 of earnings. Hence, benefits will be reduced to zero when 50 percent of earnings is equal to $12,000—which occurs when earnings are $24,000. The general relation is:

Guarantee = Tax rate × Break-even level

The fact that the break-even level is completely determined by the guarantee and the tax rate creates a vexing problem. To make a real dent in the poverty problem, the guarantee must be placed fairly close to the poverty line. But then any moderate tax rate will push the break-even level far *above* the poverty line. As a result, families who are not considered "poor" (although they are certainly not rich) will also receive benefits. For example, a low tax rate of 33⅓ percent means that some benefits are paid to families whose income is as high as three times the guarantee level.

The solution seems obvious: raise the tax rate to bring the guarantee and the break-even level closer together. But then the incentive to work shrinks, and with it the principal rationale for the NIT in the first place. So the NIT is no panacea for the ills of the welfare system. Difficult choices must still be made.

The Negative Income Tax and Work Incentives   The NIT should increase work incentives for welfare recipients. However, we have just seen that a number of families who are now too well off to collect welfare inevitably would become eligible for NIT payments. For these people, the NIT imposes work disincentives by subjecting them to the relatively high NIT tax rate. Government-sponsored experiments back in the 1960s found that recipients of NIT benefits did in fact work less than nonrecipients, but only by a slight amount.

Largely because of its superior work incentives, economists believe that an NIT is a more efficient way to redistribute income than the existing multi-faceted welfare system. If this view is correct, then replacing the current welfare system with an NIT would lead to both more equality *and* more efficiency. But this does not mean that equalization would become cost-free. There is still a trade-off: By increasing equality, we still diminish the nation's output.

The Negative Income Tax and Reality   The NIT is often mistakenly viewed as an "academic" idea that does not exist in practice. But, in fact, America has two important programs that strongly resemble an NIT. One is the Food Stamps program already mentioned. Food Stamp benefits decline as earnings rise, and Food Stamps are used like cash in many poor neighborhoods. Hence, Food Stamp benefits look very much like the NIT plan illustrated in Table 4.

The second program is an important feature of the income tax code called the Earned Income Tax Credit (EITC). It works as follows. As earnings rise from zero to some threshold (which was $11,340 in 2006 for a worker with two children), the federal government supplements the earnings of the working poor by giving them what amounts to a grant that is proportional to their earnings. But once earnings pass a second threshold ($14,810 in 2006), the government starts taking this grant back, just as an NIT would. The EITC dates back to 1975 but was made substantially more generous in 1993. It is now America's biggest income-support program, reaching over 22 million families.

OTHER POLICIES TO COMBAT INEQUALITY

If we take the broader view that society's objective is not just to eliminate poverty but to reduce income disparities, then the fact that many nonpoor families would receive benefits under an NIT is perhaps not a serious drawback. After all, unless the plan is outlandishly generous, these families' incomes will still fall well below the average. Even so, the NIT is largely thought of as an antipoverty program, not as a tool for general income equalization.

The Personal Income Tax

By contrast, the federal personal income tax *is* thought of as a way to promote greater equality. Indeed, it is probably given far more credit in this regard than it actually deserves. Because the income tax is *progressive*, it takes a larger share of income from the rich than from the poor.[3] Thus, incomes *after* tax are distributed more equally than incomes *before* tax. But the actual amount of redistribution achieved by the personal income tax is quite small—and even that was reduced by the tax cuts of 2001–2004.

Death Duties and Other Taxes

Taxes on inheritances and estates levied by both states and the federal government also equalize incomes. In this case, they seem clearly aimed at limiting the incomes of the rich, or at least at limiting their ability to transfer this largesse from one generation to the next. But the amount of money involved is too small to make much difference to the overall income distribution. Total receipts from estate and gift taxes by all levels of government provide less than 1 percent of total tax revenues.

Nonetheless, the federal estate tax became a hot political issue in 2001 when President Bush proposed to eliminate it. That proposal passed Congress, but in a rather unusual form. Under current law, the estate tax is being phased out in stages between now and 2010. But then it will miraculously reappear in 2011! Of course, virtually no one expects that to happen. So it is a good bet that the estate tax law will be changed again in the coming years. Exactly how is not so clear.

Most experts agree that the many other taxes in the U.S. system—including sales taxes, payroll taxes, and property taxes—are decidedly regressive as a group. On balance, the evidence seems to suggest that:

The U.S. tax system as a whole is only slightly progressive.

POLICIES TO COMBAT DISCRIMINATION

The policies we have just considered are all based on taxes and transfer payments—on moving dollars from one set of hands to another. A quite different approach has been used to fight *discrimination*: Governments have made it *illegal* to discriminate.

Perhaps the major milestone in the war against discrimination was the *Civil Rights Act of 1964*, which outlawed many forms of discrimination and established the *Equal Employment Opportunity Commission (EEOC)*. When you read in a want ad that the company is "an equal opportunity employer," the firm is proclaiming its compliance with this and related legislation.

---

[3] For definitions of progressive, proportional, and regressive taxes, see Chapter 18.

POLICY DEBATE

Should Affirmative Action Be Abolished?

Affirmative action has always been controversial. It became a particularly hot political issue in the 1990s, as conservative politicians reacted to what they perceived to be one of the chief grievances of the "angry white male."

A number of critics believe that affirmative action has outlived its usefulness. It is time, they say, to rely on "race-blind" standards that judge each person on his or her individual merits. Any other system of selection is unfair, they insist, especially when affirmative action programs devolve into rigid quotas by race or sex—as they frequently do.

Although no federal laws were changed, an important 1995 Supreme Court ruling in *Adarand* v. *Pena* set new and tougher standards for federal affirmative action programs. This ruling prompted President Clinton to order a comprehensive review of federal programs that favored minorities in such matters as hiring and awarding contracts. Although a few programs were cut back or eliminated, the review generally concluded that the United States was still so far from being a "color-blind" society that affirmative action was still needed, and the president continued to defend affirmative action against Republican efforts to eliminate it.

Some state governments, however, went much farther than the federal government. California and Texas, for example,

abolished several affirmative action programs at their state universities. (In California, this action followed a contentious statewide referendum on the matter.) When they did, minority enrollments plummeted so dramatically that a few opponents of affirmative action had well-publicized second thoughts.

The issue remains open. Few people actually like affirmative action—it offends many people's sense of fairness. But a majority of Americans continue to believe it is necessary to redress a centuries-long imbalance.

SOURCE: © Jason Reed/Reuters/Corbis

Originally, policy makers sought to attack the problem by outlawing discrimination in rates of pay and in hiring standards—and by devoting resources to enforcing these provisions. Some progress in reducing discrimination by race and sex undoubtedly was made between 1964 and the early 1970s. But many people felt the pace was too slow. One reason was that discrimination in the labor market proved to be more subtle than was first thought. Only rarely could officials find definitive proof that unequal pay was being given for equal work, because determining when work was "equal" turned out to be a formidable task.

To combat this problem, a new approach was added to the antidiscrimination arsenal. Firms and other organizations with suspiciously small representations of minorities or women in their workforces were required not just to end discriminatory practices but also to demonstrate that they were taking **affirmative action** to remedy this imbalance. That is, they had to *prove* that they were making efforts to locate members of minority groups and females and then to hire them if they were qualified.

Affirmative action refers to active efforts to locate and hire members of under-represented groups.

This approach to fighting discrimination was controversial from the start, and it remains so to this day. Critics, including President Bush and many Republicans in Congress, claim that affirmative action amounts to numerical quotas and compulsory hiring of unqualified workers simply because they are black or female. If this allegation is true, it exacts a toll on economic efficiency. Proponents of affirmative action—including former President Clinton and many Democrats—argue that affirmative action is needed to redress past wrongs and to prevent discriminatory employers from claiming that they are unable to find qualified minority or female employees. (See the box on affirmative action.)

The difficulty revolves around the impossibility of deciding who is "qualified" and who is not based on *purely objective criteria*. What one person sees as government coercion to hire an unqualified applicant to fill a quota, another sees as a discriminatory employer being forced to mend his or her ways. Nothing in this book, or anywhere else, will teach you which view is correct in any particular instance.

The controversy over affirmative action once again illustrates *the trade-off between equality and efficiency*. Putting more women and members of minority groups into high-paying jobs would certainly make the income distribution more equal. Supporters of affirmative action seek that result. But if affirmative action disrupts industry and requires firms to replace "qualified" white males with other, "less qualified" workers, the nation's productivity will suffer. Opponents of affirmative action are disturbed by these potential efficiency losses. How far should these programs be pushed? A good question, but one without a good answer.

■ A LOOK BACK

We have now completed three chapters on the distribution of income. So this may be an opportune moment to pause and see how this analysis relates to our central theme: *What does the market do well, and what does it do poorly?*

We have learned that a market economy relies on the marginal productivity principle to assign an income to each individual. In so doing, the market attaches high prices to scarce factors and low prices to abundant ones, and therefore guides firms to use society's resources *efficiently*. This ability is one of the market's great strengths.

However, by attaching high prices to some factors and low prices to others, the market mechanism may create a distribution of income that is quite unequal. Some people wind up fabulously rich, while others wind up miserably poor. For this reason, the market has been widely criticized for centuries for doing a rather poor job of distributing income in accord with commonly held notions of *fairness* and *equity*.

On balance, most observers feel that both the praise and the criticism are well justified: The market mechanism is extraordinarily good at promoting efficiency but not very good at promoting equality. As we said at the outset, the market has both virtues and vices.

SUMMARY

1. The United States declared a "War on Poverty" in 1964, and within a decade the fraction of families below the official **poverty line** had dropped substantially. Today, the poverty rate is higher than it was in the 1970s.

2. In the United States today, the richest 20 percent of households receive over 50 percent of the income, whereas the poorest 20 percent of households receive less than 3 1/2 percent. These numbers reflect a considerable increase in inequality since about 1980. The U.S. income distribution also appears to be more unequal than those of most other industrial nations.

3. Individual incomes differ for many reasons. Differences in natural abilities, in the desire to work hard and to take risks, in schooling and experience, and in inherited wealth all account for income disparities. **Economic discrimination** also plays a role. All of these factors, however, explain only part of the inequality that we observe. A portion of the rest is due simply to good or bad luck, and the balance is unexplained.

4. There is a trade-off between the goals of reducing inequality and enhancing economic efficiency. Namely, policies that help on the equality front normally harm efficiency, and vice versa.

5. Because of this trade-off, there is in principle an optimal degree of inequality for any society. Society finds this optimum in the same way that a consumer decides how much to buy of different commodities: The trade-off tells us how costly it is to "purchase" more equality, and preferences then determine how much should be "bought." However, because people have different value judgments about the importance of equality, they disagree over the ideal amount of equality.

6. Whatever goal for equality is selected, society can gain by using more efficient redistributive policies because such policies let us "buy" any given amount of equality at a lower price in terms of lost output. Economists claim, for example, that a **negative income tax** is an efficient redistributive tool.

7. But the negative income tax is no panacea for all inequality-related problems. Its primary virtue is the way it preserves incentives to work. But if this goal is accomplished by keeping the tax rate low, then either the minimum guaranteed level of income will have to be low or many non-poor families will become eligible to receive benefits.

8. The goal of income equality is also pursued through the tax system, especially through the progressive federal income tax and death duties. But other taxes are typically regressive, so the tax system as a whole is only slightly progressive.

9. Discrimination has been attacked by making it illegal, rather than through the tax and transfer system. But simply declaring discrimination to be illegal is much easier than actually ending discrimination. The **trade-off between equality and efficiency** applies once again: Strict enforcement of **affirmative action** will certainly reduce discrimination and increase income equality, but it may do so at a cost in terms of economic efficiency.

KEY TERMS

Poverty line   447

Absolute and relative concepts of poverty   448

Economic discrimination   452

Trade-off between equality and efficiency   453

Temporary Assistance to Needy Families (TANF)   455

Food stamps   456

Negative income tax (NIT)   456

Earned income tax credit (EITC)   457

Civil Rights Act of 1964   458

Equal Employment Opportunity Commission (EEOC)   458

Affirmative action   459

TEST YOURSELF

1. Define the poverty rate. Does it rise or fall during recessions?

2. Since the official poverty line was set at $3,000 in 1964, prices have risen by about a factor of six. If the poverty line was adjusted only for inflation, what would it be now? How does that compare with the actual poverty line?

DISCUSSION QUESTIONS

1. Discuss the "leaky bucket" analogy (page 455) with your classmates. What maximum amount of income would you personally allow to leak from the bucket in transferring money from the rich to the poor? Explain why people differ in their answers to this question.

2. Suppose you were to design a negative income tax system for the United States. Pick a guaranteed income level and a tax rate that seem reasonable to you. What break-even level of income is implied by these choices? Construct a version of Table 4 for the plan you have just devised.

3. Suppose the War on Poverty were starting anew and you were part of a presidential commission assigned the task of defining the poor. Would you choose an absolute or a relative concept of poverty? Why? What would be your specific definition of poverty?

4. Discuss the concept of the "optimal amount of inequality." What are some of the practical problems in determining how much inequality really is optimal?

5. A number of conservative politicians and economists advocate replacing the progressive income tax with a "flat tax" that would apply the same, low tax rate to all income above a certain exempt amount. One argument against making this change is that the distribution of income has grown much more unequal since the 1970s. Does the evidence support that view? Is it a decisive argument against a flat tax? How is the trade-off between equality and efficiency involved here?

APPENDIX: *The Economic Theory of Discrimination*

Although discrimination is often thought of as a noneconomic topic, economic analysis can actually tell us quite a bit about its economic effects. This appendix uses some of the analysis we have provided in previous chapters to shed light on two specific questions:

1. Must *prejudice*, which we define as arising when one group dislikes associating with another group, lead to *economic discrimination* as defined in the chapter (unequal pay for equal work)?
2. Do "natural" economic forces tend either to erode or to exacerbate discrimination over time?

Exactly *who* is prejudiced or discriminatory turns out to be critical to the answers, as we will now see.

DISCRIMINATION BY EMPLOYERS

Most attention seems to focus on discrimination by employers, so let us start there. What happens if, for example, some firms refuse to hire blacks? Figure 2 will help us find the answer. Panel (a) pertains to firms that discriminate; Panel (b) pertains to firms that do not. Supply and demand curves for labor in each market appear in the figure, based on the analysis of Chapter 20. We suppose that the two demand curves are identical.

However, the supply curve in market (b) must be farther to the right than the supply curve in market (a) because both whites *and* blacks can work in market (b), whereas only whites can work in market (a). The result is that wages will be lower in market (b) than they are in market (a). Because all the blacks are forced into market (b), we conclude that employers discriminate against them in the economic sense of that word.

But now consider the situation from the *employers'* point of view. Firms in market (a) pay more for labor (W_a

is greater than W_b), so any nondiscriminatory firms in market (b) have a cost advantage. As we learned in earlier chapters, the forces of competition will shift more and more of the total market to the low-cost (nondiscriminatory) producers, eventually driving the discriminators out of business. Of course, this only happens if there is effective competition. If the discriminating firm in market (a) has a protected monopoly, it will be able to stay in business. But it will still pay for the privilege of discriminating by earning lower monopoly profits than it otherwise would (because it will pay higher wages than necessary).

DISCRIMINATION BY FELLOW WORKERS

As we see, competitive forces tend to reduce discrimination over time *if* employers are the source of discrimination. Such optimistic conclusions do not follow, however, if workers—rather than employers—are prejudiced. Consider what happens, for example, if men object to having women as their supervisors. If male workers will not give their full cooperation, female supervisors will be less effective than male supervisors and hence will earn lower wages. Here prejudice *does* lead to discrimination. Furthermore, in this case, firms that put women into supervisory positions will be at a competitive *disadvantage* relative to firms that do not. So market forces will not erode discrimination.

STATISTICAL DISCRIMINATION

A final type of discrimination, called **statistical discrimination**, may be the most stubborn of all. And it can exist even when there is no prejudice. Let us look at an impor-

Statistical discrimination is said to occur when the productivity of a particular worker is estimated to be low just because that worker belongs to a particular group (such as women).

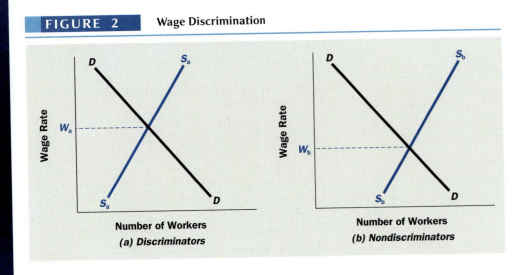

FIGURE 2	Wage Discrimination

(a) Discriminators

(b) Nondiscriminators

Number of Workers

Are Women Better Workers?

In the piece excerpted here, economist Audrey Freedman argues that a female employee can be a better bargain than a male, even though only women request pregnancy leaves and it is mainly women who miss workdays for child care reasons.

It is undeniable . . . that women, not men, take pregnancy leaves. It is also undeniable that women are the primary nurturers in a family. They are the most likely to be responsible for the care and support of children, as well as their elderly parents. If we stop there . . . women in business are more costly than men.

But the built-in bias of that analysis is the failure to account for far more costly drains on corporate productivity from behavior that is more characteristic of men than of women.

For example, men are more likely to be heavy users of alcohol. This gender-related habit causes businesses to suffer excessive medical costs, serious performance losses, and productivity drains. Yet, the male-dominated corporate hierarchy most often chooses to ignore these "good old boy" habits.

Drug abuse among the fast-movers of Wall Street seems to be understood as a normal response to the pressures of taking risks with other people's money. The consequences in loss of judgment are tolerated. They are not calculated as a male-related cost of business. . . .

In addition, in our culture, lawlessness and violence are found far more often among men than women. The statistics on criminals and prison population are obvious, yet we seem to be unable to recognize these as primarily male behaviors.

A top executive of a major airline once commented to me that his company's greatest problem is machismo in the cockpit—pilots and copilots fighting over the controls. There is an obvious solution: Hire pilots from that half of the population that is less susceptible to the attacks of rage that afflict macho males.

SOURCE: ©1986 Etta Hulme. Reprinted by permission of Etta Hulme and the *Fort Worth Star Telegram*.

SOURCE: Audrey Freedman, "Those Costly 'Good Old Boys,'" *The New York Times*, July 12, 1989, p. A23. Copyright 1989 by the New York Times Company. Reprinted by permission.

tant example. It is, of course, a biological fact that only women give birth. It is also a fact that most working women who have babies leave their jobs for a while to care for their newborns. Employers recognize both facts. What they cannot know, however, is *which* women of child-bearing age will leave the labor force for this reason.

Suppose three candidates apply for a job that requires a long-term commitment. Susan plans to quit after a few years to raise a family. Jane does not plan to have any children. Jack is a man. If he knew all the facts, the employer might not want Susan, but would be equally happy with either Jane or Jack. But the employer cannot differentiate between Susan and Jane. He therefore presumes that either one, being a young woman, is more likely than Jack to quit to raise a family. So he hires Jack, even though Jane is just as good a prospect. Thus Jane is a victim of statistical discrimination.

Lest it be thought that this example actually justifies discrimination against women on economic grounds, it should be noted that most women return to work within six months after childbirth. Furthermore, women typically have less absenteeism and job turnover for nonpregnancy health reasons than men do. The box "Are

Women Better Workers?" argues that employers often fail to take these other sex-related differences into account and thus mistakenly favor men.

■ THE ROLES OF THE MARKET AND THE GOVERNMENT

In terms of the two questions with which we began this appendix, we conclude that different types of discrimination lead to different answers. Prejudice will often, but not always, lead to economic discrimination, and discrimination may occur even in the absence of prejudice. Finally, the forces of competition tend to erode some, but not all, of the inequities produced by discrimination.

However, the victims of discrimination are not the only losers when discrimination occurs. Society also loses whenever discriminatory practices impair economic efficiency. Thus reasonable antidiscrimination policies should be able to enhance both equality and efficiency. For this reason, most observers believe that we should not rely on market forces *alone* to combat discrimination. The government has a clear role to play.

SUMMARY

1. Prejudice by employers will result in discrimination in rates of pay and in partial segregation of the workplace. However, the forces of competition should erode this type of discrimination.

2. Prejudice by fellow workers will result in wage discrimination, and perhaps even in segregated work places. But competition will not erode this type of discrimination.

3. Discrimination may also arise even when there is no prejudice. This is called **statistical discrimination**.

KEY TERM

Statistical discrimination   462

VI

THE MACROECONOMY: AGGREGATE SUPPLY AND DEMAND

Macroeconomics is the headline-grabbing part of economics. When economic news appears on the front page of your daily newspaper or is reported on the nightly television news, you are most likely reading or hearing about some macroeconomic development in the national or world economy. The Federal Reserve has just raised interest rates. Inflation remains low. Jobs are scarce—or plentiful. The federal government's budget is in deficit. The euro is rising in value. These developments are all macroeconomic news stories. But what do they mean?

Part VI begins your study of macroeconomics. It will first acquaint you with some of the major concepts of macroeconomics—things that you hear about every day, such as gross domestic product (GDP), inflation, unemployment, and economic growth (Chapters 22 and 23). Then it will introduce the basic theory that we use to interpret and understand macroeconomic events (Chapters 24 through 27). By the time you finish Chapter 27—which is only six chapters away—those newspaper articles should make a lot more sense.

AN INTRODUCTION TO MACROECONOMICS

Where the telescope ends, the microscope begins. Which of the two has the grander view?

VICTOR HUGO

By time-honored tradition, economics is divided into two fields: *microeconomics* and *macroeconomics*. These inelegant words are derived from the Greek, where *micro* means something small and *macro* means something large. Chapters 3 and 4 introduced you to microeconomics. This chapter does the same for macroeconomics.

How do the two branches of the discipline differ? It is *not* a matter of using different tools. As we shall see in this chapter, supply and demand provide the basic organizing framework for constructing macroeconomic models, just as they do for microeconomic models. Rather, the distinction is based on the issues addressed. For an example of a macroeconomic question, turn to the next page.

CONTENTS

ISSUE: *Was It George Bush's Fault?*

One of the major domestic issues in the 2004 presidential race was the American economy's poor record of job creation during George W. Bush's term of office. In fact, President Bush was the first president since Herbert Hoover during the Great Depression of the 1930s to stand for reelection with a net *decline* in the total number of Americans at work during his administration. Throughout the 2004 campaign, challenger John Kerry blamed the incumbent president for the weak job market performance. President Bush countered that the job losses early in his term were caused by the collapse of the stock market, by the 9/11 terrorist attacks, and by other factors beyond his control.

Who was right? The voters at that point seemed to side with Mr. Bush. But as we will see, first in this chapter and then throughout Parts VI and VII, there is no simple answer to the question. Although the economic policies of a president can influence the number of jobs created by the economy, they are by no means the only influence.

■ DRAWING A LINE BETWEEN MACROECONOMICS AND MICROECONOMICS

In microeconomics, the spotlight is on *how individual decision-making units behave.* For example, the dairy farmers of Chapter 4 are individual decision makers; so are the consumers who purchase the milk. How do they decide which actions are in their own best interests? How are these millions of decisions coordinated by the market mechanism, and with what consequences? Questions such as these lie at the heart of microeconomics.

Although Plato and Aristotle might wince at the abuse of their language, microeconomics applies to the decisions of some astonishingly large units. The annual sales of General Electric and General Motors, for example, exceed the total production of many nations. Yet someone who studies GE's pricing policies is a microeconomist, whereas someone who studies inflation in a small country like Monaco is a macroeconomist. The micro-macro distinction in economics is certainly not based solely on size.

What, then, is the basis for this long-standing distinction? The answer is that, whereas microeconomics focuses on the *decisions of individual units*, no matter how large, macroeconomics concentrates on *the behavior of entire economies*, no matter how small. Microeconomists might look at a single company's pricing and output decisions. Macroeconomists study the overall price level, unemployment rate, and other things that we call *economic aggregates*.

■ Aggregation and Macroeconomics

An "economic aggregate" is simply an *abstraction* that people use to describe some salient feature of economic life. For example, although we observe the prices of gasoline, telephone calls, and movie tickets every day, we never actually see "the price level." Yet many people—not just economists—find it meaningful to speak of "the cost of living." In fact, the government's attempts to measure it are widely publicized by the news media each month.

Among the most important of these abstract notions is the concept of *domestic product*, which represents the total production of a nation's economy. The process by which real objects such as software, baseballs, and theater tickets are combined into an abstraction called total domestic product is **aggregation,** and it is one of the foundations of macroeconomics. We can illustrate it by a simple example.

An imaginary nation called Agraria produces nothing but foodstuffs to sell to consumers. Rather than deal separately with the many markets for pizzas, candy bars, hamburgers, and so on, macroeconomists group them all into a single abstract "market for output." Thus, when macroeconomists announce that output in Agraria grew 10 percent last year, are they referring to more potatoes or hot dogs, more soybeans or green peppers? The answer is: They do not care. In the aggregate measures of macroeconomics, output is output, no matter what form it takes.

Aggregation means combining many individual markets into one overall market.

The Foundations of Aggregation

Amalgamating many markets into one means ignoring distinctions among different products. Can we really believe that no one cares whether the national output of Agraria consists of $800,000 worth of pickles and $200,000 worth of ravioli rather than $500,000 each of lettuce and tomatoes? Surely this is too much to swallow. Macroeconomists certainly do not believe that no one cares; instead, they rest the case for aggregation on two foundations:

1. Although the *composition* of demand and supply in the various markets may be terribly important for *some* purposes (such as how income is distributed and the diets people enjoy), it may be of little consequence for the economy-wide issues of growth, inflation, and unemployment—the issues that concern macroeconomists.

2. During economic fluctuations, markets tend to move up or down together. When demand in the economy rises, there is more demand for potatoes *and* tomatoes, more demand for artichokes *and* pickles, more demand for ravioli *and* hot dogs.

Although there are exceptions to these two principles, both seem serviceable enough as approximations. In fact, if they were not, there would be no discipline called macroeconomics, and a full-year course in economics could be reduced to a half-year. Lest this cause you a twinge of regret, bear in mind that many people believe that unemployment and inflation would be far more difficult to control without macroeconomics—which would be a lot worse.

The Line of Demarcation Revisited

These two principles—that the composition of demand and supply may not matter for some purposes, and that markets normally move together—enable us to draw a different kind of dividing line between microeconomics and macroeconomics.

In macroeconomics, we typically assume that most details of resource allocation and income distribution are relatively unimportant to the study of the overall rates of inflation and unemployment. In microeconomics, we generally ignore inflation, unemployment, and growth, focusing instead on how individual markets allocate resources and distribute income.

To use a well-worn metaphor, a macroeconomist analyzes the size of the proverbial economic "pie," paying scant attention to what is inside it or to how it gets divided among the dinner guests. A microeconomist, by contrast, assumes that the pie is of the right size and shape, and frets over its ingredients and who gets to eat it. If you have ever baked or eaten a pie, you will realize that either approach alone is a trifle myopic.

Economics is divided into macroeconomics and microeconomics largely for the sake of pedagogical clarity: We can't teach you everything at once. But in reality, the crucial interconnection between macroeconomics and microeconomics is with us all the time. There is, after all, only one economy.

SUPPLY AND DEMAND IN MACROECONOMICS

Whether you are taking a course that concentrates on macroeconomics or one that focuses on microeconomics, the discussion of supply and demand in Chapter 4 served as an invaluable introduction. Supply and demand analysis is just as fundamental to macroeconomics as it is to microeconomics.

A Quick Review

Figure 1 shows two diagrams that should look familiar from Chapter 4. In Figure 1(a), we find a downward-sloping demand curve, labeled *DD,* and an upward-sloping supply curve, labeled *SS.* Because the figure is a multipurpose diagram, the "Price" and "Quantity" axes do not specify any particular commodity. To start on familiar terrain, first imagine that this graph depicts the market for milk, so the vertical axis measures the price of milk and the horizontal axis measures the quantity of milk demanded and supplied. As we know, if nothing interferes with the operation of a free market, equilibrium will be at point E with a price P_0 and a quantity of output Q_0.

Next, suppose something happens to shift the demand curve outward. For example, we learned in Chapter 4 that an increase in consumer incomes might do that. Figure 1(b) shows this shift as a rightward movement of the demand curve from D_0D_0 to D_1D_1. Equilibrium shifts from point E to point A, so both price and output rise.

FIGURE 1

Two Interpretations of a Shift in the Demand Curve

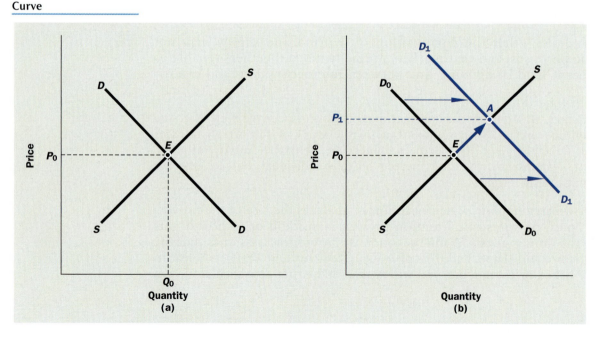

Price / P_0 / Q_0 / Quantity / (a)

Price / P_1 / P_0 / Quantity / (b)

Moving to Macroeconomic Aggregates

Now let's switch from microeconomics to macroeconomics. To do so, we reinterpret Figure 1 as representing the market for an abstract object called "domestic product"—one of those economic aggregates that we described earlier. No one has ever seen, touched, or eaten a unit of domestic product, but these are the kinds of abstractions we use in macroeconomic analysis.

Consistent with this reinterpretation, think of the price measured on the vertical axis as being another abstraction—the overall price index, or "cost of living."[1] Then the curve DD in Figure 1(a) is called an **aggregate demand curve,** and the curve SS is called an **aggregate supply curve.** We will develop an economic theory to derive these curves explicitly in Chapters 24 through 27. As we shall see there, the curves have rather different origins from the microeconomic counterparts we encountered in Chapter 4.

The **aggregate demand curve** shows the quantity of domestic product that is demanded at each possible value of the price level.

The **aggregate supply curve** shows the quantity of domestic product that is supplied at each possible value of the price level.

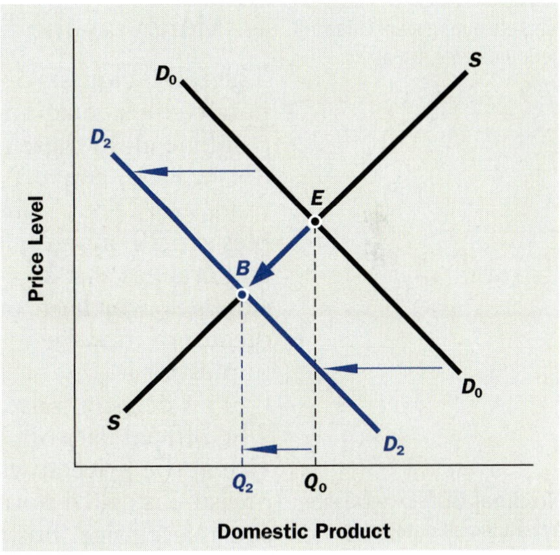

Inflation

With this macroeconomic reinterpretation, Figure 1(b) depicts the problem of **inflation.** We see from the figure that the outward shift of the aggregate demand curve, whatever its cause, pushes the price level up. If aggregate demand keeps shifting out month after month, the economy will suffer from inflation—meaning a sustained increase in the general price level.

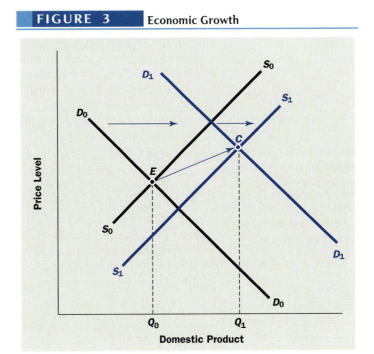

FIGURE 2 An Economy Slipping into a Recession

Recession and Unemployment

The second principal issue of macroeconomics, recession and unemployment, also can be illustrated on a supply-demand diagram, this time by shifting the demand curve in the opposite direction. Figure 2 repeats the supply and demand curves of Figure 1(a) and in addition depicts a leftward shift of the aggregate demand curve from D_0D_0 to D_2D_2. Equilibrium now moves from point E to point B so that domestic product (total output) declines. This is what we normally mean by a **recession**—a period of time during which production falls and people lose jobs.

FIGURE 3 Economic Growth

Economic Growth

Figure 3 illustrates macroeconomists' third area of concern: the process of economic growth. Here the original aggregate demand and supply curves are, once again, D_0D_0 and S_0S_0, which intersect at point E. But now we consider the possibility that *both* curves shift to the right over time, moving to D_1D_1 and S_1S_1, respectively. The new intersection point is C, and the blue arrow running from point E to point C shows the economy's growth path. Over this period of time, domestic product grows from Q_0 to Q_1.

---

[1] The appendix to Chapter 23 explains how such price indexes are calculated.

GROSS DOMESTIC PRODUCT

Inflation refers to a sustained increase in the general price level.

A **recession** is a period of time during which the total output of the economy declines.

Gross domestic product (GDP) is the sum of the money values of all final goods and services produced in the domestic economy and sold on organized markets during a specified period of time, usually a year.

Up to now, we have been somewhat cavalier in using the phrase "domestic product." Let's now get more specific. Of the various ways to measure an economy's total output, the most popular choice by far is the **gross domestic product,** or **GDP** for short—a term you have probably encountered in the news media. GDP is the most comprehensive measure of the output of all the factories, offices, and shops in the United States. Specifically, it is the sum of the *money values* of all *final* goods and services *produced* in the *domestic* economy within the year.

Several features of this definition need to be underscored.[2] First, you will notice that:

We add up the money values of things.

■ Money as the Measuring Rod: Real versus Nominal GDP

The GDP consists of a bewildering variety of goods and services: computer chips and potato chips, tanks and textbooks, ballet performances and rock concerts. How can we combine all of these into a single number? To an economist, there is a natural way to do so: First, convert every good and service into *money* terms, and then add all the money up. Thus, contrary to the cliché, we *can* add apples and oranges. To add 10 apples and 20 oranges, first ask: How much *money* does each cost? If apples cost 20 cents and oranges cost 25 cents, then the apples count for $2 and the oranges for $5, so the sum is $7 worth of "output." The market *price* of each good or service is used as an indicator of its *value* to society for a simple reason: *Someone* is willing to pay that much money for it.

Nominal GDP is calculated by valuing all outputs at current prices.

This decision raises the question of what prices to use in valuing different outputs. The official data offer two choices. Most obviously, we can value each good and service at the price at which it was actually sold. If we take this approach, the resulting measure is called **nominal GDP,** or *GDP in current dollars.* This seems like a perfectly sensible choice, but it has one serious drawback as a measure of output: Nominal GDP rises when prices rise, even if there is no increase in actual production. For example, if hamburgers cost $2.00 this year but cost only $1.50 last year, then 100 hamburgers will contribute $200 to this year's nominal GDP whereas they contributed only $150 to last year's nominal GDP. But 100 hamburgers are still 100 hamburgers—output has not grown.

For this reason, government statisticians have devised alternative measures that correct for inflation by valuing goods and services produced in *different* years at the *same* set of prices. For example, if the hamburgers were valued at $1.50 each in both years, $150 worth of hamburger output would be included in GDP *in each year*. In practice, such calculations can be quite complicated, but the details need not worry us in an introductory course. Suffice it to say that, when the calculations are done, we

Real GDP is calculated by valuing outputs of different years at common prices. Therefore, real GDP is a far better measure than nominal GDP of changes in total production.

obtain **real GDP** or *GDP in constant dollars.* The news media often refer to this measure as "GDP corrected for inflation." Throughout most of this book, and certainly whenever we are discussing the nation's output, we will be concerned with *real* GDP.

The distinction between nominal and real GDP leads us to a working definition of a *recession* as a period in which *real* GDP declines. For example, between the fourth quarter of 2000 and the third quarter of 2001, America's last recession, nominal GDP *rose* from $9,954 billion to $10,135 billion, but real GDP *fell* from $9,888 billion to $9,871 billion. In fact, it has become conventional to say that a recession occurs when real GDP declines for two or more consecutive quarters.

---

[2] Certain exceptions to the definition are dealt with in the appendix to Chapter 25. Some instructors may prefer to take up that material here.

■ What Gets Counted in GDP?

The next important aspect of the definition of GDP is that:

The GDP for a particular year includes only goods and services produced within the year. Sales of items produced in previous years are explicitly excluded.

For example, suppose you buy a perfectly beautiful 1985 Thunderbird from a friend next week and are overjoyed by your purchase. The national income statistician will not share your glee. She counted that car in the GDP of 1985, when it was first produced and sold, and will never count it again. The same is true of houses. The resale values of houses do not count in GDP because they were counted in the years they were built.

Next, you will note from the definition of gross domestic product that:

Only final goods and services count in the GDP.

The adjective *final* is the key word here. For example, when Dell buys computer chips from Intel, the transaction is not included in the GDP because Dell does not want the chips for itself. It buys them only to manufacture computers, which it sells to consumers. Only the computers are considered a final product. When Dell buys chips from Intel, economists consider the chips to be **intermediate goods.** The GDP excludes sales of intermediate goods and services because, if they were included, we would wind up counting the same outputs several times.[3] For example, if chips sold to computer manufacturers were included in GDP, we would count the same chip when it was sold to the computer maker and then again as a component of the computer when it was sold to a consumer.

Next, note that:

The adjective *domestic* in the definition of GDP denotes production within the geographic boundaries of the United States.

Some Americans work abroad, and many American companies have offices or factories in foreign countries. All of these people and businesses produce valuable outputs, but none of it counts in the GDP of the United States. (It counts, instead, in the GDPs of the other countries.) On the other hand, quite a few foreigners and foreign companies produce goods and services in the United States. All that activity does count in our GDP.[4]

Finally, the definition of GDP notes that:

For the most part, only goods and services that pass through organized markets count in the GDP.

This restriction, of course, excludes many economic activities. For example, illegal activities are not included in the GDP. Thus, gambling services in Atlantic City are part of GDP, but gambling services in Chicago are not. Garage sales, although sometimes lucrative, are not included either. The definition reflects the statisticians' inability to measure the value of many of the economy's most important activities, such as housework, do-it-yourself repairs, and leisure time. These activities certainly result in currently produced goods or services, but they all lack that important measuring rod—a market price.

Final goods and services are those that are purchased by their ultimate users.

An **intermediate good** is a good purchased for resale or for use in producing another good.

SOURCE: From *The Wall Street Journal*—Permission, Cartoon Features Syndicate.

"More and more, I ask myself what's the point of pursuing the meaning of the universe if you can't have a rising GNP."

---

[3] Actually, there is another way to add up the GDP by counting a portion of each intermediate transaction. This is explained in the appendix to Chapter 25.

[4] There is another concept, called gross *national* product, which counts the goods and services produced by all Americans, regardless of where they work. For consistency, the outputs produced by foreigners working in the United States are not included in GNP. In practice, the two measures—GDP and GNP—are very close.

This omission results in certain oddities. For example, suppose that each of two neighboring families hires the other to clean house, generously paying $1,000 per week for the services. Each family can easily afford such generosity because it collects an identical salary from its neighbor. Nothing real has changed, but GDP goes up by $104,000 per year. If this example seems trivial, you may be interested to know that, according to one estimate made several years ago, America's GDP might be a stunning 44 percent higher if unpaid housework were valued at market prices and counted in GDP.[5]

Limitations of the GDP: What GDP Is Not

Now that we have seen in some detail what the GDP *is*, let's examine what it *is not*. In particular:

Gross domestic product is not a measure of the nation's economic well-being.

The GDP is not intended to measure economic well-being and does not do so for several reasons:

Only Market Activity Is Included in GDP   As we have just seen, a great deal of work done in the home contributes to the nation's well-being but is not counted in GDP because it has no price tag. One important implication of this exclusion arises when we try to compare the GDPs of developed and less developed countries. Americans are always amazed to hear that the per-capita GDPs of the poorest African countries are less than $250 per year. Surely, no one could survive in America on $5 per week. How can Africans do it? Part of the answer, of course, is that these people are terribly poor. But another part of the answer is that:

International GDP comparisons are vastly misleading when the two countries differ greatly in the fraction of economic activity that each conducts in organized markets.

This fraction is relatively large in the United States and relatively small in the poorest countries. So when we compare their respective measured GDPs, we are not comparing the same economic activities. Many things that get counted in the U.S. GDP are not counted in the GDPs of very poor nations because they do not pass through markets. It is ludicrous to think that these people, impoverished as they are, survive on what an American thinks of as $5 per week.

A second implication is that GDP statistics take no account of the so-called underground economy—a term that includes not just criminal activities, but also a great deal of legitimate business that is conducted in cash or by barter to escape the tax collector. Naturally, we have no good data on the size of the underground economy. Some observers, however, think that it may amount to 10 percent or more of U.S. GDP—and much more in some foreign countries.

GDP Places No Value on Leisure   As a country gets richer, its citizens normally take more and more leisure time. If that is true, a better measure of national well-being that includes the value of leisure would display faster growth than conventionally measured GDP. For example, the length of the typical workweek in the United States fell steadily for many decades, which meant that growth in GDP systematically *underestimated* the growth in national well-being. But lately this trend has stopped, and may even have reversed. (See "Are Americans Working More?")

---

[5] Ann Chadeau, "What Is Households' Non-Market Production Worth?" *OECD Economic Studies*, 18, 1992, pp. 85–103.

Are Americans Working More?

According to conventional wisdom, the workweek in the United States is steadily shrinking, leaving Americans with more and more leisure time to enjoy. But a 1991 book by economist Juliet Schor pointed out that this view was wrong: Americans were really working longer and longer hours. Her findings were both provocative and controversial at the time. But since then, the gap between the typical American and European workweeks has widened.

> In the last twenty years the amount of time Americans have spent at their jobs has risen steadily. . . . Americans report that they have only sixteen and a half hours of leisure a week, after the obligations of job and household are taken care of. . . . If present trends continue, by the end of the century Americans will be spending as much time at their jobs as they did back in the nineteen twenties.
>
> The rise in worktime was unexpected. For nearly a hundred years, hours had been declining. . . . Equally surprising, but also hardly recognized, has been the deviation from Western Europe. After progressing in tandem for nearly a century, the United States veered off into a trajectory of declining leisure, while in Europe work has been disappearing. . . . U.S. manufacturing employees currently work 320 more hours [per year]—the equivalent of over two months—than their counterparts in West

Germany or France. . . . We have paid a price for prosperity. . . . We are eating more, but we are burning up those calories at work. We have color televisions and compact disc players, but we need them to unwind after a stressful day at the office. We take vacations, but we work so hard throughout the year that they become indispensable to our sanity.

SOURCE: © Comstock Images/Getty Images

SOURCE: Juliet B. Schor, *The Overworked American* (New York: Basic Books; 1991), pp. 1–2, 10–11.

"Bads" as Well as "Goods" Get Counted in GDP   There are also reasons why the GDP *overstates* how well-off we are. Here is a tragic example. Disaster struck the United States on September 11, 2001. No one doubts that this made the nation worse off. Thousands of people were killed. Buildings and businesses were destroyed. Yet the disaster almost certainly raised GDP. The government spent more for disaster relief and cleanup, and later for reconstruction. Businesses spent more to rebuild and repair damaged buildings and replace lost items. Even consumers spent more on clean up and replacing lost possessions. No one imagines that America was better off after 9/11, despite all this additional GDP.

Wars represent an extreme example. Mobilization for a war fought on some other nation's soil normally causes a country's GDP to rise rapidly. But men and women serving in the military could be producing civilian output instead. Factories assigned to produce armaments could instead be making cars, washing machines, and televisions. A country at war is surely worse off than a country at peace, but this fact will not be reflected in its GDP.

Ecological Costs Are Not Netted Out of the GDP   Many productive activities of a modern industrial economy have undesirable side effects on the environment. Automobiles provide an essential means of transportation, but they also despoil the atmosphere. Factories pollute rivers and lakes while manufacturing valuable commodities. Almost everything seems to produce garbage, which creates serious disposal problems. None of these ecological costs are deducted from the GDP in an effort to give us a truer measure of the *net* increase in economic welfare that our economy produces. Is this omission foolish? Not if we remember that national income statisticians are trying to measure economic activity conducted through organized markets, not national welfare.

Now that we have defined several of the basic concepts of macroeconomics, let us breathe some life into them by perusing the economic history of the United States.

THE ECONOMY ON A ROLLER COASTER

Growth, but with Fluctuations

The most salient fact about the U.S. economy has been its seemingly limitless *growth*; it gets bigger almost every year. Nominal gross domestic product in 2006 was around $13¼ trillion, more than 25 times as much as in 1959. In Figure 4, the black curve shows that extraordinary upward march. But, as the discussion of nominal versus real GDP suggests, a large part of this apparent growth was simply inflation. Because of higher prices, the *purchasing power* of each 2006 dollar was less than one fifth of each 1959 dollar. Corrected for inflation, we see that *real GDP* (the red curve in the figure) was only about 4½ times greater in 2006 than in 1959.

Another reason for the growth of GDP is population growth. A nation becomes richer only if its GDP grows *faster* than its population. To see how much richer the United States has actually become since 1959, we must divide real GDP by the size of the population to obtain **real GDP per capita**—which is the blue line in Figure 4. It turns out that real output per person in 2006 was roughly 2.7 times as much as in 1959. That is still not a bad performance.

If aggregate supply and demand grew smoothly from one year to the next, as was depicted in Figure 3, the economy would expand at some steady rate. But U.S. economic history displays a far less regular pattern—one of alternating periods of rapid and slow growth that are called *macroeconomic fluctuations*, or sometimes just *business*

Real GDP per capita is the ratio of real GDP divided by population.

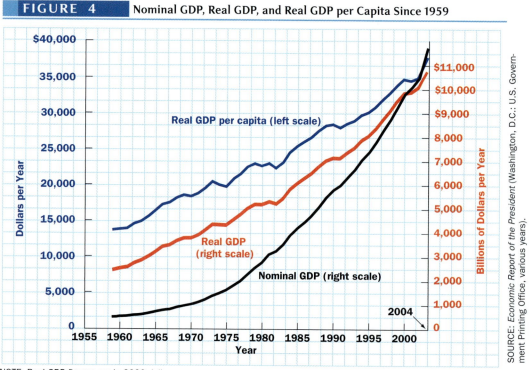

FIGURE 4   Nominal GDP, Real GDP, and Real GDP per Capita Since 1959

NOTE: Real GDP figures are in 2000 dollars.

SOURCE: *Economic Report of the President* (Washington, D.C.: U.S. Government Printing Office, various years).

cycles. In some years—five since 1959, to be exact—real GDP actually declined.[6] Such *recessions*, and their attendant problem of rising unemployment, have been a persistent feature of American economic performance—one to which we will pay much attention in the coming chapters.

The bumps encountered along the American economy's historic growth path stand out more clearly in Figure 5, which displays the same data in a different way and extends the time period back to 1870. Here we plot not the *level* of real GDP each year but, rather, its *growth rate*—the percentage change from one year to the next. Now the booms and busts that delight and distress people—and swing elections—stand out clearly. For example, the fact that real GDP grew by over 7 percent from 1983 to 1984 helped ensure Ronald Reagan's landslide reelection. Then, from 1990 to 1991, real GDP actually fell by 1 percent, which helped Bill Clinton defeat George H. W. Bush. On the other hand, weak economic growth from 2000 to 2004 did not prevent George W. Bush's reelection.

Inflation and Deflation

The history of the inflation rate depicted in Figure 6 on the next page also shows more positive numbers than negative ones—more inflation than **deflation**. Although the price level has risen nearly 16-fold since 1869, the upward trend is of rather recent vintage. Prior to World War II, Figure 6 shows periods of inflation and deflation, with little or no tendency for one to be more common than the other. Indeed, prices in 1940 were barely higher than those at the close of the Civil War. However, the figure does show some large gyrations in the inflation rate, including sharp bursts of inflation during and immediately after the two world wars and dramatic deflations in the 1870s, the 1880s, 1921–1922, and 1929–1933. Recently, as you can see, inflation has been both low and stable.

Deflation refers to a sustained decrease in the general price level.

| **FIGURE 5** | **The Growth Rate of U.S. Real Gross Domestic Product since 1870** |

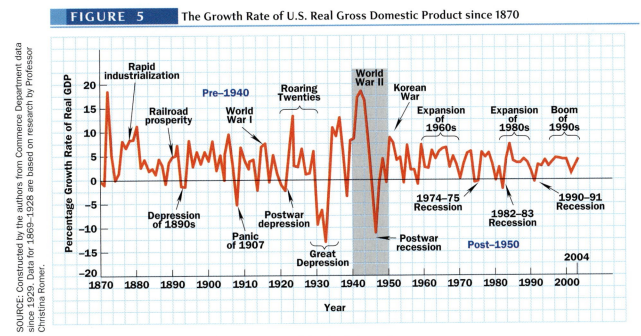

SOURCE: Constructed by the authors from Commerce Department data since 1929. Data for 1869–1928 are based on research by Professor Christina Romer.

Does the growth rate look smoother to the right of the shaded area?

---

[6] The 2001 recession was so mild that real GDP for the full year 2001 was actually higher than in 2000.

| FIGURE 6 | The Inflation Rate in the United States since 1870 |

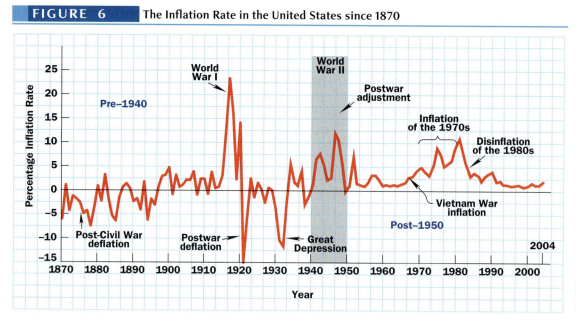

SOURCE: Constructed by the authors from Commerce Department data since 1929. Data for 1869–1928 are based on research by Professor Christina Romer.

In sum, although both real GDP, which measures the economy's output, and the price level have grown a great deal over the past 137 years, neither has grown smoothly. The ups and downs of both real growth and inflation are important economic events that need to be explained. The remainder of Part VI, which develops a model of aggregate supply and demand, and Part VII, which explains the tools the government uses to try to manage aggregate demand, will build a macroeconomic theory designed to do precisely that.

■ The Great Depression

As you look at these graphs, the Great Depression of the 1930s is bound to catch your eye. The decline in economic activity from 1929 to 1933 indicated in Figure 5 was the most severe in our nation's history, and the rapid deflation in Figure 6 was extremely unusual. The Depression is but a dim memory now, but those who lived through it—including some of your grandparents—will never forget it.

Human Consequences   Statistics often conceal the human consequences and drama of economic events. But in the case of the Great Depression, they stand as bitter testimony to its severity. The production of goods and services dropped an astonishing 30 percent, business investment almost dried up entirely, and the unemployment rate rose ominously from about 3 percent in 1929 to 25 percent in 1933—one person in four was jobless! From the data alone, you can conjure up pictures of soup lines, beggars on street corners, closed factories, and homeless families. (See "Life in 'Hooverville.'")

The Great Depression was a worldwide event; no country was spared its ravages. It literally changed the histories of many nations. In Germany, it facilitated the ascendancy of Nazism. In the United States, it enabled Franklin Roosevelt to engineer one of the most dramatic political realignments in our history and to push through a host of political and economic reforms.

Life in "Hooverville"

During the worst years of the Great Depression, unemployed workers congregated in shantytowns on the outskirts of many major cities. With a heavy dose of irony, these communities were known as "Hoovervilles," in honor of the then-president of the United States, Herbert Hoover. A contemporary observer described a Hooverville in New York City as follows:

> It was a fairly popular "development" made up of a hundred or so dwellings, each the size of a dog house or chickencoop, often constructed with much ingenuity out of wooden boxes, metal cans, strips of cardboard or old tar paper. Here human beings lived on the margin of civilization by foraging for garbage, junk, and waste lumber. I found some . . . picking through heaps of rubbish they had gathered before their doorways or cooking over open fires or battered oilstoves. Still others spent their days improving their rent-free homes . . . Most of them, according to the police, lived by begging or trading in junk; when all else failed they ate at the soup kitchens or public canteens . . . They lived in fear of being forcibly removed by the authorities, though the neighborhood people in many cases helped them and the police tolerated them for the time being.

SOURCE: © Culver Pictures

SOURCE: Mathew Josephson, *Infidel in the Temple* (New York: Knopf; 1967), pp. 82–83.

A Revolution in Economic Thought   The worldwide depression also caused a much-needed revolution in economic thinking. Until the 1930s, the prevailing economic theory held that a capitalist economy occasionally misbehaved but had a natural tendency to cure recessions or inflations by itself. The roller coaster bounced around but did not run off the tracks.

But the stubbornness of the Great Depression shook almost everyone's faith in the ability of the economy to correct itself. In England, this questioning attitude led John Maynard Keynes, one of the world's most renowned economists, to write *The General Theory of Employment, Interest, and Money* (1936). Probably the most important economics book of the twentieth century, it carried a rather revolutionary message. Keynes rejected the idea that the economy naturally gravitated toward smooth growth and high levels of employment, asserting instead that if pessimism led businesses and consumers to curtail their spending, the economy might be condemned to years of stagnation.

In terms of our simple aggregate demand–aggregate supply framework, Keynes was suggesting that there were times when the aggregate demand curve shifted inward—as depicted in Figure 2 on page 471. As that figure showed, the consequence would be declining output and deflation.

This doleful prognosis sounded all too realistic at the time. But Keynes closed his book on a hopeful note by showing how certain government actions—the things we now call monetary and fiscal policy—might prod the economy out of a depressed state. The lessons he taught the world then are among the lessons we will be learning in the rest of Part VI and in Part VII—along with many qualifications that economists have learned since 1936. These lessons show how governments can manage their economies so that recessions will not turn into depressions and depressions will not last as long as the Great Depression.

SOURCE: © Corbis

John Maynard Keynes

While Keynes was working on *The General Theory*, he wrote his friend George Bernard Shaw that, "I believe myself to be writing a book on economic theory which will largely revolutionize . . . the way the world thinks about economic problems." In many ways, he was right.

From World War II to 1973

The government's **fiscal policy** is its plan for spending and taxation. It can be used to steer aggregate demand in the desired direction.

The Great Depression finally ended when the United States mobilized for war in the early 1940s. As government spending rose to extraordinarily high levels, it gave aggregate demand a big boost. Thus, **fiscal policy** was (accidentally) being used in a big way. The economy boomed, and the unemployment rate fell as low as 1.2 percent during the war.

Figure 1(b) on page 470 suggested that spending spurts such as this one should lead to inflation. But much of the *potential* inflation during World War II was contained by price controls. With prices held below the levels at which quantity supplied equaled quantity demanded, shortages of consumer goods were common. Sugar, butter, gasoline, cloth, and a host of other goods were strictly rationed. When controls were lifted after the war, prices shot up.

A period of strong growth marred by several recessions after the war then gave way to the fabulous 1960s, a period of unprecedented—and noninflationary—growth that was credited to the success of the economic policies that Keynes had prescribed in the 1930s. For a while, it looked as if we could avoid both unemployment and inflation, as aggregate demand and aggregate supply expanded in approximate balance (as depicted in Figure 3 on page 471). But the optimistic verdicts proved premature on both counts.

Inflation came first, beginning about 1966. Its major cause, as it had been so many times in the past, was high levels of wartime spending. The Vietnam War pushed aggregate demand up too fast. Later, unemployment also rose when the economy ground to a halt in 1969. Despite a short and mild recession, inflation continued at 5 to 6 percent per year. Faced with persistent inflation, President Richard Nixon stunned the nation by instituting wage and price controls in 1971, the first time this tactic had ever been employed in peacetime. The controls program held inflation in check for a while. But inflation worsened dramatically in 1973, mainly because of an explosion in food prices caused by poor harvests around the world.

The Great Stagflation, 1973–1980

In 1973 things began to get much worse, not only for the United States, but for all oil-importing nations. A war between Israel and the Arab nations precipitated a quadrupling of oil prices by the Organization of Petroleum Exporting Countries (OPEC). At the same time, continued poor harvests in many parts of the globe pushed world food prices higher. Prices of other raw materials also skyrocketed. By unhappy coincidence, these events came just as the Nixon administration was lifting wage and price controls. Just as had happened after World War II, the elimination of controls led to a temporary acceleration of inflation as prices that had been held artificially low were allowed to rise. For all these reasons, the inflation rate in the United States soared above 12 percent during 1974.

Stagflation is inflation that occurs while the economy is growing slowly ("stagnating") or in a recession.

Meanwhile, the U.S. economy was slipping into what was, up to then, its longest and most severe recession since the 1930s. Real GDP fell between late 1973 and early 1975, and the unemployment rate rose to nearly 9 percent. With both inflation and unemployment unusually virulent in 1974 and 1975, the press coined a new term—**stagflation**—

to refer to the simultaneous occurrence of economic *stag*nation and rapid in*flation.* Conceptually, what was happening in this episode is that the economy's aggregate supply curve, which normally moves outward from one year to the next, shifted *inward* instead. When this happens, the economy moves from a point like *E* to a point like *A* in Figure 7. Real GDP declines as the price level rises.

Thanks to a combination of government actions and natural economic forces, the economy recovered. Unfortunately, stagflation came roaring back in 1979 when the price of oil soared again. This time, inflation hit the astonishing rate of 16 percent in the first half of 1980, and the economy sagged.

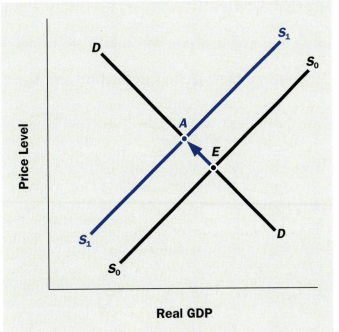

FIGURE 7

The Effects of an Adverse Supply Shift

Reaganomics and Its Aftermath

Recovery was under way when President Ronald Reagan assumed office in January 1981, but high inflation seemed deeply ingrained. The new president promised to change things with a package of policies—mainly large tax cuts—that, he claimed, would both boost growth and reduce inflation.

However, the Federal Reserve under Paul Volcker was already deploying **monetary policy** to fight inflation—which meant using excruciatingly high interest rates to deter spending. So while inflation did fall, the economy also slumped—into its worst recession since the Great Depression. When the 1981–1982 recession hit bottom, the unemployment rate was approaching 11 percent, the financial markets were in disarray, and the word *depression* had reentered the American vocabulary. The U.S. government also acquired chronically large budget deficits, far larger than anyone had dreamed possible only a few years before. This problem remained with us for about fifteen years.

The recovery that began in the winter of 1982–1983 proved to be vigorous and long lasting. Unemployment fell more or less steadily for about six years, eventually dropping below 5.5 percent. Meanwhile, inflation remained tame. These developments provided an ideal economic platform on which George H. W. Bush ran succeed Reagan—and to continue his policies.

But, unfortunately for the first President Bush, the good times did not keep rolling. Shortly after he took office, inflation began to accelerate a bit, and Congress enacted a deficit-reduction package (including a tax increase) not entirely to the president's liking. Then, in mid-1990, the U.S. economy slumped into another recession—precipitated by yet another spike in oil prices before the Persian Gulf War. When the recovery from the 1990–1991 recession proved to be sluggish, candidate

Monetary policy refers to actions taken by the Federal Reserve to influence aggregate demand by changing interest rates.

Bill Clinton hammered away at the lackluster economic performance of the Bush years. His message apparently resonated with American voters.

Clintonomics: Deficit Reduction and the "New Economy"[7]

Although candidate Clinton ran on a platform that concentrated on spurring economic growth, the yawning budget deficit forced President Clinton to concentrate on deficit reduction instead. A politically contentious package of tax increases and spending cuts barely squeaked through Congress in August 1993, and a second deficit-reduction package passed in 1997. Transforming the huge federal budget deficit into a large surplus turned out to be the crowning achievement of Clinton's economic policy.

Whether by cause or coincidence, the national economy boomed during President Clinton's eight years in office. Business spending perked up, the stock market soared, unemployment fell rapidly, and even inflation drifted lower. Why did all these wonderful things happen at once? Some optimists heralded the arrival of an exciting "New Economy"—a product of globalization and computerization—that naturally performs better than the economy of the past.

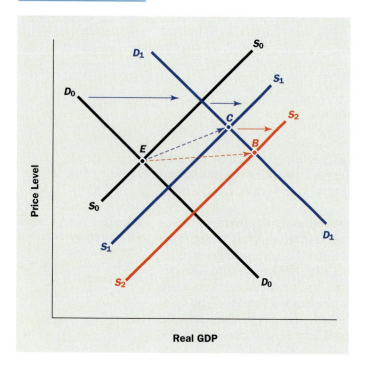

FIGURE 8

The Effects of a Favorable Supply Shift

Real GDP

The new economy was certainly an alluring vision. But was it real? Most mainstream economists would answer: yes and no. On the one hand, advances in computer and information technology did seem to lead to faster growth in the second half of the 1990s. In that respect, we did get a "New Economy." But something more mundane also happened: A variety of transitory factors pushed the economy's aggregate supply curve outward at an unusually rapid pace between 1996 and 1998. When this happens, the expected result is faster economic growth and lower inflation, as Figure 8 shows.

Figure 8 takes the graphical analysis of economic growth from Figure 3 and adds a new aggregate supply curve, S_2S_2, which lies to the right of S_1S_1. With supply curve S_2S_2 instead of S_1S_1, the economy moves from point E not just to point C, as in the earlier figure, but all the way to point B. Comparing B to C, we see that the economy winds up both farther to the right (that is, it grows faster) and lower (that is, it experiences less inflation). That, in a nutshell, is how our simple aggregate demand–aggregate supply framework explains this episode of recent U.S. economic history.

The Bush Economy and the 2004 Election

The Clinton boom ended around the middle of 2000—just before the election of President George W. Bush. Real GDP grew very slowly in the second half of 2000 and then actually *declined* for two quarters of 2001. Ironically, it was the first recession in the United States in ten years—when President Bush's father was in office.

---

[7] One of the authors of this book was a member of President Clinton's original Council of Economic Advisers.

The tax cut of 2001 turned out to be remarkably well timed, however, and the war on terrorism led to a burst of government spending. Both of these components of fiscal policy helped shift the aggregate demand curve outward, thereby mitigating the recession. (Refer back to Figure 1(b) on page 470.) The Federal Reserve under Alan Greenspan also lowered interest rates to encourage more spending. The recession ended late in 2001. But the recovery was extremely weak until the spring of 2003, when growth finally picked up—remaining strong until 2006. The tax cuts of 2001–2003, however, brought back large budget deficits—a problem that remains with us today.

? ISSUE REVISITED: *Was It George Bush's Fault?*

As we noted at the start of this chapter, the weak economy proved to be one of the major issues of the 2004 presidential election. Total employment in the United States fell from early 2001 right through the summer of 2003, and then turned up rather weakly at first. The Kerry campaign naturally blamed the poor jobs performance on George Bush. Then, when job growth finally accelerated in 2004, the incumbent president argued that his tax cuts deserved the credit. Who was right?

In fact, there were elements of both truth and exaggeration in both men's claims. And you will be in a much better position to form your own opinion after you have studied the coming chapters. But, in a nutshell, the tax cuts clearly did help boost aggregate demand and employment. That said, most objective observers agree that (a) tax cuts of that magnitude could have been better designed to boost aggregate demand, and (b) the 2003 War in Iraq—which was certainly not *economic* policy— proved to be a major drag on the economy. Nonetheless, the voters gave President Bush a second term. In that sense, he was not "blamed" (or not blamed too much) for the poor record of job creation.

■ THE PROBLEM OF MACROECONOMIC STABILIZATION: A SNEAK PREVIEW

This brief look at the historical record shows that our economy has not generally produced steady growth without inflation. Rather, it has been buffeted by periodic bouts of unemployment or inflation, and sometimes it has been plagued by both. We have also hinted that government policies may have had something to do with this performance. Let us now expand upon and systematize this hint.

To provide a preliminary analysis of **stabilization policy,** the name given to government programs designed to shorten recessions and to counteract inflation, we can once again use the basic tools of aggregate supply and demand analysis. To facilitate this discussion, we have reproduced as Figures 9 and 10 two diagrams found earlier in this chapter, but we now give them slightly different interpretations.

Stabilization policy is the name given to government programs designed to prevent or shorten recessions and to counteract inflation (that is, to *stabilize* prices).

■ Combating Unemployment

Figure 9 offers a simplified view of government policy to fight unemployment. Suppose that, in the absence of government intervention, the economy would reach an equilibrium at point E, where the aggregate demand curve D_0D_0 crosses the aggregate supply curve SS. Now if the output corresponding to point E is too low, leaving many workers unemployed, *the government can reduce unemployment by increasing aggregate demand.* Subsequent chapters will consider in detail how this is done. But our brief historical review has already mentioned three methods:

FIGURE 9

Stabilization Policy to
Fight Unemployment

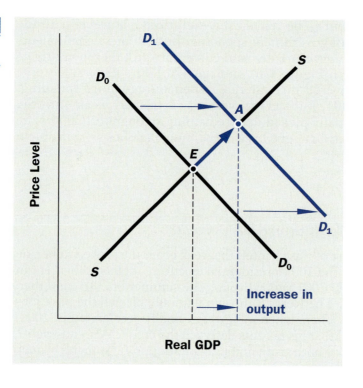

Real GDP

Congress can spend more or reduce taxes ("fiscal policy"), and the Federal Reserve can lower interest rates ("monetary policy"). In the diagram, any of these actions would shift the demand curve outward to D_1D_1, causing equilibrium to move to point A. In general:

Recessions and unemployment are often caused by insufficient aggregate demand. When such situations occur, fiscal or monetary policies that successfully augment demand can be effective ways to increase output and reduce unemployment. But they also normally raise prices.

◼ Combating Inflation

The opposite type of demand management is called for when inflation is the main macroeconomic problem. Figure 10 illustrates this case. Here again, point E, the intersection of aggregate demand curve D_0D_0 and aggregate supply curve SS, is the equilibrium the economy would reach in the absence of government policy. But now suppose the price level corresponding to point E is considered "too high," meaning that the price level would be rising too rapidly if the economy were to move to point E. A government program that reduces demand from D_0D_0 to D_2D_2 (for example, a reduction in government spending) can keep prices down and thereby reduce inflation. Thus:

FIGURE 10

Stabilization Policy to
Fight Inflation

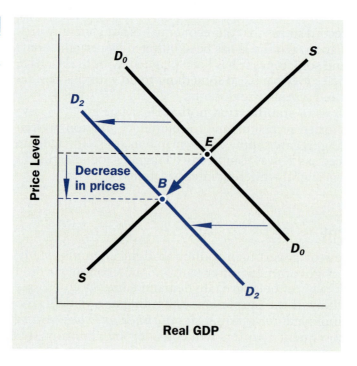

Real GDP

Inflation is frequently caused by aggregate demand racing ahead too fast. When this is the case, fiscal or monetary policies that reduce aggregate demand can be effective anti-inflationary devices. But such policies also decrease real GDP and raise unemployment.

This, in brief, summarizes the *intent* of stabilization policy. When aggregate demand fluctuations are the source of economic instability, the government can limit both recessions and inflations by pushing aggregate demand ahead when it would otherwise lag, and restraining it when it would otherwise grow too quickly.

■ Does It Really Work?

Can the government actually stabilize the economy, as these simple diagrams suggest? That is a matter of some debate—a debate that is important enough to constitute one of our *Ideas for Beyond the Final Exam.*

We will deal with the pros and cons in Part VII. But a look back at Figures 5 and 6 (pages 477–478) may be instructive right now. First, cover the portions of the two figures that deal with the period after 1940, the portions from the shaded area rightward in each figure. The picture that emerges for the 1870–1940 period is that of an economy with frequent and sometimes quite pronounced fluctuations.

Now do the reverse. Cover the data before 1950 and look only at the postwar period. There is indeed a difference. Instances of negative real GDP growth are less common and business fluctuations look less severe. Although government policies have not achieved perfection, things do look much better.

When we turn to inflation, however, matters look rather worse. Gone are the periods of deflation and price stability that occurred before World War II. Prices now seem only to rise. This quick tour through the data suggests that something *has* changed. The U.S. economy behaved differently from 1950 to 2006 than it did from 1870 to 1940.

IDEAS FOR BEYOND THE FINAL EXAM

Although controversy over this point continues, many economists attribute this shift in the economy's behavior to lessons the government has learned about managing the economy—lessons you will be learning in Part VII. When you look at the prewar data, you see the fluctuations of an unmanaged economy that went through booms and recessions for "natural" economic reasons. The government did little about either. When you examine the postwar data, on the other hand, you see an economy that has been increasingly managed by government policy—sometimes successfully and sometimes unsuccessfully. Although the recessions are less severe, this improvement has come at a cost: The economy appears to be more inflation-prone than it was in the more distant past. These two changes in our economy may be connected. But to understand why, we will have to provide some relevant economic theory.

We have, in a sense, spent much of this chapter running before we have learned to walk—that is, we have been using aggregate demand and aggregate supply curves extensively before developing the theory that underlies them. That is the task before us in the rest of Part VI.

SUMMARY

1. Microeconomics studies the decisions of individuals and firms, the ways in which these decisions interact, and their influence on the allocation of a nation's resources and the distribution of income. Macroeconomics looks at how entire economies behave and studies the pressing social problems of economic growth, inflation, and unemployment.

2. Although they focus on different subjects, microeconomics and macroeconomics rely on virtually identical tools. Both use the supply and demand analysis introduced in Chapter 4.

3. Macroeconomic models use abstract concepts like "the price level" and "gross domestic product" that are derived by combining many different markets into one. This process is known as **aggregation;** it should not be taken literally but rather viewed as a useful approximation.

4. The best specific measure of the nation's economic output is **gross domestic product (GDP),** which is obtained by adding up the money values of all **final goods and services** produced in a given year. These outputs can be evaluated at current market prices (to get **nominal GDP**) or at some

fixed set of prices (to get **real GDP**). Neither **intermediate goods** nor transactions that take place outside organized markets are included in GDP.

5. GDP measures an economy's production, not the increase in its well-being. For example, the GDP places no value on housework, other do-it-yourself activities, or leisure time. On the other hand, even commodities that might be considered as "bads" rather than "goods" are counted in the GDP (for example, activities that harm the environment).

6. America's economic history shows steady growth punctuated by periodic **recessions**—that is, periods in which real GDP declined. Although the distant past included some periods of falling prices **(deflation)**, more recent history shows only rising prices **(inflation)**.

7. The Great Depression of the 1930s was the worst in U.S. history. It profoundly affected both our nation and countries throughout the world. It also led to a revolution in economic thinking, thanks largely to the work of John Maynard Keynes.

8. From World War II to the early 1970s, the American economy exhibited steadier growth than in the past. Many observers attributed this more stable performance to the implementation of the **monetary and fiscal policies** (collectively called **stabilization policy**) that Keynes had suggested. At the same time, however, the price level seems only to rise—never to fall—in the modern economy. The economy seems to have become more "inflation-prone."

9. Between 1973 and 1991, the U.S. economy suffered through several serious recessions. In the first part of that period, inflation was also unusually virulent. This unhappy combination of economic stagnation with rapid inflation was nicknamed **"stagflation."** Since 1982, however, inflation has been low and has dropped recently.

10. The United States enjoyed a boom in the 1990s, and unemployment fell to its lowest level in thirty years. Yet inflation also fell. One explanation for this happy combination of rapid growth and low inflation is that the **aggregate supply curve** shifted out unusually rapidly.

11. One major cause of inflation is that aggregate demand may grow more quickly than does aggregate supply. In such a case, a government policy that reduces aggregate demand may be able to stem the inflation.

12. Recessions often occur because aggregate demand grows too slowly. In this case, a government policy that stimulates demand may be an effective way to fight the recession.

KEY TERMS

Aggregation   469

Aggregate demand curve   471

Aggregate supply curve   471

Inflation   472

Recession   472

Gross domestic product (GDP)   472

Nominal GDP   472

Real GDP   472

Final goods and services   473

Intermediate good   473

Real GDP per capita   476

Deflation   477

Fiscal policy   480

Stagflation   480

Monetary policy   481

Stabilization policy   483

TEST YOURSELF

1. Which of the following problems are likely to be studied by a microeconomist and which by a macroeconomist?

   a. The rapid growth of Microsoft

   b. Why unemployment in the United States rose from 2000 to 2001

   c. Why Japan's economy grew faster than the U.S. economy in the 1980s, but slower in the 1990s

   d. Why college tuition costs have risen so rapidly in recent years

2. Use an aggregate supply and demand diagram to study what would happen to an economy in which the aggregate supply curve never moved while the aggregate demand curve shifted outward year after year.

3. Which of the following transactions are included in gross domestic product, and by how much does each raise GDP?

   a. Smith pays a carpenter $25,000 to build a garage.

   b. Smith purchases $5,000 worth of materials and builds himself a garage, which is worth $25,000.

   c. Smith goes to the woods, cuts down a tree, and uses the wood to build himself a garage that is worth $25,000.

   d. The Jones family sells its old house to the Reynolds family for $200,000. The Joneses then buy a newly constructed house from a builder for $250,000.

   e. You purchase a used computer from a friend for $100.

f. Your university purchases a new mainframe computer from IBM, paying $50,000.

g. You win $300 in an Atlantic City casino.

h. You make $300 in the stock market.

i. You sell a used economics textbook to your college bookstore for $30.

j. You buy a new economics textbook from your college bookstore for $60.

DISCUSSION QUESTIONS

1. You probably use "aggregates" frequently in everyday discussions. Try to think of some examples. (Here is one: Have you ever said, "The students at this college generally think . . ."? What, precisely, did you mean?)

2. Try asking a friend who has not studied economics in which year he or she thinks prices were higher: 1870 or 1900? 1920 or 1940? (In both cases, prices were higher in the earlier year.) Most young people think that prices have always risen. Why do you think they have this opinion?

3. Give some reasons why gross domestic product is not a suitable measure of the well-being of the nation. (Have you noticed newspaper accounts in which journalists seem to use GDP for this purpose?)

THE GOALS OF MACROECONOMIC POLICY

When men are employed, they are best contented.

BENJAMIN FRANKLIN

Inflation is repudiation.

CALVIN COOLIDGE

Someone once quipped that you could turn a parrot into an economist by teaching him just two words: supply and demand. And now that you have been through Chapter 4 and Chapter 22, you see what he meant. Sure enough, economists think of the process of *economic growth* as having two essential ingredients:

Inputs are the labor, machinery, buildings, and other resources used to produce outputs.

Outputs are the goods and services that the economy produces.

- The first ingredient is *aggregate supply*. Given the available supplies of **inputs** like labor and capital, and the technology at its disposal, an economy is able to produce a certain volume of **outputs,** measured by GDP. This *capacity to produce* normally increases from one year to the next as the supplies of inputs grow and the technology improves. The theory of aggregate supply will be our focus in Chapters 24 and 27.
- The second ingredient is *aggregate demand*. How much of the capacity to produce is actually *utilized* depends on how many of these goods and services people and businesses want to *buy*. We begin building a theory of aggregate demand in Chapters 25 and 26.

CONTENTS

Growth policy refers to government policies intended to make the economy grow faster in the long run.

Corresponding to these two ingredients, economists visualize a dual task for those who make macroeconomic policy. First, *policy should create an environment in which the economy can expand its productive capacity rapidly*, because that is the ultimate source of higher living standards. This first task is the realm of **growth policy,** and it is taken up in the next chapter. Second, *policy makers should manage aggregate demand so that it grows in line with the economy's capacity to produce*, avoiding as much as possible the cycles of boom and bust that we saw in the last chapter. This is the realm of *stabilization policy*. As we noted in the last chapter, inadequate growth of aggregate demand can lead to high *unemployment*, while excessive growth of aggregate demand can lead to high *inflation*. Both are to be avoided.

Thus, the goals of macroeconomic policy can be summarized succinctly as *achieving rapid but relatively smooth growth with low unemployment and low inflation*. Unfortunately, that turns out to be a tall order. In chapters to come, we will explain why these goals cannot be attained with machine-like precision, and why improvement on one front often spells deterioration on another. Along the way, we will pay a great deal of attention to both the *causes* of and *cures* for sluggish growth, high unemployment, and high inflation.

But before getting involved in such weighty issues of theory and policy, we pause in this chapter to take a close look at the three goals themselves. How fast can—or should—the economy grow? Why does a rise in unemployment cause such social distress? Why is inflation so loudly deplored? The answers to some of these questions may seem obvious at first. But, as you will see, there is more to them than meets the eye.

The chapter is divided into three main parts, corresponding to the three goals. An appendix explains how inflation is measured.

PART 1: THE GOAL OF ECONOMIC GROWTH

To residents of a prosperous society like ours, economic growth—the notion that standards of living rise from one year to the next—seems like part of the natural order of things. But it is not. Historians tell us that living standards barely changed from the Roman Empire to the dawn of the Industrial Revolution—a period of some sixteen centuries! Closer in time, per capita incomes have tragically declined in most of the former Soviet Union and some of the poorest countries of Africa in recent decades. Economic growth is *not* automatic.

Growth is also a very slow, and therefore barely noticeable, process. The typical American propably will consume about 2 percent more goods and services in 2007 than he or she did in 2006. Can you perceive a difference that small? Perhaps not, but such tiny changes, when compounded for decades or even centuries, transform societies. During the twentieth century, for example, living standards in the United States increased by a factor of more than seven—which means that your ancestors in the year 1900 consumed roughly 14 percent as much food, clothing, shelter, and other amenities as you do today. Try to imagine how your family would fare on one seventh of its current income.

PRODUCTIVITY GROWTH: FROM LITTLE ACORNS . . .

Small differences in growth rates make an enormous difference—*eventually*. To illustrate this point, think about the relative positions of three major nations—the United States, the United Kingdom, and Japan—at two points in history: 1870 and 1979. In 1870, the United States was a young, upstart nation. Although already among the most prosperous countries on earth, the United States was in no sense yet a major power. The United Kingdom, by contrast, was the preeminent economic and military power of the world. The Victorian era was at its height, and the sun never set on the

The Wonders of Compound Interest

Growth rates, like interest rates, *compound* so that, for example, ten years of growth at 3 percent per year leaves the economy *more than* 30 percent larger. How much more? The answer is 34.4 percent. To see how we get this figure, start with the fact that $100 left in a bank account for one year at 3 percent interest grows to $103, which is 1.03 × $100. If left for a second year, that $103 will grow another 3 percent—to 1.03 × $103 = $106.09, which is already more than $106. Compounding has begun.

SOURCE: © Corbis

Notice that 1.03 × $103 is $(1.03)^2$ × $100. Similarly, after three years the original $100 will grow to $(1.03)^3$ × $100 = $109.27. As you can see, each additional year adds another 1.03 growth factor to the multiplication. Now returning to answer our original question, after ten years of compounding, the depositor will have $(1.03)^{10}$ × $100 = $134.39 in the bank. Thus her balance will have grown by 34.4 percent. By identical logic, an economy growing at 3 percent per year for ten years will expand 34.4 percent in total.

You may not be impressed by the difference between 30 percent and 34.4 percent. If so, follow the logic for longer periods. After 20 years of 3 percent growth, the economy will be 80.6 percent bigger (because $(1.03)^{20}$ = 1.806), not just 60 percent bigger. After 50 years, cumulative growth will be 338 percent, not 150 percent. And after a century, it will be 1,822 percent, not just 300 percent. Now we are talking about large discrepancies! No wonder Einstein once said, presumably in jest, that compounding was the most powerful force in the universe.

The arithmetic of growth leads to a convenient "doubling rule" that you can do in your head. If something (the money in a bank account, the GDP of a country, and so on) grows at an annual rate of *g* percent, how long will it take to double? The approximate answer is 70/*g*, so the rule is often called "the Rule of 70." For example, at a 2 percent growth rate, something doubles in about 70/2 = 35 years. At a 3 percent growth rate, doubling takes roughly 70/3 = 23.33 years. Yes, small differences in growth rates can make a large difference.

British Empire. Meanwhile, somewhere across the Pacific was an inconsequential island nation called Japan. In 1870, Japan had only recently opened up to the West and was economically backward.

Now fast-forward more than a century. By 1979, the United States had become the world's preeminent economic power, Japan had emerged as the clear number two, and the United Kingdom had retreated into the second rank of nations. Obviously, the Japanese economy grew faster than the U.S. economy during this century, while the British economy grew more slowly, or else this stunning transformation of relative positions would not have occurred. But the magnitudes of the differences in growth rates may astound you.

Over the 109-year period, GDP per capita in the United States grew at a 2.3 percent compound annual rate while the United Kingdom's growth rate was 1.8 percent—a difference of merely 0.5 percent per annum, but compounded for more than a century. And what of Japan? What growth rate propelled it from obscurity into the front rank of nations? The answer is just 3.0 percent, a mere 0.7 percent per year faster than the United States. These numbers show vividly what a huge difference a 0.5 or 0.7 percentage point change in the growth rate makes, *if sustained for a long time.*

Economists define the *productivity* of a country's labor force (or **"labor productivity"**) as the amount of output a typical worker turns out in an hour of work. For example, if output is measured by GDP, productivity would be measured by GDP divided by the total number of hours of work. It is the growth rate of productivity that determines whether living standards will rise rapidly or slowly.

Labor productivity is the amount of output a worker turns out in an hour (or a week, or a year) of labor. If output is measured by GDP, it is GDP per hour of work.

PRODUCTIVITY GROWTH IS (ALMOST) EVERYTHING IN THE LONG RUN As we pointed out in our list of *Ideas for Beyond the Final Exam,* only rising productivity can raise standards of living in the long run. Over long periods of time, small differences in rates of productivity growth compound like interest in a bank account and can make an enormous difference to a society's prosperity. Nothing contributes more to material well-being, to the reduction of poverty, to increases in leisure time, and to a country's ability to finance education, public health, environmental improvement, and the arts than its productivity growth rate.

IDEAS FOR BEYOND THE FINAL EXAM

ISSUE: *Is Faster Growth Always Better?*

How fast should the U.S. economy, or any economy, grow? At first, the question may seem silly. Isn't it obvious that we should grow as fast as possible? After all, that will make us all richer. For the most part, economists agree; faster growth is generally preferred to slower growth. But as we shall see in a few pages, further thought suggests that the apparently naive question is not quite as silly as it sounds. Growth comes at a cost. So more may not always be better.

THE CAPACITY TO PRODUCE: POTENTIAL GDP AND THE PRODUCTION FUNCTION

Potential GDP is the real GDP that the economy would produce if its labor and other resources were fully employed.

The **labor force** is the number of people holding or seeking jobs.

The economy's **production function** shows the volume of output that can be produced from given inputs (such as labor and capital), given the available technology.

Questions like how fast our economy can or should grow require quantitative answers. Economists have invented the concept of **potential GDP** to measure the economy's normal capacity to produce goods and services. Specifically, potential GDP is the real gross domestic product (GDP) an economy *could* produce if its **labor force** were fully employed.

Note the use of the word *normal* in describing capacity. Just as it is possible to push a factory beyond its normal operating rate (by, for example, adding a night shift), it is possible to push an economy beyond its normal full-employment level by working it very hard. For example, we observed in the last chapter that the unemployment rate dropped as low as 1.2 percent under abnormal conditions during World War II. So when we talk about employing the labor force fully, we do not mean a measured unemployment rate of zero.

Conceptually, we estimate potential GDP in two steps. First, we count up the available supplies of labor, capital, and other productive resources. Then we estimate how much *output* these *inputs* could produce if they were all fully utilized. This second step—the transformation of inputs into outputs—involves an assessment of the economy's *technology*. The more technologically advanced an economy, the more output it will be able to produce from any given bundle of inputs—as we emphasized in Chapter 3's discussion of the production possibilities frontier.

To help us understand how technology affects the relationship between inputs and outputs, it is useful to introduce a tool called the **production function**—which is simply a mathematical or graphical depiction of the relationship between inputs and outputs. We will use a graph in our discussion.

For a given level of technology, Figure 1 shows how output (measured by real GDP on the vertical axis) depends on labor input (measured by hours of work on the horizontal axis). To read these graphs, and to relate them to the concept of potential GDP,

SOURCE: Bureau of Labor Statistics. Data pertain to the nonfarm business sector.

FIGURE 1

The Economy's Production Function

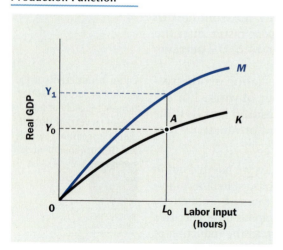

(a) Effect of better technology

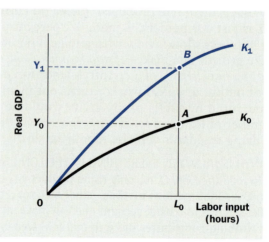

(b) Effect of more capital

begin with the black curve *OK* in Panel (a), which shows how GDP depends on labor input, *holding both capital and technology constant.* Naturally, output rises as labor inputs increase as we move outward along the curve *OK,* just as you would expect. If the country's labor force can supply L_0 hours of work when it is fully employed, then *potential GDP* is Y_0 (see point *A*). If the technology improves, the production function will shift upward— say, to the blue curve labeled *OM*—meaning that the *same* amount of labor input will now produce *more* output. The graph shows that potential GDP increases to Y_1.

Now what about capital? Panel (b) shows two production functions. The black curve OK_0 applies when the economy has some lower capital stock, K_0. The higher, blue curve OK_1 applies when the capital stock is some higher number, K_1. Thus, the production function tells us that potential GDP will be Y_0 if the capital stock is K_0 (see point *A*) but Y_1 if the capital stock is K_1 instead (see point *B*). Once again, this relationship is just what you expect: The economy can produce *more* output with the *same* amount of labor if workers have more capital to work with.

You can hardly avoid noticing the similarities between the two panels of Figure 1: Better technology, as in Panel (a), or more capital, as in Panel (b), affects the production function in more or less the same way. In general:

Either more capital or better technology will shift the production function upward and therefore raise potential GDP.

THE GROWTH RATE OF POTENTIAL GDP

With this new tool, it is but a short jump to potential growth rates. If the *size* of potential GDP depends on the size of the economy's labor force, the amount of capital and other resources it has, and its technology, it follows that the *growth rate* of potential GDP must depend on:

- The growth rate of the labor force
- The growth rate of the nation's capital stock
- The rate of technical progress

To sharpen the point, observe that real GDP is, by definition, the product of the total hours of work in the economy times the amount of output produced per hour— what we have just called *labor productivity:*

GDP = Hours of work × Output per hour = Hours of work × Labor productivity.

For example, in the United States today, using very rough numbers, GDP is about $13 trillion and total hours of work per year are about 245 billion. Thus labor productivity is roughly $13 trillion/245 billion hours = $53 per hour.

How fast can the economy increase its productive capacity? By transforming the preceding equation into growth rates, we have our answer: The growth rate of potential GDP is the *sum* of the growth rates of labor input (hours of work) and labor productivity:[1]

Growth rate of potential GDP = Growth rate of labor input + Growth rate of labor productivity

In the United States in recent decades, labor input has been increasing at a rate of about 1 percent per year. But labor productivity growth, which was very slow until the mid-1990s, has leaped upward since then—averaging about 2.8 percent per annum from 1995 to 2004 . Together, these two figures imply an estimated growth rate of potential GDP in the 3.8 percent range.

---

[1] You may be wondering about what happened to capital. The answer, as we have just seen in our discussion of the production function, is that one of the main determinants of potential GDP, and thus of labor productivity, is the amount of capital that each worker has to work with. Accordingly, the role of capital is incorporated into the productivity number.

TABLE 1
Recent Growth Rates of Real
GDP in the United States

Years	Growth Rate per Year
1994–1996	3.1%
1996–1998	4.3
1998–2000	4.1
2000–2002	1.2
2002–2004	3.2
2004–2006	3.3
1994–2006	**3.3**

SOURCE: U.S. Department of Commerce.

Do the growth rates of potential GDP and actual GDP match up? The answer is an important one to which we will return often in this book:

Over long periods of time, the growth rates of actual and potential GDP are normally quite similar. But the two often diverge sharply over short periods owing to cyclical fluctuations.

Table 1 illustrates this point with some recent U.S. data. Since 1994, GDP growth rates over two-year periods have ranged from as low as 1.2 percent per annum to as high as 4.3 percent. Over the entire 12-year period, GDP growth averaged 3.3 percent, which is probably pretty close to current estimates of the growth rate of potential GDP.

The next chapter is devoted to studying the *determinants* of economic growth and some *policies* that might speed it up. But we already know from the production function that there are two basic ways to boost a nation's growth rate—other than faster population growth and simply working harder. One is accumulating more capital. Other things being equal, a nation that builds more capital for its future will grow faster. The other way is by improving technology. When technological breakthroughs are coming at a fast and furious pace, an economy will grow more rapidly. We will discuss both of these factors in detail in the next chapter. First, however, we need to address the more basic question posed earlier in this chapter.

ISSUE REVISITED: *Is Faster Growth Always Better?*

It might seem that the answer to this question is obviously yes. After all, faster growth of either labor productivity or GDP per person is the route to higher living standards. But exceptions have been noted.

For openers, some social critics have questioned the desirability of faster economic growth as an end in itself, at least in the rich countries. Faster growth brings more wealth, and to most people the desirability of wealth is beyond question. "I've been rich and I've been poor. Believe me, honey, rich is better," singer Sophie Tucker once told an interviewer. And most people seem to share her sentiment. To those who hold this belief, a healthy economy is one that produces vast quantities of jeans, pizzas, cars, and computers.

Yet the desirability of further economic growth for a society that is already quite wealthy has been questioned on several grounds. Environmentalists worry that the sheer increase in the volume of goods imposes enormous costs on society in the form of pollution, crowding, and proliferation of wastes that need disposal. It has, they argue, dotted our roadsides with junkyards, filled our air with pollution, and poisoned our food with dangerous chemicals.

Some psychologists and social critics argue that the never-ending drive for more and better goods has failed to make people happier. Instead, industrial progress has transformed the satisfying and creative tasks of the artisan into the mechanical and dehumanizing routine of the assembly-line worker. In the United States, it seems to be driving people to work longer and longer hours. The question is whether the vast outpouring of material goods is worth all the stress and environmental damage. In fact, surveys of self-reported happiness show that residents of richer countries are no happier, on average, than residents of poorer countries.

But despite this, most economists continue to believe that more growth is better than less. For one thing, slower growth would make it extremely difficult to finance programs that improve the quality of life—including efforts to protect the environment. Such programs are costly, and economic growth makes the additional resources available. Second, it would be difficult to prevent further economic growth even if we were so inclined. Mandatory controls are abhorrent to most Americans; we cannot order people to stop being inventive and hard working. Third, slower economic growth would seriously hamper efforts to eliminate poverty—both within our own country and throughout the world. Much of the earth's population still lives in a state of extreme want. These unfortunate people are far less interested in clean air and fulfillment in the workplace than they are in more food, better clothing, and sturdier shelters.

All that said, economists concede that faster growth is not *always* better. One important reason will occupy our attention later in Parts VI and VII: An economy that grows too fast may generate inflation. Why? You were introduced to the answer at the end of the last chapter: Inflation rises when *aggregate demand* races ahead of *aggregate supply*. In plain English, an economy will become inflationary when people's demands for goods and services expand faster than its capacity to produce them. So we probably do not want to grow faster than the growth rate of potential GDP, at least not for long.

Should society then seek the maximum possible growth rate of *potential* GDP? Well, maybe not. After all, more rapid growth does not come for free. We have noted that building more capital is one good way to speed the growth of potential GDP. But the resources used to manufacture jet engines and computer servers could be used to make home air conditioners and video games instead. Building more capital imposes an obvious cost on a society: The citizens must consume less today. This point does not constitute a brief against investing for the future. Indeed, most economists believe we need to do more of that. But we must realize that faster growth through capital formation comes at a cost—an *opportunity cost*. Here, as elsewhere, you don't get something for nothing.

▦ PART 2: THE GOAL OF LOW UNEMPLOYMENT

We noted earlier that actual GDP growth can differ sharply from potential GDP growth over periods as long as several years. These *macroeconomic fluctuations* have major implications for employment and unemployment. In particular:

> When the economy grows more *slowly* than its potential, it fails to generate enough new jobs for its ever-growing labor force. Hence, *the unemployment rate* rises. Conversely, GDP growth *faster* than the economy's potential leads to a *falling unemployment rate*.

The **unemployment rate** is the number of unemployed people, expressed as a percentage of the labor force.

High unemployment is socially wasteful. When the economy does not create enough jobs to employ everyone who is willing to work, a valuable resource is lost. Potential goods and services that might have been produced and enjoyed by consumers are lost forever. This lost output is the central economic cost of high unemployment, and we can measure it by comparing actual and potential GDP.

That cost is considerable. Table 2 summarizes the idleness of workers and machines, and the resulting loss of national output, for some of the years of lowest economic activity in recent decades. The second column lists the civilian unemployment rate, and thus measures unused labor resources. The third lists the percentage of industrial capacity that U.S. manufacturers were actually using, which indicates the extent to which plant and equipment went unused. The fourth column estimates the shortfall between potential and actual real GDP. We see that unemployment has cost the people of the United States as much as an 8.1 percent reduction in their real incomes.

Although Table 2 shows extreme examples, our inability to utilize all of the nation's available resources was a persistent economic problem for decades. The red line in Figure 2 shows actual real GDP in the United States from 1954 to 2006, while the black line shows potential GDP. The graph makes it clear that actual GDP has fallen short of potential GDP more often than it has exceeded it, especially during the 1973–1993 period. In fact:

> A conservative estimate of the cumulative gap between actual and potential GDP over the years 1974 to 1993 (all evaluated in 2000 prices) is roughly $1,750 billion. At 2006 levels, this loss in output as a result of unemployment would be over two months worth of production. And there is no way to redeem those losses. The labor wasted in 1992 cannot be utilized in 2006.

TABLE 2

The Economic Costs of High Unemployment

Year	Civilian Unemployment Rate	Capacity Utilization Rate	Real GDP Lost Due to Idle Resources
1958	6.8%	75.0%	4.8%
1961	6.7	77.3	4.1
1975	8.5	73.4	5.4
1982	9.7	71.3	8.1
1992	7.5	79.4	2.6
2003	6.0	73.4	2.2

SOURCES: Bureau of Labor Statistics, Federal Reserve System, and Congressional Budget Office.

FIGURE 2

Actual and Potential GDP in the United States since 1954

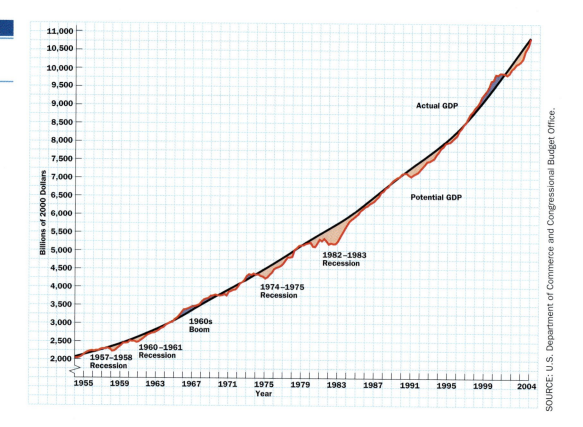

THE HUMAN COSTS OF HIGH UNEMPLOYMENT

If these numbers seem a bit dry and abstract, think about the human costs of being unemployed. Years ago, job loss meant not only enforced idleness and a catastrophic drop in income, it often led to hunger, cold, ill health, even death. Here is how one unemployed worker during the Great Depression described his family's plight in a mournful letter to the governor of Pennsylvania:

> I have been out of work for over a year and a half. Am back almost thirteen months and the landlord says if I don't pay up before the 1 of 1932 out I must go, and where am I to go in the cold winter with my children? If you can help me please for God's sake and the children's sakes and like please do what you can and send me some help, will you, I cannot find any work. . . . Thanksgiving dinner was black coffee and bread and was very glad to get it. My wife is in the hospital now. We have no shoes to were [sic]; no clothes hardly. Oh what will I do I sure will thank you.[2]

Nowadays, unemployment does not hold quite such terrors for most families, although its consequences remain dire enough. Our system of unemployment insurance (discussed later in this chapter) has taken part of the sting out of unemployment, as have other social welfare programs that support the incomes of the poor. Yet most families that still suffer painful losses of income and, often, severe noneconomic consequences when a breadwinner becomes unemployed.

Even families that are well protected by unemployment compensation suffer when joblessness strikes. Ours is a work-oriented society. A man's place has always been in the office or shop, and lately this has become true for women as well. A worker forced into idleness by a recession endures a psychological cost that is no less real for our inability to measure it. Martin Luther King Jr. put it graphically: "In our society, it is

---

[2] From *Brother, Can You Spare a Dime? The Great Depression 1929–1933*, by Milton Meltzer, p. 103. Copyright 1969 by Milton Meltzer. Reprinted by permission of Alfred A. Knopf, Inc.

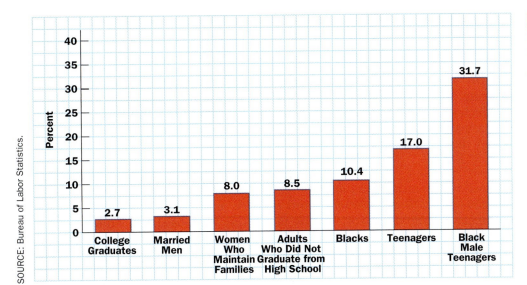

FIGURE 3

Unemployment Rates for Selected Groups, 2004

SOURCE: Bureau of Labor Statistics.

murder, psychologically, to deprive a man of a job. . . . You are in substance saying to that man that he has no right to exist."[3] High unemployment has been linked to psychological and physical disorders, divorces, suicides, and crime.

It is important to realize that these costs, whether large or small in total, are distributed most unevenly across the population. In 2005, for example, the unemployment rate among all workers averaged 5.1 percent. But, as Figure 3 shows, 10 percent of black workers were unemployed, as were 8 percent of women who maintained families. For teenagers, the situation was worse still, with unemployment at 16.6 percent, and that of black male teenagers 33.3 percent. College graduates had the lowest rate—2.3 percent. Overall unemployment varies from year to year, but these relationships are typical:

In good times and bad, married men suffer the least unemployment and teenagers suffer the most; nonwhites are unemployed much more often than whites; blue-collar workers have above-average rates of unemployment; well-educated people have below-average unemployment rates.[4]

It is worth noting that unemployment in the United States has been much lower than in most other industrialized countries in recent years. For example, during 2003, when the U.S. unemployment rate averaged 6.0 percent, the comparable figures were 6.9 percent in Canada, 9.3 percent in France, 8.8 percent in Italy, and 9.7 percent in Germany.[5]

COUNTING THE UNEMPLOYED: THE OFFICIAL STATISTICS

We have been using unemployment figures without considering where they come from or how accurate they are. The basic data come from a monthly survey of about 60,000 households conducted for the U.S. Bureau of Labor Statistics. The census taker asks several questions about the employment status of each member of the household and, on the basis of the answers, classifies each person as *employed, unemployed,* or *not in the labor force.*

The Employed   The first category is the simplest to define. It includes everyone currently at work, including part-time workers. Although some part-timers work less

---

[3] Quoted in Coretta Scott King (ed.), *The Words of Martin Luther King* (New York: Newmarket Press; 1983), p. 45.

[4] Unemployment rates for men and women are about equal.

[5] The numbers for foreign countries are based (approximately) on U.S. unemployment concepts.

than a full week by choice, others do so only because they cannot find suitable full-time jobs. Nevertheless, these workers are counted as employed, even though many would consider them "underemployed."

The Unemployed   The second category is a bit trickier. For persons not currently working, the survey first determines whether they are temporarily laid off from a job to which they expect to return. If so, they are counted as unemployed. The remaining workers are asked whether they actively sought work during the previous four weeks. If they did, they are also counted as unemployed.

Out of the Labor Force   But if they failed to look for a job, they are classified as *out of the labor force* rather than unemployed. This seems a reasonable way to draw the distinction—after all, not *everyone* wants to work. Yet there is a problem: Research shows that many unemployed workers give up looking for jobs after a while. These so-called **discouraged workers** are victims of poor job prospects, just like the officially unemployed. But when they give up hope, the measured unemployment rate—which is the ratio of the number of unemployed people to the total labor force—actually declines.

Involuntary part-time work, loss of overtime or shortened work hours, and discouraged workers are all examples of "hidden" or "disguised" unemployment. People concerned about such phenomena argue that we should include them in the official unemployment rate because, if we do not, the magnitude of the problem will be underestimated. Others, however, argue that measured unemployment overestimates the problem because, to count as unemployed, potential workers need only *claim* to be looking for jobs, even if they are not really interested in finding them.

Sticking with the official data, Figure 4 displays an interesting recent development. After climbing for about twenty-five years, the percentage of the American population at work has declined sharply from 2000 until 2004. The reasons include both rising unemployment and more discouraged workers. Figure 4 goes a long way toward explaining why Americans were so unhappy with the state of the job market in 2003 and 2004.

A **discouraged worker** is an unemployed person who gives up looking for work and is therefore no longer counted as part of the labor force.

TYPES OF UNEMPLOYMENT

Providing jobs for those willing to work is one principal goal of macroeconomic policy. How are we to define this goal?

FIGURE 4

Civilian Employment as a Percentage of Civilian Population, 1975–2004.

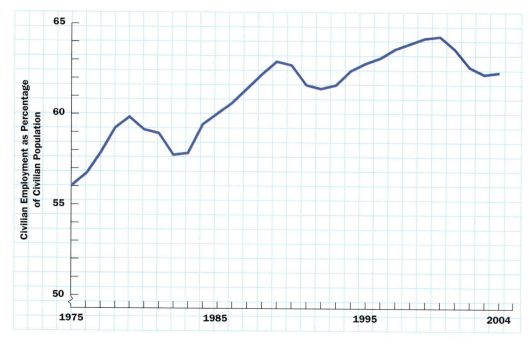

SOURCE: Bureau of Labor Statistics

POLICY DEBATE

Does the Minimum Wage Cause Unemployment?

Elementary economic reasoning—summarized in the simple supply-demand diagram to the right—suggests that setting a minimum wage (*W* in the graph) above the free-market wage (*w* in the graph) must cause unemployment. In the graph, unemployment is the horizontal gap between the quantity of labor supplied (point *B*) and the quantity demanded (point *A*) at the minimum wage. Indeed, the conclusion seems so elementary that generations of economists took it for granted. The argument seems compelling. Indeed, earlier editions of this book, for example, confidently told students that a higher minimum wage must lead to higher unemployment.

But some surprising economic research published in the 1990s cast serious doubt on this conventional wisdom.* For example, economists David Card and Alan Krueger compared employment changes at fast-food restaurants in New Jersey and nearby Pennsylvania after New Jersey, but not Pennsylvania, raised its minimum wage in 1992. To their surprise, the New Jersey stores did *more* net hiring than their Pennsylvania counterparts. Similar results were found for fast-food stores in Texas after the federal minimum wage was raised in 1991, and in

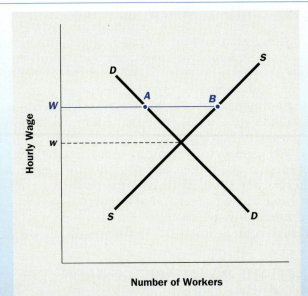

Number of Workers

California after the statewide minimum wage was increased in 1988. In none of these cases did a higher minimum wage seem to reduce employment—in contrast to the implications of simple economic theory.

The research of Card and Krueger, and of others who reached similar conclusions, was controversial from the start, and remains so. Thus, a policy question that had been deemed closed now seems to be open: Does the minimum wage really cause unemployment?

Resolution of this debate is of more than academic interest. In 1996, President Clinton recommended and Congress passed an increase in the federal minimum wage—justifying its action, in part, by the new research suggesting that unemployment would not rise as a result. In the 2004 presidential campaign, Senator Kerry advocated another increase in the minimum wage, a policy that President Bush opposed. Research can have consequences.

*See David Card and Alan Krueger, *Myth and Measurement: The New Economics of the Minimum Wage* (Princeton, N.J.: Princeton University Press; 1995).

We have already noted that a zero measured unemployment rate would clearly be an *incorrect* answer. Ours is a dynamic, highly mobile economy. Households move from one state to another. Individuals quit jobs to seek better positions or retool for more attractive occupations. These and other decisions produce some minimal amount of unemployment—people who are literally between jobs. Economists call this **frictional unemployment**, and it is unavoidable in our market economy. The critical distinguishing feature of frictional unemployment is that it is short-lived. A frictionally unemployed person has every reason to expect to find a new job soon.

A second type of unemployment can be difficult to distinguish from frictional unemployment but has very different implications. **Structural unemployment** arises when jobs are eliminated by changes in the economy, such as automation or permanent changes in demand. The crucial difference between frictional and structural unemployment is that, unlike frictionally unemployed workers, structurally unemployed workers cannot realistically be considered "between jobs." Instead, their skills and experience may be unmarketable in the changing economy in which they live. They are thus faced with either prolonged periods of unemployment or the necessity of making major changes in their skills or occupations.

The remaining type of unemployment, **cyclical unemployment**, will occupy most of our attention. Cyclical unemployment rises when the level of economic activity declines, as it does in a recession. Thus, when macroeconomists speak of maintaining "full employment," they mean limiting unemployment to its frictional and structural components—which means, roughly, producing at potential GDP. A key question, therefore, is: How much measured unemployment constitutes full employment?

Frictional unemployment is unemployment that is due to normal turnover in the labor market. It includes people who are temporarily between jobs because they are moving or changing occupations, or are unemployed for similar reasons.

Structural unemployment refers to workers who have lost their jobs because they have been displaced by automation, because their skills are no longer in demand, or because of similar reasons.

Cyclical unemployment is the portion of unemployment that is attributable to a decline in the economy's total production. Cyclical unemployment rises during recessions and falls as prosperity is restored.

HOW MUCH EMPLOYMENT IS "FULL EMPLOYMENT"?

Full employment is a situation in which everyone who is willing and able to work can find a job. At full employment, the measured unemployment rate is still positive.

President John F. Kennedy was the first to commit the federal government to a specific numerical goal for unemployment. He picked a 4 percent target, but that goal was subsequently rejected as being unrealistically ambitious. When the government abandoned the 4 percent unemployment target in the 1970s, no new number was put in its place. Instead, we have experienced a long-running national debate over exactly how much measured unemployment corresponds to **full employment**—a debate that continues to this day.

In the early 1990s, many economists believed that full employment came at a measured unemployment rate as high as 6 percent. But others disputed that estimate as unduly pessimistic. As it happened, real-world events decisively rejected the notion that the full-employment unemployment rate was 6 percent. The boom of the late 1990s pushed the unemployment rate below 5 percent by the summer of 1997, and it remained there every month until September 2001—even falling as low as 3.9 percent in 2000. All this left economists guessing where full employment might be. Official government reports issued in 2006 estimated the full-employment unemployment rate to be roughly 5 percent, but no one was totally confident in such estimates.

UNEMPLOYMENT INSURANCE: THE INVALUABLE CUSHION

Unemployment insurance is a government program that replaces some of the wages lost by eligible workers who lose their jobs.

One major reason why America's unemployed workers no longer experience the complete loss of income that devastated so many during the 1930s is our system of **unemployment insurance**—one of the most valuable institutional innovations to emerge from the trauma of the Great Depression.

Each of the fifty states administers an unemployment insurance program under federal guidelines. Although the precise amounts vary, the average weekly benefit check in 2004 was about $262, which amounted to approximately 50 percent of average earnings. Although a 50 percent drop in earnings still poses serious problems, the importance of this 50 percent income cushion can scarcely be exaggerated, especially because it may be supplemented by funds from other welfare programs. Families that are covered by unemployment insurance rarely go hungry or are dispossessed from their homes when they lose their jobs.

Eligibility for benefits varies by state, but some criteria apply quite generally. Only experienced workers qualify, so persons just joining the labor force (such as recent college graduates) or reentering after prolonged absences (such as women returning to the job market after years of child rearing) cannot collect benefits. Neither can those who quit their jobs, except under unusual circumstances. Also, benefits end after a stipulated period of time, normally six months. For all of these reasons, only some 37 percent of the roughly 8.1 million people who were unemployed in an average week in 2004 actually received benefits.

The importance of unemployment insurance to the unemployed is obvious. But significant benefits also accrue to citizens who never become unemployed. During recessions, billions of dollars are paid out in unemployment benefits. And because recipients probably spend most of their benefits, unemployment insurance limits the severity of recessions by providing additional purchasing power when and where it is most needed.

> The unemployment insurance system is one of several cushions built into our economy since 1933 to prevent another Great Depression. By giving money to those who become unemployed, the system helps prop up aggregate demand during recessions.

Although the U.S. economy is now probably "depression-proof," this should not be a cause for too much rejoicing, for the many recessions we have had since the 1950s—most recently in 2001—amply demonstrate that we are far from "recession-proof."

The fact that unemployment insurance and other social welfare programs replace a significant fraction of lost income has led some skeptics to claim that unemployment is no longer a serious problem. But the fact is that unemployment insurance is just what the name says—an *insurance* program. And insurance can never prevent a catastrophe from occurring; it simply spreads the costs among many people instead of letting all of the costs fall on the shoulders of a few unfortunate souls. As we noted earlier, unemployment robs the economy of output it could have produced, and no insurance policy can insure society against such losses.

> Our system of payroll taxes and unemployment benefits spreads the costs of unemployment over the entire population. But it does not eliminate the basic economic cost.

In that case, you might ask, why not cushion the blow even more by making unemployment insurance much more generous, as many European countries have done? The answer is that there is also a downside to unemployment insurance. When unemployment benefits are very generous, people who lose their jobs may be less than eager to look for new jobs. The right level of unemployment insurance strikes an appropriate balance between the benefit of supporting the incomes of unemployed people and the cost of raising the unemployment rate a bit.

PART 3: THE GOAL OF LOW INFLATION

Both the human and economic costs of inflation are less obvious than the costs of unemployment. But this does not make them any less real, for if one thing is crystal clear about inflation, it is that people do not like it.

With inflation very low for years now, inflation barely registers as a problem in national public opinion polls. But when inflation was high, it often headed the list—generally even ahead of unemployment. Surveys also show that inflation, like unemployment, makes people unhappy. Finally, studies of elections suggest that voters penalize the party that occupies the White House when inflation is high. The fact is beyond dispute: People dislike inflation. The question is, why?

> The **purchasing power** of a given sum of money is the volume of goods and services that it will buy.

INFLATION: THE MYTH AND THE REALITY

At first, the question may seem ridiculous. During inflationary times, people pay higher prices for the same quantities of goods and services they had before. So more and more income is needed just to maintain the same standard of living. Is it not obvious that this erosion of **purchasing power**—that is, the decline in what money will buy—makes everyone worse off?

Inflation and Real Wages

This would indeed be the case were it not for one very significant fact. The wages that people earn are also prices—prices for labor services. During a period of inflation, wages also rise. In fact, the average wage typically rises more or less in step with prices. Thus, contrary to popular myth, workers as a group are not usually victimized by inflation.

> The purchasing power of wages—what is called the **real wage rate**—is not systematically eroded by inflation. Sometimes wages rise faster than prices, and sometimes prices rise faster than wages. In the long run, wages tend to outstrip prices as new capital equipment and innovation increase output per worker.

Figure 5 illustrates this simple fact. The blue line shows the rate of increase of prices in the United States for each year since 1948, and the black line shows the rate of increase of wages. The difference between the two, shaded in red in the diagram, indicates the rate of growth of *real* wages. Generally, wages rise faster than prices, reflecting the

SOURCE: The *Wall Street Journal*–Permission, Cartoon Features Syndicate.

"Sure, you're raising my allowance. But am I actually gaining any purchasing power?"

> The **real wage rate** is the wage rate adjusted for inflation. Specifically, it is the nominal wage divided by the price index. The real wage thus indicates the volume of goods and services that the nominal wages will buy.

Calculating the Real Wage: A Real Example

The *real* wage shows not how many dollars a worker is paid for an hour of work (that is called the *nominal* wage), but rather the *purchasing power* of that money. It indicates what an hour's worth of work can buy. As noted in the definition of the real wage in the margin, we calculate the real wage by *dividing* the nominal wage by the price level. The rule is:

$$\text{Real wage} = \frac{\text{Nominal wage}}{\text{Price level}}$$

Here's a concrete example. Between 1998 and 2003, the average hourly wage in the United States rose from $13 to $15.35, an increase of 18 percent over five years. Sounds pretty good for American workers. But over those same five years, the Consumer Price Index (CPI), the most commonly-used index of the price level, rose by almost 13 percent, from 163 to 184. This means that the real wages in the two years were:

$$\text{Real wage in 1998} = \frac{\$13.00}{163} = .0798$$

$$\text{Real wage in 1998} = \frac{\$15.35}{184} = .0834$$

for an increase of just 4.5 percent over the five years, which is much less than 13 percent.[6]

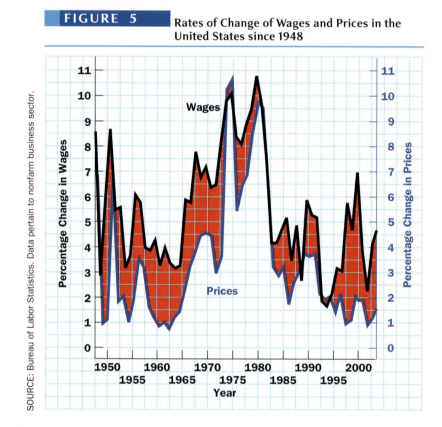

FIGURE 5   Rates of Change of Wages and Prices in the United States since 1948

SOURCE: Bureau of Labor Statistics. Data pertain to nonfarm business sector.

steady advance of labor productivity; therefore, real wages rise. But this is not always the case; the graph shows several instances in which inflation outstripped wage increases.

The feature of Figure 5 that virtually jumps off the page is the way the two lines dance together. Wages normally rise rapidly when prices rise rapidly, and they rise slowly when prices rise slowly. But you should not draw any hasty conclusions from this association. It does not, for example, imply that rising prices *cause* rising wages or that rising wages *cause* rising prices. Remember the warnings given in Chapter 1 about trying to infer causation just by looking at data. But analyzing cause and effect is not our purpose right now. We merely want to dispel the myth that inflation inevitably erodes real wages.

---

[6] As explained in the appendix, it is conventional to multiply index numbers by 100, which would make the two real wage numbers 7.98 and 8.34, respectively. That does not alter the percentage change.

Why is this myth so widespread? Imagine a world without inflation in which wages are rising 2 percent per year because of the increasing productivity of labor. Now imagine that, all of a sudden, inflation sets in and prices start rising 3 percent per year but nothing else changes. Figure 5 suggests that, with perhaps a small delay, wage increases will accelerate to 2 + 3 = 5 percent per year.

Will workers view this change with equanimity? Probably not. To each worker, the 5 percent wage increase will be seen as something he earned by the sweat of his brow. In his view, he *deserves* every penny of his 5 percent raise. In a sense, he is right because "the sweat of his brow" earned him a 2 percent increment in real wages that, when the inflation rate is 3 percent, can be achieved only by increasing his money wages by 5 percent. An economist would divide the wage increase in the following way:

Reason for Wages to Increase	Amount
Higher productivity	2%
Compensation for higher prices	3%
Total	5%

But the worker will probably keep score differently. Feeling that he earned the entire 5 percent raise by his own merits, he will view inflation as having "robbed" him of three fifths of his just deserts. The higher the rate of inflation, the more of his raise the worker will feel has been stolen from him.

Of course, nothing could be farther from the truth. Basically, the economic system rewards the worker with *the same 2 percent real wage increment for higher productivity, regardless of the rate of inflation.* The "evils of inflation" are often exaggerated because people fail to understand this point.

The Importance of Relative Prices

A related misperception results from failure to distinguish between a *rise in the general price level* and a change in **relative prices,** which is a rise in one price relative to another. To see the distinction most clearly, imagine first a *pure inflation* in which *every* price rises by 10 percent during the year, so that relative prices do not change. Table 3 gives an example in which the price of movie tickets increases from $6.00 to $6.60, the price of candy bars from 50 cents to 55 cents, and the price of automobiles from $9,000 to $9,900. After the inflation, just as before, it will still take 12 candy bars to buy a movie ticket, 1,500 movie tickets to buy a car, and so on. A person who manufactures candy bars in order to purchase movie tickets is neither helped nor harmed by the inflation. Neither is a car dealer with a sweet tooth.

But real inflations are not like this. When there is 10 percent general inflation—meaning that the "average price" rises by 10 percent—some prices may jump 20 percent or more while others actually fall.[7] Suppose that, instead of the price increases

> An item's **relative price** is its price in terms of some other item rather than in terms of dollars.

TABLE 3
Pure Inflation

Item	Last Year's Price	This Year's Price	Increase
Candy bar	$0.50	$0.55	10%
Movie ticket	6.00	6.60	10
Automobile	9,000	9,900	10

---

[7] How statisticians figure out "average" price increases is discussed in the appendix to this chapter.

	TABLE 4		
	Real-World Inflation		
Item	Last Year's Price	This Year's Price	Increase
Candy bar	$0.50	$0.50	0%
Movie ticket	6.00	7.50	25
Automobile	9,000	9,450	5

shown in Table 3, prices rise as shown in Table 4. Movie prices go up by 25 percent, but candy prices do not change. Surely, candy manufacturers who love movies will be disgruntled because it now costs 15 candy bars instead of 12 to get into the theater. They will blame inflation for raising the price of movie tickets, even though their real problem stems from the *increase in the price of movies relative to candy*. (They would have been hurt as much if movie tickets had remained at $6 while the price of candy fell to 40 cents.)

Because car prices have risen by only 5 percent, theater owners in need of new cars will be delighted by the fact that an auto now costs only 1,260 movie admissions—just as they would have cheered if car prices had fallen to $7,560 while movie tickets remained at $6. However, they are unlikely to attribute their good fortune to inflation. Indeed, they should not. What has actually happened is that *cars became cheaper relative to movies*.

Because real-world inflations proceed at uneven rates, relative prices are always changing. There are gainers and losers, just as some would gain and others lose if relative prices were to change without any general inflation. Inflation, however, gets a bad name because losers often blame inflation for their misfortune, whereas gainers rarely credit inflation for their good luck.

Inflation is not usually to blame when some goods become more expensive relative to others.

These two kinds of misconceptions help explain why respondents to public opinion polls often cite inflation as a major national issue, why higher inflation rates depress consumers, and why voters express their ire at the polls when inflation is high. But not all of the costs of inflation are mythical. Let us now turn to some of the real costs.

◼ INFLATION AS A REDISTRIBUTOR OF INCOME AND WEALTH

We have just seen that the *average* person is neither helped nor harmed by inflation. But almost no one is exactly average! Some people gain from inflation and others lose. For example, senior citizens trying to scrape by on pensions or other fixed incomes suffer badly from inflation. Because they earn no wages, it is little solace to them that wages keep pace with prices. Their pension incomes do not.[8]

This example illustrates a general problem. Think of pensioners as people who "lend" money to an organization (the pension fund) when they are young, expecting to be paid back with interest when they are old. Because of the rise in the price level during the intervening years, the unfortunate pensioners get back dollars that are worth less in purchasing power than those they originally loaned. In general:

Those who lend money are often victimized by inflation.

---

[8] The same is not true of Social Security benefits, which are automatically increased to compensate recipients for changes in the price level.

Although lenders may lose heavily, borrowers may do quite well. For example, homeowners who borrowed money from banks in the form of mortgages back in the 1950s, when interest rates were 3 or 4 percent, gained enormously from the surprisingly virulent inflation of the 1970s. They paid back dollars of much lower purchasing power than those that they borrowed. The same is true of other borrowers.

Borrowers often gain from inflation.

Because the redistribution caused by inflation generally benefits borrowers at the expense of lenders,[9] and because both lenders and borrowers can be found at every income level, we conclude that:

Inflation does not systematically steal from the rich to aid the poor, nor does it always do the reverse.

Why, then, is the redistribution caused by inflation so widely condemned? Because its victims are selected capriciously. No one legislates the redistribution. No one enters into it voluntarily. The gainers do not earn their spoils, and the losers do not deserve their fate. Moreover, inflation robs particular classes of people of purchasing power year after year—people living on private pensions, families who save money and "lend" it to banks, and workers whose wages and salaries do not adjust to higher prices. Even if the average person suffers no damage from inflation, that fact offers little consolation to those who are its victims. This is one fundamental indictment of inflation.

Inflation redistributes income in an arbitrary way. Society's income distribution should reflect the interplay of the operation of free markets and the purposeful efforts of government to alter that distribution. Inflation interferes with and distorts this process.

■ REAL VERSUS NOMINAL INTEREST RATES

But wait. Must inflation always rob lenders to bestow gifts upon borrowers? If both parties see inflation coming, won't lenders demand that borrowers pay a higher interest rate as compensation for the coming inflation? Indeed they will. For this reason, economists draw a sharp distinction between *expected* inflation and *unexpected* inflation.

What happens when inflation is fully expected by both parties? Suppose Diamond Jim wants to borrow $1,000 from Scrooge for one year, and both agree that, in the absence of inflation, a fair rate of interest would be 3 percent. This means that Diamond Jim would pay back $1,030 at the end of the year for the privilege of having $1,000 now.

If both men expect prices to increase by 6 percent, Scrooge may reason as follows: "If Diamond Jim pays me back $1,030 one year from today, that money will buy less than what $1,000 buys today. Thus, I'll really be *paying him* to borrow from me! I'm no philanthropist. Why don't I charge him 9 percent instead? Then he'll pay back $1,090 at the end of the year. With prices 6 percent higher, this will buy roughly what $1,030 is worth today. So I'll get the same 3 percent increase in purchasing power that we would have agreed on in the absence of inflation and won't be any worse off. That's the least I'll accept."

Diamond Jim may follow a similar chain of logic. "With no inflation, I was willing to pay $1,030 one year from now for the privilege of having $1,000 today, and Scrooge was willing to lend it. He'd be crazy to do the same with 6 percent inflation. He'll want to charge me more. How much should I pay? If I offer him $1,090 one year from now, that will have roughly the same purchasing power as $1,030 today, so I won't be any worse off. That's the most I'll pay."

This kind of thinking may lead Scrooge and Diamond Jim to write a contract with a 9 percent interest rate—3 percent as the increase in purchasing power that

---

[9] By the same token, *deflation* generally benefits lenders at the expense of borrowers, because the borrowers must pay back money of greater purchasing power.

Diamond Jim pays to Scrooge and 6 percent as compensation for expected inflation. Then, if the expected 6 percent inflation actually materializes, neither party will be made better or worse off by inflation.

This example illustrates a general principle. The 3 percent increase in purchasing power that Diamond Jim agrees to turn over to Scrooge is called the **real rate of interest.** The 9 percent contractual interest charge that Diamond Jim and Scrooge write into the loan agreement is called the **nominal rate of interest.** The nominal rate of interest is calculated by adding the *expected rate of inflation* to the real rate of interest. The general relationship is:

Nominal interest rate = Real interest rate + Expected inflation rate

Expected inflation is added to compensate the lender for the loss of purchasing power that the lender expects to suffer as a result of inflation. Because of this:

> Inflation that is accurately predicted need not redistribute income between borrowers and lenders. If the *expected* rate of inflation that is embodied in the nominal interest rate matches the *actual* rate of inflation, no one gains and no one loses. However, to the extent that expectations prove incorrect, inflation will still redistribute income.[10]

It need hardly be pointed out that errors in predicting the rate of inflation are the norm, not the exception. Published forecasts bear witness to the fact that economists have great difficulty in predicting the rate of inflation. The task is no easier for businesses, consumers, and banks. This is another reason why inflation is so widely condemned as unfair and undesirable. It sets up a guessing game that no one likes.

■ INFLATION DISTORTS MEASUREMENTS

So inflation imposes costs on society because it is difficult to predict. But other costs arise even when inflation is predicted accurately. Many such costs stem from the fact that people are simply unaccustomed to thinking in inflation-adjusted terms and so make errors in thinking and calculation. Many laws and regulations that were designed for an inflation-free economy malfunction when inflation is high. Here are some important examples.

■ Confusing Real and Nominal Interest Rates

People frequently confuse *real* and *nominal* interest rates. For example, most Americans viewed the 12 percent mortgage interest rates that banks charged in 1980 as scandalously high but saw the 6 percent mortgage rates of 2004 as great bargains. In truth, with inflation around 2 percent in 2004 and 10 percent in 1980, the real interest rate in 2004 (about 4 percent) was above the bargain-basement real rates in 1980 (about 2 percent).

■ The Malfunctioning Tax System

The tax system is probably the most important example of inflation illusion at work. The law does not recognize the distinction between nominal and real interest rates; it simply taxes *nominal* interest regardless of how much real interest it represents. Similarly, **capital gains**—the difference between the price at which an investor sells an asset and the price that she paid for it—are taxed in nominal, not real, terms. As a result, our tax system can do strange things when inflation is high. An example will show why.

Between 1981 and 2003, the price level roughly doubled. Consider some stock that was purchased for $20,000 in 1981 and sold for $35,000 in 2003. The investor actu-

*The **real rate of interest** is the percentage increase in purchasing power that the borrower pays to the lender for the privilege of borrowing. It indicates the increased ability to purchase goods and services that the lender earns.*

*The **nominal rate of interest** is the percentage by which the money the borrower pays back exceeds the money that she borrowed, making no adjustment for any decline in the purchasing power of this money that results from inflation.*

*A **capital gain** is the difference between the price at which an asset is sold and the price at which it was bought.*

---

[10] *Exercise:* Who gains and who loses if the inflation turns out to be only 4 percent instead of the 6 percent that Scrooge and Diamond Jim expected? What if the inflation rate is 8 percent?

ally *lost* purchasing power while holding the stock because $20,000 of 1981 money could buy roughly what $40,000 could buy in 2003. Yet because the law levies taxes on nominal capital gains, with no correction for inflation, the investor would have been taxed on the $15,000 *nominal* capital gain—even though she suffered a *real* capital loss of $5,000.

Many economists have proposed that this (presumably unintended) feature of the law be changed by taxing only real capital gains, that is, capital gains in excess of inflation. To date, Congress has not agreed. This little example illustrates a pervasive and serious problem:

> Because it fails to recognize the distinction between nominal and real capital gains, or between nominal and real interest rates, our tax system levies high, and presumably unintended, tax rates on capital income when there is high inflation. Thus the laws that govern our financial system can become counterproductive in an inflationary environment, causing problems that were never intended by legislators. Some economists feel that the high tax rates caused by inflation discourage saving, lending, and investing—and therefore retard economic growth.

Thus, failure to understand that high *nominal* interest rates can still be low *real* interest rates has been known to make the tax code misfire, to impoverish savers, and to inhibit borrowing and lending. And it is important to note that *these costs of inflation are not purely redistributive.* Society as a whole loses when mutually beneficial transactions are prohibited by dysfunctional legislation.

Why, then, do such harmful laws stay on the books? The main reason appears to be a lack of understanding of the difference between real and nominal interest rates. People fail to understand that it is normally the *real* rate of interest that matters in an economic transaction because only that rate reveals how much borrowers pay and lenders receive *in terms of the goods and services that money can buy.* They focus on the high *nominal* interest rates caused by inflation, even when these rates correspond to low real interest rates.

> The difference between real and nominal interest rates, and the fact that the real rate matters economically whereas the nominal rate is often politically significant, are matters that are of the utmost importance and yet are understood by very few people—including many who make public policy decisions.

■ OTHER COSTS OF INFLATION

Another cost of inflation is that rapidly changing prices make it risky to enter into long-term contracts. In an extremely severe inflation, the "long term" may be only a few days from now. But even moderate inflations can have remarkable effects on long-term loans. Suppose a corporation wants to borrow $1 million to finance the purchase of some new equipment and needs the loan for 20 years. If inflation averages 2 percent over this period, the $1 million it repays at the end of 20 years will be worth $672,971 in today's purchasing power. But if inflation averages 5 percent instead, it will be worth only $376,889.

Lending or borrowing for this long a period is obviously a big gamble. With the stakes so high, the outcome may be that neither lenders nor borrowers want to get involved in long-term contracts. But without long-term loans, business investment may become impossible. The economy may stagnate.

Inflation also makes life difficult for the shopper. You probably have a group of stores that you habitually patronize because they carry the items you want to buy at (roughly) the prices you want to pay. This knowledge saves you a great deal of time and energy. But when prices are changing rapidly, your list quickly becomes obsolete. You return to your favorite clothing store to find that the price of jeans has risen drastically. Should you buy? Should you shop around at other stores? Will they have also raised their prices? Business firms have precisely the same problem with their suppliers. Rising prices force them to shop around more, which imposes costs on the firms and, more generally, reduces the efficiency of the entire economy.

THE COSTS OF LOW VERSUS HIGH INFLATION

The preceding litany of the costs of inflation alerts us to one very important fact: *Predictable inflation is far less burdensome than unpredictable inflation.* When is inflation most predictable? When it proceeds year after year at a modest and more or less steady rate. Thus, the *variability of the inflation rate* is a crucial factor. Inflation of 3 percent per year for three consecutive years will exact lower social costs than inflation that is 2 percent in the first year, zero in the second year, and 7 percent in the third year. In general:

Steady inflation is more predictable than variable inflation and therefore has smaller social and economic costs.

But the *average level of inflation* also matters. Partly because of the inflation illusions mentioned earlier and partly because of the more rapid breakdown in normal customer relationships that we have just mentioned, steady inflation at 6 percent per year is more damaging than steady inflation at 3 percent per year.

Economists distinguish between *low inflation*, which is a modest economic problem, and *high inflation*, which can be a devastating one, partly on the basis of the average level of inflation and partly on its variability. If inflation remains steady and low, prices may rise for a long time, but at a moderate and fairly constant pace, allowing people to adapt. For example, inflation in the United States has been remarkably steady since 1991, never dropping below 1.6 percent nor rising above 3.4 percent.

Very high inflations typically last for short periods of time and are often marked by highly variable inflation rates from month to month or year to year. In recent decades, for example, countries ranging from Argentina to Israel to Russia have experienced bouts of inflation exceeding 100 percent or even 1,000 percent per year. (See "Hyperinflation and the Piggy Bank" on the next page.) Each of these episodes severely disrupted the affected country's economy.

The German hyperinflation after World War I is perhaps the most famous episode of runaway inflation. Between December 1922 and November 1923, when a hard-nosed reform program finally broke the spiral, wholesale prices in Germany increased by almost 100 million percent! But even this experience was dwarfed by the great Hungarian inflation of 1945–1946, the greatest inflation of them all. For a period of one year, the *monthly* rate of inflation averaged about 20,000 percent. In the final month, the price level skyrocketed 42 quadrillion percent!

If you review the costs of inflation that have been discussed in this chapter, you will see why the distinction between low and high inflation is so fundamental. Many economists think we can live rather nicely in an environment of steady, low inflation. No one believes we can survive very well under extremely high inflation.

When inflation is steady and low, the rate at which prices rise is relatively easy to predict. It can therefore be taken into account in setting interest rates. Under high inflation, especially if prices are rising at ever-increasing or highly variable rates, this is extremely difficult, and perhaps impossible, to do. The potential redistributions become monumental, and lending and borrowing may cease entirely.

Any inflation makes it difficult to write long-term contracts. Under low, creeping inflation, the "long term" may be twenty years, or ten years, or five years. By contrast, under high, galloping inflation, the "long term" may be measured in days or weeks. Restaurant prices may change daily. Airfares may go up while you are in flight. When it is impossible to enter into contracts of any duration longer than a few days, economic activity becomes paralyzed. We conclude that:

The horrors of hyperinflation are very real. But they are either absent in low, steady inflations or present in such muted forms that they can scarcely be considered horrors.

Hyperinflation and the Piggy Bank

Whereas mild inflations are barely noticeable in everyday life, hyperinflation makes all sorts of normal economic activities more difficult and transforms a society in strange and unexpected ways. This article, excerpted from the *New York Times,* illustrates some of the problems that hyperinflation created for Nicaraguans in 1989.

> For generations, Nicaraguans have guarded their savings in piggy banks. . . . But no longer. In a country where inflation recently reached 161 percent for a 2-week period, a penny saved is a penny spent. "No one wants a bank now," said a potter who has given over his kilns to making beer mugs. "We've given up even making them."
>
> The demise of the piggy bank is only the least of the complications that have vexed the public as inflation and government efforts to combat it have sent the value of the Nicaraguan córdoba fluctuating wildly . . .

SOURCE: © The Image Bank/Getty Images

That kind of uncertainty has left the banking system in shambles, despite savings accounts that offer up to 70 percent interest a month. . . . And it has left a legacy of quirks that now extends throughout the country's daily life. . . .

In many parts of the country, enterprising mechanics have converted the nation's once-precious stock of coins into something more valuable: metal washers to fit the nuts and bolts of rapidly deteriorating machinery. . . .

In Managua, it is still necessary to deposit a copper-colored 1-córdoba coin to make a pay phone call. But . . . not everybody even remembers what a 1-córdoba coin looks like, and fewer still actually own one. That is probably just as well for the phone system, because if anyone bothered to carry the coins, they could make about 26,250 phone calls for a dollar. . . .

SOURCE: Mark A. Uhlig, "Is Nicaraguan Bank an Endangered Species?" *New York Times,* June 22, 1989, p.2. Copyright © 1989 by the New York Times Company. Reprinted by permission.

LOW INFLATION DOES NOT NECESSARILY LEAD TO HIGH INFLATION

We noted earlier that inflation is surrounded by a mythology that bears precious little relation to reality. It seems appropriate to conclude this chapter by disposing of one particularly persistent myth: that low inflation is a slippery slope that invariably leads to high inflation.

There is neither statistical evidence nor theoretical support for the belief that low inflation inevitably leads to high inflation. To be sure, inflations sometimes speed up. At other times, however, they slow down.

Although creeping inflations have many causes, runaway inflations have occurred only when the government has printed incredible amounts of money, usually to finance wartime expenditures. In the German inflation of 1923, the government finally found that its printing presses could not produce enough paper money to keep pace with the exploding prices. Not that it did not try—by the end of the inflation, the *daily* output of currency exceeded 400 quadrillion marks! The Hungarian authorities in 1945–1946 tried even harder: The average growth rate of the money supply was more than 12,000 percent *per month*. Needless to say, these are not the kind of inflation problems that are likely to face industrialized countries in the foreseeable future.

But that does not mean there is nothing wrong with low inflation. We have spent several pages analyzing the very real costs of even modest inflation. A case against moderate inflation can indeed be built, but it does not help this case to shout slogans like "Creeping inflation always leads to galloping inflation." Fortunately, it is simply not true.

These children in Germany during the hyperinflation of the 1920s are building a pyramid with cash, worth no more than the sand or sticks used by children elsewhere.

SOURCE: © Camera Press/Globe Photos, Inc.

SUMMARY

1. Macroeconomic policy strives to achieve rapid and reasonably stable growth while keeping both unemployment and inflation low.

2. Only rising productivity can raise standards of living in the long run. And seemingly small differences in productivity growth rates can compound to enormous differences in living standards. This is one of our *Ideas for Beyond the Final Exam*.

3. The **production function** tells us how much output the economy can produce from the available supplies of labor and capital, given the state of technology.

4. The growth rate of **potential GDP** is the sum of the growth rate of the **labor force** plus the growth rate of **labor productivity**. The latter depends on, among other things, technological change and investment in new capital.

5. Over long periods of time, the growth rates of actual and potential GDP match up quite well. But, owing to macroeconomic fluctuations, the two can diverge sharply over short periods.

6. Although some psychologists, environmentalists, and social critics question the merits of faster economic growth, economists generally assume that faster growth of potential GDP is socially beneficial.

7. When GDP is below its potential, unemployment is above "full employment." High unemployment exacts heavy financial and psychological costs from those who are its victims, costs that are borne quite unevenly by different groups in the population.

8. **Frictional unemployment** arises when people are between jobs for normal reasons. Thus, most frictional unemployment is desirable.

9. **Structural unemployment** is due to shifts in the pattern of demand or to technological change that makes certain skills obsolete.

10. **Cyclical unemployment** is the portion of unemployment that rises when real GDP grows more slowly than potential GDP and falls when the opposite is true.

11. Today, after years of extremely low unemployment, economists are unsure where full employment lies. Some think it may be at a measured unemployment rate near 5 percent.

12. **Unemployment insurance** replaces about one half of the lost income of unemployed persons who are insured. But fewer than half of the unemployed actually collect benefits, and no insurance program can bring back the lost output that could have been produced had these people been working.

13. People have many misconceptions about inflation. For example, many believe that inflation systematically erodes **real wages** and blame inflation for any unfavorable changes in relative prices. Both of these ideas are myths.

14. Other costs of inflation are real, however. For example, inflation often redistributes income from lenders to borrowers.

15. This redistribution is ameliorated by adding the expected rate of inflation to the interest rate. But such expectations often prove to be inaccurate.

16. The **real rate of interest** is the **nominal rate of interest** minus the **expected rate of inflation**.

17. Because the real rate of interest indicates the command over real resources that the borrower surrenders to the lender, it is of primary economic importance. But public attention often is riveted on nominal rates of interest, and this confusion can lead to costly policy mistakes.

18. Because nominal—not real—**capital gains** and interest are taxed, our tax system levies heavy taxes on income from capital when inflation is high.

19. Low inflation that proceeds at moderate and fairly predictable rates year after year carries far lower social costs than does high or variable inflation. But even low, steady inflations entail costs.

20. The notion that low inflation inevitably accelerates into high inflation is a myth with no foundation in economic theory and no basis in historical fact.

KEY TERMS

Inputs   489

Outputs   489

Growth policy   490

Economic growth   490

Labor productivity   491

Potential GDP   492

Labor force   492

Production function   492

Unemployment rate   495

Discouraged workers   498

Frictional unemployment   499

Structural unemployment   499

Cyclical unemployment   499

Full employment   500

Unemployment insurance   500

Purchasing power   501

Real wage rate   501

Relative prices   503

Redistribution by inflation   504

Real rate of interest   506

Nominal rate of interest   506

Expected rate of inflation   506

Capital gain   506

TEST YOURSELF

1. Two countries start with equal GDPs. The economy of Country A grows at an annual rate of 2 percent while the economy of Country B grows at an annual rate of 3 percent. After 25 years, how much larger is Country B's economy than Country A's economy? Why is the answer *not* 25 percent?

2. If output rises by 35 percent while hours of work increase by 40 percent, has productivity increased or decreased? By how much?

3. Most economists believe that from 1994 to 2000, actual GDP in the United States grew faster than potential GDP. What, then, should have happened to the unemployment rate over those six years? Then, from 2000 to 2003, actual GDP likely grew slower than potential GDP. What should have happened to the unemployment rate over those three years. (Check the data on the inside back cover of this book to see what actually happened.)

4. Country A and Country B have identical population growth rates of 1.1 percent per annum, and everyone in each country always works 40 hours per week. Labor productivity grows at a rate of 2 percent in Country A and a rate of 2.5 percent in Country B. What are the growth rates of potential GDP in the two countries?

5. What is the *real interest rate* paid on a credit-card loan bearing 14 percent nominal interest per year, if the rate of inflation is
   a. zero?
   b. 3 percent?
   c. 6 percent?
   d. 12 percent?
   e. 16 percent?

6. Suppose you agree to lend money to your friend on the day you both enter college at what you both expect to be a zero *real* rate of interest. Payment is to be made at graduation, with interest at a fixed *nominal* rate. If inflation proves to be *lower* during your college years than what you both had expected, who will gain and who will lose?

DISCUSSION QUESTIONS

1. If an earthquake destroys some of the factories in Poorland, what happens to Poorland's potential GDP? What happens to Poorland's potential GDP if it acquires some new advanced technology from Richland, and starts using it?

2. Why is it not as terrible to become unemployed nowadays as it was during the Great Depression?

3. "Unemployment is no longer a social problem because unemployed workers receive unemployment benefits and other benefits that make up for most of their lost wages." Comment.

4. Why is it so difficult to define *full employment?* What unemployment rate should the government be shooting for today?

5. Show why each of the following complaints is based on a misunderstanding about inflation:
   a. "Inflation must be stopped because it robs workers of their purchasing power."
   b. "Inflation makes it impossible for working people to afford many of the things they were hoping to buy."
   c. "Inflation must be stopped today, for if we do not stop it, it will surely accelerate to ruinously high rates and lead to disaster."

APPENDIX *How Statisticians Measure Inflation*

■ INDEX NUMBERS FOR INFLATION

Inflation is generally measured by the change in some index of the general price level. For example, between 1974 and 2004 the Consumer Price Index (CPI), the most widely used measure of the price level, rose from 49.3 to 188.9—an increase of 283 percent. The meaning of the *change* is clear enough. But what are the meanings of the 49.3 figure for the price level of 1974 and the 188.9 figure for 2004? Both are **index numbers.**

An **index number** expresses the cost of a market basket of goods relative to its cost in some "base" period, which is simply the year used as a basis of comparison.

Because the CPI currently uses 1982–1984 as its base period, the CPI of 188.9 for 2004 means that it cost $188.90 in 2004 to purchase the same basket of several hundred goods and services that cost $100 in 1982–1984.

Now in fact, the particular list of consumer goods and services under scrutiny did not actually cost $100 in 1982–1984. When constructing index numbers, by convention the index is set at 100 in the base period. This conventional figure is then used to obtain index numbers for other years in a very simple way. Suppose that the budget needed to buy the roughly 350 items included in the CPI was $2,000 per month in 1982–1984 and $3,778 per month in 2004. Then the index is defined by the following rule:

$$\frac{\text{CPI in 2004}}{\text{CPI in 1982–1984}}$$
$$= \frac{\text{Cost of market basket in 2004}}{\text{Cost of the market basket in 1982–1984}}$$

Because the CPI in 1982–1984 is set at 100:

$$\frac{\text{CPI in 2004}}{100} = \frac{\$3,778}{\$2,000} = 1.889$$

or

$$\text{CPI in 2004} = 188.9$$

Exactly the same sort of equation enables us to calculate the CPI in any other year. We have the following rule:

$$\textbf{CPI in given year} = \frac{\textbf{Cost of market basket in given year}}{\textbf{Cost of market basket in base year}} \times \textbf{100}$$

Of course, not every combination of consumer goods that cost $2,000 in 1982–1984 rose to $3,778 by 2004. For example, a color TV set that cost $400 in 1983 might still have cost $400 in 2004, but a $400 hospital bill in 1983 might have ballooned to $2,000. The index number problem refers to the fact that there is no perfect cost-of-living index because no two families buy precisely the same bundle of goods and services, and hence no two families suffer precisely the same increase in prices. Economists call this **the index number problem:**

When relative prices are changing, there is no such thing as a "perfect price index" that is correct for every consumer. Any statistical index will understate the increase in the cost of living for some families and overstate it for others. At best, the index can represent the situation of an "average" family.

■ THE CONSUMER PRICE INDEX

The **Consumer Price Index (CPI),** which is calculated and announced each month by the Bureau of Labor Statistics (BLS), is surely the most closely watched price index. When you read in the newspaper or see on television that the "cost of living rose by 0.2 percent last month," chances are the reporter is referring to the CPI.

The **Consumer Price Index (CPI)** is measured by pricing the items on a list representative of a typical urban household budget.

To know which items to include and in what amounts, the BLS conducts an extensive survey of spending habits roughly once every decade. As a consequence, the *same* bundle of goods and services is used as a standard for ten years or so, whether or not spending habits change.[11] Of course, spending habits do change, and this variation introduces a small error into the CPI's measurement of inflation.

A simple example will help us understand how the CPI is constructed. Imagine that college students purchase only three items—hamburgers, jeans, and movie tickets—and that we want to devise a cost-of-living index (call it SPI, or "Student Price Index") for them. First, we would conduct a survey of spending habits in the base year. (Suppose it is 1983.) Table 5 represents the hypothetical results. You will note that the frugal students of that day spent only $100 per month: $56 on hamburgers, $24 on jeans, and $20 on movies.

Table 6 presents hypothetical prices of these same three items in 2004. Each price has risen by a different amount, ranging from 25 percent for jeans up to 50 percent for hamburgers. By how much has the SPI risen?

---

[11] Economists call this a *base-period weight index* because the relative importance it attaches to the price of each item depends on how much money consumers actually chose to spend on the item during the base period.

TABLE 5
Results of Student Expenditure Survey, 1983

Item	Average Price	Average Quantity Purchased per Month	Average Expenditure per Month
Hamburger	$ 0.80	70	$56
Jeans	24.00	1	24
Movie ticket	5.00	4	20
Total			$100

TABLE 6
Prices in 2004

Item	Price	Increase over 1983
Hamburger	$1.20	50%
Jeans	30.00	25
Movie ticket	7.00	40

TABLE 7
Cost of 1983 Student Budget in 2004 Prices

70 Hamburgers at $1.20	$84
1 pair of jeans at $30	30
4 movie tickets at $7	28
Total	$142

Pricing the 1983 student budget at 2004 prices, we find that what once cost $100 now costs $142, as the calculation in Table 7 shows. Thus, the SPI, based on 1983 = 100, is

$$\text{SPI} = \frac{\text{Cost of budget in 2004}}{\text{Cost of budget in 1983}} \times 100 = \frac{\$142}{\$100} \times 100 = 142$$

So, the SPI in 2004 stands at 142, meaning that students' cost of living has increased 42 percent over the 21 years.

■ USING A PRICE INDEX TO "DEFLATE" MONETARY FIGURES

One of the most common uses of price indexes is in the comparison of monetary figures relating to two different points in time. The problem is that, if there has been inflation, the dollar is not a good measuring rod because it can buy less now than it did in the past.

Here is a simple example. Suppose the average student spent $100 per month in 1983 but $140 per month in 2004. If there was an outcry that students had become spendthrifts, how would you answer the charge?

The obvious answer is that a dollar in 2004 does not buy what it did in 1983. Specifically, our SPI shows us that it takes $1.42 in 2004 to purchase what $1 would purchase in 1983. To compare the spending habits of students in the two years, we must divide the 2004 spending figure by 1.42. Specifically, *real* spending per student in 2004 (where "real" is defined by 1983 dollars) is:

$$\text{Real spending in 2004} = \frac{\text{Nominal spending in 2004}}{\text{Price index of 2004}} \times 100$$

Thus:

$$\text{Real spending in 2004} = \frac{\$140}{142} \times 100 = \$98.59$$

This calculation shows that, despite appearances to the contrary, the change in nominal spending from $100 to $140 actually represented a small *decrease* in real spending.

This procedure of dividing by the price index is called **deflating**, and it serves to translate noncomparable monetary figures into more directly comparable real figures.

Deflating is the process of finding the real value of some monetary magnitude by dividing by some appropriate price index.

A good practical illustration is the real wage, a concept we have discussed in this chapter. As we saw in the boxed insert on page 494, we obtain the real wage by dividing the nominal wage by the price level.

■ USING A PRICE INDEX TO MEASURE INFLATION

In addition to deflating nominal magnitudes, price indexes are commonly used to measure *inflation*, that is, the *rate of increase* of the price level. The procedure is straightforward. The data on the inside back cover (column 13) show that the CPI was 49.3 in 1974 and 44.4 in 1973. The ratio of these two numbers, 49.3/44.4, is 1.11, which means that the 1974 price level was 11 percent greater than the 1973 price level. Thus, the *inflation rate* between 1973 and 1974 was 11 percent. The same procedure holds for any two adjacent years. Most recently, the CPI rose from 184 in 2003 to 188.9 in 2004. The ratio of these two numbers is 188.9/184 = 1.027, meaning that the inflation rate from 2003 to 2004 was 2.7 percent.

■ THE GDP DEFLATOR

In macroeconomics, one of the most important of the monetary magnitudes that we have to deflate is the nominal gross domestic product (GDP).

The price index used to deflate nominal GDP is called the **GDP deflator**. It is a broad measure of economy-wide inflation; it includes the prices of all goods and services in the economy.

Our general principle for deflating a nominal magnitude tells us how to go from nominal GDP to real GDP:

$$\text{Real GDP} = \frac{\text{Nominal GDP}}{\text{GDP deflator}} \times 100$$

As with the CPI, the 100 simply serves to establish the base of the index as 100, rather than 1.00.

Some economists consider the GDP deflator to be a better measure of overall inflation than the Consumer Price Index. The main reason is that the GDP deflator is based on a broader market basket. As mentioned earlier, the CPI is based on the budget of a typical urban family. By contrast, the GDP deflator is constructed from a market basket that includes *every* item in the GDP—that is, every final good and service produced by the economy. Thus, in addition to prices of consumer goods, the GDP deflator includes the prices of airplanes, lathes, and other goods purchased by businesses—especially computers, which fall in price every year. It also includes government services.

For this reason, the two indexes rarely give the same measure of inflation. Usually the discrepancy is minor. But sometimes it can be noticeable, as in 2000 when the CPI recorded a 3.4 percent inflation rate over 1999 while the GDP deflator recorded an inflation rate of only 2.2 percent.

SUMMARY

1. Inflation is measured by the percentage increase in an **index number** of prices, which shows how the cost of some basket of goods has changed over a period of time.

2. Because relative prices are always changing, and because different families purchase different items, no price index can represent precisely the experience of every family.

3. The **Consumer Price Index (CPI)** tries to measure the cost of living for an average urban household by pricing a typical market basket every month.

4. Price indexes such as the CPI can be used to **deflate** nominal figures to make them more comparable. Deflation amounts to dividing the nominal magnitude by the appropriate price index.

5. The inflation rate between two adjacent years is computed as the percentage change in the price index between the first year and the second year.

6. The **GDP deflator** is a broader measure of economy-wide inflation than the CPI because it includes the prices of all goods and services in the economy.

KEY TERMS

Index number   512

Index number problem   512

Consumer Price Index   512

Deflating   513

GDP deflator   513

TEST YOURSELF

1. Below you will find the yearly average values of the Dow Jones Industrial Average, the most popular index of stock market prices, for four different years. The Consumer Price Index for each year (on a base of 1982-1984 = 100) can be found on the inside back cover of this book. Use these numbers to deflate all five stock market values. Do real stock prices always rise every decade?

Year	Dow Jones Industrial Average
1970	753
1980	891
1990	2,679
2000	10,735

2. Below you will find nominal GDP and the GDP deflator (based on 2000=100) for the years 1984, 1994, and 2004.

   a. Compute real GDP for each year.

   b. Compute the percentage change in nominal and real GDP from 1984 to 1994, and from 1994 to 2004.

   c. Compute the percentage change in the GDP deflator over these two periods.

GDP Statistics	1984	1994	2004
Nominal GDP (Billions of dollars)	3,933	7,072	11,735
GDP deflator	67.6	90.3	108.3

3. Fill in the blanks in the following table of GDP statistics:

	2002	2003	2004
Nominal GDP	10,481		11,735
Real GDP	10,083	10,398	
GDP deflator		105.7	108.2

4. Use the following data to compute the College Price Index for 2004 using the base 1982 = 100.

Item	Price in 1982	Quantity per Month in 1982	Price in 2004
Button-down shirts	$10	1	$25
Loafers	25	1	55
Sneakers	10	3	35
Textbooks	12	12	40
Jeans	12	3	30
Restaurant meals	5	11	14

5. Average hourly earnings in the U.S. economy during several past years were as follows:

1970	1980	1990	2000
$3.23	$6.66	$10.01	$13.75

Use the CPI numbers provided on the inside back cover of this book to calculate the real wage (in 1982–1984 dollars) for each of these years. Which decade had the fastest growth of money wages? Which had the fastest growth of real wages?

6. The example in the appendix showed that the Student Price Index (SPI) rose by 42 percent from 1983 to 2004. You can understand the meaning of this better if you do the following:

a. Use Table 5 to compute the fraction of total spending accounted for by each of the three items in 1983. Call these values the "expenditure weights."

b. Compute the weighted average of the percentage increases of the three prices shown in Table 6, using the expenditure weights you just computed.

You should get 42 percent as your answer. This shows that "inflation," as measured by the SPI, is a weighted average of the percentage price increases of all the items that are included in the index.

ECONOMIC GROWTH: THEORY AND POLICY

Once one starts to think about . . . [differences in growth rates among countries], it is hard to think about anything else.

ROBERT E. LUCAS, JR., 1995 NOBEL PRIZE WINNER IN ECONOMICS

Why do some economies grow rapidly while others grow slowly—or not at all? As the opening quotation suggests, there is probably no more important question in all of economics. From 1990 to 2004, according to the World Bank, the American economy grew at a 3.2 percent annual rate, while China's grew 10.3 percent per year and Russia's *declined* (on average) by 1.7 percent per year. Those are very large differences. What factors account for the disparities?

The discussion in Chapter 23 of the goal of economic growth focused our attention on two crucial but distinct tasks for macroeconomic policy makers, both of which are quite difficult to achieve:

- *Growth policy:* Ensuring that the economy sustains a high long-run growth rate of potential GDP (although not necessarily the *highest possible* growth rate).
- *Stabilization policy:* Keeping actual GDP reasonably close to potential GDP in the short run, so that society is plagued by neither high unemployment nor high inflation.

This chapter is devoted to the theory of economic growth and to the policies that this theory suggests.

Corresponding to the two tasks listed just above, there are two ways to think about what is to come in this and subsequent chapters. In discussing *growth policy* in this chapter, we will study the factors that determine an economy's *long-run* growth rate of *potential GDP*, and we will consider how policy makers can try to speed it up. When we turn to *stabilization policy*, starting in the next chapters, we will investigate how and why *actual GDP* deviates from potential GDP in the *short run* and how policymakers can try to minimize these deviations. Thus the two views of the macroeconomy complement one another.

CONTENTS

PUZZLE: *Why Does College Education Keep Getting More Expensive?*

Have you ever wondered why the cost of a college education rises more rapidly than most other prices year after year? If you have not, your parents surely have! And it's not a myth. Between 1978 and 2006, the component of the Consumer Price Index (CPI) that measures college tuition costs rose by almost 750 percent—compared to about 205 percent for the overall CPI. That is, the *relative* price of college tuition increased massively.

Economists understand at least part of the reason, and it has little, if anything, to do with the efficiency (or lack thereof) with which colleges are run. Rather, it is a natural companion to the economy's long-run growth rate. Furthermore, there is good reason to expect the relative price of college tuition to keep rising, and to rise more rapidly in faster-growing societies. Economists believe that the same explanation for the unusually rapid growth in the cost of attending college applies to services as diverse as visits to the doctor, theatrical performances, and restaurant meals—all of which also have become relatively more expensive over time. Later in this chapter, we shall see precisely what this explanation is.

SOURCE: © Jose L. Pelaez, Inc, Corbis

THE THREE PILLARS OF PRODUCTIVITY GROWTH

As we learned in the previous chapter, the growth rate of potential GDP is the *sum* of the growth rates of *hours of work* and *labor productivity*. It is hardly mysterious that an economy will grow if its people keep working harder and harder, year after year. And a few societies have followed that recipe successfully for relatively brief periods of time. But there is a limit to how much people can work or, more important, to how much they want to work. In fact, people typically want more leisure time, not longer hours of work, as they get richer. In consequence, the natural focus of growth policy is on enhancing productivity—on working *smarter* rather than working *harder*.

The last chapter introduced a tool called the *production function*, which tells us how much *output* the economy can produce from specified *inputs* of labor and capital, given the state of *technology*. The discussion there focused on two of the three main determinants of productivity growth:[1]

- The rate at which the economy builds up its stock of *capital*
- The rate at which *technology* improves

Before introducing the third determinant, let us review how these first two pillars work.

---

[1] If you need review, see pages 486–488 of Chapter 23.

■ Capital

Figure 1 resembles Figure 1 of the last chapter (see page 492). The lower curve $0K_1$ is the production function when the capital stock is some low number, K_1. Its upward slope indicates, naturally enough, that larger quantities of labor input produce more output. (Remember, technology is held constant in this graph.) The middle curve $0K_2$ is the production function corresponding to some larger capital stock, K_2, and the upper curve $0K_3$ pertains to an even larger capital stock, K_3.

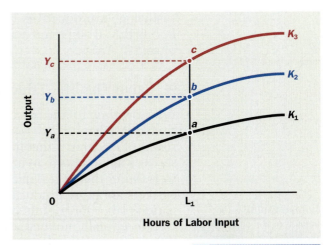

FIGURE 1

Production Functions
Corresponding to Three
Different Capital Stocks

To keep things simple at first, suppose hours of work do not grow over time, but rather remain fixed at L_1. However, the nation's businesses invest in new plant and equipment, so the capital stock grows from K_1 in the first year to K_2 in the second year and K_3 in the third year. Then the economy's capacity to produce will move up from point a in year 1 to point b in year 2 and point c in year 3. Potential GDP will therefore rise from Y_a to Y_b to Y_c. Because hours of work do not change in this example (by assumption), every bit of this growth comes from rising *productivity*, which is in turn due to the accumulation of more capital.[2] In general:

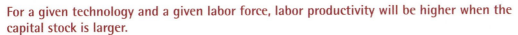

For a given technology and a given labor force, labor productivity will be higher when the capital stock is larger.

This conclusion is hardly surprising. Employees who work with more capital can obviously produce more goods and services. Just imagine manufacturing a desk, first, with only hand tools, then with power tools, and finally with all the equipment available in a modern furniture factory. Or think about selling books from a sidewalk stand, in a bookstore, or over the Internet. Your productivity would rise in each case. Furthermore, workers with *more* capital are almost certainly blessed with *newer*—and, hence, *better*—capital as well. This advantage, too, makes them more productive. Again, compare one of Henry Ford's assembly-line workers of a century ago to an autoworker in a Ford plant today.

■ Technology

In Chapter 23, we saw that a graph like Figure 1 can also be used to depict the effects of *improvements in technology*. So now imagine that curves $0K_1$, $0K_2$, and $0K_3$ all correspond to the *same* capital stock, but to *different* levels of technology. Specifically, the economy's technology improves as we move up from $0K_1$ to $0K_2$ to $0K_3$. The graphical (and commonsense) conclusion is exactly the same: Labor becomes more productive from year 1 to year 2 to year 3, so improving technology leads directly to growth. In general:

For given inputs of labor and capital, labor productivity will be higher when the technology is better.

Once again, this conclusion hardly comes as a surprise—indeed, it is barely more than the definition of technical progress. When we say that a nation's technology improves, we mean, more or less, that firms in the country can produce more output from the same inputs. And of course, superior technology is a major factor behind the

---

[2] Because productivity is the ratio Y/L, it is shown on the graph by the *slope* of the straight-line connecting the origin to point a, or point b, or point c. Clearly, that slope is rising over time.

vastly higher productivity of workers in rich countries versus poor ones. Textile plants in North Carolina, for example, use technologies that are far superior to those employed in Africa.

■ Labor Quality: Education and Training

It is now time to introduce the third pillar of productivity growth, the one not mentioned in Chapter 23: *workforce quality*. It is generally assumed—and supported by reams of evidence—that more highly educated workers can produce more goods and services in an hour than can less well-educated workers. And the same lesson applies to training that takes place outside the schools, such as on the job: Better-trained workers are more productive. The amount of education and training embodied in a nation's labor force is often referred to as its stock of **human capital.**

Human capital is the amount of skill embodied in the workforce. It is most commonly measured by the amount of education and training.

Conceptually, an increase in human capital has the same effect on productivity as does an increase in physical capital or an improvement in technology, that is, the same *quantity* of labor input becomes capable of producing more output. So we can use the ever-adaptable Figure 1 for yet a third purpose—to represent increasing *workforce quality* as we move up from $0K_1$ to $0K_2$ to $0K_3$. Once again, the general conclusion is obvious:

For a given capital stock, labor force, and technology, labor productivity will be higher when the workforce has more education and training.

This third pillar is another obvious source of large disparities between rich nations, which tend to have well-educated populations, and poor nations, which do not. So we can add a third item to our list of the principal determinants of a nation's productivity growth rate:

• The rate at which *workforce quality* (or "human capital") is improving

In the contemporary United States, average educational attainment is high and workforce quality changes little from year to year. But in some rapidly developing countries improvements in education can be an important engine of growth. For example, average years of schooling in South Korea soared from less than five in 1970 to more than nine in 1990, which contributed mightily to South Korea's remarkably rapid economic development.

Although there is no unique formula for growth, the most successful growth strategies of the post–World War II era, beginning with the Japanese "economic miracle," made ample use of all three pillars. Starting from a base of extreme deprivation after World War II, Japan showed the world how a combination of high rates of investment, a well-educated workforce, and the adoption of state-of-the-art technology could catapult a poor nation into the leading ranks within a few decades. The lessons were not lost on the so-called Asian Tigers—including Taiwan, South Korea, Singapore, and Hong Kong—which developed rapidly using their own versions of the Japanese model. Today, a number of other countries in Asia, Eastern Europe, and Latin America are trying to apply variants of this growth formula.

■ LEVELS, GROWTH RATES, AND THE CONVERGENCE HYPOTHESIS

Notice that, where productivity *growth rates* are concerned, it is the *rates of increase* of capital, technology, and workforce quality that matter, rather than their current *levels*. The distinction is important.

Productivity *levels* are vastly higher in the rich countries—that is why they are called rich. The wealthy nations have more bountiful supplies of capital, more highly skilled workers, and superior technologies. Naturally, they can produce more output per hour of work. Table 1 shows, for example, that an hour of labor in France in 1998 produced 98 percent as much output as an hour of labor in the United States, whereas the corresponding figure for Peru was only 15 percent

But the *growth rates* of capital, workforce skills, and technology are not necessarily higher in the rich countries. For example, Country A might have abundant capital, but the amount may be increasing at a snail's pace, whereas in Country B capital may be scarce but growing rapidly. When it comes to determining the long-run growth rate, it is the *growth rate* rather than the current *levels* of these underpinnings of the country's well-being that matter.

In fact, GDP per hour of work actually grew faster in several countries that have lower average incomes than the United States. For example, Table 1 shows that productivity in Ireland, France, Germany, and the United Kingdom all grew faster than the United States. Why? While a typical Irish worker in 1973 had less physical and human capital than a typical American worker, and used less advanced technology, the capital stock, average educational attainment, and level of technology probably all *increased* faster in Ireland than in the United States.

The level of productivity in a nation depends on its supplies of human and physical capital and the state of its technology. But the growth rate of productivity depends on the rates of increase of these three factors.

The distinction between productivity levels and productivity growth rates may strike you as a piece of boring arithmetic, but it has many important practical applications. Here is a particularly striking one:

If the productivity growth rate is higher in poorer countries than in richer ones, then poor countries will close the gap on rich ones. The so-called **convergence hypothesis** suggests that this is what normally happens.

The Convergence Hypothesis: The productivity growth rates of poorer countries tend to be higher than those of richer countries.

The idea behind the convergence hypothesis, as illustrated in Figure 2, is that productivity growth will typically be faster where the initial level of productivity is lower. In this hypothetical example, the poorer country starts out with a per-capita GDP of $2,000, just one fifth that of the richer country. But the poor country's real GDP per capita grows faster, so it gradually narrows the relative income gap.

Why might we expect convergence to be the norm? In some poor countries, the supply of capital may be growing very rapidly. In others, educational attainment may be rising quickly, albeit from a low base. But the main reason to expect convergence in the long run is that *low-productivity countries should be able to learn from high-productivity countries* as scientific and managerial know-how spreads around the world.

A country that is operating at the technological frontier can improve its technology only by

TABLE 1

Productivity Levels and Productivity Growth Rates in Selected Countries

Country	GDP per Hour of Work 1973 (as percentage of U.S. GDP)	GDP per Hour of Work 1998 (as percentage of U.S. GDP)	Growth Rate
United States	**100**	**100**	**1.5**
France	76	98	2.5
United Kingdom	67	79	2.2
Germany	62	77	2.4
Argentina	45	39	0.9
Ireland	41	78	4.1
Mexico	38	29	0.5
Peru	26	15	−0.7
Brazil	24	23	1.2

SOURCE: Angus Maddison, *The World Economy: A Millennial Perspective*, OECD, 2001, pp. 352–353.

The **convergence hypothesis** holds that nations with low levels of productivity tend to have high productivity growth rates, so that international productivity differences shrink over time.

FIGURE 2

The Convergence Hypothesis

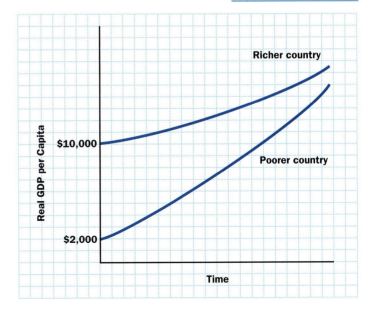

TABLE 2

GDP per Capita and GDP Growth Rates in Selected Poor Countries

Country	GDP per Capita, 2004*	GDP Growth Rate, 1990–2004
Belarus	$2,355	0.6%
Russia	4,104	−1.7
Ukraine	1,367	−4.5
Venezuela	4,214	0.8
Haiti	455	−1.2
Burundi	91	−1.1
Sierra Leone	201	−2.5

* In current U.S. dollars.

SOURCE: World Bank, World Development Indicators, 2006.

innovating. It must constantly figure out ways to do things better than it was doing them before. By comparison, a less advanced country can boost its productivity simply by *imitating*, by adopting technologies that are already in common use in the advanced countries. Not surprisingly, it is much easier to "look it up" than to "think it up."

Modern communications assist the convergence process by speeding the flow of information around the globe. The Internet was invented mainly in the United States, but it quickly spread to almost every corner of the world. Likewise, advances in human genomics and stem-cell research are now originating in some of the most advanced countries, but they are communicated rapidly to scientists all over the world. A poor country that is skilled at importing scientific and engineering advances from the rich countries can achieve very rapid productivity growth. Indeed, when Japan was a poor nation, successful imitation was one of its secrets to getting rich. India and China appear to be trying that now.

Unfortunately, not all poor countries seem able to participate in the convergence process. For a variety of reasons (some of which will be mentioned later in this chapter), a number of developing countries seem incapable of adopting and adapting advanced technologies. In fact, Table 1 shows that per-capita incomes in some of these nations actually grew more slowly than in the rich countries over the quarter-century covered by the table. Labor productivity in Mexico and Brazil both grew slower than that of the United States, and Peru's productivity actually declined. Sadly, this kind of decline is not all that unusual. Real incomes have stagnated or even fallen in some of the poorest countries of the world, especially in Africa and many of the formerly communist countries (see Table 2). Convergence certainly cannot be taken for granted.

Technological laggards can, and sometimes do, close the gap with technological leaders by imitating and adapting existing technologies. Within this "convergence club," productivity growth rates *are higher where productivity* levels *are lower. Unfortunately, some of the world's poorest nations have been unable to join the club.*

GROWTH POLICY: ENCOURAGING CAPITAL FORMATION

A nation's **capital** is its available supply of plant, equipment, and software. It is the result of past decisions to make *investments* in these items.

Investment is the *flow* of resources into the production of new capital. It is the labor, steel, and other inputs devoted to the *construction* of factories, warehouses, railroads, and other pieces of capital during some period of time.

Capital formation is synonymous with investment. It refers to the process of building up the capital stock.

Let us now see how the government might spur growth by working on these three pillars, beginning with capital.

First, we need to clarify some terminology. We have spoken of the supply of **capital,** by which we mean the volume of plant (factories, office buildings, and so on), equipment (drill presses, computers, and so on), and software currently available. Businesses *add* to the existing supply of capital whenever they make **investment** expenditures—purchases of new plant, equipment, and software. In this way, the *growth* of the capital stock depends on how much businesses spend on investment. That is the process called **capital formation**—literally, forming new capital.

But you don't get something for nothing. Devoting more of society's resources to producing investment goods generally means devoting fewer resources to producing consumer goods. A *production possibilities frontier* like those introduced in Chapter 3 can be used to depict the nature of this trade-off—and the choices open to a nation. Given its technology and existing resources of labor, capital, and so on, the country can in principle select one of the points on the production possibilities frontier shown as curve AICD in Figure 3. If it picks a point like C, its citizens will enjoy many consumer goods, but it will not be investing much for the future. *So it will grow slowly.* If, on the other hand, it selects a point like I, its citizens will consume less today, but its higher level of investment means *it will grow more quickly*. Thus, at least within limits, the amount of capital formation and growth can be chosen.

Now suppose the government wants the capital stock to grow faster, that is, it wants to move from a point like C toward a point like I in Figure 3. In a capitalist, market economy such as ours, private businesses make almost all investment decisions—how many factories and office buildings to build, how many drill presses and computers to purchase, and so on. To speed up the process of capital formation, the government must somehow persuade private businesses to invest more. But how?

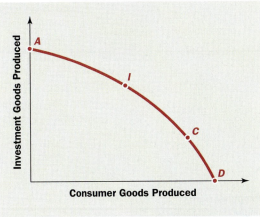

Interest Rates   The most obvious way to increase investment by private businesses is to lower real interest rates. When real interest rates fall, investment normally rises. Why? Because businesses often borrow to finance their investments, and the real interest rate indicates how much firms must pay for that privilege. An investment project that looks unattractive at an interest rate of 10 percent may look highly profitable if the firm has to pay only 6 percent.

> The amount that businesses invest depends on the real interest rate they pay to borrow funds. The lower the real rate of interest, the more investment there will be.

In subsequent chapters, we will learn how government policy, especially monetary policy, influences interest rates—which gives policy makers some leverage over private investment decisions. That relationship, in fact, is why monetary policy will play such a crucial role in subsequent chapters. But we might as well come clean right away: For reasons to be examined later, the government's ability to control interest rates is imperfect. Furthermore, the rate of interest is only one of several determinants of investment spending. So policymakers have only a limited ability to affect the level of investment by manipulating interest rates.

Tax Provisions   The government also can influence investment spending by altering various provisions of the tax code. For example, President George W. Bush and Congress agreed in 2003 to reduce the tax rate on capital gains—the profit earned by selling an asset for more than you paid for it. Perhaps the major argument for lowering capital gains taxes was the claim, much disputed by the critics, that it would lead to greater investment spending. In addition, the United States imposes a tax on corporate profits and can reduce that tax to spur investment as well. There are other, more complicated tax provisions relating to investment, too.[3] To summarize:

> The tax law gives the government several ways to influence business spending on investment goods. But influence is far from total control.

Technical Change   Technology, which we have listed as a separate pillar of growth, also drives investment. New business opportunities suddenly appear when a new product such as the mobile telephone is invented, or when a technological breakthrough makes an existing product much cheaper or better, as happened with Internet services in the 1990s. In a capitalist system, entrepreneurs pounce on such opportunities—building new factories, stores, and offices, and buying new equipment. Thus, if the government can figure out how to spur technological progress (a subject discussed later in this chapter), those same policies will probably boost investment.

---

[3] But any kind of a tax cut will reduce government revenue. Unless that revenue is made up by a spending cut or by some other tax, the government's budget deficit will rise—which will also affect investment. We will study that channel in Chapter 32.

The Growth of Demand   High growth itself can induce businesses to invest more. When demand presses against capacity, executives are likely to believe that new factories and machinery can be employed profitably—and that creates strong incentives to build new capital. Thus it was no coincidence that investment soared in the United States during the boom years of the 1990s, collapsed when the economy slowed precipitously in 2000–2001, and then revived again starting in 2003. By contrast, if machinery and factories stand idle, businesses may find new investments unattractive. In summary:

> High levels of sales and expectations of rapid economic growth create an atmosphere conducive to investment.

This situation creates a kind of virtuous cycle in which high rates of investment boost economic growth, and rapid growth boosts investment. Of course, the same process can also operate in reverse—as a vicious cycle: When the economy stagnates, firms do not want to invest much, which damages prospects for further growth.

Political Stability and Property Rights   There is one other absolutely critical determinant of investment spending that Americans simply take for granted.

A business thinking about committing funds to, say, build a factory faces any number of risks. Construction costs might run higher than estimates. Interest rates might rise. Demand for the product might prove weaker than expected. The list goes on and on. These are the normal hazards of entrepreneurship, an activity that is not for the faint-hearted. But, at a minimum, business executives contemplating a long-term investment want assurances that their property will not be taken from them for capricious or political reasons. Republican businesspeople in the United States do not worry that their property will be seized if the Democrats win the next election. Nor do they worry that court rulings will deprive them of their **property rights** without due process.

By contrast, in many less well-organized societies, the rule of law is regularly threatened by combinations of arbitrary government actions, political instability, anticapitalist ideology, rampant corruption, or runaway crime. Such problems have posed serious impediments to long-term investment in many poor countries throughout history. They are among the chief reasons these countries have remained poor. And the litany of problems that threaten property rights is not just a matter of history—these issues remain relevant in countries as different as Russia, much of Africa, and parts of Latin America today. Where businesses fear that their property may be expropriated, a drop in interest rates of, say, two percentage points will not encourage much investment.

Needless to say, the strength of property rights, adherence to the rule of law, the level of corruption, and the like are not easy to measure. Anyone who attempts to rank countries on such criteria must make many subjective judgments. Nevertheless, some results from one heroic attempt to do so are displayed in Table 3. The relative rankings of the various countries is roughly what you might expect.

Property rights are laws and/or conventions that assign owners the rights to use their property as they see fit (within the law)—for example, to sell the property and to reap the benefits (such as rents or dividends) while they own it.

TABLE 3

Selected Countries Ranked by Respect for Property Rights

Country	Rating*
Switzerland	100
Canada	98
United States	95
Japan	93
Italy	82
United Kingdom	78
South Korea	74
Brazil	68
Mexico	59
India	59
Sudan	31

* Average over the years 1986–1995.

SOURCE: Web site accompanying R. Hall and C. Jones, "Why Do Some Countries Produce So Much More Output per Worker Than Others?", *Quarterly Journal of Economics*, February 1999, http://elsa.berkeley.edu/~chad/HallJones400.asc. The index is constructed by a private company, Political Risk Services, and is based on the degree of law and order, the quality of the bureaucracy, the risk of expropriation, and the risk of government repudiation of contracts.

GROWTH POLICY: IMPROVING EDUCATION AND TRAINING

Numerous studies in many countries support the view that more-educated and better-trained workers earn higher wages. Economists naturally assume that people who earn more are more productive. Thus, more education and training presumably contribute to higher productivity. Although private institutions play a role in the educational process, in most societies the state bears the primary responsibility for educating the population. So *educational policy* is an obvious and critical component of growth policy.

To Grow Fast, Get the Institutions Right

A few years ago, the World Bank surveyed the ways the governments of around one hundred countries either encourage or discourage market activity. Its conclusion, as summarized in *The Economist*, was that "when poor people are allowed access to the institutions richer people enjoy, they can thrive and help themselves. A great deal of poverty, in other words, may be easily avoidable."

The World Bank study highlighted the importance of making simple institutions accessible to the poor—such as protection of property rights (especially over land), access to the judicial system, and a free and open flow of information—as key ingredients in successful economic development. *The Economist* put it graphically:

If it is too expensive and time-consuming, for example, to open a bank account, the poor will stuff their savings under the mattress. When it takes 19 steps, five months and more than an average person's annual income to register a new business in Mozambique, it is no wonder that aspiring, cash-strapped entrepreneurs do not bother.

The Bank's conclusion reminded many people of the central message of a best-selling 2000 book by Peruvian economist and businessman Hernando de Soto—who found to his dismay that, in his own country, it took 700 bureaucratic steps to obtain legal title to a house!

SOURCES: "Now, think small," *The Economist* September 15, 2001, pp. 40–42. Hernando de Soto, *The Mystery of Capital: Why Capitalism Triumphs in the West and Fails Everywhere Else* (New York: Basic Books), 2000.

A modern industrial society is built more on brains than on brawn. Even ordinary blue-collar jobs often require a high school education. For this reason, policies that raise rates of high school attendance and completion and, perhaps more importantly, improve the *quality* of secondary education can make genuine contributions to growth. Unfortunately, such policies have proven difficult to devise and implement. In the United States, for example, the debate over how to improve our public schools goes on and on, with no resolution in sight.

Finally, if knowledge is power in the information age, then sending more young people to college and graduate school may be crucial to economic success. It is well documented that the earnings gap between high school and college graduates in the United States has risen dramatically since the late 1970s. One graphical depiction of this rising disparity is shown in Figure 4. It shows clearly that the job market is rewarding the skills acquired in college more generously than ever before. To the extent that high wages reflect high productivity, low-cost tuition (such as that paid at many state colleges and universities), student loans to low-income families, and other policies to encourage college attendance may yield society rich dividends.

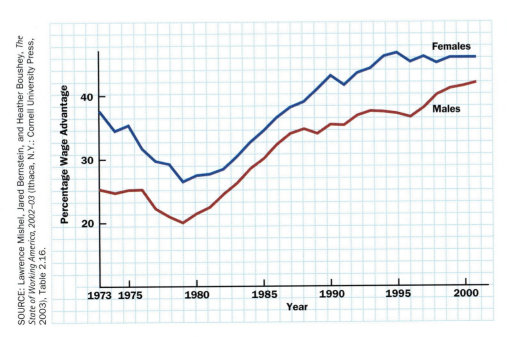

SOURCE: Lawrence Mishel, Jared Bernstein, and Heather Boushey, *The State of Working America, 2002–03* (Ithaca, N.Y.: Cornell University Press, 2003), Table 2.16.

FIGURE 4

Wage Premium for College Graduates over High School Graduates

Devoting more resources to education should, therefore, raise an economy's growth rate. By suitable reinterpretation, Figure 3 (on page 523) can again be used to illustrate the trade-off between present and future. Because expenditures on education are naturally thought of as *investments* in *human* capital, just think of the vertical axis now as representing educational investments. If a society spends more on them and less on consumer goods (thus moving from point C toward point I), it should grow faster.

But education is not a panacea for all an economy's ills. Education in the former Soviet Union was, at least in some respects, probably outstanding. Ultimately, however, it proved insufficient to prevent the Soviet economy from falling ever further behind the capitalist economies in terms of economic growth.

On-the-job training may be just as important as formal education in raising productivity, but it is less amenable to influence by the government. For the most part, private businesses decide how much, and in what ways, to train their workers. Various public policy initiatives—ranging from government-run training programs, to subsidies for private-sector training, to mandated minimum training expenditures by firms—have been tried in various countries with mixed results. In the United States, mandates have been viewed as improper interferences with private business decisions, and government training programs (other than those in the Armed Forces) have not been terribly successful.

On-the-job training refers to skills that workers acquire while at work, rather than in school or in formal vocational training programs.

GROWTH POLICY: SPURRING TECHNOLOGICAL CHANGE

Our third pillar of growth is *technology*, or getting more output from given supplies of inputs. Some of the most promising policies for speeding up the pace of technical progress have already been mentioned:

More Education   Although some inventions and innovations are the product of dumb luck, most result from the sustained application of knowledge, resources, and brainpower to scientific, engineering, and managerial problems. We have just noted that more educated workers appear to be more productive per se. In addition, a society is likely to be more innovative if it has a greater supply of scientists, engineers, and skilled business managers who are constantly on the prowl for new opportunities. Modern growth theory emphasizes the pivotal role in the growth process of committing more human, physical, and financial resources to the acquisition of knowledge.

High levels of education, especially scientific, engineering, and managerial education, contribute to the advancement of technology.

There is little doubt that the United States leads the world in the quality of its graduate programs in business and in many of the scientific and engineering disciplines. As evidence of this superiority, one need only look at the tens of thousands of foreign students who flock to our shores to attend graduate school. It seems reasonable to suppose that America's unquestioned leadership in scientific and business education contributes to our leadership in productivity. On this basis, many economists endorse policies designed to induce more bright young people to pursue scientific and engineering careers. Some well-known examples of such incentives include scholarships, fellowships, and research grants.

More Capital Formation   We are all familiar with the fact that the latest versions of cell phones, PCs, personal digital assistants (PDAs), and even televisions embody new features that were unavailable a year or even six months ago. The same is true of industrial capital. Indeed, new investment is the principal way in which the latest technological breakthroughs are hard-wired into the nation's capital stock. As we mentioned in our earlier discussion of capital formation, newer capital is normally better capital. In this way:

High rates of investment contribute to rapid technical progress.

So all of the policies we discussed earlier as ways to bolster capital formation can also be thought of as ways to speed up technical progress.

Research and Development   But there is a more direct way to spur **invention** and **innovation**: devote more of society's resources to **research and development (R&D)**.

Driven by the profit motive, American businesses have long invested heavily in industrial R&D. According to the old saying, "Build a better mousetrap, and the world will beat a path to your door." And innovative companies in the United States and elsewhere have been engaged in research on "better mousetraps" for decades. Polaroid invented instant photography, Xerox developed photocopying, and Apple pioneered the desktop computer. Boeing improved jet aircraft several times. Pharmaceutical companies have discovered many new, life-enhancing drugs. Intel has developed generation after generation of ever-faster microprocessors. The list goes on and on.

All these companies and others have spent untold billions of dollars on R&D to discover new products, to improve old ones, and to make their industrial processes more efficient. While many research dollars are inevitably "wasted" on false starts and experiments that don't pan out, numerous studies have shown that the average dollar invested in R&D has yielded high returns to society. Heavy spending on R&D is, indeed, one of the keys to high productivity growth.

The U.S. government supports and encourages R&D in several ways. First, it subsidizes private R&D spending through the tax code. Specifically, the Research and Experimentation Tax Credit reduces the taxes of companies that spend more money on R&D.

Second, the government sometimes joins with private companies in collaborative research efforts. The Human Genome Project may be the best-known example of such a public–private partnership (some called it a race!), but there also have been cooperative ventures in new automotive technology, alternative energy sources, and elsewhere.

Last, and certainly not least, the federal government has over the years spent a great deal of taxpayer money directly on R&D. Much of this spending has been funneled through the Department of Defense. But the National Aeronautics and Space Administration (NASA), the National Science Foundation, the National Institutes of Health, and many other agencies have also played important roles. Inventions as diverse as atomic energy, advanced ceramic materials, and the Internet were originally developed in federal laboratories. Federal government R&D spending in fiscal year 2006 amounted to roughly $134 billion, more than half of which went through the Pentagon.

Our multipurpose Figure 3 again illustrates the choice facing society. Now interpret the vertical axis as measuring investments in R&D. Devoting more resources to R&D—that is, choosing point I rather than point C—leads to less current consumption but more growth.

Invention is the act of discovering new products or new ways of making products.

Innovation is the act of putting new ideas into effect by, for example, bringing new products to market, changing product designs, and improving the way in which things are done.

Research and development (R&D) refers to activities aimed at inventing new products or processes, or improving existing ones.

■ THE PRODUCTIVITY SLOWDOWN AND SPEED-UP IN THE UNITED STATES

Around 1973, productivity growth in the United States suddenly and mysteriously slowed down—from the rate of about 2.8 percent per year that had characterized the 1948–1973 period to about 1.4 percent thereafter (see Figure 5 on the next page). Hardly anyone anticipated this productivity slowdown. Then, starting around 1995, productivity growth suddenly speeded up again—from about 1.4 percent per year during the 1973–1995 period back to about 2.8 percent since then (see Figure 5 again). Once again, the abrupt change in the growth rate caught most people by surprise.

Recall from the discussion of compounding in Chapter 23 that a change in the growth rate of around 1½ percentage points, if sustained for decades, makes an enormous difference in living standards. So understanding these two major events is of critical importance. Yet even now, more than thirty years later, economists remain puzzled about the 1973 productivity slowdown, and the reasons behind the 1995 productivity speed-up are only partly understood. Let us see what economists know about these two episodes.

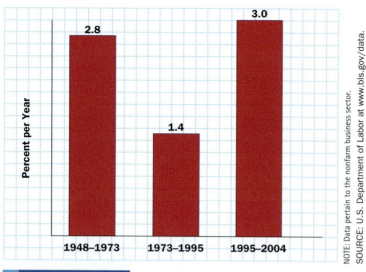

FIGURE 5

Average Productivity Growth Rates in the United States, 1948–2006

NOTE: Data pertain to the nonfarm business sector.
SOURCE: U.S. Department of Labor at www.bls.gov/data.

The Productivity Slowdown, 1973–1995

The productivity slowdown after 1973 was certainly a disconcerting development, and economists have been struggling to explain it ever since. Among the leading candidate explanations are:

Lagging Investment During the 1980s and early 1990s, many people suggested that inadequate investment was behind America's productivity problem. Countries such as Germany and Japan, these critics observed, saved and invested far more than Americans did, thereby equipping their workers with more modern equipment that boosted labor productivity. U.S. tax policy, they argued, should create stronger incentives for business to invest and for households to save.

Although the argument was logical, the facts have not treated it kindly. For example, the share of U.S. GDP accounted for by business investment did not actually decline during the period of slow productivity growth. Nor did the contribution of capital formation to growth fall. (See the box on growth accounting on the next page.)

High Energy Prices A second explanation begins with a tantalizing fact: The productivity slowdown started around 1973, just when the Organization of Petroleum Exporting Countries (OPEC) jacked up the price of oil. As a matter of logic, higher oil prices should reduce business use of energy, which should make labor less productive. Furthermore, productivity growth fell just at the time that energy prices rose, not just in the United States but all over the world—which is quite a striking coincidence.

Once again, the argument sounds persuasive—until you remember another important fact: Energy prices dropped sharply in the mid-1980s, but productivity growth did not revive. So the energy explanation of the productivity slowdown has many skeptics.

Inadequate Workforce Skills Could it be that the skills of the U.S. labor force failed to keep pace with the demands of new technology after 1973? Although workforce skills are notoriously difficult to measure, there was and is a widespread feeling that the quality of education in the United States has declined. For example, SAT scores peaked in the late 1960s and then declined for about 20 years.[4] Yet standard measures such as school attendance rates, graduation rates, and average levels of educational attainment have all continued to register gains. Clearly, the proposition that the quality of the U.S. workforce declined is at least debatable.

A Technological Slowdown? Could the pace of innovation have slowed in the 1973–1995 period? Most people instinctively answer "no." After all, the microchip and the personal computer were invented in the 1970s, opening the door to what can only be called a revolution in computing and information technology (IT). Workplaces were transformed beyond recognition. Entirely new industries (such as those related to PCs and Internet services) were spawned. Didn't these technological marvels raise productivity by enormous amounts?

The paradox of seemingly rapid technological advance coupled with sluggish productivity performance puzzled economists for years. How could the contribution of technology to growth have *fallen*? A satisfactory answer was never given. And then, all of a sudden, the facts changed.

---

[4] The SAT was rescaled about ten years ago to reflect this decline in average scores.

Growth Accounting in the United States

In this chapter, we have learned that labor productivity (output per hour of work) rises because more capital is accumulated, because technology improves, and because workforce quality rises. The last of these three pillars is quantitatively unimportant in the modern United States because average educational attainment has been high for a long time and has not changed much recently. But the other two pillars are very important.

The table breaks down the growth rate of labor productivity into its two main components over three different periods of time. We see that the productivity slowdown after 1973 was entirely accounted for by slower technological improvement; the contribution of capital formation did not decline at all.* Similarly, the productivity speed-up after 1995 was almost entirely accounted for by faster technical progress.

	1948–1973	1973–1995	1995–2004
Growth rate of labor productivity	**2.8%**	**1.4%**	**3.0%**
Contribution of capital formation	0.9	1.0	1.1
Contribution of technology	1.9	0.4	1.9

Note: Totals may not add up due to rounding.
SOURCE: Bureau of Labor Statistics at www.bls.gov/data.

*Changes in workforce quality, which are very small, are included in the technology component.

■ The Productivity Speed-up, 1995–??

Figure 5 shows that productivity growth speeded up remarkably after 1995, rising from about 1.4 percent per annum before that year to about 2.8 percent since. This time, the causes are better understood—and most of them relate to the IT revolution.

Surging Investment   Bountiful new business opportunities in the IT sector and elsewhere, coupled with a strong national economy, led to a surge in business investment spending in the 1990s. Business investment as a percentage of real GDP rose from 9.1 percent in 1991 to 14.6 percent in 2000, and most of that increase was concentrated in computers, software, and telecommunications equipment. We have observed several times in this chapter that the productivity growth rate should rise when the capital stock grows faster—and it did in the late 1990s. But then investment fell when the stock market began to crash in 2000. So over the entire 1995–2004 period, the table in the box above shows only a very modest contribution of capital formation to higher productivity growth.

Falling Energy Prices?   For part of this period, especially the years 1996–1998, energy prices were falling. By the same logic used earlier, falling energy prices should have enhanced productivity growth. But, as we noted earlier, this argument did not seem to work so well when energy prices fell in the 1980s. Why, then, should we believe it for the 1990s?

Advances in Information Technology   We seem to be on safer ground when we look to technological progress, especially in computers and semiconductors, to explain the speed-up in productivity growth. First, innovation seemed to explode in the 1990s. Computers became faster and much, much cheaper—as did telecommunications equipment and services. Corporate intranets became commonplace. The Internet grew from a scientific curiosity into a commercial reality, and so on. We truly entered the Information Age.

Second, it probably took American businesses some time to learn how to use the computer and telecommunications technologies that were invented and adopted between, say, 1980 and the early 1990s. It was only in the late 1990s, some observers argue, that U.S. industry was positioned to reap the benefits of these advances in the form of higher productivity. Such long delays are not unprecedented. Research has shown, for example, that it took a long time for the availability of electric power at the end of the nineteenth century to contribute much to productivity growth. Like electric power, computers were a novel input to production, and it may have taken years for prospective users to find the most productive ways to employ them.

In summary:

Two of the three main pillars of productivity growth—technological change and, for a while, capital formation—seem to do a credible job of explaining why productivity accelerated in the United States after 1995.

PUZZLE RESOLVED:
Why the Relative Price of College Tuition Keeps Rising

Earlier in this chapter, we observed that the relative prices of services such as college tuition, medical care, and theater tickets seem to rise year after year. And we suggested that one main reason for this perpetual increase is tied to the economy's long-run growth rate. We are now in a position to understand precisely how that mechanism works. Rising productivity is the key. The argument is based on three simple ideas.

Idea 1 It stands to reason, and is amply demonstrated by historical experience, that *real wages tend to rise at the same rate as labor productivity.* This relationship makes sense: Labor normally gets paid more when and where it produces more. Thus real wages will rise most rapidly in those economies with the fastest productivity growth.

Idea 2 Although average labor productivity in the economy increases from year to year, *there are a number of personally provided services for which productivity (output per hour) cannot or does not grow.* We have already mentioned several of them. Your college or university can increase the "productivity" of its faculty by increasing class size, but most students and parents would view that as a decrease in educational quality. Similarly, a modern doctor takes roughly as long to give a patient a physical as his counterparts did 25 or 50 years ago. It also takes *exactly* the same time for an orchestra to play one of Beethoven's symphonies today as it did in Beethoven's time.

There is a common ingredient in each of these diverse examples: The major sources of higher labor productivity that we have studied in this chapter—more capital and better technology—are completely or nearly irrelevant. It still takes one lecturer to teach a class, one doctor to examine a patient, and four musicians to play a string quartet—just as it did one hundred years ago. Saving on labor by using more and better equipment is more or less out of the question.[5] These so-called *personal services* stand in stark contrast to, say, working on an automobile assembly line or in a semiconductor plant, or even to working in service industries such as telecommunications—all instances in which both capital formation and technical progress regularly raise labor productivity.

Idea 3 *Real wages in different occupations must rise at similar rates in the long run.* This point may sound wrong at first: Haven't the wages of computer programmers risen faster than those of school teachers in recent years? Yes they have, and that is the market's way of attracting more young people into computer programming. But in the long run, these growth rates must (more or less) equilibrate, or else virtually no one would want to be a school teacher any more.

Now let's bring the three ideas together. College teachers are no more productive than they used to be, but autoworkers are (Idea 2). But in the long run, the real wages of college teachers and autoworkers must grow at roughly the same rate (Idea 3), which is the economy-wide productivity growth rate (Idea 1). As a result, wages of

---

[5] However, some people foresee a world in which some aspects of education and medical care are delivered long distance over the Internet. We'll see!

college teachers and doctors will rise *faster* than their productivity does, and so their services must grow ever more expensive compared to, say, computers and phone calls.

That is, indeed, the way things seem to have worked out. Compared to the world in which your parents grew up, computers and telephone calls are now very cheap while college tuition and doctors' bills are very expensive. The same logic applies to the services of police officers (two per squad car), baseball players (nine per team), chefs, and many other occupations where productivity improvements are either impossible or undesirable. All of these services have grown much more expensive over the years. This phenomenon has been called the **cost disease of the personal services.**

Ironically, the villain of the piece is actually the economy's strong productivity growth. If manufacturing and telecommunications workers did *not* become more productive over time, their real wages would not rise. In that case, the real wages of teachers and doctors would not have to keep pace, so their services would not have to grow ever more expensive. Paradoxically, the enormous productivity gains that have blessed our economy and raised our standard of living also account for the problem of rising tuition costs. In the most literal sense, we are the victims of our own success.

> According to the **cost disease of the personal services**, service activities that require direct personal contact tend to rise in price relative to other goods and services.

GROWTH IN THE DEVELOPING COUNTRIES[6]

Ernest Hemingway once answered a query of F. Scott Fitzgerald's by agreeing that, yes, the rich *are* different—they have more money! Similarly, whereas the main determinants of economic growth—increases in capital, improving technology, and rising workforce skills—are the same in both rich and poor countries, they look quite different in what is often called the Third World. This chapter has focused on growth in the industrialized countries so far. So let us now review the three pillars of productivity growth from the standpoint of the developing nations.

The Three Pillars Revisited

Capital We noted earlier that many poor countries are poorly endowed with capital. Given their low incomes, they simply have been unable to accumulate the volumes of business capital (factories, equipment, and the like) and public capital (roads, bridges, airports, and so on) that we take for granted in the industrialized world. In a super-rich country like the United States, $100,000 or more worth of capital stands behind a typical worker, while in a poor African country the corresponding figure may be less than $500. No wonder the American worker is vastly more productive than his African counterpart.

But accumulating more capital can be exceptionally difficult in the developing world. We noted earlier that rich countries have a *choice* about how much of their resources to devote to current consumption versus investment for the future. (See Figure 3 on page 523.) But building capital for the future is a far more difficult task in poor countries, where much of the population may be living on the edge and have little if anything to save for the future. For this reason, it has long been believed that **development assistance**, sometimes called *foreign aid*, is a crucial ingredient for growth in the developing world. Indeed, the *World Bank* was established in 1944 precisely to make low-interest development loans to poor countries.

Development assistance has always been controversial. Critics of foreign aid argue that the money is often not well spent. Without honest and well-functioning governments, well-defined property rights, and so on, they argue, the developing countries

> **Development assistance** ("foreign aid") refers to outright grants and low-interest loans to poor countries from both rich countries and multinational institutions like the World Bank. The purpose is to spur economic development.

---

[6] This section can be skipped in shorter courses.

The Millennium Development Goals

To celebrate the arrival of the new millennium in 2000, the member states of the United Nations established an ambitious set of *Millennium Development Goals* to be achieved by the year 2015. Where the goals are numerical, they refer to conditions in the year 1990 as the starting point for measurement. The twelve goals fall under eight categories:

1. Poverty and hunger
   Halve the proportion of people living on less than $1 a day.
   Halve the proportion of people who suffer from hunger.

2. Education
   Ensure that both boys and girls achieve universal primary education.

3. Gender equality
   Eliminate gender disparities at all levels of education.

4. Child mortality
   Reduce the under-five mortality rate by two thirds.

5. Maternal health
   Reduce maternal mortality by three quarters.

6. Disease
   Reverse the spread of HIV/AIDS.

7. Environment
   Halve the proportion of people without access to potable water.
   Significantly improve the lives of at least 100 million slum dwellers.
   Reverse the loss of environmental resources.

8. Global partnership for development
   Raise official development assistance.
   Expand market access for poor countries' exports.

---

cannot and will not make good use of the assistance they receive. Supporters of foreign aid counter that the donor countries have been far too stingy. The United States, for example, donates only about 0.1 percent of its GDP each year. Can grants that amount to $60 per person—which is a fairly typical figure for the recipient countries—really be expected to make much difference? In 2000, as part of an agreed set of ambitious new development goals, the wealthy members of the United Nations pledged to increase their assistance to the developing nations. (See the box "The Millennium Development Goals.")

Technology   You need only visit a poor country to see that the level of technology is generally far below what we in the West are accustomed to. In principle, this handicap should be easy to overcome. As we noted in our discussion of the convergence hypothesis, people in poor countries don't have to invent anything; they can just adopt technologies that have already been invented in the rich countries. And indeed, a number of formerly-poor countries have followed this strategy with great success. South Korea, which was destitute in the mid-1950s, is a prime example.

But as we observed earlier, many of the developing nations, especially the poorest ones, have been unable to join this "convergence club." They may lack the necessary scientific and engineering know-how. They may be short on educated workers. They may be woefully undersupplied with the necessary infrastructure, such as transportation and communications systems. Or they may simply be plagued by incompetent or corrupt governments. Whatever the reasons, they have been unable emulate the technological advances of the West.

There are no easy solutions to this problem. One common suggestion is to encourage **foreign direct investment** by **multinational corporations.** Industrial giants like Toyota (Japan), IBM (United States), Siemens (Germany), and others bring their advanced technologies with them when they open a factory in a developing nation. They can train local workers and improve local transportation and communications networks. But, of course, these companies are *foreign*, and they come to make a *profit*—both of which may cause resentment in the local population.

Foreign direct investment is the purchase or construction of real business assets—such as factories, offices, and machinery—in a foreign country.

Multinational corporations are corporations, generally large ones, which do business in many countries. Most, but not all, of these corporations have their headquarters in developed countries.

For this and other reasons, many developing countries have not always welcomed foreign investment. In addition, multinationals are rarely tempted to open factories in the poorest developing countries, such as those in sub-Saharan Africa, where skilled labor is in short supply, transportation systems may be inadequate, and governments are often unstable and unreliable.

Education and Training   Huge discrepancies exist between the average levels of educational attainment in the rich and poor countries. Table 4 shows some data on average years of schooling in selected countries, both developed and developing. The differences are dramatic—ranging from a high of 12.3 years in the United States to less than 5 years in India and less than 2 years in the Sudan. In most industrialized countries, universal primary education and high rates of high school completion are already realities. But in many poor countries, even completing grade school may be the exception, leaving rudimentary skills such as reading, writing, and basic arithmetic in short supply. In such cases, expanding and improving primary education—including keeping children in school until they reach the age of twelve—may be among the most cost-effective growth policies available. The problem is particularly acute in many traditional societies, where women are second-class citizens—or worse. In such countries, the education of girls may be considered unimportant or even inappropriate.

TABLE 4	
Average Educational Attainment in Selected Countries, 2000*	
United States	**12.3**
Canada	11.4
South Korea	10.5
Japan	9.7
United Kingdom	9.4
Italy	7.0
Mexico	6.7
India	4.8
Brazil	4.6
Sudan	1.9

* For people older than twenty-five years of age
SOURCE: Web site accompanying R. Barro and J.-W. Lee, "International Data on educational Attainment: Updates and Implications," CID Working paper No. 42, Harvard University, 2000, http://www.cid.harvard.edu/ciddata/ciddata.html

■ Some Special Problems of the Developing Countries

Accumulating capital, improving technology, and enhancing workforce skills are common ingredients of growth in rich and poor countries alike. But Third World countries also must contend with some special handicaps to growth that are mostly absent in the West.

Geography   Americans often forget how blessed we are geographically. We live in a temperate climate zone, on a land mass that has literally millions of acres of flat, fertile land that is ideal for agriculture. The fact that our nation literally stretches "from sea to shining sea" also means we have many fine seaports. Contrast this splendid set of geographical conditions with the situation of the world's poorest region: sub-Saharan Africa. Many African nations are landlocked and/or terribly short on arable land.

Health   People in the rich countries rarely think about such debilitating tropical diseases as malaria. But they are rampant in many developing nations, especially in Africa. The AIDS epidemic, of course, is ravaging the continent. Although improvements in public health are important in all countries, they are literally matters of life and death in the poorest nations. And there is a truly vicious cycle here: Poor health is a serious impediment to economic growth, and poverty makes it hard to improve health standards.

Governance   Complaining about the low quality of government is a popular pastime in many Western democracies. Americans do it every day. But most governments in industrialized nations are paragons of virtue and efficiency compared to the governments of some (but not all) developing nations. As we have noted in this chapter, political stability, the rule of law, and respect for property rights are all crucial requirements for economic growth. By the same token, corruption and over-regulation of business are obvious deterrents to investment. Lawlessness, tyrannical rule, and war are even more serious impediments. Unfortunately, too many poor nations have been victimized by a succession of corrupt dictators and tragic wars. It need hardly be said that those conditions are not exactly conducive to economic growth.

■ FROM THE LONG RUN TO THE SHORT RUN

Most of this chapter has been devoted to explaining and evaluating the factors underpinning the growth rate of *potential* GDP. Over long periods of time, the growth rates of actual and potential GDP match up pretty well. But, just like people, economies do not always live up to their potential. As we observed in the previous chapter, GDP in the United States often diverges from potential GDP as a result of macroeconomic fluctuations. Sometimes it is higher; sometimes it is lower. Indeed, whereas this chapter has studied the factors that determine the rate at which the GDP of a particular country *grows* from one year to the next, we know that GDP occasionally *shrinks*—during periods we call *recessions*. To study these fluctuations, we must supplement the long-run theory of *aggregate supply*, which we have just described, with a short-run theory of *aggregate demand*—a task that begins in the next chapter.

SUMMARY

1. More **capital,** improved workforce quality (which is normally measured by the amount of education and training), and better technology all raise labor productivity and therefore shift the production function upward. They constitute the three main pillars of growth.

2. The growth rate of labor productivity depends on the rate of capital formation, the rate of improvement of workforce quality, and the rate of technical progress. So growth policy concentrates on speeding up these processes.

3. **Capital formation** can be encouraged by low real interest rates, favorable tax treatment, rapid technical change, rapid growth of demand, and a climate of political stability that respects **property rights.** Each of these factors is at least influenced by policy.

4. Policies that increase education and training—the second pillar of growth—can be expected to make a country's workforce more productive. They range from universal primary education to post-graduate fellowships in science and engineering.

5. Technological advances can be encouraged by more education, by higher rates of **investment,** and also by direct expenditures—both public and private—on **research and development (R&D).**

6. The **convergence hypothesis** holds that countries with lower productivity levels tend to have higher productivity growth rates, so that poor countries gradually close the gap on rich ones.

7. One major reason to expect convergence is that technological know-how can be transferred quickly from the leading nations to the laggards. Unfortunately, not all countries seem able to benefit from this information transfer.

8. Productivity growth slowed precipitously in the United States around 1973, and economists are still not sure why.

9. Productivity growth in the United States has speeded up again since 1995, probably mainly as a result of the information technology (IT) revolution.

10. Because many personal services—such as education, medical care, and police protection—are essentially handicraft activities that are not amenable to labor-saving innovations, they suffer from a **cost disease** that makes them grow ever more expensive over time.

11. The same three pillars of economic growth—capital, technology, and education—apply in the developing countries. But on all three fronts, conditions are much more difficult there—and improvements are harder to obtain.

12. The rich countries try to help with all three pillars by providing **development assistance,** and **multinational corporations** sometimes provide capital and better technology via **foreign direct investment.** But both of these mechanisms are surrounded by controversy.

13. Growth in many of the poor countries is also held back by adverse geographical conditions and/or corrupt governments.

KEY TERMS

Human capital   520

Convergence hypothesis   521

Capital   522

Investment   522

Capital formation   522

Property rights   524

On-the-job training   526

Invention   527

Innovation   527

Research and development (R&D)   527

Cost disease of the personal services   531

Development assistance   531

Foreign direct investment   532

Multinational corporations   532

TEST YOURSELF

1. The table below shows real GDP per hour of work in four imaginary countries in the years 1995 and 2005. By what percentage did labor productivity grow in each country? Is it true that productivity *growth* was highest where the initial *level* of productivity was the lowest? For which countries?

	Output per Hour	
	1995	2005
Country A	$40	$48
Country B	$25	$35
Country C	$ 2	$ 3
Country D	$ 0.50	$ 0.60

2. Imagine that new inventions in the computer industry affect the growth rate of productivity as follows:

Year of Invention	Following Year	5 Years Later	10 Years Later	20 Years Later
0%	−1%	0%	+2%	+4%

Would such a pattern help explain U.S. productivity performance since the mid-1970s? Why?

3. Which of the following prices would you expect to rise rapidly? Why?

   a. cable television rates

   b. football tickets

   c. Internet access

   d. household cleaning services

   e. driving lessons

4. Two countries have the production possibilities frontier (PPF) shown in Figure 3 on page 523. But Consumia chooses point C, whereas Investia chooses point I. Which country will have the higher PPF the following year? Why?

5. Show on a graph how capital formation shifts the production function. Use this graph to show that capital formation increases labor productivity. Explain in words why labor is more productive when the capital stock is larger.

DISCUSSION QUESTIONS

1. Explain the different objectives of (long-run) growth policy versus (short-run) stabilization policy.

2. Explain why economic growth might be higher in a country with well-established property rights and a stable political system compared with a country where property rights are uncertain and the government is unstable.

3. Chapter 23 pointed out that, because faster capital formation comes at a cost (reduced current consumption), it is possible for a country to invest too much. Suppose the government of some country decides that its businesses are investing too much. What steps might it take to slow the pace of capital formation?

4. Explain why the best educational policies to promote faster growth might be different in the following countries.

   a. Mozambique

   b. Brazil

   c. France

5. Comment on the following: "Sharp changes in the volume of investment in the United States help explain both the productivity slowdown in 1973 and the productivity speed-up in 1995."

6. Discuss some of the pros and cons of increasing development assistance, both from the point of view of the donor country and the point of view of the recipient country.

AGGREGATE DEMAND AND THE POWERFUL CONSUMER

Men are disposed, as a rule and on the average, to increase their consumption as their income increases, but not by as much as the increase in their income.

JOHN MAYNARD KEYNES

T he last chapter focused on the determinants of *potential GDP*—the economy's capacity to produce. We turn our attention now to the factors determining *actual GDP*—how much of that potential is actually utilized. Will the economy be pressing against its capacity, and therefore perhaps also having trouble with inflation? Or will there be a great deal of unused capacity, and therefore high unemployment?

The theory that economists use to answer such questions is based on the concepts of aggregate demand and supply that we first introduced in Chapter 22. The last chapter examined the long-run determinants of *aggregate supply*, a topic to which we will return in Chapter 27. In this chapter and the next, we will construct a simplified model of *aggregate demand* and learn the origins of the aggregate demand curve.

While aggregate supply rules the roost in the long run, Chapter 22's whirlwind tour of U.S. economic history suggested that the strength of aggregate demand holds the key to the economy's condition in the short run. When aggregate demand grows briskly, the economy booms. When aggregate demand is weak, the economy stagnates.

The model we develop to understand aggregate demand in this chapter and the next will teach us much about this process. But it is too simple to deal with policy issues effectively, because the government and the financial system are largely ignored. We remedy these omissions in Part VII, where we give government spending, taxation, and interest rates appropriately prominent roles. The influence of the exchange rate between the U.S. dollar and foreign currencies is then considered in Part VIII.

CONTENTS

ISSUE: *Demand Management and the Ornery Consumer*

In Chapter 22, we suggested that the government sometimes wants to shift the aggregate demand curve. It can do so a number of ways. One direct approach is to alter its own spending, becoming extravagant when private demand is weak or miserly when private demand is strong. Alternatively, the government can take a more indirect route, by using taxes and other policy tools to influence *private* spending decisions. Because consumer expenditures constitute more than two-thirds of gross domestic product, the consumer presents the most tempting target.

A case in point arose after the 2000 election, when the long boom of the 1990s ended abruptly and economic growth in the United States slowed to a crawl. President George W. Bush and his economic advisers decided that consumer spending needed a boost, and Congress passed a multiyear tax cut in 2001. One provision of the tax cut gave taxpayers an advance *rebate* on their 2001 taxes.[1] Checks ranging as high as $600 went out starting in July 2001. There should be no mystery about how changes in personal taxes are expected to affect consumer spending. Any reduction in personal taxes leaves consumers with more after-tax income to spend; any tax increase leaves them with less. The linkage from taxes to spendable income to consumer spending seems direct and unmistakable, and, in a certain sense, it is.

Yet the congressional debate over the tax bill sent legislators and journalists scurrying to the scholarly evidence on a similar episode twenty-six years earlier. In the spring of 1975, as the U.S. economy hit a recessionary bottom, Congress enacted a tax rebate to spur consumer spending. But that time consumers did not follow the wishes of the president and Congress. They saved a substantial share of their tax cuts, rather than spending them. As a result, the economy did not receive the expected boost.

Perhaps the legislators should have taken the 1975 episode to heart. Early estimates of the effects of the 2001 rebates suggested that consumers spent relatively little of the money they received. Thus, in a sense, history repeated itself. But why? Why did these two temporary tax cuts seem to have so little effect? This chapter attempts to provide some answers. But before getting involved in such complicated issues, we must build some vocabulary and learn some basic concepts. Then we will see what may have gone wrong in 1975 and 2001.

AGGREGATE DEMAND, DOMESTIC PRODUCT, AND NATIONAL INCOME

Aggregate demand is the total amount that all consumers, business firms, and government agencies spend on final goods and services.

First, some vocabulary. We have already introduced the concept of *gross domestic product* as the standard measure of the economy's total output.[2]

For the most part, firms in a market economy produce goods only if they think they can sell them. **Aggregate demand** is the total amount that all consumers, business firms, government agencies, and foreigners wish to spend on U.S. final goods and services. The downward-sloping aggregate demand curve of Chapter 22 alerted us to the fact that *aggregate demand is a schedule, not a fixed number*—the actual numerical value of aggregate demand depends on the price level. Several reasons for this dependence will emerge in coming chapters.

But the level of aggregate demand also depends on a variety of other factors—such as consumer incomes, various government policies, and events in foreign countries. To understand the nature of aggregate demand, it is best to break it up into its major components, as we do in this chapter.

Consumer expenditure (C) is the total amount spent by consumers on newly produced goods and services (excluding purchases of new homes, which are considered investment goods).

Consumer expenditure (*consumption* for short) is simply the total value of all consumer goods and services demanded. Because consumer spending constitutes more

---

[1] While these checks were called "rebates" at the time, suggesting that they were a return of some of the taxes paid in 2000, they were actually first installments on the tax cuts enacted in 2001.
[2] See Chapter 22, pages 472–476.

than two-thirds of total spending, it is the main focus of this chapter. We represent it by the letter C.

Investment spending, represented by the letter I, was discussed extensively in the last chapter. It is the amount that firms spend on factories, machinery, software, and the like, plus the amount that families spend on new houses. Notice that this usage of the word *investment* differs from common parlance. Most people speak of *investing* in the stock market or in a bank account. But that kind of investment merely swaps one form of financial asset (such as money) for another form (such as a share of stock). When economists speak of *investment*, they mean instead the purchase of some *new, physical asset,* such as a drill press, a computer, or a house. The distinction is important here because it is only the economists' kinds of investments that constitute direct additions to the demand for newly-produced goods.

The third major component of aggregate demand, **government purchases** of goods and services, includes items such as paper, computers, airplanes, ships, and labor bought by all levels of government. We use the symbol G for this variable.

The final component of aggregate demand, **net exports,** is simply defined as U.S. exports *minus* U.S. imports. The reasoning here is simple. Part of the demand for American goods and services originates beyond our borders—as when foreigners buy our wheat, software, and banking services. So to obtain total demand for U.S. products, these goods and services must be added to U.S. domestic demand. Similarly, some items included in C and I are made abroad. Think, for example, of beer from Germany, cars from Japan, and shirts from Malaysia. These must be subtracted from the total amount demanded by U.S. consumers if we want to measure total spending *on U.S. products.* The addition of exports, X, and the subtraction of imports, IM, leads to the following shorthand definition of aggregate demand:

Aggregate demand is the sum $C + I + G + (X - IM)$.

The last concept we need for our vocabulary is a way to measure the total *income* of all individuals in the economy. It comes in two versions: one for before-tax incomes, called **national income,** and one for after-tax incomes, called **disposable income.**[3] The term *disposable income,* which we will abbreviate DI, is meant to be descriptive—it tells us how much consumers actually have available to spend or to save. For that reason, it will play a prominent role in this chapter and in subsequent discussions.

Investment spending (I) is the sum of the expenditures of business firms on new plant and equipment and households on new homes. Financial "investments" are not included, nor are resales of existing physical assets.

Government purchases (G) refer to the goods (such as airplanes and paper clips) and services (such as school teaching and police protection) purchased by all levels of government.

Net exports, or $X - IM$, is the difference between exports (X) and imports (IM). It indicates the difference between what we sell to foreigners and what we buy from them.

SOURCE: From *The Wall Street Journal.* Permission, Cartoon Features Syndicate

"When I refer to it as disposable income, don't get the wrong idea."

THE CIRCULAR FLOW OF SPENDING, PRODUCTION, AND INCOME

Enough definitions. How do these three concepts—domestic product, total expenditure, and national income—interact in a market economy? We can answer this best with a rather elaborate diagram (Figure 1 on the next page). For obvious reasons, Figure 1 is called a *circular flow diagram.* It depicts a large tube in which an imaginary fluid circulates in a clockwise direction. At several points along the way, some of the fluid leaks out or additional fluid is injected into the tube.

Let's examine this system, beginning on the far left. At point 1 on the circle, we find consumers. Disposable income (DI) flows into their pockets, and two things flow out: consumption (C), which stays in the circular flow, and saving (S), which "leaks out." This outflow depicts the fact that consumers normally spend less than they earn and save the balance. The "leakage" to saving, of course, does not disappear; it flows into the financial system via banks, mutual funds, and so on. We defer consideration of what happens inside the financial system to Chapters 29 and 30.

National income is the sum of the incomes that all individuals in the economy earned in the forms of wages, interest, rents, and profits. It excludes government transfer payments and is calculated before any deductions are taken for income taxes.

Disposable income (DI) is the sum of the incomes of all individuals in the economy after all taxes have been deducted and all transfer payments have been added.

---

[3] More detailed information on these and other concepts is provided in the appendix to this chapter.

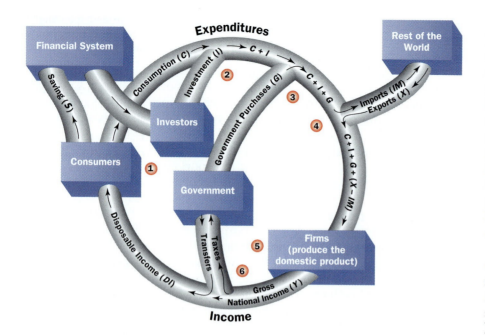

FIGURE 1

The Circular Flow of
Expenditures and
Income

The upper loop of the circular flow represents expenditures, and as we move clockwise to point 2, we encounter the first "injection" into the flow: investment spending (I). The diagram shows this injection as coming from "investors"—a group that includes both business firms and home buyers.[4] As the circular flow moves past point 2, it is bigger than it was before: Total spending has increased from C to $C + I$.

At point 3, there is yet another injection. The government adds its demand for goods and services (G) to those of consumers and investors ($C + I$). Now aggregate demand has grown to $C + I + G$.

The next leakage and injection come at point 4. Here we see export spending entering the circular flow from abroad and import spending leaking out. The net effect of these two forces may increase or decrease the circular flow, depending on whether net exports are positive or negative. (In the United States today, they are strongly negative.) In either case, by the time we pass point 4, we have accumulated the full amount of aggregate demand, $C + I + G + (X - IM)$.

The circular flow diagram shows this aggregate demand for goods and services arriving at the business firms, which are located at point 5. Responding to this demand, firms produce the domestic product. As the circular flow emerges from the firms, however, we rename it *gross national income.* Why? The reason is that, except for some complications explained in the appendix:

National income and domestic product must be equal.

Why is this so? When a firm produces and sells $100 worth of output, it pays most of the proceeds to its workers, to people who have lent it money, and to the landlord who owns the property on which the plant is located. All of these payments represent *income* to some individuals. But what about the rest? Suppose, for example, that the firm pays wages, interest, and rent totaling $90 million and sells its output for $100 million. What happens to the remaining $10 million? The firm's owners receive it as *profits.* Because these owners are citizens of the country, their incomes also count in national income.[5] Thus, when we add up all the wages, interest, rents, *and profits* in the economy to obtain the *national income,* we must arrive at the *value of output.*

The lower loop of the circular flow diagram shows national income leaving firms and heading for consumers. But some of the flow takes a detour along the way. At point 6, the government does two things. First, it siphons off a portion of the national income in the form of *taxes.* Second, it adds back government **transfer payments,** such as unemployment compensation and Social Security benefits, which government agencies give to certain individuals as outright *grants* rather than as payments for goods or services rendered.

Transfer payments are sums of money that the government gives certain individuals as outright grants rather than as payments for services rendered to employers. Some common examples are Social Security and unemployment benefits.

---

[4] You are reminded that expenditure on housing is part of *I*, not part of *C*.

[5] Some of the income paid out by American companies goes to noncitizens. Similarly, some Americans earn income from foreign firms. This complication is discussed in the appendix to this chapter.

By subtracting taxes from gross domestic product (GDP) and adding transfer payments, we obtain disposable income:[6]

$$DI = \text{GDP} - \text{Taxes} + \text{Transfer payments}$$
$$= \text{GDP} - (\text{Taxes} - \text{Transfers})$$
$$= Y - T$$

where Y represents GDP and T represents taxes *net of transfers* or simply *net taxes*. Disposable income flows unimpeded to consumers at point 1, and the cycle repeats.

Figure 1 raises several complicated questions, which we pose now but will not try to answer until subsequent chapters:

- Does the flow of spending and income grow larger or smaller as we move clockwise around the circle? Why?
- Is the output that firms produce at point 5 (the GDP) equal to aggregate demand? If so, what makes these two quantities equal? If not, what happens?

The next chapter provides the answers to these two questions.

- Do the government's accounts balance, so that what flows in at point 6 (net taxes) is equal to what flows out at point 3 (government purchases)? What happens if they do not balance?

This important question is first addressed in Chapter 28 and then recurs many times, especially in Chapter 32, which discusses budget deficits and surpluses in detail.

- Is our international trade balanced, so that exports equal imports at point 4? More generally, what factors determine net exports, and what consequences arise from trade deficits or surpluses?

We take up these questions in the next two chapters and then deal with them more fully in Part VIII.

However, we cannot dig very deeply into any of these issues until we first understand what goes on at point 1, where consumers make decisions. So we turn next to the determinants of consumer spending.

■ CONSUMER SPENDING AND INCOME: THE IMPORTANT RELATIONSHIP

Recall that we started the chapter with a puzzle: Why did consumers respond so weakly to tax rebates in 2001 and 1975? An economist interested in predicting how consumer spending will respond to a change in income taxes must first ask how consumption (C) relates to disposable income (DI), for a tax increase obviously decreases after-tax income, and a tax reduction increases it. This section, therefore, examines what we know about how consumer spending is influenced by changes in disposable income.

Figure 2 on the next page depicts the historical paths of C and DI for the United States since 1929. The association is extremely close, suggesting that consumption will rise whenever disposable income rises and fall whenever income falls. The vertical distance between the two lines represents personal saving: disposable income minus consumption. Notice how little saving consumers did during the Great Depression of the 1930s, where the two lines are very close together, and how much they did during World War II, when many consumer goods were either unavailable or rationed. The low volume of saving in recent years is also notable.

Of course, knowing that C will move in the same direction as DI is not enough for policy planners. They need to know *how much* one variable will go up when the other rises a given amount. Figure 3 presents the same data as in Figure 2, but in a way designed to help answer the "how much" question.

---

[6] This definition omits a few minor details, which are explained in the appendix.

FIGURE 2

Consumer Spending
and Disposable Income

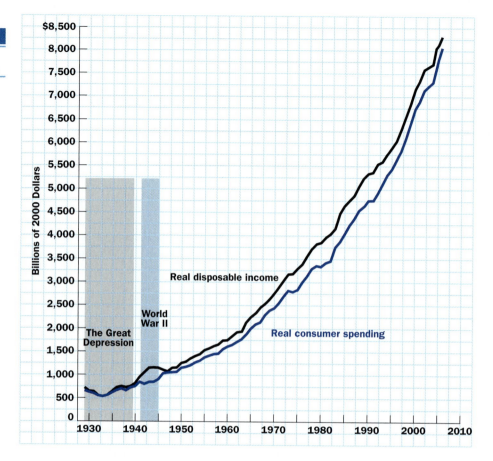

A **scatter diagram** is a graph showing the relationship between two variables (such as consumer spending and disposable income). Each year is represented by a point in the diagram, and the coordinates of each year's point show the values of the two variables in that year.

Economists call such pictures **scatter diagrams,** and they are very useful in predicting how one variable (in this case, consumer spending) will change in response to a change in another variable (in this case, disposable income). Each dot in the diagram represents the data on *C* and *DI* corresponding to a particular year. For example, the point labeled "1996" shows that real consumer expenditures in 1996 were $5,619 billion (which we read off the vertical axis), while real disposable incomes amounted to $6,081 billion (which we read off the horizontal axis). Similarly, each year from 1929 to 2006 is represented by its own dot in Figure 3.

To see how such a diagram can assist fiscal policy planners, imagine that it is 1963 and Congress is contemplating a tax cut. (In fact, Congress did cut taxes in 1964.) Legislators want to know how much additional consumer spending may be stimulated by tax cuts of various sizes. To assist your imagination, the scatter diagram in Figure 4 removes the points for 1964 through 2006 that appear in Figure 3; after all, these data were unknown in 1963. Years prior to 1947 have also been removed because, as Figure 2 showed, both the Great Depression and wartime rationing disturbed the normal relationship between *DI* and *C*. With no more training in economics than you have right now, what would you suggest?

One rough-and-ready approach is to get a ruler, set it down on Figure 4, and sketch a straight line that comes as close as possible to hitting all the points. That has been done for you in the figure, and you can see that the resulting line comes remarkably close to touching all the points. The line summarizes, in a very rough way, the normal relationship between income and consumption. The two variables certainly appear to be closely related.

The *slope* of the straight line in Figure 4 is very important.[7] Specifically, we note that it is:

---

[7] To review the concept of *slope*, see the appendix to Chapter 1, pages 15–16.

FIGURE 3

Scatter Diagram of
Consumer Spending
and Disposable Income

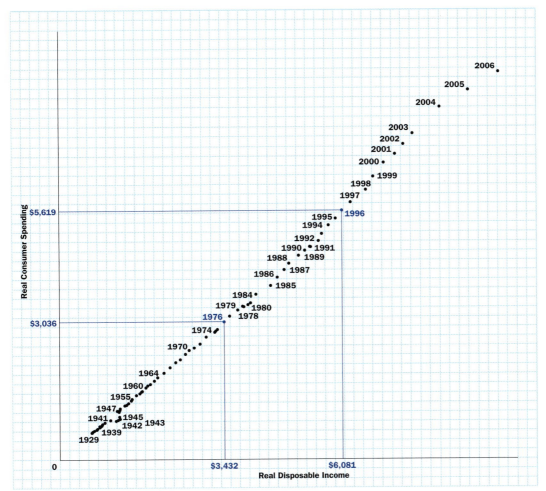

NOTE: Figures are in billions of 2000 dollars.

$$\text{Slope} = \frac{\text{Vertical change}}{\text{Horizontal change}} = \frac{\$180 \text{ billion}}{\$200 \text{ billion}} = 0.90$$

Because the horizontal change involved in the move from *A* to *B* represents a rise in disposable income of $200 billion (from $1,300 billion to $1,500 billion), and the corresponding vertical change represents the associated $180 billion rise in consumer spending (from $1,180 billion to $1,360 billion), the slope of the line indicates how consumer spending responds to changes in disposable income. In this case, we see that each additional $1 of income leads to 90 cents of additional spending.

Now let us return to tax policy. First, recall that each dollar of tax cut increases disposable income by exactly $1. Next, apply the finding from Figure 4 that each additional dollar of disposable income increases consumer spending by about 90 cents. The conclusion is that a tax cut of, say, $9 billion—which is what happened in 1964—would be expected to increase consumer spending by about $9 × 0.9 = $8.1 billion.

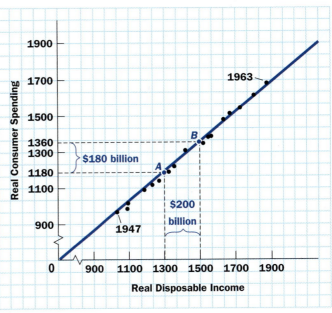

NOTE: Figures are in billions of 2000 dollars.

THE CONSUMPTION FUNCTION AND THE MARGINAL PROPENSITY TO CONSUME

The **consumption function** shows the relationship between total consumer expenditures and total disposable income in the economy, holding all other determinants of consumer spending constant.

The **marginal propensity to consume (MPC)** is the ratio of changes in consumption relative to changes in disposable income that produce the change in consumption. On a graph, it appears as the slope of the consumption function.

It has been said that economics is just systematized common sense. So let us now organize and generalize what has been a completely intuitive discussion up to now. One thing we have discovered is the apparently close relationship between consumer spending, C, and disposable income, DI. Economists call this relationship the **consumption function.**

A second fact we have gleaned from these figures is that the *slope* of the consumption function is quite constant. We infer this constancy from the fact that the straight line drawn in Figure 4 comes so close to touching every point. If the slope of the consumption function had varied widely, we could not have done so well with a single straight line.[8] Because of its importance in applications such as the tax cut, economists have given this slope a special name—the **marginal propensity to consume,** or **MPC** for short. The MPC tells us how much more consumers will spend if disposable income rises by $1.

$$\text{MPC} = \frac{\text{Change in } C}{\text{Change in } DI \text{ that produces the change in } C}$$

The MPC is best illustrated by an example, and for this purpose we turn away from U.S. data for a moment and look at consumption and income in a hypothetical country whose data come in nice round numbers—which facilitates computation.

Columns (1) and (2) of Table 1 show annual consumer expenditure and disposable income, respectively, from 2001 to 2006. These two columns constitute the consumption function, and they are plotted in Figure 5. Column (3) in the table shows the marginal propensity to consume (MPC), which is the slope of the line in Figure 5; it is derived from the first two columns. We can see that between 2003 and 2004, DI rose by $400 billion (from $4,000 billion to $4,400 billion) while C rose by $300 billion (from $3,300 billion to $3,600 billion). Thus, the MPC was:

$$\text{MPC} = \frac{\text{Change in } C}{\text{Change in } DI} = \frac{\$300}{\$400} = 0.75$$

As you can easily verify, the MPC between any other pair of years in Table 1 is also 0.75. This relationship explains why the slope of the line in Figure 4 was so crucial in estimating the effect of a tax cut. This slope, which we found there to be 0.90, is simply the MPC for the United States. The MPC tells us how much *additional* spending

TABLE 1			
Consumption and Income in a Hypothetical Economy			
Year	(1) Consumption, C	(2) Disposable Income, DI	(3) Marginal Propensity to Consume, MPC
2001	$2,700	$3,200	
2002	3,000	3,600	0.75
2003	3,300	4,000	0.75
2004	3,600	4,400	0.75
2005	3,900	4,800	0.75
2006	4,200	5,200	0.75

Note: Amounts are in billions of dollars..

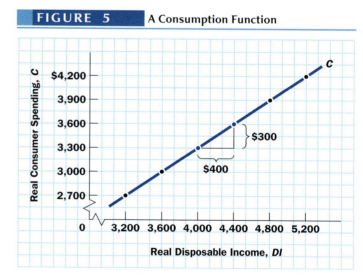

FIGURE 5   A Consumption Function

[8] Figure 4 is limited to seventeen years of data, so try fitting a single straight line to all of the data in Figure 3. You will find that you can do remarkably well.

will be induced by each dollar *change* in disposable income. For each $1 of tax cut, economists expect consumption to rise by $1 times the marginal propensity to consume.

> To estimate the initial effect of a tax cut on consumer spending, economists must first estimate the MPC and then multiply the amount of the tax cut by the estimated MPC.[9] Because they never know the true MPC with certainty, their prediction is always subject to some margin of error.

FACTORS THAT SHIFT THE CONSUMPTION FUNCTION

Unfortunately for policy planners, the consumption function does not always stand still. Recall from Chapter 4 the important distinction between a *movement along* a demand curve and a *shift* of the curve. A demand curve depicts the relationship between quantity demanded and *one* of its many determinants—price. Thus a change in price causes a *movement along the demand curve*. But a change in any other factor that influences quantity demanded causes a *shift of the entire demand curve*.

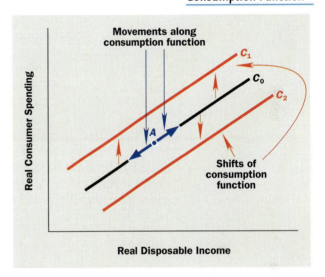

FIGURE 6

Shifts of the Consumption Function

Because factors other than disposable income influence consumer spending, a similar distinction is vital to understanding real-world consumption functions. Look back at the definition of the consumption function in the margin of page 544. A change in disposable income leads to a *movement along the consumption function* precisely because the consumption function depicts the relationship between C and DI. Such movements, which are what we have been considering so far, are indicated by the blue arrows in Figure 6.

But consumption also has other determinants, and a change in any of them will *shift the entire consumption function*—as indicated by the red arrows in Figure 6. Such shifts account for many of the errors in forecasting consumption. To summarize:

> Any change in disposable income moves us along a given consumption function. A change in any of the other determinants of consumption shifts the entire consumption schedule (see Figure 6).

Because disposable income is far and away the main determinant of consumer spending, the real-world data in Figure 3 come *close* to lying along a straight line. But if you use a ruler to draw such a line, you will find that it misses a number of points badly. These deviations reflect the influence of the "other determinants" just mentioned. Let us see what some of them are.

Wealth   One factor affecting spending is consumers' *wealth*, which is a source of purchasing power in addition to income. Wealth and income are different things. For example, a wealthy retiree with a huge bank balance may earn little current *income* when interest rates are low. But a high-flying investment banker who spends every penny of the high income she earns will not accumulate much *wealth*.

To appreciate the importance of the distinction, think about two recent college graduates, each of whom earns $40,000 per year. If one of them has $100,000 in the bank, and the other has no assets at all, whom do you think will spend more? Presumably the one with the big bank account. The general point is that current income

---

[9] The word *initial* in this sentence is an important one. The next chapter will explain why the effects discussed in this chapter are only the beginning of the story.

is not the only source of spendable funds; households can also finance spending by cashing in some of the wealth they have previously accumulated.

One important implication of this analysis is that the stock market can exert a major influence on consumer spending. A stock market boom adds to wealth and thus raises the consumption function, as depicted by the shift from C_0 to C_1 in Figure 6. That is what happened in the late 1990s, when the stock market soared and American consumers went on a spending spree. Correspondingly, a collapse of stock prices, like the one that occurred in 2000–2002, should shift the consumption function down (see the shift from C_0 to C_2).

The Price Level   Stocks are hardly the only form of wealth. People hold a great deal of wealth in forms that are fixed in money terms. Bank accounts are the most obvious example, but government and corporate bonds also have fixed face values in money terms. The purchasing power of such **money-fixed assets** obviously declines whenever the price level rises, which means that the asset can buy less. For example, if the price level rises by 10 percent, a $1,000 government bond will buy about 10 percent less than it could when prices were lower. This is no trivial matter. Consumers in the United States hold money-fixed assets worth well over $8 *trillion*, so that each 1 percent rise in the price level reduces the purchasing power of consumer wealth by more than $80 billion, a tidy sum. This process, of course, operates equally well in reverse, because a decline in the price level would increase the purchasing power of money-fixed assets.

The Real Interest Rate   A higher real rate of interest raises the rewards for saving. For this reason, many people believe it is "obvious" that higher real interest rates must encourage saving and therefore discourage spending. Surprisingly, however, statistical studies of this relationship suggest otherwise. With very few exceptions, they show that interest rates have virtually no effect on consumption decisions in the United States and other countries. Hence, in developing our model of the economy, we will assume that changes in real interest rates do not shift the consumption function. (See "Using the Tax Code to Spur Saving.")

Future Income Expectations   It is hardly earth-shattering to suggest that consumers' expectations about their *future* incomes should affect how much they spend today. This final determinant of consumer spending holds the key to resolving the puzzle posed at the beginning of the chapter: Why did tax policy designed to boost consumer spending apparently fail in 1975 and again in 2001?

ISSUE REVISITED: *Why the Tax Rebates Failed in 1975 and 2001*

To understand how expectations of future incomes affect current consumer expenditures, consider the abbreviated life histories of three consumers given in Table 2. (The reason for giving our three imaginary individuals such odd names will be apparent shortly.) The consumer named "Constant" earned $100 in each of the years considered in the table. The consumer named "Temporary" earned $100 in three of the four years, but had a good year in 1975. The consumer named "Permanent" enjoyed a permanent increase in income in 1975 and was therefore clearly the richest.

Now let us use our common sense to figure out how much each of these consumers might have spent in 1975. Temporary and Permanent had the same income that year. Do you think they spent the same amount? Not if they had some ability to foresee their future incomes, because Permanent was richer in the long run.

Now compare Constant and Temporary. Temporary had 20 percent higher income in 1975 ($120 versus $100), but only 5 percent more over the entire four-year

---

*A **money-fixed asset** is an asset whose value is a fixed number of dollars.*

POLICY DEBATE

Using the Tax Code to Spur Saving

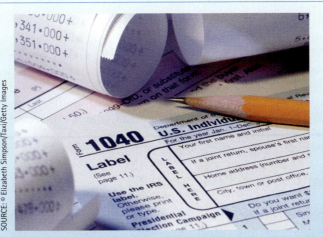

SOURCE: © Elizabeth Simpson/Taxi/Getty Images

Compared to the citizens of virtually every other industrial nation, Americans save very little. Many policy makers consider this lack of saving to be a serious problem, so they have proposed numerous changes in the tax laws to increase incentives to save. In 2001, for example, Congress expanded Individual Retirement Accounts (IRAs), which allow taxpayers to save tax-free. In 2003, the taxation of dividends was reduced. Further tax incentives for saving, it seems, are proposed every year.

All of these tax changes are designed to increase the after-tax return on saving. For example, if you put away money in a bank at a 5 percent rate of interest and your income is taxed at a 30 percent rate, your after-tax rate of return on saving is just 3.5 percent (70 percent of 5 percent). But if the interest is earned tax-free in an IRA,

you get to keep the full 5 percent. Over long periods of time, this seemingly small interest differential compounds to make an enormous difference in returns. For example, $100 invested for 20 years at 3.5 percent interest grows to $199. But at 5 percent, it grows to $265. Members of Congress who advocate tax incentives for saving argue that lower tax rates will induce Americans to save more.

This idea seems reasonable and has many supporters. Unfortunately, the evidence runs squarely against it. Economists have conducted many studies of the effect of higher rates of return on saving. With very few exceptions, they detect little or no impact. Although the evidence fails to support the "common sense" solution to the undersaving problem, the debate goes on. Many people, it seems, refuse to believe the evidence.

period ($420 versus $400). Do you think his spending in 1975 was closer to 20 percent above Constant's, or closer to 5 percent above it? Most people guess the latter.

The point of this example is that consumers very reasonably decide on their current consumption spending by looking at their long-run income prospects. This should come as no surprise to a college student. You are probably spending more than you earn this year, but that does not make you a foolish spendthrift. On the contrary, you know that your college education gives you a strong expectation of much higher incomes in the future, and you are spending with that idea in mind.

To relate this example to the failure of the 1975 income tax cut, imagine that the three rows in Table 2 represent the entire economy under three different government policies. Recall that 1975 was the year of the temporary tax cut. The first row (Constant) shows the unchanged path of disposable income in the absence of any tax cut. The second (Temporary) shows an increase in disposable income attributable to a tax cut for one year only. The bottom row (Permanent) shows a policy that increases DI in every future year by cutting taxes permanently in 1975. Which of the two lower rows do you imagine would have generated more consumer spending in 1975? The bottom row (Permanent), of course. What we have concluded, then, is this:

TABLE 2					
Incomes of Three Consumers					
	Incomes in Each Year				
Consumer	1974	1975	1976	1977	Total Income
Constant	$100	$100	$100	$100	**$400**
Temporary	100	120	100	100	**420**
Permanent	100	120	120	120	**460**

Permanent cuts in income taxes cause greater increases in consumer spending than do temporary cuts of equal magnitude.

The application of this analysis to the 1975 and 2001 tax rebates is immediate. The 1975 tax cut was advertised as a one-time increase in after-tax income, like that experienced by Temporary in Table 2. No future income was affected, so consumers did not increase their spending as much as government officials had hoped. Ironically, the 2001 tax rebate checks actually represented the first installment of a projected permanent tax reduction. But they were so widely advertised as a one-time event that most people receiving the checks probably thought they were temporary.

We have, then, what appears to be a general principle, backed up by both historical evidence and common sense. Permanent changes in income taxes have more significant effects on consumer spending than do temporary ones. This conclusion may seem obvious, but it is not a lesson you would have learned from an introductory textbook thirty years ago. It is one that we learned the hard way, through bitter experience.

THE EXTREME VARIABILITY OF INVESTMENT

Next, we turn to the most *volatile* component of aggregate demand: investment spending.[10] While consumer spending follows movements in disposable income quite closely, investment spending swings from high to low levels with astonishing speed. For example, when real GDP in the United States slowed abruptly from a 3.7 percent growth rate in 2000 to a sluggish 0.8 percent rate in 2001, a drop of about 3 percentage points, the growth rate of real investment spending dropped from 5.7 percent to *minus* 7.9 percent, a swing of over 13 percentage points. What accounts for such dramatic changes in investment spending?

Several factors that influence how much businesses want to invest were discussed in the previous chapter, including interest rates, tax provisions, technical change, and the strength of the economy. Sometimes these determinants change abruptly, leading to dramatic variations in investment. But perhaps the most important factor accounting for the volatility of investment spending was not discussed much in Chapter 24: the *state of business confidence*, which in turn depends on *expectations about the future*.

Although confidence is tricky to measure, it does seem obvious that businesses will build more factories and purchase more new machines when they are optimistic. Correspondingly, their investment plans will be very cautious if the economic outlook appears bleak. Keynes pointed out that psychological perceptions such as these are subject to abrupt shifts, so that fluctuations in investment can be a major cause of instability in aggregate demand.

Unfortunately, neither economists nor, for that matter, psychologists have many good ideas about how to *measure*—much less *control*—business confidence. So economists usually focus on several more objective determinants of investment that are easier to quantify and even influence—factors such as interest rates and tax provisions.

THE DETERMINANTS OF NET EXPORTS

Another highly variable source of demand for U.S. products is foreign purchases of U.S. goods—our *exports*. As we observed earlier in this chapter, we obtain the *net* contribution of foreigners to U.S. aggregate demand by subtracting *imports*, which is the portion of domestic demand that is satisfied by foreign producers, from our exports to get *net exports*. What determines net exports?

---

[10] We repeat the warning given earlier about the meaning of the word *investment*. It *includes* spending by businesses and individuals on newly produced factories, machinery, and houses. But it *excludes* sales of used industrial plants, equipment, and homes as well as purely financial transactions, such as the purchases of stocks and bonds.

National Incomes

Although both exports and imports depend on many factors, the predominant one is *income levels in different countries*. When American consumers and firms spend more on consumption and investment, some of this new spending goes toward the purchase of foreign goods. Therefore:

Our imports rise when our GDP rises and fall when our GDP falls.

Similarly, because our *exports* are the *imports* of other countries, our exports depend on *their* GDPs, not on our own. Thus:

Our exports are relatively insensitive to our own GDP, but are quite sensitive to the GDPs of other countries.

Putting these two ideas together leads to a clear implication: When our economy grows faster than the economies of our trading partners, our net exports tend to shrink. Conversely, when foreign economies grow faster than ours, our net exports tend to rise. Events since the 1990s illustrate this point dramatically. When the U.S. economy stagnated between 1990 and 1992, our net exports rose from −$55 billion to −$16 billion. (Remember, −16 is a *larger* number than −55!) Since then, growth in the United States has generally outstripped growth abroad, and U.S. net exports have plummeted from −$16 billion to −$619 billion in 2005.

Relative Prices and Exchange Rates

Although GDP levels here and abroad are important influences on a country's net exports, they are not the only relevant factors. International prices matter, too.

To make things concrete, let's focus on trade between the United States and Japan. Suppose American prices rise while Japanese prices fall, making U.S. goods more expensive *relative to Japanese goods*. If American consumers react to these new relative prices by buying more Japanese goods, U.S. *imports rise*. If Japanese consumers react to the same relative price changes by buying fewer American products, U.S. *exports fall*. Both reactions reduce America's *net* exports.

Naturally, a decline in American prices (or a rise in Japanese prices) does precisely the opposite. Thus:

A rise in the prices of a country's goods will lead to a reduction in that country's net exports. Analogously, a decline in the prices of a country's goods will raise that country's net exports. Similarly, price increases abroad raise the home country's net exports, whereas price decreases abroad have the opposite effect.

This simple idea holds the key to understanding how exchange rates among the world's currencies influence exports and imports—an important topic that we will consider in depth in Chapters 35 and 36. The reason is that exchange rates translate foreign prices into terms that are familiar to home country customers—their own currencies.

Consider, for example, Americans interested in buying Japanese cars that cost ¥3,000,000. If it takes ¥100 to buy a dollar, these cars cost American buyers $30,000. But if the dollar is worth ¥150, those same cars cost Americans just $20,000, and consumers in the United States are likely to buy more of them. These sorts of responses help explain why American automakers lost market share to Japanese imports when the dollar rose against the yen in the late 1990s.

HOW PREDICTABLE IS AGGREGATE DEMAND?

We have now learned enough to see why economists often have difficulty predicting aggregate demand. Consider the four main components, starting with consumer spending.

Because wealth affects consumption, forecasts of spending can be thrown off by unexpected movements of the stock market or by poor forecasts of future prices. It may also be difficult to anticipate how taxpayers will view changes in the income tax law. If the government says that a tax cut is permanent (as for example, in 1964), will consumers take the government at its word and increase their spending accordingly? Perhaps not, if the government has a history of raising taxes after promising to keep them low. Similarly, when (as in 1975) the government explicitly announces that a tax cut is temporary, will consumers always believe the announcement? Or might they greet it with a hefty dose of skepticism? Such a reaction is quite possible if there is a history of "temporary" tax changes that stayed on the books indefinitely.

Swings in investment spending are even more difficult to predict, partly because they are tied so closely to business confidence and expectations. Developments abroad also often lead to surprises in the net export account. Even the final component of aggregate demand, government purchases (G), is subject to the vagaries of politics and to sudden military and national security events such as 9/11.

We could say much more about the determinants of aggregate demand, but it is best to leave the rest to more advanced courses. For we are now ready to apply our knowledge of aggregate demand to the construction of the first model of the economy. Although it is true that income determines consumption, the consumption function in turn helps to determine the level of income. If that sounds like circular reasoning, read the next chapter!

SUMMARY

1. **Aggregate demand** is the total volume of goods and services purchased by consumers, businesses, government units, and foreigners. It can be expressed as the sum $C + I + G + (X - IM)$, where C is consumer spending, I is investment spending, G is **government purchases**, and $X - IM$ is **net exports.**

2. Aggregate demand is a schedule: The aggregate quantity demanded depends on (among other things) the price level. But, for any given price level, aggregate demand is a number.

3. Economists reserve the term **investment** to refer to purchases of newly produced factories, machinery, software, and houses.

4. Gross domestic product is the total volume of final goods and services produced in the country.

5. **National income** is the sum of the before-tax wages, interest, rents, and profits earned by all individuals in the economy. By necessity, it must be approximately equal to domestic product.

6. **Disposable income** is the sum of the incomes of all individuals in the economy after taxes and transfers. It is the chief determinant of **consumer expenditures.**

7. All of these concepts, and others, can be depicted in a circular flow diagram that shows expenditures on all four sources flowing into business firms and national income flowing out.

8. The close relationship between consumer spending (C) and disposable income (DI) is called the **consumption function.** Its slope, which is used to predict the change in

consumption that will be caused by a change in income taxes, is called the **marginal propensity to consume (MPC).**

9. Changes in disposable income move us along a given consumption function. Changes in any of the other variables that affect C shift the entire consumption function. Among the most important of these other variables are total consumer wealth, the price level, and expected future incomes.

10. Because consumers hold so many **money-fixed assets,** they lose purchasing power when prices rise, which leads them to reduce their spending.

11. The government often tries to manipulate aggregate demand by influencing private consumption decisions, usually through changes in the personal income tax. But this policy did not work well in 1975 or 2001.

12. Future income prospects help explain why. The 1975 tax cut was temporary and therefore left future incomes unaffected. The 2001 tax cut was also advertised as a one-time event.

13. Investment is the most volatile component of aggregate demand, largely because it is closely tied to confidence and expectations.

14. Policy makers cannot influence confidence in any reliable way, so policies designed to spur investment focus on more objective, although possibly less important, determinants of investment—such as interest rates and taxes.

15. Net exports depend on GDPs and relative prices both domestically and abroad.

KEY TERMS

Aggregate demand   538

Consumer expenditure (C)   538

Investment spending (I)   539

Government purchases (G)   539

Net exports (X − IM)   539

C + I + G + (X − IM)   539

National income   539

Disposable income (DI)   539

Circular flow diagram   539

Transfer payments   540

Scatter diagram   542

Consumption function   544

Marginal propensity to consume (MPC)   544

Movements along versus shifts of the consumption function   545

Money–fixed assets   546

Temporary versus permanent tax changes   547

TEST YOURSELF

1. What are the four components of aggregate demand? Which is the largest? Which is the smallest?

2. Which of the following acts constitute *investment* according to the economist's definition of that term ?

    a. Intel builds a new factory to manufacture semi-conductors.

    b. You buy 100 shares of Intel stock.

    c. A small chipmaker goes bankrupt, and Intel purchases its factory and equipment.

    d. Your family buys a newly constructed home from a developer.

    e. Your family buys an older home from another family. (*Hint:* Are any *new* products demanded by this action?)

3. On a piece of graph paper, construct a consumption function from the data given below and determine the MPC.

Year	Consumer Spending	Disposable Income
1998	$1,200	$1,500
1999	1,440	1,800
2000	1,680	2,100
2001	1,920	2,400
2002	2,160	2,700

4. In which direction will the consumption function shift if the price level rises? Show this on your graph from the previous question.

DISCUSSION QUESTIONS

1. Explain the difference between *investment* as the term is used by most people and *investment* as defined by an economist?

2. What would the circular flow diagram (Figure 1) look like in an economy with no government? Draw one for yourself.

3. The marginal propensity to consume (MPC) for the United States as a whole is roughly 0.90. Explain in words what this means. What is your personal MPC at this stage in your life? How might that change by the time you are your parents' age?

4. Look at the scatter diagram in Figure 3. What does it tell you about what was going on in this country in the years 1942 to 1945?

5. What is a consumption function, and why is it a useful device for government economists planning a tax cut?

6. Explain why permanent tax cuts are likely to lead to bigger increases in consumer spending than are temporary tax cuts.

7. In 2001 and again in 2003, Congress enacted changes in the tax law designed to promote saving. If such saving incentives had been successful, how would the consumption function have shifted?

8. **(More difficult)** Between 1990 and 1991, real disposable income (in 2000 dollars) barely increased at all, owing to a recession. (It rose from $5,324 billion to $5,352 billion.) Use the data on real consumption expenditures given on the inside back cover of this book to compare the change in *C* to this $28 billion change in *DI*. Explain why dividing the two does *not* give a good estimate of the marginal propensity to consume.

APPENDIX *National Income Accounting*

The type of macroeconomic analysis presented in this book dates from the publication of John Maynard Keynes's *The General Theory of Employment, Interest, and Money* in 1936. But at that time, there was really no way to test Keynes's theories because the necessary data did not exist. It took some years for the theoretical notions used by Keynes to find concrete expression in real-world data.

The system of measurement devised for collecting and expressing macroeconomic data is called national income accounting.

The development of this system of accounts ranks as a great achievement in applied economics, perhaps as important in its own right as was Keynes's theoretical work. Without it, the practical value of Keynesian analysis would be severely limited. Economists spent long hours wrestling with the many difficult conceptual questions that arose as they translated the theory into numbers. Along the way, some more-or-less arbitrary decisions and conventions had to be made. You may not agree with all of them, but the accounting framework that was devised, though imperfect, is eminently serviceable.

■ DEFINING GDP: EXCEPTIONS TO THE RULES

We first encountered the concept of **gross domestic product (GDP)** in Chapter 22.

Gross domestic product (GDP) is the sum of the money values of all final goods and services produced during a specified period of time, usually one year.

However, the definition of GDP has certain exceptions that we have not yet noted.

First, the treatment of government output involves a minor departure from the principle of using market prices. Unlike private products, the "outputs" of government offices are not sold; indeed, it is sometimes even difficult to define what those outputs are. Lacking prices for outputs, national income accountants fall back on the only prices they have: prices for the inputs from which the outputs are produced. Thus:

Government outputs are valued at the cost of the inputs needed to produce them.

This means, for example, that if a clerk at the Department of Motor Vehicles who earns $16 per hour spends one-half hour torturing you with explanations of why you cannot get a driver's license, that particular government "service" increases GDP by $8.

Second, some goods that are produced during the year but not yet sold are nonetheless counted in that year's GDP. Specifically, goods that firms add to their *inventories* count in the GDP even though they do not pass through markets.

National income statisticians treat inventories as if they were "bought" by the firms that produced them, even though these "purchases" do not actually take place.

Finally, the treatment of investment goods runs slightly counter to the rule that GDP includes only final goods. In a broad sense, factories, generators, machine tools, and the like might be considered to be intermediate goods. After all, their owners want them only for use in producing other goods, not for any innate value that they possess. But this classification would present a real problem. Because factories and machines normally are never sold to consumers, when would we count them in GDP? National income statisticians avoid this problem by defining investment goods as final products demanded by the *firms* that buy them.

Now that we have a more complete definition of what the GDP is, let us turn to the problem of actually measuring it. National income accountants have devised three ways to perform this task, and we consider each in turn.

■ GDP AS THE SUM OF FINAL GOODS AND SERVICES

The first way to measure GDP seems to be the most natural, because it follows so directly from the circular flow diagram (Figure 1). It also turns out to be the most useful definition for macroeconomic analysis. We simply add up the final demands of all consumers, business firms, government, and foreigners. Using the symbols Y, C, I, G, and $(X - IM)$ as we did in the chapter, we have:

$$Y = C + I + G + (X - IM)$$

The I that appears in the actual U.S. national accounts is called **gross private domestic investment.** We will explain the word *gross* presently. *Private* indicates that government investment is considered part of G, and *domestic* means that machinery sold by American firms to foreign companies is included in exports rather than in I (investment).

Gross private domestic investment includes business investment in plant, equipment, and software; residential construction; and inventory investment.

We repeat again that *only* these three things are *investment* in national income accounting terminology.

As defined in the national income accounts, investment includes only newly produced capital goods, such as machinery, factories, and new homes. It does not include exchanges of existing assets.

The symbol *G*, for government purchases, represents the volume of *current goods and services purchased by all levels of government*. Thus, all government payments to its employees are counted in *G*, as are all of its purchases of goods. Few citizens realize, however, that *the federal government spends most of its money, not for purchases of goods and services, but rather on transfer payments*—literally, giving away money—either to individuals or to other levels of government.

The importance of this conceptual distinction lies in the fact that *G* represents the part of the national product that government uses up for its own purposes—to pay for armies, bureaucrats, paper, and ink—whereas transfer payments merely shuffle purchasing power from one group of citizens to another. Except for the administrators needed to run these programs, real economic resources are not used up in this process.

In adding up the nation's total output as the sum of $C + I + G + (X - IM)$, we sum the shares of GDP that are used up by consumers, investors, government, and foreigners, respectively. Because transfer payments merely give someone the capability to spend on *C*, it is logical to exclude transfers from our definition of *G*, including in *C* only the portion of these transfer payments that consumers spend. If we included transfers in *G*, the same spending would get counted twice: once in *G* and then again in *C*.

The final component of GDP is net exports, which are simply exports of goods and services minus imports of goods and services. Table 3 shows GDP for 2006, in both nominal and real terms, computed as the sum of $C + I + G + (X - IM)$. Note that the numbers for net exports in the table are actually negative. We will say much more about America's trade deficit in Part VIII.

■ GDP AS THE SUM OF ALL FACTOR PAYMENTS

We can count up the GDP another way: by *adding up all incomes in the economy*. Let's see how this method handles some typical transactions. Suppose General Electric builds a generator and sells it to General Motors for $1 million. The first method of calculating GDP simply counts the $1 million as part of *I*. The second method asks: What incomes resulted from producing this generator? The answer might be something like this:

Wages of GE employees	$400,000
Interest to bondholders	50,000
Rentals of buildings	50,000
Profits of GE stockholders	100,000

The total is $600,000. The remaining $400,000 is accounted for by inputs that GE purchased from other companies: steel, circuitry, tubing, rubber, and so on. But if we traced this $400,000 back even further, we would find that it is accounted for by the wages, interest, and rentals paid by these other companies, *plus* their profits, *plus* their purchases from other firms. In fact, for *every* firm in the economy, there is an accounting identity that says:

$$\text{Revenue from sales} = \begin{cases} \text{Wages paid} + \\ \text{Interest paid} + \\ \text{Rentals paid} + \\ \text{Profits earned} + \\ \text{Purchases from other firms} \end{cases}$$

Why must this always be true? Because profits are the balancing item; they are what is *left over* after the firm has made all other payments. In fact, this accounting identity really reflects the definition of profits: sales revenue less all costs.

Now apply this accounting identity to *all firms in the economy*. Total purchases from other firms are precisely what we call *intermediate goods*. What, then, do we get if we subtract these intermediate transactions from both sides of the equation?

$$\begin{array}{l}\text{Revenue from sales minus} \\ \text{Purchases from other firms}\end{array} = \begin{cases} \text{Wages paid} + \\ \text{Interest paid} + \\ \text{Rentals paid} + \\ \text{Profits earned} \end{cases}$$

TABLE 3		
Gross Domestic Product in 2006 as the Sum of Final Demands		
Item	Nominal Amount*	Real Amount†
Personal consumption expenditures (*C*)	$ 9,269	$8,091
Gross private domestic investment (*I*)	2,213	1,946
Government purchases of goods and services (*G*)	2,527	1,998
Net exports (*X − IM*)	−763	−618
Exports (*X*)	1,466	1,303
Imports (*IM*)	2,229	1,921
Gross domestic product (Y)	**13,247**	**11,164**

*In billions of current dollars.
†In billions of 2000 dollars.
SOURCE: U.S. Department of Commerce. Totals do not add up precisely due to rounding and method of deflating.

On the right-hand side, we have the sum of all factor incomes: payments to labor, land, and capital. On the left-hand side, we have total sales minus sales of intermediate goods. This means that we have sales of *final goods*, which is precisely our definition of GDP. Thus, the accounting identity for the entire economy can be rewritten as follows:

GDP = Wages + Interest + Rents + Profits

This definition gives national income accountants another way to measure the GDP.

Table 4 shows how to obtain GDP from the sum of all incomes. Once again, we have omitted a few details in our discussion. By adding up wages, interest, rents, and profits, we obtain only $10,707 billion, whereas GDP in 2006 was $13,247 billion. When sales taxes, excise taxes, and the like are added to the sum of wages, interest, rents, and profits, we obtain what is called **national income**—the sum of all factor payments, including indirect business taxes.

> **National income** is the sum of the incomes that all individuals in the country earn in the forms of wages, interest, rents, and profits. It includes indirect business taxes, but excludes transfer payments and makes no deduction for income taxes.

Notice that national income is a measure of the factor incomes of all Americans, regardless of whether they work in this country or somewhere else. Likewise, incomes earned by foreigners in the United States are excluded from (our) national income. We will return to this distinction shortly.

But, reading down Table 4, we next encounter a new concept: **net national product (NNP)**, a measure of *production*. For reasons explained in the chapter, NNP is conceptually identical to national income. However, in practice, national income accountants estimate *income* and *production* independently; and so the two measures are never precisely equal. The difference in 2006 was just $2.5 billion, or just 0.02 percent of NNP; it is called the statistical discrepancy.

Moving further down the table, the only difference between NNP and **gross national product (GNP)** is **depreciation** of the nation's capital stock. Thus the adjective "net" means excluding depreciation and "gross" means including it. GNP is thus a measure of *all* final production, making no adjustment for the fact that some capital is used up each year, and thus needs to be replaced. NNP deducts the required replacements to arrive at a net production figure.

> **Depreciation** is the value of the portion of the nation's capital equipment that is used up within the year. It tells us how much output is needed just to maintain the economy's capital stock.

TABLE 4
Gross Domestic Product in 2006 as the Sum of Incomes

Item	Amount
Compensation of employees (wages)	**$7,490**
plus	
Net interest	**509**
plus	
Rental income	**77**
plus	
Profits	**2,631**
Corporate profits	1,616
Proprietors' income	1,015
plus	
Indirect business taxes and misc. items	**995**
equals	
National income	11,702
plus	
Statistical discrepancy	**−2**
equals	
Net national product	**11,700**
plus	
Depreciation	1,577
equals	
Gross national product	**13,277**
minus	
Income received from other countries	**666**
plus	
Income paid to other countries	**636**
equals	
Gross domestic product	**13,247**

Note: Amounts are in billions of dollars.
SOURCE: U.S. Department of Commerce. Totals do not add up precisely due to rounding.

From a conceptual point of view, most economists feel that NNP is a more meaningful indicator of the economy's output than is GNP. After all, the depreciation component of GNP represents the output that is needed just to repair and replace worn-out factories and machines; it is not available for anybody to consume.[11] Therefore, NNP seems to be a better measure of production than GNP.

Alas, GNP is much easier to measure because depreciation is a particularly tricky item. What fraction of his tractor did Farmer Jones "use up" last year? How much did the Empire State Building depreciate during 2006? If you ask yourself these difficult questions, you will understand why most economists believe that we can measure GNP more accurately than NNP. For this reason, most economic models are based on GNP.

---

[11] If the capital stock is used for consumption, it will decline, and the nation will wind up poorer than it was before.

The final two adjustments that bring us to GDP return to a fact mentioned earlier. Some American citizens earn their incomes abroad, and some of the payments made by American companies are paid to foreign citizens. Thus, to obtain a measure of total production in the U.S. *domestic* economy (which is GDP) rather than a measure of the total production by U.S. *nationals* (which is GNP), we must *subtract* the income that Americans receive for factors supplied abroad and *add* the income that foreigners receive for factors supplied here. The net of these two adjustments is a very small number, as Table 4 shows. Thus, GDP and GNP are almost equal.

In Table 4, you can hardly help noticing the preponderant share of employee compensation in total factor payments—about 70 percent. Labor is by far the most important factor of production. The return on land is under 1 percent of factor payments, and interest accounts for almost 5 percent. Profits account for the remaining 25 percent, although the size of corporate profits (just 15 percent of GDP in 2006) is much less than the public thinks. If, by some magic stroke, we could convert all corporate profits into wages without upsetting the economy's performance, the average worker would get a raise of about 22 percent!

■ GDP AS THE SUM OF VALUES ADDED

It may strike you as strange that national income accountants include only *final* goods and services in GDP. Aren't *intermediate* goods part of the nation's product? Of course they are. The problem is that, if all intermediate goods were included in GDP, we would wind up double- and triple-counting certain goods and services and therefore get an exaggerated impression of the actual level of economic activity.

To explain why, and to show how national income accountants cope with this difficulty, we must introduce a new concept, called *value added*.

The **value added** by a firm is its revenue from selling a product minus the amount paid for goods and services purchased from other firms.

The intuitive sense of this concept is clear: If a firm buys some inputs from other firms, does something to them, and sells the resulting product for a price higher than it paid for the inputs, we say that the firm has "added value" to the product. If we sum up the values added by all firms in the economy, we must get the total value of all final products. Thus:

GDP can be measured as the sum of the values added by all firms.

To verify this fact, look back at the accounting identity at the bottom of page 553. The left-hand side of this equation, sales revenue minus purchases from other firms, is precisely the firm's value added. Thus:

Value added = Wages + Interest + Rents + Profits

Because the second method we gave for measuring GDP is to add up wages, interest, rents, and profits, we see that the value-added approach must yield the same answer.

The value-added concept is useful in avoiding double-counting. Often, however, intermediate goods are difficult to distinguish from final goods. Paint bought by a painter, for example, is an intermediate good. But paint bought by a do-it-yourselfer is a final good. What happens, then, if the professional painter buys some paint to refurbish his own garage? The intermediate good becomes a final good. You can see that the line between intermediate goods and final goods is a fuzzy one in practice.

If we measure GDP by the sum of values added, however, we need not make such subtle distinctions. In this method, every purchase of a new good or service counts, but we do not count the entire selling price, only the portion that represents value added.

To illustrate this idea, consider the data in Table 5 and how they would affect GDP as the sum of final products. Our example begins when a farmer who grows soybeans sells them to a mill for $3 per bushel. This transaction does *not* count in the GDP, because the miller does not purchase the soybeans for her own use. The miller then grinds up the soybeans and sells the resulting bag of soy meal to a factory that produces soy sauce. The miller receives $4, but GDP still has not increased because the ground beans are also an intermediate product. Next, the factory turns the beans into soy sauce, which it sells to your favorite Chinese restaurant for $8. Still no effect on GDP.

But then the big moment arrives: The restaurant sells the sauce to you and other customers as a part of your meals, and you eat it. At this point, the $10 worth of soy sauce becomes part of a final product and *does* count in the GDP. Notice that if we had also counted the three intermediate transactions (farmer to miller, miller to factory, factory to restaurant), we would have come up with $25—2½ times too much.

TABLE 5			
An Illustration of Final and Intermediate Goods			
Item	Seller	Buyer	Price
Bushel of soybeans	Farmer	Miller	$3
Bag of soy meal	Miller	Factory	4
Gallon of soy sauce	Factory	Restaurant	8
Gallon of soy sauce used as seasoning	Restaurant	Consumers	10
			Total: $25
Addendum: Contribution to GDP $10			

Why is it too much? The reason is straightforward. Neither the miller, the factory owner, nor the restaurateur values the product we have been considering *for its own sake*. Only the customers who eat the final product (the soy sauce) have increased their material well-being, so only this last transaction counts in the GDP. However, as we shall now see, value-added calculations enable us to come up with the right answer ($10) by counting only *part* of each transaction. The basic idea is to count at each step only the contribution to the value of the ultimate final product that is made at that step, excluding the values of items produced at other steps.

Ignoring the minor items (such as fertilizer) that the farmer purchases from others, the entire $3 selling price of the bushel of soybeans is new output produced by the farmer; that is, the whole $3 is value added. The miller then grinds the beans and sells them for $4. She has added $4 minus $3, or $1 to the value of the beans. When the factory turns this soy meal into soy sauce and sells it for $8, it has added $8 minus $4, or $4 more in value. Finally, when the restaurant sells it to hungry customers for $10, a further $2 of value is added.

The last column of Table 6 shows this chain of creation of value added. We see that the total value added by all four firms is $10, exactly the same as the restaurant's selling price. This is as it must be, for only the restaurant sells the soybeans as a final product.

TABLE 6
An Illustration of Value Added

Item	Seller	Buyer	Price	Value Added
Bushel of soybeans	Farmer	Miller	$3	$3
Bag of soy meal	Miller	Factory	4	1
Gallon of soy sauce	Factory	Restaurant	8	4
Gallon of soy sauce used as seasoning	Restaurant	Consumers	10	2
		Total:	$25	$10

Addendum: Contribution to GDP

Final Products	$10
Sum of values added	$10

SUMMARY

1. **Gross domestic product (GDP)** is the sum of the money values of all final goods and services produced during a year and sold on organized markets. There are, however, certain exceptions to this definition.

2. One way to measure the GDP is to add up the final demands of consumers, investors, government, and foreigners: $GDP = C + I + G + (X - IM)$.

3. A second way to measure the GDP is to start with all factor payments—wages, interest, rents, and profits—that constitute the **national income** and then add indirect business taxes and **depreciation**.

4. A third way to measure the GDP is to sum up the **values added** by every firm in the economy (and then once again add indirect business taxes and depreciation).

5. Except for possible bookkeeping and statistical errors, all three methods must give the same answer.

KEY TERMS

National income accounting   552

Gross domestic product (GDP)   552

Gross private domestic investment (I)   552

National income   554

Net national product (NNP)   554

Depreciation   554

Value added   555

TEST YOURSELF

1. Which of the following transactions are included in the gross domestic product, and by how much does each raise GDP?

   a. You buy a new Honda, made in the United States, paying $18,000.

   b. You buy a new Toyota, imported from Japan, paying $18,000.

   c. You buy a used Cadillac, paying $3,000.

   d. America Online spends $100 million to increase its Internet capacity.

   e. Your grandmother receives a Social Security check for $1,200.

   f. Chrysler manufactures 1,000 automobiles at a cost of $12,000 each. Unable to sell them, the company holds the cars as inventories.

g. Mr. Black and Mr. Blue, each out for a Sunday drive, have a collision in which their cars are destroyed. Black and Blue each hire a lawyer to sue the other, paying the lawyers $3,000 each for services rendered. The judge throws the case out of court.

h. You sell a used computer to your friend for $100.

2. The following outline provides a complete description of all economic activity in Trivialand for 2004. Draw up versions of Tables 3 and 4 for Trivialand showing GDP computed in two different ways.[12]

   i. There are thousands of farmers but only two big business firms in Trivialand: Specific Motors (an auto company) and Super Duper (a chain of food markets). There is no government and no depreciation.

   ii. Specific Motors produced 1,000 small cars, which it sold at $6,000 each, and 100 trucks, which it sold at $8,000 each. Consumers bought 800 of the cars, and the remaining 200 cars were exported to the United States. Super Duper bought all the trucks.

   iii. Sales at Super Duper markets amounted to $14 million, all of it sold to consumers.

   iv. All farmers in Trivialand are self-employed and sell all of their wares to Super Duper.

   v. The costs incurred by all of Trivialand's businesses were as follows:

	Specific Motors	Super Duper	Farmers
Wages	$3,800,000	$4,500,000	$ 0
Interest	100,000	200,000	700,000
Rent	200,000	1,000,000	2,000,000
Purchases of food	0	7,000,000	0

3. **(More difficult)** Now complicate Trivialand in the following ways and answer the same questions. In addition, calculate national income and disposable income.[13]

   a. The government bought 50 cars, leaving only 150 cars for export. In addition, the government spent $800,000 on wages and made $1,200,000 in transfer payments.

   b. Depreciation for the year amounted to $600,000 for Specific Motors and $200,000 for Super Duper. (The farmers had no depreciation.)

   c. The government levied sales taxes amounting to $500,000 on Specific Motors and $200,000 on Super Duper (but none on farmers). In addition, the government levied a 10 percent income tax on all wages, interest, and rental income.

   d. In addition to the food and cars mentioned in Test Yourself Question 2, consumers in Trivialand imported 500 computers from the United States at $2,000 each.

DISCUSSION QUESTIONS

1. Explain the difference between final goods and intermediate goods. Why is it sometimes difficult to apply this distinction in practice? In this regard, why is the concept of value added useful?

2. Explain the difference between government spending and government purchases of goods and services (G). Which is larger?

3. Explain why national income and gross domestic product would be essentially equal if there were no depreciation.

---

[12] In Trivialand, net national product and net domestic product are the same. So there are no entries corresponding to "income received from other countries" or "income paid to other countries," as in Table 4.

[13] In this context, disposable income is *national income* plus transfer payments minus taxes.

DEMAND-SIDE EQUILIBRIUM: UNEMPLOYMENT OR INFLATION?

A definite ratio, to be called the Multiplier, can be established between income and investment.

JOHN MAYNARD KEYNES

Let's briefly review where we have just been. In Chapter 22, we learned that the interaction of aggregate demand and aggregate supply determines whether the economy stagnates or prospers, whether our labor and capital resources are fully employed or unemployed. In Chapter 25, we learned that aggregate demand has four components: consumer expenditure (C), investment (I), government purchases (G), and net exports ($X - IM$). It is now time to start building a theory that puts all the pieces together so we can see where the aggregate demand and aggregate supply curves come from.

Our approach is sequential. Because it is best to walk before you try to run, we begin in this chapter by assuming that the price level, the rate of interest, and the international value of the dollar are all constant. None of these assumptions is true, of course, and we will dispense with them all in subsequent chapters. But we reap two important benefits from making these unrealistic assumptions now. First, they enable us to construct a simple but useful model of how the strength of aggregate demand influences the level of gross domestic product (GDP)—a model we will use to derive specific numerical solutions. Second, this model gives us an initial answer to a question of great importance to policymakers: Can we expect the economy to achieve full employment if the government does not intervene?

CONTENTS

ISSUE: *Why Does the Market Permit Unemployment?*

Economists are fond of pointing out, with some awe, the amazing achievements of free markets. Without central direction, they somehow get businesses to produce just the goods and services that consumers want—and to do so cheaply and efficiently. If consumers want less meat and more fish, markets respond. If people subsequently change their minds, markets respond again. Free markets seem able to coordinate literally millions of decisions effortlessly and seamlessly.

Yet for hundreds of years and all over the globe, market economies have stumbled over one particular coordination problem: the periodic bouts of mass unemployment that we call *recessions* and *depressions*. Widespread unemployment represents a failure to coordinate economic activity in the following sense. If the unemployed were hired, they would be able to buy the goods and services that businesses cannot sell. The revenues from those sales would, in turn, allow firms to pay the workers. So a seemingly straightforward "deal" offers jobs for the unemployed and sales for the firms. But somehow this deal is not made. Workers remain unemployed and firms get stuck with unsold output.

Thus, free markets, which somehow manage to get rough diamonds dug out of the ground in South Africa and turned into beautiful rings that grooms buy for brides in Los Angeles, cannot seem to solve the coordination problem posed by unemployment. Why not? For centuries, economists puzzled over this question. By the end of the chapter, we will be well on the way toward providing an answer.

THE MEANING OF EQUILIBRIUM GDP

We begin by putting the four components of aggregate demand together to see how they interact, using as our organizing framework the circular flow diagram from the last chapter. In doing so, we initially ignore the possibility, raised in earlier chapters, that the government might use monetary and fiscal policy to steer the economy in some desired direction. Aside from pedagogical simplicity, there is an important reason for doing so. One of the crucial questions surrounding stabilization policy is whether the economy would *automatically* gravitate toward full employment if the government simply left it alone. Contradicting the teachings of generations of economists before him, Keynes claimed it would not. But Keynes's views remain controversial to this day. We can study the issue best by imagining an economy in which the government never tried to manipulate aggregate demand, which is just what we do in this chapter.

To begin to construct a simple model of the size of the economy, we must first understand what we mean by *equilibrium GDP*. Figure 1, which repeats Figure 1 from the last chapter, is a circular flow diagram that will help us do this. As explained in the last chapter, total *production* and total *income* must be equal. But the same need not be true of total spending. Imagine that, for some reason, the total expenditures made after point 4 in the figure, $C + I + G + (X - IM)$, exceed the output produced by the business firms at point 5. What happens then?

Because consumers, businesses, government, and foreigners together are buying more than firms are producing, businesses will start taking goods out of their warehouses to meet customer demand. Thus, inventory stocks will fall—which signals retailers that they need to increase their orders and manufacturers that they need to step up production. Consequently, output is likely to rise.

At some later date, if evidence indicates that the high level of spending is not just a temporary aberration, either manufacturers or retailers (or both) may also respond to buoyant sales performances by raising their prices. Economists therefore say that neither output nor the price level is in **equilibrium** when total spending exceeds current production.

The definition of *equilibrium* in the margin tells us that the economy cannot be in equilibrium when total spending exceeds production, because falling inventories

Equilibrium refers to a situation in which neither consumers nor firms have any incentive to change their behavior. They are content to continue with things as they are.

demonstrate to firms that their production and pricing decisions were not quite appropriate.[1] Thus, because we normally use GDP to measure output:

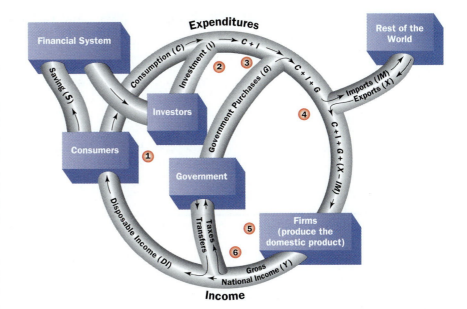

Expenditures

Financial System

Rest of the World

Saving (S)

Consumption (C)

Investment (I)

2   3   C + I

C + I + G

Imports (IM)
Exports (X)

Investors

Government Purchases (G)

4

C + I + G + (X − IM)

Consumers

1

Government

Firms (produce the domestic product)

5

Disposable Income (DI)

Taxes
Transfers

6

Gross National Income (Y)

Income

The equilibrium level of GDP on the demand side cannot be one at which total spending exceeds output because firms will notice that they are depleting their inventory stocks. Firms may first decide to increase production sufficiently to meet the higher demand. Later they may decide to raise prices.

FIGURE 1

The Circular Flow Diagram

Now imagine the other case, in which the flow of spending reaching firms falls short of current production. Unsold output winds up as additional inventories. The inventory pile-up signals firms that either their pricing or output decision was wrong. Once again, they will probably react first by cutting back on production, causing GDP to fall (at point 5 in Figure 1). If the imbalance persists, they may also lower prices to stimulate sales. But they certainly will not be happy with things as they are. Thus:

The equilibrium level of GDP on the demand side cannot be one at which total spending is less than output, because firms will not allow inventories to pile up. They may decide to decrease production, or they may decide to cut prices in order to stimulate demand.

We have now determined, by process of elimination, the only level of output that is consistent with people's desires to spend. We have reasoned that GDP will *rise* whenever it is less than total spending, $C + I + G + (X − IM)$, and that GDP will fall whenever it exceeds $C + I + G + (X − IM)$. Equilibrium can occur, then, only when there is just enough spending to absorb the current level of production. Under such circumstances, producers conclude that their price and output decisions are correct and have no incentive to change. We conclude that:

The **equilibrium level of GDP on the demand side** is the level at which total spending equals production. In such a situation, firms find their inventories remaining at desired levels, so they have no incentive to change output or prices.

Thus, the circular flow diagram has helped us to understand the concept of equilibrium GDP and has shown us how the economy is driven toward this equilibrium. It leaves unanswered, however, three important questions:

- How large is the equilibrium level of GDP?
- Will the economy suffer from unemployment, inflation, or both?
- Is the equilibrium level of GDP on the demand side also consistent with firms' desires to produce? That is, is it also an equilibrium on the *supply* side?

The first two questions will occupy our attention in this chapter; the third is reserved to the next chapter.

■ THE MECHANICS OF INCOME DETERMINATION

Our first objective is to determine precisely the equilibrium level of GDP on the demand side. To make the analysis more concrete, we turn to a numerical example.

---

[1] All the models in this book assume, strictly for simplicity, that firms seek constant inventories. Deliberate inventory changes are treated in more advanced courses.

TABLE 1					
The Total Expenditure Schedule					
(1)	(2)	(3)	(4)	(5)	(6)
GDP (Y)	Consumption (C)	Investment (I)	Government Purchases (G)	Net Exports (X – IM)	Total Expenditure
4,800	3,000	900	1,300	−100	**5,100**
5,200	3,300	900	1,300	−100	**5,400**
5,600	3,600	900	1,300	−100	**5,700**
6,000	3,900	900	1,300	−100	**6,000**
6,400	4,200	900	1,300	−100	**6,300**
6,800	4,500	900	1,300	−100	**6,600**
7,200	4,800	900	1,300	−100	**6,900**

An **expenditure schedule** shows the relationship between national income (GDP) and total spending.

FIGURE 2

Construction of the Expenditure Schedule

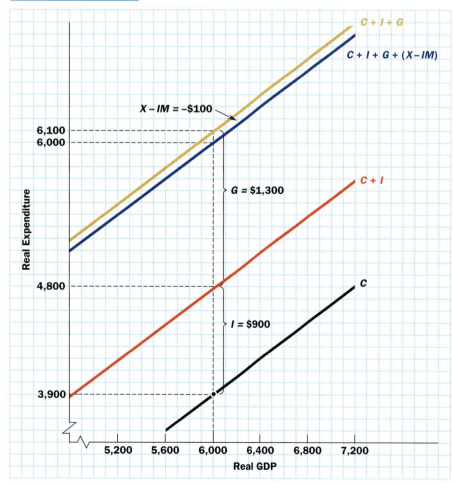

NOTE: Figures are in billions of dollars per year.

Specifically, we examine the relationship between total spending and GDP in the hypothetical economy we introduced in the last chapter.

Columns (1) and (2) of Table 1 repeat the consumption function that we first encountered in Table 1 of Chapter 25 (see page 544). They show how consumer spending, C, depends on GDP, which we symbolize by the letter Y. Columns (3) through (5) provide the other three components of total spending, I, G, and $X - IM$, through the simplifying assumptions that each is just a fixed number regardless of the level of GDP. Specifically, we assume that investment spending is $900 billion, government purchases are $1,300 billion, and net exports are −$100 billion—meaning that in this hypothetical economy, as in the United States at present, imports exceed exports.

By adding Columns (2) through (5), we calculate $C + I + G + (X - IM)$, or total expenditure, which appears in Column (6) of Table 1. Columns (1) and (6) are highlighted in blue to show how total expenditure depends on income. We call this relationship the **expenditure schedule.**

Figure 2 shows the construction of the expenditure schedule graphically. The black line labeled C is the consumption function; it plots on a graph the numbers given in Columns (1) and (2) of Table 1.

The red line, labeled $C + I$, displays our assumption that investment is fixed at $900 billion. It lies a fixed distance (corresponding to $900 billion) above the C line. If investment were not always $900 billion, the two lines would either move closer together or grow farther apart. For example, our analysis of the determinants of investment spending suggested that I might be larger when GDP is higher. Such added investment as GDP rises—which is called **induced investment**—would give the resulting $C + I$ line a steeper slope than the C line. But we ignore that possibility here for simplicity.

The gold line, labeled $C + I + G$, adds government purchases. Because they are assumed to be $1,300 billion regardless of the size of GDP, gold line is parallel to the red line and $1,300 billion higher.

Finally, the blue line labeled $C + I + G + (X - IM)$ adds in net exports. It is parallel to the gold line and $100 billion lower, reflecting our assumption that net exports are always −$100 billion. Once again, if imports depended on GDP, as the previous chapter suggested, the $C + I + G$ and $C + I + G + (X - IM)$ lines would not be parallel. We deal with this more complicated case in Appendix B to this chapter.

We are now ready to determine demand-side equilibrium in our hypothetical economy. Table 2 presents the logic of the circular flow argument in tabular form. The first two columns reproduce the expenditure schedule that we have just constructed. The other columns explain the process by which the economy approaches equilibrium. Let us see why a GDP of $6,000 billion must be the equilibrium level.

Consider first any output level below $6,000 billion. For example, at output level $Y = \$5,200$ billion, total expenditure is $5,400 billion, as shown in Column (2). This is $200 billion more than production. With spending greater than output, as noted in Column (3), inventories will fall (see Column (4)). As the table suggests in Column (5), this will signal producers to raise their output. Clearly, then, no output level below $Y = \$6,000$ billion can be an equilibrium, because output is too low.

A similar line of reasoning eliminates any output level above $6,000 billion. Consider, for example, $Y = \$6,800$ billion. The table shows that total spending would be $6,600 billion if output were $6,800 billion, so $200 billion would go unsold. This would raise producers' inventory stocks and signal them that their rate of production was too high.

Just as we concluded from our circular flow diagram, equilibrium will be achieved only when total spending, $C + I + G + (X - IM)$, exactly equals GDP, Y. In symbols, our condition for equilibrium GDP is:

$$Y = C + I + G + (X - IM)$$

Table 2 shows that this equation holds only at a GDP of $6,000 billion, which must be the equilibrium level of GDP.

Induced investment is the part of investment spending that rises when GDP rises and falls when GDP falls.

Figure 3 on the next page depicts the same conclusion graphically, by adding a 45° line to Figure 2. Why a 45° line? Recall from the appendix to Chapter 1 that a 45° line marks all points on a graph at which the value of the variable measured on the horizontal axis (in this case, GDP) equals the value of the variable measured on the vertical axis (in this case, total expenditure).[2] Thus, the 45° line in Figure 3 shows all the points at which output and spending are equal—that is, where $Y = C + I + G + (X - IM)$. *The 45° line therefore displays all the points at which the economy can possibly be in demand-side equilibrium,* for firms will be content with current output levels only if total spending equals production.

		TABLE 2		
		The Determination of Equilibrium Output		
(1) Output (Y)	(2) Total Spending [C + I + G + (X − IM)]	(3) Balance of Spending and Output	(4) Inventory Status	(5) Producer Response
4,800	5,100	Spending exceeds output	Falling	Produce more
5,200	5,400	Spending exceeds output	Falling	Produce more
5,600	5,700	Spending exceeds output	Falling	Produce more
6,000	**6,000**	**Spending = output**	**Constant**	**No change**
6,400	6,300	Output exceeds spending	Rising	Produce less
6,800	6,600	Output exceeds spending	Rising	Produce less
7,200	6,900	Output exceeds spending	Rising	Produce less

NOTE: Amounts are in billions of dollars.

Now we must compare these *potential* equilibrium points with the *actual* combinations of spending and output that are consistent with the current behavior of consumers and investors. That behavior is described by the $C + I + G + (X - IM)$ line in Figure 3, which shows how total expenditure varies as income changes. *The economy will always be on the expenditure line* because only points on the $C + I + G + (X - IM)$ line describe the spending plans of consumers and investors. Similarly, *if the economy is in equilibrium, it must be on the 45° line.* As Figure 3 shows, these two requirements imply that the only viable equilibrium is at point E, where the $C + I + G + (X - IM)$ line intersects the 45° line. Only this point is consistent with

[2] If you need review, see the appendix to Chapter 1, especially pages 16–17.

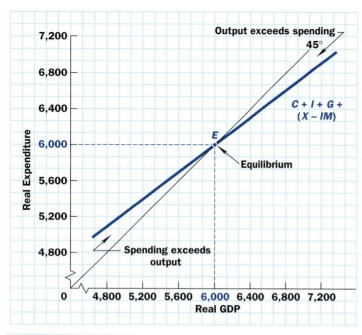

NOTE: Figures are in billions of dollars per year.

both equilibrium and people's actual desires to consume and invest.

Notice that to the left of the equilibrium point, E, the expenditure line lies *above* the 45° line. This means that total spending exceeds total output, as we have already noted. Hence, inventories will be falling and firms will conclude that they should increase production. Thus, production will rise toward the equilibrium point, E. The opposite is true to the right of point E. Here spending falls short of output, inventories rise, and firms will cut back production—thereby moving closer to E.

In other words, whenever production is *above* the equilibrium level, market forces will drive output *down*. And whenever production is *below* equilibrium, market forces will drive output *up*. In either case, deviations from demand-side equilibrium will gradually be eliminated.

Diagrams such as Figure 3 will recur so frequently in this and the next several chapters that it will be convenient to have a name for them. We call them **income-expenditure diagrams,** because they show how expenditures vary with income, or simply **45° line diagrams.**

◼ THE AGGREGATE DEMAND CURVE

An **income–expenditure diagram,** or **45° line diagram,** plots total real expenditure (on the vertical axis) against real income (on the horizontal axis). The 45° line marks off points where income and expenditure are equal.

Chapter 22 introduced aggregate demand and aggregate supply curves relating aggregate quantities demanded and supplied to the price level. The expenditure schedule graphed in Figure 3 is certainly *not* the aggregate demand curve, for we have yet to bring the price level into our discussion. It is now time to remedy this omission and derive the aggregate demand curve.

To do so, we need only recall something we learned in the last chapter. As we noted on page 546, households own a great deal of *money-fixed assets* whose real value declines when the price level rises. The money in your bank account is a prime example. If prices rise, it will buy less. Because of that fact, consumers' *real* wealth declines whenever the price level rises—and that affects their spending. Specifically:

Higher prices decrease the demand for goods and services because they erode the purchasing power of consumer wealth. Conversely, lower prices increase the demand for goods and services by enhancing the purchasing power of consumer wealth.

For these reasons, a change in the price level will shift the entire consumption function. To represent this shift graphically, Figure 4 repeats Figure 6 from the previous chapter. It shows that:

A higher price level leads to lower real wealth and therefore to less spending *at any given level of real income.* Thus, a higher price level leads to a lower consumption function (such as C_1 in Figure 4), and a lower price level leads to a higher consumption function (such as C_2 in Figure 4).

Because students are sometimes confused by this point, it is worth repeating that the depressing effect of the price level on consumer spending works through real *wealth,* not through real *income.* The consumption function is a relationship between *real consumer income* and *real consumer spending.* Thus, any decline in real income, regardless of its cause, moves the economy leftward *along a fixed consumption function;* it does not shift the consumption function.[3] By contrast, a decline in *real wealth* will *shift the entire consumption function downward,* meaning that people spend less at any given level of real income.

In terms of the 45° line diagram, a rise in the price level will therefore pull down the consumption function depicted in Figure 2, and hence will pull down the total expenditure schedule as well. Conversely, a fall in the price level will raise both the C and $C + I + G + (X - IM)$ schedules in the diagram. The two panels of Figure 5 illustrate both of these shifts.

How, then, do changes in the price level affect the equilibrium level of real GDP on the demand side? Common sense says that, with lower spending, equilibrium GDP should fall, and Figure 5 shows that this conclusion is correct. Panel (a) shows that a rise in the price level, by shifting the expenditure schedule downward, leads to a reduction in the equilibrium quantity of real GDP demanded from Y_0 to Y_1. Conversely, Panel (b) shows that a fall in the price level, by shifting the expenditure schedule upward, leads to a rise in the equilibrium quantity of real GDP demanded from Y_0 to Y_2. In summary:

A rise in the price level leads to a lower equilibrium level of real aggregate quantity demanded. This relationship between the price level and real GDP (depicted in Figure 6) is precisely what we called the aggregate demand curve in earlier chapters. It comes directly from the 45° line diagrams in Figure 5. Thus, points E_0, E_1, and E_2 in Figure 6 correspond precisely to the points bearing the same labels in Figure 5.

The effect of higher prices on consumer wealth is just one of several reasons why the aggregate demand curve slopes downward. A second reason comes from international trade. In Chapter 25's discussion of the determinants of net exports (see pages 548–549), we pointed out that higher U.S. prices (holding foreign prices constant) will depress exports (X) and stimulate imports (IM). That means that, other things

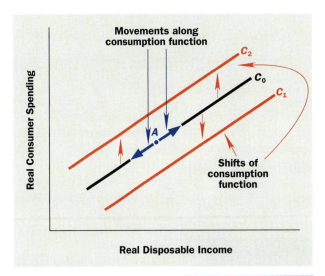

Movements along consumption function

Shifts of consumption function

FIGURE 4

Shifts of the Consumption Function

FIGURE 5

The Effect of the Price Level on Equilibrium Aggregate Quantity Demanded

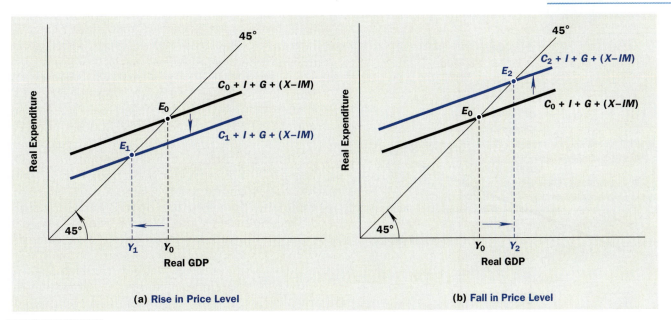

(a) **Rise in Price Level**

(b) **Fall in Price Level**

---

[3] This is true even if a rise in the price level lies behind the decline in real income.

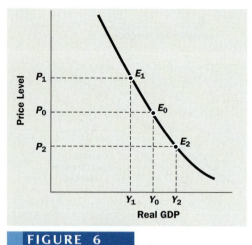

FIGURE 6

The Aggregate Demand
Curve

equal, a higher U.S. price level will reduce the $(X - IM)$ component of total expenditure, thereby shifting the $C + I + G + (X - IM)$ line downward and lowering real GDP, as depicted in Figure 5(a).

Later in this book, after we have studied interest rates and exchange rates, we will encounter still more reasons for a downward-sloping aggregate demand curve. All of them imply that:

An income-expenditure diagram like Figure 3 can be drawn only for a specific price level. At different price levels, the $C + I + G + (X - IM)$ schedule will be different and, hence, the equilibrium quantity of GDP demanded will also differ.

As we shall now see, this seemingly technical point about graphs is critical to understanding the genesis of unemployment and inflation.

■ DEMAND-SIDE EQUILIBRIUM AND FULL EMPLOYMENT

We now turn to the second major question posed on page 561: Will the economy achieve an equilibrium at full employment without inflation, or will we see unemployment, inflation, or both? This question is a crucial one for stabilization policy, for if the economy always gravitates toward full employment *automatically*, then the government should simply leave it alone.

In the income-expenditure diagrams used so far, the equilibrium level of GDP demanded appears as the intersection of the expenditure schedule and the 45° line, regardless of the GDP level that corresponds to full employment. However, as we will see now, when equilibrium GDP falls above potential GDP, the economy probably will be plagued by inflation, and when equilibrium falls below potential GDP, unemployment and recession will result.

This remarkable fact was one of the principal messages of Keynes's *General Theory of Employment, Interest, and Money.* Writing during the Great Depression, it was natural for Keynes to focus on the case in which equilibrium falls short of full employment, leaving some resources unemployed. Figure 7 illustrates this possibility. A vertical line has been drawn at the level of *potential GDP*, a number that depends on the kinds of *aggregate supply* considerations discussed at length in Chapter 24—and to which we will return in the next chapter. Here, potential GDP is assumed to be $7,000 billion. We see that the $C + I + G + (X - IM)$ curve cuts the 45° line at point E, which corresponds to a GDP ($Y = \$6,000$ billion) *below* potential GDP. In this case, the expenditure curve is too low to lead to full employment. Such a situation has characterized the U.S. economy since the 2001 recession.

An equilibrium below potential GDP can arise when consumers or investors are unwilling to spend at normal rates, when government spending is low, when foreign demand is weak, or when the price level is "too high." Any of these events would depress the $C + I + G + (X - IM)$ curve. Unemployment must then occur because not enough output is demanded to keep the entire labor force at work.

FIGURE 7

A Recessionary Gap

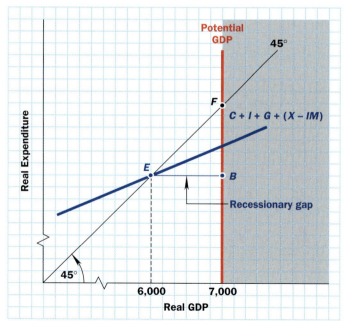

NOTE: Figures are in billions of dollars per year.

The distance between the *equilibrium* level of output demanded and the *full-employment* level of output (that is, potential GDP) is called the **recessionary gap**; it is shown by the horizontal distance from point *E* to point *B* in Figure 7. Although the figure is entirely hypothetical, real-world gaps of precisely this sort were shown shaded in pink in Figure 2 of Chapter 23 (page 496). They have been a pervasive feature of U.S. economic history.

Figure 7 clearly shows that full employment can be reached only by raising the total expenditure schedule to eliminate the recessionary gap. Specifically, the $C + I + G + (X - IM)$ line must move upward until it cuts the 45° line at point *F*. Can this happen without government intervention? We know that a sufficiently large drop in the price level can do the job. But is that a realistic prospect? We will return to this question in the next chapter, after we bring the supply side into the picture, for we cannot discuss price determination without bringing in *both* supply *and* demand. First, however, let us briefly consider the other case—when equilibrium GDP exceeds full employment.

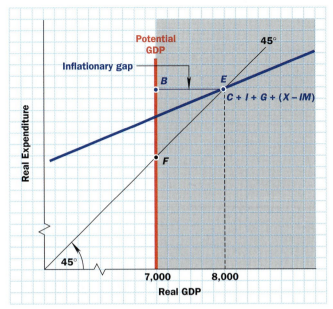

NOTE: Figures are in billions of dollars per year.

Figure 8 illustrates this possibility, which many people believe characterized the U.S. economy in the boom years of the late 1990s. Now the expenditure schedule intersects the 45° line at point *E*, where GDP is $8,000 billion. But this exceeds the full-employment level, $Y = \$7,000$ billion. A case such as this can arise when consumer or investment spending is unusually buoyant, when foreign demand is particularly strong, when the government spends too much, or when a "low" price level pushes the $C + I + G + (X - IM)$ curve upward.

To reach an equilibrium at full employment, the price level would have to rise enough to drive the expenditure schedule *down* until it passed through point *F*. The horizontal distance *BE*—which indicates the amount by which the quantity of GDP demanded exceeds potential GDP—is now called the **inflationary gap**. If there is an inflationary gap, a higher price level or some other means of reducing total expenditure is necessary to reach an equilibrium at full employment. Rising prices will eventually pull the $C + I + G + (X - IM)$ line down until it passes through point *F*. Real-world inflationary gaps were shown shaded in blue in Figure 2 of Chapter 23 (page 496). In sum:

The **recessionary gap** is the amount by which the equilibrium level of real GDP falls short of potential GDP.

The **inflationary gap** is the amount by which equilibrium real GDP exceeds the full-employment level of GDP.

> Only if the price level and spending plans are "just right" will the expenditure curve intersect the 45° line precisely at full employment, so that neither a recessionary gap nor an inflationary gap occurs.

Are there reasons to expect this outcome? Does the economy have a self-correcting mechanism that automatically eliminates recessionary or inflationary gaps and propels it toward full employment? And why do inflation and unemployment sometimes rise or fall together? We are not ready to answer these questions yet because we have not yet brought *aggregate supply* into the picture. However, it is not too early to get an idea about why things can go wrong during a recession.

■ THE COORDINATION OF SAVING AND INVESTMENT

To do so, it is useful to pose the following question: Must the full-employment level of GDP be a demand-side equilibrium? Decades ago, economists thought the answer was yes. Since Keynes, most economists believe the answer is "not necessarily."

To help us see why, Figure 9 offers a simplified circular flow diagram that ignores exports, imports, and the government. In this version, income can "leak out" of the circular flow only at point 1, where consumers save some of their income. Similarly, lost spending can be replaced only at point 2, where investment enters the circular flow.

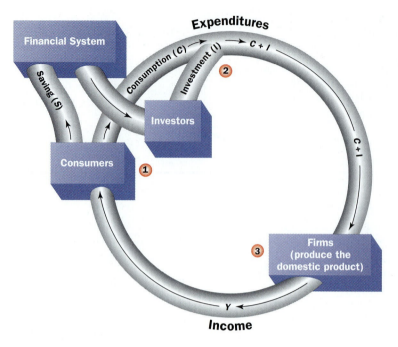

FIGURE 9

A Simplified Circular Flow

What happens if firms produce exactly the full-employment level of GDP at point 3 in the diagram? Will this income level be maintained as we move around the circle, or will it shrink or grow? The answer is that full-employment income will be maintained *only* if the spending by investors at point 2 exactly balances the saving done by consumers at point 1. In other words:

The economy will reach an equilibrium at full employment on the demand side only if the amount that consumers wish to save out of their full-employment incomes happens to equal the amount that investors want to invest. If these two magnitudes are unequal, full employment will not be an equilibrium.

Thus, the basic answer to the puzzle we posed at the start of this chapter is:

The market will permit unemployment when total spending is too low to employ the entire labor force.

Now, how can that occur? The circular flow diagram shows that, if saving exceeds investment at full employment, the total demand received by firms at point 3 will fall short of total output because the added investment spending will not be enough to replace the leakage to saving. With demand inadequate to support production at full employment, GDP must fall below potential. There will be a recessionary gap. Conversely, if investment exceeds saving when the economy is at full employment, then total demand will exceed potential GDP and production will rise above the full-employment level. There will be an inflationary gap.

Now, this discussion does nothing but restate what we already know in different words.[4] But these words provide the key to understanding why the economy sometimes finds itself stuck above or below full employment, for *the people who invest are not the same as the people who save.* In a modern capitalist economy, investing is done by one group of individuals (primarily corporate executives and homebuyers), whereas saving is done by another group.[5] It is easy to imagine that their plans may not be well coordinated. If they are not, we have just seen how either unemployment or inflation can occur.

A **coordination failure** occurs when party A would like to change his behavior if party B would change hers, and vice versa, and yet the two changes do not take place because the decisions of A and B are not coordinated.

IDEAS FOR BEYOND THE FINAL EXAM

Neither of these problems would arise if the acts of saving and investing were perfectly coordinated. While perfection is never attainable, the analysis in the accompanying box, "Unemployment and Inflation as Coordination Failures," raises a tantalizing possibility. If both high unemployment and high inflation arise from **coordination failures**, might the government be able to do something about this problem? Keynes suggested that it could, by using its powers over monetary and fiscal policy. His idea, which is one of our *Ideas for Beyond the Final Exam*, we be will examined in detail in later chapters. But even the simple football analogy described in the box reminds us that a central authority may not find it easy to solve a coordination problem.

CHANGES ON THE DEMAND SIDE: MULTIPLIER ANALYSIS

We have just learned how demand-side equilibrium depends on the consumption function and the amounts spent on investment, government purchases, and net ex-

---

[4] In symbols, our equilibrium condition without government or foreign trade is $Y = C + I$. If we note that Y is also the sum of consumption plus saving, $Y = C + S$, then it follows that $C + S = C + I$, or $S = I$, is a restatement of the equilibrium condition.

[5] In a modern economy, not only do households save, but businesses also save in the form of retained earnings. Nonetheless, households are the ultimate source of the saving needed to finance investment.

Unemployment and Inflation as Coordination Failures

The idea that unemployment stems from a *lack of coordination* between the decisions of savers and investors may seem abstract. But we encounter coordination failures in the real world quite frequently. The following familiar example may bring the idea down to earth.

Picture a crowd watching a football game. Now something exciting happens and the fans rise from their seats. People in the front rows begin standing first, and those seated behind them are forced to stand if they want to see the game. Soon everyone in the stadium is on their feet.

But with everyone standing, no one can see any better than when everyone was sitting. And the fans are enduring the further discomfort of being on their feet. (Never mind that stadium seats are uncomfortable!) Everyone in the stadium would be better off if everyone sat down. Sometimes this happens. But the crowd rises to its feet again on every exciting play. There is simply no way to coordinate the individual decisions of tens of thousands of football fans.

Unemployment poses a similar coordination problem. During a deep recession, workers are unemployed and businesses cannot sell their wares. Figuratively speaking, everyone is "standing" and unhappy about it. If only the firms could agree to hire more workers, those newly employed people could afford to buy more of the goods and services the firms want to produce. But, as at the football stadium, there is no central authority to coordinate these millions of decisions.

SOURCE: © Jonathan Nourok/PhotoEdit

The coordination failure idea also helps to explain why it is so difficult to stop inflation. Virtually everyone prefers stable prices to rising prices. But now think of yourself as the seller of a product. If all other participants in the economy would hold their prices steady, you would happily hold yours steady, too. But, if you believe that others will continue to raise their prices at a rate of, say, 5 percent per year, you may find it dangerous not to increase your prices apace. Hence, society may get stuck with 5 percent inflation even though everyone agrees that zero inflation is better.

---

ports. But none of these is a constant of nature; they all change from time to time. How does equilibrium GDP change when the consumption function shifts or when I, G, or $(X - IM)$ changes? As we will see now, the answer is simple: *by more!* A remarkable result called the **multiplier** says that a change in spending will bring about an *even larger* change in equilibrium GDP on the demand side. Let us see why.

> The **multiplier** is the ratio of the change in equilibrium GDP (Y) divided by the original change in spending that causes the change in GDP.

■ The Magic of the Multiplier

Because it is subject to abrupt swings, investment spending often causes business fluctuations in the United States and elsewhere. So let us ask what would happen if firms suddenly decided to spend more on investment goods. As we shall see next, such a decision would have a *multiplied* effect on GDP, that is, each $1 of additional investment spending would add *more* than $1 to GDP.

To see why, refer first to Table 3, which looks very much like Table 1. The only difference is that we assume here that firms now want to invest $200 billion more than previously—for a total of $1,100 billion. As indicated by the blue numbers, only income level $Y = \$6,800$ billion is an equilibrium on the demand side of the economy now, because only at this level is total spending, $C + I + G + (X - IM)$, equal to production (Y).

The *multiplier* principle says that GDP will rise by *more than* the $200 billion increase in investment. Specifically, the multiplier is defined as the ratio of the change in equilibrium GDP (Y) to the

TABLE 3					
Total Expenditure after a $200 Billion Increase in Investment Spending					
(1)	(2)	(3)	(4)	(5)	(6)
Income (Y)	Consumption (C)	Investment (I)	Government Purchases (G)	Net Exports ($X - IM$)	Total Expenditure
4,800	3,000	1,100	1,300	−100	5,300
5,200	3,300	1,100	1,300	−100	5,600
5,600	3,600	1,100	1,300	−00	5,900
6,000	3,900	1,100	1,300	−100	6,200
6,400	4,200	1,100	1,300	−100	6,500
6,800	**4,500**	**1,100**	**1,300**	**−100**	**6,800**
7,200	4,800	1,100	1,300	−100	7,100

Note: Figures are in billions of dollars per year.

original change in spending that caused GDP to change. In shorthand, when we deal with the multiplier for investment (I), the formula is:

$$\text{Multiplier} = \frac{\text{Change in } Y}{\text{Change in } I}$$

Let us verify that the multiplier is, indeed, greater than 1. Table 3 shows how the new expenditure schedule is constructed by adding up C, I, G, and $(X - IM)$ at each level of Y, just as we did earlier—only now $I = \$1,100$ billion rather than $900 billion. If you compare the last columns of Table 1 (page 562) and Table 3, you will see that the new expenditure schedule lies uniformly above the old one by $200 billion.

Figure 10 depicts this change graphically. The curve marked $C + I_0 + G + (X - IM)$ is derived from the last column of Table 1, while the higher curve marked $C + I_1 + G + (X - IM)$ is derived from the last column of Table 3. The two expenditure lines are parallel and $200 billion apart.

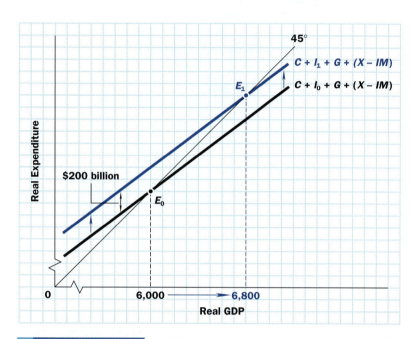

NOTE: Figures are in billions of dollars per year.

FIGURE 10

Illustration of the Multiplier

So far things look just as you might expect. But one more step will bring the multiplier rabbit out of the hat. Let us see what the upward shift of the expenditure line does to equilibrium income. In Figure 10, equilibrium moves outward from point E_0 to point E_1, or from $6,000 billion to $6,800 billion. The difference is an increase of $800 billion in GDP. All this from a $200 billion stimulus to investment? That is the magic of the multiplier.

Because the change in I is $200 billion and the change in equilibrium Y is $800 billion, by applying our definition, the multiplier is:

$$\text{Multiplier} = \frac{\text{Change in } Y}{\text{Change in } I} = \frac{\$800}{\$200} = 4$$

This tells us that, in our example, each additional $1 of investment demand will add $4 to equilibrium GDP!

This result does, indeed, seem mysterious. Can something be created from nothing? Let's first check that the graph has not deceived us. The first and last columns of Table 3 show in numbers what Figure 10 shows graphically. Notice that equilibrium now comes at $Y = \$6,800$ billion, because only at that point is total expenditure equal to production (Y). This equilibrium level of GDP is $800 billion higher than the $6,000 billion level found when investment was only $900 billion. Thus, a $200 billion rise in investment does indeed lead to an $800 billion rise in equilibrium GDP; the multiplier really is 4.

Demystifying the Multiplier: How It Works

The multiplier result seems strange at first, but it loses its mystery once we recall the circular flow of income and expenditure and the simple fact that one person's spending is another person's income. To illustrate the logic of the multiplier and see why it is exactly 4 in our example, think about what happens when businesses decide to spend $1 million on investment goods.

Suppose that Microhard—a major corporation in our hypothetical country—decides to spend $1 million on a new office building. Its $1 million expenditure goes to construction workers and owners of construction companies as wages and profits. That is, the $1 million becomes their *income*.

But the construction firm's owners and workers will not keep all of their $1 million in the bank; instead, they will spend most of it. If they are "typical" consumers, their spending will be $1 million times the marginal propensity to consume (MPC). In our example, the MPC is 0.75, so assume they spend $750,000 and save the rest. *This $750,000 expenditure is a net addition to the nation's demand for goods and services, just as Microhard's original $1 million expenditure was.* So, at this stage, the $1 million investment has already pushed GDP up by some $1.75 million. But the process is by no means over.

Shopkeepers receive the $750,000 spent by construction workers, and they in turn also spend 75 percent of their new income. This activity accounts for $562,500 (75 percent of $750,000) in additional consumer spending in the "third round." Next follows a fourth round in which the recipients of the $562,500 spend 75 percent of this amount, or $421,875, and so on. At each stage in the spending chain, people spend 75 percent of the additional income they receive, and the process continues—with consumption growing in every round.

Where does it all end? Does it all end? The answer is that, yes, it does eventually end—with GDP a total of $4 million higher than it was before Microhard built the original $1 million office building. The multiplier is, indeed, 4.

Table 4 displays the basis for this conclusion. In the table, "Round 1" represents Microhard's initial investment, which creates $1 million in income for construction workers. "Round 2" represents the construction workers' spending, which creates $750,000 in income for shopkeepers. The rest of the table proceeds accordingly; each entry in Column (2) is 75 percent of the previous entry. Column (3) tabulates the running sum of Column (2).

We see that after 10 rounds of spending, the initial $1 million investment has mushroomed to $3.77 million—and the sum is still growing. After 20 rounds, the total increase in GDP is over $3.98 million—near its eventual value of $4 million. Although it takes quite a few rounds of spending before the multiplier chain nears 4, we see from the table that it hits 3 rather quickly. If each income recipient in the chain waits, say, two months before spending his new income, the multiplier will reach 3 in only about ten months.

Figure 11 provides a graphical presentation of the numbers in the last column of Table 4. Notice how the multiplier builds up rapidly at first and then tapers off to approach its ultimate value (4 in this example) gradually.

Although this is only a hypothetical example, the same thing occurs every day in the real world. For instance, a burst of new housing creates a multiplier effect on everything from appliances and furniture to carpeting and insulation. Similarly, when a large company such as Ford makes an investment in a developing country, the multiplier effect boosts business activity in many sectors.

TABLE 4		
The Multiplier Spending Chain		
(1) Round Number	(2) Spending in This Round	(3) Cumulative Total
1	$1,000,000	$1,000,000
2	750,000	1,750,000
3	562,500	2,312,500
4	421,875	2,734,375
5	316,406	3,050,781
6	237,305	3,288,086
7	177,979	3,466,065
8	133,484	3,599,549
9	100,113	3,699,662
10	75,085	3,774,747
⋮	⋮	⋮
20	4,228	3,987,317
⋮	⋮	⋮
"Infinity"	0	4,000,000

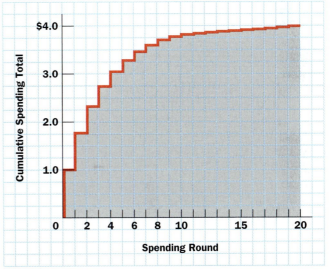

NOTE: Amounts are in millions of dollars.

FIGURE 11

How the Multiplier Builds

Algebraic Statement of the Multiplier

Figure 11 and Table 4 probably make a persuasive case that the multiplier eventually reaches 4. But for the remaining skeptics, we offer a simple algebraic proof.[6] Most of

---

[6] Students who blanch at the sight of algebra should not be put off. Anyone who can balance a checkbook (even many who cannot!) will be able to follow the argument.

you learned about something called an *infinite geometric progression* in high school. This term refers to an infinite series of numbers, each one of which is a fixed fraction of the previous one. The fraction is called the *common ratio*. A geometric progression beginning with 1 and having a common ratio of 0.75 looks like this:

$$1 + 0.75 + (0.75)^2 + (0.75)^3 + \ldots$$

More generally, a geometric progression beginning with 1 and having a common ratio R would be:

$$1 + R + R^2 + R^3 + \ldots$$

A simple formula enables us to sum such a progression as long as R is less than 1.[7] The formula is:[8]

Sum of infinite geometric progression $= \dfrac{1}{1 - R}$

We now recognize that the multiplier chain in Table 4 is just an infinite geometric progression with 0.75 as its common ratio. That is, each \$1 that Microhard spends leads to a $(0.75) \times \$1$ expenditure by construction workers, which in turn leads to a $(0.75) \times (0.75 \times \$1) = (0.75)^2 \times \$1$ expenditure by the shopkeepers, and so on. Thus, for each initial dollar of investment spending, the progression is:

$$1 + 0.75 + (0.75)^2 + (0.75)^3 + (0.75)^4 + \ldots$$

Applying the formula for the sum of such a series, we find that:

$$\text{Multiplier} = \frac{1}{1 - 0.75} = \frac{1}{0.25} = 4$$

Notice how this result can be generalized. If we did not have a specific number for the marginal propensity to consume, but simply called it MPC, the geometric progression in Table 4 would have been:

$$1 + \text{MPC} + (\text{MPC})^2 + (\text{MPC})^3 + \ldots$$

This progression uses the MPC as its common ratio. Applying the same formula for summing a geometric progression to this more general case gives us the following general result:

Oversimplified Multiplier Formula

$$\text{Multiplier} = \frac{1}{1 - \text{MPC}}$$

We call this formula "oversimplified" because it ignores many factors that are important in the real world. You can begin to appreciate just how unrealistic the oversimplified formula is by considering some real numbers for the U.S. economy. The MPC is over 0.95. From our oversimplified formula, then, it would seem that the multiplier should be at least:

$$\text{Multiplier} = \frac{1}{1 - 0.95} = \frac{1}{0.05} = 20$$

In fact, the actual multiplier for the U.S. economy is less than 2. That is quite a discrepancy!

---

[7] If R exceeds 1, no one can possibly sum it—not even with the aid of a modern computer—because the sum is not a finite number.

[8] The proof of the formula is simple. Let the symbol S stand for the (unknown) sum of the series:

$S = 1 + R + R^2 + R^3 + \ldots$

Then, multiplying by R,

$RS = R + R^2 + R^3 + R^4 + \ldots$

By subtracting RS from S, we obtain:

$S - RS = 1$ or $S = \dfrac{1}{1 - R}$

This disagreement does not mean that anything we have said about the multiplier so far is incorrect. Our story is simply incomplete. As we progress through this and subsequent chapters, you will learn why the multiplier in the U.S. is less than 2 even though the country's MPC is over 0.95. One such reason relates to *international trade*—in particular, the fact that a country's imports depend on its GDP. We deal with this complication in Appendix B to this chapter. A second factor is *inflation*, a complication we will address in the next chapter. A third factor is *income taxation*, a point we will elaborate in Chapter 28. The last important reason arises from the *financial system* and, after we discuss money and banking in Chapters 29 and 30, we will explain how the financial system influences the multiplier in Chapter 31. As you will see, each of these factors *reduces* the size of the multiplier. So:

> Although the multiplier is larger than 1 in the real world, it cannot be calculated with any degree of accuracy from the oversimplified formula. The actual multiplier is much lower than the formula suggests.

■ THE MULTIPLIER IS A GENERAL CONCEPT

Although we have used business investment to illustrate the workings of the multiplier, it should be clear from the logic that *any* increase in spending can kick off a multiplier chain. To see how the multiplier works when the process is initiated by an upsurge in consumer spending, we must distinguish between two types of change in consumer spending.

To do so, look back at Figure 4 on page 565. When C rises because income rises— that is, when consumers move outward *along a fixed consumption function*—we call the increase in C an **induced increase in consumption**. (See the blue arrows in the figure.) When C rises because the entire consumption function *shifts upward* (such as from C_0 to C_2 in the figure), we call it an **autonomous increase in consumption**. The name indicates that consumption changes *independently* of income. The discussion of the consumption function in Chapter 25 pointed out that a number of events, such as a change in the value of the stock market, can initiate such a shift.

If consumer spending were to rise autonomously by $200 billion, we would revise our table of aggregate demand to look like Table 5. Comparing this new table to Table 3, we note that each entry in Column (2) is $200 billion *higher* than the corresponding entry in Table 3 (because consumption is higher), and each entry in Column (3) is $200 billion *lower* (because in this case investment is only $900 billion).

Column (6), the expenditure schedule, is identical in both tables, so the equilibrium level of income is clearly Y = $6,800 billion once again. The initial rise of $200 billion in consumer spending leads to an eventual rise of $800 billion in GDP, just as it did in the case of higher investment spending. In fact, Figure 10 (page 570) applies directly to this case once we note that the upward shift is now caused by an autonomous change in C rather than in I. The multiplier for autonomous changes in consumer spending, then, is also 4 (= $800/$200).

The reason is straightforward. It does not matter who injects an additional dollar of spending into the economy—business investors or consumers. Whatever the source of the extra dollar, 75 percent of it will be respent if the MPC is 0.75, and the recipients of this second round of spending will, in turn, spend 75 percent of their additional income, and so on. That continued spending constitutes the multiplier process. Thus a $200 billion increase in government purchases (G) or in net exports (X − IM) would have the same multi-

An **induced increase in consumption** is an increase in consumer spending that stems from an increase in consumer incomes. It is represented on a graph as a movement along a fixed consumption function.

An **autonomous increase in consumption** is an increase in consumer spending without any increase in consumer incomes. It is represented on a graph as a shift of the entire consumption function.

TABLE 5					
Total Expenditure after Consumers Decide to Spend $200 Billion More					
(1)	(2)	(3)	(4)	(5)	(6)
			Government	Net	
Income	Consumption	Investment	Purchases	Exports	Total
(Y)	(C)	(I)	(G)	(X − IM)	Expenditure
4,800	3,200	900	1,300	−100	5,300
5,200	3,500	900	1,300	−100	5,600
5,600	3,800	900	1,300	−100	5,900
6,000	4,100	900	1,300	−100	6,200
6,400	4,400	900	1,300	−100	6,500
6,800	**4,700**	**900**	**1,300**	**−100**	**6,800**
7,200	5,000	900	1,300	−100	7,100

Note: Figures are in billions of dollars per year.

plier effect as depicted in Figure 10. The multipliers are identical because the logic behind them is identical.

The idea that changes in G have multiplier effects on GDP will play a central role in the discussion of government stabilization policy that begins in Chapter 28. So it is worth noting here that:

Changes in the volume of government purchases of goods and services will change the equilibrium level of GDP on the demand side in the same direction, but by a multiplied amount.

To cite a recent example, when the 9/11 tragedy struck in 2001, the government immediately began spending more on rescue and cleanup operations, and soon was spending even more on the military and homeland security. The G component of $C + I + G + (X-IM)$ soared, which had a multiplier effect on GDP.

Applying the same multiplier idea to exports and imports teaches us another important lesson: Booms and recessions tend to be transmitted across national borders. Why is that? Suppose a boom abroad raises GDPs in foreign countries. With rising incomes, foreigners will buy more American goods—which means that U.S. exports will increase. But an increase in our exports will, via the multiplier, raise GDP in the United States. By this mechanism, rapid economic growth abroad contributes to rapid economic growth here. And, of course, the same mechanism also operates in reverse. Thus:

The GDPs of the major economies are linked by trade. A boom in one country tends to raise its imports and hence push up exports and GDP in other countries. Similarly, a recession in one country tends to pull down GDP in other countries.

■ THE MULTIPLIER AND THE AGGREGATE DEMAND CURVE

One last mechanical point about the multiplier: Recall that income-expenditure diagrams such as Figure 3 (page 564) can be drawn only for a given price level. Different price levels lead to different total expenditure curves. This means that our oversimplified multiplier formula indicates *the increase in real GDP demanded that would occur if the price level were fixed.* Graphically, this means that it measures the *horizontal shift* of the economy's aggregate demand curve.

Figure 12 illustrates this conclusion by supposing that the price level that underlies Figure 3 is $P = 100$. The top panel simply repeats Figure 10 (page 570) and shows how an increase in investment spending from $900 to $1,100 billion leads to an increase in GDP from $6,000 to $6,800 billion.

The bottom panel shows two downward-sloping aggregate demand curves. The first, labeled $D_0 D_0$, depicts the situa-

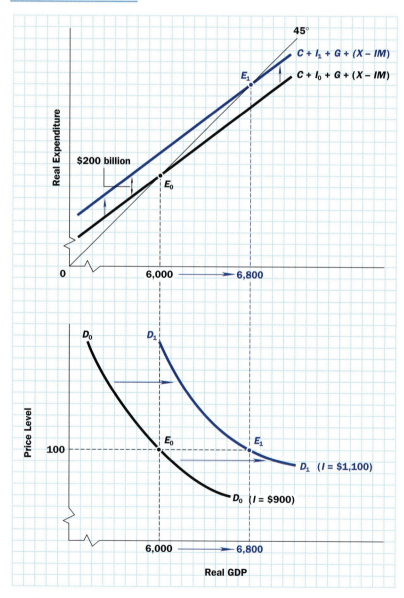

FIGURE 12

Two Views of the Multiplier

NOTE: Figures are in billions of dollars per year.

tion when investment is $900 billion. Point E_0 on this curve indicates that, at the given price level ($P = 100$), the equilibrium quantity of GDP demanded is $6,000 billion. It corresponds exactly to point E_0 in the top panel. The second aggregate demand curve, D_1D_1, depicts the situation after investment has risen to $1,100 billion. Point E_1 on this curve indicates that the equilibrium quantity of GDP demanded when $P = 100$ has risen to $6,800 billion, which corresponds exactly to point E_1 in the top panel.

As Figure 12 shows, the horizontal distance between the two aggregate demand curves is exactly equal to the increase in real GDP shown in the income-expenditure diagram—in this case, $800 billion. Thus:

An autonomous increase in spending leads to a horizontal shift of the aggregate demand curve by an amount given by the oversimplified multiplier formula.

So everything we have just learned about the multiplier applies to *shifts of the economy's aggregate demand curve*. If businesses decide to increase their investment spending, if the consumption function shifts upward, or if the government or foreigners decide to buy more goods, then the aggregate demand curve moves horizontally to the right—as indicated in Figure 12. If any of these variables move downward instead, the aggregate demand curve moves horizontally to the left.

Thus, the economy's aggregate demand curve cannot be expected to stand still for long. Autonomous changes in one or another of the four components of total spending will cause it to move around. But to understand the *consequences* of such shifts of aggregate demand, we must bring the *aggregate supply* curve back into the picture. That is the task for the next chapter.

SUMMARY

1. The **equilibrium level of GDP on the demand side is** the level at which total spending just equals production. Because total spending is the sum of consumption, investment, government purchases, and net exports, the condition for equilibrium is $Y = C + I + G + (X - IM)$.

2. Income levels below **equilibrium** are bound to rise because, when spending exceeds output, firms will see their inventory stocks being depleted and will react by stepping up production.

3. Income levels above equilibrium are bound to fall because, when total spending is insufficient to absorb total output, inventories will pile up and firms will react by curtailing production.

4. The determination of the equilibrium level of GDP on the demand side can be portrayed on a convenient **income-expenditure diagram** as the point at which the **expenditure schedule**—defined as the sum of $C + I + G + (X - IM)$—crosses the 45° line. The 45° line is significant because it marks off points at which spending and output are equal—that is, at which $Y = C + I + G + (X - IM)$, which is the basic condition for equilibrium.

5. An income-expenditure diagram can be drawn only for a specific price level. Thus, the equilibrium GDP so determined depends on the price level.

6. Because higher prices reduce the purchasing power of consumers' wealth, they reduce total expenditures on the 45° line diagram. Equilibrium real GDP demanded is therefore lower when prices are higher. This downward-sloping relationship is known as the **aggregate demand curve.**

7. Equilibrium GDP can be above or below **potential GDP,** which is defined as the GDP that would be produced if the labor force were fully employed.

8. If equilibrium GDP exceeds potential GDP, the difference is called an **inflationary gap.** If equilibrium GDP falls short of potential GDP, the resulting difference is called a **recessionary gap.**

9. Such gaps can occur because of the problem of **coordination failure:** The saving that consumers want to do at full-employment income levels may differ from the investing that investors want to do.

10. Any **autonomous increase in expenditure** has a multiplier effect on GDP; that is, it increases GDP by more than the original increase in spending.

11. The **multiplier** effect occurs because one person's additional expenditure constitutes a new source of income for another person, and this additional income leads to still more spending, and so on.

12. The multiplier is the same for an autonomous increase in consumption, investment, government purchases, or net exports.

13. A simple formula for the multiplier says that its numerical value is $1/(1 - MPC)$. This formula is too simple to give accurate results, however.

14. Rapid (or sluggish) economic growth in one country contributes to rapid (or sluggish) growth in other countries because one country's imports are other countries' exports.

KEY TERMS

Equilibrium   560

Expenditure schedule   562

Induced investment   563

$Y = C + I + G + (X - IM)$ 563

Income-expenditure (or 45° line) diagram   564

Aggregate demand curve   564

Full-employment level of GDP (or potential GDP)   566

Recessionary gap   567

Inflationary gap   567

Coordination of saving and investment   567

Coordination failure   568

Multiplier   569

Induced increase in consumption   573

Autonomous increase in consumption   573

TEST YOURSELF

1. From the following data, construct an expenditure schedule on a piece of graph paper. Then use the income-expenditure (45° line) diagram to determine the equilibrium level of GDP.

Income	Consumption	Investment	Government Purchases	Net Exports
$3,600	$3,220	$240	$120	$40
3,700	3,310	240	120	40
3,800	3,400	240	120	40
3,900	3,490	240	120	40
4,000	3,580	240	120	40

Now suppose investment spending rises to $260, and the price level is fixed. By how much will equilibrium GDP increase? Derive the answer both numerically and graphically.

2. From the following data, construct an expenditure schedule on a piece of graph paper. Then use the income-expenditure (45° line) diagram to determine the equilibrium level of GDP. Compare your answer with your answer to the previous question.

Income	Consumption	Investment	Government Purchases	Net Exports
$3,600	$3,280	$180	$120	$40
3,700	3,340	210	120	40
3,800	3,400	240	120	40
3,900	3,460	270	120	40
4,000	3,520	300	120	40

3. Suppose that investment spending is always $250, government purchases are $100, net exports are always $50, and consumer spending depends on the price level in the following way:

Price Level	Consumer Spending
$ 90	$740
95	720
100	700
105	680
110	660

On a piece of graph paper, use these data to construct an aggregate demand curve. Why do you think this example supposes that consumption declines as the price level rises?

4. **(More difficult)**[9] Consider an economy in which the consumption function takes the following simple algebraic form:

$$C = 300 + 0.75DI$$

and in which investment (I) is always $900 and net exports are always $-$100. Government purchases are fixed at $1,300 and taxes are fixed at $1,200. Find the equilibrium level of GDP, and then compare your answer to Table 1 and Figure 2. (*Hint:* Remember that disposable income is GDP minus taxes: $DI = Y - T = Y - 1,200$.)

5. **(More difficult)** Keep everything the same as in Test Yourself Question 4 *except* change investment to $I = $1,100. Use the equilibrium condition $Y = C + I + G + (X - IM)$ to find the equilibrium level of GDP on the demand side. (In working out the answer, assume the price level is fixed.) Compare your answer to Table 3 and Figure 10. Now compare your answer to the answer to Test Yourself Question 4. What do you learn about the multiplier?

6. **(More difficult)** An economy has the following consumption function:

$$C = 200 + 0.8DI$$

The government budget is balanced, with government purchases and taxes both fixed at $1,000. Net exports are $100. Investment is $600. Find equilibrium GDP.

What is the multiplier for this economy? If G rises by $100, what happens to Y? What happens to Y if both G and T rise by $100 at the same time?

---

[9] The answer to this question is provided in Appendix A to this chapter.

7. Use both numerical and graphical methods to find the multiplier effect of the following shift in the consumption function in an economy in which investment is always $220, government purchases are always $100, and net exports are always −$40. (*Hint:* What is the marginal propensity to consume?)

Income	Consumption before Shift	Consumption after Shift
$1,080	$ 880	$ 920
1,140	920	960
1,200	960	1,000
1,260	1,000	1,040
1,320	1,040	1,080
1,380	1,080	1,120
1,440	1,120	1,160
1,500	1,160	1,200
1,560	1,200	1,240

DISCUSSION QUESTIONS

1. For over twenty years now, imports have consistently exceeded exports in the U.S. economy. Many people consider this imbalance to be a major problem. Does this chapter give you any hints about why? (You may want to discuss this issue with your instructor. You will learn more about it in later chapters.)

2. Look back at the income-expenditure diagram in Figure 3 (page 564) and explain why some level of real GDP other than $6,000 (say, $5,000 or $7,000) is *not* an equilibrium on the demand side of the economy. Do not give a mechanical answer to this question. Explain the economic mechanism involved.

3. Does the economy this year seem to have an inflationary gap or a recessionary gap? (If you do not know the answer from reading the newspaper, ask your instructor.)

4. Try to remember where you last spent a dollar. Explain how this dollar will lead to a multiplier chain of increased income and spending. (Who received the dollar? What will he or she do with it?)

APPENDIX A *The Simple Algebra of Income Determination and the Multiplier*

The model of demand-side equilibrium that the chapter presented graphically and in tabular form can also be handled with some simple algebra. Written as an equation, the consumption function in our example is

$$C = 300 + 0.75DI$$
$$= 300 + 0.75(Y - T)$$

because, by definition, $DI = Y - T$. This is simply the equation of a straight line with a slope of 0.75 and an intercept of $300 - 0.75T$. Because $T = 1,200$ in our example, the intercept is -600 and the equation can be written more simply as follows:

$$C = -600 + 0.75Y$$

Investment in the example was assumed to be 900, regardless of the level of income, government purchases were 1,300, and net exports were -100. So the sum $C + I + G + (X - IM)$ is

$$C + I + G + (X - IM) = -600 + 0.75Y + 900 + 1,300 - 100$$
$$= 1,500 + 0.75Y$$

This equation describes the expenditure curve in Figure 3. Because the equilibrium quantity of GDP demanded is defined by

$$Y = C + I + G + (X - IM)$$

we can solve for the equilibrium value of Y by substituting $1,500 + 0.75Y$ for $C + I + G + (X - IM)$ to get

$$Y = 1,500 + 0.75Y$$

To solve this equation for Y, first subtract $0.75Y$ from both sides to get

$$0.25Y = 1,500$$

Then divide both sides by 0.25 to obtain the answer:

$$Y = 6,000$$

This, of course, is precisely the solution we found by graphical and tabular methods in the chapter.

We can easily generalize this algebraic approach to deal with any set of numbers in our equations. Suppose that the consumption function is as follows:

$$C = a + bDI = a + b(Y - T)$$

(In the example, $a = 300$, $T = 1,200$, and $b = 0.75$.) Then the equilibrium condition that $Y = C + I + G + (X - IM)$ implies that

$$Y = a + bDI + I + G + (X - IM)$$
$$= a - bT + bY + I + G + (X - IM)$$

Subtracting bY from both sides leads to

$$(1 - b)Y = a - bT + I + G + (X - IM)$$

and dividing through by $1 - b$ gives:

$$Y = \frac{a - bT + I + G + (X - IM)}{1 - b}$$

This formula is valid for any numerical values of a, b, T, G, I, and $(X - IM)$ (so long as b is between zero and 1).

From this formula, it is easy to derive the oversimplified multiplier formula algebraically and to show that it applies equally well to a change in investment, autonomous consumer spending, government purchases, or net exports. To do so, suppose that *any* of the symbols in the numerator of the multiplier formula increases by one unit. Then GDP would rise from the previous formula to:

$$Y = \frac{a - bT + I + G + (X - IM) + 1}{1 - b}$$

By comparing this expression with the previous expression for Y, we see that a one-unit change in any component of spending changes equilibrium GDP by

$$\text{Change in } Y = \frac{a - bT + I + G + (X - IM) + 1}{1 - b}$$
$$- \frac{a - bT + I + G + (X - IM)}{1 - b}$$

or

$$\text{Change in } Y = \frac{1}{1 - b}$$

Recalling that b is the marginal propensity to consume, we see that this is precisely the oversimplified multiplier formula.

TEST YOURSELF

1. Find the equilibrium level of GDP demanded in an economy in which investment is always $300, net exports are always -$50, the government budget is balanced with purchases and taxes both equal to $400, and the consumption function is described by the following algebraic equation:

$$C = 150 + 0.75DI$$

(*Hint:* Do not forget that $DI = Y - T$.)

2. Referring to Test Yourself Question 1, do the same for an economy in which investment is $250, net exports are zero, government purchases and taxes are both $400, and the consumption function is as follows:

$$C = 250 + 0.5DI$$

3. In each of these cases, how much saving is there in equilibrium? (*Hint:* Income not consumed must be saved.) Is saving equal to investment?

4. Imagine an economy in which consumer expenditure is represented by the following equation:

$$C = 50 + 0.75DI$$

Imagine also that investors want to spend $500 at every level of income ($I = \$500$), net exports are zero ($X - IM = 0$), government purchases are $300, and taxes are $200.

a. What is the equilibrium level of GDP?

b. If potential GDP is $3,000, is there a recessionary or inflationary gap? If so, how much?

c. What will happen to the equilibrium level of GDP if investors become optimistic about the country's future and raise their investment to $600?

d. After investment has increased to $600, is there a recessionary or inflationary gap? How much?

5. Fredonia has the following consumption function:

$$C = 100 + 0.8DI$$

Firms in Fredonia always invest $700 and net exports are zero, initially. The government budget is balanced with spending and taxes both equal to $500.

a. Find the equilibrium level of GDP.

b. How much is saved? Is saving equal to investment?

c. Now suppose that an export-promotion drive succeeds in raising net exports to $100. Answer (a) and (b) under these new circumstances.

DISCUSSION QUESTIONS

1. Explain the basic logic behind the multiplier in words. Why does it require b, the marginal propensity to consume, to be between zero and one?

2. (**More difficult**) What would happen to the multiplier analysis if $b = 0$? If $b = 1$?

APPENDIX B *The Multiplier with Variable Imports*

In the chapter, we assumed that net exports were a fixed number, -100 in the exmaple. In fact, a nation's imports vary along with its GDP for a simple reason: Higher GDP leads to higher incomes, some of which is spent on foreign goods. Thus:

Our imports rise as our GDP rises and fall as our GDP falls.

Similarly, our *exports* are the *imports* of other countries, so it is to be expected that our exports depend on *their* GDPs, not on our own. Thus:

Our exports are relatively insensitive to our own GDP, but are quite sensitive to the GDPs of other countries.

This appendix derives the implications of these rather elementary observations. In particular, it shows that once we recognize the dependence of a nation's imports on its GDP:

International trade lowers the value of the multiplier.

To see why, we begin with Table 6, which adapts the example of our hypothetical economy to allow imports to depend on GDP. Columns (2) through (4) are the same as in Table 1; they show C, I, and G at alternative levels of

GDP. Columns (5) and (6) record revised assumptions about the behavior of exports and imports. Exports are fixed at $650 billion regardless of GDP. But imports are assumed to rise by $60 billion for every $400 billion rise in GDP, which is a simple numerical example of the idea that imports depend on GDP. Column (7) subtracts imports from exports to get net exports, $(X - IM)$, and Column (8) adds up the four components of total expenditure, $C + I + G + (X - IM)$. The equilibrium, you can see, occurs at $Y = \$6,000$ billion, just as it did in the chapter.

Figures 13 and 14 display the same conclusion graphically. The upper panel of Figure 13 shows that exports

				TABLE 6			
			Equilibrium Income with Variable Imports				
(1) Gross Domestic Product (Y)	(2) Consumer Expenditures (C)	(3) Investment (I)	(4) Government Purchases (G)	(5) Exports (X)	(6) Imports (IM)	(7) Net Exports ($X - IM$)	(8) Total Expenditure [$C + I + G + (X - IM)$]
4,800	3,000	900	1,300	650	570	+80	5,280
5,200	3,300	900	1,300	650	630	+20	5,520
5,600	3,600	900	1,300	650	690	−40	5,760
6,000	3,900	900	1,300	650	750	−100	6,000
6,400	4,200	900	1,300	650	810	−160	6,240
6,800	4,500	900	1,300	650	870	−220	6,480
7,200	4,800	900	1,300	650	930	−280	6,720

Note: Figures are in billions of dollars per year.

FIGURE 13   The Dependence of Net Exports on GDP

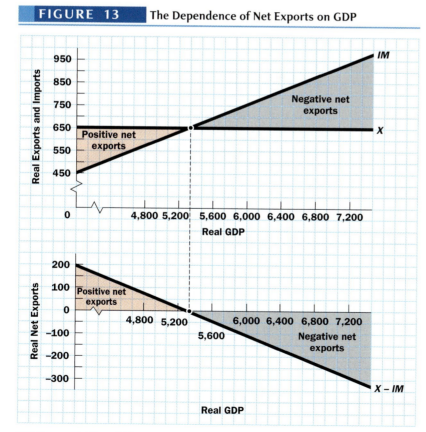

NOTE: Figures are in billions of dollars per year.

are fixed at $650 billion regardless of GDP, whereas imports increase as GDP rises, just as in Table 6. The difference between exports and imports, or net exports, is positive until GDP approaches $5,300 billion and negative once GDP surpasses that amount. The bottom panel of Figure 13 shows the subtraction explicitly by displaying *net exports*. It shows clearly that:

Net exports decline as GDP rises.

Figure 14 carries this analysis over to the 45° line diagram. We begin with the familiar $C + I + G + (X - IM)$ line in black. Previously, we simply assumed that net exports were fixed at -$100 billion regardless of GDP. Now that we have amended our model to note that net exports decline as GDP rises, the sum $C + I + G + (X - IM)$ rises more slowly than we previously assumed. This change is shown by the blue line. Note that it is less steep than the black line.

Let us now consider what happens if exports rise by $160 billion while imports remain as in Table 6. Table 7 shows that equilibrium now occurs at a GDP of $Y = \$6,400$ billion. Naturally, higher exports have raised

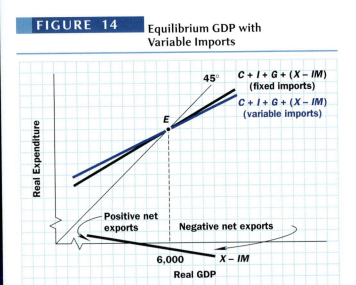

FIGURE 14   Equilibrium GDP with Variable Imports

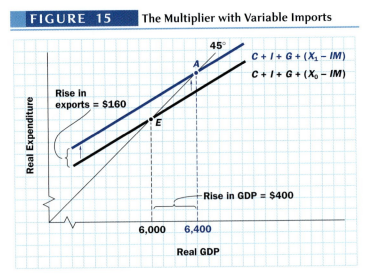

FIGURE 15   The Multiplier with Variable Imports

TABLE 7

Equilibrium Income after a $160 Billion Increase in Exports

(1) Gross Domestic Product (Y)	(2) Consumer Expenditures (C)	(3) Investment (I)	(4) Government Purchases (G)	(5) Exports (X)	(6) Imports (IM)	(7) Net Exports $(X - IM)$	(8) Total Expenditure $[C + I + G + (X - IM)]$
4,800	3,000	900	1,300	810	570	+240	5,440
5,200	3,300	900	1,300	810	630	+180	5,680
5,600	3,600	900	1,300	810	690	+120	5,920
6,000	3,900	900	1,300	810	750	+60	6,160
6,400	**4,200**	**900**	**1,300**	**810**	**810**	**0**	**6,400**
6,800	4,500	900	1,300	810	870	-60	6,640
7,200	4,800	900	1,300	810	930	-120	6,800

Note: Figures are in billions of dollars per year.

domestic GDP. But consider the magnitude. A $160 billion increase in exports (from $650 billion to $810 billion) leads to an increase of $400 billion in GDP (from $6,000 billion to $6,400 billion). So the multiplier is 2.5 (= $400/$160).[10]

This same conclusion is shown graphically in Figure 15, where the line $C + I + G + (X_0 - IM)$ represents the original expenditure schedule and the line $C + I + G + (X_1 - IM)$ represents the expenditure schedule after the $160 billion increase in exports. Equilibrium shifts from point E to point A, and GDP rises by $400 billion.

Notice that the multiplier in this example is 2.5, whereas in the chapter, with net exports taken to be a fixed number, it was 4. This simple example illustrates a general result: *International trade lowers the numerical value of the multiplier.* Why is this so? Because, in an open economy, any autonomous increase in spending is partly dissipated in purchases of foreign goods, which creates additional income for *foreigners* rather than for domestic citizens.

Thus, international trade gives us the first of what will eventually be several reasons why the oversimplified multiplier formula overstates the true value of the multiplier.

[10] *Exercise:* Construct a version of Table 6 to show what would happen if imports rose by $160 billion at every level of GDP while exports remained at $650 billion. You should be able to show that the new equilibrium would be $Y = $5,600.

SUMMARY

1. Because imports rise as GDP rises, while exports are insensitive to (domestic) GDP, net exports decline as GDP rises.

2. If imports depend on GDP, international trade reduces the value of the multiplier.

TEST YOURSELF

1. Suppose exports and imports of a country are given by the following:

GDP	Exports	Imports
$2,500	$400	$250
3,000	400	300
3,500	400	350
4,000	400	400
4,500	400	450
5,000	400	500

Calculate net exports at each level of GDP.

2. If domestic expenditure (the sum of $C + I + G$ in the economy described in Test Yourself Question 1) is as shown in the following table, construct a 45° line diagram and locate the equilibrium level of GDP.

GDP	Domestic Expenditures
$2,500	$3,100
3,000	3,400
3,500	3,700
4,000	4,000
4,500	4,300
5,000	4,600

3. Now raise exports to $650 and find the equilibrium again. How large is the multiplier?

DISCUSSION QUESTION

1. Explain the logic behind the finding that variable imports reduce the numerical value of the multiplier.

27

SUPPLY-SIDE EQUILIBRIUM: UNEMPLOYMENT *AND* INFLATION?

We might as well reasonably dispute whether it is the upper or the under blade of a pair of scissors that cuts a piece of paper, as whether value is governed by [demand] or [supply].

ALFRED MARSHALL

Chapter 26 has taught us that the position of the economy's total expenditure $(C + I + G + (X - IM))$ schedule governs whether the economy will experience a recessionary or an inflationary gap. Too little spending leads to a *recessionary gap*. Too much leads to an *inflationary gap*. Which sort of gap actually occurs is of considerable practical importance, because a recessionary gap translates into *unemployment* while an inflationary gap leads to *inflation*.

But the tools provided in Chapter 26 cannot tell us which sort of gap will arise because, as we learned, the position of the expenditure schedule depends on the price level—and the price level is determined by *both* aggregate demand *and* aggregate supply. So this chapter has a clear task: to bring the supply side of the economy back into the picture.

Doing so will put us in a position to deal with the crucial question raised in earlier chapters: Does the economy have an efficient self-correcting mechanism? We shall see that the answer is "yes, but": Yes, but it works slowly. The chapter will also enable us to explain the vexing problem of *stagflation*—the simultaneous occurrence of high unemployment *and* high inflation—which plagued the economy in the 1980s.

CONTENTS

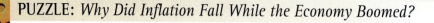

PUZZLE: *Why Did Inflation Fall While the Economy Boomed?*

For years, economists have talked about the agonizing trade-off between inflation and unemployment—a notion that made its first appearance in Chapter 1's list of *Ideas for Beyond the Final Exam* and which will be discussed in detail in Chapter 33. Very low unemployment is supposed to make the inflation rate rise. Yet the stunning success of the U.S. economy from 1996 through the middle of 2000 seemed to belie this idea. The unemployment rate fell to about 4 percent of the labor force, the lowest rate in thirty years. But inflation did not rise; in fact, it *fell* for part of this period. How can we explain this marvelous conjunction of events—extremely low unemployment coupled with falling inflation? Does it mean—as many critics said at the time—that standard economic theory does not apply to the "New Economy"? Before this chapter is over, we shall have some answers.

■ THE AGGREGATE SUPPLY CURVE

In earlier chapters, we noted that aggregate demand is a schedule, not a fixed number. The quantity of real gross domestic product (GDP) that will be demanded depends on the price level, as summarized in the economy's *aggregate demand curve*. The same point applies to *aggregate supply:* The concept of aggregate supply does not refer to a fixed number, but rather to a schedule (an *aggregate supply curve*).

The volume of goods and services that profit-seeking enterprises will provide depends on the prices they obtain for their outputs, on wages and other production costs, on the capital stock, on the state of technology, and on other things. The relationship between the price level and the quantity of real GDP supplied, *holding all other determinants of quantity supplied constant*, is called the economy's **aggregate supply curve.**

Figure 1 shows a typical aggregate supply curve. It slopes upward, meaning that, as prices rise, more output is produced, *other things held constant*. Let's see why.

The **aggregate supply curve** shows, for each possible price level, the quantity of goods and services that all the nation's businesses are willing to produce during a specified period of time, holding all other determinants of aggregate quantity supplied constant.

■ Why the Aggregate Supply Curve Slopes Upward

Producers are motivated mainly by profit. The profit made by producing an additional unit of output is simply the difference between the price at which it is sold and the unit cost of production:

Profit per unit = Price − Cost per unit

The response of output to a rising price level—which is what the slope of the aggregate supply curve shows—depends on the response of costs. So the question is: Do costs rise along with selling prices, or not?

The answer is: Some do, and some do not. Many of the costs that firms incur for labor and other inputs remain fixed for periods of time—although certainly not forever. For example, workers and firms often enter into long-term labor contracts that set nominal wages one to three years in advance. Even where no explicit contracts exist, wage rates typically adjust only annually. Similarly, a variety of material inputs are delivered to firms under long-term contracts at prearranged prices.

This fact is significant because firms decide how much to produce by comparing their selling prices with their costs of production. If the selling prices of the firm's products rise while its wages and other factor costs are fixed, production becomes more profitable, and firms will presumably produce more.

An Aggregate Supply Curve

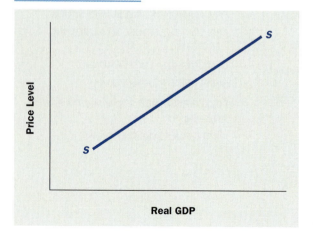

A simple example will illustrate the idea. Suppose that, given the scale of its operations, a particular firm needs one hour of labor to manufacture an additional gadget. If the gadget sells for $9, workers earn $8 per hour, and the firm has no other costs, its profit on this unit is:

Profit per unit = Price − Cost per unit
= $9 − $8 = $1

If the price of the gadget then rises to $10, but wage rates remain constant, the firm's profit on the unit becomes:

Profit per unit = Price − Cost per unit
= $10 − $8 = $2

With production more profitable, the firm presumably will supply more gadgets.

The same process operates in reverse. If selling prices fall while input costs remain relatively fixed, profit margins will be squeezed and production cut back. This behavior is summarized by the upward slope of the aggregate supply curve: Production rises when the price level (henceforth, P) rises, and falls when P falls. In other words:

> The aggregate supply curve slopes upward because firms normally can purchase labor and other inputs at prices that are fixed for some period of time. Thus, higher selling prices for output make production more attractive.[1]

The phrase "for some period of time" alerts us to an important fact: The aggregate supply curve may not stand still for long. If wages or prices of other inputs change, as they surely will during inflationary times, then the aggregate supply curve will shift.

■ Shifts of the Aggregate Supply Curve

We have concluded so far that, holding constant the levels of wages and other input prices, there is an upward-sloping aggregate supply curve relating the price level to aggregate quantity supplied. Now let's consider what happens when input prices change.

The Nominal Wage Rate   The most obvious determinant of the aggregate supply curve's position is the *nominal wage rate*. Wages are the major element of cost in the economy, accounting for more than 70 percent of all inputs. Because higher wage rates mean higher costs, they spell lower profits at any given prices. That relationship explains why companies have sometimes been known to dig in their heels when workers demand large wage increases. For example, several large supermarket chains in California took a well-publicized strike in 2004 rather than give in to their workers' demands.[2]

Returning to our example, consider what would happen to a gadget producer if the nominal wage rate rose to $8.75 per hour while the gadget's price remained $9. Profit per unit would decline from $1 to

$$\$9.00 - \$8.75 = \$0.25.$$

With profits thus squeezed, the firm would probably cut back on production.

Thus, a wage increase leads to a decrease in aggregate quantity supplied at current prices. Graphically, the aggregate supply curve *shifts to the left* (or inward), as shown in Figure 2. In this diagram, firms are willing to supply $6,000 billion in goods and services at a price level of 100 when wages are low (point *A*). But after wages increase,

---

[1] There are both differences and similarities between the *aggregate* supply curve and the *microeconomic* supply curves studied in Chapter 4. Both are based on the idea that quantity supplied depends on how output prices move relative to input prices. The aggregate supply curve pertains to the behavior of *the overall price level*, however, whereas a microeconomic supply curve pertains to the *price of some particular commodity*.

[2] This particular strike was not initiated by workers asking for higher wages. Rather, the companies said they needed to *reduce* wages in order to compete with Wal-Mart.

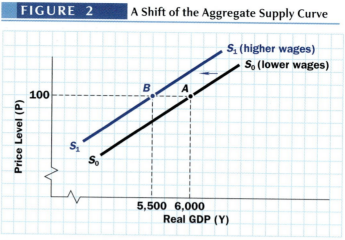

FIGURE 2   A Shift of the Aggregate Supply Curve

NOTE: Amounts are in billions of dollars per year.

the same firms are willing to supply only $5,500 billion at this price level (point *B*). By similar reasoning, the aggregate supply curve will shift to the right (or outward) if wages fall.

> An increase in the money wage rate shifts the aggregate supply curve *inward*, meaning that the quantity supplied at any price level *declines*. A decrease in the money wage rate shifts the aggregate supply curve *outward*, meaning that the quantity supplied at any price level *increases*.

The logic behind these shifts is straightforward. Consider a wage increase, as indicated by the blue line in Figure 2. With selling prices fixed at 100 in the illustration, an increase in the nominal wage means that wages rise *relative to prices*. In other words, the *real wage rate* rises. It is this increase in the firms' real production costs that induces a contraction of quantity supplied—from *A* to *B* in the diagram.

Prices of Other Inputs   In this regard, wages are not unique. An increase in the price of *any* input that firms buy will shift the aggregate supply curve in the same way. That is:

> The aggregate supply curve is shifted inward by an increase in the price of any input to the production process, and it is shifted outward by any decrease.

The logic is exactly the same.

Although producers use many inputs other than labor, the one that has attracted the most attention in recent decades is energy. Increases in the prices of imported energy, such as those that took place most recently from 2004 into 2006, push the aggregate supply curve inward—as shown in Figure 2. By the same token, decreases in the price of imported oil, such as the ones we enjoyed in parts of 2006, shift the aggregate supply curve in the opposite direction—outward.

Technology and Productivity   Another factor that can shift the aggregate supply curve is the state of technology. The idea that technological progress increases the **productivity** of labor is familiar from earlier chapters. Holding wages constant, any increase of productivity will *decrease* business costs, improve profitability, and encourage more production.

Productivity is the amount of output produced by a unit of input.

Once again, our gadget example will help us understand how this process works. Suppose the price of a gadget stays at $9 and the hourly wage rate stays at $8, but gadget workers become more productive. Specifically, suppose the labor input required to manufacture a gadget decreases from one hour (which costs $8) to three-quarters of an hour (which costs $6). Then profit per unit rises from $1 to

$$\$9 - (\tfrac{3}{4})\,\$8 = \$9 - \$6 = \$3.$$

The lure of higher profits should induce gadget manufacturers to increase production—which is, of course, why companies constantly strive to raise their productivity. In brief, we have concluded that:

Improvements in productivity shift the aggregate supply curve outward.

We can therefore interpret Figure 2 as illustrating the effect of a *decline* in productivity. As we mentioned in Chapter 24, a slowdown in productivity growth was a persistent problem for the United States for more than two decades.

Available Supplies of Labor and Capital   The last determinants of the position of the aggregate supply curve are the ones we studied in Chapter 24: The bigger the economy—as measured by its available supplies of labor and capital—the more it is capable of producing. Thus:

As the labor force grows or improves in quality, and as investment increases the capital stock, the aggregate supply curve shifts *outward* to the right, meaning that more output can be produced at any given price level.

So, for example, the investment boom of the 1990s, by boosting the supply of capital, left the U.S. economy with a greater capacity to produce goods and services—that is, it shifted the aggregate supply curve outward.

These factors, then, are the major "other things" that we hold constant when drawing an aggregate supply curve: nominal wage rates, prices of other inputs (such as energy), technology, labor force, and capital stock. A change in the price level moves the economy *along a given supply curve*, but a change in any of these determinants of aggregate quantity supplied *shifts the entire supply schedule.*

■ EQUILIBRIUM OF AGGREGATE DEMAND AND SUPPLY

Chapter 26 taught us that the price level is a crucial determinant of whether equilibrium GDP falls below full employment (a "recessionary gap"), precisely at full employment, or above full employment (an "inflationary gap"). We can now analyze which type of gap, if any, will occur in any particular case by combining the aggregate supply analysis we just completed with the aggregate demand analysis from the last chapter.

Figure 3 displays the simple mechanics. In the figure, the aggregate demand curve *DD* and the aggregate supply curve *SS* intersect at point *E*, where real GDP (*Y*) is $6,000 billion and the price level (*P*) is 100. As can be seen in the graph, at any higher price level, such as 120, aggregate quantity supplied would exceed aggregate quantity demanded. In such a case, there would be a glut on the market as firms found themselves unable to sell all their output. As inventories piled up, firms would compete more vigorously for the available customers, thereby forcing prices down. Both the price level and production would fall.

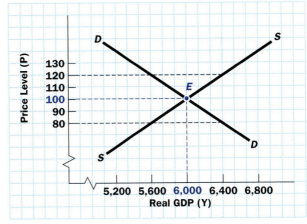

NOTE: Amounts are in billions of dollars per year.

FIGURE 3

Equilibrium of Real GDP and the Price Level

At any price level lower than 100, such as 80, quantity demanded would exceed quantity supplied. There would be a shortage of goods on the market. With inventories disappearing and customers knocking on their doors, firms would be encouraged to raise prices. The price level would rise, and so would output. Only when the price level is 100 are the quantities of real GDP demanded and supplied equal. Therefore, only the combination of *P*=100, *Y*= $6,000 is an equilibrium.

Table 1 illustrates the same conclusion by using a tabular analysis similar to the one used in the previous chapter. Columns (1) and (2) constitute an aggregate demand

TABLE 1
Determination of the Equilibrium Price Level

(1) Price Level	(2) Aggregate Quantity Demanded	(3) Aggregate Quantity Supplied	(4) Balance of Supply and Demand	(5) Prices will be:
80	$6,400	$5,600	Demand exceeds supply	Rising
90	6,200	5,800	Demand exceeds supply	Rising
100	**6,000**	**6,000**	**Demand equals supply**	**Unchanged**
110	5,800	6,200	Supply exceeds demand	Falling
120	5,600	6,400	Supply exceeds demand	Falling

Note: Quantities are in billions of dollars.

schedule corresponding to curve *DD* in Figure 3. Columns (1) and (3) constitute an aggregate supply schedule corresponding to aggregate supply curve *SS*.

The table clearly shows that equilibrium occurs only at $P = 100$ and $Y = \$6,000$. At any other price level, aggregate quantities supplied and demanded would be unequal, with consequent upward or downward pressure on prices. For example, at a price level of 90, customers demand $6,200 billion worth of goods and services, but firms wish to provide only $5,800 billion. In this case, the price level is too low and will be forced upward. Conversely, at a price level of 110, quantity supplied ($6,200 billion) exceeds quantity demanded ($5,800 billion), implying that the price level must fall.

INFLATION AND THE MULTIPLIER

To illustrate the importance of the *slope* of the aggregate supply curve, we return to a question we posed in the last chapter: What happens to equilibrium GDP if the aggregate demand curve shifts outward? We saw there that such changes have a *multiplier* effect, and we noted that the actual numerical value of the multiplier is considerably smaller than suggested by the oversimplified multiplier formula. One of the reasons, variable imports, emerged in an appendix to that chapter. We are now in a position to understand a second reason:

Inflation reduces the size of the multiplier.

The basic idea is simple. In Chapter 26, we described a multiplier process in which one person's spending becomes another person's income, which leads to further spending by the second person, and so on. But this story was confined to the *demand* side of the economy; it ignored what is likely to be happening on the *supply* side. The question is: As the multiplier process unfolds, will the additional demand be taken care of by firms without raising prices?

If the aggregate supply curve slopes upward, the answer is no. More goods will be provided only at *higher* prices. Thus, as the multiplier chain progresses, pulling income and employment up, prices will rise in tandem. This development, as we know from earlier chapters, will reduce net exports and dampen consumer spending because rising prices erode the purchasing power of consumers' wealth. As a consequence, the multiplier chain will not proceed as far as it would have in the absence of inflation.

How much inflation results from the rise in demand? How much is the multiplier chain muted by inflation? The answers to these questions depend on the slope of the economy's aggregate supply curve.

For a concrete example, let us return to the $200 billion increase in investment spending used in Chapter 26. There we found (see especially Figure 10 on page 570) that $200 billion in additional investment spending would eventually lead to $800 billion in additional spending *if the price level does not rise*—that is, *it tacitly assumed that the aggregate supply curve was horizontal.* But that is not so. The slope of the aggregate supply curve tells us how any expansion of aggregate demand gets apportioned between higher output and higher prices.

In our example, Figure 4 shows the $800 billion rightward shift of the aggregate demand curve, from D_0D_0 to D_1D_1, that we derived from the oversimplified multiplier formula in Chapter 26. We see that, as the economy's equilibrium moves from point E_0 to point E_1, real GDP does not rise by $800 billion. Instead, prices rise, which cancels out part of the increase in quantity demanded. As a result, output rises from $6,000 billion to $6,400 billion—an increase of only $400 billion. Thus, in the example, inflation reduces the multiplier from $800/$200 = 4 to $400/$200 = 2. In general:

As long as the aggregate supply curve slopes upward, any increase in aggregate demand will push up the price level. Higher prices, in turn, will drain off some of the higher real demand by eroding the purchasing power of consumer wealth and by reducing net exports. Thus, inflation reduces the value of the multiplier below that suggested by the oversimplified formula.

Notice also that the price level in this example has been pushed up (from 100 to 120, or 20 percent) by the rise in investment demand. This, too, is a general result:

As long as the aggregate supply curve slopes upward, any outward shift of the aggregate demand curve will cause some rise in prices.

The economic behavior behind these results is certainly not surprising. Firms faced with large increases in quantity demanded at their original prices respond to these changed circumstances in two natural ways: They raise production (so that real GDP rises), and they also raise prices (so the price level rises). But this rise in the price level, in turn, reduces the purchasing power of the bank accounts and bonds held by consumers, and they, too, react in the natural way: They cut down on their spending. Such a reaction amounts to a movement *along* aggregate demand curve D_1D_1 in Figure 4 from point A to point E_1.

Figure 4 also shows us exactly where the oversimplified multiplier formula goes wrong. By ignoring the effects of the higher price level, the oversimplified formula erroneously supposes that the economy moves horizontally from point E_0 to point A—which it would do only if the aggregate supply curve were horizontal. As the diagram clearly shows, output does not actually rise this much, which is one reason why the oversimplified formula exaggerates the size of the multiplier.

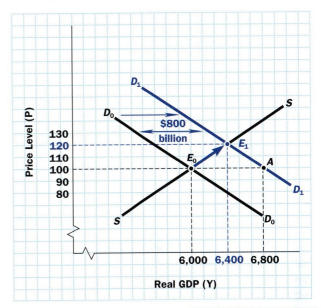

NOTE: Amounts are in billions of dollars per year.

FIGURE 4

Inflation and the Multiplier

RECESSIONARY AND INFLATIONARY GAPS REVISITED

With this understood, let us now reconsider the question we have been deferring: Will equilibrium occur at, below, or beyond potential GDP?

We could not answer this question in Chapter 26 because we had no way to determine the equilibrium price level, and therefore no way to tell which type of gap, if any, would arise. The aggregate supply and demand analysis summarized in Figure 3 and Table 1 now gives us what we need. But we find that our answer is still the same: Anything can happen.

The reason is that Figure 3 tells us nothing about where *potential* GDP falls. The factors determining the economy's capacity to produce were discussed extensively in Chapter 24. But that analysis might leave potential GDP above the $6,000 billion equilibrium level or below it. Depending on the locations of the aggregate demand and aggregate supply curves, then, we can reach equilibrium *beyond* potential GDP (an inflationary gap), *at* potential GDP, or *below* potential GDP (a recessionary gap). All three possibilities are illustrated in Figure 5 on the next page.

The three upper panels duplicate diagrams that we encountered in Chapter 26. (Recall that each income-expenditure diagram considers *only* the demand side of the economy by holding the price level fixed.) Start with the upper-middle panel, in which the expenditure schedule $C + I_1 + G + (X - IM)$ crosses the 45° line exactly at potential GDP—which we take to be $7,000 billion in the example. Equilibrium is at point E, with neither a recessionary nor an inflationary gap. Now suppose that total expenditures either *fall* to $C + I_0 + G + (X - IM)$ (producing the upper-left diagram) or *rise* to $C + I_2 + G + (X - IM)$ (producing the upper-right diagram). As we read across the

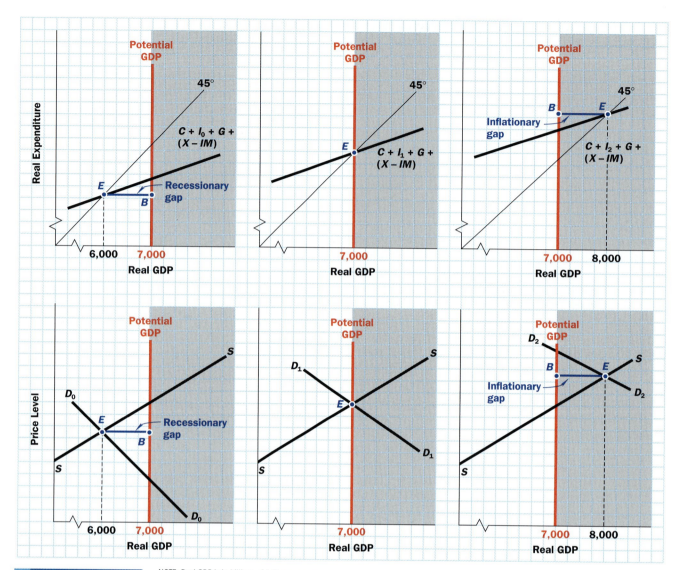

NOTE: Real GDP is in billions of dollars per year.

FIGURE 5

Recessionary and Inflationary Gaps Revisited

page from left to right, we see equilibrium occurring with a recessionary gap, at full employment, or with an inflationary gap—depending on the position of the $C + I + G + (X − IM)$ line.[3] In Chapter 26, we learned of several variables that might shift the expenditure schedule up and down in this way. One of them was the price level.

The three lower panels portray the same three cases differently—in a way that can tell us what the price level will be. These diagrams consider *both* aggregate demand *and* aggregate supply, and therefore determine *both* the equilibrium price level *and* the equilibrium GDP at point E—the intersection of the aggregate supply curve *SS* and the aggregate demand curve *DD*. But the same three possibilities emerge nonetheless.

In the lower-left panel, aggregate demand is too low to provide jobs for the entire labor force, so we have a recessionary gap equal to distance EB, or $1,000 billion. This situation corresponds precisely to the one depicted on the income-expenditure diagram immediately above it.

In the lower-right panel, aggregate demand is so high that the economy reaches an equilibrium well beyond potential GDP. An inflationary gap equal to BE, or $1,000 billion, arises, just as in the diagram immediately above it.

---

[3] These three diagrams hold potential GDP at $7,000 billion and vary the expenditure schedule. You can draw equivalent diagrams by holding the $C + I + G + (X − IM)$ line constant and changing the presumed level of potential GDP. Try it as an exercise.

In the lower-middle panel, the aggregate demand curve D_1D_1 is at just the right level to produce an equilibrium at potential GDP. Neither an inflationary gap nor a recessionary gap occurs, as in the diagram just above it.

It may seem, therefore, that we have simply restated our previous conclusions. But, in fact, we have done much more. For now that we have studied the determination of the equilibrium price level, we are able to examine how the economy adjusts to either a recessionary gap or an inflationary gap. Specifically, because wages are fixed in the short run, any one of the three cases depicted in Figure 5 can occur. But, in the long run, wages will adjust to labor market conditions, which will shift the aggregate supply curve. It is to that adjustment that we now turn.

■ ADJUSTING TO A RECESSIONARY GAP: DEFLATION OR UNEMPLOYMENT?

Suppose the economy starts with a recessionary gap—that is, an equilibrium *below* potential GDP—as depicted in the lower-left panel of Figure 5. Such a situation might be caused, for example, by inadequate consumer spending or by anemic investment spending. From 2001 through 2004, most observers believe the United States was in just such straits—for the first time in a decade. And in Japan, recessionary gaps have been the norm since the early 1990s. What happens when an economy experiences a recessionary gap?

With equilibrium GDP below potential, jobs will be difficult to find. The ranks of the unemployed will exceed the number of people who are jobless because of moving, changing occupations, and so on. In the terminology of Chapter 23, the economy will experience a considerable amount of *cyclical unemployment*. Businesses, by contrast, will have little trouble finding workers, and their current employees will be eager to hang on to their jobs.

Such an environment makes it difficult for workers to win wage increases. Indeed, in extreme situations, wages may even fall—thereby shifting the aggregate supply curve *outward*. (Recall that an aggregate supply curve is drawn for a *given* money wage.) But as the aggregate supply curve shifts outward—eventually moving from S_0S_0 to S_1S_1 in Figure 6—prices decline and the recessionary gap shrinks. By this process, deflation gradually erodes the recessionary gap—leading the economy to an equilibrium at potential GDP (point F in Figure 6).

But there is an important catch. In our modern economy, this adjustment process proceeds slowly—painfully slowly. Our brief review of the historical record in Chapter 22 showed that the history of the United States includes several examples of *deflation* before World War II but none since then. Not even severe recessions have forced average prices and wages down—although they have certainly slowed their rates of increase to a crawl. The only protracted episode of deflation in an advanced economy since the 1930s is the recent experience of Japan.

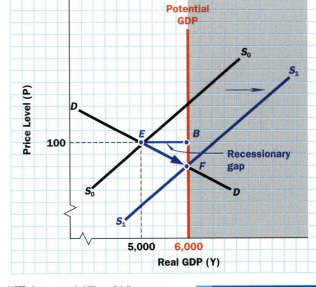

NOTE: Amounts are in billions of dollars per year.

FIGURE 6

The Elimination of a Recessionary Gap

Exactly why wages and prices rarely fall in our modern economy is a subject of intense debate among economists. Some economists emphasize institutional factors such as minimum wage laws, union contracts, and a variety of government regulations that place legal floors under particular wages and prices. Because most of these institutions are of recent vintage, this theory successfully explains why wages and prices fall less frequently now than they did before World War II. But only a small minority of the U.S. economy is subject to legal restraints on wage and price cutting. So it seems doubtful that legal restrictions can take us very far in explaining sluggish wage-price adjustments in the United States. In Europe, however, these institutional factors may be far more important.

Other observers suggest that workers have a profound psychological resistance to accepting a wage reduction. This theory certainly has the ring of truth. Think how you would react if your boss announced he was cutting your hourly wage rate. You might quit, or you might devote less care to your job. If the boss suspects you will react this way, he may be reluctant to cut your wage. Nowadays, genuine wage reductions are rare enough to be newsworthy. But although no one doubts that wage cuts can damage morale, this psychological theory has one major drawback: It fails to explain why the psychological resistance to wage cuts apparently started only after World War II. Until a satisfactory answer to this question is provided, many economists will remain skeptical of this hypothesis.

A third explanation is based on a fact we emphasized in Chapter 22—that business cycles have been less severe in the postwar period than they were in the prewar period. As workers and firms came to realize that recessions would not turn into depressions, the argument goes, they decided to wait out the bad times rather than accept wage or price reductions that they would later regret.

Yet another theory is based on the old adage, "You get what you pay for." The idea is that workers differ in productivity, but that the productivities of individual employees are difficult to identify. Firms therefore worry that they will lose their best employees if they reduce wages—because these workers have the best opportunities elsewhere in the economy. Rather than take this chance, the argument goes, firms prefer to maintain high wages even in recessions.

Other theories also have been proposed, none of which commands a clear majority of professional opinion. But regardless of the cause, we may as well accept it as a well-established fact that wages fall only sluggishly, if at all, when demand is weak.

The implications of this rigidity are quite serious, for a recessionary gap cannot cure itself without some deflation. And if wages and prices will not fall, recessionary gaps like *EB* in Figure 6 will linger for a long time. That is:

> **When aggregate demand is low, the economy may get stuck with a recessionary gap for a long time. If wages and prices fall very slowly, the economy will endure a prolonged period of production below potential GDP.**

Does the Economy Have a Self-Correcting Mechanism?

Now a situation like that described earlier would, presumably, not last forever. As the recession lengthened and perhaps deepened, more and more workers would be unable to find jobs at the prevailing "high" wages. Eventually, their need to be employed would overwhelm their resistance to wage cuts.

Firms, too, would become increasingly willing to cut prices as the period of weak demand persisted and managers became convinced that the slump was not merely a temporary aberration. Prices and wages did, in fact, fall in many countries during the Great Depression of the 1930s, and they have fallen in Japan for about a decade, albeit very slowly.

Nowadays, however, political leaders of both parties believe that it is folly to wait for falling wages and prices to eliminate a recessionary gap. They agree that government action is both necessary and appropriate under recessionary conditions. Nevertheless, vocal—and highly partisan—debate continues over how much and what kind of intervention is warranted. One reason for the disagreement is that the **self-correcting mechanism** does operate—if only weakly—to cure recessionary gaps.

The economy's **self-correcting mechanism** refers to the way money wages react to either a recessionary gap or an inflationary gap. Wage changes shift the aggregate supply curve and therefore change equilibrium GDP and the equilibrium price level.

An Example from Recent History: Deflation in Japan

Fortunately for us, recent U.S. history offers no examples of long-lasting recessionary gaps. But the world's second-largest economy does. The Japanese economy was consistently weak from the early 1990s until very recently—including several recessions. As a result, Japan experienced persistent recessionary gaps for over a decade. Unsurprisingly, Japan's modest inflation rate evaporated and turned into a small *deflation* rate. Qualitatively, this is just the sort of behavior the theoretical model of the self-correcting mechanism predicts. But it took a very long time! Hence, the practical policy question is: How long can a country afford to wait?

■ ADJUSTING TO AN INFLATIONARY GAP: INFLATION

Let us now turn to what happens when the economy finds itself *beyond* full employment—that is, with an *inflationary gap* like that shown in Figure 7. When the aggregate supply curve is S_0S_0 and the aggregate demand curve is DD, the economy will initially reach equilibrium (point E) with an inflationary gap, shown by the segment BE.

Some economists believe that such a situation prevailed in the United States in early 2006, though this is hotly debated. What should happen under such circumstances? As we shall see now, the supertight labor market should produce an inflation that eventually eliminates the inflationary gap, although perhaps in a slow and painful way. Let us see how.

When equilibrium GDP exceeds potential GDP, jobs are plentiful and labor is in great demand. Firms are likely to have trouble recruiting new workers or even holding onto their old ones as other firms try to lure workers away with higher wages.

Rising wages add to business costs, which shift the aggregate supply curve *inward*. As the aggregate supply curve moves from S_0S_0 to S_1S_1 in Figure 7, the inflationary gap shrinks. In other words, inflation eventually erodes the inflationary gap and brings the economy to an equilibrium at potential GDP (point F).

There is a straightforward way of looking at the economics underlying this process. Inflation arises because buyers are demanding more output than the economy can produce at normal operating rates. To paraphrase an old cliché, there is too much demand chasing too little supply. Such an environment encourages price hikes.

Ultimately, rising prices eat away at the purchasing power of consumers' wealth, forcing them to cut back on consumption, as explained in Chapter 25. In addition, exports fall and imports rise, as we learned in Chapter 26. Eventually, aggregate quantity demanded is scaled back to the economy's capacity to produce—graphically, the economy moves back along curve DD from point E to point F. At this point the self-correcting process stops. In brief:

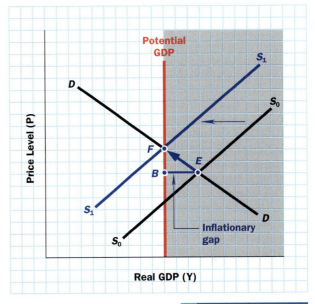

FIGURE 7

The Elimination of an Inflationary Gap

If aggregate demand is exceptionally high, the economy may reach a short-run equilibrium above full employment (an *inflationary gap*). When this occurs, the tight situation in the labor market soon forces wages to rise. Because rising wages increase business costs, prices increase; there is inflation. As higher prices cut into consumer purchasing power and net exports, the inflationary gap begins to close.

As the inflationary gap closes, output falls and prices continue to rise. When the gap is finally eliminated, a long-run equilibrium is established with a higher price level and with GDP equal to potential GDP.

This scenario was precisely what many economists expected to occur in 1998 and 1999. Because they believed that the U.S. economy had an inflationary gap in 1997 and 1998, they expected inflation to rise. But it did not. Why not? We will have the answer in just a few more pages.

But first we repeat an important caveat: *The self-correcting mechanism takes time* because wages and prices do not adjust quickly. Thus, while an inflationary gap sows the seeds of its own destruction, the seeds germinate slowly. So, once again, policymakers may want to speed up the process.

Demand Inflation and Stagflation

Simple as it is, this model of how the economy adjusts to an inflationary gap teaches us a number of important lessons about inflation in the real world. First, Figure 7 reminds us that the real culprit is an *excess of aggregate demand* relative to potential GDP. The aggregate demand curve is initially so high that it intersects the aggregate supply curve well beyond full employment. The resulting intense demand for goods and labor pushes prices and wages higher. Although aggregate demand in excess of potential GDP is not the only possible cause of inflation, it certainly is the cause in our example.

Nonetheless, business managers and journalists may blame inflation on rising wages. In a superficial sense, of course, they are right, because higher wages do indeed lead firms to raise product prices. But in a deeper sense they are wrong. Both rising wages and rising prices are symptoms of the same underlying malady: too much aggregate demand. Blaming labor for inflation in such a case is a bit like blaming high doctor bills for making you ill.

Second, notice that output *falls* while prices *rise* as the economy adjusts from point *E* to point *F* in Figure 7. This is our first (but not our last) explanation of the phenomenon of **stagflation**—the conjunction of in*flation* and economic *stag*nation. Specifically:

> **Stagflation** is inflation that occurs while the economy is growing slowly or having a recession.

A period of stagflation is part of the normal aftermath of a period of excessive aggregate demand.

It is easy to understand why. When aggregate demand is excessive, the economy will temporarily produce beyond its normal capacity. Labor markets tighten and wages rise. Machinery and raw materials may also become scarce and so start rising in price. Faced with higher costs, business firms quite naturally react by producing less and charging higher prices. That is stagflation.

A U.S. Example

The stagflation that follows a period of excessive aggregate demand is, you will note, a rather benign form of the dreaded disease. After all, while output is falling, it nonetheless remains above potential GDP, and unemployment is low. The U.S. economy last experienced such an episode at the end of the 1980s.

The long economic expansion of the 1980s brought the unemployment rate down to a fifteen-year low of 5 percent by March 1989. Almost all economists believed at the

A Tale of Two Graduating Classes: 2000 Versus 2003

Timing matters in life. The college graduates of 2000 could hardly have asked for better luck. The unemployment rate dropped to 4.1 percent in May 2000—roughly, the lowest level in a generation—and employers were literally scrambling for new hires. Starting salaries rose, many graduating seniors had numerous job offers, and some firms even offered $10,000–$20,000 bonuses to students who signed on the dotted line!

Three years later, the job market for the Class of 2003 was rather different. U.S. economic growth had slowed to a crawl, and then to a halt. Companies that had stocked up on recent college grads in the tight labor markets of 1998–2000 found themselves with more employees than they knew what to do with in 2002 and 2003. They were not eager to hire more. Bonuses and other "perks" disappeared; job offers became scarcer. With the unemployment rate around 6 percent in May and June of 2003, the job market was far from the worst ever. But it was nothing like the glory days of 2000.

SOURCE: © Felicia Martinez/PhotoEdit

time that 5 percent was below the full-employment unemployment rate, that is, that the U.S. economy had an *inflationary gap*. As the theory suggests, inflation began to accelerate—from 4.4 percent in 1988 to 4.6 percent in 1989 and then to 6.1 percent in 1990.

In the meantime, the economy was stagnating. Real GDP growth fell from 3.5 percent during 1989 to 1.8 percent in 1990 and down to -0.5 percent in 1991. Inflation was eating away at the inflationary gap, which had virtually disappeared by mid-1990, when the recession started. Yet inflation remained high through the early months of the recession. The U.S. economy was in a *stagflation* phase.

Our overall conclusion about the economy's ability to right itself seems to run something like this:

> The economy does, indeed, have a self-correcting mechanism that tends to eliminate either unemployment or inflation. But this mechanism works slowly and unevenly. In addition, its beneficial effects on either inflation or unemployment are sometimes swamped by strong forces pushing in the opposite direction (such as rapid increases or decreases in aggregate demand). Thus, the self-correcting mechanism is not always reliable.

◼ STAGFLATION FROM A SUPPLY SHOCK

We have just discussed the type of stagflation that follows in the wake of an inflationary boom. However, that is not what happened when unemployment and inflation both soared in the 1970s and early 1980s. What caused this more virulent strain of stagflation? Several things, though the principal culprit was rising energy prices.

In 1973, the Organization of Petroleum Exporting Countries (OPEC) quadrupled the price of crude oil. American consumers soon found the prices of gasoline and home heating fuels increasing sharply, and U.S. businesses saw an important cost of doing business—energy prices—rising drastically. OPEC struck again in the period 1979–1980, this time doubling the price of oil. Then the same thing happened again, albeit on a smaller scale, when Iraq invaded Kuwait in 1990. Most recently, oil prices surged for several years in a row during this decade for a combination of reasons, including war and instability in the Middle East, supply disruptions, and rapidly-growing demand in China.

Higher energy prices, we observed earlier, shift the economy's aggregate supply curve *inward* in the manner shown in Figure 8. If the aggregate supply curve shifts inward, as it surely did following each of these "oil shocks," production will decline. To reduce demand to the available supply, prices will have to rise. The result is the worst of both worlds: falling production and rising prices.

This conclusion is shown graphically in Figure 8, which shows an aggregate demand curve, *DD*, and two aggregate supply curves. When the supply curve shifts inward, the economy's equilibrium shifts from point *E* to point *A*. Thus, output falls while prices rise—exactly our definition of stagflation. In sum:

FIGURE 8

Stagflation from an Adverse Shift in Aggregate Supply

> Stagflation is the typical result of adverse shifts of the aggregate supply curve.

The numbers used in Figure 8 are meant to indicate what the big energy shock in late 1973 might have done to the U.S. economy. Between 1973 (represented by supply curve S_0S_0 and point *E*) and 1975 (represented by supply curve S_1S_1 and point *A*), it shows real GDP falling by about 1.5 percent, while the price level rises more than 13 percent over the two years. The general lesson to be learned from the U.S. experience with supply shocks is both clear and important:

> The typical results of an adverse supply shock are lower output and higher inflation. This is one reason why the

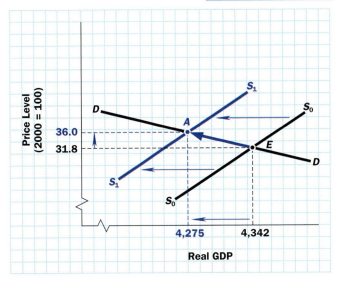

NOTE: Amounts are in billions of dollars per year.

world economy was plagued by stagflation in the mid-1970s and early 1980s. And it can happen again if another series of supply-reducing events takes place.

■ APPLYING THE MODEL TO A GROWING ECONOMY

You may have noticed that ever since Chapter 22 we have been using the simple aggregate supply and aggregate demand model to determine the equilibrium *price level* and the equilibrium *level of real GDP*, as depicted in several graphs in this chapter. But in the real world, neither the price level nor real GDP remains constant for long. Instead, both normally rise from one year to the next.

The growth process is illustrated in Figure 9, which is a scatter diagram of the U.S. price level and the level of real GDP for every year from 1972 to 2006. The labeled points show the clear upward march of the economy through time—toward higher prices and higher levels of output.

This upward trend is hardly mysterious, for both the aggregate demand curve and the aggregate supply curve normally shift to the right each year. Aggregate supply grows because more workers join the workforce each year and because investment and technology improve productivity (Chapter 24). Aggregate demand grows because a growing population generates more demand for both consumer and investment goods and because the government increases its purchases (Chapters 25 and 26), We can think of each point in Figure 9 as the intersection of an aggregate supply curve and an aggregate demand curve for that particular year. To help you visualize this idea, the curves for 1984 and 1993 are sketched in the diagram.

Figure 10 is a more realistic version of the aggregate supply and demand diagram which illustrates how our theoretical model applies to a growing economy. We have chosen the numbers so that the black curves D_0D_0 and S_0S_0 roughly represent the year 2002, and the blue curves D_1D_1 and S_1S_1 roughly represent 2003—except that we use nice round numbers to facilitate computations. Thus, the equilibrium in 2002 was at point *A*, with a real GDP of $10,000 billion (in 2000 dollars) and a price level of 104. A year later, the equilibrium was at point *B*, with real GDP at $10,320 billion and the price level at 106. The red arrow in the diagram shows how equilibrium moved from 2002 to 2003. It points upward and to the right, meaning that both prices and output increased. In this case, the economy grew by 3.2 percent and prices rose about 1.9 percent, which is close to what actually happened in the United States over that year.

FIGURE 9

The Price Level and Real GDP Output in the United States, 1972–2006

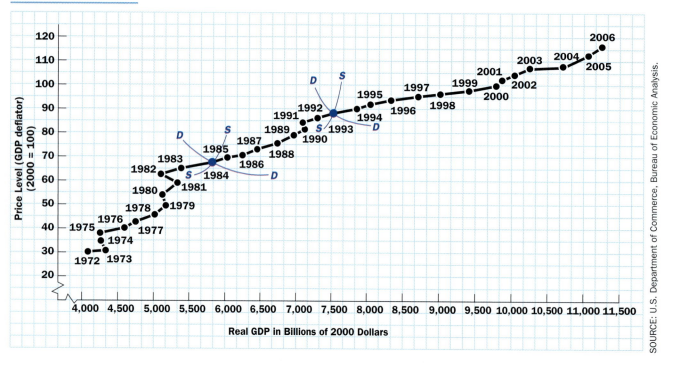

SOURCE: U.S. Department of Commerce, Bureau of Economic Analysis.

■ Demand-side Fluctuations

Let us now use our theoretical model to rewrite history. Suppose that aggregate demand grew *faster* than it actually did between 2002 and 2003. What difference would this have made to the performance of the U.S. economy? Figure 11 provides answers. Here the black demand curve D_0D_0 is exactly the same as in the previous diagram, as are the two supply curves, indicating a given rate of aggregate supply growth. But the blue demand curve D_2D_2 lies farther to the right than the demand curve D_1D_1 in Figure 10. Equilibrium is at point A in 2002 and point C in 2003. Comparing point C in Figure 11 with point B in Figure 10, we see that *both* output *and* prices would have increased more over the year—that is, the economy would have experienced faster *growth* and more *inflation*. This is generally what happens when the growth rate of aggregate demand speeds up.

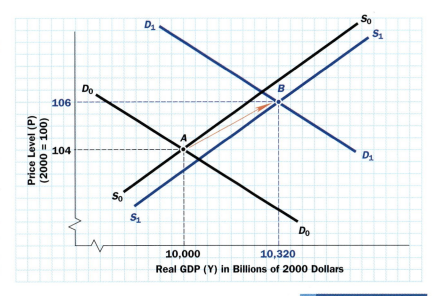

FIGURE 10

Aggregate Supply and Demand Analysis of a Growing Economy

For any given growth rate of aggregate supply, a faster growth rate of aggregate demand will lead to more inflation and faster growth of real output.

Figure 12, on the next page, illustrates the opposite case. Here we imagine that the aggregate demand curve shifted out *less* than in Figure 10. That is, the blue demand curve D_3D_3 in Figure 12 lies to the left of the demand curve D_1D_1 in Figure 10. The consequence, we see, is that the shift of the economy's equilibrium from 2002 to 2003 (from point A to point E) would have entailed *less inflation* and *slower growth* of real output than actually took place. Again, that is generally the case when aggregate demand grows more slowly.

For any given growth rate of aggregate supply, a slower growth rate of aggregate demand will lead to less inflation and slower growth of real output.

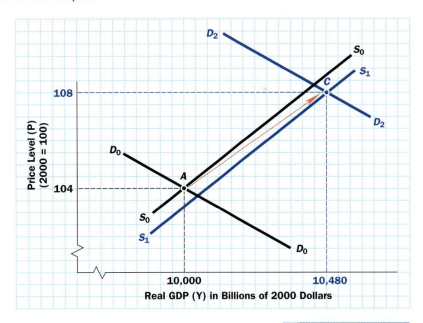

FIGURE 11

The Effects of Faster Growth of Aggregate Demand

Putting these two findings together gives us a clear prediction:

If fluctuations in the economy's real growth rate from year to year arise primarily from variations in the rate at which *aggregate demand* increases, then the data should show the most rapid inflation occurring when output grows most rapidly and the slowest inflation occurring when output grows most slowly.

Is it true? For the most part, yes. Our brief review of U.S. economic history back in Chapter 22 found that most episodes of high inflation came with rapid growth. But not all. Some surges of inflation resulted from the kinds of supply shocks we have considered in this chapter.

■ Supply-side Fluctuations

As a historical example, let's return to the events of 1973 to 1975 that were considered in Figure 8 (page 595), but now add in something we ignored there: While the aggregate supply curve was shifting *inward* because of the oil shock, the aggregate

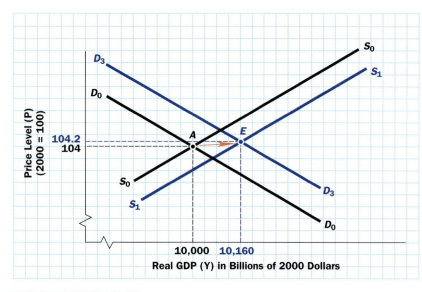

demand was shifting *outward*. In Figure 13, the black aggregate demand curve D_0D_0 and aggregate supply curve S_0S_0 represent the economic situation in 1973. Equilibrium was at point E, with a price level of 31.8 (based on 2000 = 100) and real output of $4,342 billion. By 1975, the aggregate demand curve had shifted out to the position indicated by the blue curve D_1D_1, but the aggregate supply curve had shifted *inward* from to the blue curve S_1S_1. The equilibrium for 1975 (point B in the figure) therefore wound up to the left of the equilibrium point for 1973. Real output declined slightly (although less than in Figure 8) and prices—led by energy costs—rose rapidly (more than in Figure 8).

FIGURE 12

The Effects of Slower Growth of Aggregate Demand

What about the opposite case? Suppose the economy experiences a *favorable* supply shock, as it did in the late 1990s, so that the aggregate supply curve shifts *outward* at an unusually rapid rate.

Figure 14 depicts the consequences. The aggregate demand curve shifts out from D_0D_0 to D_1D_1 as usual, but the aggregate supply curve shifts all the way out to S_1S_1. (The dotted line indicates what would happen in a "normal" year.) So the economy's equilibrium winds up at point B rather than at point C. Compared to C, point B represents *faster economic growth* (B is to the right of C) and *lower inflation* (B is lower than C). In brief, the economy wins on both fronts: Inflation falls while GDP grows rapidly, as happened in the late 1990s.

FIGURE 13

Stagflation from an Adverse Supply Shock

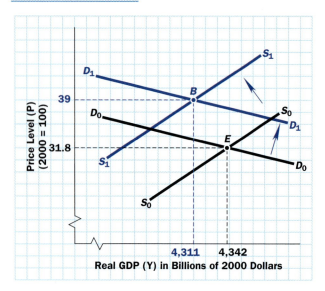

FIGURE 14

The Effects of a Favorable Supply Shock

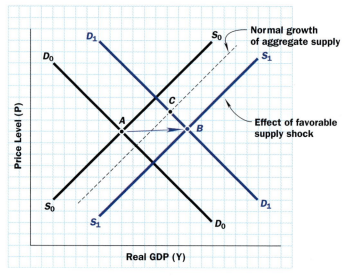

Combining these two cases, we conclude that:

If fluctuations in economic activity emanate mainly from the supply side, higher rates of inflation will be associated with *lower* rates of economic growth.

PUZZLE RESOLVED: *Explaining the Roaring Nineties*

The situation depicted in Figure 14 holds the key to understanding why the U.S. economy performed so marvelously in the late 1990s. As we observed at the beginning of this chapter, inflation *fell* while unemployment was extremely low, leading many observers to proclaim that some of the most basic precepts of macroeconomics no longer applied in the "New Economy."

What really happened? Several things, but one of them was a favorable oil shock. The world oil market weakened in 1997 and 1998, and oil prices plummeted from about $26 per barrel to just $11 per barrel. This sharp drop in the price of oil constituted a favorable supply shock that shifted the aggregate supply curve outward—just as shown in Figure 14. So U.S. economic growth speeded up while inflation declined. In addition, productivity accelerated in the late 1990s—as we discussed in Chapter 24—and this constituted another favorable supply shock. Thus, America enjoyed the happy combination of falling unemployment and declining inflation at the same time.

Lucky? Yes. But mysterious? No. What was happening was that the economy's aggregate supply curve was shifting outward much faster than it normally does. As we know from turning our previous analysis of adverse supply shocks in the opposite direction:

Favorable supply shocks tend to push output up and reduce inflation. It was mainly favorable supply shocks, including a speedup in productivity growth, which accounted for the stunningly good news in the late 1990s.

A ROLE FOR STABILIZATION POLICY

Chapter 25 emphasized the volatility of investment spending, and Chapter 26 noted that changes in investment have multiplier effects on aggregate demand. This chapter took the next step by showing how shifts in the aggregate demand curve cause fluctuations in *both* real GDP *and* prices—fluctuations that are widely decried as undesirable. It also suggested that the economy's self-correcting mechanism works, but slowly, thereby leaving room for government stabilization policy to improve the workings of the free market. Can the government really accomplish this goal? If so, how? These are some of the important questions for Part VII.

SUMMARY

1. The economy's **aggregate supply curve** relates the quantity of goods and services that will be supplied to the price level. It normally slopes upward to the right because the costs of labor and other inputs remain relatively fixed in the short run, meaning that higher selling prices make input costs relatively cheaper and therefore encourage greater production.

2. The position of the aggregate supply curve can be shifted by changes in money wage rates, prices of other inputs, technology, or quantities or qualities of labor and capital.

3. The **equilibrium price level** and the **equilibrium level of real GDP** are jointly determined by the intersection of the economy's aggregate supply and aggregate demand schedules.

4. Among the reasons why the oversimplified multiplier formula is wrong is the fact that it ignores the inflation that is caused by an increase in aggregate demand. Such **inflation decreases the multiplier** by reducing both consumer spending and net exports.

5. The equilibrium of aggregate supply and demand can come at full employment, below full employment (a **recessionary gap**), or above full employment (an **inflationary gap**).

6. The economy has a **self-correcting mechanism** that erodes a recessionary gap. Specifically, a weak labor market reduces wage increases and, in extreme cases, may even drive wages down. Lower wages shift the aggregate supply curve outward. But it happens very slowly.

7. If an inflationary gap occurs, the economy has a similar mechanism that erodes the gap through a process of inflation. Unusually strong job prospects push wages up, which shifts the aggregate supply curve to the left and reduces the inflationary gap.

8. One consequence of this self-correcting mechanism is that, if a surge in aggregate demand opens up an inflationary gap, the economy's subsequent natural adjustment will lead to a period of **stagflation**—that is, a period in which prices are rising while output is falling.

9. An inward shift of the aggregate supply curve will cause output to fall while prices rise—that is, it will produce stagflation. Among the events that have caused such a shift are abrupt increases in the price of foreign oil.

10. Adverse supply shifts like this plagued the U.S. economy when oil prices skyrocketed in 1973–1974, in 1979–1980, and again in 1990, leading to stagflation each time.

11. But things reversed in 1997–1998, when falling oil prices and rising productivity shifted the aggregate supply curve out more rapidly than usual, thereby boosting real growth and reducing inflation simultaneously.

12. Inflation can be caused either by rapid growth of aggregate demand or by sluggish growth of aggregate supply. When fluctuations in economic activity emanate from the demand side, prices will rise rapidly when real output grows rapidly. But when fluctuations in economic activity emanate from the supply side, curve, output will grow slowly when prices rise rapidly.

KEY TERMS

Aggregate supply curve   584

Productivity   586

Equilibrium of real GDP and the price level   587

Inflation and the multiplier   588

Recessionary gap   589

Inflationary gap   589

Self-correcting mechanism   592

Stagflation   594

TEST YOURSELF

1. In an economy with the following aggregate demand and aggregate supply schedules, find the equilibrium levels of real output and the price level. Graph your solution. If full employment comes at $2,800 billion, is there an inflationary or a recessionary gap?

Aggregate Quantity Demanded	Price Level	Aggregate Quantity Supplied
$3,200	90	$2,750
3,100	95	2,900
3,000	100	3,000
2,900	105	3,050
2,800	110	3,075

Note: Amounts are in billions of dollars.

2. Suppose a worker receives a wage of $20 per hour. Compute the real wage (money wage deflated by the price index) corresponding to each of the following possible price levels: 85, 95, 100, 110, 120. What do you notice about the relationship between the real wage and the price level? Relate your finding to the slope of the aggregate supply curve.

3. Add the following aggregate supply and demand schedules to the example in Test Yourself Question 2 of Chapter 26 (page 578) to see how inflation affects the multiplier.

(1) Price Level	(2) Aggregate Demand When Investment Is $240	(3) Aggregate Demand When Investment Is $260	(4) Aggregate Supply
90	$3,860	$4,060	$3,660
95	3,830	4,030	3,730
100	3,800	4,000	3,800
105	3,770	3,970	3,870
110	3,740	3,940	3,940
115	3,710	3,910	4,010

Draw these schedules on a piece of graph paper.

a. Notice that the difference between Columns (2) and (3), which show the aggregate demand schedule at two different levels of investment, is always $200. Discuss how this constant gap of $200 relates to your answer in the previous chapter.

b. Find the equilibrium GDP and the equilibrium price level both before and after the increase in investment. What is the value of the multiplier? Compare that to the multiplier you found in Test Yourself Question 2 of Chapter 26.

4. Use an aggregate supply and demand diagram to show that multiplier effects are smaller when the aggregate supply curve is steeper. Which case gives rise to more inflation—the steep aggregate supply curve or the flat one? What happens to the multiplier if the aggregate supply curve is vertical?

DISCUSSION QUESTIONS

1. Explain why a decrease in the price of foreign oil shifts the aggregate supply curve outward to the right. What are the consequences of such a shift?

2. Comment on the following statement: "Inflationary and recessionary gaps are nothing to worry about because the economy has a built-in mechanism that cures either type of gap automatically."

3. Give two different explanations of how the economy can suffer from stagflation.

4. Why do you think wages tend to be rigid in the downward direction?

5. Explain in words why rising prices reduce the multiplier effect of an autonomous increase in aggregate demand.

VII

FISCAL AND MONETARY POLICY

Part VI constructed a framework for understanding the macroeconomy. The basic theory came in three parts. We started with the determinants of the long-run growth rate of potential GDP in Chapter 24, added some analysis of short-run fluctuations in aggregate demand in Chapters 25 and 26, and finally considered short-run fluctuations in aggregate supply in Chapter 27. Part VII *uses* that framework to consider a variety of public policy issues—the sorts of things that make headlines in the newspapers and on television.

At several points in earlier chapters, beginning with our list of *Ideas for Beyond the Final Exam* in Chapter 1, we suggested that the government may be able to manage aggregate demand by using its *fiscal and monetary policies*. Chapters 28–30 pick up and build on that suggestion. You will learn how the government tries to promote rapid growth and low unemployment while simultaneously limiting inflation—and why its efforts do not always succeed. Then, in Chapters 31–33, we turn explicitly to a number of important controversies related to the government's *stabilization policy*. How should the Federal Reserve do its job? Why is it considered so important to reduce the budget deficit? Is there a trade-off between inflation and unemployment?

By the end of Part VII, you will be in an excellent position to understand some of the most important debates over national economic policy—not only today but also in the years to come.

28

MANAGING AGGREGATE DEMAND:
FISCAL POLICY

Next, let us turn to the problems of our fiscal policy. Here the myths are legion and the truth hard to find.

JOHN F. KENNEDY

I n the model of the economy we constructed in Part VI, the government played a rather passive role. It did some spending and collected taxes, but that was about it. We concluded that such an economy has only a weak tendency to move toward an equilibrium with high employment and low inflation. Furthermore, we hinted that well-designed government policies might enhance that tendency and improve the economy's performance. It is now time to expand on that hint—and to learn about some of the difficulties that must be overcome if stabilization policy is to succeed.

We begin in this chapter with **fiscal policy.** The next three chapters take up the government's other main tool for managing aggregate demand, *monetary policy.*

The government's **fiscal policy** is its plan for spending and taxation. It is designed to steer aggregate demand in some desired direction.

CONTENTS

ISSUE: *Aggregate Demand, Aggregate Supply, and the Tax-Cut Debate of 2004*

During the 2004 presidential campaign, Democratic challenger John Kerry advocated repeal of some of the tax cuts that President Bush and the Republicans had enacted during Mr. Bush's first term. In particular, Senator Kerry wanted to roll back the tax cuts for taxpayers earning more than $200,000 per year. Bush supporters argued that doing so would damage economic growth in two ways: by reducing consumer spending (and, thus, aggregate demand), and by impairing incentives to earn more income (thus reducing aggregate supply).

Kerry supporters rejected both claims. With regard to aggregate supply, they argued that the alleged incentive effects of lower tax rates were minuscule. With regard to aggregate demand, they made two arguments: First, that wealthy taxpayers would not spend much of the money they received from their tax cuts anyway, and second, that eliminating the tax cuts for the rich would enable the government to spend more on health care. On balance, they maintained, aggregate demand would rise, not fall.

The debate over the Bush tax cuts thus revolved around three concepts that we will study in this chapter:

- the multiplier effects of tax cuts versus higher government spending
- the multiplier effects of different types of tax cuts (e.g., those for the poor versus those for the rich)
- the incentive effects of tax cuts.

By the end of the chapter, you will be in a much better position to form your own opinion on this important public policy issue.

INCOME TAXES AND THE CONSUMPTION SCHEDULE

To understand how taxes affect equilibrium gross domestic product (GDP), we begin by recalling that taxes (T) are *subtracted* from gross domestic product (Y) to obtain disposable income (DI):

$$DI = Y - T,$$

and that disposable income, not GDP, is the amount actually available to consumers, and is therefore the principal determinant of consumer spending (C). Thus, *at any given level of GDP*, if taxes rise, disposable income falls—and hence so does consumption. What we have just described in words is summarized graphically in Figure 1:

> Any increase in taxes shifts the consumption schedule *downward*, and any tax reduction shifts the consumption schedule *upward*.

Of course, if the C schedule moves up or down, so does the $C + I + G + (X - IM)$ schedule. And we know from Chapter 26 that such a shift will have a multiplier effect on aggregate demand. So it follows that:

> An increase or decrease in taxes will have a mutiplier effect on equilibrium GDP on the demand side. Tax reductions increase equilibrium GDP, and tax increases reduce it.

So far, this analysis just echoes our previous analysis of the multiplier effects of government spending. But there is one important difference. Government purchases of goods and services add to total spending *directly*—through the G

FIGURE 1

How Tax Policy Shifts the Consumption Schedule

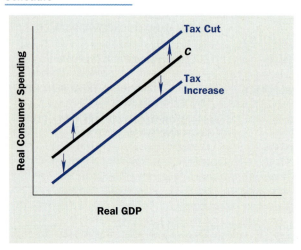

component of $C + I + G + (X - IM)$. But taxes reduce total spending only *indirectly*—by lowering disposable income and thus reducing the C component of $C + I + G + (X - IM)$. As we will now see, that little detail turns out to be quite important.

THE MULTIPLIER REVISITED

To understand why, let us return to the example used in Chapter 26, in which we learned that the multiplier works through a chain of spending and respending, as one person's expenditure becomes another's income. In the example, the spending chain was initiated by Microhard's decision to spend an additional $1 million on investment. With a marginal propensity to consume (MPC) of 0.75, the complete multiplier chain was:

$$\$1,000,000 + \$750,000 + \$562,500 + \$421,875 + \dots.$$
$$= \$1,000,000 (1 + 0.75 + (0.75)^2 + (0.75)^3 + \dots)$$
$$= \$1,000,000 \times 4 = \$4,000,000.$$

Thus, each dollar originally spent by Microhard eventually produced $4 in additional spending.

The Tax Multiplier

Now suppose the initiating event was a $1 million *tax cut* instead. As we just noted, a tax cut affects spending only *indirectly*. By adding $1 million to disposable income, it increases consumer spending by $750,000 (assuming again that the MPC is 0.75). Thereafter, the chain of spending and respending proceeds exactly as before, to yield:

$$\$750,000 + \$562,500 + \$421,875 + \dots.$$
$$= \$750,000 (1 + 0.75 + (0.75)^2 + \dots)$$
$$= \$750,000 \times 4 = \$3,000,000.$$

Notice that the mutiplier effect of each dollar of tax cut is 3, not 4. The reason is straightforward. Each new dollar of additional autonomous spending—regardless of whether it is C or I or G—has a multiplier of 4. But each dollar of tax cut creates only 75 cents of new consumer spending. Applying the basic expenditure multiplier of 4 to the 75 cents of first-round spending leads to a multiplier of 3 for each dollar of tax cut. This numerical example illustrates a general result:[1]

The multiplier for changes in taxes is smaller than the multiplier for changes in government purchases because not every dollar of tax cut is spent.

Income Taxes and the Multiplier

But this is not the only way in which taxes force us to modify the multiplier analysis of Chapter 26. If the volume of taxes collected depends on GDP—which, of course, it does in reality—there is another.

To understand this new wrinkle, return again to our Microhard example, but now assume that the government levies a 20 percent *income tax*—meaning that individuals pay 20 cents in taxes for each $1 of income they receive. Now when Microhard spends $1 million on salaries, its workers receive only $800,000 in *after-tax* (that is, disposable) income. The rest goes to the government in taxes. If workers spend 75 percent of the $800,000 (because the MPC is 0.75), spending in the next round will be only $600,000. Notice that this is only *60 percent* of the original expenditure, not *75 percent*—as was the case before.

---

[1] You may notice that the tax multiplier of 3 is the spending multiplier of 4 times the marginal propensity to consume, which is 0.75. See Appendix B for an algebraic explanation.

Thus, the multiplier chain for each original dollar of spending *shrinks* from

$$1 + 0.75 + (0.75)^2 + (0.75)^3 + \ldots = \frac{1}{1 - 0.75} = \frac{1}{0.25} = 4$$

in Chapter 26's example to

$$1 + 0.6 + (0.6)^2 + (0.6)^3 + \ldots = \frac{1}{(1 - 0.6)} = \frac{1}{0.4} = 2.5$$

now. This is clearly a large reduction in the multiplier. Although this is just a numerical example, the two appendixes to this chapter show that the basic finding is quite general:

The multiplier is reduced by an income tax because an income tax reduces the fraction of each dollar of GDP that consumers actually receive and spend.

We thus have a third reason why the oversimplified multiplier formula of Chapter 26 exaggerates the size of the multiplier: It ignores income taxes.

REASONS WHY THE OVERSIMPLIFIED FORMULA OVERSTATES THE MULTIPLIER

1. It ignores variable imports, which reduce the size of the multiplier.
2. It ignores price-level changes, which reduce the multiplier.
3. It ignores income taxes, which also reduce the size of the multiplier.

FIGURE 2

The Multiplier in the Presence of an Income Tax

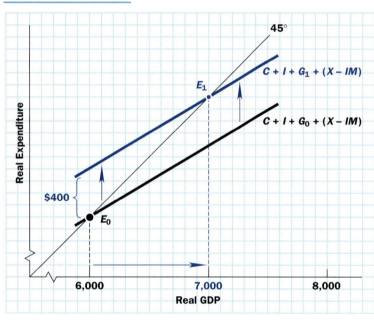

NOTE: Figures are in billions of dollars per year.

The last of these three reasons is the most important in practice.

This conclusion about the multiplier is shown graphically in Figure 2, which can usefully be compared to Figure 10 of Chapter 26 (page 570). Here we draw our $C + I + G + (X - IM)$ schedules with a slope of 0.6, reflecting an MPC of 0.75 and a tax rate of 20 percent, rather than the 0.75 slope we used in Chapter 26. Figure 2 then illustrates the effect of a \$400 billion increase in government purchases of goods and services, which shifts the total expenditure schedule from $C + I + G_0 + (X - IM)$ to $C + I + G_1 + (X - IM)$. Equilibrium moves from point E_0 to point E_1—a GDP increase from $Y = \$6,000$ billion to $Y = \$7,000$ billion. Thus, if we ignore for the moment any increases in the price level (which would further reduce the multiplier), a \$400 billion increment in government spending leads to a \$1,000 billion increment in GDP. So, when a 20 percent income tax is included in our model, the multiplier is only \$1,000/\$400 = 2.5, as we concluded above.

Thus, we now have noted two different ways in which taxes modify the multiplier analysis:

- Tax changes have a smaller multiplier effect than spending changes by government or others.
- An income tax reduces the multipliers for *both* tax changes *and* changes in spending.

Automatic Stabilizers

The size of the multiplier may seem to be a rather abstract notion with little practical importance. But that is not so. Fluctuations in one or another of the components of total spending—*C, I, G,* or *X − IM*—occur all the time. Some come unexpectedly; some are even difficult to explain after the fact. We know from Chapter 26 that any such fluctuation will move GDP up or down by a multiplied amount. If the multiplier is smaller, GDP will be less sensitive to such shocks—that is, the economy will be less volatile.

Features of the economy that reduce its sensitivity to shocks are called **automatic stabilizers.** The most obvious example is the one we have just been discussing: the personal income tax. The income tax acts as a shock absorber because it makes disposable income, and thus consumer spending, less sensitive to fluctuations in GDP. As we have just seen, when GDP rises, disposable income (*DI*) rises *less* because part of the increase in GDP is siphoned off by the U.S. Treasury. This leakage helps limit any increase in consumption spending. When GDP falls, *DI* falls less sharply because part of the loss is absorbed by the Treasury rather than by consumers. So consumption does not drop as much as it otherwise might. Thus, the much-maligned personal income tax is one of the main features of our modern economy that helps ensure against a repeat performance of the Great Depression.

But our economy has other automatic stabilizers. For example, Chapter 23 discussed the U.S. system of unemployment insurance. This program serves as an automatic stabilizer as well: When GDP drops and people lose their jobs, unemployment benefits prevent disposable incomes from falling as dramatically as earnings do. As a result, unemployed workers can maintain their spending better, and consumption fluctuates less than employment does.

The list could continue, but the basic principle remains the same: Each automatic stabilizer serves, in one way or another, as a shock absorber, thereby lowering the multiplier. And each does so quickly, without the need for any decision maker to take action. In a word, they work *automatically*.

A case in point arose when the U.S. economy sagged in the early part of this decade. The budget deficit naturally rose as tax receipts came in lower than had been expected. While there was much hand-wringing over the rising deficit, most economists viewed it as a good thing in the short run: The automatic stabilizers were propping up spending, as they should.

■ Government Transfer Payments

To complete our discussion of multipliers for fiscal policy, let us now turn to the last major fiscal tool: *government transfer payments*. Transfers, as you will remember, are payments to individuals that are not compensation for any direct contribution to production. How are transfers treated in our models of income determination—like purchases of goods and services (*G*) or like taxes (*T*)?

The answer to this question follows readily from the circular flow diagram on page 540 or the accounting identity on page 541. The important thing to understand about transfer payments is that they intervene between gross domestic product (*Y*) and disposable income (*DI*) in precisely the *opposite* way from income taxes. They add to earned income rather than subtract from it.

Specifically, starting with the wages, interest, rents, and profits that constitute national income, we *subtract* income taxes to calculate disposable income. We do so because these taxes represent the portion of incomes that consumers *earn* but never *receive*. But then we must *add* transfer payments because they represent sources of income that are *received* although they were not *earned* in the process of production. Thus:

Transfer payments function basically as negative taxes.

As you may recall from Chapter 25, we use the symbol *T* to denote taxes *minus* transfers. Thus giving consumers $1 in the form of transfer payments is treated in the 45° line diagram as a $1 decrease in taxes.

ISSUE REVISITED: *The Bush-Kerry Debate over Taxes and Spending*

What we have learned already has some bearing on the debate between George Bush and John Kerry in 2004. Remember that Kerry wanted to rescind Bush's tax cuts for wealthy taxpayers and spend the funds on government health insurance programs. We have learned that the multiplier for *T* is *smaller* than the multiplier for *G*. That means that an increase in government spending balanced by an equal increase in taxes—which is what Kerry proposed—should *raise* total spending.[2]

Next, consider Kerry's claim that the portions of the Bush tax cuts that went to wealthy individuals would not stimulate much spending. This assertion assumes that the rich have very low marginal propensities to consume, as many people naturally assume. Remember, a lower MPC leads to a lower multiplier. But the data actually suggest that the rich are spendthrifts—just like the rest of us! That said, poor families probably do have extremely high MPCs, so tax cuts for the poor would probably give rise to larger multipliers than tax cuts for the rich.

PLANNING EXPANSIONARY FISCAL POLICY

We will have more to say about the Bush-Kerry debate later. But first imagine you were a member of the U.S. Congress trying to decide whether to use fiscal policy to stimulate the economy in 2001—and, if so, by how much. Suppose the economy would have a GDP of $6,000 billion if the government simply reenacted last year's budget. Suppose further that your goal is to achieve a fully employed labor force, and that staff economists tell you that reaching this target requires a GDP of approximately $7,000 billion. Finally, just to keep the calculations simple, imagine that the price level is fixed. What sort of budget should you vote for?

This chapter has taught us that the government has three ways to raise GDP by $1,000 billion. Congress can close the recessionary gap between actual and potential GDP by:

- Raising government purchases
- Reducing taxes
- Increasing transfer payments

Figure 3 illustrates the problem, and its cure through higher government spending, on our 45° line diagram. Figure 3(a) shows the equilibrium of the economy if no changes are made in the budget. With an expenditure multiplier of 2.5, you can figure out that an additional $400 billion of government spending will be needed to push GDP up by $1,000 billion and eliminate the gap ($400 × 2.5 = $1,000).

So you might vote to raise *G* by $400 billion, hoping to move the *C* + *I* + *G* + (*X* − *IM*) line in Figure 3(a) up to the position indicated in Figure 3(b), thereby achieving full employment. Or you might prefer to achieve this fiscal stimulus by lowering taxes. Or you might opt for more generous transfer payments. The point is that a variety of budgets are capable of increasing GDP by $1,000 billion. Figure 3 applies equally well to any of them. President George W. Bush favored tax cuts, which is the tool the U.S government relied on in 2001. Especially after the September 11 terrorist attacks, encouraging consumers to spend their tax cuts became a national priority.

SOURCE: © R. J. Matson, *Roll Call*

---

[2] Some of the additional expenditures proposed by Kerry were actually transfer payments rather than government purchases. That part would have the same multiplier as taxes. Furthermore, Bush and his supporters claimed that Kerry's spending proposals exceeded his tax-increasing proposals.

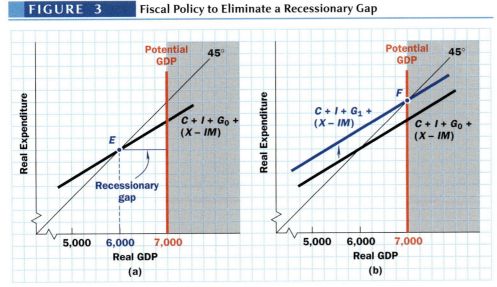

FIGURE 3   Fiscal Policy to Eliminate a Recessionary Gap

NOTE: Figures are in billions of dollars per year.

PLANNING CONTRACTIONARY FISCAL POLICY

The preceding example assumed that the basic problem of fiscal policy is to close a recessionary gap, as was the case in 2001. But only two years earlier, in 1999, many economists believed that the major macroeconomic problem in the United States was just the opposite: Real GDP exceeded potential GDP, leading to an inflationary gap. And some people believe that an inflationary gap emerged again in 2006. In such a case, government would wish to adopt more restrictive fiscal policies to reduce aggregate demand.

It does not take much imagination to run our previous analysis in reverse. If an inflationary gap would arise from a continuation of current budget policies, contractionary fiscal policy tools can eliminate it. By cutting spending, raising taxes, or by some combination of the two, the government can pull the $C + G + I + (X - IM)$ schedule down to a noninflationary position and achieve an equilibrium at full employment.

Notice the difference between this way of eliminating an inflationary gap and the natural self-correcting mechanism that we discussed in the last chapter. There we observed that, if the economy were left to its own devices, a cumulative but self-limiting process of inflation would eventually eliminate the inflationary gap and return the economy to full employment. Here we see that we need not put the economy through the inflationary wringer. Instead, a restrictive fiscal policy can avoid inflation by limiting aggregate demand to the level that the economy can produce at full employment.

THE CHOICE BETWEEN SPENDING POLICY AND TAX POLICY

In principle, fiscal policy can nudge the economy in the desired direction equally well by changing government spending or by changing taxes. For example, if the government wants to expand the economy, it can raise G or lower T. Either policy would shift the total expenditure schedule upward, as depicted in Figure 3(b), thereby raising equilibrium GDP on the demand side.

In terms of our aggregate demand and supply diagram, either policy shifts the aggregate demand curve outward, as illustrated in the shift from D_0D_0 to D_1D_1 in Figure 4 on the next page. As a result, the economy's equilibrium moves from point E to point A. Both real GDP and the price level rise. As this diagram points out:

> **Any combination of higher spending and lower taxes that produces the same aggregate demand curve leads to the same increases in real GDP and prices.**

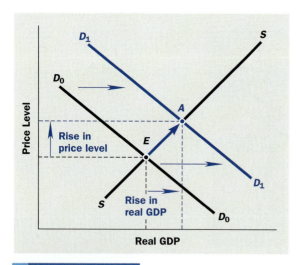

FIGURE 4

Expansionary Fiscal
Policy

*"Free gifts to every kid in the world?
Are you a Keynesian or something?"*

SOURCE: From *The Wall Street Journal*—Permission,
Cartoon Features Syndicate

How, then, do policy makers decide whether to raise spending or to cut taxes? The answer depends mainly on how large a public sector they want to create—a major issue in the long-running debate in the United States over the proper size of government.

The small-government point of view, typically advocated by conservatives, says that we are foolish to rely on the public sector to do what private individuals and businesses can do better on their own. Conservatives believe that the growth of government interferes too much in our everyday lives, thereby curtailing our freedom. Those who hold this view can argue for *tax cuts* when macroeconomic considerations call for expansionary fiscal policy (as President Bush did), and for *lower public spending* when contractionary policy is required.

An opposing opinion, expressed most often by liberals, holds that something is amiss when a country as wealthy as the United States has such an impoverished public sector. In this view, America's most pressing needs are not for more fast food and video games but, rather, for better schools, more efficient public transportation systems, and cleaner and safer city streets. People on this side of the debate believe that we should *increase* spending when the economy needs stimulus and pay for these improved public services by *increasing taxes* when it is necessary to rein in the economy.

The use of fiscal policy for economic stabilization is sometimes erroneously associated with a large and growing public sector—that is, with "big government." This need not be so.

Individuals favoring a smaller public sector can advocate an active fiscal policy just as well as those who favor a larger public sector. Advocates of bigger government should seek to expand demand (when appropriate) through higher government spending and contract demand (when appropriate) through tax increases. By contrast, advocates of smaller government should seek to expand demand by cutting taxes and reduce demand by cutting expenditures.

ISSUE REDUX: *Bush versus Kerry*

The choice between fiscal stimulus via tax cuts or fiscal stimulus via spending played a central role in the Bush-Kerry debate during the 2004 presidential campaign. President Bush staunchly defended his tax cuts, partly on the grounds that "small government" is better than "big government." His challenger argued that providing health insurance coverage to more Americans was a higher priority than providing tax cuts for the well-to-do. At the time, the voters apparently sided with Mr. Bush, although polling during the 2006 midterm elections suggested they were having second thoughts.

SOME HARSH REALITIES

The mechanics outlined so far in this chapter make the fiscal policy planner's job look pretty simple. The elementary diagrams suggest, rather misleadingly, that policy makers can drive GDP to any level they please simply by manipulating spending and tax programs. It seems they should be able to hit the full-employment bull's eye every time. In fact, a better analogy is to a poor rifleman shooting through dense fog at an erratically moving target with an inaccurate gun and slow-moving bullets.

The target is moving because, in the real world, the investment, net exports, and consumption schedules constantly shift about as expectations, technology, events abroad, and other factors change. For all of these reasons and others, the policies decided on today, which will take effect at some future date, may no longer be appropriate by the time that future date rolls around.

The second misleading feature of our diagrams (the "inaccurate gun") is that we do not know multipliers with the precision of our examples. Although our best guess may be that a $20 billion increase in government purchases will raise GDP by $35 billion (a multiplier of 1.75), the actual outcome may be as little as $20 billion or as much as $50 billion. It is therefore impossible to "fine-tune" every wobble out of the economy's growth path. Economic science is simply not that precise.

A third complication is that our target—full-employment GDP—may be only dimly visible, as if through a fog. For example, with the unemployment rate hovering around 4.5 percent in 2006 and 2007, there was a vigorous debate over whether the U.S. economy was above or below full employment.

A fourth complication is that the fiscal policy "bullets" travel slowly: Tax and spending policies affect aggregate demand only after some time elapses. Consumer spending, for example, may take months to react to an income tax cut. Because of these time lags, fiscal policy decisions must be based on *forecasts* of the future state of the economy. And no one has yet discovered a foolproof method of economic forecasting. The combination of long lags and poor forecasts may occasionally leave the government fighting the last inflation just as the new recession gets under way.

And, finally, the people aiming the fiscal "rifle" are politicians, not economic technicians. Sometimes political considerations lead to policies that deviate markedly from what textbook economics would suggest. And even when they do not, the wheels of Congress grind slowly.

In addition to all of these operational problems, legislators trying to decide whether to push the unemployment rate lower would like to know the answers to two further questions. First, since either higher spending or lower taxes will increase the government's budget deficit, what are the long-run costs of running large budget deficits? This is a question we will take up in depth in Chapter 32. Second, how large is the inflationary cost likely to be? As we know, an expansionary fiscal policy that reduces a recessionary gap by increasing aggregate demand will lower unemployment. But, as Figure 4 reminds us, it also tends to be inflationary. This undesirable side effect may make the government hesitant to use fiscal policy to combat recessions.

Is there a way out of this dilemma? Can we carry on the battle against unemployment without aggravating inflation? For almost thirty years, a small but influential minority of economists, journalists, and politicians have argued that we can. They call their approach "supply-side economics." The idea helped sweep Ronald Reagan to smashing electoral victories in 1980 and 1984 and was revived under President George W. Bush. Just what is supply-side economics?

■ THE IDEA BEHIND SUPPLY-SIDE TAX CUTS

The central idea of supply-side economics is that certain types of tax cuts will increase aggregate supply. For example, taxes can be cut in ways that raise the rewards for working, saving, and investing. *If people actually respond to these incentives*, such tax cuts will increase the total supplies of labor and capital in the economy, thereby increasing aggregate supply.

Figure 5, on the next page, illustrates the idea on an aggregate supply and demand diagram. If policy measures can shift the economy's aggregate supply to position S_1S_1, then prices will be lower and output higher than if the aggregate supply curve remained at S_0S_0. Policy makers will have reduced inflation and raised real output at the same time—as shown by point B in the figure. The trade-off between inflation and unemployment will therefore have been defeated. That is the goal of supply-side economics.

What sorts of policies do supply-siders advocate? Here is a sample of their long list of recommended tax cuts:

Lower Personal Income Tax Rates   Sharp cuts in personal taxes were the cornerstone of the economic strategy of George W. Bush, just as they had been for Ronald Reagan

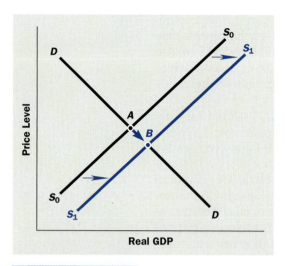

FIGURE 5

The Goal of Supply-Side
Tax Cuts

twenty years earlier. Since 2001, tax rates on individuals have been reduced in stages, and in several ways. The four upper tax bracket rates, which were 39.6 percent, 36 percent, 31 percent, and 28 percent when President Bush assumed office, have been reduced to 35 percent, 33 percent, 28 percent, and 25 percent, respectively. In addition, some very low income taxpayers have seen their tax rate fall from 15 percent to 10 percent. Lower tax rates, supply-siders argue, augment the supplies of both labor and capital.

Reduce Taxes on Income from Savings   One extreme form of this proposal would simply exempt from taxation all income from interest and dividends. Because income must be either consumed or saved, doing this would, in effect, change our present personal income tax into a tax on consumer spending. Several such proposals for radical tax reform have been considered in Washington over the years, but never adopted. However, Congress did reduce the tax rate on dividends to just 15 percent in 2003. And since then, both President Bush and a number of Democrats have proposed additional tax preferences for saving.

Reduce Taxes on Capital Gains   When an investor sells an asset for a profit, that profit is called a *capital gain*. Supply-siders argue that the government can encourage more investment by taxing capital gains at lower rates than ordinary income. This proposal was last acted upon in 2003, when the top rate on capital gains was cut to 15 percent.

Reduce the Corporate Income Tax   By reducing the tax burden on corporations, proponents argue, the government can provide both greater investment incentives (by raising the profitability of investment) and more investable funds (by letting companies keep more of their earnings). Ironically, this piece of supply-side economics was advocated by the Democratic candidate, Senator Kerry, during the 2004 campaign.

FIGURE 6

A Successful Supply-
Side Tax Reduction

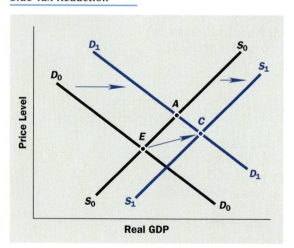

Let us suppose, for the moment, that a successful supply-side tax cut is enacted. Because *both* aggregate demand *and* aggregate supply increase simultaneously, the economy may be able to avoid the inflationary consequences of an expansionary fiscal policy shown in Figure 4 (page 612).

Figure 6 illustrates this conclusion. The two aggregate demand curves and the initial aggregate supply curve S_0S_0 carry over directly from Figure 4. But now we have introduced an additional supply curve, S_1S_1, to reflect the successful supply-side tax cut depicted in Figure 5. The equilibrium point for the economy moves from E to C, whereas with a conventional demand-side tax cut it would have moved from E to A. As compared with point A, which reflects only the demand-side effects of a tax cut, output is higher and prices are lower at point C.

A good deal, you say. And indeed it is. The supply-side argument is extremely attractive in principle. The question is: Does it work in practice? Can we actually do what is depicted in Figure 6? Let us consider some difficulties.

■ Some Flies in the Ointment

Critics of supply-side economics rarely question its goals or the basic idea that lower taxes improve incentives. They argue, instead, that supply-siders exaggerate the beneficial effects of tax cuts and ignore some undesirable side effects. Here is a brief rundown of some of their main objections.

Small Magnitude of Supply-Side Effects   The first objection is that supply-siders are simply too optimistic: No one really knows how to do what Figure 5 shows. Although it is easy, for example, to design tax incentives that make saving more *attractive* financially, people may not actually respond to these incentives. In fact, most of the statistical evidence suggests that we should not expect much from tax incentives for saving. As the economist Charles Schultze once quipped: "There's nothing wrong with supply-side economics that division by 10 couldn't cure."

Demand–Side Effects   The second objection is that supply-siders ignore the effects of tax cuts on aggregate demand. If you cut personal taxes, for example, individuals *may possibly* work more. But they *will certainly* spend more.

The joint implications of these two objections appear in Figure 7. This figure depicts a *small* outward shift of the aggregate supply curve (which reflects the first objection) and a *large* outward shift of the aggregate demand curve (which reflects the second objection). The result is that the economy's equilibrium moves from point E (the intersection of S_0S_0 and D_0D_0) to point C (the intersection of S_1S_1 and D_1D_1). Prices rise as output expands. The outcome differs only a little from the straight "demand-side" fiscal stimulus depicted in Figure 4.

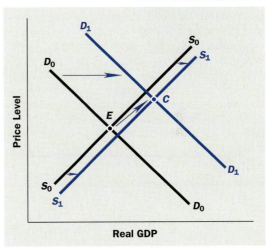

FIGURE 7

A More Pessimistic View of Supply-Side Tax Cuts

Problems with Timing   Investment incentives are the most promising type of supply-side tax cuts. But the benefits from greater investment do not arrive by overnight mail. In particular, the *expenditures* on investment goods almost certainly come before any *expansion of capacity*. Thus, supply-side tax cuts have their primary short-run effects on aggregate demand. Effects on aggregate supply come later.

Effects on Income Distribution   The preceding objections all pertain to the likely effects of supply-side policies on aggregate supply and demand. But a different problem bears mentioning: Most supply-side initiatives increase income inequality. Indeed, some tilt toward the rich is an almost inescapable corollary of supply-side logic. The basic aim of supply-side economics is to increase the incentives for working and investing—that is, to increase the gap between the rewards of those who succeed in the economic game (by working hard, investing well, or just plain being lucky) and those who fail. It can hardly be surprising, therefore, that supply-side policies tend to increase economic inequality.

Losses of Tax Revenue   You can hardly help noticing that most of the policies suggested by supply-siders involve cutting one tax or another. Thus supply-side tax cuts are bound to raise the government budget deficit. This problem proved to be the Achilles' heel of supply-side economics in the United States in the 1980s. The Reagan tax cuts left in their wake a legacy of budget deficits that took fifteen years to overcome. Opponents now argue that President George W. Bush's tax cuts have put us in a similar position: The tax cuts used up the budget surplus and turned it into a large deficit.

ISSUE: *Kerry and Bush Once More*

Several of the items on the preceding list played prominent roles in the 2004 presidential campaign. The Kerry camp argued that the Bush tax cuts had very small supply-side incentive effects, were unfair because they went mainly to the well-to-do, and were the primary cause of the large budgets deficits that emerged in 2002. Bush supporters countered that the tax cuts substantially improved the economy's efficiency, that it was fair to give the largest tax cuts to those who pay the highest taxes, and that the Bush tax cuts were not the major cause of the budget deficit—which they blamed on the 2001 recession and the spending required after September 11, 2001.

Supply-Side Economics and Presidential Elections

As we have mentioned, Ronald Reagan won landslide victories in 1980 and 1984 by running on a supply-side platform. But in 1992, candidate Bill Clinton attacked supply-side economics as "trickle-down economics," arguing that it had failed. He emphasized two of the drawbacks of such a fiscal policy: the effects on income inequality and on the budget deficit. The voters apparently agreed with him.

The hallmark of Clintonomics was, first, reducing the budget deficit that Clinton had inherited from the first President George Bush, and second, building up a large surplus. This policy succeeded—for a while. The huge budget deficit turned into a large surplus, the economy boomed, and Clinton, like Reagan before him, was reelected.

But in the 2000 presidential election, the voters once again switched their allegiance. During the campaign, Democratic candidate Al Gore promised to continue the "fiscal responsibility" of the Clinton years, while Republican candidate George W. Bush echoed Reagan by offering large tax cuts. Bush won in what was virtually a dead heat. Then, in 2004, John Kerry ran against the incumbent George Bush on what amounted to a promise to roll back some of the Bush tax cuts and return to Clintonomics. Bush won again.

So which approach do American voters prefer? They appear to be fickle! But one thing is clear: The debate over fiscal policy played a major role in each of the last seven presidential elections, and it will probably do so in 2008 again.

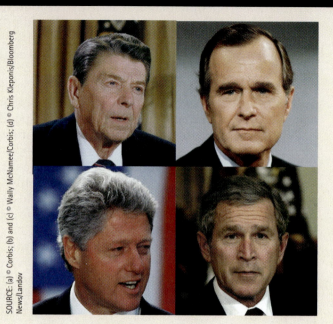

SOURCE: (a) © Corbis; (b) and (c) © Wally McNamee/Corbis; (d) © Chris Kleponis/Bloomberg News/Landov

■ Toward an Assessment of Supply-Side Economics

On balance, most economists have reached the following conclusions about supply-side tax initiatives:

1. The likely effectiveness of supply-side tax cuts depends on what kinds of taxes are cut. Tax reductions aimed at stimulating business investment are likely to pack more punch than tax reductions aimed at getting people to work longer hours or to save more.

2. Such tax cuts probably will increase aggregate supply much more slowly than they increase aggregate demand. Thus, supply-side policies should not be regarded as a substitute for short-run stabilization policy but, rather, as a way to promote (slightly) faster economic growth in the long run.

3. Demand-side effects of supply-side tax cuts are likely to overwhelm supply-side effects in the short run.

4. Supply-side tax cuts are likely to widen income inequalities.

5. Supply-side tax cuts are almost certain to lead to larger budget deficits.

Some people will look over this list and decide in favor of supply-side tax cuts; others, perusing the same facts, will reach the opposite conclusion. We cannot say that either group is wrong because, like almost every economic policy, supply-side economics has its pros and cons and involves value judgments that color people's conclusions.

Why, then, did so many economists and politicians react so negatively to supply-side economics as preached and practiced in the early 1980s? The main reason seems to be that the claims made by the most ardent supply-siders were clearly excessive. Naturally, these claims proved wrong. But showing that wild claims are wild does not eliminate the kernel of truth in supply-side economics: Reductions in marginal tax rates *do* improve economic incentives. Any specific supply-side tax cut must be judged on its individual merits.

SUMMARY

1. The government's **fiscal policy** is its plan for managing aggregate demand through its spending and taxing programs. This policy is made jointly by the president and Congress.

2. Because consumer spending (C) depends on disposable income (DI), and DI is GDP minus taxes, any change in taxes will shift the consumption schedule on a 45° line diagram. Such shifts in the consumption schedule have multiplier effects on GDP.

3. The multiplier for changes in taxes is smaller than the multiplier for changes in government purchases because each $1 of tax cuts leads to less than $1 of increased consumer spending.

4. An income tax reduces the size of the multiplier.

5. Because an income tax reduces the multiplier, it reduces the economy's sensitivity to shocks. It is therefore considered an **automatic stabilizer**.

6. Government transfer payments are like negative taxes, rather than like government purchases of goods and services, because they influence total spending only indirectly through their effect on consumption.

7. If the multipliers were known precisely, it would be possible to plan a variety of fiscal policies to eliminate either a recessionary gap or an inflationary gap. Recessionary gaps

can be cured by raising G or cutting T. Inflationary gaps can be cured by cutting G or raising T.

8. Active stabilization policy can be carried out either by means that tend to expand the size of government (by raising either G or T when appropriate) or by means that reduce the size of government (by reducing either G or T when appropriate).

9. Expansionary fiscal policy can mitigate recessions, but it also raises the budget deficit.

10. Expansionary fiscal policy also normally exacts a cost in terms of higher inflation. This last dilemma has led to a great deal of interest in "supply-side" tax cuts designed to stimulate aggregate supply.

11. **Supply-side tax cuts** aim to push the economy's aggregate supply curve outward to the right. When successful, they can expand the economy and reduce inflation at the same time—a highly desirable outcome.

12. But critics point out at least five serious problems with supply-side tax cuts: They also stimulate aggregate demand; the beneficial effects on aggregate supply may be small; the demand-side effects occur before the supply-side effects; they make the income distribution more unequal; and large tax cuts lead to large budget deficits.

KEY TERMS

Fiscal policy   605

Effect of income taxes on the multiplier   607

Automatic stabilizer   609

Supply–side tax cuts   613

TEST YOURSELF

1. Consider an economy in which tax collections are always $400 and in which the four components of aggregate demand are as follows:

GDP	Taxes	DI	C	I	G	(X − IM)
$1,360	$400	$960	$720	$200	$500	$30
1,480	400	1,080	810	200	500	30
1,600	400	1,200	900	200	500	30
1,720	400	1,320	990	200	500	30
1,840	400	1,440	1,080	200	500	30

Find the equilibrium of this economy graphically. What is the marginal propensity to consume? What is the multiplier? What would happen to equilibrium GDP if government purchases were reduced by $60 and the price level remained unchanged?

2. Consider an economy similar to that in the preceding question in which investment is also $200, government purchases are also $500, net exports are also $30, and the

price level is also fixed. But taxes now vary with income and, as a result, the consumption schedule looks like the following:

GDP	Taxes	DI	C
$1,360	$320	$1,040	$810
1,480	360	1,120	870
1,600	400	1,200	930
1,720	440	1,280	990
1,840	480	1,360	1,050

Find the equilibrium graphically. What is the marginal propensity to consume? What is the tax rate? Use your diagram to show the effect of a decrease of $60 in government purchases. What is the multiplier? Compare this answer to your answer to Question 1 above. What do you conclude?

3. Return to the hypothetical economy in Question 1, and now suppose that *both* taxes and government purchases are increased by $120. Find the new equilibrium under the as-

sumption that consumer spending continues to be exactly three quarters of disposable income (as it is in Question 1).

4. Suppose you are put in charge of fiscal policy for the economy described in Question 1 above. There is an inflationary gap, and you want to reduce income by $120. What specific actions can you take to achieve this goal?

5. Now put yourself in charge of the economy in Question 2 above, and suppose that full employment comes at a GDP of $1,840. How can you push income up to that level?

DISCUSSION QUESTIONS

1. The federal budgets for national defense and homeland security both rose rapidly after the September 11 attacks. How would GDP in the United States have been affected if this higher spending on national security led to:

    a. larger budget deficits?

    b. less spending elsewhere in the budget, so that total government purchases remained the same?

2. Explain why G has the same multiplier as I, but taxes have a different multiplier.

3. If the government decides that aggregate demand is excessive and is causing inflation, what options are open to it? What if the government decides that aggregate demand is too weak instead?

4. Which of the proposed supply-side tax cuts appeals to you most? Draw up a list of arguments for and against enacting such a cut right now.

5. **(More difficult)** Advocates of lower taxes on capital gains argue that this type of tax cut will raise aggregate supply by spurring business investment. But, of course, any increase in investment spending will also raise aggregate demand. Compare the effects on aggregate supply, aggregate demand, and tax revenues of three different ways to cut the capital gains tax:

    a. Reduce capital gains taxes on *all* investments, including those that were made before tax rates were cut.

    b. Reduce capital gains taxes only on investments made after tax rates are cut.

    c. Reduce capital gains taxes only on certain types of investments, such as corporate stocks and bonds.

    Which of the three options seems most desirable to you? Why?

APPENDIX A *Graphical Treatment of Taxes and Fiscal Policy*

Most of the taxes collected by the U.S. government—indeed, by all national governments—rise and fall with GDP. In some cases, the reason is obvious: *Personal* and *corporate income tax* collections, for example, depend on how much income there is to be taxed. *Sales tax* receipts depend on GDP because consumer spending is higher when GDP is higher. However, other types of tax receipts—such as property taxes—do not vary with GDP. We call the first kind of tax **variable taxes** and the second kind **fixed taxes.**

This distinction is important because it governs *how* the consumption schedule shifts in response to a tax change. If a *fixed tax* is increased, disposable income falls by the *same* amount regardless of the level of GDP. Hence, the decline in consumer spending is the same at every income level. In other words, the C schedule shifts downward in a parallel manner, as was depicted in Figure 1 in the chapter (page 606).

But many tax policies actually change disposable income by larger amounts when incomes are higher. That is true, for example, whenever Congress alters the tax rates imposed by the personal income tax, as it did in 2001 and 2003. Because higher tax rates decrease disposable income *more* when GDP is *higher*, the C schedule shifts down more sharply at higher income levels than at lower ones, as depicted in Figure 8. The same relation-

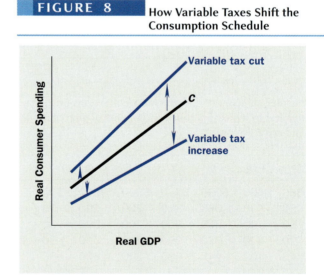

FIGURE 8   How Variable Taxes Shift the Consumption Schedule

ships apply for tax decreases, as the upward shift in the figure shows.

Figure 9 illustrates the second reason why the distinction between fixed and variable taxes is important. This diagram shows two different consumption lines. C_1 is the consumption schedule used in previous chapters; it reflects the assumption that tax collections are the same regardless of GDP. C_2 depicts a more realistic case in which

FIGURE 9   The Consumption Schedule with Fixed versus Variable Taxes

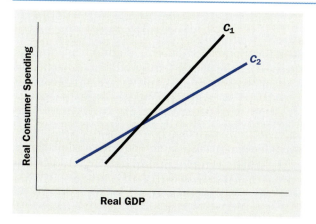

TABLE 2
The Relationship between Consumption and GDP

With Fixed Taxes ($T = \$1,200$) (from Table 1, Chapter 26)		With a 20 Percent Income Tax (from Table 1)	
Y	C	Y	C
$4,800	$3,000	$4,500	$3,000
5,200	3,300	5,000	3,300
5,600	3,600	5,500	3,600
6,000	3,900	6,000	3,900
6,400	4,200	6,500	4,200
6,800	4,500	7,000	4,500
7,200	4,800	7,500	4,800
Line C_1 in Figure 9		Line C_2 in Figure 9	

the government collects taxes equal to 20 percent of GDP. Notice that C_2 is flatter than C_1. This is no accident. In fact, as pointed out in the chapter:

Variable taxes such as the income tax flatten the consumption schedule in a 45° line diagram.

We can easily understand why. Column (1) of Table 1 shows alternative values of GDP ranging from $4.5 trillion to $7.5 trillion. Column (2) then indicates that taxes are always one-fifth of this amount. Column (3) subtracts Column (2) from Column (1) to arrive at disposable income (DI). Column (4) then gives the amount of consumer spending corresponding to each level of DI. The schedule relating C to Y, which we need for our 45° line diagram, is therefore found in Columns (1) and (4).

Notice that, in Table 1, each $500 billion increase in GDP leads to a $300 billion rise in consumer spending. Thus, the slope of line C_2 in Figure 9 is $300/$500, or 0.60, as we observed in the chapter. But in our earlier example in Chapter 26, consumption rose by $300 billion each time GDP increased $400 billion—making the slope $300/$400, or 0.75. (See the steeper line C_1 in Figure 9.) Table 2 compares the two cases explicitly. In the

TABLE 1
The Effects of an Income Tax on the Consumption Schedule

(1) Gross Domestic Product	(2) Taxes	(3) Disposable Income (GDP minus taxes)	(4) Consumption
$4,500	$ 900	$3,600	$3,000
5,000	1,000	4,000	3,300
5,500	1,100	4,400	3,600
6,000	1,200	4,800	3,900
6,500	1,300	5,200	4,200
7,000	1,400	5,600	4,500
7,500	1,500	6,000	4,800

Note: Figures are in billions of dollars per year.

Chapter 26 example, taxes were fixed at $1,200 billion and each $400 billion rise in Y led to a $300 billion rise in C—as in the left-hand panel of Table 2. But now, with taxes variable (equal to 20 percent of GDP), each $500 billion increment to Y gives rise to a $300 billion increase in C—as in the right-hand panel of Table 2.

These differences sound terribly mechanical, but the economic reasoning behind them is vital to understanding tax policies. When taxes are fixed, as in line C_1, each additional dollar of GDP raises disposable income (DI) by $1. Consumer spending then rises by $1 times the marginal propensity to consume (MPC), which is 0.75 in our example. Hence, each additional dollar of GDP leads to 75 cents more spending. But when taxes vary with income, each additional dollar of GDP raises DI by less than $1 because the government takes a share in taxes. In our example, taxes are 20 percent of GDP, so each additional $1 of GDP generates just 80 cents more DI. With an MPC of 0.75, then, spending rises by only 60 cents (75 percent of 80 cents) each time GDP rises by $1. Thus, the slope of line C_2 in Figure 9 is only 0.60, instead of 0.75.

Table 3 and Figure 10 take the next step by replacing the old consumption schedule with this new one in both the tabular presentation of income determination and the 45° line diagram. We see immediately that the equilibrium level of GDP is at point E. Here gross domestic product is $6,000 billion, consumption is $3,900 billion, investment is $900 billion, net exports are −$100 billion, and government purchases are $1,300 billion. As we know from previous chapters, full employment may occur above or below Y = $6,000 billion. If it is below this level, an inflationary gap arises. Prices will probably start to rise, pulling the expenditure schedule down and reducing equilibrium GDP. If it is above this level, a recessionary gap results, and history suggests that prices will fall only slowly. In the interim, the economy will suffer a period of high unemployment.

In short, once we adjust the expenditure schedule for variable taxes, the determination of national income proceeds exactly as before. The effects of government

(1) Gross Domestic Product Y	(2) Consumption C	(3) Investment I	(4) Government Purchases G	(5) Net Exports (X − IM)	(6) Total Expenditures C + I + G + (X − IM)
$4,500	$3,000	$900	$1,300	−$100	$5,100
5,000	3,300	900	1,300	−100	5,400
5,500	3,600	900	1,300	−100	5,700
6,000	3,900	900	1,300	−100	6,000
6,500	4,200	900	1,300	−100	6,300
7,000	4,500	900	1,300	−100	6,600
7,500	4,800	900	1,300	−100	6,900

TABLE 3 Total Expenditure Schedule with a 20 Percent Income Tax

spending and taxation, therefore, are fairly straightforward and can be summarized as follows:

> Government purchases of goods and services add to total spending *directly* through the *G* component of *C* + *I* + *G* + (*X* − *IM*). Higher taxes reduce total spending *indirectly* by lowering disposable income and thus reducing the *C* component of *C* + *I* + *G* + (*X* − *IM*). On balance, then, the government's actions may raise or lower the equilibrium level of GDP, depending on how much spending and taxing it does.

MULTIPLIERS FOR TAX POLICY

Now let us turn our attention, as in the chapter, to multipliers for tax changes. They are more complicated than multipliers for spending because they work indirectly via consumption. For this reason, we restrict ourselves to the multiplier for fixed taxes, leaving the more complicated case of variable taxes to more advanced courses. Tax multipliers must be worked out in two steps:

1. Figure out how much any proposed or actual changes in the tax law will affect consumer spending.
2. Enter this vertical shift of the consumption schedule in the 45° line diagram and see how it affects output.

To create a simple and familiar numerical example, suppose income taxes fall by a fixed amount at each level of GDP—say, by $400 billion. Step 1 instructs us to multiply the $400 billion tax cut by the marginal propensity to consume (MPC), which is 0.75, to get $300 billion as the decrease in consumer spending—that is, as the vertical shift of the consumption schedule.

Next, Step 2 instructs us to multiply this $300 billion increase in consumption by the multiplier—which is 2.5 in our example—giving $750 billion as the rise in GDP. Figure 11 verifies that this result is correct by depicting a $300 billion vertical shift of the consumption function in the 45° line diagram and noting that GDP does indeed

rise by $750 billion as a consequence—from $6,000 billion to $6,750 billion.

Notice that the $400 billion tax cut raises GDP by $750 billion, whereas the multiplier effect of the $400 billion increase in government purchases depicted in the chapter in Figure 2 (page 608) raised GDP by $1,000 billion. This is a specific numerical example of something we learned in the chapter. Because some of the change in disposable income affects *saving* rather than *spending*, a dollar of tax cut does not pack as much punch as a dollar of *G*. That is why we multiplied the $400 billion change in taxes by 0.75 to get the $300 billion shift of the *C* schedule shown in Figure 11.

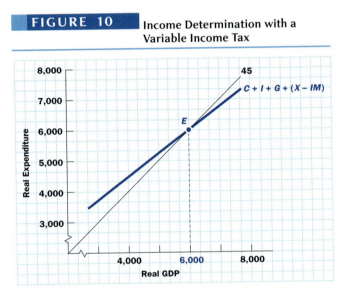

FIGURE 10 Income Determination with a Variable Income Tax

NOTE: Figures are in billions of dollars per year.

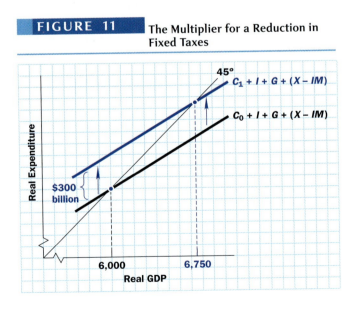

FIGURE 11 The Multiplier for a Reduction in Fixed Taxes

SUMMARY

1. Precisely *how* a tax change affects the consumption schedule depends on whether **fixed taxes** or **variable taxes** are changed.

2. Shifts of the consumption function caused by tax policy are subject to the same multiplier as autonomous shifts in *G*, *I*, or *X* − *IM*

3. Because tax changes affect *C* only indirectly, the multiplier for a change in *T* is smaller than the multiplier for a change in *G*.

4. The government's net effect on aggregate demand—and hence on equilibrium output and prices—depends on whether the expansionary effects of its spending are greater or smaller than the contractionary effects of its taxes.

KEY TERMS

Variable taxes   618

Fixed taxes   618

TEST YOURSELF

1. Which of the following is considered a fixed tax and which a variable tax?

   a. the gasoline tax

   b. the corporate income tax

   c. the estate tax

2. In a certain economy, the multiplier for government purchases is 2 and the multiplier for changes in fixed taxes is 1.5. The government then proposes to raise both spending and taxes by $100 billion. What should happen to equilibrium GDP on the demand side?

3. (**More difficult**) Suppose real GDP is $10,000 billion and the basic expenditure multiplier is 2. If two tax changes are made at the same time:

   a. fixed taxes are raised by $100 billion

   b. the income tax *rate* is reduced from 20 percent to 18 percent,

   what will happen to equilibrium GDP on the demand side?

DISCUSSION QUESTIONS

1. When the income tax rate declines, as it has in the United States recently, does the multiplier go up or down? Explain why.

2. Discuss the pros and cons of having a higher or lower multiplier.

APPENDIX B *Algebraic Treatment of Fiscal Policy*

In this appendix, we explain the simple algebra behind the fiscal policy multipliers discussed in the chapter. In so doing, we deal only with a simplified case in which prices do not change. Although it is possible to work out the corresponding algebra for the more realistic aggregate demand and supply analysis with variable prices, the analysis is rather complicated and is best left to more advanced courses.

We start with the example used both in the chapter and in Appendix A. The government spends $1,300 billion on goods and services (*G* = 1,300) and levies an income tax equal to 20 percent of GDP. So, if the symbol *T* denotes tax receipts,

$$T = 0.20Y$$

Because the consumption function we have been working with is

$$C = 300 + 0.75DI,$$

where *DI* is disposable income, and because disposable income and GDP are related by the accounting identity

$$DI = Y - T$$

it follows that the *C* schedule used in the 45° line diagram is described by the following algebraic equation:

$$C = 300 + 0.75(Y - T)$$
$$= 300 + 0.75(Y - 0.20Y)$$
$$= 300 + 0.75(0.80Y)$$
$$= 300 + 0.60Y$$

We can now apply the equilibrium condition:

$$Y = C + I + G + (X - IM)$$

Because investment in this example is $I = 900$ and net exports are -100, substituting for C, I, G, and $(X - IM)$ into this equation gives:

$$Y = 300 + 0.60Y + 900 + 1,300 - 100$$

$$0.40Y = 2,400$$

$$Y = 6,000$$

This is all there is to finding equilibrium GDP in an economy with a government.

To find the multiplier for government spending, increase G by 1 and solve the problem again:

$$Y = C + I + G + (X - IM)$$

$$Y = 300 + 0.60Y + 900 + 1,301 - 100$$

$$0.40Y = 2,401$$

$$Y = 6,002.5$$

Thus, the multiplier is $6,002.5 - 6,000 = 2.5$, as stated in the text.

To find the multiplier for an increase in fixed taxes, change the tax schedule as follows:

$$T = 0.20Y + 1$$

Disposable income is then

$$DI = Y - T = Y - (0.20Y + 1) = 0.80Y - 1$$

so the consumption function is

$$C = 300 + 0.75DI$$

$$= 300 + 0.75(0.80Y - 1)$$

$$= 299.25 + 0.60Y$$

Solving for equilibrium GDP as usual gives:

$$Y = C + I + G + (X - IM)$$

$$Y = 299.25 + 0.60Y + 900 + 1,300 - 100$$

$$0.40Y = 2,399.25$$

$$Y = 5,998.125$$

So a $1 increase in fixed taxes lowers Y by $1.875. The tax multiplier is -1.875, which is 75 percent of -2.5.

Now let us proceed to a more general solution, using symbols rather than specific numbers. The equations of the model are as follows:

$$Y = C + I + G + (X - IM) \qquad (1)$$

is the usual equilibrium condition.

$$C = a + bDI \qquad (2)$$

is the same consumption function we used in Appendix A of Chapter 26.

$$DI = Y - T \qquad (3)$$

is the accounting identity relating disposable income to GDP.

$$T = T_0 + tY \qquad (4)$$

is the tax function, where T_0 represents fixed taxes (which are zero in our numerical example) and t represents the tax rate (which is 0.20 in the example). Finally, I, G, and $(X - IM)$ are just fixed numbers.

We begin the solution by substituting Equations (3) and (4) into Equation (2) to derive the consumption schedule relating C to Y:

$$C = a + bDI$$

$$C = a + b(Y - T)$$

$$C = a + b(Y - T_0 - tY)$$

$$C = a - bT_0 + b(1 - t)Y \qquad (5)$$

Notice that a change in fixed taxes (T_0) shifts the *intercept* of the C schedule, whereas a change in the tax rate (t) changes its *slope*, as explained in Appendix A (pages 618-620).

Next, substitute Equation (5) into Equation (1) to find equilibrium GDP:

$$Y = C + I + G + (X - IM)$$

$$Y = a - bT_0 + b(1 - t)Y + I + G + (X - IM)$$

$$[1 - b(1 - t)]\, Y = a - bT_0 + I + G + (X - IM)$$

or

$$Y = \frac{a - bT_0 + I + G + (X - IM)}{1 - b(1 - t)} \qquad (6)$$

Equation (6) shows us that the multiplier for G, I, a, or $(X - IM)$ is

$$\textbf{Multiplier} = \frac{1}{1 - b(1 - t)}.$$

To see that this is in fact the multiplier, raise any of G, I, a, or $(X - IM)$ by one unit. In each case, Equation (6) would be changed to read:

$$Y = \frac{a - bT_0 + I + G + (X - IM) + 1}{1 - b(1 - t)}$$

Subtracting Equation (6) from this expression gives the change in Y stemming from a one-unit change in G, I, or a:

$$\text{Change in } Y = \frac{1}{1 - b(1 - t)}$$

In Chapter 26 (page 572), we noted that if there were no income tax ($t = 0$), a realistic value for b (the marginal propensity to consume) would yield a multiplier of 20, which is much bigger than the true multiplier. Now that we have added taxes to the model, our multiplier formula produces much more realistic numbers. Approximate values for these parameters for the U.S. economy are $b = 0.95$ and $t = \frac{1}{3}$. The multiplier formula then gives

$$\text{Multiplier} = \frac{1}{1 - 0.95(1 - \frac{1}{3})}$$

$$= \frac{1}{1 - 0.633} = \frac{1}{0.367} = 2.72$$

which is much closer to its actual estimated value—between 1.5 and 2.

Finally, we can see from Equation (6) that the multiplier for a change in fixed taxes (T_0) is:

$$\text{Tax Multiplier} = \frac{-b}{1 - b(1 - t)}$$

For the example considered in the text and earlier in this appendix, $b = 0.75$ and $t = 0.20$; so the formula gives:

$$\frac{-0.75}{1 - 0.75(1 - 0.20)} = \frac{-0.75}{1 - 0.75(0.80)}$$
$$= \frac{-0.75}{1 - 0.60} = \frac{-0.75}{0.40} = -1.875$$

According to these figures, each \$1 *increase* in T_0 *reduces* Y by \$1.875.

TEST YOURSELF

1. Consider an economy described by the following set of equations:

$$C = 120 + 0.80DI$$
$$I = 320$$
$$G = 480$$
$$(X - IM) = -80$$
$$T = 200 + 0.25Y$$

Find the equilibrium level of GDP. Next, find the multipliers for government purchases and for fixed taxes. If full employment comes at $Y = 1,800$, what are some policies that would move GDP to that level?

2. This question is a variant of the previous problem that approaches things in the way that a fiscal policy planner might. In an economy whose consumption function and tax function are as given in Question 1, with investment fixed at 320 and net exports fixed at −80, find the value of G that would make GDP equal to 1,800.

3. You are given the following information about an economy:

$$C = 0.90DI$$
$$I = 100$$
$$G = 540$$
$$(X - IM) = -40$$
$$T = \tfrac{1}{3}Y$$

   a. Find equilibrium GDP and the budget deficit.

   b. Suppose the government, unhappy with the budget deficit, decides to cut government spending by precisely the amount of the deficit you just found. What actually happens to GDP and the budget deficit, and why?

4. **(More difficult)** In the economy considered in Question 3, suppose the government, seeing that it has not wiped out the deficit, keeps cutting G until it succeeds in balancing the budget. What level of GDP will then prevail?

29

MONEY AND THE BANKING SYSTEM

[Money] is a machine for doing quickly and commodiously what would be done, though less quickly and commodiously, without it.

JOHN STUART MILL

T he circular flow diagrams of earlier chapters had a "financial system" in the upper-left corner. (Look back, for example, at Figure 1 of Chapter 26—on page 561.) Saving flowed into this system and investment flowed out. Something obviously goes on *inside* the financial system to channel the saving back into investment, and it is time we learned just what this something is.

There is another, equally important, reason for studying the financial system. The government exercises significant control over aggregate demand by manipulating *monetary policy* as well as fiscal policy. Indeed, most observers nowadays see monetary policy as the more important stabilization tool. To understand how monetary policy works (the subject of Chapters 30 and 31), we must first acquire some understanding of the banking and financial system. By the end of this chapter, you will have that understanding.

CONTENTS

ISSUE: *Why Are Banks So Heavily Regulated?*

Banking has long been one of the most heavily regulated industries in America. But the pendulum of bank regulation has swung back and forth.

In the late 1970s and early 1980s, the United States eased several restrictions on interest rates and permissible bank activities. Then, after a number of banks and savings institutions went bankrupt in the 1980s, Congress and the bank regulatory agencies cracked down with stiffer regulation and closer scrutiny. Later, the pendulum swung back in the deregulatory direction, with two landmark banking laws in the 1990s. Most restrictions on banking across state lines were lifted in 1994. And the once-strict separation of banking from insurance and investment banking was more or less ended in 1999.

So how much bank regulation is enough—or too much? To answer this question, we must first address a more basic one: Why are banks so heavily regulated in the first place?

A first reason is that the major "output" of the banking industry—*the nation's money supply—is an important determinant of aggregate demand*, as we will learn in the next chapter. Bank managers are paid to do what is best for their stockholders. But as we will see, what is best for bank stockholders may not always be best for the economy as a whole. Consequently, the government does not allow bankers to determine the money supply strictly on profit considerations.

A second reason for the extensive web of bank regulation is concern for the *safety of depositors*. In a free-enterprise system, new businesses are born and die every day; and no one other than the people immediately involved takes much notice. When a firm goes bankrupt, stockholders lose money and employees may lose their jobs. But, except for the case of very large firms, that is about all that happens.

But banking is different. If banks were treated like other firms, depositors would lose money whenever one went bankrupt. That outcome is bad enough by itself, but the real danger emerges in the case of a **run on a bank.** When depositors get nervous about the security of their money, they may all rush to cash in their accounts. For reasons we will learn in this chapter, most banks could not survive such a "run" and would be forced to shut their doors.

Worse yet, this disease is highly *contagious*. If one family hears that their neighbors just lost their life savings because their bank went broke, they are likely to rush to their own bank to withdraw their funds. In fact, that is precisely what happened in Argentina when people lost confidence in the local banks in 2002.[1]

Without modern forms of bank regulation, therefore, one bank failure might lead to another. Indeed, bank failures were common throughout most of U.S. history. (See Figure 1(a).) But since the 1930s, bank failures have been less common. (See Figure 1(b).) And they have rarely been precipitated by runs because the government has taken steps to ensure that such an infectious disease will not spread. It has done so in several ways that we will mention in this chapter.

A **run on a bank** occurs when many depositors withdraw cash from their accounts all at once.

■ THE NATURE OF MONEY

Money is so much a part of our daily existence that we take it for granted and fail to appreciate all that it accomplishes. But money is in no sense "natural." Like the wheel, it had to be invented.

The most obvious way to trade commodities is not by using money, but by **barter**—a system in which people exchange one good directly for another. And the best way to appreciate what monetary exchange accomplishes is to imagine a world without it.

Barter is a system of exchange in which people directly trade one good for another, without using money as an intermediate step.

---

[1] As will be explained in Chapter 35, the Argentine crisis had much to do with worries about the exchange rate between the Argentine peso and the U.S. dollar.

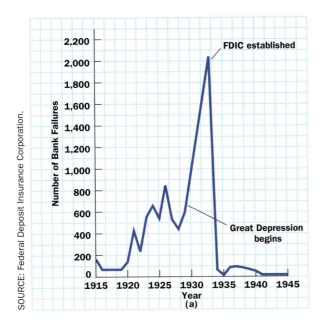

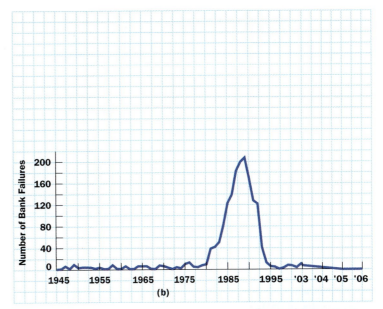

SOURCE: Federal Deposit Insurance Corporation.

FIGURE 1

Bank Failures in the
United States,
1915–2006

◼ Barter versus Monetary Exchange

Under a system of direct barter, if Farmer Jones grows corn and has a craving for peanuts, he has to find a peanut farmer, say, Farmer Smith, with a taste for corn. If he finds such a person (a situation called the *double coincidence of wants*), the two farmers make the trade. If that sounds easy, try to imagine how busy Farmer Jones would be if he had to repeat the sequence for everything he consumed in a week. For the most part, the desired double coincidences of wants are more likely to turn out to be double wants of coincidence. (See the accompanying cartoon.) Jones gets no peanuts and Smith gets no corn. Worse yet, with so much time spent looking for trading partners, Jones would have far less time to grow corn. In brief:

Money greases the wheels of exchange, and thus makes the whole economy more productive.

SOURCE: By permission of Johnny Hart and Creators Syndicate, Inc.

Dealing by Wheeling on Yap

Primitive forms of money still exist in some remote places, as this extract from an old newspaper article shows.

Yap, Micronesia—On this tiny South Pacific Island . . . the currency is as solid as a rock. In fact, it is rock. Limestone to be precise.

For nearly 2,000 years the Yapese have used large stone wheels to pay for major purchases, such as land, canoes and permission to marry. Yap is a U.S. trust territory, and the dollar is used in grocery stores and gas stations. But reliance on stone money . . . continues.

Buying property with stones is "much easier than buying it with U.S. dollars," says John Chodad, who recently purchased a building lot with a 30-inch stone wheel. "We don't know the value of the U.S. dollar."

Stone wheels don't make good pocket money, so for small transactions, Yapese use other forms of currency, such as beer. . . .

SOURCE: University of Pennsylvania Museum (58-21338)

Besides stone wheels and beer, the Yapese sometimes spend *gaw*, consisting of necklaces of stone beads strung together around a whale's tooth. They also can buy things with *yar*, a currency made from large seashells. But these are small change.

The people of Yap have been using stone money ever since a Yapese warrior named Anagumang first brought the huge stones over from limestone caverns on neighboring Palau, some 1,500 to 2,000 years ago. Inspired by the moon, he fashioned the stone into large circles. The rest is history. . . .

By custom, the stones are worthless when broken. You never hear people on Yap musing about wanting a piece of the rock.

SOURCE: Excerpted from Art Pine, "Hard Assets, or Why a Loan in Yap Is Hard to Roll Over," *The Wall Street Journal*, March 29, 1984, p. 1.

Under a monetary system, Farmer Jones gives up his corn for money. He does so not because he wants the money per se, but because of what that money can buy. Now he need simply locate a peanut farmer who wants money. And what peanut farmer does not? For these reasons, monetary exchange replaced barter at a very early stage of human civilization, and only extreme circumstances, such as massive wars and runaway inflations, have been able to bring barter (temporarily) back.

The Conceptual Definition of Money

> **Money** is the standard object used in exchanging goods and services. In short, money is the **medium of exchange.**
>
> The **medium of exchange** is the object or objects used to buy and sell other items such as goods and services.
>
> The **unit of account** is the standard unit for quoting prices.
>
> A **store of value** is an item used to store wealth from one point in time to another.

Under monetary exchange, people trade **money** for goods when they purchase something, and they trade goods for money when they sell something, but they do not trade goods directly for other goods. This practice defines money's principal role as the **medium of exchange.** But once it has become accepted as the medium of exchange, whatever serves as money is bound to serve other functions as well. For one, it will inevitably become the **unit of account**—that is, the standard unit for quoting prices. Thus, if inhabitants of an idyllic tropical island use coconuts as money, they would be foolish to quote prices in terms of seashells.

Money also may come to be used as a **store of value.** If Farmer Jones's corn sales bring in more value than he wants to spend right away, he may find it convenient to store the difference temporarily in the form of money. He knows that money can be "sold" easily for goods and services at a later date, whereas land, gold, and other stores of value might not be. Of course, if inflation is substantial, he may decide to forgo the convenience of money and store his wealth in some other form rather than see its purchasing power eroded. So money's role as a store of value is far from inevitable.

Because money may not always serve as a store of value, and because other commodities may act as stores of value, we will not include the store-of-value function as part of our conceptual definition of money. Instead, we simply label as "money" whatever serves as the medium of exchange.

What Serves as Money?

Anthropologists and historians can testify that a bewildering variety of objects have served as money in different times and places. Cattle, stones, candy bars, cigarettes,

Remaking America's Paper Money

Over the last few years, the U.S. Treasury has replaced much of America's paper money with new notes designed to be much more difficult to counterfeit. Several of the new anticounterfeiting features are visible to the naked eye. By inspecting one of the new $20 bills—the ones with the big picture of Andrew Jackson that looks like it's been through a washing machine—you can easily see several of them. (Others are harder to detect.)

Most obvious are the various shades of coloration, including the silver blue eagle to Jackson's left. Next, hold the bill up to a light, with Jackson facing you. Near the left edge, you will find some small type set vertically, rather than horizontally. If your eyesight is good, you will be able to read what it says. But, if you were a counterfeiter, you would find this line devilishly difficult to duplicate. Third, twist the bill and see how the gold numeral "20" in the lower-right corner glistens and changes color. An optical illusion? No, a clever way to make life hard on counterfeiters.

© AP/Wide World Photos

woodpecker scalps, porpoise teeth, and giraffe tails provide a few of the more colorful examples. (For another example, see the box "Dealing by Wheeling on Yap.")

In primitive or less organized societies, the commodities that served as money generally held value in themselves. If not used as money, cattle could be slaughtered for food, cigarettes could be smoked, and so on. But such **commodity money** generally runs into several severe difficulties. To be useful as a medium of exchange, a commodity must be easily divisible—which makes cattle a poor choice. It must also be of uniform, or at least readily identifiable, quality so that inferior substitutes are easy to recognize. This shortcoming may be why woodpecker scalps never achieved great popularity. The medium of exchange must also be storable and durable, which presents a serious problem for candy-bar money. Finally, because people will carry and store commodity money, it is helpful if the item is compact—that is, if it has high value per unit of volume and weight.

A **commodity money** is an object in use as a medium of exchange, but which also has a substantial value in alternative (non-monetary) uses.

All of these traits make it natural that gold and silver have circulated as money since the first coins were struck about 2,500 years ago. Because they have high value in nonmonetary uses, a lot of purchasing power can be carried without too much weight. Pieces of gold are also storable, divisible (with a little trouble), and of identifiable quality (with a little more trouble).

The same characteristics suggest that paper would make an even better money. The Chinese invented paper money in the eleventh century, and Marco Polo brought the idea to Europe. Because we can print any number on it that we please, we can make paper money as divisible as we like. People can also carry a large value of paper money in a lightweight and compact form. Paper is easy to store and, with a little cleverness, we can make counterfeiting challenging, though never impossible. (See the box on America's new $20 bills.)

Paper cannot, however, serve as commodity money because its value per square inch in alternative uses is so low. A paper currency that is repudiated by its issuer can, perhaps, be used as wallpaper or to wrap fish, but these uses will surely represent only a small fraction of the paper's value as money.[2] Contrary to the popular expression,

---

[2] The first paper money issued by the U.S. federal government, the Continental dollar, was essentially repudiated. (Actually, the new government of the United States redeemed the Continentals for 1 cent on the dollar in the 1790s.) This event gave rise to the derisive expression, "It's not worth a Continental."

Fiat money is money that is decreed as such by the government. It is of little value as a commodity, but it maintains its value as a medium of exchange because people have faith that the issuer will stand behind the pieces of printed paper and limit their production.

such a currency literally *is* worth the paper it is printed on—which is to say that it is not worth much. Thus, paper money is always **fiat money.**

Money in the contemporary United States is almost entirely fiat money. Look at a dollar bill. Next to George Washington's picture it states: "This note is legal tender for all debts, public and private." Nowhere on the certificate is there a promise, stated or implied, that the U.S. government will exchange it for anything else. A dollar bill is convertible into, say, four quarters or 10 dimes—but not into gold, chocolate, or any other commodity.

Why do people hold these pieces of paper? Because they know that others are willing to accept them for things of intrinsic value—food, rent, shoes, and so on. If this confidence ever evaporated, dollar bills would cease serving as a medium of exchange and, given that they make ugly wallpaper, would become virtually worthless.

But don't panic. This series of events is hardly likely to occur. Our current monetary system has evolved over hundreds of years, during which *commodity money* was first replaced by *full-bodied paper money*—paper certificates that were backed by gold or silver of equal value held in the issuer's vaults. Then the full-bodied paper money was replaced by certificates that were only partially backed by gold and silver. Finally, we arrived at our present system, in which paper money has no "backing" whatsoever. Like a hesitant swimmer who first dips her toes, then her legs, then her whole body into a cold swimming pool, we have "tested the water" at each step of the way—and found it to our liking. It is unlikely that we will ever take a step back in the other direction.

■ HOW THE QUANTITY OF MONEY IS MEASURED

Because the amount of money in circulation is important for the determination of national product and the price level, the government must know how much money there is. Thus we must devise some *measure* of the money supply.

Our conceptual definition of money as the medium of exchange raises difficult questions about just which items to include and which items to exclude when we count up the money supply. Such questions have long made the statistical definition of money a subject of dispute. In fact, the U.S. government has several official definitions of the money supply, two of which we will meet shortly.

Some components are obvious. All of our coins and paper money—the small change of our economic system—clearly should count as money. But we cannot stop there if we want to include the main vehicle for making payments in our society, for the lion's share of our nation's payments are made neither in metal nor in paper money, but by check.

Checking deposits are actually no more than bookkeeping entries in bank ledgers. Many people think of checks as a convenient way to pass coins or dollar bills to someone else. But that is not so. For example, when you pay the grocer $50 by check, dollar bills rarely change hands. Instead, that check normally travels back to your bank, where $50 is deducted from the bookkeeping entry that records your account and $50 is added to the bookkeeping entry for your grocer's account. (If you and the grocer hold accounts at different banks, more books get involved, but still no coins or bills will likely move.) The volume of money held in the form of checkable deposits far exceeds the volume of currency.

■ M1

So it seems imperative to include checkable deposits in any useful definition of the money supply. Unfortunately, this is not an easy task nowadays, because of the wide variety of ways to transfer money by check. Traditional checking accounts in commercial banks are the most familiar vehicle. But many people can also write checks on their savings accounts, on their deposits at credit unions, on their mutual funds, on their accounts with stockbrokers, and so on.

One popular definition of the money supply draws the line early and includes only coins, paper money, traveler's checks, conventional checking accounts, and certain other checkable deposits in banks and savings institutions. In the official U.S. statistics, this narrowly defined concept of money is called **M1.** The upper part of Figure 2 shows the composition of M1 as of December 2006.

> The narrowly defined money supply, usually abbreviated **M1,** is the sum of all coins and paper money in circulation, plus certain checkable deposit balances at banks and savings institutions.[3]

M2

But other types of accounts allow withdrawals by check, so they are also candidates for inclusion in the money supply. Most notably, *money market deposit accounts* allow their owners to write only a few checks per month but pay market-determined interest rates. Consumers have found these accounts attractive, and balances in them now exceed all the checkable deposits included in M1.

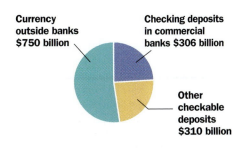

M1 = $1366 billion

In addition, many mutual fund organizations and brokerage houses offer *money market mutual funds.* These funds sell shares and use the proceeds to purchase a variety of short-term securities. But the important point for our purposes is that owners of shares in money market mutual funds can withdraw their funds by writing checks. Thus, depositors can use their holdings of fund shares just like checking accounts.

Finally, although you cannot write a check on a *savings account,* modern banking procedures have blurred the distinction between checking balances and savings balances. For example, most banks these days offer convenient electronic transfers of funds from one account to another, either by telephone or by pushing a button on an automated teller. Consequently, savings balances can become checkable almost instantly. For this reason, savings accounts are included—along with money market deposit accounts and money market mutual fund shares—in the broader definition of the money supply known as **M2.**

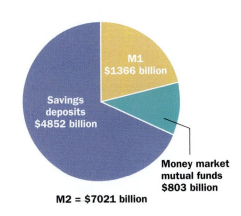

M2 = $7021 billion

SOURCE: Federal Reserve

The composition of M2 as of December 2006 is shown on the lower part of Figure 2. You can see that savings deposits predominate, dwarfing M1. Figure 2 illustrates that our money supply comes not only from banks, but also from savings institutions, brokerage houses, and mutual fund organizations. Even so, banks still play a predominant role.

FIGURE 2

Two Definitions of the Money Supply, December 2006

Other Definitions of the Money Supply

Some economists do not want to stop counting at M2; they prefer still broader definitions of money (M3, and so on), which include more types of bank deposits and other closely related assets. The inescapable problem, however, is that there is no obvious place to stop, no clear line of demarcation between those assets that *are* money and those that are merely *close substitutes* for money—so-called **near moneys.**

If we define an asset's **liquidity** as the ease with which its holder can convert it into cash, there is a spectrum of assets of varying degrees of liquidity. Everything in M1 is completely liquid, the money market fund shares and passbook savings accounts included in M2 are a bit less so, and so on, until we encounter items such as short-term government bonds, which, while still quite liquid, would not normally be included in the money supply. Any number of different *M*s can be defined—and have been—by drawing the line in different places.

And yet more complexities arise. For example, credit cards clearly serve as a medium of exchange. Should they be included in the money supply? Of course, you

> The broadly defined money supply, usually abbreviated **M2,** is the sum of all coins and paper money in circulation, plus all types of checking account balances, plus most forms of savings account balances, plus shares in money market mutual funds.
>
> **Near moneys** are liquid assets that are close substitutes for money.
>
> An asset's **liquidity** refers to the ease with which it can be converted into cash.

[3] This amount includes travelers' checks and NOW (negotiable order of withdrawal) accounts.

Is There a Smart Card in Your Future?

In the 1990s, several banks and other companies began test-marketing new forms of high-tech electronic currency, or "e-cash." One proposed form uses encrypted electronic messages to send balances from one computer to another, possibly bypassing banks entirely.

But the most commonly discussed form of e-cash—at least so far—is the so-called stored-value card. It works as follows: First, you buy a "smart card" (which looks much like a credit card) with an embedded memory chip on which your initial payment is recorded. At this point, your conventional money is transformed into electronic currency. Thereafter, you can use the cash stored on the card to make purchases simply by inserting your card into specially designed slots in vending machines and stores. When the stored value on your card is depleted, you can replenish it at an ATM.

Electronic currency raises several novel issues. For one thing, the federal government has long held a monopoly over currency issue; e-cash may erode that monopoly. For another, consumers and businesses may have privacy and safety concerns: Will their electronic transactions be safe from system errors and computer snoopers and hackers? Law enforcement agencies are also worried that large, untraceable electronic transfers of funds may prove attractive to criminals and tax evaders.

Although futurists confidently predict that these new products represent the money of the future, skeptics note that we have heard such claims before—and they have never come true. Only time will tell if the new technologies will catch on. So far, they have not.

SOURCE: © AP/Wide World Photos

say. But how much *money* does your credit card represent? Is it the amount you currently owe on the card, which may well be zero? Or is it your entire line of credit, even though you may never use it all? Neither choice seems sensible, which is one reason why economists have so far ignored credit cards in their definitions of money. And soon Americans may start using electronic money instead of cash. Money will be transferred via computer hookups or by so-called smart cards with memory chips (see "Is There a Smart Card in Your Future?").

We could mention further complexities, but an introductory course in economics is not the place to get bogged down in complex definitional issues. So we will simply adhere to the convention that:

"Money" consists only of coins, paper money, and checkable deposits.

■ THE BANKING SYSTEM

Now that we have defined money and seen how to measure it, we turn our attention to the principal creators of money—the banks. Banking is a complicated business—and getting more so. If you go further in your study of economics, you will probably learn more about the operations of banks. But for present purposes, a few simple principles will suffice. Let's start at the beginning.

■ How Banking Began

When Adam and Eve left the Garden of Eden, they did not encounter an ATM. Banking had to be invented. With a little imagination, we can see how the first banks must have begun.

When money was made of gold or other metals, it was inconvenient for consumers and merchants to carry it around and weigh and assay its purity every time they made a transaction. So the practice developed of leaving gold in a goldsmith's safe storage facilities and carrying in its place a receipt stating that John Doe did indeed own five ounces of gold. When people began trading goods and services for the goldsmiths' receipts, rather than for the gold itself, the receipts became an early form of paper money.

At this stage, paper money was fully backed by gold. Gradually, however, the goldsmiths began to notice that the amount of gold they were actually required to pay out in a day was but a small fraction of the total gold they had stored in their warehouses. Then one day some enterprising goldsmith hit upon a momentous idea that must have made him fabulously wealthy.

His thinking probably ran something like this: "I have 2,000 ounces of gold stored away in my vault, for which I collect storage fees from my customers. But I am never called upon to pay out more than 100 ounces on a single day. What harm could it do if I lent out, say, half the gold I now have? I'll still have more than enough to pay off any depositors who come in for withdrawals, so no one will ever know the difference. And I could earn 30 additional ounces of gold each year in interest on the loans I make (at 3 percent interest on 1,000 ounces). With this profit, I could lower my service charges to depositors and so attract still more deposits. I think I'll do it."

With this resolution, the modern system of **fractional reserve banking** was born. This system has three features that are crucially important to this chapter.

Fractional reserve banking is a system under which bankers keep as reserves only a fraction of the funds they hold on deposit.

Bank Profitability   By getting deposits at zero interest and lending some of them out at positive interest rates, goldsmiths made profits. The history of banking as a profit-making industry was begun and has continued to this date. *Banks, like other enterprises, are in business to earn profits.*

Bank Discretion over the Money Supply   When goldsmiths decided to keep only fractions of their total deposits on reserve and lend out the balance, they acquired the ability to *create money.* As long as they kept 100 percent reserves, each gold certificate represented exactly 1 ounce of gold. So whether people decided to carry their gold or leave it with their goldsmiths did not affect the money supply, which was set by the volume of gold.

With the advent of fractional reserve banking, however, new paper certificates appeared whenever goldsmiths lent out some of the gold they held on deposit. The loans, in effect, created new money. In this way, the total amount of money came to depend on the amount of gold that each goldsmith felt compelled to keep in his vault. For any given volume of gold on deposit, the lower the reserves the goldsmiths kept, the more loans they could make, and therefore the more money would circulate.

Although we no longer use gold to back our money, this principle remains true today. *Bankers' decisions on how much to hold in reserves influence the supply of money.* A substantial part of the rationale for modern monetary policy is, as we have mentioned, that profit-seeking bankers might not create the amount of money that is best for society.

Exposure to Runs   A goldsmith who kept 100 percent reserves never had to worry about a run on his vault. Even if all his depositors showed up at the door at once, he could always convert their paper receipts back into gold. But as soon as the first goldsmith decided to get by with only fractional reserves, the possibility of a run on the vault became a real concern. If that first goldsmith who lent out half his gold had found 51 percent of his customers at his door one unlucky day, he would have had a lot of explaining to do. Similar problems have worried bankers for centuries. *The danger of a run on the bank has induced bankers to keep prudent reserves and to lend out money carefully.* As we observed earlier, this danger is one of the main rationales for bank regulation.

◼ Principles of Bank Management: Profits versus Safety

Bankers have a reputation for conservatism in politics, dress, and business affairs. From what has been said so far, the economic rationale for this conservatism should be clear. Checking deposits are pure fiat money. Years ago, these deposits were "backed" by nothing more than a particular bank's promise to convert them into currency on demand. If people lost trust in a bank, it was doomed.

Thus, bankers have always relied on a reputation for prudence, which they achieved in two principal ways. First, they maintained a sufficiently generous level of reserves to minimize their vulnerability to runs. Second, they were cautious in making loans and investments, because any large losses on their loans would undermine their depositors' confidence.

It is important to realize that banking under a system of fractional reserves is an inherently risky business that is rendered safe only by cautious and prudent management. America's long history of bank failures (see Figure 1) bears sober testimony to the fact that many bankers were neither cautious nor prudent. Why not? Because caution is not the route to high profits. Bank profits are maximized by keeping reserves as low as possible, and by making at least some loans to borrowers with questionable credit standing who will pay higher interest rates.

The art of bank management is to strike the appropriate balance between the lure of profits and the need for safety. If a banker errs by being too stodgy, his bank will earn inadequate profits. If he errs by taking unwarranted risks, his bank may not survive at all.

■ Bank Regulation

But governments in virtually every society have decided that profit-minded bankers will not necessarily strike the balance between profits and safety exactly where society wants it. So they have thrown up a web of regulations designed to ensure depositors' safety and to control the money supply.

Deposit insurance is a system that guarantees that depositors will not lose money even if their bank goes bankrupt.

Deposit Insurance   The principal innovation that guarantees the safety of bank deposits is **deposit insurance.** Today, most U.S. bank deposits are insured against loss by the *Federal Deposit Insurance Corporation (FDIC)*—an agency of the federal government. If your bank belongs to the FDIC, as almost all do, your account is insured for up to $100,000 regardless of what happens to the bank. Thus, while bank failures may spell disaster for the bank's stockholders, they do not create concern for many depositors. Deposit insurance eliminates the motive for customers to rush to their bank just because they hear some bad news about the bank's finances. Many observers give this innovation much of the credit for the pronounced decline in bank failures after the FDIC was established in 1933—which is apparent in Figure 1.

Despite this achievement, some critics of FDIC insurance worry that depositors who are freed from any risk of loss from a failing bank will not bother to shop around for safer banks. This problem is an example of what is called the **moral hazard** problem: the general idea that, when people are well-insured against a particular risk, they will put little effort into making sure that the risk does not occur. (Example: A business with good fire insurance may not install an expensive sprinkler system.) In this context, some of the FDIC's critics argue that high levels of deposit insurance actually make the banking system less safe.

Moral hazard is the idea that people insured against the consequences of risk will engage in riskier behaviors.

Bank Supervision   Partly for this reason, the government takes several steps to see that banks do not get into financial trouble. For one thing, various regulatory authorities conduct periodic *bank examinations* to keep tabs on the financial conditions and business practices of the banks under their purview. After a rash of bank failures in the late 1980s and early 1990s (visible in Figure 1(b)), U.S. bank supervision was tightened by legislation that permits the authorities to intervene early in the affairs of financially troubled banks. Other laws and regulations *limit the kinds and quantities of assets in which banks may invest.* For example, banks are permitted to own only limited amounts of common stock. Both of these forms of regulation, and others, are clearly aimed at keeping banks safe.

Reserve Requirements A final type of regulation also has some bearing on safety but is motivated primarily by the government's desire to control the money supply. We have seen that the amount of money any bank will issue depends on the amount of reserves it elects to keep. For this reason, most banks are subject by law to minimum **required reserves.** Although banks may (and sometimes do) keep reserves in excess of these legal minimums, they may not keep less. This regulation places an upper limit on the money supply. The rest of this chapter is concerned with the details of this mechanism.

> **Required reserves** are the minimum amount of reserves (in cash or the equivalent) required by law. Normally, required reserves are proportional to the volume of deposits.

■ THE ORIGINS OF THE MONEY SUPPLY

Our objective is to understand how the money supply is determined. But before we can fully understand the process by which money is "created," we must acquire at least a nodding acquaintance with the mechanics of modern banking.

■ How Bankers Keep Books

The first thing to know is how to distinguish assets from liabilities. An **asset** of a bank is something of value that the bank *owns*. This "thing" may be a physical object, such as the bank building or a computer, or it may be a piece of paper, such as an IOU from a customer to whom the bank has made a loan. A **liability** of a bank is something of value that the bank *owes*. Most bank liabilities take the form of bookkeeping entries. For example, if you have an account in the Main Street Bank, your bank balance is a liability of the bank. (It is, of course, an asset to you.)

There is an easy test for whether some piece of paper or bookkeeping entry is a bank's *asset* or *liability*. Ask yourself a simple question: If this paper were converted into cash, would the bank receive the cash (if so, it is an asset) or pay it out (if so, it is a liability)? This test makes it clear that loans to customers are ssets of the bank (when a loan is repaid, the bank collects), whereas customers' deposits are bank liabilities (when a deposit is cashed in, the bank pays). Of course, things are just the opposite to the bank's customers: The loans are liabilities and the deposits are assets.

When accountants draw up a complete list of all the bank's assets and liabilities, the resulting document is called the bank's **balance sheet.** Typically, the value of all the bank's assets exceeds the value of all its liabilities. (On the rare occasions when this is not so, the bank is in serious trouble.) In what sense, then, do balance sheets "balance"?

They balance because accountants have invented the concept of **net worth** to balance the books. Specifically, they define the net worth of a bank to be the *difference* between the value of all its assets and the value of all its liabilities. Thus, by definition, when accountants add net worth to liabilities, the sum they get must be equal to the value of the bank's assets:

> An **asset** of an individual or business firm is an item of value that the individual or firm owns.

> A **liability** of an individual or business firm is an item of value that the individual or firm owes. Many liabilities are known as *debts*.

> A **balance sheet** is an accounting statement listing the values of all assets on the left side and the values of all liabilities and *net worth* on the right side.

> **Net worth** is the value of all assets minus the value of all liabilities.

Assets = Liabilities + Net worth

Table 1 illustrates this point with the balance sheet of a fictitious bank, Bank-a-mythica, whose finances are extremely simple. On December 31, 2004, it had only two kinds of assets (listed on the left side of the balance sheet)—$1 million in cash reserves, and $4.5 million in outstanding loans to its customers, that is, in customers' IOUs. And it had only one type of liability (listed on the right side)—

TABLE 1			
Balance Sheet of Bank-a-mythica, December 31, 2004			
Assets		Liabilities and Net Worth	
Assets		**Liabilities**	
Reserves	$1,000,000	Checking deposits	$5,000,000
Loans outstanding	$4,500,000		
Total	**$5,500,000**	**Net Worth**	
Addendum: Bank Reserves		Stockholders' equity	$500,000
Actual reserves	$1,000,000	Total	**$5,500,000**
Required reserves	1,000,000		
Excess reserves	0		

$5 million in checking deposits. The difference between total assets ($5.5 million) and total liabilities ($5.0 million) was the bank's net worth ($500,000), also shown on the right side of the balance sheet.

■ BANKS AND MONEY CREATION

Deposit creation refers to the process by which a fractional reserve banking system turns $1 of bank reserves into several dollars of bank deposits.

Let us now turn to the process of deposit creation. Many bankers will deny that they have any ability to "create" money. The phrase itself has a suspiciously hocus-pocus sound to it. But the protesting bankers are not quite right. Although any individual bank's ability to create money is severely limited, the banking system as a whole can achieve much more than the sum of its parts. Through the modern alchemy of **deposit creation**, it can turn one dollar into many dollars. But to understand this important process, we had better proceed step by step, beginning with the case of a single bank, our hypothetical Bank-a-mythica.

■ The Limits to Money Creation by a Single Bank

Excess reserves are any reserves held in excess of the legal minimum.

According to the balance sheet in Table 1, Bank-a-mythica holds cash reserves of $1 million, equal to 20 percent of its $5 million in deposits. Assume that this is the reserve ratio prescribed by law and that the bank strives to keep its reserves down to the legal minimum; that is, it strives to keep its **excess reserves** at zero.

Now let us suppose that on January 2, 2005, an eccentric widower comes into Bank-a-mythica and deposits $100,000 in cash in his checking account. The bank now has $100,000 more in cash reserves, and $100,000 more in checking deposits. But because deposits are up by $100,000, *required* reserves rise by only $20,000, leaving $80,000 in *excess* reserves. Table 2 illustrates the effects of this transaction on Bank-a-mythica's balance sheet. Tables such as this one, which show *changes* in balance sheets rather than the balance sheets themselves, will help us follow the money-creation process.[4]

Bank-a-mythica is unlikely to be happy with the situation illustrated in Table 2, for it is holding $80,000 in excess reserves on which it earns no interest. So as soon as possible, it will lend out the extra $80,000—let us say to Hard-Pressed Construction Company. This loan leads to the balance sheet changes shown in Table 3: Bank-a-mythica's loans rise by $80,000 while its holdings of cash reserves fall by $80,000.

By combining Tables 2 and 3, we arrive at Table 4, which summarizes the bank's transactions for the week. Reserves are up $20,000, loans are up $80,000, and, now that the bank has had a chance to adjust to the inflow of deposits, it no longer holds excess reserves.

TABLE 2			
Changes in Bank-a-mythica's Balance Sheet, January 2, 2005			
Assets		Liabilities	
Reserves	+$100,000	Checking deposits	+$100,000
Addendum: Changes in Reserves			
Actual reserves	+$100,000		
Required reserves	+$ 20,000		
Excess reserves	**+$ 80,000**		

[4] In all such tables, which are called *T accounts*, the two sides of the ledger must balance. This balance is required because changes in assets and changes in liabilities must be equal if the balance sheet is to balance both before and after the transaction.

TABLE 3		
Changes in Bank-a-mythica's Balance Sheet, January 3–6, 2005		
Assets		**Liabilities**
Loans outstanding	+$80,000	No change
Reserves	−$80,000	
Addendum: Changes in Reserves		
Actual reserves	−$80,000	
Required reserves	No change	
Excess reserves	**−$80,000**	

TABLE 4		
Changes in Bank-a-mythica's Balance Sheet, January 2–6, 2005		
Assets		**Liabilities**
Reserves	+$20,000	Checking deposits +$100,000
Loans outstanding	+$80,000	
Addendum: Changes in Reserves		
Actual reserves	+$20,000	
Required reserves	+$20,000	
Excess reserves	**No change**	

Looking at Table 4 and keeping in mind our specific definition of money, it appears at first that the chairman of Bank-a-mythica is right when he claims not to have engaged in the nefarious practice of "money creation." All that happened was that, in exchange for the $100,000 in cash it received, the bank issued the widower a checking balance of $100,000. This transaction does not change M1; it merely converts one form of money (currency) into another (checking deposits).

But wait. What happened to the $100,000 in cash that the eccentric man brought to the bank? The table shows that Bank-a-mythica retained $20,000 in its vault. Because this currency is no longer in circulation, it no longer counts in the official money supply, M1. (Notice that Figure 2 included only "currency outside banks.") But the other $80,000, which the bank lent out, is still in circulation. It is held by Hard-Pressed Construction Company, which probably will redeposit it in some other bank. But even before this new deposit is made, the original $100,000 in cash has supported an increase in the money supply. There is now $100,000 in checking deposits and $80,000 of cash in circulation, making a total of $180,000—whereas prior to the original deposit there was only the $100,000 in cash. The money creation process has begun.

Multiple Money Creation by a Series of Banks

Let us now trace the $80,000 in cash and see how the process of money creation gathers momentum. Suppose that Hard-Pressed Construction Company, which banks across town at the First National Bank, deposits the $80,000 into its bank account. First National's reserves increase by $80,000. But because its deposits rise by $80,000, its *required* reserves increase by only 20 percent of this amount, or $16,000. If First National Bank behaves like Bank-a-mythica, it will lend out the $64,000 of excess reserves.

Table 5 shows the effects of these events on First National Bank's balance sheet. (We do not show the preliminary steps corresponding to Tables 2 and 3 separately.) At this stage in the chain, the original $100,000 in cash has led to $180,000 in

TABLE 5

Changes in First National Bank's Balance Sheet

Assets		Liabilities	
Reserves	+$16,000	Checking deposits	+$80,000
Loans outstanding	+$64,000		
Addendum: Changes in Reserves			
Actual reserves	+$16,000		
Required reserves	+$16,000		
Excess reserves	**No change**		

TABLE 6

Changes in Second National Bank's Balance Sheet

Assets		Liabilities	
Reserves	+$12,800	Checking deposits	+$64,000
Loans outstanding	+$51,200		
Addendum: Changes in Reserves			
Actual reserves	+$12,800		
Required reserves	+$12,800		
Excess reserves	**No change**		

deposits—$100,000 at Bank-a-mythica and $80,000 at First National Bank—and $64,000 in cash, which is still in circulation (in the hands of the recipient of First National's loan—Al's Auto Shop). Thus, instead of the original $100,000, a total of $244,000 worth of money ($180,000 in checking deposits plus $64,000 in cash) has been created.

But, to coin a phrase, the bucks do not stop here. Al's Auto Shop will presumably deposit the proceeds from its loan into its own account at Second National Bank, leading to the balance sheet adjustments shown in Table 6 when Second National makes an additional loan of $51,200 rather than hold on to excess reserves. You can see how the money creation process continues.

Figure 3 summarizes the balance sheet changes of the first five banks in the chain (from Bank-a-mythica through the Fourth National Bank) graphically, based on the assumptions that (1) each bank holds exactly the 20 percent required reserves, and (2) each loan recipient redeposits the proceeds in the next bank. But the chain does not end there. The Main Street Movie Theatre, which received the $32,768 loan from the Fourth National Bank, deposits these funds into the Fifth National Bank. Fifth National has to keep only 20 percent of this deposit, or $6,553.60, on reserve and will lend out the balance. And so the chain continues.

Where does it all end? The running sums on the right side of Figure 3 show what eventually happens to the entire banking system. The initial deposit of $100,000 in cash is ultimately absorbed in bank reserves, Column (1), leading to a total of $500,000 in new deposits, Column (2), and $400,000 in new loans, Column (3). The money supply rises by $400,000 because the nonbank public eventually holds $100,000 *less* in currency and $500,000 *more* in checking deposits.

As we see, there really is some hocus-pocus. Somehow, an initial deposit of $100,000 leads to $500,000 in new bank deposits—a multiple expansion of $5 for every original dollar—and a net increase of $400,000 in the money supply. We need to understand *why* this is so. But first let us verify that the calculations in Figure 3 are correct.

If you look carefully at the numbers, you will see that each column forms a *geometric progression*; specifically, each entry is equal to exactly 80 percent of the entry before it. Recall that in our discussion of the multiplier in Chapter 25 we learned how to sum

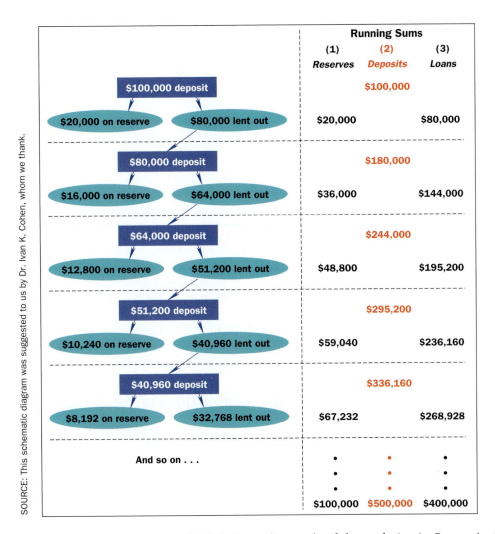

SOURCE: This schematic diagram was suggested to us by Dr. Ivan K. Cohen, whom we thank.

FIGURE 3

The Chain of Multiple Deposit Creation

an *infinite geometric progression*, which is just what each of these chains is. In particular, if the common ratio is R, the sum of an infinite geometric progression is:

$$1 + R + R^2 + R^3 + \ldots = \frac{1}{1 - R}$$

By applying this formula to the chain of checking deposits in Figure 3, we get:

$$\$100{,}000 + \$80{,}000 + \$64{,}000 + \$51{,}200 + \ldots$$
$$= \$100{,}000 \times (1 + 0.80 + 0.64 + 0.512 + \ldots)$$
$$= \$100{,}000 \times (1 + 0.80 + 0.80^2 + 0.80^3 + \ldots)$$
$$= \$100{,}000 \times \frac{1}{1 - 0.80} = \frac{\$100{,}000}{0.20} = \$500{,}000$$

Proceeding similarly, we can verify that the new loans sum to $400,000 and that the new required reserves sum to $100,000. (Check these figures as exercises.) Thus the numbers in Figure 3 are correct. Let us, therefore, think through the logic behind them.

The chain of deposit creation ends only when there are no more *excess* reserves to be loaned out—that is, when the entire $100,000 in cash is tied up in *required* reserves. That explains why the last entry in Column (1) of Figure 3 must be $100,000. But, with a reserve ratio of 20 percent, excess reserves disappear only when checking deposits expand by $500,000—which is the last entry in Column (2). Finally, because balance sheets must balance, the sum of all newly created assets (reserves plus loans) must equal the sum of all newly created liabilities ($500,000 in deposits). That leaves $400,000 for new loans—which is the last entry in Column (3).

More generally, if the reserve ratio is some number m (rather than the one-fifth in our example), each dollar of deposits requires only a fraction m of a dollar in reserves. The common ratio in the preceding formula is, therefore, $R = 1 - m$, and deposits must expand by $1/m$ for each dollar of new reserves that are injected into the system. This suggests the general formula for multiple money creation when the required reserve ratio is some number m:

OVERSIMPLIFIED MONEY MULTIPLIER FORMULA

If the required reserve ratio is some fraction, m, the banking system as a whole can convert each \$1 of reserves into \$$1/m$ in new money. That is, the so-called **money multiplier** is given by:

Change in money supply = $(1/m)$ × Change in reserves

The **money multiplier** is the ratio of newly created bank deposits to new reserves.

Although this formula correctly describes what happens in our example, it leaves out an important detail. The initial deposit of \$100,000 in cash at Bank-a-mythica constitutes \$100,000 in new reserves (see Table 2 on page 636). Applying a multiplier of $1/m = 1/0.20 = 5$ to this \$100,000, we conclude that bank deposits will rise by \$500,000—which is just what happens. But remember that the process started when the eccentric widower took \$100,000 in cash and deposited it in his bank account. Thus the public's holdings of *money*—which includes both checking deposits *and* cash—increase by only \$400,000 in this case: There is \$500,000 *more* in deposits, but \$100,000 *less* in cash.

■ The Process in Reverse: Multiple Contractions of the Money Supply

Let us now briefly consider how this deposit creation mechanism operates in reverse—as a system of deposit *destruction*. In particular, suppose that our eccentric widower returned to Bank-a-mythica to withdraw \$100,000 from his checking account and return it to his mattress, where it rightfully belongs. Bank-a-mythica's *required* reserves would fall by \$20,000 as a result of this transaction (20 percent of \$100,000), but its *actual* reserves would fall by \$100,000. The bank would be \$80,000 short, as indicated in Table 7(a).

How would the bank react to this discrepancy? As some of its outstanding loans are routinely paid off, it will cease granting new ones until it has accumulated the necessary \$80,000 in required reserves. The data for Bank-a-mythica's contraction are shown in Table 7(b), assuming that borrowers pay off their loans in cash.[5]

TABLE 7					
Changes in the Balance Sheet of Bank-a-mythica					
(a)			**(b)**		
Assets		Liabilities	Assets		Liabilities
Reserves	−\$100,000	Checking deposits −\$100,000	Reserves	+\$80,000	No change
			Loans outstanding	−\$80,000	
Addendum: Changes in Reserves			**Addendum: Changes in Reserves**		
Actual reserves	−\$100,000		Actual reserves	+\$80,000	
Required reserves	−\$20,000		Reserves required	No change	
Excess reserves	−\$80,000		Excess reserves	+\$80,000	

[5] In reality, the borrowers would probably pay with checks drawn on other banks. Bank-a-mythica would then cash these checks to acquire the reserves.

TABLE 8							
Changes in the Balance Sheet of First National Bank							
(a)				(b)			
Assets		Liabilities		Assets		Liabilities	
Reserves	−$80,000	Checking deposits	−$80,000	Reserves	+$64,000	No change	
				Loans outstanding	−$64,000		
Addendum: Changes in Reserves				**Addendum: Changes in Reserves**			
Actual reserves	−$80,000			Actual reserves	+$64,000		
Required reserves	−$16,000			Reserves required	No change		
Excess reserves	**−$64,000**			Excess reserves	**+$64,000**		

But where did the borrowers get this money? Probably by making withdrawals from other banks. In this case, assume that the funds all came from First National Bank, which loses $80,000 in deposits and $80,000 in reserves. It finds itself short some $64,000 in reserves, as shown in Table 8(a), and therefore must reduce its loan commitments by $64,000, as in Table 8(b). This reaction, of course, causes some other bank to suffer a loss of reserves and deposits of $64,000, and the whole process repeats just as it did in the case of deposit expansion.

After the entire banking system had become involved, the picture would be just as shown in Figure 3, except that all the numbers would have *minus signs* in front of them. Deposits would shrink by $500,000, loans would fall by $400,000, bank reserves would be reduced by $100,000, and the M1 money supply would fall by $400,000. As suggested by our money multiplier formula with $m = 0.20$, the decline in the bank deposit component of the money supply is $1/0.20 = 5$ times as large as the decline in reserves.

One of the authors of this book was a student in Cambridge, Massachusetts, during the height of the radical student movement of the late 1960s. One day a pamphlet appeared urging citizens to withdraw all funds from their checking accounts on a prescribed date, hold them in cash for a week, and then redeposit them. This act, the circular argued, would wreak havoc upon the capitalist system. Obviously, some of these radicals were well schooled in modern money mechanics, for the argument was basically correct. The tremendous multiple contraction of the banking system and subsequent multiple expansion that a successful campaign of this sort could have caused might have seriously disrupted the local financial system. But history records that the appeal met with little success. Checking-account withdrawals are not the stuff of which revolutions are made.

■ WHY THE MONEY CREATION FORMULA IS OVERSIMPLIFIED

So far, our discussion of the process of money creation has seemed rather mechanical. If everything proceeds according to formula, each $1 in new reserves injected into the banking system leads to a $1/m$ increase in new deposits. But, in reality, things are not this simple. Just as in the case of the expenditure multiplier, the oversimplified money multiplier is accurate only under very particular circumstances. These circumstances require that:

1. Every recipient of cash must redeposit the cash into another bank rather than hold it.
2. Every bank must hold reserves no larger than the legal minimum.

The "chain" diagram in Figure 3 can teach us what happens if either of these assumptions is violated.

Suppose first that the business firms and individuals who receive bank loans decide to redeposit only a fraction of the proceeds into their bank accounts, holding the rest in cash. Then, for example, the first $80,000 loan would lead to a deposit of less than $80,000—and similarly down the chain. The whole chain of deposit creation would therefore be reduced. Thus:

If individuals and business firms decide to hold more cash, the multiple expansion of bank deposits will be curtailed because fewer dollars of cash will be available for use as reserves to support checking deposits. Consequently, the money supply will be smaller.

The basic idea here is simple. Each $1 of cash held *inside* a bank can support several dollars (specifically, $1/m$) of money. But each $1 of cash held *outside* the banking system is exactly $1 of money; it supports no deposits. Hence, any time cash moves from inside the banking system into the hands of a household or a business, the money supply will decline. And any time cash enters the banking system, the money supply will rise.

Next, suppose bank managers become more conservative or that the outlook for loan repayments worsens because of a recession. In such an environment, banks might decide to keep more reserves than the legal requirement and lend out less than the amounts assumed in Figure 3. If this happens, banks further down the chain receive smaller deposits and, once again, the chain of deposit creation is curtailed. Thus:

If banks wish to keep excess reserves, the multiple expansion of bank deposits will be restricted. A given amount of cash will support a smaller supply of money than would be the case if banks held no excess reserves.

The latter problem afflicted Japan for many years in the 1990s and in this decade. Because they had so many bad loans on their books, Japanese bankers became super-cautious about lending money to any but their most creditworthy borrowers. So even though bank reserves soared, the money supply did not.

■ THE NEED FOR MONETARY POLICY

If we pursue these two points a bit farther, we will see why the government must regulate the money supply in an effort to maintain economic stability. We have just suggested that banks prefer to keep excess reserves when they do not foresee profitable and secure opportunities to make loans. This scenario is most likely to arise when business conditions are depressed. At such times, the propensity of banks to hold excess reserves can turn the deposit creation process into one of deposit destruction, as happened recently in both Japan and Argentina. In addition, if depositors become nervous, they may decide to hold on to more cash. Thus:

During a recession, profit-oriented banks would be prone to reduce the money supply by increasing their excess reserves and declining to lend to less creditworthy applicants—if the government did not intervene. As we will learn in subsequent chapters, the money supply is an important influence on aggregate demand, so such a contraction of the money supply would aggravate the recession.

This is precisely what happened—with a vengeance—during the Great Depression of the 1930s. Although total bank reserves grew, the money supply contracted violently because banks preferred to hold excess reserves rather than make loans that might not be repaid. And something similar has been happening in Japan for years: The supply of reserves has expanded much more rapidly than the money supply because nervous bankers have been holding on to their excess reserves.

By contrast, banks want to squeeze the maximum money supply possible out of any given amount of cash reserves by keeping their reserves at the bare minimum when the demand for bank loans is buoyant, profits are high, and secure investment opportunities abound. This reduced incentive to hold excess reserves in prosperous times means that:

> During an economic boom, profit-oriented banks will likely make the money supply expand, adding undesirable momentum to the booming economy and paving the way for inflation. The authorities must intervene to prevent this rapid money growth.

Regulation of the money supply, then, is necessary because profit-oriented bankers might otherwise provide the economy with a money supply that dances to and amplifies the tune of the business cycle. Precisely how the authorities control the money supply is the subject of the next chapter.

SUMMARY

1. It is more efficient to exchange goods and services by using **money** as a medium of exchange than by **bartering** them directly.

2. In addition to being the **medium of exchange,** whatever serves as money is likely to become the standard **unit of account** and a popular **store of value.**

3. Throughout history, all sorts of items have served as money. **Commodity money** gave way to full-bodied paper money (certificates backed 100 percent by some commodity, such as gold), which in turn gave way to partially backed paper money. Nowadays, our paper money has no commodity backing whatsoever; it is pure **fiat money.**

4. One popular definition of the U.S. money supply is **M1,** which includes coins, paper money, and several types of checking deposits. Most economists actually prefer the **M2** definition, which adds to M1 other types of checkable accounts and most savings deposits. Much of M2 is held outside of banks by investment houses, credit unions, and other financial institutions.

5. Under our modern system of fractional reserve banking, banks keep cash reserves equal to only a fraction of their total deposit **liabilities.** This practice is the key to their profitability, because the remaining funds can be loaned out at interest. But it also leaves banks potentially vulnerable to **runs.**

6. Because of this vulnerability, bank managers are generally conservative in their investment strategies. They also keep a prudent level of reserves. Even so, the government keeps a watchful eye over banking practices.

7. Before 1933, bank failures were common in the United States. They declined sharply when **deposit insurance** was instituted.

8. Because it holds only fractional reserves, the banking system as a whole can create several dollars of deposits for each dollar of reserves it receives. Under certain assumptions, the ratio of new bank deposits to new reserves will be $1/m$, where m is the **required reserve** ratio.

9. The same process works in reverse, as a system of money destruction, when cash is withdrawn from the banking system.

10. Because banks and individuals may want to hold more cash when the economy is shaky, the money supply would probably contract under such circumstances if the government did not intervene. Similarly, the money supply would probably expand rapidly in boom times if it were unregulated.

KEY TERMS

Run on a bank   626

Barter   626

Money   628

Medium of exchange   628

Unit of account   628

Store of value   628

Commodity money   629

Fiat money   630

M1   631

M2   631

Near moneys   631

Liquidity   631

Fractional reserve banking   633

Deposit insurance   634

Moral Hazard   634

Federal Deposit Insurance Corporation (FDIC)   634

Required reserves   635

Asset   635

Liability   635

Balance sheet   635

Net worth   635

Deposit creation   636

Excess reserves   636

Money multiplier   640

TEST YOURSELF

1. Suppose banks keep no excess reserves and no individuals or firms hold on to cash. If someone suddenly discovers $12 million in buried treasure, explain what will happen to the money supply if the required reserve ratio is 10 percent.

2. How would your answer to Test Yourself Question 1 differ if the reserve ratio were 25 percent? If the reserve ratio were 100 percent?

3. Use tables such as Tables 2 and 3 to illustrate what happens to bank balance sheets when each of the following transactions occurs:

   a. You withdraw $100 from your checking account to buy concert tickets.

   b. Sam finds a $100 bill on the sidewalk and deposits it into his checking account.

   c. Mary Q. Contrary withdraws $500 in cash from her account at Hometown Bank, carries it to the city, and deposits it into her account at Big City Bank.

4. For each of the transactions listed in Test Yourself Question 3, what will be the ultimate effect on the money supply if the required reserve ratio is one-eighth (12.5 percent)? Assume that the oversimplified money multiplier formula applies.

DISCUSSION QUESTIONS

1. If ours were a barter economy, how would you pay your tuition bill? What if your college did not want the goods or services you offered in payment?

2. How is "money" defined, both conceptually and in practice? Does the U.S. money supply consist of commodity money, full-bodied paper money, or fiat money?

3. What is fractional reserve banking, and why is it the key to bank profits? (*Hint:* What opportunities to make profits would banks lose if reserve requirements were 100 percent?) Why does fractional reserve banking give bankers discretion over how large the money supply will be? Why does it make banks potentially vulnerable to runs?

4. During the 1980s and early 1990s, a rash of bank failures occurred in the United States. Explain why these failures did not lead to runs on banks.

5. Each year during Christmas shopping season, consumers and stores increase their holdings of cash. Explain how this development could lead to a multiple contraction of the money supply. (As a matter of fact, the authorities prevent this contraction from occurring by methods explained in the next chapter.)

6. Excess reserves make a bank less vulnerable to runs. Why, then, don't bankers like to hold excess reserves? What circumstances might persuade them that it would be advisable to hold excess reserves?

7. If the government takes over a failed bank with liabilities (mostly deposits) of $2 billion, pays off the depositors, and sells the assets for $1.5 billion, where does the missing $500 million come from? Why?

30

MANAGING AGGREGATE DEMAND: MONETARY POLICY

Victorians heard with grave attention that the Bank Rate had been raised. They did not know what it meant. But they knew that it was an act of extreme wisdom.

JOHN KENNETH GALBRAITH

A rmed with our understanding of the rudiments of banking, we are now ready to bring money and interest rates into our model of income determination and the price level. Up to now, we have taken investment (I) to be a fixed number. But this is a poor assumption. Not only is investment highly variable, but it also depends on interest rates—which are, in turn, heavily influenced by *monetary policy*. The main task of this chapter is to explain how monetary policy affects interest rates, investment, and aggregate demand. By the end of the chapter, we will have constructed a complete macroeconomic model, which we will use in subsequent chapters to investigate a variety of important policy issues.

CONTENTS

ISSUE: *Just Why Is Ben Bernanke So Important?*

The first day of February 2006 was a momentous one in the financial world, for Alan Greenspan, who served as chairman of the Federal Reserve Board since 1987, finally retired. On that day, his replacement, Ben Bernanke, became, in the view of many, the most powerful person in the economic world.

Bernanke is a brilliant but unassuming economist who taught for years at Princeton University. But now when he speaks, people in financial markets around the world dote on his remarks with an intensity that was once reserved for utterances from behind the Kremlin walls. Why? Because, in the view of many economists, the Federal Reserve's decisions on interest rates are the single most important influence on aggregate demand—and hence on economic growth, unemployment, and inflation.

Bernanke heads America's central bank, the *Federal Reserve System*. The "Fed," as it is called, is a bank—but a very special kind of bank. Its customers are banks rather than individuals, and it performs some of the same services for them as your bank performs for you. Although it makes enormous profits, profit is not its goal. Instead, the Fed tries to manage interest rates according to what it perceives to be the national interest. This chapter will teach you how the Fed does its job and why its decisions affect our economy so profoundly. In brief, it will teach you why people listen so intently whenever Ben Bernanke speaks.

"Get a grip, Harold! Do you think Mr. Bernanke is up all night worrying about what you're going to do?"

SOURCE: ©David Brown / artizans.com

◼ MONEY AND INCOME: THE IMPORTANT DIFFERENCE

Monetary policy refers to actions that the Federal Reserve System takes to change interest rates and the money supply. It is aimed at affecting the economy.

But first we must get some terminology straight. The words *money* and *income* are used almost interchangeably in common parlance. Here, however, we must be more precise.

Money is a snapshot concept. It answers questions such as "How much money do you have right now?" or "How much money did you have at 3:32 P.M. on Friday, November 5?" To answer these questions, you would add up the cash you are (or were) carrying and whatever checkable balances you have (or had), and answer something like: "I have $126.33," or "On Friday, November 5, at 3:32 P.M., I had $31.43."

Income, by contrast, is more like a motion picture; it comes to you over a period of time. If you are asked, "What is your income?", you must respond by saying "$1,000 *per week*," or "$4,000 *per month*," or "$50,000 *per year*," or something like that. Notice that a unit of time is attached to each of these responses. If you just answer, "My income is $45,000," without indicating whether it is per week, per month, or per year, no one will understand what you mean.

That the two concepts are very different is easy to see. A typical American family has an *income* of about $45,000 per year, but its *money* holdings at any point in time (using the M1 definition) may be less than $2,000. Similarly, at the national level, nominal GDP at the end of 2006 was around $13.5 trillion, while the money stock (M1) was under $1.4 trillion.

Although money and income are different, they are certainly related. This chapter focuses on that relationship. Specifically, we will look at how the stock of *money* in existence at any moment of time influences the rate at which people earn *income*—that is, how **monetary policy** affects GDP.

■ AMERICA'S CENTRAL BANK: THE FEDERAL RESERVE SYSTEM

When Congress established the *Federal Reserve System* in 1914, the United States joined the company of most other advanced industrial nations. Until then, the United States, distrustful of centralized economic power, was almost the only important nation without a **central bank.** The Bank of England, for example, dates back to 1694.

A **central bank** is a bank for banks. The United States' central bank is the *Federal Reserve System.*

■ Origins and Structure

It was painful experiences with economic reality, not the power of economic logic, that provided the impetus to establish a central bank for the United States. Four severe banking panics between 1873 and 1907, in which many banks failed, convinced legislators and bankers alike that a central bank that would regulate credit conditions was not a luxury but a necessity. The 1907 crisis led Congress to study the shortcomings of the banking system and, eventually, to establish the Federal Reserve System.

Although the basic ideas of central banking came from Europe, the United States made some changes when it imported the idea, making the Federal Reserve System a uniquely American institution.[1] Because of the vastness of our country, the extraordinarily large number of commercial banks, and our tradition of shared state-federal responsibilities, Congress decided that the United States should have not one central bank but twelve.

Technically, each Federal Reserve Bank is a corporation; its stockholders are its member banks. But your bank, if it is a member of the system, does not enjoy the privileges normally accorded to stockholders: It receives only a token share of the Federal Reserve's immense profits (the bulk is turned over to the U.S. Treasury), and it has virtually no say in corporate decisions. In many ways, the private banks are more like customers of the Fed than owners.

Who, then, controls the Fed? Most of the power resides in the seven-member Board of Governors of the Federal Reserve System in Washington, especially in its chairman. The governors are appointed by the President of the United States, with the advice and consent of the Senate, for fourteen-year terms. The president also designates one of the members to serve a four-year term as chairman of the board, and thus to be the most powerful central banker in the world.

The Federal Reserve is independent of the rest of the government. As long as it stays within its statutory authority as delineated by Congress, it alone has responsibility for determining the nation's monetary policy. The power of appointment, however, gives the president some long-run influence over Federal Reserve policy. For example, it was President Bush who selected Ben Bernanke, a former adviser, to be the Fed's new chairman.

Closely allied with the Board of Governors is the powerful Federal Open Market Committee (FOMC), which meets eight times a year in Washington. For reasons to be explained shortly, FOMC decisions largely determine short-term interest rates and the size of the U.S. money supply. This twelve-member committee consists of the seven governors of the Federal Reserve System, the president of the Federal Reserve

"I'm sorry, sir, but I don't believe you know us well enough to call us the Fed."

---

[1] Ironically, when the European Central Bank was established in 1999, its structure was patterned on that of the Federal Reserve.

A Meeting of the Federal Open Market Committee

Meetings of the Federal Open Market Committee are serious and formal affairs. All nineteen members—seven governors and twelve reserve bank presidents—sit around a mammoth table in the Fed's cavernous but austere board room. A limited number of top Fed staffers join them at and around the table, for access to FOMC meetings is strictly controlled.

At precisely 9 A.M.—for punctuality is a high virtue at the Fed—the doors are closed and the chairman calls the meeting to order. No press is allowed and, unlike most important Washington meetings, nothing will leak. Secrecy is another high virtue at the Fed.

After hearing a few routine staff reports, the chairman calls on each of the members in turn to give their views of the current economic situation. District bank presidents offer insights into their local economies, and all members comment on the outlook for the national economy. Disagreements are raised, but voices are not. There are normally no interruptions while people talk, for politeness is another virtue. Strikingly, in this most political of cities, politics is almost never mentioned.

Once he has heard from all the others, the chairman offers his own views of the economic situation. Then he usually recommends a course of action. Members of the committee, in their turn, comment on the chairman's proposal. Most agree, though some note differences of opinion. After hearing all this, the chairman announces what he perceives to be the committee's consensus and

asks the secretary to call the roll. Only the twelve voting members answer, saying yes or no. Negative votes are rare, for the FOMC tries to operate by consensus and a dissent is considered a loud objection.

The meeting adjourns, and at precisely 2:15 P.M. a Fed spokesman announces the decision to the public. Within minutes, financial markets around the world react.

SOURCE: Courtesy of the Federal Reserve Board

Bank of New York, and, on a rotating basis, four of the other eleven district bank presidents.[2]

Central Bank Independence

Central bank independence refers to the central bank's ability to make decisions without political interference.

For decades a debate raged, both in the United States and in other countries, over the pros and cons of **central bank independence.**

Proponents of central bank independence argue that it enables the central bank to take the long view and to make monetary policy decisions on objective, technical criteria—thus keeping monetary policy out of the "political thicket." Without this independence, they argue, politicians with short time horizons might try to force the central bank to expand the money supply too rapidly, especially before elections, thereby contributing to chronic inflation and undermining faith in the country's financial system. They point to historical evidence showing that countries with more independent central banks have, on average, experienced lower inflation.

Opponents of this view counter that there is something profoundly undemocratic about letting a group of unelected bankers and economists make decisions that affect every citizen's well-being. Monetary policy, they argue, should be formulated by the elected representatives of the people, just as fiscal policy is.

The high inflation of the 1970s and early 1980s helped resolve this issue by convincing many governments around the world that an independent central bank was essential to controlling inflation. Thus, one country after another has made its central bank independent over the past 20 to 25 years. For example, the Maastricht Treaty (1992), which committed members of the European Union to both low inflation and a single

[2] Alan Blinder was the vice chairman of the Federal Reserve Board, and thus a member of the Federal Open Market Committee, from 1994 to 1996.

currency (the euro), required each member state to make its central bank independent. All did so, even though several have still not joined the monetary union. Japan also decided to make its central bank independent in 1998. In Latin America, several formerly high-inflation countries like Brazil and Mexico found that giving their central banks more independence helped them control inflation. And some of the formerly socialist countries of Europe, finding themselves saddled with high inflation and "unsound" currencies, made their central banks more independent for similar reasons. Thus, for practical purposes, the debate over central bank independence is now all but over.

The new debate is over how to hold such independent and powerful institutions *accountable* to the political authorities and to the broad public. For example, many central banks have now abandoned their former traditions of secrecy and have become far more open to public scrutiny. Some—the so-called inflation targeters—even announce specific numerical targets for inflation, thereby giving outside observers an easy way to judge the central bank's success or failure. Chairman Bernanke has even expressed interest in bringing some version of inflation targeting to the Federal Reserve.

IMPLEMENTING MONETARY POLICY: OPEN-MARKET OPERATIONS

When it wants to change interest rates, the Fed normally relies on **open-market operations.** Open-market operations either give banks more reserves or take reserves away from them, thereby triggering the sort of multiple expansion or contraction of the money supply described in the previous chapter.

How does this process work? If the Federal Open Market Committee decides that interest rates are too high, it can bring them down by providing banks with more reserves. Specifically, the Federal Reserve System would normally *purchase* a particular kind of short-term U.S. government security called a *Treasury bill* from any individual or bank that wished to sell them, paying with newly-created bank reserves. To see how this open-market operation affects interest rates, we must understand how *the market for bank reserves*, which is depicted in Figure 1 on the next page, works.

Open-market operations refer to the Fed's purchase or sale of government securities through transactions in the open market.

The Market for Bank Reserves

The main sources of supply and demand in the market on which bank reserves are traded are straightforward. On the supply side, it is the Fed that decides how many dollars of reserves to provide. The label on the supply curve in Figure 1 indicates that *the position of the supply curve depends on Federal Reserve policy*. The Fed's decision on the quantity of bank reserves is the essence of monetary policy, and we are about to consider how the Fed makes that decision.

On the demand side of the market, the main reason why banks hold reserves is something we learned in the previous chapter: Government regulations require them to do so. In Chapter 29, we used the symbol m to denote the required reserve ratio (which is 0.1 in the United States). So if the volume of transaction deposits is D, the demand for *required reserves* is simply $m \times D$. The demand for reserves thus reflects the demand for transactions deposits in banks.

The demand for bank deposits depends on many factors, but the principal determinant is the dollar value of transactions. After all, people and businesses hold bank deposits in order to conduct transactions. Real GDP (Y) is typically used as a convenient indicator of the *number* of transactions, and the price level (P) is a natural measure of the *average price* per transaction. So the volume of bank deposits, D, *and therefore the demand for bank reserves, depends on both Y and P*—as indicated by the label on the demand curve in Figure 1.

There is more to the story, however, for we have not yet explained why the the demand curve DD slopes down and the supply curve SS slopes up. The interest rate measured along the vertical axis of Figure 1 is called the **federal funds rate.** It is the rate that applies when banks borrow and lend reserves to one another. When you hear

The **federal funds rate** is the interest rates that banks pay and receive when they borrow reserves from one another.

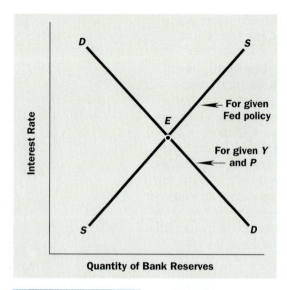

FIGURE 1

The Market for Bank Reserves

on the evening news that "the Federal Reserve today cut interest rates by ¼ of a point," it is the federal funds rate that the reporter is talking about.

Now where does this borrowing and lending come from? As we mentioned in the previous chapter, banks sometimes find themselves with either insufficient or excess reserves. Neither situation leaves banks satisfied. Keeping actual reserves below the required level of reserves is not allowed. Holding reserves in excess of requirements is perfectly legal, but since reserves pay no interest, a bank can put excess reserves to better use by lending them out rather than keeping them idle. So banks have developed an active market in which those with excess reserves lend them to those with reserve deficiencies. These bank-to-bank loans provide an additional source of *both* supply *and* demand—and one that (unlike required reserves) is interest sensitive.

Any bank that wants to borrow reserves must pay the federal funds rate for the privilege. Naturally, as the funds rate rises, borrowing looks more expensive and so fewer reserves are demanded. In a word, the demand curve for reserves (*DD*) slopes downward. Similarly, the supply curve for reserves (*SS*) slopes upward because lending reserves becomes more attractive as the federal funds rate rises.

The equilibrium federal funds rate is established, as usual, at point *E* in Figure 1—where the demand and supply curves cross. Now suppose the Federal Reserve wants to push the federal funds rate *down*. It can provide additional reserves to the market by purchasing Treasury bills (often abbreviated as *T-bills*) from banks.[3] This *open-market purchase* would shift the supply curve of bank reserves outward, from $S_0 S_0$ to $S_1 S_1$, in Figure 2. Equilibrium would therefore shift from point *E* to point *A* which, as the diagram shows, implies a lower interest rate and more bank reserves. That is precisely what the Fed does when it wants to reduce interest rates.[4]

■ The Mechanics of an Open-Market Operation

FIGURE 2

The Effects of an Open-Market Purchase

The bookkeeping behind such an open-market purchase is illustrated by Table 1, which imagines that the FOMC purchases $100 million worth of T-bills from commercial banks. When the Fed buys the securities, the ownership of the T-bills shifts from the banks to the Fed—as indicated by the black arrows in Table 1. Next, *the Fed makes payment by giving the banks $100 million in new reserves*, that is, by adding $100 million to the bookkeeping entries that represent the banks' accounts at the Fed—called "bank reserves" in the table. These reserves, shown in blue in the table, are liabilities of the Fed and assets of the banks.

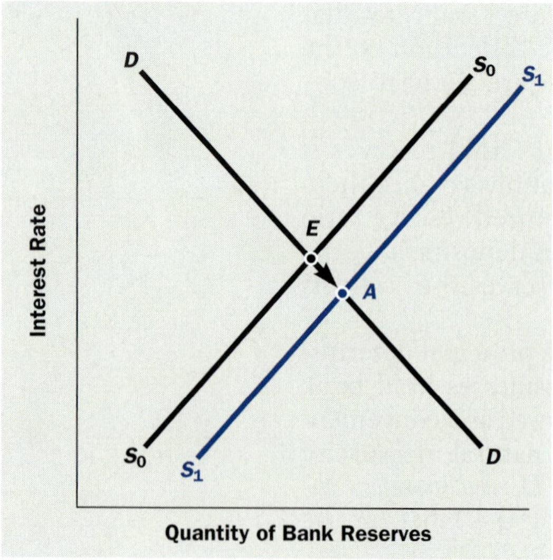

You may be wondering where the Fed gets the money to pay for the securities. It could pay in cash, but it normally does not. Instead, it manufactures the funds out of thin air or, more literally, by punching a keyboard. Specifically, the Fed pays the banks by adding the appropriate sums to the reserve accounts that the banks maintain at the Fed. Balances held in these accounts constitute bank reserves, just like cash in bank vaults. Although this process of adding to bookkeeping entries at the Federal Reserve is sometimes referred to as "printing money,"

---

[3] It is not important that banks be the buyers. Test Yourself Question 3 at the end of the chapter shows that the effect on bank reserves and the money supply is the same if bank customers purchase the securities.

[4] There are many interest rates in the economy, but they all tend to move up and down together. So, in a first course in economics, we need not distinguish one interest rate from another.

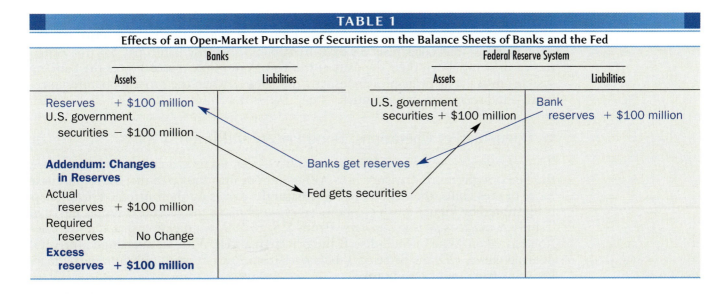

TABLE 1

Effects of an Open-Market Purchase of Securities on the Balance Sheets of Banks and the Fed

the Fed does not literally run any printing presses. Instead, it simply trades its IOUs for an existing asset (a T-bill). But unlike other IOUs, the Fed's IOUs constitute bank reserves and thus can support a multiple expansion of the money supply just as cash does. Let's see how this works.

It is clear from Table 1 that bank deposits have not increased at all—yet. So *required* reserves are unchanged by the open-market operation. But *actual* reserves are increased by $100 million. So, if the banks held only their required reserves initially, they now have $100 million in *excess reserves*. As banks rid themselves of these excess reserves by making more loans, a multiple expansion of the banking system is set in motion—just as described in the previous chapter. It is not difficult for the Fed to estimate the ultimate increase in the money supply that will result from its actions. As we learned in the previous chapter, each dollar of newly-created bank reserves can support up to $1/m$ dollars of checking deposits, if m is the required reserve ratio. In the example in the last chapter, $m = 0.20$; hence, $100 million in new reserves can support $100 million $\div$ 0.2 = $500 million in new money.

But *estimating* the ultimate monetary expansion is a far cry from *knowing it* with certainty. As we know from the previous chapter, the oversimplified money multiplier formula is predicated on two assumptions: that people will want to hold no more cash, and that banks will want to hold no more excess reserves, as the monetary expansion proceeds. In practice, these assumptions are unlikely to be literally true. So to predict the eventual effect of its action on the money supply, the Fed must *estimate* both the amount that firms and individuals will add to their currency holdings and the amount that banks will add to their excess reserves. Neither of these quantities can be estimated with utter precision. In summary:

> When the Federal Reserve wants to lower interest rates, it purchases U.S. government securities in the open market. It pays for these securities by creating new bank reserves, which lead to a multiple expansion of the money supply. Because of fluctuations in people's desires to hold cash and banks' desires to hold excess reserves, the Fed cannot predict the consequences of these actions for the money supply with perfect accuracy. But the Fed can always put the federal funds rate where it wants by buying just the right volume of securities.[5]

For this reason, in this and subsequent chapters, we will simply proceed as if the Fed controls the federal funds rate directly.

---

[5] Why? Because the federal funds rate is observable in the market every minute and hence need not be estimated. If interest rates do not fall as much as the Fed wants, it can simply purchase more securities. If interest rates fall too much, the Fed can purchase less. And these adjustments can be made very quickly.

The procedures followed when the FOMC wants to *raise* interest rates are just the opposite of those we have just explained. In brief, it *sells* government securities in the open market. This takes reserves *away* from banks, because banks pay for the securities by drawing down their deposits at the Fed. A multiple *contraction* of the banking system ensues. The principles are exactly the same as when the process operates in reverse—and so are the uncertainties.

■ Open-Market Operations, Bond Prices, and Interest Rates

The *expansionary monetary policy* action we have been using as an example began when the Fed bought more Treasury bills. When it goes into the open market to purchase more of these bills, the Federal Reserve naturally drives up their prices. This process is illustrated by Figure 3, which shows an *inward shift* of the (vertical) supply curve of T-bills *available to private investors*—from S_0S_0 to S_1S_1—indicating that the Fed's action has taken some of the bills off the private market. With an unchanged (private) demand curve, DD, the price of T-bills rises from P_0 to P_1 as equilibrium in the market shifts from point A to point B.

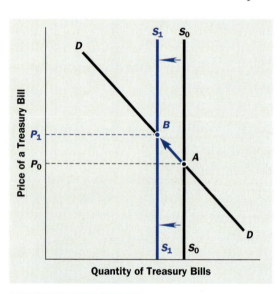

Rising prices for Treasury bills—or for any other type of bond—translate directly into falling interest rates. Why? The reason is simple arithmetic. Bonds pay a fixed number of dollars of interest per year. For concreteness, consider a bond that pays $60 each year. If the bond sells for $1,000, bondholders earn a 6 percent return on their investment (the $60 interest payment is 6 percent of $1,000). We therefore say that *the interest rate on the bond is 6 percent.* Now suppose that the price of the bond rises to $1,200. The annual interest payment is still $60, so bondholders now earn just 5 percent on their money ($60 is 5 percent of $1,200). *The effective interest rate on the bond has fallen to 5 percent.* This relationship between bond prices and interest rates is completely general:

> When bond prices rise, interest rates fall because the purchaser of a bond spends more money than before to earn a given number of dollars of interest per year. Similarly, when bond prices fall, interest rates rise.

FIGURE 3

Open-Market Purchases and Treasury Bill Prices

In fact, the relationship amounts to nothing more than two ways of saying the same thing. Higher interest rates *mean* lower bond prices; lower interest rates *mean* higher bond prices.[6] Thus Figure 3 is another way to look at the fact that Federal Reserve open-market operations influence interest rates. Specifically:

> An open-market purchase of Treasury bills by the Fed not only raises the money supply but also drives up T-bill prices and pushes interest rates down. Conversely, an open-market sale of bills, which reduces the money supply, lowers T-bill prices and raises interest rates.

■ OTHER METHODS OF MONETARY CONTROL

When the Federal Reserve System was first established, its founders did not intend it to pursue an active monetary policy to stabilize the economy. Indeed, the basic ideas of stabilization policy were unknown at the time. Instead, the Fed's founders viewed it as a means of preventing the supplies of money and credit from drying up during economic contractions, as had happened often in the pre-1914 period.

---

[6] For further discussion and examples, see Test Yourself Question 4 at the end of the chapter.

You Now Belong to a Distinctive Minority Group

When the stock market sagged from 2000 to 2003, more and more investors became attracted to bonds as a safer alternative. But an amazing number of investors do not understand even the elementary facts about bond investing—including the relationship between bond prices and interest rates.

The Wall Street Journal reported in November 2001 that "One of the bond basics about which many investors are clueless, for instance, is the fundamental seesaw relationship between interest rates and bond prices. Only 31% of 750 investors participating in the American Century [a mutual fund company] telephone survey knew that when interest rates rise, bond prices generally fall."* Imagine how many fewer, then, could explain *why* this is so.

*Karen Damato, "Investors Love Their Bond Funds—Too Much?," *The Wall Street Journal*, November 9, 2001, page C1.

SOURCE: © Sidney Harris

"When interest rates go up, bond prices go down. When interest rates go down, bond prices go up. But please don't ask me why."

■ Lending to Banks

One of the principal ways in which Congress intended the Fed to provide such insurance against financial panics was to act as a "lender of last resort." When risky business prospects made commercial banks hesitant to extend new loans, or when banks were in trouble, the Fed would step in by lending money to the banks, thus inducing them to lend more to their customers. The Fed most recently performed this role on a large scale in September 2001, when the terrorist attack on New York City literally disabled several large financial institutions. Mammoth amounts of lending to banks kept the financial system functioning and averted a panic.

The mechanics of Federal Reserve lending are illustrated in Table 2. When the Fed makes a loan to a bank in need of reserves, that bank receives a credit in its deposit account at the Fed—$5 million in the example. That $5 million represents newly-created reserves, and so expands the supply of reserves just as was shown in Figure 2. Furthermore, because bank deposits, and hence required reserves, have not yet increased, this addition to the supply of bank reserves creates *excess reserves*, which should lead to an expansion of the money supply.

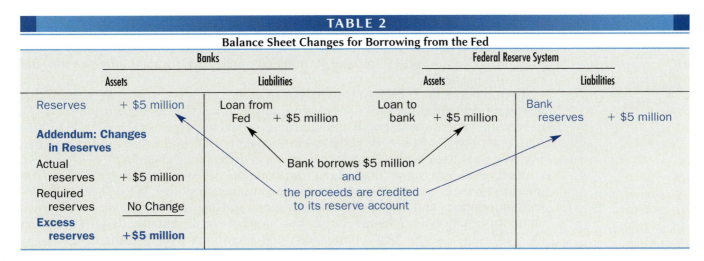

TABLE 2

Balance Sheet Changes for Borrowing from the Fed

| | Banks | | Federal Reserve System | |
	Assets	Liabilities	Assets	Liabilities
Reserves	+ $5 million	Loan from Fed + $5 million	Loan to bank + $5 million	Bank reserves + $5 million
Addendum: Changes in Reserves				
Actual reserves	+ $5 million			
Required reserves	No Change			
Excess reserves	**+$5 million**			

Bank borrows $5 million and the proceeds are credited to its reserve account

The **discount rate** is the interest rate the Fed charges on loans that it makes to banks.

Federal Reserve officials can try to influence the amount banks borrow by manipulating the *rate of interest charged on these loans*, which is known as the **discount rate.** If the Fed wants banks to have more reserves, it can reduce the interest rate that it charges on loans, thereby tempting banks to borrow more. Alternatively, it can soak up reserves by raising its rate and persuading the banks to reduce their borrowings.

But when it changes its discount rate, the Fed cannot know for sure how banks will react. Sometimes they may respond vigorously to a cut in the rate, borrowing a great deal from the Fed and lending a correspondingly large amount to their customers. At other times they may essentially ignore the change in the discount rate. So the link between the discount rate and the volume of bank reserves is apt to be quite loose.

Some foreign central banks use their versions of the discount rate *actively* as the centerpiece of monetary policy. But in the United States, the Fed lends infrequently and normally in very small amounts. Instead, it relies on open-market operations to conduct monetary policy. The Fed typically adjusts its discount rate *passively*, to keep it in line with market interest rates.

Changing Reserve Requirements

In principle, the Federal Reserve has another way to conduct monetary policy: varying the minimum required reserve ratio. To see how this works, imagine that banks hold reserves that just match their required minimums. In other words, excess reserves are zero. If the Fed decides that lower interest rates are warranted, it can reduce the required reserve ratio, thereby transforming some previously *required* reserves into *excess* reserves. No new reserves are created directly by this action. But we know from the previous chapter that such a change will set in motion a multiple expansion of the banking system. Looked at in terms of the market for bank reserves (Figure 1 on page 650), a reduction in reserve requirements shifts the demand curve *inward* (because banks no longer need as many reserves), thereby lowering interest rates. Similarly, raising the required reserve ratio will raise interest rates and set off a multiple contraction of the banking system.

In point of fact, however, the Fed has not used the reserve ratio as a weapon of monetary control for years. Current law and regulations provide for a reserve ratio of 10 percent against most transaction deposits—a figure that has not changed since 1992.

HOW MONETARY POLICY WORKS

Remembering that monetary policy actions by the Fed are almost always open-market operations, the two panels of Figure 4 illustrate the effects of *expansionary monetary policy* (an open-market purchase) and *contractionary monetary policy* (an open-market sale). Panel (a) looks just like Figure 2 on page 650. So expansionary monetary policy actions lower interest rates and contractionary monetary policy actions raise interest rates. But then what happens?

To find out, let's go back to the analysis of earlier chapters, where we learned that aggregate demand is the sum of consumption spending (C), investment spending (I), government purchases of goods and services (G), and net exports ($X - IM$). We know that *fiscal policy* controls G directly and influences both C and I through the tax laws. We now want to understand how *monetary policy* affects total spending.

Most economists agree that, of the four components of aggregate demand, investment and net exports are the most sensitive to monetary policy. We will study the effects of monetary and fiscal policy on net exports in Chapter 36, after we have learned about international exchange rates. For now, we will assume that net exports ($X - IM$) are *fixed* and focus on monetary policy's influence on investment (I).

Investment and Interest Rates

Business investment in new factories and machinery is sensitive to interest rates for reasons that were explained in earlier chapters.[7] Because the rate of interest that must be paid on borrowings is part of the cost of an investment, business executives will find investment prospects less attractive as interest rates rise. Therefore, they will spend less. Similarly, because the interest cost of a mortgage is the major component of the total cost of owning a home, fewer

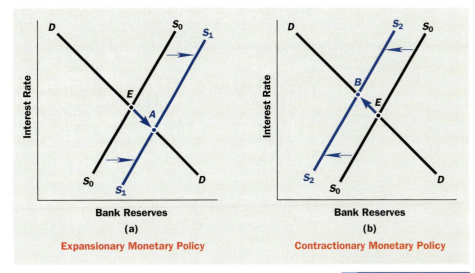

Bank Reserves
(a)
Expansionary Monetary Policy

Bank Reserves
(b)
Contractionary Monetary Policy

FIGURE 4

The Effects of Monetary Policy on Interest Rates

families will want to buy new houses when interest rates rise. Thus, higher interest rates will deter some individuals from *investment in housing*. We conclude that:

Higher interest rates lead to lower investment spending. But investment (*I*) is a component of total spending, $C + I + G + (X - IM)$. Therefore, when interest rates rise, total spending falls. In terms of the 45° line diagram of previous chapters, a higher interest rate leads to a lower expenditure schedule. Conversely, a lower interest rate leads to a higher expenditure schedule.

Figure 5 depicts this situation graphically.

Monetary Policy and Total Expenditure

The effect of interest rates on spending provides the chief mechanism by which monetary policy affects the macroeconomy. We know from our analysis of the market for bank reserves (summarized in Figure 4) that monetary policy can move interest rates up or down. Let us, therefore, outline the effects of monetary policy.

Suppose the Federal Reserve, seeing the economy stuck with high unemployment and a recessionary gap, increases the supply of bank reserves. It would normally do so by purchasing government securities in the open market, thereby shifting the supply schedule for reserves outward—as was indicated by the shift from the black line $S_0 S_0$ to the blue line $S_1 S_1$ in Figure 4(a).

With the demand schedule for bank reserves, *DD*, temporarily fixed, such a shift in the supply curve has the effect that an increase in supply always has in a free market: It lowers the price, as Figure 4(a) shows. In this case, the relevant price is the rate of interest that must be paid for borrowing reserves, *r* (the federal funds rate). So *r* falls.

Next, for reasons we have just outlined, investment spending (*I*) rises in response to the lower interest rates. But, as we learned in Chapter 26,

FIGURE 5

The Effect of Interest Rates on Total Expenditure

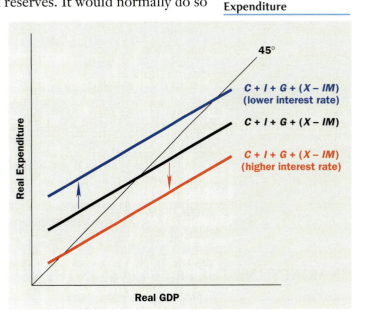

45°

$C + I + G + (X - IM)$
(lower interest rate)

$C + I + G + (X - IM)$

$C + I + G + (X - IM)$
(higher interest rate)

Real Expenditure

Real GDP

[7] See, for example, Chapter 24, page 523.

such an autonomous rise in investment kicks off a multiplier chain of increases in output and employment.

Finally, we have completed the links from the supply of bank reserves to the level of aggregate demand. In brief, monetary policy works as follows:

Expansionary monetary policy leads to lower interest rates (r), and these lower interest rates encourage investment (I), which has multiplier effects on aggregate demand.

This process operates equally well in reverse. By contracting bank reserves and the money supply, the Fed can force interest rates up, causing investment spending to fall and pulling down aggregate demand via the multiplier mechanism. This, in outline form, is how monetary influences the economy in the Keynesian model. Because the chain of causation is fairly long, the following schematic diagram may help clarify it:

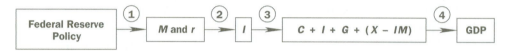

In this causal chain, Link 1 indicates that the Federal Reserve's open-market operations affect both interest rates and the money supply. Link 2 stands for the effect of interest rates on investment. Link 3 simply notes that investment is one component of total spending. Link 4 is the multiplier, relating an autonomous change in investment to the ultimate change in aggregate demand. To see what economists must study if they are to estimate the effects of monetary policy, let us briefly review what we know about each of these four links.

Link 1 is the subject of this chapter. It was depicted in Figure 4(a), which shows how injections of bank reserves by the Federal Reserve push the interest rate down. Thus, the first thing an economist must know is how sensitive interest rates are to changes in the supply of bank reserves.

Link 2 translates the lower interest rate into higher investment spending. To estimate this effect in practice, economists must study the sensitivity of investment to interest rates—a topic we first took up in Chapter 24.

Link 3 instructs us to enter the rise in I as an autonomous upward shift of the $C + I + G + (X - IM)$ schedule in a 45° line diagram. Figure 6 carries out this next step. The expenditure schedule rises from $C + I_0 + G + (X - IM)$ to $C + I_1 + G + (X - IM)$.

Finally, Link 4 applies multiplier analysis to this vertical shift in the expenditure schedule to obtain the eventual increase in real GDP demanded. This change is shown in Figure 6 as a shift in equilibrium from E_0 to E_1, which raises real GDP by $500 billion in the example. Of course, the size of the multiplier itself must also be estimated. To summarize:

The effect of monetary policy on aggregate demand depends on the sensitivity of interest rates to open-market operations, on the responsiveness of investment spending to the rate of interest, and on the size of the basic expenditure multiplier.

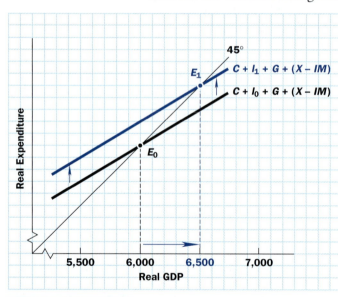

FIGURE 6

The Effect of Expansionary Monetary Policy on Total Expenditure

NOTE: Figures are in billions of dollars per year.

MONEY AND THE PRICE LEVEL IN THE KEYNESIAN MODEL

Our analysis up to this point leaves one important question unanswered: What happens to the price level? To find the answer, we must recall that aggregate demand *and* aggregate supply *jointly* determine prices and output. Our analysis of monetary policy so far has shown us how expansionary monetary policy boosts total spending: It increases the *aggregate quantity demanded at any given price level*. But to learn what happens to the price level and to real output, we must consider *aggregate supply* as well.

Specifically, when considering shifts in aggregate demand caused by *fiscal* policy in Chapter 28, we noted that an upsurge in total spending normally induces firms to increase output somewhat *and* to raise prices somewhat. This is precisely what an aggregate supply curve shows. Whether prices or real output responds more dramatically depends on the slope of the aggregate supply curve. Because this analysis of output and price responses applies equally well to monetary policy or, for that matter, to any other factor that raises aggregate demand, we conclude that:

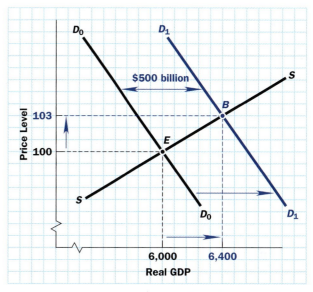

NOTE: GDP figures are in billions of dollars per year.

> **Expansionary monetary policy causes some inflation under normal circumstances. But exactly how much inflation it causes depends on the slope of the aggregate supply curve.**

The effect of expansionary monetary policy on the price level is shown graphically on an aggregate supply and demand diagram in Figure 7. In the example depicted in Figure 6, the Fed's actions lowered interest rates enough to increase aggregate demand (through the multiplier) by $500 billion. We enter this increase as a $500 billion *horizontal* shift of the aggregate demand curve in Figure 7, from D_0D_0 to D_1D_1. The diagram shows that this expansionary monetary policy pushes the economy's equilibrium from point E to point B—the price level therefore rises from 100 to 103, or 3 percent. The diagram also shows that real GDP rises by only $400 billion, which is less than the $500 billion stimulus to aggregate demand. The reason, as we know from earlier chapters, is that rising prices stifle real aggregate demand.

FIGURE 7

The Inflationary Effects of Expansionary Monetary Policy

By taking account of the effect of an increase in the money supply on the price level, we have completed our story about the role of monetary policy in the Keynesian model. We can thus expand our schematic diagram of monetary policy as follows:

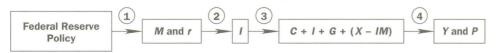

The last link now recognizes that *both* output *and* prices normally are affected by changes in interest rates and the money supply.

Application: Why the Aggregate Demand Curve Slopes Downward[8]

This analysis of the effect of monetary policy on the price level puts us in a better position to understand why higher prices reduce aggregate quantity demanded—that is, why the aggregate demand curve slopes downward. In earlier chapters, we explained this phenomenon in two ways. First, we observed that rising prices reduce the purchasing power of certain assets held by consumers, especially money and government bonds, and that falling real wealth in turn retards consumption spending. Second, we noted that higher domestic prices depress exports and stimulate imports.

There is nothing wrong with this analysis; it is just incomplete. Higher prices have another important effect on aggregate demand, through a channel that we are now in a position to understand.

---

[8] This section contains somewhat more difficult material which can be skipped in shorter courses.

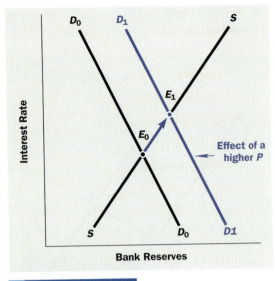

FIGURE 8

The Effect of a Higher
Price Level on the
Market for Bank
Reserves

Bank deposits are demanded primarily to conduct transactions. As we noted earlier in this chapter, an increase in the *average money cost* of each transaction—that is, a rise in the price level—will increase the quantity of deposits, and hence increase the quantity of reserves demanded. (Hence the label on the demand curve in Figure 1 on page 650.) Thus, when spending rises for any reason, the price level will also rise and more reserves will therefore be demanded at any given interest rate—that is, the demand curve in Figure 1 will shift outward to the right.

If the Fed does not increase the *supply* of reserves, this outward shift of the demand curve will force the cost of borrowing reserves—the federal funds rate—to rise, as Figure 8 shows. As we know, increases in interest rates reduce investment and, hence, reduce aggregate demand. This is the main reason why the economy's aggregate demand curve has a negative slope, meaning that aggregate quantity demanded is lower when prices are higher. In sum:

At higher price levels, the quantity of bank reserves demanded is greater. If the Fed holds the supply schedule fixed, a higher price level must therefore lead to higher interest rates. Because higher interest rates discourage investment, aggregate quantity demanded is lower when the price level is higher—that is, the aggregate demand curve has a negative slope.

■ FROM MODELS TO POLICY DEBATES

You will no doubt be relieved to hear that we have now provided just about all the technical apparatus we need to analyze stabilization policy. To be sure, you will encounter many graphs in the next few chapters. Most of them, however, repeat diagrams with which you are already familiar. Our attention now turns from *building* a theory to *using* that theory to address several important policy issues.

The next three chapters take up a trio of controversial policy debates that surface regularly in the newspapers: the debate over the conduct of stabilization policy (Chapter 31), the continuing debate over budget deficits and the effects of fiscal and monetary policy on growth (Chapter 32), and the controversy over the trade-off between inflation and unemployment (Chapter 33).

SUMMARY

1. A **central bank** is bank for banks.

2. The Federal Reserve System is America's central bank. There are 12 Federal Reserve banks, but most of the power is held by the Board of Governors in Washington and by the Federal Open Market Committee.

3. The Federal Reserve acts independently of the rest of the government. Over the past 20 to 25 years, many countries have decided that **central bank independence** is a good idea and have moved in this direction.

4. The Fed has three major monetary policy weapons: **open-market operations,** reserve requirements, and its lending

policy to banks. But only open-market operations are used frequently.

5. The Fed increases the supply of bank reserves by purchasing government securities in the open market. When it pays banks for such purchases by creating new reserves, the Fed lowers interest rates and induces a multiple expansion of the money supply. Conversely, open-market sales of securities take reserves from banks, raise interest rates, and lead to a contraction of the money supply.

6. When the Fed buys bonds, bond prices rise and interest rates fall. When the Fed sells bonds, bond prices fall and interest rates rise.

7. The Fed can also pursue a more expansionary monetary policy by allowing banks to borrow more reserves, perhaps by reducing the interest rate it charges on such loans, or by reducing reserve requirements.

8. None of these weapons, however, gives the Fed perfect control over the money supply in the short run, because it cannot predict perfectly how far the process of deposit creation or destruction will go. The Fed can, however, control the interest rate paid to borrow bank reserves, which is called the **federal funds rate**, much more tightly.

9. Investment spending (*I*), including business investment and investment in new homes, is sensitive to interest rates (*r*). Specifically, *I* is lower when *r* is higher.

10. **Monetary policy** works in the following way in the Keynesian model: Raising the supply of bank reserves leads to lower interest rates; the lower interest rates stimulate investment spending; and this investment stimulus, via the multiplier, then raises aggregate demand.

11. Prices are likely to rise as output rises. The amount of inflation caused by expansionary monetary policy depends on the slope of the aggregate supply curve. Much inflation will occur if the supply curve is steep, but little inflation if it is flat.

12. The main reason why the aggregate demand curve slopes downward is that higher prices increase the demand for bank deposits, and hence for bank reserves. Given a fixed supply of reserves, this higher demand pushes interest rates up, which, in turn, discourages investment.

KEY TERMS

Monetary policy   646

Central bank   647

Federal Reserve System   647

Federal Open Market Committee (FOMC)   647

Central bank independence   648

Open-market operations   649

Equilibrium in the market for bank reserves   649

Federal funds rate   649

Bond prices and interest rates   652

Federal Reserve lending to banks   653

Discount rate   654

Reserve requirements   654

Why the aggregate demand curve slopes downward   657

TEST YOURSELF

1. Suppose there is $120 billion of cash and that half of this cash is held in bank vaults as *required* reserves (that is, banks hold no *excess* reserves). How large will the money supply be if the required reserve ratio is 10 percent? 12½ percent? 16⅔ percent?

2. Show the balance sheet changes that would take place if the Federal Reserve Bank of New York purchased an office building from Citigroup for a price of $100 million. Compare this effect to the effect of an open-market purchase of securities shown in Table 1. What do you conclude?

3. Suppose the Fed purchases $5 billion worth of government bonds from Bill Gates, who banks at the Bank of America in San Francisco. Show the effects on the balance sheets of the Fed, the Bank of America, and Gates. (*Hint:* Where will the Fed get the $5 billion to pay Gates?) Does it make any difference if the Fed buys bonds from a bank or an individual?

4. Treasury bills have a fixed face value (say, $1000) and pay interest by selling "at a discount." For example, if a one-year bill with a $1,000 face value sells today for $950, it will pay $1,000 − $950 = $50 in interest over its life. The interest rate on the bill is therefore $50/$950 = 0.0526, or 5.26 percent.

   a. Suppose the price of the Treasury bill falls to $925. What happens to the interest rate?

   b. Suppose, instead, that the price rises to $975. What is the interest rate now?

   c. (**More difficult**) Now generalize this example. Let *P* be the price of the bill and *r* be the interest rate. Develop an algebraic formula expressing *r* in terms of *P*. (*Hint:* The interest earned is $1,000 − *P*. What is the *percentage* interest rate?) Show that this formula illustrates the point made in the text: Higher bond prices mean lower interest rates.

5. Explain what a $5 billion increase in bank reserves will do to real GDP under the following assumptions:

   a. Each $1 billion increase in bank reserves reduces the rate of interest by 0.5 percentage point.

   b. Each 1 percentage point decline in interest rates stimulates $30 billion worth of new investment.

   c. The expenditure multiplier is 2.

   d. The aggregate supply curve is so flat that prices do not rise noticeably when demand increases.

6. Explain how your answers to Test Yourself Question 5 would differ if each of the assumptions changed. Specifically, what sorts of changes in the assumptions would weaken the effects of monetary policy?

7. (**More difficult**) Consider an economy in which government purchases, taxes, and net exports are all zero, the consumption function is

$$C = 300 + 0.75Y$$

and investment spending (*I*) depends on the rate of interest (*r*) in the following way:

$$I = 1,000 - 100r$$

Find the equilibrium GDP if the Fed makes the rate of interest (a) 2 percent (*r* = 0.02), (b) 5 percent, and (c) 10 percent.

DISCUSSION QUESTIONS

1. Why does a modern industrial economy need a central bank?

2. What are some reasons behind the worldwide trend toward greater central bank independence? Are there arguments on the other side?

3. Explain why the quantity of bank reserves supplied normally is higher and the quantity of bank reserves demanded normally is lower at higher interest rates.

4. From January 2001 through June 2003, the Fed believed that interest rates needed to fall and took step after step to reduce them, eventually cutting the federal funds rate from 6.5 percent to 1 percent. How did the Fed reduce the federal funds rate? Illustrate your answer on a diagram.

5. Explain why both business investments and purchases of new homes rise when interest rates decline.

6. In the late 1990s, the federal government eliminated its budget deficit by reducing its spending. If the Federal Reserve wanted to maintain the same level of aggregate demand in the face of large-scale deficit reduction, what should it have done? What would you expect to happen to interest rates?

31

THE DEBATE OVER MONETARY AND FISCAL POLICY

The love of money is the root of all evil.

THE NEW TESTAMENT

Lack of money is the root of all evil.

GEORGE BERNARD SHAW

U p to now, our discussion of stabilization policy has been almost entirely objective and technical. In seeking to understand how the national economy works and how government policies affect it, we have mostly ignored the intense economic and political controversies that surround the actual conduct of monetary and fiscal policy. Chapters 31 through 33 cover precisely these issues.

We begin this chapter by introducing an alternative theory of how monetary policy affects the economy, known as *monetarism*. Although the monetarist and Keynesian *theories* seem to contradict one another, we will see that the conflict is more apparent than real. However, important differences *do* arise among economists over the appropriate design and execution of monetary *policy*. These differences are the central concern of the chapter. We will learn about the continuing debates over the nature of aggregate supply, over the relative virtues of monetary versus fiscal policy, and over whether the Federal Reserve should try to control the money stock or interest rates. As we will see, the resolution of these issues is crucial to the proper conduct of stabilization policy and, indeed, to the decision of whether the government should try to stabilize the economy at all.

CONTENTS

ISSUE: *Should We Forsake Stabilization Policy?*

We have suggested several times in this book that well-timed changes in fiscal or monetary policy can mitigate fluctuations in inflation and unemployment. For example, when the U.S. economy sagged after the terrorist attacks in September 2001, *both* fiscal policy *and* monetary policy turned more expansionary. These actions might be called "textbook responses," reflecting the lessons you have learned in Chapters 28 and 30.

But some economists argue that these lessons are best forgotten. In practice, they claim, attempts at macroeconomic stabilization are likely to do more harm than good. Policy makers are therefore best advised to follow fixed *rules* rather than use their best judgment on a case-by-case basis.

Nothing we have said so far leads to this conclusion. But we have not yet told the whole story. By the end of the chapter you will have encountered several arguments in favor of rules, and so you will be in a better position to make up your own mind on this important issue.

■ VELOCITY AND THE QUANTITY THEORY OF MONEY

Velocity indicates the number of times per year that an "average dollar" is spent on goods and services. It is the ratio of nominal gross domestic product (GDP) to the number of dollars in the money stock. That is:

$$Velocity = \frac{Nominal\ GDP}{Money\ stock}$$

In the previous chapter, we studied the *Keynesian* view of how monetary policy influences real output and the price level. But another, older model provides a different way to look at these matters. This model, known as the *quantity theory of money*, will be easy to understand once we introduce one new concept: **velocity.**

In Chapter 29, we learned that because barter is so cumbersome, virtually all economic transactions in advanced economies use money. Thus, if there are $10 trillion worth of transactions in an economy during a particular year, and there is an average money stock of $2 trillion during that year, then each dollar of money must have been used an average of five times during the year.

The number 5 in this example is called the *velocity of circulation*, or *velocity* for short, because it indicates the *speed* at which money circulates. For example, a particular dollar bill might be used to buy a haircut in January; the barber might use it to purchase a sweater in March; the storekeeper might then use it to pay for gasoline in May; the gas station owner could pay it out to a house painter in October; and the painter might spend it on a Christmas present in December. In this way, the same dollar is used five times during the year. If it were used only four times during the year, its velocity would be 4, and so on.

No one has data on every transaction in the economy. To make velocity an operational concept, economists need a workable measure of the dollar volume of all transactions. As mentioned in the previous chapter, the most popular choice is nominal gross domestic product (GDP), even though it ignores many transactions that use money, such as the huge volume of activity in financial markets. If we accept nominal GDP as our measure of the money value of transactions, we are led to a concrete definition of velocity as the ratio of nominal GDP to the number of dollars in the money stock. Because nominal GDP is the product of real GDP (Y) times the price level (P), we can write this definition in symbols as follows:

$$\textbf{Velocity} = \frac{\textbf{Value of transactions}}{\textbf{Money stock}} = \frac{\textbf{Nominal GDP}}{\textbf{M}} = \frac{\textbf{P} \times \textbf{Y}}{\textbf{M}}$$

The **equation of exchange** states that the money value of GDP transactions must be equal to the product of the average stock of money times velocity. That is:

$$M \times V = P \times Y$$

By multiplying both sides of the equation by M, we arrive at an identity called the **equation of exchange,** which relates the money supply and nominal GDP:

$$\textbf{Money supply} \times \textbf{Velocity} = \textbf{Nominal GDP}$$

Alternatively, stated in symbols, we have:

$$M \times V = P \times Y$$

Here we have an obvious link between the stock of money, M, and the nominal value of the nation's output, $P \times Y$. This connection is merely a matter of arithmetic, however—not of economics. For example, it does not imply that the Fed can raise nominal GDP by increasing M. Why not? Because V might simultaneously fall enough to prevent the product $M \times V$ from rising. In other words, if more dollar bills circulated than before, but each bill changed hands more slowly, total spending might not rise. Thus, we need an auxiliary assumption to change the arithmetic identity into an economic theory:

> The **quantity theory of money** transforms the equation of exchange from an arithmetic identity into an economic model by assuming that changes in velocity are so minor that velocity can be taken to be virtually constant.

You can see that if V never changed, the equation of exchange would be a marvelously simple model of the determination of nominal GDP—far simpler than the Keynesian model that took us several chapters to develop. To see this, it is convenient to rewrite the equation of exchange in growth-rate form:

$$\%\Delta M + \%\Delta V = \%\Delta P + \%\Delta Y$$

If V was constant (making its percentage change zero), this equation would say, for example, that if the Federal Reserve wanted to make nominal GDP grow by 4.7 percent per year, it need merely raise the money supply by 4.7 percent per year. In such a simple world, economists could use the equation of exchange to *predict* nominal GDP growth by predicting the growth rate of money. And policy makers could *control* nominal GDP growth by controlling growth of the money supply.

In the real world, things are not so simple because velocity is not a fixed number. But variable velocity does not necessarily destroy the usefulness of the quantity theory. As we explained in Chapter 1, all economic models make assumptions that are at least mildly unrealistic. Without such assumptions, they would not be models at all, just tedious descriptions of reality. The question is really whether the assumption of constant velocity is a useful abstraction from annoying detail or a gross distortion of the facts.

Figure 1 sheds some light on this question by showing the behavior of velocity since 1929. Note that the figure includes two different measures of velocity, labeled V_1 and V_2. Why? Recall from Chapter 29 that we can measure money in several ways, the most popular of which are M1 and M2. Because velocity (V) is simply nominal GDP divided by the money stock (M), we get a *different* measure of V for *each* measure of M. Figure 1 shows the velocities of both M1 and M2.

The **quantity theory of money** assumes that velocity is (approximately) constant. In that case, nominal GDP is proportional to the money stock.

SOURCE: Constructed by the authors; data from Bureau of Economic Analysis, Federal Reserve Board, and Robert Rasche.

FIGURE 1

Velocity of Circulation, 1929–2006

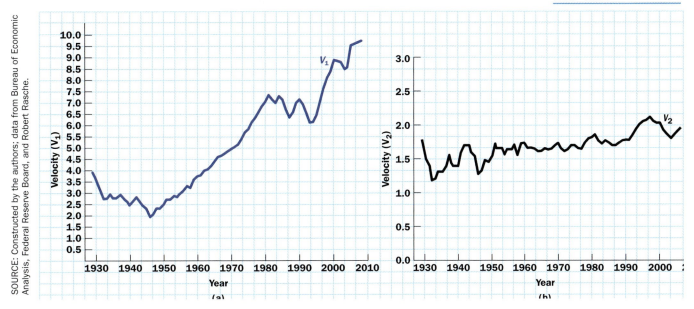

(a)

(b)

You will undoubtedly notice the stark difference in the behavior of V_1 versus V_2. V_1 is nowhere near constant; it displays a clear downward trend from 1929 until 1946, a pronounced upward trend until about 1981, and quite erratic behavior since then. V_2 is much closer to constant, but it has risen noticeably since the 1980s. Furthermore, closer examination of monthly or quarterly data reveals rather substantial fluctuations in velocity, by either measure. Because velocity is not constant in the short run, predictions of nominal GDP growth based on assuming constant velocity have not fared well, regardless of how M is measured. In a word, the strict quantity theory of money is not an adequate model of aggregate demand.

◼ Some Determinants of Velocity

Because it is abundantly clear that velocity is a variable, not a constant, the equation of exchange is useful as a model of GDP determination only if we can explain movements in velocity. What factors decide whether a dollar will be used to buy goods and services four or five or six times per year? While numerous factors are relevant, two are important enough to merit discussion here.

Efficiency of the Payments System   Money is convenient for conducting transactions, which is why people hold it. But money has one important *dis*advantage: Cash pays no interest, and ordinary checking accounts pay very little. Thus, if it were possible to convert interest-bearing assets into money on short notice and at low cost, a rational individual might prefer to use, say, credit cards for most purchases, making periodic transfers to her checking account as necessary. That way, the same volume of transactions could be accomplished with lower money balances. By definition, velocity would rise.

The incentive to limit cash holdings thus depends on the ease and speed with which it is possible to exchange money for other assets—which is what we mean by the "efficiency of the payments system." As computerization has speeded up banks' bookkeeping procedures, as financial innovations have made it possible to transfer funds rapidly between checking accounts and other assets, and as credit cards have come to be used instead of cash, the need to hold money balances has declined and velocity has risen.

In practice, improvements in the payments system pose severe practical problems for analysts interested in predicting velocity. A host of financial innovations, beginning in the 1970s and continuing right to the present day (some of which were mentioned in Chapter 29's discussion of the definitions of money), have transformed forecasting velocity into a hazardous occupation. In fact, many economists believe the task is impossible and should not even be attempted.

Interest Rates   A second key determinant of velocity is the rate of interest. The reason is implicit in what we have already said: The higher the rate of interest, the greater the *opportunity cost* of holding money. Therefore, as interest rates rise, people want to hold smaller cash balances. So the existing stock of money circulates faster, and velocity rises.

It is this factor that most directly undercuts the usefulness of the quantity theory of money as a guide for monetary policy. In the previous chapter, we learned that expansionary monetary policy, which increases bank reserves and the money supply, also decreases the interest rate. But if interest rates fall, other things being equal, velocity (V) also falls. Thus, *when the Fed raises the money supply (M), the product $M \times V$ should increase by a smaller percentage than does M itself.*

Thus, we conclude that:

Velocity is not a strict constant but depends on such things as the efficiency of the financial system and the rate of interest. Only by studying these determinants of velocity can we hope to predict the growth rate of nominal GDP from knowledge of the growth rate of the money supply.

Monetarism: The Quantity Theory Modernized

Adherents to a school of thought called **monetarism** try to do precisely that. Monetarists realize that velocity changes, but they claim that such changes are fairly *predictable*—certainly in the long run and perhaps even in the short run. As a result, they conclude that the best way to study economic activity is to start with the equation of exchange in growth-rate form:

Monetarism is a mode of analysis that uses the equation of exchange to organize and analyze macroeconomic data.

$$\%\Delta M + \%\Delta V = \%\Delta P + \%\Delta Y$$

From here, careful study of the determinants of money growth (which we provided in the previous two chapters) and of changes in velocity (which we just sketched) can be used to *predict* the growth rate of nominal GDP. Similarly, given an understanding of movements in V, controlling M can give the Fed excellent control over nominal GDP. These ideas are the central tenets of monetarism.

The monetarist and Keynesian approaches can be thought of as alternative theories of aggregate demand. Keynesians divide economic knowledge into four neat compartments marked C, I, G, and $(X - IM)$ and unite them all with the equilibrium condition that $Y = C + I + G + (X - IM)$. In Keynesian analysis, money affects the economy by first affecting interest rates. Monetarists, by contrast, organize their knowledge into two alternative boxes labeled M and V, and then use the identity $M \times V = P \times Y$ to predict aggregate demand. In the monetarist model, the role of money is not necessarily limited to working through interest rates.

The bit of arithmetic that multiplies M and V to get $P \times Y$ is neither more nor less profound than the one that adds up C, I, G and $(X - IM)$ to get Y, and certainly both are correct. The real question is which framework is more *useful* in practice. That is, which approach works better as a model of aggregate demand?

Although there is no generally correct answer for all economies in all periods of time, a glance back at Figure 1 (page 663) will show you why most economists had abandoned monetarism by the early 1990s. During the 1960s and 1970s, velocity (at least V_2) was fairly stable, which helped monetarism win many converts—in the United States and around the world. Since then, however, velocity has behaved so erratically here and in many other countries that there are few monetarists left.

Nonetheless, as we will see later in this chapter, some faint echoes of the debate between Keynesians and monetarists can still be heard. Furthermore, few economists doubt that there is a strong *long-run* relationship between M and P. They just question whether this relationship is useful in the short run. (See the box "Does Money Growth Always Cause Inflation?" on the next page.)

FISCAL POLICY, INTEREST RATES, AND VELOCITY

As we learned in the previous chapter, Keynesian economics provides a powerful and important role for *monetary* policy: An increase in bank reserves and the money supply reduces interest rates, which, in turn, stimulates the demand for investment. But *fiscal* policy also exerts a powerful influence on interest rates.

To see how, think about what happens to real output and the price level following, say, a rise in government spending. We have learned that both real GDP (Y) and the price level (P) rise, so nominal GDP certainly rises. But the previous chapter's analysis of the market for bank reserves taught us that rising prices and/or rising output—by increasing the volume of transactions—push the demand curve for bank deposits, and therefore for reserves, outward to the right. With no change in the supply of reserves, the rate of interest must rise. *So expansionary fiscal policy raises interest rates.*

POLICY DEBATE

Does Money Growth Always Cause Inflation?

Monetarists have long claimed that, in the famous words of the late Milton Friedman, "inflation is always and everywhere a monetary phenomenon." By this statement, Friedman meant that changes in the growth rate of the money supply (%ΔM) are far and away the principal cause of changes in the inflation rate (%ΔP)—in all places and at all times.

Few economists question the dominant role of rapid money growth in accounting for extremely high rates of inflation. During the German hyperinflation of the 1920s, for example, money was being printed so fast that the printing presses had a difficult time keeping up the pace! But most economists question the words "always and everywhere" in Friedman's dictum. Aren't many cases of moderate inflation driven by factors other than the growth rate of the money supply?

The answer appears to be "yes." The accompanying charts use recent U.S. history as an illustration. In the scatter diagram on the left, each point records both the growth rate of the M2 money supply and the inflation rate (as measured by the Consumer Price Index) for a particular year between 1979 and 2006. Because of the years 1979–1981, there seems to be a weak positive relationship between the two variables. But no relationship at all appears for the years 1982–2006.

Monetarists often argue that this comparison is unfair because the effect of money supply growth on inflation operates with a lag of perhaps two years. So the right hand scatter diagram compares inflation with money supply growth *two years earlier.* It tells essentially the same story. More sophisticated versions of scatter plots like these have led most economists to reject the monetarist claim that inflation and money supply growth are tightly linked.

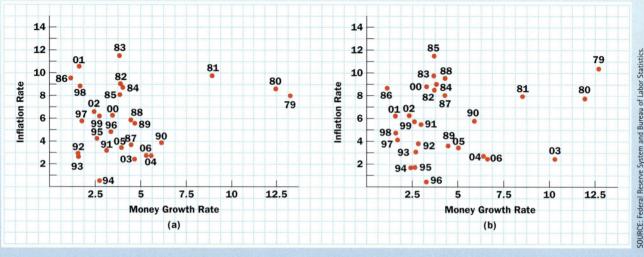

NOTE: All figures are in percent.

SOURCE: Federal Reserve System and Bureau of Labor Statistics.

If the government uses its spending and taxing weapons in the opposite direction, the same process works in reverse. Falling output and (possibly) falling prices shift the demand curve for reserves inward to the left. With a fixed supply curve, equilibrium in the market for reserves leads to a lower interest rate. Thus:

Monetary policy is not the only type of policy that affects interest rates. Fiscal policy does, too. Specifically, increases in government spending or tax cuts normally push interest rates up, whereas restrictive fiscal policies normally pull interest rates down.

The apparently banal fact that changes in fiscal policy move interest rates up and down has several important consequences. Here are two.

■ Application: The Multiplier Formula Revisited

We have just noted that expansionary fiscal policy raises interest rates. We also know that higher interest rates deter private investment spending. So when the government raises the G component of $C + I + G + (X - IM)$, one side effect will probably be a reduction in the I component. Consequently, total spending will rise by *less* than simple multiplier analysis might suggest. The fact that a surge in government demand (G) discourages some private demand (I) provides another reason why the oversimplified multiplier formula of earlier chapters, $1/(1 - MPC)$, exaggerates the size of the multiplier:

> Because a rise in G (or, for that matter, an autonomous rise in any component of total expenditure) pushes interest rates higher, and hence deters some investment spending, the increase in the sum $C + I + G + (X - IM)$ is smaller than what the oversimplified multiplier formula predicts.

Combining this observation with our previous analysis of the multiplier, we now have the following complete list of

REASONS WHY THE OVERSIMPLIFIED FORMULA OVERSTATES THE MULTIPLIER

1. It ignores variable imports, which reduce the size of the multiplier.
2. It ignores price-level changes, which reduce the size of the multiplier.
3. It ignores the income tax, which reduces the size of the multiplier.
4. It ignores the rising interest rates that accompany any autonomous increase in spending, which also reduce the size of the multiplier.

With so many reasons, it is no wonder that the actual multiplier, which is estimated to be less than two for the U.S. economy, is so much less than the oversimplified formula suggests.

◼ Application: The Government Budget and Investment

One major argument for reducing the government's budget deficit is that lower deficits should lead to higher levels of private investment spending. We can now understand why. The government reduces its deficit by engaging in *contractionary* fiscal policies—lower spending or higher taxes. As we have just seen, any such measure should *reduce* real interest rates. These lower real interest rates should spur investment spending. This simple insight will play a major role in the next chapter.

◼ DEBATE: SHOULD WE RELY ON FISCAL OR MONETARY POLICY?

The Keynesian and monetarist approaches are like two different languages. But it is well known that language influences attitudes in subtle ways. For example, the Keynesian language biases things toward thinking first about fiscal policy simply because G is a part of $C + I + G + (X - IM)$. By contrast, the monetarist approach, working through the equation of exchange, $M \times V = P \times Y$, puts the spotlight on M. In fact, years ago economists engaged in a spirited debate in which extreme monetarists claimed that fiscal policy was futile, whereas extreme Keynesians argued that monetary policy was useless. Today, such arguments are rarely heard.

Instead of arguing over which type of policy is more *powerful*, economists nowadays debate which type of medicine—fiscal or monetary—cures the patient more *quickly*. Until now, we have ignored questions of timing and pretended that the authorities noticed the need for stabilization policy instantly, decided on a course of action right away, and administered the appropriate medicine at once. In reality, each of these steps takes time.

First, delays in data collection mean that the most recent data describe the state of the economy a few months ago. Second, one of the prices of democracy is that the government often takes a distressingly long time to decide what should be done, to muster the necessary political support, and to put its decisions into effect. Finally, our $12 trillion economy is a bit like a sleeping elephant that reacts rather sluggishly to moderate fiscal and monetary prods. As it turns out, these *lags in stabilization policy*, as they are called, play a pivotal role in the choice between fiscal and monetary policy. Here's why.

The main policy tool for manipulating consumer spending (C) is the personal income tax, and Chapter 25 documented why the fiscal policy planner can feel fairly confident that each $1 of tax reduction will lead to about 90 to 95 cents of additional spending *eventually*. But not all of this extra spending happens at once.

First, consumers must learn about the tax change. Then they may need to be convinced that the change is permanent. Finally, there is simple force of habit: Households need time to adjust their spending habits when circumstances change. For all these reasons, consumers may increase their spending by only 30 to 50 cents for each $1 of additional income within the first few months after a tax cut. Only gradually will they raise their spending up to about 90 to 95 cents for each additional dollar of income.

Lags are much longer for investment (I), which provides the main vehicle by which monetary policy affects aggregate demand. Planning for capacity expansion in a large corporation is a long, drawn-out process. Ideas must be submitted and approved, plans must be drawn up, funding acquired, orders for machinery or contracts for new construction placed. And most of this activity occurs *before* any appreciable amount of money is spent. Economists have found that much of the response of investment to changes in either interest rates or tax provisions takes several *years* to develop.

The fact that C responds more quickly than I has important implications for the choice among alternative stabilization policies. The reason is that the most common varieties of fiscal policy either affect aggregate demand directly—G is a component of $C + I + G + (X - IM)$—or work through consumption with a relatively short lag, whereas monetary policy primarily affects investment. Therefore:

Conventional types of fiscal policy actions, such as changes in G or in personal taxes, probably affect aggregate demand much more promptly than do monetary policy actions.

So is fiscal policy therefore a superior stabilization tool? Not necessarily. The lags we have just described, which are beyond policy makers' control, are not the only ones affecting the timing of stabilization policy. Additional lags stem from the behavior of the policy makers themselves! We refer here to the delays that occur while policy makers study the state of the economy, contemplate which steps they should take, and put their decisions into effect.

Here monetary policy has a huge advantage. The Federal Open Market Committee (FOMC) meets eight times each year, and more often if necessary. So monetary policy decisions are made frequently. And once the Fed decides on a course of action, it executes its plan immediately by buying or selling Treasury bills in the open market.

In contrast, federal budgeting procedures operate on an annual budget cycle. Except in unusual cases, major fiscal policy initiatives can occur only at the time of the annual budget. In principle, tax laws can be changed at any time, but the wheels of Congress grind slowly and are often gummed up by partisan politics. For these reasons, it may take many months for Congress to change fiscal policy. President George W. Bush's tax cut proposal in 2001 was in some sense the proverbial exception that proves the rule. Congress passed it in record time—but that still took about four months. In sum, only in rare circumstances can the government take important fiscal policy actions on short notice. Thus:

Policy lags are normally much shorter for monetary policy than for fiscal policy.

So where does the combined effect of expenditure lags and policy lags leave us? With nothing very conclusive, we are afraid. In practice, however, most students of stabilization policy have come to believe that the unwieldy and often partisan nature of our political system make active use of fiscal policy for stabilization purposes difficult, if not impossible. Monetary policy, they claim, is the only realistic game in town, and therefore must bear the entire burden of stabilization policy.

■ DEBATE: SHOULD THE FED CONTROL THE MONEY SUPPLY OR INTEREST RATES?

Another major controversy that raged for decades focused on how the Federal Reserve should conduct monetary policy. Most economists argued that the Fed should use its open-market operations to control the rate of interest (r), which is how we have portrayed monetary policy up to now. But others, especially monetarists, insisted that the Fed should concentrate on controlling bank reserves or some measure of the money supply (*M*) instead. This debate echoes even today in Europe, where the European Central Bank (ECB), unlike the Fed, *claims* to pay considerable attention to the growth of the money supply. (Many skeptics doubt that it actually does, however.)

To understand the nature of this debate, we must first understand why the Fed cannot control both *M* and *r* at the same time. Figure 2 will help us see why. It looks just like Figure 8 of the previous chapter (see page 658), except that the horizontal axis now measures the *money supply* instead of *bank reserves*. The switch from reserves to money is justified by something we learned in earlier chapters that the money supply is "built up" from the Fed's supply of bank reserves via the process of multiple expansion.[1] As you will recall, this leads to an approximately proportional relationship between the two—meaning that if bank

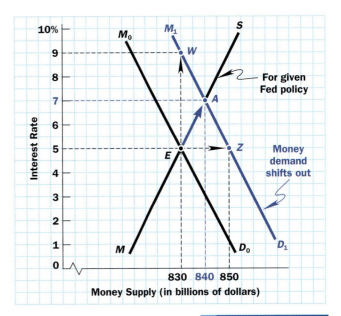

FIGURE 2

The Federal Reserve's Policy Dilemma

reserves go up by *X* percent then the money supply rises by approximately *X* percent.[2] Because *M* is basically proportional to bank reserves, anything we can analyze in the market for reserves can be analyzed in just the same way in the market for *money*—which is the market depicted in Figure 2.

The diagram shows an initial equilibrium in the money market at point *E*, where money demand curve M_0D_0 crosses money supply curve *MS*. Here the interest rate is *r* = 5 percent and the money stock is *M* = $830 billion. We assume that these are the Fed's targets: It wants to keep the money supply and interest rates just where they are.

If the demand curve for money holds still, everything works out fine. But suppose the demand for money is not so obliging. Suppose, instead, that the demand curve shifts outward to the position indicated by the blue line M_1D_1 in Figure 2. We learned in the previous chapter that such a shift might occur because output increases or because prices rise, thereby increasing the volume of transactions. Or it might happen simply because people decide to hold more bank deposits. But whatever the reason, the Fed can no longer achieve *both* of its previous targets.

If the Fed does nothing, the outward shift of the demand curve will push up both the quantity of money (*M*) and the rate of interest (*r*). Figure 2 shows these changes graphically as the move from point *E* to point *A*. If the demand curve for money shifts outward from M_0D_0 to M_1D_1, and monetary policy does not change (so the supply schedule does not move), the money stock rises to $840 billion and the interest rate rises to 7 percent.

Now suppose the Fed is targeting the money supply and is unwilling to let *M* rise. In that case, it must use *contractionary* open-market operations to prevent *M* from rising. But in so doing, it will push *r* up even higher, as point W in Figure 2 shows. After the demand curve for money shifts outward, point *E* is no longer attainable. The Fed must instead choose from among the points on the blue line M_1D_1, and point *W* is the point on this line that keeps the money supply at $830 billion. The Fed can hold *M* at $830 billion by reducing bank reserves just enough to push the money supply curve *inward* so that it passes through point *W*. (Pencil this shift in for yourself on the diagram.) But the interest rate will skyrocket to 9 percent.

Alternatively, if the Federal Reserve is pursuing an interest rate target, it might decide that the rise in *r* must be avoided. In this case, the Fed would be forced to engage in *expansionary* open-market operations to prevent the outward shift of the demand

---

[1] If you need to review this process, turn back to Chapter 29, especially pages 636–642.

[2] For further details on this proportionality relationship, including some numerical examples, see Test Yourself Question 5 at the end of this chapter.

curve for money from pushing r up. In terms of Figure 2, the interest rate can be held at 5 percent by adding just enough bank reserves to shift the money supply curve *outward* so that it passes through point Z. But doing this will push the money supply up to $850 billion. (Again, try penciling in the requisite shift of the money supply schedule.) To summarize this discussion:

> When the demand curve for money shifts outward, the Fed must tolerate a rise in interest rates, a rise in the money stock, or both. It cannot control *both* the supply of money *and* the interest rate. If it tries to keep *M* steady, then *r* will rise even more. Conversely, if it tries to stabilize *r,* then *M* will rise even more.

Two Imperfect Alternatives

For years, economists debated how a central bank should deal with its inability to control both the money supply and the rate of interest. Should it adhere rigidly to a target growth path for bank reserves and the money supply, regardless of the consequences for interest rates—which is the monetarist policy? Should it hold interest rates steady, even if that requires sharp gyrations in reserves and the money stock—which is roughly what the Fed does now? Or is some middle ground more appropriate? Let us first explore the issues and then consider what has actually been done.

The main problem with imposing rigid targets on the *supply* of money is that the *demand* for money does not cooperate by growing smoothly and predictably from month to month; instead it dances around quite a bit in the short run. This variability presents the recommendation to control the money supply with two problems:

1. It is almost impossible to achieve. Because the volume of money in existence depends on *both* the demand *and* the supply curves, keeping M on target in the face of significant fluctuations in the demand for money would require exceptional dexterity.
2. For reasons just explained, rigid adherence to money-stock targets might lead to wide fluctuations in interest rates, which could create an unsettled atmosphere for business decisions.

But powerful objections can also be raised against exclusive concentration on interest rate movements. Because increases in output and prices shift the demand schedule for money outward (as shown in Figure 2), a central bank determined to keep interest rates from rising would have to expand the money supply in response. Conversely, when GDP sagged, it would have to contract the money supply to keep rates from falling. Thus, interest rate pegging would make the money supply expand in boom times and contract in recessions, with potentially grave consequences for the stability of the economy. Ironically, this is precisely the sort of monetary behavior the Federal Reserve System was designed to prevent. Hence, if the Fed is to control interest rates, it had better formulate flexible targets, not fixed ones.

What Has the Fed Actually Done?

For most of post–World War II history, the predominant view held that the interest rate was much more important of the two targets. The rationale was that gyrating interest rates would cause abrupt and unsettling changes in investment spending, which in turn would make the entire economy fluctuate. Stabilizing interest rates was therefore believed to be the best way to stabilize GDP. If doing so required fluctuations in the money supply, so be it. Consequently, the Fed focused on interest rates and paid little attention to the money supply—which is more or less the Fed's view today as well.

During the 1960s, this prevailing view came under attack by Milton Friedman and other monetarists. These economists argued that the Fed's obsession with stabilizing interest rates actually *destabilized* the economy by making the money supply fluctuate too much. For this reason, they urged the Fed to stop worrying about fluctuations in interest rates and make the money supply grow at a constant rate from month to month and year to year.

Monetarism made important inroads at the Fed during the inflationary 1970s, especially in October 1979 when then-Chairman Paul Volcker announced a major change in the conduct of monetary policy. Henceforth, he asserted, the Fed would stick more closely to its target for money-stock growth regardless of the implications for interest rates. Interest rates would go wherever the law of supply and demand took them.

According to our analysis, this change in policy should have led to wider fluctuations in interest rates—and it did. Unfortunately, the Fed also ran into some bad luck. The ensuing three years were marked by unusually severe gyrations in the demand for money, so the ups and downs of interest rates were even more extreme than anyone had expected. Figure 3 shows just how volatile interest rates were between late 1979 and late 1982. As you might imagine, this erratic performance provoked some heavy criticism of the Fed.

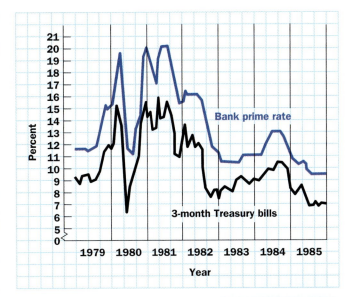

FIGURE 3

The Behavior of Interest Rates, 1979–1985

Then, in October 1982, Chairman Volcker announced that the Fed was temporarily abandoning its attempts to stick to a target growth path for the money supply. Although he did not say so, his announcement presumably meant that the Fed went back to paying more attention to interest rates. As you can see in Figure 3, interest rates did become much more stable after the change in policy. Most observers think this greater stability was no coincidence.

After 1982, the Fed gradually distanced itself from the position that the money supply should grow at a constant rate. Finally, in 1993, then-Chairman Alan Greenspan officially confirmed what many people already knew: that the Fed was no longer using the various Ms to guide policy. He strongly hinted that the Fed was targeting interest rates, especially *real* interest rates, instead—a hint that has been repeated many times since then. In truth, the Fed had little choice. The demand curve for money behaved so erratically and so unpredictably in the 1980s and 1990s that stabilizing the money stock was probably impossible and certainly undesirable. And at least so far, the Fed has shown little interest in returning to the Ms.

■ DEBATE: THE SHAPE OF THE AGGREGATE SUPPLY CURVE

Another lively debate over stabilization policy revolves around the shape of the economy's aggregate supply curve. Many economists think of the aggregate supply curve as quite flat, as in Figure 4(a) on the next page, so that large increases in output can be achieved with little inflation. But other economists envision the supply curve as steep, as shown in Figure 4(b), so that prices respond strongly to changes in output. The differences for public policy are substantial.

If the aggregate supply curve is flat, expansionary fiscal or monetary policy that raises the aggregate demand curve can buy large gains in real GDP at low cost in terms of inflation. In Figure 5(a) on the next page, stimulation of demand pushes the aggregate demand curve outward from D_0D_0 to D_1D_1, thereby moving the economy's equilibrium from point E to point A. The substantial rise in output ($400 billion in the diagram) is accompanied by only a pinch of inflation (1 percent). So the antirecession policy is quite successful.

Conversely, when the supply curve is flat, a restrictive stabilization policy is not a very effective way to bring inflation down. Instead, it serves mainly to reduce real output, as Figure 5(b) shows. Here a leftward shift of the aggregate demand curve from D_0D_0 to D_2D_2 moves equilibrium from point E to point B, lowering real GDP by $400 billion but cutting the price level by merely 1 percent. Fighting inflation by

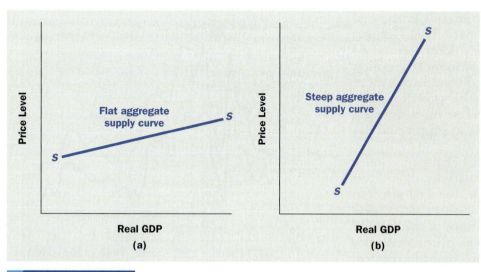

FIGURE 4

Alternative Views of the
Aggregate Supply Curve

contracting aggregate demand is obviously quite costly in this example.

Things are just the reverse if the aggregate supply curve is steep. In that case, expansionary fiscal or monetary policies will cause a good deal of inflation without boosting real GDP much. This situation is depicted in Figure 6(a) on the next page, in which expansionary policies shift the aggregate demand curve outward from D_0D_0 to D_1D_1, thereby moving the economy's equilibrium from E to A. Output rises by only $100 billion but prices shoot up 10 percent.

Similarly, contractionary policy is an effective way to bring down the price level without much sacrifice of output, as shown by the shift from E to B in Figure 6(b). Here it takes only a $100 billion loss of output (from $6,000 billion to $5,900 billion) to "buy" 10 percent less inflation.

As we can see, deciding whether the aggregate supply curve is steep or flat is clearly of fundamental importance to the proper conduct of stabilization policy. If the supply curve is flat, stabilization policy is much more effective at combating recession than inflation. If the supply curve is steep, precisely the reverse is true.

But why does the argument persist? Why can't economists just determine the shape of the aggregate supply curve and stop arguing? The answer is that supply conditions in the real world are far more complicated than our simple diagrams suggest. Some industries may have flat supply curves, whereas others have steep ones. For reasons explained in Chapter 27, supply curves shift over time. And, unlike laboratory scientists, economists cannot perform controlled experiments that would reveal the shape of the aggregate supply curve directly. Instead, they must use statistical inference to make educated guesses.

FIGURE 5

Stabilization Policy
with a Flat Aggregate
Supply Curve

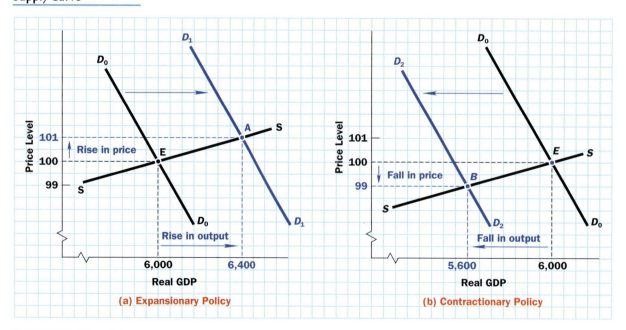

NOTE: Real GDP in billions of dollars per year.

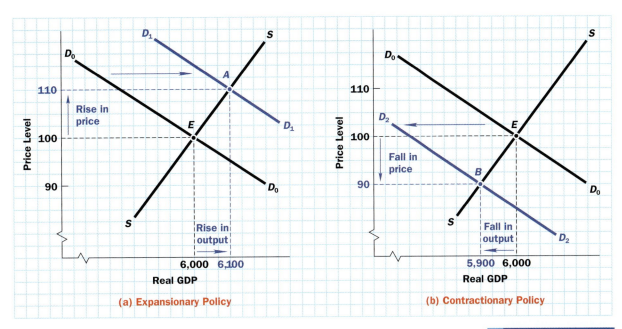

NOTE: Real GDP in billions of dollars per year.

FIGURE 6

Stabilization Policy with a Steep Aggregate Supply Curve

Although empirical research continues, our understanding of aggregate supply remains less settled than our understanding of aggregate demand. Nevertheless, many economists believe that the outline of a consensus view has emerged. This view holds that *the steepness of the aggregate supply schedule depends on the time period under consideration.*

In the very short run, the aggregate supply curve is quite flat, making Figure 5 the more relevant picture of reality. Over short time periods, therefore, fluctuations in aggregate demand have large effects on output but only minor effects on prices. In the long run, however, the aggregate supply curve becomes quite steep, perhaps even vertical. In that case, Figure 6 is a better representation of reality, so that changes in demand affect mainly prices, not output.[3] The implication is that:

> Any change in aggregate demand will have most of its effect on *output* in the short run but on *prices* in the long run.

■ DEBATE: SHOULD THE GOVERNMENT INTERVENE?

We have yet to consider what may be the most fundamental and controversial debate of all—the issue posed at the beginning of the chapter. Is it likely that government policy can successfully stabilize the economy? Or are even well-intentioned efforts likely to do more harm than good?

This controversy has raged for several decades, with no end in sight. In part, the debate is political or philosophical. Liberal economists tend to be more intervention-minded and hence more favorably disposed toward an activist stabilization policy. Conservative economists are more inclined to keep the government's hands off the economy and hence advise adhering to fixed rules. Such political differences are not surprising. But more than ideology propels the debate. We need to understand the economics.

Critics of stabilization policy point to the lags and uncertainties that surround the operation of both fiscal and monetary policies—lags and uncertainties that we have stressed repeatedly in this and earlier chapters. Will the Fed's actions have the desired effects on the money supply? What will these actions do to interest rates and spending? Can fiscal policy actions be taken promptly? How large is the expenditure multiplier? The list could go on and on.

---

[3] The reasoning behind the view that the aggregate supply curve is flat in the short run but steep in the long run will be developed in Chapter 33.

The Fed Fights Recession

The great American economic boom of the 1990s ended about midway through 2000, and the U.S. growth rate plummeted. By January 2001, the Federal Open Market Committee was alarmed enough to start cutting interest rates in an attempt to give the economy a boost. By late summer, the Fed had shaved three full percentage points off the Federal funds rate, and several members of the FOMC were beginning to think they had done enough to stimulate growth.

Then came the horrific terrorist attacks of September 11, which changed everything. The Fed worried that the shock of the attacks would not just disrupt economy activity but also damage consumer and business confidence. Six days later, at a hastily arranged telephonic meeting, it reduced the Federal funds rate by one half percentage point; and it continued to cut the rate for the rest of the year, bringing it all the way down to 1.75 percent—the lowest rate since 1961. But when the economy did not snap back, the Fed started cutting rates again, lowering the Federal funds rate to an astonishing 1 percent in June 2003—and then holding it at that extraordinarily low level for a year. Only in June 2004 did the Fed conclude that the economy was sufficiently healthy that the FOMC could safely begin to restore interest rates to more normal levels.

Federal Funds Rate, 2000–2004

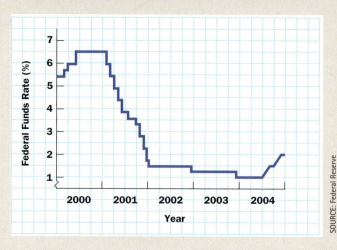

SOURCE: Federal Reserve

These skeptics look at this formidable catalog of difficulties, add a dash of skepticism about our ability to forecast the future state of the economy, and worry that stabilization policy may fail. They therefore advise both the fiscal and monetary authorities to pursue a passive policy rather than an active one—adhering to fixed rules that, although incapable of ironing out every bump in the economy's growth path, will at least keep it roughly on track in the long run.

Advocates of active stabilization policies admit that perfection is unattainable. But they are much more optimistic about the prospects for success, and they are much *less* optimistic about how smoothly the economy would function in the absence of demand management. They therefore advocate discretionary increases in government spending (or decreases in taxes) and lower interest rates when the economy has a recessionary gap—and the reverse when the economy has an inflationary gap. Such policies, they believe, will help keep the economy closer to its full-employment growth path.

Each side can point to evidence that buttresses its own view. Activists look back with pride at the tax cut of 1964 and the sustained period of economic growth that it helped to introduce. They also point to the tax cut of 1975 (which was quickly enacted at just about the trough of a severe recession), the Federal Reserve's switch to "easy money" in 1982, the Fed's expert steering of the economy between 1992 and 2000, and its quick response to the threat to the economy after September 11, 2001. Advocates of rules remind us of the government's refusal to curb what was obviously a situation of runaway demand during the 1966–1968 Vietnam buildup, its overexpansion of the economy in 1972, the monetary overkill that helped bring on the sharp recession of 1981–1982, and the inadequate antirecession policies of the early 1990s.

The historical record of fiscal and monetary policy is far from glorious. Although the authorities have sometimes taken appropriate and timely actions to stabilize the economy, at other times they clearly either took inappropriate steps or did nothing at all. The question of whether the government should adopt passive rules or attempt an activist stabilization policy therefore merits a closer look. As we shall see, the *lags* in the effects of policy discussed earlier in this chapter play a pivotal role in the debate.

■ Lags and the Rules-versus-Discretion Debate

Lags lead to a fundamental difficulty for stabilization policy—a difficulty so formidable that it has prompted some economists to conclude that attempts to stabilize economic activity are likely to do more harm than good. To see why, refer to Figure 7, which charts the behavior of both actual and potential GDP over the course of a business cycle in a hypothetical economy with no stabilization policy. At point *A*, the economy begins to slip into a recession and does not recover to full employment until point *D*. Then, between points *D* and *E*, it overshoots potential GDP and enters an inflationary boom.

The argument in favor of stabilization policy runs something like this: Policy makers recognize that the recession is a serious problem at point *B*, and they take appropriate actions. These actions have their major effects around point *C* and therefore limit both the depth and the length of the recession.

But suppose the lags are really longer and less predictable than those just described. Suppose, for example, that actions do not come until point *C* and that stimulative policies do not have their major effects until after point *D*. Then policy will be of little help during the recession and will actually do harm by overstimulating the economy during the ensuing boom. Thus:

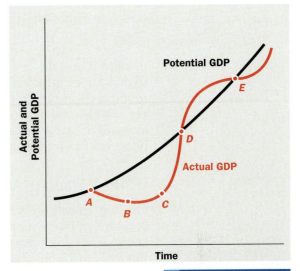

FIGURE 7

A Typical Business Cycle

In the presence of long lags, attempts at stabilizing the economy may actually succeed in destabilizing it.

For this reason, some economists argue that we are better off leaving the economy alone and relying on its natural self-corrective forces to cure recessions and inflations. Instead of embarking on periodic programs of monetary and fiscal stimulus or restraint, they advise policy makers to stick to fixed rules that ignore current economic events.

For monetary policy, we have already mentioned the monetarist policy rule: The Fed should keep the money supply growing at a constant rate. For fiscal policy, proponents of rules often recommend that the government resist the temptation to manage aggregate demand actively and rely instead on the economy's automatic stabilizers, which we discussed in Chapter 28 (see page 608).

■ DIMENSIONS OF THE RULES-VERSUS-DISCRETION DEBATE

Are the critics right? Should we forget about discretionary policy and put the economy on autopilot—relying on automatic stabilizers and the economy's natural, self-correcting mechanisms? As usual, the answer depends on many factors.

■ How Fast Does the Economy's Self-Correcting Mechanism Work?

In Chapter 27, we emphasized that the economy has a self-correcting mechanism. If recessions and inflations will disappear quickly by themselves, the case for intervention is weak. That is, if such problems typically last only a short time, then lags in discretionary stabilization policy mean that the medicine will often have its major effects only after the disease has run its course. In fact, a distinct minority of economists used precisely this reasoning to argue against a fiscal stimulus after the September 11, 2001, terrorist attacks. In terms of Figure 7, this is a case in which point *D* comes very close to point *A*.

Although extreme advocates of rules argue that this is indeed what happens, most economists agree that the economy's self-correcting mechanism is slow and not terribly reliable, even when supplemented by the automatic stabilizers. On this count, then, a point is scored for discretionary policy.

How Long Are the Lags in Stabilization Policy?

We just explained why long and unpredictable lags in monetary and fiscal policy make it hard for stabilization policy to do much good. Short, reliable lags point in just the opposite direction. Thus advocates of fixed rules emphasize the length of lags while proponents of discretion tend to discount them.

Who is right depends on the circumstances. Sometimes policy makers take action promptly, and the economy receives at least some stimulus from expansionary policy within a year after slipping into a recession. The tax cut of 2001 and the Fed's sharp monetary stimulus in the fall of 2001 are the most recent examples. Although far from perfect, the effects of such timely actions are felt soon enough to do some good. But, as we have seen, very slow policy responses may actually prove destabilizing. Because history offers examples of each type, we can draw no general conclusion.

How Accurate Are Economic Forecasts?

One way to compress the policy-making lag dramatically is to forecast economic events accurately. If we could see a recession coming a full year ahead of time (which we certainly *cannot* do), even a rather sluggish policy response would still be timely. In terms of Figure 7, this would be a case in which the recession is predicted well before point *A*.

Over the years, economists in universities, government agencies, and private businesses have developed a number of techniques to assist them in predicting what the economy will do. Unfortunately, none of these methods is terribly accurate. To give a rough idea of magnitudes, forecasts of either the inflation rate or the real GDP growth rate for the year ahead typically err by $\pm \frac{3}{4}$ to 1 percentage point. But, in a bad year for forecasters, errors of 2 or 3 percentage points are common.

Is this record good enough? That depends on how the forecasts are used. It is certainly not good enough to support so-called *fine tuning*—that is, attempts to keep the economy always within a hair's breadth of full employment. But it probably is good enough for policy makers interested in using discretionary stabilization policy to close persistent and sizable gaps between actual and potential GDP.

The Size of Government

One bogus argument that is sometimes heard is that active fiscal policy must inevitably lead to a growing public sector. Because proponents of fixed rules tend also to oppose big government, they view this growth as undesirable. Of course, others think that a larger public sector is just what society needs.

This argument, however, is completely beside the point because, as we pointed out in Chapter 28: *One's opinion about the proper size of government should have nothing to do with one's view on stabilization policy.* For example, President George W. Bush is as conservative as they come and, at least rhetorically, he is devoted to shrinking the size of the public sector.[4] But his tax-cutting initiatives in 2001–2003 constituted an extremely activist fiscal policy to spur the economy. Furthermore, most stabilization policy these days consists of monetary policy, which neither increases nor decreases the size of government.

Uncertainties Caused by Government Policy

Advocates of rules are on stronger ground when they argue that frequent changes in tax laws, government spending programs, or monetary conditions make it difficult for

---

[4] In fact, the size of the federal government has expanded rapidly during his presidency, in part because of national security concerns but also because of domestic spending.

firms and consumers to formulate and carry out rational plans. They argue that the authorities can provide a more stable environment for the private sector by adhering to fixed rules, so that businesses and consumers will know exactly what to expect.

No one disputes that a more stable environment is better for private planning. Even so, supporters of discretionary policy emphasize that *stability in the economy* is more important than *stability in the government budget* (or in Federal Reserve operations). The whole idea of stabilization policy is to *prevent* gyrations in the pace of economic activity by *causing* timely gyrations in the government budget (or in monetary policy). Which atmosphere is better for business, they ask: one in which fiscal and monetary rules keep things peaceful on Capitol Hill and at the Federal Reserve while recessions and inflations wrack the economy, or one in which government changes its policy abruptly on occasion but the economy grows more smoothly? They think the answer is self-evident. The question, of course, is whether stabilization policy can succeed in practice.

■ A Political Business Cycle?

A final argument put forth by advocates of rules is political rather than economic. Fiscal policy decisions are made by elected politicians: the president and members of Congress. When elections are on the horizon (and for members of the House of Representatives, they *always* are), these politicians may be as concerned with keeping their jobs as with doing what is right for the economy. This situation leaves fiscal policy subject to "political manipulation"—lawmakers may take inappropriate actions to attain short-run political goals. A system of purely automatic stabilization, its proponents argue, would eliminate this peril.

It is certainly *possible* that politicians could deliberately *cause* economic instability to help their own reelection. Indeed, some observers of these "political business cycles"

Between Rules and Discretion

In recent years, a number of economists and policy makers have sought a middle ground between saddling monetary policy makers with rigid rules and giving them complete discretion, as the Federal Reserve has in the United States.

One such approach is called "inflation targeting." As practiced in the United Kingdom, inflation targeting starts when an elected official (the Chancellor of the Exchequer, who is roughly equivalent to the U.S. Secretary of the Treasury) chooses a numerical target for the inflation rate—currently, this target is 2 percent for consumer prices. The United Kingdom's central bank, the Bank of England, is then bound by law to try to reach this target. In that sense, the system functions somewhat like a *rule*. However, monetary policy makers are given complete *discretion* as to how they go about trying to achieve this goal. Neither the Chancellor nor Parliament interferes with day-to-day monetary policy decisions. The Federal Reserve's new chairman, Ben Bernanke, has expressed interest in importing some aspects of inflation targeting to the United States.

Another approach is called the "Taylor rule," after Professor John Taylor of Stanford. Almost a decade ago, Taylor noticed that the Fed's interest rate decisions during the Greenspan era could be described by a simple algebraic equation. This equation, now called the Taylor rule, starts with a 2 percent *real* interest rate, and then instructs the Fed to *lower* the rate of interest in proportion to any recessionary gap, and to *raise* the interest rate in proportion to any excess of inflation above 2 percent (which is the Fed's presumed inflation goal). No central bank uses the Taylor rule as a mechanical rule; nor did Taylor intend it to be used that way. But many central banks around the world, including the Fed, find the Taylor rule useful as a benchmark to guide their decision making.

SOURCE: © Courtesy of NewsCast

The Bank of England's Monetary Policy Committee

"Daddy's not mad at you, dear—Daddy's mad at the Fed."

SOURCE: From *The Wall Street Journal*–Permission, Cartoon Features Syndicate

have claimed that several American presidents have taken full advantage of the opportunity. Furthermore, even without any insidious intent, politicians may take the wrong actions for perfectly honorable reasons. Decisions in the political arena are never clear-cut, and it certainly is easy to find examples of grievous errors in the history of U.S. fiscal policy.

Taken as a whole, then, the political argument against discretionary fiscal policy seems to have a great deal of merit. But what are we to do about it? It is unrealistic to believe that fiscal decisions could or should be made by a group of objective and nonpartisan technicians. Tax and budget policies require inherently *political* decisions that, in a democracy, should be made by elected officials.

This fact may seem worrisome in view of the possibilities for political chicanery. But it should not bother us any more (or any less) than similar maneuvering in other areas of policy making. After all, the same problem besets international relations, national defense, formulation and enforcement of the law, and so on. Politicians make all these decisions for us, subject only to sporadic accountability at elections. Is there really any reason why fiscal decisions should be different?

But monetary policy *is* different. Because Congress was concerned that elected officials focused on the short run would pursue inflationary monetary policies, it long ago gave day-to-day decisionmaking authority over monetary policy to the unelected technocrats at the Federal Reserve. Politics influences monetary policy only indirectly: The Fed must report to Congress, and the president has the power to appoint Federal Reserve governors whose views are to his liking.

ISSUE REVISITED: *What Should Be Done?*

So where do we come out on the question posed at the start of this chapter? On balance, is it better to pursue the best discretionary policy we can, knowing full well that we will never achieve perfection? Or is it wiser to rely on fixed rules and the automatic stabilizers?

In weighing the pros and cons, your basic view of the economy is crucial. Some economists believe that the economy, if left unmanaged, would generate a series of ups and downs that would be difficult to predict, but that it would correct each of them by itself in a relatively short time. They conclude that, because of long lags and poor forecasts, our ability to anticipate whether the economy will need stimulus or restraint by the time policy actions have their effects is quite limited. Consequently, they advocate fixed rules.

Other economists liken the economy to a giant glacier with a great deal of inertia. Under this view, if we observe an inflationary or recessionary gap today, it will likely still be there a year or two from now because the self-correcting mechanism works slowly. In such a world, accurate forecasting is not imperative, even if policy lags are long. If we base policy on a forecast of a 4 percent gap between actual and potential GDP a year from now, and the gap turns out to be only 2 percent, we still will have done the right thing despite the inaccurate forecast. So holders of this view of the economy tend to support discretionary policy.

There is certainly no consensus on this issue, either among economists or politicians. After all, the question touches on political ideology as well as economics, and liberals often look to government to solve social problems, whereas conservatives consistently point out that many efforts of government fail despite the best intentions. A prudent view of the matter might be that:

The case for active discretionary policy is strong when the economy has a serious deficiency or excess of aggregate demand. However, advocates of fixed rules are right that it is unwise to try to iron out every little wiggle in the growth path of GDP.

But one thing seems certain: The rules-versus-discretion debate is likely to go on for quite some time.

A Nobel Prize for the Rules-versus-Discretion Debate

In 2004, the economists Finn Kydland of Carnegie-Mellon University and Edward Prescott of Arizona State University were awarded the Nobel Prize for a fascinating contribution to the rules-versus-discretion debate. They called attention to a general problem that they labeled "time inconsistency," and their analysis of this problem led them to conclude that the Fed should follow a rule.

A close-to-home example will illustrate the basic time inconsistency problem. Suppose your instructor announces in September that a final exam will be given in December. The main purpose of the exam is to ensure that students study and learn the course materials, and the exam itself represents work for the faculty and stress for the students. So, when December rolls around, it may seem "optimal" to call off the

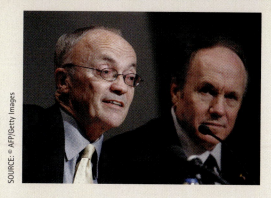

SOURCE: © AFP/Getty Images

exam at the last moment. Of course, if that started happening regularly, students would soon stop studying for exams. So actually giving the exam is the better long-run policy. One way to solve this time inconsistency problem is to adopt a simple *rule* stating that announced exams will always be given, rather than allowing individual faculty members to cancel exams at their *discretion*.

Kydland and Prescott argued that monetary policy makers face a similar time inconsistency problem. They first announce a stern anti-inflation policy (analogous to giving an exam). But then, when the moment of truth (December) arrives, they may relent because they don't want to cause unemployment (all that work and stress). Their suggested solution: The Fed and other central banks should adopt *rules* that remove period-by-period *discretion*.

SUMMARY

1. **Velocity** (V) is the ratio of nominal GDP to the stock of money (M). It indicates how quickly money circulates.

2. One important determinant of velocity is the rate of interest (r). At higher interest rates, people find it less attractive to hold money because money pays zero or little interest. Thus, when r rises, money circulates faster, and V rises.

3. **Monetarism** is a type of analysis that focuses attention on velocity and the money supply (M). Although monetarists realize that V is not constant, they believe that it is predictable enough to make it a useful tool for policy analysis and forecasting.

4. Because it increases the volume of transactions, and hence increases the demands for bank deposits and therefore bank reserves, expansionary fiscal policy pushes interest rates higher. Higher interest rates reduce the multiplier by deterring some types of spending, especially investment.

5. Because fiscal policy actions affect aggregate demand either directly through G or indirectly through C, the expenditure lags between fiscal actions and their effects on aggregate demand are probably fairly short. By contrast, monetary policy operates mainly on investment, I, which responds slowly to changes in interest rates.

6. However, the policy-making lag normally is much longer for fiscal policy than for monetary policy. Hence, when the two lags are combined, it is not clear which type of policy acts more quickly.

7. Because it cannot control the demand curve for money, the Federal Reserve cannot control both M and r. If the demand for money changes, the Fed must decide whether it wants to hold M steady, hold r steady, or adopt some compromise position.

8. Monetarists emphasize the importance of stabilizing the growth path of the money supply, whereas the predominant Keynesian view puts more emphasis on keeping interest rates on target.

9. In practice, the Fed has changed its views on this issue several times. For decades, it attached primary importance to interest rates. Between 1979 and 1982, it stressed its commitment to stable growth of the money supply. But, since then, the focus has clearly returned to interest rates.

10. When the aggregate supply curve is very flat, changes in aggregate demand will have large effects on the nation's real output but small effects on the price level. Under those circumstances, stabilization policy works well as an antirecession device, but it has little power to combat inflation.

11. When the aggregate supply curve is steep, changes in aggregate demand have small effects on real output but large effects on the price level. In such a case, stabilization policy can do much to fight inflation but is not a very effective way to cure unemployment.

12. The aggregate supply curve is likely to be relatively flat in the short run but relatively steep in the long run. Hence, stabilization policy affects mainly output in the short run but mainly prices in the long run.

13. When the lags in the operation of fiscal and monetary policy are long and unpredictable, attempts to stabilize economic activity may actually destabilize it.

14. Some economists believe that our imperfect knowledge of the channels through which stabilization policy works, the long lags involved, and the inaccuracy of forecasts make it unlikely that discretionary stabilization policy can succeed.

15. Other economists recognize these difficulties but do not believe they are quite as serious. They also place much less faith in the economy's ability to cure recessions and inflations on its own. They therefore think that discretionary policy is not only advisable, but essential.

16. Stabilizing the economy by fiscal policy need not imply a tendency toward "big government."

KEY TERMS

Velocity   662

Equation of exchange   662

Quantity theory of money   663

Effect of interest rate on velocity   664

Monetarism   665

Effect of fiscal policy on interest rates   665

Lags in stabilization policy   667

Controlling M versus controlling r 668

Rules versus discretionary policy   675

TEST YOURSELF

1. How much money by the M1 definition (cash plus checking account balances) do you typically have at any particular moment? Divide this amount into your total income over the past twelve months to obtain your own personal velocity. Are you typical of the nation as a whole?

2. The following table provides data on nominal gross domestic product and the money supply (M1 definition) in recent selected years. Compute velocity in each year. Can you see any trend? How does it compare with the trend that prevailed from 1975 to 2000?

Year	End-of-Year Money Supply (M1)	Nominal GDP
2000	$1,088	$9,817
2001	1,179	10,128
2002	1,217	10,487
2003	1,293	11,004

NOTE: Amounts are in billions.

3. Use a supply and demand diagram similar to Figure 2 to show the choices open to the Fed following an unexpected *decline* in the demand for money. If the Fed is following a monetarist policy, what will happen to the rate of interest?

4. Which of the following events would strengthen the argument for the use of discretionary policy, and which would strengthen the argument for rules?

a. Structural changes make the economy's self-correcting mechanism work more quickly and reliably than before.

b. New statistical methods are found that improve the accuracy of economic forecasts.

c. A Republican president is elected when there is an overwhelmingly Democratic Congress. Congress and the president differ sharply on what should be done about the national economy.

5. (More difficult) The money supply (M) is the sum of bank deposits (D) plus currency in the hands of the public (call that C). Suppose the required reserve ratio is 20 percent and the Fed provides $50 billion in bank reserves ($R = $50 billion).

a. First assume that people hold no currency ($C = 0$). How large will the money supply (M) be? If the Fed increases bank reserves to $R = $60 billion, how large will M be then?

b. Next, assume that people hold 20 cents worth of currency for each dollar of bank deposits, that is, $C = 0.2D$. If the Fed creates $R = $50 billion worth of reserves, how large will M be now? (*Hint*: First figure out what D must be, then add the appropriate amount of currency to get M. Remember that $M = D + C$.) If the Fed once again increases bank reserves to $R = $60 billion, how large will M be then?

c. What do you notice about the relationship between M and R?

DISCUSSION QUESTIONS

1. Use the concept of opportunity cost to explain why velocity is higher at higher interest rates.

2. How does monetarism differ from the quantity theory of money?

3. Given the behavior of velocity shown in Figure 1, would it make more sense for the Federal Reserve to formulate targets for M1 or M2?

4. Distinguish between the expenditure lag and the policy lag in stabilization policy. Does monetary or fiscal policy have the shorter expenditure lag? What about the policy lag?

5. Explain why their contrasting views on the shape of the aggregate supply curve lead some economists to argue much more strongly for stabilization policies to fight unemploy-

ment and other economists to argue much more strongly for stabilization policies to fight inflation.

6. Explain why lags make it possible that policy actions intended to stabilize the economy will actually destabilize it.

7. Many observers think that the Federal Reserve succeeded in using deft applications of monetary policy to "fine-tune" the U.S. economy into the full-employment zone in the 1990s without worsening inflation. Use the data on money

supply, interest rates, real GDP, unemployment, and the price level given on the inside back cover of this book to evaluate this claim.

8. After 2000, U.S. economic performance deteriorated. (See the data on the inside back cover of this book.) Can this decline be blamed on inferior monetary or fiscal policy? (You may want to ask your instructor about this question.)

32

BUDGET DEFICITS IN THE SHORT AND LONG RUN

Blessed are the young, for they shall inherit the national debt.

HERBERT HOOVER

Monetary policy and fiscal policy are typically thought of as tools for short-run economic *stabilization*—that is, as ways to combat either inflation or unemployment. Debates over the Federal Reserve's next interest-rate decision, or over this year's federal budget, are normally dominated by short-run considerations such as: Does the economy need to be stimulated or restrained *right now?*

But the monetary and fiscal choices the government makes today also have profound effects on our economy's ability to produce goods and services *in the future*. We began Part VI by emphasizing long-run growth, and especially the role of capital formation (see Chapters 23 and 24). But for most of Part VII, we have been preoccupied with the shorter-run issues of inflation, unemployment, and recession. This chapter integrates the two perspectives by considering both the long-run and short-run implications of fiscal and monetary policy decisions. What differences does it make if we stimulate (or restrain) the economy with fiscal or monetary policy? Should we strive to balance the budget? What are the economic virtues and vices of large budget deficits, both now and in the future?

CONTENTS

ISSUE: *Did the September 2001 Terrorist Attack Warrant Fiscal Stimulus?*

Several of these questions were brought into sharp relief by the debate over the proper macroeconomic response to the terrorist attacks of September 11, 2001. Almost immediately, many economists and politicians began calling for a fiscal stimulus that would boost spending right away. Their reasoning was that the U.S. economy, which—we now know—was in a mild recession even before the attack, might be pushed over the brink by the blow to consumer confidence and spending.

But others disagreed. Some claimed that the economy needed no further stimulus. Others argued that monetary policy was better suited to the task than fiscal policy, which should be devoted to maintaining what was then still a budget surplus. Even many supporters of fiscal stimulus worried that Congress would use the banner of "short-run stimulus" to enact tax cuts and new spending programs that would damage long-run budget prospects.

The debate quickly grew partisan and raged on for months. Republicans wanted sizable tax cuts; Democrats favored more generous benefits for the unemployed. While the two parties dickered, spending on defense and homeland security surged and the indomitable American consumer kept right on spending. So the economy held up far better than most people thought likely on September 11, 2001.

So which side was right? Did fiscal stimulus in 2001 help or hurt the U.S. economy? By the end of the chapter, you will be in an excellent position to answer this important question for yourself.

SHOULD THE BUDGET BE BALANCED? THE SHORT RUN

Americans have long been attracted by the idea of balancing the government budget year after year—so much so that they stuck to this belief both before and after Congress made a major change in the *definition* of budget balance in 1999 and then changed back just a few years later. (See "Balance the Budget? By What Definition?" on page 691.) Let us begin our examination of this idea by reviewing the basic principles of fiscal policy that we have learned so far (especially in Chapter 28) and by seeing what they say about the goal of balancing the budget.

These principles certainly do *not* imply that we should always maintain a balanced budget, much as that notion may appeal to our intuitive sense of good financial management. Rather, they instruct fiscal policy makers to focus on *balancing aggregate supply and aggregate demand*. They point to the desirability of budget *deficits* when private demand, $C + I + (X - IM)$, is too weak and of budget *surpluses* when private demand is too strong. The budget should be balanced, according to these principles, only when $C + I + G + (X - IM)$ under a balanced-budget policy approximately equals full-employment levels of output. This situation may sometimes occur, but it will not necessarily be the norm.

The reason why a balanced budget is not always advisable should be clear from our earlier discussion of stabilization policy. Consider the fiscal policy that the government would follow if its goal were to maintain a balanced budget every year. Suppose the budget was initially balanced and private spending sagged for some reason, as it did in 2001. The multiplier would pull GDP down. Because personal and corporate tax receipts fall sharply when GDP declines, the budget would automatically swing into the red. To restore budget balance, the government would then have to cut spending or raise taxes—exactly the opposite of the appropriate fiscal-policy response. Thus:

Attempts to balance the budget during recessions—as was done, say, during the Great Depression—will prolong and deepen slumps.

This is precisely what many observers feel happened to Japan when it raised taxes in a weak economy in 1997. In fact, Ryutaro Hashimoto, Japan's prime minister from 1996 to 1998, was disparagingly called the "Herbert Hoover of Japan" because he sought to reduce the budget deficit despite Japan's sinking economy.

Budget balancing also can lead to inappropriate fiscal policy under boom conditions. If rising tax receipts induce a budget-balancing government to spend more or to cut taxes, then fiscal policy will "boom the boom"—with unfortunate inflationary consequences. This possibility is one reason why few economists thought large tax cuts were wise policy in 1999, when a candidate named George W. Bush first proposed them. But by the time the Bush tax cuts were enacted in 2001, many felt they were "just what the doctor ordered" for a weak economy.

SOURCE: From *The Wall Street Journal*–Permission, Cartoon Features Syndicate

"The 'Twilight Zone' will not be seen tonight, so that we may bring you the followng special on the federal budget."

The Importance of the Policy Mix

Actually, the issue is even more complicated than we have indicated so far. As we know, fiscal policy is not the only way the government affects aggregate demand. It also influences aggregate demand through its *monetary policy*. For this reason:

The appropriate fiscal policy depends, among other things, on the current stance of monetary policy. Although a balanced budget may be appropriate under one monetary policy, a deficit or a surplus may be appropriate under another monetary policy.

An example will illustrate the point. Suppose Congress and the president believe that the aggregate supply and demand curves will intersect approximately at full employment if the budget is balanced. Then a balanced budget would seem to be the appropriate fiscal policy.

Now suppose monetary policy turns contractionary, pulling the aggregate demand curve inward to the left, as shown by the blue arrow in Figure 1, and thereby creating a recessionary gap. If the fiscal authorities wish to restore GDP to its original level, they must shift the aggregate demand curve back to its original position, D_0D_0, as indicated by the red arrow. To do so, they must either raise spending or cut taxes, thereby opening up a budget deficit. Thus, the tightening of *monetary* policy changes the appropriate *fiscal* policy from a balanced budget to a deficit, because both monetary and fiscal policies affect aggregate demand.

By the same token, a given target for aggregate demand implies that any change in *fiscal* policy will alter the appropriate *monetary* policy. For example, we can reinterpret Figure 1 as indicating the effects of reducing the budget deficit by cutting government spending. Then, if the Fed does not want real GDP to fall, it must expand the money supply sufficiently to restore the aggregate demand curve to D_0D_0.

It is precisely this change in the *mix* of policy—a smaller budget deficit balanced by easier money—that the U.S. government managed to engineer with great success in the 1990s. Congress and the Clinton administration raised taxes and cut spending, which reduced aggregate demand. But the Federal Reserve pursued a sufficiently expansionary policy to return this "lost" aggregate demand to the economy by keeping interest rates low.

So we should not expect a balanced budget to be the norm. How, then, can we tell whether any particular deficit is too large or too small? From the discussion so far, it would appear that the answer depends on the strength of private-sector aggregate demand and the stance of monetary policy. But those are not the only considerations.

FIGURE 1

The Interaction of Monetary and Fiscal Policy

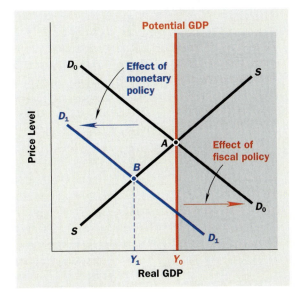

■ SURPLUSES AND DEFICITS: THE LONG RUN

One implication of what we have just said is that various *combinations* of fiscal and monetary policy can lead to the *same* level of aggregate demand, and hence to the same real GDP and price level, in the short run. For example, the government could reduce aggregate demand by raising taxes, but the Fed could make up for it by cutting interest rates. Or the reverse could happen: The government could cut taxes while the Fed raises interest rates, leaving aggregate demand unchanged. The long-run consequences of these alternative mixes of monetary and fiscal policy may be quite different, however.

In previous chapters, we learned that more expansionary fiscal policy (tax cuts or higher government spending) and tighter money should produce *higher* real interest rates and therefore *lower* investment. Thus, such a policy mix should shift the composition of total expenditure, $C + I + G + (X - IM)$, toward more G, more C (from tax cuts), and less I.[1] The expected result is less capital formation, and therefore slower growth of potential GDP. As we shall see shortly, it was precisely that policy mix—large tax cuts and very tight money—that the U.S. government inadvertently chose in the early 1980s.

But the opposite policy mix—tighter budgets and looser monetary policy—should produce the opposite outcomes: lower real interest rates, more investment, and hence faster growth of potential GDP. That was the direction U.S. macroeconomic policy took in the 1990s—with excellent results. Lowering the budget deficit and then turning it into a surplus, economists believe, was an effective way to increase the investment share of GDP, which soared from 12 percent in 1992 to 17 percent in 2000. The general point is:

The composition of aggregate demand is a major determinant of the rate of economic growth. If a larger fraction of GDP is devoted to investment, the nation's capital stock will grow faster and the aggregate supply schedule will shift more quickly to the right, accelerating growth.

International data likewise show a positive relationship between growth and the share of GDP invested. Figure 2 displays, for a set of twenty-four countries on four continents, both investment as a share of GDP and growth in per-capita output over two decades (the 1970s and 1980s). Countries with higher investment rates clearly experienced higher growth, on average.

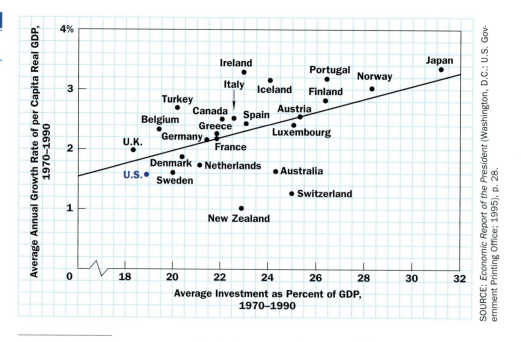

FIGURE 2

Growth and Investment in 24 Countries

SOURCE: *Economic Report of the President* (Washington, D.C.: U.S. Government Printing Office; 1995), p. 28.

---

[1] We will deal with the consequences of fiscal and monetary policy on $X - IM$ in Chapter 36.

So it appears that when we ask whether the budget should be balanced, in deficit, or in surplus, we have posed a good but complicated question. Before attempting to answer it, we need to get some facts straight.

■ DEFICITS AND DEBT: TERMINOLOGY AND FACTS

First, some critical terminology. People frequently confuse two terms that have different meanings: *budget deficits* and the *national debt*. We must learn to distinguish between the two.

The **budget deficit** is the amount by which the government's expenditures exceed its receipts during some specified period of time, usually a year. If, instead, receipts exceed expenditures, we have a **budget surplus.** For example, during fiscal year 2006, the federal government raised roughly $2.40 trillion in taxes and spent about $2.65 trillion, resulting in a deficit of about $248 billion.[2]

The **national debt,** also called the *public debt*, is the total value of the government's indebtedness at a moment in time. Thus, for example, the U.S. national debt at the end of fiscal year 2006 was about $8.45 *trillion*.

These two concepts—deficit and debt—are closely related because the government accumulates *debt* by running *deficits* or reduces its debt by running *surpluses*. The relationship between the debt and the deficit or surplus can be explained by a simple analogy. As you run water into a bathtub ("run a deficit"), the accumulated volume of water in the tub ("the debt") rises. Alternatively, if you let water out of the tub ("run a surplus"), the level of the water ("the debt") falls. Analogously, budget deficits raise the national debt, whereas budget surpluses lower it. But, of course, getting rid of the deficit (shutting off the flow of water) does not eliminate the accumulated debt (drain the tub).

The **budget deficit** is the amount by which the government's expenditures exceed its receipts during a specified period of time, usually a year. If receipts exceed expenditures, it is called a **budget surplus** instead.

The **national debt** is the federal government's total indebtedness at a moment in time. It is the result of previous budget deficits.

■ Some Facts about the National Debt

Now that we have made this distinction, let us look at the size and nature of the accumulated public debt and then at the annual budget deficit. How large a public debt do we have? How did we get it? Who owes it? Is it growing or shrinking?

To begin with the simplest question, the public debt is enormous. At the end of 2006, it amounted to just over $28,000 for every man, woman, and child in America. But just over half of this outstanding debt was held by agencies of the U.S. government—in other words, one branch of the government owed it to another. If we deduct this portion, the net national debt was about $4 trillion, or approximately $13,250 per person.

Furthermore, when we compare the debt with the gross domestic product—the volume of goods and services our economy produces in a year—it does not seem so large after all. With a GDP close to $13.5 trillion in late 2006, the net debt was only about 30 percent of the nation's yearly income. By contrast, many families who own homes owe *several years'* worth of income to the banks that granted them mortgages. Many U.S. corporations also owe their bondholders much more than 30 percent of a year's sales.

But before these analogies make you feel too comfortable, we should point out that simple analogies between public and private debt are almost always misleading. A family with a large mortgage debt also owns a home with a value that presumably exceeds the mortgage. A solvent business firm has assets (factories, machinery, inventories, and so forth) that far exceed its outstanding debt in value.

Is the same thing true of the U.S. government? No one knows for sure. How much is the White House worth? Or the national parks? And what about military bases, both here and abroad? Simply because these government assets are not sold on markets, no one really knows their true value.

---

[2] *Reminder:* The fiscal year of the U.S. government ends on September 30. Thus, fiscal year 2006 ran from October 1, 2005, to September 30, 2006.

FIGURE 3   The U.S. National Debt Relative to GDP, 1915–2006

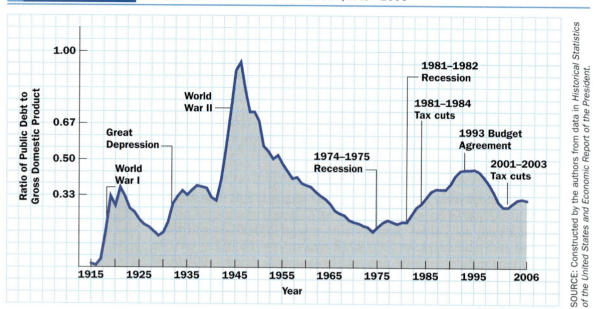

SOURCE: Constructed by the authors from data in *Historical Statistics of the United States* and *Economic Report of the President.*

Figure 3 charts the path of the *net* national debt from 1915 to 2006, expressing each year's net debt as a fraction of that year's nominal GDP. Looking at the debt *relative to GDP* is important for two reasons. First, we must remember that everything grows in a growing economy. Given that private debt has expanded greatly since 1915, it would be surprising indeed if the public debt had not grown as well. In fact, federal debt grew more slowly than did either private debt or GDP for most of the period since World War II. The years from 1980 to about 1994 stand out as an aberration in Figure 3.

Second, the debt is measured in dollars and, as long as there is any inflation, the amount of purchasing power that each dollar represents declines each year. Dividing the debt by nominal GDP, as is done in Figure 3, adjusts for both real growth and inflation, and so puts the debt numbers in better perspective.

Figure 3 shows us how and when the U.S. government acquired all this debt. Notice the sharp increases in the ratio of debt to GDP during World War I, the Great Depression, and especially World War II. Thereafter, you see an unmistakable downward trend until the recession of 1974–1975. In 1945, the national debt was the equivalent of thirteen months' national income. By 1974, this figure had been whittled down to just two months' worth.

Thus, until the 1980s, the U.S. government had acquired most of its debt either to finance wars or during recessions. As we will see later, the *cause* of the debt is quite germane to the question of whether the debt is a burden. So it is important to remember that:

Until about 1983, almost all of the U.S. national debt stemmed from financing wars and from the losses of tax revenues that accompany recessions.

But then things changed. From the early 1980s until 1993, the national debt grew faster than nominal GDP, reversing the pattern that had prevailed since 1945. This growth spurt happened with no wars and only one recession. By 1993, the debt exceeded five months' GDP—nearly triple its value in 1974. This development alarmed many economists and public figures.

At that point, the government took decisive actions to reduce the budget deficit. The ratio of debt to GDP then fell for years. But President Bush's large tax cuts reversed the trend for a few years after 2001. Lately the ratio of debt to GDP has been approximately constant.

INTERPRETING THE BUDGET DEFICIT OR SURPLUS

We have observed that the federal government ran extremely large budget deficits from the early 1980s until the mid 1990s. As Figure 4 shows, the budget deficit ballooned from $79 billion in fiscal year 1981 to $208 billion by fiscal year 1983—setting a record that was subsequently eclipsed several times. As late as fiscal year 1995, the deficit was still $164 billion. These are enormous, even mind-boggling, numbers. But what do they mean? How should we interpret them?

The Structural Deficit or Surplus

First, it is important to understand that the same fiscal program can lead to a deficit or a surplus, depending on the state of the economy. Failure to appreciate this point has led many people to assume that a larger deficit always signifies a more expansionary fiscal policy—which is not the case.

Think, for example, about what happens to the budget during a recession. As GDP falls, the government's major sources of tax revenue—income taxes, corporate taxes, and payroll taxes—all shrink because firms and people pay lower taxes when they earn less. Similarly, some types of government spending, notably transfer payments such as unemployment benefits, rise when GDP falls, because more people are out of work.

Recall that the deficit is the difference between government expenditures, which are either purchases or transfer payments, and tax receipts:

$$\text{Deficit} = G + \text{Transfers} - \text{Taxes} = G - (\text{Taxes} - \text{Transfers}) = G - T$$

Because a falling GDP leads to higher expenditure.s and lower tax receipts:

The deficit rises in a recession and falls in a boom, even with no change in fiscal policy.

Figure 5 depicts the relationship between GDP and the budget deficit. The government's fiscal program is summarized by the blue and red lines. The horizontal red line labeled G indicates that federal purchases of goods and services are approximately unaffected by GDP. The rising blue line labeled T (for taxes minus transfers) indicates that taxes rise and transfer payments fall as GDP rises. Notice that the same fiscal policy (that is, the same two lines) leads to a large deficit if GDP is Y_1, a balanced budget if GDP is Y_2, or a surplus if GDP is as high as Y_3. Clearly, the deficit itself is not a good measure of the government's fiscal policy.

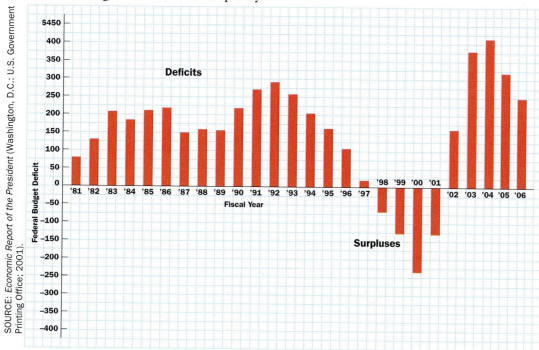

SOURCE: *Economic Report of the President* (Washington, D.C.: U.S. Government Printing Office; 2001).

Note: Amounts are in billions of dollars.

FIGURE 4

Official Fiscal-Year Budget Deficits, 1981–2006

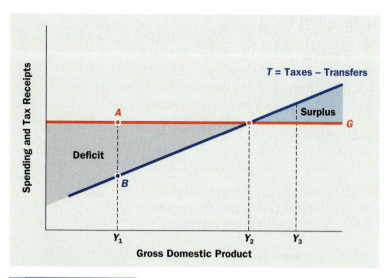

FIGURE 5

The Effect of the Economy on the Budget

The **structural budget deficit** is the hypothetical deficit we *would have* under current fiscal policies if the economy were operating near full employment.

To seek a better measure, economists pay more attention to what is called the **structural budget deficit or surplus.** This hypothetical measure replaces both the spending and taxes in the *actual* budget by estimates of how much the government *would be* spending and receiving, given current tax rates and expenditure rules, if the economy were operating at some fixed, high-employment level. For example, if the high-employment benchmark in Figure 5 was Y_2, although actual GDP was only Y_1, the structural deficit would be zero even though the actual deficit would be *AB*.

Because it is based on the spending and taxing the government *would be* doing at some fixed level of GDP, rather than on *actual* expenditures and receipts, the structural deficit does not depend on the state of the economy. It changes *only* when policy changes, *not* when GDP changes. That is why most economists view it as a better measure of the thrust of fiscal policy than the actual deficit.

This new concept helps us understand the changing nature of the large budget deficits of the 1980s, the stunning turn to surpluses in the late 1990s, and the rapid swing back to large deficits since 2001. The first two columns of data in Table 1 show both the actual surplus and the structural surplus every other year since 1981. (Most of the numbers are negative indicating *deficits*.) Because of recessions in 1983 and 1991, the actual deficit was far larger than the structural deficit in those years. But the difference between the two was negligible in 1987 and small in 1995, when the economy was near full employment, and then changed sign (the structural deficit was larger than the actual deficit) in 1997.

Four interesting facts stand out when we compare the numbers in the first and second columns. First, even though the *official* deficit was smaller in fiscal 1995 than in fiscal 1983, the *structural* deficit was larger in 1995—despite years of budget "stringency."

Second, the structural deficit rose between 1989 and 1993. It was this trend toward larger structural deficits that alarmed keen students of the federal budget. Third, the stunning $381 billion swing in the budget deficit from 1993 to 1999 (from a deficit of $255 billion to a surplus of $126 billion) far exceeds the change in the structural deficit, which fell by "only" $192 billion. This last number, which is still impressive, is a better indicator of how much fiscal policy changed during the period. Fourth, the swing from a moderate-sized structural surplus in 2001 to a large structural deficit in 2003 was both rapid and huge.

	TABLE 1			
	Alternative Budget Concepts, 1981–2005			
Fiscal Year	Total Surplus (1)	Structural Surplus (2)	On-Budget Surplus (3)	Off-Budget Surplus (4)
1981	-79	-17	-74	-5
1983	-208	-112	-208	0
1985	-212	-179	-222	+10
1987	-150	-156	-169	+19
1989	-152	-117	-205	+53
1991	-269	-150	-322	+53
1993	-255	-193	-300	+45
1995	-164	-146	-226	+62
1997	-22	-80	-103	+81
1999	+126	-1	+2	+124
2001	+127	+105	-33	+160
2003	-377	-276	-538	+160
2005	-318	-237	-493	+175

NOTE: Amounts in billions of dollars.

SOURCE: Congressional Budget Office

POLICY DEBATE

Balance the Budget? By What Definition?

As mentioned in the text, American citizens have long favored a balanced federal budget. It just *sounds* right. After all, don't most families balance their budgets? (*Answer*: No. Most families borrow to buy a house or a car.) And don't state and city governments have to balance their budgets? (*Answer*: Not by the definitions used by the federal government.)

Almost totally unnoticed by the public, Congress changed the *definition* of what a balanced budget means in 1999—and then changed in back in 2001! Traditionally, payments of Social Security benefits and the payroll tax revenues collected to finance them were segregated from other expenditures and receipts— and called *off-budget* items. But when calculating the overall budget deficit or surplus, they were *included* in a budget concept called (for obvious reasons) the *unified budget*. "Balancing the budget" meant balancing the unified budget.

But under revised accounting rules adopted in 1999, funds flowing into and out of Social Security were *excluded* from the calculation of the budget surplus or

SOURCE: © Bettmann/Corbis

deficit—leaving only so-called *on-budget* expenditures and receipts. Because the Social Security System was then (as now) running a sizable surplus, this change made "balancing the budget" much harder. Thus, two amazing things happened: Congress actually "raised the bar" for itself, and hardly anyone noticed! For example, in fiscal year 2001, the unified budget (old concept) showed a $127 billion *surplus*, but the new on-budget accounts showed a $33 billion *deficit*. (The difference, $160 billion, was the Social Security surplus.)

But it didn't last long. Seeing that it could no longer keep the budget in balance, and wanting to cut taxes, Congress changed the scorekeeping rules once again in 2001. And again, nobody seemed to notice. We are now back to the old unified budget concept, which *includes* the Social Security surplus. For example, the fiscal year 2006 books closed with an official deficit of $248 billion. But had Congress adhered to its 1999 decision to disregard Social Security, the *on-budget* deficit would have been a stunning $434 billion. Confused? That may be the idea.

◼ On-Budget versus Off-Budget Surpluses

When you read about the budget in the newspapers, you may see references to the "off-budget" surplus or deficit and the "on-budget" surplus or deficit. What do those terms mean?

Because Social Security benefits are financed by an earmarked revenue source—the payroll tax—Social Security and a few minor items have traditionally been segregated in the federal fiscal accounts. Specifically, both Social Security expenditures and the payroll tax receipts that finance them are treated as off-budget items, whereas most other expenditures and receipts are classified as on-budget. Thus:

Overall budget deficit = off-budget deficit + on-budget deficit

Because the Social Security System has been running sizable surpluses in recent years, the difference between the overall and on-budget deficits has been substantial. For example, in fiscal year 2005, the overall budget showed a $318 billion deficit (Column 1). But this was composed of a whopping $493 billion on-budget *deficit* (Column 3) less a $175 billion Social Security *surplus* (Column 4). For more on this accounting issue, see "Balance the Budget? By What Definition?"

◼ Conclusion: What Happened after 1981?

Table 1 helps us understand the remarkable rise, fall, and rise of the federal budget deficit since the 1980s. Column (1) shows the overall surplus (if positive) or deficit (if negative) every other year from 1981 to 2003, and Column (2) shows the corresponding *structural* surplus. Finally, Columns (3) and (4) break the overall surplus into its *on-budget* and *off-budget* components. The table tells the following story about the evolution of the budget deficit.

The large Reagan tax cuts in the early 1980s ballooned the budget deficit from $79 billion to $212 billion, and more than 100 percent of this deterioration was structural (see Column [2]). Late in the 1980s, the deficit started rising again—even though Social Security began to run sizable surpluses (see Column [4]). The overall deficit reached $269 billion in 1991, but then began to shrink. One reason was the burgeoning Social Security surplus, which increased by $115 between 1993 and 2001. The strong economy helped, too. Notice that the actual surplus rose more than the structural surplus. But most of the deficit-reducing "work" was on-budget and structural, as tax increases and expenditure restraint during the Clinton years finally got the budget under control—briefly, as it turned out. By 2003, a combination of large tax cuts, a burst of spending, and weaker economic growth had pushed the deficit up to a record $378 billion—a record that was topped in fiscal year 2004. But the deficit has since fallen.

■ WHY IS THE NATIONAL DEBT CONSIDERED A BURDEN?

Now that we have gained some perspective on the facts, let us consider the charge that budget deficits place intolerable burdens on future generations. Perhaps the most frequently heard reason is that *future Americans will be burdened by heavy interest payments*, which will necessitate higher taxes. But think about who will receive those interest payments: mostly the future Americans who own the bonds. Thus, one group of future Americans will be making interest payments to another group of future Americans—which cannot be a burden on the nation as a whole.[3]

But there *is* a future burden to the extent that the debt is held by foreigners. The share of the net U.S. national debt owned by foreign individuals, businesses, and governments has been rising rapidly and is now over 52 percent. Paying interest on this portion of the debt will indeed burden future Americans in a very concrete way: For years to come, a portion of America's GDP will be sent abroad to pay interest on the debts we incurred in the 1980s, 1990s, and 2000s. For this reason, many thoughtful observers are becoming concerned that the United States is borrowing too much from abroad.[4] Thus, we conclude that:

> If the national debt is owned by domestic citizens, future interest payments just transfer funds from one group of Americans to another. But the portion of the national debt owned by foreigners does constitute a burden on the nation as a whole.

Many people also worry that every nation has a limited capacity to borrow, just like every family and every business. If it exceeds this limit, it is in danger of being unable to pay its creditors and may go bankrupt—with calamitous consequences for everyone. For some countries, this concern is indeed valid and serious. Debt crises have done major damage to many countries in Latin America, Asia, and Africa over the years.

But the U.S. government need not worry about defaulting on its debt for one simple reason. *The American national debt is an obligation to pay U.S. dollars:* Each debt certificate obligates the Treasury to pay the holder so many U.S. dollars on a prescribed date. But the U.S. government is the source of these dollars. It prints them! *No nation need default on debts that call for repayment in its own currency.* If worse comes to worse, it can always print whatever money it needs to pay off its creditors.[5] This option is not open to countries whose debts call for payment, say, in U.S. dollars, as a number of Southeast Asian countries learned in 1997 and Argentina learned in 2001.

---

[3] However, the future taxes that will have to be raised to pay the interest may reduce the efficiency of the economy.

[4] We will discuss the linkages between the federal budget deficit and foreign borrowing in greater detail in Chapter 36.

[5] However, Russia astounded the financial world in 1998 by defaulting on its ruble-denominated debt.

It does not, of course, follow that acquiring more debt through budget deficits is necessarily a good idea for the United States. Nonetheless:

> There is a fundamental difference between nations that borrow in their own currency (such as the United States) and nations that borrow in some other currency (which is, normally, the U.S. dollar). The former need never default; the latter might have to.

■ BUDGET DEFICITS AND INFLATION

We now turn to the effects of deficits on macroeconomic outcomes. It often is said that deficit spending is a cause of inflation. Let us consider that argument with the aid of Figure 6, which is a standard aggregate supply and demand diagram.

Initially, equilibrium is at point A, where demand curve D_0D_0 and supply curve SS intersect. Output is $7,000 billion, and the price index is 100. In the diagram, the aggregate demand and supply curves intersect precisely at potential GDP, indicating that the economy is operating at full employment. Let us also assume that the budget is initially balanced.

Suppose the government now raises spending or cuts taxes enough to shift the aggregate demand schedule outward from D_0D_0 to D_1D_1. Equilibrium shifts from point A to point B, and the graph shows the price level rising from 100 to 106, or 6

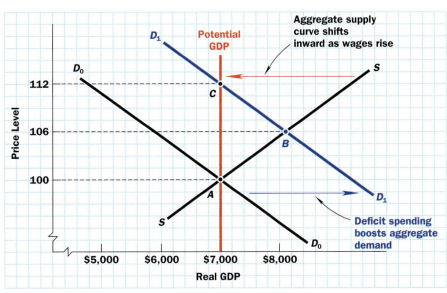

NOTE: Real GDP amounts are in billions of dollars.

FIGURE 6
The Inflationary Effects of Deficit Spending

percent. But that is not the end of the story, because point B represents an inflationary gap. We know from previous chapters that inflation will continue until the aggregate supply curve shifts far enough inward that it passes through point C, at which point the inflationary gap is gone. In this example, deficit spending will eventually raise the price level 12 percent.

Thus, the cries that budget deficits are inflationary have the ring of truth. How much truth they hold depends on several factors. One is the slope of the aggregate supply curve. Figure 6 clearly shows that a steep supply curve would lead to more inflation than a flat one. A second factor is the degree of resource utilization. Deficit spending is more inflationary in a fully employed economy (such as that depicted in Figure 6) than in an economy with lots of slack.

Finally, we must remember that the Federal Reserve's monetary policy can always cancel out the potential inflationary effects of deficit spending by pulling the aggregate demand curve back to its original position. Once again, the *policy mix* is crucial.

■ The Monetization Issue

But will the Federal Reserve always neutralize the expansionary effect of a higher budget deficit? This question brings up another reason why some people worry about the inflationary consequences of deficits. They fear that the Federal Reserve may feel compelled to "monetize" part of the deficit by purchasing some of the newly-issued government debt. Let us explain, first, why the Fed might make such purchases, and, second, why these purchases are called **monetizing the deficit.**

Deficit spending, we have just noted, normally drives up both real GDP and the price level. As we emphasized in Chapter 30, such an economic expansion shifts the

The central bank is said to **monetize the deficit** when it purchases bonds issued by the government.

demand curve for bank reserves outward to the right—as depicted by the movement from D_0D_0 to D_1D_1 in Figure 7. The diagram shows that, if the Federal Reserve takes no action to shift the supply curve, interest rates will rise as equilibrium moves from point A to point B.

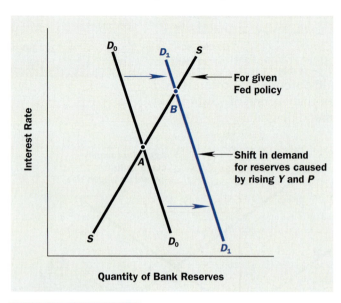

FIGURE 7

Fiscal Expansion and Interest Rates

Suppose now that the Fed does not want interest rates to rise. What can it do? To prevent the incipient rise in r, it would have to engage in *expansionary monetary policy* that creates new bank reserves, thereby shifting the supply curve for reserves outward to the right—as indicated in Figure 8. With the red supply curve S_1S_1, equilibrium would be at point C rather than at point B, leaving interest rates unchanged. Because the Federal Reserve usually pursues expansionary monetary policy by purchasing Treasury bills in the open market, deficit spending might therefore induce the Fed to buy more government debt.

But why is this process called *monetizing* the deficit? The reason is simple. As we learned in Chapter 29, giving banks more reserves generally leads, via the multiple expansion process, to an increase in the money supply. By this indirect route, then, larger budget deficits may lead to a larger money supply. To summarize:

If the Federal Reserve takes no countervailing actions, an expansionary fiscal policy that increases the budget deficit will raise real GDP and prices, thereby raising the demand for bank reserves and driving up interest rates. If the Fed does not want interest rates to rise, it can engage in expansionary open-market operations; that is, it can purchase more government debt. If the Fed does so, both bank reserves and the money supply will increase. In this case, we say that part of the deficit is *monetized.*

Monetized deficits are more inflationary than nonmonetized deficits for a simple reason: Expansionary monetary and fiscal policies *together* are more inflationary than expansionary fiscal policy *alone*. But is this a real worry? Does the Fed actually monetize any substantial portion of the deficit? Normally, it does not. The clearest evidence is the fact that the Fed managed to *reduce* inflation in the 1980s, and again in this decade, even as the government ran huge budget deficits. But monetization of deficits *has* been a serious cause of inflation in many other countries, ranging from Latin America to Russia, Israel, and elsewhere.

FIGURE 8

Monetization and Interest Rates

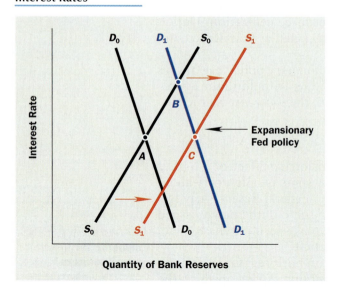

DEBT, INTEREST RATES, AND CROWDING OUT

So far, we have looked for possible problems that the national debt might cause on the *demand* side of the economy. But the real case for cutting the deficit comes on the *supply* side. In brief, large budget deficits discourage investment and therefore retard the growth of the nation's capital stock.

The mechanism is easy to understand by presuming (as is generally the case) that the Fed does not engage in any substantial monetization. We have just seen that budget deficits tend to *raise* interest rates. But we know from earlier chapters that the rate of interest (r) is a major determinant of investment spending (I). In particular, higher r leads to less I, and lower *r* leads to more *I*. The volume of investment made today will, in turn, determine how much capital we have tomorrow—and thus influence the size of our *potential* GDP. This, according to most economists, is the true sense in which a larger national debt may burden future generations and a smaller national debt may help them:

> A larger national debt may lead a nation to bequeath less physical capital to future generations. If they inherit less plant and equipment, these generations will be burdened by a smaller productive capacity—a lower potential GDP. By that mechanism, large deficits may retard economic growth. By the same logic, budget surpluses can stimulate capital formation and economic growth.

Phrasing this point another way explains why this result is often called the **crowding-out** effect. Consider what happens in financial markets when the government engages in deficit spending. When it spends more than it takes in, the government must borrow the rest. It does so by selling bonds, which compete with corporate bonds and other financial instruments for the available supply of funds. As some savers decide to buy government bonds, the funds remaining to invest in private bonds must shrink. Thus, some private borrowers get "crowded out" of the financial markets as the government claims an increasing share of the economy's total saving.

Some critics of deficit spending have taken this lesson to its illogical extreme by arguing that each $1 of government spending crowds out exactly $1 of private spending, leaving "expansionary" fiscal policy with no net effect on total demand. In their view, when *G* rises, *I* falls by an equal amount, leaving the total of *C* + *I* + *G* + (*X* − *IM*) unchanged.

Under normal circumstances, we would not expect this to occur. Why? First, moderate budget deficits push up interest rates only slightly. Second, private spending is only moderately sensitive to interest rates. Even at the higher interest rates that government deficits cause, most corporations will continue to borrow to finance their capital investments.

Furthermore, in times of economic slack, a counterforce arises that we might call the **crowding-in** effect. Deficit spending presumably quickens the pace of economic activity. That, at least, is its purpose. As the economy expands, businesses find it more profitable to add to their capacity so as to meet the greater consumer demands. Because of this *induced investment*, as we called it in earlier chapters, any increase in *G* may *increase* investment, rather than *decrease* it as the crowding-out hypothesis predicts.

The strength of the crowding-in effect depends on how much additional real GDP is stimulated by government spending (that is, on the size of the multiplier) and on how sensitive investment spending is to the improved business opportunities that accompany rapid growth. It is even conceivable that the crowding-in effect can dominate the crowding-out effect in the short run, so that *I* rises, on balance, when *G* rises.

But how can this be true in view of the crowding-out argument? Certainly, if the government borrows more *and the total volume of private saving is fixed*, then private industry must borrow less. That's just arithmetic. The fallacy in the strict crowding-out argument lies in supposing that the economy's flow of saving is really fixed. If government deficits succeed in raising output, we will have more income and therefore more saving. In that way, *both* government *and* industry can borrow more.

Which effect dominates—crowding out or crowding in? Crowding *out* stems from the increases in interest rates caused by deficits, whereas crowding *in* derives from the faster real economic growth that deficits sometimes produce. In the short run, the crowding-in effect—which results from the outward shift of the aggregate demand curve—is often the more powerful, especially when the economy is at less than full employment.

In the long run, however, the supply side dominates because, as we have learned, the economy's self-correcting mechanism pushes actual GDP toward potential GDP. When the economy is approximately at potential, the crowding-out effect takes over: Higher interest rates lead to less investment, so the capital stock and potential GDP grow more slowly. Turned on its head, this is the basic long-run argument for reducing the budget deficit: It will speed up investment and growth.

Crowding out occurs when deficit spending by the government forces private investment spending to contract.

Crowding in occurs when government spending, by raising real GDP, induces increases in private investment spending.

SOURCE: From *The Wall Street Journal*– Permission, Cartoon Features Syndicate

"Would you mind explaining again how high interest rates and the national deficit affect my allowance?"

■ The Bottom Line

Let us summarize what we have learned so far about the crowding-out controversy.

- The basic argument of the crowding-out hypothesis is sound: *Unless the economy produces enough additional saving,* more government borrowing will force out some private borrowers, who are discouraged by the higher interest rates. This process will reduce investment spending and cancel out some of the expansionary effects of higher government spending.

- But crowding out is rarely strong enough to cancel out the *entire* expansionary thrust of government spending. Some net stimulus to the economy remains.

- If deficit spending induces substantial GDP growth, then the crowding-in effect will lead to more income and more saving—perhaps so much more that private industry can borrow *more* than it did previously, despite the increase in government borrowing.

- The crowding-out effect is likely to dominate in the long run or when the economy is operating near full employment. The crowding-in effect is likely to dominate in the short run, especially when the economy has a great deal of slack.

■ THE MAIN BURDEN OF THE NATIONAL DEBT: SLOWER GROWTH

This analysis of crowding out versus crowding in helps us understand whether or not the national debt imposes a burden on future generations:

When government budget deficits take place in a high-employment economy, the crowding-out effect probably dominates. So deficits exact a toll by leaving a smaller capital stock, and hence lower potential GDP to future generations. However, deficits in an economy with high unemployment may well lead to more investment rather than less. In this case, in which the crowding-in effect dominates, deficit spending increases growth and the new debt is a blessing rather than a burden.

Which case applies to the U.S. national debt? To answer this question, let us go back to the historical facts and recall how we accumulated all that debt prior to the 1980s. The first cause was the financing of wars, especially World War II. Because this debt was contracted in a fully employed economy, it undoubtedly constituted a burden in the formal sense of the term. After all, the bombs, ships, and planes that it financed were used up in the war, not bequeathed as capital to future generations.

Yet today's Americans may not feel terribly burdened by the decisions of those in power in the 1940s, for consider the alternatives. We could have financed the entire war by taxation and thus placed the burden on consumption rather than on investment. But that choice would truly have been ruinous, and probably impossible, given the colossal wartime expenditures. Alternatively, we could have printed money, which would have unleashed an inflation that nobody wanted. Finally, the government could have spent much less money and perhaps not have won the war. Compared to these alternatives, Americans living in the 1950s and 1960s did not feel burdened by the massive deficit spending undertaken in the 1940s.

A second major contributor to the national debt prior to 1983 was a series of recessions. But these are precisely the circumstances under which budget deficits might prove to be a blessing rather than a burden. So it was only in the 1980s that we began to have the type of deficits that are truly burdensome—deficits acquired in a fully-employed, peacetime economy.

This sharp departure from historical norms is what made those budget deficits worrisome. The tax cuts of 1981–1984 blew a large hole in the government budget, and the recession of 1981–1982 ballooned the deficit even further. By the late 1980s, the U.S. economy had recovered to full employment, but a structural deficit of

$100–$150 billion per year remained. This persistent deficit was something that had never happened before. Such large structural deficits posed a real threat of crowding out and constituted a serious potential burden on future generations. After a brief interlude of budget surpluses in the late 1990s, large structural deficits reemerged a few years ago, caused by a combination of large tax cuts and rapid spending growth. Current projections foresee very large deficits "as far as the eye can see," which worries economists and budget analysts.

Let us now summarize our evaluation of the actual burden of the U.S. national debt:

- The national debt will not lead the nation into bankruptcy. But it does impose a burden on future generations when it is sold to foreigners or contracted in a fully employed, peacetime economy. In the latter case, it will reduce the nation's capital stock.

- Under some circumstances, budget deficits are appropriate for stabilization-policy purposes.

- Until the 1980s, the actual public debt of the U.S. government was mostly contracted as a result of wars and recessions—precisely the circumstances under which the new debt does not constitute a burden. However, the large deficits of the 1980s and 2000s were not mainly attributable to recessions, and are therefore worrisome.

- The shift from budget surpluses back to deficits in this decade may retard capital formation and future economic growth.

ISSUE REVISITED: *Was Fiscal Stimulus Warranted in 2001?*

We are now in a position to answer the question posed at the beginning of this chapter: Was it a good or bad idea to cut taxes in an effort to stimulate the U.S. economy after the September 2001 terrorist attacks? We can understand the nature of the debate that took place then by distinguishing between the short-run (demand side) and long-run (supply side) effects of changing what was then a modest budget surplus into a large deficit.

The terrorist attacks immediately set up fears that the U.S. economy, which was already in a mild recession, might slide downhill rapidly if consumers and businesses pulled in their horns. (Fortunately, those fears proved ill-founded.) As a short-run response, an expansionary fiscal policy consisting of both higher spending (for example, on homeland security) and tax cuts would push the aggregate demand curve outward—as shown in Figure 9. Moving from surplus to deficit in this way would cushion the recession by boosting real GDP as the economy's equilibrium shifted from point *A* to point *B*. That was why advocates of fiscal stimulus argued for quick action.

There was a long-run cost, however—as critics of fiscal stimulus reminded us. Large budget deficits would lead to higher real interest rates and hence to lower levels of private investment. That would make the nation's capital stock grow more slowly, thereby retarding the growth rate of potential GDP. This slower growth is depicted in Figure 10 on the next page, which shows budget deficits leading to a potential GDP of Y_1 instead of Y_0 in the future. With the same aggregate demand curve, *DD*, the result would be lower real GDP.

In the end, Congress argued for months and then finally passed something called a "stimulus package" in March 2002—after the recession was over. While the package had its critics, the emergency spending that followed September 11, 2001, and the first phase of the Bush tax cut (which had been enacted before the

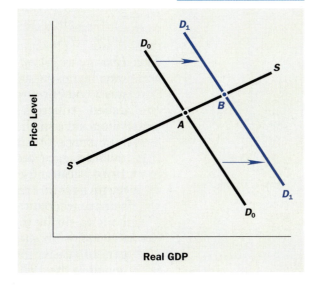

FIGURE 9

The Short-Run Effect of Larger Deficits or Smaller Surpluses

FIGURE 10

The Long-Run Effect of
Larger Deficits or
Smaller Surpluses

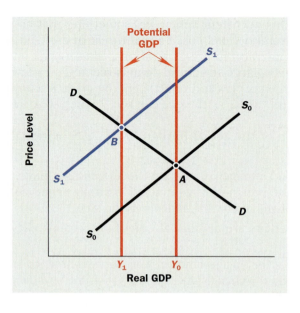

terrorist attacks) undoubtedly did stimulate the economy.

So which view was correct? Paradoxically, they both were. In the short run, aggregate demand factors dominate economic performance, and the fiscal stimulus in 2002 did provide an expansionary force just when the economy needed one. But in the long run, output gravitates toward potential GDP, no matter what happens to aggregate demand, so aggregate supply rules the roost. And because smaller surpluses deter some investment spending, they slow down the economy's potential growth rate. That is why thoughtful proponents of fiscal stimulus in 2001 urged the government to make any increases in spending or reductions in taxes temporary. We should reduce the budget surplus in the short run, they argued, but maintain it in the long run.

THE ECONOMICS AND POLITICS OF THE U.S. BUDGET DEFICIT

Given what we have learned in this chapter about the theory and facts of budget deficits, we can now address some of the major issues that have been debated in the political arena for years.

1. *Have the deficits of the 1980s, 1990s, and 2000s been a problem?* In 1981–1982, 1990–1991, and again in 2001, the U.S. economy suffered through recessions. Under such circumstances, crowding out is not a serious concern, and actions to close the deficit during or right after these recessions would have threatened the subsequent recoveries. According to the basic principles of fiscal policy, growing deficits were appropriate in each case.

   But in each case, crowding out became a more serious issue as the economy recovered toward full employment. Budget deficits should fall in such circumstances—as they did in the 1990s and from 2004 to 2006, but not in the 1980s nor in the period from 2002–2004. But instead, the structural deficit rose. Worries about the burden of the national debt, once mostly myths, became all too realistic.

2. *How did we get rid of the deficit in the 1990s?* In part, we did it the old-fashioned way: by raising taxes and reducing spending in three not-so-easy steps. There was a contentious but bipartisan budget agreement in 1990, a highly partisan deficit-reduction package in 1993 (which passed without a single Republican vote), and a smaller bipartisan budget deal in 1997.

   Taxing more and spending less produces a contractionary fiscal policy that reduces aggregate demand. This effect did not hurt the U.S. economy in the 1990s because fiscal and monetary policies were well coordinated. If fiscal policy turns contractionary to reduce the deficit, monetary policy can turn expansionary to counteract the effects on aggregate demand. In this way, we can hope to shrink the deficit without shrinking the economy. Such a change in the policy mix should also bring down interest rates, because both tighter budgets and easier money tend to have that effect. Indeed, that is just what happened in the 1990s. Interest rates fell, and the Fed made sure that aggregate demand was sufficient to keep the economy growing.

In addition, surprisingly rapid economic growth in the late 1990s generated much more tax revenue than anyone thought likely only a few years earlier. And the so-called off-budget surplus also increased. Both of these developments helped the federal budget turn rapidly from deficit into surplus.

3. *How did the surplus give way to such large deficits so rapidly?* The answer comes in three parts. First, a recession in 2001 depressed revenues. Second, the terrorist attacks of September 11, 2001, and then the wars in Afghanistan (2001) and Iraq (2003) led to a burst of spending on national defense and homeland security. Third, President Bush pushed large, multiyear tax cuts through Congress in 2001 and 2003—and has urged Congress to make them permanent. It is hardly a mystery that sharply rising expenditures and rapidly falling revenue push the budget from the black into the red.

SUMMARY

1. Rigid adherence to budget balancing would make the economy less stable, by reducing aggregate demand (via tax increases and reductions in government spending) when private spending is low and by raising aggregate demand when private spending is high.

2. Because both monetary and fiscal policy influence aggregate demand, the appropriate **budget deficit or surplus** depends on monetary policy. Similarly, the appropriate monetary policy depends on budget policy.

3. The same level of aggregate demand can be generated by different **mixes of fiscal and monetary policy**. But the composition of GDP will be different in each case. Larger budget deficits and tighter money tend to produce higher interest rates, a smaller share of investment in GDP, and slower growth. Smaller budget deficits and looser monetary policy lead to a larger investment share and faster growth.

4. One major reason for the large budget deficits of the early 1980s and early 1990s was the fact that the economy operated well below full employment. In those years, the **structural deficit,** which uses estimates of what the government's receipts and outlays would be at full employment to correct for business-cycle fluctuations, was much smaller than the official deficit.

5. The need to make future interest payments on the public debt is a burden only to the extent that the national debt is owned by foreigners.

6. The argument that a large **national debt** can bankrupt a country like the United States ignores the fact that our national debt consists entirely of obligations to pay U.S. dollars—a currency that the government can raise by increasing taxes or create by printing money.

7. Budget deficits can be inflationary because they expand aggregate demand. They are even more inflationary if they are **monetized**—that is, if the central bank buys some of the newly-issued government debt in the open market.

8. Unless the deficit is substantially monetized, deficit spending forces interest rates higher and discourages private investment spending. This process is called the **crowding-out effect.** If a great deal of crowding out occurs, then deficits impose a serious burden on future generations by leaving them a smaller capital stock with which to work.

9. But higher government spending (G) also produces a **crowding-in effect.** If expansionary fiscal policy succeeds in raising real output (Y), more investment will be induced by the higher Y.

10. Whether crowding out or crowding in dominates largely depends on the time horizon. In the short run, and especially when unemployment is high, crowding in is probably the stronger force, so higher G does not cause lower investment. But, in the long run, the economy will be near full employment, and the proponents of the crowding-out hypothesis will be right: High government spending will mainly displace private investment.

11. Larger deficits may spur growth (via aggregate demand) in the short run but deter growth (via aggregate supply and potential GDP) in the long run.

12. Whether or not deficits create a burden depends on how and why the government incurred the deficits in the first place. If the government runs deficits to fight recessions, more investment may be crowded in by rising output than is crowded out by rising interest rates. Deficits contracted to carry on wars certainly impair the future capital stock, although they may not be considered a burden for non-economic reasons. Because these two cases account for most of the debt the U.S. government contracted until the mid-1980s, that debt cannot reasonably be considered a serious burden. However, the deficits since 1984 are more worrisome on this score.

KEY TERMS

Mix of monetary and fiscal policy 685

Budget deficit 687

Budget surplus 687

National debt 687

Structural deficit or surplus 690

Monetization of deficits 693

Crowding out 695

Crowding in 695

Burden of the national debt 696

TEST YOURSELF

1. Explain the difference between the budget deficit and the national debt. If the deficit gets turned into a surplus, what happens to the debt?

2. Explain in words why the *structural* budget might show a surplus while the *actual* budget is in deficit. Illustrate your answer with a diagram like Figure 5 (page 690).

3. If the Federal Reserve begins to raise interest rates, what will happen to the government budget deficit? (*Hint:* What will happen to tax receipts and interest expenses?) If the government wants to offset the effects of the Fed's actions on aggregate demand, what might it do? How will this action affect the deficit?

DISCUSSION QUESTIONS

1. Explain how the U.S. government managed to accumulate a debt of over $8½ trillion. To whom does it owe this debt? Is the debt a burden on future generations?

2. Comment on the following: "Deficit spending paves the road to ruin. If we keep it up, the whole nation will go bankrupt. Even if things do not go this far, what right have we to burden our children and grandchildren with these debts while we live high on the hog?"

3. Newspaper reports frequently suggest that the administration (regardless of who is president) is pressuring the Fed to lower interest rates. In view of your answer to Test Yourself Question 3, why do you think that might be?

4. Explain the difference between crowding out and crowding in. Given the current state of the economy, which effect would you expect to dominate today?

5. Given the current state of the economy, what sort of fiscal-monetary policy mix seems most appropriate to you now? (*Note:* There is no one correct answer to this question. It is a good question to discuss in class.)

33

THE TRADE-OFF BETWEEN INFLATION AND UNEMPLOYMENT

We must seek to reduce inflation at a lower cost in lost output and unemployment.

JIMMY CARTER

A s early as our list of *Ideas for Beyond the Final Exam* in Chapter 1, we noted that there is a bothersome *trade-off between inflation and unemployment*: High-growth policies that reduce unemployment tend to raise inflation, and slow-growth policies that reduce inflation tend to raise unemployment. We also observed, in Chapter 31, that the trade-off looks rather different in the short run than in the long run because the aggregate supply curve is fairly flat in the short run but quite steep (perhaps even vertical) in the long run. A statistical relationship called the *Phillips curve* seeks to summarize the quantitative dimensions of the trade-off between inflation and unemployment in both the short and long runs. This chapter is about the Phillips curve.

CONTENTS

ISSUE: *Is the Trade-Off between Inflation and Unemployment a Relic of the Past?*

In the late 1990s, unemployment in the United States fell to extremely low levels—the lowest in 30 years. Yet, in stark contrast to prior experience, inflation did not rise. In fact, it fell slightly. This pleasant conjunction of events, which was nearly unprecedented in U.S. history, set many people talking about a glorious "New Economy" in which there was no longer any trade-off between inflation and unemployment. The soaring stock market, especially for technology stocks, added to the euphoria.

Is the long-feared trade-off really just a memory now? Can the modern economy speed along without fear of rising inflation? Or does faster growth eventually have inflationary consequences? These are questions the Federal Reserve was wrestling with in 2006 and 2007, and they are the central questions for this chapter. Our answers, in brief, are: no, no, and yes. And we devote most of this chapter to explaining them.

DEMAND-SIDE INFLATION VERSUS SUPPLY-SIDE INFLATION: A REVIEW

We begin by reviewing some of what we learned about inflation in earlier chapters. One major cause of inflation, although certainly not the only one, is *excessive growth of aggregate demand*. We know that any autonomous increase in spending—whether by consumers, investors, the government, or foreigners—will have a multiplier effect on aggregate demand. So each additional \$1 of C or I or G or $(X - IM)$ will lead to more than \$1 of additional demand. We also know that firms normally find it profitable to supply additional output only at higher prices. Hence, a stimulus to aggregate demand will normally pull up both real output and prices.

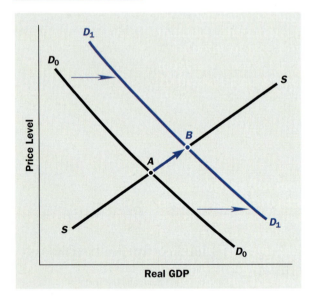

FIGURE 1

Inflation from the Demand Side

Figure 1, which is familiar from earlier chapters, reviews this conclusion. Initially, the economy is at point A, where aggregate demand curve D_0D_0 intersects aggregate supply curve SS. Then something happens to increase spending, and the aggregate demand curve shifts horizontally to D_1D_1. The new equilibrium is at point B, where both prices and output are higher than they were at A. Thus, the economy experiences both inflation and increased output. The slope of the aggregate supply curve measures the amount of inflation that accompanies any specified rise in output and therefore encapsulates the trade-off between inflation and economic growth.

But we also have learned in this book (especially in Chapter 27) that inflation does not always originate from the demand side. Anything that retards the growth of aggregate supply—for example, an increase in the price of foreign oil—can shift the economy's aggregate supply curve inward. This sort of inflation is illustrated in Figure 2, where the aggregate supply curve shifts inward from S_0S_0 to S_1S_1, and the economy's equilibrium consequently moves from point A to point B. Prices rise as output falls. We have *stagflation*.

Demand-side inflation is a rise in the price level caused by rapid growth of aggregate demand.

Supply-side inflation is a rise in the price level caused by slow growth (or decline) of aggregate supply.

Thus, although inflation can emanate from either the demand side or the supply side of the economy, a crucial difference arises between the two sources. **Demand-side inflation** is normally accompanied by rapid growth of real GDP (as in Figure 1), whereas **supply-side inflation** is normally accompanied by stagnant or even falling GDP (as in Figure 2). This distinction has major practical importance, as we shall see in this chapter.

ORIGINS OF THE PHILLIPS CURVE

Let us begin by supposing, as our brief review of U.S. macroeconomic history in Chapter 21 suggested, that most economic fluctuations are driven by gyrations in *aggregate demand*. In that case, we have just seen that GDP growth and inflation should rise and fall together. Is this what the data show?

We will see shortly, but first let us translate the prediction into a corresponding statement about the relationship between inflation and unemployment. Faster growth of real output naturally means faster growth in the number of jobs and, hence, lower unemployment. Conversely, slower growth of real output means slower growth in the number of jobs and, hence, higher unemployment. So we conclude that, if business fluctuations emanate from the demand side, unemployment and inflation should move in opposite directions: Unemployment should be low when inflation is high, and inflation should be low when unemployment is high.

Figure 3 illustrates the idea. The unemployment rate in the United States in 2004 averaged 5.5 percent (which we approximate by 5 percent in the figure), and the inflation rate was about 2.6 percent (which we approximate by 2 percent). Point B in Figure 3 records these two numbers. Had aggregate demand grown faster, inflation would have been higher and unemployment would have been lower. For the sake of concreteness, we suppose that unemployment would have been 4 percent and inflation would have been 3 percent—as shown by point A in Figure 3. By contrast, had aggregate demand grown more slowly than it actually did, unemployment would have been higher and inflation lower. In Figure 3, we suppose that unemployment would have been 6 percent and inflation would have been just 1 percent (point C). This figure displays the principal empirical implication of our theoretical model:

If fluctuations in economic activity are primarily caused by variations in the rate at which the aggregate demand curve shifts outward from year to year, then the data should show an inverse relationship between unemployment and inflation.

Now we are ready to look at real data. Do we actually observe such an inverse relationship between inflation and unemployment? More than 40 years ago, the economist A. W. Phillips plotted data on unemployment and the rate of change of money *wages* (not prices) for several extended periods of British history on a series of scatter diagrams, one of which is reproduced on the next page as Figure 4. He then sketched in a curve that seemed to "fit" the data well. This type of curve, which we now call a **Phillips curve,** shows that wage inflation normally is high when unemployment is low and is low when unemployment is high. So far, so good. These data illustrate the short run trade-off between inflation and unemployment, one of our *Ideas for Beyond the Final Exam.*

Phillips curves are more commonly constructed for price inflation; Figure 5 shows a Phillips-type diagram for the post–World War II United States. The curve appears to fit the data well. As viewed through the eyes of our theory, these facts suggest that economic

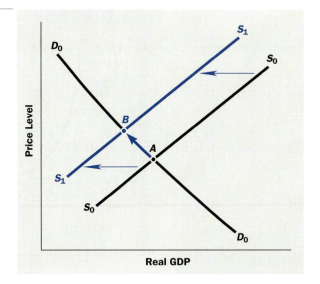

FIGURE 2

Inflation from the Supply Side

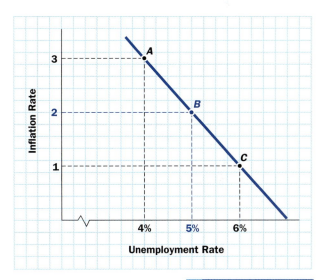

FIGURE 3

Origins of the Phillips Curve

A **Phillips curve** is a graph depicting the rate of unemployment on the horizontal axis and either the rate of inflation or the rate of change of money wages on the vertical axis. Phillips curves are normally downward sloping, indicating that higher inflation rates are associated with lower unemployment rates.

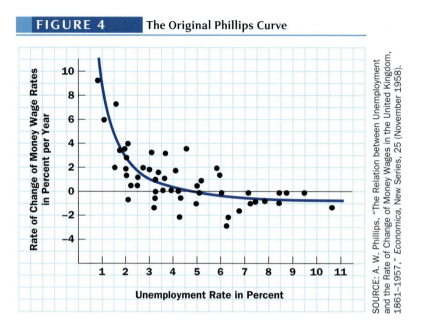

FIGURE 4 The Original Phillips Curve

SOURCE: A. W. Phillips, "The Relation between Unemployment and the Rate of Change of Money Wages in the United Kingdom, 1861–1957," *Economica*, New Series, 25 (November 1958).

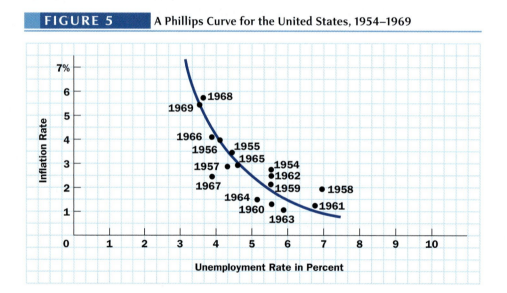

FIGURE 5 A Phillips Curve for the United States, 1954–1969

fluctuations in Great Britain between 1861 and 1913 and in the United States between 1954 and 1969 probably arose primarily from changes in the growth of aggregate demand. The simple model of demand-side inflation really does seem to describe what happened.

During the 1960s and early 1970s, economists often thought of the Phillips curve as a "menu" of choices available to policy makers. In this view, policy makers could opt for low unemployment and high inflation—as in 1969, or for high unemployment coupled with low inflation—as in 1961. The Phillips curve, it was thought, described the quantitative trade-off between inflation and unemployment. And for a number of years it seemed to work.

Then something happened. The economy in the 1970s and early 1980s behaved far worse than the Phillips curve had led economists to expect. In particular, given the unemployment rates in each of those years, inflation was astonishingly high by historical standards. This fact is shown clearly by Figure 6, which simply adds to Figure 5 the points for 1970 to 1984. So something went wrong with the old view of the Phillips curve as a menu for policy choices. But what?

SUPPLY-SIDE INFLATION AND THE COLLAPSE OF THE PHILLIPS CURVE

There are two major answers to this question, and a full explanation contains elements of each. We begin with the simpler answer, which is that much of the inflation in the years from 1972 to 1982 did not emanate from the demand side. Instead, the 1970s and early 1980s were full of adverse "supply shocks"—events such as the crop failures of 1972–1973 and the oil price increases of 1973–1974 and 1979–1980. These events pushed the economy's aggregate supply curve inward to the left, as was shown in Figure 2 (page 703). What kind of "Phillips curve" will be generated when economic fluctuations come from the supply side?

Figure 2 reminds us that output will decline (or at least grow more slowly) and prices will rise when the economy is hit by an adverse supply shock. Now, in a growing population with more people looking for jobs each year, a stagnant economy that does not generate enough new jobs will suffer a rise in unemployment. Thus, inflation and unemployment will increase at the same time:

If fluctuations in economic activity emanate from the supply side, higher rates of inflation will be associated with higher rates of unemployment, and lower rates of inflation will be associated with lower rates of unemployment.

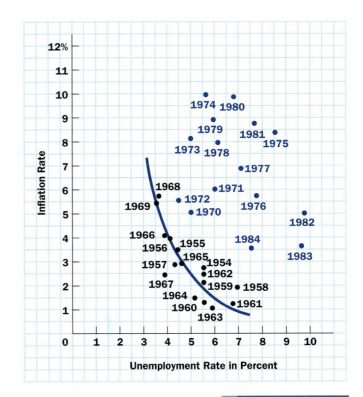

FIGURE 6

A Phillips Curve for the United States?

The major supply shocks of the 1970s stand out clearly in Figure 6. (Remember—these are real data, not textbook examples.) Food prices soared from 1972 to 1974, and again in 1978. Energy prices skyrocketed in 1973–1974, and again in 1979–1980. Clearly, the inflation and unemployment data generated by the U.S. economy in 1972–1974 and in 1978–1980 are consistent with our model of supply-side inflation. Many economists believe that supply shocks, rather than abrupt changes in aggregate demand, made the Phillips curve shift.

FIGURE 7

The Effects of a Favorable Supply Shock

Explaining the Fabulous 1990s

Now let's stand this analysis of supply shocks on its head. Suppose the economy experiences a *favorable* supply shock, rather than an adverse one, so that the aggregate supply curve shifts *outward* at an unusually rapid rate. Any number of factors—such as a drop in oil prices, bountiful harvests, or exceptionally rapid technological advance—can have this effect.

Whatever the cause, Figure 7 (which duplicates Figure 14 of Chapter 27) depicts the consequences. The aggregate demand curve shifts outward as usual, but the aggregate supply curve shifts out more than it would in a "normal" year. So the economy's equilibrium winds up at point *B* rather than

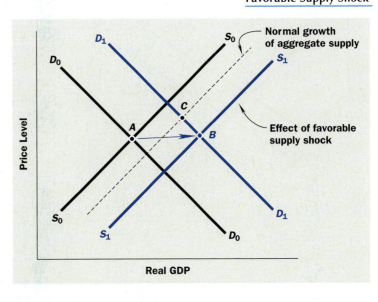

at point *C*, meaning that economic growth is *faster* (*B* is to the right of *C*) and inflation is *lower* (*B* is below *C*). Thus, inflation falls while rapid growth reduces unemployment.

Figure 7 more or less characterizes the experience of the U.S. economy from 1996 to 1998. Oil prices plummeted, lowering costs to American businesses and households. Stunning advances in technology made computer prices drop even more rapidly than usual. And the rising value of the U.S. dollar made imported goods cheaper to Americans.[1] Thus, we benefited from a series of favorable supply shocks, and the effects were just as depicted in Figure 7. The U.S. economy grew rapidly, and both inflation and unemployment fell at the same time.

ISSUE RESOLVED: *Why Inflation and Unemployment Both Declined*

We now have the answer to the question posed at the start of this chapter. We need nothing particularly new or mysterious to explain the marvelous economic performance of the second half of the 1990s. According to the basic macroeconomic theory taught in this book, favorable supply shocks should produce rapid economic growth with falling inflation. The U.S. economy did so well, in part, because we were so fortunate.

WHAT THE PHILLIPS CURVE IS NOT

So one view is that adverse supply shocks caused the stagflation of the 1970s and 1980s. But there is another view of what went wrong with the Phillips curve. It holds that policy makers misinterpreted the Phillips curve and tried to pick combinations of inflation and unemployment that were simply unsustainable.

Specifically, we have learned that the Phillips curve is a *statistical relationship* between inflation and unemployment that we expect to emerge *if business cycle fluctuations arise mainly from changes in the growth of aggregate demand*. But in the 1970s and 1980s, the curve was widely misinterpreted as depicting a number of *alternative equilibrium points* that the economy could achieve and from which policy makers could choose.

To understand the flaw in this reasoning, let us quickly review an earlier lesson. We know from Chapter 27 that the economy *self-correcting mechanism* that will cure both inflations and recessions *eventually*, even if the government does nothing. This idea is important in this context because it tells us that many combinations of output and prices cannot be maintained indefinitely. Some will self-destruct. Specifically, if the economy finds itself far from the normal full-employment level of unemployment, forces will be set in motion that tend to erode the inflationary or recessionary gap.

Figure 8 depicts the case of a recessionary gap where aggregate supply curve S_0S_0 intersects aggregate demand curve *DD* at point *A*. With equilibrium output well below potential GDP, the economy has unused industrial capacity and unsold output, so inflation will be tame. At the same time, the availability of unemployed workers eager for jobs limits the rate at which labor can push up wage rates. But wages are the main component of business costs, so when they decline (relative to what they would have been without a recession) so do costs. The lower costs, in turn, stimulate greater production. Figure 8 illustrates this process by an outward shift of the aggregate supply curve—from S_0S_0 to the blue curve S_1S_1.

FIGURE 8

The Elimination of a Recessionary Gap

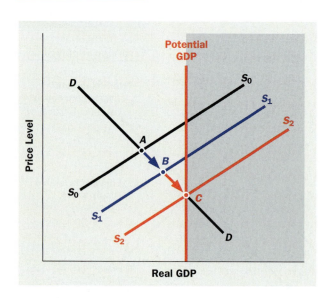

---

[1] The dollar and imports will be discussed in detail in Chapter 36.

As the figure shows, the outward shift of the aggregate supply curve brought on by the recession pushes equilibrium output up as the economy moves from point A to point B. Thus, the size of the recessionary gap begins to shrink. This process continues until the aggregate supply curve reaches the position indicated by the red curve S_2S_2 in Figure 8. Here wages have fallen enough to eliminate the recessionary gap, and the economy has reached a full-employment equilibrium at point C.[2]

We can relate this sequence of events to our discussion of the origins of the Phillips curve with the help of Figure 9, which is a hypothetical Phillips curve. Point a in Figure 9 corresponds to point A in Figure 8: It shows the initial recessionary gap with unemployment (assumed to be 6.5 percent) above full employment, which we assume to occur at 5 percent.

But we have just seen that point A in Figure 8—and therefore also point a in Figure 9—is not sustainable. The economy tends to rid itself of the recessionary gap through the disinflation process we have just described. The adjustment path from A to C depicted in Figure 8 would appear on our Phillips curve diagram as a movement toward less inflation and less unemployment—something like the red arrow from point a to point c in Figure 9.

Similarly, points representing inflationary gaps—such as point d in Figure 9—are also not sustainable. They, too, are gradually eliminated by the self-correcting mechanism that we studied in Chapter 27. Wages are forced up by the abnormally low unemployment, which in turn pushes prices higher. Higher prices deter investment spending by forcing up interest rates, and they deter consumer spending by lowering the purchasing power of consumer wealth. The inflationary process continues until the amount people want to spend is brought into balance with the amount firms want to supply at normal full employment. During such an adjustment period, unemployment and inflation both rise—as indicated by the red arrow from point d to point f in Figure 9. Putting these two conclusions together, we see that:

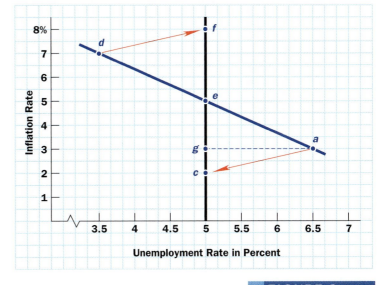

FIGURE 9

The Vertical Long-Run Phillips Curve

On a Phillips curve diagram such as Figure 9, neither points corresponding to an inflationary gap (like point d) nor points corresponding to a recessionary gap (like point a) can be maintained indefinitely. Inflationary gaps lead to rising unemployment and rising inflation. Recessionary gaps lead to falling inflation and falling unemployment.

All the points that are sustainable in the long run (such as c, e, and f) correspond to the same rate of unemployment, which is therefore called the **natural rate of unemployment**. The natural rate corresponds to what we have so far been calling the "full-employment" unemployment rate.

Thus, the Phillips curve connecting points d, e, and a is not a menu of policy choices at all. Although we can move from a point such as e to a point such as d by stimulating aggregate demand sufficiently, the economy will not be able to remain at point d. We cannot keep unemployment at such a low level indefinitely. Instead, policy makers must choose from among points such as c, e, and f, all of which correspond to the same "natural" rate of unemployment. For obvious reasons, the line connecting these points has been dubbed the **vertical long-run Phillips curve**. It is

The economy's self-correcting mechanism always tends to push the unemployment rate back toward a specific rate of unemployment that we call the **natural rate of unemployment**.

The **vertical (long-run) Phillips curve** shows the menu of inflation/ unemployment choices available to society in the long run. It is a vertical straight line at the natural rate of unemployment.

---

[2] This simple analysis assumes that the aggregate demand curve does not move during the adjustment period. If it is shifting to the right, the recessionary gap will disappear even faster, but inflation will not slow down as much. (*Exercise:* Construct the diagram for this case by adding a shift of the aggregate demand curve to Figure 8.)

this vertical Phillips curve, connecting points such as *e* and *f*, that represents the true long-run menu of policy choices. We thus conclude:

IDEAS FOR BEYOND THE FINAL EXAM

THE TRADE-OFF BETWEEN INFLATION AND UNEMPLOYMENT In the short run, it is possible to "ride up the Phillips curve" toward lower levels of unemployment by stimulating aggregate demand. (See, for example, point *d* in Figure 9.) Conversely, by restricting the growth of demand, it is possible to "ride down the Phillips curve" toward lower rates of inflation (such as point *a* in Figure 9). Thus, there is a *trade-off between unemployment and inflation in the short run.* Stimulating demand will improve the unemployment picture but worsen inflation; restricting demand will lower inflation but aggravate the unemployment problem.

However, there is no such trade-off in the long run. The economy's self-correcting mechanism ensures that unemployment will eventually return to the natural rate no matter what happens to aggregate demand. In the long run, faster growth of demand leads only to higher inflation, not to lower unemployment; and slower growth of demand leads only to lower inflation, not to higher unemployment.

FIGHTING UNEMPLOYMENT WITH FISCAL AND MONETARY POLICY

Now let us apply this analysis to a concrete policy problem—one that has often troubled policy makers in the United States and in other countries. Should the government's ability to manage aggregate demand through fiscal and monetary policy be used to combat unemployment? If so, how? To focus the discussion, we will deal with a recent, real-world example.

The unemployment rate in the United States bottomed out at 3.8 percent in April 2000, a rate that most economists thought was well below the natural rate of unemployment (something like point *d* in Figure 9). It then began to creep up gradually, and by August 2001 stood at 4.9 percent—which may be close to the natural rate (see point *e* in the figure). Then the terrorist attacks of September 11, 2001 occurred, and within a few months unemployment had risen to 5.7 percent. By December, the economy was in a position resembling point *a* in Figure 9, with a recessionary gap.

Even if fiscal and monetary policy makers did nothing, the economy's self-correcting mechanism would have gradually eroded the recessionary gap. Both unemployment and inflation would have declined gradually as the economy moved along the red arrow from point *a* to point *c* in Figure 9. Eventually, as the diagram shows, the economy would have returned to its natural rate of unemployment (assumed here to be 5 percent) and inflation would have fallen—in the example, from 3 percent to 2 percent.

This eventual outcome is quite satisfactory: Both unemployment and inflation are lower at the end of the adjustment period (point *c*) than at the beginning (point *a*). But it may take an agonizingly long time to get there. And American policy makers in 2001 did not view patience as a virtue. The Federal Reserve moved almost immediately after the terrorist attacks, cutting interest rates several times by year end. Fiscal policy reacted as well. Spending on defense and security was increased immediately after the attacks, the first phase of the 2001 tax cut kicked in, and Congress passed a small fiscal stimulus package.

According to the theory we have learned, such a large dose of expansionary fiscal and monetary policy should have pushed the economy up the short-run Phillips curve from a point like *a* toward a point like *e* in Figure 9. Compared to simply relying on the self-correcting mechanism, then, the strong stabilization policy response presumably led to a faster recovery from the 2001 recession. That was certainly the intent of the president, Congress, and the Fed. But Figure 9 points out that it also probably left us with a higher inflation rate (5 percent in the figure, about 2 percent in reality).

This example illustrates the range of choices open to policy makers: They can wait patiently while the economy's self-correcting mechanism pulls unemployment down to the natural rate—leading to a long-run equilibrium like point *c* in Figure 9. Alternatively, they can rush the process along with expansionary monetary and fiscal policy—and wind up with the same unemployment rate but higher inflation (point *e*). In what sense, then, do policy makers face a *trade-off* between inflation and unemployment? The answer illustrated by this diagram is:

The cost of reducing unemployment more rapidly by expansionary fiscal and monetary policies is a permanently higher inflation rate.

■ WHAT SHOULD BE DONE?

Should the government pay the inflationary costs of fighting unemployment? When the transitory benefit (lower unemployment for a while) is balanced against the permanent cost (higher inflation), have we made a good bargain?

We have noted that the U.S. government opted for a strong policy response in 2001. Thus two forces were at work simultaneously: The self-correcting mechanism was pulling the economy toward point *c* in Figure 9, even as the expansionary monetary and fiscal policies were pushing it toward point *e*. The net result was an intermediate path—something like the dotted line leading to point *g* in Figure 9. As the economy returned to full employment over the years from 2003 to 2006, growth was reasonably strong and inflation rose only a little.

How do policy makers make decisions like this? Our analysis highlights three critical issues on which the answer depends.

■ The Costs of Inflation and Unemployment

In Chapter 23, we examined the social costs of inflation and unemployment. Most of the benefits of lower unemployment, we concluded, translate easily into dollars and cents. Basically, we need only estimate the higher real GDP each year. However, the costs of the permanently higher inflation rate are more difficult to measure. So there is considerable controversy over the costs and benefits of using demand management to fight unemployment.

Economists and political leaders who believe that inflation is extremely costly may deem it unwise to accept the inflationary consequences of reducing unemployment faster. And indeed, a few dissenters in 2001 were worried about future inflation. Most U.S. policy makers apparently disagreed with that view, however. They decided that reducing unemployment was more important. But things do not always work out that way. In recent decades, many European governments have avoided expansionary stabilization policies rather than accept higher inflation.

■ The Slope of the Short-Run Phillips Curve

The shape of the short-run Phillips curve is also critical. Look back at Figure 9, and imagine that the Phillips curve connecting points *a*, *e*, and *d* was much steeper. In that case, the inflationary costs of using expansionary policy to reduce unemployment would be more substantial. By contrast, if the short-run Phillips curve was much flatter than the one shown in Figure 9, unemployment could be reduced with less inflationary cost.

■ The Efficiency of the Economy's Self-Correcting Mechanism

We have emphasized that, once a recessionary gap opens, the economy's natural self-correcting mechanism will eventually close it—even in the absence of any policy response. The obvious question is: How long must we wait? If the self-correcting mechanism—which works through reductions in wage inflation—is fast and reliable, high unemployment will not last very long. So the costs of waiting will be small. But if wage inflation responds only slowly to unemployment, the costs of waiting may be enormous. That has evidently been true in much of Europe, where unemployment has remained persistently high for years.

Inflation Targeting and the Philips Curve

In Chapter 31, we mentioned *inflation targeting* as a new approach to monetary policy that is gaining adherents in many countries. In practice, inflation targeting requires monetary policy makers to rely heavily on the Phillips curve. Why? Because a central bank with, say, a 2 percent inflation target is obligated to pursue a monetary policy that it believes will drive the inflation rate to 2 percent after, say, a year or two. But how does the central bank know which policy will accomplish this goal?

Knowing the proper policy with certainty is, of course, out of the question. But a central bank can use a model similar to the aggregate supply/demand model taught in this book to *estimate* how its policy choices will affect the unemployment rate, say, this year and next. Then it can use a Phillips curve to *estimate* how that unemployment path will affect inflation. In fact, that is more or less what inflation-targeting central banks from New Zealand to Sweden do.

The efficacy of the self-correcting mechanism is also surrounded by controversy. Most economists believe that the weight of the evidence points to extremely sluggish wage behavior: Wage inflation appears to respond slowly to economic slack. In terms of Figure 9, this lag means that the economy will traverse the path from *a* to *c* at an agonizingly slow pace, so that a long period of weak economic activity will be necessary to bring down inflation.

But a significant minority opinion finds this assessment far too pessimistic. Economists in this group argue that the costs of reducing inflation are not nearly so severe and that the key to a successful anti-inflation policy is how it affects people's *expectations* of inflation. To understand this argument, we must first understand why expectations are relevant to the Phillips curve.

INFLATIONARY EXPECTATIONS AND THE PHILLIPS CURVE

Recall from Chapter 27 that the main reason why the economy's aggregate supply curve slopes upward—that is, why output increases as the price level rises—is that businesses typically purchase labor and other inputs under long-term contracts that fix input costs in money terms. (The money wage rate is the clearest example.) As long as such contracts are in force, *real* wages fall as the prices of goods rise. Labor therefore becomes cheaper in real terms, which persuades businesses to expand employment and output. Buying low and selling high is, after all, the recipe for higher profits.

Table 1 illustrates this general idea in a concrete example. We suppose that workers and firms agree today that the money wage to be paid a year from now will be 10 per hour. The table then shows the real wage corresponding to each alternative inflation rate. For example, if inflation is 4 percent, the real wage a year from now will be $10.00/1.04 = $9.62. Clearly, the higher the inflation rate, the higher the price level at the end of the year and the lower the real wage.

Lower real wages provide an incentive for firms to increase output, as we have just noted. But lower real wages also impose losses of purchasing power on workers. Thus, workers are,

TABLE 1			
Money and Real Wages under Unexpected Inflation			
Inflation Rate	Price Level 1 Year from Now	Wage per Hour 1 Year from Now	Real Wage per Hour 1 Year from Now
0%	100	$10.00	$10.00
2	102	10.00	9.80
4	104	10.00	9.62
6	106	10.00	9.43

NOTE: Each real wage figure is obtained by dividing the $10 nominal wage by the corresponding price level a year later and multiplying by 100. Thus, for example, when the inflation rate is 4 percent, the real wage at the end of the year is ($10.00/104) × 100 = $9.62.

in some sense, "cheated" by inflation if they sign a contract specifying a fixed money wage in an inflationary environment.

Many economists doubt that workers will sign such contracts *if they can see inflation coming*. Would it not be wiser, these economists ask, to insist on being compensated for the coming inflation? After all, firms should be willing to offer higher money wages if they expect inflation, because they realize that higher money wages need not imply higher *real* wages.

Table 2 illustrates the mechanics of such a deal. For example, if people expect 4 percent inflation, the contract could stipulate that the wage rate be increased to $10.40 (which is 4 percent more than $10) at the end of the year. That would keep the real wage at $10 (because $10.40/1.04 = $10.00), the same as it would be under zero inflation. The other money wage figures in Table 2 are derived similarly.

TABLE 2			
Money and Real Wages under Expected Inflation			
Expected Inflation Rate	Expected Price Level 1 Year from Now	Wage per Hour 1 Year from Now	Expected Real Wage per Hour 1 Year from Now
0%	100	$10.00	$10.00
2	102	10.20	10.00
4	104	10.40	10.00
6	106	10.60	10.00

If workers and firms behave this way, and if they forecast inflation accurately, then the real wage will not decline as the price level rises. Instead, prices and wages will go up together, leaving the real wage unchanged. Workers will not lose from inflation, and firms will not gain. (Notice that, in Table 2, the expected future real wage is $10 per hour regardless of the expected inflation rate.) But then there would be no reason for firms to raise production when the price level rises. In a word, the aggregate supply curve would become vertical. In general:

> If workers can see inflation coming, and if they receive compensation for it, inflation does not erode *real* wages. But if real wages do not fall, firms have no incentives to increase production. In such a case, the economy's aggregate supply curve will not slope upward but, rather, will be a vertical line at the level of output corresponding to potential GDP.

Such a curve is shown in Panel (a) of Figure 10. Because a vertical aggregate supply curve leads to a vertical Phillips curve, it follows that even the *short-run* Phillips curve would be vertical under these circumstances, as in Panel (b) of Figure 10.[3]

If this analysis is correct, it has profound implications for the costs and benefits of fighting inflation. To see this, refer once again to Figure 9 (page 707), but now use the graph to depict the strategy of fighting inflation by causing a recession. Suppose we start at point *e*, with 5 percent inflation. To move to point *c* (representing 2 percent inflation), the economy must take a long and unpleasant detour through point *a*. Specifically, contractionary policies must push the economy down the Phillips curve toward point *a* before the self-correcting mechanism takes over and moves the economy from *a* to *c*. In words, we must endure a recession to reduce inflation.

But what if even the *short-run* Phillips curve were *vertical* rather than downward sloping? In this case, the unpleasant recessionary detour would not be necessary. It would be possible for inflation to fall without unemployment rising. The economy could move vertically downward from point *e* to point *c*.

Does this optimistic analysis describe the real world? Can we really slay the inflationary dragon so painlessly? Not necessarily, for our discussion of expectations so far has made at least one unrealistic assumption: that businesses and workers can predict inflation accurately. Under this assumption, as Table 2 shows, real wages are unaffected by inflation—leaving the aggregate supply curve vertical, even in the short run.

---

[3] Test Yourself Question 1 at the end of the chapter asks you to demonstrate that a vertical aggregate supply curve leads to a vertical Phillips curve.

A Vertical Aggregate
Supply Curve and the
Corresponding Vertical
Phillips Curve

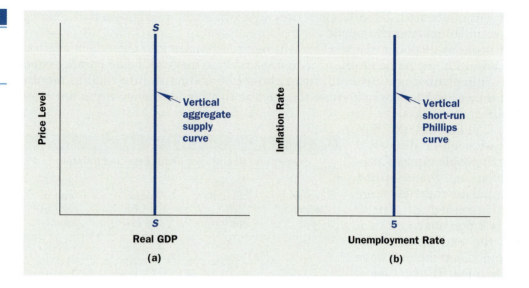

But forecasts of inflation are often inaccurate. Suppose workers underestimate inflation. For example, suppose they expect 4 percent inflation but actually get 6 percent. Then real wages will decline by 2 percent. More generally, real wages will fall if workers underestimate inflation at all. The effects of inflation on real wages will be somewhere in between those shown in Tables 1 and 2.[4] So firms will retain some incentive to raise production as the price level rises. The aggregate supply curve will retain its upward slope. We thus conclude that:

The short-run aggregate supply curve is vertical *when inflation is predicted accurately but* upward sloping *when inflation is underestimated. Thus, only* unexpectedly *high inflation will raise output, because only unexpected inflation reduces real wages.[5] Similarly, only an* unexpected *decline in inflation will lead to a recession.*

Because people often fail to anticipate changes in inflation correctly, this analysis seems to leave our earlier discussion of the Phillips curve almost intact for practical purposes. Indeed, most economists nowadays believe that the Phillips curve slopes downward in the short run but is vertical in the long run.

■ THE THEORY OF RATIONAL EXPECTATIONS

Rational expectations
are forecasts that, while not
necessarily correct, are the
best that can be made given
the available data. Rational
expectations, therefore,
cannot err systematically. If
expectations are rational,
forecasting errors are pure
random numbers.

However, a vocal minority of economists disagrees. This group, believers in the hypothesis of **rational expectations,** insists that the Phillips curve is vertical even in the short run. To understand their point of view, we must first explain what rational expectations are. Then we will see why rational expectations have such radical implications for the trade-off between inflation and unemployment.

■ What Are Rational Expectations?

In many economic contexts, people must formulate expectations about what the future will bring. For example, those who invest in the stock market need to forecast the future prices of the stocks they buy and sell. Likewise, as we have just discussed, workers and businesses may want to forecast future prices before agreeing on a money wage. Rational expectations is a controversial hypothesis about how such forecasts are made.

---

[4] To make sure you understand why, construct a version of Table 2 based on the assumption that workers expect 4 percent inflation (and hence set next year's wage at $10.40 per hour), regardless of what the actual rate of inflation is. If you create this table correctly, it will show that higher inflation leads to lower real wages, as in Table 1.

[5] To see this point, compare Tables 1 and 2.

As used by economists, a forecast (an "expectation") of a future variable is considered rational if the forecaster makes *optimal* use of all relevant information that is *available* at the time of the forecast. Let us elaborate on the two italicized words in this definition, using as an example a hypothetical stock market investor who has rational expectations.

First, proponents of rational expectations recognize that *information is limited*. An investor interested in Google stock would like to know how much profit the company will make in the coming years. Armed with such information, she could predict the future price of Google stock more accurately. But that information is simply not available. The investor's forecast of the future price of Google shares is not "irrational" just because she cannot foresee the future. On the other hand, if Google stock normally goes down on Fridays and up on Mondays, she should be aware of this fact.

Next, we have the word *optimal*. As used by economists, it means using proper statistical inference to process all the relevant information that is available before making a forecast. In brief, to have rational expectations, your forecasts do not have to be correct, but they cannot have systematic errors that you could avoid by applying better statistical methods. This requirement, although exacting, is not quite as outlandish as it may seem. A good billiards player makes expert use of the laws of physics even without understanding the theory. Similarly, an experienced stock market investor may make good use of information even without formal training in statistics.

■ Rational Expectations and the Trade-Off

Let us now see how some economists have used the hypothesis of rational expectations to deny any trade-off between inflation and unemployment—even in the short run.

Although they recognize that inflation cannot always be predicted accurately, proponents of rational expectations insist that workers will not make *systematic* errors. Remember that our argument leading to a sloping short-run Phillips curve tacitly assumed that workers are slow to recognize changes. They thus *underestimate* inflation when it is rising and *overestimate* inflation when it is falling. Many observers see such errors as a realistic description of human behavior. But advocates of rational expectations disagree, claiming that it is fundamentally illogical. Workers, they argue, will always make the best possible forecast of inflation, using all the latest data and the best available economic models. Such forecasts will sometimes be too high and sometimes too low, but they will not err systematically in one direction or the other. Consequently:

If expectations are rational, the difference between the *actual* rate of inflation and the *expected* rate of inflation (the forecasting error) must be a pure random number, that is:

Inflation = Expected inflation + a random number

Now recall that the argument in the previous section concluded that employment is affected by inflation only to the extent that inflation *differs* from what was expected. But, under rational expectations, no *predictable* change in inflation can make the *expected* rate of inflation deviate from the *actual* rate of inflation. The difference between the two is simply a random number. Hence, according to the rational expectations hypothesis, unemployment will always remain at the natural rate—except for random, and therefore totally unpredictable, gyrations due to forecasting errors. Thus:

If expectations are rational, inflation can be reduced without a period of high unemployment because the short-run Phillips curve, like the long-run Phillips curve, will be vertical.

According to the rational expectations view, the government's ability to manipulate aggregate demand gives it no ability to influence real output and unemployment because the aggregate supply curve is vertical—even in the short run. (To see why, experiment by moving an aggregate demand curve when the aggregate supply curve is vertical, as in Panel (a) of Figure 10 on page 712.) The government's manipulations of aggregate demand are planned ahead and are therefore predictable, and any *predictable* change in aggregate demand will change the *expected* rate of inflation. It will therefore leave real wages unaffected.

The government can influence output only by making *unexpected* changes in aggregate demand. But unexpected changes are not easy to engineer if expectations are rational, because people will understand what policy makers are up to. For example, if the authorities typically react to high inflation by reducing aggregate demand, people will soon come to anticipate this reaction. And *anticipated* reductions in aggregate demand do not cause *unexpected* changes in inflation.

An Evaluation

Believers in rational expectations are optimistic that we can reduce inflation without losing any output, even in the short run. Are they right?

As a piece of pure logic, the rational expectations argument is impeccable. But as is common in world of economic policy, controversy arises over how well the theoretical idea applies in practice. Although the theory has attracted many adherents, the evidence to date leads most economists to reject the extreme rational expectationist position in favor of the view that a trade-off between inflation and unemployment does exist in the short run. Here are some of the reasons.

Contracts May Embody Outdated Expectations   Many contracts for labor and other raw materials cover such long periods of time that the expectations on which they were based, although rational at the time, may appear "irrational" from today's point of view. For example, some three-year labor contracts were drawn up in 1996, when inflation had been running near 3 percent for years. It might have been rational then to expect the 1999 price level to be about 9 percent higher than the 1996 price level, and to have set wages for 1999 accordingly. By 1997, however, inflation had fallen to below 2 percent, and such an expectation would have been plainly irrational. But it might already have been written into contracts. If so, real wages wound up higher than intended, giving firms an incentive to reduce output and therefore employment—even though no one behaved irrationally.

Expectations May Adjust Slowly   Many people believe that inflationary expectations do not adapt as quickly to changes in the economic environment as the rational expectations theory assumes. If, for example, the government embarks on an anti-inflation policy, workers may continue to expect high inflation for a while. Thus, they may continue to insist on rapid money wage increases. Then, if inflation actually slows down, real wages will rise faster than anyone expected, and unemployment will result. Such behavior may not be strictly rational, but it may be realistic.

When Do Workers Receive Compensation for Inflation?   Some observers question whether wage agreements typically compensate workers for expected inflation in advance, as assumed by the rational expectations theory. More typically, they argue, wages catch up to actual inflation after the fact. If so, real wages will be eroded by inflation, as in the conventional view.

What the Facts Show   The facts have not been kind to the rational expectations hypothesis. The theory suggests that unemployment should hover around the natural rate most of the time, with random gyrations in one direction or the other. Yet this is not what the data show. The theory also predicts that preannounced (and thus expected) anti-inflation programs should be relatively painless. Yet, in practice, fighting inflation has proved very costly in virtually every country. Finally, many direct tests of the rationality of expectations have cast doubt on the hypothesis. For example, survey data on people's expectations rarely meet the exacting requirements of rationality.

But all these problems with rational expectations should not obscure a basic truth. In the long run, the rational expectations view should be more or less correct because people will not cling to incorrect expectations indefinitely. As Abraham Lincoln pointed out with characteristic wisdom, you cannot fool all the people all the time.

■ WHY ECONOMISTS (AND POLITICIANS) DISAGREE

This chapter has now taught us some of the reasons why economists may disagree about the proper conduct of stabilization policy. It also helps us understand some of the related political debates.

Should the government take strong actions to prevent or reduce inflation? You will say *yes* if you believe that (1) inflation is more costly than unemployment, (2) the short-run Phillips curve is steep, (3) expectations react quickly, and (4) the economy's self-correcting mechanism works smoothly and rapidly. These views on the economy tend to be held by monetarists and rational expectationists.

But you will say *no* if you believe that (1) unemployment is more costly than inflation, (2) the short-run Phillips curve is flat, (3) expectations react sluggishly, and (4) the self-correcting mechanism is slow and unreliable. These views are held by many Keynesian economists, so it is not surprising that they often oppose using recession to fight inflation.

The tables turn, however, when the question becomes whether to use demand management to bring a recession to a rapid end. The Keynesian view of the world—that unemployment is costly, that the short-run Phillips curve is flat, that expectations adjust slowly, and that the self-correcting mechanism is unreliable—leads to the conclusion that the benefits of fighting unemployment are high and the costs are low. Keynesians are therefore eager to fight recessions. The monetarist and rational expectationist positions on these four issues are precisely the reverse, and so are the policy conclusions.

■ THE DILEMMA OF DEMAND MANAGEMENT

We have seen that the makers of monetary and fiscal policy face an unavoidable trade-off. If they stimulate aggregate demand to reduce unemployment, they will aggravate inflation. If they restrict aggregate demand to fight inflation, they will cause higher unemployment.

But wait. Early in the chapter we learned that when inflation comes from the supply side, inflation and unemployment are *positively* correlated: They go up or down together. Does this mean that monetary and fiscal policy makers can escape the trade-off between inflation and unemployment? Unfortunately not.

IDEAS FOR BEYOND THE FINAL EXAM

> Shifts of the aggregate supply curve can cause inflation and unemployment to rise or fall together, and thus can destroy the statistical Phillips curve relationship. Nevertheless, anything that monetary and fiscal policy can do will make unemployment and inflation move in *opposite* directions because monetary and fiscal policies influence only the *aggregate demand* curve, not the *aggregate supply* curve.
>
> Thus, no matter what the source of inflation, and no matter what happens to the Phillips curve, the monetary and fiscal policy authorities still face the disagreeable trade-off between inflation and unemployment. Many policy makers have failed to understand this principle, and it is one of the *Ideas* that we hope you will remember well *Beyond the Final Exam.*

Naturally, the unpleasant nature of this trade-off has led both economists and public officials to search for a way out of the dilemma. We conclude this chapter by considering some of these ideas—none of which is a panacea.

■ ATTEMPTS TO REDUCE THE NATURAL RATE OF UNEMPLOYMENT

One highly desirable approach—if only we knew how to do it—would be to reduce the natural rate of unemployment. Then we could enjoy lower unemployment without higher inflation. The question is: How?

The most promising approaches have to do with education, training, and job placement. The data clearly show that more educated workers are unemployed less frequently than less educated ones are. Vocational training and retraining programs, if successful, help unemployed workers with obsolete skills acquire abilities that are

Why Did the Natural Rate of Unemployment Fall?

In 1995, most economists believed that the natural rate of unemployment in the United States was approximately 6 percent—and certainly not lower than 5.5 percent. If unemployment fell below that critical rate, they said, inflation would start to rise. Experience in the late 1990s belied that view. The unemployment rate dipped below 5.5 percent in the summer of 1996—and kept falling. By the end of 1998, it was below 4.5 percent. For a few months in 2001, it dipped below 4 percent. And there were still no signs of rising inflation.

One reason for such amazing macroeconomic performance was discussed in this chapter: A series of favorable supply shocks pushed the aggregate supply curve outward at an unusually rapid pace. But it also appears that the natural rate of unemployment fell in the 1990s. Why?

Economists do not have a complete answer to this question, but a few pieces of the puzzle are understood. For one thing, the U.S. working population aged—and mature workers are normally unemployed less often than are young workers. The rise of temporary-help agencies and Internet job searching capabilities helped match workers to jobs better. Ironically, record-high levels of incarceration probably reduced unemployment, because many of those in jail would otherwise probably have been unemployed. It is also believed (though difficult to prove) that the weak labor markets of the early 1990s left labor more docile, thereby driving down the unemployment rate consistent with constant inflation.

Whatever the reasons, it does appear that the United States can now sustain a lower unemployment than it could a decade ago.

currently in demand. By so doing, they both raise employment and help alleviate upward pressures on wages in jobs where qualified workers are in short supply.

Government and private job placement and counseling services play a similar role. Such programs try to match workers to jobs better by funneling information from prospective employers to prospective employees.

These ideas sound sensible and promising, but two big problems arise in implementation. First, training and placement programs often look better on paper than they do in practice, where they achieve only modest successes. Too often, people are trained for jobs that do not exist by the time they finish their training—if, indeed, the jobs ever existed.

Second, the high cost of these programs restricts the number of workers who can be accommodated, even in successful programs. For this reason, publicly-supported job training is done on a very small scale in the United States—much less than in most European countries. Small expenditures can hardly be expected to make a large dent in the natural rate of unemployment.

But many observers believe the natural rate of unemployment has fallen in the United States despite these problems. Why? One reason is that *work experience* has much in common with formal training—workers become more productive by learning on the job. As the American workforce has aged, the average level of work experience has increased, which, according to many economists, has lowered the natural rate of unemployment. (For some other possible reasons, see "Why Did the Natural Rate of Unemployment Fall?")

■ INDEXING

Indexing refers to provisions in a law or a contract whereby monetary payments are automatically adjusted whenever a specified price index changes. Wage rates, pensions, interest payments on bonds, income taxes, and many other things can be indexed in this way, and have been. Sometimes such contractual provisions are called *escalator clauses*.

Indexing—which refers to provisions in a law or contract that automatically adjust monetary payments whenever a specific price index changes—presents a very different approach to the inflation-unemployment dilemma. Instead of trying to improve the terms of the trade-off, *indexing seeks to reduce the social costs of inflation*.

The most familiar example of indexing is an escalator clause in a wage agreement. Escalator clauses provide for automatic increases in money wages—without the need for new contract negotiations—whenever the price level rises by more than a specified amount. Such agreements thus act to protect workers partly from inflation. Nowadays, with inflation so low and stable, relatively few workers are covered by escalator clauses. But they used to be more common.

Interest payments on bonds or bank accounts can also be indexed, and the U.S. government began doing so with a small fraction of its bonds in 1997. The most extensive indexing to be found in the United States today, however, appears in government transfer payments. Social Security benefits, for instance, are indexed so that retirees are not victimized by inflation.

Some economists believe that the United States should follow the example of several foreign countries and adopt a more widespread indexing system. Why? Because, they argue, it would take most of the sting out of inflation. To see how, let us review some of the social costs of inflation that we enumerated in Chapter 23.

One important cost is the capricious redistribution of income caused by unexpected inflation. We saw that borrowers and lenders normally incorporate an *inflation premium* equal to the *expected rate of inflation* into the nominal interest rate. Then, if inflation turns out to be higher than expected, the borrower has to pay the lender only the agreed-on nominal interest rate, including the premium for *expected* inflation; he does not have to compensate the lender for the (higher) *actual* inflation. Thus, the borrower enjoys a windfall gain and the lender loses out. The opposite happens if inflation turns out to be lower than expected.

But if interest rates on loans were indexed, none of this would occur. Borrowers and lenders would agree on a fixed *real* rate of interest, and the borrower would compensate the lender for whatever actual inflation occurred. No one would have to guess what the inflation rate would be.[6]

A second social cost mentioned in Chapter 23 stems from the fact that our tax system levies taxes on nominal interest and nominal capital gains. As we learned, this flaw in the tax system leads to extremely high effective tax rates in an inflationary environment. But indexing can cure this problem. We need only rewrite the tax code so that only *real* interest payments and *real* capital gains are taxed.

In the face of all these benefits, why does our economy not employ more indexing? One obvious reason is that inflation has been low for years. Indexing received much more attention in the 1970s and early 1980s, when inflation was high. A second reason is that some economists fear that indexing will erode society's resistance to inflation. With the costs of inflation so markedly reduced, they ask, what will stop governments from inflating more and more? They fear that the answer is: Nothing. Voters who stand to lose nothing from inflation are unlikely to pressure their legislators into stopping it. Opponents of indexing worry that a mild inflationary disease could turn into a ravaging epidemic in a highly indexed economy.

SUMMARY

1. Inflation can be caused either by rapid growth of aggregate demand or by sluggish growth of aggregate supply.

2. When fluctuations in economic activity emanate from the **demand side,** prices will rise rapidly when real output grows rapidly. Because rapid growth means more jobs, unemployment and inflation will be inversely related.

3. This inverse relationship between unemployment and inflation is called the **Phillips curve.** U.S. data for the 1950s and 1960s display a clear Phillips-curve relation, but data for the 1970s and 1980s do not.

4. The Phillips curve is not a menu of long-run policy choices for the economy, because the self-correcting mechanism guarantees that neither an inflationary gap nor a recessionary gap can last indefinitely.

5. Because of the self-correcting mechanism, the economy's true long-run choices lie along a **vertical long-run Phillips curve,** which shows that the so-called **natural rate of unemployment** is the only unemployment rate that can persist indefinitely.

6. In the short run, the economy can move up or down along its short-run Phillips curve. Temporary reductions in unemployment can be achieved at the cost of higher inflation, and temporary increases in unemployment can be used to fight inflation. This **short-run trade-off between inflation and unemployment** is one of our *Ideas for Beyond the Final Exam.*

7. Whether it is advisable to use unemployment to fight inflation depends on four principal factors: the relative social costs of inflation versus unemployment, the efficiency of the economy's self-correcting mechanism, the shape of the short-run Phillips curve, and the speed at which inflationary expectations are adjusted.

---

[6] For example, an indexed loan with a 2 percent real interest rate would require a 5 percent nominal interest payment if inflation were 3 percent, a 7 percent nominal interest payment if inflation were 5 percent, and so on.

8. If workers expect inflation to occur, and if they demand (and receive) compensation for inflation, output will be independent of the price level. Both the aggregate supply curve and the short-run Phillips curve are vertical in this case.

9. Errors in predicting inflation will change real wages and therefore the quantity of output that firms wish to supply. Thus, unpredicted movements in the price level will lead to a normal, upward-sloping aggregate supply curve.

10. According to the **rational expectations** hypothesis, errors in predicting inflation are purely random. As a consequence, except for some random gyrations, the aggregate supply curve is vertical even in the short run.

11. Many economists reject the rational expectations view. Some deny that expectations are "rational" and believe instead that people tend, for example, to underpredict inflation when it is rising. Others point out that contracts signed years ago may not embody expectations that are "rational" in terms of what we know today.

12. When fluctuations in economic activity are caused by shifts of the aggregate supply curve, output will grow slowly (causing unemployment to rise) when inflation rises. Hence, the rates of unemployment and inflation will be positively correlated. Many observers feel that this sort of stagflation is why the Phillips curve collapsed in the 1970s. Similarly, a series of favorable supply shocks help explain the 1990s combination of low inflation and strong economic growth.

13. Even if inflation is initiated by supply-side problems, so that inflation and unemployment rise together, the monetary and fiscal authorities still face this trade-off: Anything they do to improve unemployment is likely to worsen inflation, and anything they do to reduce inflation is likely to aggravate unemployment. (This is part of one of our *Ideas for Beyond the Final Exam*.) The reason behind it is that monetary and fiscal policy mainly influence the aggregate demand curve, not the aggregate supply curve.

14. Policies that improve the functioning of the labor market—including retraining programs and employment services—can, in principle, lower the natural rate of unemployment. To date, however, the U.S. government has enjoyed only modest success with these measures.

15. **Indexing** is another way to approach the trade-off problem. Instead of trying to improve the trade-off, it concentrates on reducing the social costs of inflation. Opponents of indexing worry, however, that the economy's resistance to inflation may be lowered by indexing.

KEY TERMS

Demand-side inflation 702

Supply-side inflation 702

Phillips curve 703

Stagflation caused by supply shocks 705

Self-correcting mechanism 706

Natural rate of unemployment 707

Vertical (long-run) Phillips curve 707

Trade-off between unemployment and inflation in the short run and in the long run 708

Rational expectations 712

Indexing (escalator clauses) 716

Real versus nominal interest rates 717

TEST YOURSELF

1. Show that, if the economy's aggregate supply curve is vertical, fluctuations in the growth of aggregate demand produce only fluctuations in inflation with no effect on output.

2. Long-term government bonds now pay approximately 5 percent nominal interest. Would you prefer to trade yours in for an indexed bond that paid a 3 percent real rate of interest? What if the real interest rate offered were 2 percent? What if it were 1 percent? What do your answers to these questions reveal about your personal attitudes toward inflation?

DISCUSSION QUESTIONS

1. When inflation and unemployment fell together in the 1990s, some observers claimed that policy makers no longer faced a trade-off between inflation and unemployment. Were they correct?

2. "There is no sense in trying to shorten recessions through fiscal and monetary policy because the effects of these policies on the unemployment rate are sure to be temporary." Comment on both the truth of this statement and its relevance for policy formulation.

3. Why is it said that decisions on fiscal and monetary policy are, at least in part, political decisions that cannot be made on "objective" economic criteria?

4. What is a Phillips curve? Why did it seem to work so much better in the period from 1954 to 1969 than it did in the 1970s?

5. Explain why expectations of inflation affect the wages that result from labor-management bargaining.

6. What is meant by "rational" expectations? Why does the hypothesis of rational expectations have such stunning implications for economic policy? Would believers in rational expectations want to shorten a recession by expanding aggregate demand? Would they want to fight inflation by reducing aggregate demand? Relate this analysis to your answer to Test Yourself Question 1.

7. It is often said that the Federal Reserve Board typically cares more about inflation and less about unemployment than the administration. If this is true, why might President Bush have worried about what the Fed might do to interest rates?

8. The year 2004 closed with the unemployment rate around $5\frac{1}{2}$ percent, real GDP rising approximately at the growth rate of potential GDP, inflation around 2 percent, and the federal budget showing a massive deficit.

   a. Give one or more arguments for engaging in expansionary monetary or fiscal policies under these circumstances.

   b. Give one or more arguments for engaging in contractionary monetary or fiscal policies under these circumstances.

   c. Which arguments do you find more persuasive?

VIII

THE UNITED STATES IN THE WORLD ECONOMY

"Globalization" became a buzzword in the 1990s—and it remains one today. Some people extol its virtues and view it as something to be encouraged. Others deplore its (real or imagined) costs and seek to stop globalization in its tracks. For example, globalization is sometimes portrayed as a threat to American workers.

We will examine several aspects of the globalization debate in Part VIII. But love it or hate it, one thing is clear: The United States is thoroughly integrated into a broader world economy. What happens in the United States influences other countries, and events abroad reverberate back here. Trillions of dollars' worth of goods and services—American computers, Chinese toys, Japanese cars—are traded across international borders each year. A vastly larger dollar volume of financial transactions—trade in stocks, bonds, and bank deposits, for example—takes place in the global economy at lightning speed.

Although we have mentioned these subjects before, we have not emphasized them. Part VIII brings international factors from the wings to center stage. Chapter 34 studies the factors that underlie *international trade*, and Chapter 35 takes up the determination of *exchange rates*—the prices at which the world's currencies are bought and sold. Then Chapter 36 integrates these international influences into our model of the macroeconomy.

If you want to understand why so many Americans are worried about international trade, why many thoughtful observers think we need to overhaul the international monetary system, or why there was so much economic turmoil in Southeast Asia, Russia, and Latin America during the last decade, read these three chapters with care.

34

INTERNATIONAL TRADE AND COMPARATIVE ADVANTAGE

No nation was ever ruined by trade.

BENJAMIN FRANKLIN

Economists emphasize international trade as the source of many of the benefits of "globalization"—a loosely-defined term that indicates a closer knitting together of the world's major economies. Of course, nations have always been linked in various ways. The Vikings, after all, landed in North America—not to mention Christopher Columbus. In recent decades, however, dramatic improvements in transportation, telecommunications, and international relations have drawn the nations of the world ever closer together economically. This process of globalization is often portrayed as something new. But in fact, it is not, as the box "Is Globalization Something New?" on the next page points out.

Economic events in other countries affect the United States for both macroeconomic and microeconomic reasons. For example, we learned in Parts VI and VII that the level of net exports is an important determinant of a nation's output and employment. But we did not delve very deeply into the factors that determine a nation's exports and imports. Chapters 35 and 36 will take up these *macroeconomic* linkages in greater detail. First, however, this chapter studies some of the *microeconomic* linkages among nations: How are patterns and prices of world trade determined? How and why do governments interfere with foreign trade? The central idea of this chapter is one we have encountered before (in Chapters 1 and 3): the *principle of comparative advantage.*

CONTENTS

Is Globalization Something New?

Few people realize that the industrialized world was, in fact, highly globalized prior to World War I, before the ravages of two world wars and the Great Depression severed many international linkages. Furthermore, as the British magazine *The Economist* pointed out a few years ago, globalization has not gone nearly as far as many people imagine.

Despite much loose talk about the "new" global economy, today's international economic integration is not unprecedented. The 50 years before the first world war saw large cross-border flows of goods, capital and people. That period of globalisation, like the present one, was driven by reductions in trade barriers and by sharp falls in transport costs, thanks to the development of railways and steamships. The present surge of globalisation is in a way a resumption of that previous trend. . . .

Two forces have been driving [globalization]. The first is technology. With the costs of communication and computing falling rapidly, the natural barriers of time and space that separate national markets have been falling too. The cost of a three-minute telephone call between New York and London has fallen from $300 (in 1996 dollars) in 1930 to $1 today . . .

The second driving force has been liberalisation. . . . Almost all countries have lowered barriers to trade. . . . [T]he ratio of trade to output . . . has increased sharply in most countries since 1950. But by this measure Britain and France are only slightly more open to trade today than they were in 1913. . . .

Product markets are still nowhere near as integrated across borders as they are within nations. Consider the example of trade between the United States and Canada, one of the least restricted trading borders in the world. On average, trade between a Canadian province and an American state is 20 times smaller than domestic trade between two Canadian provinces, after adjusting for distance and income levels.

The financial markets are not yet truly integrated either. Despite the newfound popularity of international investing, capital markets were by some measures more integrated at the start of this century than they are now. . . . [And] labour is less mobile than it was in the second half of the 19th century, when some 60m people left Europe for the New World.

SOURCE: Bettmann/Corbis

Source: "Schools Brief: One World?" from *The Economist,* October 18, 1997. Copyright © 1997 The Economist Newspaper Ltd. All rights reserved. Reprinted with permission. Further reproduction prohibited. http://www.economist.com

ISSUE: *How Can Americans Compete with "Cheap Foreign Labor"?*

Americans (and the citizens of many other nations) often want their government to limit or prevent import competition. Why? One major reason is the common belief that imports take bread out of American workers' mouths. According to this view, "cheap foreign labor" steals jobs from Americans and pressures U.S. businesses to lower wages. Such worries were prominently voiced, for example, in the 2004 presidential campaign when the Democratic candidate, Senator John Kerry, derided "Benedict Arnold CEOs" for shipping jobs abroad.

Oddly enough, the facts are grossly inconsistent with this story. For one thing, wages in most countries that export to the United States have risen dramatically in recent decades—much faster than wages here. Table 1 shows hourly compensation rates in eight countries on three continents, each expressed as a percentage of hourly compensation in the United States, in 1975 and 2005. Only workers in Mexico lost ground to American workers over this 30-year period. Labor in Europe gained substantially on their U.S. counterparts—rising in Britain, for example, from just above half the U.S. standard to above-U.S. levels. And the wage gains in Asia were nothing short of spectacular. Labor compensation in South Korea, for example, soared from just 5 percent of U.S. levels to more than half.[1] Yet, while all this was going on, American imports of automobiles from Japan, electronics from Taiwan, and textiles from Korea expanded rapidly.

---

[1] China would be an even more extreme example, but we lack Chinese data dating back to 1975.

Ironically, then, the United States' dominant position in the international marketplace *deteriorated* just as wage levels in Europe and Asia were rising closer to our own. Clearly, something other than exploiting cheap foreign labor must be driving international trade—in contrast to what the "common sense" view of the matter suggests. In this chapter, we will see precisely what is wrong with this "common sense" view.

WHY TRADE?

The earth's resources are not equally distributed across the planet. Although the United States produces its own coal and wheat, it depends almost *entirely* on the rest of the world for such basic items as rubber and coffee. Similarly, the Persian Gulf states have little land that is suitable for farming but sit atop huge pools of oil—something we are constantly reminded of by geopolitical events. Because of the seemingly whimsical distribution of the earth's resources, every nation must trade with others to acquire what it lacks.

Even if countries had all the resources they needed, other differences in natural endowments such as climate, terrain, and so on would lead them to engage in trade. Americans *could*, with great difficulty, grow their own bananas and coffee in hothouses. But these crops are grown much more efficiently in Honduras and Brazil, where the climates are appropriate.

The skills of a nation's labor force also play a role. If New Zealand has a large group of efficient farmers and few workers with industrial experience, while the opposite is true in Japan, it makes sense for New Zealand to specialize in agriculture and let Japan concentrate on manufacturing.

Finally, a small country that tried to produce every product would end up with many industries that are simply too small to utilize modern mass-production techniques or to take advantage of other economies of large-scale operations. For example, some countries operate their own international airlines for reasons that can only be described as political, not economic.

To summarize, the main reason why nations trade with one another is to exploit the many advantages of **specialization,** some of which were discussed in Chapter 3. International trade greatly enhances living standards for all parties involved because:

1. **Every country lacks some vital resources that it can get only by trading with others.**

2. **Each country's climate, labor force, and other endowments make it a relatively efficient producer of some goods and an inefficient producer of other goods.**

3. **Specialization permits larger outputs and can therefore offer economies of large-scale production.**

Specialization means that a country devotes its energies and resources to only a small proportion of the world's productive activities.

TABLE 1		
Labor Costs in Industrialized Countries as a Percentage of U.S. Labor Costs		
	1975	2005
France	73%	104%
United Kingdom	54	109
Spain	41	75
Japan	48	92
South Korea	5	57
Taiwan	6	27
Mexico	24	11
Canada	99	101

SOURCE: U.S. Bureau of Labor Statistics.

NOTE: Data are compensation estimates per hour, converted at exchange rates, and relate to production workers in the manufacturing sector.

Mutual Gains from Trade

Many people have long believed that one nation gains from trade only at the expense of another. After all, nothing new is produced by the mere act of trading. So if one country gains from a swap, it is argued, the other country must necessarily lose. One consequence of this mistaken belief was and continues to be a policy prescription calling for each country to try to take advantage of its trading partners on the (fallacious) grounds that one nation's gain must be another's loss.

Yet, as Adam Smith emphasized, and as we learned in Chapter 3, both parties must expect to gain something from any *voluntary exchange*. Otherwise, why would they agree to trade?

But how can mere exchange of goods leave both parties better off? The answer is that although trade does not increase the total output of goods, it does allow each party to acquire items better suited to its tastes. Suppose Levi has four cookies and nothing to drink, while Malcolm has two glasses of milk and nothing to eat. A trade of two of Levi's cookies for one of Malcolm's glasses of milk will not increase the total supply of either milk or cookies, but it almost certainly will make both boys better off.

By exactly the same logic, both the United States and Mexico must reap gains when Mexico voluntarily ships tomatoes to the United States in return for chemicals. In general, as we emphasized in Chapter 3:

IDEAS FOR BEYOND THE FINAL EXAM

TRADE IS A WIN-WIN SITUATION Both parties must expect to gain from any *voluntary exchange*. Trade brings about mutual gains by redistributing products so that both parties end up holding more preferred combinations of goods than they held before. This principle, which is one of our *Ideas for Beyond the Final Exam*, applies to nations just as it does to individuals.

■ INTERNATIONAL VERSUS INTRANATIONAL TRADE

The 50 states of the United States may be the most eloquent testimony to the gains that can be realized from specialization and free trade. Florida specializes in growing oranges, Michigan builds cars, California makes computers and chips, and New York specializes in finance. All of these states trade freely with one another and enjoy great prosperity. Try to imagine how much lower your standard of living would be if you consumed only items produced in your own state.

The essential logic behind international trade is no different from that underlying trade among different states; the basic reasons for trade are equally applicable within a country or among countries. Why, then, do we study international trade as a special subject? There are at least three reasons.

■ Political Factors in International Trade

First, domestic trade takes place under a single national government, whereas foreign trade always involves at least two governments. But a nation's government is normally much less concerned about the welfare of other countries' citizens than it is about its own. So, for example, the U.S. Constitution prohibits tariffs on trade among states, but it does not prohibit the United States from imposing tariffs on imports from abroad. One major issue in the economic analysis of international trade is the use and misuse of political impediments to international trade.

■ The Many Currencies Involved in International Trade

Second, all trade within the borders of the United States is carried out in U.S. dollars, whereas trade across national borders almost always involves at least two currencies. Rates of exchange between different currencies can and do change. In 1985, it took about 250 Japanese yen to buy a dollar; now it takes fewer than half that many. Variability in exchange rates brings with it a host of complications and policy problems.

■ Impediments to Mobility of Labor and Capital

Third, it is much easier for labor and capital to move about within a country than to move from one nation to another. If jobs are plentiful in California but scarce in Ohio, workers can move freely to follow the job opportunities. Of course, personal costs such as the financial burden of moving and the psychological burden of leaving friends and familiar surroundings may discourage mobility. But such relocations are not inhibited by immigration quotas, by laws restricting the employment of foreigners, or by the need to learn a new language.

There are also greater impediments to the transfer of capital across national boundaries than to its movement within a country. For example, many countries have rules limiting foreign ownership; even the United States limits foreign ownership of broadcast outlets and airlines. Foreign investment is also subject to special political risks, such as the danger of outright expropriation or nationalization after a change in government.

But even if nothing as extreme as expropriation occurs, capital invested abroad faces significant risks from exchange rate variations. An investment valued at 250 million yen is worth $2.5 million to American investors when the dollar is worth 100 yen, but it is worth only $1 million when it takes 250 yen to buy a dollar.

■ THE LAW OF COMPARATIVE ADVANTAGE

The gains from international specialization and trade are clear and intuitive when one country is better at producing one item and its trading partner is better at producing another. For example, no one finds it surprising that Brazil sells coffee to the United States and the United States exports software to Brazil. We know that coffee can be produced using less labor and other inputs in Brazil than in the United States. Likewise, the United States can produce software at a lower resource cost than can Brazil.

In such a situation, we say that Brazil has an **absolute advantage** in coffee production, and the United States has an absolute advantage in software production. In such cases, it is obvious that both countries can gain by producing the item in which they have an absolute advantage and then trading with one another.

What is much less obvious, but equally true, is that these gains from international trade still exist *even if one country is more efficient than the other in producing everything*. This lesson, the principle of **comparative advantage,** is one we first learned in Chapter 3.[2] It is, in fact, one of the most important of our *Ideas for Beyond the Final Exam*, so we repeat it here for convenience.

> One country is said to have an **absolute advantage** over another in the production of a particular good if it can produce that good using smaller quantities of resources than can the other country.

> One country is said to have a **comparative advantage** over another in the production of a particular good relative to other goods if it produces that good less inefficiently as compared with the other country.

THE SURPRISING PRINCIPLE OF COMPARATIVE ADVANTAGE Even if one country is at an absolute *dis*advantage relative to another country in the production of every good, it is said to have a *comparative advantage* in making the good at which it is *least inefficient* (compared with the other country).

The great classical economist David Ricardo (1772–1823) discovered about 200 years ago that two countries can still gain from trade, even if one is more efficient than the other in *every* industry—that is, even if one has an absolute advantage in producing every commodity.

In determining the most efficient patterns of production, it is *comparative* advantage, not *absolute* advantage, that matters. Thus a country can gain by importing a good even if that good can be produced more efficiently at home. Such imports make sense if they enable the country to specialize in producing goods at which it is *even more* efficient.

IDEAS FOR BEYOND THE FINAL EXAM

■ The Arithmetic of Comparative Advantage

Let's see precisely how comparative advantage works using a hypothetical example first suggested in Chapter 3. Table 2 gives a rather exaggerated impression of the trading positions of the United States and Japan a few years ago. We imagine that labor is the only input used to produce computers and television sets in the two countries and that the United States has an absolute advantage in manufacturing both goods. In this example, one year's worth of labor can

TABLE 2		
Alternative Outputs from One Year of Labor Input		
	In the U.S.	In Japan
Computers	50	10
Televisions	50	40

produce either 50 computers or 50 TV sets in the United States but only 10 computers or 40 televisions in Japan. So the United States is the more efficient producer of

---

[2] To review, see pages 49–50.

both goods. Nonetheless, as we will now show, it pays for the United States to specialize in producing computers and trade with Japan to get the TV sets it wants.

To demonstrate this point, we begin by noting that the United States has a comparative advantage in *computers*, whereas Japan has a comparative advantage in producing *televisions*. Specifically, the numbers in Table 2 show that the United States can produce 50 televisions with one year's labor whereas Japan can produce only 40; so the United States is 25 percent more efficient than Japan in producing TV sets. However, the United States is five times as efficient as Japan in producing computers: It can produce 50 per year of labor rather than 10. Because America's competitive edge is far greater in computers than in televisions, we say that the United States has a *comparative advantage* in computers.

From the Japanese perspective, these same numbers indicate that Japan is only slightly less efficient than the United States in TV production but drastically less efficient in computer production. So Japan's comparative advantage is in the television industry. According to Ricardo's law of comparative advantage, then, the two countries can gain if the United States specializes in producing computers, Japan specializes in producing TVs, and the two countries trade.

Let's verify that this conclusion is true. Suppose Japan transfers 1,000 years of labor out of the computer industry and into TV manufacturing. According to the figures in Table 2, its computer output will fall by 10,000 units, while its TV output will rise by 40,000 units. This information is recorded in the middle column of Table 3. Suppose, at the same time, the United States transfers 500 years of labor out of television manufacturing (thereby losing 25,000 TVs) and into computer making (thereby gaining 25,000 computers). Table 3 shows us that these transfers of resources between the two countries increase the world's production of both outputs. Together, the two countries now have 15,000 additional TVs and 15,000 additional computers—a nice outcome.

TABLE 3			
Example of the Gains from Trade			
	U.S.	Japan	Total
Computers	+25,000	−10,000	**+15,000**
Televisions	−25,000	+40,000	**+15,000**

Was there some sleight of hand here? How did *both* the United States *and* Japan gain *both* computers *and* TVs? The explanation is that the process we have just described involves more than just a swap of a fixed bundle of commodities, as in our earlier cookies-and-milk example. It also involves *a change in the production arrangements*. Some of Japan's inefficient computer production is taken over by more efficient American makers. And some of America's TV production is taken over by Japanese television companies, which are *less inefficient* at making TVs than Japanese computer manufacturers are at making computers. In this way, *world productivity* is increased. The underlying principle is both simple and fundamental:

When every country does what it can do best, all countries can benefit because more of every commodity can be produced without increasing the amounts of labor and other resources used.

■ The Graphics of Comparative Advantage

The gains from trade also can be displayed graphically, and doing so helps us understand whether such gains are large or small.

The lines *US* and *JN* in Figure 1 are closely related to the production possibilities frontiers of the two countries, but they differ in that they pretend that each country has the same amount of labor available.[3] In this case, we assume that each has 1 million person-years of labor. For example, Table 2 tells us that for each 1 million years of labor, the United States can produce 50 million TVs and no computers (point *U* in

---

[3] To review the concept of the production possibilities frontier, see Chapter 3.

Figure 1), 50 million computers and no TVs (point *S*), or any combination between (the line *US*). Similar reasoning leads to line *JN* for Japan.

America's *actual* production possibilities frontier would be even higher, relative to Japan's, than shown in Figure 1 because the U.S. population is larger. But Figure 1 is useful because it highlights the differences in *efficiency* (rather than in mere size) that determine both absolute and comparative advantage. Let's see how.

The fact that line *US* lies *above* line *JN* means that the United States can manufacture more televisions and more computers than Japan *with the same amount of labor.* This difference reflects our assumption that the United States has an *absolute* advantage in both commodities.

America's *comparative* advantage in computer production and Japan's comparative advantage in TV production are shown in a different way: by the relative *slopes* of the two lines. Look back to Table 2, which shows that the United States can acquire a computer on its own by giving up one TV. Thus, the *opportunity cost* of a computer in the United States is one television set. This opportunity cost is depicted graphically by the slope of the U.S. production possibilities frontier in Figure 1, which is $OU/OS = 50/50 = 1$.

Table 2 also tells us that the opportunity cost of a computer in Japan is four TVs. This relationship is depicted in Figure 1 by the slope of Japan's production possibilities frontier, which is $OJ/ON = 40/10 = 4$.

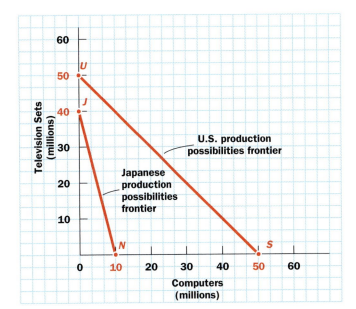

FIGURE 1

Production Possibilities Frontiers for Two Countries (per million years of labor)

> A country's *absolute* advantage in production over another country is shown by its having a higher per-capita production possibilities frontier. The difference in the *comparative* advantages between the two countries is shown by the difference in the slopes of their frontiers.

Because opportunity costs differ in the two countries, gains are possible if the two countries specialize and trade with one another. Specifically, it is cheaper, in terms of real resources forgone, for *either* country to acquire its computers in the United States. By a similar line of reasoning, the opportunity cost of TVs is higher in the United States than in Japan, so it makes sense for both countries to acquire their televisions in Japan.[4]

Notice that if the slopes of the two production possibilities frontiers, *JN* and *US*, were equal, then opportunity costs would be the same in each country. In that case, no potential gains would arise from trade. Gains from trade arise from *differences* across countries, not from similarities. This is an important point about which people are often confused. It is often argued that two very different countries, such as the United States and Mexico, cannot gain much by trading with one another. The fact is just the opposite:

> Two very similar countries may gain little from trade. Large gains from trade are most likely when countries are very different.

How the two countries divide the gains from trade depends on the prices that emerge from world trade—a complicated topic taken up in the appendix to this chapter. But we already know enough to see that world trade must, in our example, leave a computer costing more than one TV and less than four. Why? Because, if a computer bought less than one TV (its opportunity cost in the United States) on the world market, the United States would produce its own TVs rather than buying them from Japan. And if

---

[4] As an exercise, provide this line of reasoning.

a computer cost more than four TVs (its opportunity cost in Japan), Japan would prefer to produce its own computers rather than buy them from the United States.

We therefore conclude that, if both countries are to trade, the rate of exchange between TVs and computers must end up somewhere between 4:1 and 1:1. Generalizing:

If two countries voluntarily trade two goods with one another, the rate of exchange between the goods must fall in between the price ratios that would prevail in the two countries in the absence of trade.

To illustrate the gains from trade in our concrete example, suppose the world price ratio settles at 2:1—meaning that one computer costs as much as two televisions. How much, precisely, do the United States and Japan gain from world trade in this case?

Figure 2 is designed to help us visualize the answers. The red production possibilities frontiers, *US* in Panel (b) and *JN* in Panel (a), are the same as in Figure 1. But the United States can do better than line *US*. Specifically, with a world price ratio of 2:1, the United States can buy two TVs for each computer it gives up, rather than just one (which is the opportunity cost of a computer in the United States). Hence, if the United States produces only computers—point *S* in Figure 2(b)—and buys its TVs from Japan, America's *consumption possibilities* will be as indicated by the blue line that begins at point *S* and has a slope of 2—that is, each computer sold brings the United States two television sets. (It ends at point A because 40 million TV sets is the most that Japan can produce.) Because trade allows the United States to choose a point on *AS* rather than on *US*, trade opens up consumption possibilities that were simply not available before.

A similar story applies to Japan. If the Japanese produce only television sets—point *J* in Figure 2(a)—they can acquire a computer from the United States for every two TVs they give up as they move along the blue line *JP* (whose slope is 2). This result is better than they can achieve on their own, because a sacrifice of two TVs in Japan yields only one-half of a computer. Hence, world trade enlarges Japan's consumption possibilities from *JN* to *JP*.

Figure 2 shows graphically that gains from trade arise to the extent that world prices (2:1 in our example) differ from domestic opportunity costs (4:1 and 1:1 in our example). How the two countries share the gains from trade depends on the exact prices that emerge from world trade. As explained in the appendix, that in turn depends on relative supplies and demands in the two countries.

FIGURE 2

The Gains from Trade

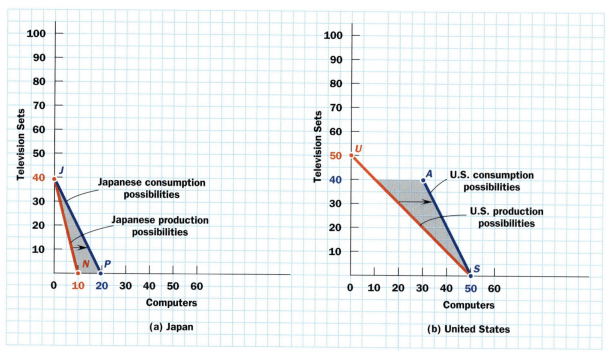

(a) Japan

(b) United States

NOTE: Quantities are in millions.

? ISSUE RESOLVED: *Comparative Advantage Exposes the "Cheap Foreign Labor" Fallacy*

The principle of comparative advantage takes us a long way toward understanding the fallacy in the "cheap foreign labor" argument described at the beginning of this chapter. Given the assumed productive efficiency of American labor, and the inefficiency of Japanese labor, we would expect wages to be much higher in the United States.

In these circumstances, one might expect American workers to be apprehensive about an agreement to permit open trade between the two countries: "How can we hope to meet the unfair competition of those underpaid Japanese workers?" Japanese laborers might also be concerned: "How can we hope to meet the competition of those Americans, who are so efficient in producing everything?"

The principle of comparative advantage shows us that both fears are unjustified. As we have just seen, when trade opens up between Japan and the United States, *workers in both countries will be able to earn higher real wages than before* because of the increased productivity that comes through specialization.

As Figure 2 shows, once trade opens up, Japanese workers should be able to acquire more TVs and more computers than they did before. As a consequence, their living standards should rise, even though they have been left vulnerable to competition from the super-efficient Americans. Workers in the United States should also end up with more TVs and more computers, so their living standards should also rise even though they have been exposed to competition from cheap Japanese labor.

These higher standards of living, of course, reflect the higher real wages earned by workers in both countries. The lesson to be learned here is elementary:

Nothing helps raise living standards more than a greater abundance of goods.

■ TARIFFS, QUOTAS, AND OTHER INTERFERENCES WITH TRADE

Despite the large mutual gains from international trade, nations often interfere with the free movement of goods and services across national borders. In fact, until the rise of the free-trade movement about 200 years ago (with Adam Smith and David Ricardo as its vanguard), it was taken for granted that one of the essential tasks of government was to *impede* trade, presumably in the national interest.

Many argued then (and many still argue today) that the proper aim of government policy was to promote exports and discourage imports, for doing so would increase the amount of money foreigners owed the nation. According to this so-called **mercantilist** view, a nation's wealth consists of the amount of gold or other monies at its command.

Obviously, governments can pursue such a policy only within certain limits. A country *must* import vital foodstuffs and critical raw materials that it cannot supply for itself. Moreover, mercantilists ignore a simple piece of arithmetic: It is mathematically impossible for *every* country to sell more than it buys, because one country's exports must be some other country's imports. If everyone competes in this game by cutting imports to the bone, then exports must go the same way. The result is that everyone will be deprived of the mutual gains from trade. Indeed, that is precisely what happens in a trade war.

After the protectionist 1930s, the United States moved away from mercantilist policies designed to impede imports and gradually assumed a leading role in promoting free trade. Over the past 50 years, tariffs and other trade barriers have come down dramatically.

In 1995, the United States led the world to complete the Uruguay Round of tariff reductions and, just before that, the country joined Canada and Mexico in the North American Free Trade Agreement (NAFTA). The latter caused a political firestorm in the United States in 1993 and 1994, with critic (and 1992 presidential candidate) Ross

Mercantilism is a doctrine that holds that exports are good for a country, whereas imports are harmful.

Liberalizing World Trade: The Doha Round

The time and place were not auspicious: an international gathering in the Persian Gulf just two months after the September 11, 2001, terrorists attacks. Nerves were frayed, security was extremely tight, and memories of a failed trade meeting in Seattle in 1999 lingered on. Yet representatives of more than 140 nations, meeting in Doha, Qatar, in November 2001, managed to agree on the outlines of a new round of comprehensive trade negotiations—one that may take years to complete.

The so-called Doha Round focuses on bringing down tariffs, subsidies, and other restrictions on world trade in agriculture, services, and a variety of manufactured goods. It also seeks greater protection for intellectual property rights, while making sure that poor countries have access to modern pharmaceuticals at prices they can afford. Reform of the World Trade Organization's own rules and procedures is also on the agenda. Perhaps most surprisingly, the United States has even promised to consider changes in its antidumping laws, which are used to keep many foreign goods out of U.S. markets. (Dumping is explained at the end of this chapter.)

Large-scale trade negotiations such as this one, involving more than 100 countries and many different issues, take years to complete. (The last one, the Uruguay Round, took seven years.) And the Doha Round almost collapsed in 2003 and again in 2006 when negotiating sessions got nowhere. In early 2007, there was a ray of hope that the contentious agricultural issues might be resolved. But no one was counting their chickens!

SOURCE: © Patrick Baz/AFT/Getty Images

Perot predicting a "giant sucking sound" as American workers lost their jobs to competition from "cheap Mexican labor." (Does that argument sound familiar?) Most of the world's trading nations are now engaged in a new multiyear round of trade talks, under guidelines adopted at an important meeting in Doha, Qatar, in 2001. (See "Liberalizing World Trade: The Doha Round.")

Modern governments use three main devices when seeking to control trade: tariffs, quotas, and export subsidies.

A tariff is a tax on imports.

A **tariff** is simply a tax on imports. An importer of cars, for example, may be charged $2,000 for each auto brought into the country. Such a tax will, of course, make automobiles more expensive and favor domestic models over imports. It will also raise revenue for the government. In fact, tariffs were a major source of tax revenue for the U.S. government during the eighteenth and nineteenth centuries—and also a major source of political controversy. But nowadays the United States is a low-tariff country, with only a few notable exceptions. However, many other countries rely on heavy tariffs to protect their industries. Indeed, tariff rates of 100 percent or more are not unknown in some countries.

A quota specifies the maximum amount of a good that is permitted into the country from abroad per unit of time.

A **quota** is a legal limit on the amount of a good that may be imported. For example, the government might allow no more than five million foreign cars to be imported in a year. In some cases, governments ban the importation of certain goods outright—a quota of zero. The United States now imposes quotas on a smattering of goods, including textiles, meat, and sugar. Most imports, however, are not subject to quotas. By reducing supply, quotas naturally raise the prices of the goods subject to quotas. For example, sugar is vastly more expensive in the United States than it is in Canada.

An export subsidy is a payment by the government to exporters to permit them to reduce the selling prices of their goods so they can compete more effectively in foreign markets.

An **export subsidy** is a government payment to an exporter. By reducing the exporter's costs, such subsidies permit exporters to lower their selling prices and compete more effectively in world trade. Overt export subsidies are minor in the United States, although a few years ago the Europeans argued successfully that certain aspects of the U.S. tax code amounted to an unfair export subsidy. Some foreign governments, however, use export subsidies extensively to assist their domestic industries—a practice that provokes bitter complaints from American manufacturers about "unfair competition." For example, years of heavy government subsidies helped the European Airbus consortium take a sizable share of the world commercial aircraft market away from U.S. manufacturers like Boeing and McDonnell-Douglas—a trend that has lately reversed.

■ Tariffs versus Quotas

Although both tariffs and quotas reduce international trade and increase the prices of domestically-produced goods, there are some important differences between these two ways to protect domestic industries.

First, under a quota, profits from the higher price in the importing country usually go into the pockets of the foreign and domestic sellers of the products. Limitations on supply (from abroad) mean that customers in the importing country must pay more for the product and that suppliers, whether foreign or domestic, receive more for every unit they sell. For example, the right to sell sugar in the United States under the tight sugar quota has been extremely valuable for decades. Privileged foreign and domestic firms can make a lot of money from quota rights.

By contrast, when trade is restricted by a tariff instead, some of the "profits" go as tax revenues to the government of the importing country. (Domestic producers also benefit, because they are exempt from the tariff.) In this respect, a tariff is certainly a better proposition than a quota from the viewpoint of the country that enacts it.

Another important distinction between the two measures arises from their different implications for productive efficiency. Because a tariff handicaps all foreign suppliers equally, it awards sales to those firms and nations that can supply the goods most cheaply—presumably because they are more efficient. A quota, by contrast, necessarily awards its import licenses more or less capriciously—perhaps in proportion to past sales or even based on political favoritism. There is no reason to expect the most efficient suppliers to get the import permits. For example, the U.S. sugar quota was for years suspected of being a major source of corruption in the Caribbean.

> If a country must inhibit imports, two important reasons support a preference for tariffs over quotas:
>
> 1. Some of the revenues resulting from tariffs go to the government of the importing country rather than to foreign and domestic producers.
> 2. Unlike quotas, tariffs offer special benefits to more efficient exporters.

■ WHY INHIBIT TRADE?

To state that tariffs provide a better way to inhibit international trade than quotas leaves open a far more basic question: Why limit trade in the first place? It has been estimated that trade restrictions cost American consumers more than $70 billion per year in the form of higher prices. Why should they be asked to pay these higher prices? A number of answers have been given. Let's examine each in turn.

■ Gaining a Price Advantage for Domestic Firms

A tariff forces foreign exporters to sell more cheaply by restricting their market access. If they do not cut their prices, they will be left with unsold goods. So in effect, the tariff amounts to government intervention to rig prices in favor of domestic producers.[5]

Not bad, you say. However, this technique works only as long as foreigners accept the tariff exploitation passively—which they rarely do. More often, they retaliate by

---

[5] For more details on this, see the appendix to this chapter.

imposing tariffs or quotas of their own on imports from the country that began the tariff game. Such tit-for-tat behavior can easily lead to a trade war in which no one gains more favorable prices but everyone loses through the resulting reductions in trade. Something like this, in fact, happened to the world economy in the 1930s, and it helped prolong the worldwide depression. Preventing such trade wars is one main reason why nations that belong to the World Trade Organization (WTO) pledge not to raise tariffs.

Tariffs or quotas can benefit particular domestic industries in a country that is able to impose them without fear of retaliation. But when every country uses them, everyone is likely to lose in the long run.

■ Protecting Particular Industries

The second, and probably more frequent, reason why countries restrict trade is to protect particular industries from foreign competition. If foreigners can produce steel or shoes more cheaply, domestic businesses and unions in these industries are quick to demand protection. And their governments may be quite willing to grant it.

The "cheap foreign labor" argument is most likely to be invoked in this context. Protective tariffs and quotas are explicitly designed to rescue firms that are too inefficient to compete with foreign exporters in an open world market. But it is precisely this harsh competition that gives consumers the chief benefits of international specialization: better products at lower prices. So protection comes at a cost.

Thinking back to our numerical example of comparative advantage, we can well imagine the indignant complaints from Japanese computer makers as the opening of trade with the United States leads to increased imports of American-made computers. At the same time, American TV manufacturers would probably express outrage over the flood of imported TVs from Japan. Yet Japanese specialization in televisions and U.S. specialization in computers is precisely what enables citizens of both countries to enjoy higher standards of living. If governments interfere with this process, consumers in both countries will lose out.

Industries threatened by foreign competition often argue that some form of protection against imports is needed to prevent job losses. For example, the U.S. steel industry has made exactly this argument time and time again since the 1960s—most recently in 2001, when world steel prices plummeted and imports surged. And the U.S. government has usually delivered some protection in response. But basic macroeconomics teaches us that there are better ways to stimulate employment, such as raising aggregate demand.

A program that limits foreign competition will be more effective at preserving employment *in the particular protected industry*. But such job gains typically come at a high cost to consumers and to the economy. Table 4 estimates some of the costs to American consumers of using tariffs and quotas to save jobs in selected industries. In every case, the costs far exceed the annual wages of the workers in the protected industries— ranging as high as $600,000 per job for the sugar quota.

Nevertheless, complaints over proposals to reduce tariffs or quotas may be justified unless something is done to ease the cost to individual workers of switching to the product lines that trade makes profitable.

TABLE 4	
Estimated Costs of Protectionism to Consumers	
Industry	Cost per Job Saved
Apparel	$139,000
Costume jewelry	97,000
Shipping	415,000
Sugar	600,000
Textiles	202,000
Women's footwear	102,000

SOURCE: Gary C. Hufbauer and Kimberly Ann Elliott, *Measuring the Costs of Protectionism in the United States* (Washington, D.C.: Institute for International Economics; January 1994), Table 1.3, pp. 12–13.

The argument for free trade between countries cannot be considered airtight if governments do not assist the citizens in each country who are harmed whenever patterns of production change drastically—as would happen, for example, if governments suddenly reduced tariff and quota barriers.

Owners of television factories in the United States and of computer factories in Japan may see large investments suddenly rendered unprofitable. Workers in those industries may see their special skills and training devalued in the marketplace. Displaced workers also pay heavy intangible costs—they may need to move to new locations and/or new industries, uprooting their families, losing old friends and neighbors, and so on. Although the *majority* of citizens undoubtedly gain from free trade, that is no consolation to those who are its victims.

To mitigate these problems, the U.S. government follows two basic approaches. First, our trade laws offer temporary protection from sudden surges of imports, on the grounds that unexpected changes in trade patterns do not give businesses and workers enough time to adjust.

Second, the government has set up **trade adjustment assistance** programs to help workers and businesses that lose their jobs or their markets to imports. Firms may be eligible for technical assistance, government loans or loan guarantees, and permission to delay tax payments. Workers may qualify for retraining programs, longer periods of unemployment compensation, and funds to defray moving costs. Each form of assistance is designed to ease the burden on the victims of free trade so that the rest of us can enjoy its considerable benefits.

> **Trade adjustment assistance** provides special unemployment benefits, loans, retraining programs, and other aid to workers and firms that are harmed by foreign competition.

■ National Defense and Other Noneconomic Considerations

A third rationale for trade protection is the need to maintain national defense. For example, even if the United States were not the most efficient producer of aircraft, it might still be rational to produce our own military aircraft so that no foreign government could ever cut off supplies of this strategic product.

The national defense argument is fine as far as it goes, but it poses a clear danger: Even industries with the most peripheral relationship to defense are likely to invoke this argument on their behalf. For instance, for years the U.S. watchmaking industry argued for protection on the grounds that its skilled craftsmen would be invaluable in wartime!

How Popular Is Protectionism?

Although the world has been moving gradually toward freer trade, its citizens are not entirely persuaded that this trend is desirable. In 1998, a Canadian polling company asked almost 13,000 people in 22 countries the following question: "Which of the following two broad approaches do you think would be the best way to improve the economic and employment situation in this country—protecting our local industries by restricting imports, or removing import restrictions to increase our international trade?" By this measure, protectionists outnumbered free traders by a narrow margin—47 percent to 42 percent, with the rest undecided. Protectionist sentiment was even stronger in the United States, where the margin was 56 percent to 37 percent.

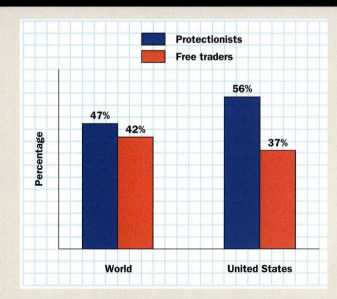

Similarly, the United States has occasionally banned either exports to or imports from nations such as Cuba, Iran, and Iraq on political grounds. Such actions may have important economic effects, creating either bonanzas or disasters for particular American industries. But they are justified by politics, not by economics. Non–economic reasons also explain quotas on importation of whaling products and on the furs of other endangered species.

■ The Infant-Industry Argument

Yet a fourth common rationale for protectionism is the so-called *infant-industry argument*, which has been prominent in the U.S. at least since Alexander Hamilton wrote his *Report on Manufactures*. Promising new industries often need breathing room to flourish and grow. If we expose these infants to the rigors of international competition too soon, the argument goes, they may never develop to the point where they can survive on their own in the international marketplace.

This argument, although valid in certain instances, is less defensible than it seems at first. Protecting an infant industry is justifiable only if the prospective future gains are sufficient to repay the up-front costs of protectionism. But if the industry is likely to be so profitable in the future, why doesn't private capital rush in to take advantage of the prospective net profits? After all, the annals of business are full of cases in which a new product or a new firm lost money at first but profited handsomely later on.

The infant-industry argument for protection stands up to scrutiny only if private funds are unavailable for some reason, despite an industry's glowing profit prospects. Even then it may make more sense to provide a government loan rather than to provide trade protection.

In an advanced economy such as ours, with well-developed capital markets to fund new businesses, it is difficult to think of legitimate examples where the infant-industry argument applies. Even if such a case were found, we would have to be careful that the industry not remain in diapers forever. In too many cases, industries are awarded protection when young and, somehow, never mature to the point where protection can be withdrawn. We must be wary of infants that never grow up.

■ Strategic Trade Policy

A stronger argument for (temporary) protection has substantially influenced trade policy in the United States and elsewhere. Proponents of this line of thinking agree that free trade for all is the best system. But they point out that we live in an imperfect world in which many nations refuse to play by the rules of the free-trade game. And they fear that a nation that pursues free trade in a protectionist world is likely to lose out. It therefore makes sense, they argue, to *threaten* to protect your markets unless other nations agree to open theirs.

The United States has followed this strategy in trade negotiations with several countries in recent years. In one prominent case, the U.S. government threatened to impose high tariffs on several European luxury goods unless Europe opened its markets to imported bananas from the Americas. A few years later, the European Union turned the tables, threatening to increase tariffs on a variety of U.S. goods unless we changed a tax provision that amounted to a subsidy to exports. In each case, a dangerous trade war was narrowly averted when an agreement was struck at the eleventh hour.

The strategic argument for protection is a difficult one for economists to counter. Although it recognizes the superiority of free trade, it argues that *threatening* protectionism is the best way to achieve that end. (See "Can Protectionism Save Free Trade?") Such a strategy might work, but it clearly involves great risks. If threats that the United States will turn protectionist induce other countries to scrap their existing protectionist policies, then the gamble will have succeeded. But if the gamble fails, protectionism increases.

Can Protectionism Save Free Trade?

In this classic column, William Safire shook off his long-standing attachment to free trade and argued eloquently for retaliation against protectionist nations.

Free trade is economic motherhood. Protectionism is economic evil incarnate. . . . Never should government interfere in the efficiency of international competition.

Since childhood, these have been the tenets of my faith. If it meant that certain businesses in this country went belly-up, so be it. . . . If it meant that Americans would be thrown out of work by overseas companies paying coolie wages, that was tough. . . .

The thing to keep in mind, I was taught, was the Big Picture and the Long Run. America, the great exporter, had far more to gain than to lose from free trade; attempts to protect inefficient industries here would ultimately cost more American jobs.

While playing with my David Ricardo doll and learning nursery rhymes about comparative advantage, I was listening to another laissez-fairy tale: Government's role in the world of business should be limited to keeping business honest and competitive. In God we antitrusted. Let businesses operate in the free marketplace.

Now American businesses are no longer competing with foreign companies. They are competing with foreign governments who help their local businesses. That means the world arena no longer offers a free marketplace; instead, most other governments are pushing a policy that can be called helpfulism.

Helpfulism works like this: A government like Japan decides to get behind its baseball-bat industry. It pumps in capital, knocks off marginal operators, finds subtle ways to discourage imports of Louisville Sluggers, and selects target areas for export blitzes. Pretty soon, the favored Japanese companies are driving foreign competitors batty.

How do we compete with helpfulism? One way is to complain that it is unfair; that draws a horselaugh. Another way is to demand a "Reagan Round" of trade negotiations under GATT, the Gentlemen's Agreement To Talk, which is equally laughable. Yet another way is to join the helpfuls by subsidizing our exports and permitting our companies to try monopolistic tricks abroad not permitted at home. But all that makes us feel guilty, with good reason.

The other way to deal with helpfulism is through—here comes the dreadful word—protection. Or, if you prefer a euphemism, retaliation. Or if that is still too severe, reciprocity. Whatever its name, it is a way of saying to the cutthroat cartelists we sweetly call our trading partners: "You have bent the rules out of shape. Change your practices to conform to the agreed-upon rules, or we will export a taste of your own medicine."

A little balance, then, from the free trade theorists. The demand for what the Pentagon used to call "protective reaction" is not demagoguery, not shortsighted, not self-defeating. On the contrary, the overseas pirates of protectionism and exemplars of helpfulism need to be taught the basic lesson in trade, which is: tit for tat.

SOURCE: © David Burnett/Contact Press Images

SOURCE: William Safire, "Smoot-Hawley Lives," *The New York Times*, March 17, 1983. Copyright © 1983 by The New York Times Company. Reprinted by permission.

■ CAN CHEAP IMPORTS HURT A COUNTRY?

One of the most curious—and illogical—features of the protectionist position is the fear of low import prices. Countries that subsidize their exports are accused of **dumping**—of getting rid of their goods at unjustifiably low prices.

Economists find this argument strange. As a nation of consumers, we should be indignant when foreigners charge us *high* prices, not *low* ones. That common-sense rule guides every consumer's daily life. Only from the topsy-turvy viewpoint of an industry seeking protection are low prices seen as being against the public interest.

Ultimately, the best interests of any country are served when its imports are as cheap as possible. It would be ideal for the United States if the rest of the world were willing to provide us with goods at no charge. We could then live in luxury at the expense of other countries.

But, of course, benefits to the United States as a whole do not necessarily accrue to every single American. If quotas on, say, sugar imports were dropped, American consumers and industries that purchase sugar would gain from lower prices. At the same

Dumping means selling goods in a foreign market at lower prices than those charged in the home market.

Unfair Foreign Competition

Satire and ridicule are often more persuasive than logic and statistics. Exasperated by the spread of protectionism under the prevailing mercantilist philosophy, the French economist Frédéric Bastiat decided to take the protectionist argument to its illogical conclusion. The fictitious petition of the French candlemakers to the Chamber of Deputies, written in 1845 and excerpted below, has become a classic in the battle for free trade.

We are subject to the intolerable competition of a foreign rival, who enjoys, it would seem, such superior facilities for the production of light, that he is enabled to inundate our national market at so exceedingly reduced a price, that, the moment he makes his appearance, he draws off all custom for us; and thus an important branch of French industry, with all its innumerable ramifications, is suddenly reduced to a state of complete stagnation. This rival is no other than the sun.

Our petition is, that it would please your honorable body to pass a law whereby shall be directed the shutting up of all windows, dormers, skylights, shutters, curtains, in a word, all openings, holes, chinks, and fissures through which the light of the sun is used to penetrate our dwellings, to the prejudice of the profitable manufactures which we flatter ourselves we have been enabled to bestow upon the country. . . .

We foresee your objections, gentlemen; but there is not one that you can oppose to us . . . which is not equally opposed to your own practice and the principle which guides your policy. . . . Labor and nature concur in different proportions, according to country and climate, in every article of production. . . . If a Lisbon orange can be sold at half the price of a Parisian one, it is because a natural and gratuitous heat does for the one what the other only obtains from an artificial and consequently expensive one. . . .

Does it not argue the greatest inconsistency to check as you do the importation of coal, iron, cheese, and goods of foreign manufacture, merely because and even in proportion as their price approaches zero, while at the same time you freely admit, and without limitation, the light of the sun, whose price is during the whole day at zero?

SOURCE: © Culver Pictures

SOURCE: F. Bastiat, *Economic Sophisms* (New York: G. P. Putnam's Sons; 1922).

time, however, owners of sugar fields and their employees would suffer serious losses in the form of lower profits, lower wages, and lost jobs—losses they would fight fiercely to prevent. For this reason, politics often leads to the adoption of protectionist measures that we would likely reject on strictly economic criteria.

? A Last Look at the "Cheap Foreign Labor" Argument

The preceding discussion reveals the fundamental fallacy in the argument that the United States *as a whole* should fear cheap foreign labor. The average American worker's living standard must *rise*, not fall, if other countries willingly supply their products to us more cheaply. As long as the government's monetary and fiscal policies succeed in maintaining high levels of employment, how can we possibly lose by getting world products at bargain prices? This is precisely what happened to the U.S. economy in the late 1990s: Even though imports poured in at low prices, unemployment in the United States was at its lowest rate in a generation.

We must add some important qualifications, however. First, our macroeconomic policy may not always be effective. If workers displaced by foreign competition cannot find new jobs, they will indeed suffer from international trade. But high unemployment reflects a shortcoming of the government's monetary and fiscal policies, not of its international trade policies.

Second, we have noted that an abrupt stiffening of foreign competition can hurt U.S. workers by not allowing them adequate time to adapt to the new conditions. If change occurs fairly gradually, workers can be retrained and move on to the industries that now require their services. Indeed, if the change is slow enough, normal attrition may suffice. But competition that inflicts its damage overnight is certain to impose real costs on the affected workers—costs that are no less painful for being temporary. That is why our trade laws make provisions for people and industries damaged by import surges.

In fact, the economic world is constantly changing. The recent emergence of China and other formerly third-world countries, for example, has created new competition for workers in America and other rich nations—competition they never imagined when they signed up for jobs that may now be imperiled by international trade. It is not irrational, and it is certainly not protectionist, for countries like the United States to use trade adjustment assistance and other tools to cushion the blow for these workers.

But these are, after all, only qualifications to an overwhelming argument. They call for intelligent monetary and fiscal policies and for transitional assistance to unemployed workers, not for abandonment of free trade. In general, the nation as a whole need not fear competition from cheap foreign labor.

In the long run, labor will be "cheap" only where it is not very productive. Wages will be high in countries with high labor productivity, and this high productivity will enable those countries to compete effectively in international trade despite high wages. It is thus misleading to say that the United States held its own in the international marketplace until recently *despite* high wages. Rather, it is much more accurate to note that the higher wages of American workers were a result of higher worker productivity, which gave the United States a major competitive edge.

Remember, in this matter it is *absolute* advantage, not *comparative* advantage, that counts. The country that is most efficient in producing every output can pay its workers more in every industry.

SUMMARY

1. Countries trade for many reasons. Two of the most important are that differences in their natural resources and other inputs create discrepancies in the efficiency with which they can produce different goods, and that specialization offers greater economies of large-scale production.

2. Voluntary trade will generally be advantageous to both parties in an exchange. This concept is one of our *Ideas for Beyond the Final Exam.*

3. International trade is more complicated than trade within a nation because of political factors, differing national currencies, and impediments to the movement of labor and capital across national borders.

4. Two countries will gain from trade with each other if each nation exports goods in which it has a **comparative advantage.** Even a country that is inefficient across the board will benefit by exporting the goods in whose production it is *least inefficient.* This concept is another of the *Ideas for Beyond the Final Exam.*

5. When countries specialize and trade, each can enjoy consumption possibilities that exceed its production possibilities.

6. The "cheap foreign labor" argument ignores the principle of comparative advantage, which shows that real wages (which determine living standards) can rise in both importing and exporting countries as a result of **specialization.**

7. **Tariffs** and **quotas** aim to protect a country's industries from foreign competition. Such protection may sometimes be advantageous to that country, but not if foreign countries adopt tariffs and quotas of their own in retaliation.

8. From the point of view of the country that imposes them, tariffs offer at least two advantages over quotas: some of the gains go to the government rather than to foreign producers, and they provide greater incentive for efficient production.

9. When a nation eliminates protection in favor of free trade, some industries and their workers will lose out. Equity then demands that these people and firms be compensated in some way. The U.S. government offers protection from import surges and various forms of **trade adjustment assistance** to help those workers and industries adapt to the new conditions.

10. Several arguments for protectionism can, under the right circumstances, have validity. They include the national defense argument, the infant-industry argument, and the use of trade restrictions for strategic purposes. But each of these arguments is frequently abused.

11. **Dumping** will hurt certain domestic producers, but it benefits domestic consumers.

KEY TERMS

"Cheap foreign labor" argument 724

Imports 725

Exports 725

Specialization 725

Mutual gains from trade 725

Absolute advantage 727

Comparative advantage 727

Mercantilism 731

Tariff 732

Quota 732

Export subsidy 732

Trade adjustment assistance 735

Infant–industry argument 736

Strategic trade policy 736

Dumping 737

TEST YOURSELF

1. The following table describes the number of yards of cloth and barrels of wine that can be produced with a week's worth of labor in England and Portugal. Assume that no other inputs are needed.

	In England	In Portugal
Cloth	8 yards	12 yards
Wine	2 barrels	6 barrels

   a. If there is no trade, what is the price of wine in terms of cloth in England?

   b. If there is no trade, what is the price of wine in terms of cloth in Portugal?

   c. Suppose each country has 1 million weeks of labor available per year. Draw the production possibilities frontier for each country.

   d. Which country has an absolute advantage in the production of which good(s)? Which country has a comparative advantage in the production of which good(s)?

   e. If the countries start trading with each other, which country will specialize and export which good?

   f. What can be said about the price at which trade will take place?

2. Suppose that the United States and Mexico are the only two countries in the world and that labor is the only productive input. In the United States, a worker can produce 12 bushels of wheat *or* 2 barrels of oil in a day. In Mexico, a worker can produce 2 bushels of wheat *or* 4 barrels of oil per day.

   a. What will be the price ratio between the two commodities (that is, the price of oil in terms of wheat) in each country if there is no trade?

   b. If free trade is allowed and there are no transportation costs, which commodity would the United States import? What about Mexico?

   c. In what range would the price ratio have to fall under free trade? Why?

   d. Picking one possible post-trade price ratio, show clearly how it is possible for both countries to benefit from free trade.

DISCUSSION QUESTIONS

1. You have a dozen shirts and your roommate has six pairs of shoes worth roughly the same amount of money. You decide to swap six shirts for three pairs of shoes. In financial terms, neither of you gains anything. Explain why you are nevertheless both likely to be better off.

2. In the eighteenth century, some writers argued that one person in a trade could be made better off only by gaining at the expense of the other. Explain the fallacy in this argument.

3. Country A has a cold climate with a short growing season, but a highly skilled labor force. (Think of Finland.) What sorts of products do you think it is likely to produce? What are the characteristics of the countries with which you would expect it to trade?

4. After the removal of a quota on sugar, many U.S. sugar farms go bankrupt. Discuss the pros and cons of removing the quota in the short and long runs.

5. Country A has a mercantilist government that believes it is always best to export more than it imports. As a conse-

quence, it exports more to Country B every year than it imports from Country B. After 100 years of this arrangement, both countries are destroyed in an earthquake. What were the advantages or disadvantages of the surplus to Country A? To Country B?

6. Under current trade law, the president of the United States must report periodically to Congress on countries engaging in unfair trade practices that inhibit U.S. exports. How would you define an "unfair" trade practice? Suppose Country X exports much more to the United States than it imports, year after year. Does that constitute evidence that Country X's trade practices are unfair? What would constitute such evidence?

7. Suppose the United States finds Country X guilty of unfair trade practices and penalizes it with import quotas. So U.S. imports from Country X fall. Suppose, further, that Country X does not alter its trade practices in any way. Is the United States better or worse off? What about Country X?

APPENDIX *Supply, Demand, and Pricing in World Trade*

As noted in the text, price determination in a world market with free trade depends on supply and demand conditions in each of the countries participating in the market. This appendix works out some of the details in a two-country example.

When applied to international trade, the usual supply-demand model must deal with (at least) *two demand curves:* that of the exporting country and that of the importing country. In addition, it may also involve *two supply curves*, because the importing country may produce part of its own consumption. (For example, the U.S., which is the world's biggest importer of oil, nonetheless produces quite a bit of domestic oil.) Furthermore, equilibrium does *not* take place at the intersection point of *either* pair of supply-demand curves. Why? Because if the two countries trade at all, the exporting nation must supply more than it demands while the importing nation demands more than it supplies.

All three of these complications are illustrated in Figure 3, which shows the supply and demand curves of a country that *exports* wheat in Panel (a) and of a country that *imports* wheat in Panel (b). For simplicity, we assume that these countries do not deal with anyone else. Where will the two-country wheat market reach equilibrium?

Under free trade, the equilibrium price must satisfy two requirements:

1. The quantity of wheat *exported* by one country must equal the quantity of wheat *imported* by the other country, for that is how *world* supply and demand balance.

2. The price of wheat must be the same in both countries.[6]

In Figure 3, these two conditions are met at a price of $2.50 per bushel. At that price, the distance *AB* between what the exporting country produces and what it consumes equals the distance *CD* between what the importing country consumes and what it produces. This means that the amount the exporting country wants to sell at $2.50 per bushel exactly equals the amount the importing country wants to buy at that price.

At any higher price, producers in both countries would want to sell more and consumers in both countries would want to buy less. For example, if the price rose to $3.25 per bushel, the exporter's quantity supplied would rise from *B* to *F* and its quantity demanded would fall from *A* to *E*, as shown in Panel (a). As a result, more wheat would be available for export—*EF* rather than *AB*. For exactly the same reason, the price increase would cause higher production and lower sales in the importing country, leading to a reduction in imports from *CD* to *GH* in Panel (b).

But this means that the higher price, $3.25 per bushel, cannot be sustained in a free and competitive international market. With export supply *EF* far greater than import demand *GH*, there would be pressure on price to fall back toward the $2.50 equilibrium price. Similar reasoning shows that no price below $2.50 can be sustained. Thus:

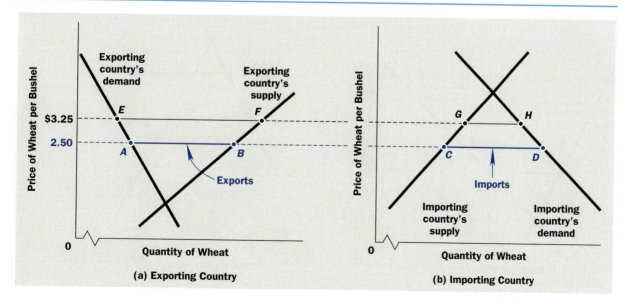

FIGURE 3   Supply-Demand Equilibrium in the International Wheat Trade

(a) Exporting Country

(b) Importing Country

---

[6] To keep things simple, we ignore such details as the costs of shipping wheat from one country to the other.

In international trade, the equilibrium price is the one that makes the exporting country want to export exactly the amount that the importing country wants to import. Equilibrium will thus occur at a price at which the horizontal distance *AB* in Figure 3(a) (the excess of the exporter's quantity supplied over its quantity demanded) is equal to the horizontal distance *CD* in Figure 3(b) (the excess of the importer's quantity demanded over its quantity supplied). At this price, the *world's* quantity demanded equals the *world's* quantity supplied.

■ HOW TARIFFS AND QUOTAS WORK

However, as noted in the text, nations do not always let free markets operate. Sometimes they intervene with quotas that limit imports or with tariffs that make imports more expensive. Although both tariffs and quotas restrict supplies coming from abroad and drive up prices, they operate slightly differently. A tariff works by raising prices, which in turn cuts the quantity of imports demanded. The sequence associated with a quota is just the reverse—a restriction in supply forces prices to rise.

The supply and demand curves in Figure 4 illustrate how tariffs and quotas work. Just as in Figure 3, the equilibrium price of wheat under free trade is $2.50 per bushel (in both countries). At this price, the exporting country produces 125 million bushels—point *B* in Panel (a)—and consumes 80 million (point *A*). So its exports are 45 million bushels—the distance *AB*. Similarly, the importing country consumes 95 million bushels—point *D* in Panel (b)—and produces only 50 million (point *C*), so its imports are also 45 million bushels—the distance *CD*.

Now suppose the government of the importing nation imposes a *quota* limiting imports to 30 million bushels. The free-trade equilibrium with imports of 45 million bushels is now illegal. Instead, the market must equilibrate at a point where both exports and imports are only 30 million bushels. As Figure 4 indicates, this requirement leads to different prices in the two countries.

Imports in Panel (b) will be 30 million bushels—the distance *QT*—only when the price of wheat in the importing nation is $3.25 per bushel, because only at this price will quantity demanded exceed domestic quantity supplied by 30 million bushels. Similarly, exports in Panel (a) will be 30 million bushels—the distance *RS*—only when the price in the exporting country is $2.00 per bushel. At this price, quantity supplied exceeds quantity demanded in the exporting country by 30 million bushels. Thus, the quota *raises* the price in the importing country to $3.25 and *lowers* the price in the exporting country to $2.00. In general:

An import quota on a product normally reduces the volume of that product traded, raises the price in the importing country, and reduces the price in the exporting country.

A tariff can accomplish exactly the same restriction of trade. In our example, a quota of 30 million bushels led to a price that was $1.25 higher in the importing country than in the exporting country ($3.25 versus $2.00). Suppose that, instead of a quota, the importing nation imposes a $1.25 per bushel *tariff*. International trade equilibrium then must satisfy the following two requirements:

FIGURE 4   Quotas and Tariffs in International Trade

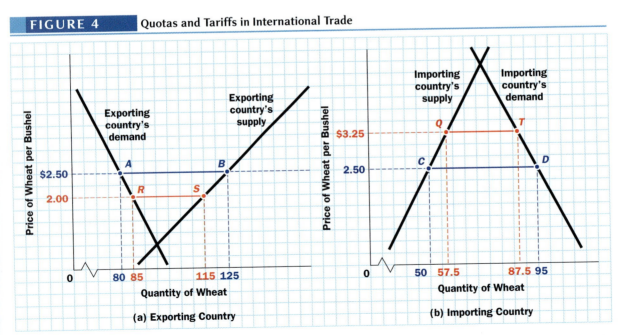

(a) Exporting Country

(b) Importing Country

NOTE: Quantities are in millions of bushels.

1. The quantity of wheat *exported* by one country must equal the quantity of wheat *imported* by the other, just as before.
2. The price that consumers in the importing country pay for wheat must *exceed* the price that suppliers in the exporting country receive by the amount of the *tariff* ($1.25 in this example).

By consulting the graphs in Figure 4, you can see exactly where these two requirements are met. If the exporter produces at S and consumes at R, while the importer produces at Q and consumes at T, then exports and imports are equal (at 30 million bushels), and the two domestic prices differ by exactly $1.25. (They are $3.25 and $2.00.) What we have just discovered is a general result of international trade theory:

Any restriction of imports that is accomplished by a quota normally can also be accomplished by a tariff.

In this case, the tariff corresponding to an import quota of 30 million bushels is $1.25 per bushel.

We mentioned in the text that a tariff (or a quota) forces foreign producers to sell more cheaply. Figure 4 shows how this works. Suppose, as in Panel (b), that a $1.25 tariff on wheat raises the price in the importing country from $2.50 to $3.25 per bushel. This higher price drives down imports from an amount represented by the length of the red line CD to the smaller amount represented by the blue line QT. In the exporting country, this change means an equal reduction in exports, as illustrated by the change from AB to RS in Panel (a).

As a result, the price at which the exporting country can sell its wheat is driven down—from $2.50 to $2.00 in the example. Meanwhile, producers in the importing country, which are exempt from the tariff, can charge $3.25 per bushel. Thus, as noted in the text, a tariff (or a quota) can be thought of as a way to "rig" the domestic market in favor of domestic firms.

SUMMARY

1. The prices of goods traded between countries are determined by supply and demand, but one must consider explicitly the demand curve and the supply curve of *each* country involved. Thus the equilibrium price must make the excess of quantity supplied over quantity demanded in the exporting country equal to the excess of quantity demanded over quantity supplied in the importing country.

2. When trade is restricted, the combinations of prices and quantities in the various countries that are achieved by a quota can also be achieved by a tariff.

3. Tariffs or quotas favor domestic producers over foreign producers.

TEST YOURSELF

1. The following table presents the demand and supply curves for microcomputers in Japan and the United States.

Price per Computer	Quantity Demanded in U.S.	Quantity Supplied in U.S.	Quantity Demanded in Japan	Quantity Supplied in Japan
1	90	30	50	50
2	80	35	40	55
3	70	40	30	60
4	60	45	20	65
5	50	50	10	70
6	40	55	0	75

NOTE: Price and quantity are in thousands.

a. Draw the demand and supply curves for the United States on one diagram and those for Japan on another one.

b. If the United States and Japan do not trade, what are the equilibrium price and quantity in the computer market in the United States? In Japan?

c. Now suppose trade is opened up between the two countries. What will be the equilibrium price in the world market for computers? What has happened to the price of computers in the United States? In Japan?

d. Which country will export computers? How many?

e. When trade opens, what happens to the quantity of computers produced, and therefore employment, in the computer industry in the United States? In Japan? Who benefits and who loses *initially* from free trade?

35

THE INTERNATIONAL MONETARY SYSTEM: ORDER OR DISORDER?

Cecily, you will read your Political Economy in my absence. The chapter on the Fall of the Rupee you may omit. It is somewhat too sensational.

MISS PRISM IN OSCAR WILDE'S *THE IMPORTANCE OF BEING EARNEST*

Miss Prism, the Victorian tutor, may have had a better point than she knew. In the summer of 1997, the Indonesian rupiah (not the Indian rupee) fell and economic disaster quickly followed. The International Monetary Fund rushed to the rescue with billions of dollars and pages of advice. But its plan failed, and some say it may even have helped precipitate the bloody riots that led to the fall of the Indonesian government.

This chapter does not concentrate on such sensational political upheavals. Rather, it focuses on a seemingly mundane topic: how the market determines rates of exchange among different national currencies. Nevertheless, events in Southeast Asia in 1997–1998, in Brazil and Russia in 1998–1999, and in Turkey and Argentina in 2001–2002 have amply demonstrated that dramatic exchange rate movements can have severe human as well as financial consequences. Even in the United States, some people are now worried about a possible decline in the value of the dollar. This chapter and the next will help us understand why.

CONTENTS

PUZZLE: *Why Has the Dollar Been Sagging?*

Many observers speak of "American exceptionalism." One way in which America differs from other countries is that its media and citizens pay little attention to the international value of its currency. So you may have missed the fact that the U.S. dollar, which was worth almost 1.2 euros as recently as February 2002 fell to a low of around 0.73 euro in December 2004. (As this book goes to press, the dollar is worth about 0.74 euro.) In most countries, a 40 percent decline in the exchange rate in less than two years would have been headline news—almost daily. But in the United States, it rarely got off the financial pages.

But it happened nonetheless. A 40 percent decline is a large drop. What caused the dollar to fall so far? Will it fall again? Does the decline signal some deep-seated problem with the U.S. economy? We will learn some of the answers to these and related questions in this chapter. But to do that, we first need to understand what determines exchange rates.

WHAT ARE EXCHANGE RATES?

We noted in the previous chapter that international trade is more complicated than domestic trade. There are no national borders to be crossed when, say, California lettuce is shipped to Massachusetts. The consumer in Boston pays with *dollars*, just the currency that the farmer in Modesto wants. If that same farmer ships her lettuce to Japan, however, consumers there will have only Japanese yen with which to pay, rather than the dollars the farmer in California wants. Thus, for international trade to take place, there must be some way to convert one currency into another. The rates at which such conversions are made are called **exchange rates.**

The **exchange rate** states the price, in terms of one currency, at which another currency can be bought.

There is an exchange rate between every pair of currencies. For example, one British pound is currently the equivalent of about $1.96. The exchange rate between the pound and the dollar, then, may be expressed as roughly "$1.96 to the pound" (meaning that it costs $1.96 to buy a pound) or about "51 pence to the dollar" (meaning that it costs 0.51 of a British pound to buy a dollar).

Exchange rates vis-à-vis the United States dollar have changed dramatically over time. In a nutshell, the dollar soared in the period from mid-1980 to early 1985, fell relative to most major currencies from early 1985 until early 1988, and then fluctuated with no clear trend until the spring of 1995. From then until early 2002, the dollar was mostly on the rise. Then, from February 2002 through December 2004, the dollar reversed course and fell steadily. And since December 2004, the dollar has been relatively stable, on balance. (However, most economist expect it to fall further.) This chapter seeks to explain such currency movements.

A nation's currency is said to **appreciate** when exchange rates change so that a unit of its currency can buy more units of foreign currency.

Under our present system, currency rates change frequently. When other currencies become more expensive in terms of dollars, we say that they have **appreciated** relative to the dollar. Alternatively, we can look at this same event as the dollar buying less foreign currency, meaning that the dollar has **depreciated** relative to another currency.

A nation's currency is said to **depreciate** when exchange rates change so that a unit of its currency can buy fewer units of foreign currency.

What is a depreciation to one country must be an appreciation to the other.

For example, if the cost of a pound *rises* from $1.50 to $2.00, the cost of a U.S. dollar in terms of pounds simultaneously *falls* from 67 pence to 50 pence. The United Kingdom has experienced a currency *appreciation* while the United States has experienced a currency *depreciation*. In fact, the two mean more or less the same thing. As you may have noticed, these two ways of viewing the exchange rate are reciprocals of one another, that is, $1/1.5 = 0.67$ and $1/2 = 0.50$. And of course, when a number goes up, its reciprocal goes down.

When many currencies are changing in value at the same time, the dollar may be appreciating with respect to one currency but depreciating with respect to another. Table 1 offers a selection of exchange rates prevailing in July 1980, February 1985, June 1995, April 2002, and April 2007, showing how many dollars or cents it cost at

TABLE 1
Exchange Rates with the U.S. Dollar

Country	Currency	Symbol	Cost in Dollars					
			July 1980	Feb. 1985	June 1995	April 2002	April 2005	April 2007
Australia	dollar	$	$1.16	$0.74	$0.72	$0.53	$0.77	$0.83
Canada	dollar	$	0.87	0.74	0.73	0.63	$0.82	0.89
France	franc	FF	0.25	0.10	0.20	*	*	*
Germany	mark	DM	0.57	0.30	0.71	*	*	*
Italy	lira	L	0.0012	0.00049	0.0061	*	*	*
Japan	yen	¥	0.0045	0.0038	0.0118	0.0076	0.0092	0.0084
Mexico	new peso	$	44.0†	5.0†	0.16	0.11	0.09	0.09
Sweden	krona	Kr	0.24	0.11	0.14	0.10	0.14	0.15
Switzerland	franc	S.Fr.	0.62	0.36	0.86	0.60	0.83	0.83
United Kingdom	pound	£	2.37	1.10	1.59	1.44	1.88	2.00
—	euro	€	—	—	—	0.88	1.29	1.36

NOTE: Exchange rates are in U.S. dollars per unit of foreign currency.

*These exchange rates were locked together at the start of the euro in January 1999.

†On January 1, 1993, the peso was redefined so that 1,000 old pesos were equal to one new peso. Hence, the numbers 44 and 5 listed for July 1980 and February 1985 were actually 0.044 and 0.005 on the old basis.

SOURCE: International Financial Statistics and *The Wall Street Journal.*

each of those times to buy each unit of foreign currency. Between February 1985 and April 2002, the dollar *depreciated* sharply relative to the Japanese yen and most European currencies. For example, the British pound rose from $1.10 to $1.44. During that same period, however, the dollar *appreciated* dramatically relative to the Mexican peso; it bought about 0.2 pesos in 1985 but more than 9 in 2002.[1]

Although the terms "appreciation" and "depreciation" are used to describe movements of exchange rates in free markets, a different set of terms is employed to describe decreases and increases in currency values that are set by government decree. When an officially set exchange rate is altered so that a unit of a nation's currency can buy fewer units of foreign currency, we say that a **devaluation** of that currency has occurred. When the exchange rate is altered so that the currency can buy more units of foreign currency, we say that a **revaluation** has taken place. We will say more about devaluation and revaluation shortly, but first let's look at how the free market determines exchange rates.

A **devaluation** is a reduction in the official value of a currency.

A **revaluation** is an increase in the official value of a currency.

■ EXCHANGE RATE DETERMINATION IN A FREE MARKET

In 1999, eleven European countries adopted a new common currency, the euro. But why does a euro now cost about $1.30 and not $1 or $1.60? In a world of **floating exchange rates,** with no government interferences, the answer would be straightforward. Exchange rates would be determined by the forces of supply and demand, just like the prices of apples, computers, and haircuts.

In a leap of abstraction, imagine that the dollar and the euro are the only currencies on earth, so the market need determine only one exchange rate. Figure 1 on the next page depicts the determination of this exchange rate at the point (denoted *E* in the figure) where demand curve *DD* crosses supply curve *SS*. At this price ($1.30 per euro), the number of euros demanded is equal to the number of euros supplied.

Floating exchange rates are rates determined in free markets by the law of supply and demand.

In a free market, exchange rates are determined by supply and demand. At a rate below the equilibrium level, the number of euros demanded would exceed the number supplied, and the price of a euro would be bid up. At a rate above the equilibrium level, quantity supplied would exceed quantity demanded, and the price of a euro would fall. Only at the equilibrium exchange rate is there no tendency for the exchange rate to change.

---

[1] In fact, the dollar bought about 200 pesos in February 1985, but that is because the old peso was replaced by a new peso in January 1993, which moved the decimal point three places.

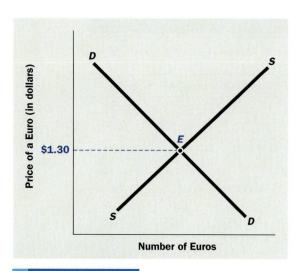

FIGURE 1

Determination of
Exchange Rates in a
Free Market

As usual, supply and demand determine price. But in this case, we must ask: Where do the supply and demand come from? Why does anyone demand a euro? The answer comes in three parts:

- *International trade in goods and services.* This factor was the subject of the previous chapter. If, for example, Jane Doe, an American, wants to buy a new BMW, she will first have to buy euros with which to pay the car dealer in Munich.[2] Thus Jane's demand for a European car leads to a demand for European currency. In general, *demand for a country's exports leads to demand for its currency.*[3]
- *Purchases of physical assets such as factories and machinery overseas.* If IBM wants to buy a small French computer manufacturer, the owners will no doubt want to receive euros. So IBM will first have to acquire European currency. In general, *direct foreign investment leads to demand for a country's currency.*
- *International trade in financial instruments such as stocks and bonds.* If American investors want to purchase Italian stocks, they will first have to acquire the euros that the sellers will insist on for payment. In this way, demand for European financial assets leads to demand for European currency. Thus, *demand for a country's financial assets leads to demand for its currency.* In fact, nowadays the volume of international trade in financial assets among the major countries of the world is so large that it swamps the other two sources of demand.

Now, where does the supply come from? To answer this question, just turn all of these transactions around. Europeans who want to buy U.S. goods and services, make direct investments in the United States, or purchase U.S. financial assets will have to offer their euros for sale in the foreign-exchange market (which is mainly run through banks) to acquire the needed dollars. To summarize:

The *demand* for a country's currency is derived from the demands of foreigners for its export goods and services and for its assets—including financial assets, such as stocks and bonds, and real assets, such as factories and machinery. The *supply* of a country's currency arises from its imports, and from foreign investment by its own citizens.

To illustrate the usefulness of even this simple supply and demand analysis, think about how the exchange rate between the dollar and the euro should change if Europeans become attracted by the prospects of large gains on the U.S. stock markets. To purchase U.S. stocks, foreigners will first have to purchase U.S. dollars—which means selling some of their euros. In terms of the supply-demand diagram in Figure 2, the increased desire of Europeans to acquire U.S. stocks would shift the supply curve for euros out from S_1S_1 (the black line in the figure) to S_2S_2 (the blue line). Equilibrium would shift from point E to point A, and the exchange rate would fall from $1.30 per euro to $1.00 per euro. Thus the increased supply of euros by European citizens would cause the euro to *depreciate* relative to the dollar. (This is precisely what happened during the U.S. stock market boom of the late 1990s.)

EXERCISE Test your understanding of the supply and demand analysis of exchange rates by showing why each of the following events would lead to an appreciation of the euro (a depreciation of the dollar) in a free market:

1. American investors are attracted by prospects for profit on the German stock market.

---

[2] Actually, she will not do so because banks generally handle foreign exchange transactions for consumers. An American bank probably will buy the euros for her. Even so, the effect is exactly the same as if Jane had done it herself.

[3] See Discussion Question 2 at the end of this chapter.

2. A recession in Italy cuts Italian purchases of American goods.
3. Interest rates on government bonds rise in France but are stable in the United States. (*Hint:* Which country's citizens will be attracted to invest by high interest rates in the other country?)

To say that supply and demand determine exchange rates in a free market is at once to say everything and to say nothing. If we are to understand the reasons why some currencies appreciate whereas others depreciate, we must look into the factors that move the supply and demand curves. Economists believe that the principal determinants of exchange rate movements differ significantly in the short, medium, and long runs. So in the next three sections, we turn to the analysis of exchange rate movements over these three "runs," beginning with the short run.

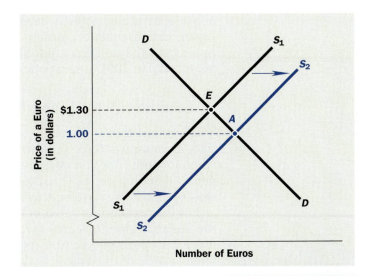

FIGURE 2

The Effect of a Foreign Stock Market Boom on the Exchange Rate

Interest Rates and Exchange Rates: The Short Run

Most experts in international finance agree that interest rates and financial flows are the major determinants of exchange rates—certainly in the short run, and probably in the medium run as well. Specifically, one variable that often seems to call the tune in the short run is *interest rate differentials*. A multitrillion-dollar pool of so-called *hot money*—owned by banks, investment funds, multinational corporations, and wealthy individuals of all nations—travels rapidly around the globe in search of the highest interest rates.

As an example, suppose British government bonds pay a 5 percent rate of interest when yields on equally safe American government securities rise to 7 percent. British investors will be attracted by the higher interest rates in the United States and will offer pounds for sale in order to buy dollars, planning to use those dollars to buy American securities. At the same time, American investors will find it more attractive to keep their money at home, so fewer pounds will be demanded by Americans.

When the demand schedule for pounds shifts inward and the supply curve shifts outward, the effect on price is predictable: The pound will depreciate, as Figure 3 shows. In the figure, the supply curve of pounds shifts outward from S_1S_1 to S_2S_2 when British investors seek to sell pounds in order to purchase more U.S. securities. At the same time,

FIGURE 3

The Effect of a Rise in U.S. Interest Rates

American investors wish to buy fewer pounds because they no longer desire to invest as much in British securities. Thus, the demand curve shifts inward from D_1D_1 to D_2D_2. The result, in our example, is a depreciation of the pound from $1.90 to $1.60. In general:

Other things equal, countries that offer investors higher rates of return attract more capital than countries that offer lower rates. Thus, a rise in interest rates often will lead to an appreciation of the currency, and a drop in interest rates will lead to a depreciation.

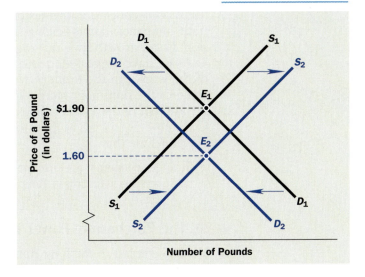

Think of interest rate differentials, in this context, as standing in for the relative returns on all sorts of financial assets in the two countries. In the late 1990s and the early part of this decade, prospective returns on American assets rose well

above comparable returns in most other countries—especially those in Europe and Japan. In consequence, foreign capital was attracted here, American capital stayed at home, and the dollar soared. Similarly, if a nation suffers from capital flight, as Argentina did in 2001, it must offer extremely high interest rates to attract foreign capital.

Economic Activity and Exchange Rates: The Medium Run

The medium run is where the theory of exchange rate determination is most unsettled. Economists once reasoned as follows: Because consumer spending increases when income rises and decreases when income falls, the same thing is likely to happen to spending on imported goods. So *a country's imports will rise quickly when its economy booms and rise only slowly when its economy stagnates.*

For the reasons illustrated in Figure 4, then, a boom in the United States should shift the *demand* curve for euros *outward* as Americans seek to acquire more euros to buy more European goods. And that, in turn, should lead to an appreciation of the euro (depreciation of the dollar). In the figure, the euro rises in value from $1.30 to $1.40.

However, if Europe was booming at the same time, Europeans would be buying more American exports, which would shift the *supply* curve of euros outward. (Europeans must offer more euros for sale to get the dollars they want.) On balance, the value of the dollar might rise or fall. It appears that what matters is whether exports are growing faster than imports.

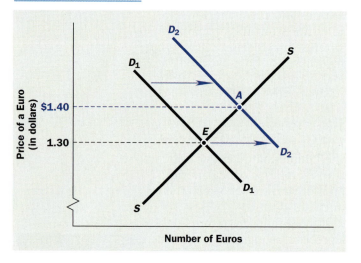

A country whose aggregate demand grows faster than the rest of the world's normally finds its imports growing faster than its exports. Thus, its demand curve for foreign currency shifts outward more rapidly than its supply curve. *Other things equal,* that will make its currency depreciate.

This reasoning is sound—so far as it goes. And it leads to the conclusion that a "strong economy" might produce a "weak currency." But the three most important words in the preceding paragraph are "other things equal." Usually, they are not. Specifically, a booming economy will normally offer more attractive prospects to investors than a stagnating one—higher interest rates, rising stock market values, and so on. This difference in prospective investment returns, as we noted earlier, should attract capital and boost its currency value.

So there appears to be a kind of tug of war. Thinking about trade in goods and services leads to the conclusion that faster growth should *weaken* the currency. But thinking about trade in financial assets (such as stocks and bonds) leads to precisely the opposite conclusion: Faster growth should *strengthen* the currency. Which side wins this tug of war?

As we have suggested, it is usually no contest—at least among the major currencies of the world. In the modern world, the evidence seems to say that trade in financial assets is the dominant factor. For example, rapid growth in the United States in the second half of the 1990s was accompanied by a sharply *appreciating* dollar even though U.S. imports soared, as investors from all over the world brought funds to America. We conclude that:

Stronger economic performance often leads to currency *appreciation* because it improves prospects for investing in the country.

The Purchasing-Power Parity Theory: The Long Run

We come at last to the long run, where an apparently simple principle ought to govern exchange rates. As long as goods can move freely across national borders, exchange rates should eventually adjust so that the same product costs the same amount of money, whether measured in dollars in the United States, euros in Germany, or yen in Japan—except for differences in transportation costs and the like. This simple statement forms the basis of the major theory of exchange rate determination in the long run:

> The *purchasing-power parity theory of exchange rate determination* holds that the exchange rate between any two national currencies adjusts to reflect differences in the price levels in the two countries.

An example will illustrate the basic truth in this theory and also suggest some of its limitations. Suppose German and American steel is identical and that these two nations are the only producers of steel for the world market. Suppose further that steel is the only tradable good that either country produces.

Question: If American steel costs $180 per ton and German steel costs 144 euros per ton, what must be the exchange rate between the dollar and the euro?

Answer: Because 144 euros and $180 each buy a ton of steel, the two sums of money must be of equal value. Hence, each euro must be worth $1.25. Why? Any higher price for a euro, such as $1.50, would mean that steel would cost $216 per ton (144 euros at $1.50 each) in Germany but only $180 per ton in the United States. In that case, all foreign customers would shop for their steel in the United States—which would increase the demand for dollars and decrease the demand for euros. Similarly, any exchange rate below $1.25 per euro would send all the steel business to Germany, driving the value of the euro up toward its purchasing-power parity level.

EXERCISE Show why an exchange rate of $1 per euro is too low to lead to an equilibrium in the international steel market.

The purchasing-power parity theory is used to make long-run predictions about the effects of inflation on exchange rates. To continue our example, suppose that steel (and other) prices in the United States rise while prices in Europe remain constant. The purchasing-power parity theory predicts that the euro will appreciate relative to the dollar. It also predicts the amount of the appreciation. After the U.S. inflation, suppose that the price of American steel is $216 per ton, while German steel still costs 144 euros per ton. For these two prices to be equivalent, 144 euros must be worth $216, or one euro must be worth $1.50. The euro, therefore, must have risen from $1.25 to $1.50.

> According to the purchasing-power parity theory, differences in domestic inflation rates are a major cause of exchange rate movements. If one country has higher inflation than another, its exchange rate should be depreciating.

For many years, this theory seemed to work tolerably well. Although precise numerical predictions based on purchasing-power parity calculations were never very accurate (see "Purchasing Power Parity and the Big Mac" on the following page), nations with higher inflation did at least experience depreciating currencies. But in the 1980s and 1990s, even this rule broke down. For example, although the U.S. inflation rate was consistently higher than both Germany's and Japan's, the dollar nonetheless rose sharply relative to both the German mark and the Japanese yen from 1980 to 1985. The same thing happened again between 1995 and 2002. Clearly, the theory is missing something. What?

Many things. But perhaps the principal failing of the purchasing-power parity theory is, once again, that it focuses too much on trade in goods and services. Financial assets such as stocks and bonds are also traded actively across national borders—and in vastly greater dollar volumes than goods and services. In fact, the astounding *daily* volume of foreign exchange transactions exceeds $1.5 trillion, which is more than an entire *month's* worth of world trade in goods and services. The vast majority of these transactions are financial. If investors decide that, say, U.S. assets are a better bet than Japanese assets, the dollar will rise, even if our inflation rate is well above Japan's. For this and other reasons:

Purchasing–Power Parity and the Big Mac

Since 1986, *The Economist* magazine has been using a well-known international commodity—the Big Mac—to assess the purchasing-power parity theory of exchange rates, or as the magazine once put it, "to make exchange-rate theory more digestible."

Here's how it works. In theory, the local price of a Big Mac, when translated into U.S. dollars by the exchange rate, should be the same everywhere in the world. The following numbers show that the theory does not work terribly well.

For example, although a Big Mac costs an average of $3 in the United States, it sold for about 10.3 yuan in China. Using the offi-

cial exchange rate of about 8.2 yuan to the dollar, that amounted to just $1.26. Thus, according to the hamburger parity theory, the yuan was grossly undervalued.

By how much? The price in China was just 42 percent of the price in the United States ($1.26/$3.00). So the yuan was 58 percent below its Big Mac parity—and therefore should appreciate. The other numbers in the table have similar interpretations.

True Big Mac aficionados may find these data helpful when planning international travel. But can deviations from Big Mac parity predict exchange rate movements? Surprisingly, they can.

When the economist Robert Cumby studied Big Mac prices and exchange rates in 14 countries over a ten-year period, he found that deviations from hamburger parity were transitory. Their "half-life" was just a year, meaning that 50 percent of the deviation tended to disappear within a year. Thus the undervalued currencies in the accompanying table would be predicted to appreciate during 2005, whereas the overvalued currencies would be expected to depreciate.

Deviations from Big Mac Purchasing Power Parity, December 2004

Country	Big Mac Prices (converted to dollars)	Percent Over (+) or Under (−) Valuation Against Dollar
United States	**$3.00**	—
Switzerland	5.46	+82%
Euro area	3.75	+25
Great Britain	3.61	+20
Canada	2.60	−13
Japan	2.50	−17
Mexico	2.12	−29
Brazil	1.99	−34
Russia	1.49	−50
China	1.26	−58

Most economists believe that other factors are much more important than relative price levels for exchange rate determination in the short run. But in the long run, purchasing-power parity plays an important role.

■ Market Determination of Exchange Rates: Summary

You have probably noticed a theme here: International trade in financial assets certainly dominates short-run exchange rate changes, may dominate medium-run changes, and also influences long-run changes. We can summarize this discussion of exchange rate determination in free markets as follows:

1. We expect to find *appreciating* currencies in countries that offer investors *higher rates of return* because these countries will attract capital from all over the world.

2. To some extent, these are the countries that are *growing faster* than average because strong growth tends to produce attractive investment prospects. However, such fast-growing countries will also be importing relatively more than other countries, which tends to pull their currencies *down*.

3. Currency values generally will appreciate in countries with *lower inflation rates* than the rest of the world's, because buyers in foreign countries will demand their goods and thus drive up their currencies.

Reversing each of these arguments, we expect to find *depreciating* currencies in countries with relatively high inflation rates, low interest rates, and poor growth prospects.

WHEN GOVERNMENTS FIX EXCHANGE RATES: THE BALANCE OF PAYMENTS

Some exchange rates today are truly floating, determined by the forces of supply and demand without government interference. Many others are not. Furthermore, some people claim that exchange rate fluctuations are so troublesome that the world would be better off with fixed exchange rates. For these reasons, we turn next to a system of **fixed exchange rates,** or rates that are set by governments.

Naturally, under such a system the exchange rate, being fixed, is not closely watched. Instead, international financial specialists focus on a country's *balance of payments*—a term we must now define—to gauge movements in the supply of and demand for a currency.

To understand what the balance of payments is, look at Figure 5, which depicts a situation that might represent, say, Argentina in the winter of 2001–2002—an overvalued currency. Although the supply and demand curves for pesos indicate an equilibrium exchange rate of $0.50 to the peso (point *E*), the Argentine government is holding the rate at $1.00. Notice that, at $1 per peso, more people supply pesos than demand them. In the example, suppliers offer to sell 8 billion pesos per year, but purchasers want to buy only 4 billion.

This gap between the 8 billion pesos that some people wish to sell and the 4 billion pesos that others wish to buy is what we mean by Argentina's **balance of payments deficit**—4 billion pesos (or $4 billion) per year in this hypothetical case. It appears as the horizontal distance between points *A* and *B* in Figure 5.

How can governments flout market forces in this way? Because sales and purchases on any market must be equal, the excess of quantity supplied over quantity demanded—or 4 billion pesos per year in this example—must be bought by the Argentine government. To purchase these pesos, it must give up some of the foreign currency that it holds as reserves. Thus, the Bank of Argentina would be losing about $4 billion in reserves per year as the cost of keeping the peso at $1.

Naturally, this situation cannot persist forever, as the reserves eventually will run out. This is the fatal flaw of a fixed exchange rate system. Once speculators become convinced that the exchange rate can be held for only a short while longer, they will sell the currency in massive amounts rather than hold on to money whose value they expect to fall. That is precisely what began to happen to Argentina in 2001. Lacking sufficient reserves, the Argentine government succumbed to market forces and let the peso float in early 2002. It promptly depreciated.

For an example of the reverse case, a severely undervalued currency, we can look at contemporary China. Figure 6 on the next page depicts demand and supply curves for Chinese yuan that intersect at an equilibrium price of 15 cents per yuan (point *E* in the diagram). Yet, in the example, we suppose that the Chinese authorities are holding the rate at 12 cents. At this rate, the quantity of yuan demanded (1,000 billion) greatly exceeds the quantity supplied (600 billion). The difference is China's **balance of payments surplus,** shown by the horizontal distance *AB*.

China can keep the rate at 12 cents only by selling all the additional yuan that foreigners want to buy—400 billion yuan per year in this example. In return, the country must buy the equivalent amount of U.S. dollars ($48 billion). All of this activity serves to increase China's reserves of U.S. dollars. But notice one important difference between this case and the overvalued peso:

Fixed exchange rates are rates set by government decisions and maintained by government actions.

FIGURE 5

A Balance of Payments Deficit

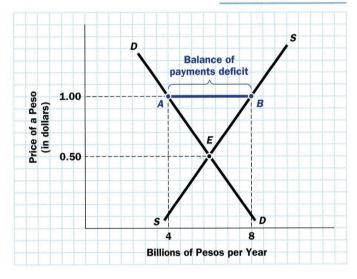

The **balance of payments deficit** is the amount by which the quantity supplied of a country's currency (per year) exceeds the quantity demanded. Balance of payments deficits arise whenever the exchange rate is pegged at an artificially high level.

The **balance of payments surplus** is the amount by which the quantity demanded of a country's currency (per year) exceeds the quantity supplied. Balance of payments surpluses arise whenever the exchange rate is pegged at an artificially low level.

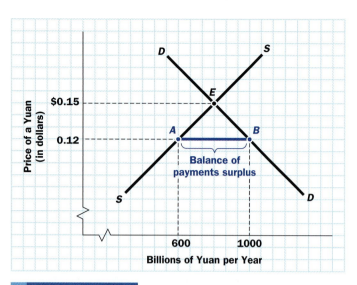

FIGURE 6

A Balance of Payments Surplus

The **current account** balance includes international purchases and sales of goods and services, cross-border interest and dividend payments, and cross-border gifts to and from both private individuals and governments. It is approximately the same as net exports.

The **capital account** balance includes purchases and sales of financial assets to and from citizens and companies of other countries.

The accumulation of reserves rarely will force a central bank to revalue in the way that losses of reserves can force a devaluation.

This asymmetry is a clear weakness in a fixed exchange rate system. In principle, an exchange rate disequilibrium can be cured either by a *devaluation* by the country with a balance of payments deficit or by an upward *revaluation* by the country with a balance of payments surplus. In practice, though, only deficit countries are forced to act.

Why do surplus countries refuse to revalue? One reason is often a stubborn refusal to recognize some basic economic realities. They tend to view the disequilibrium as a problem only for the deficit countries and, therefore, believe that the deficit countries should take the corrective steps. This view, of course, is nonsense in a worldwide system of fixed exchange rates. Some currencies are overvalued *because* some other currencies are undervalued. In fact, the two statements mean exactly the same thing.

The other reason why surplus countries resist upward revaluations is that such actions would make their products more expensive to foreigners and thus cut into their export sales. This, in fact, is presumed to be the main reason why China maintains an undervalued currency despite the protestations of many other nations. China's leaders believe that vibrant export industries are the key to growth and development.

The balance of payments comes in two main parts. The **current account** totes up exports and imports of goods and services, cross-border payments of interest and dividends, and cross-border gifts. It is close, both conceptually and numerically, to what we have called net exports $(X - IM)$ in previous chapters. The United States has been running large current account deficits for years.

But that represents only one part of our balance of payments, for it leaves out all purchases and sales of assets. Purchases of U.S. assets by foreigners bring foreign currency to the United States, and purchases of foreign assets cost us foreign currency. Netting the capital flows in each direction gives us our surplus or deficit on **capital account.** In recent years, this part of our balance of payments has registered persistently large *surpluses* as foreigners have acquired massive amounts of U.S. assets.

In what sense, then, does the overall balance of payments balance? There are two possibilities. If the exchange rate is *floating*, all private transactions—current account plus capital account—must add up to zero because dollars purchased = dollars sold. But if, instead, the exchange rate is *fixed*, as shown in Figures 5 and 6, the two accounts need not balance one another. Government purchases or sales of foreign currency make up the surplus or deficit in the overall balance of payments.

A BIT OF HISTORY: THE GOLD STANDARD AND THE BRETTON WOODS SYSTEM

It is difficult to find examples of strictly fixed exchange rates in the historical record. About the only time exchange rates were truly fixed was under the old gold standard, at least when it was practiced in its ideal form.[4]

The Classical Gold Standard

The **gold standard** is a way to fix exchange rates by defining each participating currency in terms of gold and allowing holders of each participating currency to convert that currency into gold.

Under the **gold standard**, governments maintained fixed exchange rates by an automatic equilibrating mechanism that went something like this: All currencies were de-

---

[4] As a matter of fact, although the gold standard lasted (on and off) for hundreds of years, it was rarely practiced in its ideal form. Except for a brief period of fixed exchange rates in the late nineteenth and early twentieth centuries, governments periodically adjusted exchange rates even under the gold standard.

fined in terms of gold; indeed, some were actually made of gold. When a nation ran a balance of payments *deficit*, it had to *sell gold* to finance the deficit. Because the domestic money supply was based on gold, losing gold to foreigners meant that the money supply fell *automatically*, which raised interest rates. The higher interest rates attracted foreign capital. At the same time, this restrictive "monetary policy" pulled down output and prices, which discouraged imports and encouraged exports. The balance of payments problem quickly rectified itself.

This automatic adjustment process meant, however, that under the gold standard no nation had control of its domestic monetary policy. An analogous problem arises in any system of fixed exchange rates, regardless of whether it makes use of gold:

Under fixed exchange rates, monetary policy must be dedicated to pegging the exchange rate. It cannot, therefore, be used to manage aggregate demand.

The gold standard posed one other serious difficulty: The world's commerce was at the mercy of gold discoveries. Major gold finds would mean higher prices and booming economic conditions, through the standard monetary-policy mechanisms that we studied in earlier chapters. When the supply of gold failed to keep pace with growth of the world economy, prices had to fall in the long run and employment had to fall in the short run.

The Bretton Woods System

The gold standard collapsed for good amid the financial chaos of the Great Depression of the 1930s and World War II. Without it, the world struggled through a serious breakdown in international trade.

As the war drew to a close, representatives of the industrial nations, including John Maynard Keynes of Great Britain, met at a hotel in Bretton Woods, New Hampshire, to devise a stable monetary environment that would restore world trade. Because the United States held the lion's share of the world's reserves at the time, these officials naturally turned to the dollar as the basis for the new international economic order.

The Bretton Woods agreements reestablished fixed exchange rates based on the free convertibility of the U.S. dollar into gold. The United States agreed to buy or sell gold to maintain the $35 per ounce price that President Franklin Roosevelt had established in 1933. The other signatory nations, which had almost no gold in any case, agreed to buy and sell *dollars* to maintain their exchange rates at agreed-upon levels.

The Bretton Woods system succeeded in refixing exchange rates and restoring world trade—two notable achievements. But it also displayed the flaws of any fixed exchange rate system. Changes in exchange rates were permitted only as a last resort—which, in practice came to mean that the country had a chronic *deficit* in the balance of payments of sizable proportions. Such nations were allowed to *devalue* their currencies relative to the dollar. So the system was not really one of fixed exchange rates but, rather, one in which rates were "fixed until further notice." Because devaluations came only after a long run of balance of payments deficits had depleted the country's reserves, these devaluations often could be clearly foreseen and normally had to be large. Speculators therefore saw glowing opportunities for profit and would "attack" weak currencies with waves of selling.

A second problem arose from the asymmetry mentioned earlier: Deficit nations could be forced to devalue while surplus nations could resist upward revaluations. Because the value of the U.S. dollar was fixed in terms of gold, the United States was the one nation in the world that had no way to devalue its currency. The only way the dollar could fall was if the surplus nations would revalue their currencies upward. But they did not adjust frequently enough, so the United States developed an overvalued currency and chronic balance of payments deficits.

The overvalued dollar finally destroyed the Bretton Woods system in 1971, when President Richard Nixon unilaterally ended the game by announcing that the United States would no longer buy or sell gold at $35 per ounce.

ADJUSTMENT MECHANISMS UNDER FIXED EXCHANGE RATES

Under the Bretton Woods system, devaluation was viewed as a last resort, to be used only after other methods of adjusting to payments imbalances had failed. What were these other methods?

We encountered most of them in our earlier discussion of exchange rate determination in free markets. Any factor that *increases the demand* for, say, Argentine pesos or that *reduces the supply* will push the value of the peso upward—if it is free to adjust. But if the exchange rate is pegged, the balance of payments deficit will shrink instead. (Try this for yourself using Figure 5 on page 753.)

Recalling our earlier discussion of the factors that underlie the demand and supply curves, we see that one way a nation can shrink its balance of payments deficit is to *reduce its aggregate demand*, thereby discouraging imports and cutting down its demand for foreign currency. Another is to *lower its rate of inflation*, thereby encouraging exports and discouraging imports. Finally, it can *raise its interest rates* to attract more foreign capital.

In other words, deficit nations are expected to follow restrictive monetary and fiscal policies *voluntarily*, just as they would have done *automatically* under the classical gold standard. However, just as under the gold standard, this medicine is often unpalatable.

A surplus nation could, of course, take the opposite measures: pursuing *expansionary* monetary and fiscal policies to increase economic growth and *lower* interest rates. By increasing the supply of the country's currency and reducing the demand for it, such actions would reduce that nation's balance of payments surplus. But surplus countries often do not relish the inflation that accompanies expansionary policies, and so, once again, they leave the burden of adjustment to the deficit nations. The general point about fixed exchange rates is that:

> Under a system of fixed exchange rates, a country's government loses some control over its domestic economy. Sometimes balance of payments considerations may force it to contract its economy in order to cut down its demand for foreign currency, even though domestic needs call for expansion. At other times, the domestic economy may need to be reined in, but balance of payments considerations suggest expansion.

That was certainly the case in Argentina in 2002, when interest rates soared to attract foreign capital, and the government pursued contractionary fiscal policies to curb the country's appetite for imports. Both contributed to a long and deep recession. Argentina took the bitter medicine needed to defend its fixed exchange rate for quite a while. But high unemployment eventually led to riots in the streets, toppled the government, and persuaded the Argentine authorities to abandon the fixed exchange rate.

WHY TRY TO FIX EXCHANGE RATES?

SOURCE: © *The New Yorker* Collection 1971, Ed Fisher from cartoonbank.com. All Rights Reserved.

"Then it's agreed. Until the dollar firms up, we let the clamshell float."

In view of these and other problems with fixed exchange rates, why did the international financial community work so hard to maintain them for so many years? And why do some nations today still fix their exchange rates? The answer is that floating exchange rates also pose problems.

Chief among these worries is the possibility that freely floating rates might prove to be highly variable rates, thereby adding an unwanted element of risk to foreign trade. For example, if the exchange rate is $1.25 to the euro, then a Parisian dress priced at 200 euros will cost $250. But should the euro appreciate to $1.40, that same dress would cost $280. An American department store thinking of buying the dress may need to place its order far in advance and will want to know the cost *in dollars*. It may be worried about the possibility that the value of the euro will rise, making the dress cost more than $250. And such worries might inhibit trade.

There are two responses to this concern. First, freely floating rates might prove to be fairly stable in practice. Prices of most ordinary goods and services, for example, are determined by supply and demand in free markets and do not fluctuate unduly. Unfortunately, experience since 1973 has dashed this hope. Exchange rates have proved to be extremely volatile, which is why some observers now favor greater fixity in exchange rates.

A second possibility is that speculators might relieve business firms of exchange rate risks—for a fee, of course. Consider the department store example. If each euro costs $1.25 today, the department store manager can assure herself of paying exactly $250 for the dress several months from now by arranging for a speculator to deliver 200 euros to her at $1.25 per euro on the day she needs them. If the euro appreciates in the interim, the speculator, not the department store, will take the financial beating. Of course, if the euro depreciates, the speculator will pocket the profits. Thus, speculators play an important role in a system of floating exchange rates.

The widespread fears that speculative activity in free markets will lead to wild gyrations in prices, although occasionally valid, are often unfounded. The reason is simple.

> To make profits, international currency speculators must *buy* a currency when its value is low (thus helping to support the currency by pushing up its demand curve) and *sell* it when its value is high (thus holding down the price by adding to the supply curve). This means that successful speculators must come into the market as *buyers* when demand is weak (or when supply is strong) and come in as *sellers* when demand is strong (or supply is scant). In doing so, they help limit price fluctuations. Looked at the other way around, speculators can *destabilize* prices only if they are systematically willing to lose money.[5]

Notice the stark—and ironic—contrast to the system of fixed exchange rates in which speculation often leads to wild "runs" on currencies that are on the verge of devaluation—as happened in Mexico in 1995, several Southeast Asian countries in 1997–1998, Brazil in 1999, and Argentina in 2001. Speculative activity, which may well be *destabilizing* under fixed rates, is more likely to be *stabilizing* under floating rates.[6]

We do not mean to imply that speculation makes floating rates trouble-free. At the very least, speculators will demand a fee for their services—a fee that adds to the costs of trading across national borders. In addition, speculators will not assume *all* exchange rate risks. For example, few contracts on foreign currencies last more than, say, a year or two. Thus, a business cannot easily protect itself from exchange rate changes over periods of many years. Finally, speculative markets can and do get carried away from time to time, moving currency rates in ways that are difficult to understand, that frustrate the intentions of governments, and that devastate some people—as happened in Mexico in 1995 and in Southeast Asia in 1997.

Despite all of these problems, international trade has flourished under floating exchange rates. So perhaps exchange rate risk is not as burdensome as some people think.

■ THE CURRENT "NONSYSTEM"

The international financial system today is an eclectic blend of fixed and floating exchange rates, with no grand organizing principle. Indeed, it is so diverse that it is often called a "nonsystem."

Some currencies are still pegged in the old Bretton Woods manner. One prominent example is China, which maintains a nearly-fixed value for its currency by standing ready to buy or sell U.S. dollars as necessary. (In recent years, it has been buying steadily and in large volume.) A few small countries, such as Panama and Ecuador, have taken the more extreme step of actually adopting the U.S. dollar as their domestic currencies. Other nations tie their currencies to a hypothetical "basket" of several currencies, rather than to a single currency.

More nations, however, let their exchange rates float, although not always freely. Such floating rates change slightly on a day-to-day basis, and market forces determine the basic trends, up or down. But governments do not hesitate to intervene to moderate

---

[5] See Test Yourself Question 4 at the end of the chapter.

[6] After their respective currency crises in 1995 and 1999, both Mexico and Brazil floated their currencies. Each weathered the subsequent international financial storms rather nicely. But Argentina, with its fixed exchange rate, struggled.

exchange movements whenever they feel such actions are appropriate. Typically, interventions are aimed at ironing out what are deemed to be transitory fluctuations. But sometimes central banks oppose basic exchange rate trends. For example, the Federal Reserve and other central banks sold dollars aggressively in 1985 to push the dollar *down*, and then bought dollars in 1994 and 1995 to push the dollar *up*. As we will discuss in the next chapter, the Japanese acquired hundreds of billions of dollars earlier in this decade trying to prevent the yen from floating up too much. The terms *dirty float* or *managed float* have been coined to describe this mongrel system.

■ The Role of the IMF

The International Monetary Fund (IMF), which was established at Bretton Woods in 1944, examines the economies of all its member nations on a regular basis. When a country runs into serious financial difficulties, it may turn to the Fund for help. The IMF typically provides loans, but with many strings attached. For example, if the country has a large current account deficit—as is normally the case when countries come to the IMF—the Fund will typically insist on contractionary fiscal and monetary policies to curb the country's appetite for imports. Often, this mandate spells recession.

During the 1990s, the IMF found itself at the epicenter of a series of very visible economic crises: in Mexico in 1995, in Southeast Asia in 1997, in Russia in 1998, and in Brazil in 1999. In 2001, Turkey and Argentina ran into trouble and appealed to the IMF for help. Although each case was different, they shared some common elements.

Most of these crises were precipitated by the collapse of a fixed exchange rate pegged to the U.S. dollar. In each case, the currency plummeted, with ruinous consequences. Questions were raised about the country's ability to pay its bills. In each case, the IMF arrived on the scene with lots of money and advice, determined to stave off default. In the end, each country suffered through a severe recession—or worse.

The IMF's increased visibility naturally brought it increased criticism. Some critics complained that the Fund set excessively strict conditions on its client states, requiring them, for example, to cut their government budgets and raise interest rates during recessions—which made bad economic situations even worse.

Other critics worried that the Fund was serving as a bill collector for banks and other financial institutions from the United States and other rich countries. Because the banks loaned money irresponsibly, these critics argued, they deserved to lose some of it. By bailing them out of their losses, the IMF simply encouraged more reckless behavior in the future.

Suggestions for reform are everywhere (see the box "Does the International Monetary System Need Reform?"), and some minor changes have been made in the IMF's procedures. But the debate rages on.

■ The Volatile Dollar

As mentioned earlier, floating exchange rates have not proved to be stable exchange rates. No currency illustrates this point better than the U.S. dollar. (See Figure 7.) As Table 1 showed, in July 1980 a U.S. dollar bought less than 2 German marks, about 4 French francs, and about 830 Italian lire. Then it started rising like a rocket (see Figure 7). By the time it peaked in February 1985, the mighty dollar could buy more than 3 German

FIGURE 7

The Ups and Downs of the Dollar

NOTE: Exchange rate relative to major currencies, March 1973 = 100.

POLICY DEBATE

Does the International Monetary System Need Reform?

Robert Rubin, America's former Treasury secretary, wants to "modernize the architecture of the international financial markets." Eisuke Sakakibara, Japan's top international finance official, is thinking of a "Bretton Woods II." Alan Greenspan, chairman of the Federal Reserve, wants to review the "patchwork of arrangements" governing international finance. After East Asia's crisis, activism is in the air. . . .

It is easy to see why. . . . Policymakers worry that today's financial architecture, designed at Bretton Woods in 1944 for a world of limited capital mobility, may not be capable of dealing with an ever more global capital market. For international finance has been revolutionised. Formerly closed economies have cast off controls and embraced foreign funds. Better technology and financial innovation have made it easy to move money instantaneously.

The benefits are obvious: the expansion of private flows to developing countries. . . . But vast inflows can quickly become huge outflows. And financial crises can spread overnight between apparently unconnected markets. The five worst-affected Asian economies (South Korea, Indonesia, Thailand, Malaysia, and the Philippines) received $93 billion of private capital flows in 1996. In 1997 they saw an outflow of $12 billion.

[One] reform to reinforce capital markets is better regulation. . . . Countless banking crises—in rich and poor countries alike—have shown that the combination of free capital flows and badly regulated banks is disastrous. . . . Others go much further, arguing that a global capital market needs global financial regulation, not a hotch-potch of national supervisors of varying quality. . . .

For many conservatives, particularly in America's Congress, the answer is to curb, or even eliminate, the IMF. It is the prospect of bail-outs, they argue, that encourages governments to profligacy and investors to recklessness. . . .

SOURCE: © Cvinai Dithajohn/EPA/Landov

For those who see East Asia's crisis primarily as one of panic, . . . far more urgent is the need to control the capital flows themselves. . . . For those who are uneasy with the speed with which funds flow around the globe, the perennial idea of a tax on currency transactions has surfaced again. . . .

With such an array of possible reforms, it is hardly surprising that international officials are confused and uncertain [whereas] their political masters demand quick action.

Authors' note: Politicians may have wanted "quick action" in 1998, but few of the items on this list have actually happened. The debate goes on.

---

marks, about 10 French francs, and more than 2,000 Italian lire. Such major currency changes affect world trade dramatically.

The rising dollar was a blessing to Americans who traveled abroad or who bought foreign goods—because foreign prices, when translated to dollars by the exchange rate, looked cheap to Americans.[7] But the arithmetic worked just the other way around for U.S. firms seeking to sell their goods abroad; foreign buyers found everything American very expensive.[8] It was no surprise, therefore, that as the dollar climbed our exports fell, our imports rose, and many of our leading manufacturing industries were decimated by foreign competition. An expensive currency, Americans came to learn, is a mixed blessing.

From early 1985 until early 1988, the value of the dollar fell even faster than it had risen. The cheaper dollar curbed American appetites for imports and alleviated the plight of our export industries, many of which boomed. However, rising prices for imported goods and foreign vacations were a source of consternation to many American consumers.

Over the following seven years, the overall value of the dollar did not change very much—although there was a small downward drift. Then, in the spring of 1995, the dollar began another sizable ascent which lasted until early 2002. After that, as we noted earlier in this chapter, the dollar fell for about 2 years and has been roughly

---

[7] *Exercise:* How much does a 100-euro hotel room in Paris cost in dollars when the euro is worth $1.25? $1? 80 cents?

[8] *Exercise*: How much does a $55 American camera cost a German consumer when the euro is worth $1.20? $1? 80 cents?

stable since. All in all, the behavior of the dollar has been anything but boring. Fortunes have been made and lost speculating on what it will do next.

■ The Birth of the Euro

As noted earlier, floating exchange rates are no panacea. One particular problem confronted the members of the European Union (EU). As part of their long-range goal to create a unified market like that of the United States, they perceived a need to establish a single currency for all member countries—a monetary union.

The process of convergence to a single currency took place in steps, more or less as prescribed by the Treaty of Maastricht (1992), over a period of years. Member nations encountered a number of obstacles along the way. But to the surprise of many skeptics, all such obstacles were overcome, and the euro became a reality on schedule. Electronic and checking transactions in 11 EU nations were denominated in euros rather than in national currencies in 1999, the number of participating countries has risen to 13, and euro coins and paper money were introduced successfully in 2002. Each of these transformations went remarkably smoothly.

The establishment of the euro was a great economic experiment that marked a giant step beyond merely fixing exchange rates. A government can end a fixed exchange rate regime at any time. And, as we have seen, speculators sometimes break fixed exchange rates even when governments want to maintain them. But the single European currency was created by an international treaty and is more or less invulnerable to speculative attack because it *abolished* exchange rates among the participating nations. Just as there has long been no exchange rate between New York and New Jersey, now there is no exchange rate between Germany and France. Monetary unions may create other problems, but exchange rate instability should not be one of them.

PUZZLE RESOLVED: *Why the Dollar Rose and then Fell*

What we have learned in this chapter helps us understand what brought the dollar down between 2002 and 2004. The story actually begins well before that.

During the Great Boom of the late 1990s, the United States was *the* place to invest. Funds poured in from all over the world to purchase American stocks, American bonds, and even American companies—especially in the information technology field. Yahoo! was indeed a fitting name for the age. As we have learned in this chapter, the rising demand for U.S. assets should have bid up the price of U.S. currency—and it did (see Figure 7 again).

But the soaring dollar sowed the seeds of its own destruction. Two of its major effects were (a) to make U.S. goods and services look much more expensive to potential buyers abroad and (b) to make foreign goods look much cheaper to Americans. So our imports grew much faster than our exports. In brief, we developed a huge *current account deficit* (which is roughly exports *minus* imports) to match our large *capital account surplus*.

The Internet bubble, of course, started to burst in 2000, pulling the stock market down with it. Then the September 11, 2001, terrorist attacks raised doubts about the strength of the U.S. economy. For these and other reasons, foreign investors apparently began to question the wisdom of holding so many American assets. With the U.S. current account still deeply in the red, and the foreign demand for U.S. capital sagging, there was only way for the (freely floating) dollar to go: down. And so it did. Most economists think the dollar must decline further in order to whittle our current account deficit down to size.

"His mood is pegged to the dollar"

SUMMARY

1. **Exchange rates** state the value of one currency in terms of other currencies, and thus translate one country's prices into the currencies of other nations. Exchange rates therefore influence patterns of world trade.

2. If governments do not interfere by buying or selling their currencies, exchange rates will be determined in free markets by the usual laws of supply and demand. Such a system is said to be based on **floating exchange rates.**

3. Demand for a nation's currency is derived from foreigners' desires to purchase that country's goods and services or to invest in its assets. Under floating rates, anything that increases the demand for a nation's currency will cause its exchange rate to **appreciate.**

4. Supply of a nation's currency is derived from the desire of that country's citizens to purchase foreign goods and services or to invest in foreign assets. Under floating rates, anything that increases the supply of a nation's currency will cause its exchange rate to **depreciate.**

5. Purchasing-power parity plays a major role in very-long-run exchange rate movements. The **purchasing-power parity theory** states that relative price levels in any two countries determine the exchange rate between their currencies. Therefore, countries with relatively low inflation rates normally will have appreciating currencies.

6. Over shorter periods, however, purchasing-power parity has little influence over exchange rate movements. The pace of economic activity and, especially, the level of interest rates exert greater influences.

7. Capital movements are typically the dominant factor in exchange rate determination in the short and medium runs. A nation that offers international investors higher interest rates, or better prospective returns on investments, will typically see its currency appreciate.

8. An exchange rate can be fixed at a nonequilibrium level if the government is willing and able to mop up any excess of quantity supplied over quantity demanded, or provide any excess of quantity demanded over quantity supplied. In the first case, the country is suffering from a **balance of payments deficit** because of its overvalued currency. In the second case, an undervalued currency has given it a **balance of payments surplus.**

9. The **gold standard** was a system of **fixed exchange rates** in which the value of every nation's currency was fixed in terms of gold. This system created problems because nations could not control their own money supplies and because the world could not control its total supply of gold.

10. After World War II, the gold standard was replaced by the **Bretton Woods system,** in which exchange rates were fixed in terms of U.S. dollars, and the dollar was in turn tied to gold. This system broke up in 1971, when the dollar became chronically overvalued.

11. Since 1971, the world has moved toward a system of relatively free exchange rates, but with plenty of exceptions. We now have a thoroughly mixed system of "dirty" or "managed" floating, which continues to evolve and adapt.

12. Floating rates are not without their problems. For example, importers and exporters justifiably worry about fluctuations in exchange rates.

13. Under floating exchange rates, investors who speculate on international currency values provide a valuable service by assuming the risks of those who do not wish to speculate. Normally, speculators stabilize rather than destabilize exchange rates, because that is how they make profits.

14. The U.S. dollar rose dramatically in value from 1980 to 1985, making our imports cheaper and our exports more expensive. From 1985 to 1988, the dollar tumbled, which had precisely the reverse effects. Then the dollar climbed again between 1995 and 2002, leading once again to a large trade imbalance. From 2002 to 2004, the dollar fell again.

15. The European Union has established a single currency, the euro, for most of its member nations.

KEY TERMS

Exchange rate 746

Appreciation 746

Depreciation 746

Devaluation 747

Revaluation 747

Floating exchange rates 747

Purchasing-power parity theory 751

Fixed exchange rates 753

Balance of payments deficit and surplus 753

Current account 754

Capital account 754

Gold standard 754

Bretton Woods system 755

International Monetary Fund (IMF) 758

"Dirty" or "managed" float 758

TEST YOURSELF

1. Use supply and demand diagrams to analyze the effect of the following actions on the exchange rate between the dollar and the yen:

   a. Japan opens its domestic markets to more foreign competition.

   b. Investors come to believe that values on the Tokyo stock market will fall.

   c. The Federal Reserve cuts interest rates in the United States.

   d. The U.S. government, to help settle the problems of the Middle East, gives huge amounts of foreign aid to Israel and her Arab neighbors.

   e. The United States has a recession while Japan booms.

   f. Inflation in the United States exceeds that in Japan.

2. For each of the following transactions, indicate how it would affect the U.S. balance of payments if exchange rates were fixed:

   a. You spent the summer traveling in Europe.

   b. Your uncle in Canada sent you $20 as a birthday present.

   c. You bought a new Honda, made in Japan.

   d. You bought a new Honda, made in Ohio.

   e. You sold some stock you own on the Tokyo Stock Exchange.

3. Suppose each of the transactions listed in Test Yourself Question 2 was done by many Americans. Indicate how each would affect the international value of the dollar if exchange rates were floating.

4. We learned in this chapter that successful speculators buy a currency when demand is weak and sell it when demand is strong. Use supply and demand diagrams for two different periods (one with weak demand, the other with strong demand) to show why this activity will limit price fluctuations.

DISCUSSION QUESTIONS

1. What items do you own or routinely consume that are produced abroad? From what countries do these items come? Suppose Americans decided to buy fewer of these things. How would that affect the exchange rates between the dollar and these currencies?

2. If the dollar appreciates relative to the euro, will the German camera you have wanted become more or less expensive? What effect do you imagine this change will have on American demand for German cameras? Does the American demand curve for euros, therefore, slope upward or downward? Explain.

3. During the first half of the 1980s, inflation in (West) Germany was consistently lower than that in the United States. What, then, does the purchasing-power parity theory predict should have happened to the exchange rate between the mark and the dollar between 1980 and 1985? (Look at Table 1 to see what actually happened.)

4. How are the problems of a country faced with a balance of payments deficit similar to those posed by a government regulation that holds the price of milk above the equilibrium level? (*Hint:* Think of each in terms of a supply-demand diagram.)

5. Under the old gold standard, what do you think happened to world prices when a huge gold strike occurred in California in 1849? What do you think happened when the world went without any important new gold strikes for 20 years or so?

6. Explain why the members of the Bretton Woods conference in 1944 wanted to establish a system of fixed exchange rates. What flaw led to the ultimate breakdown of the system in 1971?

7. Suppose you want to reserve a hotel room in London for the coming summer but are worried that the value of the pound may rise between now and then, making the room too expensive for your budget. Explain how a speculator could relieve you of this worry. (Don't actually try it. Speculators deal only in very large sums!)

8. In 2003 and 2004, market forces raised the international value of the Japanese yen. Why do you think the government of Japan was unhappy about this currency appreciation? (*Hint:* Japan was trying to emerge from a recession at the time.) If they wanted to stop the yen's appreciation, what actions could the Bank of Japan (Japan's central bank) and the Federal Reserve have taken? Why might the central banks have failed in this attempt?

36

EXCHANGE RATES AND THE MACROECONOMY

No man is an island, entire of itself.

JOHN DONNE

S urveying the problems afflicting a number of the world's economies in the late 1990s, then-Federal Reserve Chairman Alan Greenspan declared that the United States could not long remain an "oasis of prosperity" in a troubled world. The nations of the world are indeed locked together in an uneasy economic union. Fluctuations in foreign growth, inflation, and interest rates profoundly affect the U.S. economy. Economic events that originate in our country reverberate around the globe. Anyone who ignores these international linkages cannot hope to understand how the world economy works.

The macroeconomic model we developed in earlier chapters does not go far enough because it ignores such crucial influences as exchange rates and international financial movements. The previous chapter showed how major macroeconomic variables such as gross domestic product (GDP), prices, and interest rates affect exchange rates. In this chapter, we complete the circle by studying how changes in the exchange rate affect the domestic economy. Then we bring international capital flows into the picture and learn how monetary and fiscal policy work in an **open economy**. In particular, we build a model suitable for a *large open* economy with *substantial capital flows* and a *floating exchange rate*—in short, a model meant to resemble the United States.

An **open economy** is one that trades with other nations in goods and services, and perhaps also trades in financial assets.

CONTENTS

ISSUE: *Should the U.S. Government Try to Stop the Dollar from Falling?*

For years, economists predicted that America's huge—and growing—trade deficits would eventually drive the international value of the U.S. dollar down. In the early months of 2002, the prophecy started to come true, and the greenback began an irregular decline that lasted about two years. As we observed in the previous chapter, the decline against the euro amounted to 40 percent—and many observers believe there is more to come.

As the dollar fell, the U.S. economy recovered from the 2001 recession, and generally grew much faster than either Europe or Japan. By early 2004, both the European and Japanese governments were complaining that their businesses were losing export markets to the Americans, which was damaging European and Japanese growth. They urged the United States government to stop the dollar's decline. But the United States insisted that currency values should be "flexible," determined in world markets by the forces of supply and demand that we studied in the previous chapter. And the dollar kept on falling.

Who was right? We will examine this question as the chapter progresses.

INTERNATIONAL TRADE, EXCHANGE RATES, AND AGGREGATE DEMAND

We know from earlier chapters that a country's net exports, $(X - IM)$, are one component of its aggregate demand, $C + I + G + (X - IM)$. It follows that an autonomous increase in exports or decrease in imports has a multiplier effect on the economy, just like an increase in consumption, investment, or government purchases.[1] Figure 1 depicts this conclusion on an aggregate demand and supply diagram. A rise in net exports shifts the aggregate demand curve outward to the right, pushing equilibrium from point A to point B. Both GDP and the price level therefore rise.

But what increases net exports? One factor mentioned in Chapter 25 was a rise in foreign incomes. If foreign economies boom, their citizens are likely to spend more on a wide variety of products, some of which will be American exports. Thus, Figure 1 illustrates the effect on the U.S. economy of more rapid growth in foreign countries. Similarly, a recession abroad would reduce U.S. exports and shift the U.S. aggregate demand curve inward. Thus, as we learned in Chapter 26:

Booms or recessions in one country tend to be transmitted to other countries through international trade in goods and services.

One other important determinant of net exports was mentioned in Chapter 25, but not discussed in depth: the relative prices of foreign and domestic goods. This idea involves a simple application of the law of demand. Namely, if the prices of the goods of Country X rise, people everywhere will tend to buy fewer of them—and more of the goods of Country Y. As we will see next, this simple idea holds the key to understanding how exchange rates affect international trade.

FIGURE 1

The Effects of Higher Net Exports

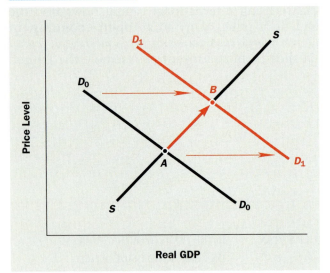

Relative Prices, Exports, and Imports

First assume—just for this short section—that exchange rates are *fixed*. What happens if the prices of American goods fall while, say, Japanese prices are constant? With U.S.

---

[1] An appendix to Chapter 26 showed that international trade lowers the numerical value of the multiplier. Autonomous changes in C, I, G, and $(X - IM)$ all have the same multiplier.

products now less expensive *relative to Japanese products*, both Japanese and American consumers will buy more American goods and fewer Japanese goods. As a result, America's exports will rise and its imports will fall, adding to aggregate demand in this country. Conversely, a rise in American prices (relative to Japanese prices) will *decrease* U.S. net exports and aggregate demand. Thus:

A *fall* in the relative prices of a country's exports tends to *increase* that country's net exports and hence to raise its real GDP. Analogously, a *rise* in the relative prices of a country's exports will *decrease* that country's net exports and GDP.

Precisely the same logic applies to changes in Japanese prices. If Japanese prices rise, Americans will export more and import less. So $X - IM$ will rise, boosting GDP in the United States. Figure 1 applies to this case without change. By similar reasoning, falling Japanese prices decrease U.S. net exports and depress our economy. Thus:

Price increases for foreign products raise a country's net exports and hence its GDP. Price decreases for foreign products have the opposite effects.

The Effects of Changes in Exchange Rates

From here it is a simple matter to figure out how changes in exchange rates affect a country's net exports, for *currency appreciations or depreciations change international relative prices.*

Recall that the basic role of an exchange rate is to convert one country's prices into another country's currency. Table 1 uses two examples of U.S.–Japanese trade to remind us of this role. Suppose the dollar depreciates from 120 yen to 100 yen. Then, from the American consumer's viewpoint, a television set that costs ¥30,000 in Japan goes up in price from $250 (that is, 30,000/120) to $300. To Americans, it is just as if Japanese manufacturers had raised TV prices by 20 percent. Naturally, Americans will react by purchasing fewer Japanese products, so American imports will decline.

Now consider the implications for Japanese consumers interested in buying American personal computers that cost $1,000. When the dollar falls from 120 yen to 100 yen, they see the price of these computers falling from ¥120,000 to ¥100,000. To them, it is just as if American producers had offered a 16.7 percent markdown. Under such circumstances, we expect U.S. sales to the Japanese to rise, so U.S. exports should increase. Putting these two findings together, we conclude that:

A currency *depreciation* should *raise* net exports and therefore *increase* aggregate demand. Conversely, a currency *appreciation* should *reduce* net exports and therefore *decrease* aggregate demand.

The aggregate supply and demand diagram in Figure 2 illustrates this conclusion. If the currency depreciates, net exports rise and the aggregate demand curve shifts outward from D_0D_0 to D_1D_1. Both prices and output rise as the economy's equilibrium moves from E_0 to E_1. If the currency appreciates, everything operates in reverse: Net exports fall, the aggregate demand curve shifts inward to D_2D_2, and both prices and output decline.

This simple analysis helps us understand why the U.S. trade deficit grew so enormously in the late 1990s and early 2000s. We learned in the previous chapter that the international value of the dollar began to

TABLE 1
Exchange Rates and Home Currency Prices

		¥30,000 Japanese TV Set		$1,000 U.S. Home Computer	
Exchange Rate		Price in Japan	Price in the U.S.	Price in the U.S.	Price in Japan
$1 = 120 yen		¥30,000	$250	$1,000	¥120,000
$1 = 100 yen		¥30,000	$300	$1,000	¥100,000

FIGURE 2

The Effects of Exchange Rate Changes on Aggregate Demand

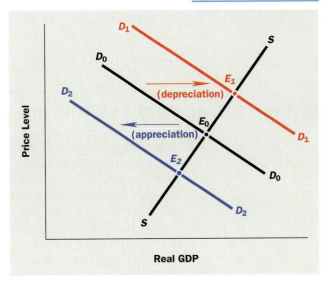

climb in 1995. According to the reasoning we have just completed, within a few years such an appreciation of the dollar should have boosted U.S. imports and damaged U.S. exports. That is precisely what happened. In constant dollars, American imports soared by over 40 percent between 1997 and 2002, while American exports rose by only 7 percent. The result was that a $105 billion net export deficit in 1997 turned into a monumental $472 billion deficit by 2002.

■ AGGREGATE SUPPLY IN AN OPEN ECONOMY

So far we have concluded that a currency depreciation increases aggregate demand and that a currency appreciation decreases it. To complete our model of macroeconomics in an open economy, we turn now to the implications of international trade for *aggregate supply.*

Part of the story is already familiar to us. As we know from previous chapters, the United States, like all economies, purchases some of its productive inputs from abroad. Oil is only the most prominent example. We also rely on foreign suppliers for metals such as titanium, raw agricultural products such as coffee beans, and thousands of other items used by American industry. When the dollar depreciates, these imported inputs cost more in U.S. dollars—just as if foreign prices had risen.

The consequence is clear: With imported inputs more expensive, American firms will be forced to charge higher prices at any given level of output. Graphically, this means that *the aggregate supply curve will shift upward* (or inward to the left).

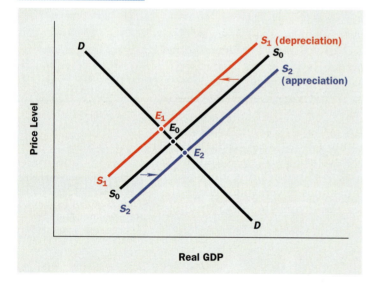

Real GDP

When the dollar *depreciates,* the prices of imported inputs rise. The U.S. aggregate supply curve therefore shifts *inward,* pushing up the prices of American-made goods and services. By exactly analogous reasoning, an *appreciation* of the dollar makes imported inputs cheaper and shifts the U.S. aggregate supply curve *outward,* thus pushing American prices down. (See Figure 3.)

Beyond this, a depreciating dollar has additional inflationary effects that do not show up on an aggregate demand and supply diagram, which depicts *the price of gross domestic product* on its vertical axis. Most obviously, prices of imported goods are included in U.S. price indexes like the Consumer Price Index (CPI). So when the dollar prices of Japanese cars, French wine, and Swiss watches increase, the CPI goes up *even if no American prices rise.* For this and other reasons, the inflationary impact of a dollar depreciation is greater than that indicated by Figure 3.

■ THE MACROECONOMIC EFFECTS OF EXCHANGE RATES

Let us now put aggregate demand and aggregate supply together and think through the macroeconomic effects of changes in exchange rates.

First, suppose the international value of the dollar falls. Referring back to the red lines in Figures 2 and 3, we see that this depreciation will shift the aggregate demand curve *outward* and the aggregate supply curve *inward.* The result, as Figure 4 shows, is that the U.S. price level certainly rises. But whether real GDP rises or falls depends on whether the supply or demand shift is the dominant influence. The evidence strongly suggests that aggregate *demand* shifts are usually larger, so we expect GDP to rise. Hence:

A currency depreciation is inflationary and probably also expansionary.

The intuitive explanation for this result is clear. When the dollar falls, foreign goods become more expensive to Americans. That effect is directly inflationary. At the same time, aggregate demand in the United States is stimulated by rising net exports. As long as the expansion of demand outweighs the adverse shift of the aggregate supply curve brought on by currency depreciation, real GDP should rise.

But wait. By this reasoning, the massive depreciations of several Southeast Asian currencies in 1997 and 1998 should have given these economies tremendous boosts. Instead, the so-called Asian Tigers suffered horrific slumps—as did Mexico when the peso tumbled in 1995. Why? The answer is that our simple analysis of aggregate supply and demand omits a detail that, although unimportant for the United States, is critical in many developing nations.

Countries that borrow in foreign currency will see their debts increase whenever their currencies fall in value. For example, an Indonesian business that borrowed $1,000 in July 1997, when $1 was worth 2,500 rupiah, thought it owed 2.5 million rupiah. But when the dollar suddenly became worth 10,000 rupiah, the company's debt skyrocketed to 10 million rupiah. Many businesses found themselves unable to cope with their crushing debt burdens and simply went bankrupt. So although currency depreciation is expansionary in the United States, it was sharply contractionary in Indonesia.

Returning to rich countries such as the United States, let's now reverse direction, and look at what happens when the currency *appreciates*. In this case, net exports *fall* so the aggregate demand curve shifts *inward*. At the same time, imported inputs become cheaper, so the aggregate supply curve shifts *outward*. Both of these shifts are shown in Figure 5. Once again, as the diagram shows, we can be sure of the movement of the price level: It falls. Output also falls if the demand shift is larger than the supply shift, as is likely. Thus:

A currency appreciation is disinflationary and probably also contractionary.

This analysis explains why many economists and financial experts cringed when the yen and the euro appreciated relative to the dollar in 2002–2004. Japan, in particular, was already experiencing deflation and very slow growth. The last thing it needed, they argued, was a decrease in aggregate demand.

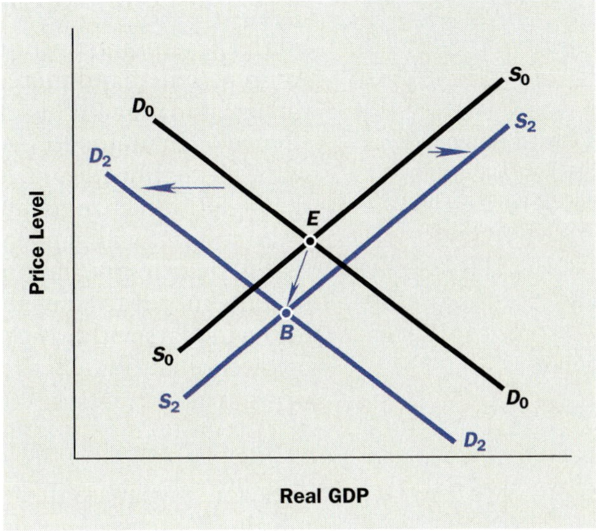

Interest Rates and International Capital Flows

One important piece of our international economic puzzle is still missing. We have analyzed international trade in goods and services in some detail, but we have ignored international movements of *capital*.

For some nations, this omission is inconsequential because they rarely receive or lend international capital. But things are quite different for the United States because the vast majority of international financial flows involve either buying or selling assets whose values are stated in U.S. dollars. In addition, we cannot hope to understand the origins of the various international financial crises since the 1990s without incorporating capital flows into our analysis. Fortunately, given what we have just learned about the effects of exchange rates, this omission is easily rectified.

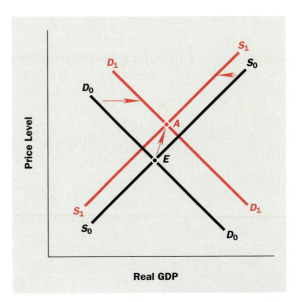

FIGURE 4

The Effects of a
Currency Depreciation

FIGURE 5

The Effects of a
Currency Appreciation

Recall from the previous chapter that interest rate differentials and capital flows are typically the most important determinants of exchange rate movements. Specifically, suppose interest rates in the United States rise while foreign interest rates are unchanged. We learned in the previous chapter that this change in relative interest rates will attract capital to the United States and cause the dollar to appreciate. This chapter has just taught us that an appreciating dollar will, in turn, reduce net exports, prices, and output in the United States—as indicated in Figure 5. Thus:

A rise in interest rates tends to contract the economy by appreciating the currency and reducing net exports.

Notice that this conclusion has a familiar ring. When we studied monetary policy in Chapter 30, we observed that higher interest rates deter investment spending and hence reduce the I component of $C + I + G + (X - IM)$. Now, in studying an open economy with **international capital flows,** we see that higher interest rates also reduce the $X - IM$ component. Thus, *international capital flows strengthen the negative effects of interest rates on aggregate demand.*

> **International capital flows** are purchased and sales of financial assets across national borders.

If interest rates fall in the United States, or rise abroad, everything we have just said is turned in the opposite direction. The conclusion is:

A decline in interest rates tends to expand the economy by depreciating the currency and raising net exports.

EXERCISE Provide the reasoning behind this conclusion.

FISCAL AND MONETARY POLICIES IN AN OPEN ECONOMY

We are now ready to use our model to analyze how fiscal and monetary policies work when capital is internationally mobile and the exchange rate floats. Doing so will teach us how international economic relations modify the effects of stabilization policies that we learned about in earlier chapters. Fortunately, no new theoretical apparatus is necessary; we need merely remember what we have learned in the chapter up to this point. Specifically:

- A rise in the domestic interest rate leads to capital *inflows*, which make the exchange rate *appreciate*. A currency appreciation *reduces* aggregate demand and *raises* aggregate supply (see Figure 5).
- A fall in the domestic interest rate leads to capital *outflows*, which make the exchange rate *depreciate*. A currency depreciation *raises* aggregate demand and *reduces* aggregate supply (see Figure 4).

Fiscal Policy Revisited

With these points in mind, suppose the government cuts taxes or raises spending. Aggregate demand increases, which pushes up both real GDP and the price level in the usual manner. This effect is shown as the shift from D_0D_0 to the red line D_1D_1 in Figure 6. In a **closed economy,** that is the end of the story. But in an *open economy* with international capital flows, we must add in the macroeconomic effects that work through the exchange rate. We do this by answering two questions.

> A **closed economy** is one that does not trade with other nations in either goods or assets.

First, what will happen to the exchange rate? We know from earlier chapters that a fiscal expansion pushes up interest rates. At higher interest rates, American securities become more attractive to foreign investors, who go to the foreign exchange markets to buy dollars with which to purchase them. This buying pressure drives up the value of the dollar. Thus, at least for a rich country that can easily sell its bonds on the world market:

A fiscal expansion normally makes the exchange rate appreciate.

Second, what are the effects of a higher dollar? We know that when the dollar rises in value, American goods become more expensive abroad and foreign goods become cheaper here. So exports fall and imports rise, driving down the $X - IM$ component of aggregate demand. The fiscal expansion thus winds up increasing both America's *capital account surplus* (by attracting foreign capital) and its *current account deficit* (by reducing net exports). In fact, the two must rise by equal amounts because, under floating exchange rates, it is always true that:[2]

Current account surplus + Capital account surplus = 0

Because a fiscal expansion leads in this way to a trade deficit, many economists believe that the large U.S. trade deficits of the 1980s were a side effect of the large tax cuts made early in the decade—and that the tax cuts of 2001–2003 once again pushed the trade deficit up. We will return to that issue shortly.

For now, note that the induced rise in the dollar will shift the aggregate supply curve *outward* and the aggregate demand curve *inward*, as we saw in Figure 5. Figure 6 adds these two shifts (in blue) to the effect of the original fiscal expansion (in red). The final equilibrium in an open economy is point C, whereas in a closed economy it would be point B. By comparing points B and C, we can see how international linkages change the picture of fiscal policy that we painted earlier in the book.

Two main differences arise. First, a higher exchange rate makes imports cheaper and thereby offsets part of the inflationary effect of a fiscal expansion. Second, a higher exchange rate reduces the expansionary effect on real GDP by reducing $X - IM$. Here we have a new kind of "crowding out," different from the one we studied in Chapter 32. There we learned that an increase in G will crowd out some *private investment* spending by raising interest rates. Here an increase in G, by raising both interest rates and the exchange rate, crowds out *net exports*. But the effect is the same: The fiscal multiplier is reduced. Thus, we conclude that:

International capital flows reduce the power of fiscal policy.

Table 2, which shows actual U.S. data, suggests that this new international variety of crowding out was much more important than the traditional type of crowding out in the 1980s. Between 1981 and 1986, the share of investment in GDP barely changed despite the rise in the shares of both consumer spending and government purchases. Only the share of net exports, $X - IM$, fell—from +0.2 percent to −2.8 percent.

American economists learned an important lesson in the 1980s. In 1981, many economists worried that large government budget deficits would crowd out private investment. By the end of the decade, most were more concerned that deficits were crowding out net exports and producing a massive trade deficit.

FIGURE 6

A Fiscal Expansion in an Open Economy

TABLE 2

Percentage Shares of Real GDP in the United States, 1981 and 1986

Year	C	I	G	X − IM
1981	64.5%	14.3%	20.5%	0.2%
1986	67.3	14.5	21.2	−2.8
Change	+2.8	+0.2	+0.7	−3.0

NOTE: Totals do not add up because of rounding and deflation.

■ Monetary Policy Revisited

Now let us consider how *monetary policy* works in an open economy with floating exchange rates and international capital mobility. To remain consistent with the history of the 1980s, we consider a *tightening*, rather than a loosening, of monetary policy.

---

[2] If you need review, turn back to Chapter 36, page 763-776.

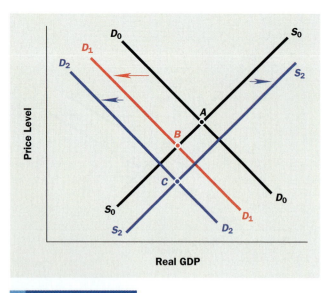

A Monetary Contraction
in an Open Economy

As we know from earlier chapters, contractionary monetary policy *reduces* aggregate demand, which lowers both real GDP and prices. This situation is shown in Figure 7 by the shift from D_0D_0 to the red line D_1D_1, and it looks like the exact opposite of a fiscal expansion. Without international capital flows, that would be the end of the story.

But in the presence of internationally mobile capital, we must also think through the consequences for interest rates and exchange rates. As we know from previous chapters, a monetary contraction *raises* interest rates—just like a fiscal expansion. Hence, tighter money attracts foreign capital into the United States in search of higher rates of return. The exchange rate therefore *rises*. The appreciating dollar encourages imports and discourages exports; so $X - IM$ falls. America therefore winds up with an inflow of capital and an increase in its trade deficit.

In Figure 7, the two effects of the exchange rate appreciation appear in blue: aggregate supply shifts *outward* and aggregate demand shifts *inward*. This time, as you can see in the figure:

International capital flows increase the power of monetary policy.

In a closed economy, higher interest rates *reduce investment* spending, *I*. In an open economy, these same higher interest rates also appreciate the currency and reduce *net exports*, $X - IM$. Thus, the effect of monetary policy is enhanced.

It may seem puzzling that capital flows *strengthen* monetary policy but *weaken* fiscal policy. The explanation of these contrasting results lies in their effects on interest rates. The main international repercussion of either a fiscal *expansion* or a monetary *contraction* is to raise interest rates and the exchange rate, thereby crowding out net exports. But that means that the initial effects of a fiscal expansion on aggregate demand are *weakened*, whereas the initial effects of a monetary contraction are *strengthened*.

■ INTERNATIONAL ASPECTS OF DEFICIT REDUCTION

We have now completed our theoretical analysis of the macroeconomics of open economies. Let us put the theory to work by applying it to the events of the 1990s, when fiscal policy was tightened and monetary policy was eased. Should reducing the budget deficit (or raising the surplus) strengthen or weaken the dollar?

As discussed in Chapter 32, the U.S. government transformed its mammoth budget deficit into a notable surplus during the 1990s by raising taxes and cutting expenditures. Column (1) of Table 3 reviews the predicted effects of a fiscal contraction: It should lower real interest rates, make the dollar depreciate, reduce real GDP, and be less disinflationary than normal because of the falling dollar. This information is recorded by entering + signs for increases and − signs for decreases.

Eliminating the budget deficit reduced aggregate demand. But the Federal Reserve restored the missing demand by lowering interest rates so that the economy would not suffer a slump. According to the analysis in this chapter, such a monetary expansion should lower real interest rates, make the dollar depreciate, raise real GDP, and be a bit more inflationary than usual because of the falling dollar. These effects are recorded in Column (2) of Table 3.

TABLE 3

Expected Effects of Policy

Variable	(1) Fiscal Contraction	(2) Monetary Expansion	(3) Combination
Real interest rate	−	−	−
Exchange rate	−	−	−
Net exports	+	+	+
Real GDP	−	+	?
Inflation	−	+	?

Column (3) puts the two pieces together. We conclude that a policy mix of fiscal *contraction* and monetary *expansion* should reduce interest rates strongly, push down the value of the dollar, and strongly stimulate our foreign trade. The net effects on output and inflation are uncertain, however: The balance depends on whether the fiscal contraction overwhelms the monetary expansion, or vice versa.

What actually happened? First, interest rates did fall, just as predicted. The rate on ten-year U.S. government bonds dropped from almost 7 percent in late 1992 to just over 4.5 percent in December 1998, and by 1998 American households were enjoying the lowest home mortgage rates since the 1960s. Second, the U.S. economy expanded rapidly between 1992 and 1998; apparently, the monetary stimulus overwhelmed the fiscal contraction. Third, inflation fell despite such rapid growth. As we explained in Chapter 27, one major reason was a series of favorable supply shocks that pushed inflation down.

But what about the exchange rate and international trade? Here the theory did less well. The dollar generally declined from 1993 to 1995, just as the theory predicts. But then it turned around and rose sharply from 1995 to 1998, just when the budget deficit was turning into a surplus. America's trade performance was even more puzzling. According to the theory, a lower budget deficit should have led to a lower exchange rate, and therefore to a smaller **trade deficit.** But, in fact, America's real net exports sagged from just $-\$16$ billion in 1992 to $-\$204$ billion in 1998. What went wrong?

> A country's **trade deficit** is the excess of its imports over its exports. If, instead, exports exceed imports, the country has a **trade surplus.**

■ The Loose Link between the Budget Deficit and the Trade Deficit

To answer this question, let's explore the connection between the budget deficit and the trade deficit in more detail. To do so, we need one simple piece of arithmetic.

Begin with the familiar equilibrium condition for GDP in an open economy:

$$Y = C + I + G + (X - IM)$$

Because GDP can either be spent, saved, or taxed away,[3]

$$Y = C + S + T$$

Equating these two expressions for Y gives

$$C + I + G + (X - IM) = C + S + T$$

Finally, subtracting C from both sides and bringing the I and G terms over to the right-hand side leads to an accounting relationship between the trade deficit and the budget deficit:

$$X - IM = (S - I) - (G - T)$$

Notice that this equation is a matter of *accounting*, not economics. It must hold in *all* countries at *all* times, and it has nothing to do with any particular economic theory. In words, it says that a trade deficit—a *negative* value of $(X - IM)$—can arise from one of two sources: a government budget deficit (G larger than T) or an excess of investment over saving (I larger than S).

Now let's apply this accounting relationship to actual U.S. events in the 1990s. As we know, the government deficit, $G - T$, fell precipitously. Other things equal, that should have *reduced* the trade deficit. But other things were not equal. The equation reminds us that the balance between saving and investment matters, too. As shares of GDP, business investment boomed while household saving declined from 1992 to 1998. So $S - I$ moved sharply in the negative direction. And that change, as our equation shows, should *raise* the trade deficit (reduce net exports).

---

[3] If you do not see why, recall that GDP equals disposable income (DI) plus taxes (T), $Y = DI + T$, and that disposable income can either be consumed or saved, $DI = C + S$. These two definitions together imply that $Y = C + S + T$.

In brief, taken by itself, deficit reduction would have increased net exports. But in reality, sharp changes in private economic behavior—specifically, less saving and more investment—overwhelmed the government's actions and made net exports fall instead. The link from the budget deficit to the trade deficit can be a loose one.

IS THE TRADE DEFICIT A PROBLEM?

The preceding explanation suggests that the United States' large trade deficits over the past decade are a symptom of a deeper trouble: The nation as a whole—including both the government and the private sector—has been consuming more than it has been producing for years. The United States has therefore been forced to borrow the difference from foreigners. The trade deficit is just the mirror image of the required capital inflows.

Those who worry about trade deficits point out that these capital inflows create debts on which interest and principal payments must be made in the future. In this view, we Americans have been mortgaging our futures to finance higher consumer spending.

But another, quite different, interpretation of the trade deficit is possible. Suppose foreign investors come to see the United States as an especially attractive place to invest their funds. Then capital will flow here, not because Americans need to *borrow* it, but because foreigners are eager to *lend* it. The desire of foreigners to acquire American assets should push the value of the dollar up, which should in turn push America's net exports down. In that case, the trade deficit would still be the mirror image of the capital inflows. But it would signify America's economic *strength*, not its weakness.

Each view has elements of truth, but the second raises a critical question: How long can it go on? As long as the United States continues to run large trade deficits, foreigners will have to continue to accumulate large amounts of U.S. assets—one way or another. As we noted in the previous chapter, starting in 2002 private investors abroad began concluding that they had acquired about all the American assets they wanted. That would have marked the day of reckoning for the United States but for one important fact: The governments of Japan and China decided to buy hundreds of billions of dollars (selling equivalent amounts of their own currencies) rather than let the yen and the yuan appreciate. These large *government* capital inflows allowed the U.S. to continue to run mammoth trade deficits.

ON CURING THE TRADE DEFICIT

How can we cure our foreign trade problem and end our addiction to foreign borrowing? There are four basic ways.

Change the Mix of Fiscal and Monetary Policy

The fundamental equation

$$X - IM = (S - I) - (G - T)$$

Suggests that a *decrease in the budget deficit* (that is, shrinking $G - T$) would be one good way to reduce the trade deficit. According to the analysis in this chapter, a reduction in G or an increase in T would lead to lower real interest rates in the United States, a depreciating dollar, and, eventually, a smaller trade deficit.

When the government curtails its spending or raises taxes, aggregate demand falls. If we do not want the shrinking budget deficit to slow economic growth, we must therefore compensate for it by providing monetary stimulus. Like contractionary fiscal policy, expansionary monetary policy lowers interest rates, depreciates the dollar, and should therefore help reduce the trade deficit. So the policy recommendation actually amounts to tightening *fiscal* policy and loosening *monetary* policy.

As we have just noted, the U.S. government—after years of vacillation—changed the policy mix decisively in this direction in the 1990s. But our trade deficit rose anyway because private investment spending soared while private saving stagnated. Then, starting in 2001, the federal budget turned rapidly from a substantial surplus to a record-high deficit, which pushed the trade deficit up further. What else might work?

More Rapid Economic Growth Abroad

One factor behind the growing U.S. trade deficit is that the economies of many foreign nations—the customers for our exports—have grown more slowly than the U.S. economy. If foreign economies would grow faster, the U.S. government has frequently argued, they would buy more American goods, thereby raising U.S. exports and reducing our trade deficit. So we have regularly urged our major trading partners to stimulate their economies and to open their markets more to American goods—but with only modest success. When the U.S. economy slowed down in 2000–2001, our trade deficit did recede a bit—albeit temporarily. But no one thought that was a very good remedy.

Raise Domestic Saving or Reduce Domestic Investment

Our fundamental equation calls attention to two other routes to a smaller trade deficit: more saving or less investment.

The U.S. personal saving rate (saving as a share of disposable income) has hit postwar lows in recent years. The *minus* 1 percent saving rate recorded in 2006 was the lowest since the Great Depression of the 1930s! If Americans would simply save more, we would need to borrow less from abroad. This solution, too, would lead to a cheaper dollar and a smaller trade deficit.

The trouble is that no one has yet found a reliable way to induce Americans to save more. The government has implemented a variety of tax incentives for saving, and more are suggested every year. But little evidence suggests that any of them has worked. Instead, large increases in stock market wealth in the second half of the 1990s, and then in housing wealth in the early 2000s, convinced Americans that it was prudent to save *even less* than they used to.

If the other cures for our trade deficit fail to work, the deficit may cure itself in a particularly unpleasant way: by reducing U.S. domestic investment. The 2001 recession accomplished this to some extent, reducing the share of investment in real GDP from 17.7 percent in 2000 to 15.1 percent in 2003. (It also curbed our appetite for imports.) That effect was only temporary, however, and the longer-run problem mentioned above remains: If our trade deficit persists, we will have to borrow more and more from foreigners who, at some point, will start demanding higher interest rates. At best, higher interest rates will lead to lower investment in the United States. At worst, interest rates will skyrocket, and we will experience a severe recession.

Protectionism

We have saved the worst remedy for last. One seemingly obvious way to cure our trade deficit is to limit imports by imposing stiff tariffs, quotas, and other protectionist devices. We discussed protectionism, and the reasons why almost all economists oppose it, in Chapter 34. Despite the economic arguments against it, protectionism has an undeniable political allure. It seems, superficially, to "save American jobs," and it conveniently shifts the blame for our trade problems onto foreigners.

In addition to depriving us and other countries of the benefits of comparative advantage, protectionism might not even succeed in reducing our trade deficit, however. One reason is that other nations may retaliate. If we erect trade barriers to reduce our imports,

"But we're not just talking about buying a car—we're talking about confronting this country's trade deficit with Japan."

IM will fall. But if foreign countries erect corresponding barriers to our exports, *X* will fall, too. On balance, our *net* exports, *X – IM*, may or may not improve. But world trade will surely suffer. This game may have no winners, only losers.

Even if other nations do not retaliate, tariffs and quotas may not improve the U.S. trade deficit much. Why? If they succeed in reducing American spending on imports, tariffs and quotas will thereby reduce the supply of dollars on the world market—which will push the value of the dollar up. A rising dollar, of course, would hurt U.S. exports and encourage more imports. The fundamental equation

$$X - IM = (S - I) - (G - T)$$

reminds us that protectionism can raise *X – IM* only if it raises the budget surplus, raises saving, or reduces investment.[4]

CONCLUSION: NO NATION IS AN ISLAND

The poet John Donne wrote that "no man is an island." Similarly, no nation is isolated from economic developments elsewhere on the globe. Instead, we live in a world economy in which the fates of nations are intertwined. The major trading countries are linked by exports and imports, by capital flows, and by exchange rates. What happens to national income, prices, and interest rates in one country affects other nations. No events make this point clearer than the international financial crises that erupt from time to time (see the previous chapter).

As we noted in Chapter 35, one root cause of almost all of these crises was the countries' decisions to fix their exchange rates to the U.S. dollar. Unfortunately for nations such as Thailand, Indonesia, and South Korea, the dollar rose spectacularly from 1995 to 1997. With their exchange rates tied to the dollar, the Thai baht, the Indonesian rupiah, and the Korean won automatically appreciated relative to most other currencies—making their exports more costly. Soon these one-time export powerhouses found themselves in an unaccustomed position: running large trade deficits.

Then the crisis hit, and all four of these countries watched their currencies tumble in value. The sharp depreciations restored their international competitiveness, but it also impoverished many of their citizens. Naturally, the shrinking Asian economies curbed their appetites for American goods, so our exports to the region fell—which contributed to further deterioration in the U.S. trade deficit.

Thus, a primarily American development (the rise of the dollar) harmed the Asian economies, and then a primarily Asian development (deep recessions in the Asian tigers) hurt the U.S. economy. The nations of the world are indeed linked economically.

? ISSUE REVISITED: *Should the U.S. Let the Dollar Fall?*

Recall the question with which we began this chapter: Should the U.S. let the dollar fall or try to stop it? Remember that a falling dollar boosts exports and growth in the United States but *reduces* exports and growth in, say, Europe and Japan. With economic growth in both Japan and Europe already slow, it was easy to understand why foreign leaders wanted the U.S. government to stop, or at least slow down, the dollar's rapid descent in 2004.

But it was also easy to understand why the United States was not eager to do so, especially in an election year, because a falling dollar could reasonably be expected to help the United States grow faster—even if that meant that Europe and Japan would grow slower. Even today, with the election long over, the United States is looking to a cheaper dollar to reduce its trade deficit.

Unfortunately, there is no way to avoid this conflict of interests. A cheaper dollar means a dearer euro and a dearer yen. For better or for worse, we all live in one world.

---

[4] Here tariffs, which raise revenue for the government, have a clear advantage over quotas, which do not.

SUMMARY

1. The nations of the world are linked together economically because national income, prices, and interest rates in one country affect those in other countries. They are thus **open economies.**

2. Because one country's imports are another country's exports, rapid (or sluggish) economic growth in one country contributes to rapid (or sluggish) growth in other countries.

3. A country's net exports depend on whether its prices are high or low relative to those of other countries. Because exchange rates translate one country's prices into the currencies of other countries, the exchange rate is a key determinant of net exports.

4. If the currency depreciates, net exports rise and aggregate demand increases, thereby raising both real GDP and the price level. A depreciating currency also reduces aggregate supply by making imported inputs more costly.

5. If the currency appreciates, net exports fall and aggregate demand, real GDP, and the price level all decrease. An appreciating currency also increases aggregate supply by making imported inputs cheaper.

6. **International capital flows** respond strongly to rates of return on investments in different countries. For example, higher domestic interest rates lead to currency appreciations, and lower interest rates lead to depreciations.

7. Contractionary monetary policies raise interest rates and therefore make the currency appreciate. Both the higher interest rates and the stronger currency reduce aggregate demand. Hence, international capital flows make monetary policy more powerful than it would be in a closed economy.

8. Expansionary fiscal policies also raise interest rates and make the currency appreciate. But in this case, the international repercussions cancel out part of the demand-expanding effects of the policies. Hence, international capital flows make fiscal policy less powerful than it would be in a closed economy.

9. Because eliminating the budget deficit in the 1990s combined tighter fiscal policy with looser monetary policy, it lowered interest rates. That should have pushed the dollar down and led to a smaller **trade deficit** in the United States. However, changes in private economic behavior—specifically, lower saving and higher investment—offset the presumed international effects of deficit reduction and the trade deficit kept growing.

10. Budget deficits and trade deficits are linked by the fundamental equation $X - IM = (S - I) - (G - T)$.

11. It follows from this equation that the U.S. trade deficit must be cured by some combination of lower budget deficits, higher savings, and lower investment.

12. Protectionist policies might not cure the U.S. trade deficit because (a) they will make the dollar appreciate and (b) they may provoke foreign retaliation.

KEY TERMS

Open economy 763

Net exports 764

Exchange rate 764

Appreciation 765

Depreciation 765

International capital flows 768

Closed economy 768

Trade deficit 771

Budget deficits and trade deficits 771

$X - IM = (S - I) - (G - T)$ 771

TEST YOURSELF

1. Use an aggregate supply-demand diagram to analyze the effects of a currency appreciation.

2. Explain why $X - IM = (S - I) - (G - T)$. Now multiply both sides of this equation by -1 to get

$$IM - X = (I - S) + (G - T)$$

and remember that the trade deficit, $IM - X$, is the amount we have to borrow from foreigners to get

Borrowing from foreigners $= (I - S) + (G - T)$.

Explain the common sense behind this version of the fundamental equation.

3. **(More difficult)** Suppose consumption and investment are described by the following:

$$C = 150 + 0.75DI$$
$$I = 300 + 0.2Y - 50r$$

Here DI is disposable income, Y is GDP, and r, the interest rate, is measured in percentage points. (For example, a 5 percent interest rate is $r = 5$.) Exports and imports are as follows:

$$X = 300$$
$$IM = 250 + 0.2Y$$

Government purchases are $G = 800$, and taxes are 20 percent of income. The price level is fixed and the central bank uses its monetary policy to peg the interest rate at $r = 8$.

a. Find equilibrium GDP, the budget deficit or surplus, and the trade deficit or surplus.

b. Suppose the currency appreciates and, as a result, exports and imports change to

$$X = 250$$
$$IM = 0.2Y$$

Now find equilibrium GDP, the budget deficit or surplus, and the trade deficit or surplus.

DISCUSSION QUESTIONS

1. For years, the U.S. government has been trying to get Japan and the European Union to expand their economies faster. Explain how more rapid growth in Japan would affect the U.S. economy.

2. If inflation is lower in Germany than in Spain (as it is), and the exchange rate between the two countries is fixed (as it is, because of the monetary union), what is likely to happen to the balance of trade between the two countries?

3. Explain why a currency depreciation leads to an improvement in a country's trade balance.

4. Explain why American fiscal policy is less powerful and American monetary policy is more powerful than indicated in the closed-economy model described earlier in this book.

5. Given what you now know, do you think it was a good idea for the United States to adopt a policy mix of tight money and large government budget deficits in the early 1980s? Why or why not? What were the benefits and costs of reversing that policy mix in the 1990s?

6. In 2001, 2002, and 2003, Congress passed the series of tax cuts that President Bush had requested. What effect did this policy likely have on the U.S. trade deficit? Why?

7. In 2004, the international value of the yen rose somewhat. This development was viewed with alarm in Japan. Why?

GLOSSARY

Ability-to-pay principle The ability-to-pay principle of taxation refers to the idea that people with greater ability to pay taxes should pay higher taxes. (p. 386)

Absolute advantage One country is said to have an absolute advantage over another in the production of a particular good if it can produce that good using smaller quantities of resources than can the other country. (p. 727)

Abstraction Abstraction means ignoring many details so as to focus on the most important elements of a problem. (p. 9)

Affirmative action Affirmative action refers to active efforts to locate and hire members of underrepresented groups. (p. 459)

Agents Agents are people hired to run a complex enterprise on behalf of the principals, those whose benefit the enterprise is supposed to serve. (p. 323)

Aggregate demand Aggregate demand is the total amount that all consumers, business firms, and government agencies spend on final goods and services. (p. 538)

Aggregate demand curve The aggregate demand curve shows the quantity of domestic product that is demanded at each possible value of the price level. (pp. 471, 564)

Aggregate supply curve The aggregate supply curve shows, for each possible price level, the quantity of goods and services that all the nation's businesses are willing to produce during a specified period of time, holding all other determinants of aggregate quantity supplied constant. (pp. 471, 584)

Aggregation Aggregation means combining many individual markets into one overall market. (p. 489)

Allocation of resources Allocation of resources refers to the society's decisions on how to divide up its scarce input resources among the different outputs produced in the economy and among the different firms or other organizations that produce those outputs. (p. 48)

Antitrust policy Antitrust policy refers to programs and laws that preclude the deliberate creation of monopoly and prevent powerful firms from engaging in related "anticompetitive practices." (p. 275)

Applied research Applied research is research whose goal is to invent or improve particular products or processes, often for profit. Note, however, that the military and government health-related agencies provide examples of not-for-profit applied research. (p. 352)

Appreciate A nation's currency is said to appreciate when exchange rates change so that a unit of its currency can buy more units of foreign currency. (pp. 746, 765)

Arbitration Arbitration occurs during collective bargaining when a neutral individual is appointed with the power to decide the issues and force both parties to accept his decisions. (p. 441)

Asset An asset of an individual or business firm is an item of value that the individual or firm owns. (p. 635)

Automatic stabilizer An automatic stabilizer is a feature of the economy that reduces its sensitivity to shocks, such as sharp increases or decreases in spending. (p. 609)

Autonomous increase in consumption An autonomous increase in consumption is an increase in consumer spending without any increase in consumer incomes. It is represented on a graph as a shift of the entire consumption function. (p. 573)

Average physical product (APP) The average physical product (APP) is the total physical product (TPP) divided by the quantity of input. Thus, APP = TPP/X where X = the quantity of input. (p. 130)

Average revenue (AR) The average revenue (AR) is total revenue (TR) divided by quantity. (p. 160)

Average tax rate The average tax rate is the ratio of taxes to income. (p. 381)

Backward-bending A supply curve of labor is backward-bending when a rise in an initially low wage leads to a rise in quantity of labor supplied, but a rise in a wage that was already high reduces the amount supplied. (p. 429)

Balance of payments deficit The balance of payments deficit is the amount by which the quantity supplied of a country's currency (per year) exceeds the quantity demanded. Balance of payments deficits arise whenever the exchange rate is pegged at an artificially high level. (p. 753)

Balance of payments surplus The balance of payments surplus is the amount by which the quantity demanded of a country's currency (per year) exceeds the quantity supplied. Balance of payments surpluses arise whenever the exchange rate is pegged at an artificially low level. (p. 753)

Balance sheet A balance sheet is an accounting statement listing the values of all assets on the left side and the values of all liabilities and net worth on the right side. (p. 635)

Barriers to entry Barriers to entry are attributes of a market that make it more difficult or expensive for a new firm to open for business than it was for the firms already present in that market. (p. 219)

Barter Barter is a system of exchange in which people directly trade one good for another, without using money as an intermediate step. (p. 626)

Basic research Basic research refers to research that seeks to provide scientific knowledge and general principles rather than coming up with any specific marketable inventions. (p. 352)

Beneficial or detrimental externality An activity is said to generate a beneficial or detrimental externality if that activity causes incidental benefits or damages to others not directly involved in the activity and no corresponding compensation is provided to or paid by those who generate the externality. (p. 314)

Benefits principle The benefits principle of taxation holds that people who derive benefits from a service should pay the taxes that finance it. (p. 387)

Bilateral monopoly A bilateral monopoly is a market situation in which there is both a monopoly on the selling side and a monopsony on the buying side. (p. 440)

Bond A bond is simply an IOU sold by a corporation that promises to pay the holder of the bond a fixed sum of money at the specified *maturity* date and some other fixed amount of money (the *coupon* or *interest payment*) every year up to the date of maturity. (p. 180)

Budget deficit The budget deficit is the amount by which the government's expenditures exceed its receipts during a specified period of time, usually a year. If receipts exceed expenditures, it is called a budget surplus instead. (pp. 687, 771)

Budget line, household The budget line for a household graphically represents all possible combinations of two commodities that it can purchase, given the prices of the commodities and some fixed amount of money at its disposal. (p. 99)

Budget line, firm A firm's budget line is the locus of all points representing every input combination of inputs that the producer can afford to buy with a given amount of money and given input prices. (p. 150)

Budget surplus The budget surplus is the amount by which the government's receipts exceed its expenditures during a specified period of time, usually a year. If expenditures exceed receipts, it is called a budget deficit instead. (p. 687)

Bundling Bundling refers to a pricing arrangement under which the supplier offers substantial discounts to customers if they buy several of the firm's products, so that the price of the bundle of products is less than the sum of the prices of the products if they were bought separately. (p. 281)

Burden of a tax The burden of a tax to an individual is the amount one would have to be given to be just as well off with the tax as without it. (p. 388)

Capital A nation's capital is its available supply of plant, equipment, and software. It is the result of past decisions to make *investments* in these items. (pp. 403, 522)

Capital account The capital account balance includes purchases and sales of financial assets to and from citizens and companies of other countries. (p. 754)

Capital formation Capital formation is synonymous with investment. It refers to the process of building up the capital stock. (p. 522)

Capital gain A capital gain is the difference between the price at which an asset is sold and the price at which it was bought. (p. 506)

Capitalism Capitalism is an economic system in which most of the production process is controlled by private firms operating in markets with minimal government control. The investors in these firms (called "capitalists") own the firms. (p. 337)

Cartel A cartel is a group of sellers of a product who have joined together to control its production, sale, and price in the hope of obtaining the advantages of monopoly. (p. 243)

Central bank A central bank is a bank for banks. The United States' central bank is the *Federal Reserve System*. (p. 647)

Central bank independence Central bank independence refers to the central bank's ability to make decisions without political interference. (p. 648)

Closed economy A closed economy is one that does not trade with other nations in either goods or assets. (pp. 24, 768)

Collective bargaining Collective bargaining is the process of negotiation of wages and working conditions between a union and the firms in the industry. (p. 440)

Commodity money A commodity money is an object in use as a medium of exchange, but which also has a substantial value in alternative (nonmonetary) uses. (p. 629)

Common stock A common stock (also called a share) of a corporation is a piece of paper that gives the holder of the stock a share of the ownership of the company. (p. 180)

Comparative advantage One country is said to have a comparative advantage over another in the production of a particular good *relative to other goods* if it produces that good less inefficiently as compared with the other country. (pp. 49, 727)

Complements Two goods are called complements if an increase in the quantity consumed of one increases the quantity demanded of the other, all other things remaining constant. (p. 117)

Concentration of an industry Concentration of an industry measures the share of the total sales or assets of the industry in the hands of its largest firms. (p. 276)

Concentration ratio A concentration ratio is the percentage of an industry's output produced by its four largest firms. It is intended to measure the degree to which the industry is dominated by large firms. (p. 277)

Consumer expenditure Consumer expenditure (C) is the total amount spent by consumers on newly produced goods and services (excluding purchases of new homes, which are considered investment goods). (p. 539)

Consumer Price Index (CPI) The Consumer Price Index (CPI) is measured by pricing the items on a list representative of a typical urban household budget. (p. 512)

Consumer's surplus Consumer's surplus is the difference between the value to the consumer of the quantity of Commodity X purchased and the amount that the market requires the consumer to pay for that quantity of X. (p. 300)

Consumption function The consumption function shows the relationship between total consumer expenditures and total disposable income in the economy, holding all other determinants of consumer spending constant. (p. 544)

Convergence hypothesis The convergence hypothesis holds that nations with low levels of productivity tend to have high productivity growth rates, so that international productivity differences shrink over time. (p. 521)

Coordination failure A coordination failure occurs when party A would like to change his behavior if party B would change hers, and vice versa, and yet the two changes do not take place because the decisions of A and B are not coordinated. (p. 568)

Corporation A corporation is a firm that has the legal status of a fictional individual. This fictional individual is owned by a number of persons, called its *stockholders*, and is run by a set of elected officers and a board of directors, whose chairman is often also in a powerful position. (p. 179)

Correlated Two variables are said to be correlated if they tend to go up or down together. Correlation need not imply causation. (p. 11)

Cost disease of the personal services The cost disease of the personal services is the tendency of the costs and prices of these services to rise persistently faster than those of the average output in the economy. (pp. 328, 531)

Credible threat A credible threat is a threat that does not harm the threatener if it is carried out. (p. 254)

Cross elasticity of demand The cross elasticity of demand for product X to a change in the price of another product, Y, is the ratio of the percentage change in quantity demanded of X to the percentage change in the price of Y that brings about the change in quantity demanded. (p. 117)

Cross licensing Cross licensing of patents occurs when each of two firms agrees to let the other use some specified set of its patents, either at a price specified in their agreement or in return for access to the other firm's patents. (p. 346)

Cross-subsidization Cross-subsidization means selling one product of the firm at a loss, which is balanced by higher profits on another of the firm's products. (p. 267)

Crowding in Crowding in occurs when government spending, by raising real GDP, induces increases in private investment spending. (p. 695)

Crowding out Crowding out occurs when deficit spending by the government forces private investment spending to contract. (p. 695)

Current account The current account balance includes international purchases and sales of goods and services, cross-border interest and dividend payments, and cross-border gifts to and from both private individuals and governments. It is approximately the same as net exports. (p. 754)

Cyclical unemployment Cyclical unemployment is the portion of unemployment that is attributable to a decline in the economy's total production. Cyclical unemploy-

ment rises during recessions and falls as prosperity is restored. (p. 499)

Deflating Deflating is the process of finding the real value of some monetary magnitude by dividing by some appropriate price index. (p. 513)

Deflation Deflation refers to a sustained decrease in the general price level. (p. 477)

Demand curve A demand curve is a graphical depiction of a demand schedule. It shows how the quantity demanded of some product will change as the price of that product changes during a specified period of time, holding all other determinants of quantity demanded constant. (p. 58)

Demand schedule A demand schedule is a table showing how the quantity demanded of some product during a specified period of time changes as the price of that product changes, holding all other determinants of quantity demanded constant. (p. 58)

Demand-side inflation Demand-side inflation is a rise in the price level caused by rapid growth of aggregate demand. (p. 702)

Depletable A commodity is depletable if it is used up when someone consumes it. (p. 318)

Deposit creation Deposit creation refers to the process by which a fractional reserve banking system turns $1 of bank reserves into several dollars of bank deposits. (p. 636)

Deposit insurance Deposit insurance is a system that guarantees that depositors will not lose money even if their bank goes bankrupt. (p. 634)

Depreciate A nation's currency is said to depreciate when exchange rates change so that a unit of its currency can buy fewer units of foreign currency. (p. 746)

Depreciation Depreciation is the value of the portion of the nation's capital equipment that is used up within the year. It tells us how much output is needed just to maintain the economy's capital stock. (p. 554)

Derived demand The derived demand for an input is the demand for the input by producers as determined by the demand for the final product that the input is used to produce. (p. 402)

Devaluation A devaluation is a reduction in the official value of a currency. (p. 747)

Development assistance Development assistance ("foreign aid") refers to outright grants and low-interest loans to poor countries from both rich countries and multinational institutions like the World Bank. The purpose is to spur economic development. (p. 531)

Direct controls Direct controls are government rules that tell organizations or individuals what processes or raw materials they may use or what products they are permitted to supply or purchase. (p. 366)

Direct taxes Direct taxes are taxes levied directly on people. (p. 381)

Discounting, or computing the present value The process that has been invented for making the magnitudes of payments at different dates comparable to one another is called discounting, or computing the present value. (p. 419)

Discount rate The discount rate is the interest rate the Fed charges on loans that it makes to banks. (p. 654)

Discouraged worker A discouraged worker is an unemployed person who gives up looking for work and is therefore no longer counted as part of the labor force. (p. 498)

Disposable income Disposable income (*DI*) is the sum of the incomes of all individuals in the economy after all taxes have been deducted and all transfer payments have been added. (p. 539)

Division of labor Division of labor means breaking up a task into a number of smaller, more *specialized* tasks so that each worker can become more adept at a particular job. (p. 48)

Dominant strategy A dominant strategy for one of the competitors in a game is a strategy that will yield a higher payoff than any of the other strategies that are possible for her, no matter what choice of strategy is made by her competitors. (p. 250)

Dumping Dumping means selling goods in a foreign market at lower prices than those charged in the home market. (p. 737)

Economic discrimination Economic discrimination occurs when equivalent factors of production receive different payments for equal contributions to output. (p. 452)

Economic model An economic model is a simplified, small-scale version of some aspect of the economy. Economic models are often expressed in equations, by graphs, or in words. (p. 11)

Economic profit Economic profit equals net earnings, in the accountant's sense, minus the *opportunity costs* of capital and of any other inputs supplied by the firm's owners. (pp. 159, 211, 414)

Economic rent Economic rent is any portion of the payment to labor or any other input that does not lead to an increase in the amount of labor supplied. (pp. 408, 432)

Economies of scale Economies of scale are savings that are obtained through increases in quantities produced. Scale economies occur when an X percent increase in input use raises output by *more than X* percent, so that the more the firm produces, the lower its per-unit costs become. (pp. 142, 264)

Economies of scope Economies of scope are savings that are obtained through simultaneous production of many different products. They occur if a firm that produces many commodities can supply each good more cheaply than a firm that produces fewer commodities. (p. 267)

Efficiency A set of outputs is said to be produced efficiently if, given current technological knowledge, there is no way one can produce larger amounts of any output without using larger input amounts or giving up some quantity of another output. (p. 47)

Efficient allocation of resources An efficient allocation of resources is one that takes advantage of every opportunity to make some individuals better off in their own estimation while not worsening the lot of anyone else. (p. 288)

Elastic demand curve A demand curve is elastic when a given percentage price change leads to a larger percentage change in quantity demanded. (p. 112)

Emissions permits Emissions permits are licenses issued by government specifying the maximum amount the license holder is allowed to emit. The licenses are restricted to permit a limited amount of

emission in total. Often, they must be purchased from the government or on a special market. (p. 369)

Entrepreneur An entrepreneur is an individual who organizes a new business firm, particularly a firm that offers new products or new productive technology. (p. 340)

Entrepreneurship Entrepreneurship is the act of starting new firms, introducing new products and technological innovations, and, in general, taking the risks that are necessary to seek out business opportunities. (p. 400)

Equation of exchange The equation of exchange states that the money value of GDP transactions must be equal to the product of the average stock of money times velocity. That is: $M \times V = P \times Y$ (p. 662)

Equilibrium An equilibrium is a situation in which there are no inherent forces that produce change. Changes away from an equilibrium position will occur only as a result of "outside events" that disturb the status quo. (pp. 65, 560)

Excess burden The excess burden of a tax to an individual is the amount by which the burden of the tax exceeds the tax that is paid. (p. 388)

Excess reserves Excess reserves are any reserves held in excess of the legal minimum. (p. 636)

Exchange rate The exchange rate states the price, in terms of one currency, at which another currency can be bought. (pp. 746, 764)

Excludable A commodity is excludable if someone who does not pay for it can be kept from enjoying it. (p. 318)

Expansion path The expansion path is the locus of the firm's cost-minimizing input combinations for all relevant output levels. (p. 151)

Expenditure schedule An expenditure schedule shows the relationship between national income (GDP) and total spending. (p. 562)

Export subsidy An export subsidy is a payment by the government to exporters to permit them to reduce the selling prices of their goods so they can compete more effectively in foreign markets. (p. 732)

Externality An activity is said to generate a beneficial or detrimental externality if that activity causes incidental benefits or damages to others not directly involved in the activity, and no corresponding compensation is provided to or paid by those who generate the externality. (pp. 314, 335, 358)

45° line Rays through the origin with a slope of 1 are called 45° lines because they form an angle of 45° with the horizontal axis. A 45° line marks off points where the variables measured on each axis have equal values. (p. 17)

45° line diagram An income-expenditure diagram, or 45° line diagram, plots total real expenditure (on the vertical axis) against real income (on the horizontal axis). The 45° line marks off points where income and expenditure are equal. (p. 564)

Factors of production Inputs or factors of production are the labor, machinery, buildings, and natural resources used to make outputs. (pp. 22, 399)

Federal funds rate The federal funds rate is the interest rates that banks pay and receive when they borrow reserves from one another. (p. 649)

Fiat money Fiat money is money that is decreed as such by the government. It is of little value as a commodity, but it maintains its value as a medium of exchange because people have faith that the issuer will stand behind the pieces of printed paper and limit their production. (p. 649)

Final goods and services Final goods and services are those that are purchased by their ultimate users. (p. 473)

Fiscal federalism Fiscal federalism refers to the system of grants from one level of government to the next. (p. 386)

Fiscal policy The government's fiscal policy is its plan for spending and taxation. It can be used to steer aggregate demand in the desired direction. (pp. 480, 605, 685)

Fixed cost A fixed cost is the cost of an input whose quantity does not rise when output goes up, one that the firm requires to produce any output at all. The total cost of such indivisible inputs does not change when the output changes. Any other cost of the firm's operation is called a variable cost. (p. 130)

Fixed exchange rates Fixed exchange rates are rates set by government decisions and maintained by government actions. (p. 753)

Fixed taxes Fixed taxes are taxes that do not vary with the level of GDP. (p. 618)

Floating exchange rates Floating exchange rates are rates determined in free markets by the law of supply and demand. (p. 747)

Foreign direct investment Foreign direct investment is the purchase or construction of real business assets—such as factories, offices, and machinery—in a foreign country. (p. 532)

Fractional reserve banking Fractional reserve banking is a system under which bankers keep as reserves only a fraction of the funds they hold on deposit. (p. 633)

Frictional unemployment Frictional unemployment is unemployment that is due to normal turnover in the labor market. It includes people who are temporarily between jobs because they are moving or changing occupations, or are unemployed for similar reasons. (p. 499)

Full employment Full employment is a situation in which everyone who is willing and able to work can find a job. At full employment, the measured unemployment rate is still positive. (p. 500)

GDP deflator The price index used to deflate nominal GDP is called the GDP deflator. It is a broad measure of economy-wide inflation; it includes the prices of all goods and services in the economy. (p. 513)

Gold standard The gold standard is a way to fix exchange rates by defining each participating currency in terms of gold and allowing holders of each participating currency to convert that currency into gold. (p. 754)

Government purchases Government purchases (G) refer to the goods (such as airplanes and paper clips) and services (such as school teaching and police protection) purchased by all levels of government. (p. 539)

Gross domestic product (GDP) Gross domestic product (GDP) is the sum of the money values of all final goods and services produced in the domestic economy and sold on organized markets during a speci-fied period of time, usually a year. (pp. 23, 338, 472)

Gross private domestic investment (I) Gross private domestic investment includes business investment in plant, equipment, and software; residential construction; and inventory investment. (p. 552)

Growth policy Growth policy refers to government policies intended to make the economy grow faster in the long run. (p. 490)

Herfindahl-Hirschman Index (HHI) The Herfindahl-Hirschman Index (HHI) is an alternative and widely used measure of the degree of concentration of an industry. It is calculated, in essence, by adding together the squares of the market shares of the firms in the industry, although the smallest firms may be left out of the calculation because their small market share numbers have a negligible effect on the result. (p. 277)

High-tech (high-technology) A high-tech (high-technology) firm or industry is one whose products, equipment and production methods utilize highly advanced technology that is constantly modified and improved. Examples are the aerospace, scientific instruments, computer, communications, and pharmaceutical industries. (p. 343)

Horizontal equity Horizontal equity is the notion that equally situated individuals should be taxed equally. (p. 386)

Human capital Human capital is the amount of skill embodied in the workforce. It is most commonly measured by the amount of education and training. (p. 520)

Human capital theory Human capital theory focuses on the expenditures that have been made to increase the productive capacity of workers via education or other means. It is analogous to investment in better machines as a way to increase their productivity. (p. 433)

Incidence of a tax The incidence of a tax is an allocation of the burden of the tax to specific individuals or groups. (p. 389)

Income effect The income effect of a rise in wages is the resulting rise of workers' purchasing power that enables them to afford more leisure. (p. 429)

Income elasticity of demand Income elasticity of demand is the ratio of the percentage change in quantity demanded to the percentage change in income. (p. 116)

Income-expenditure diagram An income-expenditure diagram, or 45° line diagram, plots total real expenditure (on the vertical axis) against real income (on the horizontal axis). The 45° line marks off points where income and expenditure are equal. (p. 564)

Increasing returns to scale Production is said to involve economies of scale, also referred to as increasing returns to scale, if, when all input quantities are increased by X percent, the quantity of output rises by more than X percent. (p. 142)

Index fund An index fund is a mutual fund that chooses a particular stock price index and then buys the stocks (or most of the stocks) that are included in the index. The value of an investment in an index fund depends on what happens to the prices of all stocks in that index. (p. 185)

Indexing Indexing refers to provisions in a law or a contract whereby monetary payments are automatically adjusted whenever a specified price index changes. Wage rates, pensions, interest payments on bonds, income taxes, and many other things can be indexed in this way, and have been. Sometimes such contractual provisions are called *escalator clauses*. (p. 716)

Index number An index number expresses the cost of a market basket of goods relative to its cost in some "base" period, which is simply the year used as a basis of comparison. (p. 512)

Index number problem When relative prices are changing, there is no such thing as a "perfect price index" that is correct for every consumer. Any statistical index will understate the increase in the cost of living for some families and overstate it for others. At best, the index can represent the situation of an "average" family. (p. 512)

Indifference curve An indifference curve is a line connecting all combinations of the commodities that are equally desirable to the consumer. (p. 101)

Indirect taxes Indirect taxes are taxes levied on specific economic activities. (p. 381)

Induced increase in consumption An induced increase in consumption is an increase in consumer spending that stems from an increase in consumer incomes. It is represented on a graph as a movement along a fixed consumption function. (p. 573)

Induced investment Induced investment is the part of investment spending that rises when GDP rises and falls when GDP falls. (p. 563)

Industrial Revolution The Industrial Revolution is the stream of new technology and the resulting growth of output that began in England toward the end of the eighteenth century. (p. 336)

Inelastic demand curve A demand curve is inelastic when a given percentage price change leads to a smaller percentage change in quantity demanded. (p. 112)

Inferior good An inferior good is a commodity whose quantity demanded falls when the purchaser's real income rises, all other things remaining equal. (p. 95)

Inflation Inflation refers to a sustained increase in the general price level. Inflation occurs when prices in an economy rise rapidly. The rate of inflation is calculated by averaging the percentage growth rate of the prices of a selected sample of commodities. (pp. 181, 472)

Inflationary gap The inflationary gap is the amount by which equilibrium real GDP exceeds the full-employment level of GDP. (pp. 567, 589)

Innovation Innovation is the process that begins with invention and includes improvement to prepare the invention for practical use and marketing of the invention or its products. (pp. 339, 415, 527)

Input-output analysis Input-output analysis is a mathematical procedure that takes account of the interdependence among the economy's industries and determines the amount of output each industry must provide as inputs to the other industries in the economy. (p. 297)

Inputs Inputs or factors of production are the labor, machinery, buildings, and natural resources used to make outputs. (pp. 22, 489)

Interest Interest is the payment for the use of funds employed in the production of capital; it is measured as the percent per

year of the value of the funds tied up in the capital. (p. 404)

Interest rate The interest rate is the amount that borrowers currently pay to lenders per dollar of the money borrowed—it is the current market price of a loan. (p. 181)

Intermediate good An intermediate good is a good purchased for resale or for use in producing another good. (p. 473)

International capital flows International capital flows are purchases and sales of financial assets across national borders. (p. 768)

Invention Invention is the act of discovering new products or new ways of making products. (pp. 339, 415, 527)

Investment Investment is the *flow* of resources into the production of new capital. It is the labor, steel, and other inputs devoted to the *construction* of factories, warehouses, railroads, and other pieces of capital during some period of time. (pp. 403, 522)

Investment in human capital Investment in human capital is any expenditure on an individual that increases that person's future earning power or productivity. (p. 424)

Investment spending Investment spending (*I*) is the sum of the expenditures of business firms on new plant and equipment and households on new homes. Financial "investments" are not included, nor are resales of existing physical assets. (p. 539)

Invisible hand The invisible hand is a phrase used by Adam Smith to describe how, by pursuing their own self-interests, people in a market system are "led by an invisible hand" to promote the well-being of the community. (p. 56)

Kinked demand curve A kinked demand curve is a demand curve that changes its slope abruptly at some level of output. (p. 298)

Labor force The labor force is the number of people holding or seeking jobs. (p. 492)

Labor productivity Labor productivity is the amount of output a worker turns out in an hour (or a week, or a year) of labor. If output is measured by GDP, it is GDP per hour of work. (p. 491)

Labor union A labor union is an organization made up of a group of workers (usually with the same specialization, such as plumbing or costume design, or in the same industry). The unions represent the workers in negotiations with employers over issues such as wages, vacations, and sick leave. (p. 435)

Laissez-faire Laissez-faire refers to a situation in which there is minimal government interference with the workings of the market system. The term implies that people should be left alone in carrying out their economic affairs. (p. 293)

"Law" of demand The "law" of demand states that a lower price generally increases the amount of a commodity that people in a market are willing to buy. Therefore, for most goods, market demand curves have negative slopes. (p. 96)

"Law" of diminishing marginal utility The "law" of diminishing marginal utility asserts that additional units of a commodity are worth less and less to a consumer in money terms. As the individual's consumption increases, the marginal utility of each additional unit declines. (p. 87)

Law of supply and demand The law of supply and demand states that in a free market the forces of supply and demand generally push the price toward the level at which quantity supplied and quantity demanded are equal. (p. 66)

Liability A liability of an individual or business firm is an item of value that the individual or firm owes. Many liabilities are known as *debts*. (p. 635)

Limited liability Limited liability is a legal obligation of a firm's owners to pay back company debts only with the money they have already invested in the firm. (p. 180)

Liquidity An asset's liquidity refers to the ease with which it can be converted into cash. (p. 631)

Long run The long run is a period of time long enough for all of the firm's current commitments to come to an end. (p. 129)

M1 The narrowly defined money supply, usually abbreviated M1, is the sum of all coins and paper money in circulation, plus certain checkable deposit balances at banks and savings institutions.3 (p. 631)

M2 The broadly defined money supply, usually abbreviated M2, is the sum of all coins and paper money in circulation, plus all types of checking account balances, plus most forms of savings account balances, plus shares in money market mutual funds. (p. 631)

Marginal analysis Marginal analysis is a method for calculating optimal choices—the choices that best promote the decision maker's objective. It works by testing whether, and by how much, a small change in a decision will move things toward or away from the goal. (p. 88)

Marginal land Marginal land is land that is just on the borderline of being used—that is, any land the use of which would be unprofitable if the farmer had to pay even a penny of rent. (p. 409)

Marginal physical product (MPP) The marginal physical product (MPP) of an input is the increase in total output that results from a one-unit increase in the input quantity, holding the amounts of all other inputs constant. (pp. 131, 400)

Marginal private benefit (MPB) The marginal private benefit (MPB) is the share of an activity's marginal benefit that is received by the persons who carry out the activity. (p. 315)

Marginal private cost (MPC) The marginal private cost (MPC) is the share of an activity's marginal cost that is paid for by the persons who carry out the activity. (p. 315)

Marginal profit Marginal profit is the addition to total profit resulting from one more unit of output. (p. 163)

Marginal propensity to consume (MPC) The marginal propensity to consume (MPC) is the ratio of changes in consumption relative to changes in disposable income that produce the change in consumption. On a graph, it appears as the slope of the consumption function. (p. 544)

Marginal revenue (MR) Marginal revenue (MR) is the addition to total revenue resulting from the addition of one unit to total output. Geometrically, marginal revenue is the slope of the total revenue curve at the pertinent output quantity. Its formula is $MR_1 = TR_1 - TR_0$, and so on. (p. 160)

Marginal revenue product (MRP) The marginal revenue product (MRP) of an input is the money value of the additional sales that a firm obtains by selling the marginal physical product of that input. (pp. 132, 400)

Marginal revenue product of labor (MRP$_L$) The marginal revenue product of labor (MRP$_L$) is the increase in the employer's total revenue that results when it hires an additional unit of labor. (p. 424)

Marginal social benefit (MSB) The marginal social benefit (MSB) of an activity is the sum of its marginal private benefit (MPB) plus its incidental benefits (positive or negative) that are received by others, and for which those others do not pay. (p. 315)

Marginal social cost (MSC) The marginal social cost (MSC) of an activity is the sum of its marginal private cost (MPC) plus its incidental costs (positive or negative) that are borne by others who receive no compensation for the resulting damage to their well-being. (p. 315)

Marginal tax rate The marginal tax rate is the fraction of each *additional* dollar of income that is paid in taxes. (p. 381)

Marginal utility The marginal utility of a commodity to a consumer (measured in money terms) is the maximum amount of money that she or he is willing to pay for *one more unit* of that commodity. (p. 86)

Market demand curve A market demand curve shows how the total quantity of some product demanded by *all* consumers in the market during a specified period of time changes as the price of that product changes, holding all other things constant. (p. 95)

Market system A market system is a form of economic organization in which resource allocation decisions are left to individual producers and consumers acting in their own best interests without central direction. (p. 50)

Maximin criterion The maximin criterion requires you to select the strategy that yields the maximum payoff on the assumption that your opponent will do as much damage to you as he or she can. (p. 252)

Mediation Mediation takes place during collective bargaining when a neutral individual is assigned the job of persuading the two parties to reach an agreement. (p. 441)

Medium of exchange Money is the standard object used in exchanging goods and services. In short, money is the medium of exchange. (p. 628)

Mercantilism Mercantilism is a doctrine that holds that exports are good for a country, whereas imports are harmful. (p. 731)

Minimum wage law A minimum wage law imposes a floor on wages and prohibits employers from paying their workers less than that amount. (p. 435)

Misallocated resources Resources are misallocated if it is possible to change the way they are used or the combination of goods and services they produce and thereby make consumers better off. (p. 313)

Mixed economy A mixed economy is one with some public influence over the workings of free markets. There may also be some public ownership mixed in with private property. (p. 36)

Monetarism Monetarism is a mode of analysis that uses the equation of exchange to organize and analyze macroeconomic data. (p. 665)

Monetary policy Monetary policy refers to actions taken by the Federal Reserve to influence aggregate demand by changing interest rates. (pp. 481, 646, 685)

Monetize the deficit The central bank is said to monetize the deficit when it purchases bonds issued by the government. (p. 693)

Money Money is the standard object used in exchanging goods and services. In short, money is the medium of exchange. (p. 628)

Money-fixed asset A money-fixed asset is an asset whose value is a fixed number of dollars. (p. 546)

Money multiplier The money multiplier is the ratio of newly created bank deposits to new reserves. (p. 640)

Monopolistic competition Monopolistic competition refers to a market in which products are heterogeneous but which is otherwise the same as a market that is perfectly competitive. (p. 237)

Monopoly power Monopoly power (or market power) is the ability of a business firm to earn high profits by raising the prices of its products above competitive levels and to keep those prices high for a substantial amount of time. (p. 264)

Monopoly profits Monopoly profits are any excess of the profits earned persistently by a monopoly firm over and above those that would be earned if the industry were perfectly competitive. (p. 223)

Monopsony A monopsony is a market situation in which there is only one buyer. (p. 440)

Moral hazard Moral hazard refers to the tendency of insurance to discourage policyholders from protecting themselves from risk. (pp. 322, 634)

Multinational corporations Multinational corporations are corporations, generally large ones, which do business in many countries. Most, but not all, of these corporations have their headquarters in developed countries. (p. 532)

Multiplier The multiplier is the ratio of the change in equilibrium GDP (Y) divided by the original change in spending that causes the change in GDP. (p. 569)

Mutual fund A mutual fund, in which individual investors can buy shares, is a private investment firm that holds a portfolio of securities. Investors can choose among a large variety of mutual funds, such as stock funds, bond funds, and so forth. (p. 184)

Nash equilibrium A Nash equilibrium results when each player adopts the strategy that gives her the highest possible payoff if her rival sticks to the strategy he has chosen. (p. 252)

National debt The national debt is the federal government's total indebtedness at a moment in time. It is the result of previous budget deficits. (p. 687)

National income National income is the sum of the incomes that all individuals in the country earn in the forms of wages, interest, rents, and profits. It includes indirect business taxes, but excludes transfer payments and makes no deduction for income taxes. (p. 539)

National income accounting The system of measurement devised for collecting and expressing macroeconomic data is called national income accounting. (p. 552)

Natural monopoly A natural monopoly is an industry in which advantages of large-scale production make it possible for a single firm to produce the entire output of the market at lower average cost than a number of firms, each producing a smaller quantity. (p. 220)

Natural rate of unemployment The economy's self-correcting mechanism always tends to push the unemployment rate back toward a specific rate of unemployment that we call the natural rate of unemployment. (p. 707)

Near moneys Near moneys are liquid assets that are close substitutes for money. (p. 631)

Net exports Net exports, or $X - IM$, is the difference between exports (X) and imports (IM). It indicates the difference between what we sell to foreigners and what we buy from them. (pp. 539, 764)

Net national product (NNP) Net national product (NNP) is a measure of production. NNP is conceptually identical to national income. However, in practice, national income accountants estimate income and production independently; and so the two measures are never precisely equal. (p. 554)

Net worth Net worth is the value of all assets minus the value of all liabilities. (p. 635)

Nominal GDP Nominal GDP is calculated by valuing all outputs at current prices. (p. 472)

Nominal rate of interest The nominal rate of interest is the percentage by which the money the borrower pays back exceeds the money that she borrowed, making no adjustment for any decline in the purchasing power of this money that results from inflation. (p. 506)

Oligopoly An oligopoly is a market dominated by a few sellers, at least several of which are large enough relative to the total market to be able to influence the market price. (p. 241)

On-the-job training On-the-job training refers to skills that workers acquire while at work, rather than in school or in formal vocational training programs. (p. 526)

Open economy An open economy is one that trades with other nations in goods and services, and perhaps also trades in financial assets. (pp. 24, 763)

Open-market operations Open-market operations refer to the Fed's purchase or sale of government securities through transactions in the open market. (p. 649)

Opportunity cost The opportunity cost of some decision is the value of the next best alternative that must be given up because of that decision (for example, working instead of going to school). (pp. 4, 41)

Optimal decision An optimal decision is one that best serves the objectives of the decision maker, whatever those objectives may be. It is selected by explicit or implicit comparison with the possible alternative choices. The term *optimal* connotes neither approval nor disapproval of the objective itself. (pp. 41, 156)

Origin (of a graph) The "0" point in the lower-left corner of a graph where the axes meet is called the origin. Both variables are equal to zero at the origin. (p. 14)

Outputs The outputs of a firm or an economy are the goods and services it produces. (pp. 22, 489)

Outsourcing Outsourcing is the hiring of workers in foreign counties by U.S. firms to do work formerly carried out in the U.S. (p. 442)

Patent A patent is a privilege granted to an inventor, whether an individual or a firm, that for a specified period of time prohibits anyone else from producing or using that invention without the permission of the holder of the patent. (p. 219)

Payoff matrix A payoff matrix shows how much each of two competitors (players) can expect to earn, depending on the strategic choices each of them makes. (p. 249)

Per-capita income Per-capita income in an economy is the average income of all people in that economy. (p. 336)

Perfect competition Perfect competition occurs in an industry when that industry is made up of many small firms producing homogeneous products, when there is no impediment to the entry or exit of firms, and when full information is available. (p. 200)

Perfectly contestable A market is perfectly contestable if entry and exit are costless and unimpeded. (p. 256)

Phillips curve A Phillips curve is a graph depicting the rate of unemployment on the horizontal axis and either the rate of inflation or the rate of change of money wages on the vertical axis. Phillips curves are normally downward sloping, indicating that higher inflation rates are associated with lower unemployment rates. (p. 703)

Plowback Plowback (or retained earnings) is the portion of a corporation's profits that management decides to keep and reinvest in the firm's operations rather than paying out as dividends to stockholders. (p. 182)

Pollution charges Pollution charges (taxes on emissions) are taxes that polluters are required to pay. The amount they pay depends on what they emit and in what quantities. (p. 366)

Portfolio diversification Portfolio diversification means inclusion of a number and variety of stocks, bonds, and other such items in an individual's portfolio. If the individual owns airline stocks, for example, diversification requires the purchase of a stock or bond in a very different industry, such as breakfast cereal production. (p. 184)

Potential GDP Potential GDP is the real GDP that the economy would produce if its labor and other resources were fully employed. (p. 492)

Poverty line The poverty line is an amount of income below which a family is considered "poor." (p. 447)

Predatory pricing Predatory pricing is pricing that threatens to keep a competitor out of the market. It is a price that is so low that it will be profitable for the firm that adopts it only if a rival is driven from the market. (p. 279)

Price cap A price cap is a ceiling above which regulators do not permit prices to rise. The cap is designed to provide an efficiency incentive to the firm by allowing it to keep part of any savings in costs it can achieve. (p. 270)

Price ceiling A price ceiling is a maximum that the price charged for a commodity cannot legally exceed. (p. 70)

Price discrimination Price discrimination is the sale of a given product at different prices to different customers of the firm, when there are no differences in the costs of supplying these customers. Prices are also discriminatory if it costs more to supply one customer than another, but they are charged the same price. (p. 227)

(Price) elasticity of demand The (price) elasticity of demand is the ratio of the *percentage* change in quantity demanded to the *percentage* change in price that brings about the change in quantity demanded. (p. 109)

Price floor A price floor is a legal minimum below which the price charged for a commodity is not permitted to fall. (p. 73)

Price leadership Under price leadership, one firm sets the price for the industry and the others follow. (p. 245)

Price taker Under perfect competition, the firm is a price taker. It has no choice but to accept the price that has been determined in the market. (p. 201)

Price war In a price war, each competing firm is determined to sell at a price that is lower than the prices of its rivals, usually regardless of whether that price covers the pertinent cost. Typically, in such a price war, Firm A cuts its price below Firm B's price; B retaliates by undercutting A; and so on and on until some of the competitor firms surrender and let themselves be undersold. (p. 246)

Principals Agents are people hired to run a complex enterprise on behalf of the principals, those whose benefit the enterprise is supposed to serve. (p. 323)

Principle of increasing costs The principle of increasing costs states that as the production of a good expands, the opportunity cost of producing another unit generally increases. (p. 44)

Private good A private good is a commodity characterized by both depletability and excludability. (p. 318)

Process innovation A process innovation is an innovation that changes the way in which a commodity is produced. (p. 350)

Producer's surplus The producer's surplus from a sale is the difference between the market price of the item sold and the lowest price at which the supplier would be willing to provide the item. (p. 300)

Product innovation A product innovation is the introduction of a good or service that is entirely new or involves major modifications of earlier products. (p. 350)

Production function The economy's production function shows the volume of output that can be produced from given inputs (such as labor and capital), given the available technology. (p. 490)

Production indifference curve A production indifference curve (sometimes called an *isoquant*) is a curve showing all the different quantities of two inputs that are just sufficient to produce a given quantity of output. (p. 149)

Production indifference map A production indifference map is a graph whose axes show the quantities of two inputs that are used to produce some output. A curve in the graph corresponds to some given quantity of that output, and the different points on that curve show the different quantities of the two inputs that are just enough to produce the given output. (p. 18)

Production possibilities frontier The production possibilities frontier is a curve that shows the maximum quantities of outputs it is possible to produce with the available resource quantities and the current state of technological knowledge. (pp. 43, 313)

Productivity Productivity is the amount of output produced by a unit of input. (pp. 336, 586)

Progressive tax A progressive tax is one in which the average tax rate paid by an individual rises as income rises. (pp. 36, 381)

Property rights Property rights are laws and/or conventions that assign owners the rights to use their property as they see fit (within the law)—for example, to sell the property and to reap the benefits (such as rents or dividends) while they own it. (p. 524)

Proportional tax A proportional tax is one in which the average tax rate is the same at all income levels. (p. 381)

Public good A public good is a commodity or service whose benefits are *not depleted* by an additional user and from which it is generally difficult or *impossible to exclude* people, even if the people are unwilling to pay for the benefits. (p. 318)

Purchasing power The purchasing power of a given sum of money is the volume of goods and services that it will buy. (p. 501)

Pure monopoly A pure monopoly is an industry in which there is only one supplier of a product for which there are no close substitutes and in which it is very difficult or impossible for another firm to coexist. (p. 218)

Quantity demanded The quantity demanded is the number of units of a good that consumers are willing and can afford to buy over a specified period of time. (p. 57)

Quantity supplied The quantity supplied is the number of units that sellers want to sell over a specified period of time. (p. 61)

Quantity theory of money The quantity theory of money assumes that velocity is (approximately) constant. In that case, nominal GDP is proportional to the money stock. (p. 663)

Quota A quota specifies the maximum amount of a good that is permitted into the country from abroad per unit of time. (p. 732)

Random walk The time path of a variable such as the price of a stock is said to constitute a random walk if its magnitude in one period (say, May 2, 2005) is equal to its value in the preceding period (May 1, 2005) plus a completely random number. That is: Price on May 2, 2005 = Price on May 1, 2005 + Random number, where the random number (positive or negative) can be obtained by a roll of dice or some such procedure. (p. 191)

Ratchet A ratchet is an arrangement that permits some economic variable, such as investment or advertising, to increase, but prevents that variable from subsequently decreasing. (p. 349)

Rational expectations Rational expectations are forecasts that, while not necessarily correct, are the best that can be made given the available data. Rational expectations, therefore, cannot err systematically. If expectations are rational, forecasting errors are pure random numbers. (p. 712)

Ray through the origin (or Ray) Lines whose Y-intercept is zero have so many special uses in economics and other disciplines that they have been given a special name: a ray through the origin, or a ray. (p. 17)

Real GDP Real GDP is calculated by valuing outputs of different years at common prices. Therefore, real GDP is a far better measure than nominal GDP of changes in total production. (p. 472)

Real GDP per capita Real GDP per capita is the ratio of real GDP divided by population. (p. 476)

Real rate of interest The real rate of interest is the percentage increase in purchasing power that the borrower pays to the lender for the privilege of borrowing. It indicates the increased ability to purchase goods and services that the lender earns. (p. 717)

Real wage rate The real wage rate is the wage rate adjusted for inflation. Specifically, it is the nominal wage divided by the price index. The real wage thus indicates the volume of goods and services that the nominal wages will buy. (p. 501)

Recession A recession is a period of time during which the total output of the economy declines. (pp. 24, 472)

Recessionary gap The recessionary gap is the amount by which the equilibrium level of real GDP falls short of potential GDP. (pp. 567, 589)

Regressive tax A regressive tax is one in which the average tax rate falls as income rises. (p. 381)

Regulation Regulation of industry is a process established by law that restricts or controls some specified decisions made by the affected firms; it is designed to protect the public from exploitation by firms with monopoly power. Regulation is usually carried out by a special government agency assigned the task of administering and interpreting the law. That agency also acts as a court in enforcing the regulatory laws. (p. 265)

Relative price An item's relative price is its price in terms of some other item rather than in terms of dollars. (p. 503)

Rent seeking Rent seeking refers to unproductive activity in the pursuit of economic profit—in other words, profit in excess of competitive earnings. (p. 322)

Required reserves Required reserves are the minimum amount of reserves (in cash or the equivalent) required by law. Normally, required reserves are proportional to the volume of deposits. (p. 635)

Research and development (R&D) Research and development (R&D) is the activity of firms, universities, and government agencies that seeks to invent new products and processes and to improve those inventions so that they are ready for the market or other users. (pp. 342, 527)

Resources Resources are the instruments provided by nature or by people that are used to create goods and services. Natural resources include minerals, soil, water, and air. Labor is a scarce resource, partly because of time limitations (the day has only 24 hours) and partly because the number of skilled workers is limited. Factories and machines are resources made by people. These three types of resources are often referred to as *land, labor,* and *capital.* They are also called *inputs* or *factors of production.* (p. 40)

Retained earnings Plowback (or retained earnings) is the portion of a corporation's profits that management decides to keep and reinvest in the firm's operations rather than paying out as dividends to stockholders. (p. 182)

Revaluation A revaluation is an increase in the official value of a currency. (p. 747)

Run on a bank A run on a bank occurs when many depositors withdraw cash from their accounts all at once. (p. 626)

Sales maximization A firm's objective is said to be sales maximization if it seeks to adopt prices and output quantities that make its total revenue (its "sales"), rather than its profits, as large as possible. (p. 246)

Scatter diagram A scatter diagram is a graph showing the relationship between two variables (such as consumer spending and disposable income). Each year is represented by a point in the diagram, and the coordinates of each year's point show the values of the two variables in that year. (p. 542)

Self-correcting mechanism The economy's self-correcting mechanism refers to the way money wages react to either a recessionary gap or an inflationary gap. Wage changes shift the aggregate supply curve and therefore change equilibrium GDP and the equilibrium price level. (pp. 592, 707)

Shift in a demand curve A shift in a demand curve occurs when any relevant variable other than price changes. If consumers want to buy *more* at any and all given prices than they wanted previously, the demand curve shifts to the right (or outward). If they desire *less* at any given price, the demand curve shifts to the left (or inward). (p. 59)

Short run The short run is a period of time during which some of the firm's cost commitments will not have ended. (p. 129)

Shortage A shortage is an excess of quantity demanded over quantity supplied. When there is a shortage, buyers cannot purchase the quantities they desire at the current price. (p. 65)

Slope of a budget line The slope of a budget line is the amount of one commodity that the market requires an individual to give up to obtain one additional unit of another commodity without any change in the amount of money spent. (p. 102)

Slope of a curved line The slope of a curved line at a particular point is defined as the slope of the straight line that is tangent to the curve at that point. (p. 16)

Slope of an indifference curve The slope of an indifference curve, referred to as the marginal rate of substitution (MRS) between the commodities, represents the maximum amount of one commodity that the consumer is willing to give up in exchange for one more unit of another commodity. (p. 102)

Slope of a straight line The slope of a straight line is the ratio of the vertical change to the corresponding horizontal change as we move to the right along the line or, as it is often said, the ratio of the "rise" over the "run." (p. 15)

Specialization Specialization means that a country devotes its energies and resources to only a small proportion of the world's productive activities. (p. 725)

Speculation Individuals who engage in speculation deliberately invest in risky assets, hoping to obtain profits from future changes in the prices of these assets. (p. 190)

Stabilization policy Stabilization policy is the name given to government programs designed to prevent or shorten recessions and to counteract inflation (that is, to *stabilize* prices). (p. 483)

Stagflation Stagflation is inflation that occurs while the economy is growing slowly ("stagnating") or in a recession.(pp. 480, 594, 705)

Statistical discrimination Statistical discrimination is said to occur when the productivity of a particular worker is estimated to be low just because that worker belongs to a particular group (such as women) (p. 462)

Sticky price A price is called sticky if it does not change often even when there is a moderate change in cost. (p. 249)

Stock option A stock option is a contract that permits its owner to buy a specified quantity of stocks of a corporation at a future date, but at the price specified in the contract rather than the stock's market price at the date of purchase. (p. 323)

Stock price index A stock price index, such as the S&P 500, is an average of the prices of a large set of stocks. These stocks are selected to represent the price movements of the entire stock market, or some specified segment of the market, and the chosen set is rarely changed. (p. 185)

Store of value A store of value is an item used to store wealth from one point in time to another. (p. 628)

Structural budget deficit The structural budget deficit is the hypothetical deficit we *would have* under current fiscal policies if the economy were operating near full employment. (p. 690)

Structural unemployment Structural unemployment refers to workers who have lost their jobs because they have been displaced by automation, because their skills are no longer in demand, or because of similar reasons. (p. 499)

Substitutes Two goods are called substitutes if an increase in the quantity consumed of one cuts the quantity demanded of the other, all other things remaining constant. (p. 117)

Substitution effect The substitution effect of a wage increase is the resulting incentive to work more because of the higher relative reward to labor. (p. 428)

Supply curve A supply curve is a graphical depiction of a supply schedule. It shows how the quantity supplied of some product will change as the price of that product changes during a specified period of time, holding all other determinants of quantity supplied constant. (p. 62)

Supply curve of a firm The supply curve of a firm shows the different quantities of output that the firm would be willing to supply at different possible prices during some given period of time. (p. 206)

Supply curve of an industry The supply curve of an industry shows the different quantities of output that the industry would supply at different possible prices during some given period of time. (p. 207)

Supply-demand diagram A supply-demand diagram graphs the supply and demand curves together. It also determines the equilibrium price and quantity. (p. 64)

Supply schedule A supply schedule is a table showing how the quantity supplied of some product changes as the price of that product changes during a specified period of time, holding all other determinants of quantity supplied constant. (p. 61)

Supply-side inflation Supply-side inflation is a rise in the price level caused by slow growth (or decline) of aggregate supply. (p. 702)

Surplus A surplus is an excess of quantity supplied over quantity demanded. When there is a surplus, sellers cannot sell the quantities they desire to supply at the current price. (p. 65)

Takeover A takeover is the acquisition by an outside group (the raiders) of a controlling proportion of a company's stock. When the old management opposes the takeover attempt, it is called a *hostile takeover attempt*. (p. 189)

Tangent A tangent to the curve is *straight* line that *touches*, but does not *cut*, the curve at a particular point. (p. 16)

Tariff A tariff is a tax on imports. (p. 732)

Tax deduction A tax deduction is a sum of money that may be subtracted before the taxpayer computes his or her taxable income. (p. 382)

Tax exempt A particular source of income is tax exempt if income from that source is not taxable. (p. 382)

Tax loophole A tax loophole is a special provision in the tax code that reduces taxation below normal rates (perhaps to zero) if certain conditions are met. (p. 382)

Tax shifting Tax shifting occurs when the economic reactions to a tax cause prices and outputs in the economy to change, thereby shifting part of the burden of the tax onto others. (p. 390)

Technology trading Technology trading is an arrangement in which a firm voluntarily makes its privately owned technology available to other firms either in exchange for access to the technology of the second company or for an agreed-upon fee. (p. 353)

Theory A theory is a deliberate simplification of relationships used to explain how those relationships work. (p. 11)

Theory of dual labor markets The theory of dual labor markets emphasizes that labor is supplied in two types of market, one with high wages and promising promotion opportunities and the other with low wages and dead-end jobs. (p. 434)

Total physical product (TPP) The firm's total physical product (TPP) is the amount of output it obtains in total from a given quantity of input. (p. 130)

Total profit The total profit of a firm is its net earnings during some period of time. It is equal to the total amount of money the firm gets from sales of its products (the firm's total revenue) minus the total amount that it spends to make and market those products (total cost). (p. 158)

Total revenue The total revenue of a supplier firm is the total amount of money it receives from the purchasers of its products, without any deduction of costs. (p. 159)

Total utility The total utility of a quantity of a good to a consumer (measured in money terms) is the maximum amount of money that he or she is willing to give up in exchange for it. (p. 86)

Trade adjustment assistance Trade adjustment assistance provides special unemployment benefits, loans, retraining programs, and other aid to workers and firms that are harmed by foreign competition. (p. 735)

Trade deficit A country's trade deficit is the excess of its imports over its exports. If, instead, exports exceed imports, the country has a trade surplus. (p. 771)

Trade surplus A country's trade surplus is the excess of its exports over its imports. If, instead, imports exceed exports, the country has a trade deficit. (p. 771)

Transfer payments Transfer payments are sums of money that the government gives certain individuals as outright grants rather than as payments for services rendered to employers. Some common examples are Social Security and unemployment benefits. (pp. 36, 540)

Unemployment insurance Unemployment insurance is a government program that replaces some of the wages lost by eligible workers who lose their jobs. (p. 500)

Unemployment rate The unemployment rate is the number of unemployed people, expressed as a percentage of the labor force. (p. 495)

Unit of account The unit of account is the standard unit for quoting prices. (p. 628)

Unit-elastic demand curve A demand curve is unit-elastic when a given percentage price change leads to the same percentage change in quantity demanded. (p. 112)

Value added The value added by a firm is its revenue from selling a product minus the amount paid for goods and services purchased from other firms. (p. 555)

Variable A variable is something measured by a number; it is used to analyze what happens to other things when the size of that number changes (varies). (p. 14)

Variable cost A variable cost is a cost whose total amount changes when the quantity of output of the supplier changes. (pp. 130, 204)

Variable taxes Variable taxes are taxes that vary with the level of GDP. (p. 618)

Velocity Velocity indicates the number of times per year that an "average dollar" is spent on goods and services. It is the ratio of nominal gross domestic product (GDP) to the number of dollars in the money stock. That is:

$$\text{Velocity} = \frac{\text{Nominal GDP}}{\text{Money stock}} \quad \text{(p. 662)}$$

Vertical equity Vertical equity refers to the notion that differently situated individuals should be taxed differently in a way that society deems to be fair. (p. 386)

Vertical (long-run) Phillips curve The vertical (long-run) Phillips curve shows the menu of inflation/unemployment choices available to society in the long run. It is a vertical straight line at the natural rate of unemployment. (p. 707)

Y-intercept The Y-intercept of a line or a curve is the point at which it touches the vertical axis (the Y-axis). The X-intercept is defined similarly. (p. 16)

Zero-sum game A zero-sum game is one in which exactly the amount one competitor gains must be lost by other competitors. (p. 253)

INDEX

Selected U.S. Macroeconomic Data, 1929–2004

Year	(1) Gross Domestic Product	(2) Personal Consumption Expenditure	(3) Gross Private Domestic Investment	(4) Government Purchases	(5) Net Exports	(6) Gross Domestic Product	(7) Personal Consumption Expenditure	(8) Gross Private Domestic Investment	(9) Government Purchases	(10) Net Exports	(11) Real GDP per capita
	(in billions of dollars)					(in billions of chained 2000 dollars)[a]					(In chained 2000 dollars)
1929	103.6	77.4	16.5	9.4	0.4	865.2	661.4	91.3	120.6	−9.4	7,099
1933	56.4	45.9	1.7	8.7	0.1	635.5	541.0	17.0	129.2	−10.2	5,056
1939	92.2	67.2	9.3	14.8	0.8	950.7	729.1	77.4	196.0	−4.7	7,256
1945	223.1	120.0	10.8	93.0	−0.8	1786.3	902.7	67.0	1152.9	−26.8	12,766
1950	293.8	192.2	54.1	46.8	0.7	1777.3	1152.8	227.7	405.3	−9.0	11,717
1955	414.8	258.8	69.0	86.5	0.5	2212.8	1385.5	256.2	640.7	−14.3	13,389
1960	526.4	331.7	78.9	111.6	4.2	2501.8	1597.4	266.6	715.4	−12.7	13,840
1965	719.1	443.8	118.2	151.5	5.6	3191.1	2007.7	393.1	861.3	−18.9	16,420
1970	1038.5	648.5	152.4	233.8	4.0	3771.9	2451.9	427.1	1012.9	−52.0	18,391
1971	1127.1	701.9	178.2	246.5	0.6	3898.6	2545.5	475.7	990.8	−60.6	18,771
1972	1238.3	770.6	207.6	263.5	−3.4	4105.0	2701.3	532.1	983.5	−73.5	19,555
1973	1382.7	852.4	244.5	281.7	4.1	4341.5	2833.8	594.4	980.0	−51.9	20,484
1974	1500.0	933.4	249.4	317.9	−0.8	4319.6	2812.3	550.6	1004.7	−29.4	20,195
1975	1638.3	1034.4	230.2	357.7	16.0	4311.2	2876.9	453.1	1027.4	−2.4	19,961
1976	1825.3	1151.9	292.0	383.0	−1.6	4540.9	3035.5	544.7	1031.9	−37.0	20,822
1977	2030.9	1278.6	361.3	414.1	−23.1	4750.5	3164.1	627.0	1043.3	−61.1	21,565
1978	2294.7	1428.5	438.0	453.6	−25.4	5015.0	3303.1	702.6	1074.0	−61.9	22,526
1979	2563.3	1592.2	492.9	500.8	−22.5	5173.4	3383.4	725.0	1094.1	−41.0	22,982
1980	2789.5	1757.1	479.3	566.2	−13.1	5161.7	3374.1	645.3	1115.4	12.6	22,666
1981	3128.4	1941.1	572.4	627.5	−12.5	5291.7	3422.2	704.9	1125.6	8.3	23,007
1982	3255.0	2077.3	517.2	680.5	−20.0	5189.3	3470.3	606.0	1145.4	−12.6	22,346
1983	3536.7	2290.6	564.3	733.5	−51.7	5423.8	3668.6	662.5	1187.3	−60.2	23,146
1984	3933.2	2503.3	735.6	797.0	−102.7	5813.6	3863.3	857.7	1227.0	−122.4	24,593
1985	4220.3	2720.3	736.2	879.0	−115.2	6053.7	4064.0	849.7	1312.5	−141.5	25,382
1986	4462.8	2899.7	746.5	949.3	−132.7	6263.6	4228.9	843.9	1392.5	−156.3	26,024
1987	4739.5	3100.2	785.0	999.5	−145.2	6475.1	4369.8	870.0	1426.7	−148.4	26,664
1988	5103.8	3353.6	821.6	1039.0	−110.4	6742.7	4546.9	890.5	1445.1	−106.8	27,514
1989	5484.4	3598.5	874.9	1099.1	−88.2	6981.4	4675.0	926.2	1482.5	−79.2	28,221
1990	5803.1	3839.9	861.0	1180.2	−78.0	7112.5	4770.3	895.1	1530.0	−54.7	28,429
1991	5995.9	3986.1	802.9	1234.4	−27.5	7100.5	4778.4	822.2	1547.2	−14.6	28,007
1992	6337.7	4235.3	864.8	1271.0	−33.2	7336.6	4934.8	889.0	1555.3	−15.9	28,556
1993	6657.4	4477.9	953.4	1291.2	−65.0	7532.7	5099.8	968.3	1541.1	−52.1	28,940
1994	7072.2	4743.3	1097.1	1325.5	−93.6	7835.5	5290.7	1099.6	1541.3	−79.4	29,741
1995	7397.7	4975.8	1144.0	1369.2	−91.4	8031.7	5433.5	1134.0	1549.7	−71.0	30,128
1996	7816.9	5256.8	1240.3	1416.0	−96.2	8328.9	5619.4	1234.3	1564.9	−79.6	30,881
1997	8304.3	5547.4	1389.8	1468.7	−101.6	8703.5	5831.8	1387.7	1594.0	−104.6	31,886
1998	8747.0	5879.5	1509.1	1518.3	−159.9	9066.9	6125.8	1524.1	1624.4	−203.7	32,833
1999	9268.4	6282.5	1625.7	1620.8	−260.5	9470.3	6438.6	1642.6	1686.9	−296.2	33,904
2000	9817.0	6739.4	1735.5	1721.6	−379.5	9817.0	6739.4	1735.5	1721.6	−379.5	34,753
2001	10128.0	7055.0	1614.3	1825.6	−367.0	9890.7	6910.4	1598.4	1780.3	−399.1	34,660
2002	10487.0	7376.1	1579.2	1956.6	−424.9	10074.8	7123.4	1560.7	1857.9	−472.1	34,955
2003	11004.0	7760.9	1665.8	2075.5	−498.1	10381.3	7355.6	1628.8	1909.4	−518.5	35,666
2004	11735.0	8229.9	1927.3	2183.9	−606.2	10841.9	7632.5	1843.5	1946.5	−583.7	36,882

[a] Components do not add up to GDP due to chain method of deflation.
[b] Persons 14 years and older for 1929–1945; thereafter, persons 16 years and older.
[c] Moody's Aaa rating.
[d] Trade–weighted average of broad group of U.S. trading partners.
[e] National income and product accounts basis; calendar years.